THE BIRTHING OF THE NEW TESTAMENT

New Testament Monographs, 1

Series Editor
Stanley E. Porter

THE BIRTHING OF THE NEW TESTAMENT

The Intertextual Development of
the New Testament Writings

Thomas L. Brodie

SHEFFIELD PHOENIX PRESS

2004

Copyright © 2004, 2006 Sheffield Phoenix Press

First published in hardback, 2004
First published in paperback, 2006

Published by Sheffield Phoenix Press
Department of Biblical Studies, University of Sheffield
Sheffield S10 2TN

www.sheffieldphoenix.com

All rights reserved.
No part of this publication may be reproduced or transmitted in any form or by any means, electronic or mechanical, including photocopying, recording or any information storage or retrieval system, without the publishers' permission in writing.

A CIP catalogue record for this book
is available from the British Library

Typeset by Forthcoming Publications
Printed by Lightning Source

ISBN 1-905048-03-3 (hardback)
ISBN 1-905048-66-1 (paperback)
ISSN 1747-9606

*To a new generation
facing a new desert
awaiting the dawn*

Contents

List of Tables	xv
Preface	xix
Acknowledgments	xxii
Abbreviations	xxiii
General Summary of the Volume	xxvii
Map of Travel Times	xxxi

PART I
GENERAL INTRODUCTION: ANCIENT WRITING AND ITS CONTEXT

Orientational Introduction to Chapters 1–9:
The Written Page and its Social Context — 2

Chapter 1
   The Greco-Roman Tradition: Writing as Rhetorical Imitation — 3

Chapter 2
   The Biblical Tradition: Writing as Rewriting — 23

Orientational Conclusion to Chapters 1 and 2 — 31

Chapter 3
   The Biblical Tradition: Narrative as Poetic Art—The Case of Judges — 32

Chapter 4
   The Biblical Tradition: Narrative as Poetic Art—The Elijah–Elisha Narrative as a Unified Interpretive Synthesis — 39

Chapter 5
   Criteria for Judging Literary Dependence — 43

Chapter 6
   Oral Tradition: Wonderfully Plausible but Radically Problematic — 50

Chapter 7
   Schools, Synagogues, and Vibrant Scripture-Related Communities: Towards a Writing-Oriented Paradigm — 63

Chapter 8
   Roads and Travel: From a Paradigm of Multi-Faceted Isolation to a Paradigm of Communication — 72

Chapter 9
   Judaism's New Community: Religious Experience, and Adaptation of Institutions—Including Scripture — 76

PART II
THE OVERALL PICTURE: INITIAL EVIDENCE

Orientational Introduction to Chapters 10–26 — 82

Unit 1. *The Central Thesis: Proto-Luke, Septuagint-Based* — 83

Chapter 10
The Central Thesis: An Early Version of Luke–Acts—
Investigation, A Closer Look, and Three Key Arguments — 84

Chapter 11
Proto-Luke: The Argument from Coherence,
Especially from Eightfold Structure — 97

Unit 2. *An Auxiliary Thesis: Proto-Luke as Based on* Logia *and Epistolography* — 107

*Orientational Introduction to Chapters 12–14: An Auxiliary Thesis—
The Literary Line from Matthew's* Logia *to 1 Corinthians to Proto-Luke* — 108

Chapter 12
Matthew's *Logia* (Sayings from Matthew 5 and 11):
Deuteronomy-Based, Unified, Verifiable — 109

Chapter 13
1 Corinthians as Systematically Adapting the Pentateuch,
Especially Deuteronomy: An Exploratory Survey — 125

Chapter 14
Luke's Use of 1 Corinthians: The Supper Texts
(1 Corinthians 11.16-34; Luke 22.14-30) — 138

Orientational Conclusion to Chapters 10–14 — 144

Unit 3. *The Central Thesis Expanded: Mark* — 145

Orientational Introduction to Chapters 15–18 — 146

Chapter 15
Mark's Sources: The Elijah–Elisha Narrative — 147

Chapter 16
Mark's Sources: Mark and Proto-Luke—An Overview — 154

Chapter 17
Mark's Sources: Mark and Proto-Luke, Episode by Episode—
One Component, Not a Systematic Proof — 159

Chapter 18
Mark's Sources: Mark and the Epistles—
Peter's Central Maxims (1 Peter 2.18–3.17) as One Component
of Mark 10.1-45: An Exploration — 189

Unit 4. *The Central Thesis Expanded: Matthew* — 196

Chapter 19
Matthew's Twofold Expansion of Mark: Using Proto-Luke,
the *Logia*, and the Greatest Discourses — 197

Orientational Introduction to Chapters 20–21 — 204

Chapter 20
Vivid, Positive, Practical: The Systematic Use of Romans
in Matthew 1–7—An Exploratory Survey — 206

Chapter 21
The Use of Romans in Matthew 8.1–17.20:
An Exploratory Survey Continued — 219

Chapter 22
Fish, Temple Tithe, and Remission: The God-Based
Generosity of Deuteronomy 14–15 as One Component
of the Community Discourse (Matthew 17.22–18.35) — 236

Chapter 23
Deuteronomy 23–34 as One Component
in Matthew's Elaboration of Mark (Matthew 19–28) — 249

Unit 5. *The Central Thesis Expanded: John and Luke–Acts* — 253

Chapter 24
John's Use of Matthew, Mark, and Proto-Luke — 254

Chapter 25
Luke and Acts — 258

Chapter 26
General Conclusion to the Entire Volume
and a Sketch of Possible Implications — 275

PART III
PROTO-LUKE AS SEPTUAGINT-BASED (ARGUMENT 1): SUPPORTING EVIDENCE

*Orientational Introduction to Chapters 27–54: Proto-Luke's Systematic
Dependence on the Septuagint—Towards Elaborating the Argument* — 282

Unit 6. *Proto-Luke's Use of the Elijah–Elisha Narrative* — 283

Chapter 27
The Introduction to the Elijah–Elisha Narrative
(1 Kings 16.29–17.1) as One Positivized Component
of the Introduction to Luke–Acts (Luke 1.5-17) — 284

Unit 7. *Proto-Luke and Elijah–Elisha:*
The Prophets and the Women — 290

Orientational Introduction to Chapters 28–32: The Prophets and the Women — 291

Chapter 28
Not Q But Elijah: The Saving of the Centurion's Servant
(Luke 7.1-10) as an Internalization of the Saving of the Widow
and Her Child (1 Kings 17.1-16) — 294

Chapter 29
The Raising of the Widow's Son (1 Kings 17.17-24; Luke 7.11-17) — 302

Chapter 30
Again Not Q: Luke 7.18-35 as an Acts-Oriented Transformation
of the Vindication of the Prophet Micaiah (1 Kings 22.1-38) — 312

Chapter 31
Luke 7.36-50 as an Internalization of 2 Kings 4.1-37 — 325

Chapter 32
A People Gathering Around the Prophet: Luke 8.1-3
as a Women-Oriented Distillation of Part of 1 Kings 18 — 339

Unit 8. *Proto-Luke and Elijah–Elisha: Journey to Jerusalem* — 346

Orientational Introduction to Chapters 33–36: The Mission-Filled
Journey to Death/Assumption—Elijah's Journey to the Jordan (1 Kings 19;
2 Kings 1–3) and Jesus' Journey to Jerusalem (Luke 9.51–10.20;
Luke 22–Acts 2) — 347

Chapter 33
The Departure for Jerusalem (Luke 9.51-56) as a Rhetorical Imitation
of Elijah's Departure for the Jordan (2 Kings 1.1–2.6) — 351

Chapter 34
Yet Again, Not Q: Jesus' Three Sayings to Would-Be
Followers (Luke 9.57-62) as a Distillation of Elijah's
Three-Part Journey to Horeb (1 Kings 19) — 359

Chapter 35
The Post-Ascent Missions of the Fifty and of Elisha (2 Kings 2.16–Ch. 3)
as Components of the Mission of the Seventy (Luke 10.1-20) — 365

Chapter 36
Elijah's Crossing, Ascending, and Spirit-Giving (2 Kings 2.7-15)
as a Framework for the Center of Proto-Luke (Luke 22–Acts 2
[Except 22.31-65]) — 377

Unit 9. *Proto-Luke and Elijah–Elisha: Crises and Expansion* — 383

Orientational Introduction to Chapters 37–39:
The Use of the Elijah–Elisha Narrative in Acts 5–8 — 384

Chapter 37
  Old Testament Rapaciousness, Especially by Ahab and Jezebel
  (1 Kings 21 and 20.1-21), as one Component of the Story of Ananias
  and Sapphira (Acts 5.1-11) — 385

Chapter 38
  The Accusing and Stoning of Naboth (1 Kings 21.8-13)
  as One Component of the Stephen Text (Acts 6.9-14; 7.58a) — 391

Chapter 39
  The Prestigious Foreign Charioteer Who Heeds the Prophet,
  and a Money-Minded Follower: 2 Kings 5 as One Component
  of Acts 8.9-40 — 402

Unit 10. *Proto-Luke and Elijah–Elisha: The Damascus Attacker* — 418

Orientational Introduction to Chapters 40–43: Upheaval
and Breakthrough (2 Kings 6–13; Paul and Peter, Acts 9–11),
and Some Final Pieces — 419

Chapter 40
  Struck Down, Temporarily Blinded, and Prophetically Commissioned:
  The Two Damascus-Based Attacks (1 Kings 20.22-34; 2 Kings 6.8-23)
  and the Two Commissionings (2 Kings 8.7-15; 9.1-13) as Components
  in Paul's Conversion from Attacker to Commissioned (Acts 9.1-19a) — 421

Chapter 41
  The (Attempted) Killings and the Restoration:
  2 Kings 9.14–Ch. 13 as One Component of Acts 9.19b-43 — 429

Chapter 42
  Amid Hunger and Famine: Good News for Outsiders (Acts 10–11) — 436

Chapter 43
  The Final Pieces of the Puzzle — 443

Orientational Conclusion to Chapters 41–43 — 446

Unit 11. *Proto-Luke and Judges* — 447

Orientational Introduction to Chapters 44–52: Domesticated Wars—
An Introduction to Luke's Reworking of Judges — 448

Chapter 44
The Mission to Gentile Territory: Judges 1.1–3.6
as a Skeletal Framework for Acts 13–14   449

Chapter 45
Escaping the Royal Guard: Ehud's Overcoming
of Eglon (Judges 3.7-31) as a Framework for Peter's Escape
from Herod (Acts 12)   458

Chapter 46
The Prophetess, the Fall and Piercing, and the Song: Judges 4–5
as One Component of the Infancy Narrative (Luke 1–2)   464

Chapter 47
Judges 6–12 as One Component of Luke 16.1–18.8   467

Chapter 48
From the Infancy Narrative to the Final Gathering:
The Story of Samson (Judges 13–16) as a Frame
for Proto-Luke (Luke 1.5–2.52; Acts 9.32–15.21)   489

Chapter 49
The Search for a True Home (With God): Zacchaeus's Search
for Jesus (Luke 19.1-10) as 'A Diminutive Model' of the Danites'
Marred Search for a Home with a Shrine (Judges 17–18)   497

Chapter 50
The Lonely Journey and the Knowing: The 'Passion'
of the Woman (Judges 19) as One Component
of the Passion Narrative (Luke 23.50–24.53)   503

Chapter 51
The Civil War against Benjamin (Judges 20) as Part of the Background
for Gamaliel's 'Anti-War' Speech (Acts 5.33-42)   510

Chapter 52
Deathly Betrothal: The Conclusion of Judges (Judges 21)
as One Component of the Last Supper (Luke 22.1-30)   513

Orientational Conclusion to Chapters 49–52   519

Unit 12. Proto-Luke and Chronicles, Ezra, Nehemiah   520

Chapter 53
A New Temple and a New Law: The Chronicler-Based Aspect
of Luke 1.1–4.22a   521

Chapter 54
Proto-Luke: Summarizing Argument 1—The Distinctive Use
of the Old Testament   536

Contents xiii

PART IV
APPENDICES: FURTHER, EXPLORATORY ASPECTS
OF NEW TESTAMENT INTERTEXTUALITY

Unit 13. *Proto-Luke*   540

Appendix 1
Proto-Luke: Reviewing Aspects of the History of Research
and Rethinking the Arguments   541

Appendix 2
1 Corinthians as One Component of Luke–Acts   545

Appendix 3
The Use of 2 Chronicles 10–36 in Acts 4–15: An Exploration   567

Appendix 4
The Trials and Death of the Just Man (Wisdom 1–5) as One Component
of the Trial and Death of Jesus (Luke 22.66–23.49)   573

Unit 14. *The Triple Intertextuality of the Epistles*   584

Appendix 5
The Triple Intertextuality of the Epistles: An Introduction   585

Appendix 6
The Use of Daniel in 1 Corinthians: An Exploration   595

Appendix 7
The Use of Tobit in 1 Corinthians   600

Appendix 8
Epistolary Interdependence: Proposal for Research—
The Case of 1 Thessalonians   605

Bibliography   607

Index of Primary Biblical References   640
Index of Select Subjects   647
Index of Authors   650

List of Tables

1.	The Structure of Judges	34
2.	The Eightfold Elijah–Elisha Narrative	40
3.	Use of the Elijah–Elisha Narrative in Luke–Acts	94
4.	Luke's Use of Judges	95
5.	Luke's Use of Chronicles–Ezra–Nehemiah (Luke 1.1–4.27)	95
6.	Luke–Acts' Combined Use of Elijah–Elisha, Judges, and Chronicles	96
7.	The Eight Units of Proto-Luke (Simplified)	100
8.	The Eight Units of Proto-Luke: a. Proto-Luke, Part I (Gospel): Diptychs 1–4; b. Proto-Luke, Part II (Acts 1.1–15.35): Diptychs 5–8	102-103
9.	The *Logia*/Sayings in English (based on the *Logoi*/Deuteronomy)	110
10.	The *Logia* as a Synthesis of the *Logoi* (Deuteronomy): Overall Outline	112
11.	Deuteronomy (1; 7.1–10.11) and Five Beatitudes (Matthew 5.5-9)	113
12.	Deuteronomy (4–6; 10–26) and Five Antitheses (Matthew 5.21-44)	116
13.	Deuteronomy, Sirach, and the *Logia*: Initial Outline	120
14.	Sirach 51 and Matthew 11.25-30	121
15.	From Qumran, Cave 4: An Arrangement of Sapiential Sayings, in Hebrew (4Q525)	123
16.	Genesis 1.1–4.16	128
17.	1 Corinthians 6.12–7.11; 8.1-13	129
18.	Justice in Deuteronomy 1 and 1 Corinthians 6.1-11	130
19.	Conduct in Deuteronomy 23–28 and 1 Corinthians 9.4-18	131
20.	Walking with God (Deuteronomy 2.1–4.40; 1 Corinthians 7.17–8.6)	133
21.	Deuteronomy as One Component of 1 Corinthians: An Exploratory Outline	134
22.	Community Crises and Leadership	135
23.	The Supper Texts in Paul and Luke	140
24.	Proto-Luke and Mark: Initial Outline	156
25.	Proto-Luke and Mark: Detailed Outline	159
26.	Proto-Luke and Mark: Beginnings	163
27.	Proto-Luke and Mark: Luke 7; Mark 1. Some Details	165
28.	Proto-Luke and Mark: Acts 9.31–15.35; Mark 2–7	166
29.	Proto-Luke and Mark: Acts 10.1–11.26; Mark 2.13–3.12	168
30.	Proto-Luke and Mark: Commissionings (Acts 1; 13; Mark 3)	170
31.	Proto-Luke and Mark: Commissionings in Detail	171
32.	Proto-Luke and Mark: Clash with Satan (Acts 13; Mark 4)	171
33.	Proto-Luke and Mark: The Word (Acts 13.1-52; Mark 4)	172
34.	Proto-Luke and Mark: The Upheaval/Storm	173
35.	Proto-Luke and Mark: Herod; the Sea (Acts 12; 4; Mark 6)	175
36.	Proto-Luke and Mark: Adapting to Gentiles (Acts 15; Mark 7.1-37)	176
37.	Proto-Luke and Mark: Crisis; Breakthrough (Acts 6–9; Mark 8)	178
38.	Proto-Luke and Mark: Journey (Luke 9–24; Acts 2–9; Mark 9–16)	180
39.	Proto-Luke and Mark: Luke 22–23; Mark 11.8-25	183

40.	Proto-Luke and Mark: Disputing in Jerusalem (Acts 3–4; Mark 11.27–12.33)	184
41.	Proto-Luke and Mark: On the Ground; Confronted (Acts 9; Mark 14.32-71)	187
42.	Central Maxims (1 Peter 2.18–3.17; Mark 10.1-45)	190
43.	Romans and Matthew 1.1–17.20: General Outline	204
44.	Romans 1.1–2.16; 9.6–10.13; Matthew 1–7	208-10
45.	Romans 2.17–9.5; 10.14–16.27; Matthew 8.1–17.20	220
46.	Deuteronomy and Matthew 17.22–18.35	240
47.	John 3–11 and Acts 16–21	268
48.	Beginnings: Two Striking Couples (1 Kings 16.29–17.1; Luke 1.5-17)	285
49.	The Commanding Healing Word (1 Kings 17.1-16; Luke 7.1-10)	295
50.	The Widow's Son (1 Kings 17.17-24; Luke 7.11-17)	302
51.	Seeking a True Prophet (1 Kings 22; Luke 7.18-35)	316
52.	The Indebted Women (2 Kings 4.1-37; Luke 7.36-50)	329
53.	The People Gathered around the Prophet (1 Kings 18; Luke 8.1-3; Acts 14.8-18)	341
54.	As Death Looms, Departure for Assumption (2 Kings 1.1–2.6; Luke 9.51-56)	352
55.	The Difficult Journey (1 Kings 19; Luke 9.57-62)	361
56.	The Difficult Journey: Aspects of Linguistic Continuity and Fusion	362
57.	The Sending and the Great Struggle (2 Kings 2.16–3.27; Luke 10.1-20)	366
58.	The Taking Up to Heaven (2 Kings 2.11; Luke 24.51; Acts 1.9-10)	379
59.	Greed and Fraud (1 Kings 21 and 20.1-21; Acts 5.1-11)	387
60.	Naboth and Stephen	393
61.	Naaman and the Ethiopian (2 Kings 5; Acts 8.9-40)	404
62.	The Great Man (2 Kings 5.1, 3-5a, 11-13; Acts 8.9-10)	405
63.	The Damascus Attacker (1 Kings 20; 2 Kings 6–9; Acts 9.1-19a)	422-23
64.	Opening the Eyes (2 Kings 6.15-19; Acts 9.3, 6-8)	626
65.	Death and Restoration (2 Kings 9.14–11.20; Acts 9.19b-31)	430-32
66.	Good News amid a Foreign Army (2 Kings 6.24–7.20; Acts 10.1–11.18)	438
67.	Moving into New Territory (Judges 1.1–3.6; Acts 13–14)	450
68.	Escaping the Royal Guard (Judges 3.7-11; Acts 12.1-23)	459
69.	Judges 6–12 as One Component of Luke 16.1–18.8	467
70.	Decisive Gideon and the Steward (Judges 6.1–8.3; Luke 16.1-9)	468-69
71.	Rags and Riches: Gideon (Judges 8.4-35), and Lazarus (Luke 16.19-31)	469-70
72.	Reversal of Abimelech's Evil Kingdom (Judges 9; Luke 17.11-37)	470-71
73.	The Maverick Judge and the Woman (Judges 10.1–12.7; Luke 18.1-8)	471
74.	The Night Action (Judges 7.9-25; Luke 2.8-20, 25-35): Initial Summary Outline	475
75.	The Night Action (Judges 7; Luke 2): A Closer Comparison	476
76.	The Samson Story as a Frame (Judges 13–16; Luke 1–2; Acts 9.52–15.21)	490
77.	The Final Gathering (Judges 16.23-31; Acts 15.6-21)	495
78.	Seeking a True Home (Judges 17–18; Luke 19.1-9)	498
79.	Passion and Death: A Reversal (Judges 19; Luke 23.50–24.53)	504
80.	Judges 21 as One Thread in the Last Supper Text (Luke 22.1-30)	514
81.	Chronicles–Ezra–Nehemiah and Luke 1.1–4.22a: General Outline	522
82.	Preparation for the Davidic Reign (1 Chronicles 1–10; Luke 1.1-25)	524
83.	Priestly Service and Song (1 Chronicles 15–16; Luke 1.57-60)	526
84.	Prelude to a (New) Temple (1 Chronicles 21–22; Luke 2.1-20)	527

85.	Temple People and Piety (1 Chronicles 23–29; Luke 2.21-38)	528
86.	Taking Possession of the Temple (1 Chronicles 5–9; Luke 2.41-52)	530
87.	The Year, the Leaders	531
88.	Rebuilding Society	532
89.	1 Corinthians as One Component of Luke 22.1–Acts 15.35	546
90.	Block 1. 1 Corinthians 1–5 and Acts 1.1–5.11: General Outline	548
91.	Christ and the Temple Building (1 Corinthians 3.10-17; Acts 3.1-8; 4.11-12, 16)	557
92.	Block 2. Justice and Related Issues	560
93.	The Passover Mystery	563
94.	The Supper Texts	564
95.	The Death of the Just Man (Wisdom 1–5; Luke 22.66–23.49): An Outline—Incomplete and Simplified	576
96.	Confronting the Mindless (Jeremiah 5.21-25; Galatians 3.1-5)	591
97.	Episodes of Contrast and Conflict: The Judgment of the World (Daniel 1–6, 13, 14; 1 Corinthians 1–4)	595
98.	The Prophetic Visions of Building and Triumph (Daniel 7–12; 1 Corinthians 14–15)	595
99.	The Story of Tobit	600

Preface

In September 1972, while preparing for biblical examinations, I was struck by curious similarities between Deuteronomy and Matthew, and then by a variety of other long-distance connections, including strong continuities between the Elijah–Elisha narrative and Luke–Acts. It was a month that would color my life, leading me to spend decades moving over and back across very diverse parts of the Bible, from Genesis to the epistles.

When the examinations were over I looked more closely at the texts—I bought a Septuagint and started ploughing through unfamiliar Greek—and it slowly emerged that the connections were genuine. While the range of reference of the New Testament authors was often vast, even encyclopedic, they kept drawing on biblical narrative, especially on the foundational biblical history, Genesis–2 Kings ('the Primary History'), and above all on the Torah, particularly Deuteronomy, the book which encompasses the climactic discourses of the greatest of the ancient prophets, and which stands literally at the centre of Genesis–2 Kings. Some of the New Testament writers also made decisive use of the Elijah–Elisha account, the prophet-centered drama that intrudes climactically near the end of the Primary History.

At one level, of course, connections between the two Testaments are clear. The New Testament writers frequently cite the older scriptures, especially the Psalms and prophets. It is a centuries-old commonplace that 'the old is fulfilled in the new'. However, the dependence that was emerging in the slow trawl through the Septuagint was of a different kind, a dependence that was massive but unacknowledged. The evidence was indicating that the use of older texts had at least two levels: (1) overt or explicit: an obvious level, often poetic, especially from the Psalms and prophets; and (2) covert or implicit: an unacknowledged use of less poetic texts, especially of the Primary History. The two uses seemed to complement one another. The covert level, often consisting of less poetic texts, supplied many of the basic building materials. The overt level—the occasional quotations—provided a colorful way of expressing those underlying materials. What was important was that beneath the surface of the New Testament there lay a base of older texts, a dependence that was largely unseen or unacknowledged.

The idea of implicit connections between texts was not new. In 1955, for instance, C.F. Evans indicated that the centre of Luke's gospel had made heavy use of Deuteronomy. Raymond E. Brown maintained that the best literary models for the gospels consist of the lives of the prophets, especially the life of Elisha (1971: 86-104). James M. Robinson (1971a) showed that there is some form of link between some sayings of Matthew and some sayings of 1 Corinthians.

These observations were extremely valuable, but they were vague. Evans did not articulate the nature of the dependence between Luke and Deuteronomy. Brown seemed more interested in the general figures of Elijah and Elisha than in the actual text that describes them. And Robinson used a term that was also unclear—trajectory.

My own terminology was likewise deficient. I tended to use the phrase 'creative rewriting'. The term was so strange that when I first submitted a short article on the topic, the 're' got lost in the process of editing/typesetting, and the article appeared as 'Creative Writing…' (Brodie 1978). In the Summer of 1980, when I showed some of my work to

Joseph A. Fitzmyer, he asked if what I was claiming fitted into any ancient literary practice. It was a sobering moment. I was not able to answer him, and I began to realize that I would have to start again.

Since then help has arrived. Ideas or emphases that had been undeveloped have begun to blossom. These include: the literary dimension of the Bible; the role of the Septuagint; ancient rhetoric, including imitation; various ideas about midrash, inner-biblical hermeneutics, and rewritten Bible; and the vast burgeoning field of intertextuality. As a result, it is now frequently possible to unravel the genealogies of texts, the ways they depend on one another.

In the case of the New Testament, each writing builds on older scriptures and on preceding New Testament texts, particularly on the texts that precede immediately. They also build on many other background writings—ancient, Greco-Roman, contemporary—and they reflect a specific historical and social setting. Thus the New Testament is Christ-centered, but it expresses its vision of Christ through existing writings, especially through the ancient God-centered scriptures.

The purpose of this work is to outline the literary development of several of the New Testament writings and, while doing so, to unravel the Synoptic Problem—the well-known puzzle about the relationship between the first three gospels ('the Synoptics').

'Outline' is the key word. The New Testament is like a vast complex tapestry, and one volume cannot try to unravel all the levels of textual weaving. This work does indeed look closely at some levels of some texts, but the volume has already become bulky, and for several reasons it is appropriate, necessary even, to keep a focus on leading threads and to provide just an outline. This then is the goal: an outline that hopefully can be tested and developed by others.

The work has four parts:
I. General Introduction: Ancient Writing and its Context (Chapters 1–9)
II. The Overall Picture: Initial Evidence (Chapters 10–26)
III. Proto-Luke as Septuagint-Based (Argument 1): Supporting Evidence (Chapters 27–54)
IV. Appendices: Further, Exploratory Aspects of New Testament Intertextuality (Appendices 1–8)

The essence of this volume lies in Part II, in the outline of the overall picture of how the New Testament developed, from Matthew's brief *Logia* ('sayings/oracles') to Luke–Acts. The reader who is pressed for time can concentrate on this section, especially on Chapter 10.

However, the foundational argument for the entire presentation is in Part III, in the slow episode-by-episode demonstration of how one section of Luke–Acts—about twenty-five chapters—has a distinctive dependence on the Old Testament. Logically, this argument comes first, yet there are advantages to beginning with the overall picture—especially with Chapter 10.

The general conclusion to the entire volume is in Chapter 26.

The Appendices, giving exploratory aspects of further evidence, represent a small step on a research process that will require many years.

Several sections or aspects of this volume have already been published in identical or varied form. Published materials include essentially three chapters from the General Introduction (Chapters 1, 4, 5), seven from Part II (Chapters 11, 12, 13, 14, 20, 22, 24), ten from Part III (Chapters 28, 29, 30, 31, 33, 34, 38, 39, 47, 53), and part of Appendix 2 (see bibliography, Brodie). Until now it has not seemed possible to place the pieces together so that they form a single thesis.

This thesis requires patience. Tracing literary threads is slow work, and the ways of weaving vary greatly. Patience is also necessary for another reason. Biblical studies are plagued by a premature rush towards historical issues, without taking the necessary time to do the detailed preliminary literary homework.[1] Apart from a very brief sketch of possible history-related responses, this study stays with a thesis that is literary. When this literary thesis has been verified, then, and not till then, let the historical implications be considered.

---

1. This is true even in monumental multi-volume works, otherwise meticulous, such as those of Meier 1991–2001, and Dunn 2003b.

Acknowledgments

This book has dominated my life and it is not possible to acknowledge all who have contributed to its composition. It has become interwoven with all that I have met—all that led me to stumble over the idea, all who have encouraged it, all who by their criticism or opposition have forced me to keep trying to clarify and refine it. The Dominicans have been generous—the Sisters in Etrepagny, Normandy, who gave me hospitality in the early 1970s, and, beginning with Damian Byrne in Trinidad, successive colleagues who allowed me time and freedom, including the Dominican community in dear old Limerick.

Others too have been generous and patient—particularly my friends and family, especially my mother. One's nineties, it seems, can be a time of special spirit and grace.

The final years of writing and editing received particular help from David Noel Freedman, Pam Fox Kuhlken, Cheryl Exum, David Clines, and especially Duncan Burns and Peig McGrath, both of whom often stayed up late guiding the proofs into becoming a book.

Abbreviations

...	Indicates intermittent reference
??/?	Indicates uncertainty
AASF DHL	Annales Academiae Scientiarum Fennicae. Dissertationes Humanarum Litterarum
AB	Anchor Bible
ABD	David Noel Freedman (ed.), *The Anchor Bible Dictionary* (New York: Doubleday, 1992)
ABRL	Anchor Bible Reference Library
Acts' Setting	B.W. Winter A.D. Clarke (eds.) *The Book of Acts in Its First Century Setting*. I. *Ancient Literary Setting* (Grand Rapids: Eerdmans, 1993)
AGJU	Arbeiten zur Geschichte des antiken Judentums und des Urchristentums
ALBO	Analecta lovaniensia biblica et orientalia
ALL	*Archiv für lateinische Lexicographie und Grammatik*
AnBib	Analecta biblica
ANET	James B. Pritchard (ed.), *Ancient Near Eastern Texts Relating to the Old Testament* (Princeton: Princeton University Press, 1950)
ANRW	Hildegard Temporini and Wolfgang Haase (eds.), *Aufstieg und Niedergang der römischen Welt: Geschichte und Kultur Roms im Spiegel der neueren Forschung* (Berlin: W. de Gruyter, 1972–)
ASNU	Acta seminarii neotestamentici upsaliensis
AThANT	Abhandlungen zur Theologie des Alten und Neuen Testaments
ATS	Arbeiten zu Text und Sprache im alten Testament
BA	*Biblical Archaeologist*
BASOR	*Bulletin of the American Schools of Oriental Research*
BBB	Bonner biblische Beiträge
BEATAJ	Beiträge zur Erforschung des alten Testaments und des antiken Judentums
BETL	Bibliotheca ephemeridum theologicarum lovaniensium
BHT	Beiträge zur historischen Theologie
Bib	*Biblica*
BibOr	Biblica et orientalia
BIOSCS	*Bulletin of the International Organization for Septuagint and Cognate Studies*
BJS	Brown Judaic Studies
BTB	*Biblical Theology Bulletin*
BZ	*Biblische Zeitschrift*
BZAW	Beihefte zur *ZAW*
CBA	Catholic Biblical Association [of America]
CBQ	*Catholic Biblical Quarterly*
CBQMS	*Catholic Biblical Quarterly*, Monograph Series
CBRA	Collectanea Biblica et Religiosa Antiqua
ConBNT	Coniectanea biblica, New Testament
ConNT	Coniectanea Neotestamentica
CRBS	*Currents in Research: Biblical Studies*
CRINT	Compendia rerum iudaicarum ad Novum Testamentum
Crucial Bridge	T.L. Brodie, *The Crucial Bridge: The Elijah-Elisha Narrative as an Interpretive Synthesis of Genesis-Kings and a Literary Model for the Gospels* (Collegeville, MN: Liturgical Press, 2000)
CTSA	Catholic Theological Society of America
DBSup	*Dictionnaire de la Bible, Supplément*
EBB	*Elenchus bibliographicus biblicus*

EBib	Etudes bibliques
EH	Europäische Hochschulschriften
EKKNT	Evangelisch-Katholischer Kommentar zum Neuen Testament
ETL	*Ephemerides theologicae lovanienses*
ExpTim	*Expository Times*
Four Gospels	F. Van Segbroeck *et al.* (eds.), *The Four Gospels* (Festschrift Frans Neirynck; BETL, 100; 3 vols.; Leuven: University/Peeters, 1992)
FRLANT	Forschungen zur Religion und Literatur des Alten und Neuen Testaments
FthSt	Frankfurter theologische Studien
GTA	Göttinger theologische Arbeiten
HE	Eusebius, *Historia ecclesiastica*
HSM	Harvard Semitic Monographs
HTKNT	Herders theologischer Kommentar zum Neuen Testament
HTS	*Harvard Theological Studies*
HUCA	*Hebrew Union College Annual*
IBS	*Irish Biblical Studies*
IDBSup	*IDB*, Supplementary Volume
Int	*Interpretation*
JAAR	*Journal of the American Academy of Religion*
JBC	*The Jerome Biblical Commentary* (ed. R.E. Brown *et al.*; London: Geoffrey Chapman, 1968)
JBL	*Journal of Biblical Literature*
JHC	*Journal of Higher Criticism*
JJS	*Journal of Jewish Studies*
JR	*Journal of Religion*
JSNT	*Journal for the Study of the New Testament*
JSNTSup	*Journal for the Study of the New Testament*, Supplement Series
JSOT	*Journal for the Study of the Old Testament*
JSOTSup	*Journal for the Study of the Old Testament*, Supplement Series
KJV	King James version
LCL	Loeb Classical Library
LD	Lectio divina
LSJ	H.G. Liddell, Robert Scott and H. Stuart Jones, *Greek–English Lexicon* (Oxford: Clarendon Press, 9th edn, 1968)
NCCHS	*A New Catholic Commentary on Holy Scripture* (ed. R. Fuller *et al.*; London Thomas Nelson, 1969)
NJBC	*The New Jerome Biblical Commentary* (ed. R.E. Brown *et al.*; London: Geoffrey Chapman, 1990)
NovTSup	*Novum Testamentum*, Supplements
NT	New Testament
NTAbh	Neutestamentliche Abhandlungen
NTS	*New Testament Studies*
OBO	Orbis biblicus et orientalis
OCD	*Oxford Classical Dictionary*
ÖKT	Ökumenischer-taschenbuch Kommentar
OSTGU	Oriental Society Transactions, Glasgow University
OT	Old Testament
OTL	Old Testament Library
PCB	*Peake's Commentary on the Bible* (ed. M. Black *et al.*; London: Thomas Nelson, 1962)
PIBA	*Proceedings of the Irish Biblical Association*
RB	*Revue biblique*
REL	*Revue des Etudes Latines*
RevQ	*Revue de Qumran*
RHPR	*Revue d'histoire et de philosophie religieuses*
SANT	Studien zum Alten und Neuen Testament
SBL	Society of Biblical Literature
SBLASP	SBL Abstracts and Seminar Papers
SBLDS	SBL Dissertation Series

SBLSP	*SBL Seminar Papers* (Atlanta: Scholars Press)
SBT	Studies in Biblical Theology
SHANE	Studies in the History of the Ancient Near East
SJOT	*Scandinavian Journal of the Old Testament*
SJT	*Scottish Journal of Theology*
SNTA	Studiorum Novi Testamenta Auxilia
SNTS	Studiorum Novi Testamenti Societas
SNTSMS	Society for New Testament Studies Monograph Series
ST	*Studia theologica*
StdHREC	Studies in the History and Religion of Early Christianity
Str–B	[Hermann L. Strack and] Paul Billerbeck, *Kommentar zum Neuen Testament aus Talmud und Midrasch* (6 vols.; Munich: Beck, 1922–61)
SUNT	Studien zur Umwelt des Neuen Testaments
THKNT	Theologischer Handkommentar zum Neuen Testament
TLZ	*Theologische Literaturzeitung*
TRu	*Theologische Rundschau*
TS	*Theological Studies*
TU	Texte und Untersuchungen
UF	*Ugarit-Forschungen*
USQR	*Union Seminary Quarterly Review*
VT	*Vetus Testamentum*
VTSup	*Vetus Testamentum*, Supplements
WMANT	Wissenschaftliche Monographien zum Alten und Neuen Testament
WUNT	Wissenschaftliche Untersuchungen zum Neuen Testament
ZNW	*Zeitschrift für die neutestamentliche Wissenschaft*
ZTK	*Zeitschrift für Theologie und Kirche*

General Summary of the Volume

1. Background

Two features of recent research are particularly important to this study. The first is the publication of a critical edition of Q—the hypothetical sayings-source thought to have been used by Matthew and Luke (Robinson, Hoffmann and Kloppenborg [eds.] 2000). The new clarity concerning the hypothesis provides an improved opportunity for judging whether it should be retained or replaced. Rather than engaging Q directly, this study generally concentrates on offering an alternative hypothesis, one that in the long term is hopefully more verifiable and more encompassing.

The second feature is the new awareness of intertextuality. There is increasing evidence that writings, especially ancient writings, depend on earlier texts. This applies also to the New Testament, to the ways New Testament books are connected to one another and to other writings, especially the Old Testament/Septuagint. Criteria now exist for judging literary dependence and for tracing literary relationships and developments.

The purpose of this volume is to apply these criteria to the New Testament writings.

2. The Thesis

This volume's central thesis is that within Luke–Acts lies a stream of passages, a total of about twenty-five chapters, that stands apart. Three reasons indicate this apartness: (1) these passages have a distinctive intertextual dependence on the Septuagint, a dependence indicated by a wide range of verifiable connections; (2) the passages form a specific unity, coherent and complete, with a clear structure that is modeled precisely on one of the great prophetic histories of the Old Testament, the Elijah–Elisha narrative (1 Kgs 16.29–2 Kgs 13); (3) when this specific unity is seen on its own, it explains other New Testament data, especially about the gospels.

The stream of passages may be summarized under the following headings:
1. Jesus' infancy narrative: Luke 1–2.
2. Jesus' early ministry: 3.1–4.22a (except 3.7-9; 4.1-13); 7.1–8.3.
3. Jesus' journey to Jerusalem: 9.51–10.20; 16.1-9, 19-31; 17.11–18.8; 19.1-10.
4. Jesus' death and resurrection: chs. 22–24 (except 22.31-65).

1. The church's beginnings: Acts 1.1–2.42.
2. The church's early ministry: 2.43–5.42.
3. The church's move away from Jerusalem: 6.1–9.30.
4. The church's transformation, integrating the Gentiles: 9.31–15.35.

The simplest, best explanation for this Old Testament-related phenomenon is that it is the long-sought first version of Luke–Acts, what some scholars call Proto-Luke. The central thesis, therefore, is that Proto-Luke, with its heavy dependence on the Old Testament, underlies the development of the gospels.

This volume's auxiliary thesis is that Proto-Luke, apart from using the Old Testament directly, also presupposed an arrangement of *logia* ('sayings'), and used at least one major epistle—1 Corinthians. The *logia*, now found within Matthew 5 and 11, are largely based on Deuteronomy. These auxiliary sources clarify the nature of Proto-Luke, and they also clarify its influence—its foundational role in the development of the other gospels.

Once Proto-Luke is in place, it becomes relatively easy to understand how the other gospels emerged, each building on all that preceded: first Mark; then Matthew; next John; and finally Luke–Acts. This relationship between the gospels makes the Q hypothesis unnecessary. The systematic relationship of Proto-Luke to the Septuagint gives it a verifiability which Q does not have.

The overall picture is of a central line of scriptural dependence running from the foundation of Old Testament narrative (Genesis–Kings) into the heart of the New Testament:

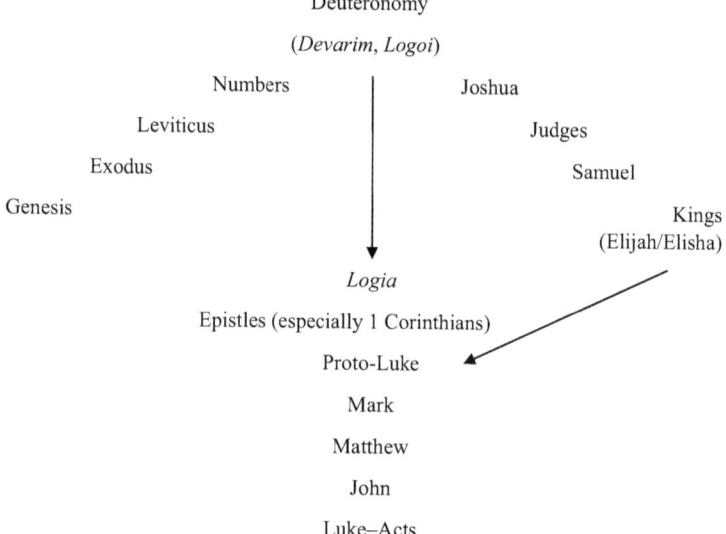

This is the literary backbone. The full pattern of dependence is far more complex, with influences from other writings and from the intense social and historical events of the first century.

Matthew's *Logia*, for instance, does not rely on Deuteronomy alone; it colors the sayings with wisdom from Ben Sirach. Others do something similar; they use Genesis–Kings, but they combine it with something else, and they improve the wording through echoes or quotes from the prophets or Psalms—poetic language which, through its universal nature, tends to open out the sometimes-restricted language of prose.

But the literary backbone has advantages: it is simple; it is subject to verification; and it provides an anchor for other New Testament discussions, including discussions of history.

The key background scriptural texts—Deuteronomy and the Elijah–Elisha narrative—are themselves complementary. Deuteronomy consists of the climactic discourses of the greatest prophet. The Elijah–Elisha narrative tells of prophets who sometimes echoed Moses. Within the Bible's foundational narrative (Genesis–Kings), Deuteronomy and Elijah–Elisha constitute, respectively, the center and the final prophetic interlude. Deuteronomy, at the center, is like the peak of a pyramid (Freedman 1991), and the use of Deuteronomy opens the way to the incorporation of material from the whole corpus of Genesis–2 Kings.

3. Demonstrating the Thesis

a. *The General Introduction (Chapters 1–9)*

The General Introduction sets the scene. The opening chapters (Chapters 1–4) highlight key aspects of ancient writing, especially the pervasive practice of reworking existing texts, and the presence of a central quality of artistry. However, detecting sources is often difficult, so it is necessary to set out criteria for judging literary dependence (Chapter 5). The criteria fall under three headings: external plausibility; significant similarities; and the intelligibility of the differences.

Chapter 6 distinguishes between orality—a central quality of ancient writing—and dependence on oral tradition. Concerning oral tradition, this chapter also distinguishes between history and myth—between oral tradition for which there is historical evidence, and oral tradition that fits into the background of the Jewish myth of an oral tradition reaching back to Moses.

Chapters 7–8 survey institutions and conditions that suggest that writers worked in communication with one another, not in isolation. Finally, Chapter 9 indicates aspects of the early Christian community: on the one hand, their unique spiritual experience; on the other, their continuity with older institutions, including the older scriptures.

b. *The Central Thesis: Proto-Luke (Chapters 10–14)*

Chapters 10–14 are pivotal to the whole volume. They set forth both the central thesis, based on Proto-Luke's use of the Old Testament (Chapters 10–11 [Unit 1]), and the auxiliary thesis, concerning Proto-Luke's relationship to some *New Testament* texts, namely Matthew's *Logia*, and 1 Corinthians (Chapters 12–14 [Unit 2]).

Chapter 10 lays the foundation for discussing Proto-Luke. First, it surveys the step-by-step process of the investigation, from initial observations about Luke–Acts' general connection with the Septuagint, to the final conclusion about the distinctive connection between the Septuagint and part of Luke–Acts—a part to be named Proto-Luke. Second, the chapter zeroes in on some of Proto-Luke's methods of adaptation. And finally, Chapter 10 summarizes the three key arguments supporting the Proto-Luke hypothesis:

Argument 1:   Distinctive dependence on the Septuagint
Argument 2:   Unity of content and structure
Argument 3:   Subsequent verification: the hypothesis works; it clarifies gospel origins.

Argument 1, being very extensive, receives a special space: Chapters 27–54 (Part III). These chapters are an episode-by-episode demonstration of dependence on the Old Testament.

Chapter 11 presents Argument 2.

Before proceeding to Argument 3—Proto-Luke's role in the development of the gospels—it is useful to take account of further elements underlying Proto-Luke itself, particularly Matthew's *Logia* and at least one epistle, 1 Corinthians (Chapters 12–14 [Unit 2]).

The arguments establishing Matthew's *Logia* (Chapter 12) are of the same nature as those for Proto-Luke: (1) distinctive dependence on the Old Testament, in this case Deuteronomy; (2) coherence of content and structure; (3) subsequent verification.

Chapter 13 indicates that what is true of Matthew's *Logia* is also true of 1 Corinthians: it depends hugely on Deuteronomy, though in a different way; and there are initial indications that 1 Corinthians depends also on Matthew's *Logia*. In other words, the epistle used both a text (Matthew's *Logia*) and the source behind the text (Deuteronomy).

Chapter 14 develops the sequence. On the basis of the supper texts (1 Cor. 11.16-34; Lk. 22.14-30), the chapter shows that Proto-Luke transformed the written text of 1 Corinthians. (Other evidence corroborates this. See Appendix 2.)

These chapters (12–14) reveal something of the complexity of Proto-Luke, its blending of Old Testament sources and New Testament writings. They also show, through Proto-Luke's reworking of 1 Corinthians, that it is not only Old Testament texts that are transformed; so are those belonging to the New Testament.

c. *From Proto-Luke to the Four Gospels and Acts (Chapters 15–25)*

Chapters 15–25 outline how the process of transforming continued. Proto-Luke, and the transforming of Proto-Luke, provide an entry to the other gospels and Acts (Argument 3).

Chapters 15–18 (Unit 3): The gospel that is most immediately indebted to Proto-Luke is Mark. Mark obviously has it own distinct sources, genre, and theology. But is also draws heavily on Proto-Luke and on Proto-Luke's sources. Instead of two parts centered on an assumption into heaven, Mark gives a text that is centered on a transfiguration. Instead of a second part that is largely concerned with the disciples (much of Acts 1.1–15.35), Mark reshapes the Acts episodes concerning the disciples, and places them in the life of Jesus (there are abundant connecting details). Instead of using the Elijah–Elisha narrative as a basis for a form of historiography, he uses it for a genre that is closer to biography (again there are numerous connections). And there are indications of Mark's use of at least one epistle (1 Peter).

Chapters 19–23 (Unit 4): Matthew expanded Mark, partly by using Mark's sources, including Proto-Luke, but especially by deuteronomizing Mark—by using Deuteronomy and its discourses as a model for a new form of gospel. The influence of the Mosaic book is extensive. Canonical Matthew also incorporated the *Logia*, and used at least one epistle (Romans).

Chapter 24: Matthew's discourses in turn provided a partial model for John, and John also used Matthew's sources, especially Mark.

Chapter 25: Finally, canonical Luke–Acts expanded Proto-Luke in a way that developed and synthesized earlier accounts of Jesus. In the course of this synthesizing, canonical Luke–Acts reshaped the Sermon on the Mount into the Sermon on the Plain—a bold act, but perfectly understandable in the context of ancient intertextuality. The relationship between Matthew and Luke—Matthew adapted Proto-Luke, and Matthew in turn was reshaped by canonical Luke—explains most of the similarities that give rise to the theory of Q.

The Appendices consider other aspects of New Testament intertextuality, especially in the epistles.

d. *Overall Summary and Conclusion (Chapter 26)*

This volume does not deal with issues of history and theology, not even with trying to decide whether the author of Luke–Acts is also the author of Proto-Luke. Such issues are important, but they would need a whole other volume. It is not practical to attempt to discuss them fully now. The only thing given here, in the overall summary and conclusion (Chapter 26), is a minuscule sketch of some of the possible categories of response to the intertextual nature of the New Testament.

Map of Travel Times

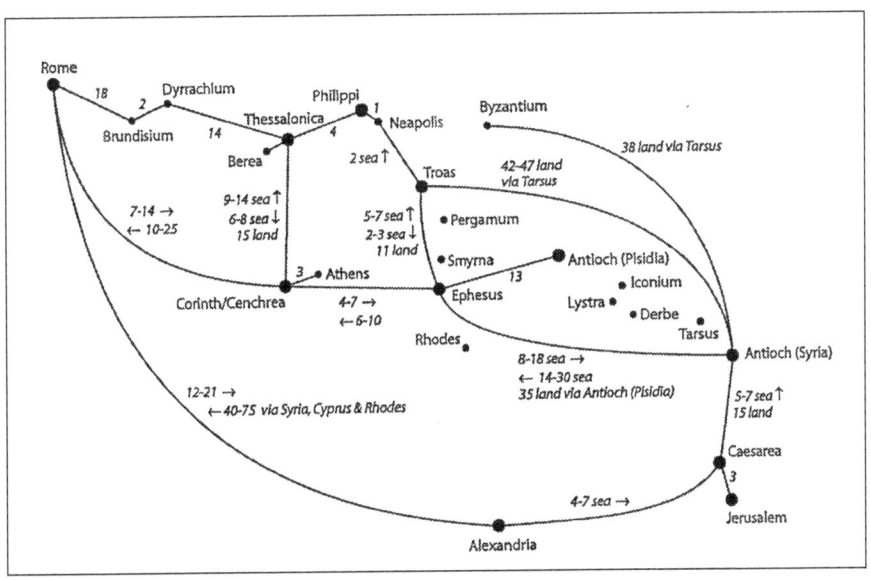

'Average' Travel Times (in Days) in the Ancient Mediterranean

Assumptions: (1) clear sailing routes and Roman roads, (2) good weather and a fair wind, (3) minimal stopovers, (4) ships, and (5) land travel by foot at a rate of 20 miles per day.

> The churches from A.D. 30 to 70 had the motivation and the means to communicate often and in depth with each other... News and information could be spread relatively quickly between the congregations in the great cities of the empire, and from there into the surrounding regions... Many churches were less than a week's travel away from a main hub in the Christian network.
>
> —Michael B. Thompson, 'The Holy Internet'[1]

---

1. 'The Holy Internet: Communication Between Churches in the First Century Generation', in Richard Bauckham, *The Gospel for All Christians: Rethinking the Gospel Audiences* (Grand Rapids: Eerdmans, 1998), pp. 49-70, especially p. 61 (map) and p. 68 (quote).

Part I

General Introduction: Ancient Writing and Its Context

Orientational Introduction to Chapters 1–9:
The Written Page and its Social Context

This general introduction (Chapters 1–9) sets the scene for discussing the writing of the New Testament.

At first, in Chapters 1–5, the focus is on the written page. These five chapters give an overview of key aspects of the whole ancient phenomenon of writing: the nature of texts, the relationships between them, and the criteria for tracing those relationships. In discussing the Old Testament, emphasis is given to texts that are important to this study—Deuteronomy, Judges, the Elijah–Elisha narrative, and Chronicles.

Then, Chapter 6, the focus shifts from the page to something behind it—the notion of oral tradition. Oral communication is central to life, and was doubly so in ancient times, particularly in Judaism. Yet, though its ethos and rhythms pervade the New Testament, it does not account for how the New Testament was written. It is necessary, therefore, before proceeding, to assess the claims of oral tradition.

Finally, in Chapters 7–9, the focus moves away from the page itself to aspects of the social contexts in which the page lived and flourished: in schools and synagogues; in a world of relatively easy communication; and among those who became known as Christians—a religious movement that, despite its radicalism and uniqueness, retained and adapted many of Judaism's institutions, including its central writings.

1

The Greco-Roman Tradition: Writing as Rhetorical Imitation[*]

> From five centuries before Christ up to the 19th century older texts are regarded as normative for later texts... We, in the 20th century, find it hard to let go of our ideal of creativity and originality, and it is difficult or even impossible for us to accept a definition of art as 'the perfect imitation'.
>
> —Ellen van Wolde (1989: 44, 45)

Before looking at the literature of the New Testament it is first necessary to look at literature as a whole, literature as it was composed in the larger Greco-Roman world. The purpose of this chapter is to indicate that the Greco-Roman practice of literary imitation provides at least a partial guide to the evangelists' way of reworking and transforming various texts, especially the Old Testament. The chapter consists of six parts: (1) the broad context within which imitation is to be examined; (2) the theory of imitation; (3) the practice of imitation; (4) imitation and historiography; (5) the Old Testament and the likelihood of Luke's use of imitation; (6) the Synoptic Problem and the need to cope with authorial complexity.

1. *Imitation: The Broad Context*

There are two fundamental differences between the way literary texts are composed in modern times and the way in which they were composed by Greco-Roman writers.

The first difference is largely concerned with content. Unlike modern writers, who usually manifest the Romantic 'preoccupation with otherness' and who seek novel content that is new and different, previous writers, even till around 1800 CE, were generally extremely careful to preserve, at least in some way, the heritage passed on from preceding generations (Ong 1971: 255-83 [255-61]). No ancient text advocates or manifests sheer innovation. Examples of preservation and re-use range from the Babylonian reworking of the Sumerian heritage to Milton's sifting and recasting of the Homeric-based epic tradition.[1]

The reason for this deep-seated custom of preservation and re-use seems to lie, in part at least, in a feeling that existing knowledge, stored largely in precious handwritten texts, was not to be taken for granted but was to be penetrated and clarified. This feeling lasted until about 1800, that is, until the continued use of the printing press, especially as manifested in the French *Encyclopédie* (1751–72), finally led to a situation in which ancient knowledge was taken for granted.[2]

---

[*] This chapter is a revision of 'Greco-Roman Imitation of Texts...', in C.H. Talbert (ed.), *Luke–Acts: New Perspectives* (New York: Crossroad, 1984), pp. 17-46.

1. See Lambert 1960: 2, 6: 'The ancients constantly rewrote old texts... The (Babylonian) *Descent of Ishtar*, to take the obvious example, is nothing but a free rewriting of the Sumerian *Descent of Inanna*'. See also Greene 1963: 363-418; Bowra 1945: 194-247 (195-97).

2. Ong 1971: 276-79. It has also been argued by French philosopher M. Foucault in his analysis of the presuppositions of knowledge (knowledge's substratum or 'archaeology') (Foucault 1966 [ET 1970]),

Whatever the full reasons, the fact is that, until 1800, writing, including original writing, involved a strong element of preservation.

Among the Greeks this widespread feeling for preserving was sharpened by a particular appreciation of the value of imitating.[3] The general idea of imitation, *mimēsis*, enjoyed immense prestige, for it was used by Plato to describe the whole world of nature (the natural world is a *mimēsis* of the eternal unchanging world) and by Aristotle, who said that imitation was natural to human beings, to describe all of art (art imitates nature).[4] However, it was Isocrates, Aristotle's older contemporary, who used this prestigious word precisely with reference to verbal composition: in verbal composition, said Isocrates, the student should imitate his teacher.[5] Thus it became customary among Greco-Roman writers to speak not of a process of preserving, but of a process of imitating. Imitation then is not only a question of style; it is, above all, a question of content. It was acceptable not only because the general tendency was to preserve the heritage of the past but also because that heritage was not copyrighted or individualized, but was rather regarded as common property.[6] What was not acceptable was sheer invention, the fabrication of plots or myths that were unrelated to the common traditions.[7] One had to show solid roots. Quintilian (c. 95 CE) sums up a long tradition when he comments that 'although invention came first and is all-important, it is expedient to imitate whatever has been invented with success'.[8]

---

that until 1800 it was presumed that writings communicated, not so much humanity and humanity's doings, as a whole natural order, something permanent of which humanity was just a part. Writings, therefore, were not occasional things; they were truly representative, representative even of the deepest reality (pp. 32-59 [ET pp. 17-45]). This was particularly the case with the greatest classical and biblical writings; these texts had been uniquely close to representing the natural order. Any writer then who wished to express reality would have to build carefully on previous writers.

But around 1800, the idea of *humanity* became detached from that of *a natural order*, and, thus detached, humanity was seen as something not of permanence and order but of changing time—of history (pp. 229-33 [ET pp. 217-21]). There had of course always been historical writing—but with the presupposition that even the description of specific events or individual acts were representative of a greater order. In 1800, however, the focus shifted to people in their individuality and to the detail of specific moments, and consequently a new importance was given to history. Thus Foucault (p. 232 [ET p. 220]) refers to this shift of presuppositions as a change from order to history ('cette mutation...de l'Ordre à l'Histoire').

3. The study of imitation has been rather in abeyance in recent times. The *Oxford Classical Dictionary* (*OCD*) did not deal with it directly, and the *Princeton Encyclopedia of Poetry and Poetics* (Preminger [ed.] 1975) begins its treatment of imitation by noting that it is only now that the term is coming back after its banishment in the nineteenth century. The following studies are particularly useful: Fiske 1920: 14-63, 476-91; White 1935: 3-19; Reiff 1959; Greene 1982: 54-80 (I am grateful to Professor Greene of Yale for providing a section of his manuscript before its publication). See also Clark 1951; Steiner 1975: 253-55; Kennedy 1980: 116-19. Auerbach (1953) is not immediately relevant to this study.

4. On *mimēsis* in Plato, see McKeon 1936: 3-16. See especially Plato, *Republic* 3.392D–394C; 4.500C-E. Plato's thought also provided some of the environment for the New Testament emphasis on the ethical imitation of Christ (Thysman 1966: 140). On *mimēsis* in Aristotle, see McKeon 1936: 16-26. See, for example, Aristotle, *Physics* 2.2.194a22, 2.8.199a15-17; *Poetics* 9.1451b9; on imitation as natural to humans, see *Poetics* 4.1448b4-23.

5. Isocrates, *Against the Sophists* 17-18.

6. See especially Isocrates, *Panegyricus* 8-9; Horace, *Ars Poetica* 131. See Fiske 1920: 39-40; White 1935: 6-7.

7. Isocrates, for instance, praises 'not those who seek to speak on subjects on which no one has spoken before' but those who speak on established subjects in a new and better way (*Panegyricus* 10). And Callimachus (hymn 5 ['On the Bath of Pallas'], 56) proclaims: 'The account (*mythos*) is not my own; it is from others'. See Fiske 1920: 33-34; White 1935: 6.

8. Quintilian, *Institutio Oratoria* (trans. H.E. Butler; LCL; Cambridge: Harvard University Press, 1960), 10.2.1.

The second difference between ancient and modern writers is somewhat more concerned with form. Unlike modern writing, which is generally geared to the eye, to being seen on the page, previous writing was largely geared to the ear, to being read aloud (Ong 1971: 1-22 [1-4]). This aural aspect was a development of the concern for sound that prevailed in times of purely oral communication (Ong 1977: 214-16). There are three periods: that of textless oral communication (before the advent of writing); that in which writing after its invention continued to be pervaded by the rhythms and formulas of oral communication (c. 3000 BCE–1800 CE); and the modern period, which began with people like the Romantic poet Samuel Taylor Coleridge and was furthered especially by the New Criticism of the 1950s, in which the text very often loses almost all traces of orality and in which the reader, in order to understand the text, has to see it on the page (Ong 1977: 213-29 [216]). The essential point is that until about 1800, writing was significantly oral in form, so that the formulary style of, say, Edmund Spenser's *Faerie Queene* is basically that of oral performance, and Tudor prose style contains many of the traits of oral speech (Webster 1976; Ong 1971: 23-47; Ong 1977: 195-99).

Among the Greeks, the general pervasiveness of oral rhythms was developed and refined through the precise craft of rhetoric, especially through the rhetorical teaching of Isocrates and Aristotle.[9] Rhetoric was directed toward improving oral delivery, especially in the law courts and public assemblies, but since speeches were often written beforehand and because, in any case, literature reflected oral patterns, the rules of rhetoric became the rules of literary composition.[10] The deliberateness of the process of composition was captured partly in the word 'text'—a word which, coming as it does from the Latin *texere*, 'to weave', suggests something woven; and in ancient Greece and Rome, writing was sometimes compared to the craft of weaving a fabric (Scheid and Svenbro 1996: 141-55). Thus the weaving of texts—the composition of literature—became of crucial importance for the rhetorician.[11] Nor was rhetoric confined to one type of literature. On the contrary, to an extent that is now difficult to imagine, rhetoric pervaded the system of education and almost every kind of writing, even poetic.[12] Long after the fall of Rome, rhetoric so maintained its influence that eventually it could be said that rhetoric 'encapsulated the most ancient, central, and pervasive tradition of verbalization and of thought known to mankind at least in the West' (Ong 1977: 214).

The pervasiveness of oral traits in ancient texts may at times cause confusion: it may lead to the premature conclusion that a particular text is dependent on oral tradition. But that does not follow. All that follows is that the text, whatever its origin, is aural, that it has been composed with a view to oral delivery.[13] Dependence on oral tradition must be shown on grounds other than the orality of the text.

9. On rhetoric, see Kennedy 1980: 3-160.
10. See Lesky 1966: 590: 'Isocrates achieved his strongest influence in the realm of Greek literature through his perfection of attic literary prose'.
11. Thus the rhetorician's reading matter as outlined by Quintilian consists of the whole range of Greco-Roman literature (*Inst. Orat.* 10.1).
12. For a summary of the way rhetoric pervaded Greco-Roman education, especially in the first century CE, and for references to the key works on education by M.P. Nilsson, H.I. Marrou, and D.L. Clark, see Kurz 1980b: 192-94. On the supremacy of rhetoric, see Dalton 1962: 438-524; Baldwin 1924: 224-25.
13. The orality of the Mishnah, for instance, does not prove that the text depends on oral tradition. As Neusner (1979: 59-75 [66]) comments: 'The sole fact in our hands is that Mishnah has been so formulated as to facilitate memorization'. Nor does the orality of Hebrew poetry prove its oral origin; see the review of Stuart 1976 by Cooper 1979. Parry (1971) and Lord (1964) have rightly pointed to the profound orality of Homeric verse, but their conclusion that such orality indicates an origin that is oral and not written is much disputed. R. Lattimore (1951: 37), for instance, admires Parry's work but does not know what conclusion to draw. Lesky (1966: 73) shows even greater ambiguity.

The essential point from all that has been said is that Greco-Roman writing, in varying degrees, was both imitative and rhetorical (oral-aural). Nor were these two elements unrelated to one another. Rather, it is through one that we may better understand the other. It was in the context of teaching rhetoric and of learning from other rhetorician-writers that imitation was emphasized and refined. As Cicero said, speaking in the context of imitation: 'Let this then be my first counsel, that we show the student [of rhetoric] whom to copy'.[14]

Therefore, our first and rather general conclusion is that in Greco-Roman literary composition the form or forms may have been largely oral, following various traits of oral verbalization, but both the form and especially the content were significantly determined by a desire to preserve the work of previous artists or, more precisely, to imitate previous literature. However, this broad conclusion needs refinement and illustration. It is therefore necessary to examine both the theory and practice of imitation more closely. First, the theory.

2. Literary Imitation: The Theory

There is no single clear-cut theory of literary imitation. This is due in part to the fact that the subject matter is not always clearly defined: literary imitation is frequently treated in conjunction with the idea of imitation in general, particularly pedagogic imitation.[15] It is also due to the fact that the subject matter is inherently difficult: insofar as literary imitation is concerned with the translation and interpretation of texts, it partakes in the general complexity and elusiveness of hermeneutical theory. We are dealing with an art, not an exact science.[16]

What is found among Greco-Roman writers, therefore, is not a single coherent theory but a series of descriptions and metaphors concerning various aspects of imitation. These references indicate first of all that imitation is a multi-faceted concept comprising different activities. The activities include:

Imitation of a teacher or of a living artist. This type of living contact was especially helpful to the beginner. Among the Greeks it was emphasized particularly by Isocrates,[17] and among the Romans, by Cicero.[18]

Reading. No single teacher or model could match the store of good verbal composition to be found in books, so reading was regarded as indispensable. Horace, for instance, recommended the incessant reading of the Greeks 'by day and…by night'.[19] Dionysius of Halicarnassus emphasized that constant reading imparts affinity of style.[20] Quintilian regarded careful, repeated reading as a prelude to imitation.[21]

Paraphrase. Paraphrase was of different kinds, sometimes staying very close to the original and at other times involving considerable changes. Quintilian advised that paraphrase

---

14. Cicero, *De Oratore* 2.21.90.
15. See Quintilian, *Inst. Orat.* 10.2.2-4.
16. For a study of the inherent artistry and complexity of language and interpretation, see Steiner 1975: 110-47 (especially 110-15), 220-35, 274-301, 460-62.
17. *Against the Sophists* 17-18; *Antidosis* 175, 301-303.
18. Cicero, *De Oratore* 2.21.89-90.
19. Horace, *Ars Poetica* 268-69.
20. Dionysius of Halicarnassus, *On Imitation* Frag. 6 Us.
21. Quintilian, *Inst. Orat.* 10.1.19-20. See Fiske 1920: 36-37.

(*paraphrasis*) should have a touch of daring, that it should compress and expand with considerable freedom.[22] Isocrates recommended that the same text be paraphrased again and again in different ways.[23]

Inventive imitation. Most Greco-Roman writing involved a tense blend of *imitatio* and *inventio* (creativity), a combining of old material with new. Thus, while Quintilian took it for granted that a large part of art consists of imitation (*artis pars magna contineatur imitatione*), he also realized that sheer imitation is not sufficient (*imitatio per se ipsa non sufficit*) and pointed out that every art involves *inventio* not only at its inception but also throughout its continuing existence.[24] Much of what Greco-Roman writers have to say about imitation is concerned precisely with this rather unpredictable blending of fidelity and creativity, a subject to which we must return later.

Emulation. From the beginning, imitation was accompanied by a certain spirit of rivalry or emulation (Gk., *zēlos*; Lat., *emulatio*), by a desire to transform the subtext or model text into a text that would be as good as the first or even better. Isocrates engaged in and invited rivalry.[25] Dionysius of Halicarnassus spoke as often of emulation as he does of imitation.[26] This spirit of emulation seems to have been motivated by a desire not so much to destroy as to fulfill, to move from the old text to a text that would be nearer to the contemporary world and to a certain ideal of perfection. Isocrates advised the abandonment of any literary field in which perfection had been attained.[27] Phaedrus stated that in a spirit not of envy but of emulation he brought to perfection the work of Aesop.[28] Quintilian hoped that continued striving would finally result in the birth of the perfect orator (*illum oratorem perfectum*).[29] In addition to this rather idealistic striving for literary perfection, there was also a certain nationalistic rivalry, which impelled Roman writers to equal and surpass their older Greek counterparts.

Contamination. Contaminatio consisted of fusing several texts or parts of texts into a new unity. The idea was to select and synthesize the best elements of a tradition. Dionysius of Halicarnassus advocated that the writer isolate and imitate specific strengths of several previous writers.[30] Cicero spoke admiringly of a painter who used five models in order to draw one figure.[31] (Later, however, Cicero felt it better to use only one model.[32]) Quintilian also, realizing that each model has flaws, advocated a process of selection and spoke admiringly of the way Cicero, through constant imitation, had combined in himself 'the force (*vim*) of Demosthenes, the copious flow (*copiam*) of Plato and the charm (*iucunditatem*) of Isocrates'.[33]

Such, in brief, are the main activities associated with the general practice of imitation. Now it is necessary to examine more closely the most crucial of these activities—namely,

22. Quintilian, *Inst. Orat.* 1.9.2.
23. Isocrates, *Panegyricus* 7-8. See Fiske 1920: 36-37.
24. Quintilian, *Inst. Orat.* 10.2.1, 4-8.
25. Isocrates, *Panegyricus* 8.1.88. See White 1935: 11-12; Fiske 1920: 40-50.
26. See, e.g., Dionysius, *Lysias* 3-4.
27. Isocrates, *Panegyricus* 3-6.
28. Aesop, *Fables*, i, prologue; iv, 20; ii, epilogue.
29. Quintilian, *Inst. Orat.* 10.2.9.
30. Dionysius of Halicarnassus, *The Ancient Orators* 4; see also *Lysias* 13.
31. Cicero, *De Inventione* 2.1-5.
32. Cicero, *De Oratore* 2.22.93.
33. Quintilian, *Inst. Orat.* 10.2.14-15, 24; 10.1.108.

inventive imitation, the process that combines the basic elements of imitation and creativity.

When Greco-Roman theorists spoke of imitation, they generally referred to inventive imitation. Their comments indicate that such imitation involved two moments: meditation and transformation. 'Meditation' refers to the various ways of getting inside the source text(s): Dionysius of Halicarnassus advocated a careful comparative analysis of several authors, and he spoke of inspecting the text.[34] Cicero referred to the wholehearted contemplation (*omni animo intueretur*) of a living model.[35] Quintilian advocated an inspection of the text (*introspectis penitus virtutibus*) that would see beyond its superficial aspect to its underlying qualities.[36] For Longinus, who wrote perhaps around 80 CE, a source text is something with which one becomes deeply involved—it is like a body one wrestles with, a vapour one is impregnated by, or a light which opens a path to the self.[37]

'Transformation' refers to the various creative processes by which the text is given a new form, a new kind of existence. The extent of this transformation is often considerable (see White 1935: 9-11). At least three authors—Cicero, Quintilian and Horace—explicitly discouraged word-for-word adaptation.[38] Horace furthermore advised the imitator to avoid well-worn easy paths or a mode of imitating that is constricted and rule-bound.[39] Far from being a slave, the imitator can be a pioneer, one who uses old material to break new ground.[40] A number of writers compared the work of the imitator to the way the bee collects material from different flowers and transforms it into something new.[41] Seneca used the image of honey-making and also compared the imitated source to food which has to be totally digested and transformed before it becomes part of the body, and to a father whose likeness to his son is largely hidden.[42] He also compared the blending of many sources with the blending of many voices in a chorus.[43]

The conclusion from this brief survey of virtually all known extant sources is that imitation is not a narrow category of literary dependence. It is, rather, a whole world of transformation, the broad context within which diverse writers combine tradition and innovation. It is not tidy and predictable. On the contrary, since it is a complex arena of artistry, it allows for constant surprises.

3. Literary Imitation: The Practice

Imitation was extremely widespread. A brief survey of the main categories of literary art shows that it pervaded almost every one of them. In lyric poetry it is found in Rome's leading lyric authors, Catullus (84–54 BCE)[44] and Horace (65–8 BCE) (Balme 1969: 50-61). As Horace put it, he 'made Aeolian song at home in Italian poetry'.[45] Yet his way of

---

34. Dionysius of Halicarnassus, *The Ancient Orators* 4; see also Kennedy 1980: 348.
35. Cicero, *De Oratore* 2.21.89.
36. Quintilian, *Inst. Orat.* 10.2.16.
37. Longinus, *On the Sublime* 13.2–14.1.
38. Cicero, *De Optimo Genere Oratorum* 14; *De Finibus* 3.4.15; Quintilian, *Inst. Orat.* 1.9.2; Horace, *Ars Poetica* 133.
39. Horace, *Ars Poetica* 131-32, 134-35.
40. Horace, *Epistle to Maecenas* 1.19.21-34; Lucretius, *De Rerum Natura* 4.1-5.
41. Horace, *Odes* 4.2.27-32; Seneca, *Letters* 84.3, 5. For a history of the analogy of the bee, see von Stackelberg 1956.
42. Seneca, *Letters* 84.5-8.
43. Seneca, *Letters* 84.9.
44. On Catullus, see Balme 1969: 46-50.
45. Horace, *Odes* 3.30.13-14.

transmuting that ancient Greek heritage was rather novel. He did it, as he himself says, 'by arts not hitherto imparted'.[46]

In pastoral poetry, forms of imitation are found in the most outstanding Latin work, that of Virgil. His *Eclogues* are significantly indebted to the pioneering pastoral poetry of Theocritus, a Sicilian (c. 300–260 BCE), so that it may be said of the eighth *Eclogue*: 'Out of the Theocritean material Virgil has created something quite new, a kind of didactic pastoral' (Coleman 1969: 117).

In didactic poetry, the leading Latin works show complex forms of imitation. *De Rerum Natura* of Lucretius (c. 94–55 BCE) involves a fusion and synthesis of several Greek sources (Cox 1969: 134-45 [143]), and Virgil's *Georgics* reacts to and reflects the work of Lucretius (Cox 1969: 145-53).

In comedy, the leading Roman writers are Plautus (died c. 186 BCE) and Terence (c. 190–160 BCE). Again there is considerable indebtedness to the Greek precedent, particularly to the comedies of Menander (c. 341–290 BCE). Greek scenes are given a Roman setting or ethos, and different Greek plays or scenes are fused (*contaminatio*) into a new unity.[47]

Within satire, which was primarily a Roman genre, the pioneering work of Lucilius (died c. 101 BCE) had considerable influence on the *Satires* of Horace, but Horace regarded Lucilius's work as slow-flowing muddy water that needed to be purified, and so his mode of imitation was crisp and critical (Higginbotham 1969: 227; see also Fiske 1920). Horace provided a model for some of the work of Persius (34–62 CE), and Persius in turn helped, to some degree at least, to pave the way for the biting satires of Juvenal (c. 60–130 CE) (Higginbotham 1969: 238-42).

In tragic drama, the surviving evidence indicates that Roman writers—authors such as Ennius (239–169 BCE), Accius (c. 170–90 BCE), and Ovid (43 BCE–17 CE)—made massive use of their Greek predecessors. In Seneca (c. 4 BCE–56 CE), the only Roman tragic dramatist whose work has not largely perished, this indebtedness is powerfully evident: Seneca's plays involve a systematic reshaping of the works of Aeschylus, Sophocles, and Euripides (see especially F.J. Miller 1907: 455-96).

In epic poetry we encounter the most esteemed and powerful work of the first century CE, the apex of Roman literary achievement—Virgil's *Aeneid* (completed around 19 BCE). Here the use of imitation is comprehensive and complex. The *Aeneid* synthesizes and reshapes the best of previous dramatic and epic writers, whether Greek, Alexandrian, or Roman, but, above all, it involves a systematic rethinking and Romanizing of the foundational work of Homer.[48] In C.G. Hardie's summary (1970: 1126), Virgil's debt to Homer 'ranges from overall structure, the compositional device of retrospective narrative...the adaptation of whole episodes, games...catalogues...to the transformation of incidents, the imitation of similes...and of turns of thought or phrase'.

The list of indebtedness is almost monotonous, but it acts as a corrective to the widespread modern presupposition that literary originality and excellence largely exclude indebtedness.

It is not possible, at least in a few pages, to illustrate in detail the many modes of adaptation used in the widespread practice of imitation. All that can be given are a few samples. At the risk of over-simplifying, these adaptations are put here under precise headings: elaboration, compression, fusion, substitution of images, positivization, internalization, form-change.

---

46. Horace, *Odes* 4.9.3. See Leishman 1956: 89-110 (102-105).
47. Harriott 1969: 201, 215-22; see also *OCD*, Plautus, Terence.
48. On Virgil's general use of sources, see Conington 1963: II, xix-xliv; Lee 1981. On Virgil and Homer, see Conway 1931; and especially Knauer 1979.

a. *Elaboration*

When Euripides described Hippolytus's fatal chariot accident, he spent one line on Hippolytus's head.[49] 'And his dear head [was] pounded on the rocks'. Five centuries later, Seneca elaborated in vivid detail:[50]

> The ground was reddened with a trail of blood;
> His head was dashed from rock to rock, his hair
> Torn off by thorns, his handsome face despoiled
> By flinty stones; wound after wound destroyed
> For ever that ill-fated comeliness.

b. *Compression or Synthesis*

Euripides describes in some detail the ominous thunder that preceded Hippolytus's accident:[51]

> When we were entering the lonely country
> The other side of the border, where the shore
> Goes down to the Saronic Gulf, a rumbling
> Deep in the earth, terrible to hear
> Growled like the thunder of Father Zeus.

Seneca, writing for Romans, omitted the references to Greek geography and gods (Zeus). However, he grasped the essence of the text and speeded it up:[52]

> At once a peal of thunder broke across the sea.

A rather different form of compression is *distillation*, that is, the procedure of isolating the significant. It is a procedure that is found, for instance, in Ovid's *Metamorphoses*—in his ability to isolate and highlight the crucial elements in old narratives.[53]

c. *Fusion/Conflation*

More complex than simple compression is the process of turning two or more elements into one new complex element. As the news of Hippolytus's death is announced, Euripides speaks of different people: the chorus is *tearful*, and the messenger has a *sorrowful face*.[54] Seneca omitted the outmoded convention of the chorus but attributed to the messenger a *tearful sorrowful face*.[55] In Homer's text, Menelaus *broke his sword in combat* and Diomed *left his sword*, but in Virgil, a single character, Turnus, mistakenly *left his own sword* and *broke in combat* the sword he took.[56] A more general form of fusion is found in the way Virgil, in large part, combined both the battles of Achilles (the *Iliad*) and the wanderings of Odysseus (the *Odyssey*) in Aeneas.[57]

---

49. Euripides, *Hippolytus*, scene vi, 1238 (from *The Complete Greek Tragedies*, III [trans. D. Grene; ed. D. Grene and R. Lattimore; Chicago and London: University of Chicago Press, 1959]).

50. Seneca, *Phaedra*, Act 4, 1092-96 (trans. E.P. Watling, *Seneca: Four Tragedies and Octavia* [Harmondsworth: Penguin, 1966]).

51. Euripides, *Hippolytus* 6.1199-1203.

52. Seneca, *Phaedra* 4.1007-1008.

53. For a summary and bibliography, see *OCD*, Ovid. On Ovid's careful but complex use of sources in *Metamorphoses*, see especially Otis 1966: 1-3, 45-49, 346-94. According to Otis, 'Ovid never imitates literally' (p. 366). Note also Anderson 1972: 6-17 (on Ovid's plan and sources), and pp. 34-35 (select bibliography).

54. Euripides, *Hippolytus* 6.1142-52.

55. Seneca, *Phaedra* 4.989-90.

56. For an analysis, see Conway 1931: 156.

57. For a summary of Virgil's fusing of different Homeric characters into single characters of the *Aeneid*, see Knauer 1979: 342-43.

d. *Substitution of images*

Catullus followed Sappho closely yet felt free not only to add and omit but also to substitute new images of his own. Thus, whereas Sappho had spoken of a jealous passion,

> Which has made my heart (*kardia*) flutter in my breast

Catullus substituted:

> Which robs me of all my senses (*omnis sensus*);

and while Sappho had said,

> I see *nothing* with my eyes,

Catullus wrote:

> The light of my eyes is covered with 'twin night'.[58]

e. *Positivization*

The *Iliad*, from its very first line, is largely dominated by the theme of the anger of Achilles. At one point he promises to maintain his quest for vengeance:

> As long as breath remains in my bosom
> And my good knees have their strength.[59]

In place of this permanent vengefulness, Virgil put the permanent devotedness of Aeneas: he promises to honor the memory of his love of a woman (Dido):

> While I remember who I am
> And while the breath still governs this frame.[60]

This radical rewriting is an example not only of positivization (turning something negative into something positive, a fairly frequent procedure in Virgil), but also of internalization—replacing emphasis on something external (the knees, symbols of physical strength) by emphasis on the internal (the memory and sense of identity).[61]

f. *Internalization*

A more complex example of internalization occurs in Seneca's version of the reaction of Hippolytus's angry father to the news of the accident. Where Euripides had written,[62]

> For hatred of the sufferer I was glad
> At what you told me. *Still he was my son.*
> As such I have reverence for him and the Gods:
> I neither sorrow nor rejoice at this thing.

Seneca wrote,[63]

> *O potent nature*
> How strong a bond of blood is thine to tie
> A parent's heart. Even against our will
> *We know and love thee.* As my son was guilty,
> I wished him dead; as he is lost, I mourn him.

---

58. For primary references and for further analysis and details, see Balme 1969: 47-50.
59. Homer, *Iliad* 9.609 (trans. Conway 1931: 157).
60. Virgil, *Aeneid* 4.336 (trans. Conway 1931: 157).
61. On Virgil's emphasis on peace (as opposed to Homer's emphasis on war), see Miles 1976. Positivization does not mean that everything in Virgil is positive. Dido's heartbroken self-immolation is negative (it is an intimation of the eventual fall of her city). But Virgil does reverse many of Homer's negative elements.
62. Euripides, *Hippolytus* 6.1257-60.
63. Seneca, *Phaedra* 4.1119-23.

The italics have been added to the foregoing excerpts in order to clarify the complex relationship of the texts. Seneca has taken the central section of the father's reaction—his recognition, despite his anger, of his relationship to his son and his consequent *reverence* both for *sonship* and the *gods*—and changed it into an *awe-filled recognition* of *nature* and *parenthood*. In doing so he spelled out some of the basic internal factors of parenthood: a bond of blood, a heart that is tied, and—despite the opposition of the will—knowledge and love. Then, in the last line and a half, Seneca synthesized the opening and closing lines of Euripides' text: the gladness at Hippolytus's suffering becomes 'I wished him dead'; and the rather mechanical 'I neither sorrow nor rejoice' becomes the more deeply felt 'I mourn him'.[64]

Internalization was far more than a literary technique. It was concerned with literature's central content, with moving the human story from the external world to the internal—to internal qualities and developments. The roots of this process lie deep in Greek culture and are probably seen most clearly in the tendency, especially among the Ionian thinkers, to change the focus of interest from the gods to what goes on within people,[65] and in the partial replacement of the warlike heroism of the Homeric tradition with the quiet heroism of Socrates.[66] Virgil, who was apparently the most esteemed writer of imperial Rome, carried this process of internalization further, for not only did he imitate and rival Homer in every way, but he consistently sought to replace the warlike Homeric heroes with the image of a hero who could indeed fight fiercely but who was above all a man of internal qualities—*pius Aeneas*. Further instances of the process of internalization may be found, for instance, in two of the most outstanding writers of the New Testament period—Seneca and Tacitus. Thus, when Tacitus was describing even such a well known event as the coup which brought Otho to power in 69 CE, he did not hesitate to describe the onlooking populace through a formula which reflected a stereotyped description of a crowd, but he adapted that description so that it focused on factors that were internal—the crowd's silent emotions.[67] And as regards Seneca's adaptations of Euripides, written about 60 CE, 'Seneca's tragedies...are modulations of Euripides... Drawing on aspects of technique latent in Euripides, Seneca wholly internalizes the action' (Steiner 1975: 431).

Internalization is of special interest because it provides a partial analogue for the way in which the biblical tradition, particularly the New Testament, moves the focus inward, from law to spirit, from external traditions to internal dispositions, and from an external temple to a spiritualized one.[68]

g. *Form-Change*
In *Epode X*, Horace wishes an evil omen on the voyage of his critic Maevius: 'With an evil omen (*mala...alite*) the ship is unmoored and departs, carrying the stinking Maevius: South Wind, remember to lash each side with wild waves...' Not only does Horace's colourful curse seem to involve a careful transformation of a somewhat similar curse written centuries earlier by Archilochus (c. 700 BCE), but it also involves a careful adaptation of a particular poetic form called the *propempticon*, which consisted of a farewell

---

64. For some further notes on Seneca's internalization of Euripides, see Steiner 1975: 431-33.
65. See Gusdorf 1967: 24-33. More briefly, see Gusdorf 1974: 1171. Sappho put unique emphasis on the internal world of feeling (Bowra 1945: 950) and to that extent she is sometimes regarded as having been among the first poets to turn the epic quest inward to the subjective self.
66. See Adkins 1960: 33, 57, 259-315 (259); Havelock 1978: 137, 307.
67. Tacitus, *Hist.*, I, 40.
68. Fraeyman 1947. The internalization begun by Proto-Luke was continued by Mark—what may be called spiritualization—and was further developed in the spiritual gospel of John.

with words of *good omen*. Horace's procedure was radical, subversive almost, but it was typical of the way in which imitation combined careful continuity with bold novelty.[69]

These examples are useful but limited. In order to get a better idea of the richness and complexity of imitation, it is necessary to examine the total procedure of particular authors. Virgil and Ovid, for instance, particularly in their epic poems the *Aeneid* and the *Metamorphoses*, show an extraordinary capacity for combining a variety of sources and methods of adaptation.

The conclusion that emerges from this brief survey of poetry and drama is that imitation was widespread and varied. It was used on texts that were contemporary or recent, but among the Romans it was used particularly to appropriate and reinterpret the texts that were often considered normative—those of ancient Greece. It seems reasonable, in fact, to accept G. Kennedy's conclusion that 'all of Latin literature is in origin an imitation of Greek' (1980: 118).

4. *Imitation and Historiography*

Is it possible that what applied to literature in general did not apply to history and to the related subject of biography?[70] After all, it is a fact of modern studies and a presupposition of most modern readers that literature and history are usually quite distinct disciplines, taught by different university departments and discussed at different conventions. It is also true that, unlike many poets and dramatists, historians such as Thucydides and Livy spoke of real historical events and characters. Furthermore, even though most ancient historiographers did not discuss sources and source criticism, there were a number of writers who stressed the need for adherence to precise facts and to trustworthy sources. Lucian of Samosata (c. 120–180 CE), for instance, emphasized that 'the historian's sole task is to tell it as it happened (*hós eprachthé eipein*)... He should for preference be an eyewitness, but if not, listen to those who tell the least impartial story.'[71] Arrian (c. 140 CE), in writing his history of Alexander, told that he chose two sources that seemed to narrate 'what actually happened' (*hōs synēnéchthē*) and where these two sources were in conflict he selected the one that seemed 'most trustworthy and most worth telling' (...*pistotera...axiaphegetotera*).[72] Philostratus (c. 200 CE), in prefacing his life of Apollonius, claimed that he was intent on giving a precise chronicle of the man's words, and that he had chosen his sources with discrimination, rejecting unreliable accounts, while combining various reputable sources into a stylized synthesis.[73]

---

69. For further discussion of Horace's procedure in the *Epodes*, see Balme 1969: 50-55. On the larger question of form-change in general, see Ovid's *Metamorphoses*, especially 1.1-4.

70. On the relatedness of ancient history and biography, see C. Turner 1969: 328-34). Both Talbert (1977: 16-17) and Hengel (1980: 15-16) suggest that there is a clear distinction between the genres of history and biography. It is indeed possible to cite individual works that are quite distinct from one another in genre, but on the whole this distinction does not hold. Even Plutarch's *Lives* at times seems more interested in history than in biography; see Pelling 1980: 136-37. Hengel's contention that the gospels consist of biographical reminiscences (*apomnémoneumata*) may at first sound quite plausible (1980: 27-29); but, apart from the apologetically oriented evidence of Justin, it rests largely on Hengel's own bland assertion —made despite an admission that we do not know how oral tradition actually worked—that Jesus' brief activity in Galilee 'provided *a wealth of firmly fixed and permanent impressions*' (1980: 22-24 [24] [emphasis added]). In this way, without any significant argumentation, Hengel prejudges a fundamental issue—the nature of the ultimate sources behind the text.

71. Lucian, *How to Write History*, paragraphs 39, 47.
72. Arrian, *Anabasis* 1.1-2.
73. Philostratus, *Apollonius* 1.2-3.

Though real events were often recorded and someone like Lucian could call for factual reporting, the general practice of history was heavily influenced by factors other than the bare events. These other factors, sometimes overlapping, consisted particularly of poetry, rhetoric, and drama:

Poetry. In a world where poetry and history writing are so separated, it is difficult to imagine how the two were frequently interwoven in ancient times. Poetry in fact was linked with several areas of knowledge: it was through what is known as didactic poetry that Hesiod (c. 700 BCE) sought to communicate his far-reaching message of justice, that Empedocles (c. 493–433 BCE) taught his doctrine of the four elements of the universe, that Aratus (c. 315–240 BCE) taught astronomy, and that Lucretius (c. 95–55 BCE) gave new life to Epicurean philosophy (see Cox 1969: 124-45). But poetry had a special link with history. The two outstanding works of Greco-Roman literature, Homer's *Iliad/Odyssey* and Virgil's *Aeneid*, consisted precisely of an extraordinary blend of history and poetry. Herodotus (c. 450 BCE) was known as the father of history, but his work consisted largely of Homeric-type stories. When Ennius (239–169 BCE) wrote a history of Rome, he did so in poetry.

In fact Lucian's call for factual reporting was largely a protest against blending poetry and history: 'Every single person is writing history… Such writers seem unaware that history has aims and rules different from poetry and poems. In the case of the latter, liberty is absolute and there is one law—the will of the poet.'[74] Indeed Lucian felt so overwhelmed by the pervasiveness of the poetic approach that he compared himself to the lonely and cynical Diogenes.[75] It is possible, of course, that Lucian overstated the problem, but the frequent intermingling of history and poetry seems undoubted, and it is in this context that one better understands Quintilian's statement that history is close to poetry and is a kind of prose poem: *Historia…est enim proxima poetis et quodammodo carmen solutum*.[76]

Rhetoric. Given the pervasiveness of rhetoric, it is not surprising that it should be found in the writing of history. Rhetoric is found first of all in a close follower of Isocrates, Timaeus of Tauromenian (c. 356–260 BCE). It reappears in some Roman writers, and does so with particularly questionable effect in Valerius Antias (c. 90 BCE), who 'fully observed the Isocratean canons of (in fact) plausibly detailed mendacity'.[77] And the history of Valerius's contemporary, Q. Claudius Quadrigenarius, 'had as its primary purpose the entertainment of the reader' (Martin 1981: 18). Coelius Antipater's influential monograph on the Second Punic War (written 120 BCE) is strewn with rhetoric and fiction (Martin 1981: 17). Particularly significant is Cicero's linking of rhetoric and history and his declaration that history demands, above all, a rhetorical treatment: *historia…opus unum oratorium maxime*.[78] It is the teaching of Cicero that inspired the method of Livy, and even though Livy often worked from the careful Polybius, he also drew on the plausibly detailed scenarios of Valerius Antias.

---

74. Lucian, *How to Write History*, paragraph 8.
75. Lucian, *How to Write History*, paragraph 3.
76. Quintilian, *Inst. Orat.* 10.1.31. With regard to the Old Testament it also seems to be a mistake to regard poetry as being quite distinct from history. Thus von Rad (1962: I, 109) believes that 'a large part of even the historical traditions of Israel has to be regarded as poetry', and Kugel (1981: 302) argues that 'the concepts of poetry and prose correspond to no precise distinction in the Bible and that their sustained use has been somewhat misleading about the nature and form of different sections of the Bible'.
77. Badian (1966: 21) remarks that 'the tradition of Roman historiography made plausible lying easy'.
78. Cicero, *De Legibus* 1.5.

Drama. The mingling of drama and history may be discerned at the very roots of the recounting of Greek history: in the opening book of the *Iliad* (1.53-303, the bitter confrontation between Achilles and Agamemnon) and again in Herodotus (particularly in the scene in which Xerxes is depicted as debating the question of invading Greece, 7.4-19). Something similar may be found in Ctesias of Cnidos (c. 400 BCE), a writer who depended on Herodotus, but it is in later writers such as Duris (c. 340–260 BC) and Phylarchus (born c. 210 BCE) that history in large part is turned into dramatic tragedy; or in other words, into a narrative specifically designed to evoke pity and horror.

Therefore it seems reasonable to conclude that a considerable portion of Greco-Roman historiography was governed largely by the norms of rhetoric, poetry, and drama.

Within this general context it is useful to look more closely at a front-rank historian such as Livy. Though he sometimes shows a fairly close verbal similarity to the sober Polybius, he generally exercised considerable freedom.[79] In particular, he tended to idealize and to dramatize. Thus, where Polybius had reported that after the Trasimene defeat, both people and Senate were in confusion, Livy drew a sharp and dramatic contrast between the panic (*terror ac tumultus*) of the general population and the cool counsel-taking of the Senate.[80] P.G. Walsh summarizes his literary methods (P.G. Walsh 1961: 190):

> He utilizes one main source, reorganizes the structural arrangement, and introduces new material to achieve more dramatic effects. He compresses or omits the less interesting content, using as criteria the purpose of his work and the interests of his audience. Then in addition to these literary aims of *enargeia* [graphic presentation to achieve dramatic effect] and *syntomia* [compression], he seeks to fulfil his historian's duties of *saphéneia* [clarification] and *pithanotés* [credibility in narration].

His affinity with poetry is particularly clear in his opening books. At that point 'his narration...has poetical colour and style: it is the prose epic of Rome, ranking with the *Aeneid*'.[81] Therefore Livy, no less than historians who were more obscure, lived in a world that was heavily influenced by rhetoric, drama, and poetry.

It is also useful to look at a front-rank biographer such as Plutarch. Like Livy, he seems to have drawn on sources of very different quality. His lives of Agis and Cleomenes, for instance, were largely based on Phylarchus, a writer who himself had drawn heavily on the sensationally dramatic accounts of Duris.[82] Like Livy, and despite his wide reading, he seems to have used one basic source at a time (Pelling 1980), but he felt free to employ bold processes of adaptation: compression and rephrasing; conflation (or fusion) of similar items; and compression and rearrangement of time sequences. Another technique of Plutarch was transference: he moved items from one character to another—a procedure akin to the fusion of characters already noted in Seneca's and Virgil's elaboration or expansion of an underdeveloped source through fabrication of a context or of circumstantial detail.[83] This procedure is similar too to that found in the poetry of Lucretius (see Kenney 1972: 12-24), and to Cicero's way of providing a new context for traditional mythical material (see C.L. Thompson 1979–80: 143-52). Plutarch also felt free to interpret an event and its motivation first in one way, then in another, so that it suited his general argument. When he was describing a defeat, such as that of Pompey at Tharsalus,

---

79. On Ctesias, Duris, and Phylarchus, see Lesky 1966: 623-23, 764-66.
80. For example compare Livy 33.39-40, and Polybius 18.49-51.
81. *OCD*, Livy.
82. See *OCD*, Duris, Phylarchus.
83. On compression and rephrasing in Plutarch, see Cadbury 1927: 161-63. On the other techniques, see Pelling 1980: 127-31.

he turned it in some ways into a tragic drama (Pelling 1980: 131-35). In general, therefore, Plutarch's method of composition showed considerable freedom, a freedom that at times resembles that of a poet or dramatist.

Is it possible that, within the general idea of historiography, there was one stream of writing, that of Thucydides and his later admirers—Dionysius of Halicarnassus, Polybius, Sallust, Tacitus—which was exempt from the pervasiveness of rhetorical and literary considerations? After all, when Lucian of Samosata appealed for matter-of-fact reporting, he expressed his admiration for Thucydides.[84] Were Thucydides and his followers different then; were they a breed apart?

To some extent they were. As one analyst put it: 'Thucydides and Polybius [are]... untypical and exceptional'.[85] They usually avoided excesses. But they were not exempt. The difficulty is seen first of all with regard to Thucydides himself. He wrote of contemporary events and there can be little doubt that from some points of view he was well informed. Yet while Lesky insists that Thucydides was scrupulously accurate, he concedes that at times he was concerned with what was typical rather than with what actually happened, and that Pericles' magnificent oration over the fallen, for instance, was Thucydides' own composition, a work of art that contrasts in ideal images the traditions of Sparta and Athens (Lesky 1966: 454-81 [459, 461, 463, 466, 473]). But Cornford's *Thucydides Mythistoricus* is much more radical: it contends that as Thucydides watched the terrible Peloponnesian War drag on and on, he increasingly began to depict it as a tragedy, and so his history is written as though it were a Greek tragic drama (Cornford 1907). Cornford's criticism, though possibly overstated, seems to be essentially accurate. Furthermore, Thucydides' style 'has a poetical and archaistic flavour'.[86] Nor was he free of rhetoric. In fact, during the two centuries following his death, it was primarily his more lavish rhetorical traits that were noted and imitated (C. Turner 1969: 306). And his later admirers also knew rhetoric. The historical work of Dionysius of Halicarnassus has been called 'a vast exercise in *mimēsis*'.[87] Sallust rejected the rhetorical methods of Cicero but not rhetoric as such; and in fact his historical works, modeled largely on Thucydides, may be characterized as 'rhetorical monographs' (C. Turner 1969: 307). In this context, it is understandable that he should indulge in imitation. He thought little of taking a speech that Demosthenes had delivered against Philip and using it, in adapted form, to condemn Sulla.[88] And he also indulged in the sophisticated literary procedure of deliberately using a rather archaic vocabulary—a procedure, incidentally, which was 'a significant feature of much of Roman historiography'.[89]

An example not only of Thucydides' dramatic style but also of the way he was imitated by subsequent historians may be found in the recurring image of the battle spectators. Just as Thucydides, in describing the momentous sea battle in Syracuse Harbor (413 BCE), suddenly launched into an elaborate description of the intense emotion of the spectators on the shore, so Polybius, when describing a daring naval escapade in a Sicilian harbor (250 BCE), suddenly switched attention to the intense emotion of the spectators,[90] and so in turn

---

84. Lucian, *How to Write History*, paragraph 139.
85. Gabba 1981: 50. Butterfield 1981: 118-37 (136-37) rightly emphasizes the achievement of Thucydides but does not make clear that Thucydides' method was not followed by most subsequent Greco-Roman writers.
86. *OCD*, Thucydides (2).
87. *OCD*, Dionysius (7).
88. Sulla, *Hist.* 1.55.24.
89. Martin 1981: 21. For an analysis of the rationale behind archaism, see Steiner 1975: 333-53. For a survey and analysis of archaism of style and content as found in works written in Greek c. 60–240 CE, see Bowie 1970.
90. Thucydides, *Hist.* 7.71.1-4; Polybius, *Hist.* 1.44.5.

Tacitus, when describing the decisive clash in the Roman Forum between the supporters of Galba and those of Otho (69 CE), suddenly switched the attention to the onlooking populace:[91]

> The basilicas and the temples around were packed with spectators of the woeful scene (*lugubri prospectu*). No word was uttered either by the people or the plebs; dismay sat on every face, and every ear was turned to listen. There was no uproar, there was no calm, only a silence like that of some great terror or some mighty passion (*magni metus et magnae irae*).

As in Polybius's text, the spectators consist of the mass of the city's population (*populi aut plebis*, 'the people or the plebs'), and the picture is quite compact. But the quality of the emotion has been further simplified, so that the population is like an audience watching a tragedy. In describing an earlier stage in the day's tumult, Tacitus had explicitly compared the city's entire population to a clamorous circus crowd, but now that same audience is, as it were, gripped in tragedy.[92] Furthermore, Tacitus's description, when compared with those of Thucydides and Polybius, involves a process of internalization: the crowd makes no sound and the ultimate focus of the narrative is on what goes on inside a person.

The essential point is not only that Thucydides painted a highly dramatic picture of battle spectators but also that subsequent writers adapted that picture to their own circumstances. There are several other examples of the same procedure. We find varied but related pictures of warnings against tyrants, exhortations before battle, the way a nation wins friends, the bad conscience engendered by tyranny, and the ravages of civil war.[93] One could add further examples (C. Turner 1969), but the complexity of the practice of reworking sources is simply not known. Thus in the case of Tacitus, while some critics believe that he weighted his evidence as carefully as a modern historian, others hold that he 'has done little more than transmute by *stylistic alchemy* a pre-existing literary source' (Martin 1981: 11 [my emphasis]). The truth may be midway between these extremes (Martin 1981), but what is certain is that the question of the origin and nature of Tacitus's text may not be studied in isolation from preceding histories and from the general practice of imitation. It is also useful to bear in mind that Tacitus's *Dialogue on Oratory* (ch. 2), which explicitly claims to be a report of a factual conversation filled with lifelike pictures of the speakers concerned, turns out, on analysis, to be an artistic composition that is largely, if not entirely, a work of fiction modeled considerably on the writings of Cicero.[94]

Summing up, one may say that the ancient practice of 'history' was something quite distinct from the modern discipline that bears the same name. In Michel Foucault's terms (see above, n. 2), ancient historiography was more about representing a natural *ordre* than about the modern concept of *histoire*. In varying degrees, history-writing has been governed by practices that were literary rather than 'scientific'—rhetoric, poetry, drama, the invention of speeches, pragmatic instruction or moralizing, and archaizing. Hence, even though ancient history contained a wealth of factual information, it was not exempt from the norms of the composition of literature, one of which was imitation.

It seems reasonable, therefore, when inquiring about the composition of an ancient work—even one that is history-like—to ask whether, to some degree at least, it is the result of a process of imitation. It is in this context that we turn to the question of whether Luke–Acts involves a process of imitating the Septuagint.

---

91. Tacitus, *Hist.* 1.40 (*The Histories of Tacitus* [trans. G.G. Ramsay; London: John Murray, 1915], pp. 47-48).
92. Tacitus, *Hist.* 1.32.
93. For further details see C. Turner 1969: 311-21.
94. For a discussion, see Atkins 1934: II, 177-96 (182-85, 194).

5. *The Old Testament and the Likelihood of Luke's Use of* Imitatio

While this study deals with all four gospels, it gives central importance to Luke–Acts, particularly to that part of Luke–Acts—'Proto-Luke'—which has a distinctive dependence on the Old Testament/Septuagint. It is therefore appropriate even in this broad introductory chapter, to give special attention to Luke's possible imitation of the Septuagint.

Two distinct arguments seem to indicate that Luke–Acts does not involve the use of *imitatio*:

1. In the course of history, Luke–Acts and the other New Testament texts have enjoyed unparalleled popularity and power and have been 'canonized' in a way that sets them apart from most other writings of the first century CE. This apartness, or uniqueness, might seem to indicate that the New Testament documents are not to be grouped with other ancient writings, nor were they governed either by the prevailing general rules of literary composition or by the specific practice of imitation.

    Neo-orthodox theology, particularly as propounded by Karl Barth, so emphasized the transcendence of the Word of God and its discontinuity with the human word that further attention was given to the idea of the *uniqueness* and *apartness* of the Bible.[95] When this idea of *theological* apartness was taken over by Rudolf Bultmann, it contributed to his idea of *literary* apartness, that is, to the idea that there is a considerable discontinuity between the gospels and the other literature of the first century (Bultmann 1963: 6). Such discontinuity does not encourage the idea that the gospels were composed according to prevailing literary methods.[96]

2. Hermann Gunkel's theory of oral traditions and forms—a theory taken up by Bultmann and reinforced apparently by his general theology of the Word and particularly of the spoken word which engenders faith—suggested that the origin and composition of the gospels is to be sought in an *oral* rather than a *literary* context. Redaction criticism, though it emphasized the work of the final author, has done little to deny the formative influence of oral tradition.

But these two arguments cannot stand. The uniqueness of the New Testament texts, as emphasized by the first argument, does not mean that they did not share the basic literary traits of first-century writings. After all, the uniqueness of Christ among humans occurs in a context of solidarity with positive human traits and therefore it is altogether appropriate that the central Christian literature should be in solidarity with the positive traits of human literature.

As for Gunkel's theory of oral tradition, it has been shown to have been built on an anthropology that is fundamentally flawed.[97] It is not surprising, therefore, that form criticism, which tries to build on a presupposition of oral tradition, should sometimes be severely criticized.[98] The problems surrounding the appealing idea of oral tradition will be examined later in greater detail (Chapter 6). Suffice for the moment to say that it is no longer possible simply to assume that the development of a gospel text is to be sought in a way that is primarily oral rather than literary. The literary explanation deserves an equal hearing.

---

95. See, for instance, Barth 1936: I, Part I, 51-399.
96. For further aspects of this argument, see Talbert 1977: 4-8.
97. See Warner 1979; Rogerson 1974: 57-65; Wolf 1980. On the question of the possible oral transmission of the gospel, see the discussion between A.B. Lord and C.H. Talbert in Walker, Jr (ed.) 1978: 33-102 (99).
98. For example, see Schmithals 1980; Schillebeeckx 1979: 92-95.

1. The Greco-Roman Tradition

There are, in fact, some positive indications that Luke's text involves imitation of previous texts or at least imitation of parts of the Old Testament. First of all, there is considerable evidence not only that Luke was a *littérateur* but also that he employed specifically Hellenistic modes of writing, including various techniques of Hellenistic rhetoric.[99] But it would have been almost impossible to receive literary and rhetorical training that did not include the practice of imitation. Imitation, as already indicated in this chapter, was a basic starting point—often *the* basic starting point—of rhetorical and literary composition. It is therefore probable that Luke was practiced in imitation.

Second, it appears that Luke regarded the Old Testament in general as being, in some basic sense, a normative text. At crucial points, he emphasizes the fundamental continuity between the Old Testament and his own narrative: in the programmatic Nazareth speech (Lk. 4.16-30), in the climactic ch. 24 (24.25-27, 44), and in the culminating Roman speech (Acts 28.17-29 [especially 28.23]). Since writers of the Roman period tended to use *normative* texts (i.e. classical Greek texts) precisely as objects of imitation, it is not a priori unlikely that Luke should have imitated the Old Testament.

Third, there are, de facto, signs of literary continuity between Luke and the Old Testament—continuity of literary genre,[100] of narrative technique (see Kurz 1980c; 1980a), and of vocabulary and style.[101] In fact, Luke's style has been described as a *mimēsis* of the style of the Septuagint.[102] More specifically, it has been contended that large areas of Luke's text show a relationship to various prolonged Old Testament narratives, particularly to the Elijah–Elisha account, a relationship of both systematic, detailed dependence and of careful, consistent adaptation (Brodie 1981d). In other words, there is evidence that Luke's acceptance of the Old Testament as normative is not just general assent to some disembodied theological ideas but also involves a close and creative interaction with the body of the Old Testament, with the text as text.

Altogether, therefore, there is both an a priori probability of Luke's practice of imitation, and a de facto practice of his adopting a normative text in a way that corresponds, broadly at least, to the actual practice of imitation. Such a combination of prior probability and de facto similarity constitutes a noteworthy case. It does not mean that everything Luke did with the Old Testament is to be explained exclusively in terms of imitation, but it establishes at least a significant probability that the practice of imitation is an important clue in unraveling Luke's use of the Old Testament.

6. The Synoptic Problem and the Need to Cope with Authorial Complexity

The discussion of Luke's use of sources cannot be isolated from the Synoptic Problem and from questions such as whether Luke's way of using the Old Testament is different from his way of using Mark. It would be extremely helpful for tracing particular processes of imitating or using sources if we could decide beforehand that there are, say, four basic techniques Luke is likely to have employed, and if we could specify further that two of these techniques were used with ancient texts (the Old Testament) and the other two with more recent sources such as Mark.

---

99. For references and discussion, see especially Kurz 1980b; 1990: 171-89; Satterthwaite 1993.

100. The fact that the genre of the gospels is in some significant respects similar to that of Greco-Roman biographies (see Talbert 1977; Alexander 1993) or historical monographs (Palmer 1993) does not take away from the fact that in other important respects the genre of the gospels, and particularly of Luke–Acts, is strikingly close to some of the Old Testament histories; see Brown 1971: 97-99; 1977: 561; Brodie 1979; Barr and Wentling 1980; Hengel 1980: 30-32; Talbert 1980: 137; Rosner 1993.

101. For summaries of the evidence, see Haenchen 1971: 72-77; and especially Fitzmyer 1981: 113-18.

102. Plümacher 1972: 38-72 (63-64); Horton 1978: 1-23 (17-18).

But we do not have a clear-cut field of possibilities. This is the core of the problem that faces us. The fact that Luke–Acts has affinities not only with ancient historiography and biography but also with the ancient novel[103] is an indicator of the complexity of its genre. The novel was particularly complex, a mixture of fact and fiction that 'acted as a literary collecting-basin and admitted features from other genres'.[104] And with regard to modes of adaptation and composition, Dionysius of Halicarnassus (c. 60–5 BCE) provides a reminder of the individuality of each author:[105]

> I assert without any hesitation that there are many specific differences of composition and that they cannot be brought into a comprehensive view or within a precise enumeration; I think too that, as in personal appearance, so also in literary composition, each of us has an individual character.

Or, as literary critic George Steiner says about the various ways of reusing texts in literature as a whole: 'We find innumerable possibilities… *It is up to us to recognise and reconstruct the particular force of relation*' (Steiner 1975: 425 [my emphasis]).

Thus, it is quite inadequate to approach the problem of Luke's sources and the larger question of the Synoptic Problem with a narrow list of preset categories based on some rather narrow selection of, say, historiographical narratives. The difficult task of recognizing and reconstructing the particular relationship between two texts is best undertaken by someone who is aware of the startling variety and complexity that may be employed in the use of sources. Discovery is rarely the result of working with rules that are clear and well established.[106]

On this issue—the need for sensivity to diverse ways of using sources—the Synoptic Problem is its own worst enemy. Since the problem is largely stated, or laid out (e.g. in Aland's *Synopsis*), on the basis of the obvious verbal similarities among the first three gospels, and since many students of the New Testament receive their formative training in text comparison on the basis of a synopsis like Aland's, researchers often develop an implicit expectation that whatever progress is to be made on the Synoptic Problem is to be made on the basis of comparing texts that show obvious verbal similarity. But obvious verbal similarity, however useful, is only one of several possible relationships between texts. The fact that the evangelists sometimes used sources in a way that retained a considerable amount of obvious verbal similarity does not mean that they did not also use methods that were complex and subtle, ways that removed almost all verbal similarities, ways that corresponded to the degree of transformation implied in the descriptions and metaphors that are used concerning imitation: inspection, contemplation, following a light, pioneering, wrestling, impregnation, honey-making, chorus-making, digestion, generation, emulation, and contamination. There is not much point in rendering homage to the literary artistry of the evangelists unless an effort is made to articulate the full dimensions of what is meant by 'literary artistry'. Such articulation must take account of many different ways of using sources.

As the discussion of New Testament sources stands at the moment, when the comparison of texts proves difficult, there is a tendency to 'explain' the difficulty by appealing to some unknown quantity—an oral tradition that is not defined, or a document (e.g. Q, a Signs Source) that is lost. These hypotheses imply a complexity of sources rather than a

---

103. See Praeder 1981. Note also the view of O'Day (1982: 10-11). On the much-disputed origins of the ancient novel, see *OCD*, 'Novel (Greek)'.

104. *OCD*, 'Novel (Greek)'.

105. Dionysius of Halicarnassus, *De Compositione Verborum* 21.

106. For an analysis of the process of problem solving and of discovery, see Polanyi 1958: 120-24 (123). On the priority of paradigms over clear rules, see Kuhn 1970: 43-51.

complexity in the authors' methods. They may have a certain validity, but part of the reason they seem relatively successful is precisely because, being unknown quantities, they can be made to fill almost any gap in any solution. Furthermore, the question arises as to whether they represent both a process of unwitting avoidance of analysis of authorial complexity and a reassertion of a rather simplistic view of the evangelists' literary artistry.

Allowance for authorial complexity opens the way to connecting extant texts. It would appear, for instance, when account is taken of such modes of adaptation as compression, internalization, and form-change, that the triple 'call' of Lk. 9.57-62 involves a pithy synthesis of the different kinds of calls found in 1 Kings 19.[107] But are there no categories of adaptation that would cast light on Luke's possible use of Matthew? If, for instance, so sensitive an artist as Ovid could subvert and compress his revered older contemporary, Virgil,[108] why could not Luke's Sermon on the Plain be a subversion of or, at least, a compressed revision of Matthew's Sermon on the Mount? As already suggested, one of the main effects of postulating Q and oral traditions is to drive so many wedges between the two gospels that the literary solution is never fully investigated. In other words, the postulating of Q and of oral traditions has helped to isolate Luke from the other canonical material. For a long time, the formulation of the Synoptic Problem was so narrow that it even isolated Luke from Acts. That has been rectified—studies on Luke–Acts are now common—but the problem of isolation continues, particularly with regard to John and the Johannine epistles. John's gospel is left out of the Synoptic Problem largely because it does not conform to the criterion of obvious verbal similarity.

But is there no category of poetry, fiction, or historiography that could resolve the question of John's possible dependence on Mark? And is there no category of adaptation that would clarify G. Volkmar's contention that Mark renders Paul's theology into narrative form?[109]

To suggest the possibility of a direct literary link between the gospels and the epistles may at first seem far-fetched. However, given the fact that secular writers did not work in isolation from one another and from their predecessors but rather that it was accepted as 'expedient to imitate whatever has been invented with success',[110] it seems unlikely within the relatively small but communicative Christian body that writers should have been unable or unwilling to imitate and emulate the Old Testament and one another. This is particularly true of Luke who was so conscious both of the Old Testament and of the need for gathering sources (see Lk. 1.1-4) and who is regarded as a writer in the Hellenistic mould. Would a researcher like Luke who wanted to highlight Paul and his preaching set to work without bothering to get copies of Paul's epistles?[111] In what corner was he marooned that he did not know of these documents? In what literary impoverishment did this elegant writer live that he could not get copies of them? The general lack of obvious verbal parallelism between Luke and the epistles proves nothing. The epistles are different in form (or genre) from historiography, and so, before being absorbed into historiography, they would have to be transformed. As Cadbury remarked once about the relationship between two writers: 'the material of one writer is transferred to another without any acknowledgement and with almost complete change of diction' (Cadbury 1927: 163). Nor

---

107. See Chapter 34 (cf. Brodie 1981d: 216-27).
108. Compare Ovid, *Metamorphoses* 12.39-63 with Virgil, *Aeneid* 4.173-97; see Zumwalt 1977; F.J. Miller 1927–28: 36-39.
109. Volkmar 1876. On Volkmar, see Wildemann 1983. See also Schmithals 1980: 179-85.
110. Quintilian, *Inst. Orat.* 10.2.1.
111. For a review of the discussion about Luke's possible use of Paul's epistles, see Enslin 1970.

does Luke's different theological emphasis prove anything. In a world of literary artists there is room for—indeed, there is need for—complementarity and variety. Perhaps the relationship of the epistles to Luke may yet be explained, largely, through such concepts as positivization, digestion, and emulation. And perhaps it is through similar imitative concepts that progress may be made on the Synoptic Problem as a whole.

7. Conclusion

Poetry and drama may seem peripheral to the search for Lukan sources and New Testament sources in general. Perhaps they are, but we do not know. What we do know is that sustained efforts to unravel New Testament sources on the basis of appeals to hypothetical lost documents and traditions have largely failed. Some basic dynamic seems to be missing. Since the New Testament documents, *to a degree not yet defined*, consist of artistry and poetry, it is surely not outlandish to suggest that the dynamic has something to do with poetic inventiveness and imitation. Authors such as Livy and Plutarch may indeed provide partial guidance to unraveling the New Testament use of sources, but to confine oneself to such models is to prejudice the basic question—the nature of the New Testament text.

Obviously the only effective way of showing the relevance of poetic methods of imitation and transformation to the writings of Luke is by giving concrete examples. These are given in Chapters 27–53 (in Part III of this volume).

Apart from thus suggesting categories of adaptation that may lead to the recognition of sources, Greco-Roman literature also gives certain negative indications, warnings against using a rather superficial aspect of the text as a guide to the nature of its source. Archaic language (e.g. Semitisms, or the use of Hebrew words) is not a reliable indicator of an old or a Semitic source, since archaizing was a well-known feature of Hellenistic historiography. Nor is detail a reliable indicator of historicity, for the careful describing of vivid details, whether details of narrative, topography, or personality, is as much the sign of a poet or dramatist as of a factual historian. Seneca and Tacitus were both capable of writing detail that was striking but fictitious. And of course, as already explained, orality is not a reliable indicator of dependence on oral tradition.

As a general conclusion, therefore, it may be said that just as the history and sociology of the Greco-Roman world are vital to New Testament studies, so is a study of Greco-Roman literature. Ultimately, of course, each literary relationship must be examined on its own. As Dionysius of Halicarnassus suggested, each author's mode of composition is as unique as one's personal appearance. Hence, while a study of Greco-Roman literature may broaden the mind and indicate possibilities for reshaping sources and comparing texts, the decisive step consists of being able to bring to the task an appropriate blend of sympathetic imagination and scholarly control, a sensitivity which allows for each author's artistic individuality.

2

The Biblical Tradition:
Writing as Rewriting

The reshaping or rewriting of texts was not limited to Greco-Roman imitation. It was central also to the biblical tradition, in several genres. However, rather than survey many diverse genres, as in the previous chapter, this chapter will begin to focus on the genre that is of prime interest for this study—prose narrative. Consequently the chapter will deal largely with examples from the two great narrative bodies of the Old Testament—from the Primary History (Genesis–2 Kings) and from the later history (Chronicles–Ezra–Nehemiah). The first example, from the Chronicles–Ezra–Nehemiah complex, is Chronicles; and the second, from the Genesis–2 Kings material, is Deuteronomy. Following these two examples, the chapter then discusses some broader aspects of the Jewish tradition.

1. *Introduction: The Old Testament: Use of Outside Sources*

Biblical writers followed their own literary tradition, distinct from that of the outside world, from Mesopotamia, Egypt, Greece, and Rome. But distinctness is not separation. Their ancient stories, wanderings and wisdom were interwoven with the history and literature of Mesopotamia and Egypt. And, particularly after Alexander's all-embracing conquests, Hellenism was inescapable. The pressure from Hellenism emerges, for instance, in Ben Sira (c. 180) (Kieweler 1992), and even more acutely in Daniel and 1 and 2 Maccabees.[1] The likelihood, therefore, is that the relationship with the larger literary world was a blend of kinship and distinctness.

One aspect of this distinctness was the apparent absence of theory. Unlike Greco-Roman writers, the biblical authors did not say what they were doing; they did not compose explicit works on literary criticism. Discovering their procedure requires a slow process of comparison and analysis.

Absence of theory did not mean less practice. If anything, the biblical labyrinth appears more dense than in Greco-Roman writers.[2] The sweep of the Old Testament authors was encyclopedic. Their content indicates that they combed through all available sources from creation and flood stories such as those of Mesopotamia to the wisdom literature of Egypt (Heidel 1951; O'Brien and Major 1982; Bryce 1979).

At times, it is difficult to know the nature of these authors' dependence on older material, difficult to discern whether it was oral or written, direct or indirect (Heidel 1951: 82, 139). But in other instances, the connection is reasonably clear. The stories set in Egypt—for instance, those involving Joseph and Moses—reflect the stories of current Egyptian literature (Irvin 1977). The account of Moses' birth seems to depend on the account of the

---

1. There is some evidence even of far-reaching linguistic influence as reflected in J. Yahudi's (1982) startling title, *Hebrew is Greek*.
2. Fishbane (1985) in particular has indicated that biblical writers reworked earlier texts with both freedom and ingenuity.

birth of Sargon (*ANET*: 119). And the admonitions of Prov. 22.17–24.22 are based closely on an Egyptian wisdom work, *The Instruction of Amen-em-ope* (Scott 1965: xxxv).

However, even when the dependence is close it is never slavish. For instance, the use of the wisdom literature shows that foreign material is adapted to Israel's own faith and situation (for detailed examples, see Bryce 1979: 57-134; Brodie 1981d: 54-58).

The overall impression, from an initial sounding of the biblical writers' relationship to surrounding cultures and literatures, is that while there is distinctness, there is also continuity. Neighboring literatures were not excluded, but neither were they accepted uncritically. Rather, in a delicate process of adaptation or rewriting, they were refashioned in light of Israel's traditions and experiences.

2. *Chronicles*

Apart from Israel's reworking of foreign materials there is a further vast phenomenon: as the biblical authors composed new works, they tended to incorporate earlier biblical writings. This is most obvious in Chronicles' adaptation of Samuel–Kings (or a variation on Samuel–Kings),[3] but incorporation occurs in many other diverse instances. This reworking of earlier texts is sometimes called 'midrash', but since there is a dispute about the meaning of the term, especially whether its reference to scripture must be explicit (Porton 1979: 112; 1985: 5), it is usually better to avoid it.

One of the first modern people to sense clearly the vastness and complexity of the way biblical writings depend on each other was Renée Bloch in the 1950s. She used the term midrash, but realized that she was entering new territory, almost completely unexplored: '*domaine encore à peu près complètement inexploré*' (1957: 1279).

The problem in discerning the mode of using sources exists even in the case of Chronicles—a situation where, because of the massive obvious similarities with the history in Kings, it should be relatively easy to see what the author is doing, and what the method and purpose are. But research on Chronicles suggests that the authorship was not a pedantic process of cut-and-paste (for a summary, see North 1990: 23.4; Duke, 1990: 11-28; Kleinig 1994: 47-49). In Bloch's view (1957: 1271), the Chronicler's work was an effort to sift Israel's history and adapt it to the needs of the moment; she called it '*une méditation sur l'histoire*'. T. Willi (1972: 233) described it as 'prophetic exegesis' of Kings. For P. Welten (1973: 204) the idea of exegesis does not do justice to the Chronicler's freedom; what is distinctive of the Chronicler is precisely the combination of apparent opposites: the literal following of an established text and free creativity (p. 205). Chronicles then can be described, along with the book of Judith, as 'free parabolic historiography' (p. 206).

Meditation (Bloch), exegesis (Willi), parabolic historiography (Welten). The perceptions vary, but there is considerable agreement that Chronicles is some form of 'the reinterpretation of history' (W. Riley 1993: especially 26-36).

As for the difficulty in categorizing Chronicles, part of the elusiveness seems to lie in the fact that the work is rhetorical and as such belongs to the world of art. As R.K. Duke summarizes, in concluding his rhetorical analysis (1990: 150-51):

> The Chronicler was faced with the situation of how to reshape and reformulate traditional material… Although changing, rearranging, and omitting traditional material, the Chronicler avoided obtrusive contradictions… [He] painted his account in bold, contrasting colors… With skill and artistry [he] retold the story of Israel in such a way as to set forth a world-view and

---

3.   At times, especially in using 1 and 2 Samuel, Chronicles seems closer to the Septuagint than to the Hebrew text so that 'most scholars now agree that…the Chronicler did not follow the [Hebrew] MT of Samuel but another text which was also used by the translators of the [Greek] LXX' (Kleinig 1994: 47).

an ideology for action within that world... [The] Books of Chronicles exemplify artistic persuasion.

In this brief survey, there is an advantage in starting with Chronicles: despite the difficulty of categorizing it, there is no doubt about it being a rewriting, a deliberate reworking of earlier texts. But perhaps it is unique; perhaps the phenomenon of deliberate rewriting does not occur elsewhere, at least not in the foundational Genesis–2 Kings narrative. It is necessary, therefore, to look at another example.

3. *Deuteronomy*

Standing at the center of a well-coordinated Primary History (Genesis–Kings), Deuteronomy is like the peak of a literary pyramid (Freedman 1991: 11):

```
                    Deuteronomy
              Numbers      Joshua
          Leviticus           Judges
       Exodus                    Samuel
    Genesis                         Kings
```

Showing Deuteronomy as literally central to Old Testament narrative heightens awareness of the book's significance.

On the question of sources, the case of Deuteronomy is more difficult than that of Chronicles; its use of sources is far more complex. Deuteronomy, in fact, is like a theological *summa*. In the words of W. Moran (1969: 259, par. 225a):

> It is a *summa theologica*, an original synthesis, and in many respects a bold one, of Israel's sacred traditions, customs and institutions. The patriarchs and God's promise to them of progeny and land, the exodus, the revelation of Sinai-Horeb, the desert wanderings, the taking of Canaan, sacred festivals, ritual and worship, the law of sanctuary and city-gate, judge, priest, prophet, king, holy war, covenant—Dt brings them all together, stripping many to their barest essence, refracting others in the prism of its special concerns, but...imparting to all a profound unity in its vision of God and his people. It is a theology rooted in the present, a theology of reform, born in a crisis of faith. Though it is strongly traditional, it is not antiquarian; it reasserts the validity of ancient beliefs and practices, but it does not hesitate to adapt, change, even boldly innovate.

The most basic problem is to find the nature of the link between Deuteronomy and (some of) its sources. In Chronicles' use of Kings (or a version of Kings) the nature of the link is clear: literary dependence. In Deuteronomy, such direct literary dependence is not as obvious, yet there are some clear similarities, for instance, with Exodus, especially 'the Book of the Covenant' (Exod. 21–23). In detail:

Exodus	Deuteronomy
21.1-11	15.12-18
21.12-14	19.1-13
21.16	24.7
22.16-17	22.28-29
22.21-24	24.17-22
22.25	23.19-20
22.26-27	24.10-13
22.29-30	15.19-23
22.31	14.3-21
23.1	19.16-21
23.2-3, 6-8	16.18-20
23.4-5	22.1-4

23.9	24.17-18
23.10-11	15.1-11
23.12	5.13-15
23.13	6.13
23.14-17	16.1-17
23.19a	26.2-10
23.19b	14.21b

Given Chronicles' dependence on Kings, the question arises as to whether Deuteronomy depends on Exodus. Did the Deuteronomic author know Exodus and rework it?

Several commentators have said yes, the link is literary. Von Rad, however, saw it otherwise. Having listed a series of shared laws, he gave an alternative explanation: oral tradition (1966: 29). But this idea of oral tradition had been borrowed, without close examination, from Gunkel (see Groves 1987: 17-21, 25-27, 33), and von Rad never explained how oral tradition works, or how it could actually account for the data. It was all part of his valuable but vague idea of contemporization (or 'actualization', *Vergegenwärtigung*) (Groves 1987: 7, 17-21, 205).

M. Weinfeld, however, having compared Deuteronomy with two types of extra-biblical literature—wisdom and historical—concluded that it was dependent on both, but that the dependence was not slavish: 'Deuteronomy had been composed by scribes and wise men… The similarity in the formulation of the Deuteronomic Covenant and the Assyrian treaties led me to infer that trained scribes…transferred literary patterns from the political sphere …to the religious' (1972: vii).

Soon afterwards, in 1979, C.M. Carmichael published an analysis of another instance of Deuteronomy's use of sources, this time a source that was closer to home. The case centered around a striking phenomenon: within Deuteronomy there is a series of laws concerning women, but instead of referring to general situations, as laws usually do, they are strangely specific, sometimes odd.

The puzzle is largely resolved when it is realized that the situations in the Deuteronomic laws correspond to the specific difficulties of many of the women in Genesis.

In outline:

Genesis	Deuteronomy
Rachel, Leah, Dinah (29.9-30a; 31.26-50; ch. 34)	Procedures for absorbing foreign women (21.10-14)
Leah (29.30b–30.24; 48.1–49.28)	The less-loved wife and right of her first-born (21.15-17)
Dinah (Sarah, Leah) (largely ch. 34)	The bad mixing of breeds; women who are treated as harlots or who act as such; adultery; treatment of a woman who has been betrothed or raped (22.10-29)
Bilhah (35.21-22)	Prohibition against sleeping with one's father's woman (23.1)
The daughters of Lot (19.30-38)	The marginalized status of bastards, Ammonites and Moabites (23.3-4)
Sarah (12.10-20; ch. 20)	Giving away a wife and taking her back (24.1-4)
Tamar (ch. 38)	What a woman may do to enforce the levirate law (25.4-10)

The order of the laws in Deuteronomy is roughly the same as the order of the women in Genesis (only Sarah and the daughters of Lot break the pattern). Some of the women's

2. The Biblical Tradition

situations are complex—especially those of Sarah, Leah, and Dinah—so they are reflected two or three times in Deuteronomy's laws.

The women in Genesis often fared badly, and the overall effect of the corresponding Deuteronomic laws is to counter such bad treatment. A survey of the texts shows several precise connections, so much so that Carmichael concludes that the link is literary:

> Certain laws in the Deuteronomic legislation are about many of the women we meet in the book of Genesis. One does not expect legislation to have this kind of relationship to literary traditions. Laws, apparently, are just not constructed this way… [Yet] instead of having to infer what the problems were in real life, we can point to them in written sources known to us. (Carmichael 1979: 1, 4)

When one tests Carmichael more closely by scrutinizing the first two alleged connections (between Deut. 21.10-17 and Rachel, Leah, and Dinah), the result confirms his thesis; virtually every element of Deut. 21.10-17 is reflected in the corresponding Genesis account (Brodie 1981d: 39-46).

Carmichael's research does not resolve the complex problem of the composition of Deuteronomy, but it unveils a corner of it.

Six years after Carmichael's work, the veil was lifted further in M. Fishbane's *Biblical Interpretation in Ancient Israel* (1985). This is the single work that has done most to begin unraveling the threads of literary dependence and adaptation within the Old Testament. The reference in the title is to inner-biblical exegesis, or the interpretation of one text by another. Apart from the interpretive role of scribal comments and corrections, Fishbane distinguishes three main types of exegesis: legal, haggadic (concerning narrative), and mantological (concerning dreams and oracles).

In examining legal exegesis, Fishbane touches the Exodus–Deuteronomy puzzle. He does not appeal to oral tradition. Instead, his detailed analysis points in another direction:

> Deut. 22.1-2 takes over the old regulation of Exod. 23.4 […Deuteronomy] is more complexly formulated and more nationalistic in focus… It has broadened…the older regulation …in several directions. (p. 177)

> The numerous and precise topical and verbal correspondences…make it clear that Deut. 7 is dependent upon Exod. 23 20-33… Deut. 7.1-26 is a deuteronomic expansion of its Exodus source. (p. 201)

> Two entirely distinct rules [Exod. 22.30 and 23.19…] are combined as one rule in Deut. 14.21… The recombination…is also a transformation…by the infusion of…deuteronomic theology. (p. 229)

> The terrain which begins to emerge is immense: 'a vast store of hermeneutical techniques'. (p. 14)

Within this store two ideas are particularly significant: transformation and synthesis. 'Transformation' has a leading role (1985: 1, 318, 383, 465, 500, 543) and it refers to multiple kinds of change, including ways in which a text may be (i) spiritualized, (ii) nationalized or (iii) nomicized (adapted to the Torah) and ethicized (1985: 426).

'Synthesis' refers to the combining of diverse texts: 'Synthetic exegesis…operates on the basis of textual comparison or association of different sorts' (p. 250). Daniel's prayer (Dan. 9.4-20), for instance, combines an oracle from Jeremiah (Jer. 25.9-12) with a picture of curses from Leviticus (Lev. 26.27-45) with the result that the Leviticus text has been 'exegetically reworked through a *recontextualization* of its content' (p. 489).

Fishbane has confirmed what commentators before von Rad suspected or presumed: Deuteronomy is dependent on Exodus. And given the findings of Weinfeld and Carmichael—as well as a suggestion about some relationship to prophetic material (Brodie

1978: 35-37)—light begins to dawn on the long-standing puzzle of the origin of Deuteronomy. This final book of the Pentateuch may indeed have used old traditions, but it also used known biblical writings, and it combined and adapted them to its own purposes. By 1991 Weinfeld (p. 19) was able to draw a straightforward conclusion: 'Critical work in Deuteronomy has indicated that this book depends on the preceding books of the Pentateuch'.

The idea that Deuteronomy is the result of a very deliberate literary procedure has received further confirmation in a study of its rhetorical nature (Lenchak 1993). Lenchak's conclusion, based especially on Moses' last discourse, is that Deuteronomy 'is a prime candidate for rhetorical criticism' (1993: xi), since its nature is rhetorical (p. 233).

Thus what is true of Chronicles—that it is a rewriting, and that it is rhetorical (Duke 1990)—is also true, though in a very different way, of Deuteronomy.

4. *Deuteronomy: The Tip of a Wider Old Testament Phenomenon of Reworking Texts*

The change in the perception of Deuteronomy is part of a larger phenomenon: the sense of how Old Testament texts were composed has begun to shift. Elements of this shift have been present for some time, for instance in the contention that the Pentateuch is dependent on written prophecy (H.H. Schmid 1977: 38-39; Brodie 1981b). But now that perspective has gained new momentum. J. Van Seters (1994b), for instance, indicates at length that much of the picture of Moses in Exodus–Numbers is heavily indebted to prophetic biography. Apparently the same applies to Genesis: it is heavily indebted to the Major Prophets (Brodie 2001c: 433-46). There are indications also that Genesis–2 Kings as a whole comes from a setting that is literary or scribal.[4] And in research on the prophets, there is increasing evidence of the literary nature of the texts and of the literary connections between various texts.[5]

This idea of literary connection between texts finds particular emphasis in André Chouraqui (1975). Having spent decades translating the Bible into French, Chouraqui formed an impression (1975: 455), reminiscent of R. Bloch's impression, in dealing with midrash, of an unexplored world:

> What were the writing techniques of the inspired authors of Israel? I believe that we have scarcely begun to glimpse them. This art corresponded to a science which was very rigorous, traditional…an art of symphonic composition where each word, each letter, has connections which continue through the entire account; [there is] even a kind of arithmetic of words. It is known that in the neighbouring civilizations…writing sometimes constituted a veritable cryptogram… As far as the Hebrews are concerned, the techniques of expression have not yet been fully deciphered. [The biblical writers] had a writing art to which we do not now have the keys. The structure of the language is extraordinarily wrought, even to the detail of the letters… There are internal harmonies between words, even between letters; there are stunning balances (*équilibres bouleversants*). A biblical text was 'assembled' with the same exactitude, the same precision, as is used today in assembling the elements of a computer or a missile.

---

4. T.L. Thompson 1992: 356; P.R. Davies 1992. Note also Goulder 1993b.

5. Between some Old Testament books, there are several curious connections: for example, Obadiah with other prophetic writings (Wehrle 1987: 365-71); Joel with diverse biblical texts (Bergler 1988: 131-333); Jeremiah with Ezekiel (Vieweger 1993); Isa. 65.25 with Isa. 11.6-11 (van Ruiten 1992). In varying degrees, particularly in the case of Ezekiel and Jeremiah (Vieweger 1993: 64-69), these connections suggest far-reaching direct literary dependence. There is also a certain literary unity, at least redactional, between the twelve minor prophets, thus raising 'questions [that] have received little attention in Old Testament research' (Nogalski 1993: 1).

Whatever the details of Hebrew composition, whatever the details of dependence, the essential point is clear: the case of Deuteronomy suggests an origin that in large part is not only literary but also dependent on literary sources which are known. Given that Deuteronomy is so embedded in the Genesis–2 Kings corpus—it culminates the Pentateuch and colors all of Joshua–2 Kings—the reworking and combining of texts is not some far-flung oddity. It is at the center of Old Testament narrative.

5. *Later Jewish Writing: Rewritten Bible and Prophetic History*

In 1961 Geza Vermes used the term 'rewritten Bible' to describe the work of several Jewish authors who, around the turn of the era, rendered the biblical narratives into a new form. *Genesis Apocryphon* (c. first century BCE), gives an elaborate reworking of Genesis 1–15. In J.A. Fitzmyer's description (1971: 11), *Genesis Apocryphon* is 'an example of late Jewish writing, strongly inspired by the canonical stories of the patriarchs, but abundantly enhanced with imaginative details'.

The imaginative details are not sheer fabrication. The description of Sarah's beauty (*Gen. Apoc.* 20.1-7), for instance, while absent from Genesis, corresponds broadly with the descriptions of the woman's beauty in the Canticle of Canticles (Cant. 4.1-7; 5.9–6.1; 7.1-9). What appears to be present, therefore, is not just a rewriting of Genesis, but a combining of Genesis with other material. The book of Wisdom has aspects of the same process: while engaging Hellenism it reworks Genesis and Exodus 1–15 (see Schwenk-Bressler 1991).

Apart from *Genesis Apocryphon* there are several other instances of rewritten Bible. D.J. Harrington (1986) lists *Jubilees*, *The Assumption/Testament of Moses*, the Qumran *Temple Scroll*, Josephus's *Jewish Antiquities*, and Pseudo-Philo's *Biblical Antiquities*.

The 'rewritten Bible', however, is not a clear category. *Genesis Apocryphon*, for example, is sometimes called a 'haggadic midrash'. But the meaning is much the same as 'rewritten Bible', and the latter term is clearer and is generally less likely to suggest a definite category of literature. Harrington, for instance, is particularly careful to avoid the idea of a definite category. Even while using the term 'rewritten Bible', he maintains (1986: 243) that 'each piece of literature has to be approached on its own terms', and he implies (1986: 242) that it would be better to refer to each of the various documents as 'a free rewriting of [a] part...of Israel's sacred history'. Because of this essential openness of the term 'rewriting', it is appropriate to apply it to books like Deuteronomy and Chronicles.

The idea of the free reworking of history is not unique to the rewritten Bible. A further sense of the same freedom occurs in another turn-of-the-era group of writings: the *Pesharim*, or 'Interpretations', discovered at Qumran. These are fifteen section-by-section commentaries on biblical books, mostly on the prophets. Each section has three parts: the biblical text, the formula introducing the interpretation, and the interpretation itself. Thus concerning Hab. 1.6a the text reads:

> 'For behold I am raising up the Chaldeans,
> that bitter and hasty nation'.
> *The interpretation* of it concerns the Kittim [= Romans],
> who are swift and vigorous in battle so as to destroy many...

This brief example touches a basic underlying belief: history can be read in such a way that it speaks directly to the present. Anyone with a sense of historical accuracy would say the prophet Habakkuk was speaking about the ancient Babylonians ('the Chaldeans'), but for the Qumran interpreter the reference is to the Kittim or Romans. M. Horgan comments (1979: 229): 'The pesher is an interpretation made known by God to a selected interpreter of a mystery revealed by God to the biblical prophet concerning history'. Thus the prophets were not writing for their own times. Rather, what they said was like an apocalypse or a revelation about a later stage of history.

The *pesharim* show four main kinds of adaptation:

1. *Contemporization/Actualization.* The ancient context is left aside and the action is depicted as occurring among new people and circumstances.
2. *Word-Play.* Occasionally, instead of dealing with the whole text, the interpreter singles out a basic word, root or idea, and elaborates on it.
3. *Metaphorical Identification.* For example, the Babylonians are the Romans, Lebanon is the council of the community, the righteous is the Qumran Teacher of Righteousness, and the wicked is the Wicked Priest.
4. *Elaboration.* This refers to both the elaboration that is inherent in interpretation, and also to specific instances of elaboration such as building on isolated words.

These two groups of writings—the rewritten Bible and the prophetic 'Interpretations'—treat history and biblical interpretation in a way that does not accord with historical criticism. For them, history can be freely reshaped, whether into a new form of the past (the rewritten Bible) or into a past that refers to what is new (the *pesharim*). They do not have the sense of history as an unchanging objective reality. Rather, history is something that in diverse ways is interwoven with the present.

6. Conclusion

In summarizing some Jewish methods of interpretation from Genesis to Qumran it is easier to say first what they do not do: they do not follow historical-critical methods. This may seem obvious, yet it needs to be said, for it provides the background of another basic principle: the evangelists do not follow historical-critical methods. While it is generally easy to accept the freedom of ancient Jewish writers, there is often a presumption that the evangelists are different. Not that anyone expects the evangelists to be scientific historians, but it is often forgotten that they are rooted in a world of multi-faceted interpretation, and that they have as much right as any other ancient interpreter to adapt the biblical text radically to their own message.

Having said what ancient biblical interpretation was not—not critically historical—the question remains of what it was. This, however, is not easy to answer. Even such a relatively clear case as Chronicles' use of Kings has been difficult for scholars to categorize.

Rather than attempt to delineate clear categories, it seems better to suggest some working principles. The first is that there seems to be no limit to the ways in which an interpreter may use a biblical source. At times the dependence may be clear, but on other occasions, such as Deuteronomy's use of the women stories in Genesis, it may involve a form change (e.g. from story to law) and may be subtle.

A further related principle has already been formulated by D. Harrington (1986: 243): 'each piece of literature has to be approached on its own terms'. Examples from ancient Israel may provide partial models for the biblical interpretation of the evangelists, but each gospel has to be allowed its own mode of interpretation.

The mode of interpretation implied in most gospel synopses is one that involves much verbal similarity. To some degree that is also the case with Chronicles; there is much verbal similarity with other biblical books. But the other major example, Deuteronomy, indicates a mode of interpretation, of rewriting, which is much less obvious, much more complex. Both examples are important. The diversity found in Chronicles and Deuteronomy provides an important background for the diversity of reworkings in the gospels.

Orientational Conclusion to Chapters 1 and 2

Taken together, Chapters 1 and 2 confirm what others have often briefly stated: ancient writers built on the work of earlier writers and did so even within the biblical tradition, although one cannot say in advance how a particular writer will do so. Dionysius of Halicarnassus (c. 30 BCE) and Daniel Harrington (1986) are in agreement that each author's mode of composition is distinct. All one can do is learn from examples and be attentive to what the author is doing.

However, before embarking on literary comparisons, or before making claims of literary dependence on specific sources, it is appropriate to take further preparatory steps. The first such step is to seek an appreciation of Old Testament narrative in its own right, particularly the narrative of the Primary History.

3

The Biblical Tradition: Narrative as Poetic Art—
The Case of Judges

> The Samson story...a superb masterpiece of Hebrew narrative art...is structured at all the compositional levels with an almost architechtonic tightness.
>
> —Jichan Kim (1993: 424)

Having surveyed aspects of composition both in Greco-Roman literature at large and in biblical narrative, it is now necessary to look more closely at the nature of Old Testament narrative. Appreciation of a text's nature increases the likelihood of understanding its use. Since Judges and the Elijah–Elisha narrative are used significantly in Luke's gospel they provide appropriate examples. This chapter concentrates on Judges.

The understanding of the book of Judges has recently undergone a transformation. Previously regarded as a kind of scrap-heap of diverse historical objects, most of them rusted almost beyond recognition, it has now emerged as a striking work of art, something which, while echoing elements of past history, has art's orientation toward more permanent truth. The transformation in understanding did not come quickly. There had indeed always been those, artists especially, who found inspiration from Judges. But historical criticism raised serious questions about the unity of the book, and those questions were tenacious.

The problem is that at one level, Judges looks old and muddled. Many of its elements have an ancient flavor, but the whole does not seem to fit well together. It has two introductions, its treatment of the various judges is very uneven, and its conclusion appears to consist of two appendices. It claims to cover 410 years but this claim does not fit other historical data (Mayes 1974).

Nonetheless, Judges seemed helpful to historians. The apparent tension between the central episodes and the general framework appeared to be a clue to the formation of the book, and thus to history. So, for many years, historians combed through Judges in search of elements from the distant past. This approach occurs, for instance, in the volume by J.M. Miller and J.H. Hayes (1986).[1] These two authors indicated that one can distinguish between the book's framework, which to them seems 'artificial and schematic', and its various episodes, episodes which 'originally had to do with localized affairs...[and which] have a more authentic ring' (1986: 90). The fact that these episodes apparently conflict with the (allegedly editorial) framework indicates that 'the narratives were already well established in Israel's folk memory when they were incorporated into the Genesis–II Kings corpus' (1986: 90).

On the basis of these perceptions, Miller and Hayes believe that Judges can function as a foundation or 'a tentative starting point' for history (1986: 91):

> While these narratives will not, unfortunately, provide a basis for reconstructing any kind of detailed historical sequence of people and events, they probably do offer a reasonably accurate impression of the general sociological, political and religious circumstances that existed among the early Israelite tribes.

---

1. A somewhat similar approach appears in Halpern 1988.

3. The Case of Judges

The purpose stated here is modest; Miller and Hayes seek to indicate only a minimum degree of history. Such modesty is not only appropriate, it is disarming; it suggests a sense of balance, and so implies a stance that is reasonable and agreeable.

But balance presupposes that all the evidence has been weighed. The problem here is whether the greatest weight of evidence has been omitted: whether, in the pursuit of a necessary historical quest, Miller and Hayes have bypassed the essence of Judges—its literary nature—and whether, in bypassing that essence, they are misreading the book and thus undermining their own investigation.

Apparent confusion could indeed be a reflection of diverse historical traditions. The more confusion, the easier it is to invoke such concepts as oral tradition and folk memory, particularly if these concepts are not defined. For that reason, much biblical history thrives on apparent confusion. But perhaps the confusion is superficial. Is it not possible, asks Robert Alter (1981: 133), that 'the biblical writers...had certain notions of unity rather different from our own?'

Already in the 1960s and '70s, ideas about the apparent confusion in Judges began to give way to a view of its integrated artistic nature. In B.G. Webb's summary (1987: 25): 'The work of Smend and Veijola taken together suggests that the opening and closing sections of the book are much more closely integrated...into its central section than was recognized by Noth and Richter'. In fact, even as early as 1961, L. Alonso-Schökel was speaking of Judges as art. (For reviews of research, see Webb 1987: 13-38; Preuss 1993: 254-64; on Samson, see Kim 1993: 1-114.)

But it was after the late 1970s that thoroughgoing analysis of the text began to reveal the full extent of the coherence and sophistication of Judges. Three authors are particularly representative and significant—J.C. Exum (1976, 1980, 1981), B.G. Webb (1987) and J. Kim (1993). Together they indicate that Judges, far from consisting of an artificial framework and ill-fitting episodes, is in fact a unified work of sophisticated literary art. Once the text is seen in this way, it becomes impossible to distinguish between artificial and authentic content, and it is correspondingly more difficult to invoke such elusive and debatable entities as folk memory. Thus the emphasis in reading Judges moves from history to art. ('Art' is a more appropriate term than 'fiction'. As plain English, 'fiction' tends to trivialize; 'art' reflects an engagement with truth.)

It does not seem possible, at this stage, to say whether the New Testament writers knew as much about Judges as modern researchers—maybe less, maybe much more since they had advantages over modern readers. But if modern researchers are to be open to the New Testament writers and various uses of the older text, then it is better to know as much as possible about that text, especially about its basic unity and nature. For this reason, it is worthwhile to examine Judges more closely.

The unity and nature of Judges may be placed under two headings: basic elements and the role of women. First the basic elements.

1. *The Unity of Judges: Basic Elements*

It is usually agreed that Judges consists of introductory material (1.1–3.6); a series of episodes which have been fitted into a unifying framework (3.7–16.31); and concluding material (chs. 17–21). It is also generally agreed that both the introductory material and the concluding material are twofold.

However, these elements are more orderly than may at first appear. Rather than speak of two introductions and two conclusions it is more accurate to speak of a two-part introduction and a two-part conclusion. In complementary ways, the two parts of the introduction provide indications of the coming problems (1.1–2.5; 2.6–3.6). The two parts of the conclusion (chs. 17–18; chs. 19–21) are in many ways overlapping pictures of chaos, and they provide resounding confirmation that Israel's problems are profound.

Furthermore, within the two parts of the introduction it is the second which is more explicit and emphatic concerning the extent of the problems to come; a good deal of the first part of the introduction seems quite positive (cf. 1.1-17). Similarly, within the two parts of the conclusion, it is the second—a story involving a devastating civil war—which illustrates most powerfully the depths to which Israel has sunk. Thus, at various levels both in the overall relationship between 1.1–3.6 and chs. 17–21, and in the relationships within the two introductions and within the two conclusions, there is a general pattern of intensification.[2] Since the elements which are being intensified are negative, the general impression is one of decline and fall.

Just as there are two introductions and two conclusions, so there is a basic two-part pattern within the central episodes (3.7–16.31). First, these central episodes increase in quantity and intensity from Othniel to Gideon (3.7–8.32), and then, starting with a larger quantity, they increase from Abimelech (from 8.33) to the longest story of all, that of Samson (chs. 13–16). Since the elements being intensified are often negative, the general picture again is one of decline.

The pattern of repetition and intensification is summarized in Table 1 (the horizontal lines on the right reflect increasing volume).

Table 1. *The Structure of Judges*

First Introduction (1.1–2.5):	an intimation of future problems	
Second Introduction (2.6–3.6):	a clearer indication of future problems	
First Series of Judges		
OTHNIEL	(3.7-11)	—
EHUD (plus Shamgar)	(3.12-31)	——
DEBORAH/JAEL	(chs. 4–5)	———
GIDEON	(6.1–8.32)	————
Second Series of Judges		
ABIMELECH (plus Tola, Jair)	(8.33–10.5)	——
JEPHTHAH (plus Ibzan, Elon, Abdon)	(10.6–12.15)	———
SAMSON	(chs. 13–16)	————
First conclusion (chs. 17–18)	cultic chaos	
Second conclusion (chs. 19–21)	total moral chaos	

The process of intensification may be seen in the quantity of the text. By and large the stories of the main characters become increasingly longer. Similarly with regard to the minor characters whose stories are told in three increasingly large groupings (Shamgar, 4.31; Tola, Jair, 10.1-5; Ibzan, Elon, Abdon, 12.8-15). And while the first story (Shamgar) is shortest of all, the final one (Abdon) is the longest.

---

2. On the centrality of intensification in Hebrew poetic composition, see Alter 1985: 10-26, 62-84. As Alter indicates (pp. 6-7), what is true of Hebrew poetry is true also, 'in many instances', of Hebrew literary prose. H.-W. Jüngling (1981: 114), in analyzing Judg. 19, refers explicitly to a process of *Intensivierung*.

The essence of the decline is the deteriorating relationship between Israel and God. At first, in the case of Othniel, the process of cry and response—Israel cries for help, and God responds—works like a dream (3.7-11). In fact, the story tells of almost nothing else, and however brief, it refers to God's response in triple form (3.9-11). With Ehud it also works smoothly. God's response is mentioned twice and again it is immediate (3.15, 28). In the story of Deborah, the response is once more effective, dramatically so; but, for the first time, between the account of the cry and that of the response there is a momentary pause (4.3). In the Gideon story the plight of Israel reaches a new level of suffering (6.1-6) and the cry is answered not by an immediate response but with a stern rebuke (6.7-10). As Webb comments (1987: 157), 'It is clear that the appeal is being abused and that Yahweh is beginning to lose patience with Israel'.

The Abimelech episode, perhaps because of its special link with the Gideon story, does not tell of the kind of plight which usually provokes the cry and response, but when the cry recurs in the Jephthah story, the initial reaction, once again, is not response but rebuke and refusal (10.10-14). Finally, in the story of Samson, 'the Israelites show little sign of even *wanting* to be rescued... Samson does not want to fight the Philistines; he wants to intermarry with them' (Webb 1987: 163). It is left to God, by whatever means, to move Samson to fight (e.g. cf. 13.25; 14.4, 6, 19; 15.14).

A further major symptom of decline is that the process of delivering Israel from danger becomes increasingly twisted, and what emerges more and more is not salvation but self-destruction and civil war. The first three stories tell of clear-cut victories, but in Deborah's song there are indications of tribal disunity, and one town, Meroz (of Naphthali), receives an ominous curse (5.14-23). After that, the situation worsens. Gideon exacts vengeance on Succoth and Penuel (8.13-17). Abimelech kills his half-brothers and brings internal disorder. Jephthah kills his own only child. Samson becomes swallowed up in the conflict and eventually kills himself. Finally, there is the self-destructive war (chs. 19–21).

The fact that continuity is not limited to the episodes' framework becomes even clearer when the plots and motifs of the episodes are analyzed and compared. A single sentence of two clauses tells that Othniel overcame the king of Edom (3.10). In a more elaborate narrative it is told that Ehud killed the king of Moab, and that he won a victory over ten thousand Moabites (3.12-30). Then comes a yet more elaborate account, of the victory of Barak's ten thousand men over the Canaanites and of Jael's killing of Sisera (ch. 4). The killing of Sisera is such that it is a complex variation on the killing of the king of Moab (see Alonso-Schökel 1961: 148-67). And so on. Each episode, however new and independent it may look at first sight, turns out to be intricately interwoven with what precedes and what follows. Even the minor characters are fitted into this fabric. The one striking detail about Shamgar, for instance, his use of an unorthodox weapon, the ox-goad (3.31), helps to set the scene for Jael's use of the tent-peg (Webb 1987: 137). And the tragedy of Jephthah's killing of his unmarried daughter is highlighted by the immediate recounting of the story of Ibzan, the judge whose distinguishing feature was his abundance of sons and daughters, and especially his exchanging of daughters in marriage (12.8-10) (Webb 1987: 161).

This interweaving of plot and motif builds up first to the story of Gideon, and then climactically to that of Samson, the story which, to a significant degree, both varies that of Gideon and synthesizes many of the elements of the earlier episodes (Webb 1987: 164-65). However, as the juxtaposing of Jephthah and Ibzan suggests, the continuity frequently consists of contrast, and, when the story of Samson is complete, with its account of being delivered to one's enemies, it turns out to be a reversal of that of Othniel.

A detailed analysis of the longest judge story, concerning Samson, strengthens the evidence of unity. In Exum's judgment this story 'exhibits a sophisticated literary patterning'

(Exum 1981: 3). And subsequent detailed analysis has confirmed that judgment (Kim 1993: 424).

Overall, therefore, strong evidence suggests that the text of Judges is unified and sophisticated.

2. *The Unity of Judges: The Role of Women*

Central to Judges are the women, a fact first highlighted by M. Bal (1988). In fact, the pattern of decline is reflected most graphically in the decline in the fate of its women. First there is Achsah (1.12-15). Though to some degree subject to her father Caleb and her husband Othniel—they are the two outstanding leaders of 1.1–2.6 and 3.7-11—she manages nonetheless to move them according to her will. Later, the two generals, Sisera and Barak, are overcome in diverse ways by Deborah and especially by Jael (chs. 4–5). And in an episode that is complementary to that of Sisera and Jael, a woman of Thebez crushes the head of Abimelech with a millstone (9.50-55).

But the victory of the woman of Thebez is much less spectacular than that of Jael. The account is brief and the actual killing is completed by Abimelech's own armor-bearer, and in the subsequent clash, it is the man of arms who wins: Jephthah the 'valiant warrior' kills his daughter (11.1).

Samson's ongoing battle with the Philistines revolves around his relationship with three Philistine women. The first, his wife, is killed in the hostilities (15.6). The second is a harlot with whom he sleeps, and whom, along with her Philistine compatriots, he surprises with a midnight show of overwhelming strength (16.1-3). The third, the beloved Delilah, achieves the Philistines' goal of overpowering him, but in the end, the Philistines and their god are devastated (16.4-31). Thus, through his dealings with all three, he ultimately leaves a trail of destruction behind him.

Finally, the terrible violence of the civil war is caused by horrendous violence towards a woman (ch. 19).

Thus, having begun with a brief introductory portrait of a woman who is calmly confident and full of life, which is part of the connotation of the springs which Achsah obtains (1.12-15), and having expanded that impression in the story of Deborah and Jael, the narrative spirals downward into stories of women who are increasingly stricken. Achsah's role is echoed in later episodes (Gros Louis 1974: 144-45) and ultimately all the women's portraits combine into a single picture of descent into tragedy. Only at the end, and then in a rough way, is there a suggestion of relief and reversal: as the daughters of Shiloh dance at the feast, they are carried off forcefully yet peacefully to become brides in rebuilt towns (Judg. 21.15-23).

Hence, while granting the need for further research,[3] once again it seems reasonable to conclude that the diverse episodes of women are interwoven to form a coherent pattern.

---

3. Investigation is necessary, for instance, concerning the sexual content or overtones which occur in several episodes and images. For R. Alter, the detail of the killing of Ehud has something 'hideously sexual' (1981: 39) and Jael with her deadly tent-peg is a 'sexual assailant' (1985: 49). The Jael scene is such that the tent-peg does in fact have sexual overtones, and Webb, though without emphasizing the sexual connotation, connects the driving of the tent-peg through the head with other elements: Ehud's sword, which comes from the thigh and enters the belly; the ox-goad used by Shamgar; and the pin with which Delilah fastens Samson's hair (Webb 1987: 136, 164, 178). There are sexual connotations also in the portrait of Achsah, the woman who enters marriage with an apparent abundance of water (1.12-15), and more obviously, in the account of Jepthah's daughter bewailing her virginity. Given these connections, and given that Webb (1987: 41) speaks of Judges as involving 'a dense network of interlocking motifs', the connections between the following elements may be worth investigating: the ox-goad (3.31), the tent-peg

3. *The Origin of Judges*

Judges contains ancient elements and evokes the distant past, a time when judges came and went.

The story goes on and on, apparently for centuries. In those days, there was no king. The entire account has a flavor of 'Once upon a time in old wild Israel…'

Yet one cannot be sure that the book is as old as its initial appearance suggests. There are diverse reasons for doubt. The first is the phenomenon of literary archaism, making writings sound old. Among Greco-Roman writers at least, archaism was a deliberate literary art (Klotz 1907; Craig 1927; Callebat 1964; G. Williams 1978). Something of the same archaizing practice prevailed in the Near East. The scribe, for instance, who wrote about King Nabonidus of Babylon 'pushed the story back a thousand years' (Conteneau 1966: 213).

A second reason for questioning the antiquity of Judges is that when it is taken as a whole—and given its tight unity it cannot be judged reliably except as a whole—it suits the time of the fall of Judah, the time of exile and restoration.

A connection with the fall of Judah may be seen first of all in its central pattern, its picture of decline and fall. The question arises as to whether this picture, set in the days when there was no king, should be connected with another time of kingless confusion during the fall and Babylonian captivity. In Webb's words (1987: 202), 'The narrator speaks as one who has seen kingship come and go'. The synthesizing picture of Samson, for instance, insofar as it emphasizes that it was God and not Dagon who gave him into the power of the Philistines, is like a variation on a theme of the exilic prophets (p. 165).

A further connection with the exile may be seen in the women. From the confident Judahite at the beginning (1.9-15) to the ravaged Judahite at the end (ch. 19), these women appear to constitute a multi-image portrayal of the decline and fall of Israel, especially of Judah. That the women are in some way representative of the people seems likely. For instance, the three Philistine women in the Samson story seem representative. Their roles are closely interwoven with the roles of the Philistines as a whole. And it is hardly an accident that the ravaging of the Judahite is followed by a picture of mass killing among the people (chs. 19–20); the fates of the woman and the people are interwoven. She is representative.[4] And while the increasingly sad fate of the women evokes the fall of Judah, the final incident, concerning the daughters of Shiloh, suggests a process of restoration (cf. 21.23-24).

For these reasons, there is a suspicion that the book was written after the exile. What is certain is that until such questions and possibilities are faced, and until literary studies on the text are taken into account, the book of Judges cannot be used as a source for the eleventh century.

(4.21), the peg or pin (16.13), the tower (9.52), the millstone (9.53), the mill (16.21), the elements of water (feminine) and fire (masculine; cf. the fire motif in ch. 9, especially 9.52), the fire torches inside the water pitchers (7.16), the torches between the tails of the foxes (15.4), the ass and the ox (cf. ass and water, 1.14-15; use of the ox-goad, 3.31; use of the jawbone of the ass and water, 15.15-20), the storming of the gates and the two posts (16.1-3).

Apart from the debatable details, the more crucial question is whether the idea or suggestion of sexuality, often found in the core of the episodes, should be linked with the images of women (including men's abuse of women) and with the framing ideas of fidelity and harlotry.

4. The role of the woman as representative of the people does not exclude the idea that, as P. Trible implies (1984: 64-87), the Judahite is in some way a symbol of suffering womanhood. Like the Suffering Servant, with whom Trible (1984: 64) compares the Judahite, she seems to have diverse levels of signification.

4. The Nature of Judges: Conclusion

While it is difficult to be sure about Judges' date of origin, there is considerable clarity about its nature. It is an intricate work of art, a multi-episodic history-like parable which spirals downward, and which intimates, long before the event, the decline and captivity of Judah. This assessment accords with its traditional Jewish classification not as 'historical', but as 'prophetical', as one of 'the Former Prophets'.

The artistic and prophetic character of Judges does not preclude the use of the book as an aid in reconstructing historical conditions, including sociological conditions. But history, no matter how pressing its agenda or how limited its claims, cannot bypass the artistic and prophetic nature of the text. For instance, there is no way that Samson, whose story is both a reversal and an intricate synthesis of all of the central episodes (all the other judges), can be described adequately and reliably as 'a hero remembered in folk tales for his strength, the trouble he caused the Philistines, and his practical jokes' (Hayes and Miller 1986: 94). The only Samson known to us, the one in the book of Judges, is a magnificent reminder of a floundering tragicomic Israel being delivered into captivity where the people rediscover the ability to call on God.

The picture of Samson is a work of art. If that picture is perceived as second-rate history, the essence of the art is lost and with it, the essence of the narrative. Instead of being a portrayal of some form of greater or more permanent truth, Judges becomes reduced to a collection of historical oddities that would be of little interest to an evangelist. What is essential, therefore, is not to exclude the historical approach to Judges but to set it on a surer foundation. Its place is within the larger context of artistry and prophecy that is established by the very nature of the text. It is with this larger dimension of artistry and prophecy that Proto-Luke was primarily concerned, and so he used Judges with corresponding freedom, with a sense that it is an artistic work with deep meaning, a prophetic work waiting for fulfillment, waiting to be rendered into a new form of expression.

The concept of timeless art is essential. Some texts are time-bound. One cannot use a detailed account of Hannibal's march towards Rome, elephants and all, as a basis for describing the Allied invasion of Normandy. Hannibal's march was very specific; its details were tied to a precise time and place. Imposing such details on the events of 1944 would be a distortion.

But if among the accounts of Hannibal's campaign there was a reflective poem written by a soldier on the night before battle, then, regardless of how many local details it included, it could be very appropriate for describing how many young soldiers felt facing Normandy. The old poem has a timeless quality. It is primarily art, not history. Likewise Judges. Despite all its colorful detail, it has a quality of timeless art. It lends itself to adaptation for a later era.

4

The Biblical Tradition: Narrative as Poetic Art—
The Elijah–Elisha Narrative as a Unified Interpretive Synthesis

In 1994, when this chapter was first written, it began as follows: 'Nobody has yet done for the Elijah–Elisha narrative what authors such as Exum, Webb and Kim did for Judges—rescue it from alleged fragmentation and show the coherence of the present text. Yet there are indications that such coherence exists.'

Faced with this lacuna, the present chapter set out to investigate the possible unity of the prophetic narrative (1 Kgs 16.29–2 Kgs 13). The result was unforeseen: the chapter expanded into a small book: *The Crucial Bridge: The Elijah–Elisha Narrative as an Interpretive Synthesis of Genesis–Kings and as a Literary Model for the Gospels* (2000). Among the book's conclusions, two are central:

1. The entire narrative (1 Kgs 16.29–2 Kgs 13) forms an eightfold unity.
2. The narrative synthesizes the rest of Genesis–Kings (except some Mosaic law).

Details aside, the essence of these ideas is as follows.

1. *The Narrative (1 Kings 16.29–2 Kings 13)*
Forms a Precise Eightfold Unity

There are at least three general features that suggest that the Elijah–Elisha narrative forms a unity: succession, prophecy, and healing. Succession refers to one of the text's most obvious aspects: it forms a succession narrative; its account of how Elisha succeeds Elijah fits into a broader pattern of succession stories that usually constitute a certain unity. Prophecy also binds the text: every episode of the Elijah–Elisha narrative, including those not dealing directly with Elijah and Elisha themselves, is concerned with prophets or prophecy. Even the murderous excesses of Jehu and Athaliah (2 Kgs 9–11) fall within the scope of what has been prophesied. And, taken as a whole, the Elijah–Elisha narrative emphasizes healing in a way that, within the Old Testament, is unique.

However, apart from these general indications, there is a feature which is more precise: the entire Elijah–Elisha narrative consists of eight diptychs: two-part texts in which the first part is complemented by the second. The most obvious example is the opening story of the drought (1 Kgs 16.29–ch. 18): the account consists essentially of the introduction to the drought (16.29–ch. 17) and, after a long time, of the drought's conclusion (ch. 18). There are other aspects of complementarity. For instance, Ahab and Jezebel, first pictured as godless and criminal (16.29-33), are introduced in the second part of the diptych as even worse—as murderers (18.4-14). Furthermore, the first part's emphasis on God's power over water (ch. 17) is balanced in the second part by God's power over fire (18.20-40). And so on, both in this diptych and in seven others. The eight diptychs fall into two fours, like two great dramas. See Table 2.[1]

---

1. For commentary on Table 2, see Brodie 2000: 6-27.

Table 2. *The Eightfold Elijah–Elisha Narrative*

Drama One: Elijah
1. *Drought and a Woman: Amid Evil, the Word Gives New Life* (1 Kgs 16.29–ch. 18) Ahab, Jezebel: evil. Drought begins. The word gives life (16.29–ch. 17) Ahab, Jezebel: killers. Drought will end. Carmel: more life, especially water (ch. 18) 2. *Death Threatens* (chs. 19–20) Jezebel threatens Elijah. Elijah, at Horeb, hears and revives. Purposeful return (ch. 19) Aram threatens Ahab. Ahab victorious but only half hears. Depressed return (ch. 20) 3. *Death Comes Closer* (chs. 21–22) Jezebel manipulates a lying court. Naboth murdered; punishment foretold (ch. 21) Spirit manipulates court prophets. Battle: Ahab killed; punishment fulfilled (ch. 22) 4. *The Two Faces of Death: Fall and Assumption* (2 Kgs 1–2) Ahaziah's fall and illness: death as an implacable descent (ch. 1) Elijah's assumption: death as an ascent (ch. 2)
Drama Two: Elisha
5. *War, Drought, Women: Amid Evil/Want, the Word Gives New Life* (2 Kgs 3–4) Warring kings (in Moab). The Moabite king kills his son (ch. 3) Women in want. The women save their sons (ch. 4) 6. *Arameans (Naaman; Hazael): Distant Shadows of Death* (chs. 5–8) Naaman and Aramean raiders: hearing and seeing; not killing (5.1–6.23) Aramean invaders and Hazael: mis-hearing God, and not seeing; killing (6.24–ch. 8) 7. *Jehu: The Word Brings Death* (chs. 9–10) Jehu kills three leaders: Israel's king; Judah's king; Jezebel (ch. 9) Jehu kills three groups: Israel's royalty; Judah's royalty; Baalites (ch. 10) 8. *As Death Closes In: Temple-Based Restoration* (chs. 11–13) Amid death, life within the temple. Arms! Athaliah dies. King restored (ch. 11) The temple is renewed. Elisha's arms. Elisha dies. Israel restored (chs. 12–13)

The number of verses in the various diptychs is as follows:

The Elijah drama:	30/46	21/43	29/54	18/25	Total: 266
The Elisha drama:	27/44	50/59	37/36	20/47	Total: 320

Generally, within each diptych, the second part is longer; and, in the Elijah–Elisha as a whole, the second drama, concerning Elisha, is also longer.

The organization into eight diptych units (in two fours) is not only precise; it is also meaningful. In biblical symbolism, four signifies completeness: four winds; four ends of the earth; four rivers of Genesis 2; fourfold encampment around the ark (Num. 2). Two fours indicates a completeness that is overflowing.

What is essential is that the Elijah–Elisha narrative—a text which at first sight may seem to be a collection of materials that are diverse and unrelated—turns out on closer inspection to be a closely constructed unity.

2. *The Elijah–Elisha Narrative as an Interpretive Synthesis of Genesis–Kings*

It has often been said that Elijah, particularly when he visits Horeb (1 Kgs 19), reflects the figure of Moses. This is true, yet it is just a small part of much larger truth: the entire Elijah–Elisha narrative reflects the rest of the Primary History (Genesis–Kings). Genesis, especially its flood, is distilled and refracted in the opening account of the drought (1 Kgs 16.29–ch. 18); the two leading images—flood and drought—are like two sides of the same coin. As already suggested, the story of Moses, especially its Sinai scenes—Exodus–Deuteronomy, except some Mosaic law—is compressed largely into the story of Elijah at the mountain (1 Kgs 19). The subsequent story of invasion (Joshua), especially the invading of Jericho, is refracted into the subsequent story of being invaded (1 Kgs 20); again, the two leading features—invading and being invaded—are like two sides of the same coin. The lawless ethos of the book of Judges— 'in those days there was no king in Israel' —is reflected in Ahab's *de facto* abdication of power to his murderous wife (1 Kgs 21); and the way in which she acts, taking over power and killing, synthesizes aspects of characters in Judges, particularly aspects of Deborah and Jael.

And so on. Apart from some Mosaic law, every leading book or collection of books in the Primary History is mirrored in the Elijah–Elisha narrative, in the same order. Eventually, the final years (2 Kgs 18–25), especially the temple-centered reform of the young Josiah, are reflected in the final episodes of the Elisha story (2 Kgs 11–13), particularly in the temple-centered reform of the young Joash.

This systematic distilling and transformation of the Primary History is not completely unique. There is a partial analogy for it in the way that 1 and 2 Chronicles distills and adapts Genesis–Kings. But while 1 and 2 Chronicles employs a form of rewriting that is reasonably straightforward, the Elijah–Elisha narrative reflects the texts in a way that is more complex, a way that changes the images.

The role of the Elijah–Elisha narrative within the Primary History is somewhat like that of a tower within a church complex. The tower stands somewhat apart, and was probably almost the last part to be constructed, yet it is an integral part of the larger complex. Furthermore the tower can express or interpret the larger body of buildings. Certainly the Elijah–Elisha narrative expresses and interprets the Primary History. It carries out several hermeneutical moves, including the following:

1. The centuries-long procession of patriarchs and kings gives way to an emphasis on the word, especially the prophetic word and the ministers of the prophetic word, prophets (Chronicles moves the emphasis to priests). Accompanying this move away from the glory of kings and towards the role of the word, there is a general tendency to pay greater attention to what is going on within ordinary people, whether stick-gatherers, or stewards, or lepers. Thus, to some degree at least, there is a move towards a greater emphasis on what is internal.

2. The idea of life after death—muted in most of the Primary History—comes more clearly to the fore, especially in the central, defining, picture of Elijah going up to heaven, and in the three accounts of people being raised from the dead (obscurely, 1 Kgs 17.17-24; more clearly, 2 Kgs 4.18-20; and 2 Kgs 13.21, clearest of all).

3. The greater emphasis on ordinary people finds an echo in the very form of the writing: in the Elijah–Elisha narrative there is a shift from historiography towards biography. Not that the accounts of Elijah and Elisha are biographical, but, in genre, they are closer to biography.

3. *The Nature of the Elijah–Elisha Narrative: Conclusion*

The stories of Elijah and Elisha do not consist of two loosely related collections of curious prophetic tales. Rather, they are closely unified into eight diptychs (two fours) and taken together they form a powerful systematic interpretation of the whole flow of ancient biblical history. History is mirrored so that its essence comes to the surface, shifting from figures of glory to lives that are more ordinary, and to a greater sense of the ways in which ordinary life can be nourished: through the prophetic word; through greater attention to a dimension that is more internal; through healing people back to life; and, finally, through a process of life-giving that challenges even death.

4. *Elijah–Elisha and Luke*

This summary of the nature and unity of the Elijah–Elisha narrative helps explain why Proto-Luke chose it as a foundational model and why he used it as freely as he did. The prophetic narrative was not a secondary collection of poorly fitting stories. Rather, it was a synthesis of the great issues of life and death and, most significantly, of the people's foundational history. If Proto-Luke wanted to make a fresh synthesis of the history of the *word* and of the *history of the people*, the Elijah–Elisha narrative went far in showing how to do it.

But, particularly because the Elijah–Elijah literary model was prophetic, filtering Israel's past history into a new prophetic and artistic form, and evoking a reality greater than itself, Proto-Luke was not bound by the old shape; on the contrary, he developed it with freedom. Prophecy was designed not for stagnation but for fulfillment. In the new figures of Jesus and his disciples the old prophets would reach that fulfillment.

However, claiming that Proto-Luke used this or that Old Testament narrative cannot be done without further analysis. It is necessary to clarify the criteria for claiming literary dependence.

5

Criteria for Judging Literary Dependence

> The [writer] need not cite [the] source-text [but…] can treat it in a limitless variety of perspectives…from interlinear translation…to the faintest most arcane of allusions… It is up to us to recognize and reconstruct the particular force of relation.
> —George Steiner (1975: 424-25)

Among all the aids for the study of literature, there has been none that summarizes the criteria for judging literary dependence. The result, especially in biblical studies, is a lack of focus on a basic aspect of method. There are indeed many studies of specific cases of literary influence, including studies of criteria for identifying Q (Bergemann 1993; Denaux 1995), but there is no general guide about diagnosing such cases. Steiner's words bear repeating: 'it is up to us'.

This lack of a general guide is symptomatic of a greater malaise: modern literary studies, including some biblical studies, are so deeply post-Romantic—so imbued with the sense that authorship means originality—that the study of direct literary dependence has never been a clear priority. On the contrary, literary dependence is regarded as something to worry about (cf. Harold Bloom's 1973 *The Anxiety of Influence*). In fact, influence is so alien to the modern sense of authorship that some modern poetic circles have difficulty in accepting T.S. Eliot as a real poet: he is too indebted to older writings.[1] As E. Van Wolde (1989: 45) said of the twentieth century, 'it is difficult or even impossible for us to accept a definition of art as "the perfect imitation"'. In some deep way, the discerning of literary dependence is not on the modern mental agenda.

Given this lack, claims to literary dependence—particularly if they are new—fall into a vacuum. Most researchers, even if they are widely read and open-minded, are not practiced in handling such claims. And if the mental habit has never been established, it is difficult to apply it suddenly. The problem is aggravated in reviewing books or articles. Reviewing tends to be a speedy process, but literary indebtedness is often dense and subtle—highly resistant to speed. Virgil, for instance, apparently composed the *Georgics* at the rate of less than a line a day (Hardie 1970: 1125). At times, literary dependence looks far-fetched and complicated and out of control. Therefore the understandable response is to turn away from the phenomenon either by rejecting its possible validity or more simply by ignoring it.

Such can be the fate even of such recognized scholarship as that of F. Neirynck. Neirynck (1984) put forward a strong case, balanced and detailed, indicating that John's resurrection narrative depends on the Synoptics. But some researchers, otherwise fine scholars, who followed Neirynck and who knew of his work simply did not engage him; they did not get involved with the detail of the evidence (cf. Brodie 1993b: 27). It is much easier to invoke something missing (a background or document) or to focus attention on other issues than to wrestle with the evidence in all its weight and detail.

---

1. On Eliot's use of sources, see Murray 1991b: especially 9-14. On poetic composition, cf. Murray 1991a: 50.

The problem of judging dependence is particularly acute in biblical studies—far more than in classical or Renaissance writings where broad connections and dates are clearer, and there is a sense of who precedes whom. But in biblical research the situation is one of deep uncertainty. Within the Old Testament there are two foundational bodies of literature —the Primary History (Genesis–Kings) and the prophets—but, for many scholars, it is not clear whether there is dependence between them, and still less what the direction of that possible dependence might be. In the New Testament there are also two main bodies of literature—the gospels and the epistles—but again it is not clear if there is dependence between them. The situation of the gospels is particularly isolated. While most scholars regard Matthew and Luke as depending on Mark, there is uncertainty not only about Mark and John but about the gospels as a whole. As a group, as a genre, they are unique; at times they seem almost to come from nowhere, depending on no other literature.

If this situation is to be redressed, insofar as it is possible, criteria must be established. The burden for establishing such criteria lies with the one claiming dependence. If that person does not indicate the criteria clearly—which is often the case—there is little room for complaint when readers do not engage the evidence.

The task is not easy. The problem concerns art, not science, and at times the criteria or the ways of applying them are inadequate. But progress can be made. It is not sufficient, however, to establish criteria which are positive. It is also necessary also to identify some principles which can cause confusion—explanations which, instead of resolving the uncertainty, compound it. The positive criteria come first, then the principles which mislead.

1. *Positive Criteria*

There are three main kinds of indications that one text depends on another: external plausibility, internal similarities, and the intelligibility of the differences.

a. *External Plausibility (Context)*

There is no point in trying to show that the Genesis deluge account depends on those of the West Indies, or that Luke's history is modeled on the fourth-century accounts of Eusebius. The relationships of time and space exclude such possibilities. Nor is it a promising task, just because Paul's eucharistic words (1 Cor. 11.23-27) are very similar to those of Luke (22.14-20), to try to show that Paul depended on Luke. Almost all calculations indicate that Paul wrote first.

Dependence can be invoked only if external factors make such dependence plausible. If ancient writers ignored predecessors, and if Luke, for instance, was culturally isolated—someone who had learned basic writing from a relative at home and who apparently had never traveled or learned Greco-Roman rhetoric or read the Old Testament—then one could not plausibly suggest that he had systematically transformed the Elijah–Elisha narrative or the book of Judges. But if dependence on earlier writings was the norm, if Luke apparently traveled and if there is conclusive evidence that he knew rhetoric and imitated the Septuagint, then the idea of an imitative transformation becomes much more credible.

b. *Significant Similarities*

(1) *Similarity of theme.* Erich Segal's brief novel *Love Story* is vastly different from *Romeo and Juliet* and is perhaps is in no way dependent on it, but at least the stories share a common theme, and so there is an immediate affinity that does not exist between, say, *Love Story* and *Macbeth*.

Similarity of theme can be an initial clue to dependence between writings. Usually it proves nothing; themes tend to be too general for drawing conclusions. But similarity of theme can set the stage for a more probing investigation.

In the case of Luke and the Elijah–Elisha narrative, the similarity of theme is striking. The idea of 'the great prophet', so central in the Old Testament text, pervades much of Luke's work—so much so that the Lukan Jesus is often described precisely as 'a prophet'.

In the case of Judges, the similarity is not as clear, and if Judges is read as a collection of old, rough, stories, then it remains alien to Luke. But if Judges is a work of art—if its recurring figure of the woman concerns the ravages of sin and the fall and suffering of Judah—then it has an immediate affinity with Luke's concern for sin, suffering, and the marginalized.

(2) *Pivotal leads or clues.* Even if the relationship between two texts is complex or obscure, the author may give some key indication of the link between the two. As mentioned earlier, the example of Elijah and/or Elisha appears in two leading texts: the opening speech (Lk. 1.5-25; see 1.17) and Jesus' inaugural speech (Lk. 4.16-27). And the two most elaborately described judges, Samson and Gideon—Samson fills four complete chapters (chs. 13–16), Gideon three (chs. 6–8)—are likewise strongly reflected in leading scenes: the two annunciations which set the whole drama in motion reflect first the story of Samson (Lk. 1.5-25; cf. Judg. 13.2-7) and then that of Gideon (Lk. 1.26-38; cf. Judg. 6.11-24, 33-40). If the stories of the two most conspicuous judges are reflected so clearly at the beginning of the work, then it is plausible to ask whether the author engaged Judges as a whole.

(3) *Action/plot.* Similarity of action can be a strong clue to literary dependence. The fact that both Elijah and Jesus are taken up to heaven, for instance, does not of itself prove dependence but, given the unusualness of the action, it calls for investigation. If the incident is surrounded in both texts by other similar actions then suspicion of dependence grows. Likewise, little follows from the fact that Elijah and Jesus raise a widow's son, but when the narratives go on to say that Elijah and Jesus both gave the son back to the mother, then the matter deserves closer scrutiny.

(4) *Completeness.* If only some passages from a possible source appear to be reflected in the finished writing, then a problem arises about the nature of the relationship between the texts. Why should some be missing? And does this absence cast some doubt on the relationship to the rest? A classic example is the impression, at first sight, that Luke does not contain a large segment of Mark (6.44–8.27). But if all the passages of the possible source are reflected in some coherent way in the final text, then the case for direct dependence is strengthened. Proto-Luke, for instance, not only uses the Elijah–Elisha narrative and Judges; in his own way, he uses *all* of these texts. Such completeness is no accident. It indicates systematic dependence.

(5) *Order.* When random elements occur in two documents in the same order the similarity requires explanation. Similarity of order does not occur easily. If two people, independently of each other, arrange the numbers 1 to 5 at random, the chance that they will arrange them in the same order is less than one in a hundred. If the numbers are 1 to 10, the chance is less than one in a million.

Acts 1–5, for example, not only has a whole series of elements which it shares with 1 Corinthians 1–5, but it also has them in almost exactly the same order. It does not seem possible to explain this phenomenon except by literary dependence.

(6) *Linguistic details.* One of the features of the evangelists' use of sources is that, even when radically transforming sources, they maintain a slight but steady undercurrent of

detailed similarity, often linguistic similarity. Sometimes the order or rarity of these detailed similarities is such that the best explanation seems to be direct dependence. For instance, the drama of the man born blind (Jn 9) involves a thorough reworking of the center of Mark (8.11–9.8), yet each of the six scenes in John 9 contains some detail or details which link it to its Markan counterpart in a way that is always unusual and sometimes unique.

(7) *Complex coherence.* Some texts, as well as containing similarity, also contain complexity—not a complexity that is meaningless or confused but one that is coherent. Again in John 9 this is true: the relationship to Mk 8.11–9.8 is one of complex coherence. Coherence, however, especially in its more complex forms, does not happen accidentally and cannot be explained through oral processes; there is a degree of complexity which oral tradition cannot handle. As W. Ong (1977: 254) says in a related context, 'closer plotting requires writing'. Thus in many cases of complex coherence, the most realistic explanation is literary dependence.

c. *The Intelligibility of the Differences*
The differences between texts may be misleading; they may give the false impression that one text cannot possibly depend on the other. But differences, no matter how great, do not decide the issue. The purpose of writing, as distinct from copying, is to say something that is in some way different. Difference, therefore, is of the essence of writing.

There is no limit on how different a writer can be from predecessors. Even the most sacred text can be rewritten or reversed: 'It was said to you of old... But I say...' As already seen, the books called 'the rewritten Bible' contain 'a free rewriting of [a] part...of Israel's sacred history' (D. Harrington 1986: 242).

The issue, therefore, when comparing texts is not whether there are differences, but whether the differences are intelligible. Even the writings of Gandhi, in the hands of someone perverse, could be turned to perverse purposes. Generally, however, the dynamic is not perversity but creativity. In comparing Ezekiel with John 10, for instance, Bultmann (1971: 367) points to the dissimilarities and decides against dependence. But for Brown (1966: 397) these dissimilarities are not decisive; rather the issue is 'whether there is sufficient similarity to suggest that the Old Testament supplied the raw material for...[a] creative reinterpretation'.

Creative reinterpretation is central to the discussion. It is creative reinterpretation which first causes the differences, and it is the concept of creative reinterpretation which subsequently makes them intelligible.

The decisive issue, however, is not whether the differences are great, but whether they are intelligible. For instance, Matthew's conclusion to the walking on the water (16.22-33) is radically different from that of his source (Mk 6.45-52), but, within the context of Matthew's larger strategy, the difference is understandable. The sinful couple in Acts 5 is guilty not of incest, as in 1 Corinthians 5, but of fraud—again a major difference, but one which accords with the larger Lukan emphasis on possessions. Jesus' refusal to call down destructive fire from heaven (Lk. 9.54-55) is in direct contrast to Elijah's killing of over one hundred soldiers (2 Kgs 1), but the difference fits with Luke's wider portrayal of Jesus. Likewise with the other warlike incidents in the Old Testament: they have been transformed to accord with a different strategy, a focus not on a specific *land* but on the *kingdom of God*. What counts, then, is not difference, but intelligibility.

2. Principles that Can Mislead

In assessing evidence about literary dependence, there are a number of factors that sometimes mislead or cause confusion:

a. *Some Connections are Weak*

Total analysis is virtually impossible, and so in almost every comparative analysis of two texts there are points where the comparison is uncertain and the connections are weak, obscure, questionable, or apparently non-existent. Insistence on what is weak, whether by the one presenting the comparison or by someone questioning it, obscures the decisive issue: Are there strong arguments?

The overall strength of the chain of literary lineage depends not on the weakest link, but on a whole series of chains. That some are weak does not matter as long as there are enough that are strong.

Weaknesses occur in an analysis not only because total analysis is almost impossible, but also because the analyst makes mistakes or is inexperienced. For instance, my dissertation on Luke–Acts and the Elijah–Elisha narrative (Brodie 1981d) is wrong on one whole episode (Acts 8.1b-8; see 1981d: 289-301) and weak on others. Again, however, the issue is not whether there are mistakes but whether there is enough strong evidence to make the overall connection credible, or at least to make it worthy of further study. What the investigator needs, therefore, is the ability to sift through evidence that is weak or misleading and to see whether there are a few good leads, or at least one.

b. *The Differences Preclude Dependence and Point to a Shared Tradition*

There are times when, even if two writings show clear similarity and difference, direct dependence may not in fact be the explanation. Perhaps instead of borrowing directly, they both used a shared source and interpreted it differently (see, for instance, Ellis 1957: 79).

This is possible, and cannot be directly disproved. But it is a gratuitous claim and cannot be proved. And since it bears the burden of proof—it claims documents that no one has ever seen or traditions for which there is no reliable evidence—it is in the weaker position.

One of the results of this claim to a third entity is that it avoids the phenomenon of direct dependence and thereby avoids dealing directly with the problem: the difference between the two documents. At a superficial level it makes the problem easier. The difference, with all its difficulty and richness, disappears under the cover of a third, unproven element. The moment in which the difference occurs is pushed into an inaccessible background.

Removing the difficulty can create the illusion that the difficulty has been solved. But it has not. To avoid claiming: 'A changed B', this theory says, 'A changed C, and possibly B changed C as well'. But these hypothetical changes are no more plausible than A's changing of B. The problem will not go away: at some stage, someone changed a source significantly. If that change is accepted in principle—in fact it is unavoidable—then why not accept it immediately? The simplest hypothesis that accounts for the data is to say 'A changed B'.

The old proverb applies: 'Things should not be multiplied without necessity'.

c. *The Similarity May be Due to General Familiarity Rather than Direct Literary Dependence*

If someone absorbs the works of, say, Pascal or Dickens, it is likely that at a later stage the thoughts and phrases of these authors will reappear in the person's speech and writing. Much of the process is unconscious and it is not a question of direct literary dependence.

This does indeed happen and it may lead to the conclusion that identifying direct literary dependence is almost impossible.

The conclusion that follows, however, is not that identifying literary dependence is impossible but that the researcher needs to be doubly careful. The positive criteria, given above, need to be applied rigorously, checking not only for broad similarities, style, and occasional phrases and details, but also for the whole range of factors which might indicate direct dependence—from external plausibility to the sequence of details to instances of complex coherence.

d. *The Similarity Does Not Correspond to Model X (e.g. Matthew–Mark), Therefore, There is No Dependence*
If a researcher's imagination is dominated by just a few basic models of literary dependence—for example, Matthew/Luke's use of Mark, or Josephus's use of known sources—then more complex cases may not receive the patient attention they need. In practice, in New Testament studies, just a few models dominate, especially Matthew's way of using Mark. Thus, one implicit reason for rejecting John's use of Mark is John's deviation from the method used by Matthew. But exclusion of an obvious method does not mean something did not happen. Certainty that there was no shooting does not mean certainty that there was no murder.

e. *Complex Structures Do Not Presuppose Literary Usage*
Anthropological studies indicate that the human mind, quite apart from writing, has inbuilt structures and is capable of handling difficult sagas.[2] Illiterate Zulus, for instance, speak a language which is wonderfully complex and orderly. Consequently, structure and complexity do not necessarily depend on conscious effort or on deliberate literary strategy. Like the case of the person who unconsciously reproduces aspects of an author, the presence of innate structure may lead to the conclusion that one can never be sure about deliberate literary strategy and dependence.

But again the more careful conclusion is not to abandon the investigation but to try harder: to apply rigorously the criteria for dependence, to work with both hypotheses—independence and dependence—for a sufficiently long time that one gets inside them and tests them at length and in detail, preferably for years. There are many problems and limitations with the two-source theory of the Synoptic Gospels, for instance, but many of those who have worked for a long time with the hypothesis that Matthew or Luke used Mark believe not only that the theory of dependence on Mark works, but also that their continuous application of the theory brings ever more supportive evidence in its favor. Likewise, when one is faced with a complex structure or a complex dependence, it is sometimes necessary to work at length with the details to see whether perhaps the literary explanation is the more reliable. This issue, however, touches on a wider discussion: the role of oral tradition.

f. *The Similarity is Due to Oral Tradition*
Oral tradition (discussed in Chapter 6 at greater length) is capable of remembering things in diverse ways, sometimes with great accuracy, sometimes with considerable changes. Since figures such as Elijah and Elisha were popular in Jewish tradition at the time of Jesus, oral tradition is the first and most obvious explanation of why the story of Jesus reflects diverse aspects of these two great prophets. The literary explanation, on the other hand, involves another hypothesis, complex and subtle, presupposing manuscripts and

---

2. Linguistic theory seeks 'to account for the rapidity and uniformity of language learning, and the remarkable complexity and range of the generative grammars that are the product of language learning' (Chomsky 1965: 28).

writing equipment and implying a process which is expensive and self-conscious—a far cry from the picture of the open-air prophet and his band of disciples. The oral tradition hypothesis, therefore, is the easier explanation of the data, and it is closer to the spirit and ethos of the gospel.

The most obvious problem with this view is that even if oral tradition played an important role, it cannot explain all the gospel data. The heart of Matthew and Luke—in their use of Mark—reveals a highly literate and deliberate process involving manuscripts and writing equipment. And the rest of Matthew and Luke—the non-Markan parts—are generally regarded as implying further manuscripts. Gospel composition, therefore, must come to terms with the whole complex apparatus of writing. The role of the literary process is certain.

The role of the oral process, however, is unclear. It is indeed true that, at first sight, the uncertainty of oral tradition broadly corresponds with the apparent uncertainty of the way the Elijah–Elisha tradition appears in the gospels. But first sight is not accurate enough. It was not first sight that established the dependence of Matthew and Luke on Mark; it was years of detailed testing. And when Luke and the Elijah–Elisha narrative are tested at length—allowance being made for the transformative christianization of the older writing—the same conclusion begins to emerge: the relationship between the texts is so consistent, detailed, and coherently complex, that the only adequate explanation is that of direct literary dependence.

Still, lest oral tradition haunt the investigation, it is necessary to deal with it.

6

Oral Tradition: Wonderfully Plausible but Radically Problematic

When Gunkel introduced research into *literary forms (genres)*, he not only stimulated a change of method but also challenged a model. What he writes in his introduction to Genesis [1901] illustrates the imaginative side of his model. His predecessors, he says, envisaged the text as though it were a work produced in an office whereas he pictured for himself a storyteller, surrounded by his listeners, retelling old stories. He saw a community assembled for their typical, regularly recurring gatherings making use of a repertoire of works composed for these occasions.

—Luis Alonso-Schökel (1985: 6)

To think that the Hebrews were simple people who, under their tents, recounted stories which were later put in writing or [to think] that the biblical books are the echo of purely oral traditions is to lose the sense of the Bible ('avoir de la Bible une conception aberrante'). A text like Genesis is magnificently crafted ('magnifiquement surélaboré'). It is not only written, it is written as no one ever wrote. I do not know, in all the world's literature, a text that makes use of such word technique, of such science of expression, of so much art.

—André Chouraqui (1975: 455)

The relationship of the New Testament to oral tradition is twofold, almost contradictory. On the one hand, the New Testament paints a *picture* in which oral tradition is primary and pervasive. This applies to the various accounts of Jesus, the disciples, the apostles' preaching and even to the epistles, especially Paul's explicit appeals to tradition (1 Cor. 11.23; 15.1-3). On the other hand, the picture itself is *written*. Discussions about the formation of the New Testament often refer to oral tradition, but the idea is unclear, and it is controverted.[1]

The purpose of the present chapter is to stand back from the complex detail of the discussion and to try to follow the underlying logic. Concentration on this logic will not do justice to the larger contribution of those involved, especially of Gunkel and Bultmann, but it is a necessary procedure if the idea of oral tradition is to be clarified. The analysis indicates that in the question of the composition of the New Testament, the idea of oral tradition is new, unfounded, unworkable, and unnecessary.

1. *Oral Tradition as New*

Oral communication is as old as humanity, and it is portrayed also in the New Testament, especially in the preaching of Jesus and the apostles. In that sense the idea of oral tradition is old and central to the New Testament. The issue here is not about the portrayal's content but about its origin: how the New Testament itself was formed.

---

1. See, for instance, Halverson: 1994; Koester: 1994. Note, also, Byrskog 1994: 155-65. Byrskog's work is closely related to that of B. Gerhardsson.

6. Oral Tradition

There was a time when the gospels were seen as the product of writing—of competent authors using some ancient form of pen and writing materials. It was presumed that the evangelists had either been present at many of the events they described (like Matthew and John) or had received their information from authoritative sources (Mark from Peter, and Luke perhaps partly from Paul). Historical criticism before 1900 questioned these authoritative identifications, but the basic picture of gospel composition remained relatively simple. The time-gap between the essential events and the gospels was generally reckoned at not more than fifty or sixty years. An evangelist, even if absent during the original events, would have been able to speak directly to eye-witnesses or to use first-hand writings. Whatever the details, however great or small the degree of history, the essential process was presumed to be one of writing, inspired writing.

But in the twentieth century an essentially new idea was introduced: oral tradition. Contrary to the way people see most books, ancient and modern, the gospels came to be regarded as the product not so much of writing but of an oral process that essentially had nothing to do with the world of pens and writing materials.

The new idea had sometimes been mentioned before 1900—for instance, by J. Wellhausen (1876: 9)—but, as the quotation from Alonso-Schökel indicates, it was H. Gunkel who used it as a model and who thus introduced it to the center of biblical studies. This he did particularly through his commentary on Genesis (1901).

The contrast between Gunkel and Chouraqui is sharp. Through decades of painstaking translation, Chouraqui managed, even before literary studies of the Bible reached their present level, to appreciate Genesis as writing that was artistic and sophisticated, but Gunkel looked at Genesis and saw something other than mature writing. Gunkel's perception was different not only from Chouraqui (who followed him) but from his own predecessors, from scholars who in their own way also treated Genesis as writing, as literature: '[Gunkel] not only stimulated a change of method but also challenged a model' (Alonso-Schökel 1985: 6). In effect, he gave the twentieth century a new paradigm.

Within a few years, this new idea 'form-criticism' began to appear in New Testament studies. Gunkel (1901: xix) had implied that his analysis could be applied to the life of Jesus, but the person who actually made the application was Wellhausen. Wellhausen's conclusions—published in a series of commentaries and introductions to the gospels, 1905–11—were later summarized by R. Bultmann:[2]

> The oldest tradition consisted almost entirely of small fragments...and did not present a continuous story of...Jesus. When these fragments were collected they were connected so as to form a continuous narrative... [Wellhausen] showed not only that the evangelists' narratives... were secondary, but also that oral tradition was steadily producing more and more new sayings of Jesus'.

The change of paradigm was soon adopted by K.L. Schmidt. In 1919 he used Gunkel's model to distinguish between Mark's framework, which Schmidt reckoned came from the evangelist, and Mark's various units, which Schmidt assigned to oral tradition (1919: v).

Soon M. Dibelius (1919) and Bultmann (1921) reiterated the emphasis on oral tradition. And so a new idea of the gospels emerged: they are not really literature, not the work of literary people. At one point Bultmann described the gospels, or at least the Synoptics, as 'unliterary'.[3]

The result is that the gospels have become strongly associated with oral tradition. In the words of H. Wansbrough (1991: 9), 'An emphasis on...oral tradition...has been one of the

---

2. Bultmann 1926: 340-44. Cf. R.J. Thompson 1970: 110.
3. '*Unliterarisch*'. See Bultmann 1931: 7.

salient contributions of the twentieth century to the study of the gospels'. Wansbrough accepts this emphasis as valid but his comment is revealing: the role allotted to oral tradition is largely a twentieth-century innovation.

2. *Oral Tradition as Unfounded*

From one point of view, the idea of oral tradition is plausible. Since the dawn of humanity there has been oral communication; and so it will be until human history ceases. Furthermore, with oral communication comes some form of oral tradition. Even a brief sentence involves communication, a process of handing something over to another, and the reporting of that sentence begins to build an extended chain. Oral communication, therefore, including oral tradition, is not something unusual. It is part of the fabric of life. Oral communication is like the air which a writer breathes. It is inevitable, then, that to some extent the New Testament depends on oral communication.

The problem is to what extent. Do the gospels merely reflect an oral atmosphere or is their indebtedness to oral tradition more central to their composition?

A writing's dependence on oral communication may entail any of three basic aspects.

a. *Minimum*

At the very least, writing inevitably uses some words and phrases from daily speech, and almost invariably reflects something of the ethos of daily communication. The computer textbook, for example, no matter how obscure, contains some phrases from daily speech.

b. *Form*

The whole form of the text is governed by oral communication. The writer largely thinks through the patterns of oral communication, and the writing is geared to oral communication; it is composed, not so much for the eye—as is the case with the computer textbook—but for the ear, to be heard (Ong 1971: 1-22 [1-4]). To some degree this form of dependence may be found in modern writing, especially in the writing of speeches, but it was uniquely strong in ancient composition when writing was a relatively new medium; it not only lived completely in the shadow of oral communication, but was also largely governed by rhetoric. Rhetoric was the art of speaking, but it became also the art of writing, with the result that speaking and writing were inextricably interwoven. As indicated earlier (Chapter 1), rhetoric pervaded the educational system[4] and almost every kind of writing.[5] In the words of W.J. Ong (1971: 214), rhetoric 'encapsulated the most ancient, central, and pervasive tradition of verbalization and of thought known to mankind at least in the West'. In this sense *all ancient literature is oral*, including the Greco-Roman classics and the Bible.

c. *Content*

This refers to the writer's basic message: the central story and its meaning. The writer's story comes not from personal observation or from other writings, but through listening to oral accounts and writing them down. The nature of these oral accounts may vary. In some classifications they are divided into *oral history* (informal, e.g., personal experiences) and *oral literature* (more formal, e.g., old legends and stories which have been handed on in oral tradition) (Lord 1978: 33-35).

---

4. For a summary of the way rhetoric pervaded Greco-Roman education, especially in the first century CE, and for references to the key works on education by M.P. Nilsson, H.I. Marrou, and D.L. Clark, see Kurz 1980b: 192-94.

5. On the supremacy of rhetoric, see Dalton 1962: 438-524; Baldwin 1924: 224-25.

6. Oral Tradition

The difference between the second and third degrees of dependence is clear in the well-known example of Virgil. Virgil's poetic thought patterns and modes of expression were massively influenced by the orality of his era; he wrote for the ear; his epic was being read aloud even during his lifetime. The foundation of his central story, however, the account of Aeneas, did not come from oral sources; it came from his copy of Homer. Oral communications may have contributed to his variations on that story, but the essential story was based on an earlier writing, not on oral tradition. His dependence on oral means, therefore, was essentially of the second kind, concerning form, not of the third, concerning content.

Gunkel's claim was of the third kind: Genesis is oral literature. It depends on oral tradition not only for its form but also for its central content.

To set Gunkel's claim about Genesis in context, it is necessary to mention some earlier claims. Before 1900 there had been two pivotal ideas about oral tradition: the old Jewish idea of an oral tradition going back to God's giving the Law to Moses; and the anthropological idea about the way stories are handed down in societies which do not rely on writing.

The Jewish idea of tradition does not come from the Old Testament; according to the Old Testament, God gave the law to Moses in one medium: writing. But later, the idea developed of what J. Neusner calls a 'myth' that God had also given the law through a second medium: oral tradition (Neusner 1985: 1):

> Judaism maintains that when Moses received the Torah from God at Mount Sinai, it came in two media. One was the Torah in writing. The other was the…'oral Torah'…mean[ing]…the 'memorized Torah';… The Mishnah…is the first document of that part of the Torah that in Jewish myth came to Israel in the medium of memory.

It is not certain when exactly the Jewish people began to invoke this authoritative tradition, but there is considerable evidence—for example in Philo, in the gospels (Mk. 7.3; Mt. 1.2), and in Josephus—that it already existed in the first century CE (Safrai 1987: 39-40).

The second, anthropological, idea was developed in the eighteenth and primarily the nineteenth century in studies of non-literate societies and in the collecting of stories that previously had been orally preserved and transmitted. In the twentieth century, study of this phenomenon continued, especially in work such as that of M. Parry and A.B. Lord.[6]

It is understandable that the Jewish rabbis ascribed their Mishnah, written around 200 CE, to Moses-based oral tradition. It invested their new writing with great authority. But it is not clear why Gunkel ascribed Genesis to oral tradition of the anthropological kind; why, when faced with the same text as Chouraqui, he started talking about primitive communities.

The basic reason given by Gunkel is that the stories of Genesis are not *history* but *sagas*. And sagas depend on oral tradition (Gunkel 1901: i, xl). When Gunkel says that sagas depend on oral tradition, he is essentially right. Those before him who gathered and recorded oral traditions often classified the various stories and legends as 'sagas'. So the word 'saga' was associated with oral tradition.

The problem is with the classification. How, in the first place, does Gunkel know that Genesis consists of sagas? Because, as Gunkel saw it, there are only two possibilities, histories and sagas (*Geschichte* and *Sage*), and, as Gunkel asserts, Genesis could not possibly be history.

The reason for this assertion is given in the opening lines of his commentary (p. i), under the heading, 'Genesis is a Collection (*Sammlung*) of Sagas':

---

6. For references, see Lord 1978: 33-35; Talbert 1978: 93-94; Foley 1988: especially 19-56.

Are the accounts (*Erzälungen*) of Genesis stories or sagas (*Geschichte oder Sage*)? For the modern historian this question is no longer a question, yet it is important to make clear the grounds for this modern position. History writing (*Geschichtsschreibung*) is no innate art of the human spirit, but has emerged in the course of human history, at a particular point of development (*an einem bestimmten Punke der Entwicklung*). Uncultured peoples (*Die uncultivierten Völker*) do not write history.

The rest is detail. Gunkel did not allow that there are two kinds of history: modern ('scientific') and ancient (historiography, as in Herodotus or Genesis–Kings). His unreal dilemma —history or saga?—had opened the way for his classification of Israel as 'uncultured', and, once that was done, the notion of oral tradition became more plausible. All he needed to clinch the argument was to indicate some apparent similarities between Genesis and sagas.

The next step was to postulate that, in its oral form, Genesis had originally existed in fragments, in isolated incidents. The reasoning here is not immediately clear. It is true that Genesis and sagas (and many other compositions, including some films) consist partly of short episodes or incidents, but how does that prove that the episodes originally existed separately?

In trying to clarify Gunkel's logic, part of the problem is that 'he was not the most exact of writers. He was capable of defining a term or stating a principle in one paragraph, and then of contradicting it soon after' (Rogerson 1974: 57). In this case—concerning the hypothesis that the episodes were originally separate from one another—the answer lies essentially in the way Gunkel imagines the detail of the oral process, particularly his ideas about the mental capacity of the people. The brevity of the short episodes

> corresponds to the art of the story-teller and the hearer's ability to absorb. The oldest story-tellers were not able to set forth complex works of art... Rather, the old times (*die alte Zeit*) were satisfied with giving very small products (*ganz kleinen Produkten*) that would fill something less than half an hour. And when the story was ended, the hearer's fantasy was fully satisfied and his ability to absorb exhausted. (Gunkel 1901: xxi)

Again, they were uncultured people. The same reason which first led Gunkel to attribute Genesis to oral tradition also led him to imagine that the people could cope only with little episodes; so the tradition could have existed only in isolated stories, in fragments. Genesis, rather than being an integral writing, is a collection (*Sammlung*), or rather a collection of collections.

The final step was to rearrange the fragments, or episodes. Partly because of his ideas about the original isolation of the episodes, and also because of the documentary theory (as in Wellhausen and others), Gunkel's commentary freely rearranged Genesis.

In his third edition (1910), Gunkel seemed to strengthen his argument. He referred to a brief article by A. Olrik concerning criteria for identifying dependence on oral tradition, but there were two problems about this procedure: despite referring to Olrik's article, Gunkel apparently did not regard it as important; and Olrik's criteria were not reliable in themselves (Warner 1979: 330-35).

Warner's conclusions (1979: 327, 335) seem warranted: 'The basis of Gunkel's argument [is]…a developmental theory of history [… He gives] no reason to assume that the narratives of Genesis bear any close resemblance to orally transmitted data at all.'

E. Nielsen is also unfavorable in his assessment of Gunkel's approach: Gunkel's Genesis commentary 'not only…rearrange[s]…the material… but the reader is constantly aware of the way in which the 'mature Western European' presents the naïve attitude of the 'childish Oriental' towards nature…God, etc.' (Nielsen 1954: 11). Given such an attitude, it becomes more understandable how, even when faced with a superb writing, magnificently crafted, Gunkel's imagination jumped to something naïve or simple. Alonso-Schökel's wording is significant: Gunkel 'pictured for himself a storyteller… He saw a community.'

This jump—picturing communities—subsequently entered biblical studies, including New Testament studies. In the case of John's gospel, the picturing of communities became particularly unpredictable ('science fiction') (see Kügler 1984).

Nielsen agrees with the idea of oral tradition, but he is no more successful than Gunkel had been in showing how biblical narratives presuppose an oral background. When he finally examines an Old Testament narrative (Gen. 6–9), his work consists essentially not of giving positive indications of dependence on oral tradition but of criticizing the Documentary Hypothesis (Nielsen 1954: 93-103).

To some degree Gunkel's claim is understandable. He felt that certain aspects of Genesis—some of the data—corresponded to oral literature, to the sagas which anthropologists had gathered from oral sources.

Some of the data. That is the essence of the confusion. In a sense, Gunkel was right. Genesis is encyclopedic and antiquarian; it filters the world's history and legends even back to the days when there were giants on the earth. Given such a mass of data, it was easy to find some data which seemed to correspond in some way to oral literature. Besides, once he understood the question as a choice between someone sitting in an office and a storyteller—another version of his unreal dilemma—there was little doubt which way he would go. And so the fateful path was taken: on the fortieth page of his commentary, Gunkel starts talking about the foundational role of oral tradition. And behind the oral tradition were, not authors, but communities.

At a stroke, biblical writers, as real writers, had been virtually eliminated. Gunkel had created an atmosphere in which it would become easy to accept that Mark was clumsy and that John's gospel was isolated, confused, and open to rearrangement.

The first half of the twentieth century surrendered to his influence. The second half, while still paying him homage—some of it justified—strove to recover the reality of authorship. The first step was redaction criticism, raising the evangelists above the level of mere collectors. Then came modern literary criticism, a discipline that, despite the danger of imposing alien modern ideas on ancient writers, contributed insights to the artistry of the biblical writers. Finally, there is an emerging emphasis on ancient rhetoric. This is literary criticism of a more appropriate kind, and as the evidence grows for its use in the Bible, especially in the New Testament, the biblical books emerge more and more as the work of genuine writers, namely literary artists.

Many New Testament scholars have now reached the conclusion that the gospels are fine writings. While moving ahead, the paradigm is coming full circle. The idea of 'genuine literature' has returned and, as it does, Gunkel's invoking of 'oral processes', unclear from the beginning, now looks even more inappropriate.

On what basis, then, is it possible to go on claiming oral tradition? The essential argument of W.H. Kelber is that ancient writing was particularly influenced by oral culture and rhythms (1992: 30-31). Kelber is right, but what he says applies to *all* ancient writings; they all reflect the rhythms of oral speech. That does not prove that all authors depended on oral tradition; it simply means they wrote for the ear rather than the eye. What Kelber is talking about—and it is an aspect of the gospels worth highlighting—is the second degree of dependence on orality, dependence of form and of thought pattern. But this is not to be confused with the third degree, dependence of central content. Kelber never shows that the gospels are indebted to oral tradition in a way that other ancient writings are not.

Perhaps the most systematic effort to apply logic to the claim for oral tradition was that of A.B. Lord (1978). He endeavored to show how some of the patterns of oral literature also occur in biblical texts, such as the gospels. He may be partly right, but that does not prove the case; to some degree, similar patterns can be shared by diverse literatures. As C.H. Talbert indicated in replying to Lord, some of the same patterns occur in literary biographies (1978: 94). In other words, the patterns which Lord claims are oral, are in fact literary, and found in genuine literature. More of what Lord attributes to oral influence can be more fully accounted for by what R. Alter (1981: 51-52) calls 'literary conventions'. And the fact that the gospels largely consist of episodes fits into a literary pattern—'the cult of the episode'.[7] B. Bryan's conclusion about Mark makes the necessary distinction: Mark, a *bios*, is pervasively oral (meant to be read aloud), but it is not oral literature (it is not the written form of a *bios* that had been composed orally) (Bryan 1993: 152-53).

Claims about oral tradition continue, but the basis for the idea remains confused. For B. Gerhardsson the basic argument is straightforward (1986: 49-50):

> It is very striking that Jesus himself did not write. He was a man who spoke. He talked to people, he preached orally, taught orally, made mighty acts with his oral word etc. Nothing indicates that Jesus wrote down one single logion, parable or speech. Nor is it indicated that he incited cooperators or disciples to write or that he dictated to them. The verbal tradition that Jesus himself initiated, was *oral*.
>
> As for the disciples, it is nowhere mentioned that they took notes or carried notebooks... The disciples remember, ponder and discuss Jesus and his words and deeds.

This argument is clear. But Genesis 1 is equally clear that the world was made in seven days. One cannot reliably argue from the narrative to a historical fact. Gerhardsson's argument presupposes that the gospels are of a specific nature—that they are essentially historical. What Gerhardsson's argument proves is that—regardless of what happened historically—the picture painted in the gospels is one in which the method of communication is oral. In other words, the conclusion is not about history but about a gospel picture, about literary art and its theological implications. The historical questions about Jesus and the gospels' origins must be answered on other grounds.

The kind of logic used by Gerhardsson recurs in the work of the Jesus Seminar:[8]

> Jesus wrote nothing, as far as we know. We do not know for certain that Jesus could write; we are not even positive that he could read, in spite of suggestions in the gospels that he could. His followers were technically illiterate, so writing did not become part of the Christian movement until persons like Paul became involved.
>
> Jesus taught his followers orally. He was a traveling sage who traded in wisdom, the counterpart of the travelling merchant who traded in soft and hard goods. Jesus taught his disciples as he moved about, and his words were first passed around by word of mouth. The gospels portray Jesus as one who speaks, not as one who writes.

In a sense this is correct. The gospels do indeed portray Jesus as a speaker, not as a writer. Furthermore, the Seminar is admirable in its search for clear rules about trying to trace sayings to an oral period and in its use of modern anthropology to trace how oral tradition works.[9] The problem is not with oral rules and modern anthropology, but with the relevance of such information to the gospels.

The Seminar confuses diverse levels of dependence on orality. It uses the difference between ancient oral culture and modern print culture—a real difference—to make a

---

7. See Williams 1978: 246-53 (246): 'The *Metamorphoses* of Ovid [died 17 BCE] was a model of the greatest influence for at least a century in many ways but especially in its exemplary structure. It consists of more or less disconnected episodes, which the poet with great wit and ingenuity, has welded into a *perpetuum carmen*...' The gospels are not poetry, but they are composite, and as such they are capable of absorbing diverse features of several genres. Ovid was the leading poet of Rome. It is a symptom of his stature that St Augustine, at a crucial moment, imitated him; see Mahon 1989.

8. Funk, Hoover, and the Jesus Seminar 1993: 27.

9. Funk, Hoover, and the Jesus Seminar 1993: 25-34.

division between an oral Jesus and writing.[10] But our evidence for Jesus is in writing, and no matter what portrait of Jesus that writing gives, one may not, logically, jump from the writing to the historical reality of an oral Jesus. Words on a page, no matter what they say, do not of themselves constitute a particular kind of person.

There are only two ways one may assert such an oral Jesus: by establishing the essential historical reliability of the gospels, or by presupposing an oral Jesus. The Seminar does not establish the historical reliability of the gospels; on the contrary, it treats the gospels' historicity with unpredictability. Its assertion of an oral Jesus, therefore, is a presupposition.

Something similar is true of James D.G. Dunn. He makes an impassioned plea for attention to oral tradition, but his case is based on a presumption: 'We simply cannot escape from *a presumption of orality* for the first stage of the Jesus tradition' (2003a: 157). Dunn does not discuss how ancient writers composed their texts. His leading example of a text allegedly shaped by oral tradition (Lk. 7.1-10; cf. Mt. 8.1-13; Jn 4.46-54) is in fact heavily dependent on the text of the Elijah–Elisha narrative.[11]

For H. Koester (1994: 293-97), the claim to oral tradition is based not on the picture painted clearly in the gospels but on something which is not mentioned in the gospels at all: the pivotal role of the communities:

> Christianity began as a religious movement that established its distinctive interior structures by the creation of a ritual and a story... Paul...received a tradition of an oral version... (1 Cor. 11.23b). The organization of the new communities was accomplished...by sayings... transmitted in the oral tradition... Writings that were later called 'gospels' came into existence as alternative forms of the continuing oral tradition...

This is very plausible, but it is also quite unproven. As Koester implies (1994: 293-94) it rests on a form-critical presupposition, 'the presupposition that the beginning and the continuation of the tradition were the early Christian community and that therefore the oral use of materials from and about Jesus...was the congenial life situation of everything that was remembered from and about Jesus'. As with other claims about oral tradition, Koester's theory fits some of the data—notably a particular reading of 1 Corinthians—and it privileges that reading at the expense of a whole world of evidence, especially literary evidence.

The difficulty of reading 1 Corinthians is seen, for instance, in Paul's reference to receiving (from the Lord) and 'handing on' (*para-didómi*, 1 Cor. 11.13; 15.3). The language used here 'is the language of tradition in the technical sense, and corresponds to that which had been established in Judaism' (Barrett 1971: 264). In other words, Paul's language about a process of 'handing on' falls within the language of the broader Jewish claim to tradition, the tradition which Neusner identified as a myth (Neusner 1985: 1).

So when Paul invokes tradition going back to the Lord, one cannot be sure whether this call is an appeal to a historical tradition related to Jesus and a community, or whether, as his language suggests, he is using and adapting the general Jewish idea about tradition going back to Moses and God. Paul's language is itself general; he gives no details about the source and workings of the tradition.

The claim that Paul is connecting tradition to Jesus (and/or to some specific Jesus-based process) rather than to Moses (and the Lord) is not reliable. As a rule, 1 Corinthians relates very few sayings from the historical Jesus (Neirynck 1996), but it shows signs of systematic dependence on the Book of Moses—the Pentateuch (Brodie 1996).

As with Gerhardsson, what Koester's reading of 1 Corinthians indicates is not something historical but something artistic and theological; not that Paul was historically within

---

10. Funk, Hoover, and the Jesus Seminar 1993: 4.
11. Dunn 2003b: 212-16. See Brodie 1992b. See Chapter 28 below.

a line of oral tradition, but that 1 Corinthians paints such a picture, a picture which, through the Jewishness of Paul's terms, fits into a larger Jewish claim to mythical tradition. Whether, historically, Paul was or was not within a specific oral tradition must be decided on other grounds.

Koester's case is further weakened by his own view that the gospel materials are largely a community creation. If the gospels are so suspect historically, then on what basis is one so sure of the historical reliability of a particular reading of an epistle? It is not only the gospels which are artistic, rhetorical. Evidence grows that, to some degree, something similar is true of the epistles.

Therefore, in the end, the claim that Paul drew on a specific oral tradition is not convincing. Given the increasing evidence for the literary and rhetorical nature of the New Testament documents, it is not reasonable to use a questionable reading of one epistle as a basis for imposing a paradigm on New Testament literature as a whole.

What is essential is that, from Gunkel to Kelber to Koester, there are no reliable arguments for claiming that the gospels depend on oral tradition.

3. *Oral Tradition as Unworkable*

Even if the foundation of a theory or hypothesis is not clear, that does not necessarily mean that it is to be discounted. It may still be useful as a working hypothesis. The question therefore is whether, in New Testament studies, the theory of oral tradition works.

Bultmann's explanation of how communities create oral tradition was very simple: 'The literature...springs out [*entspringt*] of definite conditions and wants of life' (1931: 4). Bultmann never explained how this springing process works. As G.B. Caird would later remark (1976: 138), 'It is very easy to use a phrase like "a period of oral transmission" without stopping to envisage what exactly it means'. Oral tradition, usually undefined, can become a stop-gap in almost any theory which has problems.[12]

When C.H. Dodd was faced with the idea of oral tradition as drawn from Old Testament studies—the passing on of stories from generation to generation—he did not see how it could apply; there was not enough time; the New Testament period was 'less than a normal human lifetime' (Dodd 1963: 6).

Dodd's solution was to accept the idea of oral tradition, but to change it. The community, he said, did not create the stories. It simply modified what it received: 'The materials ...were already in existence as an unarticulated wealth of recollections and reminiscences of the words and deeds of Jesus—mixed, it may be, with the reflections and interpretations of his followers' (1963: 171). Thus Dodd re-established a link with Jesus—a mixed link.

Hengel's model, rather than being mixed, is fixed: he asserts that Jesus' brief activity in Galilee 'provided a wealth of firmly fixed and permanent impressions' (1980: 24).

The two models—the mixed and the fixed—are quite different, yet both sound plausible. But despite plausibility, they lack evidence. Hengel's claim is a bland assertion; without any significant argumentation, he prejudges a fundamental issue about the nature of the ultimate sources behind the text.

It is to the credit of B. Gerhardsson that, despite his above-mentioned presuppositions, he realized the idea of oral tradition needed clarification and that he proposed a specific model of how oral tradition could work. According to Gerhardsson, Jesus used meticulous rabbinical methods of teaching and transmitting, methods with exact processes of memorization and writing; these processes of memory and manuscript underlie the gospel.[13]

---

12. See even the fine dissertation of Friedrichsen 1992: 214, 315.
13. Gerhardsson 1961. One of the Gerhardsson's insights, reflected both in his own writings and in the

J.A. Fitzmyer praised Gerhardsson's work but indicated that to a significant degree it does not fit the data because its rigidity does not allow for the central phenomenon of the differences between the Synoptic Gospels.[14] Fitzmyer therefore added two further factors, effectively two stages: 'the well-known process in oral-tradition by which a nucleus story is eventually embellished and modified', and 'theological formulation' (Fitzmyer 1962: 445-46). This implies three stages:
1. Jesus' teaching.
2. An oral-tradition process that embellishes and modifies.
3. The evangelist's theological formulation.

At first sight the three-stage model is impressive. The reference to 'the well-known process in oral-tradition' appears not only to deal with the oral-tradition debate but to do so in a way that is easy and familiar, almost self-evident. Furthermore, because the three stages are distinct, they seem capable of accounting for almost anything from the history of Jesus to the theology of the evangelist. What is not accounted for by one stage will surely be accounted for by another, or by some combination of stages.

The problem again, as with Gerhardsson's theory, is that the model does not account for the data. There are more things in the gospels than are allowed for in this three-stage theory. In the case of Luke, for example, the gospel's literary quality so pervades the text that it does not fit easily into any of the three stages. Another is Luke's detailed reworking of Old Testament stories. For instance, the first conclusion of B. Koet about Luke's reworking of the scriptures is that it is systematic (Koet 1989: especially 141-43). There is also a problem with John; despite claims that John depends on several stages, there is evidence that the whole gospel is a thorough literary unity, complex and coherent (see Stibbe 1992; Brodie 1993a). A solution to the problem is to expand the role of the third stage so that it no longer consists just of adding formulation but comes closer to the idea of thoroughgoing authorship. But the more one does that, the more the earlier stages begin to crumble.

It is a symptom of the uncertainty in the field that in 1983 Kelber could publish a major study with a whole new thesis: the world of oral transmission is radically different from that of the (literary) gospels; in fact, the gospels betrayed the oral tradition (Kelber [ed.] 1983). As for the detailed workings of Jesus' oral tradition, Kelber pictured it as unpredictable, like the stock market or a runaway proliferation of tracks (Kelber [ed.] 1983). Kelber's central thesis received some initial criticism[15] but it was not until 1994 that it suffered a more devastating judgment: after lengthy analysis, J. Halverson concluded that Kelber's ingenious thesis is 'a house of cards' (1994: 194).

There have been further suggestions for trying to clarify the workings of oral tradition. P.J.J. Botha, for instance, claimed that the dynamics of rumor as described in social science, seem to correspond to the New Testament data 'in parts' (1993: 209). Botha seems to be right, but 'in parts' is not enough. The dynamics among the gospels are so many and complex that parts of those data will correspond to almost any model. That is

---

work of Byrskog (1994: especially 35-196), is that the gospels' picture of Jesus—an authoritative teacher who instructs his disciples—is part of a much larger Jewish tradition, one which is rooted in earlier writings and which continues into the writings of the rabbis. This is an important feature of the gospel presentation, but despite the vividness and centrality of this teacher–disciple picture in Gerhardsson's presentation of the gospel data, there is still no clear reason for converting it into reliable history. On the post-1961 refining of Gerhardsson's position, both by Gerhardsson himself and by R. Riesner, see Byrskog 1994: 17-19.

14. Fitzmyer 1962: 442-57. Others have criticized Gerhardsson's work severely; for references see Cook's review (1980); note especially the critique of Neusner 1971: 6-7; see also Kelber's review (1980).

15. For reviews, see Boomershine 1985; Brodie 1984b; Dunn 1986.

why so many diverse models—Bultmann, Dodd, Gerhardsson, Fitzmyer, Botha—can appear credible. The theories really do correspond to data. But not to all the data.

The inability of diverse models to explain the data has been further illustrated by B.W. Henaut's analysis of Mark 4 (Henaut 1993). As Henaut concludes: 'It is far more difficult to prove...that oral tradition lies behind this particular text than has been commonly acknowledged' (1993: 305).

The difficulty surrounding Mark 4 reflects a larger problem. Mark, generally regarded as the first gospel, is the crucial testing ground for tracing tradition (including oral tradition), but the tracing process does not work. Major efforts to distinguish tradition from redaction have been at such odds with one another as to suggest that, on the tradition question at least, Markan research sometimes seemed to be in a cul-de-sac (Luz 1980).

The conclusion seems unavoidable: in practice, thus far at least, the hypothesis of oral tradition has proved unworkable.

4. *Oral Tradition as Unnecessary*

Even if a hypothesis is unclear in its foundation, and even if in practice there are serious difficulties with getting it to work, perhaps in some way it is still the only apparent response to a real need. It is appropriate therefore to ask whether the hypothesis of oral tradition is necessary to New Testament studies.

The reasons for regarding oral tradition as necessary inevitably overlap with the grounds for claiming it in the first place. The main reasons for seeing it as necessary seem to be:
- The gospel text follows the rhythms of oral speech.
- The variations between the gospels correspond to the variations that occur in oral communication.
- Oral tradition seems to offer a link to historicity; it fills the gap between Jesus and the writing of the gospels.
- Oral tradition is embedded in the fabric of New Testament studies, in the prevailing paradigm, and, for the moment at least, there is no alternative paradigm to replace it.
- Gospel imagery is generally not about schools and writing but about people speaking, often in the open air, in an ethos of simplicity. Such simplicity corresponds with the simplicity suggested by oral tradition.

These arguments, however, do not provide solid reasons for holding to the centrality of oral tradition. Briefly:
- Oral rhythms do not require reliance on oral tradition. The following of oral rhythms is a quality not only of oral communication but of much writing, especially ancient writing. Someone sitting silently at a computer can compose in oral rhythms with a view to being heard by the ear.
- At first sight, some correspondence indeed exists between the variations that occur in oral communication and those that occur in the gospels. But when one looks more closely, one finds that the variations are much more deliberate; they are not haphazard as in oral communication. Matthew's variations on Mark, for instance, are not accidental. They are the result of the coherent strategy and theology of a scribe, a writer.
- Oral tradition may or may not assure more historicity. From a historical point of view, the ideal is that the evangelist is an eye-witness to the gospel events—thus needing no tradition whatever—or else speaks directly to such a witness. Interjecting an unpredictable chain of communication into a period of less than a lifetime has the effect not of promoting claims to history, but of dissipating them.

In any case, it is not appropriate that the desire for a particular type of historical conclusion should predetermine the idea of how the gospels were composed. If the idea of oral tradition is to stand, it must stand on its own inherent merits.
- It is true that oral tradition has been embedded in the fabric of New Testament studies, that it has been central to the prevailing paradigm. But that situation is changing rapidly. The literary approach, despite its teething problems—its occasional obscurity, pretentiousness, and narrowness—is not an esoteric game. Rather, the literary approach provides the context which, when developed, offers the best prospect for future research. It restores the writings to their role as literature, even sacred literature, and it does not exclude theology and historical investigation. On the contrary, it sets history and theology on a firmer footing.
- It is true that a sense of simplicity corresponds at least in part to the ethos of the gospel and to its pictures of people who very often have little to do with the world of writing. However, the fact that a scene is rustic need not mean that the artist who portrays it is rustic. A film, for instance, may portray rural life but be produced in the countryside by city dwellers using highly technical methods. Likewise, the simplicity portrayed in the gospels need not indicate the way the gospels were composed.

If the gospels' rusticity does not stem from its mode of transmission then what it its origin?

There are at least four factors that may have contributed to the impression of rusticity. First, there is *the classic ideal of the pastoral* (or bucolic) represented in a whole genre of Greco-Roman literature and given new prominence and vitality by the leading writer of the era, Virgil (in the *Eclogues*). To some degree, there was also a nostalgia for the pastoral in Israel's tradition (Brown 1966: 397). The gospels' evoking of simplicity may be partly an adaptation of that ideal. To some degree the classical tradition also idealized a certain simplicity of life, as seen for instance in the portrayal of Socrates, a portrayal which seems to have influenced the genre of Luke–Acts (Alexander 1993).

Second, rusticity corresponds partly to *the Jewish ideal of an oral tradition*. Even though the ideal of an oral tradition going back to Moses and God did not correspond strictly to history, it was apparently accepted among first-century Jews and it generated an atmosphere in which a picture of oral communication (and tradition, as in 1 Corinthians) seemed appropriate. To some degree, the New Testament picture may be an imitation or emulation of that ideal.

Third, *religion's ambivalence towards writing* tends to promote an image of rusticity. Religion uses writing, but it also realizes that the world of books can become stagnant, unreal, pretentious, or might even become a false god. The Word of God, however, stands above all writings. In a crisis, saints would sell their books to feed the poor, and Aquinas would refer to his own writings as straw.

Fourth, *the literary models closest to the gospels*—the Old Testament narratives to which they constantly refer—generally highlighted people who portrayed or evoked a certain simplicity, or who illustrated that the lack of simplicity was dangerous. The stories of Elijah and Elisha in particular, despite their wars, have influenced something of the gospels' tone and setting. Even the geographic limits of Jesus' ministry—from Syria to Jerusalem—are roughly the same as those of the full Elijah–Elisha narrative (as far as 2 Kgs 13). In combining simplicity with reminders of divinity, these two prophets provide a partial precedent for the ethos of the gospels.

These four factors may not all be at work in the formation of the gospels, but they illustrate a basic truth: without invoking communities and oral tradition, it is possible to find other explanations for the gospels' picture of simplicity. The oral-tradition hypothesis is not necessary.

5. Conclusion

For most of the twentieth century, the theory of an oral tradition was present in biblical studies. Its newness is not a problem; and even the confusion (as in Gunkel) surrounding its foundation does not necessarily mean it has no value. But when a theory is unworkable and unnecessary, then it is no longer merely unhelpful; it is a real hindrance, a constant source of confusion concerning the origin and nature of the gospels.

It is time to adapt the role attributed to orality. Orality, including the atmosphere of oral transmission, does correspond to something within the gospels. But it has been taken out from them, and, like a genie released from its place. It tends to take control of the situation. The task now in discussing the New Testament is not to eliminate orality, but to restore it to its place, to see all its vitality not as something *behind* the text, but as something *inside* it (or, as others say, *in front of* it). If the concept of orality can be turned around in this way, then, instead of being a distraction from the gospels, orality can be a way of appreciating them more fully.

7

Schools, Synagogues, and Vibrant Scripture-Related Communities: Towards a Writing-Oriented Paradigm

> Written prophecy is not secondary [to spoken prophecy]... The Old Testament had writers who were genuinely prophetic.
> —H. Utzschneider (1989: 17)
>
> Scribes are the main figures behind biblical tradition. In fact, we owe them the Bible, the entire Bible.
> —E. Lipiński (1988: 157)

In diverse ways, all the preceding chapters have emphasized writing: its modes of interdependence (Chapters 1, 2 and 5), as well as its artistry in Old Testament narratives (Chapters 3 and 4). And if oral tradition is excluded as a workable hypothesis (Chapter 6), then the role which such tradition might have played in the process of composition must now be played by writing.

This places a burden on the idea of writing. It implies not only a developed writing industry, but also some kind of communication between diverse writers.

The purpose of this chapter is to ask whether such a communication industry is plausible. There is no point in claiming that Proto-Luke used several biblical books, and that other writers then combined a refashioned Proto-Luke with further texts, unless such a process of writing and communication had some kind of precedent in history.

To speak of writing and communication means, in effect, to propose that there was some form of community of writers. This does not necessarily mean that they all lived in the same place, though some degree of being together is not to be excluded. It simply means that there was communication and understanding between them.

Having just cast radical doubt on Gunkel's primitive communities (and the many Johannine communities), it may seem ironic now to start talking of a community of writers. But the claim being made here is quite limited, and it is better grounded than Gunkel's claim. It is limited because it does not attempt to describe the community, locate it, or even say that the members were all in one place. It is better grounded—and this is the crucial difference—because we possess specific objects (artifacts), namely a series of diverse but interconnected writings. The easiest explanation for the origin of these writings is that they came from diverse people, many of whom were in communication with one another. In other words, the claim to a community of writers is based on the given fact that there is a 'community' of writings. Ultimately, the idea of a writing community is simply a way of saying that many of the New Testament authors were in communication with each other.

Is it plausible to suggest the existence of such a community of writers and to invest it with such importance?

To set the scene for discussing writers and communities of writers, it is necessary to review the historical background.

1. Israel: Living in a World of Writing and Communication

Of all the places in the world where writing was available, Israel's location was ideal. The development of writing had not come easily. Writing is not something secondary or weak. It is one of the great inventions in history, perhaps the greatest. Proverbially it is even mightier even than the sword. Intelligent people lived throughout much of the world for millennia before finally, in the Fertile Crescent, shortly before 3000 BCE, the breakthrough came: cuneiform in southern Mesopotamia (Sumer) and hieroglyphics in Egypt. It revolutionized such areas as commerce, communication, recording, and story-telling. The spread of writing to the rest of the world has often been slow, but it lost little time in encompassing the central territory between Mesopotamia and Egypt, a fact reflected in the finds at Byblos, just north of Israel.

Apparently, it was precisely the central territory around Phoenicia that gave writing its crucial development: the alphabet, around 1500 BCE. And apparently it was also from the area of Phoenicia that, around 1000 BCE, the alphabet spread to the fateful neighbors—the Greeks (Lemaire 1992: VI, 999-1000).

The importance of writing may have varied from one area to another. Within Mesopotamia and Egypt, the scribe was the one who, more than any other, could keep records and communicate, and so, apart from functioning as an interpreter or serving in the temple, his place was often like that of a unique cabinet minister, a kind of state secretary. Thus, writing—especially cuneiform and hieroglyphics—though known only to a few specialists, was not something peripheral to a realm. The writer was a crucial figure and would remain so as writing developed (Légasse 1992: XII, 244-53).

There were scribes in Israel, as elsewhere in the ancient Near East, both before and after the exile, but so far it has not been possible to determine which generations of scribes were most influential in forming the biblical writings. Lipiński (1988) and Légasse (1992: XII, 253-58), for instance, quote Genesis–Kings to establish the role of pre-exilic scribes, but T.L. Thompson (1992) and P.R. Davies (1992: 87) place the composition of Genesis–Kings after the exile, thus making it difficult to use Genesis–Kings reliably as a source for pre-exilic conditions. What all four authors accept, however, is that whatever the dating, scribes were crucial to the composition of the biblical texts. Lipiński (1988: 157) regards the scribes as foundational, and attributes everything to them. Recalling the role of scribes, Légasse (1992: XII, 262) agrees ('Lipiński...est tout à fait justifiée...'). P.R. Davies (1992: 106-109) in effect also agrees and spells out the importance of the scribes.

What is essential is that the people of Israel/Judea, whatever their history, lived in the center of the most literate area of the world. It is not surprising then that in due time, the Jewish people would become known as 'the People of the Book'.

Some degree of communication is linked to writing, not only because writing is itself a means of communication, but also because it is an ingenious invention which depended on significant contact for its spreading. The Greeks did not capture the alphabet over a glass of beer or by raiding a library. Some form of patient communication was needed. Thus, writing by its nature tended to establish a network.

2. Writing's Association with Schools/Communities

To a large degree writers could not work in isolation. The industry was so complex and cumbersome—learning the art, finding manuscripts and materials, copying manuscripts one by one—that it flourished best if there was cooperation.

One form of cooperation was the building of libraries. Even when writing was cuneiform such institutions were ambitious: 'These libraries [in Babylonia, Nineveh, Ebla,

Ugarit, etc.] tried to collect most of the technical, legal, and literary texts known in their times (history, astronomy, religion, myths, etc.) so that they could be easily consulted; eventually catalogues of the titles of the texts were compiled to make consultation easier' (Lemaire 1992: 1004).

Egyptian libraries, using hieroglyphic script, and more compact than those using cuneiform, were sometimes located near temples. They tended to be vulnerable, as seen in the burning of the library in Alexandria. Apparently there were libraries also in Jerusalem (2 Macc. 2.13-15) but these too were vulnerable. Jewish libraries have not survived apart from Qumran (Lemaire 1992: 1004-1005).

As well as being associated with libraries, writing was also associated with schools. To a significant extent, in fact, schools were centers of writing. It is appropriate, therefore, in seeking how writing functioned, to survey the working of the schools. The surest place to begin, because more information is available, is with the widespread Greek system.

Hellenistic schools had four main structures (Alexander 1992: V, 1005):
1. Individual tuition.
2. Individual teacher, many students.
3. Multi-teacher.
4. Multi-center.

Individual tuition was the basis of the whole system. Schooling on any kind of a mass scale would not come until the late Roman Empire when the state began to take some responsibility for education. Therefore the foundation was individual instruction, often from father to son, handing on the precious and prestigious heritage; or people might send their child (generally their son) to a specific teacher to learn a specific subject. This individual process tended to generate two elements: imitation and tradition: the student would imitate the teacher, and might in turn hand on the teaching to another generation.

Individual teachers sometimes attracted several students in such a way that together they would form a kind of school community and would often follow the ideals of imitation, emulation, and friendship. The emulation (or rivalry) was sometimes with students of other teachers.

The two further school structures were more complex: the multi-teacher, and the multi-center. The *multi-teacher* school was a place where several teachers or researchers worked together in pursuit of a common goal. 'A wide degree of variation is possible here, from the high-powered research organizations of the Theophrastus or the Alexandrian Museum to the religiously committed brotherhood of Pythagoras or Epicurus' (Alexander 1992: V, 1005).

More complex still was the school which was *multi-centered*. Such an institution reflected the fact that

> a number of small groups in different localities [were]...conscious of belonging to the same sect or movement: the 'school' here means an agglomeration of geographically scattered groups professing adherence to the same ideals and teaching tradition. This kind of grouping is mainly associated with certain philosophical schools, particularly that of Epicurus. (Alexander 1992: V, 1005)

The different types of schools tended to teach diverse subjects. Individual tuition was almost indispensable if one wanted to learn a craft or a practical skill. In this case tuition was a form of practical apprenticeship where instruction was oral rather than written. But in many traditions from ancient Mesopotamia to modern Iran individual tuition could concentrate on teaching skills that were scribal. To some degree individual tuition—the personal process of imitation and transmission—was a paradigm for the whole process of teaching, even for the teaching that occurred in a more complex setting.

The one-teacher schools were particularly dedicated to mainstream literary education, in other words to *rhetoric*, the core of public discourse. This Greece-based rhetoric was not something specialized or localized; after 400 BCE it was 'the central component in the higher education of the free-born...[and] Athens was the educational mecca for the whole Mediterranean world' (Alexander 1992: V, 1007). So, when someone as gifted as Isocrates (436–338) taught rhetoric, large numbers came, and together they formed their own distinctive school.

The more complex schools, whether multi-teacher or multi-centered, were generally interested not so much in rhetoric (frequently career-oriented) as in mature research and reflection, often with an emphasis on philosophy, religion, and morality (Alexander 1992: V, 1007). Plato, in fact, resisted concentration on rhetoric, at least at the level of higher education; rhetoric was taken for granted, and Plato's goal was philosophy (Alexander 1992: V, 1007).

Some schools were well known (see especially Culpepper 1975). In southern Italy, towards 500 BCE, Pythogoras established a group that combined two aspects—religious community and a scientific school (Alexander 1992: V, 1007; Culpepper 1975: 48-54). Other schools also contained a complex order. Socrates may indeed have moved freely, untied to structures, but, in 387 Plato bought land near Athens and built a school there, the Academy, which would last a thousand years, and which, somewhat like the Pythagoreans, emphasized philosophy and frugal life. Aristotle set out to rival the Academy and, in 335 BCE, in a grove given by the Athenians, established the Lyceum, similar in some ways to the Academy. In turn Epicurus bought a house and garden in Athens in 306. His school was more withdrawn and more monastic than the Academy or the Lyceum, but in another sense it was outgoing, sending members to establish groups in many other places, and eventually forming a worldwide network of communities (Culpepper 1975: 117-21).

The Epicureans' journeying did not occur is a vacuum. The whole Mediterranean was a crossroads. In the fourth century BCE, the Mediterranean saw 'a proliferation of small schools' and 'a tradition of mobility' (Alexander 1992: V, 1007). Later, when there was a 'tendency for teachers to congregate in certain cultural centers, notably Athens, Alexandria and Tarsus, mobility...became characteristic of students as much as teachers' (p. 1007). The impression, again, is one of multi-faceted communication.

What is essential in this survey of schools is that it gives some idea of the ethos in which much writing took place. It shows, for instance, that it was in schools that two of the greatest writers in antiquity, Aristotle and Plato, carried out their work. It also suggests how schooling, including writing, was not a world of narrow intellectualism or self-centered curiosity. In varying degrees, a whole lifestyle was involved, and imitation was a guiding principle. In Plato's school the students even imitated his stoop (Culpepper 1975: 67).

In sum, the school tended towards being a community, but since schools were also associated with mobility, with diversity of people, sometimes with a multiplicity of centers, the notion of community could be very flexible.

3. *Writing's Association with Synagogues*

Apparently pre-exilic Israel did not have a school system. Education took place largely in the family and in the work-place, and, for most people, work did not involve writing.

Some researchers have claimed otherwise. The discoveries of pre-exilic inscriptions, some apparently scribbled, have led to a hypothesis about the existence of ancient Israelite schools and the connection between these schools and biblical texts (Lemaire 1981: especially 85), but the evidence for this hypothesis is quite insufficient; writing remained a specialization, and ancient Israel was probably no more literate than other areas in the Fertile Crescent (Haran 1988: especially 95; Puech 1988a: especially 202-203).

In post-exilic times, it does not seem possible to determine the degree of literacy among the Jewish people. Lemaire (1992: VI, 1005) suggests there was an efficient school system, but again his thesis seems unsubstantiated.

However, at some stage during or after the exile, a particular type of Jewish school or center did begin to flourish: the synagogue (a Greek word, meaning a bringing together or assembly). While the Hellenistic world witnessed a proliferation of small rhetorical schools, the Jewish people experienced a proliferation of synagogues. It is not clear whether the two phenomena—rhetorical schools and synagogues—are in any way connected. Synagogues were found not only in the diaspora but also in Galilee and Judea. Jerusalem alone is said to have had hundreds of them: 365 in the late Second Temple period, and 480 in the time of Vespasian (69-79 CE) (Meyers 1992: 252).

Some sense of an individual synagogue emerges from the following inscription (first century CE):

> Theodotus, son of Vettenos, the priest and archisynagogos, son of a archisynagogos and grandson of a archisynagogos, who built the synagogue for purposes of reciting the Law and studying the commandments, and as a hotel with chambers and waters installations, to provide for the needs of itinerants from abroad...
>
> This echoes aspects already mentioned about writings and schools: the transmission from father to son, and the fact of itinerancy or mobility. But the primary purpose of the synagogue is its connection with something written: the Law. Josephus echoes the same emphasis—the synagogue's focus on Scripture reading and study. (Meyers 1992: 252)

If writings were central to the synagogue and if synagogues proliferated as apparently they did, then at the heart of Judaism, writing was a massive process.

To some degree, the situation is reflected in the case of Philo and his great literary output. The details of how Philo wrote are not clear, whether, for instance, he spent his time in the great library, or in the synagogue, or at home, or in some other type of school or library. It may be, for instance, that his writings were used 'in a synagogue-school where Philo taught the higher vision of scripture to a select group' (Culpepper 1975: 211). What is certain is that, in his exposition of scripture, he did not live in isolation. He worked among writings and students of writing. Even if all the work attributed to him is his own—rather than the work of a school (as was once suggested)—it nonetheless comes from within the context of schools, or at least from within the schooling tradition of the synagogue. In Alexander's words (1992: V, 1010): 'Philo himself located the bulk of his scholastic activity within the sabbath-day teaching of the synagogues, which he describes (in an intentional comparison with the Greek philosophical schools) as "schools of Moses"'. It is not only the two greatest Greek philosophers therefore who wrote in schools; so did Philo in his own way. Thus, among both Greeks and Jews, some of the greatest writing was done in schools.

4. Biblical Writings and Schools/Communities

If writing was often associated with schools, it is reasonable to ask whether the same is true of biblical writing.

In the course of research into individual biblical books or corpora, several claims have been made that these writings reflect the work not just of individuals but of a series of writers in some form of school or community.

M. Weinfeld, faced with the rhetorical continuity between Deuteronomy and the diverse Deuteronomic literature, used the title, *Deuteronomy and the Deuteronomic School* (1972). The idea of a school—several writers/scribes working in cooperation or continuity—

seemed to be the obvious way to account for the data, and this school involved 'persons who had at their command a vast reservoir of literary material...[persons] skilled with the pen and the book' (Weinfeld 1972: 177-78). Nor was this school monolithic. On the contrary, the changes in the Deuteronomic material 'points to a continuous ideological and literary development...and attests to the dynamism of the school' (Weinfeld 1972: 4).

P. Davies (1992), however, goes further. The logic that led Weinfeld to invoke a distinct group, a school, for the Deuteronomic work applies to '*all* of the biblical literature' (1992: 109). For Davies (1992: 106), the origin of literature goes back to a literate class, and 'in the case of the biblical literature a class which exercises its profession through an institution, namely a scribal school'. What causes Davies (1992: 107) to invoke a school is the complexity of the work of composition: 'The production of scrolls containing histories, cultic poems, wise sayings and oracles is not an individual hobby. Such work requires a professional class with time, resources and motivation to write. In some cases, it implies access to official archives.'

In New Testament studies, K. Stendahl spoke of 'the school of St. Matthew and its use of the Old Testament' (1954). Stendahl claimed a school both because the form-critical account of Matthew, as found for instance in M. Dibelius' emphasis on preaching, does not fit the data in Matthew (1954: 13-19), and also because Matthew's use of the Old Testament resembles that of a particular school, namely Qumran, with its Habakkuk commentary (1954: 31). Furthermore, a scribe does not work in isolation:

> How does a Christian scribe fit into the context of his church?... If we owe the gospel to a converted rabbi, we must suppose that he was not working entirely alone, but that he took an active part in the life of the church where he lived and served. That is tantamount to saying that there was a school at work in the church of Matthew. (1954: 30)

Stendahl's thesis has received strong criticism (especially by B. Gärtner: 1955), yet the work of Matthew continues to be connected with aspects of the world of writing. Matthew's setting has been described as 'a scribal community' (Wire 1991). Matthew himself was 'thoroughly familiar with the Old Testament and with Jewish traditions of its interpretation' (Cope 1976: 130). In the view of D.E. Orton (1989: 38, 175), Matthew's sense of the scribe is essentially positive; and Matthew sees himself as standing in the tradition not only of the prophets but also of the apocalyptic scribes; he evokes both Ben Sira and Qumran, and his work falls within a tradition of creative 'charismatic' exegesis.

In the case of Luke, it has long been acknowledged that he is a writer in the Greco-Roman mold, someone who was trained in rhetoric and who imitated several aspects of the Greek Old Testament. His background, therefore, is that of rhetorical schooling. Furthermore, while Luke imitated the Old Testament, he also appears to reflect various aspects of Greco-Roman historiography and biography, especially the kind of intellectual biography which was associated with the schools and with the recounting of the life of Socrates. In the words of L.C.A. Alexander (1993: 31), 'The school traditions lying behind the literary texts are of great significance for Acts'. This does not prove that Luke worked with a school, but it shows that the experiences and traditions of schools were not alien to him. On the contrary, he seems to have been very much at home in them.

The Johannine writings have often been attributed to a school. R.A. Culpepper (1975: 4) traces the actual phrase 'school of John' back to Renan (1863) but shows also that the idea of Johannine disciples or of a Johannine circle had been suggested even before that. After Renan the idea recurs in several scholars, among them Lightfoot (1875–76), Martineau (1891), Bartlett (1899), von Weizsäcker (1899), Schmiedel (who spoke of a community of writers, 1908), Scott (who visualized writers working together in the same neighbourhood, 1908), Jackson (who distinguished an inner circle of writers from a larger school, 1918), Charles (who said diverse writers were 'master and pupil, or...pupils of the same master, or...members of the same school', 1920) (Culpepper 1975: 4-13). B.H. Streeter (1924: 460) was skeptical: in art and philosophy, a school 'comes into existence [only] when there is a considerable body of work by the founder which serves as a model and a standard for the pupils'. But C.H. Dodd (1937), while not using the word 'school', helped to re-establish the idea, and later authors, including C.K. Barrett, B. Lindars and R.E. Brown, strengthened it (Culpepper 1975: 18, 23, 26, 29).

In subsequent Johannine studies (1976–88), the search for the old idea of a school was overtaken by the search for a distinct community (see Brodie 1993b: 15-20). This hypothesis of a distinct community derived from a different starting-point and it turned into a process that, in the words of J.L. Martyn (SBL meeting, Anaheim, CA, 19 November 1989), became like a genie out of control.

But the original arguments for a school remain. Among these arguments, the following are particularly significant (cf. Culpepper 1975: xvii-xviii, 264-90):

1. The Johannine writings show such a curious relationship of similarities and dissimilarities that it seems reasonable to assume that the writers worked together in communication or in community—and so, in some form of school.
2. John's use of the Old Testament suggests a use of writings such as might be found in a school.
3. The ethos of the Johannine writings, especially the central and exemplary role of the leading figure (the Beloved Disciple), corresponds to the ethos of actual schools.

With regard to Paul, the epistles bearing his name present a puzzle that in some ways is similar to that of the Johannine writings: a series of works seems to come from one person but those works sometimes shows such dissimilarities that it may be better, in some instances, to think of a school. Such, for instance, is the conclusion of P. Müller (1988) concerning 2 Thessalonians and Colossians.

This idea of Paul's association with some kind of school is reinforced by his use of the Old Testament. Analysis of Paul's use of the scripture by scholars such as R.B. Hays (1989) and especially by D.A. Koch (1986) indicates that Paul engaged whole books and that he was in the presence of elaborate manuscripts (Hays 1989: 14-21 [16]; Koch 1986: 92-104, 284).

What emerges, therefore, is that from Matthew to Revelation much of the New Testament is either associated with scribes, or diverse writings, or some kind of school—or with some combination of these elements.

5. Proposal: One Key Network of Writers among the Early Believers

In the preceding list of opinions, one of the guiding principles is that where a number of books have an obvious mixture of similarity and difference—the Deuteronomic history, the Johannine writings, the Pauline corpus—the explanation lies in the work of a school, that is, a community of writers. As members of the same community, the writers maintain continuity, but as individual writers they have their own specific contributions and formulations.

If that principle applies to the bodies of writings mentioned above—the Deuteronomic, Johannine, and Pauline—then it also applies to the three Synoptics. Given the Synoptics' mixture of similarity and difference, there was obviously some kind of close communication between them. Furthermore, if John used the Synoptic Gospels—an idea finding increasing support (Neirynck 1984; Denaux [ed.] 1992; Brodie 1993b; Dundenberg 1994)—

then John becomes part of the larger gospel group of writers, and with him (in communication/community with him) are the rest of the Johannine group. If, in addition, some of these gospel writers knew some of Paul's epistles—an idea for which there is significant evidence (Goulder 1989: 132-46; Brodie 1993b: 128-34)—then what emerges is not a series of unrelated schools, but effective communication among all the main strands of New Testament writing. In some sense there was one key community of writers.

Writings were not unattainable. In L.C.A. Alexander's analysis, there were ample means of writing and copying (1997: 88-91). Consequently what was written was generally widely available. Alexander (p. 91) quotes Plato's *Phaedrus*: 'Once a thing is put into writing, the composition, whatever it may be, drifts all over the place…' And on the basis of later evidence (second century CE) Alexander (p. 92) concludes: 'What is central and primary is the expectation that books are for sharing'. Such evidence gives further context to the idea that there was one key community or network of writers.

It is not clear whether this school was localized (multi-teacher) or dispersed (multi-center), but it seems to have had one central inspiration: Jesus Christ, the 'foundation' emphasized by Paul (1 Cor. 3.11).

The proposal of this chapter, therefore, is that much of the New Testament comes from a community such as that at Qumran—a community of vision, integrity, scholarship, and solidarity—but without Qumran's restriction to one place.

It has often been noted that there are similarities between the community at Qumran and the early church, particularly the church described in Acts (see Brown 1990: 78, 109). This discussion suggests a further similarity: the importance of writing. The caves in the area contained the remains of hundreds of manuscripts. Cave 4 alone had fragments of over 500 manuscripts. The writings were focused on two main areas: the old scriptures and the new community. These two areas were closely related because the writings for the new community were themselves heavily scriptural. An obvious example is the commentary on Habakkuk, found in Cave 1. This work is 'a free interpretative commentary…adapting the thought of the book to the Qumran community' (Brown 1990: 80-95, especially 86-88).

These features of Qumran—a community process of writing, and the writing's dual nature (telling of the new community, yet scripture-based)—provide a partial precedent for the proposal being made here.

One of the basic differences between the Qumran writing process and the community effort which produced much of the New Testament is that the New Testament group, instead of retreating into the desert, went out to the world and to Greco-Roman culture. In dealing with that world, they often challenged it or rebelled against it, but they did not leave it. While they followed the practice found in Qumran of searching and adapting the scriptures, they also learned from the literature and literary methods of the wider world.

6. *Conclusion*

The thesis of this book is that much of the New Testament, especially the Gospels and Acts, depends heavily on scripture-based writing (rather than on oral tradition), and that, within the context of the larger church, the writers were in communication or in some form of community.

The idea of scripture-based writing and communication is quite different from the image of the New Testament as being heavily influenced by wandering preachers—free spirits who carried no clutter such as old scripture manuscripts or writing materials, and without the need to coordinate with other people.

The image of the free spirit is in fact at the center of the New Testament, for instance, in Galatians 1–3, but that is not a reliable indicator of how the text was composed. A sculpture of a figure who seems utterly free may itself be the product of the most studied art. Galatians, it turns out, is heavily rhetorical and carefully crafted (Betz 1979). And the figure of the free Jesus who never writes can likewise be the product of the most studied writing.

In tracing composition, therefore, the determining factor is not what is portrayed but the evidence regarding the process of composition. If the sculptor's studio reveals books about imitating earlier artists and several models that resemble the seemingly spontaneous work, then it becomes clear that for all its genius and inspiration, the artistry is studied and imitative.

Likewise in the case of the gospels. The issue is not whether the gospels are works of genius and inspiration that portray God-based freedom. They are. The issue is whether they developed in a world where the basis of writing was the imitating and reworking of earlier texts, and whether it is possible to identify a specific writing or writings that actually served as an initial model for the composition of the gospels.

The purpose of these introductory chapters has been to show that the world of the gospels was a place where writers did indeed imitate and rewrite earlier texts. There were also initial signs that specific writings—in particular the Elijah–Elisha narrative—could have served as actual models. And the present chapter indicates that—within libraries, schools, and synagogues, from Athens to Qumran—writing was a shared endeavor.

There is ample justification, then, for asking whether the composition of the gospels is due largely to writers who, within a vibrant church, were scripture-based and cooperative.

8

Roads and Travel:
From a Paradigm of Multi-Faceted Isolation
to a Paradigm of Communication

Twentieth-century New Testament research tended to work with a paradigm of fragmentation and isolation. The presence of this paradigm was scarcely noticeable. Few researchers referred to it explicitly, yet it pervaded the discipline. There was emphasis on communities but little sense that the communities were in communication, or that the various New Testament writers may have known one another or one another's work. The gospels, for instance, were often connected with genres such as history and biography, yet as a group they often seemed apart, even isolated.

The isolating of the gospels as a group was part of a larger phenomenon of isolation. First, within each gospel, the idea of isolation was applied to specific passages. Particularly among the Synoptics, the various episodes or sayings were often regarded as somehow separate from each other, or at least as only loosely connected like the parts of a necklace.

Furthermore, apart from the isolation of specific passages, research isolated the evangelists from each other. In the most popular theory of gospel origins, the only evangelist's work known to any of the others was that of Mark; his gospel was seen as available to Matthew and Luke. But, in this view, Matthew and Luke did not know one another's work.

John's gospel was sometimes treated as even more solitary and fragmented. Twentieth-century research frequently claimed that the author did not know any of the other gospels and that major sections of his own work do not hang together. In an effort to tie John to something, a whole series of hypotheses emerged about very diverse Johannine communities.

The idea of isolation has other aspects: Luke, the roving *littérateur* who wrote so much about Paul and who collected documents including Mark and even the elusive Q, was said not to have a copy of any of Paul's epistles. In other words, Luke was a roving writer who collected documents, including obscure ones, but who was isolated from all the documents written by his subject.

As for Q itself, the hypothetical sayings source, this was connected primarily to the Gospel of Thomas, a document probably written well after it. So again, apart from some general suggestions about broad contexts or traditions, Q was left in isolation. It had little specific literary context.

Proto-Luke, the hypothetical short version of Luke or Luke–Acts, was also isolated. It was initially connected to a background that was 'Semitic', but this background remained vague. There was no clear connection with any other writing.

Overall, therefore, scholarship has often placed the gospel writings and writers in a world of non-communication. Their works were fragmented within themselves; they were largely fragmented from each other; and they were also largely fragmented from literature as a whole.

Further research is needed on why this model or paradigm achieved such a grip. To some degree, the problem was one of basic information. In Old Testament studies, for instance, earlier researchers simply were not acquainted with Mesopotamian literature and so it was not possible to recognize the Bible's indebtedness to such literature. But there may have been other reasons that were more subtle. Was a role played, for example, by some form of Romanticism—whether the old idealism of ancient pastoral poetry, the newer idealism of Rousseau and the Romantic poets, or a religion-related idealism about simple faith? In these and other forms of idealism, there is a tendency to regard truth not as something given by another person—not something communicated, imitated, taught, preached, or read—but as something coming from within the individual, from a primitive noble instinct, and therefore especially from private experience. Truth—whether personal or national—is all the purer if it is one's own. Isolation is noble. Simplicity is godly. Indebtedness to foreign influence spoils the nobility of one's heritage. Technology, including the complex craft of writing, is suspect.

The complexity of the problem may be illustrated by the case of classical Greece, a situation where the isolation was corporate rather than individual.

1. *From Isolation to Communication: Classical Greece*

Of all the cultural blossomings the world has ever known, perhaps none has been more striking than that of ancient Greece. First came the great epic poets, Homer and Hesiod (c. 700 BCE); then the more personal lyric poets, including Sappho and Pindar; and next, particularly in the fifth century, a vast flowering in diverse disciplines, including geography, history, drama, rhetoric, architecture, mathematics, art, philosophy, and physics.

Curiously, later scholarship, particularly in the nineteenth century, came to regard this blossoming as occurring essentially in isolation. It was said that what happened in classical Greece came from within. It was 'the Greek miracle'.

Both biblical and classical scholars seemed eager to maintain this idea of isolation or separation. Biblical scholars, convinced they had a unique understanding of God and God's revelation in history, did not wish to see that uniqueness diminished, and therefore had no wish to see it as dependent on outside influences. And scholars of Greek, convinced that they were dealing with a unique understanding of humanity—something they elevated to the level of 'Classic'—likewise did not want to see their unique heritage as contaminated by outside influences, especially by the murky East, 'the Orient'.

Greek scholars recognized, of course, that writing had come from the east. Formed around 3000 BCE in Mesopotamia (as cuneiform) and Egypt (as hieroglyphics), writing had developed from simple uses—in trade, administration, tomb inscriptions, formulaic chronicles—and had become the vehicle for important literature. Egypt, for instance, saw the emergence of wisdom literature and of short stories. Mesopotamia's literature was even greater and included the *Epic of Gilgamesh*, the *Atrahasis Epic* and a famous account of creation, the *Enuma Elish*. Still, classical scholarship kept Greek in its cocoon. Greek after all, was West. And East and West could never meet.

Then, slowly at first, the fiction of isolation began to break. In 1936, R.E. Dodds of Oxford appealed to classicists to study 'that world culture against which Greek culture arose and from which it was never completely isolated save in the minds of scholars' (Dodds 1936: 11, cited in L.H. Feldman 1996: 13).

In the United States, it fell to Cyrus Gordon—installed near Boston in 1956 in his custom-built Department of Mediterranean Studies at Brandeis University—to proclaim, decades-long, often like a voice in the wilderness, that indeed Greece was not isolated; that scholars of the Near East were neglecting 'the Mediterranean factor'. The Mediterranean, far from keeping Greece isolated from its eastern neighbors, functioned, in fact, like a central magnet and a linking highway (Lubetski and Gottlieb 1996: 7).

However, it was Walter Burkert of Zurich who not only stated the principle but also spelled out the details. In *The Orientalizing Revolution* (1984 [ET 1992]) he showed how facet after facet of early Greek culture (the archaic age) was dependent on the Orient. In particular, significant links emerged between the great Mesopotamian epics (*Gilgamesh*, and *Atrahasis*) and the epics of Homer, especially the *Odyssey* (Burkert 1992: 88-127). More recently, others have added further evidence (see especially Morris 1992, cited in L.H. Feldman 1996).

News of this breakthrough has been slow in spreading. The 1993 Presidential Address by L. Koenen to the American Philological Association warned that 'we can no longer look at early Greece in isolation' (see the summary in L.H. Feldman 1996: 13) and the Address went on: 'What is known to researchers, however, does not always reach the classroom, and the general public is hardly aware that our picture of ancient cultures, and in particular, of early Greek culture, has undergone dynamic changes'.

2. *From Isolation to Communication: The Emergence of Intertextuality*

Recent decades have seen the development of the term 'intertextuality'. The word is primarily anthropological; it refers to interaction between whole cultures. Intertextuality 'has nothing to do with matters of influence by one writer on another, or with the sources of a literary work; it does, on the other hand, involve the components of a *textual system* such as the novel, for instance. It is defined...as the transposition of one or more *systems* of signs upon another, accompanied by a new articulation of the enunciative and denotative position.'[1]

However, partly because of research on intertextuality in the broad anthropological sense, literary scholars have become more attuned to the influence of one particular written text on another, and so the term 'intertextuality' is now frequently used precisely to refer to the relationship between written texts.

Insofar as the emphasis on 'intertextuality' heightens awareness of literary connections, the term is welcome. But insofar as the term obscures ancient terms and phenomena, it is to be treated with caution. Dale C. Allison's *The Intertextual Jesus: Scripture in Q* (2000), takes 'intertextual' in a broad sense as referring to allusions, and on that basis Allison produces a valuable map of the way the Q material alludes to other texts.

However, the kernel of ancient writing was not in allusions; it was in taking hold of entire books and transforming them systematically. Virgil did not just *allude* to Homer; he swallowed him whole. And there are comparable systematic transformations within the Bible. Allusions and quotations were often little more than decorations and embellishments.

3. *From Isolation to Communication: A Shift in New Testament Research*

Whatever the full reasons that made the implicit idea of isolation so powerful, the latter half of the twentieth century brought a change. New Testament research began to make fresh kinds of connections. Redaction criticism (c. 1950s), for instance, indicated some degree of coherence between the gospels' smallest units. Modern literary criticism (c. 1970s), drawing partly on modern theory, went further. It indicated that the unity in biblical

---

1. Roudiez 1980: 15. On the history and meaning of the term 'intertextuality', see Culler 1981: 100-18; on Julia Kristeva, originator of the term, see Roudiez 1980: 1-20; Lechte 1994: 141-44.

8. Roads and Travel

narrative, including the gospels, is not just editorial; it goes deeper. The gospels may be read as stories or coherent narrative. And Greco-Roman rhetorical criticism (c. 1980s) indicated that both the epistles and gospels are strongly shaped by ancient literary criticism: rhetoric. Thus, diverse parts of the New Testament documents have begun to come together, and the New Testament as a whole has begun to re-enter the larger world of literature.

Furthermore there has been an increasing realization that in the ancient world, and especially in the Roman Empire, communications were good. Roads were well-built, ships were frequent, and, as a result, travel was relatively easy—essentially as easy as until the modern era (for travel times, see the map on p. xxxi). An analysis of early Christian data and of first-century travel and communications has led M.B. Thompson to conclude:

> The churches from A.D. 30 to 70 had the motivation and the means to communicate often and in depth with each other... News and information could spread relatively quickly between the congregations in the great cities of the empire, and from there into the surrounding regions... Many churches were less than a week's travel away from a main hub in the Christian network. (M.B. Thompson 1998: 68)

Even between some of the churches that were furthest apart—Rome and Jerusalem—communications appear to have been close (Brown and Meier 1983: 90). Communications among Christians were such that Thompson's governing image is not that of isolated communities but of what he calls 'the holy internet' (M.B. Thompson 1998).

R. Bauckham, in the course of arguing that the gospels were written not for specific communities but for all Christians, reaches a similar conclusion: 'The early Christian movement was a network of communities in constant communication with each other, by messengers, letters, and movements of leaders and teachers—moreover, a network around which *Christian literature circulated easily, quickly, and widely*' (Bauckham 1998: 44 [my emphasis]). The details of such a process—how ancient books were produced and circulated—has been spelled out by L.C.A Alexander (1998).

Given this background of oral and written communication, it is plausible that the New Testament authors knew of many other writings and that, if they wished, could get copies of them.

9

Judaism's New Community: Religious Experience, and Adaptation of Institutions—Including Scripture

> Bias in favor of the textually defined and the theologically correct has profoundly affected the academic study of earliest Christianity, with the dual result that the beginnings of Christianity remain religiously *terra incognita* and that much of what the earliest Christian texts talked about is simply ignored.
>
> —L.T. Johnson (1998: 3)

The purpose of this brief chapter is to summarize some aspects of the group who became known as 'Christians'. The history of their development is elusive. It is generally agreed that the accounts in the gospels and Acts are heavily theological and so one has to be careful about treating these accounts as factual history. The epistles seem to offer a basis for reconstructing a life of Paul and the lives of the first urban Christians, but as the scripture-based nature of the epistles becomes clearer, such reconstructions appear hazardous.

The emphasis here is not on their history as a whole but simply on some key aspects, particularly the foundational element of spiritual experience and two institutional elements, namely rituals and writings.

1. *The Uncharted Kernel: Spiritual Experience*

In modern religious studies the heart of the matter—spiritual experience—receives little attention. Scholars such as S. Schneiders, for instance, have had to struggle to establish spirituality as an appropriate topic for academic discussion (Schneiders 1986; 1989; 1993; 1994; 1998).

In a somewhat similar way the academic study of early Christianity has paid little attention to spiritual experience. It is indeed uncharted territory, *terra incognita*. The emphasis of academic study has been on history and theology, elements that seem measurable, rather than on the elusive world of experiences which are personal, even unquantifiable.

The character of such experiences is total, intense and outgoing. In the wording of L.T. Johnson (1998: 60) religious experience is 'a response to that which is perceived as ultimate, involving the whole person, characterized by a peculiar intensity, and issuing in action'.

Within the New Testament the presence of this phenomenon is not something rare or marginal. On the contrary the emphasis on religious experience is central and strong. Even by the standards of ancient religious texts 'the New Testament is remarkable...for its high proportion of...discourse about experience' (Johnson 1998: 4).

The experience involves power—not social or personal power, but a power that is given from within (Johnson 1998: 7):

> It is a power that comes from outside those touched by it and is transmitted to them from another, to whom it properly belongs. The power transmitted to them reaches external expression in various 'wonders and signs' including healings and exorcisms and gifts of ecstatic

speech. But it is also said to be at work in the internal transformation of human freedom... The only term adequate to define the extraordinary combination of characteristics ascribed to such power is *transcendent*.

Johnson's study of early Christians' religious experience is far from being complete or definitive. Yet he has made a key contribution. He has shifted the spotlight to a foundational feature of early Christianity.

So, when one speaks of early Christian history and the context of the New Testament, it is appropriate to allow that much of the energy underlying the emergence of the first Christians came from deep religious experience. The historical details surrounding that phenomenon remain largely unexplored and elusive, yet the reality of the phenomenon itself seems undeniable. It is appropriate, then, when one asks about the earliest Christians, to visualize a group who had a great inner energy, an energy ultimately rooted in the transcendent divinity.

But experience and energy do not work in a vacuum. The positive yearnings of a suppressed population, for instance, ultimately flow not into untrammeled individualism but into certain structures: rituals, and writings such as anthems and constitutions. One of the key features of religious experience—and one that distinguishes it from the aesthetic experience of beauty—is that it flows out into the world, into interaction with other people. Thus it leads almost inevitably to the formation of various practical ways of sharing life in institutions, including the setting up of central rituals and writings.[1]

It is appropriate, then, when looking at the history of the early Christians to move from the foundational level of religious experience to the further level of the development of institutions.

2. *Institutions: Continuity but with Change*

In the accounts of Christian origins some institutions receive a special role. The emphasis on baptism, for instance, stands like a landmark near the beginning of all four gospels and 1 Corinthians (Mt. 3.13-17; Mk 1.9-11; Lk. 3.21-22; Jn 1.26-34; 1 Cor. 1.13-16); and the eucharist receives even greater prominence, generally near the end of the gospels and 1 Corinthians (Mt. 26.26-29; Mk 14.22-25; Lk. 22.14-20; 1 Cor. 11.17-34; cf. Jn 6.52-58).

The role of these two institutions is such that they seem distinctive and innovative; and to some extent they are. Yet they are rooted in Judaism. In the central case of the eucharist there is continuity with the Essene meal, but with major differences. Observance of the Law provided purity—a clean space as it were in which to live—and for the Essenes this purity was concentrated particularly in the ritual meal. The meal, along with its rite of access—baptism—was effective in imparting purity. However, impurity, especially death, was powerful, and so to keep the impurity of death at bay, the Law had to be observed carefully. But then, according to Nodet and Taylor (1998: 441), the power of the Law and death were challenged:

> Like any other system of rational organization, the Law exists...to create a boundary within which life can go on; it does this by...actions that put the performer in touch with God, who is their author. In the case of the Essenes...everything comes together in sharing in the community meal, called 'purity', with its overtones of worship. This notion of (Levitical) purity is essential: everything has to be ritually pure, and the participant must be free from sin, as sin always entails ritual impurity... The source of all impurity is death...

---

1. One of the tensions in Johnson's study (1998) is that having embarked on an analysis of religious experience he spends much of the later part of the book dealing with shared rituals: baptism and the eucharist (1998: 69-103, 137-79). His work is useful, but it has been surpassed by a more extended study, namely Nodet and Taylor 1998.

> Into this context breaks the kerygma, which is concise in its formulation and biblical in its content: Christ's resurrection is a victory—unhoped for but verified by experience—of life over death, and, by analogy, of the pure over the impure. Concretely, the foreigner and the Gentile…and…the impurity of women, cease to be dangerous, and communion is possible. Still more concretely, history and persecution are no longer to be feared, since death has been vanquished… Once all that is projected on to the 'purity', in which the role of bread and wine has been stressed, the whole system turns completely around, beginning with what is most central: forgiveness is now stronger than sin, an outcome that is nothing short of scandalous. It needs only a change of vocabulary, in terms of the kerygma, for the eucharistic elements to become a sign of resurrection and power.

Aspects of this portrayal need clarification. For instance, it is not clear concerning which was challenged first—death or the Law. And the roots of the kerygma—along with the uncharted territory of religious experience—remain obscure. Yet, the overall Nodet/Taylor thesis is strong: the institutions of the new community—which, like the Essenes, saw itself as a new Israel (Nodet and Taylor 1998: 392-97; Stegemann 1998: 139-210 [164-66])—consist largely of profound adaptations of the institutions of the older Israel.

The essence of the Nodet/Taylor thesis is relatively simple: 'The central elements of Christianity in their entirety, including the eucharist, the cross and the system of excommunication, are directly derived from Jewish sects of the most traditional type claiming to represent the renewal of the true Covenant, especially in Galilee' (1998: 437). Associated with the eucharist is the baptismal rite which gave access to it, and this rite too is an adaptation of earlier Jewish practice (pp. 86-88).

3. *The Writings*

What is true of ritual is also true of another institution: the central scriptures. The writings of the early Christians were not primarily ad hoc responses to local crises or communities. They consist, like the rituals, of profound adaptations of the writings of Judaism, particularly of the Greek form of these writings—the Septuagint.

To some degree this is clear and widely acknowledged. The New Testament refers frequently to the older scriptures. But recent scholars have come to a new awareness: the older scriptures are not just citations or allusions that function like adjuncts, buttresses, or cherries on the top. Rather they are constitutive; to a large degree they form the body itself. In the epistles, for instance, 'the "determinate subtext plays…a constitutive role" in shaping [the] literary production'.[2] And in Luke–Acts the author's 'deliberate composition in Septuagintal Greek and his conviction that his story was the fulfilment of the Old Testament imply that as a continuation, Luke–Acts represents *sacred narrative*' (Sterling 1992: 363).

This continuation broke new ground. Like their contemporaries, early Christian writers as a whole valued antiquity and invoked tradition,

> but the past was not simply idealised, depicted as golden and by nature superior to what came later… Christian intellectuals of various shades developed highly sophisticated hermeneutical rules in order to read the Jewish Scriptures in the light of this [messianic] coming, which represented a radical *caesura* in world history. Most Jews, of course, hotly disputed this vision of history… Christian hermeneutical behaviour thus reflects a radical change of attitude towards the past, and quite a new approach to the Scriptures. This change of attitude is tantamount to a revolution. (Stroumsa 1998: 13)

---

2. Hays 1989: 16, quoting Greene 1982: 51; cf. Koch 1986: 92-101, 284; Stockhausen 1989.

The purpose of this book is partly to outline the beginning of that revolution—the process by which the earliest Christians adapted the older writings. This outline does not account for the roots of Christianity. But it indicates how, as Christianity expanded, it developed one of its key institutions—the writings which, in effect, would form a kind of constitution.

They did not aim for a legal document. The multiplicity of texts—epistles and especially gospels—was probably a deliberate way of preventing any one version from becoming a source of fixation. Why the early Christians limited the number of canonical gospels to four is difficult to say. Some scholars invoke petty politics, but the more probable reason is some form of foundational vision, like a simple central sense that the gospel should mirror the four corners of the earth.

Such features—deliberate diversity, and the central symbolism of four—are themselves central to the old scriptures. The Hebrew writings are pervaded by diversity; they are dialectic and dialogical (see Brueggemann 1997: especially 83-84, 317). And the use of four as a symbol of completeness or universalism occurs in leading texts: four rivers of Eden (Gen. 2); four directions around the ark in the desert (Num. 2); and four of several features in the foundational vision of Ezekiel (Ezek. 1).

Whatever the details, the central conclusion is clear. Emerging Christianity, with all its religious experience, was marked by a profound adaptation of Jewish institutions. One of those Jewish institutions was its scriptural heritage. The Christians took that heritage and reshaped it radically to a new prophetic vision, a new understanding of human beings and of the divinity that encompasses the world.

Part II

The Overall Picture: Initial Evidence

Orientational Introduction to Chapter 10–26

Part II (Chapters 10–26) implies a process of writing which began with Matthew's *Logia* and with epistolography, and which then moved through five stages of prose narrative: Proto-Luke, Mark, Matthew, John, and Luke–Acts. The initial evidence indicates that the process was one of dialectical continuity: the writers generally built on the foundation laid by those who preceded them, especially those who preceded them immediately, but they did so through a form of dialogue or dialectic—through developing a further point of view.

The presentation consists of three sections:
1. The central thesis: Proto-Luke, especially Proto-Luke's use of the Old Testament (Chapters 10–11 [Unit 1]).
2. An auxiliary thesis: Aspects of Proto-Luke's New Testament background, namely Matthew's *Logia*, and epistolography (Chapters 12–14 [Unit 2]).
3. Once Proto-Luke and its background are in place: an outline of the development of Mark, Matthew, John, and Luke-Acts (Chapters 15–25 [Units 3–5]).

A final chapter gives the overall summary and conclusions (Chapter 26).

Unit 1. The Central Thesis: Proto-Luke, Septuagint-Based

10

The Central Thesis:
An Early Version of Luke–Acts

Having seen the general context of writing, especially how texts were bound with rewriting, artistry, and communication, it is time now to look at one set of writings—the New Testament.

Ideally, in tracing the development of the New Testament one should begin with its oldest writings, generally reckoned to be either some collection of sayings or some epistles. But the beginning of something is not necessarily the most practical point of entry; often it is easier to observe a phenomenon when it has reached an advanced stage. In the case of the New Testament, one of the most effective ways of observing some of its underlying dynamics is by examining Luke–Acts.[1] Luke–Acts provides a strong clue to its own literary origin, and opens the way to understanding other New Testament developments.

The central thesis of this volume is as follows. Within Luke–Acts is a stream of texts—a total of about 25 chapters—with a distinctive relationship to the Septuagint/LXX, so distinctive that that it is reasonable to conclude that these chapters once existed alone, as a first short version of Luke–Acts. This short version falls into eight sections:[2]

1. Jesus' infancy narrative (Lk. 1–2).
2. Jesus' early ministry (3.1–4.22a [except 3.7-9; 4.1-13]; 7.1–8.3).
3. Jesus' journey to Jerusalem (9.51–10.20; 16.1-9, 19-31; 17.11–18.8; 19.1-10).
4. Jesus' death and resurrection (chs. 22–24 [except 22.31-65]).
5. The church's beginnings (Acts 1.1–2.42).
6. The church's early ministry (2.43–5.42).
7. The church's move away from Jerusalem (6.1–9.30).
8. The church's transformation, integrating the Gentiles (9.31–15.35).

The essence of this idea is not new. Many researchers have suggested that Luke–Acts once existed in a shorter form,[3] but there was no way of identifying reliably which passages belonged to that version. Now, however, the distinctive relationship to the LXX acts as a verifiable identifying mark. The situation is somewhat like that of sorting out the origin of, say, a large number of lions: some carry telltale traces of a specific area, so it is possible to distinguish those that have come from that area.

Once it is reasonably clear that these texts constitute the first version of Luke–Acts, other issues become easier to manage.

This chapter looks at three aspects of establishing Luke's first version: the sequence of the logic underlying the investigation, some of Luke's methods of adaptation, and the three key arguments.

---

1. For a discussion of the general relationship between Luke and Acts, see Pervo 1999 and Marshall 1999.
2. For Greek text of Proto-Luke, see Brodie 2002: 2-46.
3. See Appendix 1.

1. *Luke's First Version: The Sequence of Logic Underlying the Investigation*

The General Introduction (Chapters 1–9) set the scene: ancient authors built on existing texts. In literary studies, this is a first principle, verified repeatedly and without major exception.[4] The subsequent process of investigation has several steps:

(1) In seeking to reconnect the New Testament writings to their literary background, a substantial clue is found in Luke–Acts: several of its general features reflect the Greek version of the Old Testament (LXX), so much so that Luke–Acts has been described as a *mimésis* or literary imitation of the LXX (Plümacher 1972), and as a continuation of the LXX (Sterling 1992: 352-63 [363]). Indebtedness to the LXX does not exclude significant indebtedness to several other kinds of sources,[5] but within the complex body of Luke's writing, it is the LXX that supplies the backbone.

(2) When this clue or lead is followed—when the general relationship to the LXX is examined closely—more specific connections begin to emerge. The most striking of these is a unique link to the Elijah–Elisha narrative (1 Kgs 16.29–2 Kgs 13.25). In the entire world of ancient literature, Luke–Acts and the Elijah–Elisha narrative are the only texts that consist of two balancing parts bridged by an assumption into heaven.

(3) The connection to Elijah and Elisha is confirmed by explicit references in leading passages. In Luke's opening scene, the first ancient name mentioned by the visiting angel is 'Elijah' (Lk. 1.17). And in Luke's account of Jesus' inaugural speech at Nazareth, Jesus invokes the examples of both Elijah and Elisha (Lk. 4.25-27).

(4) The connection to the Old Testament account of Elijah and Elisha is further confirmed by central thematic links. For instance, in common with the old prophet-centered narrative, Luke–Acts has a special emphasis on the role of *prophecy* and the *Word*. More than in other gospels, Jesus is the prophet (Lk. 7.16, 'a great prophet'). And Acts, to a significant degree, is a history of the Word.[6] Both texts also share such elements as: healing; raising the dead; widows, army officers, exotic foreign government ministers in chariots; rich and poor; and a conspicuous turning point when the great prophet sets off to walk towards assumption.[7] Other connections involve reversal. For instance, Elijah calls down fire, but Jesus reverses the proposal (2 Kgs 1.10; Lk. 9.55). The Elijah–Elisha narrative subtly leads *towards* an emphasis on the temple (2 Kgs 11–12), but Luke–Acts leads *away* from it. Both texts begin with thumbnail sketches of couples who are heavily involved with worship, but while the backgrounds of Ahab and Jezebel are virtually unspeakable (1 Kgs 16.29-34), the credentials of Zechariah and Elizabeth are impeccable (Lk. 1.5-10— the details will be discussed later). Thus, the overall relationship between the narratives seems to be a thought-provoking blend of continuity and reversal.

(5) Whole Lukan episodes are colored by Old Testament episodes. For instance, the killing of Stephen—accused by false witnesses and then stoned to death (Acts 6.19-14; 7.58a)—contains detailed similarities with the false accusing and stoning of Naboth

---

4. See especially Chapters 1–4. The tragedy of Gunkel and Bultmann, scientifically speaking, is that despite their wonderful talents and contributions, they violated this first principle. Partly because of regarding the people as 'uncultivated' (Gunkel 1901: i) and the gospels as 'unliterary' (Bultmann 1931: 7), they effectively severed the fundamental relationship between biblical texts and the larger world of earlier writing, and left the biblical books stranded and fragmented (see Chapter 6).

5. Luke's text is colored, for instance, by Greco-Roman prologues, Hellenistic historiography, and other ancient texts. See Moessner (ed.) 1999, especially the articles by L.C.A. Alexander, D.D. Schmidt, V.K. Robbins, D.P. Moessner, W. Kurz, C.R. Holladay, G.E. Sterling, D.L. Balch, E. Plümacher, C.H. Talbert and J.H. Hayes, and D. Marguerat.

6. See, for instance, Haenchen 1971: 98.

7. For a summary of some themes and motifs in the Elijah–Elisha narrative, see Brodie 2000: 70-76.

(1 Kgs 21.8-13). There are numerous adaptations and important differences, but all of these differences are intelligible; they make sense in light of the requirements of Luke's narrative (Brodie 1983a: 417-32). The continuity between the texts is clear, but the Old Testament passage has been *expanded* to provide a framework for a larger body of material (for the Stephen narrative). In other cases, the Old Testament episode is *contracted or distilled*.

(6) Whole Lukan chapters are grounded, episode by episode, on passages from the Old Testament, especially from the Elijah–Elisha narrative. For instance, the four major episodes of Luke 7—the healing of the centurion's servant, the raising of the widow's son, the discussion about the Baptist, and the forgiving of the woman—are all based significantly on four episodes from the Elijah–Elisha narrative (Brodie 1992b; 1986a; 1994; 1983b).

(7) Luke's use of the Elijah–Elisha text is systematic, complete.[8] Each Old Testament episode is used in some form, and essentially used only once. The analysis of this phenomenon, this systematic refashioning of passage after passage, requires considerable space. (See Chapters 27–54 [Part III of this volume]).

(8) To a significant degree, Luke keeps the Old Testament order. Having begun at the beginning (using Ahab and Jezebel as foils for Zechariah and Elizabeth), he generally uses the first half of the Old Testament narrative in composing the gospel, and the second half in Acts. (For details of completeness and order, see Table 3 at the end of this chapter.)

(9) The Lukan texts involved in this systematic reworking of the Elijah–Elisha narrative form an intermittent patchwork extending from Luke 1 to Acts 14.[9] Taken on their own, these texts lack coherence.

(10) The patchwork of texts based on the Elijah–Elisha narrative is inextricably interwoven with a larger fabric involving the use of other texts, especially Judges and the Chronicler's History. Some such phenomenon was to be expected. It is clear from the opening scene of the angel's annunciation in the temple that, quite apart from the use of the Elijah–Elisha narrative, other influences are at work. The two annunciations which introduce Luke's infancy narrative have clear echoes of the two angelic annunciations which introduce Gideon and Samson, characters who, in the structure of Judges, occupy central positions (see Chapter 3). In other words, the annunciations concerning the leading characters of Judges have been used to form the annunciations concerning John and Jesus—the leading characters in early Luke.

(11) Further analysis shows that Luke has used the entire book of Judges. As with the Elijah–Elisha narrative, Luke's transformation of Judges is systematic, complete, essentially non-repetitive, and maintaining aspects of the original order. (See Table 4 at the end of this chapter.) For analysis of Luke's use of Judges, passage after passage, see Chapters 44–52 (in Part III of this volume).

(12) At times, as in the opening scene (Lk. 1.5-26), the systematic use of Judges overlaps with the influence of the Elijah–Elisha narrative (the two sources are conflated), but in other instances, the use of Judges breaks new ground. It adds to the patchwork of texts already established by the use of the Elijah–Elisha narrative. In particular (as Table 4 shows), it extends the patchwork to include virtually all of Luke 1–2 and Acts 12.1–15.21.

(13) This broader patchwork of texts—including the Judges-based material—still lacks coherence.

---

8. The idea of systematic dependence on the Old Testament is not new. See Koet (1989: 141): '[Luke] tends towards a treatment of the Scriptures that we would nowadays call systematic: a well thought out, organized and coherent way of dealing with the Scriptures (cf. Luke 1.3)'. Cf. aspects of systematic use in the epistles (Koch 1986: 92-101; Hays 1989: 14-21.

9. As Table 3 implies, the passages are: Lk. 1.1-17; 7.1–8.3; 9.51–10.20; 18.1-8; 19.1-10; Lk. 22–Acts 2 (except Lk. 22.31-65); Acts 5.1-11; 6.9-14; 7.58; 8.9–11.30; 14.8-18.

(14) Inextricably interwoven with the use of Elijah–Elisha and Judges is a further source, the temple-centered Chronicler's History (taking this term in a broad sense to include 1 and 2 Chronicles, Ezra, and Nehemiah). Beginning with the annunciation scenes, the text of Luke 1–2 is regularly colored by aspects of 1 and 2 Chronicles. The way of using Chronicles is not the same as the way of using Elijah and Judges; it is much more compressed or distilled, a reflection perhaps of Chronicles' own method of occasionally employing extreme compression of sources. The use of Ezra and Nehemiah, on the other hand, is somewhat easier to see; it extends into most of Luke 3 and 4. The sense of moral and social renewal which pervades the books of Ezra and Nehemiah is reflected systematically in the arrival and preaching of John and Jesus (Lk. 3.1–4.22a). As Ezra and Nehemiah sought, for instance, to correct border-crossing marriages (Ezra 9–10; Neh. 9), so John condemns the transgressive marriage of Herod (Lk. 3.19-20). And as returned Ezra solemnly read the Law to the people (Neh. 8) so Jesus returns to Nazareth and solemnly reads Isaiah to the people (Lk. 4.14-22a). On the basis of dependence on the Chronicler's History, the Nazareth scene ends with the people's approval (4.22a).[10]

(15) As with the Elijah–Elisha text and Judges, the overall pattern is systematic: complete, non-repetitive, and maintaining much of the Old Testament order. Apart from one major block (2 Chron. 10–36), the entire Chronicler's History is synthesized into Lk. 1.1–4.22a. (See Table 5.)

(16) The use of the major block (2 Chron. 10–36, the later history of the temple) remains obscure. Apparently it was distilled in a complex way to form one component in Luke's account of the church's break from the temple and the Law—Acts 4.1–15.35. (See Appendix 3.)

(17) As with Judges, the use of the Chronicler's History breaks new ground. It adds further to the patchwork of texts, particularly by including most of Lk. 3.1–4.22a and by reaching as far as Acts 15.35.[11]

(18) The extended patchwork of texts, a larger fabric of about 25 chapters, consists of the following: Lk. 1.1–4.22a (except 3.7-9; 4.1-13); 7.1–8.3; 9.51–10.20; 16.1-9, 19-31; 17.11–18.8; 19.1-10; chs. 22–24 (except 22.31-65); and Acts 1.1–15.35.

(19) These texts form a distinct group; they have a systematic relationship to a specific set of interwoven sources. This does not prove that they ever existed separately, but it does set them apart.

(20) When this larger fabric is removed from Luke Acts and viewed on its own, it shows profound unity—coherence of both theme and plot (Chapter 11).

(21) The unity includes an orderly structure of eight sections. As already indicated above, these sections may be designated approximately as follows:

1. Jesus' infancy narrative (Lk. 1–2).
2. Jesus' early ministry (3.1–4.22a [except 3.7-9; 4.1-13]; 7.1–8.3).
3. Jesus' journey to Jerusalem (9.51–10.20; 16.1-9, 19-31; 17.11–18.8; 19.1-10).
4. Jesus' death and resurrection (chs. 22–24 [except 22.31-65]).
5. The church's beginnings (Acts 1.1–2.42).
6. The church's early ministry (2.43–5.42).
7. The church's move away from Jerusalem (6.1–9.30).
8. The church's transformation, integrating the Gentiles (9.31–15.35).

(22) The unity is confirmed further by another phenomenon: beginning with the infancy narrative, each of the eight units consists of a diptych (Chapter 11).

---

10. The pattern of dependence does not include the vipers speech (Lk. 3.7-9), the temptations (4.1-13), or the rejection at Nazareth (Lk. 4.22b-30). For details, see Brodie 1979. (Or see Chapter 53, below).

11. Inclusion of all of Acts 1.1–15.35 will be confirmed later on other grounds. See Chapter 11 on the unity of Proto-Luke; cf. Appendices 2 and 3.

(23) This structure—eight units, each a diptych—corresponds precisely to the structure of the Elijah–Elisha narrative (Brodie 2000: 6-27).

(24) Luke's use of the Elijah–Elisha narrative is eminently understandable. The account of the two great prophets is itself an interpretive synthesis of the Bible's foundational history (Genesis–Kings) (Brodie 2000: 29-97). For a historiographer like Luke, who wanted to build on Old Testament historiography, the Elijah–Elisha presented a ready-made synthesis, an ideal starting-point.

(25) The 25 chapters correspond significantly to some of the long-standing proposals for the shape of Proto-Luke. The eightfold narrative, modeled especially on the Elijah–Elisha account, corroborates these Proto-Luke theories, and gives them a more solid foundation—not vague Semitism but Septuagintism.[12] When Feine first attempted, on the basis of Semitism, to trace those areas of Luke–Acts which constituted Proto-Luke, he identified a series of texts running intermittently from Luke 1 to Acts 12. Feine's followers (e.g. Gaston 1970) went slightly further; they traced the Semitism as far as the council of Jerusalem (Acts 15.35). When the criterion is adjusted—when instead of Semitism one seeks Septuagintism (the systematic use of the LXX)—then, as already seen, the footprints become clearer. Apart from the occasional echoes of the LXX which occur throughout all of Luke–Acts, there are 25 chapters which form a distinctive line of LXX-based texts extending intermittently from Luke 1 to Acts 15.35. For further details on Proto-Luke, see Appendix 1.

(26) The hypothesis works. When the 25 chapters are seen as a separate entitiy, grounded on a synthesis of Old Testament narrative and New Testament epistolography, the development and sequence of the four canonical gospels becomes much more understandable. This will be outlined below.

In conclusion, then, this distinct fabric (25 chapters) stands apart, and is most easily understood as a separate document—the first version of Luke–Acts. For practical purposes it may be called Proto-Luke.

It is not immediately clear, nor is it very important in a study that is literary rather than historical, whether the author of Proto-Luke is identical to the author of canonical Luke–Acts. For practical purposes the authorship of both texts may often be attributed to 'Luke', but sometimes it is useful to distinguish 'Proto-Luke' from 'canonical Luke'

---

12. Around 1890 two new terms emerged in New Testament research—Q in 1890 (see Neirynck 1978) and Proto-Luke, or at least the concept of Proto-Luke, in 1891 (Feine 1891). Both terms designated hypothetical documents which, if real, had a major role in the gospels' formation. But so far it has not been possible to identify reliably the nature and content of these documents. In the case of Proto-Luke, essentially two methods, two criteria, have been used in trying to trace its shape: (1) *The identification of Semitism* (using Luke–Acts alone). The Proto-Luke hypothesis started with Paul Feine's observation that parts of Luke–Acts are distinctly Semitic. This led to the idea that Luke–Acts had two stages: an early Semitic stage, Proto-Luke; and a later, more hellenistic, stage, giving the present Luke–Acts. To distinguish the original Proto-Luke, it seemed that what was needed was to go carefully through Luke–Acts and identify those parts of the text which were markedly Semitic. But, in practice, working with Luke–Acts alone, it was not possible to be sure which texts were Semitic and which were not; often the distinction was not clear, and so the project floundered. (2) *Comparison with Mark* (using Luke and Mark—c. 1920s). A varied theory of Proto-Luke began with the observation that, if the Markan material is removed from Luke's gospel (especially from Luke's Passion Narrative), Luke's account still forms an essentially complete gospel—so much so that Luke, before using Mark, seems to have had a gospel of his own, a proto-gospel. But the first argument, using the criterion of Semitism—in other words, tracing the parts that are heavily Semitic—is not to be abandoned. What is necessary is an adjustment of the criterion: *instead of Semitism identify Septuagintism.* (Lukan studies have generally shown alleged Semitisms to be Septuagintisms.) The LXX is not at all vague; it is a specific book that can be checked in detail.

2. A Closer Look at Luke's First Version:
Motivation, and Diverse Methods of Adaptation

Proto-Luke's overall motivation for using scripture in Luke–Acts is a matter for further research, yet, as with canonical Luke–Acts, one may say that the author 'conceived of his work as the *continuation* of the LXX...[as the] fulfilment of the promises of the Old Testament'.[13] The prologue refers to 'fulfilling' (*pléro-phoreó*), to 'the beginning' (*arché*) and to 'the word' (*logos*, Lk. 1.1-2), thus suggesting, among other things, that the account of Jesus involves a fulfilling of the Word which was present from the beginning.[14]

Luke's motivation for focusing on specific texts is somewhat clearer. Elijah held a special role in Jewish memory,[15] and, as indicted earlier, the Elijah–Elisha narrative was a synthesis of Judaism's foundational historiography. The Chronicler's History also distilled ancient history, but with greater emphasis on the temple—an emphasis that suited an author who highlighted Jerusalem. And the intensifying suffering in Judges is like the story of the fall and suffering of Judah—a theme well suited to the story of Jesus and his fateful journey to Jerusalem.[16]

In this study, the motivation, the *why*, is less important than the *how*—the methods by which Proto-Luke reworked existing texts, especially the LXX.

The presupposition underlying this thesis is that the author of Proto-Luke had access to diverse ways of adapting sources. He was not bound by one or two particular modes of reworking sources; not bound, for instance, to the near-verbatim methods sometimes used later by canonical Matthew and canonical Luke when they incorporated Mark. Such word-for-word reworking had its place in ancient writing, but it was by no means the only way. As already seen, in discussing 'transformation', some leading writers expressly discouraged word-for-word adaptation (see Chapter 1, 'Literary Imitation: The Theory').

Luke had many options available. There were very diverse ways of reworking existing texts, and it is necessary to make allowance for the individual methods used by each writer (see Chapters 1, 2 and 4). The literary methods of Greco-Roman writers and Jewish writers differed little,[17] and, in any case, as a Hellenistic-style writer who engaged the Jewish scriptures, Luke was close to both.

What counts is not whether a particular method of adapting Scripture seems strange by modern standards, but whether it is plausible in the context of antiquity, and whether there is evidence that it was actually used.

Details of how Proto-Luke used some Septuagintal texts are given in the episode-by-episode analysis (in Part III of this volume). The analysis is not complete, but it is sufficient to indicate a strong systematic connection between Proto-Luke and the LXX.

Some initial aspects of Proto-Luke's methods need to be mentioned at this point.

---

13. Sterling 1992: 363 (cf. Koet 1989: 156). For discussion of how God's ancient promises work out in Luke–Acts, see Tannehill 1999.

14. For references regarding Luke's prologue and theology of salvation, see nn. 1 and 6, above.

15. Elijah stood out like a beacon: 'Despite...Isaiah, Jeremiah, Ezekiel, by far the most popular and from the point of view of Jewish hopes and aspirations, the most important is Elijah' (L.H. Feldman 1994: 61).

16. Some writers apparently saw Judges as having a special role. Pseudo-Philo's *Biblical Antiquities*, generally dated to the later part of the first century CE, 'is a biblical history from Adam to the death of Saul. Its treatment however is very uneven... The central focus of the work is on the period of the Judges, constituting approximately 40 percent of the work' (L.H. Feldman 1988: 59). In the words of B. Halpern-Amaru (1994: 94), Pseudo-Philo apparently 'used Judges as his base'.

17. For instance, citation techniques among Greco-Roman writers and Jewish writers were virtually identical. See Stanley 1992: 337.

a. *The Lukan Text and Elijah–Elisha: Overall Relationship*
The process of tracing the overall relationship between Luke–Acts and Elijah–Elisha varies in difficulty. Some instances of dependence (Naboth/Stephen; the raising of the widow's son) are relatively easy to detect, and as one works with them they begin to reveal the details of how Luke–Acts adapts Old Testament episodes. It thereby becomes somewhat easier to detect what is going on in more complex cases.

For instance, immediately before the accounts of raising a widow's son, both the Old Testament and Luke tell of saving someone who was about to die: Elijah saves the widow and her son from dying (1 Kgs 17.2-16), and Jesus saves the centurion's slave from dying (Lk. 7.1-10). The obvious difference is so great—a poor widow and a powerful centurion (one gathering sticks; the other building a synagogue)—that, even though both are devout foreigners, the two texts do not seem to merit comparison. There is nothing in the Elijah story about centurions.

True, but it suits Luke's narrative to have a centurion figure. Acts 10 will highlight the decisive role of Cornelius, the centurion whose openness to the word merited baptism. The centurion figure of Luke 7, with his openness to the Word ('Say but the word'), prepares for the pivotal openness of Cornelius.

Luke's changing of characters—substituting a centurion for a widow—may be described as a form of *transference*. It is taboo in modern history writing, but not in ancient historiography (Chapter 1, 'Imitation and Historiography').

Luke has also changed the relationship: one is mother and son; the other is centurion and slave. But the presence of a slave, rather than a son, also suits Luke's larger purpose: it enables him to highlight something internal—an inner love which is surprising. Mother–son love is to be expected, but master–slave concern requires something else, something beyond a primal physical bond. Such a dimension suits Luke; he wants to emphasize inner qualities. Within the larger unity of Luke 7, the centurion's love and faith prepares the way for the love and faith of the repentant woman (7.36-50, especially 7.42, 50). Furthermore, shifting the focus towards what is internal is in line with what the Elijah–Elisha narrative itself had already done: move the focus from various external kingdoms to the deeper reality of God's word—to something more internal. This change towards *internalization* is also in line with Greco-Roman practices (Chapter 1, 'Literary Imitation: The Practice'). In making the change Luke brings the process of internalization, begun in the Elijah–Elisha narrative, to a new level, to a fulfillment.

If the Old Testament text is read as strict history such a change is unwarranted. But if it is heavily poetic then it may be adapted to a later time. It is in fact adapted, so Luke's methods emerge slowly. Sometimes Jesus does what Elijah or Elisha had done; but, as seen concerning calling down fire from heaven, at other times Jesus reverses the Old Testament. In general, as with the deathly fire, Luke positivizes: he changes what seems negative to an image that is more positive. Luke's procedures of reversal and positivization may seem highhanded or far-fetched, but they have strong precedents.[18]

The same procedures—reversal and positivization—are used in dealing with the very beginning of the Elijah–Elisha narrative, the introductory picture of Ahab and Jezebel (1 Kgs 16.29-34). The Old Testament picture has been turned around to help build the positive picture of Zechariah and Elizabeth (Lk. 1.5-25, especially 1.5-17). All that was negative in Ahab and Jezebel, especially their gross (Baalite) distortion of worship, has been adapted—reversed—to form an introduction that is deeply positive, especially concerning worship in the Jerusalem temple. Jeze*bel* daughter of Eth*baal* was like an

---

18. On reversal of scripture in Paul, for instance, see Pate 2000. On positivization, see Chapter 1, 'Literary Imitation: The Practice' (pp. 8-13).

incarnation of Baalite worship. But Elizabeth is introduced as like an incarnation of someone related to true worship—she is 'a descendant of Aaron' (for details, see Chapter 27).

Both introductions are effective. They provide powerful settings for the entry of God's Word, but while the Old Testament picture is negative, Luke has turned it around into something positive. The result of his adaptations is that the three major episodes at the beginning of the Elijah account all find an equivalent in the gospel:

Negative couple:
Scene set for entry of God's word in Elijah (1 Kgs 16.29-34).
The foreign widow and son doomed to die, but saved (1 Kgs 17.1-16).
The raising of the widow's son (1 Kgs 17.17-24).

Positive couple:
Scene set for entry of angel, invoking Elijah (Lk. 1.5-25).
The foreign centurion and the doomed slave who is saved (Lk. 7.1-10).
The raising of the widow's son (Lk. 7.11-17).

And so it goes on. Every major passage of the Elijah–Elisha narrative finds an equivalent in Luke–Acts. One episode is exceptional. The centre-piece of the Elijah–Elisha narrative, concerning Elijah's departure and ascent (2 Kgs 1.7-15), has been opened out as it were so that it forms a framing device for several chapters at the centre of Proto-Luke (cf. Lk. 22–Acts 2). Otherwise, as Table 3 indicates, each Old Testament text generally influences just one text of Proto-Luke.

In summary, the Elijah–Elisha narrative made at least three diverse contributions to Luke–Acts. First, through its various episodes, it provided components for a specific stream of texts running intermittently from Luke 1 to Acts 14. Second, as a two-part narrative, it acted as a unique general model for Luke–Acts: two balancing parts centered on an assumption. Third, and most basic of all, it provided a bridge between the central tradition of Old Testament historiography (the Primary History) and the central text of New Testament historiography (Luke–Acts).

b. *The Lukan Text and Judges*
In dealing with Judges, the New Testament adapts the order in three major areas—the beginning (Judg. 1–3), the highpoint (the Samson story, Judg. 12–16), and the conclusion (war and peace, Judg. 20–21).

1. The beginning becomes the beginning of the end. The ancient Israelite engagement with the nations (Judg. 1–3) provides one component in introducing and describing Paul's missionary journey (Acts 12–14).
2. The highpoint opens out to form a framing device. The first half of the Samson story, dealing with annunciation and youth (Judg. 13–14) underlies the infancy narrative (Lk. 1–2); and its later part, dealing with his dying triumph over adversity (Judg. 15–16) colors the picture of the church's often-painful expansion (Acts 9.32–15.21).
3. The end, concerning war and peace, is rearranged freely: the war (Judg. 20) underlies the concluding war-related talk of Gamaliel (Acts 5.33-42); and the peace (Judg. 21) contributes to the last supper (Lk. 22.1-30).

The use of the remaining twelve chapters of Judges (4–12 and 17–19) follows essentially the order of Judges itself. (See the references in italics in Table 4.) The only partial exception to this orderly arrangement is the Gideon story (Judg. 6–8): aspects of this account, notably the angel's annunciation and the night action (Judg. 6.11-24, 33-40; 7.9–8.3), have been used in Luke's infancy narrative.

c. *The Lukan Text and the Chronicler*

There is an obvious appropriateness in using Chronicles to build the infancy narrative (Lk. 1–2); both texts emphasize the temple. And Proto-Luke generally maintains the order of the older writing. Yet, the specific connections between Luke 1–2 and Chronicles are relatively difficult to detect. Some readers may find it better, on this issue, to suspend judgment until the larger picture clarifies and until there is more time for close analysis.

While the beginning of Chronicles (1 Chron. 1 to 2 Chron. 9) was used at the beginning of Proto-Luke (Lk. 1–2), the later part (2 Chron. 10–36) was apparently used at the end (Acts 4.1–15.35). Here also, but in a different way, an Old Testament text is opened out to provide a framing device in composing a new work.

d. *Aspects of Adaptation: Summary*

In using the three key Old Testament sources, Luke generally stays *one on one*: he uses one Old Testament episode as a (partial) basis for one New Testament episode. He also tends to maintain the Old Testament order (see Tables 3–5). However, occasionally he disperses or synthesizes (he scatters one Old Testament episode among many New Testament passages, or combines many Old Testament passages into one New Testament passage). Variations of order can generally be explained. For instance, texts may be divided up to form framing devices, or may be combined because of inherent affinities.

The three sources form a unique combination. At the beginning of the infancy narrative they are inextricably interwoven, and the systematic use of them continues through several subsequent passages right into the center of Acts.

The use of these sources does not exclude others. This is particularly true of the Passion Narrative (Lk. 22.1-30; 22.66–ch. 24), and especially of Judges. The systematic influence of Judges goes right through the heart of the gospel, and then into Acts, yet this influence, while important, is often subsidiary to other sources. At times it adds little more than a secondary tinge. Other sources, including specifically Christian sources, have filled out the text.

Luke's methods of adapting are diverse. Some have been mentioned here—transference, internalization, positivization, and reversal—but, as the introductory chapters indicate (Chapters 1, 2, 4) many others were available, and each writer could also use individual methods.

What is essential is the flexibility of Proto-Luke's methods of adaptation. On the one hand, there is systematic fidelity: in principle the source-text is absorbed completely and in order. On the other hand, there is radical transformation: depending on the needs of the new narrative, the sections of the older text are adapted to suit new faces, places, and purposes. And the methods of adaptation are many. Among others they include re-arrangement, combination, division, transference, internalization, positivization, and reversal.

3. *Luke's First Version: The Three Key Arguments*

The sequence of investigation is long, and the methods of adaptation are many, yet the basic case for Proto-Luke can be reduced to three key arguments:

a. *Argument 1. Distinctive Dependence on the LXX*

Within Luke–Acts lies a stream of texts—a total of about 25 chapters—that has a distinctive systematic dependence on the LXX, especially on the Elijah–Elisha narrative (1 Kgs 16.29–2 Kgs 13). The dependence occurs intermittently in Luke's gospel, and continuously in Acts 1.1–15.35. The distinctiveness of this stream of texts does not necessarily mean that they ever existed separately, but at some level it does set them apart.

b. *Argument 2. Unity of Content and Structure*
The distinctive stream is not muddled. On the contrary, its various texts constitute a solid unity, coherent in both content and form. In particular, the texts have a precise eightfold structure. This structure is not only unified in itself; it also corresponds exactly and uniquely to the structure of the Elijah–Elisha narrative. The clear solidity of the unity is most easily accounted for by saying that this body of material once existed as a separate unity. (Separateness is all the more credible because of the semi-separate status of the Elijah–Elisha narrative—a text that forms an interpretive synthesis of most of Judaism's foundational history.) The distinctive stream corresponds significantly to some long-held views concerning Proto-Luke, Luke's hypothetical first version, so for practical reasons it may be called Proto-Luke.

c. *Argument 3. Subsequent Verification*
The Proto-Luke hypothesis works. Once Proto-Luke is in place, it is easier to trace the development of the gospels, beginning with Mark. The development is as follows:
- Mark has its own special sources, genre, and theology, but much of it relies heavily on Proto-Luke and on Proto-Luke's sources, including the Elijah–Elisha narrative.
- Matthew then used Mark, but he also reached back to Proto-Luke, refashioning Proto-Luke to his own purposes. Matthew also used his own sources, and made particular use of Deuteronomy. Deuteronomy, with its many discourses, provided a model for a new form of gospel.
- John in turn used Matthew. Matthew's discourses provided John with a partial model; and John also used Matthew's sources, including Mark and Proto-Luke.
- Finally, canonical Luke–Acts expanded Proto-Luke in a way that developed and synthesized Mark, Matthew, and John. This new synthesis distilled the Sermon on the Mount into the Sermon on the Plain—a transformation that seems strange in the context of modern historical method, but that fits well into the writing practices of antiquity.

The relationship between Matthew and Luke (Matthew adapted Proto-Luke, and Matthew in turn was reshaped by canonical Luke) explains most of the similarities that give rise to the theory of Q.

Overall, the presence of Proto-Luke opens the way to understanding basic aspects of the four gospels and Acts. The effectiveness of the hypothesis provides a third, strong argument to support the reality of Proto-Luke.

4. Before Developing Argument 3: The Value of an Auxiliary Thesis

Having outlined the central thesis, and indicated the nature of the three main arguments, it is appropriate to develop these arguments. This will be done: Argument 1 is elaborated in Chapters 27–54 (Part III of this volume); Argument 2, in the next chapter (Chapter 11); and Argument 3, in subsequent chapters (Chapters 15–25). Readers who want to see the central thesis substantiated immediately may go directly to those chapters.

However, in reading about the development of the four gospels and Acts (Argument 3, Chapters 15–25), it is useful to take account of an auxiliary thesis concerning Matthew's *Logia* and 1 Corinthians.

So, the essential sequence of the rest of the volume is as follows: Argument 2, the unity of Proto-Luke: Chapter 11; Auxiliary thesis, the *Logia* and 1 Corinthians: Chapters 12–14; Argument 3, the development of the gospels and Acts: Chapters 15–25; General conclusion and implications: Chapter 26; Details of Argument 1, Proto-Luke's use of the LXX: Chapters 27–54 (Part III of this volume).

Table 3. *Use of the Elijah–Elisha Narrative in Luke–Acts*
(following Lukan order, with basic Old Testament order in italics)

	A Great Prophet (Luke 1.5-17; 7.1–8.3)		
1 Kgs 16.29-34	Evil couple	1.5-17	Good couple
1 Kgs 17.1-16	Saving the doomed	7.1-10	Saving the centurion's slave
1 Kgs 17.17-24	Raising a widow's son	7.1-17	Raising a widow's son
1 Kgs 22	Prophet Micaiah vindicated	7.18-35	John vindicated
2 Kgs 4.1-37	The indebted women	7.36-50	The indebted woman
1 Kgs 18	Prophets; twelve; Baal worship	8.1-3	Twelve; Acts 14.8-18, False worship
	Mission Journey to Death and Spirit (Luke 9.51–10.20; Luke 22–Acts 2)		
2 Kgs 1.1–2.6	Death; setting out for ascent	9.51-56	Setting out for death/ascent
1 Kgs 19	Journey: from desert to ploughing	9.57-62	Journey: homeless…ploughing
2 Kgs 2.16–ch. 3	Mission to cities, places. War	10.1-20	Mission to cities. Conflict
2 Kgs 2.7-15	Jordan, assumption, spirit	Lk. 22–Acts 2	Death, ascent, Spirit [omit 22.31-65]
	Expansion Problems, Some Damascus-Related (Acts 5–11)		
1 Kgs 20.1-21; 21.1-7	Greed: Ben/Ahab/Jezebel	5.1-11	Fraud: Ananias/Sapphira
1 Kgs 21.8-13	Naboth accused, stoned	6.9-14; 7.58	Stephen stoned
1 Kgs 21.14-29	Sequel to greed and prophecy	8.15-26; 2.37-38	Response by/to Peter
2 Kgs 5	Namaan; Gehazi's money	8.9-40	Simon's money; the Ethiopian
2 Kgs 6.8-23; 1 Kgs 20.22-34	Two attacks reversed	9.1-19a	Paul's attack reversed
2 Kgs 8.7–9.13	Two commissionings		…and Paul is commissioned
2 Kgs 9.14–ch 11	Murderous attacks (Jehu…)	9.19b-31	Murderous attacks on Paul
2 Kgs 12–13	Repairs, resurrection, restoration	9.32-43	Peter heals, raises (cf. 3.1-10)
2 Kgs 6.24–ch 7	Famine; good news for lepers	chs. 10–11	Hunger; good news for outsiders…
2 Kgs 4.38-44	Famine: prophets and food		…and prophets deal with famine
	Final, Rearranged Pieces (As Minor Components)		
1 Kgs 20.35-43	Ben-hadad's escape	Acts 12	Peter's escape
2 Kgs 6.1-7	Trees; lost axe restored	Lk. 19.1-10	Zacchaeus: tree, restoration
2 Kgs 8.1-6	Woman pleads for justice	Lk. 18.1-8	The widow and the judge
	Simplified Summary of Main Connections		
1 Kgs 16.29-34			Lk. 1.1-17
1 Kgs 17–18	plus 1 Kgs 22; 2 Kgs 4		Lk. 7.1–8.3
1 Kgs 19	plus 2 Kgs 1–3		Lk. 9.51–10.20; Lk. 22–Acts 2
1 Kgs 20–21	plus 2 Kgs 5		Acts 5–8
2 Kgs 6–13			Acts 9–11

'Plus' texts are not added arbitrarily. They have inherent continuities with the texts to which they are added, for example, 1 Kgs 22 and 2 Kgs 4 with 1 Kgs 17–18

Table 4. *Luke's Use of Judges*
(in Luke's order; main Old Testament order in italics)

Beginnings and Annunciations			
Judges		Luke–Acts	
chs. 13–14	Samson's beginning	Lk. 1.5–2.52	Infancy Narrative
6.11-24, 33-40	Angel	1.26-38	Annunciation
7.9–8.3	Night, light, sound	2.8-20	Night, light, sound
chs. 4–5	Deborah, Jael	1.42-55; 2.34-38	Mary, Anna
Crises, Kingdoms and Maverick Judges			
chs. 6–8 (in part)	Gideon	16.1-9, 19-31	Parables
ch. 9	Abimelech's kgm	17.11-19	The Kingdom
chs. 10–12	Judge, virgin	18.1-8	Judge, widow
chs. 17–18	Dan's shrine	19.1-10	Zacchaeus
Passion and Restoration			
ch. 21	Peace: death and love	22.1-30	Last Supper
ch. 19	A woman's Passion	23.50–24.53	Passion, Resurrection
ch. 20	War	Acts 5.33-42	Gamaliel talk of war
The Beginning (Judg. 1–3): The Beginning of the End (Acts 12–14)			
1.1–3.6	Mission	chs. 13–14	Mission
3.7-31	Oppressor dies	ch. 12	Herod
chs. 15–16	Samson's end	9.32–15.21	Mission's end

Table 5. *Luke's Use of Chronicles–Ezra–Nehemiah (Luke 1.1–4.27)*
(largely in Luke's order)[19]

Preparation for David's reign (1 Chron. 1–10).	Preparation for Jesus' Davidic reign (Lk. 1.1-25)
Nathan announces David's reign (chs. 11–12; 17)	Gabriel announces Jesus' reign (1.26-38)
The ark in the hills (ch. 13)	Mary in the hill-country (1.39-45, 56)
God gives David victory (chs. 14; 18–20)	Mary's victorious Magnificat (1.46-55)
Priestly service, sons and song (chs. 15–16)	Zechariah, his son and his song (1.57-80)
The census and the origin of the Temple (chs. 21–22)	The census and the birth of Jesus (2.1-20)
The people and piety of the Temple (chs. 23–29)	People and piety around Jesus (2.21-38)
The building of the Temple (2 Chron. 1.1–5.1)	Jesus grows up (2.39-40)
The Lord takes possession of his Temple (5.2–ch. 9)	Jesus in the Temple (2.41-52)
Life and decline of the Temple (chs. 10–36)	[cf. Acts 4–15]
The leading people, Persian and Israelite (Ezra 1–2)	Leading people, in Rome and Israel (3.1-2)
Rebuild! (Ezra 3.1–6.18; Neh. 1–4; 6–7)	Rebuild morally! (3.2c-6)
	Brood of vipers (3.7-9)
Correction of social abuses (Neh. 5)	Correction of possible abuses (3.10-14)
The people: purification and joy (chs. 10–13)	The people: expectation, purification 3.15-18)
Correcting unlawful marriages (Ezra 9–10; Neh. 9)	Correcting Herod's marriage (3.19-20)
Purification and celebration (Ezra 6.19-22)	Baptism of the Beloved (3.21-22)
Ezra…son of…son of… (Ezra 7.1-10)	Jesus…son of…son of (3.23-38)
	The temptations (4.1-13)
Ezra returns to Jerusalem (Ezra 7.11–ch. 8)	Jesus returns to Galilee (4.14-15)
Ezra reads the Law (Neh. 8)	Jesus reads Isaiah (4.16-22a)

19. The two Lukan texts in italics (3.7-9; 4.1-13) have no systematic counterpart in Chronicles and do not belong to Proto-Luke.

Table 6. *Luke–Acts' Combined Use of Elijah–Elisha,*
Judges, and Chronicles (in Lukan order)

	Lk. 1.1-4: Decision to write
Judg. 13–14: Samson's beginning	1.5–2.52: Infancy Narrative
6.11-24, 33-40: Angel	1.26-38: Annunciation
7.9–8.3: Night, light, sound	2.8-20: Night, light, sound
chs. 4–5: Deborah, Jael	1.42-55; 2.34-38: Mary, Anna
Chronicles–Ezra–Nehemiah	1.5–4.22a (except 3.7-9; 4.1-13)
1 Kgs 16.29-34: Evil couple	1.5-17: Good couple
ch. 17: Saving the doomed; widow's son	7.1-17: Centurion's slave; widow's son
ch. 22: Micaiah vindicated	7.18-35: John vindicated
2 Kgs 4.1-37: The indebted women	7.36-50: The indebted woman
1 Kgs 18: Israel; Baal worship	8.1-3: Twelve; Acts 14.8-18, False worship
2 Kgs 1.1–2.6: Death; setting out for ascent.	9.51-56: Setting out for death/ascent
1 Kgs 19: Journey: from desert to ploughing.	9.57-62: Journey: homeless…ploughing
2 Kgs 2.16-25: Mission to cities, places.	10.1-12: Mission to cities
ch. 3: Total war	10.13-20: Total clash
Judg. 6–8; Gideon	16.1-9, 19-31: Parables
ch. 9: Abimelech's kingdom	17.11-19: The Kingdom
chs. 10–12: Judge and virgin daughter	18.1-8: Judge and widow
2 Kgs 8.1-6: Woman pleads for justice	As above
Judg. 17–18: Dan's shrine	19.1-10: Zacchaeus
2 Kgs 6.1-7: Tree; lost axe restored	As above
2 Kgs 2.7-15: Jordan, assumption, spirit	Lk. 22–Acts 2: Death, ascent, Spirit [omit 22.31-65]
Judg. 21: Peace: death and love	22.1-30: Last Supper
ch. 19: A woman's Passion	23.50–24.53: Passion, Resurrection
1 Kgs 20.1-21; 21.1-7: Greed: Ben-hadad/Ahab/ Jezebel	Acts 5.1-11: Fraud: Ananias/Sapphira
	5.33-42: Gamaliel's warning of war
Judg. 20: War	6.9-14; 7.58: Stephen accused, stoned
1 Kgs 21.8-13: Naboth accused, stoned	8.15-26; 2.37-38: Response by/to Peter
21.14-29: Sequel to greed and prophecy	8.9-40: Simon's money; the Ethiopian
2 Kgs 5: Namaan; Gehazi's money	
2 Kgs 6.8-23; 1 Kgs 20.22-34: Two attacks reversed	9.1-19a: Paul's attack reversed…
2 Kgs 8.7–9.13: Two commissionings	…and Paul is commissioned
9.14–ch. 11: Murderous attacks (Jehu…)	9.19b-31: Murderous attacks on Paul
chs. 12–13: Repairs, resurrection, restoration	9.32-43: Peter heals, raises (cf. Acts 3.1-10)
2 Kgs 6.24–ch. 7: Famine; good news for lepers	chs. 10–11: Hunger; good news for outsiders….
4.38-44: Famine: prophets and food	…and prophets deal with famine
1 Kgs 20.35-43: Ben-hadad's escape	ch. 12: Peter's escape
Judg. 3.7-31: Oppressor dies	ch. 12: Herod
1.1–3.6: Mission to Canaan	chs. 13–14: Mission to the Gentiles
chs. 15–16: Samson's end	9.32–15.21: Mission's end
	15.22-35: Decision to write

11

Proto-Luke: The Argument from Coherence, Especially from Eightfold Structure

Apart from distinctive dependence on the Old Testament, there is a second argument in favor of the proposed version of Proto-Luke. It shows unity and coherence of content and, above all, coherence of structure. An initial investigation, focused on literary composition rather than theology, shows five aspects of unity. Aspects 1 and 2 concern unity of *content*. Aspects 3, 4, and 5 concern unity of *structure*.

1. *Content: A Consistent Flow*

As indicated earlier, Proto-Luke consisted of the following texts:
1. Jesus' infancy narrative (Lk. 1–2).
2. Jesus' early ministry (3.1–4.22a [except 3.7-9; 4.1-13]; 7.1–8.3).
3. Jesus' journey to Jerusalem (9.51–10.20; 16.1-9, 19-31; 17.11–18.8; 19.1-10).
4. Jesus' death and resurrection (chs. 22–24 [except 22.31-65]).
5. The church's beginnings (Acts 1.1–2.42).
6. The church's early ministry (2.43–5.42).
7. The church's move away from Jerusalem (6.1–9.30).
8. The church's transformation, integrating the Gentiles (9.31–15.35).

These texts flow into one another in a way that corresponds broadly with other biblical narratives. This does not mean that Proto-Luke, as proposed, corresponds to a canonical gospel. For instance, unlike (most of) the gospels, Proto-Luke recounts neither the transfiguration nor a climactic public entry into Jerusalem. To a considerable extent, the gospels are a new genre; but Proto-Luke, despite breaking some new ground, still belongs significantly to an old genre found in the Elijah–Elisha narrative: comprising two parts, a mix of history and biography, and strongly prophetic. The Elijah–Elisha narrative provided a skeletal framework, and Proto-Luke expanded that framework in light of other factors, especially in the light of Christian experience. Its unity, therefore, while genuine, is something other than that of a gospel. As one goes through the text, this absence of well-known gospel features may seem jolting, but, taken on its own pre-gospel terms, the narrative flows.

From 1.1 to the synagogue scene (1.1–4.22a), Proto-Luke lacks just two canonical passages—John's brood-of-vipers speech (3.7-9), plus Jesus' temptations/testing (4.1-13)—and the absence of these passages still leaves a text that is quite coherent. The viper metaphor is not essential to John's message, and the basic testing of Jesus had already been accomplished in his visit to the temple, especially in his encounter with the temple teachers (Lk. 2.41-52).

The distinctive use of the LXX stops at the positive response to Jesus' Nazareth speech (4.22a) and resumes in 7.1–8.3. This omits a major section (4.22b–ch. 6, from rejection in the synagogue to the Sermon on the Plain), yet instead of causing the text to be disjointed the effect leaves a narrative which is smooth and unified: the account of Jesus concluding his words (7.1) refers back not to the Sermon on the Plain but to the synagogue speech with its positive conclusion (4.16-22a). The transition from the synagogue speech to 7.1–8.3 is very understandable: straight from Jesus' references concerning a prophet, healing and remission (4.15-22a) to a prophet-related section (7.1–8.3) which includes episodes of healing and remission. In this section (7.1–8.3), the words said in the synagogue become reality. The positive tone of the synagogue speech is reinforced by the absence of both the vipers speech (3.7-9) and the synagogue rejection (4.22b-30).

The conclusion of 7.1–8.3, with its picture of journeying (8.1-3), provides a very appropriate transition to the next part of Proto-Luke: the death-related journey and mission that begins in 9.51 ('And it happened when the days were fulfilled for his assumption...'). The death-related journey and mission (9.51–10.20) forms a unity,[1] and particularly because of its emphasis on heaven, especially the final 'your names are written in heaven' (10.20), it also forms an appropriate transition to the subsequent twin stories: the unjust steward (16.1-9); and the rich man and Lazarus (16.19-31).

The culminating emphasis on heaven ('your names...written in heaven', 10.20) reappears in varied form at the culmination of the story of the unjust steward ('receive you into everlasting tents', 16.9). And this final verse of the story of the unjust steward (16.9) begins in a way that easily leads to the further story of the rich man ('And I say to you...', 16.9). Thus 16.9 prepares for 16.19: 'There was a certain rich man...'—itself a precise echo of the beginning of the story of the unjust steward (16.1).

The end of the story of the rich man (16.31) speaks of resurrection ('even if someone should rise from the dead'), thus matching the earlier stories' climactic references to heaven (10.20; 16.9) and also forming a balancing inclusio with the initial reference to assumption (9.51). So, from assumption (9.51) to resurrection (16.31), the entire body of material (9.51–10.20; 16.1-9, 19-31) forms a coherent unity.

The balancing allusion to 9.51, as found in 16.31, in turn prepares for a more obvious echoing of 9.51: Jesus' meeting with the ten lepers begins, 'And it happened as he was journeying to Jerusalem...' (17.11). Thus begins a panel which, apart from 18.9-43 (largely Markan), runs unbroken from the ten lepers (17.11-19) to Zacchaeus (19.1-10). This material also (17.11–18.8; 19.1-10) forms a unity. The lepers' problem of awareness—only one in ten praises God (17.11-19)—exemplifies the ensuing problem concerning awareness of God's kingdom (17.20-37). And the dynamics of that kingdom are then clarified by twin stories: first the account of the unjust judge who, despite his initial attitude, sought justice for the widow (18.1-8), and then the account of rich Zacchaeus restoring ill-gotten wealth (19.1-10). While recalling those who were lost (*apollymi*)—especially in the flood and the fire (17.27, 29; see Gen. 7 and 19)—this entire section (17.11–18.8 and 19.1-10) holds out hope to those who fight diverse odds (the leper, the widow, the arch-tax-collector). The conclusion of the Zacchaeus story pulls the section together: 'For the Son of

---

1. The unity of 9.51–10.20 needs closer examination. Unlike 7.1–8.3 with its emphasis on prophecy, 9.51–10.20 shifts the focus to journeying, especially to the ultimate journey towards death and beyond (Hades or heaven). At the beginning (9.51-56), as the days are fulfilled for Jesus to be taken up, he sets his face for his destination—*towards Jerusalem*. Next, during the journey (9.56-62), he warns would-be followers about preoccupation with home and death, and, using the image of a ploughman, he directs them instead to journey single-mindedly *towards God*. Finally (10.1-20), in a flourish of journeying, the healing mission of the seventy entails orientation *towards either hell* (*Hades*, 10.15) or *heaven* (10.20). The emphasis on heaven is repeated and vivid. It is associated with the descent of destructive fire (9.54), the throwing down of a city (10.14), and, climactically, the fall of Satan, like lightning (10.18). The final note (10.20) is positive: the names of the seventy are 'written in heaven'. For more on the unity of 9.51–10.20, see General Introduction to Chapters 33–36.

Man/Humanity came to seek and save what was lost' (*apollymi*, 19.10). Furthermore, the Zacchaeus story occurs as Jesus is 'passing through' Jericho (19.1)—one of the entry points for Jerusalem—thus evoking the end of the journeying that began in 9.51.

Proto-Luke's next event, the Passover plot and preparation (22.1-13), evokes in yet another way the journeying that began in 9.51. The emphasis on the *time* ('feast'), the *death-plot*, and the *preparation* (22.1-13) all recall the initial departure for Jerusalem—the fulfilling of the *days*; the allusion to *death*; and the sending of messengers to *prepare* (9.51-56). Thus, at one level the plot and preparation (22.1-13) forms a most appropriate sequence: Jesus' approach to Jerusalem, occurring some time after passing through Jericho, recalls his original departure (9.51-62).

But, unlike 9.51, Jerusalem is not mentioned (in 22.1-13), not explicitly.[2] Given the emphasis on Jerusalem both at the original departure and again when meeting the lepers (17.11), narrative coherence would seem to demand an account of the arrival in Jerusalem, and thus the inclusion in Proto-Luke of Jesus' public entry into Jerusalem (Lk. 19.28-40).

Yet, at this point (ch. 22), Proto-Luke's explicit use of the name 'Jerusalem' is not necessary. While the name is not given, arrival in the city is clearly implied. There is an analogy for Proto-Luke's procedure: the entire second part of John's gospel (Jn 13–21), set almost completely in Jerusalem, never uses the name.[3] What is essential for narrative coherence is not that Jerusalem be explicitly named but that Jesus clearly be understood to have arrived there.

Having recounted the supper (as far as the promise of sitting on thrones 'judging the twelve tribes of Israel', 22.1-30), Proto-Luke goes directly to the morning action when Jesus is led to the Sanhedrin (22.66)—thus skipping the denials and night action, including the arrest (22.31-65, mostly Markan). This absence of an elaborate arrest account may seem to make the sequence abrupt, but in an analogous case—bringing Stephen before the Sanhedrin (Acts 6.12)—the sequence is equally compact. Thus the omission of the denials and night action does not deprive Proto-Luke's Passion account of narrative coherence.

The second half of Proto-Luke consists of Acts 1.1–15.35, a text which, insofar as it is unbroken, may be regarded as a unity.

Overall, therefore, the designated texts from Lk. 1.1 to Acts 15.35 form a sequence which has basic narrative coherence. The text is not quite a gospel; but is has unity.

2. *Content: Continuity between the Beginning (Luke 1.1-4), Middle (Acts 1.1-5), and End (Acts 13.1–15.35, Especially 15.22-35)*

The unity of a text, particularly an ancient text, is generally reflected by the continuity between its beginning, middle, and end (Robbins 1996: 50-53). In various ways, the proposed form of Proto-Luke shows such continuity. Part of this continuity is obvious, especially between Lk. 1.1-4 and Acts 1.1-5. But the ending (Acts 13.1–15.35, especially 15.1-35) is also quite fitting. Some aspects of this appropriateness are as follows:

- The challenges to various Jews, especially in synagogues, and the Jews' increasingly hostile reactions (Acts 13.4-12, 13-43, 44-52; 14.1-7; cf. 14.19-20) is a fitting culmination of the tension which had been intimated earlier in Proto-Luke, for instance, in the quiet clash in the house of the Pharisee (Lk. 7.36-50).

---

2. In 22.3, where one might expect the place name 'Jerusalem' (*Ierousalēm*) there is a very different word, Iscariot (*Iscariōtēn*), a name which, among other things, seems related to a place, the southern town of Kerioth (Fitzmyer 1985: 620).

3. Whether Luke's omission of the name was theologically motivated, as was John's (Brodie 1993a: 27-28), is a matter for further research.

- The decision of the Jerusalem Council (Acts 15.1-21) provides a resolution for a central problem in Proto-Luke: how to move from traditional Judaism to a wider world.
- The final section, the Council's *decision to write* (Acts 15.22-35), contains an elaborate variation on the beginning, on the initial *decision to write* (Lk. 1.1-4; cf. Acts 1.1-5). The balance between these opening and closing texts (Lk. 1.1-4; Acts 15.22-35) is not even: the account of the Council's decision is more elaborate. For instance, the crucial word indicating decision, *edoxe* ('it seemed good'), appears not just once, as in Lk. 1.1-4, but three times (Acts 15.22, 25, 28). But conclusions, by their nature, whether in writings, symphonies, or fireworks, tend to be elaborate, often with a final flourish. John's conclusion, for instance, which is also concerned with writing, is threefold (Jn 19.35-36; 20.30-31; 21.24-25; Brodie 1993a: 121, 123, 125, 573). And so a threefold expansion is quite appropriate. Hence, once allowance is made for a closing flourish, the two texts (Lk. 1.1-4; Acts 15.22-35) are in balance. And the balance implies a correspondence. If the first decision to write (Lk. 1.1-4) is a beginning, then the Jerusalem decision to write (Acts 15.22-35) is most easily understood as an ending.

3. Structure: The Text's Appropriate Proportions
(Jesus: c. Ten Chapters; Disciples: c. Fifteen Chapters)

The proposed text of Proto-Luke is coherent not only in narrative content but also in structure. The first aspect of coherent structure has to do with general proportions. Like a human body, a unified text has appropriate proportions. If one part of the text is seriously disproportionate, the whole lacks unity. In the case of Proto-Luke, it may seem at first that the proposed shape is unbalanced: there are about *ten* chapters on Jesus, but virtually *fifteen* on his disciples. However, this kind of proportion—this increase in length—accords with basic aspects of biblical narrative. It corresponds broadly with the way the narrative of Genesis, for instance, tends to progress from small units to larger panels; and it accords more specifically with the proportions of one of Proto-Luke's basic models: the Elijah–Elisha narrative, a two-part narrative composed of about *eight* and *eleven* chapters (1 Kgs 16.29–2 Kgs 2; and 2 Kgs 3–13).

4. Structure: The Proposed Text Forms Eight Units (Two Fours)

The unity of the proposed text of Proto-Luke is indicated by a further feature of structure: the text falls with relative ease into eight blocks (two groups of four). See Table 7 (using simplified headings, and subdividing the units with a double slash, //):

Table 7. *The Eight Units of Proto-Luke (Simplified)*

1. Annunciations/Births	Lk. 1.1-56//1.57–ch. 2
2. Ministry: Preaching/Action	Lk. 3.1-6, 10-38; 4.14-22a//7.1–8.3
3. Death-Related Journey	Lk. 9.51–10.20; 16.1-9, 19-31//17.11–18.8; 19.1-10
4. Death/Resurrection	Lk. 22.1-30; 22.66–23.49//23.50–ch. 24
5. Spirit Promised/Given	Acts ch. 1//2.1-42
6. Ministry: Action/Preaching	Acts 2.43–4.31//4.32–ch. 5
7. Stephen Dies/Saul Reborn	Acts 6.1–8.1a//8.1b–9.30
8. Breakthrough: Peter/Paul	Acts 9.31–ch. 12//13.1–15.35

To some degree, units 1–4 are echoed in units 5–8. For instance, while unit 1 recounts the infancy of Jesus (his conception, and later his birth), unit 5 recounts the infancy of the church—its incubation (when awaiting the Spirit, Acts 1) and its birth (when the Spirit is given, Acts 2.1-42).

This structure—eight blocks/units—is not exclusive. Like a human body, a complex text has many overlapping structures, and this eightfold aspect is just one. Nor can this proposed division be discussed adequately in this short chapter. Yet, as a matter for further research, it is appropriate to indicate that such a division exists.

The use of eight as a basis for structure is significant. Comprised of two fours, eight indicates completeness (cf. four ends of the earth; four rivers in Eden, Gen. 2; four directions around the tabernacle, Num. 2).[4] Such completeness argues for the independence of these texts—the independence of Proto-Luke.

5. *The Diptych Structure of the Eight Blocks*

A basic feature of the eight blocks—and an indication of their reality—is that each consists, as it were, of two panels; each constitutes a diptych. Thus Proto-Luke consists of eight diptychs. (See Table 8 next pages.)

The basic idea of a diptych is not new to Lukan studies. It is widely recognized that Luke's infancy narrative contains diptychs; first there is a twofold account of annunciation (1.5-25, 26-38), and then a twofold account of birth (1.57-80; 2.1-40).[5] However, the obviousness of these diptychs is but the tip of a much larger phenomenon. The most basic diptych phenomenon in Luke 1–2 is not constituted by the two annunciations, nor by the two birth accounts, but by Luke 1–2 as a whole: the entire first section of the infancy narrative (1.5-56: birth announcements, plus Mary's visit to Elizabeth) is balanced by the entire second section (1.57–ch. 2: the actual births, plus various visits to the family and to Jerusalem):

Panel A (1.1-56)	*Panel B (1.57–2.52)*
John's birth foretold (1.5-25)	John's birth (1.57-80)
Jesus' birth foretold (1.26-38)	Jesus' birth (2.1-14)
Mary visits Elizabeth (1.39-56)	Visits: to the family, and to Jerusalem (2.15-52)

Diptychs vary in nature. Some are short and simple, showing two scenes that are closely similar. Others show two scenes that, instead of mirroring each other, complement one another. When introducing diptychs (Proto-)Luke does so gradually. He begins with a diptych that is short and simple: the two annunciations with their many similarities of detail (1.5-25, 26-38). Next, in the two births, there is another case, but the degree of similarity is not as great (1.57-80; 2.1-40). Then, when Luke 1–2 is viewed as a whole, there is a further diptych effect, one in which the similarity is of yet another kind: the emphasis is not on parallelism but on complementarity. Thus in dealing with Luke's diptychs, there are two broad principles: relationships between panels vary; and Luke tends to go from simple to more complex.

Part of the increasing complexity is a twofold or *spiraling* tendency towards greater volume. Thus (counting occasional half verses as units):
in diptychs 1–4 the number of verses respectively—56/70, 44/53, 54/45, 85/60; in diptychs 5–8 the number of verses respectively—26/42, 62/48, 76/70, 116/105.

Within each half of Proto-Luke, every diptych, except number 2, is longer in total volume than the one which immediately precedes it. In the case of number 2, the decrease in volume may have something to do with the idea that an old order—traditional Judaism and

---

4. On the significance of eight and of (twice) four, see especially Freedman 1995.
5. See, for instance, Stuhlmueller 1968: 24; Brown 1997: 230-31.

Table 8. *The Eight Units of Proto-Luke*

a. *Proto-Luke, Part 1 (Gospel): Diptychs 1–4*

1. Annunciation—Birth		2. Word—Action		3. To Jerusalem—To Jerusalem contd.		4. Death–Resurrection	
John's birth foretold (1.1-25)	John's birth (1.57-80)	John's word: nature miracles (3.1-6, 10-14)	Jesus' word: 'human' miracles (7.1-17)	To Jerusalem: a Samaritan village; would-be followers (9.51-62)	To Jerusalem: lepers on the way; a Samaritan. (17.11-19)	Judas approaches Jews; preparation; My body… …and the twelve (22.1-30)	Joseph approaches Pilate; preparation; the body… …and the eleven (23.50–24.12)
Jesus' birth foretold (1.26-38)	Jesus' birth (2.1-14)	Jesus' identity in principle (baptism, genealogy) (3.15-38; 4.14-15)	Jesus' identity in his miracles (John's questions) (7.18-35)	The seventy: the kingdom is near. Sodom… (10.1-20)	The coming of the kingdom: Noah, Lot, Sodom (17.20-37)	Trial. Are you…? Condemnation. Weep for the future (22.66-23.31)	To Emmaus: Are you…? Condemnation recalled. Recognition (24.13-35)
Mary visits Elizabeth (1.39-56)	Visits, especially to the temple (2.15-52)	Jesus in the synagogue: miracles; remission (4.16-22a)	Jesus in the Pharisee's house. remission (7.36-8.3)	Twin stories: the unjust steward; the rich man (16.1-9, 19-31)	Twin stories: the unjust judge; rich Zacchaeus (18.1-8; 19.1-10)	Amid criminals. Thief forgiven. Jesus dies (23.32-49)	In the midst. Proclaim forgiveness. Jesus ascends (24.36-53)

b. *Proto-Luke, Part II (Acts 1.1–15.35): Diptychs 5–8*

5. Spirit promised—Spirit given		6. Heal/speak—Punish/speak		7. Stephen's death—Saul's conversion		8. Breakthrough: Peter (and Paul)—Paul (and Peter)	
Spirit promised. To heaven (1.1-11)	Spirit given, 'dividing out'. From heaven (2.1-13)	All shared, 'divided'. Lame healed (2.43–3.10)	Sharing, none in need. Couple punished (4.32–5.11)	Murmuring. Stephen. Stephen's signs (ch. 6)	Persecution. Stephen mourned. Simon's magic (8.1b-13)	Church (Judea/Gal/Sam). Peter travels, heals/raises (9.31-43) Peter enters Caesarea (10.1-33)	Church (Antioch). Paul travels, blinds Bar-jesus (13.1-12) Paul enters synagogue (13.13-15)
The eleven praying (1.12-14)	The twelve preaching (2.14-21)	Sol's porch. (3.11-26)	Sol's porch. (5.12-16)	Speech: Patriarchs sell/buy. Moses as Egyptian (7.1-29)	?? Simony. The Ethiopian. (8.14-40)	Peter's speech; eager response. Later: Jews accept (10.34–11.8) Persecution recalled; believing; Famine foretold (11.19-30)	Paul's speech; response. Later: Jews reject (13.16-48) Persecution; believing; God gives food (13.49–14.20)
Peter: Judas is dead. (1.15-26)	Peter: Jesus is risen (2.22-42)	Peter addresses authorities. (4.1-31)	Peter addresses authorities. Saw the Lord (5.17-42)	Moses called. Killers! Sees Jesus. Killed. Saul (7.30-8.1a)	Saul called. Attempt to kill. Saul escapes (9.1-30)	Herod threatens church (12.1-5) Peter freed from shackles (12.6-17) Herod's judgement (12.18-19) Herod's assembly: no glory to God (12.20-23) Word increases (12.24-25)	Paul builds up church (21-28) Council: freed from law (15.1-18) James' judgement (15.19-21) Church assembly: recognizes Spirit (15.22-29)

the Old Testament, strong in the infancy narrative, and represented especially in John the Baptist—is fading, diminishing. The opening sequence of the fourth gospel (the seven passages in Jn 1.1–2.22) also has an initial Baptist-related slump in volume (see Brodie 1993a: 73).

This entire structure—eight diptychs (two sets of four)—finds a precedent in one of Luke's key sources, namely in the Elijah–Elisha story (see Brodie 2000). There, too, the second panel is generally longer.

a. *Initial Aspects of the Eight Diptychs*
It is useful, without going into detail—full details would require a monograph—to summarize some of the balances and complementarities within the eight diptychs, within each pair of complementary panels. The subsequent brief analysis follows the accompanying outline (Table 8).

(1) *Diptych 1: the infancy narrative (Luke 1–2) (Panel A = 1.1-56; Panel 2 = 1.57–2.52).* Complementarity here varies from simple to more complex. The initial instance, between *annunciations* (1.5-38) and *births* (1.57-2.14) is easy to see; what is foretold in one becomes reality in the other; the angel's words become flesh. However, in the case of the visits—Mary visits Elizabeth (1.39-56); later, the shepherds visit the baby, and the family visits Jerusalem twice (2.15-52)—the balance is not as obvious. Yet it is genuine. Between Mary's visit, for instance, and the later visit to Jerusalem, complementarities include the following: two ascending journeys to cities of Judea, a stay of three months/days, and a return. Furthermore, both visits connect with the temple: Mary's journey to the hill country evokes the journey of the ark to Jerusalem and to the temple (2 Sam. 6–7); and in Luke 2 the idea of journeying to the temple is explicit.

(2) *Diptych 2: ministry: preaching; miracles (Panel A = 3.1-6, 10-38; 4.14-22a; Panel B = 7.1–8.3).* The opening panel highlights the first preaching of John and Jesus; and, in broad terms, what is preached in the first panel (3.1-6, 10-38; 4.14-22) becomes reality in the second (7.1–8.3); the Word becomes action. This is clearest in the preaching of Jesus. His prophetic synagogue speech emphasizing miracles and remission (4.16-22a) becomes reality in his role as prophet (7.16, 39), in his miracles (7.1-22), and in his remission of the sinful woman (7.36-50). But there are other aspects of balance between the panels: (1) initial emphasis on authorities (Roman and Jewish), rulers (3.1-2), centurion and elders (7.2-3); (2) John as a prophetic desert preacher (initially, 3.2-6; recalled by Jesus, 7.24-27); (3) miracles of nature (3.5) are balanced by miracles in individual lives (7.4-15); (4) triple pattern of sayings about what to do (questions, 3.10-14; commands, cf. 7.6-10); (5) expectation of a prophet 'Is this he?', contrast in prophets, and in responses (3.15-20; 7.19, 28-30); (6) baptism, generation (genealogy; 'this generation'), and a teaching or wisdom that finds a response in all ('glorified by all'; 'justified by all…') (3.31-38; 4.14-15; 7.29-35).

The diptych as a whole is framed by references to Herod and Herod's steward (3.1; 8.3).

(3) *Diptych 3: to Jerusalem (Panel 1 = 9.51–10.20; 16.1-9, 19-31; Panel 2 = 17.11–18.8; 19.1-10).* There are three main areas of complementarity. First, the headline references to journeying towards Jerusalem through Samaria (9.51-52; 17.11—the balance here, extending into all the journeying in 9.51-62 and 17.11-19, involves other elements, especially meeting, sending, and awareness of [the kingdom of] God). Second, the announcing of the coming of God's kingdom (by the seventy, 10-1-20; and, in a further form, by Jesus, 17.20-37). Third, two sets of twin stories: *Panel 1 (16.1-9, 9-31)*: the unjust but decisive

steward; and the lethargic rich man; *Panel 2 (18.1-8; 19.1-10)*: the unjust but avenging judge; and the decisive rich Zacchaeus.

The texts on announcing God's kingdom (10.1-20; 17.20-37) share basic elements: (1) *a certain unworldliness*—no baggage (10.1-4); the kingdom is *entos*, 'within?' (17.1-21); (2) *a double challenge*—two places (house; city; 10.5-11); two times: Noah; Lot/Sodom (17.26-30); (3) *final woe*—Sodom and woe to the cities (10.12-16); the taking away of people (17.31-37); (4) *amid lightning*: contrasting emotions: joy (10.17-20)—and frustrated desire (17.22-25).

Generally, while Panel 1 (9.51–10.20, and 16.1-9, 19-31) focuses largely on the ultimate heavenly objective, Panel 2 (17.11–18.8, and 19.1-10) seems more concerned with the practicalities of achieving that objective.

(4) *Diptych 4: death and resurrection (Panel 1 = 22.1-30; 22.66–23.49; Panels2 = 23.50–24.53)*. As with Good Friday and Easter Sunday, so also with death and resurrection. Though apparent opposites, they form a whole. Within this unity, some complementarities are basic: two diverse emphases on the body (eucharist, 22.1-30; burial and resurrection, 23.50–24.12); diverse accounts of Jesus' sad fate (the trial, 22.66–23.31; on the Emmaus road, 24.13-35); final emphasis on forgiveness of sins (before dying, 23.32-49; before ascending, 24.36-53)

(5) *Diptych 5: spirit promised and given (Panel 1 = Acts 1, incubation; Panel 2 = Acts 2.1-42, birth)*. Somewhat like Luke 1–2, which is largely a diptych of annunciation and birth, most of Acts 1–2 constitutes a diptych of incubation and birth. The birth, however, is that of the church. The incubation occurs in Acts 1: the Spirit is promised; along with the others, Mary is again present in a receptive mode (at prayer); and, with Peter leading, the number of the twelve is restored. But it is only is only in Acts 2.1-42 when the Spirit is given that this group 'comes to birth' so to speak. It literally emerges from its enclosed space—from the upper room with the women—into the world, into the presence of a crowd which represents all nations.

There is continuity between the two pictures of the eleven/twelve grouped together: first for prayer (Acts 1.12-14) and later for preaching and prophecy (2.14-21).

Among the various complementarities between Acts 1 and Acts 2.1-42, one of the most important is the contrast in the ways Peter deals with the death of Judas (1.15-26) and the death of Jesus (2.22-42). Both of these death accounts conclude with a heart-searching response and with an increase in their number (1.23-26; 2.37-42). The final verse on solidarity with the apostles and in prayer (2.42) dovetails with aspects of the first panel (1.14, 26).

(6) *Diptych 6: Peter: action; Solomon's Porch; Sanhedrin (Panel 1 = 2.43–4.31; Panel 2 = 4.32–5.42)*. The narrative of Acts 2.43–ch. 5 centers largely around two decisive actions by Peter: the healing of the lame man (3.1-10), and the punishing of Ananias and Sapphira (5.1-11). The balance or contrast between two actions, however, is but part of a larger balance between two whole panels. First, the panels give summaries of life among the believers (2.43-47; 4.32-37). Then comes Peter's decisive action (3.1-10; 5.1-11). Next there is a focus on Solomon's Porch (3.11-26, Peter's speech; 4.12-16, a summary statement). And finally, there is an appearance before the Sanhedrin—an experience that in no way inhibits the believers (4.1-31; 5.17-42).

(7) *Diptych 7: Stephen's death; Saul's conversion/rebirth (Panel 1 = 6.1–8.1a; Panel 2 = 8.1b–9.30)*. There is an obvious continuity between Stephen and Saul; Saul approves of

Stephen's killing; the death of one introduces the other (7.58; 8.1). This explicit link, however, is but part of a larger unity: the accounts of Stephen and Saul form the two panels of a single diptych.

The balance between the panels is often complex and obscure. In simplified terms, there are three major areas of complementarity. First, the persecution which engulfed the wonder-working Stephen (Acts 6) is echoed and intensified in the persecution that led to the evangelization of Samaria (8.1b-13). Second, aspects of Stephen's speech, especially about the role of Moses as an Egyptian (7.1-29) would appear to be echoed in the pictures of Simon and the Ethiopian (8.14-40). Third, and more clearly, the culminating pictures of Moses' call and Stephen's killing (7.30–8.1a) are partly balanced by the pictures of Saul's call and the attempted killing of Saul (9.1-30).

(8) *Diptych 8: breakthrough: Peter and Paul (Panel 1 = 9.31–12.25; Panel 2 = 13.1–15.35)*. The remainder of Proto-Luke recounts two major breakthroughs: Peter's baptizing of the household of Cornelius (10.1–11.18), and Paul's mission, with its turn towards the Gentiles (13.13-48). The repeated explicit emphasis on the inclusion of the Gentiles (11.18; 13.46) helps to bind this large body of text into a unity—the last and largest diptych.

There are a number of balancing features: a general sense of the church and a journey (9.31-32; 13.1-3); initial miracles (Peter heals, 9.33-43; Paul punishes/blinds, 13.4-12); the breakthrough to the Gentiles (10.1–11.18; 13.13-48); and diverse references to persecution, believing, and famine/food (11.19-13; 13.49–14.20). The panels end with a new twist: Peter's angel-led release from shackles (12; 1-20); and the strengthened church's Spirit-led move away from the Law (14.21–15.29). Finally, there are notes on the word's increase/spread (12.24-25; 15.30-35).

6. *Conclusion*

The unity of Proto-Luke is not that of a gospel but of a document which stands halfway between Old Testament narrative and the gospels. Once Proto-Luke is treated on its own terms rather than as a gospel, its unity begins to emerge.

The overall effect of the designated gospel texts (from chs. 1–4, 7–10, 16–19, 22–24) is to portray Jesus as being like Elijah: a divine prophet, but more so—more divine, and more human. The unity of this portrait of Jesus does not correspond to that found in the later Luke, but, in comparison with the portrait of Elijah, it has its own integrity.

The unity of the proposed texts is one of both content and structure. The narrative flows, and it does so both as a whole and in its key areas (beginning, middle, and end). The proportions are appropriate. And the structure shows a coherence that is precise and complete.

The result is a strong case for unity.

And such unity indicates original separateness.

**Unit 2. An Auxiliary Thesis:
Proto-Luke as Based on *Logia* and Epistolography**

Orientational Introduction to Chapters 12–14:
An Auxiliary Thesis: The Literary Line from Matthew's
Logia to 1 Corinthians to Proto-Luke

> Paul's criticism of the wisdom of the Corinthians has parallels in Q [especially in Matt 11.25 and the Beatitudes].
>
> —James M. Robinson (1971a: 42)

> Paul was familiar with a sayings or *logia* source related to the Q-traditions…and encouraged the writing of a document that is more of less what Streeter identified as Proto-Luke… There is evidence in 1 Corinthians for Paul's knowledge of Jesus-traditions similar to the logia source; some of Paul's difficulties in Corinth stemmed from disagreements with that source; some features of Proto-Luke resemble features of Paul's message.
>
> —Peter Richardson (1987: 302)

Thus far, in discussing Proto-Luke, focus has been on its use of the Old Testament. But Proto-Luke reflected many other factors, social, historical, and literary; and one of the literary factors is particularly important—a stream of Christian writing that involved sayings and epistolography.

The idea is not new. One of the purposes of the next three chapters is to substantiate some of the ideas suggested by the observations of James Robinson and Peter Richardson—first, that there is a connection between some of Matthew's sayings and 1 Corinthians; and second, that the connection continues into Proto-Luke.

The primary way these next chapters link Matthew and 1 Corinthians is by filling in some of their background, indicating how both documents share a common root—the Torah, particularly Deuteronomy. If both New Testament documents have strong direct literary ties with Deuteronomy, it becomes more understandable that they have links with one another. Yet, there is no claim here that 1 Corinthians is linked to all of Matthew. Rather, as Robinson suggested, the link is with just some Matthean sayings. These sayings are best seen as an arrangement of Deuteronomy-based *Logia* (Chapter 12). Chapter 13 indicates that 1 Corinthians is likewise indebted to the Torah, especially to Deuteronomy.

Chapter 14 follows the trail further. The well-known similarity between the eucharistic texts of 1 Cor. 11.23-25 and Lk. 22.19-20 emerges as part of a systematic literary connection. As Peter Richardson suggested, 1 Corinthians flows into Proto-Luke; or, more simply, Proto-Luke took up 1 Corinthians and refashioned it. The process has its own coherence. If Proto-Luke's outline was modeled on the Septuagint, especially on the Elijah–Elisha narrative, it is understandable that he would be disposed towards absorbing an epistle that reflected another part of the Septuagint, the Mosaic Torah. He would use an earlier writing not only because it was related to his own Christian message, but because, in its own way, the earlier writing too was scriptural—a continuation of Scripture.

The overall picture is one of a cooperative writing process which is inspired by an extraordinary new vision but which is also firmly anchored in its scriptural heritage.

12

Matthew's *Logia* (Sayings from Matthew 5 and 11): Deuteronomy-Based, Unified, Verifiable

Within Matthew 5 and 11.25-30 lies a group of sayings that constitutes a distinct synthesis of Deuteronomy, and, to a lesser degree, of Sirach. The sayings—shown in Table 9[1] (next page)—are three-part:
1. Five Beatitudes (Mt. 5.5-9).
2. Five Antitheses, plus Prologue and Sequel (parts of Mt. 5.17-48).
3. A Call/Song of Revelation/Wisdom (Mt. 11.25b-30).

The purpose of this chapter is to indicate that these sayings, a total of about twenty-six verses, once constituted a distinct document, a separate arrangement of *logia*, oracular sayings. The main arguments are: (1) these texts have a distinct literary relationship with Deuteronomy (and Sirach); (2) the texts form a unity, with affinity to a Qumran text, and to Papias's testimony; (3) the theory works—it helps explain the development of New Testament writings.

These three arguments are akin to the main arguments for Proto-Luke; and, once the Proto-Luke hypothesis is verified, it gives precedent and support to the reality of a further Old Testament-based document. However, Matthew's *Logia*, because it does not have Proto-Luke's bulk or solid shape, is less amenable to systematic demonstration, and it may require refining. Yet, with patience, demonstration is possible. The relationship of these Matthean sayings to the Old Testament is complex, but it is precise and verifiable.

Matthew's *Logia*, when combined with Proto-Luke and Proto-Luke's literary influence, makes the prevailing hypothesis of Q unnecessary.

1. *A Distinct Synthesis of Deuteronomy and Sirach*

a. *Literary Dependence: Initial Plausibility*

The idea of a connection between Q and Ben Sirach is not new. R. Bultmann (1971: 104; 1967: 11-12) linked Sirach with the gospel discourses. And J. Robinson linked Sirach with Q (Robinson 1971b: 71).

But Sirach did not come out of a void. Its pivotal chapter (ch. 24) proclaims: 'All this is no other than the book of the covenant (*biblos diathékés*) of God most High...' (Sir. 24.23a), and it quotes Deuteronomy: '...the Law which Moses enjoined on us, the heritage for the assemblies of Jacob' (Sir. 24.23b; Deut. 33.4). Sirach, then, is grounded in the law, including Deuteronomy. Q's connection to Sirach leads to the question of Q's relationship to Deuteronomy.

Deuteronomy is eminently appropriate as a basis for arranging *logia* (Brodie 1997: 476-77). It is a summa of Jewish tradition; it is central to Jewish piety; and it contains the

---

1. For the Greek text of the *Logia*, see Brodie 2002: 128-29.

Table 9. *The Logia/Sayings in English (based on the Logoi/Deuteronomy)*

	Beatitudes	
5.5	Blessed are the gentle,	for they shall inherit the land.
5.6	Blessed are those who hunger and thirst for rightness,	for they shall be satisfied.
5.7	Blessed are the merciful,	for they shall receive mercy.
5.8	Blessed are the clean of heart,	for they shall see God.
5.9	Blessed are the peacemakers,	for they shall be called children of God.

	Law: Prelude
5.17	Do not think that I came to undo the law or the prophets; I came not to undo but to fulfill.
5.18	For amen I say to you; until heaven and earth pass, not one iota or dot will pass from the law until all is accomplished.

	Law: Antitheses
5.21	You have heard that it was said of old, 'You shall not kill, and whoever does kill shall be liable to judgment'.
5.22a	But I say to you that all who are angry with their brother shall be liable to judgment.
5.27	You have heard that it was said, 'You shall not commit adultery'. But I say to you that whoever looks at a woman with desire has already committed adultery with her in his heart.
5.33:	Again you have heard that it was said of old, 'You shall not break your oath, but shall carry out your oaths to the Lord'.
5.34	But I say to you, do not swear at all neither by heaven for it is God's throne
5.35a	nor by earth for that is his footstool.
5.38	You have heard that it was said, 'An eye for an eye and a tooth for a tooth'.
5.39a	But I say to you, do not set yourself against (the) evil (one).
5.43	You have heard that it was said, 'You shall love your neighbor and hate your enemy'.
5.44a	But I say to you, love your enemies.

	Law: Sequel
5.45	So you may become children of your father in heaven, for he raises his sun on the evil and the good and it rains on the just and the unjust.
5.48	You shall therefore be complete as your heavenly father is complete.

	Call/Cry of Revelation/Wisdom
11.25b	I thank you, father, Lord of heaven and earth for hiding these things from the wise and understanding and revealing them to infants.
11.26	Yes, father, for such was your gracious will.
11.27	All has been handed over to me by my father, and no one knows the son except the father, just as no one know the father except the son and anyone to whom the son chooses to reveal him.
11.28	Come to me all you who labor and are burdened and I will give you rest;
11.29	take my yoke upon you and learn from me for I am gentle and humble of heart and you will find rest for your souls;
11.30	for my yoke is easy and my burden is light.

climactic discourses of Israel's greatest prophet. Even the name is appropriate—*devarim* (Deut. 1.1 LXX; *logoi*). It is plausible then to connect the *Logia* to Deuteronomy.[2]

b. *Deuteronomy and Matthew: Initial Comparison*
To a significant degree Deuteronomy revolves around three elements: the *people*, *law*, and the final sense of *song* and blessing.

1. The beginning (Deut. 1) is a portrait of the *people*. Moses shows them as variously difficult, fearful, and brash—so much so that the promise of inheriting the land goes to the little ones, the new children (1.39, 'the young child shall inherit [the land]').
2. The most clearly defined *law* collections in Deuteronomy are the Decalogue (5.1-22) and the Deuteronomic Code (12.1–26.15). However, the *prelude* to the Decalogue begins as early as ch. 2, and the *sequel* (the curses and blessings) to the Deuteronomic Code extends into ch. 28. Hence the law codes dominate most of Deuteronomy 2–28.
3. The conclusion (Deut. 29–34) is like a rising *song*. First, a profound discourse on revelation (chs. 29–30, emphasizing heart and mind); then, a prolonged song of Moses (chs. 31–32); and finally, a flow of poetry (ch. 33, Moses' blessing of Israel) which ends climactically with a unique blessing: *MAKARIOS SU, Israēl* ... 'Blessed are you, Israel...' (33.29).

Between the two law codes and their sequels lies Deuteronomy 7–11, much of which (7.1–10.11) is like ch. 1—focused on the people. Hence in broad terms, Deuteronomy deals with:

1. The struggling people, later pronounced blessed (chs. 1 and 7–11).
2. The law codes, with prelude and sequels (chs. 2–6 and 12–28).
3. The finale, with song and blessing (chs. 29–34).

Turning to Matthew, one finds that of the three central emphases in Deuteronomy, two occur in Matthew 5. The emphasis on the blessed people and on the laws are reflected

---

2. Comparison of ten clarifies issues, so it is useful to compare and contrast this hypothesis with that of another researcher—B. Mack *The Lost Gospel: The Book of Q and Christian Origins* (1993). The beginning of the sayings source, as proposed here, is a shortened version of the beatitudes, essentially the same beginning as in Mack's proposal (Mack 1993: 73). Both reconstructions, Mack's and this one, then go on to the statement 'Love your enemies' (Mt. 5.44), but unlike Mack, this account first includes a shortened version of the antitheses (Mt. 5.17-48). And while Mack includes such texts as Jesus' three sayings to the would-be followers (Lk. 9.57-62), this account does not. The reason for omitting the sayings to the would-be followers is that they belong to Proto-Luke. As indicated in Chapter 34, these three sayings constitute a distillation, radical but precise, of the three exchanges in 1 Kgs 19; they are part of Proto-Luke's literary adaptation of the Elijah–Elisha narrative, and as such they do not belong to Q. Quite apart from any theory of Proto-Luke, they still would not belong to Q; they are Luke's reworking of 1 Kgs 19. The antitheses, on the other hand, reflect dependence on the laws of Deuteronomy, and so they are part of the larger literary pattern whereby much of Mt. 5 and 11.25-30 depends systematically on the books of Deuteronomy and Sirach. What is important is that the relationship of the New Testament sayings to the older books provides an element of control which is missing in much of the discussion about the shape of Q. Mack's prologue (1993: 1-11) to his version of Q is interesting, insightful, and courageous. It is an important landmark. But it lacks adequate controls; it has almost no literary moorings. There is no reference, for instance, to Luke's curious relationship to 1 Kgs 19 or to the notorious problem of Luke's perplexing minor agreements with Matthew. There is no wrestling with criteria as in Bergemann (1993) or Denaux (1995). In the end, Mack's reconstruction is yet another example of premature history which is undertaken without first resolving certain fundamental literary questions. If a reconstructed Q is to stand the test of time it will need to be anchored more firmly in the surrounding literature.

respectively in the beatitudes (5.1-16) and in the antitheses (5.17-48). The beatitudes—used liturgically on the feast of All Saints—are a form of ideal for the people. And the antitheses are like indicators for an ideal law. Deuteronomy's third major emphasis, the sense of song, occurs in Matthew 11—in Jesus' hymn of thanks, a call of revelation (Mt. 11.25b-30). Overall, then, Matthew 5 and 11.25-30 shows an initial affinity with Deuteronomy. (See outline in Table 10).

Table 10. *The* Logia *as a Synthesis of the* Logoi *(Deuteronomy): Overall Outline*

The (Blessed) People	
Israel: in crisis; weak; yet blessed (Deut. 1; 7.1–10.11)	The Blessed: the gentle are blessed (Five beatitudes) (Mt. 5.5-9)
1. Crises, so the children shall inherit the land (ch. 1)	1. The gentle shall inherit the earth (Mt. 5.5)
2. Doing the law induces God's mercy (ch. 7)	4. Those hungering/thirsting for righteousness shall be satisfied (5.6)
3. Tested heart knows God as a father and is filled (ch. 8)	2. The merciful shall receive mercy (5.7)
4. No righteousness; Moses does not eat or drink (9.1-10)	3. The pure of heart shall see God (5.8)
5. God's fierce anger is averted by Moses (9.11–10.11)	5. The peacemakers shall be called children of God (5.9)
The (New) Laws	
Prelude: 'Do not add or subtract anything' (Deut. 2.1–4.31)	Prelude: 'Not an iota or dot is to be lost' (Mt. 5.17-18)
The laws: 'Thou shalt...' (4.42–5.22; 12.1–26.15)	Renewed laws/antitheses: 'It was said, Thou shalt...' (5.21-43)
From creation was ever such heard as you heard? (4.42-33)	You have heard that it was said of old (*archaiois*) (5.21a)
Killing, not killing, anger (4.41-43; 5.18; 19.1-20; 21.1-9)	You shall not kill...liable for judgment. Whoever is angry...brother (5.21-26)
Adultery, desire (5.17, 21; 21.10-14; 22.13-30)	You shall not commit adultery. Whoever looks in desire... (5.27-30)
Vows; you must do what is vowed (23.18, 21-23)	You...must perform your oaths
To God belong heaven and earth (10.14, 17, 22)	...Do not swear at all, neither by heaven nor by earth (5.33-37)
Standing against someone...Evil... Eye for eye, tooth for tooth (19.16, 19-21)	Eye for eye, tooth for tooth... Do not set yourself against the evil one (5.38-42)
Compassion for weak (*passim*) War against enemies (ch. 20) You shall love... (6.5)	Love your neighbor and hate your enemy Love your enemy (5.43-44)
Sequel: Enemies will scatter; you will be above (26.16–ch.28, especially 28.1-14) (cf. 5.23–ch. 6; 10.12–ch. 11)	Sequel: Love enemies, so you will be children of God (5.44-48)
The Concluding Song/Hymn	
Revelation discourse; song; blessing/death (chs. 29–34)	Hymn/song of blessing and revelation (11.25b-30)

c. *Matthew and Deuteronomy: Initial Aspects of a More Detailed Comparison*

(1) *Five beatitudes (Mt. 5.5-9) as distillations of Deuteronomy 1; 7.1–10.11*. The picture of Israel (in ch. 1 and 7.1–10.11) is not flattering. The people first emerge as troublesome and untrusting—and so the promise of inheriting the land goes to the little ones, the children (ch. 1). Later (in 7.1–10.11), Israel is described as a chosen people, yet this chosen role, this blessedness, comes not from their own strength or righteousness, but from God's gift in cleansing their hearts and from Moses' role as he goes hungry and thirsty in order to bring peace. Thus their blessedness is not of their own making; it is an enigmatic gift.

This sense of enigmatic blessedness occurs also in Matthew's beatitudes, especially in the five consecutive beatitudes at the center of Matthew's text (5.5-9). See Table 11:

Table 11. *Deuteronomy (1; 7.1–10.11) and Five Beatitudes (Matthew 5.5-9)*

Deuteronomy: Israel	Matthew: The Blessed
Crises, so the children shall inherit the land (ch. 1)	The gentle shall inherit the earth (5.5)
	Those who hunger and thirst for righteousness ** shall be satisfied (5.6)
Doing the law induces God's mercy (ch. 7)	The merciful shall receive mercy (5.7)
Testing of the heart leads to knowing God * as a father ** and to being filled (ch. 8)	The pure of heart shall see God (5.8)
No righteousness; Moses does not eat or drink (9.1-10)	
God's fierce anger is averted by Moses (9.11–10.11)	The peacemakers shall be called * children of God (5.9)

In the case of Deuteronomy 8 the primary affinity is with the fourth beatitude (Mt. 5.8), but there are elements of affinity also with the second and fifth (Mt. 5.6, 9).

Most of the elements in these five beatitudes, including the general idea of blessing, are found in Deuteronomy 1 and 7.1–10.11 (*eulogeō*, 'to bless',1.11; 2.7; 7.13; 8.10; *eulogētos*, 'blessed', 7.14), but one element is missing. The beatitudes' leading word, *makarios* ('happy/blessed'), occurs only once in Deuteronomy—in Moses' climactic blessing (*Makarios su, Israēl*, 33.29), the last verse he utters before he dies (33.29). Thus the *logia* start where Moses ended—by pronouncing *makarios* over (the new) Israel. The end has become a beginning.

The affinity between the texts may now be looked at more closely.

(a) *Beatitude 1. The gentle shall inherit the land/earth (Deut. 1; Mt. 5.5)*. Deuteronomy introduces the people as variously difficult, fearful, and brash (cf. especially 1.12, 26-35, 41-43). They are so afraid to go forward and take the land that God decides to grant the land to another generation: 'For Joshua shall inherit it [the land/earth]. And every young child, who this day does not know good or evil, they shall enter there…and they shall inherit it' (*tēn gēn…hoti autos klēronomēsei autēn…autoi klēronomēsousin autēn*, 1.36, 38-39).

This corresponds closely to Mt. 5.5: 'Blessed are the gentle, for they shall inherit the land/earth' (*hoti autoi klēronomousin tēn gēn*, Mt. 5.5).

While using Deuteronomy 1, Matthew's beatitude also reflects, even more closely, the wording of Ps. 37.11. This illustrates the occasional practice—also found, for instance, in Proto-Luke (e.g. Acts 8.32-33)—of using one text as a primary source (here Deuteronomy) and another (often from the prophets or Psalms) to formulate the precise wording. What is essential is that an obvious connection with one text does not exclude dependence on another.

(b) *Beatitude 2. Fulfilling the law (of mercy) earns the mercy of God (Deut. 7; Mt. 5.7).* Deuteronomy 7 seems destructive—imposing the ban—but its basic focus, as indicated by the chapter's center, is on doing the law and receiving mercy: 'The Lord thy God...keeps covenant and mercy (*eleos*)... So keep the commandments...so that the Lord thy God shall keep for thee the covenant and the mercy (*eleos*)...and [God] will love thee and bless thee...and bless thy offspring...You will be blessed among all nations' (7.9, 12-14).

Overall, the law is largely concerned with mercy—see, for instance, the Decalogue's emphasis on sabbath rest, especially for the vulnerable (Deut. 5.12-15)—so when Deuteronomy 7 says that *doing the law brings God's mercy* it is not far from saying that *those who do mercy will receive mercy*. Nor is it very far from Mt. 5.7: 'Blessed are the merciful, for they shall receive mercy' (*ele ēmones...ele ēthēsontai*).

(c) *Beatitude 3. The tried heart remembers God (Deut. 8; Mt. 5.8).* Deuteronomy 8 deals largely with a drama of the heart—the proud heart forgets God (8.11-20, especially 8.14, 17-18), and the tested heart comes to know God (8.1-10; 8.2, literally, 'that...the things in your heart might be manifested', *hopōs...diagnōsthē ta en tē kardia sou*; 8.5: 'You shall know in your heart [*gnōsē tē kardia sou*] that, as a man disciplines [*paideuō*, "discipline/educate"] his child, so the Lord your God disciplines you'). This knowing heart presages blessing: 'You will eat and be filled and bless (*eulogeō*) the Lord your God' (8.10).

Matthew's next beatitude speaks not of knowing God but, more concretely, of seeing God: 'Blessed are the clean of heart, for they shall see God'. Yet, like Deuteronomy, the beatitude indicates that the heart which has been thoroughly tried or cleansed is aware of God.

Deuteronomy 8 also shares some elements with other beatitudes: being filled or satisfied (Deut. 8.10; Mt. 5.6), and being children of God (Deut. 8.5; Mt. 5.9; cf. Deut. 1.31).

(d) *Beatitude 4. Righteousness, hungering, and thirsting (Deut. 9.1-10; Mt. 5.6).* Israel's good fortune did not come from its own righteousness *(dikaiosynē*, Deut. 9.1-6), and when Israel was alienated from God, Moses underwent hunger and thirst to restore God's favor to it: '[for] forty days and forty nights, I ate no bread and drank no water' (Deut. 9.7-9; cf. 9.18). Thus Moses' hunger and thirst is carried out in the context of Israel's lack of righteousness.

Mt. 5.6 combines these ideas: 'Blessed are those who hunger and thirst for righteousness (*dikaiosynē*), for they shall be satisfied' (Mt. 5.6).

Beatitude 5. *Amid destructive enmity, making peace (Deut. 9.11–10.11; cf. Mt. 5.9).* Deuteronomy 9.11–10.11, set after the period of forty days, tells of breaking the covenant and extends from God's initial impulse to destroy the people (9.11-14) to renewed talk of blessing when God, relenting, decides not to destroy them (10.7-11). The intervening drama is colorful, heated, and angry (see especially Deut. 9.14, 18-20, 22). But Moses fasts and prays, and God relents and establishes Levi to pronounce blessing (*ep-euchomai*) in God's name (10.8).

The word 'peace' never occurs explicitly in this passage of Deuteronomy, yet Deuteronomy here is largely about Moses' role as peacemaker. Consequently, it has a central affinity with the next beatitude: 'Blessed are the peacemakers...'

(2) *Five antitheses (from Mt. 5.17-48) as distillations of law-texts (Deut. 2–6; 10.12–ch. 28)*. Much of Deuteronomy 2–28 (apart from 7.1–10.11) deals with the law: first with the prelude, then with the actual laws, and finally with the sequel. In simplified terms, the text may be divided as follows:
1. *Prelude* to Sinai (2.1–4.31).
2. Laws: Decalogue, Shema, and Deuteronomic code (4.32–26.15).
3. *Sequel*: blessings and curses (26.16–ch. 28).

There is obvious continuity between the law-centered block—Deuteronomy 2–28 (omitting 7.1–10.11)—and the laws or antitheses of Matthew 5 (5.17-48). Some links are clear—the references to what was said of old (at Sinai, Mt. 5.21, 33), and the explicit citing of laws which in varying degrees come from Deuteronomy (Mt. 5.21, 27, 33, 38, 43). The problem is to gain the precision to see if there is a deliberate use of Deuteronomy. One of the first suggestions of consistent dependence comes from the fact that, as in Deuteronomy, Matthew's laws have a prelude and a sequel:

*Prelude to Sinai (2.1–4.31)	* Prelude (5.17-20)
Laws: Decalogue, Shema, and Deuteronomic code (4.32–26.15)	New laws: the antitheses (5.21-44)
*Consequences: blessings, curses (26.16–ch. 28)	* Epilogue—positive consequences (5.45-48)

The texts may now be looked at more closely.

(a) *Prelude. Do not think of any undoing of the law (Deut. 2.1–4.32; Mt. 5.17-18)*. Moses' prelude gives kindred instructions about land (chs. 2–3) and law (4.1-32):

Concerning the land:	*Concerning the law:*
Respect every foot of peoples' land (2.1-25)	Respect everything in the law (4.1-14)
Fight the enemy (2.26–3.11)	Resist all idolatry (4.15-20)
The giving of the land to the people (3.12-22)	Moses' personal fate (4.21-24)
Moses' personal fate (3.23-29)	The taking of the people from the land (4.21-24)

The themes—land and law—are interwoven. Whatever the implications of this interweaving—is there, for instance, a suggestion that those who follow the law come into a space or way of being that constitutes a kind of land (though not land in the territorial sense)?—the salient point is simple: the prologue begins not with ch. 4 but with ch. 2.

Some important details in Deuteronomy's prelude find echoes in that of Matthew. In ch. 2, Moses speaks repeatedly of passing (*par-erchomai*) through the land (*gē*) until (*heōs*) coming to a specific place or event (Deut. 2.8, 13-15, 24, 27-30). Three references are particularly important:

Deut. 2.13-14:	*parēlthomen...heōs*,	'we passed...until'
Deut. 2.14:	*parēlthomen...heōs*,	'we passed...until'
Deut. 2.29:	*heōs (an) pareltho*,	'until I have passed'

In Matthew's prologue to the antitheses (Mt. 5) there are related references to the passing of heaven and earth (*gē*) and to the passing of details from the law:

Mt. 5.18:	*heōs an parelthē...gē*,	'until...earth pass'
	ou mē parelthē...nomou,	'will not pass...law'

The gospel text (*ge...nomos*, 'earth/land...law') echoes Deuteronomy's broad continuity between land and law (in 2.1–4.31), and it also contains a synthesis of some of the precise linguistic peculiarities of Deuteronomy 2. Deuteronomy had regarded the passing of the land as a prelude to the granting of the law. Matthew 5 regards the apocalyptic passing of everything (including the land/earth) as a prelude to the passing away of the law.

In Deut. 4.1-31, Moses speaks both of respecting the law meticulously (4.1-14) and of guarding against transgressing through idolatry (4.15-20): 'You shall not add to the word that I command you, and you shall not take away from it' (4.2). This extreme care for the law finds an echo in the same Matthean verse (5.18): 'not one iota, not one dot, will pass from the law...'

Even the opening 'Do not think...' (*mē nomisēte*, Mt. 5.17) is curiously similar to the opening of Moses' warning: 'Take care...lest you transgress' (*mē anomēsēte*, Deut. 4.15-16; cf. Deut. 2.5, 9, 19). And while Moses' prelude concludes with a wide, eschatological, horizon ('all these words shall come upon you at the end of days', 4.30), the gospel prelude has an even wider eschatological allusion: the passing away of heaven and earth and the accomplishing of all (5.18). Overall, Matthew's prelude echoes and synthesizes that of Deuteronomy.

(b) *The five antitheses: the laws and the new law/covenant (Deut. 4.32–ch. 6; 10.12–26.15; Mt. 5.21-44)*. This is both the easiest and most difficult area of comparison. It is easy because some connections are obvious, and so one can make an effortless first decision: Matthew's text as a whole (all six antitheses, 5.21-44, including the divorce clause) depends in some way on the Pentateuch, including Deuteronomy). But the comparison is difficult because of the complexity of the texts. Some leading connections are outlined in Table 12:

Table 12. *Deuteronomy (4–6; 10–26) and Five Antitheses (Matthew 5.21-44)*

	Deuteronomy 4.32–ch. 6; 10.12–26.15	Matthew 5.21-44
	From creation [the beginning] was ever such a word heard as you heard? (4.32-33)	You have heard that it was said to the ancients (*archai-ois*, [from *archē*, 'beginning'], 5.21a)
1.	Killing, not killing, anger (4.41-43; 5.18; 19.1-20 21.1-9)	You shall not kill...liable for judgment. Whoever is angry...brother (5.21-26)
2.	Adultery, desire (5.17, 21; 21.10-14; 22.13-30)	You shall not commit adultery. Whoever looks in desire (5.27-30)
3.	Various vows; you must do what is vowed (23.18, 21-23) To God belong heaven and earth (10.14, 17, 22)	You...must perform your oaths ...Do not swear at all, neither by heaven nor by earth (5.33-37)
4.	Standing against someone... Evil...Eye for eye, tooth for tooth (19.16, 19-21)	Eye for eye, tooth for tooth... Do not set yourself against the evil one (5.38-42)
5.	Compassion for weak (*passim*) War against enemies (ch. 20) You shall love... (6.5)	Love your neighbor and hate your enemy. Love your enemy (5.43-44)

The references to what was said in the past are not to Deuteronomy only. Three of the quotations—'You shall not kill'; 'You shall not commit adultery'; 'Eye for eye and tooth for tooth' (Deut. 5.17, 18; 19.21)—are found also in Exodus (20.13, 14; 21.24; cf. Lev.

24.20). 'You shall love your neighbor and hate your enemy', comes, partly, from Leviticus (19.18). And the citation about not swearing—'You shall not swear falsely, but shall perform your oaths to the Lord'—combines a reference to Deuteronomy (23.21) with references to three other sources (Lev. 19.12; Num. 30.2; Ps. 49.14; cf. Meier 1980: 53).

But the sharing of material with other sources does not take away from the central role of Deuteronomy. As already seen, the prologue which sets the scene for the antitheses (Mt. 5.17-20, especially 5.17-18) has a special relationship to the prologue found in Deuteronomy (2.1–4.31).

Furthermore, the partly repeated phrase which frames the various citations—'You have heard that it was said of old' (literally, 'said to the ancients', *archaioi* [from *archē*, 'beginning'])—has multiple resonances of the introduction found in Deuteronomy (4.32-33). To a significant extent, therefore, the governing framework is that of Deuteronomy.

Like Matthew 5 (5.31-32), Deuteronomy mentions divorce (Deut. 24.1-4), but apparently the divorce clause does not belong to the *Logia*. As will be seen in Chapter 19, Matthew's text at this point owes more to Mark than to Deuteronomy.

Concerning the reformulated laws, a few comments may be made, brief or exploratory.

1. 'You shall not kill' (Deut. 4.41-43; 5.18; 19.1-20; 21.1-9; Mt. 5.21-26). Apart from the Decalogue, Deuteronomy has several references to voluntary and involuntary killing, and aspects of these references may be reflected in Matthew. See, for instance, 'whoever kills' (*hos…an phoneusē*, Deut. 4.42; Mt. 5.21).
2. 'You shall not commit adultery…nor desire in your heart' (Deut. 5.18; cf. 21.10-12; Mt. 5.27-30). Deuteronomy forbade adultery and emphasized the importance of the inmost heart. Yet the Law was accommodating to the desiring gaze of warring soldiers (Deut. 21.10-12). The gospel clarifies the full implications of interior desire and thus calls for a better quality of heart and of marital fidelity.
3. 'You shall not break your oaths/pledges… Do not swear at all' (Deut. 23.22-24; cf. 10.14, 17, 22; Mt. 5.33-37). Here the law is abrogated, but the primary emphasis of the gospel is not negative; it is on the sovereignty of God.
4. 'An eye for an eye… Do not set yourself against (the) evil (one)' (Deut. 19.16-21; Mt. 5.38-42). Deuteronomy describes a false witness who 'stands against' his brother as 'evil' (19.16, 19-20), and then states, 'An eye for an eye…' (19.21). The gospel, while synthesizing a number of elements from the old text gives a new principle: it is not good to set oneself against evil, meaning perhaps that it is counter-productive to let oneself become focussd on evil.
5. 'You shall love your neighbor and hate your enemy… Love your enemy' (Deut. 6.5; 10.18-19; ch. 20; 28.7; Mt. 5.43-44). Deuteronomy has numerous references to loving God, having compassion for one's fellow Israelite, caring for the weak, and fighting enemies. It even speaks of loving the stranger (10.19). The gospel command to love one's enemy involves a synthesis and deepening of the older laws.

The overall conclusion is that the new law/covenant (Mt. 5.17-44) uses Deuteronomy as a source, even a central component.

(c) *Sequel to the laws: enemies, love, and relationship to God (Deut. 5.22–ch. 6; 10.12–ch. 11; 18.9-22; 26.16–ch. 28; Mt. 5.45-48)*. After the central code (Deut. 12.1–26.15) comes a sequel: the writing of the code and the listing of consequences, especially of curses and blessings (26.16–ch. 28). These blessings (28.1-14) promise Israel great power and prosperity, and among other things, they say:

Deut. 28.7:	'The Lord will hand over your enemies (*tous echthrous sou*)...' they shall flee seven ways before you'.
28.12:	'May the Lord open his good treasure, the heaven, to give rain (*hueton*) to your land'.
28.13:	'The Lord will make your the head and not the tail and you shalt be (*esē*) above, and you shalt not be (*esē*) below'.

Likewise, after the final antithesis (5.44), Matthew gives a sequel (Mt. 5.45-48): These texts (5.44-48) include:

Mt. 5.44:	'Love your enemies (*tous echthrous hymōn*)...'
5.45:	'and so you will become children of your father in heaven, for he raises his sun on the men and on the good, and it rains (*brechei*) on the just and unjust'.
5.48:	'You shall (*ese-sthe*) therefore be complete as your heavenly father is complete'.

The texts (Deut. 28.1-14; Mt. 5.44-48) suggests both imitation and reversal. Just as the old laws were rewritten (in the antitheses), so the account of the consequences has been reshaped, deepened. There is a new attitude to enemies, a greater sense of God's impartiality, and a realization that blessing lies not in superiority over others but in being children of God.

Apart from using this sequel (26.15–ch. 28), Matthew also uses two other sequels: the sequel to the Decalogue (5.22–ch. 6), and the sequel to the remaking of the covenant (10.12–ch. 11). It is from these, particularly from their use of the Shema (Deut. 6.4-9; 11.13-21; cf. 10.12-19), that Matthew's text draws the emphasis on love:

Deut. 6.5:	'You shalt love (*agapēseis*) the Lord...'
10.19:	'Love (*agapēsete*) the stranger...'
Mt. 5.43:	'You shalt love (*agapēseis*) your neighbor'.
5: 4:	'Love (*agapate*) your enemies'.

As sometimes occurs, part of the actual formulation ('You shalt love thy neighbor') is from another source (Lev. 19.18), but the more basic source is Deuteronomy.

Deuteronomy said to love God; but since God loved strangers, love of God meant love of strangers (10.14-22). At this point Matthew does not directly say: love God. He resolves the possible tension between the Deuteronomic commands to love both God and neighbor by fusing them into one: love your enemies and thus you will become children of a loving God. Ultimately, each writer gives only one commandment: Deuteronomy's being 'love God' (and therefore the stranger); Matthew's being 'love your enemies' (and thereby become children of God...and Godlike).

The closing (Mt. 5.48) draws not just from the sequels, but also from Deuteronomy's center, from the account of the (eschatological) prophet-like-Moses:

Deut. 18.13:	'You shall be perfect (*teleios esē*) before the Lord your God'.
Deut. 18.15:	'The Lord your God will raise up for you a prophet like (*hōs*) me...'
Mt. 5.48:	'You shall therefore be complete (*esesthe...teleoi*) as (*hōs*) your heavenly father is complete (*teleios*)'.

In Mt. 5.48 the perfection or completion is set in the context not of law but of love, and the likeness which is to be achieved is not to Moses but to God. (Moses, however, is not far from God. The same verse, Deut. 18.15, tells of God giving God's own words into the prophet's mouth, an action which recalls that God knew Moses face to face [Deut. 5.4; 34.10].)

12. *Matthew's* Logia *(Sayings from Matthew 5 and 11)* 119

(3) *Jesus' song of revelation (Mt. 11.25b-30) as a variation on Deuteronomy 29–34.*
Deuteronomy 29–34, recounting Moses' end, consists of:
1. Revelation-centered discourse (chs. 29–30) (cf. Exod. 3–34).
2. Song, with a prose introduction (chs. 3–32).
3. Blessing and death (chs. 33–34).

Among these chapters, the song (ch. 32) stands out—by length, and by poetic quality.

In Matthew also (in 11.25b-30) there is a particularly poetic section, a song which celebrates revelation. In general terms, while Deuteronomy speaks of *revelation* (chs. 29–30) and then of a *song* (chs. 31–32), Matthew gives a synthesis—a *song of revelation*.

Both texts begin with exclamations of praise to God, and they share specific words (heaven, earth, Lord, wise, understand[ing], Father—Deut. 32.1-11; Mt. 11.25-26).

The affinity is strongest in the center (Mt. 11.27, stanza two). The picture of revelation as coming from the interaction of father and son corresponds significantly to the imagery at Deuteronomy's beginning and end (Deut. 1; and in Moses' final song; Deut. 1.31; 32.6):

> 1.31: 'the Lord your God bore/nursed (*trophophoreō*) you,
> as a person (*anthrōpos*) bears his/her son (*huios*)'.
> 32.6: 'Is not this your father (*patēr*), who created you,
> who made you, and established you?'

Apart from imagery, the final part of Deuteronomy also supplies the pivotal emphasis on the content of revelation. In Moses' third and final discourse (Deut. 29–30), the focus is not on external law, but, like the new covenant of Jeremiah (Jer. 31.31-34), on a process of revelation which is internal—a process involving knowing with the heart, learning, understanding (*oida, ginōskō, syniēmi*, Deut. 29.4, 6, 9), a process which speaks of things that are hidden (*krypta*) and things that are revealed (*phanera*, 29.29).

Furthermore, the central couplet in the middle of the second stanza ('no one knows [*epi-ginōskō*] the son except the father//and no one knows [*epi-ginōskō*] the father except the son') expresses a two-way relationship. This corresponds significantly to the Deuteronomic ideas of prophetic revelation which is face-to-face (Deut. 5.4; 34.10), and, indirectly, mouth-to-mouth ('I will place my words in his mouth', Deut. 18.18). As the final lines of Deuteronomy recall, Moses was the prophet 'whom the Lord knew (*ginōskō*) face-to-face' (*egnō...prosōpon kata prosōpon*, Deut. 34.10; cf. 5.4; 18.18). Thus the Deuteronomic 'know', with its balance of 'face' and 'face', has given away in Matthew to the balance of 'know' and 'know'.

Stanza three, a call to come and learn (Mt. 11.28-30), has a distant echo of the calls to come and hear Moses' song (Deut. 31, especially 31.12-13) and the law at Sinai (Deut. 5, especially 5.1, 14, 23), but it has a more direct echo from another source—from Sirach.

d. *Matthew and Sirach: An Initial Comparison*
The main dependence on Sirach seems to involve its beginning (chs. 1–6), middle (ch. 24), and end (ch. 51). This dependence dovetails with that on Deuteronomy (see Table 13 next page).

Within the *Logia* the relative influence of Deuteronomy and Sirach varies. Initially (in the beatitudes and antitheses) Deuteronomy is primary, and Sirach secondary. Later (in the hymn) Sirach is primary, and Deuteronomy secondary.

(1) *Literary dependence on Sirach: 1. The beatitudes*. The Sirach-beatitudes link seems weak. The most obvious connection is the word *praus* ('gentle'), which is quite prominent in Sirach 1–6 (1.27; 3.17; 4.8) and which occurs near the beginning of the beatitudes (Mt. 5.5). It also occurs in the final stanza of Mt. 11.25-30.

Table 13. *Deuteronomy, Sirach, and the* Logia: *Initial Outline*

Deuteronomy	Sirach	Sayings (Matthew 5; 11.25b-30)
	The Blessed	
Children will inherit the land (ch. 1)	Wisdom, gentleness (chs. 1–6)	The gentle will inherit the land (5.5)
	The Laws	
Prelude: Passing; not changing the law (2.1–4.31)	Wisdom came forth as law, a river filled (ch. 24)	Prelude: I came not to undo the law but to fulfill…till all passes (5.17-18)
The laws and sequels (4.32–ch. 28)		New laws and sequel (5.21-48)
	The Song/Hymn	
Revelation; song (chs. 29–33)	Hymn of thanksgiving (ch. 51)	Hymn of thanks for revelation (11.25b-30)

(2) *Literary dependence on Sirach: 2. The new laws (Antitheses).* Here, too, the link with Sirach is relatively weak. However, the beginning of the prelude to the renewed law (Mt. 5.17) contains multiple echoes of Sirach's pivotal portrayal of wisdom (identified with the law) as coming forth into the world (Sir. 24.3, 23, 25, 26, 30):

Sirach: 'I came forth (*ex-ēlthon*), from the mouth of the Most High' (24.3).
'All this is the…law (*nomon*)…'
'[God] fills wisdom like the [flooded river] Pishon…
fills up (*ana-plēroō*) understanding like the Euphrates…
'and as a watercourse I came forth (*ex-ēlthon*)…' (24.23-30)
Matthew: 'Do not think that I came (*ēlthon*) to undo the law (*nomon*)…
I came (*ēlthon*) not to undo but to fulfill (*plēroō*)' (5.17)

(3) *Literary dependence on Sirach: 3. The concluding hymn.* In Jesus' hymn, where dependence on Deuteronomy is relatively weak (largely limited to the middle stanza), the role of Sirach, especially the concluding hymn (Sir. 51), is primary:

Sirach: Thanksgiving to God (51.1-12)
The quest for her—for wisdom (and the law, 51.12-22)
Invitation to wisdom (51.23-30)
Matthew: Thanksgiving for revelation (11.25-26)
Content of revelation (father-son, 11.27)
Invitation to revelation (11.28-30)

Matthew's first and third stanzas depend respectively on the beginning of the first and thirds parts of Sirach 51 (see Table 14).

While Sirach's last chapter thus provides Matthew's framework, the opening chapters (Sir. 1–6) supply many further elements of Matthew's first and third stanzas: 'Lord…of heaven…of earth' (1.1, 3); '…wisdom and understanding…revealed' (*sophia kai synesis…apekalyphthē*, 1.4, 6); gracious will (*eudokia*, 1.27; 2.16); 'gentle(ness)…heart… humble/humility' (1.27; 2.17; 3.17, 18; 4.7, 8); 'Choose…wisdom…you will labor (*kopiaō*) a little…you will find rest (*heurēseis tēn anapausin*) in her' (6.19, 27).

Thus the first and third stanzas (Mt. 11.25-26, 28-30) reflect the beginning and end of Sirach, especially of Sirach 51, but the second stanza, more dependent on Deuteronomy, is different. It sees revelation as coming not from feminine wisdom (as implied in the middle of Sir. 51), but from the interaction of father and son. In blending the sources, Sirach's central image of *feminine* wisdom (51.13-22) has been replaced by the Deuteronomy-based imagery of *father* and *son*.

Overall, then, Sirach strongly influences Jesus' hymn, and it has a significant role also in the portrayal of the new laws, or at least in the prelude (Mt. 5.17). In the beatitudes, this influence looks weak, yet the strong link of Sirach 1–6 with the gentleness theme of Jesus' hymn adds weight to the apparent link between Sirach 1–6 and the gentleness idea near the beginning of the beatitudes. The gentleness, so linked in Sirach 1–6 and Mt. 11.29, becomes a frame for the combined sayings (Mt. 5 and 11.25-30). The influence of Sirach in Mt. 11.25-30 does not rule out the influence of other wisdom writings, particularly of the book of Wisdom.

The general conclusion concerning Matthew 5 and 11.25-30, is that, when taken together, they incorporate a distinctive distillation of the whole length of Deuteronomy and Sirach, and so they have their own unity and identity. At some level that distillation of *logia* stands apart.

Table 14. *Sirach 51 and Matthew 11.25-30*

51.1-2:	*Exomologēsomai soi, kyrie...*	'I will thank you, Lord...
	Exomologoumai tō onomati sou hoti...	I thank your name because...'
51.23-27:	*Eggisate pros me, a-pai-deut-oi...*	'Approach me you uninstructed...
	kai hai psychai hymōn dipsōsi...	and your souls are thirsty...
	ton trachēlon hymōn hypothete hypo zygon	put your neck under the yoke
	...oligon e-kopi-asa	...little have I labored
	...kai heuron...pollēn anapausin.	and found...much rest'.
11.25:	*Exomologoumai soi, pater, kyrie...hoti....*	'I thank you, Father, Lord...because...'
11.28-30:	*Deute pros me pantes hoi kopi-ōntes...*	'Come to me all you who labor
	kai anapausō hymas	and I will give you rest.
	arate ton zygon mou eph' hymas...	Take my yoke upon you...
	kai heurēsete anapausin tais psychais hymōn	and you will find rest for your souls;
	ho gar zygos mou...	for my yoke...'

2. *A Coherent Unit, in Accord with Qumran and Papias*

The Deuteronomy/Sirach sayings from Matthew 5 and 11 are not jumbled. They form a unity, not the square solid unity of Proto-Luke, but a unity nonetheless. The details of this unity are a matter for further research, but some aspects are immediately clear.

The five beatitudes—an unbroken sequence from Mt. 5.5-9—are centered on mercy, and framed by concepts of deeply rooted belonging (inheriting the land; being called children of God).

The beatitudes are refracted in various ways in the five antitheses. Concepts like mercy and belonging open the way for the antitheses' constructive challenge to the Law. In variant form, what was central to the beatitudes, the emphasis on mercy, becomes the framework for the antitheses—not being angry with a brother, and loving enemies.

The focus on 'heaven and earth', which first appears in the prelude to the antitheses, reappears at the antitheses' center, and again at the beginning of the concluding call or hymn. Closeness to God, which first appears in the beatitudes, recurs more expansively in the antitheses, and blossoms even more fully in the final call.

The overall impression is of a poetic composition which is unusually dense, resonant, and pregnant with meaning. It engages the Law and daily realities, including anger, adultery, revenge, hatred, sun, rain, and weariness, yet from the blessedness at the beginning, it spirals towards an increasing sense of closeness to God. And the form of the sayings spirals equally: first, the fivefold monotone of the beatitudes, calm yet arresting; then, the more tension-packed fivefold rhythm of the antitheses; and finally, when the tension has been resolved, the emergence into a rhythm which, while breaking the bounds of the earlier poetic language, brings the whole to a new level of resolution and peace.

a. *A Precedent from Qumran (4Q525)*

In seeking the pattern and nature of a sayings source, it helps if, apart from tracing its relationship to relatively long texts (such as Deuteronomy and Sirach), one can first locate it within a genre of shorter texts, texts of length roughly equal to its own. To some degree, for instance, this collection of *logia* may be compared to the small collections of sayings in the book of Proverbs (Prov. 24.23-34; 30.1–31.9); or its use of beatitudes may be compared to Sirach (Sir. 14.1-2, 20-21).

However, there is a closer analogue in manuscript 525 from Cave 4 in Qumran. This document (4Q525) is sometimes referred to 'a collection of beatitudes', but that designation is over-simplified and somewhat misleading. The document in fact contains *an arrangement of sayings* concerning *beatitudes, law*, and *wisdom*. There is no reliable evidence that its sayings were collected rather than composed and arranged by the writer. The beginning of the scroll (or scroll section) seems to designate the contents as wisdom sayings.

This arrangement of sayings, discovered in September 1952,[3] was partly published in 1988 and more fully in 1991 (Puech 1988b: 66; 1991). It has now been translated into English (1992).[4]

The text (Table 15) consists essentially of three parts:
1. Five beatitudes (four containing antithetical parallelism: ולוא, 'and do/does not').
2. Focus on the law (law/torah described in wisdom terms) (with antithetical emphasis in the middle ('does not forsake…abandon…forget…reject').
3. A direct appeal: 'Listen to me…' (truncated in the surviving manuscript).

Both texts (4Q525 and Matthew's *Logia*) contain five positive beatitudes, but the later text (the *Logia*), instead of balancing the positive with an antithetical negative, seeks to go further, to spell out the implication or consequences of its beatitudes: 'for they shall…'.

The texts then shift from beatitudes to the law (Qumran, torah; the *Logia*: *nomos*), but neither of them takes the law in a way that is legalistic, set in stone. Qumran, while praising the law's ways and admonishments, nonetheless moves it to a new context, that of wisdom, and in effect describes the law in terms of wisdom femininity. The *Logia*, while assuring fulfillment of the law, nonetheless also moves it to a new context, the context of a new voice: 'It was said to you… But I say…' By the end of the *Logia* this new voice will sound clearly like that of wisdom (especially in the final 'Come to me…') yet in the *Logia* the move away from the old formulation is sharper. The emphasis on antithesis, a common feature of much Hebrew poetry, now comes more clearly to the fore: 'But I say…' Instead of a woman image which is implied (Qumran), the *Logia* give an image which is explicit but very different: whoever looks at a woman with desire commits adultery of the heart. This simultaneously steps back from facile engagement with a woman, even engagement that is internal, but implicitly advocates looking at a woman in another way, with the deepest respect.

In their third parts the texts shift gears. As the Qumran manuscript breaks off, it moves into direct speech, that of wisdom calling to her children: 'Children, listen to me…'. And the final part of the *Logia* text (from Mt. 11) becomes more like the voice of intermediary

---

3. For an account of the discovery, see de Vaux *et al.* (1977: VI, 2-5). For subsequent developments, see, for instance, Vermes 1994: 1-25.
4. Fitzmyer 1992a. See also G.J. Brooke 1989; De Roo 1997.

wisdom, a wisdom which first looks up to God ('I thank you, father...') and then out to people ('Come to me...'). The explicit imagery of the *Logia* is significantly masculine ('father...son') yet the most fundamental emphasis is not on men but on relationship, relationship which has a feminine quality.[5]

Table 15. *From Qumran, Cave 4: An Arrangement of Sapiential Sayings, in Hebrew (4Q525 [Adapted from Puech 1991; Fitzmyer 1992a; Vermes 1997: 24])*

Beatitudes
[Blessed is the one who speaks truth] with a pure heart and does not (ולוא) slander with his tongue. Blessed are those who cling to her statutes and do not (ולוא) cling to paths of iniquity. Blessed are those who rejoice in her and do not (ולוא) babble about paths of iniquity. Blessed are those who search for her with clean hands and do not (ולוא) seek after her with a deceitful heart. Blessed is the man who has attained wisdom
Law
and walks by the law (תורה, torah) of the Most High and fixes his heart on her ways,   gives heed to her admonishments delights al[way]s in her chastisements, and does not (ולוא) forsake her in the stress of [his] trou[bles]; (who) in time of distress does not (ו...לוא) abandon her and does not (ולוא) forget her [in days of] fear, and in the affliction of his soul does not (ו...לוא) reject [her]. For on her he meditates, and in his anguish he ponders [on the law]; and in all his existence [he considers] her and [puts her before] his eyes   so as not to walk in the paths of [ ] [ ] his [ ] together, and he perfects his heart for her [ ] [and she will put a crown upon] his [hea]d and make him sit with kings [ ] he will *pr*[ ] brothers [ ] [ ] [   ]
Wisdom's Call
[And now, children, listen to me, and] turn [n]ot away from...

b. *Congruence with the Testimony of Papias*

The idea that Matthew composed a seminal arrangement of sayings corresponds with Eusebius's account of the testimony of Papias, bishop of Hierapolis, c. 125 CE (Eusebius, *Historia ecclesiastica* 3.39.16):

> Matthew arranged/compiled (*synetaxato*) the sayings/oracles (*logia*) in the Hebrew/Aramaic language/style/mode (*Hebraidi dialectō*), and each translated/interpreted (*hērmēneusen*) them as best he could (*hōs ēn dunatos*).

---

5. This conclusion—the primary shift was not from feminine imagery to masculine, but from feminine imagery to relationship—was worked out with the help of A. Dornan, J. Powell, and V. Warren.

It is not certain exactly what Matthew is supposed to have done. *Synetaxato* is ambiguous (arranged or compiled?); and so is *dialecto*—it could either refer to the language (Hebrew/Aramaic) or simply to the style of composition (Hebraic/Semitic). *Logia* is the plural of *logion* ('saying/oracle'), frequently referring to short sayings that originate from a divinity.

One thing, however, is clear: the *Logia* were difficult. Those who dealt with them hermeneutically had to wrestle with them as best they could. The most likely meaning of *hermēneuō* is 'interpret' (rather than just 'translate'); 'interpret' is suggested not only by the difficulty but also by a preceding paragraph in which Papias uses *hermeneia* to mean 'interpretation' (*HE* 3.39.3).

As well as being difficult, the *Logia* were the object of considerable attention; 'each' points to an undefined number of interpreters. The picture, therefore, is one of several people wrestling with difficult sayings.

It is not possible, on the basis of what was said about Papias, to describe the contents of the purported *Logia*. Yet, for what it is worth, Papias's testimony does fit the Deuteronomy/Sirach *logia* of Matthew 5 and 11.

3. *The Theory Works: It Helps Explain New Testament Writings*

In the final analysis, the idea of Matthew's *Logia*—Deuteronomy-based and seminal—will stand or fall on the basis of one criterion: Does it work? Does it help explain the development of the New Testament? This is a question that will need years of research. However, even at this stage, there is some evidence that it does.

The pre-eminence of Deuteronomy in a seminal text such as Matthew's *Logia* helps explain Deuteronomy's leading role in other New Testament writings such as 1 Corinthians, canonical Matthew, and Luke's gospel.

The method used in composing Matthew's *Logia*—the transforming and combining of diverse writings, one from the Torah (Deuteronomy), another from later scriptural writings (Sirach)—provides a precedent for aspects of other New Testament texts.

The *Logia*'s relationship to the Law—respectful, yet antithetical—corresponds significantly with many debates in the New Testament writings.[6] In particular, the antithetical formulation is akin to the reversal technique found, for instance, in Galatians' use of certain Deuteronomic material (see Pate 2000).

The connections between some of Matthew's saying and 1 Corinthians (Robinson 1971a: 40-44; cf. Richardson 1987) become more understandable if an arrangement of Matthew's sayings once existed as a separate seminal document.

4. *Conclusion*

As a document, Matthew's *Logia* is brief, and therefore not as susceptible as Proto-Luke to prolonged systematic demonstration. Yet its main supporting arguments are essentially like those of Proto-Luke, and all three are significant. It has a strong consistent literary relationship to the great book of Deuteronomy. It reflects internal coherence, as well as congruence with other texts (Qumran) and traditions (Papias). And it shows signs of helping explain central aspects of the development of the New Testament. As such it is a worthwhile working hypothesis.

---

6. The disputatious nature of the New Testament must also be seen in the context of the broader context of the disputatious/dialectic nature of the Old Testament (Brueggemann 1997).

13

1 Corinthians as Systematically Adapting the Pentateuch, Especially Deuteronomy: An Exploratory Survey

1. *Introduction*

Like Matthew's *Logia*, 1 Corinthians used Deuteronomy systematically. It did what the *Logia* had done, but more so. On the one hand it pushed the interpretive process further back, back into Deuteronomy's own roots and contexts, particularly into the Pentateuch. On the other hand, it brought the process of interpretation forward, transforming the Pentateuch so that it spoke to Corinth and to the contemporary world.

This view is not altogether new. For some time now, the literary study of Paul's epistles has been advancing on two main fronts—Greco-Roman and scriptural. On the Greco-Roman side it has become clear, particularly through the work of G.A. Kennedy, H.D. Betz, A.J. Malherbe, and M.M. Mitchell that Paul, far from being an isolated writer, was attuned both to the writing methods of his day (rhetoric) as well as to the whole 'canon' of popular philosophers.[1] In Malherbe's words (1989: 5), 'It is now recognized that Platonists, Peripatetics, Cynics, Stoics, Epicureans and Pythagoreans must all come under consideration'.

On the scriptural side, there has been a similar widening of horizons.[2] D.A. Koch (1986), R.B. Hays[3] and C.K. Stockhausen (1989; 1993) have led the way in showing that Paul's relationship to the Jewish scriptures was not something distant and narrow—as if he were limited to explicit citations which, plucked from memory or anthologies,[4] acted merely as an external buttress for his own already-constituted message. Rather, he had access to whole books—written texts which he had before his eyes—and, by a process of transformation, used these books as constitutive of his message, as central to his own writings.[5] This view that scripture was formative to Paul's writing has recently received support from other writers, especially from B.R. Rosner (1994), S. Hafemann (1996), R.E. Ciampa (1998), and C.M. Pate (2000).[6]

The general purpose of this chapter is to suggest that, as with the popular philosophers, Pauline studies need to consider the whole range of the scriptures. The more specific purpose here is to indicate that 1 Corinthians drew directly on broad areas of the Pentateuch, especially on Deuteronomy. Yet, though this pentateuchal element is important—constitutive, as Koch and Hays would say—it is no more than one component. Allowance

---

1. Kennedy 1984; Betz (especially 1979); Malherbe (especially 1986, 1989); Mitchell 1993.
2. For reviews of research, see Ellis 1957: especially 2-9, 76-82; 1991: 54-74.
3. Hays 1989: especially 14-21; see also 1993: especially 70-96.
4. For Ellis (1978: 213-16), 1 Cor. 1–2 uses pre-existing expositions of scriptural texts; but the contrary thesis of Mitchell (1993: 65-111), concerning the text's unity of composition, is much stronger and is not dependent on the invoking of hypothetical documents.
5. Koch 1986: 92-101, 284; Hays 1989: 14-21, especially 16. (Note Hays 1989: 35, 'Scripture broods over [Romans]'). Though Hays speaks of 'intertextuality', he does not regard this word as indispensable (1993: 81). It would probably be appropriate, and perhaps fruitful, to connect his work with the Jewish phenomenon of 'rewritten scripture' and with the Greco-Roman rhetorical idea of competitive *imitatio*.
6. For a review of studies on Paul's use of Scripture, see Ciampa 1998: 12-20.

must also be made for later writings, including especially Daniel, Tobit, and Sirach, and for several factors from Paul's own experience and situation.

To some degree, Paul's dependence on the Pentateuch is obvious. In 1 Corinthians 10, he explicitly takes some events from Exodus and Numbers (10.1-13) as well as elements of Leviticus (10.14-22) and he adapts them, sometimes in ways that are 'fanciful...and... startling',[7] to Christ and the Corinthian church. If the center of the Pentateuch can be contemporized so freely in ch. 10, then perhaps variations on the same procedure occur elsewhere.

The investigative method is one of trial and error.[8] However, the obvious or explicit citations may sometimes provide a lead or indication of a wider dependence. Such is the case in 1 Cor. 10.1-13; the brief quotation (from Exod. 32.6, in 1 Cor. 10.7) is but one element from a much broader (and obvious) reference to Exodus and Numbers.

A similar phenomenon occurs in 1 Corinthians 6–8: the obvious allusion to Gen. 2.24 ('the two will be one flesh', 1 Cor. 6.16) proves to be just one part of a broader use of Gen. 1.1–4.16 (the two creation accounts and two sin accounts). The affinity begins in 6.12-20 —a passage which Barrett entitles 'The Root of the Trouble' (Barrett 1971: 143)—and continues in 7.1-11 and 8.1-13. (Compare Tables 16 and 17 [pp. 128-29].) The details are debatable, yet it does not seem possible that so many links are coincidental.

Likewise with Deuteronomy. 1 Corinthians has just two obvious quotations from Deuteronomy: 5.13 ('Drive out the evil one...'; cf. Deut. 13.6; 17.7; 19.19; 22.21, 24; 24.7), and 9.9 ('You must not muzzle the ox...'; cf. Deut. 25.4), but both these quotations are tips of scriptural icebergs.[9] The 'drive out' text (1 Cor. 5.13) is immediately followed by a passage (6.1-11, justice and the kingdom) which is heavily indebted to Deuteronomy 1, and the 'ox' text (9.9) occurs in a section (1 Cor. 9.3-18, Paul's *apologia*) which draws systematically on Deuteronomy 23–28. (See Tables 18 and 19 [pp. 130-31].)

A comparison of the texts indicates that Paul has transformed Deuteronomy, a finding which gives new force to Koch's conclusions.[10] Transformation is first of all seen in the reworking of Deuteronomy 1. This chapter (Deut. 1) tells largely of two events: the appointment of wise men and judges (1.9-18); and the faithlessness which causes a division between those who will and those who will not inherit the promised land (1.19-46). Paul uses these elements for his own purposes. The appointment of wise men and judges (1.9-18) is adapted to the situation in Corinth: to the need for the community to appoint its own wise judge (1 Cor. 6.1-6). And the division between those who will and will not inherit the promised land (1.19-46) provides a framework for the division between those who will and will not inherit the kingdom of God (1 Cor. 6.7-11).

---

7. Hays 1989: 91. Hanson (1974: 225) vindicates Paul's use of scripture but admits that at first sight it often appears 'strange'.

8. From a strictly logical viewpoint which seeks to trace historical developments from their beginning, one should start by clarifying Paul's *Vorlage* (see Koch 1986: 48-88; Stanley 1988: 3-5; 1992: 31-32). In Septuagintal and Pauline studies this clarifying of the *Vorlage* must remain a long-term objective, but such an historical judgment, however desirable, is probably best postponed, or at least kept tentative, until more data have been gathered, in other words, until some of Paul's many other connections with the LXX (apart from obvious quotations) have been traced.

9. A similar phenomenon is found in the use of Deuteronomy by Matthew. The clear allusion to the Deuteronomic law about two or three witnesses (Mt. 18.16; cf. Deut. 17.6; 19.15) is linked to a wider dependence on Deut. 14–15; see Chapter 22, below. Likewise in Luke's use of the Elijah–Elisha Narrative—'and he gave him to his mother' (Lk. 7.15; cf. 1 Kgs 17.23)—is but part of a broader dependence on 1 Kgs 17.17-24, and the reference to calling down fire from heaven (Lk. 9.54; cf. 2 Kgs 1.7-14) is part of the reworking of all of 2 Kgs 1.1–2.6; see Chapters 29 and 33.

10. For Koch (1986: 198), Paul's freedom 'signalisiert einen grundsätzlichen Wandel im Verständnis der Schrift'.

Furthermore, while the idea of justice is important in Deuteronomy 1—see especially 'judge justly' (*dikaiōs*, 1.17)—Paul gives it a new prominence. Partly because of the situation of the early Christians, and partly because of his own general emphasis on justification,[11] he brings justice to the center. He uses variations on the word 'justice' (*adikoi, adikeō, dikaioō*, 'unjust, do wrong, justify') to knit the whole text (6.1-11) into a literary and theological unity. One aspect of this unity is the idea of a transition from injustice to justification.

Paul's distinctive unity, in this case his emphasis on justice, helps explain aspects of his procedure. While following Deuteronomy, he is subjecting it to the requirements of his own justice-related message.

Paul also makes detailed adaptations. At almost every stage he abbreviates, sometimes distilling the older text to its essence and giving it a new application or meaning. And he sometimes plays with the wording. In reworking the appointment of wise men and judges (Deut. 1.9, 12-15), for instance, *ou dynēsomai* ('I cannot') becomes one factor in forming *ouk...dynēsetai* ('Is there no one who can?').

Concerning Moses' climactic appeal against injustice (against 'recognizing faces', Deut. 1.17), Paul makes a basic rearrangement. He takes the text from the end and places it at the beginning of his own address.[12] The appeal against unjust judgment (Deut. 1.17a) becomes an appeal against going to judgment before the unjust (1 Cor. 6.1).

The rest of Deut. 1.17 is equally transformed. Judging small and great (1.17b) becomes judging what is greatest (the world) and smallest (or least, 6.2b). And the idea that judgment belongs to God (*theos*, 1.17c) is applied to mean that judgment belongs to God's people (the saints/holy ones, *hagioi*, 6.2a).

In dealing with the second part of Deuteronomy 1 (concerning those who will and will not inherit the land, 1.19-46) Paul again rearranges. He takes what is last in the Deuteronomic passage—the account of how the rebellious unbelievers were thoroughly defeated by the Amorites (1.40-46, especially 1.42-46)—and sets it at the beginning of the second part of his own text: 'It is a complete defeat for you that you do...injustice' (6.7-8). In Deuteronomy, disbelief leads to defeat; in Paul, injustice (Paul's preferred emphasis) implies moral defeat. The defeat, therefore, has become internal or spiritual.

The remaining sections (Deut. 1.21, 26, 35, 37 and 1.36, 38-39; 1 Cor. 6.9-10 and 6.11) give a contrast between those who will and will not inherit the land (Deuteronomy) or kingdom (Paul). Here too Paul moves the emphasis from rebellious disbelief to the idea of justice: the unjust will not inherit the kingdom, but those who have been justified will.

These final verses (6.9-11) illustrate how Deuteronomy supplies just one component. Paul not only changes 'land' to 'kingdom'; he also adds a list of those who will not inherit that kingdom. And in describing implicitly those who will inherit, he speaks not of 'new children' (Deut. 1.39) but of those who have been 'washed...sanctified...justified in the name of the Lord Jesus...' (1 Cor. 6.11)—a richness of description which is specifically Christian and which at one level at least surpasses Deuteronomy. Overall, therefore, Paul has moved beyond Deuteronomy 1. Yet, in another sense, he never left it.

Switching now to Deuteronomy 23–28 and Paul's *apologia* (1 Cor. 9.3-18), one finds a different method of using the Mosaic text. The first difference is in the use of the obvious quotation. In 1 Cor. 5.13 dependence on Moses is unacknowledged; but in 1 Cor. 9.8-10a, it is acknowledged, and lavishly.

---

11. For Conzelmann (1975: 107), *dikaioō* in 1 Cor. 6.11 'has the full sense of the Pauline concept of justification'.

12. A similar procedure—moving the end of the subtext to the beginning of the final text—occurs occasionally in Luke; see, for example, Chapter 33.

Table 16. *Genesis 1.1–4.16*

God Made All…and Food	
1.1	God made heaven and earth.
1.4, 31	God saw that it was good (*kalon*)…very good.
2.1-3	Heaven and earth were finished and all…all…all (*pas…pantōn…pantōn*).
2.9	God made to grow…every (*pan*) tree…good for food (*kalon eis brōsin*)… and the tree of learning the knowledge (*eidenai gnōston*) of good and evil.
2.16	God said, 'Of every (*pantos*) tree eat the food (*brōsei phagē*). but of the tree of knowledge (*ginōskein*)…do not eat (*phagesthe*)'.
Man and Woman	
2.18	It is not good (*kalon*) for the man to be alone.
2.24	A man will…join (*kollaō*) to his wife, and the two will become one flesh.
3.1	Now the serpent was the most cunning (*phronimos*) of all… and said to the woman, 'Why did God say, Do not eat (*esthiō*)…'
3.3	The woman: 'God said, Do not touch (*me hapsēsthe*) it…'
Eating and Knowledge	
3.6	[When] you eat (*phagēte*)…you will be like gods (*theoi*) knowing (*ginōskontes*).
3.7	The woman saw that the tree was good for food (*eis brosin*)…and she ate (*ephagon*) and gave to the man…and he ate (*ephagon*)…and they knew (*egnōsan*).
3.11	God….the tree I said you should not eat, have you eaten (*phagein… ephages*)?
3.12	Adam: 'The woman…gave me…and I ate (*ephagon*)'.
3.13	The woman: 'The serpent tricked me and I ate (*ephagon*)'.
My Brother's Guardian?	
3.22	God: 'The man has become like one of us knowing (*ginōskein*)…and now…lest…he eat and live for ever (*mēpote…phagē…eis ton eiōna*)…'
4.2	Adam knew his wife; she bore Cain…and his brother (*ton adelphou autou*).
4.7	God to Cain: 'Have you not…sinned (*hamartanō*)'. [First sin word in Genesis.]
4.9	God to Cain: 'Where is your brother (*ho adelphos sou*)?'
4.10	Cain: 'Am I my brother's guardian (*mē…tou adelphon mou*)?'.

13. *1 Corinthians and the Pentateuch*

Table 17. *1 Corinthians 6.12–7.11; 8.1-13*

	All and Food—God Unmakes
6.12-13	All things (*panta*) are lawful for me but not all things (*panta*) are helpful. All things (*panta*)... Food (*brōmata*) for the stomach and the stomach for food (*brōmasin*)... These God will bring to nothing (*ho theos katargēseo*). The body...
	Man and Woman
6.16	Do you not know that he that is joined (*kollaō*) to a prostitute becomes one body; for, it says, the two will be one flesh.
6.17	But he who is joined (*kollaō*) to the Lord becomes one spirit with him.
6.18	Flee prostitution. Every sin (*hamartēma*) [First sin word in 1 Corinthians]... But in prostitution a person sins (*hamartanō*) against his own body.
7.1	It is good (*kalon*) for a man not to touch (*mē haptesthai*) a woman.
7.5	Come together again lest Satan tempt you...
7.10	A woman should not separate from a man...and a man should not dismiss the woman.
	Eating and Knowledge
8.1-3	Idol sacrifices: we know we all have knowledge (*gnōsin*). Knowledge (*gnōsis*) inflates... If anyone thinks he knows something, he does not yet know as he ought to know (*egnōkenai...egnō...gnōnai*). Whoever loves God is known (*egnōstai*)...
8.4	So, concerning the food (*brōsis*)...there is only one God.
8.5	Though there are many so-called 'gods' (*theoi*) either in heaven or on earth...
8.6	But for us there is one God from whom all (*panta*)...through whom all (*panta*)...
8.7	Yet not all have this knowledge (*gnōsis*). Some...eat (*esthiō*)...
8.8	Food (*brōma*) does not... If we eat... If we do not eat (*phagōmen... phagōmen*).
8.10	For if someone sees you, with knowledge (*gnōsis*)...might he not eat (*esthein*).
	Lest My Brother Perish
8.11	And so through your knowledge (*gnōsis*) the brother (*ho adelphos*) perishes.
8.12	Thus sinning against your brothers (*hamartontes eis tous adelphous*)...
8.13	If food scandalizes my brother (*ton adelphon mou*), I will not eat meat for ever (*ou mē phagō...eis ton aiōna*).

Table 18. *Justice in Deuteronomy 1 and 1 Corinthians 6.1-11*

Deuteronomy 1	1 Corinthians 6.1-11
Avoid Judgment among the Unjust	
	1. 'You…go to judgment (*krinesthai*) before the unjust (*adikōn*). 3. Do you not know that the holy (*hagioi*) shall judge (*krinousin*) the world? [= Judgment belongs to the holy ones]. 2. If by you the world (*kosmos*) is judged (*krinetai*), are you unworthy to judge what is smallest (*elachistōn*)? (6.1-2)
Appoint the Wise…and Judge	
'I cannot (*ou dynēsomai*) carry you alone… Give yourselves wise men (*sophous*)…' So I took from you (*ex hymōn*) wise men man (*sophous*)… and set them over you (*eph'hymōn*) as rulers…and instructors to beyour judges (*kritais*)' (1.9, 12-15)	'Is it that there is not (*ouk*) among you (*en hymin*) one wise (*sophos*) who is able (*dynēsetai*) to judge (*dia-krinai*)
Judge among Brothers	
'I told the judges, "Hear your brothers (*ana meson tōn adelphōn*) and judge justly (*krinate dikaiōs*) between a man and his brother or the alien with him" (*ana meson andros kai ana meson adelphou kai ana meson prosēlytou autou*)' (1.16)	between his brothers (*ana meson tou adelphou autou*), but brother goes to judgment against brother (*adelphos meta adelphou krinetai*)' (6.5-6).
Avoid Unjust Judgment	
1. 'Do not recognize faces in judgment (*en krinei*) [= Do not judge unjustly]. 2. Judge (*krineis*) small (*mikron*) and great (*megan*) alike 3. Do not shrink before a face, because judgment (*krisis*) belongs to God (*theou*)' (1.17)	
Complete Moral Defeat	
	'It is a complete defeat (*holōs hēttēma*) for you that you…do injustice' (6.7-8).
Inheriting the Land/Kingdom: Those Who Will Not…	
'Enter, inherit (*klēronomeō*) the land' (1.8). 'Go up, inherit (*klēronomeō*)… Do not fear… But you disobeyed/disbelieved (*apeitheō*)…' The Lord, angry, said: 'Not one will enter… (*oude…ou*) (1.21, 26, 35, 37).	'Do you not know that the unjust (*adikoi*) will not inherit (*klēronomeō*) the kingdom of God… Neither…nor…nor……nor… (*oute…oute…oute*) will inherit (*klēronomeō*) the kingdom of God' (6.9-10)
…And Those Who Will	
'But (*plēn*) Caleb…Joshua shall inherit (*klēronomeō*) it, and every new (*neos*) child who knows not good or evil…will inherit (*klēronomeō*) it' (1.36, 38-39).	'And such were some of you. But (*alla*) you have been washed…sanctified… justified in the name of the Lord Jesus and in the Spirit…' (6.11)
Moral Failure Leading to Complete Defeat	
'"Do not go up… You will be destroyed…" But… rebelling, you went up… And the Amorites came out to meet you, and like a swarm of bees pursued you, and they struck you down from Seir to Hormah' (1.42-44)	

Table 19. *Conduct in Deuteronomy 23–28 and 1 Corinthians 9.4-18*

Deuteronomy 23–28	1 Corinthians 9.4-18
Food, Wife, and War	
'If you go through your neighbor's vineyard, you may eat (*fagē*)' (23.25)	'Do we not have the right to eat (*fagein*) and drink?' (9.4)
[Next verse] 'If someone takes a wife (*gunaika*)…' (24.1)	'Do we not have the right to take around a wife (*adelphēn gunaika*)?' (9.5)
'If someone takes a wife, he will not go out to war (*polemon*), not will any thing be laid on him; he will be free' (24.5)	'Who goes soldiering (*strateuetai*) at his own expense?' (9.7a)
The Vineyard and the Ox	
'When you gather [the fruit] (*trugaō*) of your vineyard (*ampelōna*)…' (24.21)	'Who plants a vineyard (*ampelōna*) and does not eat of its fruit?' (9.7b)
'You must not muzzle the ox that treads out the corn (*ou kēmōseis boun aloōnta*)' (25.4)	'Do I say these things on human authority? Does not the law say these things too? For in the law of Moses it is written, "You must not muzzle the ox that treads out the corn (*ou kēmōseis boun aloōnta*)". Is it about oxen God is concerned? Or is he not speaking entirely for our sake? It was written for our sake…' (9.8-10a)
The Good Announcement (Exodus/Gospel) and the Altar	
'You will go to the priest (*hierea*)… and say, "I announce (*An-aggellō*)…" The priest (*hiereus*) will take…and set before the altar (*thusiastērion*). Then…say, "My father was…in Egypt …And the Lord saw our humiliation… hardship…affliction…and led us out"…' And rejoice (*eu-franthēsē*)…' (26.1-11)	'We endure all…not to obstruct the gospel (*eu-aggelion*) of Christ. You know that those who minister holy things (*hiera*) eat from the holy place (*hierou*), that those attending the altar (*thusiastēriō*) share from the altar. So [we] should live by the gospel (*eu-aggelion*)' (9.12c-14)
The Writing of these Things	
'Keep the[se] laws… Today the Lord has…made you a…people—a name and a boast (*kauchēma*)…Write (*grapseis… grapseis*) all the words of the law…' (26.16–27.8)	'I did not write (*egrapsa*) these things that it be otherwise… Better…to die than…[lose] my boast (*kauchēma*)' (9.15)
Woe and Reward	
Curses: 'Cursed (*epikataratos*) be he who does not do…the law' (27.[9-]26)	'Woe (*ouai*) to me if I do not preach the gospel' (9.16b)
Blessings, blessed (*eulogai…eulogēmenos*): You will be rich and powerful (28.1-14)	My reward…reward (*misthon…misthos*): to give the gospel free of charge, not using my right (9.17-18)

The more general difference is that in 1 Corinthians 9, Paul seems to look not so much for synthesis as for representative samples. He ranges across several disparate chapters and picks out elements which seem either intrinsically important or particularly suited to his own purpose.

Yet he retains some element of synthesis. While much of Deuteronomy 23–25 is concerned with protecting the vulnerable, Paul is concerned with defense (*apologia*, 1 Cor. 9.3). In Deuteronomy the idea of protecting or defending is implicit; in Paul it is distilled and explicit—and it applies not to vulnerable people in ancient Israel but to himself and his preaching of the gospel to a cosmopolitan city.

Apart from the use of Deuteronomy 1 in 1 Corinthians 6, there is some use of Deuteronomy 2–4 in parts of 1 Corinthians 7 and 8. (See Table 20.) However, the mode of dependence is again different—no longer a dependence of considerable detail (as in using Deut. 1) but one of broad outline (and a few details). Apparently just as Paul has diverse ways of making obvious quotations (Koch 1986: 21-23), so he has diverse ways of absorbing whole passages.

The evidence suggests that Paul is systematically distilling Deuteronomy. (This may seem startling but it has at least partial analogues in the use of Deuteronomy by Matthew and Luke[13]). If this is indeed the case—thus far he has used aspects of chs. 1–4, 7–9, and 23–28—then it is appropriate to check all of Deuteronomy for possible use in 1 Corinthians.

The initial results of such a full-length check are summarized in Table 21 below [p. 134]. In one way, this outline is very unsatisfactory. Apart from being incomplete and simplified, it is often tentative. And most correspondences are unproven. (Proving them all would require a monograph). Yet, given the apparently detailed dependence of 1 Cor. 6.1-11 on Deuteronomy 1, and given also Koch's contention that Paul used whole biblical books, the tentative outline seems useful for further research.

The process of trial and error leads also to Numbers. This book deals largely with the community (*synagōgē*): with its idealized form (Num. 1–10), with its divisive crises (Num. 11–19, especially chs. 11–14, 16–17), and with its overcoming of deathly obstacles (Num. 20–36). In dealing with a community and its struggles, Numbers has a broad affinity with 1 Corinthians.

Direct literary dependence occurs in at least one area. The account of how the leaders, especially Moses, handled the various crises (Num. 11–17, especially chs. 11–14 and 16–17), has provided one component in Paul's account of leaders, including himself (1 Cor. 3.1–5.8) (see Table 22 below [p. 135]). Some connections in the outline are debatable, especially those with question marks (??). Yet, overall, the similarities seem far beyond the range of coincidence. The idea that Paul is transforming a written source may also help explain his obscure allusion, midway through the text, to 're-schematizing' (*meta-schēma-tizō*)[14] and to keeping to what is written (4.6).

Paul does in fact reshape the crisis texts (Num. 11–17). He reduces the episodes to their essence, and instead of using the climactic moments immediately—the series of divine descents or appearances (Num. 11.25; 12.5; 14.10; 16.19; 17.7)—he gathers them and reshapes them to form components for describing the appearances of the risen Jesus (1 Cor. 15.5-8).

Part of Paul's text (4.14-21) combines Numbers with Deuteronomy—a complexity which makes analysis more challenging, but which accords with Hays's reference to

---

13. See Chapters 22, 23, and 25; and Moessner 1989: especially 81-288.
14. On the foreground, as opposed to the possible background, of 4.6 see Hall 1994.

authors who 'bind themselves to their authenticating [literary] model with particularly intricate knots' (1989: 16).

Table 20. *Walking with God (Deuteronomy 2.1–4.40; 1 Corinthians 7.17–8.6)*

Deuteronomy 2.1–4.40	1 Corinthians 7.17–8.6
Journey on as God has assigned, respecting different inheritances (*en klērō…en klērō…en klērō…*) (triple structure, about Edom Moab and Ammon) (2.1-23)	Walk in life as God has assigned, not worrying about diverse callings (*eklēthē…eklēthē…eklēthē…*) (triple structure, about circumcised, non-circumcised, and slaves) (7.17-24)
The total wars against Sihon and Og will 'spread trembling and fear through all nations under heaven' (2.24–3.11, especially 2.25)	Virgins—in the context of 'the eschatological woes that are impending over the world' (C.K. Barrett 1971: 175) (7.25-34)
Exact assignment of places (3.12-17) Future crossing of the Jordan and Moses' demise (3.18-28)	??
??	Relationships: seemly decisions (7.35-34) Marital bonds—until death (7.39-40)
Framing references to Moses as entrusted by the Lord God to teach the commandments (4.1-4, 14)	Framing references to Paul who has no command but is worthy by the Lord and God to give an opinion (7.25, 40)
The Israelites have unique wisdom and understanding (4.5-8), yet they must guard soul and heart (4.9-13)	Concerning idols: all have knowledge, but it is love which builds; and love brings knowledge (8.1-3). ??
Idolatry > negative results (4.15-31). (4.16-19: Do not idolize creation)	Idols are not real (8.4a)
The uniqueness of God's revelation and God's self; there is no other (4.32-40 [4.37, God's love])	The uniqueness of God, from whom comes all (creation) (8.4b-6)

Moving on in Deuteronomy one soon finds another area of affinity: the description of the Israelite people and Moses (Deut. 7–9) has echoes in the description of the Corinthians and Paul (1 Cor. 1.25–2.5; 4.14-21): In minimal outline:

Deuteronomy 7–9	*1 Corinthians 1.25–2.5; 4.14-21*
God has chosen you above people who were stronger, not because you were many, for you were the least of all peoples (ch. 7; 9.1-6)	Not many of you are wise, but God chose the foolish…the weak to confound the strong so that all flesh should not boast (1.25-31)
Having encountered God on the mountain, I came down to you, sinners; and I fell prostrate—in fasting, and fear and prayer (9.7-29)	When I came to you proclaiming God I did not come with lofty wisdom— but in weakness and fear and trembling (2.1-5)
Remember the way the Lord led you, as a man would bring up his son (ch. 8)	I admonish you, as beloved children, and I sent Timothy, my beloved child, to remind you of my ways (4.14-21)

Table 21. *Deuteronomy as One Component of 1 Corinthians: An Exploratory Outline*

Deuteronomy		1 Corinthians	
ch. 1 2.1–4.40 4.32–ch. 5/ Exod. 19	Judges; inherit the land. Assigned inheritances; one God. Horeb/Sinai: the great, solemn, revelation; God's descent to Israel. Moses as mediator.	6.1-11 7.17–8.6 ??	Justice; inherit the kingdom. Assigned callings; one God. Cf. aspects of 15.1-5—the great New Testament revelation, solemnly announced. Appearances. Paul as mediator.
ch. 6 chs. 7, 9 ch. 8 10.1-11 chs. 10–11	*Shema* (total love). The weak; Moses' fear, prayer. Remember the way—like a son. Tablets, ark, Aaron, Levi, Moses. *Shema*/love, and the two ways.	1.25–2.5 4.13-21	Cf. ch. 13? The weak; Paul's fear… Son will remind you of my way. ?? Cf. ch. 13?
chs. 12–15 16.1-8 16.9–18.8 18.9-22 chs. 19–23 chs. 23–28	Worship, idols, clean, tithes. Passover and unleavened bread. Feasts; worship abuses, leaders. Sorcery, the prophet, falsehood. Revenge, war, fornication… Protecting, 'credo', writing.	5.6-8 14.20-21 9.4-18	?? Christ our Passover ?? Strange tongues. Cf. 15.4, 12-14?? ?? Paul's *apologia*
29.1-13	Second covenant—to know God. Exod. 12-13: Passover lamb/night. Isaiah 53: The Servant, like a lamb, handed over for our sins.	11.23-26	New covenant—to remember me. The night, the meal. The handing over. […for our sins, 15.3].
29.14-29 30.1-10 30.11-20	Warnings. From dispersal to reunion. Love, not in the sky; two ways. The future (30.19-20)	11.27-34 ch. 12 ch. 13	Warnings. From division to union. Love—not angels' tongues. Love's future (13.8-13)
31.1-8 31.9-13 31.14-22 31.23-30	Journeys of Moses and Joshua Writing, reading, learning. God's descent; the curses. Be a man; gather all.	16.1-13 14.26-40 16.21-22 14.20-25	Journeys of Paul and Timothy Learning, recognizing, writing. ?? Anathema. Maranatha. Be not children; all gathered.
32.1-25 32.26-42 32.43-52 ch. 33 ch. 34	The one God; remember past generations; Jacob/Israel sacrificed to idols. The God of all restrains for the people's sake. Homage to God. Say all to all the people of Israel—it is their life. Israel's tribes: God's blessings, especially on worshipping Levi, and glorious Joseph with hair on his head. Moses' end, burial.	10.14-15, 18-20, 22 10.23-24, 26-27 10.31-33 11.2-15 15.3-4	Flee idols; consider historic Israel; sacrifice, idols. 'All' is restrained because of God and the other's sake. Glory to God. I please all people in all ways—to save them. The human race (men and women). God's glory, especially praying. Christ's death, burial.

13. *1 Corinthians and the Pentateuch*

Table 22. *Community Crises and Leadership*

Numbers 11–17	1 Corinthians 3.1–5.8
Nursing the Community: The Need for Spirit and the Test of Fire (Numbers 11 and 16; 1 Corinthians 3.1-17)	
God's fire burns in punishment (11.1-3) The people want meat (*krea*) (11.4-9) Moses cannot conceive, birth, and nurse the meat-seeking people (11.10-15) The *pneuma*—first divine, and then bearing deadly meat (11.16-35)	Paul cannot speak to the church as *pneumatikoi*—but as flesh-oriented (*sarkinoi, sarkikoi*). So he has fed them with milk (3.1-3)
Rebellion (against leaders) is tested and punished by fire (ch. 16)	Division (about leaders, 3.4-9); fire will test and punish (3.10-17)
Pretentiousness, the Faithful Servant, and Judgment (Numbers 12; 1 Corinthians 3.18–4.5)	
Miriam, Aaron claim God's word (12.1-2). Moses as supremely humble (*praus*, 12.3)	?? Thinking oneself wise (3.18-23)
Moses: servant (*therapeuēn*), hearing God face to face, is faithful in God's house (*en oikō mou pistos*) 12.7-8	We: servants (*hypēretai*)…and stewards (*oikonomoi*) of God's secrets. A steward is to be faithful (*oikonomois…pistos*) (4.1-2)
Sin, ignorance, punishment (12.9-15)	?? Conscience and judgment (4.3-5)
	I adapted (*metaschēmatizō*) these things to myself and Apollos…that you learn, 'Keep to what is written' (4.6)
The Apostoloi *May Die but a 'Child' Will Guide* (Numbers 13–14; 1 Corinthians 4.9-17)	
Twelve sent out (*apostellō*) to see if the people are strong or weak, few or many… (13.1-20) A generation will die (cf. 13.25–14.38; 17.27)	We apostles (*apostoloi*) are a show, condemned to die (4.9); we are fools but you are wise, we are weak but you are strong… (4.10)
But the children…with me (*all'…ta tekna…met' emou*, 14.23 LXX) But my servant/child (*pais*) Caleb… I will lead him into the land (14.24)	But as you [are my]…children (*all' hōs tekna mou…*). So I sent you Timothy, my son (*teknon*) …to remind you of my ways (4.14-17)
Coming with Speed and Power, and with a Rod (Numbers 17; 1 Corinthians 4.18-21)	
Aaron runs quickly (*tachōs*) and stops the plague (17.1-15) Aaron's branch (*rabdon*) (17.16-26)	I will come…quickly (*tacheōs*)… in power. Do I come with a rod (*rabdon*) or in…humility (*praütēs*) (4.18-21)?
Offence, Sacrifice and Removing the Offender (Numbers 15; 1 Corinthians 5.1-8)	
Sacrifice, dough, atonement (15.1-29) Getting rid of an offender (15.30-36) [Chapters 9; 18–19: Passover, sacrifices.]	Remove the offender. New dough. Christ, our Passover, has been sacrificed (5.1-8)

The process of combining seems to occur especially in the final or climactic moments of a text. Thus, the closing verse of ch. 4 (4.21) combines in Paul two of the key features of Moses and Aaron: humility (Num. 12.3) and the *rabdon* of authority (Num. 17.16-26).[15]

Paul also combines Deuteronomy with Genesis. The divorce text, for instance (1 Cor. 7.10-11), seems to reflect aspects of both Gen. 2.24 and Deut. 24.1-4. Likewise, the reference to the one God as source of all (creation) (1 Cor. 8.1-6) may reflect aspects of both Genesis 1–2 and Deut. 4.5-40. And these same Pauline texts may also reflect aspects of Corinth, including Corinthian slogans. Apparently Paul's method was to bring the heart of the old sacred writings to the centre of contemporary culture.

Ideally this analysis should also examine the relationship of 1 Corinthians to Leviticus, the book which was literally the center of the Pentateuch. But that is left to further research.

2. *Conclusion*

The outlines given here need extensive testing and explaining, yet it seems better, at least as a working hypothesis, to allow that they may reflect a systematic engagement of the Pentateuch, and especially of Deuteronomy. Such a conclusion not only avoids invoking an unlikely degree of coincidence; it also accords with the increasing evidence about the broadness and deliberateness of Paul's frame of reference (including popular philosophers, rhetoric, and whole written scripture books). This conclusion also accords with the broad foundational scope of the theology in 1 Corinthians.[16]

Paul teaches indirectly. While apparently focused on a specific occasion (the details of the Corinthian community), he is also carrying out, quite deliberately, a major literary and theological task: transforming the Torah.

Though Paul apparently drew on all five books of the Pentateuch, it has seemed easiest, in tracing his sources, to find links with Deuteronomy, as though he accorded Deuteronomy a special role.

It is possible to account for Paul's focus on Deuteronomy by recalling Deuteronomy's status as a synthesis of many of the Jewish scriptures and traditions, including traditions from the earlier books of the Pentateuch.

But there is a further explanation, namely that the epistle is continuing the *Logia*'s process of transforming scripture, especially Deuteronomy. This explanation is corroborated by the apparent connections between the gospel sayings and 1 Corinthians (see the quotes from J. Robinson and P. Richardson in the Introduction to Chapters 12–14). The next task for research—but not for this volume—will be to compare Matthew's *Logia* and 1 Corinthians directly.

Pending such research, some tentative observations may be useful.

In broad terms the *Logia* and 1 Corinthians may be divided into three main areas—people, laws, and a revelatory conclusion:

		Logia	*1 Corinthians*
1.	The people/community:	Beatitudes	A community struggling for peace (chs. 1–4)
2.	Laws—old and new:	Antitheses	Problems and diverse directives (chs. 5–10)
3.	Revelatory conclusion:	Great cry/call	Eucharist, love, resurrection, journeys (chs. 11–16)

---

15. For other apparent final combinings, see 1 Cor. 3.16-17 (cf. Num. 11.29-35 and 16.24-35), and 1 Cor. 4.19-20 (cf. Num. 16.28-30 and 17.11-15). The testing fire (1 Cor. 3.10-17) depends not only on Num. 11 and 16 (see top of Table 22) but also on a whole 'combination of traditional motifs'; see Hollander 1994: 104.

16. 1 Corinthians contains 'part of the foundations of christian theology'; see Murphy-O'Connor 1979: ix.

13. *1 Corinthians and the Pentateuch*

Like the *Logia*, 1 Corinthians uses a diverse mix of older texts: the *Logia* blends Deuteronomy with Sirach, and 1 Corinthians blends Pentateuchal books with texts that are much later (see Appendices 6 and 7). In addition, both texts—the *Logia* and 1 Corinthians—involve a combination of the sapiential and eschatological.

It seems worth researching whether Paul used Sirach. For instance, should Paul's attitude to women (1 Cor. 5–7) be linked to Sirach (9.1-9; 23.16-27; 25.13–26.18; 42.9-14)? Or should Paul's picture of himself in his *apologia* (1 Cor. 9.3-12, especially 9.10b-12) be linked to Sirach's portrait of the contemplative student (Sir. 38.24–39.11)? The problem is complicated by Sirach's own indebtedness to Deuteronomy.

Whatever the details, there are significant initial indications that 1 Corinthians, as well as sharing aspects of the *Logia*'s sources and methods, also drew directly on the *Logia* text itself.

The supper text (1 Cor. 11.17-34) is in continuity with both 'Christ our Passover has been sacrificed' (cf. 5.6-8) and Christ's death 'for our sins' (15.1-4). (11.17-34 and ch. 5 share substantial elements [coming together; Christ's death; judgment] and linguistic details.) As these three texts are interwoven among themselves, so their scriptural roots also are interwoven. Passover ideas occur in both 5.6-8 and 11.23-26; and Servant ideas (Isa. 53) occur in both 11.23-26 and 15.1-4.

14

Luke's Use of 1 Corinthians:
The Supper Texts (1 Corinthians 11.16-34; Luke 22.14-30)*

1 Corinthians served two basic roles. On the one hand, it interpreted the ancient scriptures for Corinth and the contemporary world. On the other hand, it provided a crucial component for another writer who used historiography for a somewhat similar purpose. Proto-Luke's continuity with ancient scripture was somewhat clearer than that of 1 Corinthians, and his historiographical form had a distinct purpose, but he too wanted to write his account of Christ in a way that would adapt the ancient scriptures. The epistle provided a partial model, and it also provided a rich source.

The purpose of this chapter is to indicate that Proto-Luke absorbed and refashioned 1 Corinthians. The topic is extensive and complex; so it is better at this point simply to illustrate the phenomenon, and to keep further discussion until later (Appendix 2).

The idea of the evangelists' indebtedness to the epistles is not new or vague. Scholars have given evidence for connections that are quite specific. According to W. Schenk, for instance, 'Mark shows familiarity with Paul's epistles' (Schenk 1992: 903). M.-E. Boismard maintains that Mark uses Pauline words and themes (Boismard and Benoit 1972: II, 23-23). P. Rolland seems to go further: 'Mark has nourished himself on the letters of Paul …and Peter' (Rolland 1992: 778). The present writer also has made some proposals, four altogether, one for each of the evangelists:

1. Mark: Mark 10 has distilled the practical admonitions at the center of 1 Peter.[1]
2. Matthew: Matthew 1–7, especially the Sermon on the Mount, drew on Romans.[2]
3. John: John 17, with its broad vision of unity, synthesizes much of Ephesians (Brodie 1993b: 128-34).
4. Luke: Acts 1–5, on community unity, reverses the disunity in 1 Corinthians 1–5.[3]

The proposal to link Luke with 1 Corinthians is not new. In 1989 M.D. Goulder indicated a literary connection between Luke's text and some epistles, especially on 1 Corinthians.[4]

In fact, in the case of Luke it is very hard to build a credible scenario in which the evangelist, while writing about Paul, would not bother trying to acquire copies of Paul's epistles. Luke was not a self-taught scribbler marooned on some distant desert island. Even if Luke is located as far west as Rome or as far east as Antioch, he is still within a few weeks of Corinth. If he is located in Greece, as is sometimes done, then his distance from Corinth is just a matter of days. Furthermore, he was a *littérateur*; he dealt with writings, and he carefully reviewed sources (Lk. 1.3). In chronicling Jesus, he searched for

---

* This chapter is a variation on a paper first delivered at the Claremont conference on mimesis and intertextuality (1998) and subsequently published as 'Towards Tracing the Gospels' Literary Indebtedness to the Epistles' (Brodie 2001d).

1. Brodie 1980. See Chapter 18, below.
2. Brodie 1993c. See Chapter 20, below.
3. Brodie 1995a. See Appendix 2.
4. Goulder 1989: 129-46. See also the review of the discussion in Enslin 1970.

sources on Jesus; he used the works (or sources) of other evangelists. Would he do less for Paul? Would he write so much about Paul and never bother getting a copy of any of Paul's own writings?[5]

Luke's use of 1 Corinthians is particularly understandable. Among all the New Testament epistles, its implied picture of a community is uniquely vibrant. And its ideas are foundational—'part of the foundations of christian theology' (Murphy-O'Connor 1979: ix). If Luke wanted an authoritative sense of an early community, he could hardly do better than absorb 1 Corinthians.

It is disputed, of course, whether Luke's was Paul's travelling companion; and theologically, Luke and Paul are often regarded as quite different, even incompatible.[6] On closer inspection, however, the objections of history and theology are not convincing. The decisive historical question here is not whether Luke travelled with Paul but whether Luke had access to any of Paul's epistles.

Similarly with theological differences. The issue is not whether there are theological differences but whether the differences are intelligible. On the question of Luke and Paul, J.C. Beker implied that in fact the theological gap *is* intelligible: Luke has 'redesigned' Paul's theology in view of a later situation; 'within the overall perspective of Luke's salvation-history and the problems he needs to address, his portrayal of Paul becomes intelligible' (Beker 1993: 517, 519). And L.T. Johnson's brief comparative study of 'salvation' tends to confirm Luke–Paul theological continuity (Johnson 1993). The issue then is not difference but intelligibility.

Given the basic plausibility of Luke having access to an epistle such as 1 Corinthians it is appropriate to look more closely at the question. The test case here concerns the supper texts.

1. *The Supper Texts (1 Corinthians 11.16-34; Luke 22.14-30)*

The kernel thesis here is that Proto-Luke reversed and reshaped the account of abuses at supper (1 Cor. 11.16-34) to form one component for the account of Jesus' last supper (Lk. 22.14-30). The elements of Paul's version have been adapted to a new context; and the process of reversal means that at times the relationship between the texts is one of sharp contrast.[7]

The texts may be outlined in five sections (see Table 23 next page). The order of the two texts is essentially the same. However, in section 4 the square brackets indicate a variation: Luke's reshaping *combines* two kindred passages, namely the initial reference to problems (11.16-19, including, curiously, the preceding reference to contentiousness, 11.16) and the later reference to further problems (11.30-32). Also, there are some minor variations of order within sections 2 and 3. The overall process of reversal and contrast is particularly acute in section 1. The following section-by-section analysis is not meant to be exhaustive; it is preliminary to further research.

---

5. The problem about the relation to Luke to the epistles touches another puzzle, that of the sources of Acts. Despite much research these sources have remained unidentified; see Dupont 1964; Haenchen 1971: 24-34, 81-90; Grässer 1976; 1977: 41; Schneider 1980: 82-89; Conzelmann 1987: xxxvi-xl.

6. For discussion, see Fitzmyer 1981: 47-51. On Luke's portrait of Paul as theologically incompatible with the epistles, see Vielhauer 1968: 33-50; Haenchen 1971: 112-16.

7. The procedure is akin to that used in transforming the account of Corinthian divisions (1 Cor. 1–5) to form a central component in describing the church's unity (Acts 1–5). See Appendix 2.

Table 23. *The Supper Texts in Paul and Luke*

1 Corinthians 11.16-19	Luke 22.14-30
1. *Coming Together*	
Coming together to eat. Each for himself. Regarding the church of God as nothing No praise (11.20-22)	Reclining together to eat. Desiring to eat with others. Fulfillment in the kingdom of God Giving thanks (22.14-17a)
2. *Eucharist*	
Eucharist. *Do this…declaring the death of the Lord **until he comes (11.23-26)	*Eat this…I clearly imply my death **'until the kingdom of God comes'. Eucharist (22.17b-20)
3. *Guilty Participant*	
Guilty eater. Examine yourself. ** Condemnation (11.27-29)	Treacherous table companion ** Woe. Examining themselves (22.21-23)
4. *Problems of Contentiousness and Worldliness*	
[Problems: Contention; divisions (11: 16-19)] Judgment: so not to be like the world (11.30-32)	Problems: Contention. Who is greater? Do not be like the kings (22.24-27)
5. *Solidarity: Not Judged, but Judging*	
Solidarity in waiting. Eating and not being condemned (11.33-34)	Solidarity in staying. Eating and judging (22.28-30)

2. *Analysis*

a. *Section 1. Coming Together—Issues: Otherness; Positiveness; Praise/Thanks (1 Corinthians 11.20-22; Luke 22.14-17)*
Both Paul and Luke begin by telling of people assembling to eat (1 Cor. 11.20; Lk. 22.14), yet the scenes they describe are opposites:
- The Corinthian coming together is *not* for the Lord's supper (1 Cor. 11.20), but Luke, in contrast, has a sense of appropriate timing and decorum, a sense of harmony (Jesus 'reclined', 'when the hour had come', and 'the apostles with him', Lk. 22.14).
- In Corinth, each gives preference to their own supper, so that while one is hungry, another gets drunk (1 Cor. 11.21); but Luke is precisely the opposite: Jesus has a deep desire to eat with the others, and his readiness is not for drunkenness but for suffering (Lk. 22.15).
- The Corinthian eaters regard 'the church of God' as nothing (*kataphroneō*, 'despise/ regard as nothing') (1 Cor. 11.22a), but as Jesus eats, he has an opposite attitude: he looks towards a fulfillment (*pleroō*, 'fulfill') in 'the kingdom of God' (Lk. 22.16). Luke's use of 'kingdom' rather than 'church' is part of a larger pattern of emphasizing the imagery and language of kings and kingdoms.
- Given the Corinthian situation, Paul refuses to give praise ('In this I do not praise [*epaineō*]', 1 Cor. 11.22b). But Jesus does give a form of praise: taking the cup, he gives thanks (*eucharisteō*, Lk. 22.17a). Luke's version of praise is thus more elevated, and he adapts this thanksgiving ('And…having given thanks…') so that it flows into what follows—concerning the eucharist.

b. *Section 2. Eucharist, and Declaring the Death of the Lord...Until the coming of the Lord/Kingdom of God (1 Corinthians 11.23-26; Luke 22.17b-20)*
As is well known, Paul's account of the institution of the eucharist (1 Cor. 11.23-25a) occurs also in Luke (22.19-20). The verbatim similarity, while explainable through a common liturgy, is also consistent with a form of imitation known in secular contexts as 'sacramental' (Hays 1989: 173-75).

Paul's preliminary reference to the night Jesus was betrayed (1 Cor. 11.23) finds an elaborate counterpart in Luke's pre-supper account of the plot to betray Jesus (Lk. 22.1-6).

Paul's subsequent reference to the eucharist as declaring the death of the Lord ('you *declare the death of the Lord* until he comes', 1 Cor. 11.26) finds a Lukan counterpart in Jesus' declaration, implicit but solemn, of his own death ('*For I tell you, I shall not drink*...until the kingdom of God comes', Lk. 22.18). Luke's further phrasing—looking forward not to *the coming of the Lord* but to *the coming of the kingdom of God*—is a further illustration of his preference for the language of kings and the kingdom. Luke also avoids repeating 'in memory of me', and he adapts the order slightly: he places the declaration of death before rather than after the basic eucharistic account. Part of the effect of this adaptation is to build a narrative that flows smoothly.

c. *Section 3. The Guilty Eater: Self-Examination, and Condemnation (1 Corinthians 11.27-29; Luke 22.21-23)*
Having spoken of sharing the eucharist, both Paul and Luke turn to a specific problem: eucharistic sharing which is unworthy. Paul does not specify any individual: 'whoever eats unworthily' is 'guilty of the body and blood of the Lord' (1 Cor. 11.27). Luke gives a particular instance but without giving a name: 'the hand of my betrayer is with me at the table' (22.21). The single word 'betrayer' captures both the unworthiness and the guilt.

The topic of the unworthy eater leads Paul to two remarks: the participant's need for self-examination (1 Cor. 11.28); and condemnation of the unworthy ('he eats...condemnation to himself', 1 Cor. 11.29). These two features—self-examination and condemnation—likewise appear in Luke, in reverse order: 'woe to that man...' (Lk. 22.22); and the participants began to examine themselves ('they began to debate among themselves which of them it might be', 22.23). Luke's text is more specific and dramatic; and the adaptation of order again helps to build a smooth narrative. The picture of the apostles in debate leads easily to the next development: contentiousness.

d. *Section 4. Problems: Especially Contentiousness, Division, and Worldliness (1 Corinthians 11.16-19 and 11.30-32; Luke 22.24-27)*
In the context of the eucharist, Paul focuses on problems at two main points: near the beginning when he refers to contentiousness, aggravation, and division (1 Cor. 11.16-19); and now, in the aftermath of condemning the unworthy eater (11.30-32). He evokes people who are variously laid low ('weak/sick, ill, sleeping/dead') and speaks of the need not to be like the world ('that we may not be condemned with the world').

In reworking these two problem-related texts, Luke conflates them, and thus concentrates most of the problems into a single brief scene of the disciples debating about who is greatest (Lk. 22.24-27). Without attempting to trace all the details of Luke's adaptation, it is possible to indicate some main correspondences:

- Contentious/contentiousness (*philoneikos*, 1 Cor. 11.16; *philoneikia*, Lk. 22.24). Neither of these words occurs elsewhere in the New Testament.
- The Corinthian tendency, when people are together, to become *worse* (rather than *better*, 1 Cor. 11.17) seems partly reflected in the way the apostles' discussion leads to a focus on who is *greater*. In both texts this slide towards trouble ('worse',

'greater') is offset implicitly by setting the negativity with the framework of two opposing comparative adjectives ('better', 'younger'): not better but worse (1 Cor. 11.17); not so, but let the greater be like the younger (Lk. 22.26a).

Two elements are particularly elusive:
- The Corinthian tendency towards divisions and factions (1 Cor. 11.18-19) may, perhaps, be part of the background for Luke's contrasting picture of leaders as servants (Lk. 22.26b). Divisions are generally led by people who set themselves above others. One of the opposites for such a leader is a servant.
- Likewise Paul's reference to peoples as variously laid low—weak/sick, ill, asleep/dead (1 Cor. 11.30)—may, perhaps, be part of the background for Luke's contrast between the servant and the one who is reclining (22.27).

The need to be unlike the world, to avoid being judged with the world (1 Cor. 11.32), finds a fairly elaborate counterpart in Luke's reference to the need to be unlike the kings of the nations (22.26). Luke has kept the basic idea of being unlike the world, but he again employs the imagery of kings and kingdoms. And instead of being focused towards the end—judgment—he is focused towards conduct here and now, towards an ongoing, historical quality. While Paul sets this contrast with the world in a part of his text that is climactic and final, Luke uses it in an opposite but complementary way: as a beginning, the beginning of Jesus' brief speech.

Paul's brief reference to self-judgment (1 Cor. 11.31) apparently has been conflated with other parts of Luke—with the apostles' debate among themselves (Lk. 22.23) and with the final emphasis on judgment (Luke 30).

The overall impression concerning the presentation of the problems is that Luke has rendered Paul's many diverse images into a form that is simpler, clearer, and more vivid.

e. Section 5. Conclusion: Solidarity (Waiting/Staying), and Eating in a Way that Avoids Condemnation (1 Corinthians 11.33-34; Luke 22.28-30)
Paul finally goes on to call for solidarity in waiting (that brothers wait for each other in eating, 1 Cor. 11.33), and Luke also gives an image of solidarity in staying, namely staying with Jesus in his temptations (22.28). Then, while Paul speaks of eating so as to avoid condemnation (1 Cor. 11.34), Luke shows eating and the avoidance of condemnation as occurring in a kingdom: in the kingdom the apostles eat, and, far from being condemned, they are the judges (22.29-30). In other words, the picture of eating and escaping judgment (Paul) is adapted to become a picture of eating and judging (Luke).

2. Conclusion

There are many clear differences between the two supper accounts (1 Cor. 11.16-34; Lk. 22.14-30). Yet there are also strong reasons for seeing a literary link between the two texts.

First, there is the extrinsic plausibility: Luke, as someone interested in sources, the early church, and Paul, could have sought access to a copy of 1 Corinthians. Given the ease of first-century communications, acquiring such a copy would have been relatively easy.

Second, there are the consistent similarities. Both texts deal not only with the same broad theme, but also with several of the same specific motifs. Furthermore, they do this with completeness: for every significant portion of the Pauline text there is a corresponding feature in Luke. In addition, they essentially follow the same order. As indicated earlier, the chance that five elements will occur in the same order in two unrelated texts is less than one in a hundred. Variations of order, when they occur in the supper texts, are minor, yet precise. Finally, there are several correspondences of detail.

Third, there is the intelligibility of the differences. The idea of transforming an existing text—however alien to modern procedure—finds plausibility in the context of literary imitation and theological redesigning. The imitator could change the earlier text and also vary the modes of transformation. On the one hand, Luke's verbatim similarity concerning the words of institution corresponds to what has been called the 'sacramental' mode of imitation. On the other hand, the major differences in describing the larger supper scene correspond to the need to adapt the rather negative Corinthian account to the context of the life of Jesus and to Luke's general practice of setting out a positive vivid ideal.

In the end, there are two possible explanations of the data: either an extraordinary series of coincidences, or, more simply, that Luke the *littérateur* used a literary method; in other words, the chronicler of the church and of Paul used one of Paul's letters to a church. It is reasonable, then, to conclude that the Corinthian account constituted one of Luke's sources, and provided him with one component for his gospel account of the last supper.

Luke's use of the supper text is not an isolated phenomenon. There is evidence that Proto-Luke also uses the rest 1 Corinthians (see Appendix 2). Taken together these links indicate that Proto-Luke's systematic approach to sources is not limited to the Septuagint. It applies also to at least one major epistle.

Orientational Conclusion to Chapters 10–14:
The Nature of Proto-Luke

The central thesis of this volume, summarized in Chapter 10, maintains that Proto-Luke, while expressing its Christian vision, draws *directly* on the Septuagint, particularly on the Elijah–Elisha narrative and structure. Thus, what is generally said of Luke–Acts as a whole—that it is a continuation of the Septuagint—applies even more strongly to Proto-Luke.

The auxiliary thesis—concerning continuity between Matthew's *Logia*, 1 Corinthians, and Proto-Luke—confirms and complements Proto-Luke's relationship to the Old Testament. The epistle (1 Corinthians) reflects contemporary Corinth, but it is so strongly indebted to the Torah—and to some degree to the Deuteronomy-based *Logia*—that Proto-Luke's use of it brings further, *indirect* continuity with the Old Testament.

Thus the theses converge: Proto-Luke uses the Old Testament directly; and by absorbing New Testament writings that have a strong Old Testament base, he also draws on the Old Testament indirectly.

The diversity of Proto-Luke's methods of adaptation (mentioned in Chapter 10) is confirmed by his reworking of the supper text from 1 Corinthians.

However, these diverse methods are not only confirmed; they are also given a new application, namely to New Testament material. The transformations wrought on the old Scriptures, may also be wrought on documents that are new, even on a major epistle bearing the name of Paul. This development, the radical reshaping of New Testament material, clarifies further the nature of Proto-Luke.

It also sets the scene for how Proto-Luke itself will be transformed.

Unit 3. The Central Thesis Expanded: Mark

Orientational Introduction to Chapters 15–18

Once Proto-Luke is in place—Proto-Luke itself as well as its dependence on both the Old Testament and an epistle—the question of Mark's origin becomes less elusive. It emerges that all three sources—Proto-Luke, the Old Testament (especially the Elijah–Elisha narrative), and the epistles—have been used in Mark's composition. This does not mean that they explain Mark fully; they are simply components, yet their role is important. A treatment of that role occupies four chapters of the present study, as follows:

Chapter 15: Mark's Sources: The Elijah–Elisha Narrative.
Chapter 16: Mark's Sources: Mark and Proto-Luke—An Overview.
Chapter 17: Mark's Sources: Mark and Proto-Luke, Episode by Episode—One Component, Not a Systematic Proof.
Chapter 18: Mark's Sources: Mark and the Epistles—Peter's Central Maxims (1 Peter 2.18–3.17) as One Component of Mark 10.1-45: An Exploration.

15

Mark's Sources:
The Elijah–Elisha Narrative

1. *The Quest for Mark's Origin*

The quest for the origin of Mark's gospel has been long and complex. Originally, the gospel bore no name; 'According to Mark' was attached in the second century. The name connects with New Testament references to Mark (1 Pet. 5.13) and John Mark (Acts 12.12, 25; 13.5-13; 15.37-39; Col. 4.10; Phlm. 24; 2 Tim. 4.11).

There is no tradition that Mark knew Jesus; so Mark—presuming Mark really was the author's name—apparently relied on other sources. There is an ancient claim (by second-century Papias, recorded by Eusebius, *Historia ecclesiastica* 3.39.15) that Mark learned from Peter, and there have been modern claims that he used oral tradition or a non-extant earlier gospel.[1] But these claims to oral tradition or a non-extant gospel, however plausible at first sight, are unverifiable. One cannot check on a distant tradition that is purely oral or on a gospel that is not extant. It is better, therefore, at least in the short term, to concentrate on verifiable written sources.

The radical difference between invoking Proto-Luke and invoking a non-extant earlier gospel is that the actual text of Proto-Luke is extant—at least insofar as every word of it has been preserved within the present Luke–Acts—and, above all, that its shape is verifiable. As proposed here, it is not something vague or lost; it is a specific part of Luke–Acts. Its crucial septuagintal background is identifiable, as is its precise diptych structure.

Before discussing Mark's sources, it is appropriate, in accordance with a hermeneutical circle in which diverse issues illuminate one another, to summarize basic aspects of the finished work—its theological vision, and genre.

2. *Mark's Theological Vision*

In Mark's view—Mark's theological vision—reality is bubbling. It is not flat or dead. God is not flat; nor is God's Son, Jesus; nor are Jesus' followers, the disciples. All three—God, Jesus, and the disciples—have a rich complexity, one flowing into the other, and the life which bubbles forth is ultimately that of God's Spirit.

Mark's primary emphasis is on *God*, or at least on God's kingdom, an immense power, positive but mysterious/secret, which is breaking forth into history—into history's ills of mind and body, even into history's convulsions and deaths.

Like God's kingdom, God's Son, Jesus, too, has great authority, but again it is mysterious so that his true identity as God's anointed (Messiah) is sometimes revealed. But often, Jesus retains that identity as something that generally speaking, is hidden—secret.

Finally, the disciples also are complex. First, they follow with enthusiasm; then, particularly as death looms, they lose their way, falling even into denial; and finally, after

---

1. For a review, see Trocmé 1975: 11-31; cf. Wenham 1984: 369; Telford 1995: 53-56; Boismard 1994.

tears of repentance, they get another chance, based this time on a new form of life—the resurrection.

The overall portrait—of God, Jesus, and the disciples—shows human history as a place of great depth. To some degree, another feature of Mark, a multi-faceted literary duality (Neirynck 1988a), may, perhaps, be a reflection of the complexity of the gospel's theological vision; the literary duality indicates theological reality—the overall depth of things. Be that as it may, for Mark, history has an explosive depth that is essentially positive, God-based.

This overall picture—history as something bubbling with an extra dimension—is the precise opposite of Toynbee's oft-cited definition: history is 'one damn thing after another'. The modern historian, quite appropriately, is on another level, not Mark's visionary level, but the level of seeing a flat sequence of events.

Occasionally the two approaches—visionary depth and modern historical flatness—have become confused. Wrede (1971), for instance, seeing the account of Jesus' half-revealed secret, reconstructed a flat history about Jesus: essentially, in Jesus' historical life, there was nothing to reveal. And other historians reconstructed a similarly flat view of the disciples: Mark wanted to show them as negative. Thus the richness of Jesus' inner secret is reduced to nothing. And there is an equal reduction of the richness of the disciples' repentance and resurrection-based new beginning. Such reductionism is like reading Ezekiel's opening vision as a guide to animal anatomy.

Despite the flattening effect of some modern history-writing, what is important is that Mark's gospel is brimming with an extra dimension: historical reality is alive—in God's kingdom, in God's Son (Jesus), and, despite sinfulness, in Jesus' disciples.

The richness of Mark's vision—dealing with more than flat history—provides a context not only for the richness of the gospel's components, but also for the freedom with which Mark handles history; the freedom, for instance, with which he reshapes the Old Testament and Proto-Luke. If Mark were primarily interested in maintaining a storyline or a historical account, then he would have reproduced far more of Proto-Luke's storyline. But precisely because he has a whole other interest in revealing a visionary depth—one which modern historians as such do not seek—then he reshapes existing narratives in order to express that vision.

3. *Genre*

Mark's theological vision helps to make the gospel what it is—to define its genre. While the vexed issue of genre is still not fully resolved,[2] the best overall approach allows role for both apocalyptic/eschatological history (Yarbro Collins 1992: 27, 34; cf. Robbins 1994: 115), and for some form of biography.[3] Apocalyptic history sees reality, especially the course of history, as dominated ultimately by God's presence and purpose—elusive but powerful. And biography captures the fact that Mark's portrayal of history is not carried out through visions of succeeding empires—as in Daniel, for instance—but primarily through the picture of one person, Jesus.

Mark's biographical aspect gives his gospel affinity with Greco-Roman biography, but the affinity is limited. Mark's biographical presentation is primarily governed not by a desire to detail a specific life, nor even by the desire to provide a model of virtue (to write an aretology), but, in accordance with his theological vision, to portray the most basic reality of history—the multi-faceted inbreaking of God's kingdom, God's word. Thus,

---

2. For discussion, see especially Telford 1995: 94-100; Yarbro Collins 1992: 1-38.
3. Burridge 1992: 258; Bryan 1993: 9-64. Mark's sources may also include Homer (McDonald 2000).

Mark introduces Jesus not with details of his background and birth, but by emphasizing that this life, this biography, is governed by factors which are beyond biography—by God's angel and prophetic word (Mk 1.1-2).

This summary of genre provides part of the context for the discussion of sources; and in turn the discernment of sources helps to clarify the issue of genre.

4. *Mark and the Old Testament, Especially the Elijah–Elisha Narrative (1 Kings 16.29–2 Kings 13)*

The Old Testament provides Mark with a broad literary starting-point. This is the mountain from which he quarried the foundation of his gospel. Mark's first word, *archē* ('beginning') is essentially the same as that of the Septuagint (Gen. 1.1). His rootedness in the Old Testament is indicated explicitly by immediately invoking Isaiah. Yet his use of scripture is not simple. The words attributed to Isaiah (Mk 1.2-3) are a synthesis of two passages from either end of the prophetic corpus: from Isaiah 40, and from Malachi 3 about sending a messenger ('Behold, I send my messenger...', Mal. 3.1). This synthesis of diverse books provides a first minimal clue to Mark's use of the old writings.[4]

Mark reflects virtually the whole range of Old Testament narrative (see especially Swartley 1994: 48-60, 96-115, 157-70, 203-15), but among these scriptures he gives a special role to the Elijah–Elisha narrative. As in the case of Proto-Luke, this procedure is understandable: the Elijah–Elisha is an interpretive synthesis for virtually the whole Primary History (Genesis–Kings) and therefore it makes sense, if one is engaging that History to take account of an earlier interpretation. The Elijah–Elisha text is like a lens, or a foundational model, through which to engage both the Primary History and other sources (Brodie 2000: especially 86-95).

The connections between Mark and the Elijah–Elisha narrative are multifaceted: genre, overall length, length of episodes, key connections, and finally, location and geographical structure.

a. *Genre*

As seen above, Mark's genre is best seen as mystery-filled history (apocalyptic history) expressed through biography. This combination of history with biography establishes a basic affinity with the Elijah–Elisha narrative.

The Elijah–Elisha narrative is itself a blending of history and biography. On the one hand it synthesizes the whole sweep of history from creation to the fall of Jerusalem, and it does so in a way which emphasizes the presence in history of a powerfully revealing divine word. Thus, history is revelatory, apocalyptic. (The mode of apocalyptic expression is not quite the same as in Daniel, but the basic portrayal of history as pervaded by a revelatory word is already present.)

On the other hand, the Elijah–Elisha narrative is also biographical. The flow of the Primary History is rendered into a form which places primary emphasis not on those who are usually regarded as history-making (kings and armies), but on two prophetic figures who are portrayed in a way that is significantly like biography. As in Mark, biography is placed at the service of history. In short, the genre of the Elijah–Elisha narrative provides a partial precedent for the genre of Mark.

---

4.   For a survey of Mark and the Old Testament, see Watts 1997: 9-28. Mark's prologue may seem less formal than that of the other evangelists, yet it fits a broad pattern: all four gospels have prologues which correspond to Greco-Roman convention (Hooker 1993: 18-28).

b. *Overall Length*

Mark is so familiar to most readers that its basic features are taken for granted. One such feature is its length; one almost presumes that this gospel has to be more or less the length it is.

But the size of histories and biographies can vary enormously. The histories of Herodotus and Thucydides, for instance, constitute extensive books (four hundred pages or more). The biblical histories of Moses and David are also very lengthy. Mark, however, is quite brief. The question arises, purely on the question of length, as to what model was used by Mark.

In so far as it is biographical, Mark might have been inspired by Greco-Roman biographies. But here, too, it is not clear what the model might have been. Xenophon's life of Socrates (*Memorabilia*) and Philo's *Life of Moses* are both quite extensive (each over a hundred full pages). Other biographies are closer to Mark's size. Those of Plutarch (c. 50–120 CE), for instance, were sometimes quite brief: he devotes about one hundred pages to Alexander, but only about thirty to Demosthenes.

In view of the great variety in the size of ancient histories and biographies, it is striking that Mark's gospel, with just sixteen chapters, is so close to the length of the Elijah–Elisha narrative, which is just over nineteen chapters (and part of those nineteen consists of formulaic padding, e.g. 2 Kgs 8.16-29; 13.1-13). Thus, in searching among ancient histories and biographies for a possible model for the length of Mark's gospel, the Elijah–Elisha narrative has a significant claim.

c. *Length of Episodes*

What is true of Mark as a whole is also true of its individual episodes. Their length, including their variations in length, is significantly close to the length of the episodes in the Elijah–Elisha narrative. Furthermore, the way in which Mark's episodes are connected—first poorly (the text is episodic), then more continuously—finds a partial precedent in the Elijah–Elisha narrative. Despite their episodic beginnings, both Mark and the Elijah–Elisha narrative conclude with continuous or near-continuous accounts of about five chapters: the traumatic Jehu–Athaliah sequence with its positive ending in the figure of Joash (2 Kgs 9–12; or 9–13); and Mark's sequence of passion and resurrection (Mk 11–16).

This progression from episodic to continuous is not linear; it is not just one straight process; rather it spirals. First, there is a gradual progression to fairly long episodes (cf. 1 Kgs 17–22; Mk 1–5); and then both texts seem to start again: to some degree they return to short episodes (e.g. 2 Kgs 2.19-22, 23-25; 4.1-7, 38-41, 42-44; Mk 6.45-52, 53-56; 7.24-30, 31-37; 8.1-10). Then these relatively short episodes give way to greater continuity; and eventually both texts expand into their respective long continuous conclusions (2 Kgs 9–13; Mk 11–16).

d. *Key Connections: Beginning, Middle, and End*

If one's research is to have an anchor amid the immense complexity of the full relationship between Mark and Old Testament narrative, it is important to focus on certain key areas. In ancient texts the key areas consisted of the beginning, middle, and end (Robbins 1996: 50-53). Like the pillars of a bridge, these three points helped carry the text.

In asking about a possible relationship between Mark and the Elijah–Elisha narrative, it is appropriate to pay special attention to these three areas. The beginning, middle, and end of Mark all show strong connections with the Elijah–Elisha narrative (for greater detail, see Chapter 5 of Brodie 2000; Gerhard Dautzenberg 1992).

15. The Elijah–Elisha Narrative 151

(1) *The beginning*. Mark's opening quotation about a messenger refers in effect to Elijah (Mk 1.2; cf. Mal. 3.1, 23). Likewise, Mark's opening episodes (1.1-20) have clear echoes of Elijah (1 Kgs 17.3, 6; 19.4-8, 19-21; 2 Kgs 1.8): the abruptness of the beginning; the wilderness; the Jordan; Elijah's appearance (cf. John); the ravens (cf. the animals in the desert); the angels; and the abrupt calling to discipleship. In this latter case—the call of the disciple/s (1 Kgs 19.19-21; Mk 1.16-20)—Jesus' call uses Elijah's call of Elisha; but Mark both simplifies and doubles the older account—building a text which has added clarity and momentum.

Still within Mark 1, the account of Jesus' healing of the leper (Mk 1.40-45) constitutes an event that in the entire Old Testament is virtually without precedent, except for the long drama of how Elisha's healed Naaman (2 Kgs 5). Mark's account is relatively brief, yet it contains similarities to 2 Kings 5 including the following: the leper takes the initiative, moving towards Elisha/Jesus; there is a question of the healer extending his hand; the cleansing of the leprosy is immediate; and there is a subsequent reference to worship (to a temple or priest).

(2) *The middle*. Mark's central episode—the transfiguration on the high mountain—has several connections with the center of the Elijah–Elisha narrative: the coming down of heavenly fire on a mountaintop (2 Kgs 1) and Elijah's fiery ascent to heaven (2 Kgs 2). One mountaintop scene is of heavenly fire (Elijah), the other of unearthly light (Mark). The Elijah–Mark connection is not only implied; it is explicit. The transfiguration and its ensuing discussion uses Elijah's name five times (Mk 9.4-13).

Furthermore, while the larger central section of Mark (especially 6.14–9.13) is largely dominated by the two accounts of the multiplication of the loaves (6.30-44; 8.1-10), the single clearest Old Testament precedent for such multiplication consists of the multiplication of loaves by Elisha (2 Kgs 4.42-44, next to the Naaman account).

Altogether, Mk 6.14–9.13 clearly echoes Elijah or Elisha several times: Herod and the opinion that John is Elijah (6.15); the miracles of the loaves (6.30-44; 8.1-10); the opinion that Jesus is Elijah (8.28); the five references during and after the transfiguration (9.4-5, 12-13). In the course of these references, Elijah's name is used seven times.

(3) *The end*. The manner of Mark's ending—abrupt and enigmatic (16.8)—partly corresponds to the end of the Elijah–Elisha narrative, particularly to the abrupt and enigmatic account of Elisha's death and burial, including the dead man's rising to life (2 Kgs 13.21). Even Mark's picture of the frightened women fleeing from the tomb is partly matched by the apparent fright of the pall-bearers and by their implied flight from the tomb of Elisha.

Furthermore, after Jesus' dying cry, '*Eloi, Eloi…*', there are two explicit references to Elijah (Mk 15.35-36) (see Dautzenberg 1992: 1088-1091).

These final details, however, are but part of a larger general similarity, noted earlier, between the continuity of Mark's long passion story (Mk 11–16) and the continuity at the end of the Elijah–Elisha narrative (2 Kgs 9–13). Within these final chapters are further connections. In particular, both narratives focus on the temple/s. The Jehu–Athaliah story (2 Kgs 9–12) is ultimately focused on some form of temple story: Jehu's high point is the terrible purging of the temple of Baal (2 Kgs 10.18-27); and Athaliah's takeover eventually centers on the temple in Jerusalem—on its takeover and renewal (2 Kgs 11–12). Despite being vastly different, Mk 11–15 does likewise; it focuses on the temple. The climax of Jesus' arrival in Jerusalem is the cleansing of the temple (Mk 11). Later, there are other temple-related events: Jesus teaches in the temple (12.35-40); Jesus speaks of the temple's impending destruction (13.1-4); the temple is an issue at his trial (14.57-58); at Jesus' death, the temple veil is sundered (15.38).

These final chapters (2 Kgs 9–13; Mk 11–16) also contain further broad similarities, including the following: anointing and conspiracy (2 Kgs 9.1-11; Mk 14.1-14); accession, with cheering, and cloaks on the ground (2 Kgs 9.12-13; Mk 11.7-10); an apparent wait before taking over (2 Kgs 9.14-21; Mk 11.11); challenging the authorities (2 Kgs 9.22–10.27; Mk 11.12–12.12); and giving money for the temple (2 Kgs 12.5-17; Mk 12.41-44).

Overall, therefore, the literary relationship is a mixture of strong differences and striking similarities. Mark is indeed radically different. The military and political aspects of the Old Testament account, instead of dominating as they do in the Old Testament, have been transformed. On the other hand, the similarities go far beyond the range of coincidence. Jehu's accession to power, especially his purging of the Baalite temple, has contributed one component to Mark's account of the cleansing of the temple. The essence of the Old Testament text has not been lost. From the point of view of prophecy, the primary purpose of anointing Jehu was religious, and in Mark's account of cleansing the temple, that purpose is maintained. The result of omitting the gory Old Testament details is not to destroy the prophetic text, but to bring out its purpose more clearly.

e. *Location and Geographic Structure*

Unlike the other evangelists, especially Luke and John, Mark's geographic structure is relatively simple, consisting of a basic north-to-south movement: Jesus moves from Galilee to Jerusalem.

This north–south structure corresponds significantly to the general structure of the Elijah–Elisha narrative. Elijah and Elisha work in (northern) Israel, but, as the narrative nears its end, the focus switches to Jerusalem and the temple (2 Kgs 11–12).

In both texts, however, there are complications. Stepping outside the basic north–south movement, Jesus sometimes goes elsewhere, particularly at the three key points:

Beginning:	The wilderness and the Jordan (Mk 1.9)
Center:	Tyre and Sidon (7.24, 31)
End:	Galilee (16.7)

The Elijah/Elisha complications also occur particularly at the three key points:

Beginning:	Elijah is east of the Jordan and in Sidon (1 Kgs 17.2-10)
Center:	Elijah is at the Jordan (2 Kgs 2)
End:	Elisha apparently faces east and Damascus (2 Kgs 13.17)

Without trying to unravel all the details, it is clear that even in the complications, there is some affinity. In general, therefore, the Elijah–Elisha narrative provides a partial precedent for Mark's geographic pattern.

5. *Conclusion*

There are several basic affinities between the Elijah–Elisha narrative and Mark: genre (mixing history and biography); overall length; length of episodes; the content of the three key points; and the geographic pattern. Even where Mark's genre is rather different from that of the Elijah–Elisha narrative—he lays greater emphasis on biography—he is continuing the trend already established by the Elijah–Elisha narrative itself when it first interpreted the Primary History through a largely biographical form.

Taken as a whole, the case for Mark's use of the Elijah–Elisha narrative is strong. First, given Mark's general engagement with the Old Testament, his use of the Elijah–Elisha narrative is eminently plausible. Second, his similarities with the prophetic narrative are significant and consistent, particularly at the three most decisive points: the beginning, middle, and end. And the differences, though great, are intelligible. For instance, it is appropriate in a life of Jesus that the cleansing of the temple—no matter how inspired by the Jehu–Athaliah story—be carried out not with the blood of others, but in a way that clarifies the religious purpose.

It is reasonable to conclude that in using literary models, Mark drew on the Elijah–Elisha narrative, on the succinct interpretive synthesis which culminates the scriptures' greatest history. No other explanation accounts so well for the data.

16

Mark's Sources: Mark and Proto-Luke—An Overview

Mark used not only the old Elijah–Elisha narrative; he also used its literary descendant—Proto-Luke. Proto-Luke supplied the basics of the story of Jesus, particularly the beginning, middle and end: at the beginning, the preparatory preaching of John the Baptist; at the centre, emphasis on the transcendental (especially assumption in Proto-Luke, and transfiguration in Mark); and at the end, Jesus' death-and-resurrection.

Yet Mark is very different from Proto-Luke. It has its own spirit-filled theological vision, and a literary form closer to biography (see Chapter 15). So—while his beginning, middle, and end secure basic continuity—his larger text rethinks the whole Proto-Lukan account. His adaptation is thorough. It is influenced not only by a partial return to the form of the Elijah–Elisha narrative, but also by other factors. Among these factors, three are particularly important: adapting Acts 1.1–15.35 to biography (to the life of Jesus), emphasizing spirit, and adapting to the requirements of narrative continuity.

1. *Adapting Acts to Biography*

In reshaping the plot of Proto-Luke, Mark's greatest change was to adapt Acts 1.1–15.35 to biography—to an account of the life of Jesus. The basic principle is not strange to New Testament research. Scholars generally agree that the history of the early church is reflected in the gospel accounts of Jesus' life. Mark followed that principle, but in a literary way. He adapted the history of the church *as told in Acts* to his account of the life of Jesus.

At times, this is relatively easy to visualize. There is a clear thematic connection, for instance, between the Jerusalem council's debate of Jewish practices (Acts 15.1-11) and Jesus' evaluation of Jewish practices (Mk 7.1-23). It is plausible that when formulating Jesus' evaluation, Mark took account of traditions such as those of the Jerusalem council.

At other times the adaptation seems far-fetched, at least by the standards of much modern reporting or writing. For instance, the account (Acts 12) of the persecution of the church by Herod (King Herod Agrippa I, 37-44 CE), has been used by Mark as one component in describing how another Herod (Tetrarch Herod Antipas, 4 BCE–39 CE), killed John the Baptist (Mk 6.14-29). Apart from the fact that the two Herods are different people, the initial sense of the two accounts (Acts 12 and Mk 6.14-29) is diverse: Acts 12 is largely about a prisoner, Peter, who escaped, while Mk 6.14-29 is largely about a prisoner who was killed.

Yet Mark apparently felt it was appropriate to shift actions about, whether from one character to another (the two Herods), or from one outcome to another (escaping; being killed). Such procedures were accepted in ancient writing practices (see Chapter 1), and despite the changes, Mark was developing the tradition, not rejecting it. Herod's persecution (Acts 12), directed toward James the brother of John and towards Peter, illustrates what the disciples have to suffer. And Mark keeps that message: 'By sandwiching these [Herod] stories in between the material about the disciples, Mark has indicated what discipleship may finally cost' (D. Harrington 1990: 41).

A further example occurs in Mark's use of the preaching to the Gentiles (Acts 9.32–15.35): Mark turns this long account around to help form the portrayal of Jesus' preaching in Galilee (Mk 2–7)—'Galilee of the Gentiles' as Matthew will explain (Mt. 4.15, adapting Isa. 8.23). For instance, the picture of Peter on the roof in Jaffa when he saw heaven opened and a heavily laden sheet being let down by the four corners (Acts 10.9-12) has been used to describe how, as Jesus was preaching, four men opened the roof and let down a paralytic (Mk 2.3-4). The purpose in both cases is to describe a break from set ways of thinking: Peter is asked to embrace a more universal sense of God's presence in dealing with both food and people (Peter has reached the sea and will soon come to Cornelius, Acts 10.6); in Mark, Jesus brings a challenging sense of God's grace (forgiveness, healing), then moves to the sea and eats with sinners (Mk 2.5-17). In other words, the church's breakthrough in dealing with outsiders—something criticized by Jews in Jerusalem (Acts 11.2)—has become a breakthrough in Jesus' conduct, particularly in his dealing with all kinds of outsiders (Mk 2.1-17). The principle of accepting outsiders, which is thought through so carefully in Acts 10–11, is applied in Mark with energy and innovation.

Mark's adaptations include a variation in structure. Proto-Luke had emphasized the center: he had used the crossing point between the two parts of his double account—the resurrection and assumption/ascension—to highlight the transcendent. Essentially Mark does likewise: he places the most dramatic manifestation of the transcendent at the center of his text—in the transfiguration (Mk 9.2-8), an event which leads to a form of raising the dead (Mk 9.26-27). Thus the transcendent is still at the center, but in a form suitable to a narrative that is more like a biography.

2. *Emphasizing Spirit*

The moving of the Spirit-led mission of the disciples back into the life of Jesus has contributed to another major change by Mark—an emphasis on spirit in the the life of Jesus. Where Proto-Luke had spoken of the Holy Spirit, Mark goes a stage further. He depicts something of the deeper domain in which the Holy Spirit works—the world of spirits and demons.

As a further element of this strange world of spirit, Mark also depicts a sense of mystery or secrecy—a sense which is found in a special way at the beginning, middle, and end of the gospel. At the beginning, this sense of mystery/secrecy is present both in the suggestion of the holy which so surrounds John that he is unworthy even to open Jesus' sandal straps, and also in the baptism (1.1-11). At the center, the transfiguration leaves the disciples not knowing what to say (9.2-8). And at the end, Jesus' death evokes a sense of God, and his resurrection leaves the women overcome (15.39; 16.1-8).

As well as being something which is outside (something by which people are surrounded), this mystery is also something within—most clearly within Jesus. Jesus carries and reflects the whole mystery. The fact that he commands silence about his identity (1.25, 34, 44) does not have to be explained by a fragile historical conjecture (such as Wrede used). The silence is part of a much larger phenomenon—historical and theological—concerning the gradual revelation of the divine secret or mystery (see Eph. 1–3, especially 3.5) (Quesnell 1969: 188-89).

By moving the emphasis towards the exploration of this vast, unseen world of spirit and mystery, Mark transforms the work of Proto-Luke. For instance, Proto-Luke's account of Jesus' first miracle, the healing of the centurion's servant (Lk. 7.1-10), shows how, through the extraordinary authority of his word, Jesus can heal. When Mark describes Jesus' first miracle, he retains aspects of first miracle in Proto-Luke, including the centrality of Jesus' authority, but he leaves aside much of the external centurion-related drama and shows Jesus' authority as focused on a different object, on an unclean spirit (Mk 1.21-28).

And so on. Mark retains pictures of Jesus as healing, but he consistently downplays many of Luke's preferred interests in order to portray the elusive world of mysterious spirit and the disciples' difficulty in grasping it.

John's gospel will recast the story of Jesus yet further so as to portray more probingly the mysterious world of the spirit/Spirit, particularly insofar as that spirit/Spirit works within the life of the disciples, yet that central theological and spiritual quest is already at work in Mark.

3. Narrative Continuity

These basic changes—adapting Acts to biography, and emphasizing Spirit—meant that Mark was involved in the construction of a new narrative, one which would make its own requirements and which would further effect the adaptation of Proto-Luke.

For instance, it is common in Mark to do things by threes. Thus, as noted in discussing the emphasis on spirit, the sense of an awesome divine presence is repeated three times in Mark: the awesomeness of God's coming (1.1-11), of the transfiguration (9.2-8), and of the death-and-resurrection (15.39; 16.1-8).

There is another pivotal triad of texts dealing with the relationship between Jesus' saving death and the quality of discipleship (particularly shared discipleship—community). These occur in connection with the three passion predictions. Each passion prediction introduces a discussion of discipleship and of some aspect of community (8.31–9.1; 9.30-50; 10.32-52).

There are also three accounts of a woman and a daughter: the haemorrhaging woman and the daughter of Jairus (5.21-43), Herodias and her daughter (6.14-29), and the Syrophoenician woman and her daughter (7.23-30).

So when Mark is adapting an episode from Proto-Luke, apart from reflecting Mark's theological interests, the adaptation will also reflect broader narrative patterns. Hence, while the picture of Jesus as taking the road to death (Lk. 9.51) is primarily reflected in a single Markan text (the second passion prediction, 9.30), aspects of it occur in all three passion predictions (8.31; 9.30; 10.32). Proto-Luke's text has been spread out—dispersed—to suit Mark's narrative (see Table 24).

Table 24. *Proto-Luke and Mark: Initial Outline*[1]

Proto-Luke	Mark
1. Beginnings. Ministry (Lk 1.1…8.3)	Beginnings. Ministry (Mk 1)
	*** Mission to Galilee (chs. 2–7)
	** Breakthrough (8.1–9.1)
	* *Transfiguration, raising (9.2-29)*
2. Journeying (9.51…16.31)	Journeying (9.30-50)
3. Teaching, trial (chs. 16…22)	Teaching, trial (chs. 10–14)
4. Death and resurrection (23.1–24.12)	Death and resurrection (chs. 15–16)
5. * *Resurrection, ascension (Lk. 24.13–Acts 1.12)*	
6. ** Teaching, trial. Breakthrough (Acts 2–9)	
7. *** Mission to the Gentiles (Acts 9.32–15.35)	

First, the beginnings—in Table 24—have obvious affinities. A good deal of what Mark says about John the Baptist and about Jesus' first actions (Mk 1.1-16) has clear similarities

---

1. Hereafter an ellipsis (…) is used to indicate intermittent reference. Thus, for example, Proto-Luke's account of beginnings and early ministry occurs within Lk. 1.1–8.3, but it does not occupy all of it.

16. Mark and Proto-Luke: An Overview

with parts of Proto-Luke (especially Lk. 3.1-6, 10-22; 4.14-15). And in a more subtle way, Mark's first ministry-related block (1.21-45, the eventful day at Capernaum), is largely based on the first ministry-related block in Proto-Luke (7.1–8.3). Thus, Mark 1 is considerably based on the part of Proto-Luke that is spread over Lk. 1.1–8.3, especially over 3.1–8.3.

The details are not as tidy. Mark 1 also depends on some elements from later parts of Luke. But its predominant dependence is on Lk. 1.1–8.3. Such details will be dealt with, partly at least, in the discussion of specific texts.

Second, the links between Lk. 9.51–24.12 and Mark are relatively easy to see, at least in their broad outline. The picture of journeying towards death, so clear in the account of Jesus setting his face towards Jerusalem (Lk. 9.51), also occurs in Mk 9.30—but in a form adapted to his own narrative, particularly his emphasis on secrecy and his use of three inter-related passion predictions (8.31-33; 9.30-32; 10.32-34).

Third, a shift towards teaching (rather than miracle) which, within Proto-Luke, occurs around Luke 16–19, also becomes noticeable in Mark around ch. 10. The parables of Luke 16, for instance—the unjust steward (16.1-9), the rich man and Lazarus (16.19-31)—deal with aspects of possessions; and, correspondingly, the most developed passage in Mark 10 concerns a rich man and possessions (10.17-31).

Fourth, later, both Proto-Luke and Mark make a further shift from Jesus' teaching to his trial. And after that they both speak of Jesus' death and resurrection (Lk. 23.1–24.12; Mk 15–16).

Fifth, Mark's use of the middle and later part of Proto-Luke (marked with asterisks in the outline, Lk. 24.13-53; Acts 1.1–15.35) is quite difficult to analyze. Mark has made use of the post-resurrection narratives (Emmaus, the appearance to the disciples in Jerusalem, the ascension, Lk. 24.23–Acts 1.12), but instead of keeping them at the end of the story of Jesus, he places them, in transformed shape, at its center (the transfiguration and the raising of the apparently dead boy, Mk 9.2-29).

Sixth, Mark's reshaping of Acts 2–9 (2.1–9.31) needs particular attention because he uses diverse parts of it in two areas. First, he takes its sense of a breakthrough (found especially in aspects of the martyrdom of Stephen and the conversion of Paul, Acts 6–9) and uses that breakthrough to help construct the account of the breakthrough in the recognition of Jesus as the Christ-who-must-suffer (Mk 8.1–9.1).

Then he takes the rest of Acts 2–9, including parts of the Stephen and Paul stories, but especially the account of how the disciples went from teaching to trial (trial by the Jews, Acts 2–5), and he uses these teaching-and-trial episodes to develop the account of the teaching and trial of Jesus (Mk 10–14). For instance, the Jews' challenge to the authority of the disciples (Acts 4.5-7, 15-22) is adapted to become one component in the account of the Jews' challenge to the authority of Jesus (Mk 11.27-33). Mark's account of Jesus' controversies with the Jews is based partly on Proto-Luke's account of the controversies recounted in Acts 2–5. And so on.

As a result of this procedure, the account which runs from Jesus' teaching to his trial (Mk 10–14) involves a combination of two areas of Proto-Luke: the initial teaching and trial of Jesus himself (Lk. 16…22) and the subsequent teaching and trial of his disciples (Acts 2–9).

Finally, seventh, the final section of Proto-Luke—the account of how Peter and Paul brought the gospel to the Gentiles (Acts 9.32–15.35)—underlies much of the account of how Jesus brought the gospel to Galilee (Mk 2–7). In other words, the mission to the Gentiles has become the mission to Galilee ('Galilee of the Gentiles'—Mt. 4.15).

4. Conclusion

Already there are some indications that Mark's text meets the criteria for dependence:

a. *External Plausibility*

If Luke knew Mark, it is plausible that Mark knew Luke. More precisely, if Luke (author of Luke–Acts) knew the Markan gospel—as is generally accepted—it is reasonable to suggest that Mark could have had knowledge of Lukan writings.

b. *Similarities*

As illustrated in the incident of the opening on/of the roof, there are close similarities of plot and detail. And there is essential completeness: virtually all of Proto-Luke finds an equivalent in Mark.

c. *Intelligibility of the Differences*

Mark is very different from Proto-Luke, but the differences are sufficiently understandable to make the overall continuity of the two texts credible. In the scene on the roof, most of the variations are intelligible as adaptations to Mark's new setting; likewise with the emphasis on transfiguration rather than on resurrection and ascension. If, as in Proto-Luke, the transcendent highpoint was to be literally at the center of his work, and thus at the center of the biography of Jesus, then it almost had to take a form other than resurrection. Again, the difference is intelligible. The well-known principle that the gospels reflect the life of the church now receives new application: Mark's gospel reflects the life of the church—but as described by Proto-Luke. And so on: inch by inch, by staying with the texts and bearing in mind the distinctness of Mark's agenda, the differences begin to make sense. The entire exercise of discerning how Mark adapted his basic source is like a radical variation on redaction criticism.

It is therefore reasonable—despite the great amount of detail that still needs to be clarified, and despite the many aspects of Mark that remain unexplained—to consider, at least as a working hypothesis, that Mark may have used Proto-Luke. No other document comes remotely as close to explaining the emergence of Mark.

17

Mark's Sources:
Mark and Proto-Luke, Episode by Episode—
One Component, Not a Systematic Proof

Having introduced Mark's use of Proto-Luke, it is now necessary to look at the texts in more detail and systematically. However, it is important to be clear about the limits of this analysis.

One component. That is the thesis: that Proto-Luke provided just one component in the writing of Mark. This analysis, therefore, does not attempt to give a complete account of Mark's origin. Nor does it attempt to give a systematic proof of the role of that one component. Only a small percentage of the similarities between Proto-Luke and Mark are indicated, and there is little attempt to develop the proof value of such similarities. There may come a point, however, when the reader will decide that the similarities are surely significant.

The question, then, is not whether Mark has been fully explained, but whether in seeking the origin of Mark, it is necessary to take account of Proto-Luke, among other factors.

The subsequent analysis follows the seventeen sections of the accompanying outline (Table 25). For instance, section 1 concerns the beginnings, especially John the Baptist (Mk 1.1-20; see Lk. 1.1…4.15); and section 2 contains the first block describing Jesus' ministry (Mk 1.21-45; Lk. 7.1–8.3). Furthermore, to improve overall clarity of presentation, the seventeen sections are divided into four Blocks, A, B, C, and D. All divisions are pragmatic and do not necessarily reflect inherent structures. Within the outline, brackets [ ] indicate rearrangement.

Table 25. *Proto-Luke and Mark: Detailed Outline*

Proto-Luke	Mark
A. BEGINNINGS AND EARLY MINISTRY (MAINLY LUKE 1.1…8.3; MARK 1)	
1. Lk. 1.1–4.22a; 9.51-56	Mk 1.1-20
John (Lk. 1; 3.1-6, 15-18; 7.27)	John (Mk 1.1-8)
Jesus is baptized (Lk. 3.21-22)	Jesus is baptized (1.9-11)
Jesus is questioned (2.39-52)	Jesus is tempted (1.12-13)
Preaching in Galilee (4.14-21)	Preaching in Galilee (1.14-15)
Call to discipleship (9.51-56)	Call of disciples (1.16-20)
2. Lk. 7.1–8.3	Mk 1.21-45
The centurion's servant (7.1-10)	The demoniac (1.21-28)
Raises a mother's son (7.11-17)	Raises a mother-in-law (1.29-31)
Many cures; tell John (7.18-23)	Many cures; don't tell (1.32-34)
Why go to the desert? (7.24-30)	Jesus goes to the desert (1.35)
Anointing by a sinner (7.36-50)	[Anointing at Bethany, 14.3-9]
Jesus travels about (8.1-3)	Jesus travels about (1.36-39)
[Ten lepers cleansed, 17.11-19]	A leper cleansed (1.40-45)

	B. Mission to the Gentiles/to Galilee (Mainly Acts 9.32–15.35; Mark 2–7)	
3.	Acts 10.1–11.26	Mk 2.1–3.12
	Call of a Roman officer (10.1-8)	The opening of the roof (2.1-12)
	The opening of heaven (10.9-16)	Call of a tax-collector (2.13-17)
	Meeting the new (10.17-23)	Breaking with the old (2.18-22)
	In Cornelius's house (10.24-48)	In the forbidden house (2.23-28)
	The Judaizers object (11.1-18)	The Pharisees' plot (3.1-6)
	Expansion to Antioch (11.19-26)	Crowds from Tyre, Sidon (3.7-12)
4.	Acts 13.1–14.3 Acts 1	Mk 3.13–4.41
	Choosing two (13.1-2) The twelve (ch. 1)	Choosing twelve (3.13-19)
	Bar-Jesus (13.4-12) Mother/brothers (1.14)	Beelzebul, mother/brothers (3.20-35)
	The discourse (13.13-52)	The parables (4.1-34)
	Upheaval, Lord's signs (14.1-3)	Storm, calmed by Jesus (4.35-41)
5.	Acts 14.4-28	Mk 5
	Healing amid pagan confusion (14.4-18)	The Gerasene demoniac.
	Paul, apparently dead, rises (14.19-20)	Jairus's daughter and
	Suffering church strengthened (14.21-28)	the suffering woman,
	[Twin miracles, 9.32-43]	two interwoven miracles.
6.	Lk. 3.23-38; 4.16-22a; 10.1-11	Mk 6
	Acts 4.23-31; 5.12-16; 11.27–ch. 12	
	Genealogy, Nazareth (3.23-38; 4.16-22a)	Nazareth, family (6.1-6)
	Mission of the seventy-two (10.1-12)	Mission of twelve (6.7-13)
	Famine… (Acts 11.27-30)	Herod and John (6.14-29)
	Herod and persecution (Acts 12)	Hunger…loaves (6.30-44)
	Persecution, the Creator (Acts 4.23-31)	Walking on water (6.45-52)
	Many cures (Acts 5.12-16)	Many cures (6.53-56)
7.	Acts 15.1-35	Mk 7
	Dispute: Jewish tradition (15.1-11)	Dispute: Pharisees' tradition (7.1-23)
	Decision for the Gentiles (15.12-21)	Jesus favors the Greek woman (7.24-30)
	The word spreads far (15.22-35)	The deaf man is opened (7.31-37)
	C. Breakthrough and Manifestation of Resurrection (Mainly Acts 6–9; Luke 24.13–Acts 1.12; Mark 8.1–9.29)	
8.	Mainly Acts 6–9	Mk 8.1–9.1
	Food crisis, the Seven (Acts 6.1-7)	Hunger, (seven) loaves (8.1-10)
	Signs incur opposition (6.8-10)	Pharisees seek signs (8.11-13)
	Stubborn hearts, ears (7.51-53)	Hard hearts…ears (8.14-21)
	'Who are you, Lord?' (9.3-7)	The blind man sees (8.22-26)
	Blinded Saul sees (9.8-12, 17-18)	'Who am I?' (8.27-30)
	Saul must suffer (9.13-16)	Jesus must suffer (8.31–9.1)
9.	Lk. 24.13–Acts 1.12	Mk 9.2-29
	The ascension (Lk. 24.50-53; Acts 1.6-11)	The transfiguration (9.2-8)
	Emmaus road confusion (Lk. 24.13-16)	Mountain descent confusion (9.9-13)
	Sadness, then recognition (24.17-49)	Weak faith, then boy raised (9.14-29)
	D. The Journey to Death (Mainly Luke 9.51…24.12; Acts 2.1–9.31; Mark 9.30–16.8)	
10.	Lk. 9.51-58; 10.13-16, 20; 16.19-31; 22.24-30	Mk 9.30-50
	Setting out to Jerusalem (9.51-56)	Journeying to death (9.30-32)
	The way (9.57-58; greatness, 22.24-30)	Greatness on the way (9.33-37)
	Those not responding (10.13-16, 20)	Those not following (9.38-41)
	The rich man in torment (16.19-31)	Scandal and hell (9.42-50)

17. *Mark and Proto-Luke, Episode by Episode*   161

11.	Lk. 16.1-9; Acts 4.32–5.11; 7.1-51; 8.31-39	Mk 10.1-31
	* Riches (Lk. 16.1-9; Acts 4.32–5.11) Stephen's scripture-based view of hardheartedness (Acts 7.1-51) * Childlike Ethiopian (8.25-40)	Divorce: scripture-based view of hardheartedness (10.1-12) * Childlike kingdom (10.13-16) * The rich man (10.17-31)
12.	Lk. 22.28-30; 19.1-10	Mk 10.32-52
	You will sit on thrones (22.28-30) Zacchaeus at Jericho (Lk. 19.1-10)	Third passion prediction (10.32-34) Sitting in glory (10.35-45) Bartimaeus at Jericho (10.46-52)
13.	Lk. 22.7-13; 23.27…43; Acts 5.17-21, 26, 33	Mk 11.1-25
	Preparing Passover (Lk. 22.7-13) To Golgotha (23.27-31, 34, 40-43) Temple clash (Acts 5.17-21, 26, 33)	Preparation for Jerusalem (11.1-7) Into Jerusalem (11.8-14, 20-25) Temple cleansed (11.15-19)
14.	Acts 2.34–5.11	Mk 11.27–ch. 12
	David and Christ (Acts 2.34-36) Resurrection sermon (3.11-26) On what authority? (4.5-7, 16-22) Jesus as cornerstone (4.8-11) There is no other name (4.12-14) ? Sharing and fraud (4.32–5.11)	[David and Christ (12.35-37)] [Resurrection question (12.18-27)] On what authority? (11.27-33) Vineyard, cornerstone (12.1-12) ?? What about Caesar? (12.13-17) The great commandment (12.28-34) ?? The scribes and the widow (12.38-44)
15.	Acts 6.14; 7.47-50; 8.1-25; Lk. 17.20–18.8	Mk 13
	Temple threatened (Acts 6.14; 7.47-50) Subsequent woes (8.1-25) Coming of Son of Humanity (Lk. 17.20-37) Widow parable: pray always (18.1-8)	Temple doomed (13.1-2) Beginning of woes (13.3-13) Son of Humanity (13.14-27) Stay alert (13.28-37)
16.	Lk. 7.36-50; 22.1-30, 65-71; Acts 4.1-4; 9.1-8, 19-30	Mk 14
	Plot: kill Jesus (Lk. 22.1-6) Sinner's anointing (Lk. 7.36-50) Passover prepared (22.7-14) Betrayal foretold (22.21-23) The Last Supper (22.15-20) Greatness dispute (22.24-30) ? Trauma near Damascus (Acts 9.1-8) Arrest of Peter, John (Acts 4.1-4) ? Before the Sanhedrin (Lk. 22.66-71) Paul's affirmations (Acts 9.19-30)	Plot: kill Jesus (14.1-2, 10-11) Anointing at Bethany (14.3-9) Passover prepared (14.12-17) Betrayal foretold (14.18-21) The Last Supper (14.22-26) [Greatness dispute (9.33-37)] Denials foretold (14.27-31) Agony in Gethsemane (14.32-42) Arrest of Jesus (14.43-50) Young man flees (14.51) Before the Sanhedrin (14.53-65) Peter's denials (14.66-72)
17.	Lk. 23.1–24.12	Mk 15.1–16.8
	Before Pilate (23.1-5, 13-16) Barabbas; sentencing (23.18-25) Herod mocks Jesus (23.6-12) The way to Golgotha (23.26-31) Crucifixion (23.32-39) The good thief (23.40-43) The death of Jesus (23.44-49) The burial of Jesus (23.50-56) The resurrection (24.1-12)	Before Pilate (15.1-5) Barabbas; sentencing (15.6-15) Soldiers mock Jesus (15.16-20) [Entry to Jerusalem (11.11-14)] Crucifixion (15.21-32) [Fig tree (11.20-25)] The death of Jesus (15.33-41) The burial of Jesus (15.42-47) The resurrection (16.1-8)

1. *Block A. Beginnings and Early Ministry (mainly Luke 1.1...8.3; Mark 1)*

a. *Section 1. From the Beginning to the First Calls (Mark 1.1-20; Luke 1; 2.39-52; 3.1-6, 10-22; 4.14-15; 9.51-56)*

Mark's opening is compact and swift. Having begun with a summary of John the Baptist (1.1-8), the evangelist immediately places the focus on Jesus—first on his baptism and temptation (1.8-12), and then on the Galilean preaching and the call of the first disciples (1.14-20). Within twenty verses, the gospel is poised for action.

In diverse ways, these twenty verses correspond with certain sections of Proto-Luke:

Luke	Mark
John (1; 3.1-6, 15-18; 7.27)	John (Mk 1.1-8)
Jesus is baptized (Lk. 3.21-22)	Jesus is baptized (1.9-11)
Jesus is questioned (2.39-52)	Jesus is tempted (1.12-13)
Preaching in Galilee (4.14-21)	Preaching in Galilee (1.14-15)
Call to discipleship (9.51-56)	Call of disciples (1.16-20)

In some cases, Mark's connections with Proto-Luke are obvious. The summary of John the Baptist (Mk 1.1-8) is like a synthesis of Proto-Luke's more elaborate account of John (cf. Lk. 1, especially 1.80; 3.1-6, 15-18; 7.27). The baptism account (Mk 1.9-11) is like a modification of the similar version in Lk. 3.20-21. And likewise the start of the Galilean preaching (Mk 1.9-11) is like a modification of a similar Proto-Lukan text (Lk. 3.14-15).

Less obvious are the origins of the temptation account (Mk 1.12-13) and the account of the call of the first disciples (Mk 1.16-20). Yet they, too, show connections with Proto-Luke. The temptation account, brief though it is—two verses—fulfills essentially the same function as the questioning of Jesus in the temple (Lk. 2.39-52): both texts are variations on the literary convention of the initiatory trial (cf. Alter 1981: 51). And the account of the call of the first disciples (Mk 1.16-20) is a development of the implicit calls which stress the cost of discipleship (Lk. 9.51-56).

Among the factors governing Mark's adaptations, two may be identified fairly easily. One is the aim of compactness (at least at this stage of the gospel). The other is the echoing of the Elijah–Elisha narrative. The summary of John the Baptist, with its distinctive reference to striking clothing (hair and leather, Mk 1.6), adapts the description of Elijah (2 Kgs 1.8). The temptation account, in which Jesus begins by having to go into the wilderness (Mk 1.12-13), adapts the account of how Elijah began by being sent into the wilderness to be fed by the ravens (1 Kgs 17.2-6; see also 1 Kgs 18.8; 19.4-8). And the call of the first disciples (Mk 1.16-20) adapts Elijah's call of Elisha (1 Kgs 19.19-21).

In adapting the call of Elisha, Mark makes one change that is particularly significant: whereas Elisha had been ploughing when he was called, the first disciples had been fishing.

A better sense of the detail of the texts may be seen in Table 26.

Mark's account of the call of the first four disciples (1.16-20) shows clear affinity not only with Lk. 9.57-62 and with the underlying call of Elisha (1 Kgs 19.19-21), but also with the list of the twelve as found in Acts 1.13. What is more difficult to trace is the shift from ploughing (as practiced by Elisha) to fishing (as practiced by the first four disciples). Part of the answer seems to lie with Jeremiah's prophecy of God sending fishermen who will fish the people up and thus open the way for the conversion of the nations (Jer. 16.16-21).

Table 26. *Proto-Luke and Mark: Beginnings*

John the Baptist	
See Lk. 1.1-5, especially 1.2 (see Gen. 1.1; Rom. 1.1)	The beginning (*archē*) of the gospel… (Mk 1.1)
Angels' annunciations (1.5-80) As it is written in Isaiah, A voice…crying… (3.4) Behold I send my angel… (7.27)	As it is written in Isaiah… Behold I send my angel… A voice…crying… (1.2-3)
…the word came to John …in the desert and he came to all the…Jordan heralding a baptism… (3.2-3) All wondered about him (3.15)	John was in the desert… heralding a baptism… (1.4) And all were baptized in the Jordan (1.5)
Elijah wore a hair cloak and a leather loincloth (2 Kgs 1.8)	John wore…camel hair… and a leather belt (1.6)
John replied…saying, 'I baptize you in water, but a stronger one is coming, whose sandal straps I am not… He will baptize you in the Holy Spirit…' (3.16)	He heralded saying, 'One stronger than I is coming… whose sandal straps I am not… For I baptize you in water, but he will baptize you in the Holy Spirit' (1.7-8)
The Baptism of Jesus	
In those days… (Lk. 2.1) …he came to Nazareth (2.51) The baptism of Jesus (3.21-22)	In those days… Jesus came from Nazareth… The baptism of Jesus (1.9-11)
The Initiatory Trial	
The development of John in the desert (1.80; cf. 2.39-40) The questioning of Jesus in the temple (2.41-52) Elijah in desert with ravens (1 Kgs 17.3-7), with angel (19.4-8) Spirit takes Elijah away (18.12)	The temptation/trial of Jesus in the desert: Spirit drives Jesus to desert… tempted by Satan for forty days was with the animals, and the angels served him (1.12-13)
Beginning the Galilean Preaching	
In the power of the Spirit Jesus returned to Galilee (4.14a); he taught in their synagogues… (4.15) At Nazareth: 'The Spirit anointed me to bring good news [gospel]… Today the scripture is fulfilled'	After John's betrayal Jesus came to Galilee heralding the gospel of God: 'The time is fulfilled… (4.15a, 16a, 18a, 21) the kingdom of God is near. Repent…believe the gospel' (1.14-15)
Uncompromising Calls to Discipleship	
Three uncompromising calls ('I will follow…Follow me…I will follow') (9.57-62) Elijah's call of Elisha (1 Kgs 19.19-21) Peter, John, James, Andrew (Acts 1.13) Fishermen of people (cf. Jer. 16.16?)	Two double peremptory calls ('Come after me') Simon, Andrew—brothers. James, John—brothers. The sea, fishermen, fishers of people (1.16-20)

b. *Section 2. The First Block Recounting Jesus' Ministry: From Capernaum to Travelling About (Luke 7.1–8.3; 17.11-19; Mark 1.21-45)*
Within Proto-Luke, the first major block describing the ministry of Jesus consists of Lk. 7.1–8.3—a unified text which, having told of a series of miracles (some of them for John the Baptist's encouragement, 7.1-35), then goes on to recount Jesus' anointing (by a sinful woman, 7.36-50) and his travelling about (8.1-3).

Within Mark, there is a corresponding opening block—the account of a full day's ministry at Capernaum (Mk 1.21-39)—but Mark has adapted the description of the anointing, turning it into a prelude of Jesus' passion (14.3-9). In summary outline:

Luke 7.1–8.3	Mark 1.21-39
The centurion's servant (7.1-10)	The demoniac (1.21-28)
Raises a mother's son (7.11-17)	Raises a mother-in-law (1.29-31)
Many cures; tell John (7.18-23)	Many cures; don't tell (1.32-34)
Why go to the desert? (7.24-30)	Jesus goes to the desert (1.35)
Anointing by a sinner (7.36-50)	[Anointing at Bethany (14.3-9)]
Jesus travels about (8.1-3)	Jesus travels about (1.36-39)
[Ten lepers cleansed (17.11-19)]	A leper cleansed (1.40-45)

Again, Mark is more compact, both in length and in visual imagery. Instead of a ministry which begins in Capernaum and then moves to Nain and beyond as in Luke, at this stage Mark concentrates all the initial action around Capernaum.

And in contrast to Proto-Luke, who even at this stage speaks considerably of John the Baptist (Lk. 7.18-38), Mark leaves John aside—John after all belongs to the old order—and he moves the emphasis towards those disciples, especially Peter, who represent the new form of discipleship (Mk 1.29-30, 36). Thus, while Mark will never recount the later activities and outward actions of the apostles and disciples as Proto-Luke did (in Acts 1.1–15.35), he is beginning to portray a deeper reality of discipleship—the way in which, even during Jesus' ministry, the disciples struggled, often vainly, to understand.

There is a further way in which Mark aims for greater depth. Instead of just recounting illnesses and cures, he portrays or evokes what lies beneath them—the twin realities of spirit and mystery.

Thus the first cure, for instance, that of the centurion's servant (Lk. 7.1-10), has been radically stripped down and reintegrated with other material to help form the account of the cure of the demoniac (the man with the unclean spirit, Mk 1.21-28). Both cures are set in Capernaum and both highlight Jesus' authority. But the focus of that authority has shifted—no longer the overcoming of deathly illness, as in Proto-Luke, but the overcoming of a negative spirit (an unclean spirit which, despite its knowledge of Jesus as the Holy One of God, throws the man into convulsions, Mk 1.23-26). In other words, instead of merely confounding the force of death (Proto-Luke), Jesus partly unmasks that force (Mark).

Having given an opening cure, both gospels then use it as part of a pair: they add another, shorter, miracle—the raising to life of the widow's son (Lk. 7.11-17) and the raising to health of Peter's mother-in-law (Mk 1.29-31). Jesus cures now not by sheer authority but by coming close to the one who is afflicted: he touches the stretcher (Lk. 7.14); he takes the hand of the woman who is in bed (Mk 1.31).

The essence of both of these later miracles is that they represent a greater human involvement by Jesus. The principle which had been established in the opening miracles—his supreme authority over the powers of evil—is now brought down to earth in human ways.

Table 27. *Proto-Luke and Mark: Luke 7; Mark 1. Some Details*

Healing by Authority	
Jesus went to Capernaum. [Jesus at Nazareth (Lk. 4.16, 22a)] Healing (centurion's servant) through word of authority (7.1-10) ('Do not bother... that you come to me')	Jesus journeyed to Capernaum. Entered synagogue, impressed. Healing (man with unclean spirit) by authority (1.21-28) ('What to me and to you? You have come to destroy us') * Amazed reaction (1.27-28)
Healing by Touch	
Next, at Nain, a mother's son was being carried out. City crowd. The Lord felt sorry for her, and approaching he touched the bier and said...'Arise'. And the dead man sat up, and began to talk (7.11-17) * Amazed reaction (7.16-17)	Then Peter's mother-in-law was down with a fever. They told him about her, and approaching he raised her having taken her hand. The fever left her, and she served them (1.29-31)
Healing Many	
He healed many from diseases and evil spirits... 'Go, tell John... [about] me: blind see... lepers are cleansed' (7.18-23)	City crowded around. He healed many ...with various diseases and expelled many demons. He did not allow them to speak because they knew about him (1.32-34) [Cleansing of a leper (1.40-45)]
The Desert and the Journeying	
Why go out to the desert? Summary of John's ministry, of reactions to him (7.24-35) Jesus is anointed (7.36-50) Jesus journeys about (8.1-3)	Jesus goes out to the desert. People's attitude to Jesus, and a summary of his ministry as he journeys about (1.35-39) [The Bethany anointing (14.3-9)]

Having thus illustrated the two central ingredients of miracles (divine authority and care for humanity), both gospels proceed to speak of miracles in large numbers: the many miracles which were to be recounted to John (Lk. 7.18-23), and the many miracles about which Jesus commanded silence (Mk 1.32-34). Mark has retained the report of many miracles but, as well as distilling it, has rendered it into a form which brings out the idea of silence and thus of secret or mystery.

The subsequent question about why people went out into the desert (Lk. 7.24) develops into a discussion of the larger question of the missions of John and Jesus (Lk. 7.24-35), and Mark distills this into the account of Jesus going out into the desert and then giving a summary account of his own mission ('...because that is why I have come', Mk 1.35, 38). Furthermore, within this brief desert scene (1.35-39), Mark combines the brief scene of Jesus travelling about (Lk. 8.1-3). (For some details of the texts, see Table 27.)

Apart from moving the anointing, at this point Mark generally follows the order of Proto-Luke. However, a few details have been relocated, particularly the amazed reaction

(Lk. 7.16-17; Mk 1.27-28), the city crowd (Lk. 7.11; Mk 1.33), and, to a lesser degree, the journeying about (Lk. 8.1-3; Mk 1.36-39).

In dealing with Luke's account of the amazed reaction (Lk. 7.16-17), Mark moves it forward to a leading position—from the end of the second episode to the end of the first (Mk 1.27-28). But he retains significant similarities:

Fear seized all and they praised God saying,	And all were amazed so that they discussed it with one another saying,
'A great prophet has arisen among us', and, 'God has visited his people'.	'What is this? A new teaching with authority', and, 'He commands unclean spirits and they obey him'.
And this word about him went out in all of Judea and all everywhere the surrounding countryside.	And his fame went out immediately to all the surrounding countryside of Galilee.

Attached at the end of the account of the eventful day in Capernaum is a story of how Jesus cleansed a leper (Mk 1.40-45). To some degree this is based on Lk. 7.1–8.3—it is like an illustration of Jesus' words 'lepers are cleansed' (Lk. 7.22)—but it also breaks out, as it were, and uses other texts. Among those the most obvious is Proto-Luke's account of the cleansing of ten lepers (Lk. 17.11-19), but there may be some dependence on the presentation in the temple (Lk. 2.21-38, with its ideas of purification, revelation, and struggle/suffering).

2. Block B. Mission to the Gentiles/to Galilee
(Mainly Acts 9.32–15.35; Mark 2–7)

The next five sections of Mark (sections 3–7, chs. 2–7) are inherently connected not only because they all develop the picture of Jesus' Galilean ministry, but also because they all make use of Proto-Luke's account of the mission of Peter and Paul to the Gentiles (Acts 9.31–15.35).

Presupposing the summary given earlier in Table 25 (sections 3–7), the relationship between Acts 9.31–15.35 and Mark 2–7 may now be summarized even more briefly (Table 28).

Table 28. *Proto-Luke and Mark: Acts 9.31–15.35; Mark 2–7*

Twin miracles (Acts 9.31-43)	
3. Accepting Gentiles (10.1–11.26)	Conflict with Jews (Mk 2.1–3.12)
Famine, Herod (11.27–ch. 12)	
4. Commissioning, Bar-Jesus, discourse, upheaval (13.1–14.3)	Commissioning, Beelzebul, parables, storm (3.13–4.41)
5. The confusion of the pagans; the suffering church (14.4-28)	The Gerasene demoniac; the suffering women (ch. 5) (Two interwoven miracles)
6.	Herod, hunger... (ch. 6)
7. Questioning traditions (15.1-35)	Questioning traditions (ch. 7)

This outline (Table 28) is a mere starting point. It simplifies the contents of the texts, omitting their distinguishing characteristics, and makes no reference to other Proto-Luke texts used by Mark. But during the subsequent discussion of individual sections, it provides a certain overview.

a. *Section 3. Breaking the Mold: Jesus' Message Breaks Jewish Boundaries and Reaches Outsiders (Acts 10.1–11.26; Mark 2.1–3.12)*

Having finished with the eventful day at Capernaum, Mark returns to Capernaum in 2.1 and the city acts as a point of departure for a fresh series of episodes which, while reaching out to new horizons and various kinds of outsiders, involve conflict with the Jews (2.1–3.6). At the end of the series, the Pharisees plot to destroy Jesus (3.1-6), but on the other hand great crowds follow him, crowds from as far away as Tyre and Sidon (3.7-12).

These barrier-breaking episodes are partly based on the account of how the conversion of Cornelius the centurion opened the way for outsiders, including those as far away as Antioch—even though such opening of barriers involved breaking out of some of the confines of Judaism (Acts 10.1–11.26).

In moving from one Capernaum-based series to another (from Mk 1.21-45 to Mk 2.1–3.12), Mark has also moved from Proto-Luke's first centurion-based block (Lk. 7.1–8.3) to his second (Acts 10.1–11.18). Like Capernaum, which was a border town and therefore a reminder of another, wider, world, the Roman centurions evoked the wider world of the day. There is a continuity between the two accounts of the centurions—the second (Acts 10.1–11.18) is like a variation and expansion of the first (7.1-10)—and so in moving from one to the other, Mark is responding to something inherent in Proto-Luke.

The Cornelius sequence 'comprises five scenes' (Dillon 1990: 58) and the subsequent expansion to Antioch (Acts 11.19-26) constitutes a sixth. Mark likewise has five consecutive scenes of tension-causing generosity (2.1–3.6, 'five conflict stories' [D. Harrington 1990: 14]), and the subsequent picture of the crowds (Mk 3.7-12) adds a sixth. The correspondence between these two series of episodes may be outlined as follows:

Acts 10.1–11.26	Mark 2.1–3.12
Call of a Roman officer (10.1-8)	The opening of the roof (2.1-12)
The opening of heaven (10.9-16)	Call of a tax-collector (2.13-17)
Meeting the new (10.17-23)	Breaking with the old (2.18-22)
In Cornelius's house (10.24-48)	In the forbidden house (2.23-28)
The Judaizers object (11.1-18)	The Pharisees' plot (3.1-6)
Expansion to Antioch (11.19-26)	Crowds from Tyre, Sidon (3.7-12)

Mark's compactness is not only in length (little more than half as long as Proto-Luke) but also in form: instead of giving one long five-scene sequence in which the conflict does not emerge explicitly until the final scene (until Acts 11.1-18), Mark places some aspect of the conflict within each scene. Thus, in Mark each brief scene has its own dramatic completeness. The element of conflict has been dispersed.

One of the effects of repeating the drama, and of repeating it with increasing intensity, is that in Mark's text the overall sense of conflict is much sharper.

A further effect of repeating the drama is that the conflict is more wide-ranging in Mark, or at least it engages more specific issues: the forgiving of sins (2.2-12), eating with tax-collectors and sinners (2.13-17), eating in a way which breaks with the old order (2.18-22), eating in a way which breaks the sabbath and which recalls David's unlawful entry into the house of God (2.23-28), and finally, confronting the synagogue authorities (3.1-6). While the Cornelius sequence established the basic principle of freedom from the restrictions of Judaism, Mark's five conflict stories apply that principle to particular questions.

Mark has distilled the Cornelius drama and, by adding new material, has built up a sequence which spells out some of the drama's implications. The details of Mark's reshaping are quite intricate. The outline (Table 29) is limited and sometimes tentative.

Table 29. *Proto-Luke and Mark: Acts 10.1–11.26; Mark 2.13–3.12*

The Call of the Outsider	
An angel visits Cornelius, a Roman officer. Implicitly this brings salvation to his house (Acts 10.1-8)	Jesus calls Levi, a tax-collector, and explicitly offers salvation to those in his house (2.13-17)
The Opening to Heaven	
Cornelius is an outsider but Peter on his roof sees heaven opened and 'outside' creatures being let down by four corners (10.9-16)	The house is inacessible but the roof is opened and a paralytic is let down by four men. Jesus forgives sins, raises up. Amazed reaction (2.1-12)
Meeting the New Order	
Peter worriedly tries to cope with the tradition-breaking vision and with the arrival of strangers, Gentiles (10.17-23)	The question of John and fasting gives way to perplexing images of newness: the bridegroom, the new garment, and the new wineskins (2.18-22)
From Jewish Law to the Forbidden House	
Peter goes to the house of the Gentile, Cornelius, and there asserts the primacy of humanity over rank and over Jewish laws. Peter's speech: Jesus, raised, forgives sins (10.24-48)	The disciples override Jewish sabbath laws and Jesus cites David's entry to the forbidden house, and he places humanity above sabbath law (2.23-28)
A More Direct Confrontation (Judaizers/Pharisees)	
Back in Jerusalem the Judaizers confront Peter about eating with Gentiles. Peter tells what happened. Amazed reaction (11.1-18)	In the synagogue they watch Jesus lest he heal on the sabbath. They plot to kill him (3.1-6)
Increasing Crowds, Advancing Revelation (Antioch/Tyre)	
The Stephen-related distress led to a scattering to Phoenicia, Cyprus, and Antioch, and those scattered spoke the word to Jews only. But some Cypriots and Cyrenians coming to Antioch spoke of Jesus to the Greeks, a great number.	[Following the death-plot,] Jesus and the disciples retreated to the sea and a great crowd followed him from Galilee, Judea, Jerusalem, Idumea, and beyond the Jordan, and around Tyre and Sidon, a great crowd.
This was heard in Jerusalem and they sent Barnabas...	Hearing what he did came to him...
for he was a good man and full of the Holy Spirit.	because he healed many...and the unclean spirits fell before him.
Barnabas brought Saul and they taught for a year in Antioch and there the disciples were first called 'Christians' (11.18-26)	And they cried out 'You are the Son of God' but he rebuked them greatly not to make him known (3.7-12)

The most obscure correspondence (under the heading of 'Meeting the New Order') is between Peter's worried meeting with the Gentiles (Acts 10.17-23) and the dense symbolism about the old and the new (the bridegroom, the new garment, and the new wine)

(Mk 2.18-22). Part of the correspondence may lie in the idea of obscurity itself—the idea of a mysterious transition which is not easily understood. In other words, faced with Peter's perplexity and difficulty, Mark, using other sources, produces further forms of perplexity.

At times, Mark's text constitutes a contrast with Acts. Jesus' rebuking, for instance, of those who were making him known as the Son of God (Mk 3.11-12) appears to be a reversal of the Barnabas-inspired teaching at Antioch (Acts 11.25-26), a reversal explained by Mark's theme of silence or secrecy. Furthermore, Mark concludes the first five episodes not with acceptance (the amazed reaction, about the giving of life, Acts 11.18), but, in stark contrast, with a plot to kill (Mk 3.6). This reflects the more tense mood of Mark's narrative. As for the amazed reaction, Mark moves it forward (somewhat as he moved it forward in the previous block [section 2 above—Lk. 7.16-17; Mk 1.27-28]) from the end of the fifth episode to a leading position at the end of the first:

Hearing this they were at peace,	[Seeing this] they were astounded,
and they glorified God saying,	and they glorified God saying,
'So God gives life-giving repentance even to the nations!' (11.18)	'We have never seen anything like this!' (2.12)

Mark also moves the essence of Peter's speech (concerning Jesus' power of resurrection and forgiveness, Acts 10.34-43; Mk 2.5-11) forward, and he combines it within the leading episode—with the amazed reaction.

b. *Section 4. The Commissioning, the Clash with Satan, and the Spread of the Word (Acts 13.1–14.3 [and Acts 1]; Mark 3.13–4.41)*
Having used the account of the church in Antioch (Acts 11.19-26) as one element in describing the far-flung crowds which accepted Jesus (Mk 3.7-12), Mark then goes on to distill the next major Antioch-related sequence:
1. The apostles Barnabas and Paul were commissioned at Antioch (Acts 13.1-3).
2. A clash in Cyprus with the diabolical Bar-jesus (Acts 13.4-12).
3. Away in the other Antioch, in a long discourse, they spread the word of God (Acts 13.13-52).

Thus, from one Antioch to another (Acts 13) are three major events: the commissioning, the diabolical clash, and the discourse (the spread of the word).

Correspondingly, Mark's own narrative goes on to show three major kinds of texts:
1. A commissioning (of the twelve, 3.13-19).
2. A clash with the devil/Beelzebul/Satan (sandwiched amid texts on Jesus' relatives, 3.20-35).
3. The spread of the word (the parables, 4.1-34).

In other words, in both texts (Acts 13; Mk 3.13–4.34) the central sequence is a commissioning, a clash with the devil, and a long section of discourse.
Attached to the end of the Antioch preaching is an account of how the apostles preached 'in the same way' in Iconium (Acts 13.1), and of how the Iconium preaching ran into a deadly upheaval: 'the unbelieving Jews stirred up and poisoned the minds of the Gentiles against the brothers' (Acts 13.2). And attached to the end of the parables is an account of how the boat ran into a frightening storm (Mk 4.35-41). In face of the Iconium upheaval, 'the Lord [working through the apostles] gave…signs and wonders' (Acts 13.3). And from the boat, Jesus calmed the storm (4.39). Thus—after the commissioning, the clash, and the discourse—both texts attach some form of upheaval or storm.

But Acts 13 is not the only part of Proto-Luke to describe a commissioning of named people. Something similar is found in Acts 1—in the account of the twelve: how they were chosen, their names (including Matthias, in place of Judas), and the way they were gathered in prayer 'with…Mary the mother of Jesus and with his brothers' (Acts 1.1-5, 12-26). One of the affinities between Acts 13 and Acts 1 is that both chapters give lists of names: the five from whom Barnabas and Saul were chosen (13.1); and the eleven (1.13).

So when Mark (in 3.19–4.41) begins to fill in the skeletal framework provided by Acts 13.1–14.3, one of the sources he uses is Acts 1. This combining process is outlined in Table 30.

Table 30. *Proto-Luke and Mark: Commissionings (Acts 1; 13; Mark 3)*

Acts 13.1–14.3	Acts 1	Mark 3.13–4.41
The commissioning of the two in Antioch (Acts 13.1-3)	The eleven and the choosing of a twelfth (Acts 1.13, 15-26)	The commissioning of the twelve by Jesus (Mk 3.13-19)
The clash with the diabolical Bar-Jesus (13.4-12)	Mary, the mother of Jesus, and his brothers (1.14)	The relatives, the Beelzebul clash, the mother and brothers (3.20-35)
The discourse (13.13-52)		The parables (4.1-34)
The upheaval, countered by the Lord's signs and wonders (14.1-3)		The storm, which is calmed by Jesus (4.35-41)

As Mark's gospel develops, its episodes tend to become longer, and its use of sources accordingly tends to rely less on the process of abbreviation.

The Antioch discourse (Acts 13.13-52) is a prolonged drama of the word—its history and the way it challenges and surprises. The parables are a series of miniature dramas, each capturing one aspect of the greater drama. Thus, as he had done in dealing with the protracted Cornelius sequence (breaking it into five conflict stories), Mark has divided the prolonged Antioch event (discourse and response), dispersing it into a series of parables. And, somewhat like the conflict stories, each parable is self-contained, yet as a group they complement one another.

The essence of the discourse and the parables is the portrayal of the spread of God's word. But Mark has made a radical change of imagery. Instead of recounting history as Paul does—by telling how Old Testament history, which is fulfilled in Jesus, demands a response of faith in the present (Acts 13.17-41)—Mark describes various phenomena of nature, especially the growing of seeds. Whatever the full motivation and sources behind Mark's change, it is not alien to Paul's speech. It takes what had been clearly implied in Paul—the emphasis on the present (the past has implications for the present)—and makes it central. Thus the word for Mark is not so much something that happened in the past; like growth in nature, it is happening all the time, a perpetual challenge. The kingdom of God is not just a memory of history, something from the time of Saul and David (Acts 13.21-22), it is a kingdom of the here and now—though shrouded in the Markan sense of secrecy or mystery (Mk 4.10-12, 26-32).

And having applied images of nature to the preaching in Antioch, Mark then applies a further image of nature to the preaching in Iconium. He renders the Iconium upheaval suffered by the community (literally, 'the brothers') into a storm suffered by those in the boat. The Iconium disturbance does not explain all of the storm scene—Mark is using other sources—but it does provide one component. Other correspondences are suggested by the outline (Table 31).

17. *Mark and Proto-Luke, Episode by Episode*

Table 31. *Proto-Luke and Mark: Commissionings in Detail*

The Commissioning of the Apostles	
In Antioch, in the church there, were prophets and teachers:	
Barnabas, Simeon called Niger, Lucius the Cyrenean, Manaen, who was raised with Herod the tetrarch, and Saul (Acts 13.1)	
As they worshipped and fasted the Holy Spirit said, 'Set apart Barnabas and Saul for the work to which I have called them'. So after fasting and praying they laid hands on them and sent them off (Acts 13.2-3)	
Jesus had chosen the apostles; they were with him (1.2, 21-22) Returning from the mountain, Matthias was added to the eleven (Acts 1.12, 26)	He went up to the mountain and called whom he willed and he made twelve to be with him… (Mk 3.13-14a),
	and that he might send them to preach and to have power to expel demons (3.14b):
In Jerusalem (1.12): Peter and John and James and Andrew,	Simon, whom he named Peter, James the son of Zebedee, and John, the brother of James, whom he named Boanerges or Sons of Thunder, and Andrew,
Philip and Thomas, Bartholomew and Matthew,	Philip and Bartholomew and Matthew and Thomas,
James son of Alphaeus and Simon the Zealot and Jude son of James [and Matthias, for Judas] (1.13)	and James son of Alphaeus and Thaddaeus and Simon the Cananaean and Judas Iscariot… (3.16-19)

At least two features of the Antioch commissioning—the elaborating of some of the names, and the implied mission to preach—reappear in Mark's account (see Table 32).

Table 32. *Proto-Luke and Mark: Clash with Satan (Acts 13; Mark 4)*

The Clash with the Devil/Satan	
Cf. The Antioch church, assembled, fasting, laying hands, invoking a higher spirit/mind (Acts 13.1-3)??	He came to the house and a crowd came together so they could not eat. When those near him heard of this they went out to take hold of him, saying he was out of his mind (Mk 3.22-23)
The mission of Paul and Barnabas to Cyprus provoked a reaction from a Jewish pseudo-prophet Bar-Jesus. But Paul, full of the Holy Spirit, confronted him:	Following the appointment of the twelve, scribes from Jerusalem said,
'Oh, full of every treachery and every wickedness, son of the Devil, enemy of all righteousness, will you not cease perverting the straight ways of the Lord? And now the hand of the Lord is on you and you shall be blind for a time…' Immediately…darkness fell on him…	'He has Beelzebul. It is in the power of demons that he casts out demons.' And calling them he said in parables, 'How can Satan cast out Satan?… No one can enter a strong man's house and take his property unless he first ties the strong man up.
	'…Whoever blasphemes against the Holy Spirit will never have forgiveness'…because they were saying, 'He has an unclean spirit'.

The perversity of the Jewish pseudo-prophet and Paul's ability to undo his Devil-based power find a partial counterpart in the perverse accusation of the Jerusalem scribes and in Jesus' ability to cast out Satan. There is an implication that both the Jewish pseudo-prophet and the Jerusalem scribes are in opposition to the Holy Spirit.

It is unclear how Mark has used the positive figure of the proconsul, Sergius Paulus (Acts 13.7-8, 12), and whence Mark drew the images of the kingdom and the house (Mk 3.24-27).

Both Proto-Luke and Mark give images of the mother and brothers:

All these were persevering together in prayer with women and with Mary, the mother of Jesus, and with his brothers (Acts 1.14)	His mother and his brothers…stood outside… And a crowd sat around him… And looking at those sitting around him in a circle he said, 'Behold my mother and my brothers…' (Mk 3.31-35)

In complementary ways both texts highlight the ideal of a human grouping which is based not so much on physical ties but on ties which are spiritual or divine (prayer; listening effectively to the word of God). Luke seems to combine both kinds of ties, but Mark introduces a sense of contrast:

Proto-Luke and Mark then highlight the Word (see Table 33).

Table 33. *Proto-Luke and Mark: The Word (Acts 13.1-52; Mark 4)*

The Mystery of the Word and of its Spread, Growth, and Revelation	
The setting: Voyage, entry to Antioch synagogue, sitting, standing to speak, 'Listen…' (Acts 13.13-16)	The open-air/natural setting: Teaching by the sea, seated in a boat listen, 'Listen…' (Mk 4.1-3a)
The history of how God cared for Israel (includings kings) and of how it developed (13.17-25)	A nature parable: the story of how a farmer sowed seed and of how it grew (4.3b-9)
Brothers, sons of Abraham, and Godfearers, 'This word of salvation is sent to us/you' (13.26)	To those around him with the twelve, 'To you is given the mystery of the kingdom of God' (4.10-11)
Interpretation of the history: Jesus fulfills history/scripture and he is now risen (13.27-37)	Interpretation of the parable: The seed is the word of God and gives forth fruit (4.13-20)
	The parable of the light which is revealed (4.21-25)
Conclusion: God's work is amazing (13.38-41)	Parable: The growth of God's kingdom is beyond understanding (4.26-29)
Almost the whole city comes to hear the word (13.42-44)	Parable: The mustard seed becomes a shelter for all (4.30-32)
Paul turns to the Gentiles—as a light to the nations (13.45-49)	
Paul is expelled from Antioch but the disciples are filled with joy and the Holy Spirit (13.50-52)	Jesus speaks in parables but explains all to the disciples in private (4.33-34)

The conclusions (Acts 13.50-52; Mk 4.33-34) suggest a division between an outside world which does not understand (which expels Paul; which sees things in parables) and an inside world which has a special sense of meaning (joy and the Holy Spirit; private explanation).

Then come images of great disturbance: upheaval in Acts, a storm in Mark (Table 34).

Table 34. *Proto-Luke and Mark: The Upheaval/Storm*

In the Iconium synagogue many believe, Jews—and Greeks (Acts 14.1)	Jesus is in the boat—and other boats were with him (Mk 4.35-36)
But unbelieving Jews stirred up and rendered evil the souls of the Gentiles against the brothers (14.2)	And a great squall developed and the waves were beating against the boat... (4.37)
So Paul stayed preaching confidently...the word of grace...	But Jesus was in the stern, asleep on a cushion... (4.38)
as...the Lord gave signs and wonders (14.3)	Then he rebuked the wind and calmed the storm (4.39)
?	And he said, Why are you afraid? Have you still no faith? (4.40)
The shepherds feared with a great fear...and said to each other... (Lk. 2.9, 15; cf. Lk. 1.66)	And they feared with a great fear, and said to each other, Who can this be?... (4.41)

There may be some correspondence between 'the Greeks' (Acts 14.1) and Mark's perplexing reference to 'other boats' (4.36). Compared with the Jews, the Greeks in a sense were secondary, other.

In the final part of calming the storm, when describing the awestruck feelings of those in the boat, Mark makes use of the awestruck reaction of the shepherds as they were surrounded by the heavenly army (Lk. 2.9, 15).

c. *Section 5. The Healing of the Pagan, and the Enlivening of the Church (Acts 14.4-28; 9.32-43; Mark 5)*

The remainder of Acts 14 (14.4-28) begins by speaking of a disruptive division (14.4-7: some were for the Jews, others for the apostles), and then it goes on to describe two main events:

1. The healing of the crippled man among the pagans—among those who in a fit of confused enthusiasm wanted to offer sacrifice to Barnabas and Paul as if the apostles were Zeus and Hermes (14.8-18).
2. The enlivening and strengthening of the suffering disciples (14.19-28). The enlivening begins in dramatic form when, amid a circle of disciples, an apparently dead Paul rises up (14.19-20), and the revived Paul then goes on to strengthen the disciples (14.22-23: putting fresh heart into them, telling them of the need to endure 'many tribulations', and appointing elders in each of the churches). Thus there is a clear contrast—the healing takes place among the pagans, and the subsequent enlivening among the disciples (in the church).

Mark used these two events—healing and enlivening—as components for the two events in ch. 5: the healing of the Gerasene demoniac (5.1-20), and the enlivening of the suffering women (the woman with the flow of blood, and Jairus's daughter, 5.21-43). In outline:

Healing amid pagan confusion (14.4-18)	The Gerasene demoniac
Paul, apparently dead, rises (14.19-20)	Jairus's daughter
Strengthens the suffering church (14.21-28)	The suffering woman

This simplified outline merely begins the complex process of tracing Mark's procedure. Much of the gospel text remains unaccounted for.

A next step is to take note of the 'twin' miracles which precede the call of the centurion, Cornelius—the healing of Aeneas who had been paralyzed in bed for eight years (Acts 9.32-35), and the raising of the dead Tabitha (Dorcas, Acts 9.36-43). They are twin because of being placed together and because of some connecting details (Peter, 'the saints', 'rise up', 'to the Lord', 9.32, 34, 35, 40-42). Mark uses this phenomenon of twin miracles as a partial basis for describing the two miracles that are interwoven: the hemorrhaging woman and Jairus's daughter. As Proto-Luke had underlined the twinning effect by using connecting details, so Mark underlines the interweaving by including shared details (daughter, twelve years, 5.23, 25, 34, 42). The twin miracles provide Mark with part of his form (insofar as they go part of the way towards the interweaving of two miracles), and they also supply a significant part of his content (the raising of Tabitha is reflected in the raising of Jairus's daughter; see especially Acts 9.37-41; Mk 5.38-42).

Mark has also drawn details from the other two centurion-associated miracles: the healing of the centurion's servant (Lk. 7.1-10), and the raising of the widow's son (Lk. 7.11-17).

Hence, in tracing the interwoven miracles of Mk 5.21-43, it is necessary to take account of at least three aspects of Proto-Luke: the enlivening of Paul and the disciples (Acts 14.19-28), and the two pairs of centurion-associated miracles (Lk. 7.1-17; Acts 9.32-43). Apparently Mark has started with the picture of how God enlivens the suffering church (Acts 14.19-28), but in portraying that church (that body of disciples), he has rendered it into the picture of suffering women, and has drawn on other accounts of how God's power enlivens sufferers.

With regard to the Gerasene demoniac (Mk 5.1-20), the origin of its composition remains difficult to trace. One component has come from the immense confusion surrounding the healing of the crippled man (Acts 14.4-18, a situation where unbelief is associated with violence and confusion, all dramatically illustrated in the violence and confusion of the demoniac).

In concluding the demoniac account (5.14-20), and especially when describing the reaction of the startled herdsmen, Mark returns once more, as he had when concluding the preceding episode (the amazed reaction of the disciples in the boat, 4.41), to the account of the shepherds (Lk. 2.8-20). Having seen the army of heaven, the shepherds went and told people; and the herdsmen, having seen the destruction of the army of hell (the legion of pigs), also went and told people.

The details of the Gerasene story are so complex and elusive (at least for the present writer) that it seems better not to attempt to indicate them here.

d. *Section 6. The Calm amid the Storm Clouds: Despite Famine and Herod, the Mission Advances (Luke 3.23-38; 4.16-22a; 10.1-11; Acts 4.23-31; 5.12-16; 11.27–ch. 12; Mark 6)*
In reworking the account of the missionary work of Peter and Paul (Acts 9.32–ch. 14), Mark had passed over one major area: the foretelling of famine and Herod's persecution of the church (Acts 11.27–ch. 12). Now, however, in ch. 6, the images of Herod and hunger become central: Herod kills John (Mk 6.14-29), and the threat of hunger, which in Acts had been circumvented by prophecy (Acts 11.27-30), is dramatically averted through the multiplication of the loaves (Mk 6.30-44).

Then, having reworked the account of the persecution by Herod, Mark goes on to the aftermath of another persecution—that of the Sanhedrin (Acts 4.23-31). The dramatic scene which followed that persecution—the calm confident prayer to the Creator of earth and sea and the Creator's dramatic response (the house shook, 4.31)—becomes one component in Mark's subsequent account of Jesus walking on the water (Mk 6.45-52). In his walking on the water, as in Acts, the Creator is indeed present.

Having used the Creator prayer (Acts 4.23-31), Mark skips the subsequent possessions-focused passage (4.32-11)—it will be used later—and then goes to the summary account of the many cures worked by Peter (5.12-16). This summary text becomes a component for Mark's next episode—the account of many cures worked by Jesus at Gennesaret (Mk 6.53-56).

The dependence of Mark 6 on Proto-Luke may be outlined as follows:

Luke–Acts	Mark
Genealogy, Nazareth (3.23-38; 4.16-22a)	Nazareth, family (6.1-6)
Mission of the seventy-two (10.1-12)	Mission of twelve (6.7-13)
Famine… (Acts 11.27-30)	Herod and John (6.14-29)
Herod and persecution (Acts 12)	Hunger…loaves (6.30-44)
Persecution, the Creator (Acts 4.23-31)	Walking on water (6.45-52)
Many cures (Acts 5.12-16)	Many cures (6.53-56)

In Proto-Luke's Nazareth scene (Lk. 4.16-22a), the response to Jesus is positive (4.22a). The Markan scene, in contrast, is more complex and negative. Mark introduces questions and several names ('the carpenter…Mary…James, Joset, Jude, Simon…his sisters', Mk 6.3). Apparently Mark, while omitting Luke's historical genealogy (Lk. 3.23-38), has substituted a family picture which is more focused on the present—more biographical.

The sending of the twelve (Mk 6.7-13) summarizes the sending out of the seventy-two (Lk. 10.1-12) and gives it a typically Markan emphasis on unclean spirits and demons. (This emphasis may involve a reflection of a somewhat similar idea in Luke's account of how the seventy-two returned, Lk. 10.18-20.)

The brief account of how the famine was foreseen by prophecy and circumvented by generosity (Acts 11.27-30) provides Mark with a starting point for the elaborate account of the transition from hunger to an abundance of loaves (6.30-44). Mark's sources for this elaboration include the return of the seventy-two (Lk. 10.17; see the return of the apostles, Mk 6.30), Psalm 23 with its picture of a shepherd and green pastures, the eucharistic tradition of breaking bread (Lk. 22.19), and above all, Elisha's multiplication of the loaves (2 Kgs 4.42-44).

In Acts 12, Herod kills James and imprisons Peter. In Mk 6.14-29, he imprisons and kills John. One of the important changes wrought by Mark is the injection of a sense of tragedy: in place of a drama of release, he portrays a drama of death. Table 35 gives some further details.

Table 35. *Proto-Luke and Mark: Herod; the Sea (Acts 12; 4; Mark 6)*

Herod	
Herod: James is killed and Peter imprisoned (Acts 12.1-5)	Herod: John imprisoned and killed (Mk 6.14-20)
Just before the decisive day, a night drama releases Peter (12.6-19). In a regal scene, Herod dies (12.20-23)	On Herod's birthday, a regal drama dooms John, and he is killed (6.21-29)
The Creator and the Sea	
Disciples return to their own (Acts 4.23)	Jesus gets the disciples to embark in the boat (Mk 6.45)
The disciples raise their voices in prayer: 'Master, you who made heaven and land and sea' (4.24)	Jesus goes to the mountain to pray (6.46). They were in the middle of the sea and he alone on land (6.47)
…there have been plots and wars against your anointed (4.25-27), but they fulfill your plan (4.28)	And seeing them worn out, for the wind was against them, he came to them… (6.48)
And now Lord, stretch out your hand to work signs and wonders. And as they were praying the place was shaken (4.29-31)	Jesus came to them and the wind became calm (6.49-52)

The account of Jesus walking on the water (Mk 6.45-52), while dependent on its own sources, especially the prayer amid persecution (Acts 4.23-31), is also partly modeled on the lines of Mark's earlier account of calming the storm (Mk 4.35-41).

e. Section 7. From Disputing about Tradition to Opening to the Gentiles (Acts 15.1-35; Mark 7)

The missionary work of Peter and Paul is followed by the Jerusalem council (Acts 15.1-35)—the event which moved from a controversy about Jewish tradition to an opening up to the Gentiles. Mark takes this and uses it first to describe a controversy about Jewish tradition (7.1-23), and then as a component for two complementary miracles: the healing of the daughter of the Gentile woman (7.24-30) and the opening of the deaf man (7.31-37). In outline:

Controversy about Jewish tradition (Acts 15.1-11)	Controversy about Pharisees' tradition (Mk 7.1-23)
The decision in favor of the Gentiles (15.12-21)	Jesus' decision in favor of the Greek woman (7.24-30)
Communication: letter, delegates spread the word afar (15.22-35)	After a long journey, the deaf man is opened (7.31-37)

While the Jerusalem drama provides the basic themes for the two miracle stories, it does not provide the narrative action, and it is not clear whence Mark drew this pair of stories. To some degree, they are modeled on the centurion-associated pairs in Proto-Luke (Lk. 7.1-17; Acts 9.32-42). And the woman's initial request (Mk 7.24-26) is somewhat like that of Jairus at the beginning of Mark's own interwoven miracles (5.21-23). For more details, see Table 36.

Table 36. *Proto-Luke and Mark: Adapting to Gentiles (Acts 15; Mark 7.1-37)*

From Jewish Restriction to Gentile Wellbeing	
People from Judea, especially Pharisees from Jerusalem, try to impose Mosaic circumcision, despite all God has done among the Gentiles (Acts 15.1-5). See 15.3: The circumcision party in Jerusalem objects to Peter's eating practice	Pharisees from Jerusalem object to the disciples' eating practice because it does not follow the traditions of the elders. But Jesus invokes the authority of both Moses and God (Mk 7.1-13)
The convening in Jerusalem: Peter stresses the priority of cleanliness of heart (15.6-11)	Jesus reconvenes the crowd: he stresses the heart, making all foods clean (7.14-23)
Central theme:	Narrative action: ?
Accepting how God first took a people from among the Gentiles, the council decides in favor of the Gentiles (15.12-21)	Jesus says it is not good to take first the children's' bread, but the Syrophoenician woman persuades him to decide in her favor (7.24-30)
Central theme:	Narrative action ?
the spreading far of the word—through writing and speech (15.22-35)	After a far journey the healing of the deaf man opens the word and spreads it abroad (7.31-37)

As usual, Mark is adapting his sources to the patterns and requirements of his own narrative. Thus, the picture of the Syrophoenician woman and her daughter (8.24-30) forms part of the larger pattern of three woman-and-daughter scenes (see the hemorrhaging woman and Jairus's daughter, 5.21-43, and Herodias and her daughter, 6.14-29).

3. Block C. The Breakthrough and the Manifestations of Resurrection (Mainly Acts 6–9; Luke 24.13–Acts 1.12; Mark 8.1–9.29)

The next two sections of Mark (sections 8 and 9; Mk 8.1–9.29) cover the center of the gospel and may be grouped together. The first, involving a breakthrough in understanding Jesus, emphasizes his future suffering and death (Mk 8.1–9.1). The second, showing him being transfigured and raising someone, implies something of his resurrection (9.2-29).

In composing these texts, Mark has used aspects of the painful breakthrough of the early church (Acts 6–9) and also the center of Proto-Luke (Lk. 24.13–Acts 1.12, a text which reflects the resurrection).

This switch to the earlier part of Acts is not completely new for Mark. In composing the end of ch. 6 (walking on water, and cures, 6.45-56), he already made some use of Acts 4–5 (praying amid persecution, 4.23-31; cures, 5.12-16).

a. *Section 8. The Wrenching Breakthrough to the Essence of Humanity: The Church Begins to Engage the World and the Disciples Begin to See Jesus (see Acts 6–9; Mark 8.1–9.1)*
It is one thing to let go of an old tradition; it is another to make one's way to a new horizon and to see new meaning. Such new insight often involves a suffering journey. If the letting go of some Jewish tradition is accomplished with relative ease at Jerusalem (Acts 15.1-35), it is only because a new insight had already been found and the disciples had already undergone a suffering journey. In Acts 6–9, Stephen's clash with the synagogue and Sanhedrin had opened the way to his own death, to a persecution which scattered the disciples, and to the shock-like conversion of Saul (6.1–9.31). By the time that journey was over, the old Jewish framework had in fact already been broken and the church was poised for the missionary work of Peter and Paul (Acts 9.32–ch. 14). The disciples would no longer be dealing just with Jews, but with all of humanity. In a sense, they were about to discover humanity.

Mark takes that basic idea—of breaking through to humanity, of discovering it—and gives it a new form; he describes a process of discovering the individual human person. Thus while Proto-Luke described a discovery in breadth, Mark describes a discovery in depth. This is part of Mark's larger procedure, exemplified in his emphasis on spirits—going from far-flung narrative to an examination of a person's depths.

This process of discovering the human person, of discerning or recognizing what lies within, is portrayed in the account of the discerning or recognition of Jesus (Mk 8.1–9.1). The account begins with a broad panorama—a multiplication account which has suggestions of universality (great crowd, seven, four, Mk 8.1-10)—and which, after turning away from the heaven-centered preoccupations of the Pharisees (8.11-13), then begins to focus on the difficult task of recognizing Jesus (8.1–9.1).

In the recognition process, the first episode concerns the slowness of the disciples in understanding the enigmatic bread (8.14-21), a slowness which indicates the difficulty of recognizing Jesus. The two-stage healing of the blind man (8.22-26) shows that insight is possible, but the man's first effort, in which he really does not see people properly (they appear as mobile plants or walking trees), indicates that even when insight does happen, it is slow. Finally, after moving to a new, Gentile-sounding place (Caesarea-Philippi), and after reporting some inadequate opinions, the disciples, led by Peter, recognize Jesus as the Christ (8.28-30).

But even Peter's understanding is inadequate, and then Jesus has to offer a long explanation of his own fate and of the fate of his disciples (8.31–9.1). It is a fate which involves death but also involves glory. The result is a revelation of what is most fearful and most hopeful—a portrayal of some of the deepest dimensions of Jesus and of humanity.

Mark uses Acts 6–9 (or parts of it at least) in composing 8.1–9.1, but his emphasis is so different that he changes his source considerably. His focus is on the two individuals who in a sense had to suffer most: Stephen the martyr, who worked signs and accused the Sanhedrin of having stubborn hearts and ears (Acts 6–7), and Saul, who fell down, blinded, and had to learn to suffer (Acts 9). The main points of dependence may be outlined as follows:

Food crisis, the Seven (Acts 6.1-7)	Hunger, (seven) loaves (8.1-10)
Signs incur opposition (6.8-10)	Pharisees seek signs (8.11-13)
Stubborn hearts, ears (7.51-53)	Hard hearts...ears (8.14-21)
'Who are you, lord?' (9.3-7)	The blind man sees (8.22-26)
Blinded Saul sees (9.8-12, 17-18)	'Who am I?' (8.27-30)
Saul must suffer (9.13-16)	Jesus must suffer (8.31–9.1)

Mark's second account of the multiplication of the loaves (8.1-10) is largely modeled on the first, Israel-oriented account (6.30-44), but it has details which give it a more universal dimension. Such universalism is already evoked in the appointment of the Seven (in its reference not only to Hebrews but also to Hellenists and in its use of the universal number seven).

Stephen's signs and wonders, however impressive, had aroused nothing but opposition from many Jews (Acts 6.8-10)—an implicit indication that such signs have limited effectiveness. Mark (8.11-13) goes further: he sees signs as Pharisees' distractions, something best left behind.

Much of the hardness of heart which Stephen found in the Sanhedrin (Acts 7.51-53) is found by Jesus in the disciples (Mk 8.14-21). For some further details, see Table 37.

Table 37. *Proto-Luke and Mark: Crisis; Breakthrough (Acts 6–9; Mark 8)*

The Food Crisis and the Increase in Numbers	
In those days there was a food crisis. So they called the multitude of the disciples together and appointed the seven—on whom the apostles, praying, laid their hands. The word spread, and the number of disciples greatly increased (Acts 6.1-7)	In those days the multitude was hungry, so calling his disciples, Jesus was told they had seven loaves. These he blessed, thus feeding the multitude, and there remained seven baskets (Mk 8.1-10)
Hardness of Heart	
Stephen to the Jews: 'You are stubborn...in heart and ears. You resist the Spirit... You have killed the Just One' (7.51-53)	'Beware of the leaven of the Pharisees... Are your hearts hard?... Having ears do you not hear? Do you not recognize the bread?' (8.14-21)
From Blindness to Sight	
Paul, blind, is led to Damascus. He cannot see, yet he sees Ananias in a vision. Later, Ananias lays hands on him and then he sees fully (9.8-12)	Jesus comes to Bethsaida and when they bring a blind man to him, he lays his hands on the man and heals him (8.22-26; cf. Mk 7.31-37)
Recognizing Jesus	
On the road to Damascus, Saul (along with his companions) has to face the question of Jesus' identity: 'Who are you...?' 'I am Jesus...' But, particularly for the companions, the answer is wrapped in mystery (9.3-7)	On the road in the region of Caesarea Philippi, the disciples are faced with the question of Jesus' identity. The answer comes from Peter, but there were other opinions and the true answer is to be a secret (8.27-30)
Fated to Suffering and Glory	
The high priest's authority threatens death, and Saul must suffer in Jesus' name (9.1-2, 13-16)	Jesus foretells death, suffering, and resurrection (8.31–9.1)

Mark's text on suffering and glory (8.31–9.1) is central to the gospel, and partly for that reason involves a synthesis of several texts from Proto-Luke, including part or all of Lk. 9.51, 55-58; 17.25, 33; Acts 9.27-28. The concluding verses, about the Son of Humanity coming in glory and about standing and seeing the kingdom of God coming in power (Mk 8.38–9.1) partly depend on the visionary witness of Stephen (Acts 6.15; 7.55-56) and on some of the ideas which frame the ascension (Acts 1.6-8, 11).

This final section (8.31–9.1) is also colored by the fact that, along with 9.30-50 and 10.32-52, it forms part of a larger three-part pattern in which a passion prediction is followed by a discussion involving some aspect of discipleship or community.

b. *Section 9. Death, Resurrection and Transformation into Heaven (Luke 24.13-53; Acts 1.1-11; Mark 9.2-29)*

The celebration of the resurrection—so vivid in Proto-Luke, particularly in the Emmaus journey (Lk. 24.13-35) and the ascension (Acts 1.6-11)—is strikingly absent in Mark. Instead Mark has taken Proto-Luke's vivid narratives and has placed them, in transmuted form, at the heart of his gospel in the accounts of the transfiguration and the raising of the boy who seemed to die (9.2-29). By doing this, he shows that the power of the resurrection belongs not just to the end of human life, but to its daily progress.

The essential dependence may be outlined as follows:

The ascension (Acts 1.6-11)	The transfiguration (Mk 9.2-8)
Confusion on the road to Emmaus (Lk. 24.13-16)	Confusion coming down from the mountain (Mk 9.9-13)
From sadness to the recognition of Jesus (24.17-49)	From weak faith to the raising of the boy (Mk 9.14-29)

Luke's narratives had already paid some attention to the attitudes of the disciples, particularly the sadness of the two who were walking to Emmaus, but Mark looks at the disciples' attitudes more closely, particularly at their inability to help the boy as well as at the father's struggle to believe.

Some of the details may be outlined as follows:

The ascension of Jesus—on a mountain, between two men in white, while the disciples look on, unsure (Acts 1.9-11; cf. Lk. 24.50-53)	The transfiguration of Jesus—on a mountain, in white, between Elijah and Moses, Peter does not know what to say (Mk 9.2-8)
On the road to Emmaus the two disciples discuss but cannot grasp the risen Jesus (Lk. 24.13-16)	Descending the mountain the three disciples discuss resurrection, but cannot understand it (9.9-13)
Disciples' loss of hope is countered by the scriptures and a recognition of the risen Jesus. Then the disciples gather together (24.17-49)	Disciples inability to deal with the unclean spirit is overcome when Jesus raises the apparently dead boy. Then the disciples gather with Jesus (9.14-29)

4. *Block D. The Journey to Death (Mainly Luke 9.51…24.12; Acts 2.1–9.31; Mark 9.30–16.8)*

The remaining eight sections of Mark (sections 10–17; from 9.30 to the end) follow fairly closely on Jesus' journey to Jerusalem (Lk. 9.51…24.12). In six of these (sections 11–16; chs. 10–14), Mark also uses Acts 2.1–9.31. The texts are outlined in Table 38 (next page). This simplified outline is not meant as a source of analysis; it is a rough general map, a reference point during subsequent discussion. (By and large, Mark uses those parts of Acts 2.1–9.31 which he had not used already.)

Table 38. *Proto-Luke and Mark: Journey (Luke 9–24; Acts 2–9; Mark 9–16)*

Luke 9.51...24.12	Acts 2.1–9.31	Mark 9.30–16.8
The journey (9.51...10.20; 16.19-31; 22.24-30)		The journey (9.30-50)
Dishonest steward (16.1-9)	Possessions (4.32–5.11), hardheartedness (7.1-51), childlike Ethiopian (8.26-40)	Hardhearted divorce, childlikeness, the rich man (10.1-30)
Zacchaeus (19.1-10)	Pentecost: passion and community (Acts 2)	Passion, community, Bartimaeus (10.31-52)
Passover preparation (22.7-13). Way to Golgotha (23.27...43)	Temple-related clash (5.17-21, 26, 33)	Preparation for Jerusalem. Way to Jerusalem. Temple cleansed (11.1-25)
Accusation about tribute to Caesar (23.2)	Preaching and controversies (2; 34-36; 3.11-26; 4.5-22) (4.32–5.11??)	Teaching and controversies (11.27–ch. 12)
Son of Humanity. Prayerfulness (17.20–18.8)	Dooming of temple induces woes (6.14; 7.57-50; 8.1-25)	Doomed temple. Woes. Son of Humanity. Alertness (ch. 13)
Anointing, supper, Sanhedrin (7.36-50; 22.1-23, 66-71)	An arrest (4.1-4). Trauma near Damascus. Paul affirms (9.1-8, 19-30)	Anointing, supper, arrest, trauma in Gethsemane, Sanhedrin, Peter denies (ch. 14)
Death and resurrection (Lk. 23.1-23, 32-56; 24.1-12)		Death and resurrection (Mk 15.1–16.8)

a. *Section 10. The Humble Journey to Death—to Heaven (Reward) or to Hell (Luke 9.51-58; 10.13–16, 20; 16.19-31; 22.24-30; Mark 9.30-50)*
Associated with death-and-resurrection is the journey which precedes it. For Luke, that journey begins when Jesus sets his face towards Jerusalem (9.51-56). The journey, as it progresses, brings a call for detachment (9.57-58), a woe-filled reminder of the Sender (10.13-16), and then opposite pictures: those whose names are written in heaven (10.20) and the rich man who ends in torment (16.19-31).

Beginning with the second passion prediction (9.30-32), Mark also has a journey towards death, and in its early stages, he uses some of the elements of the Proto-Lukan journey. In outline:

> Setting out to Jerusalem (Lk. 9.51-56)   Journeying to death (Mk 9.30-32)
> Detachment on the way (9.57-58)   Greatness on the way (9.33-37)
> Those not responding (10.13-16, 20)   Those not following (9.38-41)
> The rich man in torment (16.19-31)   Scandal and hell (9.42-50)

Unlike the open nature of Jesus' departure for Jerusalem (Lk. 9.51-56)—he even sends messengers before him—Mark's account of the journey is shrouded, typically, in secrecy. It is also adapted to be in continuity with Mark's other passion predictions (8.31; 10.32).

Mark had already used Luke's passage on the need for detachment (the cost of discipleship, 9.56-62), and so at this stage, he takes only its initial image of going along the way, and he grafts onto that image the discussion about greatness (taken from the Last Supper, Lk. 22.24-30).

In the case of the next set of passages (under the tentative headings of those not responding and those not following; Lk. 10.13-16, 20; Mk 9.38-41), the connection, if real, is subtle. The texts may be summarized as follows:

Those not responding.	Those not following.
Those working miracles—even if they are ignored—represent Jesus.	Those working miracles in my name—even if not following us—are not against me.
And they represent the one who sent him [i.e. God] (Lk. 10.13-16)	Even lesser works receive their reward [from God] (Mk 9.38-41)

Mark's reference to a reward (10.41) may be colored by Luke's mention of heaven ('your names are written in heaven', 10.20).

Instead of retelling the vivid story of the rich man in torment (Lk. 16.19-31), Mark has filtered some of its ideas and images and turned it into a general precaution about avoiding scandal and hell.

b. *Section 11. Freedom Regarding Possessions, Hardhearted Resistance to Scripture, and Childlike Receptivity (Luke 16.1-9; Acts 4.32–5.11; 7.1-51; 8.31-39; Mark 10.1-31)*
Having previously skipped the parable of how the dishonest steward decisively dealt with possessions (Lk. 16.1-9), Mark now returns to it and, having distilled it, makes it part of his own long section on possessions (Mk 10.17-30: the rich man who turned away; the difficulty caused by riches; and the rewards of renunciation). The steward, in his longing for a dwelling place (with its symbolism of a dwelling place that is eternal, Lk. 16.4, 9), had been able to let go of certain possessions (apparently of his precious commission). But the rich man who came up to Jesus and who explicitly desired eternal life could not make a similar decision.

It is at this point, in ch. 10, that Mark returns to using Acts 2.1–9.31. He will use Acts 2.1–9.31 intermittently from now until the end of ch. 14—until the account of Peter's denials (14.66-72).

Along with the possessions-related parable of the steward (Lk. 16.1-9), Mark also uses the possessions-related incidents of Acts 4.32–5.11 (the sharing of goods; the generosity of Barnabas; and the fraud of Ananias and Sapphira). The sharing of goods, as practiced by the community and Barnabas (Acts 4.32-37), is part of the challenge to the rich man (Mk 10.21). And the inability of Ananias and Sapphira to complete the transition from property-ownership to genuine sharing (Acts 5.1-11) provides part of the material for the statements about how difficult it is for the rich to enter the kingdom of God (Mk 10.23-27).

Next to the passage on possessions, Mark has episodes involving wives (10.1-12, concerning divorce) and children (10.13-16). However, the passages involving wives and children come first (before the possessions), and, in the discussion of divorce, the standing of the wives is equal to that of the husbands (10.11-12).

What is important here is that the discussion of divorce is significantly scripture-based: Moses allowed divorce only because of a hardhearted rejection of the original scriptural ideal of marriage (10.3-9). And the discussion of children 'is really about...what kind of people can expect to be part of [the kingdom]... The chief characteristic of children is receptivity' (D. Harrington 1990: 63).

In composing these passages involving hardhearted rejection of scripture and childlike receptivity, Luke apparently has used two further texts of Acts: the scripture-based speech of Stephen with its accusation of hardheartedness (Acts 7.1-51, especially 7.51) and the childlike receptivity of the Ethiopian eunuch (Acts 8.26-40, especially 8.31-39). In other words, Mark has taken Stephen's prolonged portrayal of hardheartedly rejecting God's scripture throughout history and has applied it to the rejection which occurs in one of the central realities of daily life—marriage. The connection between the Ethiopian and children is seen not only in his attitude of receptivity but also in the dependence of the Ethiopian passage on the story of Naaman (2 Kgs 5.1-14), a story in which children and childlike characters are central (2 Kgs 5.2, 13, 14—the little servant girl, the servants [*paides*], and the childlike body). The main texts may be listed as follows:

1. The challenge of relinquishing	2. Divorce: scripture-based view of riches (Lk. 16.1-9; Acts 4.32–5.11) hard-heartedness (Mk 10.1-12)
2. Stephen's scripture-based view of hard heartedness (Acts 7.1-51)	3. Childlike kingdom (10.13-16)
3. Childlike Ethiopian (8.25-40)	1. The rich man and the difficulty caused by riches (10.17-30)

c. *Section 12. The Passion, the Community, and the Saving of the Man at Jericho (Luke 19.1-10; cf. Acts 2; Mark 10.32-52)*

The later part of Mark 10 (10.31-52) has three inter-related episodes—concerning the coming passion, the community ethos, and the healing of blind Bartimaeus. The description of the coming passion sets the framework and tone for the discussion of the community ethos. And the open-mindedness of the community ethos is exemplified in the story of Bartimaeus's own humble eagerness towards Jesus and in the way the others, despite their initial intolerance, encourage him in his quest.

Some of this text (10.32-52) appears to make some use of the Pentecost scene (Acts 2). Obviously the external drama of the fiery descent of the Spirit has not been reproduced as such by Mark, but two of Pentecost's main ideas—the importance of the death-and-resurrection of Jesus, and the subsequent way in which a generous spirit can pervade a community—appear to have been incorporated into the episodes about the passion and the community spirit (Mk 10.31-45).

As usual, Mark's reshaping of his sources has been governed by the need for continuity within his own narrative—particularly continuity with the somewhat similar passion-and-community sequences which occur in the preceding chapters (predictions of the passion, followed by exchanges about discipleship, Mk 8.31–9.1; 9.30-50). In fact, to some degree, all three of these pivotal passion-and-community sequences (Mk 8.31–9.1; 9.30-50; 10.31-52) reflect something of the Pentcostal experience.

The Bartimaeus episode (Mk 10.46-52) involves a recasting of Proto-Luke's account of Zacchaeus (Lk. 19.1-10):

Zacchaeus	*Bartimaeus*
Going through Jericho: Rich Zacchaeus sought to see Jesus. He could not, because of the crowd. So he climbed a tree to see him. When Jesus came he called him. He hurried down, and received him rejoicing. Zacchaeus declares his resolution. Jesus: 'Today salvation has come to this house'.	Leaving Jericho: Blind Bartimaeus started to cry out to Jesus. Many rebuked him and told him to be silent. But he cried out all the more. Jesus stood and said, 'Call him'. He sprang up, and came to Jesus. Bartimaeus expresses his wish. Jesus: 'Go your way. Your faith has saved you'.

d. *Section 13. Jesus Enters Jerusalem (Luke 22.7-13; 23.27...43; Acts 5.17-21, 26, 33; Mark 11.1-25)*

Proto-Luke has no solemn entry to Jerusalem. However, it has a relatively long journey to crucifixion (involving Simon of Cyrene, the crowd, the weeping women, Jesus' words to the women, the two thieves and Jesus' words to the good thief, Lk. 23.26-43), and Mark uses much of this journey as one of the components for composing an account of Jesus' entry into Jerusalem.

In doing this, Mark uses Proto-Luke's account of Jesus going to the heavenly Jerusalem as a basis for describing Jesus' entry to the earthly Jerusalem. Here, as before—for instance, when he moved aspects of the resurrection to the center of the gospel—he suggests that some of the ultimate realities of Jesus' death-and-resurrection are already present in earlier stages of Jesus' life.

17. Mark and Proto-Luke, Episode by Episode

Along with Jesus' journey to death, Mark also uses some other Proto-Lukan episodes, notably the preparation for the Last Supper (which he uses in describing the preparation for the entry to Jerusalem, Lk. 22.7-13), and the temple-related clash with those around the high priest (Acts 5.17-21, 26, 23, a clash which helps form the account of the cleansing of the temple). The main texts may be outlined as follows:

Preparation for Passover (Lk. 22.7-13) Preparation for entry to Jerusalem (Mk 11.1-7)
The way to Golgotha (as distinctively Lukan, The way into Jerusalem and the incident of the
  23.27-31, 34, 40-43)   fig tree (11.8-14, 20-25)
The temple-related clash (Acts 5.17-21, 26, 33) The cleansing of the temple (11.15-19)

The account of the preparation for Passover (Lk. 22.7-13) does not provide some of the distinctive ideas in Mark's preparation for the entry to Jerusalem (11.1-7); all it provides is the form. The distinctive ideas require another source. On Mk 11.8-25, see Table 39.

Table 39. *Proto-Luke and Mark: Luke 22–23; Mark 11.8-25*

The Way to Death/Jerusalem	
As Simon, from the field, went after Jesus, a great crowd followed him in lamentation (Lk. 23.27)	Many (in celebration) lay their clothes on the way or cut branches from the fields going ahead and following him (Mk 11.8-9a)
Weep for yourselves and for your children (23.28-29)	??
Then they will begin to say (in lamentation) to the mountains, 'Fall on us, and to the hills, Cover us' (23.30)	And they were shouting (in celebration): 'Hosanna, Blessed is he who comes… Blessed is the kingdom… Hosanna in the highest' (11.9b-10)
?? (See Acts 4.1-4?)	Jesus looks around at the temple and goes out (11.11)
For if they do these things to the green tree, what will they do to the dry? (Lk. 23.31)	The cursing of the fig tree (11.12-14)
The good thief: faith, remembering, forgiveness (23.40-43; see 23.34?)	The withered fig tree: remembering, faith, forgiveness (11.20-25)
The Temple-Related Clash	
The high priest throws his hands on the apostles and puts them in prison But they escape to the temple and teach (Acts 5.17-21)	Jesus goes into the temple, throws people out, overturns the tables and seats, and teaches: 'My house shall be called…' (11.15-17)
When the authorities hear, they want to kill the apostles. But they fear the people (5.26, 33)	When the high priests hear, they seek to destroy him, but they fear the people (11.18-19)

Mark has turned the lamentation of the way of the cross into the celebration of the entry to Jerusalem. Thus, he not only moves something of the final events of Jesus' life back to an earlier stage, but he manages, as it were, to find a form of resurrection even in death.

In Acts (5.17-21, 26, 33), the actions of the high priest and those with him imply their bankruptcy as far as the temple is concerned: they remove from the temple those who could best teach in it. Mark goes further by making this idea more explicit: the bankrupt occupiers of the temple are thrown out (11.15-19).

e. *Section 14. Addressing the Jews: from Preaching to Controversies (see Acts 2.34–5.11; Mark 11.27–Ch. 12)*
Mark's account of Jesus' controversies with the Jewish authorities, from their questioning of his authority (11.27-33) to his condemnation of the scribes (12.38-44), to a significant

extent is based on the apostles' early preaching to the Jews (Acts 2–5). Initially, the preaching had been peaceful, but later it became controverted, and it is the controversial tone which dominates much of Mark's account. The relationship of the texts is roughly as follows:

```
 *  David and Christ (Acts 2.34-36).                    ———
**  Resurrection sermon (3.11-26).                      ———
    On what authority? (4.5-7, 16-22).      On what authority? (Mk 11.27-33).
    Jesus as cornerstone (4.8-11).           Vineyard, cornerstone (12.1-12).
    There is no other name (4.12-14).        ?? What about Caesar? (12.13-17).
                ———                         ** Resurrection question (12.18-27).
                 ?                              The great commandment (12.28-34).
                ———                          * David and Christ (12.35-37).
    The sharing and the fraud (4.32–5.11).   ?? The scribes and the widow (12.38-44).
```

Peter's second resurrection sermon (Acts 3.11-26) begins with a reference (from Exod. 3) to 'the God of Abraham, Isaac and Jacob'—the text Jesus uses against the Sadducees when they argue against the resurrection (Mk 12.26). For some details, see Table 40.

Table 40. *Proto-Luke and Mark: Disputing in Jerusalem*
(Acts 3–4; Mark 11.27–12.33)

The Question about the Resurrection	
Peter's speech in Solomon's portico: 'The God of Abraham, Isaac and Jacob glorified servant Jesus...whom God raised from the dead...Moses said, "The Lord will raise up a prophet from among your own brothers..."' (Acts 3.11-26)	The question about the resurrection: 'Moses wrote, "If a man's brother dies...the man must raise up children for his brother..." God said, "I am the God of Abraham...Isaac...Jacob—God of the living"' (Mk 12.18-27)
The Questioning of the Authority	
The high priests, elders, and scribes question the authority of the apostles—but they are in a dilemma (Acts 4.5-7, 16-22)	The high priests, scribes, and elders question the authority of Jesus—but Jesus catches them in a dilemma (Mk 11.27-33)
Jesus as the Cornerstone	
Peter's speech to the authorities: 'Let it be known to you and to the whole people of Israel: the healing was done in the name of Jesus whom you crucified, whom God raised; he is the rejected stone which has become the cornerstone' (Acts 4.8-11)	Jesus' parable to the authorities: The story of the vineyard and of the tenants who killed the...son. 'What will the lord of the vineyard do? He will...give it to others. Have you not read, "The stone which the builders rejected..."' (Mk 12.1-12)
No Tribute to Caesar?	
'There is no other name under heaven by which we may be saved'. The Sanhedrin saw Peter's external appearance, and were amazed (Acts 4.12-14). ?? Jesus accused of opposing the paying of tribute to Caesar (Lk. 23.2)	They questioned Jesus about tribute to Caesar. 'You do not look at a person's face...' And they were amazed at him (Mk 12.13-17)

Apart from depending on the accusation about forbidding tribute to Caesar (Lk. 23.3), Mark's text (12.13-17) seems influenced by Peter's stance before the Sanhedrin (Acts 4.12-14).

It is not clear whether or how the discussion of the great commandment (Mk 12.28-34) is dependent on some part of Acts 2–5. Nor is it clear whether Mark's contrast between the scribes who devour the houses of widows and the widow who gave so much (12.38-44) should be connected with the contrast between the generosity of the community and the fraudulence of Ananias and Sapphira (Acts 4.32–5.11). Mark had already used most of the Acts text (4.32–5.11) in describing the rich man (10.17-31), but that does not preclude using it again in a limited way and from a different viewpoint. In any case, most of Mark's scribes–widow contrast requires other sources or another explanation.

f. *Section 15. From the Temple Woes to the Coming of the Son of Humanity (Acts 6.14; 7.47-50; 8.1-25; Luke 17.20–18.8; Mark 13)*
Proto-Luke speaks of two cataclysmic events: the coming of the kingdom (Lk. 17.20-37) and the fall of the temple (Acts 6.14; 7.47-50). Both are associated with the revelation of the Son of Humanity (Lk. 17.20-24; Acts 7.56).

Mark takes these events, along with the episodes which immediately follow them, and combines them to form a cataclysmic eschatological discourse (Mk 13). In outline:

Temple threatened (Acts 6.14; 7.47-50)	Temple doomed (Mk 13.1-2)
Subsequent woes (8.1-25)	Beginning of woes (13.3-13)
Coming of Son of Humanity (17.20-37)	Son of Humanity (13.14-27)
Widow parable: pray always (18.1-8)	Stay alert (13.28-37)

Stephen's threats against the temple (Acts 6.14; 7.47-50) have been adapted to become part of a vivid statement by Jesus that the temple is doomed (Mk 13.1-2). The woes which follow Stephen's death (Acts 8.1-25)—the deadly upheaval of the church, the prosecuting zeal of Saul, the pretentious claims of Simon, the effort to subvert the Holy Spirit—have all been reshaped to become part of Mark's beginning of woes (13.3-13). Mark has also reshaped the account of the coming of the kingdom and of the Son of Humanity (Lk. 17.20-37). And the parable of the widow and the judge has also been adapted, and has been combined with the image of the fig tree, as follows:

The parable about the need to pray always and not lose heart (Lk. 18.1-8)	The image of the fig tree (see Mk 11.28-31)	Learn from the fig tree about being alert to what is coming. So be alert all the time (Mk 13.28-37)

g. *Section 16. Jesus' Passion: From the Plot to the Night Action (Luke 7.36 50; 22.1-30, 65-71; Acts 4.1-4; 9.18, 19-30; Mark 14)*
Proto-Luke's passion had moved quickly from the plot (Lk. 22.1-6) to the Last Supper (22.7-30) to the appearance before the Sanhedrin (22.66-71). Apart from one small section, the dispute about greatness (Lk. 22.24-30, already used in Mk 9.33-71), Mark 14 uses all this Proto-Lukan material, but he elaborates upon it with new episodes. Before the supper account, he inserts the anointing at Bethany (14.3-9), and on the night itself he adds three major events—Gethsemane (14.32-42), the arrest (14.43-50), and Peter's denials (14.27-31, 66-72).

The anointing at Bethany is relatively easy to account for, at least in part: it is an adaptation of the description of how Jesus was anointed by a sinful woman (Lk. 7.36-50).

The other events (Gethsemane, the arrest, and the denials) are more elusive, yet they, too, emerge as being partly on Proto-Luke. Mark has maintained the basic pattern, established in the preceding chapters (Mk 10–13), of working his way through those sections of Acts 2.1–9.31 which up to this point had not been used. Thus Mk 11.27–ch. 12 had used parts of Acts 2–5, and Mark 13 had used parts of Acts 6–8. Now, in Mark 14, he models the arrest of Jesus to some extent on the arrest of Peter and John (Acts 4.1-4), and he uses events from the life of Paul (Acts 9) as a partial basis for the account of Gethsemane and of Peter's denials. The arrangement may be outlined as follows:

Luke–Acts	Mark
Plot: kill Jesus (Lk. 22.1-6)	Plot: kill Jesus (14.1-2, 10-11)
Sinner's anointing (7.36-50)	Anointing at Bethany (14.3-9)
Passover prepared (22.7-14)	Passover prepared (14.12-17)
Betrayal foretold (22.21-23)	Betrayal foretold (14.18-21)
The Last Supper (22.15-20)	The Last Supper (14.22-26)
Greatness dispute (22.24-30)	[Greatness dispute (9.33-37)]
?	Denials foretold (14.27-31)
Trauma near Damascus (Acts 9.1-8)	Agony in Gethsemane (14.32-42)
Arrest of Peter, John (4.1-4)	Arrest of Jesus (14.43-50)
?	Young man flees (14.51)
Before the Sanhedrin (Lk. 22.66-71)	Before the Sanhedrin (14.53-65)
Paul's affirmations (Acts 9.19-30)	Peter's denials (14.66-72)

Two episodes of Mark 14 remain quite unaccounted for—the foretelling of Peter's denials (14.27-31) and the flight of the young man (14.51).

Saul's collapse near Damascus which brought him into a personal encounter with Jesus (Acts 9.1-8) has become part of the collapse in Gethsemane which brought Jesus into a prayerful encounter with the Father (Mk 14.32-42). For Saul, the encounter meant a transition from a form of death to new life, and for Jesus it meant a transition from the fear of death to a new form of life. Mark's formulation maintains continuity with the transfiguration.

The account of Jesus' appearance before the Sanhedrin (Mk 14.53-65) makes use not only of the corresponding scene in Proto-Luke (Lk. 22.66-71), but also of the appearance of Stephen before the Sanhedrin (Acts 6.11-14).

In describing Peter's repeated denials of Jesus (14.66-72), Mark uses the account of how, after his conversion, Paul repeatedly affirmed Jesus (Acts 9.19-30). At one level, Mark's adaptation accomplishes the opposite of the scene in Acts (it denies Jesus)—a reversal—but, insofar as it fulfills what Jesus had foretold, it becomes a further form of affirming Jesus.

Some of the details are outlined tentatively in Table 41.

h. *Section 17. Jesus' Death and Resurrection (Luke 23.1–24.12; Mark 15.1–16.8)*
At the end of Mark, as at the beginning, the connections with Proto-Luke are relatively easy to see. In outline:

Before Pilate (Lk. 23.1-5, 13-16)	Before Pilate (Mk 15.1-5)
Barabbas; sentencing (23.18-25)	Barabbas; sentencing (15.6-15)
Herod mocks Jesus (23.6-12)	Soldiers mock Jesus (15.16-20)
The way to Golgotha (23.26-31)	[Entry to Jerusalem (11.11-14)]
Crucifixion (23.32-39)	Crucifixion (15.21-32)
The good thief (23.40-43)	[Fig tree (11.20-25)]
The death of Jesus (23.44-49)	The death of Jesus (15.33-41)
The burial of Jesus (23.50-56)	The burial of Jesus (15.42-47)
The resurrection (24.1-12)	The resurrection (16.1-8)

Two parts of Proto-Luke (the way to Golgotha, and the good thief, Lk. 23.26-31, 40-43) were used by Mark at an earlier stage. In a further change, Mark omits the Herod scene (Lk. 23.6-12) but recasts its mockery in the scene with the soldiers (15.16-20).

17. *Mark and Proto-Luke, Episode by Episode* 187

Table 41. *Proto-Luke and Mark: On the Ground; Confronted (Acts 9; Mark 14.32-71)*

\multicolumn{3}{c}{The Damascus Trauma and the Gethsemane Agony}
Theme: fall and rise—Paul's conversion (Acts 9.1-8)	Form: see transfiguration (Mk 9.2-8)	Theme and form: Jesus' in Gethsemane. (Mk 14.32-42)
Saul comes to Damascus breathing threats, murder.		Jesus in Gethsemane feels dread, distress. ??
Journeying along a light from heaven surrounded him and falling to the ground		Going on a little he fell to the ground and he prayed…
he heard a voice saying to him 'Saul, Saul, why do you persecute me?… But rise and go…'. Those with him were speechless hearing the voice but seeing no one.		and he said 'Abba, Father…take this cup from me But not as I will…'. He came and found them sleeping…
Saul rose from the ground and opening his eyes saw nothing…		Again he found them sleeping for their eyes were heavy…
\multicolumn{3}{c}{The Arrest}
While they were speaking the priests and the commander of the temple and the Sadducees came upon them,		While he was still speaking Judas arrived with an armed crowd from the high priests and scribes and elders…
annoyed that they were teaching [in the temple] about Jesus… And they laid hands on them… (Acts 4.1-4)		And they laid hands on him… He said, 'I was with you daily teaching in the temple…' (Mk 14.43-50)
\multicolumn{3}{c}{Accused before the Sanhedrin}
Jesus before the Sanhedrin: 'Son of God! We have no more need of witnesses' (Lk. 22.66-71)	Stephen before false witnesses and the Sanhedrin (Acts 6.11-14)	Jesus before the Sanhedrin: False witnesses. 'Son of the Most High! We have no more need of witnesses' (Mk 14.53-65)
\multicolumn{3}{c}{The Affirmations and Denials}
Saul was with the Damascus disciples; he preached in the synagogues: 'Jesus is the Son of God'(Acts 9.19b-20)		Peter in the high priest's court: Maidservant: 'You were with Jesus. But he denied it' (Mk 14.66-68)
All who heard him…said, 'Is not this the destroyer', but he insisted all the more: 'This is the Christ' (9.21-22)		She said again to the bystanders, 'This is one of them'. But he again denied (14.69-70a)
In Jerusalem Saul tried to join the disciples and all feared him, not believing he is a disciple… He told them how on the road he saw the Lord and spoke to him, and how he spoke openly in the name of Jesus (9.26-27)		Later, the bystanders say to Peter, 'Truly you are one of them'. He began to curse and swear. 'I do not know this man' (14.70b-71)

5. Conclusion

As already indicated, the aim here is not a full explanation of Mark, but simply to indicate whether Proto-Luke provided one component. The evidence is affirmative:

- *External plausibility*. While it is not possible to reconstruct the background of either Mark (perhaps Rome or Syrian Antioch?) or Proto-Luke, it is plausible that Mark should have been aware of Proto-Luke's work. This is particularly so because, in diverse ways, both use the Elijah–Elisha narrative as a form of fundamental model. This is the sort of broad continuity that makes a link between the two plausible.
- *Similarities*. The similarities are multiple, diverse, and generally in the same order.
- *Intelligible differences*. The differences between Mark and Proto-Luke are radical, yet they are generally understandable. Mark's emphasis on Jesus' family (Mk 6.1-6), for instance, rather than Jesus' centuries-long genealogy (Lk. 3.23-38) becomes more understandable in light of Mark's general shift from history towards biography.

The simplest explanation of the data is that Mark had a copy of Proto-Luke—just as, at a later stage, canonical Luke had a copy of Mark.

18

Mark's Sources: Mark and the Epistles—
Peter's Central Maxims (1 Peter 2.18–3.17) as One Component
of Mark 10.1-45: An Exploration*

While Mark's first word corresponds to the first word of Genesis, his subsequent words correspond to verse 1 of the Pauline corpus (Mk 1.1, *euaggeliou Iēsou Christou*, 'gospel/ good news of Jesus Christ'; Rom. 1.1, *Christou Iēsou...euaggelion*, 'Paul, servant of Christ Jesus...appointed to the gospel of God'). And, as already noted, his initial quotation (Mk 1.2-3), blends the first and last books of the prophetic corpus (Isaiah and Malachi).

It is possible that the precision of the connections between Mark's opening (1.1-3) and three great bodies of literature—Old Testament narrative, Old Testament prophets, and the epistles—is the result of an extraordinary coincidence, like winning a draw three times in succession. There is also a simpler explanation: like many others, he had copies of the texts; and he is signaling, from the beginning, that his vision of history builds on the widest inclusion of great writings. What he is doing is literary and systematic.

Within such a context, it is appropriate to re-evaluate the many detailed connections which some scholars have shown between Mark and the epistles[1] including 1 Peter (Rolland 1992; cf. Boismard and Benoit 1972: 23-24). Boismard and Benoit (1972: 23-24), for instance, maintain that Mark uses Pauline words and themes. Likewise Schenk (1992: 903): 'Mark shows familiarity with Paul's epistles'. Rolland (1992: 778) seems to go further: 'Mark has nourished himself on the letters of Paul...and Peter'.

To test these opinions, particularly the latter view of Rolland, this chapter will compare Mark 10 with the center of 1 Peter—2.18–3.17, almost exactly the text which B. Reicke entitles 'Maxims for Daily Living' (Reicke 1964: 97). These maxims, which contain a household code, can easily be divided into three parts:

1. Suffering service (1 Pet. 2.18-25). While 1 Peter has a number of references to the idea of service (1.12; 2.16; 4.10-11), only the exhortation to slaves (2.18-25) associates service/slavery with the suffering of Christ—Christ being depicted as the suffering Servant of Isa. 52.13–ch. 53.
2. Husbands and wives (1 Pet. 3.1-7). Just as 1 Peter's exhortation to slaves is the epistle's unique mention of suffering service, so the exhortation at the beginning of ch. 3 is the epistle's only mention of husbands and wives.
3. Zealots of goodness (1 Pet. 3.8-17). This third passage has a unique stress on goodness, using the words 'good' or 'goodness' six times (3.11, 17) and speaking even of the need to be zealots of the good (3.13). This repetition of 'good' is unique, not only in 1 Peter itself, but, with the exception of Romans (ch. 7; see 13.3-4), in all the epistles.

Like 1 Peter, Mark also contains each of these basic elements just once, and, again like 1 Peter, clusters the elements together (Mk 10). In simplified outline:

---

* This chapter is an edited version of a paper delivered to the Irish Biblical Association, Bellinter Conference Centre, near Navan, 27 April 1979. Abstracted in *PIBA* 4 (1980): 98.
1. See Wildemann 1983: 314-35; Breytenbach 1992; Goulder 1992; Schenk 1992.

1 Peter 2.18–3.17	*Mark 10.1-45*
A. Slaves: like Christ, Suffering Servant (2.18-25; 3.8-9a).	
B. Wives…husbands: like Sarah, Abraham (3.1-7)	Divorce: see Moses, creation (10.1-16)
C. Practice good (3.9b-17)	The rich man and the good (10.17-31)
	Not glory but Servantlike service (10.32-45)

The fuller outline (Table 42) follows the order of 1 Peter—bringing Mk 10.32-45 forward.[2]

Table 42. *Central Maxims (1 Peter 2.18–3.17; Mark 10.1-45)*

A. SERVICE AND THE SERVANT (1 PETER 2.18-25; MARK 10.32-45)	
1. House-servants, obey masters (1 Pet. 2.18)	Be servants, not lords (Mk 10.42b-43a)
2. Accepting undeserved punishment—as did Christ (2.19-21a)	Being the slave of all—like the Son of Humanity (10.43b-45)
3. Follow his footsteps (2.21b)	On the road, Jesus walking ahead (10.32a)
4. Christ's suffering: looking back (2.22-24)	Christ's suffering: looking forward (10.32b-34)
5. Straying sheep return to shepherd (2.25)	?? Jesus calls the divided disciples (10.41-42a)
B. WIVES, HUSBANDS, AND CHILDREN (1 PETER 3.1-9A; MARK 10.1-16)	
6. Wives, as subject to husbands (3.1a)	Husband who divorce wives (10.1-2)
7. Wives: what counts is the heart (3.1b-4)	Divorce is from hardness of heart (10.3-6)
8. The precedent: Sarah and Abraham (3.5-6a)	The precedent: creation (10.7-12)
9. Women as children, weak, but heirs (3.6b-7)	Children/childlike and the kingdom (10.13-16)
10. Brotherly compassion, humility (3.8-9a)	[?? I cannot grant high seats (10.35-40)]
C. SEEKING GOODNESS (1 PETER 3.9B-17; MARK 10.17-31)	
11. The wish to inherit life (3.9b-10a)	What do I do to inherit eternal life? (10.17-18)
12. The required conduct (3.10b-11)	Keep the commandments (10.19)
13. The Lord's eyes are on the virtuous (3.12)	Jesus looks at the rich man (10.20-22)
14. The good are not harmed (3.13-14)	The rich cannot enter (10.23-27)
15. Answer questions on one's hope (3.15-17)	Peter questions Jesus (10.28-31)

1. *More Detailed Analysis (Tentative)*

a. *Block A. Suffering Service (1 Peter 2.18-25; 3.8-9a; Mark 10.32-45)*
While Peter exhorts to suffering service, Mark does the same but says it in story form—in the account of Jesus and his disciples going up to Jerusalem. An examination of the texts, section-by-section (Table 42), shows that 1 Peter has been absorbed and recast by Mark.

---

2. Apart from moving marriage and children to the front (10.1-16), Mark generally follows the order of 1 Peter. Occasional rearrangement, artificial though it seem, occurs elsewhere in the New Testament. For instance, Ephesians' use of Colossians is 'a meticulous imitative adaptation…[a] procedure…of… laboriously dissecting and reassembling passages' (W.J. Harrington 1965: 302). For comments on the relationship of 1 Pet. 2.21-24 to Mk 10.45, see Roloff 1972–73: 43, 45.

(1) *Section 1. Servants and lords (1 Peter 2.18; Mark 10.42b-43a)*. This section highlights the contrast between lords and servants and in both texts, acts as an introduction to the theme of total service.

(2) *Section 2. Total service...like that of Christ the Suffering Servant (1 Peter 2.19-21a; Mark 10.43b-45)*. Having emphasized the distance between lords and servants, both texts go on to a notion of total service beyond the demands of reason—service which accepts unjust suffering (1 Pet. 2.19-20), and which makes one the slave of all (Mk 10.43b-44). This is what gives one grace and glory (1 Peter: *charis...kleos*); this is what makes one great and first (Mark: *megas...prōtos*). And the inspiration for this service is found in Christ, the Suffering Servant who gave himself for others (1 Pet. 2.21a; Mk 10.45).

(3) *Section 3. Following his footsteps (1 Peter 2.21b; Mark 10.32a)*. Peter's image of following in the footsteps of the suffering Christ is balanced by Mark's image of the disciples following Jesus on the road to Jerusalem. Mark, however, also notes that the disciples were astonished and afraid (*ethambounto...efobounto*). These two words seem connected to the Suffering Servant theme which pervades Peter's text (2.21-25); according to the beginning of the fourth Servant Song, people are amazed and in wonder at him (Isa. 52.14-15, *ekstēsontai...thaumasontai*). In other words, what Mark seems to have done, apart from using 1 Peter directly, is to have gone back to Peter's source text (Isa. 52.13–53.12) and devised a fresh way of using it. Thus Mark's entire section on suffering and service (10.32-45) opens and closes as does the fourth Servant Song—with the astonishment and awe of the people (Isa. 52.14-15; Mk 10.32), and with the Servant giving his life for the redemption of many (Isa. 53.12; Mk 10.45).

(4) *Section 4. Christ's suffering (1 Peter 2.22-24; Mark 10.32b-34)*. Just as the Servant was innocent and willing, so is Jesus. Peter brings out this idea of innocence and willingness by quoting some words from that part of Isaiah's text which refers to the Servant's innocence and careful use or non-use of speech (Isa. 53.7-9: before his executioners 'he did not open his mouth...there was no deceit in his mouth'). In Mark, Jesus is not yet in the presence of his executioners, so his innocence, willingness, and lack of deceit are depicted in a totally different way—by speaking openly of what is going to happen to him (10.32b). The speech that accepted the suffering has become—in Mark—the speech that accepts the suffering in advance.

Peter's description (1 Pet. 2.23-24) of Christ suffering like the Servant is paralleled by Mark's picture of Jesus foretelling his sufferings. But there is more than suffering—there is death and life (1 Pet. 2.24), death and resurrection (Mk 10.34). Peter explicitly relates these death and life elements to a process within many people, within the entire community ('that we, being dead to sins, might live to integrity, by whose wounds you have been healed'). Mark brings out the involvement of many people—the community—by more subtle touches. When Jesus announces his suffering, death, and life he carefully calls the *Twelve*; he stresses that *we* are going up to Jerusalem, and that the Son of Humanity will suffer, die, and rise. (The involvement of 'the nations' in the death of the Son of Humanity [Mk 10.33-34], seems connected to the involvement of the nations in the death of the Servant [Isa. 52.15].)

(5) *Section 5. Returning to the shepherd (1 Peter 2.25; Mark 10.41-42a??)*. Peter's image of scattered sheep returning to their shepherd (see Isa. 53.6) may, perhaps, be a component in Mark's picture of the divided and angry Twelve being called back to Jesus.

In these larger sections (1 Pet. 2.18-25; 3.8-9a; Mk 10.32-45), the text of the epistle has been transformed into narrative which has a strength and identity of its own. The notion of following Christ takes on new power and vitality when it is depicted as following the Son of Humanity along the road to Jerusalem, to a city of cruel powers. The threat of internal disharmony becomes more real when it is seen in a quarrel among the Twelve. And all these elements of narrative have been blended together so that Mark's final product is not a collection of piecemeal stories each with no other purpose than to illustrate a passage of 1 Peter; rather, the narrative pieces are part of one larger narrative whole.

Thus, the passion prediction, for instance (10.32-34), while reflecting the text of 1 Peter, is so shaped that it fits into Mark's larger framework of passion predictions and a Passion Narrative. Though Mk 10.32-45 makes systematic use of 1 Peter, and though in itself it constitutes a new and unified presentation of the drama of the Suffering Servant, it can be fully understood only in the light of Mark's entire work, in the light of all his other sources, and in the light of his encompassing vision.

Just as Mark is not a slavish imitation of the form of 1 Peter, neither does it give a slavish reproduction of the epistle's thought. The content of 1 Peter is heightened or refined. Thus, while Mark is faithful to Peter's basic notion of Christ as innocent and willing to face death (1 Pet. 2.22; Mk 10.32b), Mark's image of Christ is more exalted: he is one who knows the future.

There seems to be a change, too, in the attitude to lords or masters. Peter would grant that some of them may be good and kind; Mark seems to regard all worldly powers as overbearing.

More strikingly still, Peter's notion of slavery does not appear in Mark. Nor does his repeated notion of accepting unjust suffering. Instead, these ideas of slaves and unjust suffering have been replaced by the repeated notion of voluntary service. The only slavery mentioned by Mark is the slavery of willing service to all people—not that of institutional slaves to their masters.

b. *Block B. Husbands and Wives (and Children) (1 Peter 3.1-7; Mark 10.1-16)*
(1) *Section 6. Husbands and subject wives (1 Peter 3.1a; Mark 10.1-2).* Peter assumes that men have superiority over women ('wives…submitting to… husbands') and, likewise in Mark, the Pharisees' question on divorce presupposes the privileged position of men—for while there is some dispute over the legality of dismissing a wife, the question of dismissing a husband does not arise. Initially, therefore, the link between the texts is very broad (and Mark is using other sources, especially about Jesus' traveling and teaching).

(2) *Section 7. Putting the word and heart into marriage (1 Peter 3.1b-4; Mark 10.3-9).* Peter is intent on improving the quality of marriages, especially in situations where the husband rejects the word. In Peter's view, the key to acceptance of the word is through the heart. If wives show the right kind of heart, husbands will be won over to the word. Mark, too, wants to put heart and the word into marriage. He rejects the hardness of heart which led to the Mosaic law of divorce, and he invokes God's original word concerning marriage (Gen. 1.27; 2.24). In other words, like Peter, Mark sees a connection between a good heart and acceptance of God's word, and he wants to put these things into a defective marriage situation. Both texts conclude with a little note that the idea of a heart-filled marriage is important in God's eyes (it is of great value, 1 Pet. 3.4b; it must not be broken up, Mk 10.9).

(3) *Section 8. The ideal marriage situation (1 Peter 3.5-6a; Mark 10.10-12).* In their different ways, Peter and Mark express the ideal they have been advocating: Peter, a

marriage where the wife is submissive; Mark, a picture of marriage which does not admit of divorce. Both give a double statement of this ideal (1 Peter: the holy women *submitted*...Sarah *obeyed*; Mark: Whoever *divorces*...if she *divorces*), and both connect this ideal with a special setting: Peter's ideal is a reflection of 'the holy women'; Mark's ideal is stated in 'the house' with his disciples. In other words, both relate their ideal with the believing community.[3]

While the similarities between the two wives/husbands texts seem to reflect careful literary indebtedness, there are differences which point to bold adaptation.

First, Mark extends Peter's idea of the influence of the word and heart on a marriage. Peter had implied that the word and heart should make a marriage good. Mark goes further: God's word and the true quality should not only *make* a good marriage good; they should *keep* it good; they should exclude divorce.

Second, while Peter does envisage a certain reciprocity within the marriage relationship (obedience in exchange for respect or consideration), he stresses the submissive role of women. Not so Mark. While the gospel text opens with the Pharisees assuming the superiority of the husband, the passage closes with a balancing statement which implies the equality of man and wife. This statement, given within the house, appears to be saying that, within the community at least, man and wife are equal. Mark's intention looks deliberate: his twofold statement of equality is in precise contrast to Peter's twofold emphasis on submission and obedience (1 Pet. 3.5-6b; Mk 10.10-12).

(4) *Section 9. Honor the childlike (1 Peter 3.6b-7; Mark 10.10-12)*. Mark's boldness with regard to 1 Peter is seen again in his handling of Peter's final words to husbands and wives (3.6b-7). The epistle refers to wives as 'children' and as being 'weaker'. With his statement of equality regarding divorce, Mark has already said all he wants about wives. Thus by playing on Peter's word 'children', Mark uses Peter's text as a basis for his account of Jesus and the little children. The texts have several points in common:

- The sudden introduction of the basic image of children.
- The contrast in conduct (1 Peter: between doing good and intimidation; Mark: between touching the children and rebuking).
- The strong show the weak awareness and honor (1 Peter: husbands should be aware of their wives' situation and treat these 'weaker vessels' with honor; Mark: Jesus suddenly sees what is going on and insists on letting the children through—'Do not forbid them, for of such is the kingdom of God'. Thus he is sensitive to their weakness and treats them with honor).
- Clarification of the honor due to the weak (Peter explains that the wives are due honor because of their place in the world of grace and life—'coheirs of grace and life'; Mark, too, clarifies his statement about the honor due to children. Not only do children belong to the kingdom of God, but it is *only* those who are like children who belong to it. Here, again, Mark goes beyond Peter: the epistle grants those who are physically vulnerable an equal place in the spiritual world;[4] the gospel grants them a special place; theirs is the only way).
- Finally, Peter's image of the prayers of a husband and wife, implying both human intimacy and closeness with the Lord, is recaptured in Mark's striking picture of

---

3. There may be a connection between Peter's use of 'house' to refer to the community of believers (1 Pet. 2.5; 4.17), and Mark's use of house, especially when the house appears as the place of disciples or believers (Mk 7.17, 9.28-33; 10.10).

4. Peter's recognition of women as coheirs of the grace of life, implying that women are equal to men in the spiritual world, may have been one of the factors that led Mark to extend equality into a social institution such as marriage.

human intimacy and closeness with the Lord: Jesus embraces the children and blesses them.

(5) *Section 10. The need for harmony and humility (1 Peter 3.8-9a; Mark 10.35-40??)*. Peter's brief exhortation to harmony and humility is apparently balanced by the scene in which James and John exhibit an enormous lack of those qualities and are corrected by Jesus (1 Pet. 3.8-9a; Mk 10.35-40). In other words, with its contrast between the exclusive power-seeking of the brothers and the courtesy and humility of Jesus, the Markan scene is like a living sermon on the virtues recommended by Peter.

Again, one of Mark's other sources at this point appears to have been Isaiah 53. The basic contrast between the brothers and Jesus, and their complete failure to understand to what extent he is a man of suffering rather than glory, generally corresponds to the misunderstanding surrounding the Servant (Isa. 53.1-3). In both texts, those who surround the Servant ('we' in Isa. 53.1-3 and Mk 10.37) see him in terms of power and glory—failing to appreciate the crucial role of suffering in his life.

c. *Block C. Zealots for Goodness (1 Peter 3.9b-17; Mark 10.17-31)*
Peter's rather abstract exhortation to doing good has been highly dramatized in Mark's contrast between the rich man and the disciples.

(1) *Section 11. The wish to inherit life (1 Peter 3.9b-10a; Mark 10.17-18)*. The opening exchange between Jesus and the rich man is laden with the influence of Peter's wording: the unique repetition of the word 'good'; 'in order…to inherit'; 'life'; 'do'. Yet Mark's treatment of the epistle is not slavish. Apart from producing so memorable a dramatization of Peter's idea of wishing for life, he has refined Peter's thought. He has changed the notion of life to that of eternal life; he has gone behind Peter's multifaceted ideas of goodness and pointed to the source of it all: 'No one is good but God alone'.

(2) *Section 12. The one who wishes for life must keep the commandments (1 Peter 3.10b-11; Mark 10.19)*. Peter's code of conduct from Psalm 34 is balanced in Mark by a code of conduct based on the Ten Commandments. This is a good example of Mark's combination of fidelity and creativity. Insofar as he gives an Old Testament code, he is doing as Peter had done. But insofar as he is setting up the Mosaic Commandments only to go beyond them a few verses later (10.21), he is bringing out his own thesis of the inadequacy of the Mosaic Law—just as he had earlier shown its inadequacy regarding marriage (10.4-9).

(3) *Section 13. The Lord looks on the just and answers (1 Peter 3.12; Mark 10.20-22)*. Peter's brief quotation about the Lord setting his eyes on the just and answering their prayer is paralleled by the dramatic picture of Jesus looking with love on the man who had kept the commandments, and answering his question concerning inheriting eternal life. In a very down-to-earth way, Jesus put his eyes on the just man and responded to his request. But again Mark is not simply dramatizing Peter; he is developing Peter's thought. He goes from an expression of the eyes to the love that lies behind them. And he goes from Peter's general statements about being good and just to the supreme, concrete generosity of giving everything to the poor, putting one's treasure in heaven, and following Jesus. From Peter's repeated theme of goodness, Mark goes on to clarify both its source (God alone is good) and its culmination (give all to the poor).

In Peter's text (3.12b), there is a sudden contrast in the Lord's expression: his eyes were on the just, but his face is against evildoers. In Mark, the contrast is equally sudden and much more dramatic: from Jesus' eyes of love to the rich man's crestfallen face (10.22). Again, Mark is both faithful and creative. Like Peter, he gives the contrast of facial expressions. But, probably because he does not regard the opposition between the Lord and evildoer as due to the Lord, he places the expression of rejection or opposition not on the face of the Lord, but on the face of the rich man.

(4) *Section 14. Conduct and its reward (1 Peter 3.13-14; Mark 10.23-27)*. With almost parallel phrases, Peter emphasizes that good conduct is rewarded: those who do good are not harmed, those who seek justice are blessed. Mark also produces two parallel phrases on the link between conduct and reward, but he gives the other side of the coin—the link between a bad lifestyle and a bad end: how difficult it is for the rich to enter the Kingdom of God (Mk 10.23-25). Then, just as Peter has a double warning against being fearful or upset (3.14b), so Mark twice reports the consternation of the disciples (10.24a, 26), and he implies that they should trust in God (10.27).

(5) *Section 15. Answering those who question about one's hope in Christ (1 Peter 3.15-17; Mark 10.28-31)*. Peter speaks twice of those who have set their heart/conduct on Christ (3.15a, 16b); and the gospel in turn refers twice to leaving everything and following Christ ('and followed you', 10.28; 'for my sake', 10.29). Both writers picture this Christ-centered conduct as being questioned—but in different ways: in 1 Peter it is being questioned from the outside; in Mark it is being questioned from within. Hence, there is a vast difference in the replies. In 1 Peter, the effect of the reply is to shame the skeptical outsiders; in Mark, however, the reply pours blessings on the believing insiders. But Mark does note that with the blessings come persecutions too. In other words, he does not concentrate on the hostile outsiders, but he does acknowledge that they are there and cause problems.

From the world's point of view, it is, quite simply, better not to suffer. But Peter stands this worldly principle on its head: if suffering is the way to avoid doing evil, then it is better to suffer (3.17). This idea that Christ turns values upside down seems to be reflected in Mark's cryptic phrase about the first being last and the last first (10.31).

2. Conclusion

It seems impossible to account for the relationship between the texts except by saying that Mark systematically distilled the text of 1 Peter. The relationship is far too complex and systematic to be accounted for by such a fluid link as memory or oral tradition. While using 1 Peter, Mark appears to have gone back to Isaiah's text on the Suffering Servant.

Mark's reworking of 1 Peter involves diverse developments. The epistle, for instance, shows no awareness of the Passion Narratives as found in the gospel tradition, but instead relies on Isaiah's description of the Suffering Servant. And the epistle also takes the submissiveness of slaves and women for granted. Mark, however, has another point of view. While keeping Peter's idea of the Suffering Servant, he relates the death of Jesus to a new narrative: to execution in Jerusalem. He depicts Jesus as knowing the future. And he shows a unique sensitivity not only about spiritual concepts like God, goodness, and life, but also about basic issues of society. In Mark's gospel children are treated with honor; ideally at least, riches are for the poor; slavery has been omitted; and women are seen as equal. In divorce, at least, the double standard has been removed.

Unit 4. The Central Thesis Expanded: Matthew

19

Matthew's Twofold Expansion of Mark:
Using Proto-Luke, the *Logia*, and the Greatest Discourses

1. *From* Imitatio/Emulatio *to 'Rewritten Bible'*

Matthew's dependence on Mark, while sometimes disputed, is accepted by most researchers, and so, for the purposes of this study, will be taken as a given.

Aspects of Matthew's reworking of Mark may be seen in the context of a widespread literary phenomenon which was essentially Jewish—'rewritten Bible' (see especially Vermes 1973; D. Harrington 1986). Within rewritten Bible there was great flexibility, yet Matthew's use of it signals a change from the way Proto-Luke reworked the Septuagint. Proto-Luke brought radical changes to the Old Testament storyline, thus apparently reflecting the inventive spirit of Greco-Roman *imitatio/emulatio*. The authors of rewritten Bible, however, 'take as their literary framework the flow of the biblical text itself and apparently have as their major purpose the clarification and actualization of the biblical story' (D. Harrington 1986: 239). To some degree, this was also Matthew's approach to Mark. He kept Mark's essential storyline, yet in other ways he too, like Proto-Luke, was capable of completely refashioning some sources, including the Old Testament.

In rewriting Mark, Matthew introduced a twofold expansion:

1. *Expansion of the Markan storyline* (for instance, by adding an infancy narrative).
2. *Expansion towards long discourses.*

The sources for the expansions are often designated Q and M—'M' being shorthand for 'Matthew's special sources'—but it is possible to be more specific.

As regards the storyline, Matthew's expansion depends significantly on the reworking of Proto Luke. Matthew's infancy narrative, for instance, uses Luke 1–2 as one of its components.

As regards the discourses, Matthew incorporates the Deuteronomy-based *Logia*, and reshapes leading discourses from two great figures—the Deuteronomic discourses of Moses, and Paul's epistle to the Romans. At one level, Paul is not far from Moses. As 1 Corinthians shows (see Chapter 13 above), the epistles sometimes reshape the Pentateuch, especially Deuteronomy. Sometimes Matthew uses Deuteronomy and Romans for the storyline rather than the discourses.

The discussion occupies five chapters of the present study:

Chapter 19:	Matthew's use of: Proto-Luke; the *Logia*
Chapters 20–21:	Matthew's use of Romans
Chapters 22–23:	Matthew's use of Deuteronomy

2. *Matthew's Use of Proto-Luke: One Feature*
in Expanding Mark's Story Line—An Initial Investigation

The hypothesis of Proto-Luke helps to explain important features of Matthew, especially Matthew's expansion of Mark's storyline. These expansive texts—all partly dependent on Proto-Luke—include the following (ranging from Mt. 1–2 to Mt. 23):

a. *The Infancy Narrative (Matthew 1–2)*

Proto-Luke's infancy narrative and genealogy provide part of the background for Matthew 1–2. In approximate terms, the shared elements are as follows:

- Genealogy (Mt. 1.1-17; Lk. 3.23-38).
- Annunciation and birth (Mt. 1.18-25; Lk. 1.7, 21, 26-39) (cf. Benoit and Boismard 1965: I, 4).
- The ruler who sent people to Bethlehem (Mt. 2.1-8; Lk. 2.1-6).
- Adoration by magi/shepherds (Mt. 2.9-12; Lk. 2.8-20).
- Waiting for the Lord (Mt. 2.13-15; Lk. 2.22-32).
- The fall of many in Israel (Mt. 2.16-18; Lk. 2.33-38).
- End of the search for the child; return to Nazareth (Mt. 2.19-23; Lk. 2.39-52).

Further aspects of Matthew 1–2 are provided by (Proto-Lukan) Acts, especially by Acts 7 and 12.1–13.12. For instance, Stephen's survey of Israel's history gives an importance to Abraham, Egypt, David, and Babylon that seems to be reflected in Matthew's history of Jesus (Mt. 1.2, 6, 11-12, 17; 2.2, 13-15; Acts 7.1-4, 8-9, 17-22, 29, 43, 45). Other links may be listed:

- Star and magi(cians) (Mt. 2; Acts 7.43; 8.9; 13.8).
- The plot of king Herod (Mt. 2.1-7; Acts 12.1-3).
- The foiling of the plot by an angel, Herod's murderous reaction, and his death (Mt. 2.12-19; Acts 12.6-7, 18-23).
- The return of Jesus and his Nazarene calling in accordance with what was said by the prophets, rather as Paul had returned to his strict calling in accordance with what was said to the prophets and teachers at Antioch (Mt. 2.20-23; Acts 12.24–13.3; cf. Rom. 1.1-2).

b. *Matthew 3–4*

Most of Matthew 3–4 consists of an adaptation and elaboration of the beginning of Mark (especially Mk 1.1-20, 39, and 3.7-12).

The two most notable elaborations concern John's preaching (Mt. 3.7-10, 'Brood of vipers…') and the temptation of Jesus (Mt. 4.1-11). As will be indicated later, these two elaborations—vipers and temptations—rely partly on Romans and Deuteronomy (the temptation account uses Deuteronomy explicitly, Mt. 4.4, 7, 10). However, the harshness of the 'Brood of vipers' confrontation has echoes of the confrontations of Peter with Simon the magician (Acts 8.20-23) and of Paul with Bar-Jesus (Elymas Magos, Acts 13.10-11).

c. *Matthew 8*

The miracles narrated in Matthew 8–9 are largely taken from Mark, but two of its texts are from Proto-Luke: the cure of the centurion's servant (Mt. 8.5-13; Lk. 7.1-10) and Jesus' three challenges to the would-be disciples (Mt. 8.18-22; Lk. 9.57-60). Because of his different context, Matthew omits the third challenge about not turning back from the plough(ing) (Lk. 9.61-62). In Luke, the image of ploughing, with its evoking of vitality and fruitfulness, acts as an appropriate introduction to the mission (Lk. 10.1-20). In Matthew, however, the challenges introduce not a mission but a storm, and for that topic the second challenge was more suitable. The storm was potentially deadly, and the second challenge speaks of burial and the dead (Mt. 8.21-22).

d. *Matthew 10*

The missionary discourse in Matthew 10 relies heavily on both Mark and Romans (9.1-5; 10.14–11.24), but it probably used other sources as well, particularly Proto-Luke. For instance, the image of the mission as a harvest (Mt. 9.37-38) draws on Lk. 10.2. And the picture of fleeing from one city to the next (Mt. 10.23) partly corresponds to events in Acts (8.1-5; 14.19-21).

e. *Matthew 11–13*
At one level, Matthew 11–13 deals with the difficulties and evil encountered by the kingdom/realm of God, particularly the resistance of the Jews. But rather than become engulfed in these problems, the gospel sets them in the context of the greater reality of the mystery of God's action, God's wisdom. For example, God's patience allows the bad element, the darnel, to remain in the ground for the moment (Mt. 13.24-30, 36-43). Hence, the encompassing element of Matthew 11–13 is mystery and wisdom.

Within these chapters (11–13), Matthew's most obvious indebtedness to Proto-Luke occurs in ch. 11. The portrait of the Baptist (Mt. 11.2-19) reproduces most of Lk. 7.18-35, and the condemnation of the unrepentant cities (Mt. 11.20-24) is a variation on Lk. 10.13-15.

Matthew 12 does not seem to use Proto-Luke but it is useful to look briefly at some of its main sources. With its episodes of more direct clashes with the Jews (more direct than in ch. 11) particularly concerning the sabbath and exorcism, it is a chapter which builds closely on Mark, especially Mark 3 (Mt. 12.1-32; Mk 2.23–3.6; 3.20-35).

Near the end of Matthew 12, however, where the text looks more closely at evil (Mt. 12.33-45), the nature of the reliance on Mark changes. Matthew not only switches from Mark 3 to Mark 8 (the clash with the Pharisees concerning a sign, 8.11-13) but also brings in other images, beginning with that of a tree and its fruit (Mt. 12.33).

This may suggest that Matthew is drawing on Q, but that explanation does not seem either necessary or appropriate. Matthew is using Mark quite freely and, apart from Mark, Matthew is also using Romans. This combination (the free use of Mark and of Romans) may explain part of Matthew's text. The image of the tree is found in both Mark (11.12-14, 20-25) and Romans (11.14-24), and in both cases, it has to do with the refusal of the Jews to accept the gospel—precisely the larger issue in Matthew 12.

Aspects of Matthew's text remain unexplained, including the elusive phrase 'Brood of vipers' (Mt. 12.34; cf. Mt. 3.7), but Matthew's steady dependence on Romans, plus the capacity of Mark and Romans to explain the leading image of the tree, means that there is little or no room left for invoking the importation of whole passages from Q.

Before raising any questions about Matthew 13 and Proto-Luke, it is necessary to clarify a more basic relationship—the dependence of Matthew 13 on Mark 4. The more obvious aspects of this relationship may be outlined as follows:

Mark 4	*Matthew 13*
The sower, and explanation	The sower, and explanation
The lamp	See Mt. 5.14-16
The measure	See Mt. 7.2
Seed: grows during sleep	Seed: weeds added during sleep
The mustard seed	The mustard seed
	The leaven
	The weeds explained
	The treasure
	The pearl
	The dragnet
	The householder and his storeroom

The similarity indicates that Matthew has absorbed all of Mark's text, adapting two of the parables to fit into the Sermon on the Mount, and adapting a third one—that of the seed growing by itself, even during sleep—to form a component of the parable of the weeds.

Even Matthew's distinct parables are partly adaptations or elaborations of material found in Mark. As just mentioned, the parable of the weeds builds on the parable of the seed growing during sleep. And the next longest parable—the dragnet—seems in turn to reflect aspects of the parable of the weeds. The parable of the leaven, likewise, appears to be modelled partly on the parable which precedes it—that of the mustard seed.

Matthew's way of expanding Mark's parables is clarified by the way he sometimes expands Mark's miracles. The two final miracles in Matthew 9—the healing of the two blind men (9.27-31) and of the dumb man (9.32-34)—do not have exact equivalents in Mark. Yet they are drawn from Mark. Meier (1980: 98-99) outlines the process:

> [In ch. 9] Mt needs two more miracles to round out his final trio. More specifically, he needs the healing of some blind and deaf persons, if Jesus' report in 11.5 is to reflect the foregoing narrative accurately and if the prophecy of Is 35.4-6 is to be fulfilled. Hence, in these last two miracles, Mt creates shadowy twins or 'doublets' of more substantial miracle stories in Mk, stories Mt will give in fuller form later.

Likewise, Matthew has created variations of some of Mark's parable. Thus, even more than appears at first sight, the primary source of Matthew 13 is Mark.

However, several elements remain unexplained, particularly the emphasis on evil invading God's realm, the brief picture of the woman, and, in the parables of the treasure and the pearl, the selling and buying.

Here the question arises as to whether some of these Matthean parables depend partly on Proto-Luke's picture of the church in Acts, particularly the mixture of generosity and fraud which was brought into the church by the selling activity of Barnabas, Ananias, and Saphira (Acts 4.32–5.11).

f. *Matthew 13.53–18.35*

This part of Matthew is concerned not so much with the mystery of God's realm as with some of the more down-to-earth aspects of that mystery, particularly the church.

The narrative section (Mt. 14.1–17.21) depends heavily on Mark but has been colored slightly by Romans. The discourse section (Mt. 17.22–ch. 18) on the other hand, while making some use of Mark, is very dependent on other sources including Deuteronomy 14–15 (see Chapter 22).

One of the features of these chapters is the highlighting of Peter (Mt. 14.28-33; 15.15; 16.17-19; 17.24-27; 18.21-22). References to Peter are frequent in Acts (1.1–15.35, especially chs. 1–5) and it is possible that Peter's role in the church of Acts may have contributed to his role in Matthew 14–18.

g. *Matthew 23*

The lament over Jerusalem (Mt. 23.37-39)—over its killing and stoning—seems to echo aspects of the story of Stephen, especially his death and his last words (Acts 7.47–8.1).

The hypothesis proposed here—Matthew's use of Proto-Luke—seems promising. At various important points, it provides a verifiable source for Matthean texts that otherwise have no traceable roots. Yet this analysis is quite limited. It contributes not so much a proof as an avenue of investigation. The value of that avenue can become clear only with time through a long process of scholarly testing.

3. *Matthew's Incorporation of the* Logia

As Proto-Luke was eventually expanded to form Luke–Acts, so the *Logia* were expanded to form Matthew, or at least to inspire the way Matthew developed Mark.

The original wording of the *Logia* was preserved (as was the original wording of Proto-Luke), but the text was dispersed into two places—the beginning of the Sermon on the Mount, and the gospel's central section (Mt. 11–13). And the opening sections of the *Logia,* the five beatitudes and five antitheses, were further dispersed throughout almost all of Matthew 5.

The general principle of dispersal is understandable,[1] but its detailed implementation is difficult to trace, at least in this case. The transition from, the original *Logia* to Matthew 5 needs a special study. On what basis and with what materials did the evangelist expand the five beatitudes and five antitheses into the present text? Failure to find general indications of that process of expansion would weaken the initial hypothesis of isolating the proposed *Logia.*

At an earlier stage (Chapter 12), three criteria or arguments were given for identifying the *Logia* themselves: distinctive relationship to Deuteronomy, internal unity, and effectiveness as a hypothesis. The need now is for criteria to identify *the expansions* around the *Logia*, especially to explain the origin or nature of the rest of Matthew 5. Ultimately, the two sets of criteria overlap and complement one another. The following suggestions are exploratory.

a. *Matthew 5: Criteria for Distinguishing Expansions to the* Logia

(1) *The non-Deuteronomic principle.* A distinctive relationship to Deuteronomy identifies the *Logia*, so absence of a link to Deuteronomy can help identify what was added. This principle is a blunt instrument, not always reliable; but it can be useful. (Sirach can also be a guide, but less so, since in Mt. 5—the really entangled area—its use is secondary.)

Some parts of Matthew 5 do not in fact have the same distinctive, orderly affinity with Deuteronomy as do the *Logia*, and so is more likely to have been added by the evangelist when writing the canonical gospel. Such material includes the following:

5.19-20:	Least and greatest in the kingdom; scribes; Pharisees
5.22b-26:	From 'fool' and the Sanhedrin to the prison
5.29-30:	Scandal and hell
15.35b-37:	Jerusalem and one's hair color (swearing)
5.39b-42:	The cheek; the cloak; and going the extra mile
5.44b:	Praying for persecutors
5.46-47:	Reward? Tax-collectors/Gentiles do the same

(2) *Authorial style and content.* Another principle—again a blunt instrument—is the authorial influence of the evangelist, canonical Matthew. If something is typically Matthean, then it is less likely to belong to the original Sayings. Thus, in two of the beatitudes and part of the prologue (5.3, 10, 17-18), for example, one finds the phrase *basileia tōn ouranōn* ('kingdom/realm of heaven'), something which is typically Matthean. Consequently, it seems likely, as the non/Deuteronomic principle had already suggested, that these verses do not belong to the Sayings.

Generally, the authorial principle tends to confirm the Deuteronomic principle. The texts listed above as non-Deuteronomic (5.19-20, 22b-26, 29-30, 35b-37, 39b-42, 44b, 46-47) may also be seen, with varying degrees of probability, as elaborations which reflect the authorial influence of the later evangelist.

In the case of the hymn (Mt. 11.25-30), the three stanzas are so tightly interwoven, both in themselves and in their dependence on Sirach, that it is likely they existed together as a

---

1. R.E. Brown (1961), for instance, without claiming literary connection, noted how synoptic material is dispersed in John. Dispersal occurs also at a literary level; see Brodie 1993b: 67. For a discussion of the expansion of the beatitudes in Mt. 5.3-10, see Betz 1995: 105-109.

unit in the Sayings. The only phrase that appears to have been added is the introduction ('At that time Jesus replied and said', 11.25a).

The discernment of Matthew's authorial method should be able to explain, partly at least, how the *Logia*'s concluding hymn, now in Matthew 11, became so separated from the rest of the *Logia* (in Mt. 5).[2]

To some degree, the separation of the concluding hymn is easy to understand. Once the evangelist expanded the early parts of the *Logia* (beatitudes and laws, the more Deuteronomic part) into the Sermon on the Mount, the character of the material changed. It became less a brief, enigmatic wisdom speech and more obviously an imitation of the long discourses of Moses, thus prompting Matthew to conclude it as Moses had concluded his speeches, namely with a version of the two ways (Mt. 7.24-27; cf. Deut. 30.15-20). Since it remained a climactic acclamation of God's wisdom, the hymn was given a concluding role in the next appropriate setting: in the aftermath of Matthew's next major speech when the apostolic discourse (Mt. 10) gives way (in Mt. 11) to a series of statements about divine salvation, judgment, and wisdom (cf. especially Mt. 11.19).

(3) *Dependence on Mark*. If something apparently depends on Mark—for example, the statements on scandal and hell (Mt. 5.29-30; cf. Mk 9.43-47)—the probability is that, like much else in Matthew, it was introduced by the later evangelist. In principle, this is an important criterion. The antithesis on adultery, for example, is composed of two parts: first a simple antithesis ('It was said... But I say', 5.28-28), and then a statement on scandal and hell which is heavily Markan (Mk 9.43-47).

The role of Mark in Matthew 5 is not limited to the sayings on scandal. The very next antithesis in Matthew 5 concerning divorce (5.31-32) has detailed similarities with the next major episode in Mark concerning divorce (Mk 10.1-12, especially 10.11-12). In other words, Mark's essential scandal–divorce sequence (9.42–10.12) reappears with detailed verbal similarities in Matthew 5. The implication is that the sequence, including the entire divorce antithesis (all of Mt. 5.29-32), is based not on the *Logia*, but on the evangelist's Mark-based elaboration of the *Logia*. Matthew has of course made adaptations to Mark, especially his distinctive exception to the divorce prohibition ('except for unchastity', Mt. 5.32; cf. 19.9) but the basic sequence appears to be Mark-based.

Surrounding Mark's scandal–divorce sequence is a series of phrases about teaching (9.31; cf. 9.38), greatness in relation to all (9.33-37), some antagonism surrounding Jesus' name (9.38-41), salt (9.49-50), and some further antagonism about children and the kingdom of God (10.13-16). In varying ways, all of these elements have echoes—some clear, some remote—in Matthew 5, especially in the verses which bridge the gap between the initial beatitudes and the antitheses (5.10-20). Some of these bridging verses probably come from the *Logia* (particularly the pivotal phrases about interpreting the law, 5.17-18), but the likelihood, for many of these verses, is that they partly depend on Mark 9–10.

Even the introduction to the beatitudes, the gathering of a great crowd and Jesus' ascent to the mountain (Mt. 4.23–5.2), finds a basic precedent in Mark (3.7-14).

The divorce saying (Mt. 5.31-32) illustrates the need to balance the different principles. On the one hand, this saying is clearly and uniquely Deuteronomic—built around a quotation drawn directly and exclusively from Deuteronomy (24.1)—and as such, would appear to belong to the Sayings. On the other hand, it is dependent both on Mark as a source and on Matthean authorship (as seen in the exceptive clause 'unless for unchastity'; Mt. 5.32; cf. 19.9). It seems better, therefore, as with the statements on scandal and hell, to see the

---

2. Some of the gaps between parts of Proto-Luke are also very long, especially between Lk. 9.51–10.20 and Lk. 16.

divorce saying as an elaboration which the evangelist introduced into the Sayings. In making this elaboration, he did what he sometimes did elsewhere, for example, in the temptation of Jesus, Mt. 4.1-11: he quoted from Deuteronomy. In addition, he adapted the addition to the context of the antitheses.

(4) *Dependence on other known sources.* Just as dependence on Mark can help identify an addition to the *Logia*, so can dependence on some other documents. For instance, the saying concerning the greater righteousness (Mt. 5.20) reflects Matthew's use of Romans (Rom. 10.2-4) (see Chapter 20 below). Such dependence suggests strongly that this saying is an addition to the *Logia*.

b. *Conclusion Regarding Canonical Matthew's Use of the* Logia
Further research is needed on how and why canonical Matthew expanded the *Logia*. But at least such research has a reasonably solid basis. There are good reasons for identifying the *Logia* themselves, and there are also some ways of identifying how the evangelist added to these sayings.

Orientational Introduction to Chapters 20–21:
On the Use of Romans in Matthew 1–17

Matthew's use of Romans is essentially a single phenomenon, but it is complex. To keep the discussion to manageable proportions, it is useful to divide it into two chapters (20 and 21).

Table 43 gives an overview of the contents of these two chapters. For practical purposes of comparison, the texts have been divided into seven blocks. Generally, Matthew follows the order of Romans but two blocks have been transposed. A relatively *early* block of Romans (2.17–3.20) is used quite *late* in Matthew (15.1–16.12). And a relatively *late* block of Romans (9.6–10.13) is used *early* in Matthew (in 4.1–6.18).

Table 43. *Romans and Matthew 1.1–17.20: General Outline*

Romans	Matthew
Beginnings, righteousness, wrath (1.1-18)	A. INFANCY, WRATH, RIGHTEOUSNESS (CHS. 1–3)
	B. JESUS TEMPTED; TRUE RIGHTEOUSNESS PREACHED (4.1–6.18)
God's absence and judgment (1.19–2.16)	C. GOD'S PRESENCE AND ITS IMPLICATIONS FOR HUMAN JUDGMENTS (6.19–7.27)
The Jews and the law; universal need (2.17–3.20)	
Faith leading to salvation (3.21–9.5)	D. FAITH LEADING TO SAVING MIRACLES (8.1–10.6)
The word questioned; false righteousness examined (9.6–10.13)	
Israel's anguish; wisdom; love; not judging (10.14–15.14)	E. COMING PERSECUTION; WISDOM; MERCY; LEAVING JUDGMENT TO GOD (10.7–14.36)
	F. THE PHARISEES AND THE LAW; UNIVERSAL NEED IS MET BY JESUS (15.1–16.12)
Paul's ministry; his difficult journey faithful disciples (15.15–ch. 16)	G. PETER'S MINISTRY; JESUS' FATEFUL JOURNEY; DISCIPLES, DEMONS AND FAITH (16.13–17.20)

There is at least one small exception to this neat division: the ambiguity about Abraham's children (physical descendants are not necessarily true children, or vice versa) occurs at the beginning of the fifth block of Romans (9.6-8, within 9.6–10.13) and should reappear at the beginning of the corresponding block in Matthew, the second—but in fact it is near the end of the first (in Mt. 3.9).

Within each block, Matthew generally keeps to the order of the material in Romans. However, in at least one instance, when reworking Rom. 9.9-33, he adapts the order.

Chapter 20 deals with the blocks in italics (Mt. 1–7); Chapter 21 with the rest (Mt. 8–17). The analysis is meant as a beginning rather than as a full account.

One factor is especially important: the nature of Matthew's dependence on Romans varies. In comparison with Mark, Romans is a secondary component. It is only when he wants to expand Mark, for instance in the temptation account or in the discourses, that Romans assumes a central role. More often he uses Romans simply to add some touches to the narrative of Mark.

20

Vivid, Positive, Practical: The Systematic Use of Romans in Matthew 1–7—An Exploratory Survey

In the entire New Testament, there are only two books which begin by speaking of Jesus as a descendent of David: Romans and Matthew. Romans' complex opening sentence refers to Jesus as 'God's…son who was made from the seed of David' (*huiou…genomenou ek spermatos Dauid*, Rom. 1.1-3), and Matthew begins by telling of 'the generation of Jesus Christ, son of David' (*geneseōs…huiou Dauid*, Mt. 1.3). Thus in both cases Jesus is born (*ginomai*) or generated (*genesis*) from the line of David.

The purpose of this chapter is to indicate that this Davidic detail is the tip of an iceberg: Romans is one of Matthew's sources. Matthew has taken the difficult text of Romans and in varying ways has rendered it into a form that is vivid, positive and practical.

The present chapter is intended not so much as a proof—though for some the evidence will be convincing—but as an exploratory survey providing other researchers with a useful lead.

1. *Context and Plausibility*

Much discussion of Matthew presupposes that he was unaware of Paul and of Romans. Przybylski, for instance, studied righteousness in Matthew's 'world of thought' but made no allowance for the possibility that this world may have contained some of Paul's epistles (Przybylski 1980). It is as though Paul and Matthew lived poles apart, quite out of contact.

This presupposition of Matthew's isolation is long overdue for questioning. Matthew's sources are generally reckoned to have been Mark, Q, and M—where M is 'an umbrella-term that covers different strata of tradition (varying in origin and theological viewpoint) that came to Matthew largely through his local church' (Meier 1976: 2). This is an extremely elastic hypothesis, one in which the local church acts as a filter for very diverse materials. In speaking of the scribe instructed in the kingdom of heaven, Matthew himself suggests something similar—a process of combining diverse sources, 'bringing out of his treasure things old and new' (Mt. 13.52). Such diversity does not sit well with presuppositions of isolation.

It may seem, however, that what Matthew was open to were traditions, scattered fragments, many of them oral—rather than any systematic use of whole written documents. Orality was indeed important—it pervades all ancient literature—yet Matthew did, in fact, make use of written documents. Most New Testament scholars are convinced that through a process of limited adaptation Matthew incorporated Mark. And there are indications that, by radically distilling and modernizing the text, Matthew has also made systematic use of Deuteronomy: in composing the Discourse on the Community (Mt. 17.22–18.35), he has used Deuteronomy 14 and 15 as a basis for supplementing the material in Mark (see Chapter 22).

Again, however, it may be objected that for Matthew, a copy of Deuteronomy would have been much more obtainable than a copy of Romans. Matthew may, for instance, have been in Syria, far removed from Rome. True—but he had made it his business to obtain a copy of Mark, a text which, according to many calculations, would also have had to come from Rome. If one, why not both?

Because, it may be repeated, Paul belonged to another world, and because Paul's notion of law, for instance, would have been anathema to Matthew. This objection exercises great influence, but it is not valid. As Davies writes about the background of the Sermon on the Mount: 'Paulinism was not a peculiarity in primitive Christianity but a profundity. Paul shared his faith with his predecessors, his contemporaries, and…his successors'; 'the Sermon on the Mount would not have appeared to Paul as an alien importation into the faith' (W.D. Davies 1964: 323, 366).

As for the question of the Law, it is easy to depict incompatibilities between Romans and Matthew. Romans at times seems very negative. In the course of establishing the primacy of grace over law, Paul apparently denigrates the law, and thus disparages God's traditional revelation (Rom. 2–3; 7.1–8.3). Matthew seems more positive; he inculcates 'the abiding validity of the law' (Bornkamm, Barth and Held 1963).

Emphasizing incompatibilities, however, is misleading. First, because they are overdrawn; Romans, in fact, is not so negative, nor is Matthew so positive (Mohrlang 1984: 126; see also Via 1990: 134). The complexity is underlined by Snodgross: 'Matthew's understanding of the law is an unfinished agenda. But this is also the case with *every other understanding of the law in the New Testament*' (Snodgross 1992). Second, emphasizing incompatibilities can be misleading because real differences do not exclude direct literary dependence. As seen in several preceding chapters, one of the most basic dynamics in the history of literature, especially ancient literature, was the practice of combining dependence with independence, *imitatio* with *emulatio*. And in the history of theological writing it is taken for granted that one engages people with whom one disagrees. In fact, disagreement can be an added motive for getting one's hands on someone's work.

What is important is that the basic idea of Matthew reshaping the material in Romans is not implausible. Within Christianity in general this epistle has been central; 'Rom[ans] has affected later Christian theology more than any other New Testament book' (Fitzmyer 1990: 12), and there is no reason why early Christian writers should not have appreciated its centrality. If, as is generally supposed, Matthew was writing at least ten or twenty years after the composition of Romans Meier would say a generation later (Meier 1976: 169) —it makes sense that he should take account of this central epistle. To ignore it would make him like a Catholic theologian of the 1970s, '80s or '90s who, while writing on the renewal of the Catholic Church, ignored Vatican II. Not that a latter-day theologian would follow Vatican II slavishly; there would be room, indeed need, for significant changes and adaptations.

2. *Introductory Analysis*

Matthew 1–7 interweaves two areas of Romans: 1.1–2.16 (which he subdivides into two blocks, 1.1-18 and 1.19–2.16) and 9.6–10.13. In other words, he includes two beginnings: the beginning of the epistle as a whole, and most of the beginning of the climactic central section (chs. 9–11). The relation of Romans 9–11 to the rest of the epistle has been disputed, but there is increasing agreement that it is integral to the text, even central to it (Fitzmyer 1990: 92; Ziesler 1989: 37-39). The question with which it deals—the relationship of Israel's sad fate to God's promises, God's Word—'is in the background of Paul's whole discussion' (Achtemeier 1985: 153). Hence, when Matthew combined the two beginnings, he was not doing violence to the text; in a creative way he was bringing together materials which had an inherent connection.

Romans supplies just one component. Most of Matthew's infancy narrative (Mt. 1–2), for instance, comes from other sources, and so does most of the beginning of the Sermon on the Mount (Mt. 5). The overall narrative sequence largely comes from Mark.

Yet Romans is important. The notions of wrath and righteousness which Matthew introduces into John's preaching and John's baptism of Jesus (Mt. 3.7, 8, 15) reflect significant ideas in Romans (Rom. 1.16-18). And the discussion of true righteousness (Mt. 5.20; 6.1-18) owes much to what Romans says about the inadequate righteousness of the Jews (Rom. 10.2-13).

In general, Matthew turns what seems obscure or negative in Romans into a form which is more accessible and attractive. The idea of God's anger, for instance, while reasonably clear in Paul (Rom. 1.18), is made yet more vivid by being injected into John's bitter confrontation with the 'brood of vipers' (Mt. 3.7-8). The negative righteousness of the Jews (Rom. 10.2-4) is used to formulate the exhortation to a greater, positive, righteousness among the disciples (Mt. 5.20). And Paul's heavy statement about God's absence and judgment (Rom. 1.19–2.16) is turned around to show the other, positive side of the same reality—God's care for the world, and the need to translate that care into human judgments about practical living (Mt. 6.19–7.27).

Perhaps the most difficult connection to unravel is between the temptation account (Mt. 4.1-11) and Romans 9. (As noted earlier, there has also been difficulty in relating Romans 9–11 even to the rest of the epistle.) Using Mark's brief temptation text (Mk 1.12-13) as a starting-point, Matthew has in effect rendered the questioning of God's Word (Rom. 9.9-23, 30-33) into the questioning of God's Son (Mt. 4.3-10). Without claiming to explain the adaptation fully, one may say that this involves a shifting of focus from God to humanity, and from history (the history of God's word) to the present; it is another dimension of turning something obscure into something vivid and practical.

It may be objected that most of Matthew's temptation account, as shared by Luke, came from Q. The problem is that no one knows what Q contained. As will be found in examining Luke (especially Lk. 7.1-10, 18-35; 9.57-62; see Chapters 28, 30, 34), the premature invocation of Q may distract from pursuing other avenues of investigation which are initially more difficult, but which in the long term are less conjectural and more promising.

3. *More Detailed Analysis*

The analysis follows the outline in Table 44. The division of the texts—ten sections with headings italicized—is a pragmatic arrangement; it is not meant to reflect the texts' most important structures. (The ten sections comprise three blocks, corresponding to blocks A, B, and C in Table 44.)

Table 44. *Romans 1.1–2.16; 9.6–10.13; Matthew 1–7*

A. BEGINNINGS, WRATH AND RIGHTEOUSNESS (ROMANS 1.1-18; MATTHEW 1–3)	
Infancy Narrative: Son of David and the Journey *(Romans 1.1-12; Matthew 1–2)*	
1. *The Seed of David (1.1-7)* Called…Son…seed of David …called…called (1.1-7)	*The Son of David (Mt. 1–2)* Son of David… call…call…call… (ch. 1)
Faith known in the whole world. I serve God in his Son so as to have a good way/journey to you, to give you a gift (*charisma*, 8-12)	Magi came from the east to adore him… and bring him gifts (*dōra*). They went back another way (2.1-12)

John's Ministry: God's Wrath and Righteousness *(Romans 1.13-18; 9.6-8; Matthew 3)*	
2. *Wrath revealed (1.13-18; 9.6-8)* * Paul prevented until now, wants to bear fruit (1.13-15) God's righteousness (1.16.17) God's wrath is being revealed (1.18) Abraham's seed not his children (9.6-8)	*Wrath impending (3.1-17)* [God's] wrath is impending (3.7) Bear appropriate fruit (3.8) Abraham's children from stones (3.9) * Jesus, prevented momentarily, is baptized in righteousness (3.13-17)
B. TESTING THE WORD AND SEEKING TRUE RIGHTEOUSNESS (ROMANS 9.6–10.13; MATTHEW 4.1–6.18) [ROM. 9.6-8 = MT. 3.9]	
The Temptation: A Scripture-Based Testing of God's Word/Son *(Romans 9.9-23, 30-33; Matthew 4.1-11)*	
3. *Not flesh but the word (9.9-13)*	*Not bread alone but the word (4.3-4)*
It was the word (*logos*) [of God] which gave [life] not alone to Isaac but to Jacob as it is written…	It is written not on bread alone does a human live but on every word (*rhēma*)…of God.
4. *Stumbling in Zion (9.30-33)*	*Falling down in the holy city (4.5-7)*
(Works-based) Israel stumbled as it is written… in Zion a stone to strike against.	The holy city, on the temple: Throw yourself down …for it is written …lest you strike against a stone.
5. *Pharaoh and all the earth (9.14-23)*	*All the kingdoms of the world (4.8-10)*
It is God who decides for the scripture/writing says… God's name is shown forth, through Pharaoh, in all the earth. God, potterlike, shows his glory.	He showed him all the kingdoms of the world and their glory…. Be gone…for it is written… God…alone shall you serve.
The Ministry of Paul and Jesus Includes Gentiles *(Romans 9.24-29; 10.1; Matthew 4.12-25)*	
6 *Unloved people are loved (9.24-29)*	*Darkened people see light (4.12-17)*
We, Gentiles included, are God's [transformed] people, as Hosea says. And Isaiah speaks of us twice, mentioning the sea (9.24-29)	Ministry begins by the sea, with Isaiah's words concerning the sea, the Gentiles, and the [transformed] people (4.12-17)
Brothers, I desire… 'their' salvation (10.1)	The fishermen 'brothers' (4.18-22) Jesus in 'their' synagogues (4.23)
True Righteousness: Paul's Proclamation to the World *and Jesus' Sermon on the Mount (Romans 10.2-13; 1.19–2.16: Matthew 5–7)*	
7. *Righteousness (10.2-13)*	*Righteousness (5.20; 6.1-18)*
Jews' righteousness ignores God (10.2-4)	Scribes'/Pharisees' righteousness does not enter God's realm (5.20)
Righteousness not of doing but of heart (10.5-9)	Watch that your righteousness is not in doings but in secret (6.1-4)
Whoever confesses and calls on the name of the Lord of all …will be saved (10.9-13)	When you pray… 'Our Father in heaven, may your name…forgive us…and… deliver us from evil' (6.5, 9-13)

C. God's Absence/Presence and Consequent Judgments (Romans 1.19–2.16; Matthew 6.19–ch. 7)	
8. *God is lost sight of (1.19-23)*	*Keep God in sight (6.19-24)*
• World reflects God (1.19-20) • The heart is darkened (1.21) • Confusing God and idols (1.22-23)	• Treasure God/heaven not earth (6.19-21) • Light/darkness in the body (6.22-23) • God and mammon (6.24)
9. *God abandons (1.24-32)*	*God cares (6.25-34)*
• Forgetting the Creator, they misuse their bodies (1.24-25) • Away from God, bodily misuse intensifies (1.26-27) • Away from God, intensified sin leads to death (1.28-32)	• Let God's care of [creatures] inspire your attitude to life and body (6.25-27) • God's care [for the body] shown even more clearly in providing clothing (6.28-30) • Seek the kingdom of God first, and all the rest [of life] will be added (6.31-34)
10. *God's judgment (2.1-16)*	*Judgment and discernment (Mt. 7)*
Do not judge others (2.1-3) The good God deals justly (2.4-6) One gets what one deserves (2.7-8) Anguish (*sten-*), evil, good (2.9-10) Judged with/without law (2.11-12) Just: doers, not hearers (2.13-16)	Judge not (7.1-6) The Father gives generously (7.7-11) Give as you would like to receive (7.12) Narrow (*sten-*), good, bad (7.13-20) Condemnation of the lawless (7.21-23) Hearers who do/do not (7.24-27)

a. *Block A (Matthew 1–3)*
(1) *Section 1. The seed/son of David (Romans 1.1-12; Matthew 1–2).* Matthew's infancy narrative has at least three significant points of similarity with the beginning of Romans (1.1-12):
1. The introduction of Jesus as a descendent or son of David (Rom. 1.3; Mt. 1.1, 6, 17).
2. The triple use of *kaleō* ('to call'), as an element in structuring the text. The opening salutation in Romans is framed between repeated uses of 'called' (*klētos*, Rom. 1.1, 6, 7) and the account of the birth is largely dominated by repeated references to the name by which the child is to be called (*kaleō*, Mt. 1.21, 23, 25).
3. The sudden opening of horizons to a worldwide faith and a world-evoking journey. The second section of Romans, the proemium or introduction, begins by evoking the involvement of the world—the fact that the Romans' 'faith...is spoken of in the whole world', and Paul's own plan to make a 'good journey' (*eu-hodoō*) to those who are called in Rome (Rom. 1.8-12). Matthew's second chapter, particularly in its account of the Magi, also implies a world-related faith and a good journey (they came from 'the east', and they went back safely by another 'way' (*hodos*, Mt. 2.1-12).

These similarities are sufficiently close that one cannot dismiss them immediately as coincidence. As already mentioned, Romans and Matthew are the only New Testament books which begin with references to Jesus as a descendent or son of David, and even the wording shows affinity:

        Rom. 1.3:   *huiou...genomenou ek spermatos Dauid.*
        Mt. 1.1:   *geneseōs...huiou Dauid.*

The triple use of *klētos/kaleō* occurs a number of times in the New Testament (e.g. 1 Cor. 1.1, 2, 24; Mt. 2.7, 15, 23; Lk. 1.31, 32, 35) but there appears to be no other New Testament instance in which it occurs just three times within a short passage in a form which is repetitive and structuring. Furthermore, within both Rom. 1.1, 6, 7 and Mt. 1.21, 23, 25, two of the three uses of *klētos/kaleō* are immediately associated with the name 'Jesus' (Rom. 1.1, 6; Mt. 1.21, 25).

As for the world-related faith and journey, the affinity is heightened: in both instances those who are journeying bring gifts. Paul longs to see the Romans so that he may 'impart some spiritual gift' (*charisma pneumatikon*, Rom. 1.11), and the Magi bring gifts (*dōra*) of gold, frankincense and myrrh (Mt. 2.11). The Magi's gifts are more physical, but they have a spiritual dimension; 'elsewhere in Matthew *dōron* is used exclusively and fairly often for offerings to God' (Gundry 1982: 32).

Both journeys are also connected with worship. It is on worship that Paul's journey is based (*latreuō*, 'serve', Rom. 1.9, has a cultic meaning), and it is towards worship (*proskuneō*) that the Magi's journey is directed (Mt. 2.2, 11). Thus, for both, worship is the mainspring (Lyonnet 1990: 36-42).

Obviously, Matthew is using sources other than Romans; the main content of the infancy narrative is quite independent of Paul. The combination of *kaleō* with 'Jesus', for instance, is best paralleled in Lk. 1.31 ('you shall call his name Jesus', just as in Mt. 1.21), and the description of the gifts of the Magi reflects the Old Testament (Isa. 60.2-3, 6) (Gundry 1982: 32; Schweizer 1975: 39).

Yet, however great Matthew's indebtedness to other sources, the affinity with Romans remains, and the question which must at least be asked is whether, while depending primarily on those other sources, Matthew has used the beginning of Romans as one component in structuring and coloring the infancy narrative.

(2) *Section 2. The wrath, the righteousness, and the God-based nature of the children of Abraham (Romans 1.13-18; 9.6-8; Matthew 3).* In the case of Matthew 3 (concerning John's preaching and Jesus' baptism), there is a clear comparison with the corresponding text in Mark (Mk 1.1-11), and this allows for an easier examination of how Matthew used sources. He has incorporated almost everything in Mark's text but has added several elements:

Mark 1.1-11	*Matthew 3*
John's preaching (1.1-8)	John's preaching,
	the impending wrath,
	bear fruit,
	children of Abraham? (3.1-12)
Jesus' baptism (1.9-11)	Jesus came for baptism,
	John prevented him,
	need for righteousness (3.13-17)

Most of the added elements (wrath, fruit, prevention, righteousness) are found in the very next section of Romans when Paul speaks of a fruitful visit (momentarily prevented) and of the righteousness and wrath of God (Rom. 1.13-18). And one of the other main elements concerning those who rely unduly on physical descent from Abraham (as opposed to those whose descent from Abraham is based on God) is found in Rom. 9.6-8 (when Paul speaks of the word of God).

The easiest explanation of the data is that Matthew, having used Rom. 1.1-12 in the structuring and coloring of the infancy narrative, went on to use Rom. 1.13-18 as a way of supplementing the next chapter (Mt. 3). Then, by some kind of association, he moved from the ideas of the righteousness and wrath of God (in Rom. 1.17, 18) to the idea of the word of God and the effect of God's word on becoming children of Abraham (in Rom. 9.6-8).

This does not mean that Matthew is using these various elements in the sense that they had been used by Paul. For instance, two of the leading features—righteousness and wrath

(Rom. 1.17, 18)—are used quite differently in the gospel (Mt. 3.7, 17). Instead of being directed towards the whole world (Rom. 1.18), God's wrath is now more focused on the Jewish leadership (Mt. 3.7). And the concept of righteousness becomes narrower—not so much an attribute of God (Rom. 1.17) as a certain ritual which has to be fulfilled (Mt. 3.15).

The juxtaposition of 'wrath' and 'righteousness' (*orgē* and *dikaiosunē*), as found in Rom. 3.17, 18, and Mt. 3.8, 18, is rare in the New Testament; there are two other instances in Romans (4.13, 15; 9.22, 30), but otherwise it occurs in the New Testament only twice (Jas 1.20; Rev. 19.11, 15). Consequently, when students of Matthew seek literary precedents for this wrath–righteousness combination, the first place to look is Romans.

The larger grouping of elements (wrath, righteousness, fruit, prevent) occurs nowhere in the New Testament. Hence, as in the case of the way Romans and Matthew begin (introducing Jesus as a descendant of David), the link between the texts is unique.

b. *Block B (Matthew 4.1–6.18)*
(1) *Section 3. It is the word that gives life, as it is written (Romans 9.9-13; Matthew 4.3-4).* Having moved to Romans 9 (the discussion about the word of God, and the effect of God's word on the question of being children of Abraham, Rom. 9.6-8; Mt. 3.9), Matthew now stays with that chapter; he begins to make systematic use of the rest of Romans 9.

But Matthew transforms his source. Where Paul had tested God's word—asking agonizingly whether Israel's fall meant that God's word had failed (Rom. 9.6-33)—Matthew tests God's Son (the tempting or testing of Jesus, Mt. 4.1-11). This change in the focus of the testing—from God's word to God's Son—means that while both texts scrutinize God's way of intervening in human life, Matthew's account is more vivid, and in a sense more human.

Obviously, Romans 9 is not the only source used by Matthew in describing the temptation of Jesus. For instance, he makes use of Mark's temptation account (Mk 1.12-13) and of Deuteronomy (Mt. 4.4, 7, 10; see Deut. 6.13, 16; 8.3). And he may have used other sources. But Romans 9 is one factor.

The transformation begins when Matthew distills Paul's account of how God's word of promise brought about the birth of Isaac and the life-circumstances of Jacob (in other words, the divine word gave them birth and life). Instead of repeating any of the historical details of the Romans account (Rom. 9.9-13), Matthew extracts the central principle—it is God's word which gives life—and applies it to the circumstances of the hungry Jesus when Jesus tells the Devil that a person lives not by bread alone but by God's word. Thus, the word which gave life to the ancient patriarchs has become a word which gives life in the down-to-earth circumstances of Jesus' struggle with temptation.

Despite the transformation, Matthew's deuteronomized text retains resonances of the more complex text of Romans. Some connections may be coincidence, but hardly all:

    Rom. 9.9-13: For this [is] the word (*logos*)...
            I will come
            and there will be a son.

            Not only that but (*ou monon...alla*)...
            the purpose of God...
            as it is written (*kathōs gegraptai*).

    Mt. 4.3-4:   The tempter coming to him said,
            'If you are the Son of God...'

            He replied, 'It is written (*gegraptai*),
            not on bread alone but (*ouk...monō...all'*)
            by every word (*rhēma*)...of God.'

(2) *Section 4. Stumbling Against a Stone in Zion (Romans 9.30-33; Matthew 4.5-7)*. At the end of Romans 9 Paul describes how Israel, by relying on externals, stumbled, and he uses scripture to visualize this stumbling as happening in Zion (Rom. 9.30-33). Matthew, on the other hand, effectively shows Jesus as not stumbling in Zion. When the Devil takes him to the temple pinnacle and tempts him to throw himself down, Jesus refuses. This refusal to rely on an external show constitutes a reversal of the conduct of Israel.
Again, there are significant connections of detail:

>   Rom. 9.32-33: They struck against a stone of stumbling,
>   as it is written,
>   'Behold I place in Zion
>   a stone of stumbling...'
>
>   Mt. 4.5-7:   The Devil took him to the holy city/temple...
>   'Throw yourself down, For it is written.
>   Lest you strike your foot against a stone.'

The verb 'to strike against' (*pros-koptō*) occurs only eight times in the New Testament, and apart from 1 Pet. 2.8 (and Luke's parallel, 4.11), there is no other New Testament instance where it is combined with *lithos* ('stone'). Nor is there any other instance (apart from Luke's parallel, 4.10) where it is combined with *gegraptai* ('it is written'). Both incidents are located in Zion/the holy city—lending further significance to this unique link.

(3) *Section 5. God alone decides about the earth and its kingdoms (Romans 9.4-23; Matthew 4.8-10)*. In explaining how the fall of Israel does not negate God and God's word, Paul recounts how the changing fortunes and attitudes even of Pharaoh served to show God's name through all the earth. God's sovereignty is supreme and goes out through the greatest ruler (Pharaoh) to all the earth (Rom. 9.14-18). Then Paul speaks of God as a potter who reshapes clay in order to show his glory (Rom. 9.19-24).

Matthew takes this idea—God is supreme over the whole earth and shows his glory—and turns it into the temptation of the Devil showing Jesus all the glory of the world (Mt. 4.8-9). But Jesus rejects the temptation and says that God alone is supreme (worthy of worship).

There are a number of detailed connections:

>   Rom. 9.17, 22-23: For [in] the scripture [God] says to Pharaoh,
>   (*legei gar hē graphē tō Pharao...*)
>
>   'For this I raised you up,
>
>   to show my power in you...
>   throughout all the earth...
>   God [waited]...to show his...power...
>   to make known...his glory.'
>
>   Mt. 4.8-10:   The Devil takes him again to a high mountain
>
>   and shows him
>   all the kingdoms of the world
>   and their glory...
>
>   Jesus says to him, 'Go... For it is written...
>   (*legei autō...gegraptai gar...*)'

(4) *Section 6. Isaiah and the calling of the Gentiles, of a people transformed (Romans 9.24-29; Matthew 4.12-17)*. In discussing Israel's refusal, Paul also tells of the call of the Gentiles—a call seen in the words of the prophets Hosea and Isaiah. Hosea spoke of this

call through the idea of a people being transformed (from being unloved to being loved, Rom. 9.24-26), and Isaiah, referring to other aspects of the call, alluded to the seashore and to the names of two places (Sodom and Gomorrah; Rom. 4.27-29).

Faced with these three quotations (one from Hosea and two from Isaiah), Matthew made a simple transformation. In rewriting Mark's brief account of the beginning of the Galilean ministry (Mk 1.14-15), he incorporated into the text (Mt. 4.13-16) a single passage from Isaiah which combined aspects of all three quotations.

The essence of the texts may be outlined as follows:

> Rom. 9.24-29: He called us from…among Jews…and Gentiles.
> As Hosea says:
> 'I will call not-a-people my people
> and unloved loved…'
> And Isaiah cries:
> 'Though they be as the sand of the sea…'
> And Isaiah said:
> '…we would have been as Sodom and Gomorrah.'
>
> Mt. 4.13-16: He moved to Capernaum beside the sea
> thus fulfilling the words of Isaiah:
> 'Land of Zabulun and…Naphthali,
> by the way of the sea…
> Galilee of the Gentiles.
> The people…in darkness…saw light,
> on those in death's shadow, light has dawned.'

Aspects of this correspondence are debatable. It is difficult, for instance, to be sure whether or to what extent there is a connection between 'Sodom and Gomorrah' and 'Zabulun and Naphthali'. But other features are clearer. The word-cluster shared by the two texts (*ethnoi, laos, Ēsaias, thalassa*, 'Gentiles, people, Isaiah, sea') does not occur elsewhere in the New Testament. And the pictures of the people's transformation (to love; to light) solidifies that unique link.

The subsequent passages in Matthew (the call of the four fishermen, 4.18-22, and Jesus' ministry to the multitudes, 4.23-25) depend considerably on Mark (for 4.18-22 see Mk 1.16-20, and for 4.23-25 see Mk 1.35-39; 3.7-12; 6.6b). But two details of Matthew's reworking of Mark seem to depend on the next verse of Romans when Paul speaks of his 'brothers' and 'their' salvation (Rom. 10.1). Matthew's account of the call of the fishermen uses 'brother/s' an unusual number of times (four times, as opposed to twice in Mark). And Matthew's account of Jesus' ministry begins with a reference to 'their' synagogues (Mt. 4.23)—a detail which depends primarily on Mk 1.39 ('their synagogues') but which may, perhaps, owe its position (near the beginning of Matthew's passage) to its leading position in Romans (at the beginning of Rom. 10).

Such details, however, are questionable and it is better to concentrate on what is essential: Matthew's description of Jesus as moving to the seashore and fulfilling Isaiah is uniquely linked to Rom. 9.24-29.

c. *Block C (Matthew 6.19–ch. 7)*
(1) *Section 7. Jewish righteousness does not know God (Romans 10.2-23; Matthew 5.20; 6.1-18)*. The Sermon on the Mount, however numerous or varied its sources, also drew on Romans. The connection emerges in Jesus' call for the 'greater righteousness' (Mt. 5.20):

1. 'They [the Jews] have the zeal of God, but not the knowledge. For, *not knowing the righteousness of God, they seek to establish their own*, not submitting to the righteousness of God' (Rom. 10.2-3).
2. '*Unless your righteousness exceeds that of the scribes and Pharisees*, you will not enter into the realm/kingdom of heaven' (Mt. 5.20).

The texts are unusual insofar as they both speak, implicitly at least, not just of one kind of righteousness, but of two. Furthermore, the first type of righteousness is regarded negatively and is associated with the apparently superficial side of Judaism (its zeal; its scribes and Pharisees). The other, while more elusive, is associated in both writers with the realm of God (what Matthew calls the kingdom of heaven).

Both Romans and Matthew set these two kinds of righteousness in contrast, but from a certain viewpoint, Matthew is more positive. Instead of lamenting the presence of the inadequate righteousness in the Jews, he turns his attention to the disciples and challenges them to pursue the true righteousness—of (the kingdom of) God.

Paul then goes on to speak of a righteousness based not on deeds but on the heart (Rom. 10.5-8), and shortly afterwards, Matthew calls for a righteousness which consists not of devout deeds performed to gain praise, but of an inner dedication to the God who sees in secret (Mt. 6.1-18, especially 6.1, 4, 6, 18).

In describing righteousness which is deficient, both texts are obviously similar—they refer to doing (external) actions (verb *poieō*, Rom. 10.5; Mt. 6.1). But when it comes to describing the positive kind of righteousness, they take different viewpoints (as they already had in the earlier contrast, Rom. 10.2-4; Mt. 5.20). While Paul focuses on the inner workings of the heart—the human dynamics—Matthew lays the emphasis on the accompanying transcendent element, on the divine heart so to speak, the Father who sees in secret. Both use a threefold rhythm:

The human heart:		*The corresponding divine presence:*	
Rom. 10.6:	in your heart	Mt. 6.4:	your Father who sees in secret
10.8:	in your heart	6.6:	your Father who sees in secret
10.9:	in your heart	6.18:	your Father who sees in secret
(en tē kardia sou)		*(ho patēr sou ho blepōn en tō kryptō)*	

Interwoven with this threefold pattern is an emphasis on prayer. Paul tells how the person who acknowledges ('confesses') the Lord and calls on the Lord of all will be saved (Rom. 10.9-13), and Matthew gives the Our Father—a prayer which involves both confessing and calling on the God of all (Mt. 6.9-13). Thus, Romans 10 seems to have had some influence on Matthew's formulation of the Our Father, but again, Matthew has changed the emphasis. His attention is not so much on the inner workings of the heart as on the accompanying elements of the divine presence and the interpersonal implications.

(2) *Section 8. The danger of losing sight of God (Romans 1.19-23; Matthew 6.19-24).* Matthew now returns to using Romans 1, beginning with 1.19—exactly the point at which he had previously left it.

The essence of the first section (Rom. 1.19-23) is that the world has lost sight of God. Matthew turns this negative picture around and uses it to help form a positive exhortation: Do not lose sight of God (Mt. 6.19-24).

There are three main subsections. First (Rom. 1.19-20; Mt. 6.19-21), there are two views of the ambiguity of the world. Looking downward so to speak (as he elsewhere looks inward at the heart), Paul emphasizes that the world reflects God. But Matthew, looking upward (as he elsewhere looks at the transcendent), emphasizes that concentration on the world should not cause one to lose sight of God ('Do not store treasure on earth... but in heaven').

Then Paul laments how the human heart has been darkened (Rom. 1.21). Matthew also speaks of darkness in the body, but in a typically positive variation, he sets that idea of darkness in the context of the body's light (Mt. 6.22-23).

Paul goes on to paint a very negative picture of the confusion between God and idols (Rom. 1.22-23). In yet a further positive variation, Matthew warns against any such confusion; one must choose between God and mammon (Mt. 6.24).

(3) *Section 9. God's Involvement with Life and the Body: God Cares for the Body; without God, the Body Suffers (Romans 1.24-32; Matthew 6.25-34).* At this point the presupposition of both writers is that God is involved with human life, particularly with the human body. But they emphasize diverse aspects of this truth. Paul expresses the negative side: alienation from God brings bodily abuse and death. Matthew expresses it positively: God's providential presence means care for the body and for life. In Paul, for instance, birds are negative—effectively idols which distract from God (Rom. 1.23). But in Matthew, they are positive; they are the birds 'of the heavens' and they are a reminder of God's care (Mt. 6.26).

Again, the texts have three subsections. Paul begins by saying that God's absence has led to bodily abuse (Rom. 1.24-25). Matthew expresses the complementary truth and he does so with a flourish; he speaks of God's care not only for the body, but even for the birds (Mt. 6.25-27).

Paul then intensifies his negative picture: he speaks of alienation from God as inducing even greater bodily abuse (Rom. 1.26-27). Matthew in turn intensifies the positive picture: God's care for the body extends even to clothing as seen in the lilies of the field (Mt. 6.28-30).

Finally, Paul speaks of how alienation from God leads to the loss of everything—to death (Rom. 1.28-32), what Fitzmyer (1990: 26) calls 'exclusion from the kingdom of God'. Matthew turns this around: seeking God brings life ('Seek first the kingdom…and all the rest will be added to you', Mt. 6.31-34).

(4) *Section 10. The Process of Judgment and Action (Romans 2.1-16; Matthew 7).* In the next section of Romans, particularly in 2.1-16, Paul speaks of judging and action. It is God who judges, and judgment depends on people's actions. Many commentators believe Paul's primary focus here is on the Jews, lest they be judgmental and rely on the law rather than on action.

These Pauline ideas—judgment and action—provide ideal raw material for building the Sermon's conclusion, for moving from high ideals (in Mt. 5 and 6) to practical implementation (Mt. 7). As usual, Matthew's adaptation looks beyond the Jews to a wider audience.

The texts begin with warnings about judging others (Rom. 2.1-3; Mt. 7.1-6). But there is a difference of emphasis. Paul is interested not so much in preventing the judging of others as in clarifying the implications—that all, including the one who judges, are under condemnation, under the judgment of God. Matthew, as usual, has a more positive aim: he seeks to prevent such judgment altogether. However, like Paul, he turns the would-be judge inward towards self-examination.

The texts show close similarities:

> Rom. 2.1: Whoever you are you are defenseless (*an-apologētos*) in judging;
> for in what you judge another, you condemn yourself
> (*en ho gar krineis ton heteron, seauton kata-krineis*);
> for, you who judge, you do the same.

Mt. 7.1-2: Judge not, that you may not judged;
for with what judgment you judge, you shall be judged
(*en ho gar krimati krinete, krithēsesthe*);
and in what measure you measure, it shall be measured to you
[i.e. what you measure, you receive the same].

Matthew follows closely the three phrases of Rom. 2.1. First, the image of the defenseless judge is spelled out to become the judge who is liable to judgment. Then both texts speak of judgment actually rebounding. And, finally, there are complementary pictures of being identified with what is condemned (Romans: you do the same condemned action; Matthew: you receive the same measure/condemnation).

Matthew's changes affect both the content and the form. The content has been developed. Thus, as already mentioned, the initial idea of defenselessness is spelled out or advanced to become that of being liable to judgment. And the final idea of doing 'the same' is similarly advanced so as to focus more broadly on the consequences—on receiving subsequent judgment or measure.

Matthew has also changed the form. Instead of Paul's rather obscure phraseology, he uses expressions which are balanced in wording, and which are therefore more memorable. And the final shift to the image of measuring makes the text all the more colorful.

Both writers then go on to intensify the warning against judging others. Paul continues in the same vein as before (Rom. 2.2-3), but Matthew uses colorful examples (Mt. 7.3-6, 'Why do you see the splinter…?').

The fourfold use of *krinō* ('judge'), as found in Rom. 2.1 and Mt. 7.1-2, is rare in the New Testament (a total of six times). The combination of that fourfold usage with *en hō gar* ('for in/with what'), constitutes a word-cluster which, within the New Testament, is unique.

In the subsequent texts (Rom. 2.4-16; Mt. 7.7-27), Paul speaks largely of judgment, especially God's judgment. Matthew shifts the emphasis from God to people, to practical life—to the fact that implicitly there is a judgment, almost a dualism, at work among people, and that they tend to divide into two distinct directions—one good/sincere, the other evil/superficial. These texts may be dealt with briefly, under five headings.

(a) *The gracious God gives according to one's actions (Romans 2.4-6; Matthew 7.7-11).* While speaking of judgment, Paul describes a God who is immensely generous but who is driven to anger by people's hardness of heart. Matthew turns this around, positively. The gracious God, parentlike, is driven as it were to generosity by people's asking ('Ask and it shall be given…'). In both cases, God will give or render (Rom. 2.6: *apo-dōsei;* Mt. 7.9, 10: *epi-dōsei*) according to what one has done. The evil which is spoken of in Romans ('your hard and impenitent heart') is turned around by Matthew ('you who are evil') and used as a contrast which heightens the picture of God's goodness.

(b) *Act as if what you do is what comes back to you (Romans 2.7-8; Matthew 7.12).* Still thinking of judgment, Paul summarizes the consequences of one's actions: goodness earns eternal life, but unrighteousness brings wrath. In other words, what you do is mirrored back to you in another, eschatological, form. Matthew takes this principle of mirrored action, and in effect tells hearers to act accordingly; they should act as if what they do will come back to them here and now ('Whatever you wish that people do to you, do you also…'). Thus, Matthew has turned the most basic eschatological principle into the most basic principle of practical conduct.

(c) *The narrow place and the working out of evil and good (Romans 2.9-10; Matthew 7.13-20).* Paul begins by referring to anguish, *steno-chōria*, literally 'narrowness', and then refers to the division between those who 'work evil' (*kat-ergazomenou to kakon*) and those who 'work good' (*kat-ergazomenō to agathon*). Matthew takes that concept of narrowness and adapts it to the context: he speaks of a narrow gate (*stenē pylē*) and of a division into two—between those who enter and those who do not (Mt. 7.15-20), between those doing good (*agathon*) and those who are bad (*ponēros*). As often, Matthew's version is more practical (it addresses the problem of discerning prophets) and it is more vivid (it uses the imagery of a tree and fruit).

(d) *No superficiality: God's searching judgment of the lawless (Romans 2.11-12; Matthew 7.21-23).* God's judgment, says Paul, is not made on the basis of favoritism or appearances (*prosōpo-lēmpsia*, 'social standing', 'outward appearance'), but on the basis of whether or not people sinned, with or without the law (*anomōs*). Matthew elaborates the idea of superficiality (those who by their 'Lord, Lord' expect a favorable judgment) and then describes the condemnation of those who 'work lawlessness' (*ergazomenoi tēn anomian*). (Matthew's adaptation at this point seems to heighten the importance of law; Paul judges by sin, Matthew by law.)

(e) *It is not hearing that counts but doing (Romans 2.13-16; Matthew 7.24-27).* 'It is not the hearers (*akroatai*) of the law who are just before God', says Paul, 'but the doers (*poiēsin*) of the law'. Matthew elaborates this into the vivid imagery of the two foundations: 'Everyone who hears (*akouei*) these words and does (*poiei*) them... And everyone hearing (*akouōn*) these words and not doing (*poiōn*) them...'

4. *Conclusion*

As often in comparing texts, it is important not to emphasize connections which are weak. Such emphasis, whether by the person presenting the thesis or by someone questioning it, distracts from the decisive issue: are there connections which are strong, connections which go beyond the range of coincidence?

In this case there are. First, there are all the shared details, many of them rare in the New Testament, some unique. And, beyond the details, there is a certain cumulative effect —the weight of persistent affinity. As in some other cases, in the end it is hard to escape a basic choice. Either this is a case of coincidence which goes beyond all known laws of probability, or, more simply, Matthew, as well as using a copy of Mark, used also a copy of Romans.

This conclusion, even if accepted, is but the beginning of research. Further clarification is needed about Matthew's precise modes of adaptation. Three such modes have been highlighted—rendering Romans into forms which are vivid, positive, and practical—but much remains to be done. Specific texts need to be examined in detail, and many of the more subtle literary moves have yet to be discerned. When that is done, and only when that is done, will it be possible to deal clearly with the central issue: Matthew's reworking of Paul's theology.

21

The Use of Romans in Matthew 8.1–17.20:
An Exploratory Survey Continued

The use of Romans, which has already been partly uncovered in Matthew 1–7, continues as far as Mt. 17.20. The volume of text to be examined is great—roughly thirteen chapters of Romans and almost ten of Matthew—so this analysis is not full or detailed.

The Matthean text consists of four Blocks: Blocks D, E, F, and G in Table 45 (next page). These blocks do not correspond precisely to the structure of Matthew's finished gospel but, for comparative purposes, they are useful.

Apart from 10.1-6, Block D (Mt. 8.1–10.6), the first to be examined, consists of a clearly defined Matthean block—the miracles of chs. 8–9. Many of these miracles are adapted from Mark (cf. Mk 1.29–2.22; 4.35–ch. 5; 10.46-52) or Proto-Luke (cf. Lk. 7.1-10; 9.57-62). But Matthew is not simply reproducing the texts of others. Rather, he is a theological interpreter who, by diverse adaptations, great and small, imparts new meaning to the gospel, particularly concerning Christology and faith (Bornkamm, Barth and Held 1963: 165-299).

The proposal here is that much of Matthew's message, especially about faith, is adapted from what was said about faith in Romans. In Romans, faith leads to salvation from sin and death (Rom. 3.21–ch. 8), and in Matthew's account of the miracles, faith leads to various forms of salvation, particularly freedom from sin and from diverse forms of sickness and death. What Paul described in the realm of the spirit, Matthew describes in the vivid practical world of actual lives. Thus, the miracles of Mark (and Proto-Luke) have been pressed into service to act as vehicles for an adapted version of the teaching of Paul.

At times, Mark's miracles seem to suit this purpose well—so much so that one may ask whether Mark himself reflects something of Romans. Be that as it may, Matthew gives a new use of Romans, his own distinctive reading, and it is better to concentrate on that.

The next section of Matthew, Block E (Mt. 10.7–14.36), consists of almost five chapters (Mt. 10.6–ch. 14) and it uses an equally long section of Romans (10.14–15.14). The heaviest use of the epistle occurs in Matthew 10. The discourse to the Twelve ('the apostolic discourse'), particularly its emphasis on coming persecutions, reflects much of what Paul says about the anguished situation of Israel (Rom. 10.14–11.24). Matthew uses God's treatment of Israel, as described by Paul, as a basis for describing the mission of the church.

Block E goes on to evoke God's wisdom both in God's own dealing with Israel and all of humankind (Rom. 11.25-36), and in Jesus' dealing with the cities (Mt. 11). Then, in the closing section of Block E, Matthew (chs. 12–14) incorporates aspects of Paul's long exhortation, for instance, concerning practical love (Rom. 12.1–15.14).

In the case of Block F (Mt. 15.1–16.12), it is relatively easy to see the continuity between Paul (Rom. 1.17–3.20) and Matthew (15.1–16.12). Both are concerned with unhealthy reliance on the law, and both see all of humankind as in need. Unlike Paul at this point, Matthew shows that need as being met—Jesus responds to the Canaanite woman and feeds the four thousand.

Finally, in Block G (Mt. 16.13–17.20), Matthew uses Paul's conclusion. Paul's special ministry (Rom. 15.15-21) becomes one component in describing the ministry of Peter (Mt. 16.13-20). Paul's long, difficult journey (15.22-33) contributes to the picture of the fateful journey of Jesus through death and resurrection (Mt. 16.21–17.9). And Paul's final chapter of greetings to the disciples (ch. 16) contributes one or two minimal touches to the account of expelling the demon (Mt. 17.14-20).

1. *Aspects of a More Detailed Analysis*

The texts are outlined in Table 45. The accompanying analysis is very brief—a short comment on each passage. Comments are grouped by blocks (with occasional subheadings).

Table 45. *Romans 2.17–9.5; 10.14–16.27; Matthew 8.1–17.20*

BLOCK D: FROM SIN AND DEATH TO FAITH AND SALVATION (ROMANS 3.21–9.5; MATTHEW 8.1–10.6)	
Matthew Adapts the Miracles (Matthew chs. 8–9) to Reflect Paul's Message of Faith Leading to Salvation (Romans 3.21–ch. 8)	
Not Law, but Abraham's Faith	
1. Sinners are justified by faith, not law (Rom. 3.21-31)	The leper, healed by faith, respects law (Mt. 8.1-4)
2. Abraham's faith prepares for the faith of outsiders (4.1-17)	Centurion's faith shows that those out side will join Abraham (8.5-13)
3. Aged Abraham/Sarah did not weaken, nor do we, because of Jesus; he 'was delivered for our sins, and and was raised for our justification' (4.18-25)	Jesus raises Peter's mother-in-law, and he als many; 'he took up our weaknesses and carried away our diseases' (8.14-17)
From Sin and Death to Grace	
4. Despite our sins and sufferings, Jesus has saved us (5.1-11)	Disciples face homelessness and death, but in the storm, Jesus saves (8.18-27)
5. Deliverance from sin, death (5.12-21)	The Gerasene demoniacs (8.28-34)
6. Dead to sin, raised with Jesus (6.1-14)	Paralytic: freed from sin, raised by Jesus (9.1-8)
7. Grace: freedom from sin; an analogy from marriage; the new and the old (6.15–7.6)	Joyful discipleship: Jesus came to call sinners; an analogy from marriage; old and new (9.9-17)
New Life, Sight, Revelation, and Love	
8. The law killed but the Spirit gives life (7.7–8.13)	The raising of the dead daughter and the saving of the woman (9.18-26)
9. The two spirits expressing sonship, crying 'Abba', are heirs to glory (8.14-17)	The two blind men crying 'Son of David…' receive sight/vision (9.27-31)
10. Revelation coming in creation, something unknown and unspeakable (8.18-30)	The deaf man speaks, something never known before (9.32-34)
11. God's love (8.31-39)	The compassion of Jesus (9.35-38)
Lost Israel	
12. Paul's sorrow over Israel (9.1-5)	Mission to the lost children of Israel (10.1-6)

21. The Use of Romans in Matthew 8.1–17.20

BLOCK E: THE ANGUISH, THE WISDOM, AND THE PRACTICAL LOVE (ROMANS 10.14–15.14; MATTHEW 10.7–CH. 14)	
The Anguish of Israel (Romans 10.14–11.24) is Reflected in the Missionary Trials of the Twelve (Matthew 10.7-42)	
13. Need to proclaim and be sent (Rom. 10.14-15)	Jesus sends the Twelve to proclaim the kingdom (Mt. 10.7-13)
14. Israel's rejection of the word was foretold by the prophets (10.16-21)	Jesus foretells the rejection of the mission to Israel (10.17-23)
15. God's messengers were rejected but God sustains, as with Elijah when God was replaced by Baal (11.1-4)	The disciple may be treated as badly as the Lord but that is to be expected; they called the Lord/master Beelzebul (10.24-25)
16. By God's action Israel's hearing of revelation is blocked (11.5-10)	All will be revealed. What you hear, proclaim (10.26-27)
17. The providence in Israel's fall; how much more in their fullness (11.11-12)	Fear not: even a sparrow's fall is within providence. How much more you? (10.28-31)
18. Preaching [Christ] and reconciling Israel will bring a/the (final?) resurrection to life (11.13-15)	Confessing Christ to people brings life at the final judgment (10.32-33)
19. The tree is cut (11.16-21)	Christ brings a sword (10.34-39)
20. God rewards and punishes according to conduct (11.22-24)	God rewards exactly, depending on conduct (10.40-42)
The Wisdom: The Lord's Mysterious Involvement with Humanity/the Cities, and a Hymn of Praise (Romans 11.25-32; Matthew 11)	
21. God and humankind: doing mercy through a mystery involving enmity and confinement/imprisonment (11.25-32)	Jesus and the diverse cities: Jesus does wonders but John is imprisoned and the kingdom suffers violence (11.1-24)
22. Hymn: God's mercy, wisdom (11.33-36)	Prayer: 'I thank you, Father…' (11.25-30)
The Practical Love: Paul's Exhortation (Romans 12.1–15.14) is Reflected in the Kingdom (Matthew 12–14) Love, Humility…Not Uncleanness of Spirit	
23. Offer the sacrifice of yourselves… as God's will…with mercy (12.1-8)	Sabbath and temple: 'I will mercy and not sacrifice' (12.1-8)
24. Love without hypocrisy, in view of people's needs (12.9-13)	Even on the sabbath, heal, as one would raise a fallen sheep (12.9-14)
25. Sympathize with all; do not be set on high things; beloved, it is written: Vengeance is mine… Feed your enemy Be victorious over evil (12.14-21)	Jesus heals all, and forbids them to make him known, to fulfill Isaiah: Behold…my beloved… does not quarrel or crush the bruised reed… till he brings justice to victory (12.15-21)
26. Power comes from God; to resist power is to resist God Rulers are for good, not bad They bring God's wrath on evildoers (13.1-7)	Jesus' powers reflect the kingdom of God The one not with me is against me Distinguish good and rotten/evil Every negative word will be punished (12.22-37)
27. No debts/laws, except love Love surpasses the [narrow] law (13.8-10)	?? No signs, except death and resurrection Jonah/Nineveh sees more than this [narrow?] generation (12.38-42)
28. At one time we came to belief; now salvation is closer; put away orgies, etc.(13.11-13)…	An unclean spirit goes out; time passes; it may return with greater uncleanness (12.43-45)

29.	...But put on the Lord Jesus; make no provision for the flesh (13.14)	Jesus judges not by flesh (his mother/brothers) but by listening to his word (12.46-50)
	Food: Judgment, Scandal, and Doubt	
30.	Do not judge your brother (14.1-12)	?? Leave final judgment to God (13.1-52, especially 13.24-30, 36-43, 47-50)
31.	Judge not, and avoid scandal (14.13)	Nazareth: Jesus condemned, scandalized (13.53-58)
32.	In Jesus, everything is clean (14.14)	?? John's death is framed by references to Jesus and so is integrated/'cleansed' (14.1-12)
33.	Use of food (*brōma*) is governed by love (14.15-21)	Through sympathy Jesus supplies food (*brōma*) (14.13-21, especially 14.14-15)
34.	Have faith, do not waver; receive...as Christ received you; and glorify God, Father of Jesus (14.22–15.13)	Jesus received Peter; '...little faith, why did you doubt?' They worshipped, 'You are the son of God' (15.22-33, especially 15.28-33)
	Knowledge and Mutual Help	
35.	With goodness and knowledge you admonish one another (15.14)	Knowing/recognizing Jesus, people bring others to him for healing (14.34-36)
	BLOCK F: THE JEWS/PHARISEES HAVE NO ADVANTAGE OVER THE GENTILES (ROM. 2.17–3.20; MT. 15.1–16.12)	
	The Jewish law gives no advantage over Gentiles; all are sinful and in need (Paul). Nor does the Pharisees' law help; but (more positively) Jesus meets the needs of all, Israelite and Canaanite (Matthew)	
36.	The Jews, with their law, think they are guides to the blind (2.17-29)	The Pharisees, in using the law, are blind guides (15.1-20, especially 15.13-15)
37.	In faith, the Jews are 'first'; some Jews have disbelieved, but God remains true to them (3.1-4)	The Canaanite woman comes 'after'; the house of Israel may be lost, but Jesus is sent to it (15.21-28)
38.	Jews are not excused just because their unfaithfulness glorifies God (3.5-8)	Jesus cured many and they glorified the God of Israel (15.29-31, especially 15.31)
39.	We...and all...Jews and Gentiles are in need [lit. under sin] (3.9)	All [Jews and Gentiles] have their need met, by the loaves (15.32-39)
40.	There is no good person; all the law brings is knowledge of sin (3.10-20)	The generation is evil, adulterous; as for the leaven/teaching of the Pharisees, beware (16.1-12, especially 16.4, 12)
	BLOCK G: PRE-EMINENT MINISTRY, DIFFICULT JOURNEY, AND ENGAGED DISCIPLES (ROM. 15.22–CH. 16; MT. 16.13–17.20)	
	The Ministry	
41.	Paul has a gift given by God Paul's ministry is a liturgy reflecting the full power of God He builds on a foundation (15.15-21)	Peter is blessed, from the Father On this rock Jesus will build Peter's keys reflect the power of heaven (16.13-20)
	The Journey	
42.	Paul's journey, first to Jerusalem (15.22-26)	Facing death, Jesus must go to Jerusalem (16.21-23)

43.	What Paul gives is really a debt which is due (15.27-29)	When the Son of Humanity comes, he will give according to peoples' works (16.24-28, especially 16.27)
44.	Struggling together in prayer (15.30)	Falling on their faces in [holy] fear (17.1-8, especially 17.6-7)
45.	May I be delivered from unbelievers in Judea (15.31-33)	?? The Son of Humanity will suffer through them (17.9-13, especially 17.12)
The Disciples		
46.	A list of disciples (15.1-16, 21-23); God crushes Satan (15.20), and empowers (*dunamenō*) in faith (15.25-26) (see also ch. 16)	In the presence of 'the disciples' Jesus drives out the demon In faith nothing is impossible (*adunatēsei*) (17.14-20, especially 17.18, 20)

a. *Block D (Matthew 8.1–10.6)*
(1) *Section 1. The justified sinners and the healed leper (Romans 3.21-31; Matthew 8.1-4).* All have sinned, says Paul. Justification is given not through the law, but through faith, as a gift (*dōrean*, 3.24); this gift is a demonstration (*endeixis*, 3.24) of the justification of God. Faith does not abolish the law but upholds it (3.27-31, especially 3.31).

Apparently Matthew regarded the healing of the leper (taken from Mk 1.40-45) as capable of illustrating Paul's teaching. Like sinful humanity, the leper is healed not by the law, but by faith. However, the law is not abolished but upheld: the man has to show (*deixon*, Mk 1.44; Mt. 8.4) himself to the priest and bring the gift (*dōron*, Mt. 8.4) ordered by Moses.

Matthew has adapted the notion of gift and added it to Mark's account. In Paul, 'gift' is independent of the law (justification apart from the law is a gift), but Matthew uses the gift as something which simultaneously reflects divine graciousness (in Jesus) and also the requirements of the law. Thus, Matthew achieves a slightly greater sense of continuity between the old order and the new.

(2) *Section 2. Abraham's faith is open to outsiders/non-Jews (Romans 4.1-17; Matthew 8.5-13).* Analyzing the faith of Abraham, Paul shows that it was independent of circumcision and the law, and that as such it is open not just to Jews but to all people. Thus, Abraham is the father of 'many (*pollōn*) nations' (4.17).

To illustrate Paul's idea, Matthew takes Proto-Luke's account of a non-Jew who showed faith—the centurion whose servant was sick (Lk. 7.1-10)—and rewrites it in a way that, on the one hand, *omits* and *changes* several details, and on the other, *adds* the account of how 'many (*polloi*) from the east and west' will join the patriarchs, beginning with Abraham (8.11).

(3) *Section 3. Overcoming weakness, giving life to many, and taking away our sins (Romans 4.18-25; Matthew 8.14-17).* Despite physical incapacity (his own, and Sarah's inability to be a mother), Abraham's faith did not weaken (*asthenēsas*) about the eventual working out [or fulfillment] of what had been said (*to eirēmenon*)—that he would be the father of many (*pollōn*) nations. And, adds Paul—switching the focus from Abraham to 'us'—the same applies to us. We, too, are justified by faith in God who raised Jesus 'who was put to death for our transgressions and arose (*ēgerthē*) to justify us' (*hēmōn*).

To illustrate the idea of overcoming physical inability and giving life to many, Matthew takes the account of how Jesus healed Peter's mother-in-law and exorcised many (*pollous*,

Mk 1.29-34), and he adds details which reflect Romans. In Matthew's account, Peter's mother-in-law arose (*ēgerthē*, 8.15), and at the end, Matthew switches the focus from the past to what Jesus did for 'us'. He healed, so that what was said (*to rhēthen*) by Isaiah might be fulfilled: 'He took up our weaknesses (*astheneias hēmon*) and carried away our diseases'.

By adding Isaiah's two lines of intensifying poetry ('he took up...and carried away'), Matthew reflects diverse aspects of the Romans passage, including something of the balance between Paul's final phrases ('he was put to death...and he arose').

(4) *Section 4. The meaning of faith/discipleship: the journey from powerlessness and distress to salvation (Romans 5.1-11; Matthew 8.18-27)*. Having established the centrality of faith, Paul then begins to describe what faith means, what it entails. In basic terms, it involves a transition—a passage or journey—from helplessness and distress (5.3, 6) to salvation. In fact, Paul builds up to a resounding emphasis on the idea of being saved ('we shall be saved...all the more...shall we be saved'; *sōthēsometha... sōthēsometha*, 5.9, 10). The sense of moving or journeying is heightened by the description of stages: 'suffering leads to endurance, and endurance leads to character, and character leads to hope, and hope does not disappoint us' (5.3, 4).

Matthew speaks of the same reality; he uses the calming of the storm (from Mk 4.35-41) to show the need for faith amid distress, and he turns the idea of a progression or journey into a vivid form by using the verb *akoloutheō*, 'follow'; the disciples are actively following Jesus. Not only does he insert the word 'follow' into the beginning of the storm story (Mt. 8.23), he also sets the entire storm incident in the context of challenging calls to follow Jesus (Mt. 8.18-22).

These challenging calls are adapted from the triple call appearing in Proto-Luke (Lk. 9.57-62). In dealing with Proto-Luke's three-part picture, Matthew concentrates on the two most demanding parts (those with images of homelessness and death, Lk. 9.57-60). As for the third part—more positive, with its image of ploughing (Lk. 9.61-62)—Matthew distills some of its phrases and includes them in his adaptation of the first two parts. Matthew forms a bleaker background, ending with the word 'dead' (8.22).

But this bleak background suits what follows—a storm which threatens life—and it accentuates the sense of distress. The result of this and other adaptations is that 'the need of the disciples on the sea becomes a symbol of the distresses involved in discipleship of Jesus as a whole' (Bornkamm, Barth and Held 1963: 56). While Paul described the distresses of faith in theological terms (5.3), Matthew depicts them in colorful narrative. And as a further adaptation of Mark, Matthew inserts the key Pauline word 'save' ('Lord, save [us]', *sōson*, 8.25).

(5) *Section 5. Deliverance from demons and tombs (Romans 5.12-21, from sin and death; Matthew 8.28-34, the Gadarene demoniacs)*. Paul goes on to describe how, through (*dia*) the sin of Adam, the world lay under a great weight of sin and death—until the arrival of 'the one who was to come' (5.12-14). Through (*dia*) him, through Jesus, the weight of sin and death, great though it was, was overcome and gave way to a greater presence of eternal life. In place of the condemnation of 'all', Jesus opened the way to the justification of 'all' (5.15-21, especially 5.18, 21).

To illustrate this idea of living under the weight of sin and death, Matthew uses Mark's account of the wretched man who lived among the tombs (Mk 5.1-20). Most of Matthew's text is simply an abbreviation of Mark, but some small adaptations (though not all) would seem to reflect the text of Romans. The picture of people being possessed by demons (8.28), rather than having an unclean spirit, as in Mark, may catch something of the idea of a sin which goes back to Adam (and ultimately to the devil). More concretely, the fact that people could not pass 'through that way' (*dia tēs hodou ekeinēs*, 8.28), appears to reflect Paul's repeated use of 'through' (*dia*, eleven times in 5.12-21). In other words, as in the previous passage, when Matthew introduced the word 'follow' (8.23), he has rendered Paul's ideas into vivid forms which suggest physical movement. And Matthew's account of announcing 'all' and of 'all the city' coming out (*panta...pasa*, 8.33-34) roughly coincides with Paul's repeated use of 'all' (*pantas...pantas*, 5.18).

Two details in Matthew appear to be related not to the passage directly in question (Rom. 5.1-12), but to those immediately before and after it (Rom. 5.1-11 and 6.1-14). The first detail is the reference to Jesus coming 'before the time' (*pro kairou*, 8.29). To some degree, this means that Jesus 'has destroyed the demonic powers "before the time" set by Jewish apocalyptic' (Meier 1980: 90). It may also be associated with the idea that Christ intervened 'at the due time' (*kata kairon*, Rom. 5.6). Such criss-crossing of details occurs frequently, for instance, in Proto-Luke.

The second detail concerns the demon-bearing swine that 'died in the waters' (*apethanon en tois hydasin*, 8.32, rather than 'perished in the sea' as in Mark). This appears to reflect the idea that sin died in baptism (Rom. 6.2-3, 'we died to sin...we were baptized into his death', *apethanomen... dia tou baptizmatos eis ton thanaton*).

(6) *Section 6. Leaving sin and being raised with/by Jesus (Romans 6.1-14; Matthew 9.1-8, the raising of the sinful paralytic).* Paul now speaks of leaving sin (*hamartia...hamartia... hamartias... hamartia*, 6.1, 6, 9-14) and being raised with Christ to new life. 'Christ being raised (*egertheis*)...death no longer has dominion over him' (6.9).

In depicting this, Matthew summarizes the story of the paralytic (Mk 2.1-12)—the man whose sins (*hamartiae...hamartiae...hamartias*, 9.2, 5, 6) were forgiven and whose deliverance from sin was associated with Christ raising him up. In Matthew's version, the man 'arose' (*egertheis*, 9.7) and went to his house.

(7) *Section 7. Joyful grace calls from sin: an analogy from marriage: the old and the new (Romans 6.15–7.6; Matthew 9.9-17).* Paul now describes the more positive aspects of faith, particularly grace and its effects, and he begins by saying grace means leaving sin (6.15-23). Matthew correspondingly gives a positive picture using a block of Markan texts (Mk 2.13-22) which give a picture of joy. The word 'joy' does not occur in Mark's text or in Matthew's, yet, as Meier (1980: 92) indicates, the whole Matthean section may be entitled 'The Joy of Discipleship'. Thus, Paul's reference to grace is reflected in Matthew's implication of joy.

Both writers, Paul and Matthew, show significant similarities. Both call people away from sin (away from the slavery and wages of sin, Rom. 6.15-23; Jesus' call of Matthew means that he came to call sinners, Mt. 9.9-13). Paul contrasts sin and righteousness (*hamartia* and *dikaiosynē*, 6.16); Jesus came not to call the just (*dikaious*) but sinners (*hamartōlous*, 9.13).

Then both writers give an analogy from marriage. For Paul, being bound to the law was like being married to a husband who has now died; one was bound as long (*eph' hoson*) as he lived (Rom. 7.1-5). And for Matthew, the disciples will undergo a related experience. The bridegroom will be taken away; they do not mourn as long (*eph' hoson*) as the groom is with them (Mt. 9.14-15). Matthew has adapted the spouse-related break once experienced by believers (in letting go of the law) to the later spouse-related break of having to let go of Jesus (at least at one level).

Paul and Matthew then contrast the old(ness) (*palaios/palaiotēs*) and the new(ness) (*kainos/kainotēs*)—the transition from the old way of the written law to the new life of the

Spirit (Rom. 7.6), and the need to avoid mixing old cloth with new, or old wine with new wineskins (Mt. 9.16-17).

(8) *Section 8. Doomed to death and raised to life (Romans 7.7–8.13; Matthew 9.18-26, the ruler's daughter and the hemorrhaging woman).* Paul now embarks on a complex analysis of a process of death and life. First, death: how the law killed him and his own internal conflict doomed him to death (7.7-25); then life: how Jesus' spirit brought freedom from sin and death (8.1-13). In his own words, 'sin came to life and I died' (*apethanon*, 7.9); 'who will deliver me from this body of death' (7.25); and, 'he who raised (*egeirantos*) Jesus from the dead will also give life (*zōo-poiēsei*) to your mortal bodies' (8.11).

The unity of the entire section (7.7–8.13) is suggested by how its two parts (7.5-25 and 8.1-13) come under complementary headings (Byrne 1986: 134, 148). Paul's references to himself and his dilemma appear to be representative of a larger situation, to some degree the human situation as a whole (Byrne 1986: 143; Maly 1979: 56) but particularly the Christian situation (Barrett 1957: 153). It is a section of unusual complexity and intensity.

To communicate this complexity and intensity, as well as the sense of Christ's victory over doom and death, Matthew chooses the account of how Jesus saved two interrelated figures: the woman who had been hemorrhaging for twelve years (addressed by Jesus as 'Daughter'), and the twelve-year-old daughter who actually died (Mk 5.21-43).

In biblical thought, women often represent the people, and since both women are associated with twelve (the number of Israel's tribes and of the Christian Twelve), they are doubly suited to play a representative role—and thus to reflect something of the representative role depicted by Paul.

Without attempting to analyze these complex texts, it may be noted that in Matthew, as in Romans, there is talk of dying and raising (*apethanon... ēgerthē*, 9.24, 25).

(9) *Section 9. The double cry of sonship and of vision/glory (Romans 8.14-17; Matthew 9.27-31).* Paul now describes further how the spirit works. In fact, there are two spirits, our spirit and God's Spirit, and together they leave aside any spirit of slavery and cry (*krazō*) as sons (*huioi*) with the confidence of children, 'Abba, Father'. This cry in turn opens the way to something further—future glory.

In depicting this cry of sonship which leads to glory, Matthew adapts Mark's account of how blind Bartimaeus cried (*krazō*) to Jesus, 'Son (*huios*) of David', and received not glory but at least vision—his sight (Mk 10.46-52). Glory and sight (or vision) are inherently connected. In other words, the cry of sons has given way in Matthew to a cry to Jesus as a son. And the opening of the path towards glory has become the opening of the eyes to vision and discipleship.

It seems hard to say whether Matthew's account of two men (rather than one as in Mark) is in any way a reflection of the two spirits that cry out (the human spirit and the divine Spirit).

(10) *Section 10. The revelation of something never known before (Romans 8.18-30, creation groaning to reveal and speak; Matthew 9.32-34, the healing of a dumb man).* Having spoken of the cry of the spirit, Paul then goes on to talk of a deeper cry—the groaning of creation as it comes to a new revelation (8.18-25), and the action of the Spirit as it enables the human spirit with groanings which cannot be spoken (*a-lalētos*, 8.26-27).

Matthew captures this sense of finding speech and a new utterance or revelation by telling how the dumb man was empowered to speak (*laleō*, 9.33)—an event which is without parallel in Israel, in other words, which represents a whole new stage in development or revelation. The sense of creation groaning to a new stage is reflected in a miracle which brings Israel to a new stage of God's intervention.

The Pharisees' reaction to this miracle (Mt. 9.34) is adapted from Mark (3.22), but the main body of the account is from Matthew himself, and from Rom. 8.13-30.

(11) *Section 11. God's love and the compassion of Jesus (Romans 8.31-39; Matthew 9.35-38).* Paul culminates this part of the epistle by speaking eloquently of God's love—even if 'we are reckoned as sheep (*hōs probata*) for the slaughter' (8.36). And Matthew, drawing partly on Mark (6.6, 34), culminates this part of the gospel by speaking simply but memorably of the compassion of Jesus—his healing, his shepherdlike concern ('they were...like sheep', *hōsei probata*), and his exhortation to pray to the Lord of the harvest. Both Paul and Matthew speak of this love as all-encompassing ('delivered him for us all... give us all things...In all these things...', *pantōn, panta, pasin,* Rom. 8.32, 37; 'went around all the cities and villages...healing all diseases and all illnesses', *pasas, pasan, pasan,* Mt. 9.35).

(12) *Section 12. Commitment to lost Israel (by Paul, Romans 9.1-5; by the Twelve, Matthew 10.1-6).* As he begins the discussion on the fate of Israel (Rom. 9–11), Paul expresses his immense sorrow and his readiness to give up everything for the sake of the 'Israelites' (*Israēlitai,* 9.4; cf. 9.6, *Israēl...Israēl*; His feelings, therefore, are of both loss and commitment.

To underline this idea of commitment, Matthew takes the sending of the Twelve (as found in Mk 3.13-19; 6.7) and refashions their mission so that it is directed specifically and exclusively to Israel, 'to the lost sheep of the house of Israel' (10.1-6, especially 10.5-6, *Israēl*). Thus he keeps the focus on the 'Israelites', and, in varied form, he also keeps the sense of both a loss and a commitment.

b. *Block E. The Anguish (of Israel; of the Twelve) (Romans 10.14–11.24; Matthew 10.7-42)*
(1) *Section 13. The sending and proclaiming (Romans 10.14-15; Matthew 10.7-13).* At this point, Paul turns directly to the part played by Israel, and he begins by speaking, in a general way, of the need for preachers: 'How are they to hear without a proclaimer (*kērrussōn*)? And how are they to proclaim if they have not been sent?' (10.14-15).

In reworking Mark, Matthew incorporates this idea of the need for preaching: Jesus tells the Twelve that they are to proclaim (*kērrussō*) the kingdom of God (10.7-13).

(2) *Section 14. Israel rejects the word, and becomes hostile to others (Romans 10.16-21; Matthew 10.14-23).* People do not necessarily listen to the preacher. Paul, quoting Isaiah, describes Israel as disobedient and rebellious towards the word: 'They did not obey (*ou hyp-ēkousan*)... Have they not heard (*ouk ēkousan*)?' Furthermore, they are hostile towards those who do listen: 'I will make you [Israel] jealous...I will make you angry...' (10.19).

When Matthew is rewriting Mark, he first reproduces what Mark said about people not receiving the Twelve and not hearing (*mēde akousē,* Mk 6.11; Mt. 10.14-16; cf. Lk. 10.3, 14). And then, mirroring Israel's hostility, he goes on to describe the Twelve as suffering hostility (Mt. 10.17-23).

The connection of Israel with this hostility is clear. The account begins by referring to Sanhedrins and synagogues (10.17) and concludes by speaking once more of the mission to 'Israel' (10.23). Yet Matthew reflects considerable diversity (diversity of sources and of persecutions), and all that Romans provides is one component—a literary and theological starting point.

(3) *Section 15. The disciple (like Elijah) suffers, but rejection is not complete—despite interchanging the Lord for Baal/Beelzebul (Romans 11.1-4; Matthew 10.24-25).* In discussing persecution and suffering, Paul takes the example of the plight of Elijah, of the way death-threats led the prophet to supplicate, in fact to whine, about his fate (Rom. 10.1-3; cf. 1 Kgs 19.1-14). In effect, God had told Elijah to leave his whining and to see further to God's glory and reign (Rom. 10.4; cf. 1 Kgs 19.15-21).

Matthew adapts this to the disciples. They may suffer, but it is not the end of the world; even the Lord suffered indignities, so they can expect the same (Mt. 10.24-25a).

The precise indignity suffered by the Lord—they called him Beelzebul (*Beelzeboul*)—adapts an accusation found in Mark (3.22), but it also seems to reflect Paul's account of the Elijah story. Elijah had suggested that Baal had taken over; so God had to tell him otherwise; God was still God (Rom. 11.3-4). And Jesus may be equated with Baal, and thus denied his identity as Lord, but in fact he is still the Lord. Thus the reference to Baal's apparent taking over of God (Rom. 11.3-4) has been replaced by a reference to Beelzebul's apparent taking over of Jesus (Mt. 10.25b).

(4) *Section 16. Israel's hearing is blocked (Romans 11.5-10), but let you hear and proclaim (Matthew 10.26-27).* Paul describes a contrast between a faithful remnant, who are attentive, and Israel which, through God's action, has become turned in on itself (11.8, 10: 'ears that do not hear...their eyes darkened', *ōta...akouein...skotis-thētōsan*).

Matthew concentrates on the faithful—on those who listen to Christ—and he sees them as doing the very opposite of what Israel had done. In contrast to Paul's description of 'ears that do not hear...their eyes darkened', Jesus says, 'What I tell you in darkness, say in the light, and what you hear in the ear, preach on the housetops' (*skotia...ous akouete*). In other words, the Lord who closed Israel to revelation can also open it up. Matthew emphasizes the positive, and he adds the vivid touch, 'on the housetops'.

(5) *Section 17. The providence of the fall (Romans 11.11-12; Matthew 10.28-31).* Paul speaks of Israel's fall as being providential, and then develops the idea. If Israel's falling (*pesōsin*, 11.11) is providential, how much greater is the providence that will accompany Israel's positive development, its 'fullness?'

Matthew, again more interested in Christ's followers than in Israel, applies the theme of providence to those being sent out: they should not fear; even a sparrow's falling (*peseitai*, 10.29) is providential. Then he develops that idea: if providence accompanies even a sparrow, how much more will it accompany you?

(6) *Section 18. The proclaiming of Christ brings eternal life (in the final resurrection?) (Romans 11.13-15; Matthew 10.32-33).* Paul understands that the preaching of Christ will eventually lead, through the reconciliation of Israel, to a resurrection from the dead—a reference, many would say, to the final resurrection (but see Fitzmyer 1990: 51.108).

Matthew has a similar idea: those who acknowledge or proclaim Christ will be acknowledged by Christ before God—a reference to the final judgment. In both writers, therefore, proclamation or acknowledgement of Christ leads to a form of resurrected life, but Matthew's picture, for most Christians, is more practical.

(7) *Section 19. The divine cutting (of the tree, Romans 11.16-21; by the sword, Matthew 10.34-39).* Paul now summarizes God's overall action concerning Israel and the Gentiles as that of cutting branches off a tree and grafting them on others.

Matthew, in turn, refers to Christ's entire mission ('I have come...'), and he does so with another image of cutting—that of the sword ('not to bring peace but the sword...to set a man against his father, and a daughter against her mother'). Matthew keeps the basic idea that God's word may cut across established bonds. Again, however, his focus is not on Israel, but on the practical implications for Christians, particularly with regard to family ties.

(8) *Section 20. The Lord gives appropriate retribution/rewards (Romans 11.22-24; Matthew 10.40-42).* 'Behold', says Paul, 'the kindness and severity of God: towards those who fell [Israel], severity; towards you, kindness'. But this can change. Those who had earned severity can come to deserve kindness, and vice versa. God punishes and rewards according to what people do.

Matthew adapts this in a way that is simultaneously practical, positive and vivid. He makes it practical by focusing not on the general conduct of Israel, but on the day-to-day conduct of Christians. He makes it positive by concentrating on rewards: disciples will get exact rewards for what they do ('Whoever receives a prophet will receive the reward of a prophet. Whoever receives a just man will receive the reward of a just man', 10.41). And (partly by borrowing fom Mk 9.41), he makes it vivid by illustrating it in detail, down to the example of giving a cup of cold water (10.42).

(9) *Section 21. The Lord and humanity/cities: doing wondrous mercy even amid enmity and imprisonment (Romans 11.25-32; Matthew 11.1-24).* Paul now stands back as is were and reflects on the entire realm of God—God's dealings with humankind as a whole. He sees the fate of Israel, however disruptive at one level, as ultimately contributing to the way God shows mercy to humanity: 'They are enemies for your sake... God has shut/locked up all people in unbelief that he might show mercy to all' (11.28, 32). God's mercy, in its working out, includes certain forms of enmity and imprisonment.

The following text in Matthew, largely taken from Proto-Luke (Lk. 7.18-35; 10.12-15), tells especially of Jesus' reply to John, but the image which frames the whole complex passage is that of Jesus' ministry to the cities (Mt. 11.1, 20-24). This picture of the way Jesus deals with the cities would appear to be part of Matthew's way of depicting how the Lord deals with humanity. While Paul speaks in general terms about God and humanity, Matthew tells in more vivid language of Jesus and the cities.

Into this situation, Matthew introduces Paul's ideas—that God's dispensation involves forms of enmity and imprisonment. Hence, unlike Proto-Luke (Lk. 7.18), Matthew describes John as being in prison (11.2). And, again unlike Proto-Luke (Lk. 7.28-29), Matthew tells that the kingdom of heaven suffers violence (11.12; cf. Paul, enmity). The merciful kingdom preached by Jesus (with all its healing miracles) reflects the merciful divine dispensation described by Paul.

Both texts suggest the overarching presence of a wisdom. Matthew (11.19), following Proto-Luke (Lk. 7.35), mentions it explicitly. Paul implies it, particularly by speaking of 'this mystery' (11.25).

(10) *Section 22. The prayerful praising of God's mercy and wisdom (Romans 11.33-36; Matthew 11.25-30).* Paul climaxes his analysis of God's dispensation with a poetic outburst: 'O the depths of the riches and wisdom and knowledge of God... Who could ever know the mind of the Lord...? All things are from him and through him and to him. To him be glory forever. Amen'. This passage has frequently been described as a hymn.

The next passage in Matthew is equally prayerful and poetic: 'I thank you, Father, Lord of heaven and earth, for you have hidden these things from the wise and understanding... No one knows the Son except the Father, and no one knows the Father except the Son... Come to me all of you...'.

Despite its basic affinity with Rom. 11.33-36, Matthew's text has a distinctive character, and, as already seen (Chapter 12), belongs to the Deuteronomy-based *Logia*. Perhaps the main effect of Romans was not on its wording but on its position. Placed at the end of Matthew 11, it provides a counterpart to the prayerful hymn in Romans.

(11) *Section 23. Practical action: mercy and spiritual sacrifice (Romans 12.1-8; Matthew 12.1-8)*. Paul now changes to another mode, that of practical conduct. He asks people to give themselves willingly: 'Present yourselves as a living sacrifice (*thusian*)...to discover the will (*thelēma*) of God...[doing] acts of mercy (*eleōn*)...'

To express this idea of spiritual sacrifice, Matthew uses the incident (from Mk 2.23-28) of picking grain on the sabbath, an incident which reinterprets not only the sabbath but also, especially in Matthew (cf. Mt. 12.5), the temple. Sabbath and temple are not absolutes, to be reverenced for their own sakes, but are for the sake of a greater spiritual good.

This interpretation is made explicit when Matthew adds, 'I will mercy and not sacrifice' (*Eleos thelō kai ou thusian*)—a phrase which also captures several echoes of Paul's exhortation.

(12) *Section 24. Love without hypocrisy, in view of people's needs (Romans 12.9-13; Matthew 12.9-14)*. Paul exhorts people to sincere love: 'Let love be genuine', literally, without hypocrisy, and he spells it out: 'Abhor evil, hold fast to what is good. Love one another...'. Then he tells them to care for people's 'needs' (12.9, 10, 13).

To illustrate hypocrisy, Matthew takes the incident of healing on the sabbath (Mk 3.1-6) when the authorities, under pretence of piety, used a man with a withered arm to test Jesus—thus utterly confusing good and evil. However, Matthew makes a change in the Markan account: he tells how, if necessary, a person will save a sheep which has fallen into a pit on the sabbath day (12.11). The example of the sheep appears to reflect Paul's emphasis on love. (In Mt. 9.35-35, the image of the shepherd and the sheep is used to reflect Paul's passage on God's love, Rom. 8.31-39).

(13) *Section 25. Sympathize with all...be humble and gentle (Romans 12.14-21; Matthew 12.15-21)*. Paul's next exhortation is to sympathy, humility and kindness. In depicting this Matthew makes some use of Mark's account of Jesus healing people (cf. Mk 3.7, 10, 12), but the primary way of illustrating it is through a quotation from Isaiah dealing with God's Servant. As the outline shows, there are several correspondences:
- being positive/healing with 'all' (*pantōn*, Rom. 12.14, 15, 17, 18; *pantas*, Mt. 12.15);
- reference to the beloved (*agapētoi*, Rom. 12.19; *agapētos*, Mt. 12.18);
- following or fulfilling the scriptures (Rom. 12.19; Mt. 12.17);
- avoiding vengeance/quarrelling and choosing gentleness (Rom. 12.19-20; Mt. 12.19-20a);
- bringing what is right to victory (*nika*, Rom. 12.21; *nikos*, Mt. 12.12.20b-21).

The command to silence (Mt. 12.16), which in Mark (3.16) is part of the messianic secret, would appear to serve a very different purpose in Matthew—to illustrate Paul's emphasis on humility ('Do not set your mind on high things') and to introduce the humility of the Servant.

Part of Matthew's overall strategy in this text is to show how the attitude advocated by Paul is found first of all in Jesus—a fact which strengthens the basis for adopting that attitude.

(14) Section 26. The power is from God: so avoid resistance, confusion (of good/evil), and Punishment (Romans 13.1-7; Matthew 12.22-37). 'Let every soul be subject to the higher powers', says Paul, 'for there is no power except from God'. Paul is referring to civil authorities, but he is ultimately speaking of the power of God, and so Matthew uses this text to elaborate what Mark had said about Jesus' power over demons (Mk 3.22-30).

There are four main points in common:
1. The power comes from God (Rom. 13.1; Mt. 12.22-28, especially 12.28, 'therefore the kingdom of God has come upon you').
2. To resist this power is to resist God (Rom. 13.2; Mt. 12.30, 'Whoever is not with me is against me').
3. The power is for the good, so let there be no confusion between good and evil (*agathos, kakos*, Rom. 13.3-4; Mt. 12.31-33, especially 12.33, 'good (*kalos*)... bad (*sapros*)...the tree is known by the fruit').
4. Evil will be punished (Rom. 13.5-7, the powers will bring God's wrath on evildoers; Mt. 12.34-37, especially 12.36, 'on judgment day you will render account for every thoughtless word').

(15) Section 27. Not laws or signs, only something more radical—love (Romans 13.8-10) or death-and-resurrection (Matthew 12.38-42). The analysis at this point is very tentative, perhaps wrong. Against the background of the central demands of the old law, Paul singles out love: 'Have no debts, except (*ei mē*) to love one another... Love is the fulfillment of the law'.

In Matthew (following partly on Mk 8.11-12), the background is not that of Jewish law, but the Jewish insistence on signs. Jesus will give no sign 'except (*ei mē*) the sign of the prophet Jonah'—in other words, his own death and resurrection and the willingness of foreigners like the Ninevites to hear the word.

Therefore, when faced with Paul's surpassing of legal narrowness, Matthew apparently decided to adapt Mark's account of the narrow Jewish insistence on signs. Beyond laws there is love. And beyond signs? There is resurrection—the sign of Jonah!

(16) Section 28. The passage of time, and the need for increased vigilance against darkness or uncleanness (Romans 13.11-13; Matthew 12.43-45, the return of the unclean spirit). Paul tells of the passage of time and the greater closeness of salvation, compared to 'when we first believed'. However, this calls not for complacency but for vigilance against everything to do with darkness—orgies, promiscuity, quarrelling and jealousy.

Matthew does not refer to first belief, but he does speak of the unclean spirit going forth and of the passage of time. At that stage, however, the situation is not one for complacency—the unclean spirit may come back with increased force. This warning against increased uncleanness seems to be a dramatic presentation of Paul's warning against orgies and so on.

(17) Section 29. Never mind the flesh: attend to the Lord Jesus (Romans 13.14; Matthew 12.46-50, Jesus comes before relatives). Next comes Paul's famous exhortation: 'Put on the Lord Jesus Christ and make no provision for the flesh'. Apparently as a way of illustrating this, Matthew uses Mark's account (Mk 3.31-35) of how Jesus placed listening to the word and doing God's will before family ties, in other words, before the flesh. For both Paul and Matthew, what counts is not the demands and ties of the flesh, but attending to God.

(18) Section 30. Allow diversity and leave judgment to God (Romans 14.1-12; Matthew 13.1-52, especially 13.24-30, 36-43, 47-50). On the question of diverse views about eating

meat, Paul urges that people not condemn each other but leave judgment to God, 'for we shall all have to stand before the judgment seat of God'.

Given the context of the other links between Romans and Matthew, it seems likely that this idea of leaving judgment to God has contributed to Matthew's expansion of Mark's parables (Mk 4.1-34), an expansion which lays particular emphasis on God's final judgment (Mt. 13.24-30, 36-43, 47-50) and which contains a modified idea of allowing things to be as they are, such as allowing the weeds to grow along with the wheat (13.24-30). This alleged dependence, however, needs critical testing.

(19) *Section 31. Causing scandal to one's brothers (Romans 14.13; Matthew 13.53-58).* 'Never cause...a scandal to a brother' (*adelphō, skandalon*), says Paul, and the next incident in Matthew (borrowed largely from Mk 6.1-6a) tells that when Jesus visited Nazareth, those who were close to his brothers and sisters were scandalized ('Are not his brothers...? And are not all his sisters here with us? And they were scandalized at him', *adelphoi, adelphai, eskandalizonto*, 13.56-57; also in Mk 6.3).

(20) *Section 32. In Jesus everything is clean (Romans 14.14; Matthew 14.1-2).* Paul declares that 'in the Lord Jesus (*en...Iēsou*) nothing is unclean in itself'. The next incident in Matthew is the account (taken largely from Mk 6.14-29) of the beheading of John. The notion of uncleanness is not mentioned, but in Matthew the entire account is framed by references to Jesus (*Iēsou, Iēsou*, 14.1, 12). In place of Paul's idea that what seems unclean does have a place when set in the context of Jesus, Matthew *apparently* carries out a similar process of integration on the awful act of killing John. Setting it in the context of Jesus, he incorporates it into a larger, positive reality, and however negative in itself, it ultimately contributes to the good news, the gospel.

(21) *Section 33. The use of food is governed by love (Romans 14.15-21; Matthew 14.13-21).* 'If your brother is being upset by your food (*brōma*), you are no longer walking in love', says Paul, and he goes on to elaborate this idea that love should govern the use of food.

The next incident in Matthew is very concerned with love and food—on the basis of sympathy, Jesus cures and feeds the five thousand—but the account is almost completely Markan (6.32-44). The one change that has apparently been contributed by Romans is that in Matthew, unlike Mark, the word for food is *brōma*.

(22) *Section 34. Faith and doubt: place your focus on Christ who received you, and glorify God (Romans 14.22–15.13; Matthew 15.22-33, especially 15.28-33, Peter comes to Jesus).* 'Keep your faith', continues Paul, '...but the one who has doubts is condemned' (14.22-23), and he tells the Romans to focus on Christ's example so that 'you may glorify the God and Father of our Lord Jesus Christ' (14.15.3-6). Then he urges them to accept or receive one another 'as Christ received (*pros-elabeto*) you' (15.7).

Matthew now incorporates Mark's passage about Jesus walking on the water (Mk 6.45-52), but he adds the account of Peter trying to do the same—trying to come to Jesus across the water. This addition (15.28-33) builds on Paul's exhortation to keep faith and not doubt. Peter sought to follow the example of Jesus (as Paul had urged); he went through both faith and doubt; as he floundered Jesus took or received him (*ep-elabeto*); and when he and Jesus entered the boat, the disciples effectively glorified God: 'they worshipped him saying, "Truly you are the Son of God".'

(23) *Section 35. Knowledge, goodness and mutual help (Romans 15.14; Matthew 14.34-36, Gennesaret)*. Paul now reaffirms his faith in his hearers; they are 'full of goodness…[and] all knowledge (*pasēs gnōseōs*), able also to advise one another'. This picture of knowledge and goodness, particularly towards one another, appears to have contributed to Matthew's next (Mark-based, 6.53-56) incident. At Gennesaret the people respond to Jesus with knowledge (*epi-gnontes*) and mutual goodness, they recognize him and bring to him all (*pantas*) who are unwell. Knowledge has been replaced by knowing or recognizing Jesus, and goodness and mutual admonition have been replaced by the practical action of actually bringing people to Jesus.

c. *Block F (Matthew 15.1–16.12): The Jews'/Pharisees' Law Leaves All in Need*
(1) *Section 36. The Jews/Pharisees and their law: not guides to the blind but blind guides (Romans 2.17-29; Matthew 15.1-20, especially 15.13-15)*. The Jews 'rely on the law and…are convinced that [they] are a guide for the blind' (*hodēgon…tuflōn*, Rom. 2.17, 19), but in fact, says Paul, neither the law nor circumcision will save them (2.21-28). Genuine Jewishness is something 'inward…of the heart, in the spirit' (2.29).

When Matthew is telling about the Pharisees' misunderstanding of the law—their undue reliance on externals—he uses Mark's account (Mk 7.1-23), but he also draws on Romans. Hence, unlike Mark, Matthew adds a passage which describes the Pharisees as blind guides (*hodēgoi tuflōn*, 15.13-15).

(2) *Section 37. The Jews are first; even if lost, God is faithful to them (Romans 3.1-4; Matthew 15.21-28, especially 15.13-15, the Canaanite woman)*. Despite the Jewish infidelity concerning the law, Paul insists both that the Jews retain their position of being first (*prōton*) and that God remains faithful to them.

Therefore, when Matthew is incorporating Mark's account of Jesus' attitude to a non-Jew—the Canaanite woman whose daughter was sick (Mk 7.24-30)—he makes some additions which show that the Jews still have a special position. In contrast to the Jews who are first (in Romans), the woman comes after (*opisthen*, Mt. 15.23). And in face of her insistence, Jesus asserts God's fidelity to the Jews: Israel may be lost, but it is to them that he has been sent (15.24).

(3) *Section 38. The glorification of God (Romans 3.5-8; Matthew 15.29-31, especially 15.31, cures near the sea)*. The unrighteousness of the Jews (Israel) may ultimately demonstrate God's righteousness and thus give glory to God (*theou…doxa*), but that does not excuse them, says Paul (3.5-8, especially 15.7). From this text, Matthew simply distills its most positive part—the idea of Israel or the Jews as glorifying God—and when rewriting Mark's next episode, the cures by the sea (Mk 7.31-37), he adds that those who were healed 'glorified the God of Israel' (*edoxasan ton theon Israēl*, 15.31).

(4) *Section 39. 'We' and 'all'—Jews and Gentiles (Romans 3.9; Matthew 15.32-39, especially 15.33, 37, a Gentile/universal feeding)*. Paul now concludes that 'we' Jews have no advantage over the Gentiles (*pro-echometha*, 'Are we better off?'); on the contrary 'Jews and Gentiles, all, are under sin' (*Ioudaious, Hellēnas pantas*).

The next episode in Matthew (taken from Mk 8.1-10) is the feeding of the four thousand, an account which for many commentators indicates a feeding which is symbolically universal, and therefore includes Gentiles (Viviano 1990: 42.102; cf. D. Harrington 1990: 41.51; in contrast to the numbers in the first loaves account [five loaves, twelve baskets, five thousand] those in this account all have a dimension that is eschatological or universal—three days, seven loaves, seven baskets, four thousand). It would appear, therefore, that when Matthew was faced with Paul's equalizing of all people, Jew and Gentile, he found it appropriate to reproduce a Markan text which had a universal dimension, and which implicitly included Gentiles. As often, however, the gospel text is more positive. The equality among all people is not just one of need (of being under sin) but of the need being met (all receive the loaves).

Though Paul's text is just one verse, Matthew seems to have taken two of its details, the implicit 'we' ('Are we better off?') and the 'all'. At least when compared to Mark, Matthew's text shows such details—the implicit we ('Where can we…?' *pothen hēmin*, 15.33) and the 'all' ('They all ate…', *pantes*, 15.37)

(5) *Section 40. The whole generation is sinful (Romans 3.10-20; Matthew 16.1-12, especially 16.4, 12)*. Finally, says Paul, there is not a good person left; all the law brings is knowledge of sin. And the next text in Matthew is equally condemnatory: when reworking Mark's account of Jesus' response to the Pharisees (Mk 8.11-21), Matthew inserts references to 'an unfaithful and adulterous generation' (16.4) and to the (implicitly unwholesome) teaching of the Pharisees (16.12). Thus, all the law brought was knowledge of sin, and the knowledge or teaching of the Pharisees is equally lacking in nourishment.

d. *Block G (Matthew 16.13–17.20): The Ministry, the Journey, the Disciples*
(1) *Section 41. The special ministry of Paul/Peter (Romans 15.15-21; Matthew 16.13-20, especially 16.17-19)*. In describing his own ministry, Paul mentions three major facets:
1. God has given him a grace (*charin…tou theou*, 15.16).
2. His ministry has great and divine authority (it is priestlike, widespread and backed by God's signs and wonders, 15.16-19).
3. He builds (*oikodomō*) but not on another's foundation (*ep'… hemelion*, 15.20-21).

When Matthew rewrites Mark's account of the confession of Peter (Mk 8.27-30) he ascribes to Peter a position which reflects that of Paul:
1. Peter's confession and leadership come from God (he is blessed by the heavenly Father, *makarios…patēr…en tois ouranois*, 16.17).
3. Jesus will build on him as on a rock *(epi…petra oikodomēsō*, 16.18a).
2. His authority is great and divine (keys and divine sanctions, 16.18b-20).

Paul's general terms—great authority on a personal foundation—have been made vivid by clear images: the keys of the Kingdom on a foundation of rock. Matthew has taken the account of Paul's ministry and, while depending also on other factors, has reshaped it to describe the role of Peter.

(2) *Section 42. Going to Jerusalem (Romans 15.22-26; Matthew 16.21-23)*. Paul now gives his travel plans, and though his ultimate goal is Spain, the place he highlights is Jerusalem (*eis Ierousalēm*, 15.25-26). And when Matthew incorporates Jesus' first passion prediction (from Mk 8.31-33), he adds something—he is going 'to Jerusalem' (*eis Ierosolyma*, 16.21).

(3) *Section 43. Giving what is due (Romans 15.27-29; Matthew 16.24-28, especially 16.27)*. When Paul speaks of the contribution he is bringing to Jerusalem, he emphasizes that in view of what Jerusalem has given spiritually to others, it is well-deserved; it is paying a debt.

In rewriting the account of the demands of discipleship (from Mk 8.34–9.1), Matthew inserts essentially the same idea that actions will receive their due return: 'the Son of Humanity…will reward each one according to behavior' (16.27).

(4) *Section 44. Striving together in prayer (Romans 15.30; Matthew 17.1-8, especially 17.7, the transfiguration)*. Paul asks people to strive with him in prayer on his behalf (literally, struggle or 'agonize' with him, *syn-agōnizomai*). Some of this intensity, this struggling with the divine, seems to be reflected in one of Matthew's additions to the transfiguration account (Mk 9.2-8)—in the description of the disciples falling to the ground in great fear (Mt. 17.6-7). The fear is reverential fear of the divine, and falling to the ground is like a physical form of struggling or 'agonizing'.

(5) *Section 45. Impending danger (Romans 15.31-33; Matthew 17.7-13, especially 17.12)*. Paul's main wish is that he should be delivered from the unbelievers in Jerusalem (15.31). Thus, he is facing danger, but hopes to be delivered from his enemies (*apo tōn apeithountōn en tē Ioudaia*, 'from the unbelievers in Judea', 15.31). Something of the same sense of impending danger hangs over the account of the descent from the mountain (Mk 9.9-13; Mt. 17.9-13), particularly in one of Matthew's final phrases: 'So also the Son of Humanity will suffer from them' (*hyp' autōn*, 17.12). Unlike Paul, Matthew does not continue by speaking of deliverance—perhaps because he had already just done so (in speaking of resurrection, 17.9).

(6) *Section 46. Disciples: the demon is defeated and faith empowers (Romans 16; Matthew 17.14-20, especially 17.18, 20)*. Most of Paul's final chapter deals with greetings and to some degree is like a list of disciples (16.1-16, 21-23). However, he gives a warning about trouble, saying that 'God…will soon crush Satan (*ton Satanan*) under your feet' (16.17-20), and ends by glorifying the God who empowers in faith (*dynamenō…pisteōs*, 16.25-27).

Aspects of this chapter seem to be reflected in the account of the healing of a possessed boy (Mk 9.14-29; Mt. 17.14-21). Apart from the emphasis on the presence of the disciples (Mt. 17.16, 19), there is the suggestion of defeating if not Satan at least a demon (*to daimonion*, in Matthew, 17.18), and at the very end, as in Romans, there is an emphasis on the power of faith ('If you have faith…nothing shall be impossible', *pistin…adynatēsei*, 17.20).

2. Conclusion

Some connections given in these two chapters are weak, particularly when seen out of context. For instance, one would not even inquire about a possible connection between the primacy of love (Rom. 13.8-10) and the sign of Jonah (Mt. 12.38-42) if the context did not raise the question.

On the other hand, in many instances where Matthew elaborates significantly on Mark—for instance, in the discourses (chs. 5–7, 10) or in highlighting the role of Peter (15.22-33; 16.13-20)—the connection with Romans appears strong and consistent. In other words, where Matthew is most distinctive, the connections are strong.

22

Fish, Temple Tithe, and Remission:
The God-Based Generosity of Deuteronomy 14–15 as One Component
of the Community Discourse (Matthew 17.22–18.35)

In 1970, Günther Bornkamm proposed that in investigating the problem of sources in Matthew's gospel, it is useful to focus on the discourse concerning the community (Bornkamm 1983). While maintaining that focus, the purpose of this chapter is to show that *one* of the sources used in this discourse (Mt. 17.22–18.35) consists of Deuteronomy 14–15.[1] The emphasis on 'one' is important. As Bornkamm maintains, Matthew's community discourse is 'a conglomerate of materials from very different traditions' (1983: 89). The Old Testament text has not only been synthesized and adapted, it has also been blended with other materials, many of them from the New Testament period.

1. *General Introduction to Matthew's Use of Deuteronomy*

The basic idea that Matthew used the Old Testament in diverse ways is not new. Apart from forty formal quotations, researchers have already discovered over a hundred quotations which are allusive or implicit.[2] And these usages are often both central and complex. The centrality is highlighted, for instance, in the work of Lamar Cope. When Cope reviewed this question, his basic conclusion was that it provides 'evidence of the conscious use of the Old Testament in the construction of the gospel' (Cope 1976: 121); Matthew uses several Old Testament citations as 'the structural key to the composition of the passages in which they occur' (p. 121); and 'Moses typology...shapes all of Matthew 1–7' (Allison 1993: 268).

As for the complexity of Mathew's usage, aspects of it are reflected in Goulder: 'Matthew shows himself to be a Targumist in small ways and large. He not only chooses the textual form he is going to cite, ...he not only combines one scripture with another, he also writes his own interpretation into scripture' (1974: 128). This latter idea, that Matthew incorporated his own interpretation of scripture, is central to this chapter.

Of all the Old Testament books used by Matthew, the most influential appears to have been Deuteronomy. It is from Deuteronomy, rather than from Isaiah or the Psalms, that Matthew takes the greatest number of explicit quotations (thirteen, compared to ten from Isaiah and nine from the Psalms). More than any other Old Testament book, it is Deuteronomy which provides the best precedent for Matthew's central achievement: shifting the basic tradition from narrative to discourse. As Deuteronomy once recast and expanded the

---

1. The Greek texts used for this comparison are the UBSGNT, 3rd edn (corrected), and the Cambridge critical edition of Deuteronomy. However, for the practical purpose of maintaining harmony with the majority of texts and versions, the verse numbers used here for Deut. 14.11-29 are those which the Cambridge edition places in parentheses.
2. For reviews, see van Segbroeck 1972; Goulder 1974: 123-36; Senior 1983: 37-46.

most basic Old Testament story (the exodus) into the form of discourses, so, in a modified way, Matthew has recast and expanded the basic story of Jesus into a form in which discourse prevails. He has deuteronomized Mark.

In 1974, Hubert Frankemölle proposed that Matthew's concept of the church is founded on the Old Testament picture of Israel, particularly as Israel is described in Deuteronomy and in 1 and 2 Chronicles. In Frankemölle's analysis, the essence of this similarity is that in both cases the community is grounded in the divine presence: Israel rested on its covenant with the abiding God, and the church rests on its union with the risen Christ. God was 'with' Israel, 'in the midst' of Israel, and the risen Christ is 'with' the church, and 'in the midst' of the community (cf. especially Mt. 28.20; 18.20) (1974: 27-34, 71, 79). Frankemölle drew a specific connection between *ekklēsia*, 'assembly', as found in Deuteronomy and the same word as found in Matthew (16.18; 18.17) (1984: 230).

In 1989, Joseph A. Grassi, without referring to Frankemölle, went further by stating that Matthew's dependence on Deuteronomy is not limited to the idea of the church. Rather, Matthew itself, the written gospel, is modeled on the book of Deuteronomy ('Matthew as a Second Testament Deuteronomy') (Grassi 1989). As Grassi indicates, Deuteronomy and Matthew contain several leading points of contact. Three of these are particularly important:

1. In describing the gospel, Matthew (24.14; 26.13) speaks of '*this* gospel', a phrase which is otherwise not found in the New Testament, but which finds a precedent in Deuteronomy's references to 'this book' and 'this law' (Deut. 28.58, 61; 29.20, 27; 30.10; 31.9, 24). In both documents, the unusual phrasing occurs first in the aftermath of pronouncements concerning curses/woes and coming sorrows (Deut. 28.58, 61; Mt. 24.14), and finally in the introduction to the narratives concerning death (of Moses, Deut. 31.9, 24; of Jesus, Mt. 26.13). In Grassi's analysis, what is at stake is not just a detail of phrasing but an aspect of Matthew's view of his entire gospel and of its relationship to Deuteronomy: As Deuteronomy once claimed to reflect the authoritative voice of God, so Matthew's gospel claimed to reflect the authority of God's Son.
2. The most distinctive feature in Matthew's landscape—the mountain—reflects the distinctive role of the mountain in Deuteronomy. Deuteronomy not only refers more than fifty times to the mountain, but also concludes on the mountain when Moses is about to die and God addresses him for the last time (Deut. 34). And Matthew not only sets its great opening sermon on the mountain (Mt. 4.23–7.28), but also concludes on the mountain when Jesus, speaking with the authority of God, addresses the disciples for the last time (Mt. 28.16-20).
3. One of the most important and distinctive words in Matthew's theological vocabulary, *ekklēsia*, 'church/assembly', a word which he uses three times (16.18; 18.17[twice]) but which does not occur elsewhere in the gospels, is also found also in (Greek) Deuteronomy (4.10; 9.10; 18.16; 23.1, 2, 3, 8; 32.1), though it does not occur elsewhere in the Pentateuch. In both books *ekklēsia* is associated first with the authoritative setting up of the believing community (Deut. 4.10; 9.10; 18.16; Mt. 16.18), and later, when the word is repeated, with the question of membership and exclusion (Deut. 23.1, 2, 3, 8; Mt. 18.17).

In Frankemölle's thesis, the primary continuity between Deuteronomy and Matthew is theological (rather than literary). For Grassi, however, the continuity has a markedly literary dimension.

This chapter seeks to develop one shared aspect of the preceding proposals: Matthew's discourse on the community or church (17.22–18.35) is founded not only on Deuteronomy's overall theological sense of the covenant and *ekklēsia*, and on the book of Deuteronomy as a whole, but also on a specific Deuteronomic text—on chs. 14–15.

2. *The Texts: Introductory Analysis*

Deuteronomy 14–15 is part of the Deuteronomic Code (Deut. 12.1–26.15), part, that is, of the striking amalgam of traditions and laws which stands at the center of Moses' second, great discourse (Deut. 4.21–ch. 28). It is a code which, insofar as it deals with practicalities—particularly with faith and worship, with officials, with personal relationships—helps to bring the elevated vision of Deuteronomy down to earth.

Deuteronomy 14 is concerned both with cleanliness, especially as regards animals (animals, fish, birds, 14.1-21), and also with tithing, especially for the place of worship (the temple, 14.22-29). Chapter 15 focuses on release or remission—the process of letting go (*aphiēmi*) of some form of payment or profit (repayment, money, controlling power); instead of seeking to control and enslave people, one lets them go because of God. This remission particularly applies to debtors and slaves.

There is no obvious thematic unity to these two chapters' exhortation involving animals, tithes and remission. But despite the detailed and disparate nature of some of the material, the content is never trivial. The opening two verses (Deut. 14.1-2), for instance, allude to forbidden customs which are indeed obscure, but for the Israelites, the central issue is clear: 'such customs will impair their status with their God' (G.H. Davies 1962: par. 238a). It is this factor—the link between customs and God—which seems to summarize these two chapters best. Customs (including conduct) may be diverse but they are not meaningless rituals; they are all linked to a sense of God, a sense of the holy (14.2). In the Septuagint, the explicit reference to being holy is repeated (14.21). And in varying ways, the sense of the connection between God and conduct pervades the subsequent discussion of tithes and remission. In simplified terms, therefore, Deuteronomy 14–15 may be said to deal with God-based conduct—God-based generosity.

Mathew's text is equally significant.

Matthew 17.22–18.35 is the second part of a large section of Matthew (13.53–18.35), a section which—without analyzing content in any detail—may be summarized tentatively as follows:

Narrative (13.53–17.21)
Introductory episodes (Nazareth; Herod, 13.53–14.12)
First sequence of the loaves (14.13–15.31)
Second sequence of the loaves (15.32–17.20)

Discourse (17.22–18.35)
Introductory episodes (passion; temple tax, 17.22-27)
Among disciples: The kingdom's childlike quality (18.1-14)
Among brothers: Sin and remission (18.15-35)

The section as a whole (Mt. 13.53–18.35), and particularly 17.22–18.35, is sometimes seen as focusing on the church and church administration.[3] It is within this large section that Matthew not only uses the word *ekklēsia* (16.18; 18.17) but also gives a distinctive prominence to Peter (14.28, 29; 15.15; 16.16, 18, 22, 23; 17.1, 4, 24; 18.21). Thus, in broad terms, this church-related section of Matthew functions somewhat like the Deuteronomic Code within Deuteronomy: it brings the vision down to earth; it manifests a concrete aspect of God's realm or kingdom.

---

3. See, for instance, Bacon 1930; Davies and Allison 1988: 59. For reviews of discussion on Matthew's structure, see W.G. Thompson 1970: 13-16; Davies and Allison 1988: 58-72.

The unity of 17.22–18.35 is seen not only in its emphasis on *church* but also in details which bind it into a unity or suggest togetherness. The emphasis on *togetherness* or *community* is reflected in the first, difficult phrase, *sy-strephomenōn de autōn*... ('As they were gathered together...', 17.22). By placing the word *sy-strephō* ('gather together'), at the very beginning, Matthew prepares the way for other words with some form of *syn*, 'together/with/co-' (*sym-phōneō*, 'agree [with]', 18.19; *syn-agō*, 'gather together', 18.20; *syn-doulos*, 'fellow-servant', 18.28, 29, 31, 33—a word never used by the other evangelists). The fact that some of these words occur at the beginning and end of the text (in 17.22 and in 18.28, 29, 31, 33) helps to bind the text into a unity.

Other binding details are the references to Galilee (17.22; 19.1) and the repetition near the beginning and end of the unusual phrase, *elypēthēsan sphodra* ('they were greatly saddened', 17.23; 18.31; the phrase does not otherwise occur in the New Testament).

The beginning of the text—Jesus' second prediction of death (17.22-23)—constitutes a major division within the gospel, and with its emphasis on Galilee and on forthcoming death, it is roughly the equivalent of the division which occurs in John's gospel at 7.1.

The Passion prediction may seem unrelated to the discourse on the church, but in fact it is central. It has the effect, before the discourse develops, of setting the hearers together in the shadow of Jesus' death and resurrection. The rule which follows, therefore, may be a Rule for the Congregation, a *Gemeindeordnung*, but is not some detached code. It is an extension of God's presence working in the human fate of Jesus, and it involves people to the core ('they were greatly saddened').

The temple-tax episode (17.24-27) also has an important introductory role: it emphasizes both consideration for the weak (the avoidance of scandal) and the presence of a superhuman power (as manifested in Jesus' anticipation of Peter and in his [implied] commanding of Peter and the fish, 17.25, 27). In other words, the church is not to be a place for making one's power felt. Rather, it is governed by awareness both of the weak and of the greater power of God.

Hence, as Deuteronomy 14–15, with all its diversity, is governed by an awareness of God and of holiness, Mt. 17.22–18.35 begins by showing the disciples as living in the presence of something greater than themselves.

The text (17.22–ch. 18) may now be outlined with more attention to content. The division given here into seven pericopes follows the lines of the UBSGNT:

> * *Introductory episodes (17.22-27)*
> Gathered in the shadow of Jesus' cross (passion foretold, 17.22-23)
> Reminding Peter of the weak and of Jesus' power (temple tax, 17.24-27)
>
> *The kingdom's childlike quality (18.1-14)*
> The greatest is like a child (18.1-4)
> Throw away whatever destroys the child (scandal, 18.5-9)
> God's care for the little and weak (the lost sheep, 18.10-14)
>
> * *Sin and remission (18.15-35)*
> Coping with sinners and finding life (procedure and prayer) (18.15-20)
> Reminding Peter/all about granting sinners forgiveness (18.21-35)

The asterisks indicate the two areas where there has always been the greatest difficulty in identifying Matthew's sources (Mt. 18.1-14, apart from the lost sheep passage, is heavily dependent on Mark. So is the Passion prediction, 17.22-23). It is on these two areas (17.22-27 and 18.15-35) that the present chapter concentrates.

The thesis is as follows: these texts—the temple-tax (17.24-27); sin and remission (18.15-35)—may indeed have drawn on many sources, but they are particularly dependent on Deuteronomy 14–15.

Table 46. *Deuteronomy and Matthew 17.22–18.35*

A. Animals and the Temple Payment (Deuteronomy 14.1-27; Matthew 17.24-27)		
1. You are holy; you are God's children (*huioi*) among the nations of the earth (*tēs gēs*) (Deut. 14.1-2) You are holy, not strangers (*allotrioi*) (14.21)		
2. Discriminate (clean/unclean) among animals, fish, birds (14.3-20)		
3. Give the (temple) tithe (14.22-23)		Do you pay the (temple) coin? Yes. (Mt. 17.24-25a)
	1.	In the house: among kings of the earth (*tēs gēs*), payment is not by the children (*huioi*), but by strangers (*allotrioi*) (17.25b-26)
	2.	Drawing on the first fish [i.e. without discrimination] (17.27b),
4. Take the money…go…give (14.24-27)		go…and taking the coin, give (17.27ac)
B. Sin and Remission (Deuteronomy 15.1-15: Matthew 18.15-35)		
5. If your brother has a private debt, grant him (7th year) remission (15.1-4)		If your brother sins, go and settle it with him alone (18.15a)
6. If you really hear (*ean…eisakousēte*) God, you will be rich and powerful—in contrast to many nations (*ethnoi*) (15.5-6)		If he hears (*ean…akousē*), you will gain your brother (18.15b)
7a. [Deut. 17.6; 19.15: The need for two or three witnesses]		If he does not hear, take…two or three witnesses (18.16)
7b. [Deut. 18.17: Hearing God on the day of the *ekklēsia*]. [Deut. 23.1, 2, 3: Exclusion from the *ekklēsia*]		If he does not hear them, tell the *ekklēsia*, and if he does not hear the *ekklēsia*, treat him as a heathen (*ethnikos*)… (18.17)
	10.	Remission for a brother even to 7 times? Parable: The servant who was to be sold (*prathēnai*) and who gets remission (18.21-25)
8. Do not close yourself to the needy; give whatever loan (*daneion*) he needs (15.7-8)		Be large-minded with me. And he remitted the loan (*daneion*) (18.26-27)
9. Keep secret selfishness from your heart, lest you reject remission.		Be large-minded with me. Servant refuses remission.
Your attitude would be evil (*ponēreuomai*). Your brother would cry to the Lord (*kyrios*). Avoid anything so saddening (*lypeō*), and so God will bless you in all (*pasin*) (15.9-10)		Fellow-servants were saddened (*lypeō*). And they told the Lord (*kyrios*). Evil (*ponēros*) servant I remitted all (*panta*) (18.28-32)
10. The case of a brother who is sold (*prathē*) and who, in the seventh year, gets remission (15.12)		
11. As the Lord blessed and redeemed (*eulogēsen…elutrōsato*) you, let you be generous to your indebted brother (15.11, 13-15)		You should be merciful (*eleēsai*) to your sinning brother, as I was to you (18.33-35)

Obviously, Matthew does not reproduce Deuteronomy word-for-word. It was of the essence of the New Testament message that the existing scriptures needed reinterpretation, and so Deuteronomy is reinterpreted and synthesized. Even Mark's gospel, despite all its newness and its New Testament character, had already been subjected by Matthew to a certain process of interpretation and synthesis. For instance, the episode immediately preceding the community discourse concerning the epileptic demoniac had been reduced by Matthew from sixteen verses to seven (Mt. 17.14-20; cf. Mk 9.14-29). If Mark often needed reinterpretation and synthesis, then all the more so did Deuteronomy.

Unlike Deuteronomy 14, Mt. 17.24-27 does not mention a variety of *animals* (clean and unclean) not does it refer to the *temple tithe*. But it tells the incident of the *temple tax* and the *fish*. And unlike Deuteronomy 15, Matthew 18 is not directly concerned with granting remission (*aphesis*) to debtors and slaves. But it lays great emphasis on remitting or forgiving (*aphiēmi*, 18.15, 21-22), and it illustrates forgiveness through a parable involving debtors and selling a debtor (into slavery; 18.23-35).

What emerges is that Matthew has modernized Deuteronomy 14–15, for instance, by replacing the temple tithe with an incident involving the temple-tax. But he has also done something more fundamental: in accordance with a strategy which is found elsewhere in the ancient world and in the New Testament, he has internalized the older text.[4] Where Deuteronomy was concerned with a remission which was primarily external, Matthew shifts the emphasis more clearly to the internal, to the remission which occurs within the heart.

The essence of this policy of internalization had already been indicated by Matthew in the Sermon on the Mount. The section on alms, prayer, fasting and true treasure (Mt. 6.1-21) is an emphatic statement on the importance of the internal over the external. And the antitheses (Mt. 5.20-48) showed that internalization meant a rethinking of the old scriptures. Now (17.22–18.35), as the evangelist takes old Deuteronomy from his treasure (cf. 13.52), he applies the process of internalization.

3. *More Detailed Analysis*

The following analysis goes through the outline (Table 46), section by section. Not all of Deuteronomy 14–15 is included in the outline—it is not clear whether Matthew used the ends of the chapters (14.28-29; 15.16-23)—and, besides, the outline sometimes simplifies the content of the text. Nonetheless, the outline provides a useful starting-point for analysis.

a. *Block A. Animals and the Temple Payment (Deuteronomy 14.1-27; Matthew 17.24-27)*
(1) *Section 1. A community of native children, not of strangers (Deuteronomy 14.1-2, 21; Matthew 17.25b-26).* The Greek text of Deut. 14.1-21 begins and ends by addressing the Israelites as 'a holy people' (14.2, 21), and in the context of that holiness, it speaks of the people first as sons or native-born children (*huioi*) whom God chose from all the peoples of the earth (14.1-2), and then as people whose eating habits are different from those of the foreigners or strangers (*allotrioi*). The details of the legislation are obscure but the central implication is that Israel is a people apart, a people which does not follow the practices of the nations.

In Matthew, as the scene moves to the house, there is a conversation between Jesus and Peter which refers to another sense of apartness. In the eyes of the kings of the earth, the

---

4. On internalization, see especially Chapter 1, 'Literary Imitation. The Practice'; and Chapter 31 (on Lk. 7.36-50).

native-born children (*huioi*) have a special status and, unlike the foreigners (*allotrioi*), they do not have to pay tribute.

Matthew has preserved the central image of a people apart, but has made several adaptations. The apartness is no longer based on nationhood. Rather, Matthew uses the image of national apartness as a metaphor for the apartness of a community which is based on Jesus' teaching, based on consideration for others as illustrated by the desire not to scandalize ('However, so as not to scandalize…', 17.27). In other words, Jesus and Peter (representing the church, Mt. 16.18) are indeed apart—they are the native-born children (*huioi*)—but this apartness is not something to be enforced harshly, as might happen among kingdoms which are based on human power. Instead, the sense of apartness takes second place to the desire not to hurt or scandalize people, a desire which will later be emphasized at length (18.6-9).

Matthew's other adaptations include the insertion of the idea of payment (thus suiting the discussion to the context) and highlighting the role of Peter (in accordance with the pattern of Peter-related incidents in 13.53–ch. 18).

There *may* be a balance between the Deuteronomic idea of 'the holy people' (Deut. 14.2, 21) and Matthew's image of 'the house' (Mt. 17.25b). (In 1 Pet. 2.5, for instance, those who are *holy* form a spiritual *house)*. In other words, in accordance with Matthew's overall transformation of legislation (Deut. 14.1-2, 21) into colorful conversation or narrative, he may have transformed the idea of those who are holy into the more concrete image of those who are within a particular house. In this case, the house is not a minor detail. Rather, it evokes the church and provides the setting for the subsequent discourse on the *ekklēsia*.

Verbal affinities are worth noting:

Old Testament:
14.2, *huioi…apō pantōn tōn ethnōn…tēs gēs*.
14.21, *allotriō…*

New Testament:
17.25, *tēs gēs apō tinōn…apō tōn huiōn…apō tōn allotriōn…*
17.26, *apō tōn allotriōn…huioi*.

One of the other distinctive words of the Matthean passage, *eleutheros*, 'free', occurs three times in Deuteronomy's next chapter (15.12, 13, 18). Thus, Deuteronomy 14–15 contains five of the more important words used in the brief Matthean conversation (17.25b-26, *huios, ethnos, gē, allotrios, eleutheros*, 'son, nation, land/earth, foreigner, free'). Apart from Exodus 20–21, there is no other two-chapter block either in the Old Testament or New Testament which contains these five words. (The blocks which come nearest to it, each with four of the words, are Jer. 36–37, and Jer. 41–42, LXX.) The linguistic similarity with Deuteronomy 14–15 is all the greater because apart from the five shared words, there are a number of shared details (*apo*, 'from', followed by the plural; use of the same grammatical case, e.g. *huioi*, nominative plural in both texts). Thus, Mt. 18.25b-26 has a linguistic link with Deuteronomy 14–15 such as it has with no other two chapters in the Greek Old Testament.

(2) *Section 2. The animal world: discriminating and not discriminating (Deuteronomy 14.3-20; Matthew 17.27b).* In contrast to Deuteronomy's three-fold list of clean and unclean creatures (animals, fish, birds), Matthew mentions just one, a fish, and he does so in a way that excludes any effort to discern whether the fish is clean or unclean ('take the first fish that comes up'). By keeping the central picture of the fish, Matthew has distilled the essence of the Old Testament list but, in accordance with the spirit of the New

Testament (cf. Acts 10.9-16; Mt. 15.10-20), he has effectively laid aside the distinction between clean and unclean.

At first, such a procedure may seem unlikely. Matthew is often seen as the evangelist who favors a traditional approach to the Mosaic law. Yet as J. P. Meier's study of Matthew's programmatic statement (5.17-20) shows, Matthew is ready not only to go beyond the Mosaic law but at times even to oppose it (Meier 1976: especially 123-24, 167).

In setting the scene for the subsequent discourse, therefore, the incident of the temple tax strikes a delicate balance: it combines a spirit of freedom with a sensitivity towards the weak.

(3) *Section 3. Giving the annual temple payment (Deuteronomy 14.22-23; Matthew 17.24-25a)*. Deuteronomy indicates that every year, one should take a tithe of what one's sowing yields and bring it to the place chosen by God—in other words, to the temple. In the first century, however, the annual payment to the temple was the half-shekel, and so when Peter is challenged about payment to the temple the question concerns the half-shekel. In both cases, the attitude to the payment is positive. Matthew has maintained the essence of the Old Testament picture but has updated it.

There are very few biblical instances of a command about giving a tithe or tariff for the temple. Within the Pentateuch and the gospels, the nearest equivalents are the commands about what to sacrifice (Lev. 1–5) and the offering of the pair of turtledoves or pigeons (Lk. 2.24). The similarity is therefore significant.

(4) *Section 4. The mode of payment: Take the money, go, and give (Deuteronomy 14.24-27; Matthew 17.27b)*. One of the problems envisaged by Deuteronomy is that it may not be practical to carry one's tithe all the way to the temple, and so provision is made for turning the tithe into money (*argurion*). One then takes the money in one's hand, goes, and gives it. Matthew, while sounding almost miraculous, has something of the same effect. The money (*statēr*) comes not from the yield of the land but from the fish, and the process involves going, taking, and giving. In Greek:

Old Testament:
lempsē to argurion...poreusē...dōseis...epi...sou...sou.

New Testament:
poreutheis...statēra...labōn dos...anti...sou.

Reviewing these first four sections, it may be seen that Matthew has combined the essence of the two main parts of Deuteronomy 14, the initial emphasis on *the animals, including fish* (14.1-21), and the later picture of *the land yielding tithes and thus money* (14.22-27). The result is an account of *a fish yielding money*. In writing this, Matthew no doubt used source material other than Deuteronomy, and he certainly had a purpose which surpassed the Old Testament source, yet he has managed to make use of some of even the most obscure sections of the Mosaic law. Nothing is being lost from the law—in a sense, not even a jot or a tittle.

b. *Block B. Sin and Remission (Deuteronomy 15.1-15; Matthew 18.15-35)*
At this stage, both Deuteronomy and Matthew broach the questions of sin and remission. Though Matthew prefers verbs to nouns, both books essentially use the same Greek vocabulary:

Deut. 15.9: *hamartia* ('sin')
Mt. 18.15, 21: *hamartanō* ('to sin')
Deut. 15.1, 2, 3, 9: *aphesis* ('remission/forgiveness/release')
Deut. 15.1 and Mt. 18.21, 27, 32, 35: *aphiēmi* ('to remit/forgive/let go')

But the meaning is different. Remission in Deuteronomy refers to the custom, every seven years, of remitting debts. In Matthew, it refers to remitting sins.

Yet the two diverse meanings are related. In Deuteronomy, the avoidance of remission is a sin (15.9). And in Matthew, the remitting of sins is compared to the remitting of debts. As already indicated, Matthew has taken the Old Testament idea of remitting debts and has internalized it, making it refer to interior debts—sins. A similar idea of sins as debts occurs in Matthew's wording of the Lord's Prayer (Mt. 6.12; contrast Lk. 11.4).

(1) *Section 5. If your brother needs private remission, settle it with him (Deuteronomy 15.1-4; Matthew 18.15a)*. Deuteronomy begins (15.1) with a simple reminder about remission: 'Every seven years you shall grant a remission'. The reference is to a private debt by a brother Israelite. (There is an explicit contrast between treatment of a brother and treatment of a stranger, Deut. 15.3.) The debt is financial, yet the remission has a theological dimension: it is granted in light of God's blessing and care for the poor (Deut. 15.4).

Matthew does not mention God at this stage, yet the theological dimension is more explicit: 'If your brother *sins*…' The privacy of the debt is apparently reflected in the exhortation to settle with him *alone* (Mt. 18.15a); in other words, the privacy concerning something external, the debt, has been focused on something more internal or personal, the settling between the two.

(2) *Section 6. If there is hearing, there will be gain (Deuteronomy 15.5-6; Matthew 18.15b)*. If the Israelites hear (*ean…eis-akousēte*) God's voice, they will achieve wealth and power, more than the foreign nations (Deut. 15.5-6). And, in Matthew, if the brother hears (*ean… akousē*), 'you have gained your brother'. Thus, Matthew keeps the idea that hearing leads to gain (wealth and power) but transforms the gain to refer to something more personal and internal. Even the idea of hearing becomes more personal, human: it refers not to the hearing of God but to the hearing of a fellow-human who is concerned about an offence against God.

The contrast with the foreigners (*ethnoi*) is left aside for the moment.

(3) *Section 7ab. The need to involve witnesses and the* ekklēsia *(Deuteronomy 17.6 [cf. 19.15]; 18.16 [cf. 23.1, 2, 3]; Matthew 18.16-17)*. Having internalized the notion of debt and thus raising the question of sin, Matthew now goes on to develop a strategy for dealing with sin in the community. In doing this, he is going beyond Deuteronomy 15, yet for a while he continues (18.16-17) to draw on Deuteronomic elements. First, in advocating that the sinner be confronted by one or two others (18.16), Matthew draws heavily on the Deuteronomic laws for calling witnesses (Deut. 17.6; 19.15).

Then, in involving the *ekklēsia*, it would seem, as Grassi suggested, that he drew on the corresponding idea in Deuteronomy. The primary Deuteronomic text here appears to be 18.16, the key passage concerning 'the day of *ekklēsia*' at which God told the people to listen to a human voice (the voice of a prophet who is like Moses, but from among 'your own brothers' 18.15-18). Something of the divine authority which was to be invested in the prophet-like-Moses should now be reflected in the *ekklēsia*. In other words, instead of an *ekklēsia* which was granted a divinely-authoritative figure (Deut. 18.15-18), Matthew at this point implies a certain supreme authority in the *ekklēsia* itself.

Matthew also speaks of exclusion from the *ekklēsia*, as did Deuteronomy (23.1, 2, 3), and it is at this juncture that the gospel adapts and incorporates the contrast with the foreigner: '…let him be to you as an *ethnikos*'. (Like Deut. 14–15, Mt. 17.24–18.35 implies a contrast with both strangers [*allotrioi*, Deut. 14.21; 15.3; Mt. 17.24-25] and foreigners [*ethnoi*, Deut. 14.2; 15.6; Mt. 18.17].)

The subsequent statement about the modes of the divine presence (in the binding/loosing and in the togetherness, Mt. 18.18-20) may have been influenced by the sense of divine presence and authority which surrounds the picture of the prophet-like-Moses (Deut. 18.15-22, especially 18.19-22), but at this stage, Matthew has also used other very different source material.

What is essential is that the picture of dealing with the one who is in debt/sin, while it may have involved diverse sources, also drew on Deuteronomy.

(4) *Section 8. Be open-minded about the loan (Deuteronomy 15.7-8; Matthew 18.26-27).* Speaking now of a brother in need, Deuteronomy appeals for generosity: 'Do not harden your heart, or close up your hand… Open your hands wide to him' (Deut. 15.7-8a). In Matthew's parable, there is a similar appeal. The desperately indebted servant falls in obeisance, saying, 'Be patient [literally, 'long-minded' or 'large-minded', *makro-thumeō*] with me…' (Mt. 18.26). The essential generosity of the Old Testament text has been maintained, but it has been cast into a form which both fits the flow of the parable story and lays emphasis on interior dispositions (the obeisance of the servant, and the idea of large-mindedness).

Deuteronomy continues: 'and lend to him whatever loan he needs'. Matthew tells that the *kyrios* 'was moved with compassion…and forgave the debt'. Thus, Matthew keeps the idea of a full response, giving all that is needed, but again he lays emphasis on internal dispositions.

It is useful to lay out some of the text:

> Old Testament:
> Do not harden your heart or close up your hand… Open your hand widely… And lend to him whatever loan (*daneion*) he needs.

> New Testament:
> Be large-minded with me and I will repay you all.
> And he forgave him the debt/loan (*daneion*).

The word *daneion* is Deuteronomic and rare (found only here [15.5, 8] and in 24.11). Otherwise it does not occur in the canonical books of the Old Testament, and, apart from Matthew's parable, does not otherwise occur in the New Testament.

(5) *Section 9. The rejection of remission is evil before the Lord (Deuteronomy 15.9-10; Matthew 18.28-32).* Having spoken of generosity, Deuteronomy goes on to warn about refusing it, about allowing the heart to reject remission (15.9a). Matthew takes that idea, the heart's rejection of remission, and dramatizes it in colorful detail. He tells of the forgiven servant who, on finding a fellow-servant who owed him a little, throttled him and mercilessly threw him into prison (18.28-30). But such refusal of remission is evil. In summary outline:

Refusal would make you evil, and	The fellow-servants were saddened,
he would cry to the *kyrios* against you.	and told everything to the *kyrios*.
Give without being saddened.	Then…he said, 'Evil servant…'

Matthew keeps the basic idea of the offended servant/s appealing to the *kyrios*, but sadness, instead of being a kind of afterthought associated with giving begrudgingly, is now brought forward in the drama and is seen as a leading consequence of the refusal to give. This highlighting of sadness ('they were greatly saddened', *elypēthēsan sphodra*) is of a piece with the highlighting of sadness in the passion prediction ('they were greatly saddened', *elypēthēsan sphodra*, Mt. 17.22-23; contrast Mk 9.30-32; Lk. 43b-45).

Deuteronomy then adds that, presuming one is generous concerning the year of remission and giving, 'the *kyrios* will bless you in everything...' (15.10b). Matthew reproduces this idea of the Lord giving totally, but in an adapted form: the *kyrios* said, 'I forgave you the entire debt [of 10,000 talents] because you besought me'. In other words, instead of a totality of promised blessing, Matthew depicts a totality of response already given. This adaptation accords with his larger strategy of emphasizing responsiveness to prayer (e.g. 17.20; 18.19).

Apart from 2 Sam. 13.21-22, there is no other instance either in the Old Testament or New Testament where *lypeō* ('to sadden/be sad') is combined with *ponēreuomai/ponēros* ('[to be] evil'). (In 1 Macc. 14.14, 16 the two words are further apart and are unrelated). The link, then, is virtually unique.

(6) *Section 10. The case of the brother who was for sale and who gets remission (Deuteronomy 15.12; Matthew 18.21-23).* Deuteronomy now turns to the question of someone sold into slavery. If a brother Israelite has been sold as a slave, his servitude is not to be perpetual; in the seventh year, the year of remission, he is to receive freedom (15.12).

The corresponding text in Matthew is the introduction to the parable of the unforgiving servant (18.21-25). The idea of remission in the seventh year has been used, by a kind of free association or word-play, as a basis for forming Peter's question about remission (or forgiveness) up to seven times (18.21). In other words, the old custom referring to a particular time has been adapted to refer to a particular number of times. This gives a proposal which is more suitable to a later period and to diverse people and circumstances. And Jesus' response, multiplying the seven (18.22), expands the proposal yet further.

Jesus then goes on to illustrate the idea of remission or forgiveness and he begins with a picture of a king who was about to sell an indebted servant into slavery (18.23-24).

Thus, Matthew reworks almost all the distinctive elements in the Deuteronomic passage—brother, slavery/service, remission/forgiveness, seven, selling—but in doing so, he used other sources and scriptural allusions and has subjected all these materials to the patterns and requirements of his own larger narrative, in this case, the pattern of parables involving kings (cf. 22.1-14; 25.31-46).

The procedure found here—of using the elements of Deuteronomy to build a parable—is a variation on using Deut. 14.1-2, 21 (sons, strangers, of the earth) to build the account of the conversation in the house (Mt. 17.25b-26). And the imagery of the conversation, like that of the parable, is set in the context of kings ('The kings of the earth: from whom...?').

Thus, while being faithful to the ancient scripture, even to its details, to its 'jots and tittles', Matthew also manages to subject that scripture to his own preferred New Testament imagery, in this case, the imagery of kings and the kingdom.

The combination of *pipraskō* ('to sell') with *hebdomē*... ('seventh/seventy') is otherwise virtually unknown in the Bible. (The one apparent exception is Lev. 25.20, 25, but in that case the two words are in different pericopes. 1 Macc. 1.10, 15 is textually uncertain and is even more tenuous.) It is also significant that in both Deuteronomy and Matthew the two words (*pipraskō* and *hebdomē*...) are clustered with *adelphos*, 'brother', and *doulos/douleuō* ('servant/to serve'). The only comparable word-cluster is spread across Leviticus 25, but that is a long chapter, and so one can scarcely speak of a cluster. Thus, the linguistic link between the passages is unique.

(7) *Section 11. Be kind to your indebted brother, as the Lord was to you (Deuteronomy 15.11, 13-15; Matthew 18.33-35).* In dealing first with the poor and then with slaves, Deuteronomy's command, concerning kindness and remission, is repetitious ('Therefore I

command you to do this thing', 15.11; 'Therefore I command you to do this thing', 15.15). This repetition links the two sets of commands, and this built-in link was probably one of the reasons why Matthew combined the two texts. (The built-in link between the two 'You-are-a-holy-people' texts [Deut. 14.1-2, 21] had likewise led, in Matthew, to combination [Mt. 17.25b-26].)

The result is that somewhat as Deuteronomy gives a repeated command to be kind to others, so the conclusion of the parable gives a repeated exhortation to be kind, an exhortation which in varied ways links human mercy with divine:

> The *kyrios*: You should have been merciful to your fellow-servant, as I was to you.
>
> Jesus adds: So your heavenly Father will do to you, unless you each forgive your brother…

The relationship between the two sets of double exhortations may be summarized as follows:

> Regards the poor: I command you:
> Give [remission] to your brother.
>
> Regards a slave: I command you:
> Be kind, as I was to you.   Be merciful, as I was to you.
> (The Lord delivered from Egypt)   (The *kyrios* gave him to the
>   torturers).
>
>   So will God do with you,
>   unless each forgives his brother.

Some of the connections here are extremely elusive. For instance, the reference to giving the cruel man over to the torturers must be from another source or inspiration, but it is possible that it is also meant as a kind of contrast to the Lord's act of deliverance from Egypt.

More manageable is the positive connection. The command not to shrink from giving generously to one's brother (Deut. 15.11, implying also the giving of remission [*aphesis*, 15.9]), is incorporated into Jesus' final exhortation on the need to forgive (*aphiēmi*) one's brother (Mt. 18.35).

And the later command to be generous as God was (Deut. 15.13-15) is echoed in the exhortative reproach to the servant (Mt. 18.33):

> Old Testament:
> Give him (from your) provisions…;
> as the Lord blessed you, you will give to him.
> (…*sou, katha eulogēse se kyrios*…).
>
> New Testament:
> Should you not have had mercy on your fellow-servant,
> as I had mercy on you. And the master…
> (…*sou, hōs kagō se eleēsa…kyrios*).

While it keeps the substance of the Old Testament text, this similarity involves a form of word-play.

4. *Conclusion*

In the preceding array of similarities, there are indeed some which are obscure or questionable. It is difficult, for instance, despite 1 Pet. 2.4 ('*holy* priesthood…spiritual *house*'), to know whether there is a connection between the opening emphasis on holiness (Deut. 14.2, 21) and the opening picture of the house (Mt. 17.25).

But there is a whole series of similarities which in varying ways are striking or even unique:

- *Position:* Both texts, taken in their totality, occur within the central discourse of their respective documents (within the second discourse in Deuteronomy, and within the third discourse in Matthew).
- *Broad themes*: Both texts deal with variations on the same ideas: temple payment and remission.
- *Similarities of the subsections:* Again and again, the basic elements of the Old Testament text may be found in adapted form in Matthew.
- *Order:* By and large, the order both of the themes and of the subsections is the same in both texts.
- *Linguistic continuity:* Several of the subsections share words or word-clusters which are (almost) without parallel in either testament.

Furthermore, the differences, great though they are, are not meaningless. Most of them can be accounted for through a few consistent practices: synthesis, modernization, and internalization, and through adaptation to the requirements of Matthew's new narrative. Nor are these practices alien to what is otherwise known of Matthew, both regarding his synthesizing of Mark and his bold attitude towards the Old Testament and towards internalization (cf. 5.20–6.21; 13.51-52).

Therefore, it seems reasonable to conclude that Matthew engaged not only the broad outlines of Deuteronomy, as Frankemölle and Grassi indicated, but also the down-to-earth body of the text. He has synthesized part of Deuteronomy's center and has adapted it for a new age. He has written not to destroy the law, but to fulfill it.

23

Deuteronomy 23–34 as One Component in Matthew's Elaboration of Mark (Matthew 19–28)

Having seen the dependence on Deuteronomy in Mt. 17.22–18.35, the purpose of this brief chapter is to indicate that the remainder of Matthew (chs. 19–28) continues this dependence in a modified way. What follows here is not a detailed analysis nor an attempt to prove this dependence. The idea is simply to give a working sketch.

These final ten chapters (Mt. 19–28) build systematically on seven chapters of Mark (Mk 10–16). But Matthew contains several elaborations, especially in the final discourses (Mt. 23–25). This survey concentrates on these elaborations.

There is a complicating factor which this chapter does not examine. Mark may already have used Deuteronomy, so that, quite apart from inserting extra episodes or elaborations, the mere fact of reworking Mark means that Matthew's text contains elements of Deuteronomy. This is the case, for instance, in the account of Jesus' entry to Jerusalem: Matthew's version (21.1-22) contains echoes of Deuteronomy 20 (campaigning, especially against a city), but so does the account of Mark (11.1-25). A fuller examination of Matthew's use of Deuteronomy would examine such passages. This chapter, however, does not.

The material falls under several headings:

1. *The Exclusion of* Porneia *or Gross Infidelity*
(Deuteronomy 23.3, 18-19; Matthew 19.3, 9)

The Deuteronomic concern for the quality of the assembly or *ekklēsia* involves the exclusion of anything to do with gross ecclesial infidelity. This entails the exclusion of the earnings of a cultic prostitute (*pornē*). The ruling applies no matter what vow has been taken (*pros pasan euchēn*, Deut. 23.3, 18-19). And in Matthew, Jesus forbids the breaking of the marriage bond no matter what the cause (*kata pasan aitian*, Mt. 19.3) except in the case of *porneia* (Mt. 19.9). The Deuteronomic background seems to link this vague term (*porneia*) to ecclesial infidelity, but the background does not necessarily decide the meaning in Matthew.

2. *The Hiring and Paying of Workers*
(Deuteronomy 24.14-15; Matthew 20.1-16)

Deuteronomy's rule for hiring workers seems to have been one of the elements in Matthew's parable of the vineyard laborers. Both texts share several elements:

- The poverty of the workers: strangers in the city, idle in the market place (Deut. 24.14; Mt. 20.3).
- Just payment or reward (Deut. 24.14; Mt. 20.4, 8).
- Payment by the day, to be given in the evening (Deut. 24.15; Mt. 20.4, 8).
- The worker's eager expectation of (more) payment (Deut. 24.15; Mt. 20.10).
- The worker's appeal at not being paid as expected (Deut. 24.15; Mt. 20.11).

3. *Fathers, Sons and Strangers/Outsiders*
(Deuteronomy 24.16-22; Matthew 21.28-32)

Matthew's next major addition to Mark, after the parable of the vineyard workers, is the parable of the two sons. This is partly modeled on the picture of the vineyard workers (the father sends his sons to work in his vineyard). Having spoken of the father and his sons, Jesus goes on to speak of the admission of outsiders, tax-collectors and prostitutes.

After the rule for hiring workers (24.14-15), the next texts in Deuteronomy are about fathers and sons (24.16), and about care for strangers (24.17-25).

The Deuteronomic concern about the correct allocation of culpability (between fathers and sons, 'Fathers are not to be put to death for their sons, nor sons for their fathers', 24.16), is turned around in the parable to refer to the correct allocation of credit (between the father's two sons). And God's care for the stranger (Deut. 24.17-22) is reflected in the entry of tax-collectors and prostitutes into God's kingdom (Mt. 21.31).

4. *The Marriage and the Refusal*
(Deuteronomy 25.5-10; Matthew 22.1-14)

As it happens, the next major text in Deuteronomy deals with the levirate law, the case of a man who was asked to take his brother's place in a marriage, and who, even when called, was unwilling to do so. And Matthew's next major addition to Mark is the parable of the marriage feast and of those who, even when called, were unwilling to come.

The similarities could be coincidence, and certainly Matthew contains a whole drama of complex elements which are quite absent in Deuteronomy (including apparently a distillation of wisdom's invitation to the feast, Prov. 8–9, especially 9.1-6). But if Matthew used the little pieces of legislation in Deuteronomy 24 (concerning the workers, and the fathers and sons) as starting points for parables in Matthew 20 and 21, then he was equally capable of using the much larger drama of the man who refused marriage (Deut. 25) as a starting point for building the larger parable of the marriage feast.

5. *All the Laws, Your One Lord, and Curses/Woes on Those who do not Keep the Laws*
(Deuteronomy 27; Matthew 23; cf. Mark 12.38-40)

Matthew's next elaborations of Mark are built around the brief episodes at the end of Mark 12, the condemnation of the scribes (12.38-40) and the widow's mite (12.41-44).

First, the condemnation of the scribes. Using Mark's brief condemnation text as one component, Matthew builds condemnation into a whole chapter (ch. 23), and this lengthy elaboration seems to be partly based on the curses of Deuteronomy 27. Both texts (Deut. 27 and Mt. 23), while very different in detail, share certain basic elements:

- Guarding all the written laws of Moses (Moses commands that all the laws be written, Deut. 27.1-8; Jesus commands that the disciples follow all that is taught by those who sit on the chair of Moses, Mt. 23.1-23).
- Attend to your one God/Lord (Deut. 27.9-10; Mt. 23.8-11). Moses reminds Israel to listen to God and to remember its special relationship to its God. And Jesus tells the disciples to attend to the one true master, father, and teacher.
- Curses/woes on those who do not keep the Law (Deut. 27.11-26; Mt. 23.15-36). Deuteronomy curses those who do not keep specific laws, and Jesus utters woes against the law-breaking scribes and Pharisees. In Deuteronomy's list, the emphasis seems to fall at the end. In Matthew's list, it falls both at the end and the center.

6. Wise Generosity, Blessings and Curses
(Deuteronomy 28.1-19; 30.15-20; Matthew 24.45–ch. 25; cf. Mark 12.41-44)

Matthew's next elaboration—the longest of all in this series—consists of three parables and the climactic scene of judgment. One of the features which binds these four passages into a unity is a form of moral dualism. Each parable presents a sharp division of characteristics or characters: the servant is either faithful or unfaithful (24.45-51), the ten bridesmaids either wise or foolish (25.1-13), and the servants who received the talents either good and faithful or evil and lazy (25.14-30). Finally, in the judgment, the division into two is applied to all people (25.31-46).

A further feature uniting most of these passages is the statement or implication of a division between being blessed or cursed. The faithful servant is called blessed (*makarios*, 24.46). The servants who develop the talents are told 'Well done' (*Eu...Eu*, 25.21, 23). And at judgment the just are called blessed (*eu-logēmenoi*) and the condemned are called cursed (*katēramenoi*).

Of the many components which have gone into the composition of these texts, two would appear to be the widow's mite (Mk 12.41-44) and part of Deuteronomy 28–30. As a rule, Matthew makes use of everything in Mark, but the widow's mite, as such, does not appear in Matthew, so the question arises as to whether Matthew transformed it into something else. Its most obvious links are with the the parable of the ten bridesmaids (because of the emphasis on feminine characters and wisdom) and with the servants who let go of their money.

The main connection between Matthew 24.45–ch. 25 and part of Deuteronomy 28–30 is the sense of moral division. Deuteronomy 28 begins with a contrast between being many times blessed (*eulogēmenos*, 28.3-8) and many times cursed (*epi-kataros*, 28.15-19; cf. 28.13, 15; Mt. 24.45, 47, 'The Lord will set... And/But if...'). And the sense of a climactic division between blessing and cursing, so dramatic in the scene of final judgment, finds a less dramatic precedent in Moses' final challenge to choose between life and death, between blessing and curse (Deut. 30.15-20).

While Deuteronomy 28–30 and the widow's mite thus provide a framework and starting point for Mt. 24.45–ch. 25, the rest of the material may have come from diverse sources, including other parts of Deuteronomy. The striking picture of Matthew's judgment scene, for instance, seems to involve a synthesis of elements from several areas of Deuteronomy, including chs. 5, 17, 23 and 32:

- The Sinai theophany (5.24-33), particularly: glory...we have seen...God (5.24), devouring fire (5.25), all days...forever (5.29), left...right (5.32), the land you are to possess (5.33).
- The king seated on his throne (17.18).
- Criterion of exclusion, forever, not giving food and drink (23.3-4).
- Creation and the founding and dividing of the nations (32.6-9).

7. The Closing Episode on the Mountain
(Deuteronomy 34; Matthew 28.16-20)

Within chs. 26–28, Matthew's most extensive elaboration on Mark is at the end—concerning the guard (27.62-66; 28.11-15), the meeting with the women (28.9-10), and the final scene on the mountain (28.16-20). Of these elements, the final one depends on Deuteronomy. As Grassi (1989: 23-29) has shown, Matthew's mountain finale reflects the mountain scene at the end of the life of Moses (Deut. 34).

8. Postscript: Towards Tracing Other Sources

As an example of some of some further source questions, it is useful to look briefly at Mt. 6.1-18 with its picture of the three acts of devotedness (almsgiving, prayer and fasting).

Apart from using Romans, this text may have drawn on Deuteronomy, perhaps on Deuteronomy's emphasis on a place of worship (e.g. Deut. 12). But in dealing with 6.1-18, several commentators draw attention not so much to Deuteronomy as to Tobit (Plummer 1909: 92; Meier 1980: 57).

Tobit, in fact, does seem a promising area of comparison, especially Tobit 1–3. Despite some textual complexity in Tobit—the text exists in three distinct Greek recensions (see Moore 1996: 53-60)—both Tobit and Matthew may generally be seen to share several elements:
- Righteousness in general, and the questions of reward and of what is hidden (Tob. 1.3; 2.11-14; cf. 12.1-15; Mt. 6.1-4).
- Almsgiving (Tob. 1.3, 6; 2.14; Mt. 6.2-4).
- Prayer (Tob. 3; Mt. 6.5-6).
- Fasting (cf. Tob. 2.1-10?; Mt. 6.16-18).
- Prayer in one's room (3.10-17; cf. 7.15-8.4; Mt. 6.6).

On the Our Father, see the father–child atmosphere in Tobit, and also some details:
- Father in heaven (Mt. 5.45, 48; Deut. 32.1, 6; cf. Tob. 2.3).
- Hallowed be thy name (cf. Tob. 1.4-9; Deut. 12.5).
- Thy kingdom come (cf. Tob. 1.15–2.1, changes of kings, action by the king of heaven, and the preservation of Tobit's goods in the kingly palace; also Tob. 10.1-7, 13; 13.1, 4, 7?).
- Thy will…earth, heaven (the will, like other aspects of the prayer, finds a parallel in Matthew 18 where the will is described as the will of the Father that none of the little ones be lost [Mt. 18.4]. This idea of a saving will fits Rom. 10.11-13; cf. Tob. 1.18; 2.2-4).
- Give us today our…bread (cf. Tobit and meals, Tob. 1.10-11; 2.1-5; cf. 7.9-14, S text, Tobias will not eat until he is given Sarah today and forever).
- Forgive debts (Tob. 3.1-5; cf. Mt. 18.35).
- Lead us not into temptation, but deliver us from the (evil) one (cf. Sarah's prayer concerning liberation, purity and the evil demon, Tob. 3.7-17; defeat of the demon and of immorality or *porneia*, Tob. 8.3-9; temptation, Tob. 12.3)..

Without attempting to draw conclusions, especially about details, it is reasonable to say that in studying the composition of Mt. 6.1-18 and of the Our Father, it is appropriate to include an examination of the gentle and wholesome optimism of the book of Tobit.

Unit 5. The Central Thesis Expanded: John and Luke–Acts

24

John's Use of Matthew, Mark, and Proto-Luke

Initial comparison of John with the Synoptics shows a wide range of differences and similarities. Twentieth-century research into this complex phenomenon falls into three main periods.[1]

First, before the ascendency of form criticism, a long-standing presumption prevailed: John was aware of the Synoptics and had often used them or changed them. A tradition attributed to Clement of Alexandria had implied that John had known the Synoptics but decided to go beyond them: 'Last of all, John, perceiving that the externals (*ta sōmatica*) had been made plain in the gospels...composed a spiritual gospel (*pneumatikon...evangelion*)' (Eusebius, *Historia ecclesiastica* 6.14.7). Church tradition followed suit: 'Many of the Fathers thought that the obvious differences between Jn and the Syn were to be explained by the evangelist's intention of supplementing the earlier gospels' (*JBC* 63:17). And the advent of modern criticism gave this old idea a new form: 'In the era of criticism the theory gained ground that in all common material John was dependent on the Synoptic Gospels. Indeed even Johannine scenes that had no parallel in the Synoptic tradition were sometimes explained as an amalgamation of Synoptic details' (Brown 1966: xliv).

Second, during the heyday of form criticism, majority opinion moved to the opposite view: John had not known the Synoptics; he was independent. Thus P. Gardiner-Smith (1938) reasoned that John's differences from the Synoptics preclude dependence; and, more decisively, that form criticism's idea of oral tradition provides an alternative explanation of the John–Synoptic similarities. Several other scholars, including C.H. Dodd, R.E. Brown, and R. Schnackenburg, accepted this explanation. However, Dodd saw that the appeal to oral tradition was problematic: the New Testament period was 'less than a normal human lifetime' (1963: 6). Most people, recalling distant crucial events of their own lifetime, do not disagree about the basic facts, at least not in the way John disagrees with the Synoptics. Dodd, therefore, tried to spell out what happened, and concluded that 'the...recollections...[were] mixed with reflections and interpretations' (p. 171). As a general idea, this proposal seemed eminently plausible.

Third, from about the early 1970s onwards, as form criticism came under closer scrutiny and as scholars looked more closely at the detail of the texts, majority opinion began to shift back towards the older view: John had known the Synoptics and used them. Some of the dates are as follows:

- 1971: G. Selong (1971) John's account of cleansing the temple uses the Synoptics.
- 1971: C.K. Barrett (1971) restated the general argument for dependence on Mark.
- 1974: N. Perrin of Chicago (1974: 229): the details of Jesus' trial, particularly the manner of its interweaving with Peter's denials (Jn 18.12-27), indicate that John 'must have known the gospel of Mark'.
- 1976: Some followers of Perrin: a wider study of the passion narratives corroborates Perrin's basic conclusion (Kelber [ed.] 1976).

---

1. For reviews of research, see especially Smith 1992; Neirynck 1977 and 1992.

- 1977: Frans Neirynck of Louvain (1977: 106): a detailed comparison of the resurrection accounts, including verses generally reckoned to be editorial, leads to the conclusion that '*not the traditions behind the Synoptic Gospels but the Synoptic Gospels themselves* are the sources of the Fourth Evangelist'.

1. John and the Synoptics *(1992)*

The subsequent publications and opinions have been particularly well chronicled by Neirynck (1977). The results of the next fifteen years of research (1975–90), and of a Louvain Colloquium, were published in a major 1992 volume: *John and the Synoptics* (Denaux [ed.] 1992).[2] Part of this volume discusses the possibility that those who follow Gardiner-Smith are right. Neirynck (1992: 55-59), for instance, summarizes J.D.G. Dunn's positive assessment of the role of oral tradition in forming John (Dunn 1991). But the general movement is away from that explanation. Denaux, in introducing the volume, speaks of 'a growing consensus about the hypothesis that the author of John was dependent on one or more of the Synoptic Gospels' (1992: xxii). The essay on John and Mark (by Kieffer 1992: 109-25) breaks new ground in investigating three areas—structure, sequence, and details—and concludes:

> John knew Mark (or a source very like Mark), but at the same time he used his own traditions, written or oral. The knowledge he had of the Markan tradition is more pronounced in certain chapters, for example, in John 6 and 18–19, but [this knowledge] is such that it commands numerous other aspects of Johannine composition [*elle commande de nombreux autres aspects de la composition johannique*]... There is little probability that the author of John would have reinvented structures so similar to those of Mark without any knowledge of these.
>
> Our study also shows that an oral tradition is scarcely sufficient to explain the precise contacts between John and Mark: there are too many relatively long texts where identical words follow one another in the same order, sometimes with exceptional expressions... There are... many insignificant details which are identical... Likewise, the general convergences which we have seen between the two gospels invite us to envisage relations between written documents and so probably a dependence of John on Mark. (Kieffer 1992: 125)

Recent research into John's possible use of *Matthew* is less developed. As a test case, Neirynck, having summarized that research, proposes the specifically Matthean account of the appearance to the women at the tomb: 'The parallel in Jn 20, 14-18 is substantial and shows specific contacts with Matthew' (1992: 34). The case for John's use of *Luke* is clearer: 'Most scholars accept that some kind of relationship exists between Luke and John' (Neirynck 1992: 35). But the nature of that relationship is uncertain, and, to illustrate the uncertainty, Neirynck (p. 3) quotes the view of F.L Cribbs (1979: 251): 'John may have known some form of Luke, Luke may have known some early form of John, both evangelists may have been influenced by some other common source or sources'.

Overall, therefore, the 1992 Louvain volume implies:

Concerning Mark:	The connections are multiple.
Concerning Matthew:	A connecting beachhead has been established (the resurrection appearance).
Concerning Luke:	One evangelist knew some form of the other (or the other's source).

---

2. Part of the discussion of John's sources centered on the hypothesis of a Johannine sign source. For a brief summary, see Brodie 1993b: 25-27. For detailed data and opinions, see Van Belle 1975, and especially 1994.

2. The Quest for the Origin of John's Gospel *(1993)*

In the meantime, the present writer developed the following thesis: the fourth evangelist was independent-minded, yet this independence did not exclude building carefully on earlier writers. Basically, John's gospel did what Matthew had done, only more so. First, it expanded Mark's storyline, but in a more radical way. While keeping a basic obvious continuity with Mark—the essence of Mark's beginning, middle, and end (John the Baptist; the loaves/sea; the passion; see Jn 1; 6; 18–19)—it systematically reshaped the rest of the narrative. In other words, instead of applying conventions such as those of rewritten Bible to Mark, it applied a mode of transformation which was more akin to that of *mimēsis/zēlos*. Second, it brought the writing of gospel discourses—the form so developed by Matthew—to a new level, using Matthew's own discourses as one of its sources. Third, like Matthew, it also used part of Luke–Acts (Proto-Luke); the portrayal of Nicodemus (Jn 3.1-21), for instance, is drawn partly from (Proto-)Luke's account of Gamaliel (Acts 5.17-42). John also made systematic use of the Pentateuch and of at least one epistle (Ephesians).

This thesis was proposed in *The Quest for the Origin of John's Gospel* (1993), a slender book which was written before the magesterial Louvain volume (1992) was published. John's positive theological program—the program which in effect made John so different—was set forth in a separate study.[3]

The basic difference between the Louvain volume and *The Quest* is not one of detail but of paradigm. The implicit paradigm for the Louvain volume was *primarily one of obvious similarity*—as in the Matthew–Mark relationship or rewritten Bible. The paradigm underlying *The Quest* consisted not only of current biblical studies but also involved the larger world of ancient literature, a world in which authors commonly reshaped and synthesized entire works, imitating and emulating them in such a way that *obvious similarity was the exception*.

At times, the two paradigms overlap. The essay quoted above, for instance—Kieffer on John and Mark (1992)—goes beyond details, broaching larger affinities of structure and sequence. And *The Quest*, apart from giving overall schemas for John's absorbing of whole documents, enters into the details of some specific texts, particularly where such details are not obvious (as in the test-case relationship between Jn 9 and Mk 8.11–9.8) (*The Quest*, Chapter 7 [pp. 48-66]). Both paradigms have strengths, and, while one may be more suited to a specific literary relationship, allowance must be made for both paradigms.

3. *The Test Case: John 9 and Mark 8.11–9.8*

It does not seem appropriate to repeat the arguments already available in *The Quest*.

However, in referring readers to *The Quest*, it is necessary to underline the crucial role of the test case (Chapter 7). Most reviewers avoided giving a judgment on this pivotal chapter. To some degree this avoidance is understandable. The relationship between John 9 and Mk 8.11–9.8 is complex and time-consuming; it does not follow the Matthew–Mark paradigm. Examining it sympathetically means pausing and entering a new paradigm, a new frame of reference. Yet it is not possible to reach a judgment on the book without reaching some conclusion, at least tentative, about the test case. If the test case is wrong, then it is as well to burn the book. If it is right, then the rest of the book, however dense, is worth engaging, over time.

---

3. Brodie 1993a. This commentary indicates that John's gospel is shaped partly according to the stages of human life and human believing. Cf. Weinfeld 1992.

As the evidence concerning John's relationship to the Synoptics, especially to Mark, slowly emerges and clarifies—whether in the Louvain volume or *The Quest* or elsewhere—it is becoming increasingly difficult to deny some kind of dependence.

Sometimes this acceptance of dependence is qualified. Ismo Dundenberg (1994: 214), for instance, sees the present form of John's gospel as dependent on the Synoptics, but he claims that there was an earlier form of the fourth gospel which was not dependent. R.E. Brown modified his earlier position, laying less emphasis on the concept of John's independent tradition (1966: xlv) and espousing a theory which invokes shared traditions (1997: 365): 'Mark and John shared common preGospel traditions, oral or written'. This theory is attractive, but, somewhat like Dundenberg's appeal to an earlier form of John's gospel, it postulates unknown traditions, some possibly written. In the nature of the case, such a theory cannot be disproved; it appeals to elements which are outside all scholarly control. However, from the viewpoint of logical explanation, the decisive issue is not whether this theory is right or wrong, but whether it is necessary. In scientific method, priority goes to the simplest explanation which accounts for the data. The simplest explanation for the relationship between Mark and John is that John, an acknowledged thinker and literary artist, knew Mark and adapted it to his own purposes.

The theory of 'shared common preGospel traditions, oral or written' is not only unnecessary. It is also distracting and confusing. It draws the would-be researcher into a hypothetical world which is vast and vague, a labyrinth which obscures the one thing that is certain—the finished gospels. In effect, it blocks the way towards tracing the full connection between John and Mark.

25

Luke and Acts

Majority scholarship sees the main sources of Luke's gospel as Mark, Q, and L (Luke's special materials),[1] but is less confident about designating the sources of Acts (see the introduction to Chapter 39). Even Q and L are elusive. A significant minority of researchers believes Luke used Matthew—thus accounting for their many shared passages, and thus making Q largely unnecessary.[2]

The purpose of this chapter is to indicate briefly that Luke (Deutero-Luke, the author of Luke and Acts) did indeed use Mark and Matthew, and that Luke also used a broad range of other sources, including Proto-Luke and John. Immediate attention here goes to Luke's use of the four central narratives: Proto-Luke, Mark, Matthew, and John. The later part of the chapter will broaden the inquiry. The main headings are as follows:

1. Luke's Use of Proto-Luke.
2. Luke's Use of Mark.
3. Luke's Use of Matthew.
4. Luke's Use of John.
5. Luke's Use of Deuteronomy.
6. Luke's Use of Other Sources.

1. *Luke's Use of Proto-Luke*

Luke's diverse ways of using existing gospel narratives have a clear logic: he treats the earlier ones (Proto-Luke and Mark) as set, one might almost say canonical, and the later ones (Matthew and John) as more malleable.

- Proto-Luke is reproduced unchanged. Thus,
- Mark is changed slightly.
- Matthew, especially the discourse material, is changed considerably.
- John is changed radically.

Proto-Luke has a special status. Though Luke adds to it in many ways, he does not change the wording. Thus, in a sense, Proto-Luke remains intact; it is not so much a source as a given, a fixed starting-point, like an old house which is both carefully preserved and lavishly expanded. (As already mentioned, it is not clear whether it was the same person who first built Proto-Luke and who later added to it.)

In using the other sources, however, Luke takes a different approach: he always makes changes—apparently as a matter of principle. The extent of the changes varies from miniscule to radical, but, in contrast to what frequently happens in oral transmission, he never reproduces a passage word for word. Apparently following the spirit of rhetorical imitation and Jewish midrash, he regards verbatim copying as inappropriate. Even the Our Father undergoes change (Mt. 6.9-13; Lk. 11.2-4).

---

1. See, for instance, Fitzmyer 1981: 66.
2. McNicol *et al.* (eds.) 1996. The value of this important work is obscured by its denial of Luke's dependence on Mark. See also, for instance, Green 1984.

2. Luke's Use of Mark

Most researchers agree that Luke incorporated Mark massively and systematically. However, rather than say he started with Mark and inserted his own material, it is better to say he started with Proto-Luke and inserted other material, especially Mark.

Even a glance at Luke (as distinguished from Proto-Luke) shows massive connections with Mark.[3] These connections may be summarized approximately as follows:

Mark		Luke
1.16–3.19	=	4.31–6.19
3.31–6.44	=	8.4–9.17
8.27–9.40	=	9.18-50
10.13-52	=	18.15-43
Chs. 11–13	=	19.28–ch. 21
14.26-52, 65-72	=	22.31-65

While thus reproducing most parts of the gospel, Luke omitted others. The preceding list implies that he omitted the following sections of Mark: 1.1-15 (introduction); 3.20-30; 6.45–8.26; 9.41–10.12; 14.1-25, 53-64; chs. 15–16 (conclusion/passion)

These apparent omissions give rise to an objection: if Luke left out these passages, then he did not have them, and so he did not have Mark. What he used was some other document, a document like Mark, now lost.

However, the apparent omissions do not prove that Luke did not use Mark. There are explanations for many of the missing sections. Thus, in the second and fourth omissions (Mk 3.20-30 and 9.41–10.12), some verses may be accounted for with relative ease: Luke has abbreviated them and positioned them in another sequence (see Lk. 11.15-23; 17.1-2).[4]

In the case of 6.45–8.26 (sometimes called 'the Great Omission'), 'avoidance of doublets can be at least part of the answer' (Neirynck 1990b: 11). In other words, since Mk 6.45–8.26 involves a good deal of duplication, most obviously in giving two miracles of loaves (Mk 6.30-44; 8.1-10; for further duplication, see Mally 1968: 38), Luke wanted to avoid such duplication.

Essentially the same principle—avoiding obvious duplication—seems to apply to the first and last omissions. Mark's introduction and passion narrative would have duplicated Luke's, and so he omitted them. The only major part of Mark's passion narrative that was quite different from that of Luke's was the account of the night action (Mk 14.26-72—the denials, Gethsemane, and arrest) and so Luke duly reproduced this, adapting it to the context of his own narrative (Lk. 22.31-65).

The fact that Luke does not reproduce a Markan passage, especially one involving duplication, need not mean that either Luke did not know such a text or that he omitted it completely. At times, apparently, especially in dealing with 6.45–8.26, Luke rendered the Markan text into a new form or drew on it to color other texts. Thus, Neirynck, who has begun to explore this phenomenon (1990b: 11), notes Lukan details or 'reminiscences [which] suggest that Luke knew the material in…Mark [6.45–8.26]'.

Following Neirynck's lead, other possible links are evident which are worth exploring. Luke, for instance, omits the account of the Pharisees who, in their preoccupation with multiple externals, especially concerning food, neglect the word of God (Mk 7.1-13). But he tells the story of Martha and Mary, one preoccupied with food, the other attentive to the word (Lk. 10.38-42).

---

3. For outlines see for instance, Gast 1968: 6; Neirynck 1990b: 9, 12. For discussion, see Fitzmyer 1981: 66-72.
4. For other transpositions, see Neirynck 1990b: 12; Fitzmyer 1981: 71-72.

What is essential is that despite transpositions and omissions (or apparent omissions), the balance of evidence indicates strongly that Luke incorporated Mark's gospel. The link is direct.

3. *Luke's Use of Matthew*

Researchers agree that there is also some link between Luke and Matthew. These two evangelists share much material with Mark ('the Triple Tradition'), and they share much with each other ('the Double Tradition'). The Double Tradition could be attributed to Q.

But, in attributing the Double Tradition to Q, there is a serious problem: within the Triple Tradition, there are agreements of Matthew and Luke against Mark ('the Minor Agreements'). The implication is that there was direct copying between Matthew and Luke. In Fitzmyer's view 'the…Minor Agreements [are]…the biggest chink in the armor of the modified Two-Source Theory [the theory that Matthew and Luke depended on Mark and Q but not on each other]…for it seems inexplicable that…there would be a number of—not just a coincidental few—agreements of Matthew and Luke against Mark' (1981: 72). In other words, how can Matthew and Luke agree with each other in this way if there was no contact between them?

The objection is so strong that Fitzmyer, a great scholar, does not attempt to answer it. Instead he pours gentle scorn on those who use it, appeals to authority (F. Neirynck), says it cannot be handled in a commentary, and then states that its importance has been exaggerated (1981: 72-73). Fitzmyer has 1700 pages at his disposal, but he gives no argument of his own, and no argument from his authority.

F. Neirynck's study, arguing against the objection, constitutes an elaborate work, listing and analyzing all the details.[5] In itself this study is valuable, and Fitzmyer calls it 'a stout volume' (1981: 72), but the fact that Fitzmyer does not extract any argument from it reflects the elusiveness of its logic.

Other scholars have concluded that the Minor Agreements cannot be swept aside so easily, and so a re-evaluation of the status of Q is necessary.[6]

The proposal here is that Matthew first used Proto-Luke, and later—after John had rendered Matthew and his discourses into a new form—Luke in turn adapted Matthew. This is the simplest explanation which accounts for the data.

a. *Objections to the Claim that Luke used Matthew*
In the history of research (see Neirynck 1990b: 32-34; Fitzmyer 1981: 73-75), several researchers have proposed that Luke depends on Matthew, but against this others have placed objections, mainly the following:

---

5. Neirynck 1974. For further discussion, see Strecker (ed.) 1983.
6. See N. Turner 1959: 234: 'There cannot be any other reason than literary dependence to explain these apparently irrelevant agreements'. For a classic argument against Q, see Farrer 1955. For the history of the discussion of the minor agreements, see Neirynck 1974: 11-48; Friedrichsen 1992: I, 113-215. For the data on the minor agreements, see Neirynck 1974: 55-195; Friedrichsen 1992: II, 1-296. In Neirynck's view (1974: 199) 'a great deal' of the agreements do not presuppose borrowing; they can be explained as features of the literary style of independent redactions. Friedrichsen's dissertation continues the process of seeking to explain the agreements on the basis of independent redaction; 'only a small number of more difficult cases will provide any support for an alternative source-critical solution (1992: I, 214); 'nevertheless the minor agreements will no doubt remain at the center of the discussion of the Synoptic Problem (I, 314). Goulder's article (1993a: especially 160), a response to Neirynck, is an emphatic statement that the agreements cannot be disposed of so easily; they show dependence of Luke on Mathew.

- Luke never reproduces the typically Matthean additions within the Triple Tradition: for instance, the exception clause in the divorce text (Mt. 19.9), the highlighting of Peter (as he walks on the water and receives a promise, Mt. 14.28-31; 16.16-19), and peculiarly Matthean episodes in the Passion Narrative (especially those involving Pilate—his wife's dream and his washing of his hands, Mt. 27.19, 24). If Luke depended on Matthew, would he not adopt these additions, or at least some of them?

  The same is said of smaller additions such as the public proclamation at the baptism of Jesus as Son (Mt. 3.17, 'This is…', not 'You are…', as in Mk 1.11), the naming of Simon as Peter (Mt. 4.18), and the changing of Levi's name to Matthew (Mt. 9.9). Why did Luke not follow Matthew in these little additions or changes?
- Luke also omits Matthew's extra material in the Double Tradition. Matthew's Beatitudes (5.3, 6) have 'poor in spirit' and 'hunger and thirst for righteousness', but Luke (6.20-21) has only 'poor' and 'hunger'. And Matthew's version of the Our Father is longer (Mt. 6.9-13; Lk. 11.2-4—Matthew, for instance, begins 'Our Father in heaven', but Luke simply begins, 'Father'). If Luke had had Matthew's versions, what would have motivated him to reformulate them?
- Why would Luke break up Matthew's discourses, especially a masterpiece like the Sermon on the Mount, and scatter many of its parts throughout the travel account (Lk. 9.51–ch. 19)?
- Apart from John's preaching and Jesus' temptation (Lk. 3.7-9, 17; 4.2b-13), Luke never inserts the material of the Double Tradition into the same Markan context as Matthew. If he had been reworking Matthew, would he not have respected it just as much as he respected Mark? Luke's frequent disagreement with the Matthean order is crucial in judging that Luke did not depend on Matthew.
- Analysis of the Double Tradition reveals that the more original setting is found sometimes in Luke and sometimes in Matthew. If Luke used Matthew such divergence would not occur; Matthew (but not Luke) would consistently reflect the more original setting.
- If Luke used Matthew why did he constantly omit Matthean material in episodes which lack Markan parallels: for example, the infancy and resurrection narratives?

b. *Luke's Use of Matthew Reaffirmed*
As a general principle, it is not necessary to explain every aspect of how an author used a source in order to claim literary dependence. Some matters will often remain difficult or elusive. As already seen, Luke's apparent omission of two chapters of Mark (Mk 6.45–8.26), for instance, has driven some researchers to say that Luke did not have Mark. But, while unsure of how to explain the omission, the vast majority believe that the weight of evidence indicates otherwise: Luke used Mark. Likewise with Matthew: despite some difficulties, the weight of evidence indicates direct dependence.

Before considering the six objections individually, it is necessary to mention some general guidelines:
- What is in question is not all of Luke but the second version—the material added to Proto-Luke.
- The most basic principle of *imitatio* was *emulatio*—the need not just to reproduce but to improve, to write something fresh.
- As of yet, there is no full understanding of Luke's methods and objectives. Much progress has indeed been made by authors as diverse as Conzelmann, Tannehill, Bovon, and Sterling, but much has yet to be done, and until it is, one cannot expect to be able to explain all of Luke's procedures, including all his variations on Matthew.

However, even in our present, limited state of knowledge, the objections to Luke's use of Matthew have severe limitations.

(1) *Objection 1: Luke does not reproduce the typically Matthean additions/elaborations within the Triple Tradition.* To some degree this is true, but it is part of a larger truth: in dealing with Mark and Matthew (i.e. with the Triple Tradition), Luke gives a certain priority to Mark over Matthew. (As already mentioned, there is a form of gradation in Luke's use of sources: Proto-Luke, Mark, Matthew, John.) In particular, Luke tends to keep closer to Mark's original order. Likewise, and this is the issue, he also tends to keep closer to Mark's content and thus to omit Matthew's additions to Mark's basic storyline.

Nonetheless, while this is Luke's general tendency, he sometimes does otherwise: he reproduces some of Matthew's additions to Mark. Matthew, for instance, adds the vipers speech (Mt. 3.8-10) and Jesus' triple temptation (Mt. 4.2-10), and Luke includes them in adapted form (3.7-9; 4.2b-13, 28-30). Luke does not indeed have Matthew's exceptive addition in the divorce text (taken over from Mk 10.1-12), but neither does he have the divorce text as a whole, a passage based on Mark. If, while using Mark, he omitted the main divorce passage—he retains only the conclusion (Lk. 16.18)—then it is not surprising that while using Matthew, he omits Matthew's divorce amendment.

Luke does not reproduce the Matthean episodes highlighting Peter (the sinking in the water and the promise, Mt. 14.28-31; 16.17-20) but his account of the first call of Peter portrays another form of sinking and promising (Lk. 5.1-11, especially 5.7, 10, a text based partly on Jn 21). In other words, some of the essence of Matthew's Peter-related episodes is distilled into Luke's version of the first call of Peter.

When Luke introduces Simon, he does not immediately add the name 'Peter' (as does Mt. 4.18; cf. Lk. 5.3); but a few verses later, at the critical point in the story, he does add that name (Lk. 5.8). And Luke (5.27) does not follow Matthew in giving the name 'Matthew' (Mt. 9.9) to 'Levi, the son of Alphaeus' (Mk 2.14). But he does not need to. Neither does he follow Mark in mentioning 'Alphaeus'.

Luke's omission of details involving Pilate and his wife from the Passion Narrative can largely be explained: Luke's Passion Narrative was already essentially formed in Proto-Luke. Generally, in Luke's relationship to Matthew—as in Luke's relationship to Mark—some apparent omissions do not exclude dependence. Very often the material is not omitted; it is transformed or/and relocated. The challenge is to find it.

(2) *Objection 2: Luke does not reproduce the Matthean additions/elaborations in the Double Tradition (e.g. the longer elements of the Beatitudes or the Our Father).* Luke's omissions of Matthew's extra details in the Beatitudes and the Our Father can be understood largely through the respective theological emphases of the two evangelists. Luke says 'poor' (rather than 'poor in spirit') because he has a major interest in the poor and in the distribution of possessions. He says 'hungry' (rather than 'hungry and thirsty for righteousness', *dikaiosynē*) because, like 'poor', it is tangible and brief, and because, in general, he does not share Matthew's interest in righteousness. And he says 'Father' (rather than 'Our Father in heaven'), because, again, he does not share Matthew's peculiar preference for specific words (in this case Matthew's repeated use of 'heaven', 'kingdom of heaven', and so on), and because, within his own narrative, the simple word 'Father' has a special resonance (e.g. 15.18, 21; 23.46).

(3) *Objection 3: Why would Luke break up Matthew's sermons?* Luke breaks up Matthew's long discourses for several reasons. Working with Proto-Luke, he does not have Matthew's purpose-built framework for carrying five such long discourses. Furthermore, from

the point of view of subsequent Christian readers, it would have been more pointless and boring to have Luke reproduce the entirety of Matthew's five discourses. In addition, the essence of *imitatio* was *emulatio*—the effort to improve, to go beyond what was already written, to offer something fresh. (John, for instance, did not hesitate to rewrite Matthew's discourses much more radically.) What Luke apparently offered instead of five set-piece discourses was a prolonged journey which, filled as it is with varied deeds and discourse material (9.51–ch. 19), captures something of the varied journey of life.

(4) *Objection 4: Luke does not follow Matthew's order in the way he follows Mark's; therefore he did not have Matthew*. As already stated (in dealing with Objection 1), it is true that Luke does not treat Matthew and Mark in the same way; he gives different treatment to Proto-Luke, Mark, Matthew, and John. Mark had priority over Matthew, and so while Mark's order was largely preserved, Matthew's was not—not to the same degree.

However (as will be seen briefly later), in adapting Matthew's five discourses, Luke does preserve their main pillars: the beginning, middle, and end. He begins, as Matthew does, with the beatitudes (Lk. 6.20-23; Matthew, Discourse 1); he continues later with the central parable of the sower (Lk. 8.4-15; Matthew, Discourse 3); and concludes (cf. Lk. 19.11–ch. 21) with various adaptations of Matthew's eschatological discourse (cf. Lk. 19.11–ch. 21; Matthew, Discourse 5).

Having thus preserved the essential outline framework of Matthew's discourse, Luke rearranged the rest of Matthew's material according to the requirements of his own narrative. Sometimes passages had to be located as circumstances would allow. The Sermon on the Plain (Lk. 6.20-49), for instance, was placed before the cure of the centurion's servant (Lk. 7.1-10), apparently because Lk. 7.1—which originally followed Proto-Luke's Nazareth speech (4.16-22a)—begins with a reference to the fact that Jesus had been speaking to the people. Thus, it makes an appropriate place for the insertion of a sermon. Likewise with other passages. Matthew's texts and their order were adapted to Luke's other texts and to Luke's overall schema.

(5) *Objection 5: In the Matthew/Luke relationship, priority varies; one does not have consistent priority over the other*. Therefore one does not use the other. Insofar as it is possible to detect original settings, it is appropriate that, as a general principle, some be assigned to Matthew and some to Luke. And so priority varies. Yet, this does not exclude literary dependence; it means that the literary dependence is twofold. Each gospel has a certain priority over the other: Proto-Luke preceded Matthew, and Matthew preceded Luke.

(6) *Objection 6: Why did Luke not use Matthean materials in episodes lacking Markan parallels, for example, the narratives of infancy and resurrection?* These accounts (Lk. 1–2 and 24) belonged to Proto-Luke and were already complete. Furthermore, within the initial account of Jesus, they constituted the beginning and end—key pillars, not easily changed.

c. *Survey of the Main Areas of Luke's Dependence on Matthew*
The primary way of solving the question of Luke's possible dependence on Matthew does not come through theoretically debating the intricacies of order, but through tracking down the actual dependence. This tracking process is slow and, as yet, incomplete. However, progress can be made.

Luke's greatest dependence on Matthew is in the area of the discourses, so this brief survey will concentrate on these five distinctive blocks (Mt. 4.23–ch. 7; ch. 10; ch. 13;

17.22–ch. 18; chs. 23–25). But first, it is necessary to mention two introductory texts, those involving vipers and temptations.

d. *Introductory Passages (Matthew 3.7-10; 4.1-11; Luke 3.7-9; 4.1-13, 28-30)*
Luke does not reproduce most of Matthew's introductory chapters (at least not as such). There is no need to; he already has his own infancy narrative and his own account of John's preaching.

However, in reporting John's preaching, Matthew had included an added warning ('Brood of vipers...', Mt. 3.7-10), and so Luke, seeing this new material, incorporated it almost word for word (Lk. 3.7-9)—his first insertion into Proto-Luke.

The next distinctive feature in Matthew is the triple-episode account of the temptation of Jesus (Mt. 4.1-11). Luke absorbs Matthew's account, but with a change (Lk. 4.1-13). He has taken Matthew's *second* temptation—in which the devil sets Jesus on the pinnacle of the temple and asks him to throw himself down (Mt. 4.5-7)—and he has drawn on this throwing-down image twice: he uses it as the climactic *third* temptation of his own account (Lk. 4.9-13, set in Jerusalem); and then, just after Jesus' visit to Nazareth, he uses it again, as a starting-point for describing how the hostile Jews tried to throw Jesus down from the top of the hill (Lk. 4.28-30). The result is that the account of Jesus' visit to Nazareth, which in Proto-Luke had been peaceful (Lk. 4.14-22a), is now framed between two attacks, one by the tempting devil in Jerusalem and the other by the Jews of the synagogue. The devil tried to get Jesus to throw himself down, and he would not; those in the synagogue actually tried to throw him down, and he went away.

In incorporating these two Matthean texts—John's warning and Jesus' temptation—Luke shows greater freedom with the second. This may, perhaps, be due to a sense that, before improving on Matthew, it was appropriate to acknowledge him—and thus to reproduce him almost word for word.

e. *The Sermon on the Mount (Matthew 4.23–7.29; Luke 6.17-49; 10.23-37; 11.1-13; 12.13-34)*
Luke's Sermon on the Plain (6.17-49) is largely based on Matthew's Sermon on the Mount, especially on Matthew 5 and 7. At this stage Luke does not use Matthew 6.

However, after a sequence of almost five chapters dominated by material from Proto-Luke and Mark (Lk. 7.1–10.20), Luke returns, especially in chs. 11 and 12, to the use of Matthew—beginning with Matthew 6. The two major texts of Matthew 6—concerning the forms of piety (alms, prayer, and fasting (Mt. 6.1-18) and concerning God-centeredness (Mt. 6.19-34)—occur in varied form in Lk. 11.1-13 and 12.13-31. The section on piety (Mt. 6.1-18) has been adapted so that, with the help of Mt. 7.7-11, it highlights prayer—a typically Lukan emphasis. And the section on God-centeredness (on trusting, not hoarding, Mt. 6.19-34) remains much as in Matthew, except that the warning against hoarding has been made more vivid, particularly through the parable of the rich man and the barns (Lk. 12.13-32, especially 12.16-21).

The one major section of the Sermon on the Mount which Luke seems to omit completely is the list of antitheses: 'Do not think that I came to destroy the law and the prophets... It was said to you of old...but I say' (Mt. 5.17-47). This looks like another great omission.

It is useful, however, in face of this apparent omission, to apply the Neirynck principle (Neirynck's way of dealing with Luke's 'Great Omission' from Mark [1990b: 11]): to ask whether Luke, while omitting the external form of the earlier gospel, adapted it in some way, thus preserving a reminiscence of it in another text.

It appears that he did, namely in Lk. 10.23-37 concerning the relationship of his own teaching to that of the prophets and the law: 'Many prophets wanted to...hear what you hear and never heard it... What is written in the law?' (10.23-28). In other words, in Luke, as in Matthew, Jesus does not destroy the prophets and law; he surpasses them and fulfills them. And instead of going on to give a whole list of contrasts between the old commands and the new (the antitheses, Mt. 5.21-48), Luke provides a single parable—the Good Samaritan (Lk. 10.29-37)—in which the central contrast between the old law (the priest and Levite) and a deeper goodness is unforgettably vivid.

f. *The Apostolic Discourse (Matthew 10; Luke 6.12-16; 9.1-6; 12.1-12)*
Instead of reproducing Matthew's long apostolic discourse (about the mission of the Twelve, Mt. 10.1-16, and about persecution and fearless speech, Mt. 10.17-42), Luke synthesizes the material and disperses it. The mission of the Twelve (Mt. 10.1-16), overlapping with material in Mark (3.13-19; 6.7-13), is placed in chs. 6 and 9 (Lk. 6.12-16; 9.1-6). And the themes of persecution and fearless speech (Mt. 10.17-42) occur, in reverse order, in ch. 12 (Lk. 12.1-9 and 12.11-12). Several small parts of Matthew 10 have been rearranged in Luke (for instance, 'the disciple is not greater than the master', Mt. 10.24; Lk. 6.40), but the overall situation is clear: the essential content of Matthew's apostolic discourse may be found in varied form in Luke.

g. *The Parabolic Discourse (Matthew 13; Luke 8.4-15; 13.6-9, 18-30)*
The first part of Matthew's parabolic discourse (concerning the sower, Mt. 13.1-23), is reproduced, in obvious fashion, in Lk. 8.4-15.

The second part, involving the darnel, mustard seed, yeast, and other parables (Mt. 13.24-50), is less easy to trace. Luke never speaks of darnel and of a conversation between the owner and servants about whether to let the damaged crop grow. But he speaks of a conversation between the owner and vinedresser about whether to let the barren fig tree grow (Lk. 13.6-9), and he then goes on, almost immediately, to tell the parables of the mustard seed and the yeast (Lk. 13.18-21). In other words, Luke has left aside the specific image of darnel with its teaching about a final judgment (Mt. 13.24-30, 36-43), and, using the image of a barren fig tree (drawn from Mt. 21.18-22; cf. Mk 11.12-14, 20-24), he implies a judgment which is more immediate, and—typically Luke—also implies the consequent need to repent (Lk. 13.6-9; cf. 13.5).

Matthew's other fairly long parable, the dragnet (Mt. 13.47-50), tells of sorting the fish and throwing the bad ones into a place where there is weeping and grinding of teeth. And Luke, combining the essence of the dragnet parable with other texts, immediately goes on to tell of the few who are saved and of the weeping and grinding of teeth (13.22-30).

Among the parables of Matthew 13, therefore, the only ones for which no equivalent has yet been seen in Luke are the two little parables about finding (finding the treasure and finding the pearl, Mt. 13.44-46).

h. *The Community Discourse (Matthew 17.22–ch. 18; Luke 14.25–ch. 15; cf. 9.46-48; 17.1-2)*
Matthew's discourse on the community is solemnly set in the context of Jesus—the context of his death (Mt. 17.22-23) and of his sovereignty (his knowledge and power as illustrated by the fish and coin incident, Mt. 17.24-27; see Brodie 1992b: 703). The discourse then goes on to deal with the central issues—first concerning being great or little (Mt. 18.1-10), and then concerning sin and forgiveness (18.12-35).

The essential ideas about those who are great and little may be seen with relative ease in two brief passages in Luke (9.46-48; 17.1-2).

The other part of Matthew's discourse—the solemn context and the question of the forgiveness of sin—finds its nearest Lukan equivalent in the parables on discipleship and forgiveness (Lk. 14.25–ch. 15).

The solemn context (Mt. 17.22-27), especially the opening reference to Jesus' death (17.22-23), is echoed broadly in the solemn context set by Luke (14.25-35), especially in Luke's opening reference to the cross (14.25-27 [Lk. 14.28-35 uses other source]).

The more important connection centers around forgiveness. Matthew speaks of a brother doing wrong and he tells the parables of the lost sheep and the unforgiving debtor (18.12-35). Luke converts these texts into three parables of forgiveness (Lk. 15): the lost sheep, the prodigal son, and the finding of the lost coin. This latter Lukan parable—the finding of the lost coin—draws also on Matthew's parables of finding (Mt. 13.44-46) and on the Matthean story of the coin (Mt. 17.24-27).

The details of Luke's work are complex and it is better in this work not to attempt to unravel them. The major connection needing examination is the one between the two climactic parables on forgiveness: the unforgiving servant (Mt. 18.23-35) and the prodigal son (Lk. 15.11-32). Luke has retained some of the emotional intensity of Matthew's drama about forgiveness given and refused, but he has also used other sources, apparently including one aspect of Matthew's own story of the two brothers (Mt. 21.28-32).

At one level, therefore, Matthew's community discourse remains unique, but it emerges as something which is used and reflected in Luke's portrayal of discipleship and forgiveness.

i. *The Woes and the Eschatological Discourse (Matthew 23–25; Luke 11.37-54; 12.35-48; 19.11-27; 21.5-36)*
In Matthew, Jesus' ministry concludes with three chapters about judgment: judgment against Jewish leaders (ch. 23, the woes), and final judgment (chs. 24–25, the eschatological discourse).

In using these three chapters Luke again disperses them. The first part of the eschatological discourse (Mt. 24.1-44, corresponding to Mk 13) retains in Luke the late position which it has in Matthew (Lk. 21, especially 21.4-36).

But Luke moves the two other texts—the condemnation of the Jewish leaders (Mt. 23) and the second part of the eschatological judgment (Mt. 24.45–ch. 25)—back towards the center of the gospel. Thus, he synthesizes the condemnation of the leaders into a shorter condemnation which occurs during a meal (Lk. 11.37-54; cf. Mt. 23.37-39; Lk. 13.34-35); and he distills the second part of the eschatological discourse with its increasingly long parables of readiness and judgment (Mt. 24.45–ch. 25) into two briefer exhortations about being ready for the decisive return (Lk. 12.35-48; 19.11-27).

These latter texts (Mt. 24.45–ch. 25; Lk. 12.35-48; 19.11-27) require closer scrutiny. Matthew's text has four parables: the steward, the bridesmaids, the talents, and the last judgment by the king. The first two concerning the steward and the bridesmaids (Mt. 25.45–25.13) are inverted in Luke to become the exhortations concerning the wedding feast and the steward (Lk. 12.35-38, 42-46). And the final climactic two, concerning the talents and the last judgment by the king (Mt. 25.14-46) are fused to form the climactic parable about the pounds (in place of talents) and the returning king—returning to judge (Lk. 19.11-27). In other words, instead of reproducing Matthew's dread scene of the king presiding over the last judgment (Mt. 25.31-46), Luke has distilled it and blended it with the parable of the talents or pounds.

j. *Luke Use of Matthew: Conclusion*
Luke maintains obvious resemblance with the three pivotal points of Matthew's discourses: the beginning, middle, and end. As in Matthew, his discourses begin with beatitudes and

end with an eschatological discourse and an accompanying parable of pounds or talents. And he reproduces the most obvious aspects of Matthew's central parabolic discourse, especially the parable of the sower (Lk. 8.4-15). But having thus accepted something of Matthew's overall framework, Luke works a major adaptation: he collects sections from all five of Matthew's discourses into a massive central area of intermittent discourse (Lk. 10.23–ch. 15), and he uses that as part of his portrayal of a long complex journey (Lk. 9.51–ch. 19).

Luke rarely allowed those discourses to be as long as in Matthew. He generally broke Matthew's text into more digestible units, or he interspersed them with fresh images or settings. And he adopted many of Matthew's changes to Mark.

The change is great, but so is the continuity. Every major part of Matthew's discourses is reflected in Luke. Hence, without attempting to unravel the full details of the relationship between these two gospels, it is reasonable to conclude—as the easiest way to account for the data—that Luke used Matthew.

4. *Luke's Use of John*

Researchers agree that there is some link between Luke–Acts and John.[7] The connection is particularly clear in Luke's version of the call of the first four disciples (Lk. 5.1-11). In contrast to the brief call accounts in the other Synoptics (Mt. 4.18-22; Mk 1.16-20), Luke recounts a vivid Peter-centered fishing drama which goes from catching nothing all night to catching more than can be handled—a drama which has multiple connections with John 21. Fitzmyer (1981: 560-61) notes eleven similarities.

The easiest way to account for these similarities is to say the link was direct: when Luke was absorbing Mark's account of the call he also absorbed the essential drama of John 21; he adapted the Johannine account so that it fits into the Markan text and into his own larger narrative. (This use of John 21 is compatible with some less-obvious uses of Peter-related texts from Matthew.)

It may seem strange that Luke highlighted Peter so early in his gospel—at the first call of the disciples. (Matthew and Mark do not do it until much later—Mt. 14.28-32; 16.13-20; Mk 8.27-30.) But the explanation for this strange procedure is not far away: in John's gospel there is a highlighting of Peter precisely within the call of the first disciples (Jn 1.35-42). Thus, Luke's use of John's gospel explains not only the essence of the Peter-centered drama, but also its location within the first calling of disciples.

The full details of Luke's use of John seem quite complex. There are some indications, for instance, that throughout all of Luke–Acts (excluding Proto-Luke), Luke may have used John systematically simply as a basis for adding finishing touches to material drawn from other sources. Thus the distinctive use of *legō* and *archomai* ('to say' and 'to begin') at the opening of the vipers text (Lk. 3.7-8)—the first Lukan text (Deutero-Luke, as distinct from Proto-Luke)—may be an echo of the opening verse of John (*en archē ēn ho logos*, 'In the beginning was the Word'). Likewise, the use of *plērēs* and *pleroō* ('full' and 'fill') at the beginnings of the next (Deutero-)Lukan passages (Lk. 4.1, 28, the two temptation-based texts) may reflect the use of *plērēs* and *plērōma* at the beginning of the final section of John's prologue (Jn 1.14, 16). And so on. Does *ēn didaskōn* ('he was teaching') in the next (Deutero-)Lukan passage (Lk. 4.31) echo *ēn...baptizōn* ('he was baptizing') in the next Johannine passage (Jn 1.28)? Does the distinctive use of 'Son of God' in Lk. 4.41 reflect the (textually disputed) 'Son of God' in John 1.34? And does the

---

7. For bibliography on Luke and John, see Fitzmyer 1981: 104. See also Denaux (ed.) 1992, *passim*, particularly the review of research by Neirynck (pp. 35-46).

idea of 'coming' to Jesus and trying to keep him from going away (Lk. 4.42) reflect the Johannine picture of the disciples 'coming' to Jesus and abiding with him (Jn 1.39)?

a. *The Use of John in the Later Part of Acts (Acts 15.36–ch. 28)*
Apart from using John to provide an apparent necklace of finishing touches, Luke used John in a much more substantive way, particularly in Acts 15.36–ch. 28.

Table 47. *John 3–11 and Acts 16–21*

Prison, Woman, and Official (John 3–4; Acts 16.11-34)	
* Nicodemus comes by night (3.1-21) ** John thrown into prison (3.24) The woman at the well (4.1-42)	Lydia at river; slave-girl freed from spirit and *kyrioi* (16.11-18) ** Paul thrown into prison (Acts 16.24)
Official and household believe (4.43-54)	Jailer and household are baptized (16.25-34)
Addresses to Jews and to Galileans/Gentiles (John 5–6; Acts 17)	
Jesus and Jerusalem Jews: creation goes on (ch. 5) Jesus at Galilee/Tiberias (ch. 6)	Paul and resisting Jews (Thessalonica): 'They turn the world upside down' (17.1-9) * By night to well-disposed Beroea (17.10-12) Paul at Athens (17.16-34)
Tents: Law and Spirit (John 7; Acts 18.1–19.10)	
Feast of Tents (7.1-2) Jesus teaches the law (7.14-24) Jesus speaks of the Spirit (7.37-39)	At Corinth: Paul as tentmaker (18.1-4) Dispute about the law (18.12-17) Ephesus, Apollos, the Spirit (18.18–19.10)
?? *Two Obscure Passages: Inner Spirits and Bankrupt Assemblies* ?? (John 8; Acts 19.11-41)	
Jesus as light of the world; his inner witness and identity; Jews oppose; others believe (8.12-30)??	Paul's miracles; spirits recognize Jesus and Paul but not Jews; many believe (19.11-20)??
The Jews rely on externals: 'We are the descent of Abraham' Jewish confusion Jesus, the light, leaves the temple (8.31-59)??	The Ephesians rely on idols: 'Great is Diana of the Ephesians' The Ephesian riot The Ephesian *ekklēsia* is disbanded (19.23-40)??
Lifecycle, Shepherd, and Fateful Journey (John 9.1–11.53; Acts 20.1–21.36)	
The sending, the healing, and the cycle of life (ch. 9)	The journey, the miracle, and the course of Paul's life (20.1-24)
The sheepfold and the good shepherd (10.1-21)	'You will not see my face again… Guard the flock' (20.25-38)
* Surrounded in the temple (10.22-39) Journeying towards death (11.1-16) Approaching the tomb (11.17-37) Glory; a crisis meeting (11.38-53)	Journeying towards Jerusalem (21.1-6) Approaching Jerusalem (21.7-14) Meeting: glory and crisis (21.17-26) * Paul arrested in the temple (21.27-36)

That Luke should use John differently in Acts is understandable. While engaged in expanding the gospel section of Proto-Luke, he was governed largely by the framework already laid down by the other evangelists, particularly the broad framework of the life of Jesus; and so in using them he stayed moderately close to them. But in expanding the second part of Proto-Luke—the work of the apostles—the whole world was available as a stage, and the drama could go on for many years. Consequently, other things being equal, there was greater scope for breaking new ground, for transforming texts—even those of the evangelists—into new forms, and for blending them with fresh sources.

In any case, whatever the full reasons, there are indications that Luke used John as one component in composing Acts 15.36–ch. 28, and that he transformed John into something quite new. The outline (Table 47) concentrates on one area: the continuity between John 3-11 and Acts 16-21. Double question marks (??) emphasize uncertainty.

The outline is exploratory; it is not the result of detailed analysis. This tentativeness is particularly clear in juxtaposing John 8 and Acts 19.11-41—texts which, at first sight at least, have little to link them except their obscurity.

More inviting is the affinity between the woman at the well (Jn 4.1-42) and the woman at the river, Lydia (Acts 16.11-15). Lydia is not as troubled as the woman at the well, but at one level the Lydia story extends as far as 16.40 (when the released Paul returns to her house), and within that longer text there is the account of a woman who was very troubled—the servant or slave who was being manipulated both by a spirit and by the men who owned her (Acts 16.16-18). Thus, the releasing of the Samaritan woman from her complex history finds an echo in the releasing of the enslaved woman from her plight.

John 5–6 and Acts 17 show less obvious affinity, but at least they share a broad framework. Both texts move from a concentration on Jews to a more universal audience. John goes from a relatively narrow focus on the Jerusalem Jews (Jn 5) to a scene in Galilee (Galilee of Tiberias, 6.1) which, from almost every point of view, evokes a world which is more complex and cosmopolitan (Jn 6). And in Acts 17 there is a similar shift from an initial emphasis on Jews (in Thessalonica and Beroea, 17.1-15) to the wide world of Athens (17.16-34).

Moving beyond the framework to the more important question of content, it is not easy to see much connection between John 5–6 and Acts 17; in Acts 17 there is no orderly discourse on ongoing creation (as in Jn 5). However, Acts 17 portrays Paul's opponents as shouting that the world is being turned upside down (Acts 17.6). Thus, through very different means, both texts suggest that Jesus' message affects the whole world in some radical way.

In the case of John 7 and Acts 18.1–19.10, some initial points of contact are clear: the tents, the law, and the Spirit (in the same order).

The essence of the affinity between John 9 and Acts 20.1-24 is the shared evoking of the course of human life, particularly the life of Jesus' disciples. The six scenes of John 9 are such that they suggest the advancing stages of living and believing (Brodie 1993a: 343-54). And the sense of an advancing life also appears in Paul's activity: he is on a journey leading towards Jerusalem and death; he performs a miracle which recalls the whole reality of giving life; and he refers to the course of his life with the Ephesians from the first day with them to his final farewell.

Incidentally, Luke may sometimes engage in pre-sourcing. In other words, he may base his work not so much on the immediate source, John, as on John's own previous sources (Mark or Matthew, or even the sources of Mark and Matthew). Thus, in the present case, while using John 9, he may have taken account of one of the main sources behind John 9, namely Mk 8.11–9.8.

Moving to the next episode, there is also some significant affinity between the story of Lazarus (Jn 11.1-53) and Paul's continuing journey to Jerusalem (Acts 21.1-26). The crucial element in the Lazarus story is its account of Jesus' journey towards death, for even though Lazarus is raised, the final focus of the story is the death of Jesus (Jn 11.53; see Brodie 1993a: 383-86).

b. *Summary*
What emerges, therefore, without attempting either to prove anything or even to survey all of Acts (15.36–ch. 28), is an affinity which almost seems persistent. The colorful adventures of Acts 15.36–ch. 28 may seem far removed from the calm flow of John's gospel, yet many of the most distinctive elements of John 3–11 find a counterpart in Acts 16–21. And in essentially the same order.

It is therefore appropriate, as part of a working hypothesis, to investigate whether in composing Acts 15.36–ch. 28 one component consisted of John's gospel.

5. *Luke's Use of Deuteronomy*

In 1955 C.F. Evans proposed that the central section of Luke's gospel (from the departure for Jerusalem until the parable of the Pharisee and the publican; 9.51–18.14) was arranged to match the order and contents of Deuteronomy (C.F. Evans 1955). Later researchers have generally viewed Evans's proposal as essentially valid but in need of refinement.[8]

The purpose here is to contribute in a limited way to the process of refinement, namely by clarifying the outer limits—the beginning and end—of this distinctive use of Deuteronomy.

a. *The Beginning*
There has been some uncertainty as to where Luke's central distinctive dependence on Deuteronomy begins. C.F. Evans suggested in principle that it began with the departure for Jerusalem (9.51), but the first text which he designated as actually dependent on Deuteronomy is in Luke 10 (the sending of messengers, 10.1-3, 17-20). The uncertainty is noted and amended by Swartley (1994: 151).

It seems best, in fact, to amend the beginning yet further: Luke's distinctive use of Deuteronomy commences with the parable of the Good Samaritan (10.25-37). There is indeed some affinity between Lk. 10.1-20 (or 9.51–10.20) and Deuteronomy 1, particularly in the images of traveling and sending messengers/scouts (Deut. 1.19, 22-25), but *in view of other evidence* this could simply mean that Luke has chosen a very appropriate context for locating the reworking of Deuteronomy.

The other evidence consists not only of the case for Proto-Luke, including a detailed alternative explanation for Lk. 9.51–10.20, but, above all, the unique and manifold links between the parable of the Good Samaritan and Deuteronomy, especially Deuteronomy 1—links which are altogether appropriate for a beginning. Without going into a detailed analysis, some of these links are as follows:

The parable's beginning has a curious affinity with Deuteronomy's title ('second law', *deu-tero-nomion*): 'And behold a lawyer (*idou nomikos*)... written in the law (*en tō nomō*)...' (Lk. 10.25-26). As well a using a form of the word 'law' a second time (first, 'lawyer', then, 'law', thus resonating 'second law'), the words preceding 'lawyer' and 'law' respectively, the words *i-dou...en tō* ('Behold [a lawyer]'... In the [law]'), coincide strangely with *deu-te-ro*. The impression is of word-play—in effect, a way of working the title of Deuteronomy into the beginning of the parable.

---

8. For bibliography, a summary of Evans's proposal, and an evaluation, see C.A. Evans 1994. For further evaluation, see Swartley 1994: 128-53. For a major reformulation of the Deuteronomy-based theory, see Moessner 1989: especially 260-88.

Absorbing Deuteronomy's title is followed by explicitly citing Deuteronomy's most famous text, the Shema (Lk. 10.27; Deut. 6.5). Taken together, these two features—the title and leading quotation (Lk. 10.25-27)—signal the arrival of Deuteronomy into the text.

The two main sections of the parable text—the emergence of the clear-minded lawyer (10.25-28), and the story of the attack on the way to Jericho (10.29-39)—correspond broadly but significantly with the two main episodes of Deuteronomy 1: appointing good judges (1.9-18), and suffering defeat on the journey into the land (1.19-46), a journey that will lead eventually to Jericho (Deut. 34.1, 3, 8, LXX). Thus, the parable reflects Deuteronomy's title, leading text, and opening chapter.

Other connecting details include the following:
- *klēronomeō*, 'inherit' (Lk. 10.25; Deut. 1.8, 21, 39)
- *dikaioō*, 'justify' (Lk. 10.29; Deut. 1.16, *dikaiōs*, 'justly')
- *en tō hodō...hodeuōn*, 'on the way...journeying' (10.31-32; Deut. 1.33, *en tō hodō...hodēgōn*, 'on the way...guiding')

b. *The Ending*

While it is theoretically possible that Luke's orderly use of Deuteronomy concluded with a correspondence between Luke 18 and Deuteronomy 26, the claim to such orderly use would be stronger if it included a significant part of Deuteronomy's conclusion (chs. 27–34). Generally, those who engage narratives do not ignore endings.

There is evidence, in fact, that at least some of Deuteronomy's ending was used by Luke. The very last text before the Passion Narrative, a double text which is uniquely Lukan—Jesus' call for strong vigilance, and his mountain-based teaching (Lk. 21.34-38)—has significant affinities with the last chapter of Deuteronomy (ch. 34). Shared features include:
- *Analogous literary functions*: Deuteronomy 34 concludes Deuteronomy, and Lk. 21.34-38 concludes the penultimate division of Luke's gospel.
- *Analogous human contexts*: Moses dies and Jesus is about to die.
- *Analogous immediate locations, on/to 'the mountain' (to oros)*: Moses, when about to die, goes to 'the Mountain' of Nebo in Moab (Deut. 34.1); and Jesus, though teaching in the temple, spends his final nights on 'the Mountain' of Olives (Lk. 21.37).
- *Analogous wider locations*: 'the whole land/earth'. From the mountain, Moses looks out on the whole land: 'facing Jericho... the whole land...the whole land... the whole land...the whole land' (34.1-2, *epi prosōpou Iereichō...pasan tēn gēn...*). And Jesus, just before going to the mountain, speaks of everyone 'on the face of the whole earth' (Lk. 21.35, *epi prosōpou...pasēs tēs gēs...*).
- *Death-related emphasis on vison/vigilance and strength*: when he dies, Moses is not caught unaware; he is clear-eyed and strong (Deut. 34.7); and Jesus, in this final context close to death, admonishes vigilance and strength (Lk. 21.34-36).
- *Closing emphasis on the attentiveness of all the people*: Deuteronomy closes by telling of (the people of) Israel listening to Joshua and of incomparable Moses acting in the presence of all (the people of) Israel (Deut. 34.9-12). Luke's text closes by telling of all the people getting up early to listen to Jesus (Lk. 21.38).

The basic conclusion, both in the parable of the Good Samaritan and in the picture of Jesus' final nights on 'the mountain', is that however diverse Luke's sources may have been, one important component has been drawn from Deuteronomy, especially from Deuteronomy 1 and 34.

Overall, therefore, in searching for Luke's distinctive use of Deuteronomy, it seems best on the one hand to extend the search from the parable of the Good Samaritan to Jesus' nights on the mountain (Lk. 10.25–ch. 21), and on the other hand to exclude from that search—at least as a working hypothesis—all the texts assigned to Proto-Luke. In practice this means that Luke's use of Deuteronomy is best sought within the following texts. Passages which are *clearly* related to Matthew and/or Mark are noted as such:

10.25-37:	The Lawyer, and the Good Samaritan on the way to Jericho
10.38-42:	Martha and Mary
11.1-26:	Prayer; Beelzebul (Matthean/Markan)
11.27-28:	Blessedness of hearing the word
11.29-54:	A sign? Light. Denunciations (Matthean/Markan)
12.1-21:	Hypocrisy; fear; confessing Christ; the rich fool
12.22-59:	Care; watchful servants; division; discerning time; judgment (Matthean)
13.1-17:	Repent or perish; the barren fig tree; healing a woman on the Sabbath
13.18-35:	Mustard seed; leaven; the narrow door; lament over Jerusalem (Matthean)
14.1-14:	Healing the man with dropsy; guests at a feast
14.15-35:	The great banquet; the cost of discipleship; tasteless salt (Matthean)
ch. 15:	Lost sheep (Matthean); lost coin; prodigal son
16.10-13:	Faithfulness in small things
16.14-18:	The law and the kingdom (Matthean)
17.1-10:	Sayings of Jesus (Matthean/Markan)
18.9-14:	The Pharisee and the publican
18.15-43:	Children; rich man; passion prediction; blind beggar (Matthean/Markan)
19.11-27:	Parable of the ten pounds (Matthean)
19.28–20.47:	Jerusalem, temple cleansed, authority questioned, parable of the vineyard, Caesar, question about the resurrection, David's son, scribes denounced (Matthean/Markan)
21.1-33:	Widow's mite; foretelling the end (Matthean/Markan)
21.34-38:	Vigilance, strength, and spending the last nights on the mountain

It seem likely, *a priori*, that Luke's primary use of Deuteronomy occurs in passages unique to himself, but Deuteronomy may also be used in adapting texts from other evangelists, especially from Matthew.

In the balance of the hermeneutical circle—moving over and back between broad themes and specific details—it seems that the primary need now is for greater attention to specific details. It is necessary to spell out, as precisely as possible, the literary relationship between particular passages. Later, it will be necessary to return to the broad themes.

What is important from the viewpoint of the general composition of Luke and Acts is that the Proto-Luke hypothesis does not exclude C.F. Evans's idea about Luke's distinctive dependence on Deuteronomy. Rather, identifying Proto-Luke provides a context which, in the long term, should help to clarify Evans's proposal. The following is a tentative list of connections between Deuteronomy and Luke 10–21. (Unlike other lists, this omits Proto-Lukan texts. When, in one reference, the order of details differs, the list follows the order of Deuteronomy.)

Deuteronomy	Luke	
1	10.25-37	Good Samaritan: good judiciary/lawyer; and a wounding journey
2.1-23	10.38-42	Martha, Mary: not taking the share (part/lot) of one's brother/sister
2.24–ch. 3	11.1-26	Road-related food; enemies that are powerful or superhuman; prayer
4.1-40	11.27-36	Guarding the word; a drama of light and darkness; signs and past days
4.41–ch. 6	11.37-54	The Law given (Deuteronomy) and abused (Luke)?; cf. Deut. 6.5; Lk. 10.27
7-8	12.1-34	The cost and blessings of fidelity
9-11	12.35-59	Long-term fidelity: being ready for the return of Moses/the Master
12.1-28	13.1-5	Jerusalem (implied), sacrifice, blood
12.29–ch. 13	13.6-9	Cutting out what is bad
14	?	Eating—as a holy and blessed people; cf. Lk. 14.1-24 (eating)?
15.1-18	13.10-17	Releasing the brother/sister who is bound
15.19–16.17	?	Feasting, in the place; cf. Lk. 14.1-24 (eating, places)?
16.18–17.1	13.18-30	Judgment based on justice, not on recognition
17.2-13	?	Due process and witnesses
17.14–ch. 19	13.31-35	Kings, prophets and murder
20.1–21.9	14.1-14	The feast/battle (three excuses); going to war; the animal in the trench
21.10–22.4	15	A woman; two brothers; a troublesome son; lost and found
22.5–24.5	16.10-18	Little things; man and wife
24.6–25.4, 13-19	17.1-10	Mill stones; care for brothers. Dis/service on coming from Egypt/work?
25.5-12	?	Levirate law; cf. Lk. 20.27-33 (Mk 12.18-23)
26	18.9-14	Two prayers: one humble; one (arguably) self-righteous
27–33	?	Woes, final decisions, and songs (mostly of blessings)
34	21.34-38	The finale: watching, teaching, and on the mountain

6. *Luke's Use of Other Sources*

The purpose of this brief comment on Luke's other sources is not to identify them but simply to suggest that they are many and varied. Apart from distilling whole scriptural books—as in the preceding example concerning Deuteronomy—Luke sometimes ranges far afield. For instance, in the sea voyage in Acts 27.1–28.15, 'the textual message of safety (*sōtēria*) depends on sea voyages in ancient literature'.[9] In addition, as indicated by Marianne Palmer Bonz, Luke's mode of presentation also draws in some way on a much more central stream of literature: the great epic tradition which runs from Gilgamesh and Homer into Virgil's *Aeneid*.[10] There is evidence that:

> Luke's narrative has incorporated a number of stylistic and dramatic devices characteristic of the Greco-Roman epic in general and the *Aeneid* in particular... Furthermore, Luke appears to have been inspired by epic paradigms... Above all, however, Luke–Acts appears to have drawn inspiration from heroic epic in the manner in which it creates its story as the fulfilment of divine prophecy and the accomplishment of a divine plan. (Bonz 1997: 213-15)

---

9. From the abstract of Praeder 1980. See also Kettenbach 1997.
10. See especially Bonz 1997.

Apart from incorporating aspects of epic, Luke also drew on the great tradition of historiography. In the words of Gregory Sterling,

> Like Josephus, he hellenized his native sources by moving them into the realm of Hellenistic historiography. Unable to claim chronological age for his movement, he argued that it was a continuation of Israel of old… As the narrative of fulfilment he regarded his work as sacred narrative. He thus provided Christians with a new self-definition. (Sterling 1992: 391)

Taken together, Deuteronomy, epic, and historiography reflect some of the most basic traditions of Jewish and Greco-Roman literature. In their diversity and depth, they give a telling indication of the weight and richness of Luke's sources of inspiration.

26

General Conclusion to the Entire Volume and a Sketch of Possible Implications

The rest of this work (Part III: Chapters 27–54) presents details of the foundational argument for Proto-Luke—distinctive systematic use of the Old Testament. However, before looking into these details, many readers may wish to have a sense of the conclusions and possible implications of the volume as a whole. Hence the present chapter. It is built essentially on what precedes (Chapters 1–25), including the initial General Summary and the summary in Chapter 10, and it also takes account of what follows—Part III and Part IV (Appendices).

1. *General Conclusion*

Ideally, in tracing the composition or development of the New Testament texts one should begin at the beginning, with those that seem to be oldest—the possible sayings source (Q/*logia*) and the epistles. But the debates surrounding Q are so complex and hypothetical that it has proved better to start the argument at a more manageable point of entry, namely in Luke–Acts.

Amid the myriad connections between the Old Testament and the New Testament, the most basic narrative affinity is between the respective leading histories—Luke–Acts and the Primary History (Genesis–Kings). More than any other New Testament writer, Luke gave the early Christians a self-defining history, and he did so not in literary isolation but in careful imitation of Old Testament historiography.

Luke's closeness to Old Testament historiography accords with two broad contexts: the Christian practice of adapting older Jewish institutions, and, above all, the literary practice of reworking older texts. Detecting literary dependence is often difficult but, as the study of intertextuality develops, reliable criteria are emerging.

The initial General Summary sketches this volume's central thesis: Luke–Acts first existed in a shorter version which may be called Proto-Luke. There are solid arguments for Proto-Luke:

1. It has a distinctive systematic dependence on the Old Testament (Chapter 10, and Part III [Chapters 27–54]).
2. It is thoroughly unified (Chapter 11).
3. It is very effective. More than any other hypothesis, it provides a verifiable entry to the development of the canonical gospels and to the way they built on one another, first Mark, then Matthew, next John, and finally canonical Luke–Acts (Chapters 15–17, 19, 24–25).

Apart from Proto-Luke, an earlier stream of New Testament writings provides a further entry to the gospels. These writings are Matthew's *Logia* and the epistles. Matthew's *Logia* synthesized Deuteronomy and Sirach; and many epistles followed suit, radically reshaping the older scriptures. They also reshaped one another, and in turn they themselves were absorbed into the gospels (Chapters 12–14, 18, 20–21; Appendices 5–8). The arguments for Matthew's *Logia* are essentially of the same kind as those for Proto-Luke: systematic dependence on specific Old Testament texts (Deuteronomy/Sirach); internal coherence; and effectiveness in accounting for other New Testament data.

Given these pre-gospels documents—especially Proto-Luke—the Q hypothesis becomes unnecessary. Most of the links between Matthew and Luke are explained, not by shared use of Q, but by direct interdependence—Matthew's use of Proto-Luke, and canonical Luke's use of Matthew. Further Matthew–Luke links are explained by Matthew's brief *Logia*.

The overall picture is of a central line of scriptural dependence running from the foundation of Old Testament narrative (Genesis–Kings) into the heart of the New Testament:

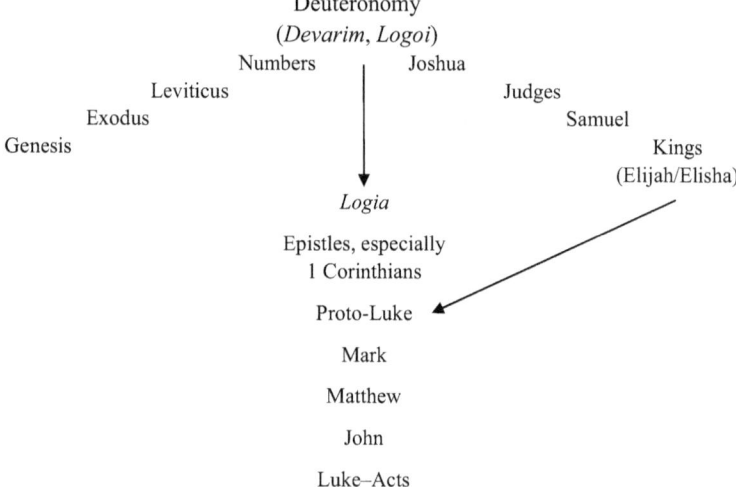

The full pattern of dependence is far more complex, and includes many diverse texts and influences, Greco-Roman and Jewish.

This outline of literary continuity may seem far from the ethos of early Christianity. The New Testament often gives an impression of rusticity and of oral tradition; and the leading New Testament figures, Jesus and Paul, are unique—hugely distinct from Old Testament leaders. Yet, while the New Testament is indeed saturated in orality—in the rhythms of oral speech—its picture of oral communication fits into the background of a wider Jewish claim, largely non-historical, concerning a whole world of oral tradition, tradition extending even back to Moses, and so New Testament suggestions of oral tradition cannot be taken at face value.

The primary advantage of the outline is that, as regards the gospels and Acts, it clarifies the issues of order and background—the order in which the gospels were written, and the indebtedness of the gospels to one another, to the epistles, and ultimately to the Old Testament.

A further advantage of this outline is that is contains no unknowns, at least in the sense that it does not appeal to any text which is out of sight. Proto-Luke and Matthew's *Logia* do not exist as separate documents, but they are known insofar as not a word of them has been lost, and they are based systematically on books that we still possess. Claims about them can be verified directly.

The greatest weakness in this outline is that it does not clarify the order and interrelationships of the epistles. The problem of the order of the epistles will not be resolved easily, but major progress can be made, particularly if the literary discussion can be separated from problems of history, especially from the problems of Pauline history and authorship. The purpose of such separation is not to neglect history but to serve it better in the long term.

2. *Historical and Theological Implications: Issues for a Future Discussion*

This volume is essentially a literary study, not directly concerned with history and theology. In principle, therefore, it would be appropriate at this point simply to conclude that there is no more to be said, at least not here not now.

However, if other researchers verify the preceding literary thesis, then issues of history and theology will inevitably arise and, even if a full discussion is not feasible at this point—a full discussion would require another volume—it seems appropriate to mention some of these historical and theological questions. The main points concern the quest for the historical Jesus, the quest for the historical Paul, and the history of Christian origins.

a. *The Quest for the Historical Jesus*

On this issue there are essentially three options: (1) carry on with the historical quest, perhaps in a modified form; (2) dismiss the figure of Jesus as an empty story, even a misleading lie; (3) rethink what the figure of Jesus means.

(1) *Carry on with the historical quest, perhaps in a modified form.* The historical quest for Jesus has proved itself extraordinarily resilient. Despite repeated failures and seriously divergent conclusions it keeps rolling forward in great periodic waves. The increasing evidence that the gospels are massively dependent on the older scriptures and on the epistles may cause some practitioners of the quest to let the matter lie, but others could say that the quest has adapted to earlier developments—such as form criticism—and that it can adapt to this also. The divergence of approach already exists in regard to the infancy narratives. Some historians see Matthew 1–2 and Luke 1–2 as so pervaded by older scriptures that it is impossible to distinguish what is historical; but others are undaunted and maintain that they can establish what happened.

(2) *Dismiss the figure of Jesus as an empty story, even a misleading lie.* Those who regard the infancy narratives as historically unreliable may now conclude that the same it true of the gospels as a whole, and on that basis may tend to discount the entire story of Jesus. In other words, the gospels, no matter how wonderful, may suddenly seem empty. And those who have long claimed that the story of Jesus is a fabrication, a lie, may see dependence on the Old Testament as providing them with fresh ammunition.

(3) *Rethink what the figure of Jesus means.* Another approach is to ask whether history is as important as it is generally claimed to be, whether the meaning of the figure of Jesus can be separated from a claim about a specific individual of the first century. Obviously, in some sense Christianity is radically historical, radically tied to a sense of God's presence in the daily events of life, but the meaning of this historicality, along with the meaning of the doctrine of the incarnation, is open to further clarification. The council of Chalcedon (451 CE), for instance, made a monumental effort to clarify the meaning of Christ, yet some theologians see its pronouncements not as the last word on Christ but as a basis for discussion. It is possible to re-envisage Christ so that he becomes once again the inspiring symbol of God?

b. *The Quest for the Historical Paul*

The task of writing a reliable biography of Paul has been overshadowed by the quest for the historical Jesus, yet it is central to the larger issue of historical research. In fact, insofar as the epistles were largely written before the gospels, the investigation of the epistles may prove to be the final testing ground in the quest for the historical Jesus. As for the quest for the life of Paul, there are again essentially three avenues of development: (1) carry on with the historical quest; (2) dismiss the portrait of Paul as a lie; (3) rethink the meaning of the portrait of Paul.

(1) *Carry on with the historical quest.* The heavy dependence of spontaneous-looking epistles on ancient scriptures may lead some scholars to wonder if it is possible to write a life of Paul. However, difficulties are not new for Pauline scholars. They have long contended with problems—for instance, with the inauthenticity of some epistles, with the apparent confusion in others, and with the tensions between the epistles and Acts. It may seem then that it is possible to continue the task of writing a biography of Paul, and the autobiographical form of some of the epistles may appear to make this task more feasible.

(2) *Dismiss the portrait of Paul as a lie.* For some historians and admirers of Paul, the dependence of the epistles on older texts may lead to disillusion, and perhaps to a great sense of loss. Others will regard it as confirmation that much of the New Testament picture of Christian origins is a fraud.

(3) *Rethink the meaning of the portrait of Paul.* Another avenue—even if Paul's biography seems elusive—is to ask whether the biblical portrait of Paul may be regarded like a piece of inspired art, something that depends for its validity not on how it occurred in history but on the inspiration that depicted it. Perhaps Paul, despite all his limitations, can become once again a symbol of groundedness in God, a beacon of authentic existence and loving freedom.

c. *The Larger Search for Christian Origins*

The scripture-based nature of many New Testament documents makes certain aspects of Christian origins more elusive, but it may also give impetus to fresh research. The following areas, for instance, seem to come into clearer focus: (1) the centrality of religious experience; (2) institutional continuity with aspects of Judaism; (3) the formation of the canon of writings.

(1) *The centrality of religious experience.* The rethinking of the historical dimension of Jesus and Paul may liberate another dimension of these great figures, namely their full religious significance, and the religious experience associated with their emergence. The Jesus of the New Testament is far more than some kind of wandering preacher or philosopher. Hidden behind the portrayals of him lies a powerful sense of a presence that transforms both creation and human life.

(2) *Institutional continuity with aspects of Judaism.* The scriptural continuity between Judaism and Christianity confirms the impression of a larger institutional continuity, and this in turn may cast light on other aspects of continuity. It is not clear, for instance, how priesthood emerged in Christianity, but part of the explanation may lie in the closeness of the New Testament to the old scriptures, particularly to the priest-related texts at the heart of the Pentateuch.

(3) *The formation of the canon of writings*. There is a puzzle about the Christian canon of scriptures—about how widely scattered writings were gathered into one collection. However, if the New Testament writings were inherently connected from the outset—with the older scriptures and with each other—then, like the assembling of a family, the process of bringing them together, or holding them together, becomes more understandable.

3. Conclusion

There is a challenge here for both historians and theologians. At times these two groups seem to stand back, waiting for one another. The theologians hesitate to advance in theology because they feel constrained by the scripture scholars' insistence on history. The scripture scholars hesitate on points of history because they feel constricted by theological doctrines. And as each group waits for the other to clear the way, there is little overall movement.

What is needed, if this literary thesis is verified by those with literary competence, is a strong dialogue of historians and theologians. The historians will have the problem of assessing the thesis' implications, and the theologians will be asked to discuss the conclusions of the historians. The theological assessment in turn can free the historians for further investigation, and thereby open the way to a yet more searching process.

> We shall not cease from exploration,
> And the end of all our exploring
> Will be to return where we started
> and know the place for the first time.
>
> —T.S. Eliot, *Four Quartets* ('Little Gidding')

Part III

The Overall Picture: Initial Evidence

Orientational Introduction to Chapters 27–54:
Proto-Luke's Systematic Dependence on the Septuagint—
Towards Elaborating the Argument

As indicated earlier, especially in the initial 'General Summary' and in Chapter 10, the primary argument for Proto-Luke (Argument 1) is the distinctive dependence of part of Luke–Acts on the Greek version of the Old Testament, the Septuagint. Logically this argument should be placed near at the beginning in this volume, but its details are so extensive that it seems better to give this argument a place of its own, and so it is now presented as Part III.

The testing and elaborating of this argument will require many years. All that can be given here are some initial data—various indications, outlines, and details. Yet, these data should be sufficient to assure the researcher that, even if the investigative journey is long, one may undertake it with confidence. There is something to be discovered.

Unit 6. Proto-Luke's Use of the Elijah–Elisha Narrative

27

The Introduction to the Elijah–Elisha Narrative (1 Kings 16.29–17.1) as One Positivized Component of the Introduction to Luke–Acts (Luke 1.5-17)

Luke's infancy narrative (Lk. 1.5–2.52) reflects the Old Testament both through a web of diverse allusions to the past, and through the systematic use of specific texts. Among the systematically used texts, three are outstanding: the beginning of the Elijah–Elisha narrative, the beginnings of the two longest judge narratives (concerning Gideon and Samson, Judg. 6–8 and 13–17), and the extended beginning of the books of Chronicles. All three kinds of Old Testament beginnings have been filtered and woven together to form the foundation of a new infancy narrative.

The present chapter concentrates on Luke's use of the beginning of the Elijah–Elisha narrative.[1] (The relationship to Judges and Chronicles will be seen later.)

The Elijah–Elisha narrative begins not only with the mention of Elijah (1 Kgs 17.1) but also with the dark foil of the sinfulness of Ahab and Jezebel, and of Hiel who rebuilt Jericho at the cost of his sons (16.29-34).[2] Luke has used the dramatic negativity of the Ahab–Jezebel introduction as a partial model for the dramatic goodness of his own introduction: the beginning of the angel's annunciation to Zechariah (1.5-25, especially 1.5-17). In particular, the sinfulness of Ahab and Jezebel is reversed in the faithfulness of Zechariah and Elizabeth. Wayward worship is mirrored in meticulous worship. What was negative in the Old Testament has been turned around to form a picture that is positive.

Luke's procedure is to be seen against the background of his larger strategies: his multifaceted imitation of the LXX, his use of the Elijah–Elisha narrative, his use of positivization (turning negative images to positive), and his orderly use of the entire first segment of the Elijah account (1 Kgs 16.29–17.24) (in Chapter 10, see 'A Closer Look').

The word 'component' is important. Within Luke's complex text—complex both in content and Old Testament dependence—the role of the Elijah–Elisha narrative is quite limited.

The following analysis follows the sixfold division in the outline (see Table 48).

1. *Section 1. In the Days of the King of Judea: A Clear-Cut Character and an Intimation of Contrast (1 Kings 16.29; Luke 1.5a)*

The texts begin by setting their respective scenes in the reign of a king of Judah:

Old Testament:
In the…reign of Jehoshaphat [king of Judah].[3] (16.29 LXX).

---

1. For the Elijah–Elisha narrative, this study uses the Cambridge edition of the LXX (Brooke *et al.* [eds.] 1930).
2. On 1 Kgs 16.29-34 as introductory, see Conroy 1996.
3. Some LXX manuscripts contain *basileōs Iouda* ('king of Judah'). The text-critical variations are complex, but they do not lessen the essential continuity between 1 Kgs 16.29–17.1 and Lk. 1.5-17.

New Testament:
In the days of Herod king of Judea... (Lk. 1.5)

Then an important character is introduced:

Old Testament:
...Ahab, son of Ambri [Omri] reigned over Israel in Samaria...

New Testament:
...there was a priest named Zechariah, of the division of Abijah...

Ahab will soon be associated with Baal and will emerge as a figure of evil and of false worship, the dark foil for much of the story of Elijah. Zechariah, however, will be seen as the very opposite—blameless and dedicated to true worship—and will help to prepare for the eventual emergence of John and Jesus.

Table 48. *Beginnings: Two Striking Couples (1 Kings 16.29–17.1; Luke 1.5-17)*

1 Kings 16.29–17.1	Luke 1.5-17
1. In the...year of Jehoshaphat [king of Judah], Ahab son of Ambri became king (16.29)	In the days of Herod king of Judea... was a priest, Zechariah of...Abijah,
	2. his wife was of the daughters of Aaron, and her name was El-i-za-beth (1.5)
3. He did evil before the Lord more than all before him...(16.30) He walked in the sins of Jeroboam, [16.33: intensification of v. 30]	Both were just before God walking in all the commandments and ordinances of the Lord, blameless (1.6)
2. he took as wife Ie-za-b-el daughter of Ie-thab-aal	
4. He served Baal and worshipped him. He set up an altar to Baal in the house of provocations in Samaria (16.31-32)	In his priesting...before God...(1.8) in the shrine of the Lord ...all the people praying (1.10) An angel stood at the altar (1.11)
	6. The angel said...He shall be great before the Lord...and shall go before him in the spirit and power of Elijah
5. In his days Hiel rebuilt Jericho at the cost of his sons (16.34)	to turn the hearts of fathers to their children (1.13-17)
6. Elijah said... 'As the Lord...of powers lives, before whom I stand, there shall not be...except by my word' (17.1)	

Within each text is an intimation of contrast: a contrast of Ahab with Jehoshaphat (later seen as essentially good; cf. 1 Kgs 22.7.29-51); and a contrast of Zechariah with Herod (later seen as evil, Lk. 23.6-11; cf. Acts 12.1-4, 18-23). But while the Old Testament lays the initial emphasis on the one who is evil and involved in false worship, Luke emphasizes the one who is blameless, practicing true worship.

What is important is that despite the stark difference between Ahab and Zechariah, both texts begin with characters who will highlight the issues of conduct and worship. Ahab will highlight these issues in a way that is negative; Zechariah in a way that is positive.

The phrase 'in the days of...' (Lk. 1.5) occurs when introducing Hiel (1 Kgs 16.34), a verse inherently connected with the introduction of Ahab (16.29) (Conroy 1996: 211). The phrase contributes to the verbal resonances:

> Old Testament:
> en...tō Iōsaphat basileuei/[basileōs Iouda]...Achaab...Ambri.
>
> 16.34:
> en tais hēmerais autou...
>
> New Testament:
> en tais hēmerais Hērōdou...
> basileōs tēs Ioudaias...Zacharias...Abia.

2. Section 2. The Woman: Wife and Daughter (Jezebel, 1 Kings 16.31b; Elizabeth, Luke 1.6)

Associated with the two men (Ahab; Zechariah) are their wives:

> Old Testament:
> He...took as wife Jezebel,
> daughter of Ethbaal, king of the Sidonians.
>
> New Testament:
> His wife was of the daughters of Aaron,
> and her name was Elizabeth.

The contrast is sharp and precise. Jezebel's father bears the name Baal; but Elizabeth's ultimate father is Aaron (Aaron's wife was called Elizabeth, Exod. 6.23). Jezebel is therefore rooted in the essence of false worship; but Elizabeth is descended from the essence of true worship, from the great high priest of Israel.

Verbal resonances:

> Old Testament:
> kai ouk ēn autō...
> kai elaben gunaika tēn Ie-za-b-el thugatera Ie-the-baal.
>
> New Testament:
> kai gunē autō ek tōn thugaterōn Aarōn
> kai to onoma autēs El-i-sa-beth.

Here—and in later texts—Luke's relationship to the Old Testament seems to involve word-play.

3. Section 3. Walking in Sin or Justice (1 Kings 16.30-31a, 33; Luke 1.6)

The Old Testament gives two pictures of Ahab's sinfulness, one *before* mentioning his wife (16.30-31a), the other *after* (16.33). These two pictures of sin are related; they have the same framing phrases ('and he did/made...'; '...more than all before him'), and they involve repetition and intensification. The sense of sin which was present before the marriage (v. 30) becomes worse afterwards. The implication: Jezebel helped to intensify his sin; in some way she was a partner in sin.

In Luke, partnership is not merely implied; it is explicit: Zechariah and Elizabeth were 'both just before God' (Lk. 1.6). This partnership is further clarified through a modification of the order: Luke has moved the female figure towards the beginning of the passage so that she and her husband are introduced together.

Again the reversal of the Old Testament is acute and precise. Instead of partners in sin and idolatry, Luke presents partners in justice and true worship. The Old Testament structure of repetition and intensification (16.30-31a, 33) is partly reflected in Luke's brief account of the devout couple (1.6): they are 'just', they follow all the 'commandments' and 'ordinances', and, climactically, they are described as 'blameless'. There are some verbal resonances:

> Old Testament:
> Ahab did evil before the Lord
> more than all...to walk in the sins...
>
> New Testament:
> They were...just before God
> walking in all the commandments and ordinances of the Lord...
>
> Old Testament:
> *epoiēsen...ponēron enōpion kuriou*
> *huper pantas...poreuesthai en tais hamartiais...*
>
> New Testament:
> *ēsan...dikaioi...enantion tou theou*
> *poreuomenoi en pasais tais entolais kai dikaiōmasin tou kuriou...*

At this point in formulating the way the couple did all that was right before God, Luke is combining aspects of 1 Kings 16 with aspects of 1 Chronicles 6 concerning the service of the Levites in the house of the Lord.

4. Section 4. Worship in the House of Baal or God
(1 Kings 16.31c-32; Luke 1.8, 10-11)

Then both narratives introduce three basic elements: worship, temple, and altar.

First, the worship. Ahab 'served' and 'worshipped' (*douleuō*, *proskuneō*) Baal (1 Kgs 16, 31c). Zechariah was 'priesting' (*hierateuō*) before God (Lk. 1.8). Luke's single verb, *hierateuō*, often translated 'serve as priest', manages to capture something of both Old Testament verbs: 'serve' and 'worship'.

Then, the temple and the altar. Ahab set up a Baalite altar in the temple (literally, 'house of provocations') which 'he built in Samaria' (1 Kgs 16.32). The Old Testament temple-and-altar picture is one of Samarian worship which is far from God—a house of provocations. Luke gives the precise opposite: a temple-and-altar picture which resonates true Jerusalem worship. The Jerusalem shrine is a house not of provocations (*prosochthismatōn*) but of people praying (*proseuchomenon*). It is attended even by God's angel; while Zechariah is in the temple (literally 'shrine'), an angel of the Lord stands by the altar (Lk. 1.9, 11).

Areas of verbal resonance:

> Old Testament:
> [*altar*] He set up an altar to Baal
> [*temple*] in the house of provocations...which he built in Samaria
>
> New Testament:
> [*temple*] ...into the shrine of the Lord...people praying...
> [*altar*] an angel of the Lord stood at the...altar
>
> Old Testament:
> *estēsen thusiastērion tō Baal*
> *en oikō tōn pros-ochthismatōn autou hon ōkodomēsen en Samaria.*

New Testament:
eis ton naon tou kuriou...pros-euchomenon...
aggelos kuriou estōs ek...tou thusiastēriou.

Luke's adjustment of the order—moving the altar to the end—allows the final emphasis to fall on the figure near the altar, namely on the angel, who now begins to speak.

5. Section 5. Fathers and Their Children (1 Kings 16.34; Luke 1.17b)

Built into the fabric of the Old Testament picture is the account of how Hiel of Bethel rebuilt Jericho at the cost of two sons: the firstborn and the youngest. An oath sworn before God had once effectively foretold that anyone rebuilding Jericho would lose his firstborn and youngest sons (Josh. 6.26), but Hiel went ahead regardless. Nothing is said of how precisely the two sons died, so the emphasis falls not on the details of their deaths but on the relation of the deaths to the ancient word of God ('according to the word of the Lord', 1 Kgs 16.34). So God's word is involved with a father bringing death on his sons.

Luke portrays the opposite: the angel foretells how the God-given spirit of Zechariah's son will 'turn the hearts of fathers to [their] children' (Lk. 1.17b). Contravening God's word meant a father brought death to his sons; but the God-given spirit has the opposite effect—it makes fathers attentive to their sons.

It is necessary here to distinguish between Luke's *raw material* and his *wording*. His wording ('turn the hearts of fathers…') is taken from a prophet (the Elijah-related prophecy of Mal. 3.23 [4.5 LXX]); but the underlying inspiration is the Hiel episode which immediately precedes the Elijah story. As will be seen later, Luke uses the same procedure elsewhere: in reshaping an Old Testament prose narrative, he sometimes expresses it through the words of poetry or prophecy.

6. Section 6. Great before the Lord:
The Power of Elijah (1 Kings 17.1; Luke 1.13-17)

The Old Testament account suddenly changes. The dark foil of the Ahab–Hiel introduction is left behind and the text erupts with the arrival of Elijah speaking God's word in a way that commands creation: water—the source of life—shall depend on Elijah's God-given word.

The New Testament has already been positive, so the sense of eruption is not as strong, yet the arrival of the angel does cause disturbance (Zechariah is disturbed and fearful, Lk. 1.12).

Then Elijah (Old Testament) and the angel (New Testament) begin to speak—the first spoken words in either the Elijah–Elisha narrative or Luke–Acts. In both cases the words are not uttered by God, yet they are divinely authoritative (spoken by Elijah in the Lord's name and by the angel of the Lord). Furthermore, the angel explicitly invokes Elijah: the future son 'shall…go before [the Lord] in the spirit and power of Elijah' (Lk. 1.15, 17). In effect, Elijah's pronouncement (17.1) provides part of the framework for the angel's elaborate announcement (1.13-17).

Some verbal echoes:

Old Testament:
kai eipen Ēliou
zē kurios ho theos tōn dunameōn...hō parestēn enōpion autou ei estai.

New Testament:
eipen...ho aggelos...
estai gar megas enōpion kuriou...enōpion autou en...dunamei Ēliou.

On a detail of order, these references to Elijah (1 Kgs 17.1; Lk. 1.17) are the first, respectively, in the books of Kings and in Luke–Acts. The continuity between their contexts—placed after descriptions of paradigmatic couples—is hardly an accident.

Unlike Elijah—whose words seem directed towards the outside world, especially towards the rainfall—the angel pays more attention to a world which is internal, towards a world of abstinence, spirit and heart (Lk. 1.15, 17). This shift—moving the emphasis towards what is internal—accords with Luke's larger strategy, found elsewhere, of internalization (or spiritualization).

7. *Summary and Conclusion*

The foregoing analysis is incomplete—an almost inevitable situation in dealing with any complex literary reworking—and Luke's dependence on 1 Kgs 16.29–17.1 is quite limited. The Ahab–Hiel introduction is only one component, and the negative energy of that component has been reversed.

Yet, however limited and reversed, the dependence on that text is certain; it is indicated by key features:

- *External plausibility*: Luke's literary imitation of the LXX, and Luke's special attention to the figures of Elijah and Elisha.
- *Persistent similarities*: from the opening words, setting the story in the reign of a king of Judea, to the final dramatic image of the power of Elijah, the two texts show a steady stream of similarities—including similarities of theme (especially concerning conduct and worship), action (plot), linguistic detail, and, to some degree, order.
- *Intelligibility of the differences*: the differences, great though they are, are not a meaningless muddle. They can largely be accounted for through specific strategies of transformation, strategies which are consistent in themselves and which Luke uses elsewhere. In particular, Luke has adapted the darkness of the Old Testament account to the requirements of his own more positive narrative.

The conclusion is simple. When Luke was modeling his two-part account along the broad lines of the Elijah–Elisha narrative, he started at the beginning. In building his complex opening scene, one of his components was the opening of the Elijah story. He took that component, adapted it to his own requirements, and integrated it with other material to form a new text which simultaneously fulfilled and surpassed the old.

Unit 7. Proto-Luke and Elijah–Elisha: The Prophets and the Women

Orientational Introduction to Chapters 28–32:
The Prophets and the Women*

The five passages of Lk. 7.1–8.3 show Jesus as a great prophet. These texts begin on a very high note—with the general, somewhat abstract idea of Jesus' all-commanding word ('Say but the word…')—and gradually they descend into the reality of Jesus' life and into his journeys along the road.
- First (7.1-10), the centurion's friends announce that Jesus' word controls life (v. 7).
- Then (7.11-17), as Jesus raises the widow's son, the people call him 'a great prophet' (v. 16).
- Next (7.18-35), in recognizing John as 'a prophet…more than a prophet', Jesus himself emerges implicitly as a more down to earth form of prophet (vv. 26, 33-34).
- Subsequently (7.36-50), as the woman anoints Jesus, the Pharisee who wonders 'if this man were a prophet' (v. 39) receives Jesus' low-key word in a way that implicitly answers his question.
- Finally (8.1-3), the brief picture of the traveling entourage shows Jesus as a prophetic preacher who descends into the thick of the action: he is going 'through cities and villages preaching and evangelizing' (8.1).

While portraying prophecy and prophets, this block (7.1–8.3) also highlights women: the widow; the woman who anoints; and the many women, including the wife of the king's steward, who, along with the twelve, accompany the preacher.

All five passages use the Elijah–Elisha narrative. The procedure is quite orderly. Having used the Chronicler to under gird Jesus' early life as far as the Nazareth speech (most of Lk. 1.1–4.22a) (see Chapter 53), and having used the introduction to Elijah (1 Kgs 16.29–17.1) to fill out his own introduction (Lk. 1.5-17) (see Chapter 27), the New Testament writer now proceeds to the next part of the Elijah account: the great drought (1 Kgs 17–18). In simplified terms the drought consists of three episodes:
1. Elijah's wondrous saving encounter with the doomed widow and son (1 Kgs 17.1-16).
2. Elijah's raising of the widow's son (1 Kgs 17.17-24).
3. The king's steward, and a twelve-based confronting of the prophets (1 Kgs 18).

Details aside for the moment, and allowing for adaptation, these three passages become important components in three parts of Lk. 7.1–8.3:
1. Saving of doomed widow and son > Saving centurion's doomed servant (7.1-10).
2. Raising of widow's son > Raising of widow's son (7.11-17).
3. King's steward, twelve, the prophets > Preaching, twelve, wife of king's steward (8.1–3).

---

* Of these five chapters, the four major ones—those dealing with Lk. 7—have already been published elsewhere as independent articles: Chapters 28 and 30 in *Irish Biblical Studies* (1992 and 1994 respectively), Chapter 29 in *New Testament Studies* (1986) and Chapter 31 in *Biblica* (1984). The articles have been revised slightly to suit the present context.

Luke's two other passages—John the prophet (Lk. 7.18-35) and the anointing woman (7.36-50)—use two later Old Testament passages, respectively the kings' search for a true prophet (1 Kgs 22) and the indebted women (2 Kgs 4.1-37). This gives a fuller picture. Italics denote dependence on the later Old Testament passages:
- Saving of the doomed (1 Kgs 17.1-16) > Saving a doomed servant (Lk. 7.1-10).
- Raising of the widow's son (1 Kgs 17.17-24) > Raising of the widow's son (Lk. 7.11-17).
- *Kings seek a true prophet (1 Kgs 22) > Are John and Jesus prophets? (Lk. 7.18-35).*
- *The indebted women (2 Kgs 4.1-37) > The sinful woman who anoints (Lk. 7.36-50).*
- Steward, twelve, prophets (1 Kgs 18) > Preaching, twelve, steward's wife (Lk. 8.1-3).

The later passages (1 Kgs 22 and 2 Kgs 4.1-37) break the orderly sequence. However, their use is not arbitrary. On the contrary, their connection with 1 Kings 17–18 is inherent. The contrast between true and false prophets, as seen in the kings' search for a true prophet (1 Kgs 22), develops a theme from 1 Kings 18. And the women of 2 Kings 4 are partly an elaborate variation on the widow of 1 Kings 17. Thus, Lk. 7.1–8.3 is founded on an orderly use of 1 Kings 17–18 and on the incorporation at its center of two related passages. The overall effect is a coherence of both theme and order.

While the five large passages thus follow an essentially orderly arrangement, smaller passages are rearranged to suit the requirements of the overall narrative. In particular, not all of 1 Kings 18 is used in the brief account of Jesus' preaching (Lk. 8.1-3). Part of the drama of resisting the false worship of Baals on Carmel (1 Kgs 18.20-40) is adapted to a much later picture: resisting the false worship of humans at Lycaonia (Acts 14.8-18).

It suited Luke's purposes to replace the account of a *mother and son* (1 Kgs 17.1-16) with that of a *centurion and servant*. The centurion–servant relationship places greater emphasis on ties that are internal rather than familial/ethnic; and the image of a centurion prepares for the later figure of Cornelius (Acts 10). (In Chapter 10, see 'A Closer Look'.)

Giving slightly more detail, the five passages may be outlined as follows:

1 Kings 17–18, 22; 2 Kings 4	*Luke 7.1–8.3*
[Evil couple; God's word in Elijah (1 Kgs 16.29–17.1)]	[Good couple; God's word…in the spirit of Elijah (1.5-57)]
The commanding word averts death for the widow and her child (1 Kgs 17.1-16)	The commanding word averts death for the centurion's servant (7.1-10)
Raising the widow's son (1 Kgs 17.17-24)	Raising the widow's son (7.11-17)
Kings seek a true prophet and Micaiah is vindicated (1 Kgs 22.1-38)	John the prophet seeks the one to come and prophecy is vindicated (7.18-35)
A woman and a creditor, and a woman's change of attitude (2 Kgs 4.1-37)	The woman who had been a sinner and the parable of the creditor (7.36-50)
Journeying; the steward; Israel's twelve; prophets clash on Baal worship (1 Kgs 18)	Journeying; twelve; steward's wife (8.1-3) (Acts 14.8-18, resisting false worship)

The next five chapters (28–32) examine the five episodes, in Lukan order, as follows:

Chapter 28: Not Q But Elijah: The Saving of the Centurion's Servant (Luke 7.1-10) as an Internalization of the Saving of the Widow and Her Child (1 Kings 17.1-16).

Chapter 29: The Raising of the Widow's Son (1 Kings 17.17-24; Luke 7.11-17).

Chapter 30: Again Not Q: Luke 7.18-35 as an Acts-Oriented Transformation of the Vindication of the Prophet Micaiah (1 Kings 22.1-38).
Chapter 31: Luke 7.36-50 as an Internalization of 2 Kings 4.1-37.
Chapter 32: A People Gathering Around the Prophet: Luke 8.1-3 as a Women-Oriented Distillation of Part of 1 Kings 18.

28

Not Q But Elijah: The Saving of the Centurion's Servant (Luke 7.1-10) as an Internalization of the Saving of the Widow and Her Child (1 Kings 17.1-16)

The account of the life-giving command which healed the centurion's servant (Lk. 7.1-10; Mt. 8.5-13; cf. Jn 4.43-54) is generally attributed to Q. In itself, this attribution is plausible, but on closer examination there is a further explanation which is less hypothetical and ultimately more credible: Luke's text involves a systematic synthesizing and christianizing of the account of the life-giving commands which were issued to and through Elijah and which warded off the threat of death (1 Kgs 17.1-16). Thus, the threat which once faced a widow and her children—the Greek is plural, 'children'—has been adapted to help form the account of the threat which faced the centurion and his servant.

Of the many adaptations wrought by Luke, two are pivotal: the figure of the widow has been replaced by that of the centurion (a move which, among other things, accords with the requirements of Luke's own narrative). And, most basic of all, the Old Testament drama has been internalized. In other words, Luke has rewritten the action so that there is a far greater sense of what is happening *within* people. In particular, the Old Testament picture of a relationship which is based on what is physical (mother and child) has been replaced by a relationship (centurion/master and slave) which depends for its quality not on what is physical but on factors which are internal—particularly on genuine appreciation and *agapē*.

Several elements in Luke's narrative cannot be accounted for through 1 Kgs 17.1-16; the Old Testament text is just one component, and Luke is also using materials which are specifically Christian. But Luke's use of that one component provides a major clue to the composition of his text.

1. *Introductory Analysis*

The Old Testament text (1 Kgs 17.1-16) occurs at the very beginning of the Elijah–Elisha narrative and it consists of two scenes. First, there is a brief account of how God's commanding word controlled all the forces of life and death (controlled the sending of Elijah ['Go... And he did so'] and controlled even the ravens so that they sustained Elijah's life, 17.1-7). Second, there is a longer description of how God's commanding word not only sustained Elijah but also averted the imminent death of a widow and her children (17.8-16). Of these two scenes, the first concerning the all-commanding word, is introductory, that is, illustrative or exemplary. The emphasis falls on the second, longer, story concerning the threatened widow and her children (see Table 49).

The New Testament text (Lk. 7.1-10) occurs at the beginning of one of Luke's distinctive chapters (ch. 7)—the chapter which 'is thematically so closely related to the [inaugural] Nazareth pericope' (Johnson 1977: 96). Thus, it has a certain leading role. And it tells how the word of Jesus turned away the imminent death of the centurion's servant. Contained within the New Testament account is a very brief scene which is both subsidiary and exemplary—that of the commanding process within the army (Lk. 7.7b, 8).

Table 49. *The Commanding Healing Word (1 Kings 17.1-16; Luke 7.1-10)*

1 Kings 17.1-16	Luke 7.1-10
1. *Exemplary/Subsidiary Scene* In nature: God's word commands all of life, and *sends* Elijah forth (17.1-7).	
2. The word comes to Elijah, and *sends* him to Sarepta (17.8-9a)	When he had completed his words… he went to Capernaum (7.1)
3. The foreign widow will care for Israel's prophet (17.9b) [She and children, about to die (17.12)]	The foreign officer whose servant is about to die, loves the Jewish people (7.2, 5)
4. Meeting the widow at the gate. (17.10a)	[Meeting a widow at a gate (7.11-12)]
5. Requests for sustenance: (17.10b-11, 13): * Elijah *calls* the widow for water; * Elijah *calls* the widow for bread; (pause, 17.12) * Elijah asks the widow for cake; the prophet's word commands many *goings, comings, doings*.	Requests for life (7.3-4, 6a): * The officer *sends* the elders * The elders ask Jesus to go (pause, 7.5) * The officer *sends* friends
6. [The widow recalls her sins (17.18)]	The officer's unworthiness (7.6b-7) *Exemplary/Subsidiary Scene:* In the army: the word commands life completely: '*Go… Come… Do…*' (17.8; cf. 7.7b)
7. Solemn pronouncement [about God]: the Lord's word assures life (17.14)	Solemn pronouncement [about response to God]: see this faith (7.9)
8. The prophetic word fulfilled: the food lasts and so the widow and her children live (17.15-16)	Jesus' word fulfilled: they find the servant well (7.10)

The essence of both accounts is that the Lord's word has complete command over life and death. Even when death is imminent, the commanding word can turn it away.

But Luke has made several adaptations. First, concerning the characters. Unlike the Old Testament, where there is a clear distinction between the Lord and the prophet, Jesus combines roles; in Luke 7 he is both Lord and prophet (7.6, 16, 29). Luke has thereby christianized the text; he has allowed the developing Christology of the New Testament era, including his own Christology, to shape his reworking of the older story.

The character of the foreign widow has also been changed, giving way to that of the foreign officer, the centurion. The larger reality which governs this change is not so much that of Christology as the requirements of Luke's own narrative, specifically Luke's emphasis on widows and officers as seen especially in the later figures of Tabitha and Cornelius (Acts 9.36–ch. 10; Tabitha is associated with several widows, and Cornelius was a centurion).[1]

1. In fact, as indicated by A. Finkel (in conversation, New Orleans, 19 November 1990) there is a sense in which Luke's entire gospel is framed by references to widows/women and soldiers: Anna and 'some soldiers' near the beginning (in 2.36; 3.14), and, near the end, the women of Jerusalem and the centurion (23.27-29, 47). The full reasons why Luke establishes this widow–officer pattern may be complex, but apart from possible historical, sociological, and theological reasons, the Old Testament provides a literary reason: the Elijah–Elisha narrative is set largely between two balancing patterns of command-and-compliance: the initial commands to the elements of creation, 1 Kgs 17; and the climactic commands, during the reign of Athaliah, for taking over the temple, 2 Kgs 11.4-16. These two patterns are focused largely

Luke's next adaptation in the characters—from child(ren) to servant (*doulos*, New Testament)—is basic to his entire procedure. As already partly indicated, it is one of the primary elements in a larger process of internalization which moves the focus away from what is external and physical (including physical relationships, even of parent and child) to the internal. The Old Testament relationship is physical, based on parenthood; the New Testament relationship, however, is based on something more internal, on the fact that, to the centurion, the servant is *entimos* ('dear', or 'highly valued')—a word which in the context, particularly the context of the centurion's love (verb, *agapaō*) for the Jews (7.5), indicates a bond that, in some way at least, is spiritual or internal.

Incidentally, this change from child(ren) to servant would seem connected to variations among the gospels. In the Hebrew original there is only one child, a son, and in Luke the servant is referred to at one point (7.7) as a boy, *pais*, meaning either 'servant' or 'child'—a form which may be read as essentially the same as the Hebrew. Matthew highlights the word *pais*, using it three times (8.5, 8, 13), and he omits *doulos* altogether. John is clearer still: though he uses *pais* once (4.51), he surrounds it with words (*paidion*, '[small] child', 4.49; *huios*, 'son', 4.46, 47, 49, 53) which unambiguously indicate that the *pais* is indeed a son.

The process of internalization which is applied to the parent–child relationship is also applied also to other aspects of the Old Testament story. Luke has so rewritten the text that one gets a far better sense of what is going on within the various characters.

As well as adapting the characters and employing internalization, Luke has also used other procedures, particularly that of fusion or conflation. One instance of fusion was already noted: the fact that, within Luke 7, Jesus is both Lord and prophet. A further instance is his integration of the introductory illustrative scene concerning the all-controlling word (1 Kgs 17.1-7) into the main story. In Luke's version the illustrative scene alludes to the army (7.7b, 8), but, while it has essentially the same illustrative function as the introductory scene in the Elijah story, it has become an inherent part of the larger story.[2]

The fact that Luke's illustrative scene is drawn from the army (rather than the sending of Elijah and the ravens, etc.) may be explained in part by the requirements of his narrative —by the inclusion, at the beginning of his account, of an army officer. More on this later.

A further aspect of Luke's procedure is his striving for vivid communication. This encompasses a number of techniques, including the effort to compose a text which is concise, clear, and explicit. He pursues this aim of vividness elsewhere—for example, in rewriting the account of the raising of the widow's son (7.11-17; cf. 1 Kgs 17.17-24)—and essentially the same procedure may be found, for instance, in the historical writings of Livy (P.G. Walsh 1961: 190).

2. *More Detailed Analysis*

The outline (Table 49) sometimes simplifies the relationship between the texts, and it does so particularly in section 5, but it provides an initial guide. The following analysis looks more closely at the eight sections of Table 49, taking them one at a time.

on a widow (1 Kgs 17) and on officers (commanders of hundreds, 2 Kgs 11.4-16). Thus, just as Proto-Luke brings the complementary stories of women (in 1 Kgs 17 and 2 Kgs 4) together in ch. 7, so, in the figures of the centurion and widow (the two opening miracles, Lk. 7.1-10 and 7.11-17), he brings together aspects of the further complementarity between the widow and the commanders (1 Kgs 17 and 2 Kgs 11).

2. A similar procedure of fusion will be seen in Proto-Luke's rewriting of the two distinct stories in 2 Kgs 4.1-37. He fuses the two accounts into one(radically synthesizing the first introductory narrative so that it falls within the larger pattern of the second (Lk. 7.36-50). The initial story concerning indebtedness (2 Kgs 4.1-7) has been absorbed into the larger story concerning finding new life (4.8-37) (see Chapter 31).

Generally, Luke stays close to the order and content of the main Old Testament story (17.1-6), but two small sections have been criss-crossed with the following stories: the meeting with the widow at the gate (1 Kgs 17.10a) has been used in the New Testament story of raising the widow's son (at Nain, Lk. 7.11-12); and part of the Old Testament story about raising the widow's son—the reference to the widow's sinfulness (1 Kgs 17.18)—has been used in describing the centurion's unworthiness, 7.6b-7).

a. *Section 1. The Commanding Word: The Lord's Word Commands Life Completely (Two Subsidiary, Illustrative Scenes, 1 Kings 17.1-7; Luke 7.8; cf. Luke 7.7b)*
While the larger texts (1 Kgs 17.1-16; Lk. 7.1-10) are primarily concerned with the encounter between the prophet and the foreigner who is threatened by death, both contain a subsidiary scene which is quite distinct: one about an obedience which involves even the ravens (at God's command the ravens feed Elijah), and the other about the obedience which operates in the army (Lk. 7.8). The essential point of both these distinctive scenes is graphically to illustrate the idea of obedience. But, as indicated earlier, while Luke maintains the central idea of the older text he adapts it to the requirements of his own narrative, in this case the requirements posed by the figure of an army officer. Thus, the scene with the ravens gives way to an army scene.

But there is a further reason why the image of the army is so suitable. As J.T. Walsh (1982: 22) has indicated, one of the pervasive structures of the Old Testament text (1 Kgs 17.1-16) is that of 'command and compliance', and within day-to-day human experience, one could scarcely find a better illustration of the dynamic of command and compliance than in the picture of a master or centurion giving orders. Three times (in vv. 2-6, 9-10a, and 13-16) the Old Testament passage uses a 'structure wherein a command or the like is given with a description of its execution following in similar words' (Walsh 1982: 21). In compact form, that is exactly what one finds in Luke. Three times there is an account of a command, and each time the execution repeats the essential word of the command: '"Go", and he goes... "Come", and he comes... "Do this", and he does it'. In other words, Luke has taken the essence of the opening, illustrative, episode—its command–compliance element—and, while synthesizing it with subsequent instances of command and compliance, has integrated it into the flow of his narrative.

In formulating this brief scene, Luke has maintained several verbal echoes of the older text, both of the opening scene with the ravens and also of the larger Old Testament picture of various goings, and comings and doings:

Old Testament:
Go...And he did (1 Kgs 17.3, 5)
...go...and he went (17.8, 10)
...go in and do according to your word, but do/make me (17.13)
And [she]...went and she did (17.15)

New Testament:
...should come/go to me; but say the word... (Lk. 7.7b)
Go and he goes...
Come and he comes...
Do this and he does it (7.8)

Old Testament:
poreuou...kai epoiēsen (1 Kgs 17.3, 5)
poreuou...kai eporeuthē (17.8, 10)
eiselthe kai poiēson kata to rēma sou, alla poiēson emoi (17.13)
kai eporeuthe...kai epoēsen (17.15)

New Testament:
...*se elthein, alla eipe logō* (Lk. 7.7b)
poreuthēti kai poreuetai
erchou kai erchetai
poiēson kai poiei (7.8)

Some of the similarities suggest an element of word-play, but the essence of the similarity indicates a straightforward process of vivid summary adaptation.

b. *Section 2. From the Word(s) to the Foreign/Border City (1 Kings 17.8-9a; Luke 7.1)*
In both texts, the main stories begin by speaking of the word(s), *rēma(ta)*, and of a move to a town which is in some way foreign—the foreign city of Sarepta, and the border town of Capernaum. In the Old Testament the word of the Lord is the cause of Elijah's going, whereas with Jesus the speaking of the words appears to be more the occasion of his going. (Since Jesus himself is the Lord, his relationship to the word is necessarily different from that of Elijah. The words are described as '*his* words'.)

c. *Section 3. The Threatened Foreigner (Widow/Officer) Who Cares for Israel (For Israel's Prophet, 1 Kings 17.9b, 12; For the Jewish People, Luke 7.2, 5)*
As indicated in the introductory analysis, the replacement of a foreign widow by a foreign officer brings Lk. 7.1-17 into line with Luke's broader pattern of widow–officer complementarity (cf. Acts 9.36–ch. 10).

The Old Testament image of nourishing the Israelite prophet gives way to that of loving the Jewish nation and building a synagogue—an adaptation which in its explicitness ('loving') and vividness (building a synagogue) corresponds to the way Luke adapts other texts. The emphasis on loving (*agapaō*), insofar as it spells out what is happening within the centurion, also adds an important element of internalization.

Even though the centurion himself is not threatened by death (as the widow is), neither is he free from the death threat. What Luke has done is shift the focus somewhat from the *physical* death which threatens the child(ren)/servant to the *inner impact* which the situation is having on the centurion. He may not be in danger himself, and the threatened person may not be his child, yet to him that person is highly valued, and therefore he is effected, but interiorly.

d. *Section 4. Meeting the Widow at the Gate (1 Kings 17.10a; Luke 11–12)*
Luke has adapted the meeting to suit the situation of the widow at Nain, and to include the presence of many onlookers, yet he has stayed close to the Old Testament text:

And...he went to Sarepta,	And...he went to a city called Nain...
to a gate of the city,	As he neared the gate of the city,
and behold there a widow woman.	behold...the son...and she was a widow.
Kai eporeuthē eis Sarepta,	*Kai...eporeuthē eis polin kaloumenēn Nain...*
eis ton pylō tēs poleōs,	*hōs de ēggisen tē pyle tēs poleōs,*
kai idou ekei gynē chēra.	*kai idou...huios...kai autē chēra.*

e. *Section 5. Sending People to Bring Sustenance/Life (1 Kings 17.10b-11, 13; Luke 7.3-4, 6a; cf. 1 Kings 17.2, 9)*
Three times Elijah asks the widow for sustenance, twice in a rather commanding way (he shouts after her, 17.10b-11) and once in an insistent plea (17.13). And three times Luke portrays a process of asking for life: twice by sending people (the centurion first sends elders and then friends, 7.3, 6a) and once by pleading strongly (the elders press Jesus to go, 7.4).

Luke's rewriting involves several changes, among them explicitly pronouncing the sendings in a form that is explicit, and placing the sendings so that they balance one another (in first and third place, rather than first and second as in the Old Testament).[3]

In depicting a double sending, Luke apparently depends not only on Elijah's double cry or call to the woman (17.10, 11), but also on God's double sending of Elijah ('Go from here… Go to…', 17.3, 8). Thus, he has fused together, in explicit form, elements which are scattered and less clear in the Old Testament:

> 1 Kings 17:
> 'Go from here…[to receive the sustenance of life]'.
> 'Go to…[receive the sustenance of life]'.
> 'He called to her…[for the sustenance of life]'.
> 'He called to her [again…for the sustenance of life]'.
>
> Luke 7:
> 'He sent elders…[to request the saving of life]'.
> 'He sent friends…[to adapt the request for life]'.

Here Luke's procedure is akin to the procedure he will employ when reworking the actions of the woman of Shunem (2 Kgs 4.8-37): the varied actions of the woman and her child are synthesized into into a more compact action by the sinful woman (Lk. 7.38) (see Chapter 31). The present case is not as strong linguistically, but it seems to accord with Luke's practice.

Unlike the Elijah story, where the various implicit sendings originate either with God or the prophet, Luke shows the sendings as coming from the centurion, a move which, like so many others, places a greater focus on what is happening *within* ordinary people, particularly within the centurion. Unlike the encounter between Elijah and the widow, where it is extremely difficult to sense the inner and interpersonal dynamics, Luke's interactions are more explicit: the centurion has a high regard for the Jews, for the elders, and for Jesus and the servant; the elders have a high regard for the centurion and they trust Jesus; and the centurion sends 'friends'—a word which highlights a world of the inner and interpersonal.

f. *Section 6. The Foreigner Recalls Sinfulness (1 Kings 17.18; Luke 7.6b-7)*
In the subsequent story, when the widow addresses the prophet who has come to her, she speaks of her sinfulness. And as Jesus is coming to the centurion, he speaks of his unworthiness:

She said to Elijah,	…saying to him,
'What have you with me,	'Lord,
man of God?	do not trouble yourself;
Have you come in to me	for I am not worthy
to recall my sins	that you come in under my roof;
and to kill my son?'	…and my boy shall be healed'.

Luke's rewriting involves several adaptations. The obscure 'What have you with me?' (*Ti emoi kai soi;*) has been replaced by something simpler, 'Do not trouble yourself [with me]'. 'Man of God' has given way to 'Lord', a title which intensifies the idea of the connection with God. The reference to the roof adds a touch of vividness. And in place of the Old Testament references to sin and death, Luke gives a rendering which, as so often in his gospel, lays the emphasis on the positive—on healing.

---

3. A similar balance between first and third occurs, for instance, in Lk. 9.57-62—between 'I will follow you…' in 9.57 and 9.61.

g. *Section 7. The Solemn Pronouncements about the Lord's Life-Giving Word (1 Kings 17.14), and About the Response of Faith to that Word (Luke 7.9)*
Elijah pronounces the word of the Lord as a *promise* to give the sustenance of life. Jesus also makes a pronouncement about the *faith* of the centurion in the granting of life. Apparently what Luke has done, rather than reproduce the *promise*, is to show the other side of the coin, the response of *faith*. Thus, once again as in the case of the sending, he has shifted the emphasis from the *action* of God to the corresponding reality *within* the centurion as part of a larger strategy of developing the older text, and particularly of portraying what is happening within people, in this case, the working of an extraordinary faith.

h. *Section 8. The Word is Fulfilled, thus bringing Continued Life (1 Kings 17.15-16; Luke 7.10)*
In the Old Testament, the sustenance of life is maintained—thus enabling the widow and her children to eat and presumably to stay alive. And in Luke, those who return to the house find that the servant is healthy. Despite its brevity, Luke's text manages, as often, to be more vivid (the house) and explicit (healthy).

3. *Conclusion*

In the preceding analysis, some of the links between the texts are obvious and strong; others are weak and more debatable. As already indicated in Chapter 5 on criteria, when assessing such evidence, it is important not to insist on what is weak. Insistence on what is weak, whether by the person presenting the evidence or by someone who is questioning it, obscures the main issue: Is there evidence which is strong—strong enough to indicate that Luke reworked 1 Kgs 17.1-16?

It appears that there is. The following factors are particularly important:
- *The broad context of Jewish and Hellenistic rewriting.* To say that Luke's text is dependent on a text which is older is not to claim something unique. Rather, it is to place Luke within the literary world of his day where the interconnectedness of texts was a commonplace.
- *The immediate context of Luke's use of the LXX.* Luke's kinship with the LXX is not a matter of dispute. This was the version of Scripture he used most, and in seeking to understand and portray how Jesus fulfilled that Scripture, Luke drew on it deeply.
- *Luke's unique affinity with the Elijah–Elisha narrative.* Luke's affinity with the Elijah–Elisha narrative in the inaugural Nazareth speech, and in the overall plan of Luke–Acts is such that there is nothing surprising in the basic idea that Lk. 7.1-10 reworks 1 Kgs 17.1-16. The likelihood of a connection between these specific texts is heightened by the fact that in varying degrees, both are leading texts. Luke 7.1-10 inaugurates a leading Lukan block, and 1 Kgs 17.1-16 inaugurates the Elijah-related drought.
- *The persistence of similarities.* In every section and at diverse levels—theme, order, details—there are persistent similarities which go well beyond the range of coincidence.
- *The understandability of the differences.* The differences are such that even though they are great, they are not a confused jumble. Rather, they show a certain coherence, and as such, they can be understood within the context of imitative rewriting, particularly within the context of some of Luke's most basic processes of adapting other texts: modernization, christianization, clarification (including vividness and explicitness), fusion, adaptation to the broader requirements of his own narrative, and, above all, internalization.

In a sense, the conclusion is simple: Luke, an acknowledged *littérateur*, employed a literary method. Furthermore, it is no longer possible, without further ado, to attribute Lk. 7.1-10 to Q. It is not reasonable to invoke an unknown document and at the same time to bypass a source which, on the basis of multiple evidence, was known to Luke and was imitated by him.

29

The Raising of the Widow's Son
(1 Kings 17.17-24; Luke 7.11-17)

Having recounted incidents about the power of the word to save those who seem doomed to die (1 Kgs 17.1-16; Lk. 7.1-10) both texts immediately go on to speak of the raising of a widow's son (1 Kgs 17.17-24; Lk. 7.11-17).

1. *Introductory Analysis*

Before looking at the texts in detail, it is useful to lay them out in summary outline (Table 50).[1] As the Table shows, each account has an element for which the other has no equivalent. Unlike the New Testament text, the Old Testament account of the raising of the son (1 Kgs 17.17-24) does not tell of meeting the widowed mother at the city gate; and unlike the Old Testament text, the New Testament does not depict the widow as professing her sinfulness or unworthiness. But, as some scholars have noted,[2] these elements do find an equivalent in the preceding episodes (1 Kgs 17.1-16; Lk. 7.1-10), in the encounter with the widow at the gate of Sarepta, and in the centurion's profession of unworthiness.

Table 50. *The Widow's Son (1 Kings 17.17-24; Luke 7.11-17)*

	1 Kings 17.17-24	Luke 7.11-17
	The Widow's Son: A Summary Outline	
1.	'It happened after this…' (17.17a)	'It happened afterwards…' (7.11a)
	[v. 10: At the gate of Sarepta, Elijah met a widow]	At the gate of Nain, Jesus meets…a widow (7.11b, 12a, c)
	The son of the widow died (17.17b)	The widow's son was dead (7.12b)
2.	The widow's sense of her sinfulness (17.18)	[7.6: The centurion professes unworthiness]
3.	Elijah carries the boy upstairs, sadly asks the Lord if he cares and breathes into the boy (17.19-21a)	The Lord felt compassion and touched the bier, and the bearers stood still (7.13-14a)
	Elijah prays to the Lord for the return of the soul of the child (17.21b)	The Lord commands the boy to rise (7.14b)
4.	And it was so and the child cried out (17.22)	'And the dead person sat up and began to talk' (7.15a)
	And he led him down 'and gave him to his mother' (17.23)	'And he gave him to his mother' (7.15b)
5.	The woman acknowledges the man of God and the word in his mouth (17.24)	All the people recognize that a great prophet of God has come, and this word went forth (7.16-17)

1. For a table of the Greek texts in full see Brodie 1986a: 252-53
2. On the meeting at the gate, see Gils 1957: 26; Schürmann 1969: 399. On the sentiments of sinfulness and unworthiness, see Dabeck 1942: 183.

In the outlined texts, there are three Lukan phrases for which the Old Testament text offers virtually no base: the two introductory balancing phrases which tell of the two crowds—the crowd with Jesus (7.11b) and the crowd with the woman (7.12b)—and the concluding phrase which tells of the *logos* going forth to two geographic designations: 'the whole of Judea' and 'all the surrounding territory' (7.17). Taken together, these phrases constitute Luke's 'landscape', the human and geographic setting of his narrative.[3]

2. *More Detailed Analysis*

This analysis concentrates on Lukan elements not already dealt with. These elements involve a systematic adaptation of the Old Testament text:

a. *Section 1. The Setting (1 Kings 17.17; Luke 7.11-12)*
The opening phrase, *en tō hexēs* ('soon afterwards'), is little more than a rewording of *meta tauta* ('after these things').

The meeting at the gate of Nain is closely modeled on the meeting at the gate of Sarepta.

b. *Section 2. The Sinfulness/Unworthiness (1 Kings 17.18; Luke 7.6b, 7b)*
Between these two texts—the widow's admission of sinfulness (1 Kgs 17.18) and the centurion's sense of unworthiness (Lk. 7.6b, 7b)—there is a relationship both of continuity and of change. The continuity is seen in the fact that for each Old Testament phrase, there is a corresponding New Testament phrase: the woman's unease at being involved with the man of God ('What is there to me and to you, man of God')[4] is balanced by the centurion's unease at the idea of involvement with Jesus ('*Kyrie*, do not bother...'); both would prefer some distance between themselves and the prophet. The idea of entering the woman's house (*eisēlthes pros me*, 'Have you come in to me...') is matched by the centurion's reluctance that Jesus should enter under his roof (*hina...mou eiselthes*, 'that you should come in...my...'). And where the woman is sensitive to the consequences of her sinfulness, *adikia*, the centurion is sensitive to the consequences of his unworthiness. Finally, while the woman presupposes that Elijah has the power of life and death over her son ('to kill my son'), the centurion presupposes that Jesus can prevent the death of his servant. Thus, between the texts, there is a precise continuity.

But there is also a fundamental change. Whereas in the Old Testament text the sense of sinfulness leads to a kind of despair, to an idea that (the man of) God is a bothersome visitor who comes to punish with death, in the New Testament text the sense of unworthiness is combined with a profound faith—with an immense reverence for the *kyrios*,[5] a

---

3. It seems noteworthy that some commentators see 'Judea' to mean the land of the Jews (as it does in 1.5; 4.44; 6.17; 23.5; Acts 2.9; 10.37), and the *perichōros*, 'surrounding territory', as a subtle suggestion of the territory beyond the Jews—in other words, as an allusion to the coming Gentile mission (see especially Schürmann 1969: n. 12, 404; note also Grunmann 1961: 161). In the same vein, one might ask if there is not also a subtle suggestion of the differentiation and union of Gentiles and Jews in the balancing references to the *ochlos polys* and the *ochlos tēs poleōs*, the 'great crowd' and the 'crowd of the city'. Such a differentiation and union are already suggested by the preceding episode in which the Jews and centurion are one in friendship and faith. In any case, the references to crowds and territories constitute Luke's landscape.

4. On *ti emoi kai soi* as a 'refusal of...involvement', see Brown 1966: 99.

5. The centurion's mode of addressing Jesus, *Kyrie* ('Sir' or 'Lord'), could, if taken in isolation, be translated simply as 'Sir'. But in the context of a story of surpassing faith, and in the context of Luke's general use of *Kyrios* as meaning 'Lord' (cf. Lk. 5.12, 17; 7.13, 19; 9.54, 61 etc.)—and it is context, above

reverence so great that one hesitates to bother him or contain him under one's roof, but also with a clear conviction that despite one's unworthiness the *kyrios* comes to heal, to save from the encroachment of death. In other words, the Old Testament picture of God visiting the sin of a mother on her child is replaced by the New Testament image of the life-giving *kyrios* as looking not on one's unworthiness but on one's faith. Of course, the Old Testament text itself, to some degree at least, goes on to correct the idea that (the man of) God has come to punish the woman's sin; after all, Elijah does revive the boy. But Luke shuns the very idea of an apparently vindictive God, and instead shows positively that the *kyrios* comes to heal. Thus, while the ultimate meaning of the two texts may not be very far apart, Luke's version is simpler; it is more positive and more explicit.

c. *Section 3. The Compassion and the Call for New Life (1 Kings 17.19-21; Luke 7.13-14)*
Also more explicit is Luke's notion of compassion. Whereas Elijah cries out in a way that *implies* compassion for the woman ('Alas', 1 Kgs 17.20), Luke uses the word itself, *esplagchnisthē* ('he felt compassion', 7.13). Here, too, is a delicate blend of continuity and change.

First of all, in both texts there is the idea that the Lord is aware of the woman's plight. In the Old Testament, Elijah cries out to the Lord whom he addresses as 'the witness of the widow' (1 Kgs 17.20a); in the New Testament, Luke gives the same idea ('And the Lord seeing her...'), but Luke's text has more brevity and immediacy. His image of the Lord as witness is more simple and vivid.

The second element in both texts, compassion, has already been mentioned. Elijah's gut sympathy for the woman is sensed not only in his general cry of lament, but especially in the fact that he has been in close physical proximity with her, dwelling with her in her house (1 Kgs 17.20b); Luke cuts through all the complications about living arrangements and gets to the core of the communication between the prophet and the woman with little more than the single word *esplagchnisthē*—a brief but explicit reference to compassion or gut sympathy. Again, therefore, Luke has distilled and explicitated the Old Testament text.

The third element in both texts involves a precise contrast. Whereas the Old Testament suggests, through Elijah's cry, that the Lord is the author of evil, the one who brings harm to the widow (1 Kgs 17.20c), the New Testament gives a clear and simple corrective: the Lord is the one who says, 'Do not cry'. Thus, as the earlier Old Testament suggestion that the Lord is vindictive was replaced by an image of the Lord as the one who heals (1 Kgs 17.18d; Lk. 7.7), now the suggestion that the Lord is harmful is replaced by an image of the Lord as the one who removes tears. Hence, in comparison both with the woman's address to the prophet (1 Kgs 17.18) and the prophet's cry to the Lord (1 Kgs 17.20), Luke's text shows a precise pattern of continuity, clarification, and correction, or at least correction of possible misunderstanding.

Returning now to Lk. 7.12b and resuming the flow of Luke's text, we find that the single word *tethnēkōs*, 'having died' or 'dead' (7.12b), is a fairly straightforward abbreviation of the Old Testament account of how the son grew sick so that eventually there was no spirit left in him (1 Kgs 17.17b). There is a similar abbreviation for the return to life: Luke's single word *egerthēti*, 'rise up', or 'be raised up'[6] (7.14), replaces the more

---

all, which gives meaning—such a translation, though partially valid, is ultimately quite inadequate. Contrast, for instance, NEB with RSV.

6. The word *egerthēti*, aorist imperative passive of *egeirō* may mean 'Get up', 'Rise up', or 'Be raised up', and, if taken in isolation, may be translated simply as 'Get up', a phrase used more of getting out of bed than of rising from the dead. But in the context of a narrative which tells of someone who is 'dead' being brought to life by 'the Lord' (cf. Lk. 7.12, 13, 15), and in the larger context of Luke's use of the passive of *egeirō* to refer to the raising of the dead (cf. 7.22; 9.7, 22; 20.37; 24.6, 34), such a translation is

complex expression about the soul (*psychē*) returning to the son (1 Kgs 17.21). Thus, the rather complex and anthropologically analytical ideas and expressions of the Old Testament are replaced by the simple but stark phraseology of death and resurrection.

In a somewhat similar way, the Old Testament description of carrying and laying out the dead son (1 Kgs 17.19) is abbreviated and transformed into phraseology that is simple and powerful. In the Old Testament, the apparently lifeless son is brought up and laid on a bed. In the New Testament, the son is being carried, already laid out, on a bier. In other words, through the single image of carrying the bier—as through the single words *tethnēkōs* and *egerthēti*—Luke manages to simplify and sharpen the focus of the narrative, to give an increased emphasis to the stark idea of death.

The details of this sharpening action are quite complex. The Old Testament describes two movements. First, there is the movement of bringing up the son and laying him out on a bed. An action such as laying someone out might, from one point of view, be seen as a stage on the road to burial. (It is difficult to say if there is any significance in the fact that *klinē*, 'bed', was also used for 'bier'.[7]) In any case, the action is reversed: in the second movement the boy is led back down (17.23a). In other words, the Old Testament description of restoring life involves a twofold movement, or, more simply, a single movement which is reversed: the boy is brought up; the boy is led down. In the New Testament there is, first, a movement which seems to be leading to burial: the dead son 'was being carried out' (7.12); but later there is the arresting of that movement: 'the bearers stopped'. Thus, in different ways both texts speak of a movement, a possibly ominous movement, which is rolled back or neutralized. But while the Old Testament uses four verbs—*elaben auton… anēnegken auton…ekomisen auton…ketēgagen auton* (17.19, 23), 'he took him…he brought him up…he laid him out to rest', and later 'he led him down'—the New Testament uses just two: *exekomizeto* (7.11), *hoi de bastazontes estēsan* (7.14), 'he was being carried out', and 'the bearers stopped'. And, as already suggested, while the Old Testament action is not only complex, but also enigmatic, the New Testament action is simple and stark.

Furthermore, when the texts, apart from speaking of carrying the son, describe the decisive physical contact between the dead person and the prophet, the Old Testament image is more complex and more laden with anthropological ideas. Elijah breathed into the boy three times (1 Kgs 17.21a); but of Jesus it is said only that 'approaching he touched the bier' (Lk. 7.14a). Again, therefore, Luke's image, in comparison to the Old Testament, has a stark simplicity, and it also has, at least at this point, a hint of serene authority, a touch that is almost majestic: 'approaching, he touched the bier, and the bearers came to a stand'.

A similar suggestion of supreme authority is found in Luke's next sentence. Unlike Elijah who is described as calling on the Lord to restore the boy's life (1 Kgs 17.21b), Jesus is depicted as the Lord who issues a sovereign command that the boy be raised: *Neaniske, soi legō egerthēti* ('Young man, I say to you, rise up', Lk. 7.14). Therefore, there is a perfect complementarity between the texts: Elijah calls on the Lord (Old Testament) and the Lord commands accordingly (New Testament). But, of course, once more Luke's wording is more simple and powerful.

---

inadequate; it loses the continuity with the general idea of resurrection, and it particularly loses the literary and theological continuity with 7.22. Contrast, for instance, JB and RSV. Similarly, the word *logos* (Lk. 7.17, 'This *logos* went forth…') is capable of several meanings, but in the context of Luke's emphasis on 'the word' and 'the word of God', it seems better to translate it as 'word' (cf. especially the nearby texts, Lk. 7.7; 8.11, and the fact that as Haenchen comments [*Acts*, 98]: 'the "word of God"…fills the time after Pentecost').

7. Cf. LS, p. 381, under *klinē*; Fitzmyer 1981: 659.

d. *Section 4. The Restoration of Life (1 Kings 17.23; Luke 7.15)*
Then the son recovered:

| And it was so | And the dead person sat up |
| and the boy cried out. | and began to talk. |

The resemblance between the texts is not only, as Schürmann (1969: 402) points out, that the son immediately breaks into utterance. There is also a structural similarity: both texts have a simple twofold composition: 'and...and...'. Also, both texts have a precise correspondence between the first part of the text and the prophetic words which preceded it: Elijah prayed that the soul might return, '*and it was so*'; Jesus commanded the young man to rise up, '*and the dead person sat up*'. But once again, while the Old Testament can only suggest the enigmatic process by which the soul returns, Luke gives the simple and stark image of the dead person, *ho nekros*, sitting up.

As already indicated, the next detail in the Old Testament—Elijah leading the boy back down—is remodeled into the image of Jesus bringing the bearers to a stand.

Then come the identical phrases: 'and he gave him to his mother'.

The subsequent Old Testament phrase, 'And Elijah said, "See your son lives"', has been rendered superfluous by the changes which Luke has already made. The mother had not been absent, as in the Old Testament story, so there was no need to say 'See'; and the idea of being alive is already contained in Luke's stark language and images of death and resurrection. Thus, at this point we may say that through Luke's adaptations the essence of the Old Testament phrase has already been absorbed into the New Testament text.

e. *Section 5. The Response to the Miracle (1 Kings 17.24; Luke 7.16-17)*
Just as in the miracle itself there is a consistent difference between the Old Testament emphasis on such basic human elements as spirit, breath, and soul, and the New Testament emphasis on such stark and powerful images as death and rising up, so in the responses to the miracles there is a corresponding difference in dramatic emphasis:

And the woman said to Elijah,	Great awe came upon all
'Now I recognize	and they glorified God saying
that you are a man of God among us	'A great prophet has been raised
and	and
the word of God in your mouth is true'.	God has visited his people'.

The Old Testament text contains a recognition of something divine, but the focus is on the human. The words of recognition are words spoken by one human being to another, and the divine element that is recognized is recognized as being in a human—in a man and in the truth of the word in his mouth. But in the New Testament text the emphasis is on the divine: the 'great awe', *phobos*, is a reaction to the presence of the holy, and the words of recognition are not those of one human to another, but of humans to God; and the words actually spoken—'A great prophet has been raised (*ēgerthē*)...' and 'God has visited...'—further emphasize the divine. Overall, while the Old Testament tends to speak a language that is subtle and suggestive—*suggestive* of death, of coming back to life, of God intervening—the New Testament speaks plainly and powerfully of death, of rising up and of God.

Of course, there are other factors at work in Luke's reshaping of the Old Testament text. Instead of giving the reaction of just one person—the woman—as in the Old Testament, he gives the reaction of 'all', an adaptation which fits both with the particular landscaping of this narrative—the crowds mentioned in 7.11 and 7.12—and with 'Luke's general predilection for "all"' (Fitzmyer 1981: 524). In fact, the 'all' is like a synthesis of the two crowds mentioned earlier. Furthermore, the outburst of awe and glorification by so many gives the effect of 'a sort of Greek-chorus-like reaction to the miracle' (Fitzmyer 1981: 659; see Schürmann 1969: 402). Insofar as this observation is accurate, it indicates that Luke is adapting Old Testament writings to some of the elements of Greek literature. As for Luke's use of the word 'prophet' at this point, it is both an explicitation of the idea suggested by the Old Testament woman that Elijah is a prophet, and it is also in line with the programmatic Nazareth speech, a speech centered on a quotation from 'the prophet Isaiah' (Lk. 4.16-22a, especially 4.18-19) which depicts Jesus as a prophet.[8]

Just as Luke's inclusion of the reaction of 'all' serves to dramatize the narrative, in a complementary way, so does his addition in 7.12 of the poignant word *monogenēs* ('only'). Or, to put it in other terms, the two words *monogenēs* and *pantes* ('only' and 'all'), give balancing dramatic effects of poignant detail and widespread glorification.

3. *Clarifying the Adaptation*

As an example of how the relationship between texts may be further clarified, it is now useful to summarize the process of adaptation.

First, on the one hand, every element of the Old Testament text has been incorporated in some form into the New Testament. On the other hand, there are elements in the New Testament text which cannot be accounted for on the basis of the Old Testament text. It follows that while Luke appears to have made systematic use of the Old Testament text, he also used other sources, or at least added other material.

Second, the main techniques which Luke uses for adapting the Old Testament text are as follows:

- *Simple rewording*: Thus, instead of *meta tauta*, Luke reads *en tō hexēs*, and instead of *pylōn*, *pylē*.
- *Geographic adaptation*: In place of foreign 'Sarepta', Luke reads 'Nain', a location which fits the flow of Luke's narrative. However, 'Capernaum' (7.1) preserves a foreign note.
- *Compression*: The rather complex Old Testament descriptions of losing life, being carried, and regaining life, are compressed into words and images that are simple and stark: *tethnēkōs*, *exekomizeto*, *egerthēti* ('dead', 'carried out', 'arise').
- *Elaboration*: The acknowledgment of one person in the Old Testament is replaced in Luke by a more elaborate picture of the acknowledgment of all. Associated with the process of elaboration is that of *addition*—inserting a broad landscape of people and places.
- *Dramatization*: The procedures of *compression* and *elaboration*, especially that of compression, are used to achieve greater dramatic effect, to build images that are more vivid and powerful.
- *Explicitation or clarification*: Where the Old Testament *suggested* that Elijah felt compassion (1 Kgs 17.24), Luke, by using the very word 'compassion' explicated the idea. And while the Old Testament woman suggested God's action, the New Testament crowds spoke more explicitly of his intervention. To some extent, the process of explicitation is connected with that of dramatization. Both help to make the text clear and striking.
- *Complementarity*: Whereas the Old Testament presents one angle of a reality, namely a cry to the Lord for life, the New Testament shows a complementary angle of that reality—the Lord commanding the restoration of life. And while the Old Testament describes the actual process of laying out the son, the New Testament,

---

8. Luke's text may also involve a reference to the raising up of a prophet as described in Deut. 18.18; see Fitzmyer 1981: 660.

looking at the corresponding action from a slightly different angle in time, views it as something already done.
- *Contrast*: While the Old Testament widow expressed fear that the man of God had come to bring death ('…to kill my son'), the centurion expressed hope that the one he addressed as *Kyrie* would restore life ('…and heal my servant'). And in place of a Lord who appears to hurt (1 Kgs 17.20), Luke shows a Lord who stops tears.

Third, Luke's principal aims or his authorial purposes in thus adapting the Old Testament text appear to be as follows:
- *Positivization*: Whereas the Old Testament might seem to suggest a negative image of God, a vindictive God who brings death, the New Testament presents the *kyrios* as inspiring hope, as one who saves.
- *Universalization*: Luke's added 'landscape' of twofold crowds and twofold territories, as well as his use of 'all', suggest that God's saving visitation is for everybody. Thus, even though in one way Luke 'nationalized' the narrative by moving it from foreign Sarepta back to Nain, and by doing so kept the explicit focus of this stage of Luke–Acts within the neat confines of the Jewish homeland, yet by subtle touches he already intimates a wider horizon.
- *Christianization*: This is the most basic adaptation of all. The entire Old Testament text has been so taken over and reworked that it fits into the fabric of the gospel narrative and into the New Testament message which sees Jesus as Lord of life and as a source of hope for all.

Summing up, it may first of all be seen that the relationship between the texts is not haphazard, but rather is consistent and systematic. Every element of the Old Testament text has been integrated and transformed in the New Testament. Second, the relationship cannot be accounted for through oral transmission. Even if one grants B. Gerhardsson's much-disputed theory concerning the popularity in first-century Judaism of various forms of oral transmission, none of the techniques of which Gerhardsson speaks—memorization, conciseness, rhythm, repetition, recitation (Gerhardsson 1979: 14-22)—accounts for a relationship that as well as being consistent and coherent, is also subtle and complex. Such coherent complexity requires a *literary* explanation. Or, as W. Ong puts it concerning a related point, 'Closer plotting demands writing' (1977: 254).

Hence, rather than invoke a mode of transmission which is doubtful and ineffective, one may account for the data, the complex relationship, by the relatively straightforward explanation that Luke had before him a copy of the text to which his work shows such affinity, the LXX, or at least a part of the LXX which contained the Elijah–Elisha narrative, and that precisely as a literary artist he transformed the text, dramatizing and christianizing the ancient narrative. In some ways such a conclusion is to be expected. It is hardly surprising that a *littérateur* should have used a literary method.[9]

4. *Luke's Literary Adaptation in Relation to Imitation*

There is considerable similarity of detail between the adaptive methods of Luke and those of the writers of his general era. Luke's fundamental idea of christianizing an Old Testament text finds a powerful precedent in Virgil's Romanizing of Homer. Virgil, for instance,

---

9. One might ask why Luke did not use an equally complex method in rewriting Mark. A full study of this question is far beyond the scope of the present study, but it may be observed that Mark differs significantly from the Elijah–Elisha narrative: its style is extremely dramatic—sharp and vivid; and of course it tells of Christ. Thus, the basic processes which Luke uses on the Elijah–Elisha narrative, those of dramatization and christianization were, in considerable part, unnecessary in rewriting Mark.

does indeed reproduce the Homeric scene which describes the climactic victory of Greece over the Trojans (*Iliad* 22), but he has so thoroughly reworked it that it becomes a victory of the Trojan survivors, a victory that opens the way to the founding of Rome (*Aeneid* 12).

One may also find in Virgil processes of contrast, positivization, and universalization. Where Homer speaks of a snake which is a religious portent of great tragedy and destruction (*Iliad* 2.308-332), Virgil, in a carefully contrasting scene, speaks of a snake which is a religious portent of all that is positive, a sign which inspires profound eagerness and joy (*Aeneid* 5.84-108). As for universalization, there is a sense in which Virgil's entire reworking of Homer may be called a process of universalization: the epic that was once focused on a relatively localized event, the Trojan war, is used as a basis for depicting the founding of what was regarded as an entire world order, the *pax Romana*. Obviously, this adaptation involves also a pervasive procedure of geographic adaptation.

Furthermore, the fact that Luke should include an entire sentence unchanged ('And he gave him to his mother') is a phenomenon for which Virgil again provides a precedent. In *Georgics* 1.375-87, for instance, there is a blending of three sources—the Greek Aratus, the Roman Varro (who had himself drawn on Aratus), and Homer. G. Williams summarizes the procedure:

> It seems that Varro kept the order of the material as used by Aratus but that he selected from it, and his 'translation' is a more or less free adaptation. Virgil recast the material of Aratus into an arrangement of his own, and he has borrowed details from Varro (including *a whole line unchanged*—a very unusual procedure and a great compliment to Varro). Virgil has also introduced a new idea based on a famous simile of Homer's (*Iliad* 2: 459-65). The result is something which is entirely Virgil's own, and forms a perfectly homogeneous unity. This is 'creative borrowing', a technique which...Virgil was to bring to perfection in his Aeneid. (Williams 1970: 57 [my emphasis])

Other aspects of Luke's work of adaptation may be found, for instance, in Livy's use of sources. Not alone does he employ both compression of sources and vividness of presentation, but, as P.G. Walsh puts it, 'Livy's technique of compression has an obvious connection with his dramatic presentation' (1961: 188). In fact, Walsh's general conclusion might well be applied to much of Luke's work:

> Livy's literary approach can thus be summarised as follows. He utilises one main source, re-organises the structural arrangement, and introduces new material to achieve more dramatic effects. He compresses or omits the less interesting content, using as criteria the purpose of his work and the interests of his audience. Then, in addition to these...aims of *enargeia* [graphic presentation] and *syntomia* [compression], he seeks...*saphēneia* [clarification] and *pithanotēs* [credibility in narration]. (1961: 190)

Thus, while Virgil supplies a precedent for Luke's general approach, Seneca, and especially Livy, provide a precedent for his more detailed techniques. Of course, this is not meant to imply that it is only in these authors that Luke's methods find a precedent. Rather, Luke's similarity to these mainstream writers is simply an indicator of his general affinity to the mainstream of Greco-Roman literature.

In view of all these arguments—not only Luke's general affinity with rhetoric and the spirit of imitation, but also his more detailed resemblances to the imitative practices of particular Greco-Roman authors—it seems reasonable to conclude that his work should be classified as an *imitatio*, or at least should be regarded as involving imitative techniques.

Does this mean that Luke's narrative is based exclusively on the Old Testament text? Apparently not. There are elements in Luke's text which cannot be explained on the basis of the older narrative. In particular it has already been noted that, unlike the Old Testament, Luke's account contains carefully balanced references to two crowds (the 'great crowd' and the 'crowd of the city') and two territories ('the whole of Judea' and 'all the surrounding territory'). If Schürmann is correct in reading the account of the word going forth to the two territories as a reference to the spread of the word among the Jews and Gentiles,[10] and if the two crowds represent a similarly delicate reference to the Jews and Gentiles—the narrative implies that they merge and become the 'all' glorifying God (Lk. 7.16a)—then Luke's text, apart from its use of 1 Kgs 17.17-24, involves also the interweaving of a specifically New Testament theme, namely the glory-filled union of Jews and Gentiles around the death-defeating word of Christ. In other words, Luke apparently has taken a basic theme of the early church—a theme that is reflected powerfully, for instance, in Eph. 1.15–ch. 2[11]—and used the Old Testament text to build it into a narrative. Thus, he does indeed have a tradition about the life-giving power of Christ but it is a tradition that is drawn more from developed Christian preaching and writing than from contact with an original single event in the life of Jesus. Hence, a major proportion of the *theological content* of Lk. 7.11-17 may be from the New Testament period, but the *narrative shape* is drawn very largely from the Old Testament. As Virgil had once adapted Homeric events so that they often centered on totally different people in the *Aeneid*, so Luke has adapted Elijah's raising of a widow's son so that it centers on Jesus.[12]

It may seem, from certain points of view, that the use of the Old Testament in Lk. 7.11-17 should be described not as an imitation but rather as a midrash. After all, the use of rather similar techniques in Luke 1–2 is often described as midrash.[13] Insofar as 'midrash' may be used broadly to refer to any adaptation or updating of the Old Testament, then Lk. 7.11-17, like Luke 1–2, as well as being called an imitation, may also be described

---

10. (Cf. Schürmann 1969: 404: '...die Zeit der Heiden deutet sich an'.

11. Eph. 1.15–ch. 2, like Lk. 7.1-17, contains two basic themes: (1) *the union of Gentiles and Jews in love and glory* (explicitly in Eph. 2, especially vv. 11-21; cf. Eph. 1.17-18; implicitly in Lk. 7.2-5, 11-12, 16-17: the love of the centurion and the Jews; the two crowds and the two territories; the 'all' who glorify God); (2) *the raising of the dead* (Eph. 1.20, the raising of Christ from the dead; Eph. 2.1, 5-6, the raising of Gentiles and Jews from the death of sin; Lk. 7.1-17, the saving of the centurion's servant from death, and the raising of the widow's son. Luke's terminology concerning the raising of the widow's son, *egerthēti kai anekathisen ho nekros* has less affinity with the Old Testament than with Paul's *egeiras auton ek nekrōn, kai kathisas*, Eph. 1.20, and *nekrous...synēgeiren kai synekathisen*, Eph. 2.5-6).

Apart from these thematic links there are also certain linguistic links. Most of the linguistic links concern words which are quite common, and they are sometimes used differently in the two texts, but they seem worth noting—at least as initial data for further work: *akousas...pistin Iēsou...agapēn/agapaō* (Eph. 1.15; cf. 2.4, Lk. 7.3-4, 9); *kyrios...Iēsous* (Eph. 1.15, 17; cf. 2.21; Lk. 7.6); *pantes* (Eph. 1.15; 2.3; cf. 1.22-23; Lk. 7.16); *doxa/doxazō* (Eph. 1.17-18; Lk. 7.16); *exousia...huptassō hypo* (Eph. 1.21; cf. 2.3; Lk. 7.8); *mellonti/ēmellen* (Eph. 1.21; Lk. 7.2); *plērōma/eplērōsen...panta...ekklēsia/laos* (Eph. 1.22-23; Lk. 7.1); *(dia)sōzē* (Eph. 2.5, 8; Lk. 7.3); *makran...eggys/eggizō* (Eph. 2.13, 17; Lk. 7.6, 12); *(pros)-elthōn* (Eph. 2.17; Lk. 7.3, 14); *oikeioi, oikodomeō, oikodome, oikia* (cf. Eph. 2.19-22; Lk. 7.5-6); *prophētēs* (Eph. 2-20; Lk. 7.16). For a survey of the question of whether Luke knew Paul's epistles, see Enslin 1970. Note also J.A. Grassi's comment (1968: 19): 'It would seem that the theology of Ephesians 2 is expressed in story form in Luke [15.11-32]'.

12. For instance, the climactic combat between Achilles and Hector (*Iliad* 22) is adapted in various ways to become the climactic combat between Aeneas and Turnus (*Aeneid* 12). For a summary of some of the instances in which Homeric roles are played by totally different characters in the *Aeneid*, see Knauer 1979: 342-43. For a summary of some of the ways in which ancient historians transferred descriptions from one character or situation to another, see C. Turner 1969: 311-21.

13. See, for instance, Laurentin 1957: 92-119; Sanders 1978. Note also the emphasis on the idea of Lukan midrash in Sanders 1975; Drury 1976: 43-45; Dumais 1976: especially 67-130. In Lk. 1–2, as in Lk. 7.11-17, Old Testament events have been adapted to suit totally different New Testament characters. Thus, for an outline of the way Luke has synthesized and adapted the Old Testament birth announcements, see Brown 1977: 156-57.

loosely as a midrash; and there is nothing inherently impossible or incongruous about the combination of Jewish and Hellenistic literary techniques.[14] But insofar as midrash strictly defined involves explicit citation and interpretation of the Old Testament[15] then neither Luke 1–2 nor Lk. 7.11-17 should be called midrash. It is largely for this reason that R.E. Brown expressed reservations about describing Luke 1–2 as a midrash (Brown 1977: 557-62 [560-61]), and that J.A. Fitzmyer, in the same context, declared the term 'midrash' 'quite unsuitable' (1981: 309). Fitzmyer does not ask if Luke 1–2 should be described technically as an *imitatio*, but it seems significant that he adopts the term 'imitative historiography' and states that 'the infancy narrative was in large part freely composed by Luke on the basis of information obtained from earlier models and *in imitation of some Old Testament motifs*'.[16] While Fitzmyer's categorization and description of Luke 1–2 thus represent something of a turning point, this chapter indicates that that categorization and description may be given greater clarity and precision through an examination of the world of *imitatio*.

The same must be said of Lk. 7.11-17: though the passage may indeed contain something of the searching spirit of midrash, it seems better that it be described as an imitation.

14. For references concerning the interaction of Hellenistic rhetoric and Jewish exegesis and argument, see Kurz 1980b: 182; Daube 1953; Hamerton-Kelly 1976; Fischel 1973; 1969; 1975.

15. For a review of the debate concerning the definition of midrash, see Porton 1979: 104-38; cf. also Le Déaut 1971.

16. Fitzmyer 1981: 309 (my emphasis). By 'imitative historiography' Fitzmyer means that 'whatever historical matter has been preserved by the…evangelists has been assimilated by them to other literary accounts, either biblical or extrabiblical'.

30

Again Not Q: Luke 7.18-35 as an Acts-Oriented Transformation of the Vindication of the Prophet Micaiah (1 Kings 22.1-38)

It has already been indicated (Chapter 28) that a text frequently attributed to Q—the healing of the centurion's servant (Lk. 7.1-10)—may in fact be explained more reliably as Luke's reworking of part of the Elijah–Elisha narrative.

The purpose of this chapter is to indicate that the same is true for Luke's account of the relative roles of John and Jesus (Lk. 7.18-35). Though often attributed to Q (it is found in Mt. 11.2-19 and consists largely of Jesus' words),[1] this passage turns out to be a reworking of the account of the vindication of the prophet Micaiah (1 Kgs 22.1-38)—a text which falls within the Elijah–Elisha narrative.

1. *The Texts: Introductory Analysis*

Unlike the episode about raising the widow's son, where some of the continuity between the texts (1 Kgs 17; Lk. 7) is obvious, in this case the initial detection of the continuity needs more attention. Consequently, it is useful first to look closely at each text in its own right.

a. *1 Kings 22*

The story of Micaiah (1 Kgs 22.1-38) is an interlude, shifting the focus away from Elijah. At first sight, this interlude may seem to have little to do with the surrounding Elijah-centered material. It begins with Ahab's warlike ambition to wrest Ramoth-gilead from Aram (22.1-4), and ends with Ahab's death—killed by a chance arrow which pierces his disguise and his armor, and which, despite efforts at further disguise (he was held upright facing the enemy), drains his blood into his chariot (22.29-38).

But, as often happens in biblical narrative, apparent interludes are integral to the story. For instance, the interlude concerning Judah and Tamar (Gen. 38) is integral to the Joseph story (Alter 1981: 5-17). Likewise, Ahab and the Aramean wars are integral to the Elijah–Elisha narrative; in varying ways they are woven through large parts of it. Furthermore, the death of Ahab—when taken in conjunction with the death of his successor Amaziah (2 Kgs 1)—forms a foil for the fate of Elijah: struck by different accidents, the two kings sink down (one draining down into his bloodied chariot, the other falling down from his balcony into his death bed), but Elijah is taken up to heaven in a chariot of fire (2 Kgs 2). Besides, the essence of 1 Kings 22 is not about *war* but about *prophecy* and its fulfillment, and about the difference between true and false prophecy. Hence, S. De Vries places this chapter under the heading 'Prophet against Prophet' (1978). This clash of prophets is not

---

1. As well as being regarded as coming from Q, Lk. 7.18-35 is also regarded at times as reflecting early traditions and the historical Jesus; see, for instance, Lambrecht 1980; Wink 1989; Vaage 1989. But other authors indicate the need for caution in attributing some of the sayings of Lk. 7.18-35 to Jesus; see, for instance, Cotter 1989. For a comparison of Lk. 7.18-35 with the Gospel of Thomas, and for a discussion of some of the rhetorical features of Luke's text, see Cameron 1990.

new in the Elijah–Elisha narrative; it takes up a basic motif from the clash on Mount Carmel (1 Kgs 18).

The importance of prophecy is introduced by Jehoshaphat, the king of Judah, who accompanies Ahab and who, unlike the disguised king of Israel, wears his royal robes.

Jehoshaphat wants honesty, and so, when faced with all the false prophets who predict success, he insists on calling a true prophet, 'a prophet of the Lord'. So they send a messenger for Micaiah.

When Micaiah comes, he stands against the pressure of the royal court with its pliant prophets, and he announces dramatically and poetically that Israel will be scattered shepherdless—leaving God's word to bring them home.

In the event, Micaiah's prophetic word is vindicated.

b. *Luke 7.18-35: Aspects of Unity, Content, and Structure*

Like 1 Kings 22, the Lukan text (7.18-35) also is a form of interlude. The emphasis shifts from Jesus, the central character of the surrounding episodes, to John. But the passage also has implications for the larger character of Jesus, and most of the text consists of Jesus' words. Hence, while Luke imitates something of the Old Testament effect of an interlude, the encompassing role of the larger character comes out clearly—more clearly than in the Old Testament.

The emphasis on John is one of the factors which brings out the unity of the text. In Talbert's words, the passage is 'held together by the focus on John' (1986: 84).

The full dimensions of the text's unity are complex and orderly. The passage falls into three parts, and each part looks at an aspect of John: his question to the healer (7.18-23), his positive prophetic role (7.24-30), and the negative reaction to him (7.31-35).[2] In simplified terms, therefore, the entire text deals with wondrous healings, positive speaking, and negative reactions.

Apart from dealing with John, these three parts share a further and deeper unity: each contains some element of division or confrontation, and together they portray an overall movement from harmony to a divisive confrontation which is intensifying:

1. At first (7.18-23) the division or confrontation is scarcely perceptible; in fact it is mentioned as something which hopefully will not occur (7.23, 'And blessed is the one who is not scandalized in me').
2. Then, in the positive address (7.24-30), it emerges clearly, but only in the closing verses which contrast the receptive people and tax-collectors with the rejection which comes from the Pharisees and lawyers (7.29-30).
3. Finally, in the negative reactions (7.31-35), the sense of confrontation is uppermost.

The sense of increasing confrontation or division governs not only the content, but also the form. The allusion to scandal at the end of the first part (7.23) contains a mild break in style; it is a beatitude ('And blessed are they...'), and as such, involves a change in form, but—in a feature which is very rare in a beatitude—it is tied to what precedes it by 'and' ('And blessed...) (Fitzmyer 1981: 668). The gap is bridged, and thus content and form correspond: the scandal is something which hopefully will not happen, and the break in style is something which is bridged. Division is evoked but avoided.

At the end of the second part, however, 'the Greek text is a bit awkward' (Fitzmyer 1981: 675) and the break is quite clear. The last two verses ('And all the people hearing...', 7.29-30) are so out of joint with what precedes them that translators sometimes place them in a separate paragraph (NEB) or in parenthesis (RSV).

2. See Fitzmyer 1981: 662. Note Karris 1990.

In the third part (7.31-35), when virtually the whole text deals with some form of rejecttion, division, or confrontation, the disjuncture is equally great, effecting not just the final verse/s but the whole text. To some degree, the whole text breaks away from the preceding parts (from 7.18-30)—causing the UBSGNT to put in its only paragraph division in 7.18-35, and the JB its only new heading.

Yet division is not the last word. Despite increasing confrontation, Luke's central emphasis is positive. Not only is the initial allusion to scandal covered over, as it were, by a beatitude (7.23), but the second picture of division contains the picture of all the people and the tax-collectors as glorifying/justifying (*dikaioō*) God (7.29-30). And even the final section closes with a similar positive idea—'wisdom is vindicated/justified (*dikaioō*) by all her children' (7.35).[3]

Luke's text (7.18-35), therefore, is a well-constructed three-part unit in which even the disjunctures contribute to the overall unity: a picture which advances from healing and positive speaking to increasing dividedness. It is a picture which, despite its negativity, ultimately vindicates God and God's wisdom.

c. *Luke 7.18-35: Continuity within Luke–Acts*

While Lk. 7.18-35 has its own distinctness, it is written so that it is in narrative continuity with the larger narrative of Luke–Acts. It builds on what precedes it and, above all, it prepares for what lies ahead.

It forms a unity, first of all, with the rest of ch. 7. On the one hand, it looks back to Lk. 7.1-17. Its opening verse refers to what has preceded ('all these things', 7.11), and, like the first verse of the preceding episode, it uses the phrase *hoi mathētai autou* ('his disciples', 7.18; cf. 7.11). More substantively, the initial emphasis in Lk. 7.18-35 concerning many wondrous healings, including the raising of the dead (7.21-22), is like an expansion or intensification of the accounts of the healing of the centurion's servant (7.1-10) and the raising of the widow's son (7.11-17). Luke 7.18-35 also continues the climactic idea of the prophet being accepted by all the people (7.26, 29; cf. 7.16).

On the other hand, Lk. 7.18-35 looks forward and prepares for the subsequent part of ch. 7. The sense of scandal and of division—especially division or contrast between the sinners (tax-collectors) and the Pharisees (7.23, 29-30)—establishes the broad background for the scandal of Simon the Pharisee and for the contrast between that Pharisee and the forgiven woman (7.36-50, especially 7.39, 44-46).[4] And the broad idea of the rejection of the prophet (7.31-34) is likewise illustrated in Simon (7.39, 44-46).

As well as being in close-knit unity with the rest of the chapter, Lk. 7.18-35 is also in continuity with much of Luke–Acts.

Continuity with *what precedes* ch. 7 is found, for instance, in the following:
The implication of someone coming (7.19; cf. 3.16).
- The sense of waiting or expecting (7.19-20; cf. 3.15).
- The Isaiah-related healings (7.21-22; cf. 4.17-18; Isa. 61.1).[5]
- The desert (7.24; cf. 1.80; 3.2).
- Sending of an angel; birth; women; kingdom (7.27-28; cf. 1.26-27, 31, 33, 42).
- All the people being baptized (7.29; cf. 3.21).
- John's abstention from wine (7.33; cf. 1.15).

The continuity of 7.18-35 with *what follows* Luke 7 is focused largely on Acts. The picture of Jesus speaking, including the reference to the unresponsive Jewish authorities

---

3. On the role of *dikaioō* in Lk. 7.29, 35, see especially Talbert 1986: 84-85.
4. For further details of this continuity, see Talbert 1986: 84-85.
5. On the close relationship of the healings in Lk. 7.21-22 to those in Isa. 61.1, see Fitzmyer 1981: 668, and especially Tannehill 1986: 78-80.

(Pharisees and lawyers; cf. 'this generation'), prepares the way for much that happens in Acts, especially for Peter's speeches.

The idea that part of Luke 7 should be a preparation for Acts finds initial backing in the very first episode of that chapter. The picture of the centurion and Jesus (Lk. 7.1-10) prepares the way for the picture of Cornelius and Peter (Acts 10).

Furthermore, the broad three-part sweep of Lk. 7.18-35 (*wonders/healings*, followed first by *positive witness* and then by an *increasing sense of confrontation*) corresponds to the broad patterns of Peter's activities, especially in Acts 2–5. The first such pattern, with great emphasis on the miraculous and virtually no confrontation (except a final ominous reference to 'this perverse generation', 2.40), occurs in Acts 2. The second, with more obvious confrontation, is in Acts 3.1–4.22. And the third, in which confrontation becomes acute, is in Acts 4.23–5.42.[6]

This kinship with Acts 2–5 casts light on a further feature of Lk. 7.18-35, namely its general similarity to a speech or sermon. Acts 2–5 is heavily colored by the speeches of Peter, and it is appropriate that Lk. 7.18-35, in foreshadowing Peter's speeches, should itself consist largely of speechlike material. This oratorical or sermonic quality has tended to reinforce the impression that Lk. 7.18-35 comes from Q, but the verifiable literary relationship with Acts 2–5 provides a less conjectural explanation of that quality.

d. *Luke 7.18-35: Relationship with 1 Kings 22.1-38*
However great the continuity of Lk. 7.18-35 with Luke–Acts, it is distinct, and this distinctness has its own sources. As already seen, despite its continuity with Acts 10, the centurion story (Lk. 7.1-10) depends significantly on distinct sources (including 1 Kgs 17.1-16).

6. A full analysis of the relationship of Lk. 7.18-35 to Acts 2–5 would be disproportionate in a chapter which is primarily focused on its relationship with 1 Kgs 22, but certain aspects may be noted briefly. Lk. 7.18-35 and Acts 2 share some basic features. First, an initial emphasis on wonders/miracles (Lk. 7.18-23; Acts 2.1-20; with just a suggestion of scandal or skepticism, Lk. 7.23; Acts 2.13). Second, positive testimony (to John and Jesus, Lk. 7.24-28; to Jesus, Acts 2.22-36), and people's reactions (divided in Luke [7.29-30]; united in Acts [2.37-41] but with a reference to 'this perverse generation'). Third, the question of unity: contrasting pictures of division (Lk. 7.31-35) and harmony (Acts 2.42-47).

In the case of Acts 3.1–4.22, there is a more obvious sense of division. The text again starts with a miracle (Acts 3.1-10), but instead of one harmonious speech and response, there are two speeches and two responses, interwoven but diverse: one involving the people (Acts 3.11-26; 4.21-22), the other the authorities (4.1-20). In Acts 4.23–ch. 5, the initial emphasis is again on something wondrous (the place shakes, 4.23-31) and later there are many more wonders and healings (4.12-16). But the sense of division is much greater; it is intimated earlier, even amid the different wonders, on a matter of property (4.32–5.11). And eventually when the apostles are arrested and beaten, and when Peter's speech becomes curt and short, this sense of division becomes explosive (5.17-42). In addition, there are more detailed links, among them the following: 'And they announced' (*kai apēggeilan*) (Lk. 7.18; Acts 4.23); calling (*proskaleō*)...disciples (Lk. 7.18; Acts 2.39; 5.40); waiting/expecting (*prosdokaō*) (Lk. 7.19; Acts 3.4); coming/arriving (*paragenomenoi*) (Lk. 7.20; Acts 5.21, 22, 25); hour (Lk. 7.21; Acts 2.15; 3.1; 5.7); multiple healings (Lk. 7.21-22; Acts 5.12-16); the lame walk (Lk. 7.22; Acts 3.1-9); this is what is written/said (in scripture) (Lk. 7.27; Acts 2.16); the kingdom of God (Lk. 7.28; Acts 1.3, 6); 'All the people...' (*pas ho laos*) (Lk. 7.29; Acts 3.9, 11); hearing and being baptized (Lk. 7.29; Acts 2.37, 38, 41); contrast between people and authorities (Lk. 7.29-30; Acts 5.26); God's plan (*boulē...theou*) (Lk. 7.30; Acts 2.23; 5.38-39); 'This (perverse) generation...' (Lk. 7.31; Acts 2.40); all her children (Lk. 7.35; Acts 2.39, 'your children and all...'). While the significance of some details is questionable, the overall conclusion is reasonably clear: the language of Lk. 7.18-35 shows continuity with Acts 2–5. Thus, there is a triple affinity between Lk. 7.18-35 and Acts 2–5: in content (wonders; positive witness; negative division/confrontation amid God's plan), in structure (threefold, intensifying), and in language. The John-related text (Lk. 7.18-35) encapsulates what is to follow in Acts.

One of the distinct sources of Lk. 7.18-35 is the story of Micaiah (1 Kgs 22).

The central link between Lk. 7.18-35 and 1 Kgs 22.1-38 is again the idea of confrontation—the idea highlighted in De Vries's title *Prophet Against Prophet* (1978). The confrontation is that which results from God's word, and which, despite rejection by some, is vindicated.

Thus, in order to build a text which will prepare for an account of God's word issuing forth in confrontation in multiple ways (Acts 2–5), Luke draws on an Old Testament text which dealt with that very topic.

Table 51. *Seeking a True Prophet (1 Kings 22; Luke 7.18-35)*

	Questioning the Lord, Repetitiously	
1.	Refrain: ask the Lord (*kyrion*). Two questions: 'Do I go or (*ē*) hold back?' 'Is there a prophet of the Lord?' (22.1-9)	John sends to the Lord (*kyrion*). One complex question, twice: 'Are you the one [prophet?] to come or (*ē*) do we wait for another?' (7.18-20)
	Fruits of False Prophecy and True: Violence and Healing	
2.	——— *Zedekiah* prophesied *goring*. Micaiah: 'I tell what God says'. *Zedekiah hit*, and the king was *hit*, in that day (22.10-14, 24-25, 34-35)	In that hour: *Healing*…and granting sight. Tell what you have seen. *Healing*, the blind see…(7.21-23) ———
	Going Forth: The Pliant Prophet and the Courtly Clothing	
3.	When Micaiah comes: 'Should I go up/forth…?' Micaiah is pliant: 'Go up/forth'. And the kings went up… one in royal clothing (22.15, 29-33)	When the messengers go: 'What did you go out…?' A reed shaken by the wind? A man in fine clothing? Such are in royal courts (7.24-25)
	True Prophecy about God Guiding People on their Way	
4.	Micaiah speaks as a real prophet in the name of the Lord, 'I have seen Israel scattered, shepherdless And God said 'Let each go home'. Did I not tell….Hear the word…' (22.16-19a)	A prophet, more than a prophet… it is written, 'Behold I send my angel before you to prepare your way before you I say to you…' Pronouncement on John (7.26-28)
5.		** God's word fulfilled in baptizing…baptizing (7.29-30)
	Sitting and Talking to One Another (Images from Complementary Worlds)	
6.	God sitting in the heavenly court: some say this and some say that (22.19b-23)	Children sitting in the marketplace, calling to one another (7.31-32)
	Eating, Drinking, Rejection…and Vindication	
7.	Micaiah's rejection; his eating and drinking. God's word will be vindicated (22.26-28) ** God's word fulfilled in washing…washing (22.36-38)	John and Jesus eating and drinking; both rejected. Wisdom is justified/vindicated (7.33-35)

As with other texts from the Elijah–Elisha narrative, Luke has left aside the ancient setting (in this case a war) and has given a contemporary, christianized version which places greater emphasis on what is positive and internal.

For instance, instead of showing how falsifying God's word leads to violence as exemplified in the false prophet Zedekiah with his iron horns that symbolize goring, Luke shows the other, positive side of the coin: God's true word/revelation brings peaceful healing as seen in Jesus. Correspondingly, the picture of going forth to war is replaced by the picture of going out into the desert.

The shift to what is more internal and closer to the human heart is sharply reflected in one dramatic adaptation. Instead of tracing the roots of perversity to a distant drama in the high heavens (the heavenly host talking back and forth, 2 Kgs 22.19b-23), Luke pictures this perversity as if it were implicitly coming from ordinary life, or an internal disposition—the unresponsiveness which is reflected in the children calling to each other in the marketplace (Lk. 7.31-32). Thus, Luke has changed a perversity which originates in the highest heavens to one which emanates from the lowliest human arena.

Both texts (1 Kgs 22.1-38 and Lk. 7.18-35) contain one declaration which is particularly prophetic and poetic: Micaiah's vision of scattered Israel being sent home in peace by God's word (1 Kgs 22.17), and Jesus' description (taken from Mal 3.1) of John as God's angel who prepares the way (Lk. 7.27). In each case, God helps people on their way, but Luke uses a picture which plays down the negative (the scattering) and which contributes to his emphasis regarding the fulfillment of Scripture. The uniqueness of these texts within their respective contexts is highlighted in the JB poetic layout.

Table 51 outlines the overall relationship between 1 Kgs 22.1-38 and Lk. 7.18-35. Generally, Luke follows the order of the Old Testament texts, but on two occasions he combines texts which are inherently related—the three texts which in various ways flow from Zedekiah's violence (22.10-14, 24-25, 34-35), and two texts about going to war (Micaiah's make-believe recommendation to go, and the actual going, 22.15, 29-33).

Furthermore, Luke has relocated the final scene of the washing/baptizing so that it concludes not the entire passage (as in 1 Kgs 22) but just its second part (7.29-30, concluding 7.24-30). Variations on such relocating of concluding verses occur in other parts of Luke. For instance, in reworking 2 Kgs 1.1–2.6 and ch. 5, Luke transposes some of the concluding verses to a much earlier position in his own text (see Chapters 33 and 39).

2. Detailed Analysis

a. *Section 1. Questioning the Lord, Repetitiously (1 Kings 22.1-9; Luke 7.18-20)*
In the first scene, the two kings express their readiness to conquer Ramoth-gilead, thus expanding the kingdom of Israel. But before embarking on this expansion, they decide to 'ask the Lord' (*ton kyrion*). First, the king of Israel asked the assembled prophets, 'Should I go to war...or refrain?', and, when the answer was a glib yes, the other king asked, 'Is there here no prophet of the Lord?' Then, after these two questions, they decide to call Micaiah.

The context in Luke is also one of expansion—not military but evangelical. The previous episode had concluded by telling that 'this word' concerning 'a great prophet' went out to all of Judea 'and all the surrounding territory' (Lk. 7.16-17). And it is precisely within this context that John calls two disciples and sends them to 'the Lord' (*ton kyrion*) to ask, 'Are you the one who is coming or should we wait for another?'

The meaning of 'the one who is coming' is unclear. On the one hand, it is continuous with the coming one announced earlier by John (in Lk. 3.16). On the other hand, in a tension that is typical of Luke's expanding text—a text full of the dynamics of prophecy and fulfillment—it builds on the preceding, explicit reference to Jesus as a great prophet (7.16, 18); it has affinities with the idea of the prophet-like-Moses (Deut. 18.18; cf. Jn 6.14); and it leads into the account of healings which imply the coming of the eschatological prophet.[7] In other words, the messengers' questions may have started with a fairly narrow presupposition about the one to come, but, like prophecy leading to something fuller, they open the way to a greater reality of the presence of the eschatological prophet. Thus, like the king's messenger, but much more so, John's two disciples are on their way to a true prophet from God.

The affinities between the texts may be outlined thus:

Context: Israel's expansion.	Context: spread of the word.
	Calls (*pros-kaleō*) two disciples;
Refrain: Ask the Lord (*kyrion*).	sends them to the Lord (*kyrion*).
Two questions:	One complex question, repeated:
Do I go or (*ē*) hold back?	Are you the coming one [prophet?]
Is there a prophet of the Lord?	or (*ē*) do we wait for another?
Call (*kaleō*) Micaiah.	

The affinities involve four areas: substance, action (plot), form, and detail. The substantive link is the quest for the true prophet of God. In both texts this quest occurs in a context which in different ways suggests an imminent expansion of God's kingdom—the ancient kingdom of Israel and the gospel kingdom of the word—and this situation of expansion or movement generates a sense of uncertainty about what to do, about whether to go with the momentum or hold back.

The plots are very different at one level—the Old Testament action is set in war and the other in profound peace—yet they involve a fundamental similarity: the one who, amid his followers, is hesitating, decides to call ([*pros-*]*kaleō*) (a) messenger/s and to send him/them to the person who is apparently the true prophet of the Lord.

There are also links in form. Both texts use questions which are specifically either/or in nature and both use repetition. The Old Testament has a repetitive refrain about asking the Lord (1 Kgs 22.5, 7, 8) and it also has two questions. Luke has a single question, but it is asked twice, repetitively, a pattern which 'gives the words a distinct rhythm' (Tannehill 1986: 79; see Schürmann 1969: 411).

Finally, there is a curious link in detail, the Old Testament reference to asking 'the Lord' helps explain the rather surprising reference to Jesus as 'the Lord' (Lk. 7.19).

But while thus maintaining manifold continuity with the Old Testament text, Luke has also made important adaptations. As so often in his reworking of the Old Testament, he has shifted the emphasis from an external drama about an external kingdom and its wars, to a world in which the focus falls more clearly on what is positive and more internal (the kingdom inaugurated by Jesus).

Furthermore, despite omitting many dramatic elements such as the armies and wars, he manages not only to build a drama of his own, but to do so in a way which is vivid and memorable. (He achieves this largely through the single striking question, which, for greater effect, is repeated.)

In addition, he has adapted the whole both to the general tradition of Jesus and in particular to the requirements of his own narrative. The sending of two messengers, for instance, rather than one, involves an adaptation to a general pattern in Luke–Acts (cf. Lk. 10.1; 22.8; Acts 3.11; 8.14). And the designation of these messengers as 'his disciples'

---

7. See Marshall 1978: 292: 'The combination of Old Testament allusions indicates that the future era of salvation has arrived, but this is especially linked with the function of Jesus as the eschatological prophet'.

likewise accords with one of Luke's larger patterns (as seen, for instance, in the preceding episode, 7.11). Even the key word *pros-dokaō* ('wait'), while it contains a close echo of the Old Testament idea of refraining/holding back (1 Kgs 22.6), also fits in also with other Lukan episodes (Lk. 3.15; Acts 3.5).

b. *Section 2. The Fruits of False Prophecy and True: Violence and Healing (1 Kings 22.10-14, 24-25, 34-35; Luke 7.21-23)*
Both texts now move from the messenger/s to a scene of prophecy: in the Old Testament, to the prophets Zedekiah and Micaiah, and in Luke, to the eschatological prophet.

The Old Testament text begins with violence. The false prophet Zedekiah uses iron horns to symbolize the idea of goring the Syrians until they are finished (1 Kgs 22.10-12), and then—following an interlude in which the focus switches to the messenger, and in which Micaiah says that he will tell what (*ha*) the Lord says (1 Kgs 22.13-14)—the picture comes back later to intensified Zedekiah-related violence: Zedekiah's hitting (*epataxen*) of Micaiah and the enemy's hitting (*epataxen*) of the king (1 Kgs 22.24-25, 34-35).

Luke's scene begins not with violence, but with peace (the picture of peaceful healing, 7.21), and then—following an interlude in which the focus switches to the messengers, and in which they are told to tell what (*ha*) they have seen [the Lord doing] (7.21a)—the picture returns to being one of further, intensified healing (7.22-23).

Thus, instead of moving from violence to intensified violence, Luke moves from peace (healings) to intensified peace. In doing this, he combines the three violent scenes of the Old Testament text, and in giving a New Testament equivalent (an opposite) he seeks, as with the questions in the previous scene, a greater sense of repetition. In approximate outline:

———	In that hour:
Zedekiah prophecies goring.	*Peaceful healing.*
The messenger goes.	The messengers are told to go.
Micaiah: I tell what God says.	Tell what you have seen/heard:
Zedekiah hit; *king is hit*,	*Further peaceful healing.*
in that day.	———

As earlier, there are multiple links. The substantive issue is the nature and testing of prophecy. The Old Testament shows the violent bankruptcy of prophecy which is false. Luke, with an eye to Acts 2–5, shows the other side of the same coin—the peaceful and healing nature of prophecy which is true.

Furthermore, despite the adaptation from war to peace, there is also continuity in the actions and form. A picture of dramatic activity (concerning wounding/healing) first gives way to an image of the journeying messenger/s and later switches back to a more intense version of the same activity.

Finally, in the timing (of war, 1 Kgs 22.25, 35; of peace, Lk. 7.21), and in the one activity which is shared (of speaking to the journeying messengers, 1 Kgs 22.13a, 14; Lk. 7.22a) there are links of detail:

Old Testament:
kai ho aggelos ho poreutheis... (22.13a)
kai eipen...ha (22.14)
tē hēmera ekeinē...en tē hēmera ekeinē (22.25, 35)

New Testament:
en ekeinē tē hōra (7.21)
kai...eipen...poreuthentes apaggeilate...ha (7.22a)

Old Testament:
And the messenger who was going...
And he said...whatever [the Lord tells]
that day...in that day

New Testament:
In that hour
And...he said... Go tell...whatever [you see the Lord doing].

Luke's use of 'hour' (rather than 'day') helps to prepare the way for the emphasis on 'hour' in Acts (2.15; 3.1; 5.7).

c. *Section 3. Going Up/Out: The Pliant Prophet and the Courtly Clothing (1 Kings 22.15, 29-33; Luke 7.24-25)*

When Micaiah first arrives (*erchomai*) and the king asks his question, Micaiah plays the role advised by the messenger of the pliant court prophet who tells the king to go forth to war (1 Kgs 22.15). In Luke, too, as the messengers go (*ap-erchomai*), there is a question about going forth—not up (to war) but out (to the desert). And there is also the image of the pliant prophet—the reed shaken by the wind. In other words, the pliant prophet who says to go forth (Old Testament) has been replaced by going forth to see the pliant prophet (New Testament).

Subsequently, when the king of Judah does go forth, he goes very explicitly in royal clothing (1 Kgs 22.29-33). And Luke immediately speaks of going forth to see someone in fine clothing found in royal courts (Lk. 7.25). Thus, where the Old Testament had spoken repeatedly of going forth to a war, Luke speaks repeatedly of going forth to a scene of peace in the desert.

Again Luke has combined related texts. The two images of going forth, though separated in 1 Kings 22 (22.15, 29-33), have been distilled and brought together in the New Testament.

And once again, as in the two previous episodes, Luke builds repetitively and memorably. Instead of *a question* about going forth and *a statement* about going forth, he gives *two similar questions* ('What did you go out...to see?', 'But what did you go out to see?').

There are also links of detail:

Old Testament: [Opening words]
kai ēlthen... (22.15)
ei anabō eis...polemon (22.15)
kai anebē...eis...eis ton...eis ton (22.29-30)
basileus...pros...basilea...kai su en-dusai ton himatismon... (22.30)

New Testament: [Opening word]
ap-elthontōn... (7.24)
ti exēlthate eis tēn erēmon... (7.24)
ti exēlthate... (7.25)
anthrōpon...ēmphi-esmenon...en himatismō...en...basileiois (7.25)

Old Testament: [Opening words]
And he came...
Will I go up to...war?
And the king...the king...went up to...to the...to the
King...to...king: You wear your robes.

New Testament: [Opening word]
As-they-were-going...
What did you go out to the desert...?
But what did you go out...?
A man clothed in robes...in kings' courts.

The word *himatismos* ('clothing/apparel/robes'), is relatively rare (32 times in the Old Testament, five times in the New Testament). Rarer still is the explicit reference to an inherent link between wearing *himatismos* and being kings or in kings' courts. Apart from the parallel text in 2 Chron. 18.29 and two debatable Solomon-related texts (1 Kgs 10.5, 25 [parr. 2 Chron. 9.4, 24]), the nearest one comes to it is in the royal wedding song (Ps. 45.8-12).

d. *Section 4. The True Prophet Reveals God's Voice that Shows the Way (1 Kings 22.16-19a; Luke 7.26-28)*
The king now tells Micaiah to stop playing the pliant prophet and to speak the truth in the name of the Lord—in other words, to speak as a real prophet (1 Kgs 22.16). And Luke in turn switches from the image of someone pliant and soft to that of 'a prophet and more than a prophet' (Lk. 7.26).

Then come two pictures of true prophets: the text's description of Micaiah (1 Kgs 22.17) and Jesus' description of John (Lk. 7.27).

They begin by implying that the true prophet's basis is God. Micaiah speaks 'the truth *in the name of God*'. And John is described as predicted in God's written word (he is 'the one of whom *it is written*'). Thus Luke keeps the sense of someone who is grounded in God, but he expresses that groundedness through one of his favorite patterns, by emphasizing the fulfillment of Scripture.

Then come the key texts. Micaiah has a vision of Israel being scattered and of God intervening to say that they should be allowed to '*go home in peace*' (1 Kgs 22.17). John's role (two balanced, repetitive phrases, quoted from Mal. 3.1) also implies that God helps people on a journey: John is God's 'messenger...who *prepares the way*...' (Lk. 7.27). In different ways, then, both prophets communicate the message about God helping people find their way, but Luke omits the negative emphasis on scattering and adapts the idea of God guiding people to his pattern concerning the fulfilling of Scripture.

Here, as in some other cases (cf. the use of Isaiah in the Nazareth speech, Lk. 4.18-19), Luke blends sources, expressing prosaic raw material (from 1 Kgs 22) through a poetic formulation (from Malachi).

Luke's text then gives a pivotal pronouncement about John: he is greater than all yet less than anyone in the kingdom of God (Lk. 7.28). However, apart perhaps from the introductory 'I say to you' (Lk. 7.28a; cf. 1 Kgs 22.18-19a, 'Did I not say to you...?', 'Hear the word...'), this pronouncement does not seem to reflect 1 Kings 22. Apparently, it comes from some other source or inspiration.

The most important links between these texts are the sudden emergence of the picture of a true prophet and the consequent picture of God as intervening to help people on their way. But there is also a very distinctive link in the form of the texts—in the way the poetic prophetic statements stand out.

e. *Section 5. God's Word Fulfilled in the Washing/Baptizing (1 Kings 22.36-38; Luke 7.29-30)*
Having inserted the pivotal pronouncement about John's status, Luke now makes a radical adaptation. He takes the final Old Testament scene about the washing of the blood-stained chariot and the harlots washing in the blood-stained pool, and uses it as a starting-point for speaking about another kind of washing: baptism, the washing which was accepted by all the people and the tax-collectors, but not by the Pharisees and lawyers.

In both texts, the image of washing is used twice. In the Old Testament, 'they washed (*apenipsan*) the chariot' and 'the harlots washed (*elousanto*)' (1 Kgs 22.38). In the New Testament, 'all the people and tax-collectors justified God, having being baptized (*baptisthentes*) with John's baptism, but the Pharisees and lawyers rejected God's plan for them, not having been baptized (*mē baptisthentes*) by him'. Once again, while adapting his source, Luke forges a text which is clearly repetitive.

What is central to these texts is not just the repeated image of material washing but the fact that this washing fulfills the word or plan of God. The Old Testament washing happened 'in accordance with the word that the Lord had spoken' (1 Kgs 22.38), and the New Testament washing 'justified God', in other words, vindicated God.[8]

However, Luke has adapted the two washing references to form a contrast, thus preparing the way for later contrasts, including that between the two thieves (Lk. 24.39-43) and especially the contrast in Acts between the people who accepted baptism, and the Jewish authorities who were in conflict with God's plan (Acts 2.37-42; 4.1-4; 5.21, 26, 38).

In different ways both texts are final or have something of a closing role. This is clear in the Old Testament; the washing concludes the basic story. But even in Luke where the larger passage will continue as far as 7.35, some authors and editors (though not all) regard the contrast between those who accepted baptism and those who did not as an interim conclusion.[9]

In any case, the essential link is that of a process of washing which, whatever its limitations, fulfills God's word or plan.

There are also some linking details. There is a correspondence between the Old Testament text's opening picture of the army's *herald telling everyone go home* (1 Kgs 22.36) and Luke's opening reference to *all the people hearing* (7.29); these two pictures may perhaps be two sides of the same coin. More precisely, the repeated phrase *eis tēn heautou... eis tēn heautou...* ('to his own...to his own...', 1 Kgs 22.36) helps explain the perplexing phrase *eis heautous* ('for themselves'?, Lk. 7.30). Luke's curious wording is sometimes regarded as reflecting Aramaic (Marshall 1978: 299). But, as it often occurs in Luke, his wording is not so much a Semitism as a Septuagintism—one which, as occasionally occurs, involves a form of word-play.[10]

f. *Section 6. Sitting and Speaking Back and Forth to Each Other: Israel's Failure Explained in Images from Opposite Worlds: From God's Heavenly Court (1 Kings 22.19b-23) and from the Human Playground (Luke 7.31-32)*

Having spoken of Israel's defeat, Micaiah goes on to give the root of that failure, and he places the root in God—in a decision taken in the heavenly court to use lying prophets to deceive Israel's king (1 Kgs 22.19b-22).

However, in looking for some parable to explain the failure or fall of the later Israel (the Jewish refusal of the gospel), Luke places the root not in God but in the human will—and its stubbornness which is evident in a children's playground (in the children's refusal to respond to what is called out, 7.31-32).

Theologically, failure and evil can either be attributed to some factor outside human control, a factor which ultimately touches God, or it can be attributed to human factors. The Old Testament gives one view and Luke gives the other. Again, Luke has given the other side of the coin, and again he places the emphasis on a factor that is more internal, closer to the human makeup. ('The fault is not in the stars but in ourselves'.)

The two scenes of the heavenly court and the children's playground have a fundamental similarity. The heavenly court is a *chorus-contra-chorum* arrangement, with God 'sitting'

---

8. On *dikaioō* as meaning 'to vindicate', see Talbert 1986: 84.
9. UBSGNT; JB; Fitzmyer 1981: 670.
10. The full details of the relationship between the washing texts (1 Kgs 22.36-38; Lk. 7.31-32) seem to be extremely intricate, and eventually could deserve a chapter to themselves. There are two main dynamics that need to be unraveled: the transformation of the images (into New Testament equivalents); and the rearrangement (and duplication) of the elements to suit Luke's repetitive pattern.

(*kathēmenon*) on the throne and all the heavenly host arranged to God's left and right. And in that situation, 'one said one thing and another said another' (1 Kgs 22.20). In the marketplace, the children are 'sitting (*kathēmenois*) and calling to one another'.

Obviously the children's song ('We played... We wailed...') has its own sources and resonances quite independent of 1 Kings 22.[11]

Yet Luke manages to echo something of the details of the heavenly converstaion. Through inquiring about how to bring down Israel's king (22.20-21), God had asked two questions (one fairly long, one short): 'Who...?', and 'By what...?' (*Tis... En tini...*). And when Jesus is wondering how to describe the later Israel's failure, he introduces his parable by asking two questions (one relatively long, one short): 'To what...?', and 'To what...?' (*Tini... Tini...*). As ever, Luke manages, even in such miniscule echoes, to build more precise repetition.[12]

g. *Section 7. The Food-and-Drink Implications of Speaking God's Word: A Picture of Rejection and Vindication (1 Kings 22.26-28; Luke 7.33-35)*

When Micaiah's word is rejected, he is imprisoned by two men and has to 'eat the bread (*esthiein...arton*) of affliction and the water of affliction'. Yet Micaiah's final statement is that God's word to him will be vindicated ('If you return...the Lord has not spoken through me').

Luke describes the eating and drinking habits of both John and Jesus: 'John...came neither eating bread (*esthiōn...arton*) nor drinking wine... The Son of Man came eating and drinking...' And both were rejected. Yet Luke's final statement is that wisdom is vindicated.

Again Luke has used repetition. He has taken the account of the eating and drinking of Micaiah and applied it in varied but repetitive ways to both John and Jesus. In the case of John, for instance, the idea of drinking is adapted to the angel's message that John would not drink wine (Lk. 1.15).

In both cases (1 Kgs 22.26-28; Lk. 7.33-35) this eating and drinking is linked with the speaking of the word of God and with rejection.

Furthermore, in both cases the final statement is of vindication. God's prophetic word to Micaiah will be shown to have been true (1 Kgs 22.28), and wisdom will be justified by 'all her children' (Lk. 7.35). In concluding this speech, Luke is following Micaiah's final statement about the vindication of God's word, but he is also preparing for the conclusion of Peter's speech about the fulfillment of God's word/promise to 'your children and to all...' (Acts 2.39). Thus, in a single brief phrase about vindication and all the children, he has managed to dovetail the closing words of both Micaiah and Peter.

3. *Conclusion*

As always in comparing Luke with an Old Testament text, some links are debatable or inadequately analyzed, and insistence on such weak links, whether by someone proposing literary dependence or someone opposing it, tends to obscure the key issue: are there links which are strong, links which go beyond the range of coincidence? If something is to be proved in court, for instance, it is often unnecessary or ill-advised to insist on every piece

---

11. For an interpretation of the children sitting in the marketplace as implying a court scene—an adult process of judgment—see Cotter 1987.

12. The indebtedness of Luke's introductory formula, *Tini... Tini*, to the *Tis... En tini* of 1 Kgs 22.20-21 does not rule out further indebtedness to other sources, such as those reflected in the rabbinical use of *Tini... Tini* (cf. Str-B, 2.8).

of evidence, strong or weak. All that is needed are a few arguments or pieces of evidence which are sufficiently strong. Even one may be enough.

In the case of Lk. 7.18-35 and 1 Kgs 22.1-38, a few arguments are strong:

1. *The context*. Everything else in Luke 7 depends on the Elijah–Elisha narrative. Given the unity of the chapter, a situation is created in which there is some likelihood that the same is true of Lk. 7.18-35. In fact, the context is such that the burden of proof begins to shift towards someone who wants to maintain otherwise.
2. *The manifold similarities*. The similarities begin with the central theme of confrontation (based on God's vindicated revelation) and then continue through a wide range of links: from the content and order of the various parts to the persistent presence of small similarities of detail.
3. *The coherence of the differences*. Though the differences are great, they are not inexplicable or jumbled. On the contrary, they can be understood as based on adaptations to the larger patterns of Luke–Acts and as coming from transformational strategies which are consistent and coherent—particularly strategies aimed at producing a text which is positive, internalized, christianized, and memorable (repetitive).

Overall, the easiest way to account for the data is through a straightforward conclusion: Luke, an acknowledged *littérateur*, used a literary method.

The explanation of Lk. 7.18-35 given here is difficult. One has to work with it. Yet this explanation is grounded systematically in known scriptural reality, and as such it is ultimately more satisfactory and less conjectural than the appeal to Q.

31

Luke 7.36-50 as an Internalization of 2 Kings 4.1-37

The purpose of this chapter is to indicate that Luke's account of the forgiving of the sinful woman (7.36-50) is modeled, largely but not exclusively, on the two women described in 2 Kgs 4.1-37: the woman who was freed from a great debt (vv. 1-7), and the Shunammite woman who received an awesome gift of life (vv. 8-37).

However, unlike the Old Testament text, with its apparent emphasis on gifts which are external, freedom from *financial* debt (vv. 1-7), and the granting of *physical* life (vv. 8-37), the gospel account stresses gifts which are primarily internal—freedom from *moral* debt and the granting of *spiritual* life. Thus, Luke's account emerges not as a slavish copy of the older text, but as a sophisticated internalization. This process of internalization, and Luke's other processes of adaptation, are to be understood not only in the context of the general New Testament emphasis on what is internal and spiritual, but also in the context of the rhetorical practice of *imitatio*.

1. *The Origin of Luke 7.36-50: A Problem in Stalemate*

The origin of Lk. 7.36-50 has always been a puzzle.[1] On some points, particularly in its image of a woman anointing Jesus, the passage is strikingly similar to the anointing stories found in Mk 14.3-9 and Jn 12.1-8.[2] (Matthew's version, 26.6-13, appears to be a minor variation on Mark's.) But while Luke sets the scene in Galilee, at a rather early stage in Jesus' ministry, the other gospels give a very different setting: Bethany, some days before Jesus' death. Besides, the basic theme of sin-and-forgiveness, which is so essential to the Lukan account, is nowhere mentioned in the Bethany account. In fact, Luke's text and context are so different from the other accounts that even though most scholars believe that Luke's gospel generally depends on Mark, many see serious objections to applying that dependence to Lk. 7.36-50.[3] Thus, from a literary point of view, Lk. 7.36-50 seems not to depend on any of the other gospels. Luke, it appears, had some source of his own, but it is not at all clear what that source might be, nor how the literary similarities between the various anointing accounts developed.

One of the usual methods of responding to the data, to the complex array of similarities and dissimilarities, is to attempt immediately to reconstruct a historical background which could explain the oddly differing accounts. Was there, in history, in Jesus' life, just one event which was handed on in different ways? Or were there two events which, in the process of transmission, became confused?

---

1. According to Sybel (1924: 185), Lk. 7.36-50 is the most difficult of all Synoptic pericopes. Bouwman (1969:172) refers to it as a '*crux interpretum notoire*'. For a brief survey of research, see Holst 1976: 435-36. For a bibliography, see Fitzmyer 1981: 693-94.
2. For a table comparing details, see Brown 1966: 450.
3. See, for instance, Streeter 1924: 210; Jeremias 1966: 99; Schürmann 1969: 441; Fitzmyer 1981: 684. The most elaborate analysis of the passage, however, that of Delobel (1966: 474-75) opts tentatively for its partial dependence on Mark.

Repeated use of this method has shown that it is not fruitful. Admittedly, it seems in some ways to be an obvious line of inquiry, and it represents a concern which ultimately must be met. But it would appear to be one of those instances where 'the historical question is posed prematurely',[4] and it certainly does not yield results. The most meticulous weighing of the data has not been able to indicate, with any decisiveness, whether there was one event or two. It is symptomatic of the inadequacy of the data for solving the problem that while Schürmann and Brown see two events, Dodd and Fitzmyer opt for one.[5]

It appears therefore that discussion of the literary and historical origin of Lk. 7.36-50 has reached a kind of stalemate. In view of this impasse, it seems appropriate to try another approach, to ask whether—like the rest of Luke 7—the anointing account depends at least in part on an imitating and reworking of the Elijah–Elisha narrative.

However, before turning to the Elijah–Elisha narrative, it is appropriate to highlight a feature that so far has been mentioned only briefly, namely internalization.

2. *Internalization*

Internalization was one of the techniques of imitation (see Chapter 1, 'Literary Imitation: The Practice'). It involved a shifting of focus from external attributes and actions to various qualities and developments that were more internal. Manifestations of this process extend from the Greeks' foundational Ionian thinkers (see Gusdorf 1967: 24-33; 1974: 1171) to Virgil with his portrayal of *pius Aeneas*. Thus, where Achilles at one point emphasizes physical strength ('As long as...my good knees have their strength'), Virgil, in a complete reshaping of the passage, depicts Aeneas as emphasizing something far more internal ('While I remember who I am').[6] The overall impression is of a literary procedure that was well established.

3. *1 Kings 4.1-37 and Luke 7.36-50: Introductory Analysis*

As one scans the Elijah–Elisha narrative, asking whether any of its episodes have anything to do with Luke's account of the sinful woman, there are a number of reasons why 2 Kgs 4.1-37 attracts attention. The first is that, like Lk. 7.36-50, its tone is significantly feminine. Few passages in the Elijah–Elisha narrative put so great an emphasis on the presence of women. Such a similarity, of course, is only a straw in the wind, yet it is not to be despised. The second is that the stories of women in 2 Kgs 4.1-37 (concerning the oil, and the raising of the son) appear, in some ways, as variations on the storiess of woman stories in 1 Kings 17;[7] in other words, as variations on the very text which Luke had already used at the beginning of ch. 7, especially in the Nain incident, 7.11-17. If Luke used the woman of 1 Kings 17 as a model for the woman of Nain (in the early part of ch. 7), then perhaps he used the related stories of 2 Kings 4 as a basis for describing the sinful woman (at the end of ch. 7). To put it another way, Luke's sensitivity to 1 Kings 17 suggests that he may have been equally sensitive to the related episodes in 2 Kings 4.

---

4. Sarason (1981: 61), analyzing the heritage of Gunkel 1901.
5. Dodd 1963: 162-73; Brown 1966: 449-51; Schürmann 1969: 441; Fitzmyer, 1981: 685-86. An examination of the items in Fitzmyer's bibliography (pp. 693-94) increases rather than alleviates the impression of stalemate.
6. Cf. *Iliad* 9.609; *Aeneid* 4.336.
7. Montgomery, for instance, speaks of parallelism and correspondences of detail between the texts (1951: 366-67). In comparison with 1 Kgs 17, 2 Kgs 4.1-37 puts greater emphasis on the initiative and role of the woman.

Then, as the texts (2 Kgs 4.1-37; Lk. 7.36-50) are examined more closely, a whole series of similarities begins to emerge. These similarities, however, are quite complex, and to grapple with them it is necessary to look at the texts more closely.

a. *2 Kings 4.1-37*

The Old Testament text consists of two stories. The first (2 Kgs 4.1-7) tells of a widow who was in debt to the point of almost forfeiting her two sons to a creditor, and who, according to the LXX, had nothing left but a little oil for anointing herself. However, she called Elisha, and, by a process which involved the pouring out of the oil, she was freed from debt.

The second story (2 Kgs 4.8-37) is striking. It is delicately controlled and highly sophisticated. The woman is a woman of rank (*gynē megalē*). She is not indebted to anyone, nor does she ask anything of Elisha. Rather, it is she who endows him, providing him with hospitality (4.8-10). Her husband, who is old, is a vague and ineffectual creature (4.9-10, 14, 18-19, 22-23). She has no children. When the prophet asks if there is anything he can do for her 'she stood before him' and made a dignified and understated declaration of independence: 'I live in the midst of my own people' (4.13). The second time Elisha calls her, her resistance is palpable. She does not come before him. Instead, 'she stood at the door' (4.15). Even when Elisha promises her a child, her reaction, much as it betrays a hidden desire, still maintains a regal formality: 'No, my lord, do not deceive your servant' (4.16).

But the miracle happens, and when the boy dies, the woman who once had stood at a distance from Elisha now seeks him out with a desperate determination. And when she finds him she throws herself at his feet, first in bitter entreaty, and later, after the boy is revived, in quiet thanksgiving.

The woman provides a powerful example of the deep transformation which had been effected by the prophet, and ultimately by God. Her body finds new life in the birth of her son. And her spirit finds new life in the realization that, however self-sufficient she may be, there is a God who grants more than she dare ask.

In different ways, therefore, both Old Testament stories tell of women who, through Elisha, found new life. The first was released from a crushing debt; the second discovered a whole new richness in life.

b. *Luke 7.36-50*

The New Testament text (Lk. 7.36-50) speaks first of a hospitable Pharisee, but then devotes most of its attention to the contrasting figure of a sinful woman who threw herself at Jesus' feet, emotionally anointed them, and thereby found forgiveness and peace.

Literary analysts,[8] while differing on details, have sometimes pointed out that there are two basic points at which the text seems to have been conflated or sewn together. First, there is the brief parable of the creditor and the two debtors (7.40-42), a parable which, because it puts forgiveness first (before love), is sometimes regarded as being at variance with the larger scene which seems to put love first—the woman's love for Jesus led to her being forgiven. Second, there are the concluding remarks by Jesus and the onlookers, remarks largely concerned with forgiveness and Jesus' authority to forgive (7.47-50), most of which appear to have been added on, as a kind of commentary, to the picture of the Pharisee and the woman. But it has never been possible to explain what exactly lies behind these apparent divisions or seams.

The problem is partly solved by comparison with 2 Kings 4.

---

8. For example, see Jülicher 1899: I, 299-300; Loisy 1924: 235; Bultmann 1963: 20-21; Schürmann 1969: 430, 434-35; Fitzmyer 1981: 684.

4. Initial Comparison

Comparison of the two texts (2 Kgs 4.1-37; Lk. 7.36-50) finally yields the following fundamental points:

The basic framework and raw material for Luke's overall text come from the story of the woman of Shunem (2 Kgs 4.8-37). Her contrasting characteristics (her initial standoffishness; her later humility and faith) have been transformed by Luke into two contrasting characters: the Pharisee and the sinful woman. The result of Luke's transformation is not to destroy the Old Testament but to clarify it, bringing out in unforgettable images what the Old Testament had suggested with subtlety.

The parable which, to some degree, seems to interrupt Luke's main text (the story of the creditor and two debtors, Lk. 7.40-42), has little to do with the story of the Shunammite. It is drawn largely from the preceding story of the creditor who was claiming the two sons (2 Kgs 4.1-7).

The final verses—the commentary (Lk. 7.47-50)—have little to do with either Old Testament story. They appear to be largely taken from some other source/s.

The essential point is that the basic divisions which have long been noticed in Luke's text correspond broadly to his fusing or conflating of different sources: his conflating of the creditor story with the Shunammite story, and his conflating of both with some other final material.

The relationship between the two texts is outlined in Table 52. The outline (which simplifies somewhat, especially by omitting Luke's final verses, 7.47-50), indicates that not all the elements of the Old Testament creditor story (2 Kgs 4.1-7) are used in the New Testament creditor story. The image of *an indebted woman pouring out anointing oil* has been, as it were, extricated or divided from the Old Testament creditor story, and has been fused or conflated with the image of *the humble woman at the prophet's feet*—whence the complex picture of *a woman anointing Jesus' feet* (Lk. 7.37-38). Furthermore, while the picture of Simon the Pharisee is modeled largely on the self-sufficient picture of the Shunammite, it is also modeled on Gehazi, the servant whose rather distant approach failed to spark life in the child. Thus, Luke's depicting of characters involves a rather complex process both of division and fusion: the Shunammite's contrasting characteristics have been divided into contrasting characters (one self-sufficient, the other humble), and each of these characters has been expanded through fusion with other characters (with the indebted woman, and with the detached servant).

To a modern historian, such dividing and fusing of characters is not only far-fetched; it is abhorrent and bizarre. In the world of literary imitation, however, it was quite acceptable. As already mentioned, the source text was treated as raw material which could be wrestled or digested into a new form. Cicero, at one point, when explaining the method of literary imitation, tells of an artist who, in order to produce one figure, drew on five models;[9] and in Virgil's *Aeneid*, for instance, we find on several occasions that figures from Homer have not only been adapted to new situations, but have also been fused together in various ways.[10] Luke's procedure, therefore, bizarre though it may seem from one point of view, from an artistic viewpoint is quite legitimate, and from a pedagogical point of view it is extremely purposeful. By dividing and fusing as he has done, Luke has rendered two stories which involve considerable length and subtlety into one single story which is concise and clear.

---

9. *De inventione* 2.2.3-4.

10. For a summary of some of the ways in which Homeric characters have been transformed and fused by Virgil, see Knauer 1979: 342-43.

Table 52. *The Indebted Women (2 Kings 4.1-37; Luke 7.36-50)*

	2 Kings 4.1-37		Luke 7.36-50
1.	An indebted woman contacts Elisha. She has only some anointing oil (4.1-2)		
2.	*Initial/Exemplary Story:* The indebtedness of the woman and her two sons is miraculously overcome (by the pouring of oil) (4.1-7)		
3.	A woman of rank regularly invites the prophet to eat and recline in a room in her house (4.8-11)		A Pharisee invites Jesus to eat and recline in his house (7.36)
		1.	A sinful woman knows of Jesus and comes with perfumed oil (7.37)
		6a.	*Sin…* The woman pours out her vitality, especially through her head, at the feet of the prophet (And she pours oil) (7.38)
4.	The hospitable woman stays within her own world and does not appreciate the power of the prophet (4.12-16)		The hospitable Pharisee stays within his own thoughts and does not appreciate Jesus' role as prophet (7.39)
			2. *Exemplary Story:* Apropos of the sinful woman, Jesus tells of two people whose debts were gratuitously cancelled (7.40-42)
5.	The woman conceives (4.17)		Simon conceives an idea of love (7.43)
6a.	*Death…* Suffering from its head, the child gives up its life on the woman's knees… And she falls at the prophet's feet (4.18-28)		
6b.	*…And restoration* Gehazi's detached approach fails. Through contact of mouth/eyes/hands, life is restored; the woman falls at Elisha's feet (4.29-37)		*…And forgiveness* Simon's approach is insufficient. The woman's tears, kisses, and anointing restore her to forgiveness at Jesus' feet (7.44-46)

5. *2 Kings 4.1-37 and Luke 7.36-50: Detailed Analysis*

The following analysis goes through the Old Testament text, section by section, as in the outline, and compares each section with some section of Lk. 7.36-50. The division of the text into such sections involves some simplification. Luke does not always work in clearly separated sections, with one section of the Old Testament being used in one section only of Luke's text. On the contrary, there is some criss-crossing of details. By and large, however, the sections do correspond.

a. *Section 1. The Indebted Woman (2 Kings 4.1-2; Luke 7.37)*
The indebted woman who appeals to Elisha has only some anointing oil. And the sinful woman who comes to Jesus brings perfumed anointing oil.

Luke's text shows three basic adaptations. First, the woman's impoverishment is not financial but moral, or internal. She is 'a sinner' (*hamartōlos*), a designation which not only reflects Luke's general concern for sinners, but particularly reflects the statement, made just a few verses earlier (Lk. 7.34), that the Son of Humanity is a friend of sinners. Thus, on the one hand, Luke is following the Old Testament, but on the other hand he is adapting it boldly to his own concerns and to the requirements of his own narrative coherence.

Second, while the anointing material in the LXX is quite modest ('some oil with which I shall anoint myself'), the New Testament anointing material is lavish—an alabaster vase of perfumed oil. Once again, what Luke has done is adapt the Old Testament text to his own narrative, to the fact that in his account the woman's bankruptcy is not financial but moral. In other words, he keeps the basic element of material for anointing but adapts it to a form more suited to the sinful woman. For lavish perfume may indeed connote a richness of love, but in the possession of a well-known sinner, it may also suggest a questionable luxuriousness.[11]

Third, while Luke maintains the two basic Old Testament elements (the indebted woman and the anointing material), the narrative line is stripped to its barest essence. Instead of giving all the details regarding the loss of her husband and the impending loss of her sons, Luke concentrates on the core of the narrative: the woman's appeal to the prophet. In fact, Luke gives no initial conversation with the woman, none at all. But, though Luke's version is spare, his wording carries echoes of the longer Old Testament text. The Old Testament woman calls Elisha because he 'knows that' her family situation was such and such, and she tells him she has nothing 'in the house' but anointing oil. The New Testament woman is also is linked by knowledge to Jesus. She 'knows that' he is 'in the house' and she brings material for anointing. These verbal echoes may be laid out thus:

Old Testament:
kai gynē...kai su egnōs hoti...en tō oikō

New Testament:
kai idou gynē...kai epignousa hoti...en tē oikia

Old Testament:
and a woman...and you know that...in the house

New Testament:
and behold a woman...and knowing that...in the house

Thus, while Luke's words reflect the Old Testament the exact context in which he uses these words is so different that we are faced not with a quotation of any kind, but apparently with some form of word-play. Such verbal similarity could possibly be coincidence, but if the phenomenon occurs several times, then it will have to be taken more seriously.

Overall, therefore, it is found that most elements of the Old Testament picture of the indebted woman are found in adapted or abbreviated form in Luke.

b. *Section 2. The Two who were Freed from Debt (2 Kings 4.1-7; Luke 7.40-42)*
While the image of the indebted woman is transformed into that of the sinner, the image of two indebted sons is transformed into that of two contrasting debtors ('Which of them will love him more?'), thus building contrast and focusing attention on the internal disposition of the two.

Though Luke's processes of internalization and abbreviation involve a change in the form of the text and in the storyline, his final text again echoes the wording of the LXX:

11. It has been suggested that the action of the woman may indicate, among other things, that the perfume had been bought with ill-gotten money; see Derrett 1970: 268.

danistēs ('creditor'), a *hapax* in the New Testament, is found only four times in the LXX, only once in the narrative books of the LXX in 2 Kgs 4.1. Nowhere else save in Lk. 7.41 and 2 Kgs 4.1 is the creditor involved with 'two' people. And the word 'to pay' (*apodounai*) in Lk. 7.42, echoes *apodou* in 2 Kgs 4.7, but is used in a rather different way.

Furthermore, there is the verbal resemblance of the initial conversations. Each of the two Old Testament stories contains an initial conversation between the prophet and the woman (2 Kgs 4.1-4 and 12-16). The essence of each conversation is that the prophet asks what he can do for the woman, or offers to do something for her (4.2, 13, 14). In Luke's text, these conversations do not occur where one might expect them—in the initial presentation of the sinful woman and of the Pharisee. But in the Lukan story of the creditor, there is an initial conversation with the Pharisee in which Jesus offers, not to *do* something, but to *say* something. This conversation has apparent verbal and/or structural echoes of both Old Testament conversations. Compare:

Old Testament (vv. 1-3):
*danistēs...duo...kai eipen...ti poiēsō soi; ti estin soi
en tō oikō...eipen pros autēn...*

New Testament:
eipen pros auton...echō soi ti eipein...duo...danistē...

Old Testament (vv. 8-16):
*Souman...Sōmaneitēn...eipen...pros autēn...ti doi poiēsai soi
en mesō...egō...oikō...ti dei poiēsai autē...ē de eipen
Mē kyrie mou, mē diapseusē tēn doulēn sou*

New Testament:
eipen pros auton, Simōn, echō soi ti eipein. Ho de, Didaskale eipe...

Old Testament (vv. 1-3):
Creditor...two...and he said... 'What shall I do for you? What do you have in the house?'...
He said to her...

New Testament:
He said to him... 'I have something to say to you...two...creditor...'

Old Testament (vv. 8-16):
Shunem...Shunammitess...he said...to her...'what shall I do for you?'
In the middle...I...live... 'What should I do for her?'... But she said,
'No, my lord, do not deceive your servant'.

New Testament:
He said to him, 'Simon, I have something to say to you'. He [said], 'Teacher, speak'.

It does not seem possible, at least in the present state of research, to form a firm judgment concerning many of the details of these similarities. What is to be said, for instance, concerning the similarity of *Simōn* to *Souman/Sōmaneitēn*? And of *Didaskale* to *Kyrie mou diapseusē...doulēn*? How far may word-play go?[12] But whatever the details, it seems reasonable, given the general similarities between the conversations, and given the general acceptability, in Luke and in other authors, of the practice of fusing or conflating,[13] to note

---

12. In the Old Testament, word-play is quite common. Among the rabbis, some forms of word-play were used in a way that to us seems 'very artificial and far-fetched'; see Lieberman 1962: 68-77 (68).

13. Thus, where Euripides speaks of Hippolytus' father as cursing and of Hippolytus and his friends as crying (*Hippolytus* 6.1166-83), Seneca gives a fused image, greatly compressed and starkly dramatic, of Hippolytus alone as cursing and crying (*Phaedra* 4.1004-1005). For further examples, see Introduction, Chapter 1, on Greco-Roman imitation.

that Jesus' initial conversation with Simon is significantly similar to Elisha's initial conversations with the Old Testament women.

c. *Section 3. The Distinguished Host Invites a Prophet (2 Kings 4.8-11; Luke 7.36)*
The second Old Testament story begins by telling how a woman of rank regularly invited Elisha to eat and rest in her house. Luke tells how a Pharisee invited Jesus to eat with him and that Jesus went in and reclined. Unlike the rather elaborate Old Testament narrative, Luke's text is brief and clear, yet its wording has significant similarities with the Old Testament wording. Compare:

> Old Testament:
> *ekratēsen auton phagein...exeklinen...phagein...klinēn...ekklinei
> kai eisēlthen...exekllinen...ekoimēthē*
>
> New Testament.:
> *ērōta...auton...hina...phagē...kai eiselthōn...kateklithē*
>
> Old Testament:
> She constrained/held him to eat...he turned aside...to eat...a bed...turn aside... and he went in...and he turned aside...and lay down.
>
> New Testament:
> He asked...him...to...eat... And going in...he reclined.

d. *Section 4. The Host's Narrow World and Narrow Perception (2 Kings 4.12-16; Luke 7.39)*
Despite her apparent outgoing hospitality, the woman of Shunem tends to stay within a rather circumscribed world, living, as she puts it, within her own people. And when the Pharisee who has called Jesus sees the wondrous encounter between the sinful woman and the prophet, his reaction is not one of receptivity but of confinement within his own narrow thoughts: 'He said in himself...' Thus, both hosts, despite their openness at one level, seem quite isolated, living in their self-sufficient worlds. But, again, Luke has internalized his source: instead of a picture of economic and social self-sufficiency (living within one's own people), he gives a picture of a self-sufficiency which is more internal (living within one's own thoughts).

Apart from internalizing, Luke also greatly compresses the narrative. Yet, despite these changes, he manages, by a kind of word-juggling, to keep a continuity with his source:

> Old Testament:
> *kai ekalesen autēn...hē de eipen, En mesō tou laou...*
>
> New Testament:
> *ho kalesas auton eipen en heautō*
>
> Old Testament:
> And he called her... But she said, 'In the middle of [my own] people...'
>
> New Testament:
> He who called him said in himself...

As well as being confined within rather narrow worlds, the two hosts are hampered by a rather narrow perception of the prophet. The woman does not realize that he can bring her childless body to new life. And the Pharisee does not realize that Jesus is bringing new life to the sinful woman. In other words, both the Shunammite and Simon focus on what is negative (the apparently lifeless body; the apparently lifeless soul), and do not appreciate the positive power of the prophet. The Shunammite senses deception: 'No, my lord, do not lie to your servant'. The Pharisee doubts that Jesus is really a prophet.

e. *Section 5. The Host Comes to a New Conception (2 Kings 4.17; Luke 7.43)*
But the woman conceived (*lambanō*) and bore a son. And the Pharisee 'conceived' the wonder of love and forgiveness: 'I suppose (*hypo-lampanō*) the one to whom he graciously forgave more'. Here, too, there is a radical internalization. Both the woman and the Pharisee break out of their confined world and, through the prophetic word, come to a new conception. But while one conception is physical, the other is of a more internal kind. And here, too, through a form of word-play (*lambanō/hypolambanō*), Luke manages to echo the Old Testament wording.

f. *Section 6. The Outpouring and the Restoration (2 Kings 4.18-37; Luke 7.38, 44-46)*
The remainder of the Old Testament text consists of two balancing sections—one dealing with the boy's dying (2 Kgs 4.18-28), the other with his restoration (4.29-37)—and just as it was necessary to take in conjunction the two Old Testament initial conversations between Elisha and the women, so now, though in a somewhat different way, these two sections have to be taken together.

The balance or complementarity of the two Old Testament sections may be seen in a number of basic features. First, there is the emphasis on the head and on bodily contact. The death began when the child complained about his head ('My head, my head'), and then he lay on his mother's knees till midday (*kai ekoimēthē epi heōs*) and died (2 Kgs 4.19-20). The restoration to life occurred when Elisha lay on the child up to seven times (*kai ekoimēthē epi...heōs*) and touched him on the head ('he put his mouth upon his mouth, and his eyes upon his eyes, and his hands upon his hands', 4.34-35). Furthermore, both sections emphasize the prophet's reclining place or couch. Just as the account of the dying tells how the woman took the dead child, laid it on the prophet's couch, shut the door and went out (4.21), so the restoration account, using very similar wording, tells that Elisha went in, saw the child laid out on his couch, and shut the door (4.32-33). Both accounts tell also of an urgent journey, full of non-stop intensity and of imperatives not to pause: after the death there is the journey of the woman to the prophet (4.22-26), and before the restoration there is the breathless journey of Gehazi for what proves to be a futile attempt to try to raise the child (4.29-31). (Gehazi did not touch the child. He simply laid a staff on his face.) Finally, both accounts conclude with the surprising image of the woman throwing herself at the feet of the prophet.

Apart from the urgent journey, a factor to be dealt with briefly later, the main elements of the two parts may be summarized thus:

> The Death (2 Kgs 4.18-28):
> a. 'My head, my head'...and he lay on her knees till midday, and he died.
> b. She took him, laid him on the prophet's couch and shut the door.
> c. She went to Elisha and threw herself at his feet.
>
> The Restoration (2 Kgs 4.29-37):
> (Gehazi's failed attempt.)
> a. Elisha saw him laid out on his couch and he shut the door.
> b. He lay on the child...mouth to mouth...eyes to eyes...hands to hands...up to seven times...and the child revived.
> c. The woman went in and threw herself at Elisha's feet.

Luke's treatment of this twofold Old Testament material is quite complex. First of all, he keeps the basic structure of two scenes, the second of which is some kind of variation on or complement of the first, and so instead of balancing scenes of death and restoration, we find balancing scenes emphasizing sin (Lk. 7.38; cf. 7.37-39) and forgiveness (Lk. 7.44-46; cf. 7.42-47). He also keeps, as a distinctive feature of the second scene, the element of failure: Gehazi failed to spark life (2 Kgs 4.31), and Simon, too, failed to produce a kind of life (Lk. 7.44-46). (We will return to this question of the failure.) But with regard to the details which are particular to each of the two Old Testament scenes, these he does not keep distinct. Rather, he fuses details of both scenes together so that these details are found in each of the two New Testament scenes.

We begin by looking at Lk. 7.38, the first account of the woman at the feet of Jesus. In some ways, it is like a synthesis of the various processes surrounding the death of the child.

> 2 Kgs 4.18-28:
> From its head the child gives up its life on its mother's knees.
> The woman lays the child on the prophet's reclining place.
> The woman throws herself at the feet of the prophet.
>
> Lk. 7.38:
> From her head (tears, hair, kisses) and with her hands, the woman pours out her vitality at the feet of the prophet.

It may be seen through careful comparison that Luke's initial description of the woman involves both an internalization (because it stresses a kind of moral dying rather than a physical dying) and a fusing of the elements from the Old Testament death scene. But it also contains details from the second Old Testament scene of the restoration: the tears, kisses, and implicit use of hands (for anointing) involve an exact transmutation of the emphasis the Old Testament restoration account puts on the eyes, mouth, and hands. And, as already indicated, insofar as it includes the use of anointing oil, Luke's description fuses and transmutes an element from the earlier story (2 Kgs 4.1-2). Thus, the first scene of the woman at Jesus' feet is a dense but precise conflation of many elements from different sources.

And the second scene is largely a variation on the first. It mentions the same diversity of elements. Yet it is quite distinct from the first, not just because it emphasizes forgiveness rather than sinfulness, but also because it includes a sustained contrast with Simon: he gave no water, but she washed with her tears; he gave no kiss, but she did not cease to kiss; he did not even freshen Jesus' face with oil (a fairly common custom);[14] but she anointed his feet—and with perfumed oil. As already indicated, this failure on the part of Simon corresponds to Gehazi's failure to arouse any spark of life in the child. It is probably not an accident that both failures—both descriptions of lifelessness—are described through a triple negative (*ouk...ouk...ouk*, 2 Kgs 4.31; Lk. 7.44-46). But while the Old Testament puts all three negatives together (there was neither sound, nor sign...and the child did not awake), Luke interweaves them clearly and powerfully into the different elements of his text (you did not...but she; you did not...but she; you did not...but she) and thus achieves a contrast which is more dramatic and sustained.

This increased sense of contrast—this greater clarity—coincides with the phenomenon noted earlier: the clear contrast which is achieved by changing the Shunammite's two characteristics into two characters. It also coincides with the aim of dramatic clarity which may be observed elsewhere in Luke and in other writers.[15]

Overall, therefore, Luke's balancing scenes of sin-and-forgiveness involve a complex and precise reworking of the Old Testament scenes of death-and-restoration.

Some additional details concerning verbal similarities may be noted. The initial designation of the woman as standing (*stasa*) at Jesus' feet as he reclined (Lk. 7.38), coincides

---

14. See Fitzmyer 1981: 691; Mt. 6.17; Str-B, 1.426-28.

15. On the relation of Luke's method of dramatization and compression to that of other writers, especially Livy, see Plümacher 1972: 111-36.

with the initial description, carefully repeated, of the Shunammite as standing in Elisha's presence in his reclining room (*estē...estē*, 7.12, 15). It is difficult to say whether the repeated references to 'this Shunammite' (*tēn Sōmaneitēn tautēn*, 2 Kgs 4.12, 36) and the phrase 'Behold that Shunammite' (*Idou dē hē Sōmaneitis ekeinē*, 4.25) are in any way reflected in 'You see this woman (*Blepeis tautēn tēn gynaika*, Lk. 7.44). Other similarities, some of which have already been suggested, may be summarized as follows:

Old Testament:
tous podas autou, 'his feet' (repeated, 4.27.37)
...*eisēlthen...eis tēn oikon*..., 'went into the house' (repeated 4.32-33)
...*ouk* ('no')...*ouk...ouk*... (4.31)

New Testament:
tous podas autou, 'his feet' (repeated, 7.38, 44-46)
...*eiselthōn/eisēlthon...eis tēn oikian*, 'going/coming...into the house' (repeated, 7.36, 44)
...*ouk* ('not')...*ouk...ouk* (7.44-46)

Whatever our judgment on some details, the number of links between the texts is remarkable.

Finally, turning to Luke's concluding verses (7.47-50, 'And so, I say to you, her sins... Go in peace'), we find, as already mentioned, that there is no dependence on 2 Kgs 4.1-37. However, Luke's use of the fairly common Old Testament dismissal form, 'Go in peace', is probably occasioned to some degree by the repeated references in 2 Kgs 4.22-26 to the woman's going/journeying (*poreu-omai*) amid greetings of peace (*eirēnē*) or wellbeing. Compare:

Old Testament:
poreusē...eirēnē...poreuou...poreusē...eirēnē...eirēnē...eirēnē...eirēnē

New Testament:
poreuou eis eirēnēn

In other words, through the use of the well-known form Luke synthesizes and transforms a rather complex Old Testament passage.

6. *Assessment of Method and Data*

As indicated earlier (Chapter 5), literary studies in general have no single established method for dealing with complex literary relationships. It is partly because of this lack of a clear method that much remains to be discovered about the use of sources.[16] Even so central and obvious a question as Milton's use of Homer and Virgil needs significant development (see Blessington 1979: especially xi).

In New Testament literary studies, the situation is somewhat worse. Not only is there an absence of a good method, but, to some degree, there is the presence of a method that is bad or at least inadequate. The use of the gospel synopsis—which is, of course, in itself, an indispensable aid—has tended to establish a method of comparing texts on the basis of something very simple: obvious verbal parallelism. Little or no effort is made to relate texts on the basis of the complex methods of transformation current in the first century. The result is that if two passages do not show fairly obvious parallelism, they are either not compared, or their complex relationship, instead of being set in a literary context, is usually accounted for on the basis of an appeal to evidence which is missing and uncontrollable: oral traditions and lost documents. Such lost traditions and documents may not

---

16. As G. Highet notes in his survey of the influence of the classics on later literature (1949: viii), 'A great deal of the territory is still quite unexplored'.

easily be discounted, but to appeal to them too readily is to bypass the possibility of complex literary dependence.

The difficulty of seeing the relationship between two texts, one of which involves a complex reshaping of the other, may be seen, as Seneca suggests (*Epistulae Morales* 84.8), in the case of a parent and a child. The offspring may be a very independent individual, and very different from the parent in many ways. A twenty-five-year-old woman may be very independent of and dissimilar from her sixty-year-old father. Yet she is composed, among other things, of what may be called a complex reworking of her father. If for some reason there is some doubt about whether the two are related, it is not sufficient simply to point to the many dissimilarities between them. Rather, the question is whether there are sufficient similarities to link the two. Are there, for instance, certain traits or marks, certain facial or bodily expressions which almost definitely point to some relationship? Are there external circumstances or details which confirm these indications?

Similarly, with regard to the way in which the New Testament involves a reworking of the Old Testament. As R.E. Brown points out (Brown 1966: 397-98), dissimilarities do not clinch the issue. Rather, the question rather is whether there are sufficient positive indications to say that the Old Testament text provided much of the raw material for the New Testament passage. And it seems that there are.

First of all, there is a certain extrinsic likelihood. Not only does Luke appear to have imitated the Old Testament in various ways, but by mentioning Elijah and Elisha as he does in the programmatic Nazareth speech (Lk. 4.16-30), he seems to indicate that these great prophets were among his primary Old Testament models. And the link with the Nazareth speech and the figures of the great prophets is rarely stronger than in Lk. 7.1–8.3.

Second, there are the inherent similarities of the texts. The tone of both passages is markedly feminine. The themes are also significantly similar: variations on the basic idea of overcoming a crushing mixture of debt and death. More decisive, however, than these general similarities are the correspondences of the many and varied actions. Virtually every element of the Old Testament narrative is found in summarized or transformed shape in the New Testament passage. Even relatively rare elements find an equivalent in Luke: the creditor, the anointing oil, the emphasis on the place where the prophet reclined, the host's standoffishness, the woman's throwing herself at the prophet's feet, the emphasis on physical contact involving head, eyes, mouth, and hands, the contrast or failure on the part of a third party. And finally, at almost every stage there are curious verbal similarities. Many of them are small details, but taken together, they form a pattern and appear to confirm the existence of a persistent literary link.

Third, there is the consistency of the dissimilarities. They do not form some haphazard mixture, at odds with one another and with general literary practice. On the contrary they reflect coherent patterns, patterns of internalization, fusion, division, compression, and clarification. And these are precisely some of the fundamental procedures of rhetorical imitation. As far as the basic variation in theme is concerned—an emphasis on sin and forgiveness rather than on death and life—this difference is quite consistent with Luke's general emphasis on the forgiveness of sinners and with his comparison of sin and forgiveness to death and life (Lk. 15.32).

It seems reasonable to conclude that Luke did indeed imitate 2 Kgs 4.1-37. Through his careful artistry the ancient scripture has been modernized and clarified by the Hellenistic method. But though the Old Testament provides the narrative basis, it does not dictate the shape of Luke's text. On the contrary, it has been subjected to the overarching interests of a new theological vision. It has been developed and christianized. In a real sense, it has been fulfilled.

It does not, however, seem reasonable to say that the link between the texts is due to oral tradition. There is no known process of oral transmission which is capable of transforming a text in a way that is so complex and coherent.[17] It is the literary explanation, and the literary explanation alone, which is capable of accounting for the data.

Luke's use of 2 Kgs 4.1-37 allows for his use of other sources. Some aspects of Luke's text seem quite independent of the Old Testament passage. This is especially true of the harmless sensuousness of the woman's actions (Lk. 7.37-38, 44-46), the theological explicitness of some of Luke's vocabulary (sinner, forgive, love, 7.37, 39, 42-43), and the conclusion, which is a kind of commentary on the whole scene (7.47-50). However, whether it is possible to trace the origin of these extra elements is not the concern of this study. It is a matter for further research.

Luke's use of Hellenistic methods of composition does not exclude his use of Jewish methods as well. The two were often interwoven[18] and Luke's apparent use of a certain form of word-play, for instance, coincides with the Jewish tradition of word-play. But it seems better that Luke's reworking of the Old Testament should not be called a midrash. 'Midrash' is often used only in cases of explicit citation and interpretation; it seems better not to use the term to describe Luke 1–2;[19] and for the same reason it seems better not to use it of Lk. 7.36-50.

Luke's imitation of the Old Testament does not rule out his inclusion of genuine history. On the available evidence it might be suggested, for instance, that Luke's particular way of reshaping the Old Testament reflects the historical reality of Jesus' relationship with Pharisees and sinners. But it does not appear possible, at least in the present state of research, to go beyond such suggestions. For the moment, it seems better to say of Lk. 7.36-50, as Fitzmyer said of Luke 1–2, that 'whatever historical matter has been preserved...has been assimilated...to other literary accounts' (Fitzmyer 1981: 309).

Luke's apparent inconsistency with regard to which comes first, love or forgiveness, seems to be due, not to muddled thinking or to an inability to control sources, but to a sensitivity to the complexity of things, to an awareness that the two interact in subtle ways.[20] It is slowly being realized that many of the apparent inconsistencies of biblical writers are symptoms, not of awkwardness, but of artistry (see especially Alter 1981), and, given Luke's established reputation as 'a consummate literary artist',[21] it seems best to see the tension which he creates in his text, much as it reflects some variety in his sources, as a careful artistic expression of the complexity of reality.

As a result of this investigation, the rootedness of Luke's text in the ancient (canonical) scriptures is considerably enhanced. Here is not the place to investigate the implications of such rootedness, but it does seem useful at least to raise a question: Does this relationship to the Old Testament mean that Luke's work was already something more than an occasional document, from the moment of its writing, before being officially designated canonical by the church? Does it mean that it already had an inherent quality of canonicity?[22]

---

17. None of the categories of oral transmission proposed, for instance, by B. Gerhardsson (1979: 14-22) are capable of explaining such a transformation. Here, as elsewhere, Ong's remark (1977: 254) is valid: 'Closer plotting requires writing'.

18. On the interaction of the two kinds of methods, see Kurz 1980b: 182.

19. For discussion, and so on, see Fitzmyer 1981: 308-309.

20. See Delobel 1966: 416, 470-74; Dupont 1980.

21. See Fitzmyer 1981: 92. It is a matter for further research to decide whether Luke's tense balancing of two complementary points of view should be related to the Lukan 'law of duality' so emphasized by Morgenthaler (1949).

22. Sterling (1992: 363) maintains that 'Luke conceived his work as the *continuation* of the LXX. His deliberate composition in Septuagintal Greek and...[as] fulfilment...imply that...Luke–Acts represents *sacred narrative*.'

In all this, no appeal has been made to the Bethany anointing (Mk 14.3-9; Mt. 26.6-13; Jn 12.1-8), and it may seem perverse to pursue the veiled Old Testament relationship while ignoring the obvious links of the Bethany texts. But the relationship to the Old Testament provides an explanation of Luke's text, which, though partial, is quite conclusive, and the relationship to the Bethany texts does not. As far as Lk. 7.36-50 is concerned, the Bethany texts, at first so inviting, do not yield results. They tend rather to distract from other possible avenues of research. It has seemed better, therefore, for the moment, to concentrate on Luke's relationship to the Old Testament.

7. Conclusion

Detailed literary comparison indicates that almost every element of the Old Testament stories of the woman in debt and of the woman who found new life (2 Kgs 4.1-37) may be found in abbreviated or transformed shape in Luke's account of the forgiving of the sinful woman (Lk. 7.36-50). The major difference between the texts is that in Luke, many actions and ideas, especially those of debt and new life, are more internal. The most reasonable explanation of the complex but coherent mixture of similarities and dissimilarities is that Luke, as a Hellenistic writer, used the commonly accepted Hellenistic practice of rhetorical imitation, including the techniques of internalization, fusion, and compression, to synthesize, clarify, and christianize the Old Testament passage.

The comparison of Lk. 7.36-50 with the Old Testament passage is considerably more conclusive than comparison with the other evangelists' account of a later anointing at Bethany.

32

A People Gathering Around the Prophet: Luke 8.1-3 as a Women-Oriented Distillation of Part of 1 Kings 18

When L.T. Johnson (1991: 134) summarized the brief account of Jesus journeying through the land with the Twelve and with the women who shared their possessions (Lk. 8.1-3), he spoke of 'a people *in nuce* gathering around the prophet'. For him the Twelve and the women are not a haphazard collection of individuals; rather, they represent a people, they are a people in a nutshell.

However, this description of 'a people gathering around the prophet', while referring to Lk. 8.1-3, can also be used of a much more dramatic scene from the Old Testament: the account of how, after some persons journeyed through the land, the people gathered around the prophet Elijah on Mt Carmel (1 Kgs 18).

The Old Testament process of gathering the people is described in stages. First, Elijah issues the call: 'Gather all Israel to me on Mt Carmel' (1 Kgs 18.19-20). Then, as the clash with the Baalites begins, the people stand by quietly (1 Kgs 18.21). Finally, after the Baalite worship has failed, the people gather in closer to Elijah, and when God sends fire, they eliminate the Baalites (1 Kgs 18.30, 40). With the Baalites gone, the nourishing rain returns.

Luke (8.1-3) has used the Old Testament picture of the gathering of the people but he has synthesized and internalized it. He has described the gathering more briefly, and the freedom which is given is not from Baal and the Baalites but from something more internal—demons. In other texts (Lk. 11.15; cf. Mt. 11.24; Mk 3.22), the expulsion of demons is explicitly linked with the Baal-related figure of Beelzebul. Thus the dramatic eradication of the Baal-related evil which beset Israel finds a more internal equivalent in the eradication of the Beelzebul-related demons which once beset some of those around Jesus.

However, Lk. 8.1-3 is not written just for its own sake. Rather it prepares for what is to come, and has been adapted for this purpose. The journeying sets the tone for future journeys, especially those to Emmaus and for others in Acts. And the overall picture of the Twelve, the women, and the sharing prepares for the women's role at the resurrection and in Acts, and also for the later sharing of possessions (Lk. 23.49; 23.55–24.11; Acts 1.13-14; 2.41-47; 4.32-37). Thus most of the material which relates to 8.1-3 occurs much later in Luke–Acts.

Likewise with 1 Kings 18. While part of it is distilled into Lk. 8.1-3, most of it is used much later in connection with the resurrection and in Acts. The initial meeting with the Spirit-empowered Elijah (1 Kgs 18.7-16), for instance, has been transformed into one small component of the resurrection-related accounts—especially the initial meetings involving the women (24.4-11) and the subsequent meeting on the road to Emmaus (Lk. 24.13-35).

The same is true of the later, dramatic episodes of 1 Kings 18 which contribute to later, dramatic scenes in Acts. The shattering, prayer-induced descent of fire from heaven (1 Kgs 18.32b-40) has provided a partial model for the fire and the prayer-induced shaking of the house (Acts 2.1-4 and especially 4.23-31). And the hectic worship by the prophets of Baal

(1 Kgs 18.17-29) has contributed to the hectic near-worship by the priests of Zeus (Acts 14.8-18).

Thus, while 1 Kings 18 contributed to the picture of the people gathering around the prophet (Lk. 8.1-3), it has also influenced later scenes at the resurrection and in Acts.

The accompanying outline (Table 53) highlights those parts of 1 Kings 18 which have contributed most to Lk. 8.1-3 (i.e. it focuses on the beginning, middle, and end of 1 Kgs 18 —vv. 1-6, 30-32a, 41-46; see Sections 1–3). The remaining parts of 1 Kings 18 (18.7-29, 32b-40), along with the corresponding texts from Luke–Acts (especially Lk. 24; Acts 4.23-31; 14.8-18), are also included in the outline, but only in the most summary fashion (sections 4–6).

The primary interest of this chapter is with Lk. 8.1-3 and its use of a portion of 1 Kings 18. The other Lukan texts (from Lk. 24 and Acts) are discussed only because, having accounted for part of 1 Kings 18, it is necessary to give at least some indication of what Luke did with the rest of that chapter. Hence, while 8.1-3 will be examined closely, the other texts will be dealt with more briefly.

1. *The Texts: Introductory Analysis*

The Old Testament account (1 Kgs 18) tells how the rain returned to the land, ending the long drought which was declared through Elijah (1 Kgs 17). The text has three main parts:

1. *A journey through the land with the king's steward* (18.1-16). King Ahab and his steward, Obadiah, travel through the land in search of water for their horses. Unlike the king who is preoccupied with his horses, the steward's deeper interest is God and God's prophets; he had devoted himself to these prophets, helping and feeding them. And in the case of the steward, the journey takes an unusual turn: it becomes a meeting with the Spirit-empowered Elijah (18.7-16).
2. *The gathering and rebuilding of the people* (18.17-40). Elijah summons all the people to Mt Carmel, and, after the failure of the Baalite worship, he rebuilds them. (He calls them close to him, and, using twelve stones representing the twelve tribes of Israel, he rebuilds the stones into an altar.) Then he calls down shattering fire. The people get rid of the Baalites.
3. *After a sevenfold vigil, the foodbearing rain returns* (18.41-46). Elijah tells Ahab to eat and drink because the rain is coming back. But the return of the rain requires a form of sevenfold vigil: as Elijah waits on Carmel, his servant, looking for signs of rain, has to go to the sea seven times. Only then does the rain come.

The New Testament text (Lk. 8.1-3) is like a summary of Jesus' ministry. Its short account may be divided into the following parts:

1. *Jesus journeys through the land* heralding the kingdom of God (8.1a).
2. *With him are the Twelve and the healed women*—women who have been cured from unclean spirits and weaknesses (8.1b-2a).
3. *The many women minister*—including Mary, freed of seven demons, and the wife of King Herod's steward (8.2b-3).

Luke's passage is a single sentence, loosely connected. It occurs in no other gospel, and so belongs to Luke alone. In fact, a number of factors—its language and style, and its role as a summary—indicate that 'the passage is best regarded as a Lucan composition as a whole' (Fitzmyer 1981: 695).

As already mentioned, Luke's summary gives a preview of what is to come in Luke 24 and Acts: the journeys, the sharing of possessions, and the role of the women. This latter feature—the role of the women—is particularly striking, so much so that Talbert (1986: 90) uses it as a heading. The emphasis on women is not new in Luke; already in his infancy narrative (chs. 1–2) he gives women a role which is prominent. Here (8.1-3), he simply continues and develops that emphasis.

In composing this picture of the people gathering around the prophet, Luke has drawn heavily on the story of Elijah. As the outline indicates, the journey through Israel's springs and wadis (1 Kgs 18.1-2, 5-6) provides some of the material for the account of Jesus journeying through the towns and villages (Lk. 8.1a). The gathering of the rebuilt people around Elijah (1 Kgs 18.30-32a) underlies the account of the Twelve and the women gathering around Jesus (Lk. 8.1b-2a). And the picture of the women ministering (Lk. 8.2b-3) involves a combining of two related texts: the nourishing role of the king's steward (1 Kgs 18.3-4) and the nourishing rain which required a sevenfold vigil (1 Kgs 18.41-46).

Table 53. *The People Gathered around the Prophet*
(1 Kings 18; Luke 8.1-3; Acts 14.8-18)

Beginning, Middle, and End of 1 Kings 18	Luke 8.1-3
The Journey	
1. And it happened (*Kai egeneto*) after (*meta*) many days: journeying through (*epi*) the land (*deuro...di-elthōmen hodon*) through (*epi...epi*) springs and wadis expecting (God-given) rain (*Kyriou...dōsō hueton*) (18.1-2, 5-6) The king's steward (*oikonomos*) nourished (*dia-trepho*) God's prophets (18.3-4)	And it happened (*Kai egeneto*) afterwards (*en tō kathexēs*), he journeyed (*di-ōdeuen*) through (*kata*) towns and villages heralding...God's kingdom (8.1a);
The People Gathered And Rebuilt	
2. * Come near (*pros...pros*) me, ** all the people. *** And he took the twelve stones/tribes and built the stones and healed (*iaomai*) the broken altar (18.30-32a)	*** and the Twelve * with (*syn*) him, ** and the women cured (*therapeuō*) from evil spirits and weaknesses (8.1b-2a)
Providing	
3. Baalites eliminated. Sevenfold vigil and foodbearing rain (18.40-46)	Mary Magdalene...freed from seven demons Herod's wife's steward (*epitropos*)... provided for them out of their possessions (*hyparchonta*) (8.2b-3)
The rest of 1 Kings 18	See Luke 24–Acts 14
4. Spirit-filled meeting (18.7-16)	Cf. Resurrection-related meetings, including women (Lk. 24, Acts)
5. Baalite worship fails (18.17-29)	Pagan worship prevented; God gives rain, nourishment (*theon...huetous didous... trophē*, Acts 14.8-18)
6. Prayer fires the altar (18.32b-39)	Prayer shakes the house (Acts 4.23-31). Sharing possessions (*hyparchonta*, 4.32-36)

2. *The Texts: Detailed Analysis*

The following analysis goes through the various sections of the outline. It concentrates first on the three sections which belong to Lk. 8.1-3, and then looks more briefly at the other three sections dealing with passages from Luke 24 and Acts.

a. *Sections Involving Luke 8.1-3*
(1) *Section 1. The journey through the land (1 Kings 18.1-2, 5-6; Luke 8.1a).* Apart from an initial promise that God will give rain, the Elijah story begins with a journey through the land: Ahab and Obadiah go through springs and wadis searching for water for the horses.

Luke 8 also begins with a journey through the land: Jesus goes through towns and villages heralding the kingdom of God.

Luke has maintained the picture of travelling through the land, but the dynamic is different: instead of a king preoccupied with horses, Jesus heralds the kingdom of God. In other words, Luke shows Jesus as seeking a kingdom or realm which is different from Ahab's kingdom of horses and raw power, based on Baal. The idea of an alternative realm was already implicit in the Old Testament when God promises rain and sends Elijah to confront Ahab. In Luke, however, that alternative realm is explicitly expressed in the familiar New Testament term 'kingdom of God'.

Luke's switch from 'springs and wadis' (Old Testament) to 'towns and villages' fits in with his larger strategies, including modernization and a more obvious focus on the human and thus on areas of greatest human habitation.

As the outline shows, Luke has included detailed resonances of the Old Testament text. Even when the evangelist replaces the threefold use of *epi* ('through'), with the single *kata* ('through'), the '*kata* is used in a distributive sense, "from town to town"' (Marshall 1978: 316). Thus, Luke's single distributive 'through' has captured the Old Testament sense of the 'through' being repeated.

(2) *Section 2. A picture of the people being rebuilt around the prophet (1 Kings 18.30-32a; Luke 8.1b-2a).* When the Baalite worship fails, Elijah gathers the people around him: 'Come near to me', he said, 'and all the people came near to him'. Then he took 'twelve stones—the number of the the tribes of Israel' and built them up, healing (*iaomai*) the altar that had been broken down. Thus, Israel is represented both in 'all the people' and in the twelve stones, and it is reconstructed, or healed, into an altar.

Luke's picture of Jesus with the Twelve and the women fits closely with the Old Testament picture of the people gathering around the prophet Elijah. Both texts refer to the people in two ways: first, symbolically through 'the twelve', and then more realistically, through 'all the people' (Old Testament) and 'certain women' (New Testament). The connection between the women and the larger community of the people is confirmed in later parts of Luke–Acts (Lk. 23.55–24.10; 24.48-49; Acts 1.13-14). In biblical symbolism, the people are sometimes represented by women (cf. Gen. 3.15; Ezek. 16; Hos. 1–3; Eph. 5.21-33; Rev. 12.1-6).

Furthermore, both texts (1 Kgs 18.30-32a; Lk. 8.1b-2a) refer to a process of restoration or healing. Elijah heals (*iaomai*) the broken altar which is representative of Israel. And Jesus cures (*therapeuō*) the women from evil spirits and weaknesses. Luke has kept the idea of a restoration, but with typical emphasis on internalization, he moves its focus from the world of external ritual (the altar) to the world which is within (the realm of spirit and weakness). Elijah restores ritual, but Jesus restores human spirits.

In describing the women's recovery, Luke speaks of two actions: how Jesus cured, and how the demons went out. While the curing broadly corresponds to the healing (or rebuilding) of the altar, the departure of the demons is closer to the elimination of Baal and the

Baalites. Together, the two actions synthesize complementary aspects of what Elijah did for the people: he rebuilt them and freed them from the Baalites.

(3) *Section 3. The king's steward and providing for the people around the prophet (1 Kings 18.3-4, 40-46; Luke 8.2b-3)*. The Old Testament narrative (1 Kgs 18) has two accounts of providing for people. First, there is a brief summary of how Obadiah, the king's steward, cares for the threatened prophets of God, nourishing them with food and drink (bread and water, 18.3-4). Later, there is a description, following the elimination of the Baalites, of how Elijah's sevenfold vigil brought back rain to the land, and, with the rain, eating and drinking (18.41-46).

Following the idea of the departure of the demons in Luke, there is an account of provision: the women provide for those around Jesus. Furthermore, these women reflect aspects of the Old Testament account of providing. Mary's demons had been seven. And Joanna is the wife of the king's steward.

The double reference to seven in ending the drought and ending the demons is hardly coincidence. Rather, there seems to some kind of balance between drought/waterlessness and demons, as though the terrible emptiness of the lack of water was balanced by the terrible effect of the demon or the lack of God. Elsewhere in the gospels, unclean spirits are explicitly associated with waterless country (Mt. 12.43; Lk. 11.24).

Easier to understand is the adaptation from the providing role played by the king's steward (Old Testament) to the providing role played by the wife of the king's steward (New Testament): Luke has used the Old Testament picture but has brought it into line with his emphasis on women.

He has also brought his text into line with other parts of Luke–Acts, especially with the picture of the community sharing their possessions (*hyparchonta*, Acts 4.32) and with the role of the women before and after the resurrection (Lk. 23.48-49; 23.55–24.10; Acts 1.13-14).

b. *Sections Involving Luke 24 and Acts*
(1) *Section 4. The spirit-filled meetings (1 Kings 18.7-16; Luke 24.4-9; cf. 24.13-35; Acts 8.26-40)*. The meeting between Obadiah and Elijah is full of reverence and spirit. As they come together, Obadiah hastens forward, falls on his face, and asks, 'Is it you, *kyrie*…?' Elijah said, *Egō* ('It is I'). And then the prophet sends Obadiah on a mission to Ahab to announce his (Elijah's) presence: 'Go, tell…"Behold Elijah"'.

But Obadiah, fearful of the king, gives a long reply (1 Kgs 18.9-14) in which he contrasts his own vulnerability to sin and death with the spirit-empowered Elijah. Elijah is capable of being anywhere—in any kingdom—and even when he is located, he can suddenly disappear: 'When I go away from you, the Spirit of the Lord will take you to a land which I do not know' (18.12).

So Elijah decides to use his spirit-power to meet Ahab: 'As the Lord of Hosts lives, before whom I stand, today I shall appear before him' (1 Kgs 18.15).

When Luke was describing various resurrection-related meetings, he colored some of his accounts with aspects of the meeting between the reverential Obadiah and the Spirit-empowered Elijah.

Thus, when the women (of Lk. 8.1-3) reappear in the resurrection account, they are somewhat like Obadiah when faced by Elijah: they fall on their faces, and then, in a variation on the impossible mission given to Obadiah, they are told to go and announce Jesus' living presence (Lk. 24.5-11). In different ways, it is precisely the extraordinary nature of the presence (of Elijah, of Jesus) which makes the two missions unworkable. Elijah's presence is so subject to the Spirit of the Lord that it does not follow human calculations about location. And the presence of the risen Jesus seems beyond all human calculations. Obadiah cannot risk such an announcement. The women do, but nobody believes them.

Later, in describing two related journeys which in different ways led to a change of heart —the walk to Emmaus (Lk. 24.13-35) and the journey of the Ethiopian (Acts 8.26-40)— Luke seems to use some further elements of Elijah's Spirit-based unpredictability to describe the appearance and disappearance of Jesus and Philip (Lk. 24.15, 31; Acts 8.29, 39-40).

Without tracing every detail, what is essential is that, beginning with the women, some of the actions in the resurrection-related narratives reflect the unique atmosphere surrounding Elijah.

(2) *Section 5. Pagan worship with animals—hectic, then stopped (1 Kings 18.17-29; Acts 14.8-18).* When the prophets of Baal on Mt Carmel attempt to offer a bull to Baal, the scene is hectic. They hobble and shout and cut themselves. But Baal does not respond, and in the presence of Elijah's mockery, the sacrifice never happens.

When Paul and Barnabas heal a lame man in Lycaonia, the scene becomes almost equally hectic. Amid great shouting, the priests of Zeus brought oxen and wanted to sacrifice them, but, because the apostles rend their garments and protest, the sacrifice never happens.

Luke has taken the attempt to offer sacrifice to Baal and, with a greater sympathy for alien worship, has used it as one component in describing the attempt to offer sacrifice to Zeus. There are many connecting details, including the following:
- The initial negative image of hobbling (*chōlaneō*, 1 Kgs 18.21) or being lame (*chōlos*, Acts 14.8), something which is despised by Elijah and healed by Paul.
- Shouting, and 'with a great voice' (*phōnē megalē*, 1 Kgs 18.24, 27-28; Acts 14.10, 15).
- The bringing of animals (1 Kgs 18.23, 25-26; Acts 14.13).
- The presence of a crowd ('all the people', 1 Kgs 18.19; 'the crowds', Acts 14.11), and, later, the place of the true prophet/apostles in the midst of that crowd (Elijah gathers the people around him, 1 Kgs 18.19, 21, 30; Paul and Barnabas rush into the crowd, Acts 14.14).
- Turning the people (with regard to God, *dia-strephō*, 1 Kgs 18.17-18; Acts 14.15, *epi-strephō*), and the role of the older generation/s in going after (*poreuomai*) other gods ('You and the house of your father left…God…going after the Baals', 1 Kgs 18.18; 'God…allowed earlier generations to go their own ways', Acts 14.15-16).
- The pagans' confuse their god with humans: the Baalites think Baal is like a human, gone away, perhaps, or asleep (1 Kgs 18.27); and the Lycaonians think their gods have come down in Paul and Barnabas (Acts 14.11, 15).
- The true God is lord of the natural elements—rain and fire (giving rain which brings nourishment, 1 Kgs 18.1, 41, Acts 14.17; and sending fire which, in diverse ways, reveals God, 1 Kgs 18.24, 38; cf. Acts 2.3).

(3) *Section 6. Prayer to the God of All, inducing fire(like) disturbance/shaking on earth (1 Kings 18.32b-39; Acts 4.23-36; cf. 2.2-4; 10.44, 46).* After the failure of the Baalite prophets, Elijah prays. He made a great trench of water (literally, 'he made a sea', *epoiēsen thalassan*, 1 Kgs 18.32b; cf. 18.35), and he cried out to heaven, calling on God to hear (18.36-37). 'And fire fell from…heaven and consumed the holocausts…and licked up the stones and the dust' (18.38).

In Acts 4, after the healing of the lame man and the subsequent confrontation with the Jewish leaders, the disciples gathered together and, praying to the God who 'made heaven and earth and the sea', they called on God to look down (4.23-30, especially 4.24, 29). 'And as they were praying, the place was shaken…and they were all filled with the Holy Spirit' (4.31).

In both cases, there is a prayer to the great God to intervene, and then there is a dramatic result—fire which consumes and which licks up the very stones and earth (Old Testament), and a Spirit-filled shaking of the house (New Testament), presumably the same house that was earlier filled with the wind which brought the Spirit-filling tongues of fire (Acts 2.1-4).

Apparently Luke has used Elijah's prayer as one component in describing the prayer of the disciples. But to some degree, he has dispersed the elements, scattering them through three Lukan accounts of the descent of the Spirit. In place of God's sending of *fire* which *fell* and hit the earth strongly (licked up the *stones and earth*), God sent *fire* (Acts 2) and shook the *house* (Acts 4), and later the Spirit *fell* (Acts 10.44). Thus the three scenes concerning the descent of the Spirit (Acts 2.1-4; 4.31; 10.44-45) reflect complementary aspects of the climactic Old Testament account of the descent of the fire on Mt Carmel.

3. *Conclusion*

Whatever the details about the use of the Carmel gathering (1 Kgs 18) in Luke 24 and Acts, there can be little doubt about the use of it in Lk. 8.1-3. Given that 8.1-3 is so thoroughly Lukan in style—some would say completely Lukan in composition—and given that other Lukan passages, especially in the preceding episodes (in Lk. 7), depend on the Elijah–Elisha narrative, it is not surprising that this text should also show such dependence.

Several factors confirm this link, not only the broad themes (the journey, the gathering, and the providing) and their order, but also the persistent similarities of detail from the opening ('And it happened after…') to the final, curious balance between, on the one hand, the Baalites and the sevenfold vigil, and on the other hand, the seven demons.

There are also many differences between the texts, but, great though they are, they are generally understandable. They reflect the fact that in reworking the Old Testament, Luke is adapting it to the Jesus tradition, to the preaching of the kingdom of God, and to Luke's own narrative and theological interests (emphasis on the internal, on the sharing of possessions, and on the role of women).

Unit 8. Proto-Luke and Elijah–Elisha: Journey to Jerusalem

Orientational Introduction to Chapters 33–36:
The Mission-Filled Journeys to Death/Assumption—Elijah's Journey to the Jordan (1 Kings 19; 2 Kings 1–3) and Jesus' Journey to Jerusalem (Luke 9.51–10.20; Luke 22–Acts 2)

So far, in his first major reworking of the Elijah–Elisha narrative (7.1–8.3), Proto-Luke has used the Old Testament text both as a frame and as a center. The opening chapters (1 Kgs 17–18) provided a *frame* (a basis for the beginning and end of Lk. 7.1–8.3); later, related material (1 Kgs 22; plus 2 Kgs 4.1-37) provided a *center* (the center of 7.1–8.3, namely 7.18-50).

Now, in constructing another block (9.51–10.20), Luke goes a step further, and reverses the process. He uses the next available episode, Elijah's journey to Horeb (1 Kgs 19), as a *center* (concerning would-be followers of Jesus' journey, Lk. 9.57-62); and he uses later, related material (2 Kgs 1–3) to form a *frame* around it. In simplified terms, highlighting the center:

2 Kings 1	>	Lk. 9.51-56: Jesus' departure for Jerusalem
1 Kings 19	>	*Lk. 9.57-62:* Would-be followers of Jesus' journey
2 Kings 2–3	>	Lk. 10.1-20: The journey/mission of seventy others

However, there is an elaboration. The Old Testament framing text (2 Kgs 1–3) has a center of its own, namely Elijah's ascent (2 Kgs 2.7-15). In fact, the ascent is the the center of the entire Elijah–Elisha narrative, and, rather than use this pivotal text just to place a frame around the center of 9.51–10.20, Luke gives it special recognition, bringing it out, as it were, and employing it as a framework for the center of his own entire work: a frame for virtually all of Luke 22–Acts 2. Thus, the ascent of Elijah (2 Kgs 2.7-15) provides an initial foundation for the elaborate events surrounding the ascent of Jesus. It is necessary, then, to add to the outline:

2 Kings 1	>	Lk. 9.51-56
1 Kings 19	>	*Lk. 9.57-62*
2 Kings 2–3	>	Lk. 10.1-20
2 Kgs 2.7-15	>	Luke 22–Acts 2

Furthermore, Luke has rearranged some details to suit the requirements of his own narrative. In particular, the account of Jesus' departure for Jerusalem (Lk. 9.51-56), while using 2 Kings 1, also uses the beginning of the following chapter—the verses which recount Elijah's departure for the Jordan (2 Kgs 2.1-6). Hence another modification:

2 Kgs 1.1–2.6	>	Lk. 9.51-56
1 Kings 19	>	*Lk. 9.57-62*
2 Kgs 2.16– ch. 3	>	Lk. 10.1-20
2 Kgs 2.7-15	>	Luke 22–Acts 2

1. *Inherent Connections*

Before comparing these Old Testament texts with Luke, it is necessary to indicate the inherent connectedness of the passages in question—1 Kings 19 with 2 Kings 1–3—and especially the connection of Lk. 9.51–10.20, as a unified text, with Luke 22–Acts 2.

a. *1 Kings 19 and 2 Kings 1–3*

Elijah's journey (1 Kgs 19) is inherently connected with a later elaborate drama, 2 Kings 1–3—three chapters that tell of the later fate and journeys of both Elijah himself and the young ploughman, Elisha (the man called in 1 Kgs 19). This inherent connection is clearest between 1 Kings 19 and 2 Kings 2, two journeys in which Elijah walks towards death. What was resolved in the first bears fruit in the second: the person who once faced death in a state of weak loneliness (1 Kgs 19) now faces the death-related crossing of the Jordan with hopeful resolve (2 Kgs 2).

Furthermore, this latter chapter (2 Kgs 2) is variously connected to those on either side (2 Kgs 1 and 3). The preceding chapter—the inglorious falling death of Ahaziah (he fell off a balcony and later died, 2 Kgs 1)— provides a foil for the glorious ascending departure of Elijah, and Elisha's subsequent mission (during the Moabite war, 2 Kgs 3) finds its origin in the spirit given to him by the departing Elijah. Thus, the journey of 1 Kings 19 links easily with 2 Kings 1–3.

b. *Luke 9.51–10.20*

The journey of Jesus (Lk. 9.57-62) is inherently connected both to the larger unity of 9.51–10.20 and with Jesus' later fate (Lk. 22–Acts 2).

The unity of 9.51–10.20 needs closer examination.

Unlike 7.1–8.3, with its emphasis on prophecy, 9.51–10.20 shifts the focus to journeying, especially to the ultimate journey towards death and beyond (Hades or heaven). At the beginning (9.51-56), as the days are fulfilled for Jesus to be taken up, he sets his face for his destination—*towards Jerusalem*. Next, during the journey (9.56-62), he warns would-be followers about preoccupation with home and death, and, using the image of a ploughman, he directs them instead to journey single-mindedly *towards God*. Finally (10.1-20), in a flourish of journeying, the healing mission of the seventy entails orientation *towards either hell* (Hades, 10.15) or *heaven* (10.20). The emphasis on heaven is not only repeated; it is also vivid: it is associated with the descent of destructive fire (9.54), the throwing down of a city (10.14), and, climactically, the fall of Satan, like lightning (10.18). The final note (10.20) is positive: the names of the seventy are 'written in heaven'.[1]

---

1. The unity of Lk. 9.51–10.20 bears further scrutiny. The mission of the seventy (Lk. 10.1-12) has obvious similarities with the mission of the Twelve (Lk. 9.1-6; Mk 6.7-13; Mt. 10.7-16) but, rather than enter prematurely into the complex, inconclusive debate about the relationships between these various mission texts, as a temporary working hypothesis it is better to concentrate on the relation of Lk. 10.1-12 to the Elijah–Elisha narrative and to Proto-Luke, particularly to Lk. 9.51-62. The entire passage (9.51–10.20) is pervaded by a sense of movement. The only indications of a slowing or stopping of that momentum occur in the context of some (partial) rejection of the kingdom of God—when the Samaritan village occasions a turning (9.55), when the unworthy disciple turns back (9.61-62), and when the woes against the unrepentant towns bring the momentum of the text to a halt (10.13-16). Apart from the broad sense of movement and mission which link 10.1-20 with 9.51-62, there are many smaller continuities, among them the following: (1) 'Seventy *others*' (10.1) echoes 'other' in 9.59, 61, and echoes also the larger sense in 9.51-62 of an expanding movement; (2) 'He sent them ahead of him' (10.1, see 9.52); (3) carry nothing for the journey (10.4, see 9.58 [no stone to sleep on]); (4) the non-receptiveness of some places (10.8, 10-16; see 9.53 [they would not receive him]); (5) the kingdom of God (10.9, 11, see 9.60, 62); (6) fire from heaven (Satan falls '*like lightning from heaven*', 10.18, see 9.54 ['Do you want us to call down *fire from heaven*...?']).

The unity of the mission of the seventy with the preceding journey is particularly striking in its final line: 'Your names are written in heaven' (10.20). It was on that note that the preceding journey had begun: Jesus' journey towards being taken up was effectively a journey that would eventually carry him to heaven (see Acts 1.10-11). Thus the entire block (9.51–10.20) begins and ends with variations on the idea of a

Many key ideas of 9.51–10.20 burst into bloom much later in Lk. 22–Acts 2. These ideas, such as days, Jerusalem, death, and heaven, re-emerge in the fifty-day period from Passover to Pentecost (Lk. 22–Acts 2). For example, the departure for Jerusalem, emphasizing the coming of the (deathly) time and the making of preparations (9.51-52), finds an elaborate down-to-earth echo in the coming of deathly Passover and the preparations for it (Lk. 22.1-13). And the entire drama of death and heaven, including heaven's fire, finds elaborate development not only in Jesus' death and ascent, but also in the heaven-sent fiery descent of the Spirit (Lk. 22.66–Acts 2).

Thus, the three passages of the journey-oriented block (9.51–10.20) are inherently linked with a long fifty-day drama at the journey's end (Lk. 22–Acts 2).

Overall, one journey (1 Kgs 19) leads to the elaborate ascent-centered drama of 2 Kings 1–3, the other (Lk. 9.51–10.20) to the elaborate ascent-centered drama of Luke 22–Acts 2.

2. *Death and Mission*

Central to both sets of texts (first, 1 Kgs 19; 2 Kgs 1–3; second, Lk. 9.51–10.20; Lk. 22–Acts 2) is the question of death. Death sometimes looks freakish or meaningless, but that is not the case with Elijah and Jesus. Elijah does indeed have a moment when death seems pointless—he simply wants to lie down and die (1 Kgs 19.1-4); but he recovers, and the movement towards death becomes a journey with a mission. Even when his prophetic journey ends after he crosses the Jordan and is taken up to heaven, there is still an emphasis on mission, at least implicitly. First, there is the abortive mission of the fifty to find Elijah (2 Kgs 2.15-18); and then there is the genuine mission of Elisha who continues the prophetic work both at home and abroad.

In the case of Jesus, there is a similar idea. His journey is accompanied by mission. As soon as he faces Jerusalem, he starts sending people out: he sends messengers ahead to Samaria (Lk. 9.52); he tells one of the would-be followers to go and announce the

journey which leads surely to heaven. Apart from the overall unity of 9.51–10.20, there is the more specific problem of the unity of 10.1-20. The elements within 10.1-20 are quite diverse: (1) the sending of the seventy (10.1); (2) instructions for the journey (10.2-7), (3) diverse towns—receptive and unreceptive (10.8-12); (4) woes against unreceptive Galilean towns (10.13-15); (5) whoever hears/rejects you hears/rejects me/my sender (10.16); (6) the return of the seventy (10.17-20).

This diversity brings two problems. Should one omit some of these topics as alien to the mission? And should one perhaps do the opposite—add some topics, especially the subsequent episode ('In that hour he rejoiced in the Holy Spirit and said, "I thank you, Father, Lord of heaven and earth…" ', 10.21-24)? The question of omitting particularly arises with the woes against the unreceptive towns (10.13-15); they 'are more like an aside or a soliloquy than an integral part of the instructions' (Fitzmyer 1981: 850). To some degree, the woes are indeed jarring. They halt the onward momentum of the text, and they suggest disjuncture. But this sense of disjuncture is appropriate: it corresponds to the content, to the disjuncture caused by rejection. A similar phenomenon was found in Lk. 7.18-35: the twist in style (especially in 7.29 and 7.31) reflected the underlying content: the message about rejection. In the present text, the woes have their place. By comparing Galilean towns with Gentile towns, they show 'the implications of Jesus' words of instruction for the Gentile mission. The passage thus contributes to the universalism of the Christian mission and evangelization' (Fitzmyer 1981: 853). As for adding Jesus' rejoicing (10.21-24), it is better not to do so. The rejoicing does indeed fit well after the account of the mission, yet its opening time-related phrase (*En autē tē hōra*…, 'In that hour…') suggests a new beginning (cf. 'In the days/year…', Lk. 1.5; 2.1; 3.1. In 2.38 ('And in that hour [Anna]…'), where there is no new beginning, the time-related phrase is preceded by 'and'). Furthermore, the rejoicing in 10.21-24 is addressed to the 'disciples'—a word never used in the account of the seventy (10.1-20). In addition, through the use of the word 'and' ('*And* a certain lawyer…', Lk. 10.25) the rejoicing is linked to what follows. It is better, therefore, to see the rejoicing as the inauguration of what follows and not as the conclusion of the mission of the seventy.

kingdom of God (9.60); and he sends the seventy others to diverse cities and places (10.1-20). Finally, the death itself becomes a starting point for assumption into heaven, and the assumption in turn becomes the starting point for the Spirit and the greatest mission of all: from Jerusalem and Samaria even to the ends of the earth (Lk. 22–Acts 2).

In both Old Testament and New Testament passages, the crucial link between death and mission is spirit. It is the spirit of the ascending Elijah which launches Elisha (2 Kgs 2.9-15), and it is the Spirit sent by the ascended Jesus which launches the disciples (Lk. 24.49; Acts 1.4-5; 2.1-4).

3. General Outline, and Aspects of Adaptation

The overall relationship of the various texts may now be outlined in slightly greater detail:

2 Kgs 1.1–2.6: Death. Impending ascent	>	Lk. 9.51-56: Jesus' impending death, ascent
1 Kgs 19: Journey: desert to ploughing	>	9.57-62: Journey: no home to ploughing
2 Kgs 2.16–ch. 3: Mission: fifty; Elisha	>	10.1-20: Mission: seventy
2 Kgs 2.7-15: Crossing Jordan; ascent; spirit	>	Luke 22–Acts 2: Jesus dies, ascends; Spirit

The degree of similarity between Luke's text and the Elijah–Elisha story varies considerably from one passage to the next. Luke seems to invert aspects of the Old Testament. While some Old Testament episodes have been reproduced and elaborated, others, particularly the Moabite war (2 Kgs 3), have been distilled to a minimum.

Among Luke's changes, one of the most pivotal is the unpacking of 2 Kgs 2.1-18, the dense passage which tells of the ascent of Elijah and which stands at the center of the entire Elijah–Elisha narrative. Instead of using this central passage to help form just a single gospel episode, Luke takes its elements and, in varying ways, disperses them, placing them in leading positions and elaborating them.

Thus, the beginning of 2 Kings 2 concerning Elijah's impending ascent (2.1-6) is moved (along with 2 Kgs 1) to an earlier stage in Luke's narrative so that it becomes a headline at the beginning of the whole journey to Jerusalem (Lk. 9.51-56).

Likewise, with the concluding part of 2 Kgs 2.1-18 concerning the abortive mission of the fifty who, after the ascent, are sent out to the places Elijah might have gone, this mission (2 Kgs 2.16-18) is adapted so that instead of being a small obscure episode it becomes a leading element in the whole mission of the seventy (Lk. 10.1-20).

The most central text of all—the kernel account of crossing the Jordan, ascending to heaven, and imparting the spirit (2 Kgs 2.7-15)—becomes a small, central component for the center of Luke–Acts (Lk. 22–Acts 2, omitting 22.31-65). The crossing of the Jordan is reflected in Jesus' death, in Jesus' ascent, and in the sending of the Spirit.

The relationships between specific texts will be examined in Chapters 33–36, following the Lukan order, as follows:

Chapter 33: The Departure for Jerusalem (Luke 9.51-56) as a Rhetorical Imitation of Elijah's Departure for the Jordan (2 Kings 1.1–2.6)

Chapter 34: Yet Again, Not Q: Jesus' Three Sayings to Would-Be Followers (Luke 9.57-62) as a Distillation of Elijah's Three-Part Journey to Horeb (1 Kings 19)

Chapter 35: The Post-Ascent Missions of the Fifty and of Elisha (2 Kings 2.16–Ch. 3) as Components of the Mission of the Seventy (Luke 10.1-20)

Chapter 36: Elijah's Crossing, Ascending, and Spirit-Giving (2 Kings 2.7-15) as a Framework for the Center of Proto-Luke (Luke 22–Acts 2 [Except 22.31-65])

33

The Departure for Jerusalem (Luke 9.51-56) as a Rhetorical Imitation of Elijah's Departure for the Jordan (2 Kings 1.1–2.6)

The origin of the departure account (Lk. 9.51-56) has always been something of a puzzle. Though the text is quite striking—it tells both of Jesus setting his face to go to Jerusalem, and of James and John wanting to call down fire from heaven—it is not at all clear whence Luke drew the account. It is not found in Mark, and apparently did not come from Q. One is left wondering whether it is derived from the hypothetical and hazy 'L' source, or whether to some degree at least, it is the result of Luke's 'free creative activity'.[1] In 1984, the puzzle received a new angle: D. Flusser suggested that much of the passage, especially 9.51-53, is derived from a Hebrew fragment (Flusser 1984).

The purpose of this chapter is to indicate that the origin of the departure account need not remain so mysterious. To a significant degree it is derived from a text which, far from being lost, is quite familiar: the account which introduces and describes the departure of Elijah for the Jordan (2 Kgs 1.1–2.6). However, unlike the Old Testament text, with its division into two episodes—one emphasizing death (2 Kgs 1), and the other, assumption (2 Kgs 2.1-6)—the Lukan text integrates the ideas of death and assumption into a single episode which is brief and relatively clear (Lk. 9.51-56). What is being proposed is that the two parts of the Old Testament text have been fused, and that the text as a whole has been reshaped, particularly through being abbreviated and improved. Luke's basic procedures of fusion, abbreviation, and improvement are to be seen as part of the rhetorical practice of imitating and emulating existing texts, especially ancient texts.

1. *Introductory Analysis*

As already partly indicated, the Old Testament text (2 Kgs 1.1–2.6) is part of a larger unit: the two-episode account which tells first of the death of the king, Ahaziah (2 Kgs 1.1-17, LXX),[2] and then of the assumption of Elijah (2 Kgs 2.1-18).

The account of the death of the king (2 Kgs 1) involves a considerable mixture of elements. After Ahaziah falls from an upper storey, he sends messengers from Samaria to Ekron to consult Baalzebub about his prospects of recovery. Elijah stops the messengers and sends them back to say that the Lord has decreed Ahaziah's death. When the king sends fifty soldiers from Samaria to apprehend Elijah, the prophet calls down fire from heaven to destroy them, but later he relents and goes into Samaria where he reiterates the decree of death. And, in accordance with the word of the Lord, Ahaziah dies.

The second episode tells of Elijah and Elisha going, stage by stage, from Gilgal to the Jordan, and it describes how, amid the muted statements and observing eyes of the prophets, Elijah was taken up to heaven.

---

1. For a discussion of 'L', of Luke's creative activity, and of the possible origin of Lk. 9, 51-56, see Fitzmyer 1981: 82-85, 826-27. See also the useful discussion of Marshall 1978: 403-404.
2. 2 Kgs 1.18 is a stereotypical addendum which adds little to the narrative.

Table 54. *As Death Looms, Departure for Assumption*
(2 Kings 1.1–2.6; Luke 9.51-56)

	2 Kings 1.1–2.6	Luke 9.51-56
		As the time is fulfilled for his taking up… (9.51a)
1a.	The king's death is divinely decreed (1.1-2a, 4, 6b, 15-17)	… Jesus sets his face to go to Jerusalem (9.51b)
2.	He sends messengers…from Samaria to Ekron…to inquire about his future (1.2b)	He sends messengers…to Samaria…to prepare for him (9.52)
3.	The messengers are turned back because of their destination (Ekron) (1.3, 5-6a)	He is not received because of his destination (Jerusalem) (9.53)
4.	The calling of fire from heaven (1.7-14)	The idea of calling fire from heaven is rejected (9.54-55)
1b.	At the time of his assumption Elijah sets out on a journey (2.1)	
5.	Elijah and Elisha go from place to place en route to the Jordan (2.2-6)	Jesus and company go to another village (en route to Jerusalem) (9.56)

The unity of these two episodes is not immediately obvious. King Ahaziah's death may seem like a freakish accident which has nothing to do with the grandiose nature of Elijah's ascent to heaven. But, as indicated earlier, particularly with reference to the story of Judah and Tamar (Gen. 38), there is increasing evidence that biblical episodes which at first sight may seem unrelated do in fact have a deep-seated unity. Something similar may be observed in the episodes concerning the king's death and Elijah's assumption. Examination of the two events begins to uncover several points of contact or contrast. Like the death, the assumption is repeatedly described as something decreed or planned by God (2 Kgs 1.4, 6, 16; 2.1, 3, 5).

The most dramatic ingredient in both accounts is fire which descends from heaven and brings death (2 Kgs 1.9-14), and fire which, in a life-giving way, sweeps someone up to heaven (2.11). And there are other interrelated points of contact: the motif of identifying or recognizing Elijah (1.17; 2.10, 12); the motif of locating the true God, the God of Elijah (1.3; 2.14); and, finally, the motif of a useless quest and of a quest involving fifty people (1.2b, 5, 9, 11, 13; 2.7, 16-18). Even the mode of death—a fall (1.2)—provides a contrast to the image of the taking up. Furthermore, as Elijah is approaching or is about to approach the places of death and assumption, the structure of the narratives is repetitious and threefold (1.9-14; 2.1-6).

Without pursuing all the details of complementarity between 2 Kings 1 and 2, it seems reasonable to draw a minimal conclusion: that, as the juxtaposing of the two episodes suggest, there is some inherent connection between them. And the best way to summarize that connection is to say that the two episodes are like complementary aspects of one reality, and that in their different ways they point to a single theme: God's power over everything, and particularly the way in which the divine word encompasses both death and life.

Turning to the New Testament text, one finds a brief description of how Jesus faced both death and assumption: 'When the time was fulfilled for his being taken up he set his face to go to Jerusalem' (Lk. 9.51). He sent messengers ahead of him and was rejected by a Samaritan village, but, despite the suggestion of James and John, he did not call down fire from heaven; instead, he rebuked them and went to another village. Luke blends the two parts of the Old Testament text. In other words, instead of leaving the reader with the problem of putting the two texts together—a problem which for most readers may be baffling—he takes the initiative in synthesizing them. A rather similar procedure is found in his reworking of the two stories in 2 Kgs 4.1-37: Luke combines the stories of two women into the single account of the repentant woman (Lk. 7.56-50). The process does not destroy the Old Testament text, but rather clarifies its meaning and, in a sense, fulfils it.

He does not, however, make use of the climactic section of the second episode: the actual assumption of Elijah (2 Kgs 2.7-18). He holds that over and uses it, in distilled form, for other purposes, particularly to provide a skeletal framework for describing the events surrounding the ascent of Jesus (Lk. 22–Acts 2).

What remains, therefore, is 2 Kgs 1.1–2.6. It is this passage which provides a foundational component for Lk. 9.51-56.

The outline (Table 54) is considerably simplified, yet, once that limitation is borne in mind, it may serve as a useful stepping-stone towards a more complete analysis.

2. *More Detailed Analysis*

a. *Section 1. The Lord's Plan/s of Death and Assumption, and the Departure (2 Kings 1.1-2a, 4, 6b, 15-17; 2.1; Luke 9.51)*

The Old Testament shows the Lord (*kyrios*) as having two plans: one for the imminent death of King Ahaziah, and the other for the taking up of Elijah. The image of someone dying is placed at the beginning and end of the chapter (2 Kgs 1.1, 17), and the decree of death is spelled out, solemnly, three times: '... Thus says the Lord... You shall surely die... You shall surely die... You shall surely die' (1.4, 6b, 15-17). It is because the references to death are so repetitious and unified that one is justified in suggesting that they be taken as a unit.

The Lord's second plan—for taking up Elijah—is recounted in 2 Kgs 2.1: 'Now when the Lord was about to take Elijah up to heaven by a whirlwind...' And the text goes on to emphasize, in an account which is almost as repetitious as the death decree, that the Lord is really going to do it (cf. 2.3, 5).

The New Testament suggests the presence of a single plan, namely for the assumption (*analēmpsis*) of Jesus: 'When the days were drawing near [literally, 'were being filled up', *en tō symplērousthai*] for him to be taken up, he set his face...' (Lk. 9.51).

Luke's text involves several adaptations. First, fusion. Instead of two plans or decrees, one for death and one for the taking up, he indicates a single plan which involves both. Of course, he does not explicitly refer to Jesus as going to his death, but the word 'assumption' is sufficiently broad to include such a meaning[3] and the setting of the face, as well as the subsequent account, indicate that he was in fact taking the road to his death.

Second, geographical adaptation. The idea of a journey, stage by stage, to a location across the Jordan (cf. 2 Kgs 1.1–2.6) is adapted to suit Jesus' journey to Jerusalem.

Third, abbreviation. Instead of the prolonged triple death decree, Luke gives a single phrase: 'he set his face'. Curiously, however, he uses the word 'face' (*prosōpon*) three times (Lk. 9.51, 52, 53)—a frequency not matched elsewhere in the New Testament. And it is also curious that Elijah had been told not to fear the face (*prosōpon*) of the man who asked him to come down to the dying king (2 Kgs 2.15). The question which arises—and which at this stage seems difficult to answer—is whether Luke took the idea of not fearing a face, turned it into that of a face which did not fear ('he set his face'), and then, in an echo of the triple death decree, used the word 'face' three times. Rather similar adaptations may be found in Luke's rewriting of other Old Testament texts.[4]

---

3. For discussion, see Fitzmyer 1981: 828, and especially Marshall 1978: 405.
4. See especially Luke's intricate reworking of certain aspects of the Naaman text, and the compact adaptation, in Lk. 3.10-16, of the threefold form of Neh. 5.1-14.

Apart from these adaptations, a number of other factors, some of them quite subtle, seem to have influenced the reworking of the source and the shaping of the final text. The actual phrasing, 'he set his face', apart from its relationship to 2 Kings 1, may also reflect some other Old Testament text.[5] Furthermore, the association of Jesus' (implied) death with the 'filling up' of time seems to be part of Luke's larger strategy of associating Jesus' death with a process of providential fulfillment (cf. Lk. 24.7, 26-27, 44-46). And there is another detail: instead of depicting the Lord as being the mere source of the plan/s, the New Testament shows the Lord (*kyrios*, 9.54) as being *personally involved* in the plan.

What is essential is that even though within the Bible as a whole there are three other references to people being taken away (Enoch in Gen. 5.24; and Elijah in 1 Macc. 2.58 and Sir. 48.9), there are no other biblical texts apart from 2 Kgs 2.1 and Lk. 9.51 which speak of the one who is soon to be assumed as journeying to the fated place. Nor are there any other biblical texts which place the image of assumption so close to the image or idea of death. The link is unique.

Even in the wording there is significant similarity:

Old Testament:
Kai egeneto en tō anagein Kyrion ton Ēleiou en synseismō hōs eis ton ouranon, kai eporeuthē

New Testament:
Egeneto de en tō symplēroustha tas hēmeras tēs analēmpseōs... tou poreuesthai

Old Testament:
And it happened,
as the Lord was going to take Elijah up to heaven in a whirlwind as it were,
that he set out...

New Testament:
Now it happened,
as the days were fulfilled for being taken up...
that he set out...

Instead of the complex idea of taking someone up to heaven in a *synseismos* ('whirlwind'), Luke has substituted the single word *analēmpsis* ('taking up'), and has then refined the phrasing so that it both synthesizes the Old Testament text and fits into the pattern of his overall work. It prepares the way for the fact that in Acts 1.2, 11, 22, Jesus is described as being 'taken up'.

b. *Section 2. The Sending of the Messengers (2 Kings 1.2b; Luke 9.52)*
Faced with the prospect of death, the king sent messengers from Samaria to Ekron to inquire about his future, more specifically to ask if he would live. And as Jesus faced Jerusalem, he also sent messengers before him, and they went into a Samaritan village to prepare for him. Thus, in different ways, both texts tell of messengers who are concerned about the future of someone who is going to die.[6]

---

5. For discussion, see Fitzmyer 1981: 828.
6. To say that the New Testament messengers are interested only in the practicalities of finding lodging does not do justice to the text. The context indicates that Jesus is journeying, not just towards a lodging place, but towards his ultimate fate. This latter idea is strengthened by the fact that the messengers are going 'before his face', a phrase which, in the context, links their mission with the setting of his face towards death. And the rejection of Jesus, 'because his face was set towards Jerusalem', reinforces the idea of a link between their mission and his facing of death. This does not deny a practical dimension to their mission, nor does it take away from the fact that, historically, the Samaritans were indeed hostile to Jerusa-

33. *The Departure for Jerusalem*   355

One may well ask why the theme of death, which is so explicit in 2 Kings 1, is rendered so cryptically in Lk. 9.51. The explanation, partly at least, seems to lie in the fact that Luke is adapting the theme to the larger requirements of his narrative. Within that narrative, death will indeed eventually become a major and explicit theme; in fact, along with the idea of resurrection and assumption, it will become, to some degree, *the* major focus of the gospel story. But for the moment it is in the distance, and it is appropriate that Luke introduce it gradually.[7] In other words, the precise reshaping of the subtext (2 Kgs 1) has been adapted to the fact that Luke has a distinct narrative focus. (The same principle will be used in his reworking of the Naboth text to describe the fate of Stephen.) Luke has taken the Old Testament text, sifted its death-related essence, and rendered it to suit the context of Jesus' journey to Jerusalem.

Apart from this thematic similarity, there are also similarities which are linguistic:

Old Testament:
Kai apesteilen aggelous… Kai eporeuthēsan eperōtēsai di' autou.

New Testament:
Kai apesteilen aggelous pro prosōpou autou kai poreuthentes eisēlthon hōs hetoimasai autō.

Old Testament:
And he sent messengers… And they went to inquire of him.

New Testament:
And he sent messengers before his face, and going they entered to prepare for him.

Some of the details of this resemblance are debatable, but others are striking. Even though the two words *apostellō* and *aggelos* ('I send' and 'messenger/angel'), are extremely common, the unbroken phrase found here, *kai apesteilen aggelous* ('and he sent messengers/angels'), does not occur elsewhere in the New Testament. Even in the Old Testament it is rare—apparently there are just five other occurrences (Judg. 9.31; 1 Sam. 19.21; 2 Sam. 3.26; 1 Chron. 19.2, 16).[8] And there is no other instance, even in the Old Testament, where the phrase 'and he sent messengers/angels' is followed by the verb *poreuomai* ('I go/journey'). Thus, ordinary as the words may be, the linguistic link between the texts is unique.

---

lem-bound travelers. But neither does that historical dimension which is now woven into the fabric of the gospel negate the fact that the present text, concerning Jesus' journey and concerning the disciples' process of preparation, connects the preparation process with Jesus' setting of his face towards death. Later events reinforce the link between preparation and death. It is probably not a coincidence that the word 'prepare' (*hetoimazō*) occurs most frequently not at the beginning of Luke's gospel but near its conclusion, in death-related contexts: in preparation for the Passover (22.8, 9, 12, 13) and for burial (23.56; 24.1). Apparently, as the Jerusalem journey begins, Luke is already intimating what the Emmaus journey will eventually say more clearly: that death has to be faced, that it is prepared for in Scripture, and, by implication, that it is something for which every traveler should be prepared (cf. Lk. 24.13-35). Whatever the final details, there are significant indications that the messengers in Luke's text, like those in the Old Testament passage, are on a mission which reflects the fact that the one who sent them is facing death.

7. The principle of gradation or gradualness seems important in much biblical composition. It appears to be present in the Pentateuch's gradual unfolding of plot and theme, and may also be present in the elusive composition of Jeremiah's steady, circular advance from the virtual absence of prose narrative (Jer. 2–6) to the increasingly vivid narrative of the final events (Jer. 32–45). It is a phenomenon which should probably be linked to the poetic process of intensification (cf. Alter 1985: 13-26, 62-84). It appears to be present in the gospel of John, a document which is frequently referred to as spiraling, and the themes of which have been described as advancing gradually 'like the waves of the rising tide' (Lacan 1957: 97). The presence of this phenomenon in Luke–Acts is suggested by the work of Tannehill (1984).

8. There are about thirty instances of very minor variations on the phrase in question (e.g. cf. Num. 20.14; 22.10; Josh. 7.22; Judg. 7.24; 11.19).

c. *Section 3. The Mission is Turned Back (2 Kings 1.3, 5-6a; Luke 9.53)*
As the king's messengers are on their way from Samaria to Ekron, Elijah stops them and rebukes them for going (*poreuomai*) to consult such an alien deity. And when Jesus comes to the village of the Samaritans, he is not received because he is going (*poreuomai*) to Jerusalem.

In both cases, the mission runs into a religious antagonism: Elijah could not accept the Ekron deity; and the Samaritans could not accept the worship of Jerusalem. Therefore, the missions were turned back. What Luke has done, then, is to take an ancient antagonism and replace it with one from the time of Jesus. (This accords with what he does elsewhere; for instance, in using the Naboth story to describe the fate of Stephen, he replaces the ancient institutions of Naboth's time with institutions from the time of Stephen.)

Of course he also makes other adaptations, particularly of abbreviation. The rather long description of turning back the Old Testament messengers is replaced by the brief phrase 'they would not receive him'. Not only does 'not receive' synthesize the essence of the Old Testament text, but it also prepares the way for the fact that those sent out later may perhaps not be received (Lk. 10.10). Once again, Luke is simultaneously synthesizing the Old Testament and adapting it to the shape of his own narrative.

d. *Section 4. Calling Fire from Heaven (2 Kings 1.7-14; Luke 9.54-55)*
When soldiers from Samaria approach Elijah, he twice calls down fire on them, but on the third occasion when the captain pleads for mercy, he relents. In the New Testament, when James and John suggest calling down fire on the Samaritans, Jesus turns and rebukes them.

Luke's account involves both drastic abbreviation and sharp reversal. But these adaptations are not without purpose: they reduce an elaborate and frightening account to a brief picture of mercy which is in accord with Luke's overall approach.

Despite these changes, the two texts show a unique resemblance. Nowhere else in the Bible is there quite the same image of calling down from heaven a fire which consumes. (The fire in Num. 16.34 is not called in the same way.) The resemblance is reinforced by the fact that in both cases the (potential) victims are from the same area, Samaria.

The verbal similarity is considerable:

> Old Testament:
> *Katabēsetai pyr ek tou ouranou kai kataphagetai* (twice)...
> *kai katebē pyr ek tou ouranou kai katephagen* (three times)...
> *kai...en-timōthētō* (twice).

> New Testament:
> *pyr katabēnai apo tou ouranou kai analōsai...epe-timēsen...*

> Old Testament:
> Fire shall descend from heaven and devour...
> and fire descended from heaven and devoured...
> [but]...let [my life] have value...

> New Testament:
> [that] fire descend from heaven and destroy...
> But...he rebuked...

Most of this similarity is easy to see: Luke has abbreviated the Old Testament wording and has replaced *kataphagetai/katephagen* ('devour'), with the synonymous *analōsai* ('destroy'). What is more difficult to judge is whether Luke's use of *epi-timaō* ('I rebuke') involves a word-play on *en-timoō* ('I honor/value'). Despite their difference in meaning, the words are related. They occur in similar contexts—towards the end of the fire-from-heaven passages (cf. 2 Kgs 1.13-14; Lk. 9.55)—and they are used for exactly the same purpose of preventing fire from descending. Seeing that fire has already twice descended, the captain of the third group pleads with Elijah to *value* him and not call down fire. And when Jesus hears that James and John are threatening to call down fire, he *rebukes* them. In other words, it is the processes of valuing (*en-timaō*) and of rebuking (*epi-timoō*) which stop the fire. The idea that Luke should play with the Old Testament wording is rendered more plausible by the fact that he does so elsewhere. Fitzmyer (1981: 828) suggests the possible presence of a form of word-play when he says that the Greek word for 'set' ('he set his face', 9.51) seems to be 'a takeoff' on a Hebrew word. However, until the entire phenomenon of word-play is studied more closely, it seems difficult to judge such details.

In any case, what is certain is that these similarities are substantial and unique.

e. *Section 5. The Journey from One Place to Another (2 Kings 2.2-6; Luke 9.56)*
In highly repetitive language, the Old Testament text tells of the journey of Elijah and Elisha: first to Bethel, then to Jericho, and finally to the Jordan. The whole purpose, of course, is to go to Elijah's place of destiny.

The New Testament text simply says that Jesus and those with him went to another village—a journey that carries him also further along the path that will eventually lead to Jericho, to Bethphage and Bethany, and to his place of destiny, Jerusalem (cf. 9.57; 10.1; 18.35; 19.1, 28-29).

The similarity between the two journeys is clear—if for no other reason than that, passing through Jericho, they both travel, stage by stage, to meet their fate.[9] But, for Luke, it is too soon in 9.51-56 to speak of Jericho. Because he will inject into his narrative an extended travel account, he holds over the reference to Jericho. Instead of saying that Jesus and his company went from one specific place to another, he simply says, in a general way, that they went to another village.

Once again, he has both abbreviated the repetitiveness of the Old Testament text and has adapted it to suit the long-term shape of his own narrative.[10]

Despite the drastic abbreviation, there is some linguistic similarity: in both texts the final brief phrases begin with 'And they journeyed...' (*kai eporeuthēsan*). The two Greek words constitute an expression which, though fairly common in the Old Testament, does not otherwise occur in the New Testament.[11]

3. *Summary of the Similarities, Differences and Adaptations*

The texts have been broken into five sections or groupings:
1. The plan/s of death and assumption (2 Kgs 1.1-2a, 4, 6b, 15-17; 2.1; Lk 9.51).
2. The sending of the messengers (2 Kgs 1.2b; Lk. 9.52).
3. The turning back of the mission (2 Kgs 1.3, 5-6a; Lk. 9.53).
4. The question of calling down fire (2 Kgs 1.7-14; Lk. 9.54-55).
5. The journeying from one place to another (2 Kgs 2.2-6; Lk. 9.56).

Such similarities are striking, particularly when they occur in essentially the same order. What is doubly striking, however, is that three of the five sections, numbers 1, 2, and 4, contain elements that are unique in the entire (Greek) Bible. Nowhere else save in these

---

9. The dependence of Lk. 9.56 on 2 Kgs 2.2-6 was first pointed out by J. Walsh in a discussion which followed the presentation of this article as a research report at the 1986 CBA meeting in Washington, DC.

10. In Walsh's opinion (see previous note) the Old Testament emphasis on being quiet about Elijah's impending assumption (cf. 2 Kgs 2.3, 5) contributes to the way Luke avoids explicitness about the impending death of Jesus.

11. It does, however, occur in the interpolated story of the adulteress (cf. Jn 7.53).

passages does one find a picture of *someone setting off for assumption*, a combining of 'and *he sent messengers*' with *poreuomai*, and an image of *calling down fire from heaven*. In addition to these unique similarities are other significant similarities of detail, some of them intriguing.

The differences are great. In comparison with Luke, the Old Testament text is long and repetitive. Furthermore, it involves not just one main character but two: King Ahaziah and Elijah. And it sets the image of departing for assumption not at the beginning of the death-related episode, but after its conclusion.

However, though the differences are indeed great, they are not jumbled or incoherent, at odds with one another and with all known literary procedures. On the contrary, they correspond to steady patters of adaptation such as modernization, abbreviation, fusion, and emulation—patterns which are common both in general imitation and in other instances where Luke imitates the Old Testament. Since these differences may be explained through the procedures of imitation, they may not be invoked to prove that imitation was not used.

4. *Conclusion*

In attempting to account for the complex range of similarities and dissimilarities, the simplest hypothesis is that Luke, being a first-century *littérateur*, employed a well-known literary procedure of the first century: he imitated part of the Old Testament account of Elijah. He used basic techniques of adaptation, and he sought, above all, to emulate the older text. In other words, he sought to produce a better account and to show that the Jesus of whom he spoke surpassed the Old Testament figure of Elijah.

Of course, one could say that it was Jesus himself who first sought to surpass Elijah. That there was some such tradition is possible and even likely (see especially Flender 1967: 33-34), but the way in which Luke has sought to express that tradition appears to be literary through the careful synthesizing and surpassing of the Elijah narrative. In fact, it is the literary explanation, and the literary explanation alone, which is capable of doing justice to the fact that many of the similarities are so unique or subtle, and to the fact that the differences, great though they are, have a certain coherence. Hence, the tradition about Jesus, whatever it was, seems to have been combined with a deliberate literary procedure.

As well as integrating a basic tradition about Jesus, Luke has also integrated certain other elements of history and tradition. For instance, he refers to James and John, and to the Samaritans' antipathy towards Jerusalem.

It is scarcely possible, however, clearly to distinguish what is historical and what is not. Rather, it seems better to say of Lk. 9.51-56 what Fitzmyer (1981: 309) said of Luke 1–2, that whatever history it reflects 'has been assimilated...to other literary accounts'.

The Old Testament text, therefore, emerges not as a complete explanation of Luke's departure account, but as one of its basic components. It does not provide an explanation of certain traditional or historical elements, nor of Luke's distinctive shaping of the material. But it does provide a framework, or a literary skeleton, and it is on the basis of that framework that Luke has built up the narrative.

To the extent that the Old Testament text accounts for Luke's narrative, the hypothesis of a lost 'L' source is less necessary, at least as far as Lk. 9.51-56 is concerned (unless L is equated with Proto-Luke). Also less necessary is the hypothesis of a lost Hebrew fragment. As so often with alleged Semitisms in Luke–Acts, the data may be accounted for as Septuagintisms.[12] Nor is it necessary to envisage Luke as creating the text freely. If his care in synthesizing 2 Kgs 1.1–2.6 is any guide, he seems to have exercised his creativity with immense discipline and fidelity.

12. See especially Fitzmyer 1981: 113-25; Richard 1980.

34

Yet Again, Not Q: Jesus' Three Sayings to Would-Be Followers (Luke 9.57-62) as a Distillation of Elijah's Three-Part Journey to Horeb (1 Kings 19)

Jesus' three sayings to would-be followers of his journey (Lk. 9.57-62; cf. Mt. 8.18-22) are generally attributed to Q. While this attribution is plausible, there is an alternative explanation of these sayings, namely that they are a christianized distillation of Elijah's three-part journey to Horeb (1 Kgs 19). Initially, this alternative explanation is more difficult to grapple with; one has to work patiently with the relationship of Jesus' saying to 1 Kings 19 rather than pull them ready-made out of Q. But in the final weighing of evidence, the relationship to 1 Kings 19 is much more reliable and more verifiable than the appeal to Q.

As already indicated in the general introduction to Chapters 33–36, Proto-Luke's distillation of Elijah's journey to Horeb (1 Kgs 19) is part of the larger systematic reworking of the Elijah–Elisha narrative, especially of 1 Kings 19 and 2 Kings 1–3. In composing the account of Jesus' departure for Jerusalem, Luke had reduced twenty-four verses (1 Kgs 1.1–2.6) to six (Lk. 9.51-56). In describing the subsequent journey, including Jesus' sayings to the would-be followers, Luke makes a similar reduction: twenty-one verses (1 Kgs 19) to six (Lk. 9.57-62).

In reworking both 2 Kgs 1.1–2.6 and 1 Kings 19, what the Elijah text supplies is one component. The journey to Horeb on its own does not account for all the elements of Lk. 9.57-62. It makes no mention, for instance, of foxes and birds, as does Lk. 9.58; it is but one of a number of components. But it is a component that is central, foundational. And even without tracing the origin of the other components, the Horeb journey is sufficient in supplying an understanding of the essential nature of the Lukan passage.

1. 1 Kings 19 and Luke 9.57-62: Introductory Analysis

a. *1 Kings 19*
Within the context of the Elijah–Elisha narrative, 1 Kings 19 is unusual. Instead of proceeding as he usually does with decisiveness and power, the prophet Elijah instead begins to waver. Suddenly, and to some degree inexplicably, he feels profoundly vulnerable. The threat of death, which he would have previously countered with the word of the living God, now assumes frightening proportions and begins to overpower him. The text consists of three sections:

1. *The desert journey (19.1-8).* Under the threat of death, Elijah journeys into the wilderness and lies down. But he is not allowed to stay where he is. An angel awakens him, first to the fact that there is food at his head, and later, in a repetitive scene, to the fact that the food is not for lying down but for journeying. And the journey is through the wilderness to the mountain of God.

2. *The death-centered Elijah is commissioned by the living God to go and anoint kings and a prophet (19.9-18).* At the mountain, Elijah is not much more outgoing than he had been in the wilderness. Twice he goes in or near a cave

(*spēlaion*), and despite all his high-flown rhetoric about jealous zeal for the God of Hosts, the basic action is that he is afraid of being killed (19.9-10, 13-14). But again, as in the wilderness, there is a twofold repetitious pattern which awakens Elijah, first to the reality of the living God (19.11-12, a theophany), and then to the need to go forth and anoint kings and a prophet so that they will bring that living reality to others (19.15-18).

3. *The call of the vigorous ploughman (19.19-21).* The sense of life which had first been indicated by the food-ministering angel and then by the living God now finds powerful expression in human life—in the image of Elisha the ploughman. In contrast to the preceding images of the desert and the cave, the picture of the ploughman is one which, of its nature, suggests energy and hope. Details accentuate this impression: there is not just one yoke of oxen but twelve; Elisha is 'in' or 'with' the oxen, a detail that associates their energy with him; and at the touch of Elijah's cloak, Elisha 'ran' after him (19.19-20a).

Here again there is a twofold repetition. Elisha's initial act of responding positively (19.19-20a) is followed immediately by a further scene in which that response is intensified (19.20b-21). Having declared 'I will follow you', he says goodbye to his father (the Greek omits his mother) and burns his oxen and plough, an action which is like burning his boats. But the repetition in this third section (the ploughman, 19.19-21) is unlike that of the preceding sections. In these earlier passages, particularly in the response of Elijah in or near the cave, the repetition is word-for-word—a reflection of Elijah's death-centered paralysis (19.9-10, 13-14). But in the third section, the two-scene portrayal of Elisha's response avoids any such mechanical repetition. Instead, in accord with the vigor of the whole passage, the action and repetition in these two brief scenes moves swiftly and with a certain unpredictability.

As a whole, therefore, 1 Kings 19 is a carefully wrought unit.[1] Against a background of desert and death, its three two-part passages increasingly build an awareness of the living God and of the need to bring word of that God to others.

b. *Luke 9.57-62*

The Lukan passage also consists largely of three two-part texts. As Jesus is on his journey, he challenges three would-be followers, and each challenge is built on an exchange which is essentially two-part.

Aside from this similarity of underlying structures, there is a similarity of substance. As implied by 9.51, the journey of Jesus is a journey towards his death. Thus, in Lk. 9.57-62 as in 1 Kings 19, there is a tension between limiting factors on the one hand, especially death, and on the other hand, an awareness of God and of the need to spread God's word.

This does not mean that Jesus is weary and frightened in the way Elijah had been. On the contrary, his implicit defiance of death and his call to announce God's kingdom means that as well as taking over positive aspects of Elijah's role—those aspects subject to God's word—he takes over the role of God's own self. It is the more negative aspects of Elijah's role—those dictated by human fear and limitation—which are taken over by the would-be followers.

Thus, the tension between the divine word and human limitation—a tension which in 1 Kings 19 is played out in a drama of considerable complexity and subtlety—is presented in Luke in a form which is clear and vivid.

---

1. The unity of 1 Kgs 19 has sometimes been contested. For instance, E.V. Nordheim (1978: 171) sees the central section as quite distinct from the rest of the chapter. But others perceive the whole chapter as a unit; see Carlson 1969; Childs 1980: 134-36.

In transforming the Old Testament text, Luke not only continues the process which he had already used in composing 9.51-56, he also follows some of the basic procedures and goals of Hellenistic rhetoric, particularly the widespread practice of simultaneously imitating (Gk. *mimésis*; Lat. *imitatio*) and surpassing (Gk. *zélos*; Lat. *emulatio*) existing texts. Nor is this transforming practice alien to the transforming spirit of ancient Jewish writers. Furthermore, in doing this, Luke achieves one of his most basic aims: to show that in Jesus the prophetic scriptures are fulfilled.

2. *1 Kings 19 and Luke 9.57-62: More Detailed Analysis*

Tables 55 and 56 (next page) indicate aspects of the relationship between the texts.

Table 55. *The Difficult Journey (1 Kings 19; Luke 9.57-62)*

A Simplified Outline	
1 Kings 19	Luke. 9.57-62
The desert journey (19.1-8) Under threat of death, Elijah lies down, but the food at his head means he must keep journeying.	*The homeless journey (9.57-58)* Journeying to his death, Jesus says that the Son of Humanity has nowhere to lay his head.
From death to anointing God's kings and prophet (19.9-18) Preoccupied by death Elijah is first met by God, and then told to go anoint God's kings and prophet.	*From burial to announcing God's kingdom (9.59-60)* Jesus first meets someone who is preoccupied by burial. Then Jesus tells him to go announce the kingdom of God.
Burning the plough (19.19-21) Reflecting his decidedness, Elisha says goodbye, and burns his plough.	*Resolute ploughing (9.61-62)* To someone preoccupied with goodbyes, Jesus speaks of ploughing and not looking back.

As Table 55 shows, Luke generally follows the order of the Old Testament episodes. However, he makes some minor rearrangements. The declaration 'I will follow you', which in 1 Kings 19 occurs dramatically at the *end* (v. 20), is found in Luke in various forms from the *beginning*:

* 'I will follow you wherever you go' (9.57)
* 'Follow me' (9.59)
* 'I will follow you wherever you go' (9.61)

A somewhat similar procedure is found in the way Lk. 9.51-56 reworks 2 Kgs 1.1–2.6. The image of assumption is taken from near the *end* of the Old Testament text (see 2 Kgs 2.1) and placed at the beginning of the New Testament passage (see Lk. 9.51); thus it achieves a certain dominance over the subsequent text. In the case of 'I will follow you' and its variations, the phrase not only has a certain dominance over the New Testament text, it also establishes a rhythm of repetition which holds the text together, moving it along and reflecting something of the repetitive aspect of the Old Testament passage.

Luke has rearranged some other details, for instance, the use of 'my father/s' (cf. 1 Kgs 19.4, 20; Lk. 9.59); but by and large, the three New Testament exchanges correspond in order to the Old Testament episodes. This correspondence may now be seen more closely.

Table 56. *The Difficult Journey: Aspects of Linguistic Continuity and Fusion*

The Journey (1 Kings 19.1-8; Luke 9.57-58)
Old Testament: *kai autos eporeuthē en tē erēmō hodon hēmeras...* (1 Kgs 19.4) *kai idou tis hēpsato autou kai eipen autō...* (19.5) *kai idou pros kephalēs...* (19.6) *akolouthēsō opisō sou...* (19.20) New Testament: *kai poreuomenōn autōn en tē hodō* *eipen tis pros auton, Akolouthēsō soi hopou...* (Lk. 9.57) *pou tēn kephalēn...* (9.58) Old Testament: And he went into the desert a day's journey [and he sat under a juniper tree]... And behold someone touched him and said to him... And behold at [his] head... I will follow after you. New Testament: And as they were going along the way someone said to him, I will follow you wherever... [holes...nests]...where [to lay] the head
Leaving Death, Work for the Living God (19.9-18; Lk. 9.59-60)
Old Testament: *kai idou rhēma Kyriou pros auton kai eipen Ti su...* (19.9) *kai idou pros auton phōnē kai eipen Ti su...* (19.13) *anastrephe...chriseis...eis basilea...eis basilea...*[v. 19] *kai apēlthen...* (19.15-16) New Testament: *Eipen de pros heteron...*[60] *su de apelthōn diaggelle tēn basilleian...* (Lk. 9. 59) Old Testament: And behold the word of the Lord [came] to him, and he said, What [are] you... And behold a voice [came] to him and said, What [are] you... Return...anoint...to be king...to be king...And he went away New Testament: He said to another...But you, going away, announce the kingdom
The Plough (1 Kgs 19.19-21; Lk. 9.61-62)
Old Testament: *autos ērotria...* *Eperripse tēn mēlōtēn autou ep' auton...opisō...opisō...opisō...* (1 Kgs 19.19-21) New Testament: *epibalōn tēn cheira ep' arotron,* *kai blepōn eis ta opisō* (Lk. 9.62) Old Testament: He was ploughing He cast his mantle upon him...after...after...after... New Testament: ...throwing the hand upon the plough, and looking to what was after [i.e. past]...

a. *The Homeless Journey (1 Kings 19.1-8; Luke 9.57-58)*
Threatened by Jezebel, the fearful Elijah journeys into the desert, but when he lies under a tree to die, mysterious food is placed at his head and he is told to keep journeying to the mountain of God. In the New Testament, Jesus tells a would-be follower that, unlike the foxes and birds, the Son of Humanity has nowhere to lay his head.

Luke has made several adaptations. The circumstantial details of the past concerning Jezebel have been omitted. He has preserved the central idea of a journey which allows no permanent resting place. The idea of lying down and finding, at one's head, food which means that one must keep going, has been abbreviated into the imagery of having nowhere to lay one's head. And in describing the absence of a resting place, the understated Old Testament implication that Elijah has to leave his resting tree (the bush under which he lay), has been replaced by the clear and vivid imagery of not having a den or a nest. Furthermore, certain elements have been added, not just the image of foxes and birds, but also the reference to the Son of Humanity.

In various ways, the Old Testament text has been abbreviated, modernized, clarified, and christianized. Yet as the chart of linguistic similarities indicates (Table 56), it still manages to fuse certain words and phrases from 1 Kings 19, retaining some detailed echoes of the older passage. Examples of fusion, some of them quite complex, may also be found elsewhere in Luke's use of the Old Testament.

b. *From Preoccupation with Death to Being Met by the Lord and Sent Forth (1 Kings 19.9-18; Luke 9.59-60)*
When Elijah is in the cave, preoccupied by destruction and death, God calls him out and speaks to him powerfully yet gently (1 Kgs 19.9-12). Then, to inaugurate a radical God-centered change, Elijah is sent to anoint two kings and a prophet (19.11-18). In Luke, the man who is preoccupied with burying his father is first spoken to by Jesus, simply yet powerfully ('Follow me'), and then he is told to *go and announce the kingdom of God*.

Again, Luke's text involves several adaptations. The complex scene of preoccupation with a widespread destruction leading to death is synthesized into the single, striking image of burying one's (dead) father.

The phrase 'my father' is itself adapted from 1 Kings 19. First, there is an allusion to the death of one's fathers ('Take my life...I am no better than my fathers...', 19.4), and later the leave-taking of one's father ('Elisha left...and said, "I will kiss my father and follow..."', 19.20). Luke fuses these into the idea of leaving one's dead father ('"...bury my father"... "Let the dead..."', 9.60).

The call and the elaborate theophany have been distilled into the simple strong invitation—'Follow me'. To some degree, the Old Testament text itself undermines or purifies the emphasis on spectacular theophanies, placing its emphasis on a gentle sound. Thus, Luke's adaptation completes that anti-spectacle tendency.

And the elaborate picture of going forth to anoint the kings and the prophet who will inaugurate a radical new God-centered order is again distilled and purified into the command to go announce the kingdom of God. To a significant extent, this process of purification is a form of christianization.

Once again, Luke uses the processes of abbreviation, modernization, clarification, and christianization. And once again, both in reworking the Old Testament references to 'my fathers/s' and in echoing other linguistic details, there is a process of fusion. At the same time, Luke is shaping the materials to the requirements of his own narrative. Thus, the second exchange is composed in such a way that it maintains and develops the basic elements of the first exchange: the element of rhythm, and the underlying theme of letting go of an undue attraction to home and to the security which home seems to offer. The third exchange will follow suit.

c. *The Resolute Ploughman (1 Kings 19.19-21; Luke 9.61-62)*
At one level, the demand of Elijah seems to be surpassed by that of Jesus. Elijah allows the ploughman to say goodbye; Jesus does not. Yet even in saying goodbye, Elisha had been extremely resolute. He had burned his plough, and by using it to cook his oxen he had given his workers an apparently extravagant meal. What Luke has done is take the resoluteness which is implicit in the Old Testament text and as with other Old Testament passages, turns it into a form which is clear and vivid.

Here, too, Luke has employed essentially the same procedures that he used in reworking the preceding sections. The new text is brief and graphic. The image of the plough is retained, but in a context which is less tied to ancient agriculture. And the explicit emphasis on 'the kingdom of God' is essentially Christian. Finally, the process of fusion, which to some degree is present in the other sections, seems at this point to be brought to a new level of complexity and sophistication. As the chart of linguistic similarities suggests, the images of Elisha *ploughing* and Elijah *casting the cloak over him* have been combined into the single image of *throwing one's hand to the plough* (*epi-ballō*, 'put' or 'throw', Lk. 9.62). And in a touch of word-play and further fusion, the resoluteness of Elisha in following *after* Elijah (*opisō...opisō...opisō*) has been turned around to refer to a resoluteness which does *not look after*—that is, backwards (*eis ta opisō*).

3. *Assessing the Evidence*

The evidence consists of a mixture of elements, some strong, some weak. As indicated earlier, the crucial question in assessing such mixed evidence is whether some of it is strong enough to conclude that Luke is dependent on the Old Testament.

It would seem that it is, particularly in view of certain key factors:
- *The broad context of ancient literary practice.* It was central to ancient Greco-Roman and Jewish authors to rework older texts. Some aspects of Luke's reworking correspond, for instance, to that of Livy, a historian who followed one basic source and rendered it into a form that was brief, clear, and vivid (Walsh 1961: 188). Luke does likewise, but he also employs a whole theology of Christian fulfillment, thus leading to a more thorough reshaping of the older text.
- The immediate context of Luke's relationship to the LXX, especially to the Elijah–Elisha narrative.
- *The wide range of the similarities*: structure, order, themes, images, linguistic details. These similarities go far beyond the range of coincidence.
- *The coherence of the differences.* The differences are not a meaningless jumble at odds with one another and with known literary practices. Rather, they follow well-established procedures for transforming and imitating texts and, in particular, they follow processes—abbreviation, modernization, clarification, christianization, and fusion—which Luke employs elsewhere in reworking the Elijah–Elisha narrative.

A further factor might be added: Luke was a *littérateur*. In the final analysis, the essential claim is very simple: a *littérateur* used a literary method.

35

The Post-Ascent Missions
of the Fifty and of Elisha (2 Kings 2.16–Ch. 3) as Components
of the Mission of the Seventy (Luke 10.1-20)

Having used the accounts of death-plus-departure (2 Kgs 1.1–2.6) and the Horeb journey (1 Kgs 19) to compose 9.51-56 and 9.57-62 respectively, Luke now comes to 2 Kgs 2.16–ch. 3 and uses it to describe a further aspect of Jesus' journey: the sending of seventy others (10.1-20).

This Old Testament text (2 Kgs 2.16–ch. 3) is complex and, partly for that reason, inherently difficult. It begins with a mission: the ascent-related sending of the fifty:
- 2.16-18: Elisha sends the fifty to all the places they think (ascended) Elijah might have gone.
- 2.19-25: Elisha deals with two diverse towns—one receptive, the other mocking.
- Ch. 3: Elisha deals with an enigmatic war in Moab.

Both missions—of the fifty and the seventy—are ascent-related. The fifty went to all the places where the (ascended) Elijah might have gone. The seventy go to all the places the ascent-bound Jesus is yet to go.

But, in comparison with the sending of the fifty, the sending of the seventy is much more elaborate and positive. As well as making his account more positive and universal, Luke has incorporated many further sources, particularly the texts which immediately follow the sending of the fifty, namely the diverse experiences with two towns (2 Kgs 2.19-25) and the enigmatic conflict (the war in Moab, 2 Kgs 3).

The incorporation of these further episodes (the diverse towns; the enigmatic conflict) is understandable. Along with the sending of the fifty, these two episodes—the towns and the conflict—represent the beginning of Elisha's prophetic ministry, his first steps as successor to Elijah. In other words, the complex launching of Elisha as successor of Elijah has contributed to the launching of the seventy as messengers or representatives of Jesus.

The mission of the fifty (2 Kgs 2.16-18) had a double purpose. Apart from going to all the places where the ascended Elijah might have gone, it also served, in practice, as a prelude to the great mission which would follow the ascent: the far-reaching mission of Elisha. Likewise with the mission of the seventy. Apart from going to all the places where the ascending Jesus was to go, it also serves in part as a prelude to the great mission which will follow the ascent of Jesus—the far-reaching mission in Acts. Thus, two central actions in the mission of the seventy—healing the receptive, and shaking off the dust of the unreceptive (Lk. 10.9, 11)—are illustrated in the course of Acts (5.15-16; 8.7; 13.51).

The role of the fifty as a prelude (to Elisha in the diverse towns) was merely implicit. Luke changes that role to become explicit—the seventy are clearly linked with the diverse towns. And by changing fifty to seventy—a number which has a greater suggestion of universalism, and which probably reflects the seventy(-two) nations of the world (Gen. 10; see Tannehill 1986: 233)—he achieves a clearer sense of inaugurating something wide and far-reaching.

Table 57. *The Sending and the Great Struggle (2 Kings 2.16–3.27; Luke 10.1-20)*

	Sending the Fifty, etc. (2 Kings 2.16–ch. 3)	Sending the Seventy (Luke 10.1-20)
1.	Elisha sent the fifty (*kai apesteilen pent-ēkonta*) to every spot in which the Lord's Spirit might have thrown Elijah [on his being taken up] (2.16-18)	The Lord sent the seventy (*hebdom-ēkonta kai apesteilen*) to every city and place in which he was to come [on the way to being taken up] (10.1)
2.	?? [Ruth among the harvesters (Ruth 2)] [cf. hurried mission of the Shunammitess and of Elisha to save a life (2 Kgs 4.22-33)]	The harvest; lambs among wolves. Greet no one on the way; say, 'Peace' (10.2-7)
	The Two Contrasting Cities	
3.	The town (*polis*) asks help from Elisha; he cures (*iaomai*) its diseased waters (2.19-22)	Whatever town (*polis*) receives you heal (*therapeuō*) the weak/sick (10.8-9)
	Boys from Bethel town (*polis*) mock Elisha, so bears come out (*ex-erchomai*) and tear them (2.23-25)	Whatever town (*polis*) does not receive you come out (*ex-erchomai*) and shake off the dust (10.10-11)
	Woeful War (against Moab) and Woeful Cities	
4.	Formulaic condemnation of Israel's king, including a reference to its original 'sin' (3.1-3)	Condemnation of cities ('Woe…'), including references to Sodom, Tyre, Sidon (10.12-14)
5.	Rebelling (*atheteō*) against me [Jehoram] involves rebelling (*atheteō*) against you [Jehoshaphat]? (3.4-7)	———
6.	Ascent (*anabainō*) and descent (*katabainō*) of the three kings ('Alas') (3.8-14)	Exaltation (*hypsoō*) and descent (*katabainō*) of the third city (10.15)
		5. Whoever rejects (*atheteō*) you rejects (*atheteō*) me (10.16)
	Total Victory over the Enemy	
		7. The seventy returned (*hypestrepsan*)
8.	What was dry is watered; SACRIFICE ascends (3.15-17, 20)	The demons are subdued; Satan falls from HEAVEN (10.17-18)
9.	Elisha gives total power (*para-didōmi… patasso pasan…*) over Moab (3.18-19, 21-26)	Jesus gives total power (*didōmi… pateō…pasan*) over the enemy (10.19)
10.	SACRIFICE of firstborn son (3.27a)	Names connected with HEAVEN (10.20)
7.	Israel returned (*epestrepsan*) (3.27b)	———

Luke has taken the mission of the fifty, which in the Old Testament is tucked almost inconspicuously between Elijah's ascent and Elijah's mission, and, by adapting it, has turned it into an introduction to the New Testament mission.

An initial conclusion, therefore, is that the sending of the seventy is based partly on the sending on the fifty (Elisha 'sent fifty', 2.17).

But the sending of the seventy is also based partly on another nearby text: the Lord's triple sending of Elijah (2 Kgs 2.1-6: 'The Lord has sent me to Bethel…to Jericho…to the Jordan', 2.2, 4, 6). Because of Luke's method of dispersing or elaborating certain key texts, God's triple sending of Elijah helps form the basis of three distinct sendings in the gospel (9.52; 10.1; 22.8). These two backgrounds—the Lord's sending of Elijah, and Elisha's sending of the fifty—are combined in the single action of Jesus, who (in Lk. 10.1) is described as 'the Lord'.

Table 57 outlines the relationship between the texts. But the material summarized in the later parts of the outline (Sections 4–10, dealing with the woeful war, 2 Kgs 3) is unusually difficult, and before examining specific sections, it seems necessary to look at the texts as a whole: 2 Kings 3, and the corresponding part of Luke (the woes to the cities and the victory of the seventy, 10.11-20).

1. *Woe and Victory: The Nature of 2 Kings 3 and Luke 10.12-20*

Before comparing the texts in any detail, it is necessary to survey the account of the war against Moab (2 Kgs 3) and the corresponding part of Luke (the mission's woes and successes, 10.13-20; cf. 10.12). Both texts are difficult. It is best to begin with a preliminary look at the text of Luke.

a. *The New Testament Text (Luke 10.13-20; cf. 10.12)*
The New Testament text (Lk. 10.13-20), which occurs within the larger unity of 9.51–10.20 (already discussed in the general introduction to Chapters 33–36) consists essentially of two parts. The first gives woes against the three unrepentant cities, and concludes with a saying about hearing and rejecting ('whoever rejects you, rejects me...', 10.13-16). These woes build on the preceding verse: the comparison with the most condemned city of all, namely Sodom (Lk. 10.12).

The second part telling of the return of the seventy suggests a great victory (demons are subjected, Satan falls from heaven, and there is power 'to tread on...the whole strength of the enemy', 10.17-20). And with the victory there is joy, not only because of the victory, but because the emissaries' names are written in heaven.

The passage (Lk. 10.13-20) has two obvious relationships: (1) with the rest of Luke–Acts, and (2) with the woes of the prophets.

First, Lk. 10.13-20 is attuned to the larger narrative of Luke–Acts. The woes may break the flowing rhythm of the mission of the seventy, but apart from being an elaboration of the theme of rejection or of not being received (10.10; cf. 9.53), they are like a variation on the rejection-related breaks in the account of the missions of John the Baptist and Jesus (Lk. 7.18-35, especially 7.29, 31). Coming like a prophetic warning at the close of Jesus' address to the seventy, they also help to prepare for Paul's prophetic warning at the close of his speech to the Jews in Pisidian Antioch, 'Look, you despisers...' (Acts 13.41)—a warning which precedes rejection (Acts 13.45). Whatever may have been the sources of the woes, these sources have been adapted in the light of Luke's larger narrative.

Likewise, Luke has adapted his sources in the account of the return of the seventy (10.17-20). The joy of their mission foreshadows the joy of those who will receive the word—particularly in Samaria (Acts 8.8), on the road to Ethiopia (Acts 8.39), and in Pisidian Antioch (Acts 13.48). Their power over Satan foreshadows the pivotal struggle against Elymas, the 'son of the devil', before going to Pisidian Antioch (Acts 13.8-11). And apart from balancing Jesus' orientation towards assumption into heaven (Lk. 9.51; Acts 1.9-11), the fact that their 'names are written in heaven' prepares also for the idea, at Pisidian Antioch, that those who believed were 'marked out for eternal life' (Acts 13.48).

The mission of the seventy not only echoes earlier missions, but it is also focused towards what is to come, especially towards the opening out to the Gentiles.

Second, Lk. 10.13-16 and the prophetic woes. A further element of Luke's text, at least in the composition of the woes (*Ouai...ouai...*, 10.13), is a partial dependence on the Old Testament use of woes (LXX *ouai*). In Fitzmyer's words (1981: 636) 'the woe-form is abundant in the LXX, and...undoubtedly provides the background for the New Testament use', and (p. 851) 'the woes against these Galilean cities can profitably be compared with such Old Testament passages as Amos 6.4-7; Mic. 2.1; Hab. 2.6-7; and Zeph. 2.5'.

Overall, the account of the seventy is well attuned to the larger narrative of Luke–Acts, yet it also reflects the prophetic tradition. This prophetic dimension opens the way for a discussion of Luke's relationship to another prophet-related text: 2 Kings 3.

b. *The Prophet Elisha and the War with Moab (2 Kings 3)*
The Old Testament text (2 Kgs 3) is about a war to regain control of Moab. Mesha, the king of Moab, had been paying massive annual tribute to Israel (100,000 lambs and the wool of 100,000 rams) and, when he rebelled, Jehoram of Israel invited Jehoshaphat of Judah to join him in a war of reconquest. The king of Edom joined also joined in.

The campaign consisted of two phases. The first lasted a week and might be summarized as 'the Rise and Fall of the Three Kings' (2 Kgs 3.1-14). They set off pretentiously (literally, they 'went up'), but they went round in circles in the desert and ended up without any water, neither for men or beasts.

'Alas' (*ō*), said the king of Israel, 'the Lord has called the three kings to hand them over to Moab' (2 Kgs 3.13).

But Jehoshaphat asked—as he had during the war to regain control of Ramoth-gilead (1 Kgs 22.7)—whether there was any prophet of the Lord, and someone spoke of Elisha and of how he had poured water. So they 'went down' to Elisha.

Elisha's entry brought in the second phase of the campaign (2 Kgs 3.15-27). To the sound of music, he told the three kings what they must have wanted to hear: that the stream bed would be filled with water and that they would totally conquer Moab.

What followed is extraordinary. The next morning at the time of sacrifice, 'behold, water came from the way of Edom' (a desert), 'and the land/earth (*gē*) was filled with water'.

When the Moabites saw the water, with the morning sun shining on it, they thought it was blood, the result of a fight among the three kings, so they came to the Israelite camp to pick up easy spoil.

But the result was disaster for Moab and its people. When the Moabites came to the Israelite camp, 'the Israelites rose and attacked the Moabites'. And even though the Moabites fled, the Israelites kept attacking them: 'and they went ahead, slaughtering the Moabites as they went'. As for the land, the devastation was complete. The invaders:
- Razed the cities.
- Threw stones into every good field 'and filled it'.
- Blocked every well.
- Cut down every good tree.

All that was left apparently—the text is obscure—were the stones of the capital, and even that was surrounded and attacked by slingers. The Moabite king tried a military gambit to get at the king of Edom, but he failed.

Finally, the king of Moab took his eldest son, the heir apparent, and offered him as a holocaust on the wall.

The result was quite extraordinary: 'There was great repentance [LXX; Hebrew: "anger/indignation"] on Israel. They went away from him, and returned to their own land' (2 Kgs 3.27).

c. *The Search for the Meaning of 2 Kings 3*

The basic problem with this story is that researchers are not sure what it is really about. It is often referred to as 'the Moabite War' and the idea of a war is corroborated in a general way by the famous Moabite Stone (now at the Louvre in Paris) in which Mesha tells how he recovered territory from Israel. Therefore, it would seem that historically there was a Moabite war.

But 2 Kings 3 does not correspond to the data on the Moabite Stone and it does not make military or political sense. If Jehoram was disturbed about losing his annual tax of 100,000 lambs and the wool of 100,000 rams, then the matter would not be solved by reducing Moab to a ruin without land, water, or trees. And how do sacrifice and holocaust either fill the land with water or turn back a slaughtering army?

One could say, of course, that the 100,000 and the utter devastation are exaggerations, that there really was not so much water, and that the offering of the heir apparent may have spurred the remnants of the Moabite army to make a decisive rally.

This is very reasonable, but it is not 2 Kings 3, and when one has finished with plausible historical scenarios, the problem of the text remains. In fact, changing the text so that it makes historical sense confirms that the biblical account, while it may contain elements of history, is not historical. It has used history or some history-like elements for another purpose.

Rather than being historical, some would see 2 Kings 3 as priestly. H. Schweizer (1974: 17-210, especially 87-90, 169-73), for example, regards the text as primarily didactical, but believes that its puzzling picture of the role of Elisha, as well as its emphasis on sacrifice and holocaust, emanate from priestly circles.

Others regard the account of the devastation of Moab as prophetical. H.-C. Schmitt (1972: 32-37), for instance, sees the text as part of a larger collection of war stories that was first composed around 750 BCE, at the time of Jeroboam II, and which, around the time of the exile, was rewritten in view of the theology of the prophets, particularly the teaching of Amos, that God does nothing without revealing his plans to the prophets (Amos 3.7).

The link with prophetic works finds confirmation in the similarities between the war to regain Moab (2 Kgs 3) and the war to regain Ramoth-gilead (1 Kgs 22). Despite the great differences between them, the second disastrous war of reconquest seems to have been modelled partly on the first, even to the point of including Jehoshaphat, whose presence in the second war is anachronistic (de Vaux 1958: 138). The Moabite War also reflects David's warlike wanderings in the desert (Brodie 2000: 56-57).

What is significant in the link with the Ramoth-gilead account (1 Kgs 22) is that that text was also not primarily about a war. Rather, it used aspects of a war story to speak about prophecy, particularly about prophetic confrontation and vindication.

If Schmitt is right that 2 Kings 3 was rewritten in light of the theology of the prophets, then it is worth asking once again what prophet or prophecy could have contributed to the picture of the utter ruin of Moab.

When one surveys the prophets—Isaiah, Jeremiah, Ezekiel, Hosea, Amos, and the others—one finds a number of texts which refer to trouble in Moab. But among them all, two stand out: Jeremiah 48 and, in a special way, Isaiah 15–16. The first four lines of Isaiah 15 are like a drumbeat announcing devastation:

>…when Ar was destroyed
>Moab was doomed
>…When Kir was destroyed
>Moab was doomed.

And then, for two full chapters, Isaiah speaks of Moab as experiencing a multi-faceted cataclysm.

Thus, the search for the meaning of 2 Kings 3 leads to the prophets, even to the heart of Isaiah's oracles concerning the nations/Gentiles. It is an area which stretches all the way from the fall of Babylon (Isa. 13–14) to a poetic apocalypse (Isa. 24–27).

This foray into the prophets may be interesting, but the topic which it touches is vast and largely unexplored. Pursuing the investigation would mean a massive digression, one which would lead not only into the heart of the prophets but also into some of the most difficult questions about the sources of Old Testament narrative.

In the present circumstances, the most realistic approach is to acknowledge that the meaning of 2 Kings 3 remains elusive and to bear in mind the possibility that it may have something to do with the wide world of the prophets.

d. *The Use of 2 Kings 3 in Luke 10.13-20*
From all that has been said, it is clear that Luke's use of 2 Kings 3 will not be easy to discern. The meaning of the Old Testament text is unclear, and within Lk. 10.13-20 it is just one factor among others, both elusive and subsidiary.

Nonetheless, as an exploratory effort it is worthwhile to attempt to discern some of the lines of its usage.

The Old Testament story might be summarized as one which changes from woe to victory. The woe occurs in the first part (2 Kgs 3.1-14) when the three kings, working without reference to God's prophet, end up pronouncing a parched 'Alas' (3.10).

But in the second half (2 Kgs 3.15-26), when Elisha calls for music and speaks in the name of the Lord, the expedition goes from woe to total victory, and it is the enemy who cry 'Alas' (3.21).

At the end, however, the total victory is tempered (apparently in a negative way) by the strange event of the son's sacrifice (3.27).

In the New Testament, there is a comparable change from woe to victory. The first part, referring to those who reject the prophetic seventy, consists of woes against three cities (Lk. 10.13-16). But in the second half (10.17-19), when the prophetic seventy return, the scene is one of joy and of total victory of a spiritual kind (demons obey, Satan is fallen, power over everything injurious, and safety from all harm).

At the end, however, the experience of total victory is tempered (in a positive way) by shifting the emphasis to the connection with heaven (Lk. 10.20).

These central ideas may be outlined as follows:

No prophet: result: 'Alas' (2 Kgs 3.1-14)	Prophetic seventy rejected: result: 'Woe' (Lk. 10.13-16)
Prophet leads: result: victory (3.15-26)	Prophetic seventy act: result: joy, victory (10.17-19)
But: victory is tempered (negatively) by sacrifice (3.20)	But: victory is tempered (positively) by the link with heaven (10.20)

Both texts (2 Kgs 3 and Lk. 10.13-20) build on what preceded them in their respective contexts. The previous accounts, about the diverse towns (some receptive, others unreceptive, 2 Kgs 2.19-25; Lk. 10.8-12), had implied two divergent reactions or ways: one leading to healing, the other to disaster (being mauled [Old Testament] or a fate worse than Sodom's [New Testament]). Now, in their own way, the accounts of the Moabite war and of the seventy suggest a deepening of that implied sense of division.

As already suggested, 2 Kings 3 is not primarily the account of a war. Rather, placed as it is at the end of the block of texts which surround the ascent of Elijah, it uses a war setting to depict a climactic divergence of woe and victory. Woe comes from pretentiously ignoring God's prophetic word; victory, on the other hand, comes from following that word.

Luke distils these ideas, and he adapts them to the prophetic mission of the seventy and to the climactic divergence which emerges from that mission between those whose rejection of the seventy brings woe, and those whose implied acceptance brings joy and victory.

Thus, the contrast of woe and victory once expressed through a war setting are now expressed through the setting of a mission. Ultimately, both texts are concerned with the spiritual dimension—with acceptance of God's word—but in Luke, that dimension is clearer.

Both texts verge on the apocalyptic. The Moabite war is like a great convulsion of nature and humanity, and the mission of the seventy expands to include everything from Sodom and Satan to serpents and heaven. Fitzmyer (1985: 860) sees Luke's reference to Satan's fall as 'indulg[ing] in a bit of apocalyptic writing'. Mattill (1979: 7) regards all of Lk. 10.1-24 as an apocalypse. This aspect of the texts requires further research.

However unrelated the texts may appear at first—one a war, the other a mission—ultimately they are closely related. In fact, the notions of mission and war are present in both; God's word implies an element of both mission and war (mission for what is good, war against what is evil). But the emphasis varies greatly; while the Old Testament emphasizes a war against an enemy, Luke, as always, lays the greater stress on the positive, and the explicit idea of overcoming an enemy is kept to a low key.

2. *More Detailed Analysis*

a. *Section 1. The Sending of the Fifty/Seventy (2 Kings 2.16-18; Luke 10.1)*
The taking up of Elijah was something so extraordinary that the prophetic groups wanted to check its reality, making sure the Spirit of the Lord had not thrown Elijah down somewhere, perhaps into the Jordan or onto some mountain or hill. So, though Elisha knew it was not necessary, he sent fifty strong men to all the places where the Lord's Spirit might have taken Elijah.

In Luke, soon after the reference to the taking up (9.51), the Lord sent seventy to all the towns and places where he was going to go (Lk. 10.1).

In both cases, people are sent to all the places which are in some way marked by the Lord and the taking up. Both missions, therefore, involve many earthly locations—just about anywhere the Lord may go—but they also point to another realm beyond ordinary life.

Unlike the Old Testament, however, where the sense of this other dimension may appear tentative—Elisha is the only one who is sure about it—the New Testament is explicit and leaves no doubt: Jesus, who is to be taken up, is Lord, and he sends the seventy, not on a negative mission (as does Elisha to counter his aides' negative attitude), but on a mission which is positive, one which will bring the heavenly realm right into people's lives.

While the Old Testament merely implies the inbreaking of the divine, the New Testament states it powerfully and positively.

Luke has made several other adaptations. The fifty have become seventy(-two)—a number which suggests something broader, more rounded, more universal (cf. Num. 11.16-17; Gen. 10). The phrasing has been brought into line with Luke's usage elsewhere, particularly with that of the preceding sending, following the reference to the taking up (e.g. 'before his face', cf. Lk. 9.52; for *ana-deiknumi*, 'appointed', cf. Acts 1.24). The use of 'others' ('seventy others') seems to be yet a further element of continuity with the preceding episodes' repeated use of 'other' in reference to would-be followers (Lk. 9.59, 61).

The sending 'in twos' is probably partly for companionship, but also for increased credibility as witnesses. One of the implied functions of the fifty was to bear witness; they verified that instead of being thrown somewhere on the earth, Elijah had been taken up by the Lord. By implication, they verified the inbreaking of the power of God. The task of the seventy was essentially the same, but was expressed more positively and explicitly: they would announce the approach of the kingdom of God. Two-by-two also echoes the flood and its implied new creation (Gen. 6.20; 9.1-17, just before the listing of the seventy nations, Gen. 10). Within the structure of Genesis, the water of the flood is counterbalanced by the fire of Sodom (Gen. 19) alluded to in Lk. 10.12. While reworking the account of devastation in 2 Kings 3, Luke is echoing more basic universal accounts of creation and devastation.

Overall, Luke has taken the low-key conclusion of the Elijah story and, by turning it around and expanding it, has made it into the introduction for the mission which is to follow.

b. *Section 2. The Urgency of the Journey (2 Kings 4.22-33; Luke 10.2-7; cf. Ruth 2??)*
Jesus' instructions for the journey (Lk. 10.2-7) are radical; they suggest having nothing, and they evoke danger, even danger of death ('lambs among wolves').

These instructions do not seem to find any detailed parallel in the journeys of 2 Kings 2. In fact, their suggestion of emissaries who are vulnerable contrasts with the characterization of the fifty (the fifty were strong or powerful, *hoioi dynameōs*, literally, 'sons of power').

The one element of 2 Kings 2 which may be reflected in the instructions is the general idea of a journey which is shadowed by death: Elijah's pre-assumption journey to the Jordan—sent by God, accompanied by Elisha, and watched by the prophets—has something of the tense balance of proximate danger and ultimate hope which is found in the journey of the seventy.

But, as regards details, the journeys of 2 Kings 2 are not helpful, and at first it may seem that in these instructions Luke has left the Elijah–Elisha narrative.

Yet some of the details are not far away. The mission of the Shunammitess—her urgent journey to rescue the life of her dead son, and Elisha's response to her (2 Kgs 4.22-33)—contains some of the elements at the center of the instructions to the seventy: greet no one on the way, repetition of the word 'peace', and entry into the house (2 Kgs 4.23, 26, 29, 32; Lk. 10.4-6).

The Elijah–Elisha narrative also provides some precedent for the idea of staying in one house (1 Kgs 17.15; 2 Kgs 4.8; see Talbert 1986: 117).

As for the rest of the instructions (especially in 10.2-3, 7-8) concerning the harvest, workers, food, and again the idea of not moving about to other households, there are some affinities with the mission of Ruth as she gleaned in the fields (Ruth 2, especially 2.2-3, 5, 8, 9, 12, 14, 16, 18, 20, 22). Like the woman of Shunem, Ruth had felt the shadow of death, and her character complements that of the Shunammitess, but whether or how Ruth's mission is really reflected in the mission of the seventy is a matter best left to further research.

What is certain is that the mission of the seventy reflects aspects of the urgency of the woman of Shunem, and so, while Luke may be blending a variety of old and new sources, one of these sources is from the Elijah–Elisha narrative.

c. *Section 3. The Two Contrasting Cities—Receptive and Unreceptive (2 Kings 2.19-25; Luke 10.8-11)*
After the sending of the fifty, 2 Kings 2 gives two contrasting accounts of Elisha's interaction with two cities (or towns). The first city is receptive, and when Elisha invokes the Lord, the Lord's word means life (2 Kgs 2.19-22, especially 2.21: 'Thus say the Lord, "I

heal (*iaomai*) these waters; no longer shall death come from them"'). But the second city, as represented by its children, is mocking, and so the word of the Lord is a curse which brings death ('And he cursed them in the name of the Lord, and two bears came out [*exēlthon*]...and tore forty-two children', 2 Kgs 2.23-24). For one city the word of the Lord brings healing and life, but for the second it brings death.

Luke in turn goes on to speak of two contrasting cities, one receptive, the other unreceptive (10.8, 10):

Whatever city you enter, and they receive you...

Whatever city you enter, and they do not receive you...

To the first city comes healing: 'Heal (*therapeuō*) those who are weak/sick' (Lk. 10.9). The fate of the second is not death, as it is in the Elisha story, but simply radical separation —coming out (*exelthontes*) they are to shake off the very dust from the city (10.10-11).

Luke has kept the basic idea of two cities giving two contrasting reactions, but he has rendered the Old Testament examples into two general instances where, by using repetition, the contrast is clearer and more universal. He has also made the text more positive: the terrible action of the bears, in coming out and mauling the boys, is replaced by the action, strong but not harmful, of coming out and shaking off the dust of the town.

d. *Section 4. Condemnation of Sin—and Reference to Ancient Sin, Making the Condemnation Stronger (2 Kings 3.1-3; Luke 10.13-14; cf. 10.12)*
The Old Testament account begins with a (Deuteronomically) stereotyped condemnation of Jehoram of Israel. Not only did he do evil (2 Kgs 3.2), but (*plēn*)—making the condemnation worse—he clung to Israel's primordial sin, the sin of Jeroboam (3.3).

Luke begins with a (prophetically) stereotyped condemnation ('Woe... Woe...') of two towns (10.13a). Not only that, but (*plēn*)—making the condemnation worse—this sin is connected with some of the most primordial sins in the Bible, those of Sodom, Tyre, and Sidon (Sodom's sin was proverbial; and the sin of Tyre had a primordial quality, Ezek. 26–28, especially 28.1-19). (Apparently Sidon was treated as one with Tyre. The two were neighboring cities of the Sidonians.)

Yet the nature of the connection with ancient sin differs in Luke. While Jehoram's sin was simply as bad as the ancient sin, that of Chorazin and Bethsaida is worse. Tyre and Sidon would have repented, and eventually Tyre and Sidon, along with Sodom, will fare better than Chorazin and Bethsaida.

Hence, Luke's condemnation is stronger, but it has a positive side. While condemning those towns which rejected Jesus, it implies that even the worst of Gentile towns will listen.

There may be some further smaller links, but it is better to concentrate on the essentials. What is present in both texts is a stereotyped condemnation of Israel. But instead of following the form of the Deuteronomistic History, Luke, even while absorbing that History, switches to the ringing style of the prophets. At the same time, he adapts it to a later situation, and to a mission which envisages the Gentiles.

e. *Section 5. Rejecting Me Means Rejecting You (2 Kings 3.4-7; Luke 10.16)*
When Mesha of Moab rebels (*atheteō*) against Israel, Jehoram makes preparations and sends out (*ex-apostellō*) to Jehoshaphat saying, 'Moab rebelled against me (*atheteō...en emoi*), will you go with me (*met' emou*)...?' (2 Kgs 3.4-7). The implication, accepted by Jehoshaphat, is that rebellion against one involves the other.

Luke has essentially the same principle: 'The one who rejects you, rejects me' (*ho athetōn hymas eme athetei*). But Luke expands the principle. First, in typical fashion, he gives the corresponding positive principle: 'The one who hears you, hears me'. Then he uses the idea of sending (*ex-apostellō*) as a starting point for bringing out the deeper implication of the rejection: 'and whoever rejects me rejects the one who sent (*apostellō*) me'. Thus, the Old Testament principle of solidarity is enriched, and it is rendered into a form which is repetitive and memorable.

f. *Section 6. The Ascent and Descent (Rise and Fall) of the Pretentious (2 Kings 3.8-14; Luke 10.15)*

The Old Testament campaign begins pretentiously: Jehoshaphat is matching strength and military pride with Jehoram: 'I am as [ready] as you are, my people as your people, my horses as your horses' (2 Kgs 3.7b), and so Jehoshaphat is ready to go. 'I will go up' (*ana-bēsomai*), he said.

They discuss how to 'go up' (again *ana-bainō*, 3.8), and off they go, three kings, with the word 'king' being solemnly repeated ('king...king... king', 3.9). But, after a week in the desert, there is a cry of 'Alas' (*Ō*) for the 'three kings' (3.10), and the three kings have to 'go down' (*kata-bainō*) to Elisha, with the word 'king' once again being solemnly repeated ('king...king...king', 3.12). The picture may be set in outline:

> I will go up...king...king...king.
> Alas (*Ō*)...three kings.
> He went down...king...king...king.

What emerges is a rise and fall centered on 'Alas'.

Worse still for the king of Israel when he goes down is that Elisha addresses him contemptuously as 'you' ('What have I to do with you [*soi*]? Go to the prophets of your father [*patros sou*]....I would not...even look at you [*se*]', 2 Kgs 3.13-14).

Luke (10.15) adapts all this to the third town, Capernaum:

> 'And you (*su*), Capernaum,
> will you be lifted (*hypsoō*) up to heaven?
> You will be brought down (*kata-bainō*) to Hades.'

As with the condemnation of sin (lack of repentance), Luke uses the content of the Deuteronomic History (2 Kgs 3), but, once again, when it comes to style (or form), he switches from that of the Deuteronomic narrative to that of the prophets.

The prophetic style which he is imitating is found especially in Isaiah's satire on the fall of the king of Babylon (Isa. 14.13-15):

> You (*su*) said...
> I will go up (*ana-bēsomai*) to heaven...
> as on a lofty mount...lofty mountains (*hypsēlō...hypsēla*)...
> But now you go down (*kata-bainō*) to Hades.

Luke's wording comes largely from Isaiah, but the underlying idea is from 2 Kings 3, and so is the slightly contemptuous tone in the 'you'.

g. *Section 7. The Abrupt Return (2 Kings 3.27b; Luke 10.17a)??*

There may, perhaps, be some correspondence between the return of the Israelite coalition and the return of the seventy:

———	The seventy returned (*hypestrepsan*)
There was great repentance	with joy
(*metamelos megas*) on Israel,	(*meta charas*),
and they went away from him	saying, 'Lord...'
and returned (*epestrepsan*)...	———

The difficulty of connecting these texts comes from two factors: they are extremely brief (thus giving little data to work with), and they occur at different stages within their respective contexts (at the very end of 2 Kgs 3, and at the very beginning of the account of the return of the seventy).

Yet there may, in fact, be a link for a number of reasons:
- Luke sometimes moves a closing or climactic Old Testament element into a leading position in his own text (e.g. in using 1.1–2.6 to form 9.51-56, he moves aspects of 2.1 to the beginning to form 9.51).
- Both groups are broad: the Israelite coalition, and the seventy.
- There is a verbal link: *epe/hype-strepsan* ('they returned').
- In both cases, the picture of advance or mission is abruptly reversed. Before the mention of the return, the Israelite coalition had been advancing unstoppably; and the seventy were still being sent out. The return comes unexpectedly.

h. *Section 8. The Lord's Name Overcomes the Waterlessness/Demons (and Sacrifice Ascending Means Satan Falling from Heaven) (2 Kings 3.15-17, 20; Luke 10.17b-18)*
When 'the hand of the Lord' comes on Elisha, he gives a command which leads to the parched land being filled with water (2 Kgs 3.15-17, 20).

And when the seventy use the Lord's name, the demons submit to them (Lk. 10.17b).

Elisha's overcoming of *waterlessness* is balanced by the seventy's overcoming of *demons*. Both are done through the Lord (through 'the hand of the Lord'; in the Lord's name), and both seem to involve variations on obedience (Elisha's challenging command is obeyed; the demons submit).

Whatever the details, the basic correspondence between demons and waterlessness is not new. It was seen earlier (Chapter 32) in the link of the spirits/demons (Lk. 8.2) with the drought (1 Kgs 18.40-46), and Luke's later text explicitly connects unclean spirits with waterless places (Lk. 11.24; cf. Mt. 12.43).

Hence, the basic idea, expressed in different ways, is that God's command (the word of the Lord) overcomes a form of death (the death implied by waterlessness, or the death implied by demons).

To this overcoming of something deathlike, both texts add a striking feature. The overcoming of waterlessness is accompanied by the ascent or going up (*ana-bainō*) of sacrifice (2 Kgs 3.20), and the overcoming of demons is associated with the falling of Satan like lightning from heaven (Lk. 10.18). The two details—the ascent of sacrifice and the fall of Satan—are like two sides of the same coin, and they accord well with the sacrifice–demon imagery of the Tobit story. Tobit's offering of burning incense drives the demon away (Tob. 6.17; 8.3).

Again Luke's wording ('falling from heaven') depends considerably on Isaiah's satire on the king of Babylon (Isa. 14.12; see Marshall 1978: 429; *pace* Fitzmyer 1981: 862).

i. *Section 9. The Total Victory: I Give You Power Over All the Enemy and Nothing Shall Hurt You (2 Kings 3.18-19, 21-26; Luke 10.19)*
'I shall give over (*para-dōsō*) Moab into your hand', says Elisha. 'You shall strike (*patassō*) every (*pasan*) strong town, every…tree…well… field…' (2 Kgs 3.18-19). And so it happens—repeating the words *patassō* and *pas* in various ways (3.21-25).

Luke also speaks of giving complete power over an enemy: 'I have given (*didōmi*) you power to tread on (*pateō*)…all (*pasan*) the strength of the enemy'. While adapting the idea of complete power to the New Testament situation, Luke synthesizes the complex Old Testament picture into a single verse and plays with the Old Testament wording.

Then both texts briefly mention that those who have just been given power over the enemy will themselves escape harm. The final Moabite rally (700 swordsmen!) tried to reach the king of Edom, but 'they were not able' (*ouk ēdun-ēth-ēsan*, 2 Kgs 3.26). 'And', says Jesus, 'nothing will ever touch you' (*ouden...ou...adik-ēsē*). Again, Luke seems to distill the Old Testament idea while playing with some of its wording.

j. *Section 10. Yet the Total Victory is Tempered by Sacrifice (2 Kings 3.27) and by the Connection with Heaven (Luke 10.20)*

The victory over Moab is tempered by the final and most enigmatic turn in the Old Testament story: the king's sacrifice of his son as a holocaust. Luke in turn tempers the idea of total victory, but he does so in a way that is clearer and more positive by referring to heaven.

One of the results of Luke's adaptation is that both references to sacrifice in 2 Kings 3 are balanced in the gospel passage with references to heaven:

Sacrifice ascends (2 Kgs 3.20)	Satan falls from heaven (Lk. 10.18)
Sacrifice of holocaust (3.27)	Your names are...in heaven (10.20)

In Luke's adaptation, therefore, sacrifice effects heaven either by removing what is negative (Satan) or establishing what is positive (one's name). Like a poet who can vary from antithetical parallelism to synonymous parallelism, Luke varies from first showing an image of what sacrifice removes (Satan) to showing later an image of what it establishes (one's name in heaven).

3. *Conclusion*

Partly because of the inherent obscurity of the Old Testament section, the full relationship between the texts is unusually elusive. Yet, despite the incompleteness of the analysis, there is sufficient data to make an assessment.

External plausibility is no problem. Given the context already established by the preceding chapter, it is not surprising that Luke should rework yet another part of the Elijah–Elisha narrative.

The similarities are complex, and the details are sometimes perplexing. But before entering the details, if one considers the similarities which are most prominent—for instance, as indicated by the four main headings in the general outline—then the overall pattern begins to fall into place. And with that broad pattern are other elements including order, completeness, and some significant verbal details.

Some differences are intelligible but not all. There is a strong residue of elements which need further explanation.

However one decides—for or against literary dependence—one's conclusion will be accompanied by a certain lack of understanding. A positive decision will not understand all the differences. A negative decision will not be able to explain the similarities. But the person who decides in favor of literary dependence has the hope that with further research and reflection more of the differences will become intelligible. Given the context of the preceding chapters, a positive decision seems to be a useful working hypothesis.

36

Elijah's Crossing, Ascending, and Spirit-Giving (2 Kings 2.7-15) as a Framework for the Center of Proto-Luke (Luke 22–Acts 2 [Except 22.31-65])

In tracing Proto-Luke's use of 2 Kings 2—the central chapter concerning the crossing, the ascending and the spirit—one comes eventually to the center of Luke–Acts. To some degree, an initial similarity is obvious. Nowhere else in all of ancient literature, save in the Elijah–Elisha narrative and in Luke–Acts, does an account of ascent/assumption bridge a two-part work. What is not immediately clear is whether that unique similarity is a coincidence or whether it is part of a larger pattern.

A larger pattern does in fact emerge. Close examination indicates that while Luke's Passion Narrative involves many diverse sources, including 1 Corinthians, 2 Kings 2 plays a kernel role, small but foundational. Particular importance goes to the center of 2 Kings 2—the account of how Elijah crossed the Jordan, was taken up, and in effect imparted his spirit (2.7-15). These three events—the crossing, the taking up, and the spirit—provide an initial framework for the center of Luke–Acts (Luke 22–Acts 2):

	Elijah	*Jesus*
1.	Elijah crosses the Jordan	Jesus dies
2.	The fiery ascent to heaven	The ascent to heaven
3.	The descent of the spirit	The fiery descent of the Spirit

The significance of crossing the Jordan may look obscure at first. At the fateful river, as fifty of the prophetic disciples stand at a distance, Elijah's cloak rends the waters, and, when Elijah ascends in fire, his spirit comes to rest on Elisha. Seeing that Elisha too can part the Jordan, the watching disciples realize that the spirit has come to rest on him, and so they come to him and bow down before him.

This crossing of the Jordan is like the bridging of death. The whole chapter (2 Kgs 2) is set in the shadow of the death of Ahaziah (2 Kgs 1) and Elijah's journey terminates his earthly life. The Jordan, therefore, is the end.

But the Jordan is overcome. Through his spirit of prophecy as he strikes the waters with his prophetic mantle, Elijah survives the Jordan. He has a spirit that is greater than death— a spirit which is passed on to Elisha and which draws the other disciples to it.

1. *More Detailed Analysis (2 Kings 2.7-15; Aspects of Luke 22–Acts 2)*

In using 2 Kings 2 Luke disperses the account; to some degree he seems to take the text in layers rather than in whole blocks or passages, as he usually does. This procedure is due presumably to the centrality of 2 Kings 2, and to its extraordinary density. This procedure makes analysis more difficult, and it means that references to this particular Old Testament text tend to overlap. The subsequent analysis therefore is limited. It does not attempt to cover all the connections between the texts, and above all it does not attempt to explain the complex way in which many details have been transformed by Luke. It simply seeks to establish the basic principle of the connection between the two sequences of events.

a. *Section 1. The Crossing of the Jordan and the Death of Jesus (2 Kings 2.7-15; cf. Luke 23.26-49)*

The role of the Elijah text in the description of Jesus' death is quite limited; it is one component. The substantive link between Elijah's crossing of the Jordan and Jesus' dying is that for both of them it is the end of normal earthly life. But there are also some similarities of detail. Both departures are surrounded by loud cries concerning the father/Father and the spirit (Jesus hands over his spirit to the Father, Lk. 23.46; and Elisha's cry of 'Father, father...' is interwoven with his desire for the spirit, 2 Kgs 2.9-12). Both also involve two processes of dividing or tearing: the prophetic mantle divides the Jordan, and Elisha tears his garments in two (2 Kgs 2.8, 12); and Jesus' death is attended by the dividing of his garments and by the rending of the temple veil (Lk. 23.34, 45). And while all this is happening, it is noted both before and afterwards that disciples of various kinds 'stood...at a distance' and watched (2 Kgs 2.7, 15; Lk. 23.35a, 49). Some of the detailed affinities are as follows:

- Handing over the spirit:

    Old Testament:
    pneumati sou ep' eme...eboa, Pater, pater... (2.9, 12)

    New Testament:
    phōnēsas phōnē megalē, Pater eis cheiras sou...to pneuma mou (23.46)

    Old Testament:
    your spirit in me...he shouted, 'Father, father...'

    New Testament:
    he cried in a loud voice, 'Father into your hands...my spirit'.

- Two dividings with/of cloth:

    Old Testament:
    elabon tēn mēlōtēn autou...kai diērethē to hydōr entha kai entha (2.8)
    kai epelabeto tōn himatiōn autou kai dierrēxen auta eis duo rhēgmata (2.12)

    New Testament:
    diamerizomenoi de ta himatia autou ebalon klēron (23.34)
    eschisthē de to katapetasma tou naou meson (23.45)

    Old Testament:
    Elijah took his mantle...and the water was divided hither and thither.
    And he took his garments and rent them in two pieces.

    New Testament:
    They cast lots dividing out his garments.
    The veil of the temple was rent in the middle.

In assessing the dividing of the garments (Lk. 23.34), it is necessary, as elsewhere in Proto-Luke, to distinguish sources from wording. The source, or one of the sources, seems to be the Elijah–Elisha text, but the wording is largely from Ps. 22.18:

- Two groups watching:

    Old Testament:
    Pentēkonta andres huioi tōn prophētōn kai estēsan ex enantias makrothen (2.7).
    Kai eiden auton hoi huioi tōn prophētōn [kai] hoi en Ierichō ex enantias... (2.15).

    New Testament:
    Kai heistēkei ho laos theōrōn (23.35).
    Heisēkeisan de pantes hoi gnōstai autō apo makrothen...horōsai tauta (23.49).

Old Testament:
Fifty prophetic disciples stood across at a distance.
And the prophetic disciples across in Jericho saw him.

New Testament:
And the people stood watching.
All those known to him stood at a distance...to see this.

b. *Section 2. The Taking Up (2 Kings 2.11; Luke 24.51; Acts 1.9-10)*
Concerning the taking up of Elijah—the most pivotal text in the whole Elijah–Elisha narrative—it is relatively easy to see how Luke has used it. On the principle of unpacking diverse layers, he draws from it twice (see Table 58).

Table 58. *The Taking Up to Heaven (2 Kings 2.11; Luke 24.51; Acts 1.9-10)*

	2 Kings 2.11	Luke 24.51	Acts 1.9-10
1.	And it came to pass that they were going along walking and talking,	And it came to pass as he was blessing them,	And as he was saying these things and they were looking on,
2.	and behold a chariot of fire and horses of fire separated (*diesteilan*) the two of them,	he was parted (*diestē*) from them,	he was lifted up and a cloud took him out of their sight,
3.	and Elijah was taken up in a whirlwind as it were to heaven	and he was carried up to heaven	And as they were looking up to heaven as he was going, behold two men stood by them in white garments and said, 'Men of Galilee, why do you stand looking to heaven?'

The main purpose of this outline is to show that each of the texts has three basic moments: (1) the time of togetherness and communication; (2) the abrupt separation; (3); the disappearance into heaven. The differences between the texts are considerable, but they may be accounted for through deliberate adaptation on Luke's part.

On the one hand, he has omitted the stupendous elements (the fiery chariot and whirlwind). This procedure is in line with the generally humble and human tone of his writing and with the picture of Jesus—in contrast to Elijah—as refusing to call down fire from heaven (Lk. 9.54-55; cf. 2 Kgs 1.9-14).

On the other hand, he has made some elaborations to suit the new Christian context and his own particular theological tendencies. Thus, the image of blessing, for instance (Lk. 24.51), is part of a larger Lukan emphasis on blessing (cf. especially Lk. 24.30, 50, 53). And the image of the two men in white garments (Acts 1.10) reflects the Christian imagery used to express the events surrounding the resurrection (cf. Lk. 24.4; Mk 16.5; Mt. 28.2-3).

What emerges, therefore, is that Luke used the skeleton of Elijah's assumption as a basis for describing the taking up of Jesus. This is corroborated by the fact that both assumptions are linked with various forms of promising the spirit/Spirit and granting it (2 Kgs 2.9-10, 15-16; Lk. 24.49; Acts 1.2, 8; 2.1-41). But again, of course, Luke's idea of the Spirit is colored and elaborated by Christian experience and reflection.

c. *Section 3. The Tumultuous Granting of the Spirit (2 Kings 2.1, 7, 11, 14, 15; Acts 2, Especially 2.1-6)*
In the wake of the taking up or ascent, it is also relatively easy to see a continuity between the incidents involving the *pneuma* (spirit/Spirit). In Acts 2, as in 2 Kings 2, the spirit is

the spirit of the one who has ascended (Elijah, 2 Kgs 2.9; Jesus, Lk. 24.49); and there are curious affinities (2 Kgs 2.1, 7, 11, 14, 15; Acts 2.1-6):

Old Testament:
syn-seismō...(2.1)   a whirlwind...
Kai pentēkonta andres...pyros...   And fifty men...fire...
dierragēsan entha kai entha...   divided hither and thither...
pneuma...epi...(2.7-15).   spirit...on....

New Testament:
Kai ...pentēkostēs...   And...Pentecost [literally, the fiftieth]...
pheromenēs pnoēs biais...   a violent wind blowing
diamerizomenoi...pyros...eph' hena hekaston   parted...fire...on each one...
pneuma...andres...(2.1-5).   Spirit...men....

d. *Conclusion to Analysis of Sections 1–3*
In the three preceding episodes (death, ascent, Spirit), many details are debatable. But the overall range of similarities goes far beyond the scope of coincidence, and it leads to the conclusion that Proto-Luke regarded the ascent of Elijah as a seminal text of great importance, a text which captured something of the fusion of heaven and earth and which could be used to describe some of the most decisive moments in the history of Jesus and his sending of the Spirit.

2. *Towards Greater Precision:*
Luke's Further Use of the Sending (2 Kings 2.1-6)

Luke's use of 2 Kings 2 helps to establish the broad link between the center of the Elijah–Elisha narrative and the center of Luke–Acts, but it does not establish fully the limits of Luke's Passion Narrative.

As a partial help towards achieving this clarity, it is useful to look more closely at Luke's further use of the Lord's initial sending of Elijah to the Jordan (2 Kgs 2.1-6: 'The Lord has sent me to Bethel...to Jericho...to the Jordan', 2.2, 4, 6). Though Luke has used this text before in composing Jesus' departure for Jerusalem (Lk. 9.51-56), he later unpacks another layer of it, dispersing it.

Because of this method of dispersing or elaborating certain key texts, God's triple sending of Elijah helps form the basis of three distinct sendings in the gospel (9.52; 10.1; 22.8). A similar complexity was noted in dealing with the sending of the seventy. It depended primarily on the sending of the fifty (2 Kgs 2.16-18), yet its first phrase, '...the Lord... sent', also drew on the initial sending (in 2 Kgs 2.1-6).

The sending (2 Kgs 2.1-6) is used carefully. As Elijah is journeying to the Jordan (2.1-6), he tells his disciple Elisha three times, with repetitive solemnity, that the Lord God had sent him on just a part of that journey. Each time he effectively offers Elisha a chance to bow out, but each time his disciple vows to stay with him. The tension and repetitiveness is heightened by the interventions of whole bands of prophetic disciples ('the brotherhood/ community of the prophets') from the towns along the route—disciples who whisper to Elisha about the impending taking away of their lord (*kyrios*) Elijah (2.3, 5).

This journey, with its triple sending and its multiple repetitions, is shadowed by a sense of mystery, and as it progresses to the Jordan it may seem almost fateful. Yet it had begun with a clear indication that the Lord is about to take Elijah up to heaven, and in their whispered way the disciples know this. 'Yes, I know', said Elisha, 'be quiet' (2 Kgs 2.3, 5).

In the repetitious account of Elijah's journey to the Jordan, the use of *apostellō* ('to send'), is explicit ('God/the Lord has sent', *Theos apestalken...Kyrios apestalken...Kyrios*

apestalken, 2 Kgs 2.2, 4, 6). And within Lk. 9.51–20.20 and Luke 22–Acts 2, Jesus sends his disciples on three missions:
- He sent (*kai apesteilen*) messengers before him to a Samaritan village to prepare for him (Lk. 9.52).
- He sent (*kai apesteilen*) the seventy before him to every town and place where he was to come (Lk. 10.1).
- He sent (*kai apesteilen*) Peter and John to go and, as he said, 'prepare the passover for us' (Lk. 22.8).

These three Lukan episodes are in such continuity of content, style, and detail that they form a certain unity. And just before the first of them, like a headline over them all, is the announcement of the imminent ascent of Jesus (Lk. 9.51)—a headline which is adapted from the opening of the ascent of Elijah (2 Kgs 2.1). In other words, Luke has taken the first scene of 2 Kings 2 (the announcement of ascent and the three repetitive sendings, 2 Kgs 2.1-6) and has used it as a repetitive framework both for the two missions which dominate Lk. 9.51–10.20, and for the final mission which inaugurates his passover (including his passion).

Furthermore, within the third area of the passover and passion, Luke has developed the phenomenon of threefold repetition in other ways: using phrases which begin the episodes of the passover and passion:

Now the feast of unleavened bread was near... (22.1)
Now the day of unleavened bread came... (22.7)
And when the hour came to pass (*egeneto*)... (22.14)
It came to pass (*egeneto*) that there was contention... (22.24)
And when day came (*egeneto*)... (22.66)

There is a triple progression with regard to the time of the passover: from being near, to the day itself, to the very hour. And even as that progression is concluding, another one begins: the coming to pass (*egeneto*) of the passover meal, of the contention during the meal, and of the fateful day of crucifixion.

These patterns of intensification and repetition, from facing Jerusalem (Lk. 9.51) to the dawning of the fateful day (22.66), form a kind of drum beat leading to death, an effect which recaptures elaborately the drum beat repetitiveness of Elijah's journey towards the Jordan.

The effect of tracing Luke's further systematic use of 2 Kgs 2.1-6 is to clarify the dimensions of Proto-Luke: it contains at least a large part of the last supper account (from Lk. 22.1 onwards) and also the event beginning at 22.66—the morning trial before the sanhedrin.

3. *Conclusion*

The overall effect of tracing Proto-Luke's use of 2 Kings 2 is that it uncovers the framework for some of the central areas of Proto-Luke. First of all, it helps to highlight the unity of the two missions at the center of Proto-Luke's gospel (Lk. 9.51–10.20—the death-shadowed mission and journey [9.51-62] and the more hope-filled mission of the seventy [10.1-20]).

The use of Elijah's ascent also helps to trace tentatively the shape of Proto-Luke's Passion Narrative. The repetitive rhythms of the triple sending (2 Kgs 2.1-6) run through the passover-related events (Lk. 22.1-30, especially 22.1, 7, 14, 24), and—having skipped a block of thirty-five verses—reappear with the dawning of the day of death (Lk. 22.66).

The area which is thus bypassed, and which would appear not to belong to Proto-Luke, is the account of some of the night events from foretelling Peter's denial to the denial itself, and including Jesus' anguished prayer and his arrest (Lk. 22.31-65).

The use of the Elijah ascent, therefore, points to a framework which, at the center of the gospel includes Lk. 9.51–10.20, and, at the center of Proto-Luke as a whole, extends from Luke 22 to Acts 2 and beyond, omitting Lk. 22.31-65.

Unit 9. Proto-Luke and Elijah–Elisha: Crises and Expansion

Orientational Introduction to Chapters 37–39:
The Use of the Elijah–Elisha Narrative in Acts 5–8*

In Acts 5–8, the reshaping of the Old Testament text continues systematically. Thus far, Proto-Luke has used everything in the Elijah–Elisha narrative as far as 2 Kings 4 except the chapters on Ben-hadad's invasion and Naboth's stoning (1 Kgs 20–21). In Acts 5–8, he first goes back to collect most of this material (1 Kgs 20–21), and then moves ahead to the next major episode—Naaman (2 Kgs 5). The resulting overall relationship (analyzed here in Chapters 37–39) is as follows:

Chapter 37:	*1 Kgs 20.1-21; 21.1-7*	Greed: Ben-hadad/Ahab/Jezebel
	∨	∨
	Acts 5.1-11	Fraud: Ananias/Sapphira
Chapter 38:	*1 Kgs 21.8-13*	Naboth accused, stoned
	∨	∨
	Acts 6.9-14; 7.58	Stephen accused, stoned
Chapter 39:	*2 Kgs 5*	Namaan; Gehazi's money
	∨	∨
	8.9-40	Simon's money; the Ethiopian

The Naboth text (1 Kgs 21) plays diverse roles. Its beginning (21.1-7) is used for Ananias/Sapphira; its center (21.8-13) for Stephen; and its conclusion (21.17-29) for some actions involving Peter (Acts 2.37-38; 8.15, 20-26). The details need refining (particularly concerning the use of 21.14-16).

As for Ben-hadad's invasion (1 Kgs 20), only the first half of the chapter is used, and only in a secondary way, concerning his greed and his defeat by the young men (20.1-21). The rest of 1 Kings 20 (Ben-hadad's attack and escape) will be used elsewhere.

Incidentally, the Greek reverses chs. 20 and 21 of 1 Kings, and perhaps that is how Luke found them. However, it seems more practical to follow the chapter numbering of the Hebrew.

---

*   Chapter 38 was originally published in the *CBQ* (1983) and Chapter 39 in *Biblica* (1986).

37

Old Testament Rapaciousness, Especially by Ahab and Jezebel (1 Kings 21 and 20.1-21), as one Component of the Story of Ananias and Sapphira (Acts 5.1-11)

It is accepted by diverse commentators that Luke's account of the fraud of Ananias and Sapphira—their deceit in holding back the price of their land (Acts 5.1-11)—is modeled partly on the account in Joshua 7 of the misappropriation by Achen (Bruce 1954: 110; Conzelmann 1972: 45; Haenchen 1971: 239). In both texts, 'there is a deceitful holding back of goods, a confrontation with God's spokesman, and the cutting off [of] the miscreants from the people by death…—similarities which suggest that Luke was using the Achen story as a rough model for his own' (Johnson 1977: 205-206).

If the Achen story supplied one component—if indeed it was 'a rough model'—perhaps other Old Testament texts supplied further components for Acts 5.1-11.

The purpose of this chapter is to indicate that a further component comes from the Elijah–Elisha narrative's two accounts of rapaciousness which follow one another in successive chapters (in 1 Kgs 20 and 21). It is within these Elijah-related chapters that one finds the concerted rapaciousness of one of the Old Testament's most notorious couples, Ahab and Jezebel, and the picture of that infamous couple has colored the presentation of Proto-Luke's deceitful couple. In other words, the Achen story may have contributed to the basic picture of misappropriation and subsequent death, but the added factor—that the man who did it was in full partnership with a woman—has drawn partly on the partnership of Ahab and Jezebel.

In contrast to the Old Testament account in which the woman, Jezebel, plays a special role in instigating evil, Luke's account of the relative responsibility of the two is much more even-handed. Sapphira may share the blame fully and may echo aspects of Jezebel, but there is no suggestion, as in the Old Testament presentation of Jezebel, that Sapphira is at the root of the evil. And while Satan is indeed present in the story of Ananias and Sapphira, he is associated first of all with Ananias ('Ananias, why has Satan filled your heart…?', Acts 5.3). Thus Luke uses the notorious Jezebel, yet apportions blame more evenly. In this sense, there is no Jezebel in Proto-Luke.

1. The Texts: Introductory Analysis

The Old Testament text consists primarily of 1 Kings 21—the story of how Ahab and Jezebel stole Naboth's vineyard. But in using the Naboth story, Luke has made two basic changes. On the one hand, he leaves aside the final sections dealing with the stoning (21.7-16), the condemning (21.17-24), and the repentance (21.27-29), and he uses them largely to describe aspects of the stoning of Stephen and its aftermath (Acts 6–8). On the other hand, he grafts on a further section dealing with the rapaciousness of Ben-hadad of Syria (1 Kgs 20.1-21).

The reason for grafting on the Ben-hadad story is fairly clear. Like the Naboth story, the Ben-hadad account begins with a greedy threat which affects not only property but also people who in diverse ways are very close (forefathers or families). The affinity between these two Old Testament stories emerges quickly:

Ahab to Naboth:
'Give me your vineyard...I will give you money...'
Naboth (in response): 'God forbid that I give you the inheritance of my fathers' (1 Kgs 21.2-3)

Ben-hadad to Ahab:
'You will give me your money...and your wives'
Ahab (responding, to the elders): 'He seeks evil, for he has sent for my wives and children' (1 Kgs 20.5, 7)

To some degree, the two stories are somewhat like two sides of the same coin. The essence of the Naboth account is that after Ahab has taken over the vineyard of the dead Naboth, Elijah 'finds' him, confronts him, and, in God's name, condemns him and Jezebel to oblivion.

The essence of the Ben-hadad story is that after Ben-hadad threatens to take everything from Ahab, a prophet intervenes and, in God's name, promises deliverance—provided Ahab relies on the young men (*paidaria*, 1 Kgs 20.14, 15, 17). Thus Ben-hadad's army suffers a great slaughter (*plēgē megalē*, 20.21).

Luke incorporates several elements and echoes from these stories. After the fraud, Peter confronts the culprits. And there is a process of 'finding' (5.10), an intervention by the young men (*neōteroi, neaniskoi*, 5.6, 10), and finally, not a great slaughter, but a great fear (*phobos megas*, 5.5, 11).

Luke's text is a small diptych. First he tells of Peter confronting Ananias (5.1-6) and then gives a similar scene of Peter confronting Sapphira (5.7-11). There are probably diverse reasons for this: Luke has a penchant for diptychs; there are two Old Testament stories; and he wants to give the woman equal time, a scene of her own.

While there are two Old Testament stories and two New Testament confrontations, the relationship is not one-to-one. When Luke is distilling the Old Testament stories, he uses aspects of *both* of them to describe the confrontation with Ananias, and he again uses some of the same aspects to describe the confrontation with Sapphira. Thus, while maintaining something of the Old Testament effect of two stories, he achieves—as often—a greater sense of repetition.

Because of Luke's adaptation of the order of the texts, the overall relationship is quite complex. Some of the main aspects are summarized in Table 59.

2. *The Texts: More Detailed Analysis*

a. *The Fraudulent Couple—A Summary of Selling and Covetous Plotting (1 Kings 21.1-3, 25; 20.1-12; Acts 5.1-2)*

Ahab's plot (to take Naboth's vineyard) is framed by two passages: the introductory account of his effort to buy it for himself (1 Kgs 21.1-3), and the concluding summary that he sold himself to do evil (21.25). Luke takes these two ideas—trying to take something for himself, and selling in a way that is evil—and combines them into the single action of Ananias: he sold and then tried to keep some of the price for himself (Acts 5.1-2).

At this point, Luke is also incorporating aspects of the Achen story (Josh. 7). In particular, the wording, 'and he misappropriated from' (*kai enosphisato apo*, Acts 5.1) is taken almost unchanged from Josh. 7.1 (*kai enosphisanto apo*, 'and they misappropriated from').

Table 59. *Greed and Fraud (1 Kings 21 and 20.1-21; Acts 5.1-11)*

Ahab and Jezebel (1 Kings 21 and 20.1-21)	*Ananias and Sapphira (Acts 5.1-11)*
1. [Summary: Ahab and Jezebel, 21.25] Ahab's attempted takeover: he tries to get Naboth's family inheritance (*klēronomia*, 21.1-3) [Ben-hadad tries to get Ahab's goods and family (20.1-12)]??	Summary: Ananias and Sapphira; Ananias's misappropriation: he gives only part (*meros*) (5.1-2)
2. Ahab's disturbance of spirit and face and body (21.4)	2a. 'Why...does your Satan-filled heart... lie to the...Spirit...to God?' (5.3-4)
	8a. Ananias' death brings great fear and the young men bury him (5.5-6)
3. Enter Jezebel, his wife (21.5) (*kai eisēlthen...hē gynē autou... kai eipen pros autēn*)	Enter Sapphrira, his wife (5.7) (*kai hē gynē autou...eisēlthen apekrithē de pros autēn*)
4. Ahab to her: 'I said to Naboth, "Give me (*Dos moi*) your vineyard for money"' (21.6)	Peter to her: 'Tell me (*eipe moi*), was it for so much [money] you gave up the land?' (...*ape-dos-the*) (5.8)
	2b. Sapphira tests the Spirit (5.9a)
5. The stoning (21.7-16)	[Stephen accused, stoned (6.9-14; 7.58)]
6. The condemning (21.17-24) [Ahab and Jezebel (21.25; see 1 above)]	[Peter descends, condemns (8.15, 20-21)]
7. The repentance (21.27-29)	[Peter's word > repentance (8.22-24; 2.37)]
8. Prophet: 'Behold...the young men'. The young men went out...' (20.13-19) And...he took all... and struck a great slaughter on Syria (20.20-21)	8b. 'Behold...' and the young men...buried her (5.9-10) And the came a great fear on the whole church and on all who heard it (5.11)

Yet it is the Ahab story which colors some of the key elements of the Ananias account. Apart from the combination of the two elements already mentioned—trying to get something for himself, and selling in a way that is evil—it is the Ahab story's conclusion (1 Kgs 21.25) which contains the distinctive account of the role of the woman:

Summary conclusion (1 Kgs 21.25):	*Summary introduction (Acts 5.1-2a):*
Ahab sold (*pipraskō*) himself to do evil as Jezebel his wife misled him.	Ananias and his wife sold (*pōleō*) ...and misappropriated from... his wife also knowing.

These two texts illustrate several of Luke's procedures. As elsewhere (e.g. in using 2 Kgs 2.1 to write Lk. 9.51), he takes a text from a relatively late position within the Old Testament and moves it, in its rewritten form, to the top of his own text—perhaps because he realized it provided material for a good opening. Consequently, Acts 5 begins with the image of selling. (Luke's choice of word, *pōleō*, builds on the use of *pōleō* a few verses earlier, in Acts 4.34.)

Luke's next idea, still following the Ahab story, is of doing evil, but he expresses this general idea through the specific image of misappropriation (taken from the story of Achen). Thus, as often, he is blending sources, taking a broad idea from one source and the specific image or wording from another.

Then, still following the Ahab story closely, there is the role of the women: Jezebel and Sapphira. Luke, however, changes the woman's image—not the instigator in evil, as in the Old Testament account, but a fully responsible partner.

Luke's further description of Ananias' actions—how he brought a 'share' (*meros*) and placed it (deceitfully) at the feet of the apostles (Acts 5.2b)—would appear, given the context, to form a rough equivalent to the effort of Ahab to get his hands on Naboth's inheritance (*klēronomia*, 1 Kgs 21.1-3). As it happens, *meros* and *klēronomia* are related terms; *meros* can refer to an inheritance (e.g. Lk. 15.12). Luke apparently juggled the Old Testament concept of taking someone's inheritance: Ahab sought to misappropriate the inheritance of another; and Ananias, in *giving* a share/inheritance, committed another form of misappropriation.

While using Ahab's effort to take Naboth's family inheritance, Luke may have also drawn on the related effort of Ben-hadad to take Ahab's own goods and family (1 Kgs 20.1-12). Thus, the attempted crime of Ananias and Sapphira would reflect something of the attempted crimes of both Ahab and Ben-hadad.

b. *The Evildoer's Disorientation in Spirit and Body (1 Kings 21.4; Acts 5.3-4)*
Ahab was so set on Naboth's vineyard that he became 'disturbed in spirit' and prostrate in body ('he lay on his bed, covered his face, and did not eat bread', 1 Kgs 21.4).

In the case of Ananias, Peter asks why Satan filled his heart to lie to the Holy Spirit and to God. In other words, Luke keeps the idea of a disorder which affects both body and spirit ('heart...Holy Spirit'), but he adapts that disorder to the more explicitly theological language of the New Testament, to the tension between Satan and God/the Holy Spirit (cf. Acts 13.9-10; Lk. 4.1-14).

Luke's adaptation—from spirit to the Holy Spirit—is related to the adaptation made earlier when speaking of the assumption: whereas the Old Testament had spoken of receiving the spirit of Elijah, Luke described receiving the Holy Spirit. Both spirit/Spirit adaptations suggest an effort by Luke to relate different phenomena (positive and negative) of the human spirit to the divine Spirit.

This episode shows one of Luke's ways of balancing the elements in his texts. On the one hand, the idea of tension with the Holy Spirit which had just been attributed to Ananias (section 2a, in the first part of the diptych, Acts 5.3-4) will also be attributed in less elaborate form to Sapphira (section 2b, in the second part, 5.9a)—thus maintaining her equal status. On the other hand, the picture of the young men carrying out the dead culprit and the consequent dread on all, a picture which occurs in greatest detail in the later Sapphira section (section 8b, 5.10-11), is now attributed, in slightly less elaborate form, to Ananias: his death causes fear and the young men bury him (section 8a, 5.5-6).

c. *The Wife Enters (1 Kings 21.5; Acts 5.7)*
As Ahab lay on his bed, face covered and not eating, Jezebel entered. And a few hours after Ananias had been buried, Sapphira entered. Both women are in a scheming mood—ready to take or keep what does not belong to them.

Luke's account is different insofar as it presupposes the death of the culprit—an element colored by the Achen story (Josh. 7.25)—so Sapphira's interlocutor is Peter, not her husband. And there is a difference concerning the woman's role in the scheming: Jezebel initiates the process; Sapphira simply maintains the scheme she had shared with her husband.

Yet some of the wording is similar:

Old Testament:
And Jezebel, his wife, entered and said to him...
(*Kai eisēlthen Iezabel hē gynē autou...kai elalēsen pros auton*)
'Why (*ti*) is your spirit (*pneuma*) disturbed?'
And he said to her (*kai eipen pros autēn*).
'Because (*hoti*)...'

New Testament:
And his wife...entered
(*kai hē gynē autou...eisēlthen*).
And Peter spoke to her (*apekrithē de pros autēn*)...
'Why (*Ti hoti*)...tempt the Spirit (*pneuma*)...?'

d. *Speaking to the Wife about Giving Land for Money (1 Kings 21.6; Acts 5.8)*
Replying to Jezebel, Ahab tells her he had asked Naboth to give his vineyard in exchange for money. And when Sapphira enters, Peter asks her if she had given the land in exchange for so much (money). Thus, Ahab's brief recalling of his original money-for-land offer is balanced by having Sapphira recall something of her land-for-money deal. There are echoes in the wording:

Old Testament:
Give me (*Dos moi*) your vineyard for money.

New Testament:
Tell me (*Eipe moi*) was it for so much [money] you gave up (*apo-dos-the*) the land?

e. *The Accusing and Stoning of Naboth/Stephen (1 Kings 21.7-16; Acts 6.9-14; 7.58)*
The next, dramatic episode about how Jezebel arranged the accusing and stoning of Naboth is not used in the story of Ananias and Sapphira. Instead, Luke adapts it in considerable detail to the account of the martyrdom of Stephen (see next Chapter).

f. *The Descending and Condemning (1 Kings 21.17-24; cf. Acts 8.15, 20-21, 26)*
The incident which follows the death of Naboth—the sending down of Elijah, especially to condemn—seems to have given some minimum coloring to the incidents which follow the death of Stephen, particularly the sending down of Peter, resulting in the condemning of Simon (Acts 8.15, 20-21), and even the sending down of Philip to meet the Ethiopian (Acts 8.26).

g. *The Repentance (1 Kings 21.27-29; Acts 8.22-24; Acts 2.37-38)*
Given the order of the episodes, Ahab's subsequent repentance seems to have had at least some minimum influence on the subsequent repentance of Simon (Acts 8.22-24), but its more obvious influence is on an earlier repentance account, in Acts 2.37-38:

Because of the word	Hearing
Ahab was pierced (*katenygē*)...	they were pierced...(*katenygēsan*).
and he put on sackcloth...	And Peter said, 'Repent...'
Ahab was pierced (*katenygē*)...	

The word 'to be pierced/stabbed' (*katanyssomai*), occurs eighteen times in the LXX. Ahab's repentance is the only brief incident in which it occurs twice, and Acts 2.37 is its only occurrence in the New Testament.

h. *Behold…the Young Men…and the Dread-Filled Effect On All (1 Kings 20.13-21; Acts 5.9b-11)*

The Old Testament text also tells the story of Ben-hadad's rapacious desire (1 Kgs 20.1-12) and of his undoing through the young men (20.13-21). The distilled essence of his rapacious desire may perhaps have been already incorporated by Luke (in conjunction with the related rapaciousness of Ahab, 21.1-3) to help form the beginning of the Ananias story (Acts 5.1-2). In any case, it is only now, at the end of the New Testament story (5.9b-11), that he makes use of the incident of the young men and their devastating effect.

The achievement of the young men in the Old Testament was to lead an attack on Ben-hadad's rapacious army (1 Kgs 20.13-19), and this attack caused great devastation on all (20.20-21).

Luke adapts this to the circumstances of Ananias and Sapphira: the young men rising up carried the culprits to their burial, and great fear fell upon all (5.5b-6 and especially 5.9b-11). Some further details may be seen in Table 59 (section 8/8b).

3. Conclusion

Some of the foregoing analysis is incomplete or debatable. It seems particularly difficult, for instance, to be sure whether or how the rapaciousness of Ben-hadad (1 Kgs 20.1-12) is incorporated into the initial presentation of Ananias (Acts 5.1-2).

But while some aspects are unsure, the overall picture is not. Luke's use of part of 1 Kings 20–21 is externally plausible. There is independent evidence that Luke's text (the story of Ananias and Sapphira) reworks the LXX (Josh. 7), and the incorporation of 1 Kings 20–21 would dovetail with that—and with Luke's earlier use of the Elijah–Elisha narrative.

The similarities, though quite limited in quantity, are striking and varied. They range from the central focus on the ownership of a field to details about the entry of the woman, and they include the subsequent puzzling entry of the young men.

The differences are largely intelligible. For instance, the purpose of the young men in Luke is not to drive out an invading army but to remove a couple, the instruments of Satan. The difference, while huge, accords with Luke's larger purpose of writing historiography (thus echoing the flow of great movements and wars) but of doing so in a way that is oriented towards individuals (biography) and towards what happens within them (internalization).

38

The Accusing and Stoning of Naboth (1 Kings 21.8-13) as one Component of the Stephen Text (Acts 6.9-14; 7.58a)

It is generally accepted that the Stephen speech, like the infancy narrative, involves a complex interweaving of Old Testament texts.[1] Hence the question arises whether other parts of the Stephen story, apart from the speech, are also dependent on the Old Testament. In other words: Could it be that just as in the infancy narratives, the use of the Old Testament is found not only in the prolonged utterances (the hymns) but also in the birth annunciations, so too in Acts the use of the Old Testament is found not only in Stephen's speech but also in the surrounding narratives concerning his being accused and stoned?

The idea that Luke used the Old Testament in some of the narrative sections of Acts is not in itself novel. As already seen (in the preceding Chapter) Luke's account of Ananias' misappropriation and punishment (Acts 5.1-11) seems to be modeled to a significant extent on the Old Testament account of the misappropriation and punishment of Achan (Josh. 7).[2] If the Ananias of Acts 5, the community's first 'criminal', could thus be modeled on an Old Testament character, then so could the Stephen of Acts 6 and 7, the community's first martyr.

It may be objected that the Stephen speech, from a literary point of view, is radically different from the narratives concerning Stephen being accused and stoned, and therefore that it is very unlikely that the use of the Old Testament should extend beyond the speech. It is true that unlike the speech, the surrounding narratives do not explicitly refer to the Old Testament, but detailed stylistic analysis of the entire Stephen story, speech and narratives, indicates that it is a literary unit—that in every place it is heavily marked by Luke's deliberate literary artistry.[3] If Luke played so strong a part in shaping the entire story, there is no reason why, having saturated the central speech with Old Testament quotations and allusions, he should not also use the Old Testament in shaping the surrounding narratives.[4] In fact, since Stephen's speech puts such emphasis on Old Testament history, it is altogether appropriate that the martyr, not only by his words, but also by other elements of his martyrdom, should reflect that history. In other words, it is appropriate that the fate of the martyr should in some way echo his speech.

---

1. See Richard 1978: 33-155; see pp. 13-31 of Richard's study, and also Kilgallen 1976: 3-26 for a review of research on the Stephen story. For further bibliography, see Schneider 1980: 431-42, 469-70.
2. Bruce 1954: 110; Haenchen 1971: 239; Conzelmann 1972: 45; Johnson 1977: 205-206. As Johnson comments, in both texts 'there is a deceitful holding back of goods, a confrontation with God's spokesman, and the cutting off the miscreants from the people by death...similarities [which]...suggest that Luke was using the Achan story as a rough model for his own'.
3. See Richard 1978: 157-242. Richard's exhaustive analysis effectively counters the idea put forward by Dibelius, Surkau, and Trocmé that the speech and the martyrdom do not fit well together stylistically. For a summary of Dibelius *et al.*, see Haenchen 1971: 287-88.
4. See Richard 1978: 238: 'That a narrative and speech should bear so many linguistic, thematic and structural connections speaks against independent sources for these texts... These parts of the Stephen story have too much in common to be the product of secondary editing.'

It may also be objected that Luke would feel constrained to give a strictly historical account of the fate of Stephen, not one that has been colored by Old Testament texts. But there is evidence that our present text concerning Stephen is something of a composite—that it involves shades both of Jesus and of Paul. With regard to Jesus, there are at least four points of similarity: being led into the Sanhedrin by the concerted leadership of the people (Acts 6.12; cf. Lk. 22.66); the accusation concerning the temple (Acts 6.14a; cf. Mk 14.57-58); the vision of the Son of Humanity (Acts 7.55, 56; cf. Lk. 22.69; Mk 14.62); and the last words (Acts 7.59-60; cf. Lk. 23.34, 46).[5] And with regard to Paul, a similarity has been noted (see Cerfaux and Dupont 1953: 73) concerning the accusation about disrespect for the Law or customs of Moses (Acts 6.13, 14b; cf. especially Acts 15.1, 5; note Acts 21.21, 28; 25.8; 28.17). As Richard concludes from an analysis of the accusations:

> The author borrows from his source—very often two or more sources—a variety of elements: quotations, terms and ideas. He then combines them to suit his purpose, adds to them, often by imitating the style or theme of the text in question, and finally, imposes upon this totality his own personal style and structural perspective... The mere fact that the author has left his redactional mark...does not rule out the use of a source. (Richard 1978: 292)

If Luke felt free to color his picture of Stephen by combining shades of both Jesus and Paul, then it is unlikely that he would have ruled out the use of any Old Testament coloring. On the contrary, given his use of the Old Testament elsewhere, such a procedure is not at all surprising.

If Luke did indeed want to describe the stoning of Stephen, the expositor of biblical history, through some narrative of that same biblical history, he could hardly have chosen a more fitting and obvious text than the account of the stoning of the faithful Naboth. For while the Old Testament has several references to the threat or law of stoning (e.g. Exod. 17.4; Lev. 20.2, 27) and has occasional references to people actually being stoned to death (e.g. Josh. 7.25, Achan; 1 Kgs 12.18, Adoram), it has only one example of the stoning to death of a really good man—Naboth.

It is important to emphasize what is *not* being claimed here. It is not being said that the account of the accusing and stoning of Stephen is simply a reworking or reshaping of the Naboth text. Rather, what is being suggested is that of the various elements and components which Luke has sifted and grafted together, *one* consists of the Naboth text. It is important, too, to try to describe the function of that component. It is an underlying framework, almost like a skeleton which, having lost its former body, is fleshed out once more until it supports a new body. Such a component is not immediately obvious, but with patient analysis a reasonable case may be made for its presence. It is with this limited claim in mind that we turn to the texts.

1. *Introductory Analysis*

The Naboth text[6] is quite repetitious. First, it tells how Jezebel wrote letters sealed with the royal seal commanding that through the popular court[7] Naboth be falsely accused and

---

5. For further details, see Richard 1978: 286-301, and especially Schneider 1980: 433.
6. In Codex Vaticanus, which is used as a basis for the Cambridge critical edition of the LXX, vv. 10b-13a of the Naboth text are omitted. This omission, however, which involves skipping from *paranomōn* in v. 10 to *paranomōn* in v. 13, may be explained as an instance of homoioteleuton; in other manuscripts (Codex Alexandrinus, Codex Basilano-Vaticanus, all the cursive manuscripts selected for preparing the Cambridge edition) vv. 10b-13a are included. The longer reading, therefore, seems to be the better.
7. The meeting which condemned Naboth, a meeting which involved the proclamation of a fast and a gathering of the leaders and people, may be described as a popular court. It was a regular part of the Old Testament system of justice. See de Vaux 1965: 153.

stoned. Then, it tells how Naboth was, in fact, falsely accused and stoned. The Stephen text is also repetitious, but it contains more variety. First, certain synagogue members arranged that Stephen be falsely accused. Then Stephen was led into the Sanhedrin and there, in somewhat varied form and with slightly varied introductions, the accusations were repeated. (The first group of accusers, the suborned men, accused Stephen of blaspheming *God* and *Moses* [Acts 6.11]; the second group, the 'false witnesses', accused him in different ways of speaking against *the holy place* and the *Law/customs of Moses* [Acts 6.13-14]. That there is continuity and repetition in the accusations is widely recognized.[8]) Because of the repetitious or doublet structure of the texts, it is useful, when setting them in parallel, to divide them into two scenes. See Table 60.[9]

Table 60. *Naboth and Stephen*

Scene 1	
1. *Conspiracy Begins (Monarchy-Based)* And she wrote a letter in the name of Ahab and sealed it with his seal and sent the letter to the elders and to the free(d)men who were dwelling with Naboth. And it was written in the letters saying, Proclaim a fast and set Naboth before the people (1 Kgs 21.8-9)	*Hostility Begins (Synagogue-Based)* But there rose up some from the synagogue (called) of the Freedmen and Cyrenians and Alexandrians and of those from Cilicia and Asia, disputing with Stephen, and they were not able to resist the wisdom and the spirit whereby he spoke (Acts 6.9-10)
2. *The Setting up of False Witnesses* And set two men, sons of transgressors, opposite him, and let them testify against him saying,	*The Suborning of Witnesses* Then they suborned men saying, We have heard him

3. *A Twofold Accusation*
He cursed [literally, blessed]
  * God
  * and king.
Lead him out and stone him
And let them lead him out and stone him and let him die (21.10)
	A Twofold Accusation
	speaking blasphemous words against
	  * Moses
	  * and God (6.11)

Scene 2	
4. *The Leaders and People Accept Manipulation* And the men of his city, the elders and the free(d)men who were dwelling in his city did as Jezebel sent to them, as it had been written in the letters which she sent to them (21.11)	*The People and Leaders are Manipulated* And they stirred up the people and the elders and the scribes.
5. *Naboth is Set before the Popular Court* And they called a fast and set Naboth before the people (21.12)	*Stephen is Led into the Sanhedrin* and coming upon [him] they seized him and led [him] to the sanhedrin. (6.12)

8. As Loisy (1920: 309) comments: 'L'accusation est donc anticipée, et elle fait doublet avec la suivante, tout comme "les hommes subornés" font double emploi avec "les faux témoins"'. In Richard's summary (1978: 287): 'Commentators...since... Loisy...view the indictments against Stephen as being two in number: concerning Moses/Law/customs and God/this place'.

9. For a table of the texts in Greek, see Brodie 1983a: 422.

6.	*The False Witness* And there came two men, sons of transgressors, and sat opposite him and bore witness against him saying,	*The Lying Witnesses* And they set up false witnesses saying,

7.	*The Twofold Accusation*
	 You cursed [literally, blessed]
	   * God
	   * and king.
		Variations on the Twofold Accusation
		 This man does not cease speaking words
		   * against this holy place
		   * and the law,
		 for we have heard him saying that this Jesus of Nazareth
		   * shall destroy this place
		   * and change the customs which Moses handed on to us. (6.13-14)
		 (Speech and its rejection [6.15–7.57])

8.	*The Stoning* And they led him out outside the city and stoned him with stones and… (21.13)	*The Stoning* And throwing [him] out outside the city they stoned [him] and… (7.58)

As laid out, the texts show major differences and striking similarities. The greatest difference is that of setting. In writing the birth-announcements, Luke did not reproduce the settings of the Old Testament birth-announcements—the institutions and circumstances of the periods of the patriarchs and judges. Instead, the settings were laid aside, and the basic pattern of the announcements was transferred, in adapted form, to the later circumstances of Zechariah and Mary. And in adapting the story of Achan (Josh. 7) to Ananias, the setting of the conquest is laid aside.

Similarly in the texts under consideration: the institutional setting which is so prominent in the Old Testament text—the monarchy, the regal letters, the popular court—is totally absent in Luke's text. Indeed, that it should be present would be odd. Instead we find that the basic process of accusing is present, but in a way that is adapted to a first-century institutional setting, that of the synagogue and sanhedrin. Thus, instead of a conspiracy which is hatched by monarchical power (1 Kgs 21.8-9), there is hostility which is synagogue-based (Acts 6.9). Instead of putting the accused before the popular court (1 Kgs 21.12), there is a picture of people leading the accused into the sanhedrin (Acts 6.12b). And instead of an accusation concerning God and the *king* (1 Kgs 21.10b, 13b) there is an accusation concerning God and *Moses/the Law*, that is, concerning God and the one whose law reigned within first-century Judaism (Acts 6.11b, 13b-14). As already noted, the later accusations against Stephen, those concerning the (holy) place and the Law, are generally regarded as involving variations of the initial accusation concerning God and Moses.

Apart from the differences that are based on the varied institutional settings, there are differences which seem to spring largely from what may be called a diverse narrative focus. The larger Old Testament text, all of 1 Kings 21, is focused not so much on the figure of Naboth as on the resulting confrontation between Elijah and the house of Ahab. The incident concerning the accusing and stoning of Naboth is little more than one passing stage in building towards that confrontation. It is told with a stony repetitiveness—the exact balance of command and fulfillment—and the cadence of the repeated words brings the incident rapidly and rather predictably to its sad conclusion.

But the accusing and stoning of Stephen is no passing incident which is rapidly told. It is a major focal point which increases gradually in intensity, a focal point which centers on a dramatic speech and culminates in a glorious death. It is this diverse focus which helps explain certain differences between the texts. Luke's mention of the wisdom and power with which Stephen spoke (Acts 6.10)—a verse which has affinities with the gospels but for which the Naboth passage provides no substantial precedent—acts as a prelude to the speech which intervenes between the accusing and stoning. In other words, in light of the importance of Stephen's speech, the type of speech which Naboth never managed to deliver, it is appropriate, at an early stage in the hostilities, that the narrative give some indication of Stephen's capacity for speech. The inclusion of Acts 6.10, therefore, is an understandable adaptation.[10]

Another difference which also seems related to the difference of narrative focus is the fact that, in comparison with the Old Testament text, Luke's account has a smaller proportion of exact repetition. Obviously, it does have some; it has a certain twofold structure. In fact, this element of repetition has led some to believe that Luke is fusing different sources.[11] But it is not, as in the Old Testament, the almost exact repetition of command-and-fulfillment. Rather, it appears as the repetition which is involved in statement-and-intensification; in other words, it is an instance where a narrative makes a statement, and later, with some new intensity, repeats that statement.[12] Such a pattern of statement-and-intensification accords with the fact that Luke's account of the accusing of Stephen is building up to a dramatic speech and death. Thus, while the rapid closing of the Naboth incident invited the predictable repetition of command-and-fulfillment, the gradually unfolding drama of Stephen invited a repetition which was one of increasing intensity.

However, it is not only the difference of narrative focus which seems to have effected Luke's shaping of the twofold account; the difference of setting may also have been a factor. For while it is quite appropriate in the context of a rather ruthless monarchy to speak of an unscrupulous command and of its literal fulfillment, such a pattern of repetition is not altogether suitable in a less authoritarian setting. Something more sophisticated is required, a mode of repetition which fits the more complex power structure constituted by the interaction of synagogue and sanhedrin. This, too, helps explain the move from a doublet of precise repetition to a doublet of increasing intensity. Whatever the precise interaction of these two factors—different narrative focus and different institutional setting—taken together they go far in explaining why Luke's twofold structure is different from that of the Naboth text.

2. More Detailed Analysis

Apart from the changes demanded by the differences of setting and of narrative focus, the correspondence between the texts is quite close.

a. *Section 1. The Beginning of Conspiracy/Hostility (1 Kings 21.8-9; Acts 6.9-10)*
While the Old Testament tells of a conspiracy which begins in the monarchy (21.8-9), Acts tells of hostilities which originate in the synagogue (Acts 6.9).[13] Incidentally, even

---

10. On the affinity of Acts 6.10 with the Synoptics, see Richard 1978: 283-85.

11. The fact that there are two distinct groups of accusers, first the suborned men, and later, before the sanhedrin, the false witnesses, has led Weiss, Wendt, Loisy, Feine, and Spitta to suggest that Luke is combining different kinds of sources, one dealing with a lynching or a popular court, the other with an orderly judicial process. For a summary of these opinion, see Haenchen 1971: 273. As Haenchen notes, the two elements do not require two sources; rather, Luke 'could portray the behaviour of the authorities as exhibiting both juridical and anarchic features'.

12. One of the features of biblical narrative consists of repetition in which there is 'some intensification or increment from one occurrence to the next'; see Alter 1981: 96.

13. Luke's mention of 'the so-called synagogue' and of five groups could be read as referring to several synagogues or to one (see Haenchen 1971: 271). Perhaps the essential point is not the number of

though Luke's picture of the synagogue has a cosmopolitan aspect which is appropriate to first-century Judaism ('Cyrenians, Alexandrians...those from Cilicia and Asia'), it begins with a puzzling reference to free(d)men (*libertinoi*), a term which is difficult to link satisfactorily with any particular first-century group,[14] but which has a curious counterpart in the Old Testament reference to the *eleutheroi*—a term which may, indeed, refer to the nobles but which literally means 'free(d)men'. In other words, at least part of the explanation for Luke's obscure reference to *Libertinoi* seems to consist of the fact that it is a Latinized[15] form of *eleutheroi*. Through such an adaptation, Luke would have kept an added thread of continuity between the conspiracy which engulfed Naboth and the hostility which broke upon Stephen. Thus Luke's text, insofar as it depicts institutional discontent expressing itself against an innocent man, does maintain continuity with the Old Testament text, but, insofar as it speaks of a cosmopolitan synagogue, it represents a radical departure from the older setting.

As already mentioned, the reference to Stephen's power of speech (Acts 6.10) finds no substantial base in the Old Testament text. It appears rather as a prelude to the long speech which is to come.

b. *Section 2. Setting Up False Witnesses (1 Kings 21.10a; Acts 6.11a)*
Instead of describing the process of suborning witnesses, as does the Old Testament (1 Kgs 21.10; cf. 21.8-9), Luke simply notes: 'then they suborned men...' (Acts 6.11a). In other words, once allowance is made for the different setting, Luke's text reads like a summary or rewording of the older text. The detail that there were two witnesses, a detail so appropriate to the Old Testament setting (cf. Deut. 17.6; 19.15), is not explicitly reproduced by Luke, but his use of the plural makes it clear that at least two people were involved. And in place of 'let them witness against him' (*katamartyrēsatōsan autou*), Luke's suborned men say 'we have heard him' (*akēkoamen autou*). The two details—witnessing against someone about what he has said and reporting what has been heard—are like different sides of the same coin, two complementary elements, and it is quite understandable that in reworking the Old Testament text, Luke should switch from one to the other.[16]

---

buildings in question, but the involvement of the institution—the synagogue. For further discussion, see Knowling 1974: 174.

14. John Chrysostom (*Homilies on Acts* 15) interprets *libertinoi* as people freed by Rome, *hoi Romaiōn apeleutheroi*. As Haenchen notes (1971: 271), it has been suggested by Schürer, Zahn, and Strathmann that *libertinoi* is a reference to those Jews (and the descendants of those Jews) who were taken to Rome by Pompey and who were afterwards released. But there is no adequate explanation of why they should have formed a distinct social group, why that group and their descendants should have remained distinct till the time of Stephen (about a century later), or why they should have particularly associated with such people as the Cyrenians and Alexandrians. M. Dibelius regarded this explanation as so weak that he proposed that *libertinōn* is a corruption of *libyōn*, 'of the Libyans' (1956: 91). Loisy seems to regard efforts at historical reconstruction as hopeless. He speaks of the reference to *libertinoi* as an 'indication obscure et indécise, comme il convient à un fragment de tradition mutilée' (1924: 307). For further discussion, see Knowling 1974: 173-74.

15. The Latinizing of *eleutheroi* may be seen as part of the larger process of changing the setting from that of a local popular court in ancient Israel to that of a first-century synagogue which is cosmopolitan in composition and which lives under the shadow of Rome.

16. The process of complementing a source-text, of switching it to show a different angle, may be found in literary processes as varied as the reworking of the wisdom of Amen-em-ope in Prov. 22.18 and Seneca's reworking of the tragedies of Euripides; see Brodie 1981d: 24-32, 58.

c. *Section 3. A Twofold Accusation (1 Kings 21.10b; Acts 6.11b)*
Whereas the Old Testament witnesses are to say that Naboth has cursed[17] God and the king (1 Kgs 21.10b), the suborned men say that Stephen has blasphemed Moses and God (Acts 6.11b). Once again, when account is taken of the different setting, Luke's text appears to be a rewording of the Old Testament narrative.

Unlike the Old Testament (21.10b), Luke at this point does not refer to stoning Stephen. This omission makes sense. For while the Old Testament doublet structure consists of command-and-fulfillment and therefore can refer twice to the stoning—first to its being commanded and later to its being carried out—the New Testament doublet structure of statement-and-intensification does not allow for such repetition. (Luke could not say that after the first accusation Stephen was stoned, and that after the later accusations he was stoned again.) Just as the difference of setting requires certain adaptations in reworking the Old Testament text, so does the difference of narrative focus and structure.

d. *Section 4. Manipulation of Leaders and People (1 Kings 21.11; Acts 6.12a)*
The Old Testament (21.11) goes on to say that the city's citizens and leaders followed the subversive plot of Jezebel, and Luke in turn tells how the plotters stirred up the people and their leaders. Obviously, once again the setting makes a difference: Luke does not allude to regal letters, and his image of the leadership (elders and scribes) involves an updating of the Old Testament image (elders and free[d]men), but the basic process of manipulating both the people and their leaders is found clearly in both texts. Incidentally, this is the first time in Acts that the people appear hostile to the followers of Jesus. Such sudden hostility may perhaps be explained historically, at least to some degree, but part of the explanation seems to lie in Luke's effort to reflect the involvement of the people in the condemning of Naboth (cf. 1 Kgs 21.9, 11, 12).

e. *Section 5. Bringing the Accused before the Court/Sanhedrin (1 Kings 21.12; Acts 6.12b)*
Just as Naboth is set before the popular court (1 Kgs 21.12), so Stephen is seized and led into the Sanhedrin (Acts 6.12b). At this point, Luke's brief text seems to combine diverse elements: the *essential action* of taking the victim and bringing him to a prejudiced trial and the *position* of that action within the text of Acts may both be accounted for through the hypothesis of Luke's use of the Naboth text. But the *wording* in Acts ('and led him into the sanhedrin') seems, as G. Schneider notes,[18] to be influenced by the description of leading Jesus into the Sanhedrin (Lk. 22.66).

f. *Section 6. False Witnesses, Saying...(1 Kings 21.13a; Acts 6.13a)*
While the Old Testament tells of the unscrupulous witnesses who allowed themselves to be used against Naboth (1 Kgs 21.13a), Luke recounts briefly that 'they set up lying witnesses'. In other words, both texts speak of manipulated witnesses, but, as in speaking of the manipulated people and leaders, Luke's version is briefer, and he emphasizes the active process of manipulating ('they stirred up...they set up', Acts 6.12a, 13a) rather than the passive compliance of those being manipulated. (The Old Testament structure of command-and-fulfillment, by its emphasis on fulfilling a command, invited a picture of

---

17. What the Hebrew literally says, and what the Greek reproduces, is that Naboth *blessed* God and the king; but that is a euphemism for saying Naboth *cursed* God and the king. (The idea of the euphemism was to avoid the use of 'curse' along with 'Yahweh'; see Gray 1970: 441). Stephen is accused of speaking blasphemous words against Moses and God (Acts 6.11). Thus, the accusation in Acts is almost an exact copy of the accusation brought against Naboth, but it avoids the use of euphemism.

18. Schneider 1980: 433. Note that Naboth too was led (1 Kgs 21.10, 13).

passive compliance. But the New Testament structure of statement-and-intensification makes less room for emphasis on passivity. Hence, Luke's more active presentation is understandable.) As E. Haenchen notes (1971: 271), Luke's mention of 'lying witnesses' reflects various Old Testament texts (cf. Prov. 14.5; 24.28; note Pss. 27.12; 35.11; Exod. 20.16; 23.1; Deut. 20.16, 18). Once again, the *basic action* which is in Luke's text, and the *positioning* of that action within the narrative, both correspond to the Naboth text, but the actual *wording* ('lying witnesses saying'), while in part owing to the Naboth text, also encompasses a phrase from other sources.

g. *Section 7. The Twofold Accusation Repeated (1 Kings 21.13b; Acts 6.13b-14)*
The Old Testament goes on to repeat the accusation about cursing God and the king (1 Kgs 21.13b; cf. 21.10b) and Acts goes on to give variations on the accusation about blaspheming God and Moses (6.13b, 14; cf. 6.11). At this stage, continuity with the Old Testament may still be discerned. In both texts the *structure* of the accusations is two-pronged, the wording involves *repetition* of an earlier accusation (cf. 1 Kgs 21.10b; Acts 6.11), and there is some continuity of *content* (the concern about 'this holy place' and the Law is partly a variation on a concern about God and Moses, and ultimately a variation on the Old Testament concern about God and the king). But such continuity is only a skeletal framework onto which other material has been grafted. And, as already indicted, this extra material has significant resemblance to the accusations brought against Jesus and Paul (see especially Mk 14.57-58; Acts 15.1. 5).

h. *Section 8. The Stoning (1 Kings 21.13c; Acts 7.58)*
Finally, there is the actual stoning. The two descriptions (21.13c; Acts 7.58a) are almost identical, but the text of Acts is slightly briefer and it manifests stylistic differences that are typically Lukan: the avoidance of unnecessary personal pronouns (*auton*), of *kai*, and of unnecessary-looking repetition.[19]

3. *Assessing the Evidence*

In comparison with the Naboth narrative, Luke's text manifests considerable differences with regard to setting and narrative focus, yet it shows also a series of striking similarities. These similarities may be outlined as follows:

General theme:
The accusing and stoning to death of a just man

General structure:
Basic twofold (doublet) arrangement

Actions (plot):
Concerted hostility
The suborning of witnesses
The two-pronged accusation
The manipulation of people and leaders
Setting the victim before the (popular) court
The false witnesses
The two-pronged accusation/s
The stoning

---

19. On Luke's stylistic tendencies, see Cadbury 1920: 83-90 (on the avoidance of repetition), 142-44 (substituting for *kai*), 151-52 (more compact sentences), 191-95 (avoidance of unnecessary personal pronouns).

38. The Accusing and Stoning of Naboth

Some details:
Repetition of 'men/witnesses...saying':
Involvement of 'the people'
Involvement of free(d)men

The data summarized do not *necessarily* lead to the conclusion that Luke used the Naboth text; one may not invoke deductive logic. After all, the similarity between the texts may be due to some freakish coincidence. But in the context of Luke's use of the Old Testament, especially of the Elijah–Elisha story, such a degree of correspondence is unlikely to be the result of coincidence. In other words, in trying to choose between coincidence and deliberate literary adaptation, Luke's practice of various kinds of deliberate literary adaptation means that we may reasonably choose deliberate adaptation rather than coincidence. It does not necessarily follow, but it seems much more probable.

Such a probability gains further weight when seen in the context of the general literary practice of the first century. The normal practice among the writers of the day was to take older works and, without naming them, to rework them into a new form. H.J. Cadbury sums up the practice:

> The predecessor's language is not retained but is paraphrased, being thus transformed into the vocabulary and mannerisms of the author who uses him. The contents of the material is identical, and often the agreement between two writers in arrangement or in occasional unusual word conclusively proves the literary relationship which the similarity of substance suggests...verbatim quotation was usually avoided...there is often no significant agreement of wording. (Cadbury 1927: 158, 160, 162)

Cadbury's summary of the Greco-Roman process of paraphrasing does not attempt to cover the more artistic forms of adaptation, the forms found in the broader Greco-Roman practice of imitation,[20] nor does it, in fact, fit all the details of the Naboth–Stephen relationship. But it provides a broad context in which that relationship may reasonably be seen as one of direct literary dependence. The fact that at times Luke makes careful use of Old Testament patterns or models tends to confirm such a view.

Luke's use of the Old Testament does not necessarily mean that his narrative should be described as a midrash. The term 'midrash', of course, is difficult to define, but there seems to be increasing support for the idea that it should be used only of the explicit citation and development of Scripture.[21] Hence, just as R.E. Brown has reservations about applying the term to the infancy narrative (1977: 557-62 [560-61]), and as J.A. Fitzmyer, speaking in the same context, declares the term 'quite unsuitable' (1981: 309), so here too it seems better to avoid the term. Luke's use of unacknowledged sources seems to belong not so much to the techniques of midrash, but to those of Greco-Roman paraphrase and imitation.

It may be objected that what we are dealing with is not direct use of the Old Testament but simply the reproduction of a general pattern for describing stoning. There is no evidence, however, for such a general pattern; none of the available references to stoning or the threat of stoning[22] contain the pattern of the Naboth and Stephen texts. Nor do any of

---

20. Cadbury's remarks about paraphrase are perfectly valid and pertinent, but if paraphrase (*paraphrasis*) is to be understood fully it should be seen as part of the larger process of imitation (Gk. *mimēsis*; Lat. *imitatio*).

21. Though the term 'midrash' may be used loosely to refer to the implicit or unacknowledged use of Scripture (e.g. see Bloch 1957), the strict use of the term refers to a process of explicit citation and commentary; see Porton 1979.

22. On the threat of stoning, see Exod. 17.4; Num. 14.10; 1 Sam. 30.6; Lk. 20.6; Jn 8.59; 10.31, 33; 11.8; Acts 5.26; 14.5. On various degrees of actual stoning, see Num. 15.32-36; 2 Sam. 16.6; 1 Kgs 12.18; Acts 14.19; 2 Cor. 11.25. For the legislation concerning stoning, see Lev. 20.27; 24.14; Deut. 13.10;

them contain, for instance, a neat two-pronged accusation concerning cursing or blaspheming 'God and king/Moses'. An appeal to unavailable evidence (in this case evidence for a general pattern) may be plausible if there are data that cannot otherwise be accounted for. But when a perfectly straightforward explanation of the data is already available (i.e. that Luke as a sophisticated *littérateur* deliberately adapted the Naboth text), the invoking of such evidence is unnecessary, and, to a considerable degree, implausible.

The impression which emerges is that, when Luke set about describing the fate of Stephen, he decided to present not so much the bare historical facts or the actual legislative procedure, but rather a picture which would emphasize the continuity between Stephen and other people or elements of sacred history. Thus, he took the bare bones of the Naboth text and grafted onto them a wide variety of other elements, elements drawn both from the Old Testament[23] and from various traditions of the first century.

The conclusion that Luke made direct use of the Old Testament text corroborates E. Richard's similar conclusion with regard to Stephen's speech.[24] If Richard is correct—and his minute analysis indicates that he has not drawn his conclusion lightly—and if the analysis presented here is correct, then a large proportion of the Stephen account (speech and narratives) is based on Luke's direct use of the Old Testament.

The question of sources other than the Old Testament is particularly important when trying to judge the historicity of the Stephen account. If Luke's text consisted exclusively of Old Testament material, then it would be difficult to speak of historicity. But it does not, and it is because there are other elements—particularly in the account of the accusing —that the question of historicity must be kept open. However, the problem is not easy, for it is precisely within the later accusations (Acts 6.13-14), in other words, within some of the matter which has least resemblance to the Old Testament and which might be used as a basis for building historicity, that we find the greatest affinity with the texts concerning Jesus and Paul. In other words, what has not been adapted from the figure of Naboth, has, to some degree at least, been borrowed from the figures of Jesus and Paul. Hence, whereas it seems advisable at this stage of research to leave the question of historicity open, it seems reasonable to conclude that whatever history is contained in Luke's account has now been profoundly interwoven with adaptations of Naboth, Jesus, and Paul.[25]

4. *Summary of Results*

A comparison of the texts (1 Kgs 21.8-13; Acts 6.9-14; 7.58a) shows major differences and considerable similarities. The differences may be accounted for largely by the fact that

---

17.2-7; 21.20; 22.20-24. The legislation in the Mishnah (*m. Sanh.* 6.1-4) does not contain any pattern significantly similar to that of Luke's text.

23. Apart from E. Haenchen's comment, already noted, that Luke's reference to 'lying witnesses' reproduces an Old Testament idea, it has also been indicated to me by A.J. Malherbe (in discussion) that Luke may have drawn on some of the legislative texts concerning stoning (Lev. 24.11-14; Num. 15.32-36; Deut. 17.2-7). This is particularly so with regard to the emphasis on the role of the witnesses (Deut. 17.7; cf. Acts 7.58b). Knowling (1974: 201) links *exō tēs poleōs* (Acts 7.58a) with Lev. 24.14. At this stage in research, it is difficult to say whether the occurrence of *apethento* in two of these texts (Lev. 24.12; Num. 15.34) and in Acts 7.58 is sheer coincidence.

24. Richard 1978: 145 states: 'The Author of Acts has utilized the biblical text directly in composing this unique history of Israel. It is the Old Testament narrative which has furnished him with the events, their sequence, their terminology, and, to a great extent, the themes exposed throughout the speech.'

25. This conclusion is rather similar to the one reached by J.A. Fitzmyer (1981: 309) with regard to the historical character of Lk. 1–2. To describe the infancy narratives he adopts the term 'imitative historiography', meaning that 'whatever historical matter has been preserved by the two evangelists has been assimilated by them to other literary accounts'.

the New Testament episode is placed in a different setting and within a narrative which has a different purpose or focus. The similarities (theme, general structure, sequence of actions, some details) are such that, rather than attribute them to coincidence, it seems reasonable to conclude that Luke has deliberately adapted or distilled the Naboth text. This conclusion is all the more plausible because rather similar adaptations are found elsewhere in Luke's work and because the adaptation of unacknowledged older sources was a general practice in the first century.

Luke's distilled form of the Naboth text is not the only element used in the account of the accusing and stoning of Naboth. Rather, it is one component, a basic framework to which Luke has grafted other elements, especially elements which have an affinity with the accusations leveled against Jesus and Paul. This grafting process is somewhat similar to the way in which the birth announcements of Luke 1–2 combine an Old Testament pattern with New Testament materials.

The conclusion that the account of the accusing and stoning points to Luke's direct use of the Old Testament corroborates E. Richard's similar conclusion with regard to Stephen's speech. It follows that the dependence of the entire Stephen story on the Old Testament is somewhat greater than has hitherto been assumed.

The historical facts concerning Stephen have been profoundly interwoven with elements drawn from the figures of Naboth, Jesus, and Paul.

Insofar as Luke uses his sources without citing them explicitly, his literary method seems closer to Greco-Roman paraphrase and imitation than to Jewish midrash.

39

The Prestigious Foreign Charioteer Who Heeds the Prophet, and a Money-Minded Follower: 2 Kings 5 as One Component of Acts 8.9-40

This chapter indicates that Luke's stories of Simon and the Ethiopian (Acts 8.9-40) are modeled largely, but not exclusively, on the Old Testament story of Naaman and Gehazi (2 Kgs 5). The Syrian commander's *physical* renewal—the cleansing of his leprosy—has been adapted to form a basis for describing the Ethiopian treasurer's internal renewal, his cleansing in baptism. The deviousness of Gehazi, his desire to use God's healing gift as a way of making money, has been adapted to depict the more internal deviation of Simon—his attempt to give money in order to have power over the gift of the Spirit, in other words, in order to have a power that was primarily internal. Thus, in describing Simon and the Ethiopian, Luke has distilled the essence of the Old Testament text, and has used that essence as a basic component, a skeletal framework, around which he has grafted other material. Luke's processes of adaptation are to be seen in the context of the rhetorical practice of *imitatio*, particularly in the context of the imitative practice of internalizing ancient texts.

The more general purpose of this chapter is to suggest that Luke's method of adapting 2 Kings 5 may provide a partial clue to an old problem, the question of the use of sources in Acts.

1. *The Sources of Acts: A Stalled Quest*

For about 200 years, researchers have battled with the problem of the sources of Acts.[1] In particular, beginning with the work of B. Königsmann in 1798, it has been asked whether its elements of diversity and duplication should be regarded as reliable indicators of a diversity of written sources.[2] The problem was more than a century old when A. Harnack, to some degree at least, did for Acts what Wellhausen had done for the Pentateuch: he gave personality to a number of hypothetical sources. Working largely on the basis of the places mentioned in the text and, to some degree, on the basis of its mention of particular people, he distinguished, among other documents, what he called the Jerusalem–Caesarea source (cf. especially 3.1–5.16; 8.5-40; 9.31–11.18; 12.1-23) and the Antioch source (cf. especially 6.1–8.4; 11.19-30; 13.1–15.35) (see especially Harnack 1908: 148-49). Aspects of this theory, particularly its idea of an Antioch source, have received a moderate amount of support.[3]

---

1. For summaries of research, see McGiffert 1922: II, 385-95; Dupont 1964; Haenchen 1971: 24-34; Kümmel 1975: 174-85; Grässer 1976: 144-46, 186-94; 1977: 41; Schneider 1980: 82-89.

2. *De fontibus commentariorum sacrorum, quae Lucae nomen praeferunt* (Altonae, 1798). For brief accounts of the earliest researchers such as W.K.L. Ziegler (1801), J.G. Eichhorn (1810), and J.C. Riehm (1821), see especially McGiffert 1922: II, 385-86, and Haenchen 1971: 24-25.

3. On the qualified acceptance of the idea of an Antioch source, especially by R. Bultmann and P. Benoit, see Dupont 1964: 62-72.

There have been several other theories, in particular that Acts (especially 1.1–15.35) consists of a reworking of a major single document dealing with the early church, and that the use of 'we' (cf. 16.10-17 etc.) indicates either a distinct source or the personal involvement of the author (see especially Dupont 1964: 17-32, 75-112).

But little agreement has been reached. It is symptomatic of the depth of the problem that while M. Dibelius, using form criticism, claimed that beneath the accounts of Paul's missionary journeys it is possible to detect an itinerary source—a source which gave the framework of Paul's itinerary (Dibelius 1923 [ET 1956]), D.H. Conzelmann sees no such source. For him the framework of the first journey (chs. 13–14), for instance, is a creation of Luke's (Conzelmann 1972: 80).

Today the state of the entire quest is not substantially different from what it was when assessed in 1960 by J. Dupont (1964: 166):

> The predominant impression is certainly very negative. Despite the most careful and detailed research, it has not been possible to define any of the sources used by the author of Acts in a way which will meet with widespread agreement among the critics.

Given this state of stalemate, it seems better to stand back from the problem and to ask a more basic question: How, in general, did ancient writers use sources? How did they compose a text? To answer this, it is necessary to take account of rhetoric, particularly the rhetorical practice of imitation (see Chapter 1).

The preceding chapters indicate that in composing his account Proto-Luke imitated and reworked the LXX, especially the Elijah–Elisha narrative. It is appropriate then in seeking the sources of Acts to search the LXX carefully.

As one sifts through the episodes of the LXX, wondering whether or to what extent they have been used in Acts, 2 Kings 5 tends to attract attention. This is a story which, in the programmatic Nazareth speech (Lk. 4.16-30, especially 4.27), Luke singles out explicitly as a kind of model. When one asks which episode, if any, in Acts, reflects the Naaman story, it is difficult not to become suspicious of the story of the Ethiopian. After all, the New Testament does not have many stories about prestigious foreigners coming in chariots. One immediately sees great differences between the stories, particularly the fact that the latter part of the Naaman story is taken up with the money-minded Gehazi, and for that there is not equivalent at all in the story of the Ethiopian. But then one notices that immediately before the Ethiopian story there is the story of Simon, someone who, in his own way, was quite money-minded. And so one's suspicions are strengthened.

It turns out that the relationship between the texts is quite complex, and to understand it, it is first necessary that the texts be summarized.

2. *2 Kings 5 and Acts 8.9-40: Introductory Analysis*

Far from being a raw miracle account, the Old Testament passage is a delicately composed narrative. It tells of an imposing man who, through his servants, came to appreciate what is small and lowly—in other words, a man who passed from one mentality to another, and who thus was healed. And, in contrast, it tells also of the exploitive servant, Gehazi.

The New Testament tells first of Simon, the man who had once been regarded as great and who was intent on maintaining some form of power, and, second, of the Ethiopian who, despite his exalted position, was eager to learn from the account of the humble Servant.

Luke has taken the contrasting mentalities or characters of Naaman and attributed them to the contrasting characters of Simon and the Ethiopian. And he also uses Gehazi as a basis for depicting Simon. Thus, the figure of Simon, as now described in Acts 8, involves a fusing of two basic elements: Naaman's initial preoccupation with greatness, and Gehazi's money-mindedness. This does not explain what is *missing* in Luke's text—the well-known problem of why, unlike Justin and Irenaeus, he says nothing of Simon as a leader of some form of heresy or gnosticism[4]—but it does help to explain a significant part of what is present.

As well as thus adapting the characters, the *dramatis personae*, Luke has also made several adaptations of content. In particular, the idea of a physical washing which cleans the body is replaced by the washing of baptism, a cleansing which is more internal.

And Gehazi's *desire* for money is replaced by Simon's *giving* of money so that he may have spiritual power. In other words, Simon's desire is more obviously in the realm of the spiritual or internal.

Thus, to a considerable extent, Luke's reworking of the Old Testament text involves a process of internalization.

For a scientific historian, such a process of adapting characters and content seems odd and far-fetched. Yet such were the practices of literary imitation, and such also were the practices which Luke himself employed elsewhere. Odd though some of these practices may appear from the point of view of scientific history, from another point of view they were acceptable.

Table 61. *Naaman and the Ethiopian (2 Kings 5; Acts 8.9-40)*

2 Kings 5	Acts 8
	1a. Simon was regarded as great (8.9-11)
	6. He offers money for the Spirit (8.17-19)
	7. Peter confronts Simon (8.20-23)
	3b. *An angel sends* Philip down to the… desert (8.26-27a)
1. Naaman, in charge of the army… …was regarded as a great man …was mighty (*dynatos*), a leper (5.1; cf. 5.3-5, 11-12)	1b. Eunuch was powerful (*dynastēs*), in charge of the treasury (8.27b) (Had come worshipping to Jerusalem)
2. Naaman brings treasure and a writing to the king; he ignores the prophet (5.6-7)	He was reading the prophet, not knowing what he was reading (8.28, 30b-31a)
3a. *Elisha sends* so Naaman may know of the prophet; he comes in his chariot (5.8-9; cf. 5.15a)	3a. *The Spirit sends* Philip to the chariot, so the Ethiopian may know the prophet (cf. 8.29-30, 34-35)
3b. *Elisha sends* an *aggelos* to say, Go (down) to the Jordan and wash (5.10)	
4. [Captured servant suggests the prophet (5.2)] Naaman wants something great from the prophet, but his servants suggest humility (5.11-13)	The prophet speaks of the Servant who was…led…in humility (8.32-33)
5. Naaman goes down, washes (5.14)	Eunuch goes down, is baptized (8.38-39)
6. Naaman offers something; Gehazi takes money for the cure (5.15b-24) (Naaman desires Israel-based worship.)	
7. Elisha confronts Gehazi (5.25-27)	

4. For a review of recent research on Simon, see Grässer 1977: 24-34. See also McLaglan Wilson 1979.

And they make sense. In effect, what Luke has done is take an Old Testament text which despite its power is rather subtle and obscure, and render it into images which are clear and which emphasize what is internal. The problem of being preoccupied with greatness, a problem which is not stated explicitly in the Old Testament, is brought out much more clearly in the figure of Simon. The value of open-mindedness, half hidden in Naaman, comes to the fore in the figure of the Ethiopian. Luke, therefore, has not written to distort the Old Testament text, but to develop it.

3. *2 Kings 5 and Acts 8.9-40: Detailed Analysis*

An initial idea of the way in which Luke has reworked the details of the Old Testament text may be found in the general outline (Table 61). In many ways the outline simplifies, omitting those verses of Acts 8.9-40 for which 2 Kings 5 seems to provide no base whatever. And it overstates some similarities. At the same time, it provides a starting-point for discussion.

The analysis given below generally follows the order of the outline. However, the section on the captured servant (2 Kgs 5.2) is not dealt with in sequence. And there are some other complicating details. By and large, though, the sequence is maintained.

a. *Section 1. A Foreign Royal Official, A Great Man (2 Kings 5.1, 3-5, 11-12; Acts 8.9-11, 27b)*

Naaman, in simplified terms, is a royal official, and is regarded as a great man. In Acts 8, Simon is regarded as great, and the Ethiopian is a royal official. On the one hand, therefore, Naaman's status as 'great' (2 Kgs 5.1), and his misguided preference for actions and objects that are great (2 Kgs 5.11-12) have been used together as one factor in characterizing the negative figure of Simon. On the other hand, Naaman's status as a foreign royal official has been used in Acts 8 to depict another foreign royal official, the Ethiopian.

These two items will be dealt with separately.

(1) *The man preoccupied with greatness (cf. 2 Kings 5.1a, 3-5a, 11-12; Acts 8.9-11).* While the general correspondence of the two texts is fairly clear—both present individuals who are unduly taken up with greatness—the correspondence of the details is quite complex. In fact, Luke's treatment of the Old Testament text is like an extended intricate word-play. The main elements of the correspondences are outlined in Table 62.

Table 62. *The Great Man (2 Kings 5.1, 3-5a, 11-13; Acts 8.9-10)*

'And Naaman, ruler of the *dynamis*,	
* was a great man before his lord,	'But a man named Simon was previously practicing magic in the city,
** and was regarded with wonder because in him the Lord gave deliverance to Syria...' (5.1a)	** astonishing the nation of Samaria, * saying that he was someone great,
From the small maid to the king, people attend to Naaman (5.3-5a)	to whom all gave heed, from small to great, saying, "This man is the *dynamis*
'call on...his God...a great thing...' (cf. 5.11-13)	of God which is called Great"' (8.9-10)

As the outline shows, the Old Testament text provides no basis for the initial description of Simon as a magician. But everything else in Luke's text seems to involve a reworking of 2 Kings 5. The word *dynamis* is changed to refer not to a force or army, but to a power of God. (However, even in the Old Testament, the *dynamis* was in some sense an instrument of God. Through it, or at least through its commander, the Lord had delivered Syria.) In varied ways, both Naaman and Simon were regarded as great. The sense of wonder at what Naaman had helped do for Syria is balanced by Samaria's sense of astonishment at the power of Simon. Both Naaman and Simon receive attention from diverse people small and great. Finally, Naaman's implicit demand for a spectacular God—for a prophet who would call publicly on his God and who would command something great (2 Kgs 5.11-13) —is balanced by the equally sensation-oriented religion proposed by Simon's pretension to be the great power of God.

The following verse in Luke (Acts 8.11), the rather repetitious account of Simon's practice of magic, may, perhaps, be inspired in part by the repetitiousness of the description of Naaman's angry reaction (2 Kgs 5.11-12).

Luke's use of the Old Testament does not rule out his use of other sources. On the contrary, given his tendency to fuse two or more texts, the use of other material is to be expected—in this case material pertaining to Simon's role in Samaria. According to Justin, the Samaritans revered Simon as the first or highest god (*1 Apol.* 26.3; *Dial.* 120.6). Presumably Luke used this and other information in giving his material its present shape.

However, from the point of view of this study, the essential point is that, whatever the extent of Luke's information about the historical Simon, his final picture of the magician, as now found in the text of Acts, includes a careful reworking of the text of 2 Kings 5. Naaman's spectacular standing and his misconception about a spectacular God, have been used to depict the spectacular standing of Simon and his misrepresentation of God as a source of spectacle.

Despite Luke's considerable adaptations, in various ways his wording echoes the Old Testament text and at times seems to play with it:

Old Testament:
archōn tēs dynameōs...ēn anēr megas...kai tethaumasmenos prosōpō hoti en autō... kai...neanida mikran...
[vv. 11-13:] *pros me pantōs exeleusetai kai epikalesetai...theou autou...megan logon*

New Testament:
anēr...pro-yp-ērchen...magan hō proseichon pantes apo mikrou heōs megalou ...hē dynamis tou theou hē kaloumenē Megalē. proseichon de autō

Old Testament:
ruler of the power...was a great man...and regarded with wonder because in him... and...a small servant girl...
[vv. 11-13:] to me by all means he will come and call on...his God...a great word...

New Testament:
a man...was previously...great, to whom all gave heed from small to great...
...the power of God called Great; and they gave heed to him.

It does not seem possible, at least at this point, to give a firm judgment on some of the similarities of detail, on whether they result from deliberate word-play. It is worth noting, however, that in Luke's description of another Simon, Simon the Pharisee (based on 2 Kgs 4), there is evidence of similar word-play.

(2) *The foreign royal official (cf. 2 Kings 5.1, 5b; Acts 8.27b).* As already seen, the picture of Naaman as commander of the *dynamis* has been used to depict Simon as a *dynamis*. But no use has so far been made of the fact that being commander-in-chief meant being a high official, close to the king, and it is that aspect of Naaman which Luke uses as a

foundational element in describing the Ethiopian. Luke's picture involves three adaptations of the Old Testament text.

First, the foreign country in question is not Syria, but Ethiopia. In other words, while the idea of a foreign country has been kept, it has been adapted so that it no longer refers to neighboring Syria but—in accordance with the overall plan of Acts ('...in...Judea and Samaria and to the ends of the earth', 1.8)—to a country which represents the ends of the earth, namely Ethiopia.

Second, the official is in charge not of the army (*dynamis*), but of the treasury. Though Luke sometimes tells of military characters (cf. the centurion and Cornelius, Lk. 7.1-10; Acts 10), this adaptation is understandable. He had already used and transformed the image of the *dynamis*. What he had not used was the idea of Naaman's treasure. For when Naaman comes to Israel, he brings not an army, but a treasure that is quite considerable— ten silver talents, 6000 pieces of gold, and ten sets of robes. How he should be able to bring so great a treasure is not explained, but his doing so is presented in the context of the approval he enjoyed from his king (2 Kgs 5.5b). Thus, instead of someone who emerges from the royal presence and brings treasure, Luke depicts someone who is over the royal treasure.

Third, the official is presented not as a leper, but as a eunuch. Without attempting to unravel the full implications of this adaptation, it has an immediate reasonableness: in some Eastern regions 'it was the general practice to have eunuchs for treasurers' (cf. Plutarch, *Demetrios* 25.5). Once Luke decided to replace the figure of a Syrian commander by that of an Ethiopian treasurer, it made sense—given the Eastern custom of frequently having eunuchs as treasurers—to describe that treasurer as a eunuch. Similarly, the figure of the Syrian king is replaced by the specifically Ethiopian figure of the Candace or queen.[5]

Thus, Luke's text keeps the basic figure of a foreign official, but replaces the setting of the Syrian monarchy with details appropriate to a new context, that of the Ethiopian monarchy. A similar phenomenon was noticed in comparing the fates of Naboth and Stephen (Chapter 38): the basic figure of a just man undergoing false accusation is preserved in the depiction of Stephen, but the institutional setting involved in the Naboth case (the ancient monarchy and popular court) has been systematically replaced by details appropriate to an institutional setting which is of more interest to Luke's account (the synagogue and Sanhedrin).

While the figure of the eunuch suits the new setting, it also suits Luke's theological theme of God's mercy for all, including those who, like eunuchs, had previously been regarded as excluded from the community (cf. Deut. 23.1-2).

The essential point is that the Ethiopian official is significantly similar to the Syrian official, and that, insofar as he is different, the differences may reasonably be seen as reflecting Luke's specific purposes, especially his purpose of indicating the spread of the word to the ends of the earth.

At this stage, it is worth noting that Luke's reworking of the Naaman story has been influenced not only by his general editorial purposes, but also by his desire to build narrative continuity with earlier parts of his own text, particularly with the Emmaus story (Lk. 24.13-35). In fact, the story of how Philip encountered the Ethiopian and explained the scriptures to him has been so shaped that, to some degree, it is like a variation on the story of how Jesus met the men on the road to Emmaus and explained the scriptures to them.[6]

---

5. As Haenchen (1971: 310) notes, 'Candace' was not a particular queen's name, but rather a title given to the Ethiopian queen mother.
6. See Grassi 1964; Lindijer 1978: II, 80-81. As well as echoing the Emmaus text, the Ethiopian story

A similar phenomenon may be seen in Luke's use of the Naboth story: he adapts it to Stephen, but does so in a way which maintains continuity with other quite distinct episodes concerning Jesus and Paul. Thus, for Luke, the Old Testament does indeed provide a basis, a foundation, but it is a text which is ultimately subordinated to a new narrative.

Despite Luke's processes of adapting, his final wording retains some echoes of the older text:

> Old Testament:
> *ho archōn tēs dynameōs...kai ho anēr ēn dynatos...*
>
> New Testament:
> *anēr...dynastēs...hos ēn epi pasēs tēs gazēs*
>
> Old Testament:
> the ruler of the power/army...and the man was powerful/strong...
>
> New Testament:
> a man...a power/authority...who was over all the treasure

b. *Section B. Royal Backing, Money and a Writing—But No Knowledge of the Prophet (2 Kings 5.6-7; Acts 8.25b, 30b-31a)*

When Naaman comes to Israel he seems to have everything in his favor: access to royalty, treasure, and even a *biblion*. *Biblion* may refer to almost anything written, including a letter or legal document, but it generally refers to a book or scroll. In this case the *biblion* is from the Syrian kings to the king of Israel, requesting a cure for Naaman. But it is useless. When the king of Israel reads it, he sees it as nonsense. The original suggestion that Naaman go to the prophet appears to be forgotten. Thus, despite royal backing, riches, and the reading of the *biblion*, Naaman has not done the one thing necessary: establish appropriate communication with the prophet.

In the New Testament, the eunuch in turn has royal backing, riches, and a process of reading. He is reading Isaiah (*ton prophētēn Ēsaian*), yet internally he is at a certain distance from the prophet; he does not really understand what he is reading.

Luke's text involves several adaptations. First, there is modernization, The royal backing has been adapted to the context of Ethiopia and to the absence of a monarchy in Israel. Thus, instead of depicting an Israelite king as reading in the presence of the foreign official, Luke describes the foreign official as doing the reading himself.

Second, there is internalization. Instead of a process of reading which is physically at a distance from Israel's prophet, Luke depicts a reading in which the distance is internal. The eunuch has Isaiah in his hands but does not understand him.

Third, there is fusion. The basic idea of reading a *biblion*, plus the quite distinct idea of being at a distance from the prophet, have been fused to become the single complex idea of reading (a *biblion* of) the prophet Isaiah[7] while being at some internal distance.

The essential point is that for both foreign officials, royal backing, treasure, and reading are not enough. They still need to communicate effectively with the prophet.

---

also involves a certain foreshadowing of the Cornelius episode (Acts 10.1–11.18). For discussion, see Grässer 1977: 34. The hypothesis that the Ethiopian story once existed on its own, in competition with the Cornelius episode (cf. Conzelmann 1972: 63), is unnecessary, and, in view of the dependence of Luke's text on 2 Kgs 5, highly unlikely. On the place of the Ethiopian story within the theological framework of Acts 8.5-11.18, see O'Toole 1983.

7. In Luke's only explicit reference to reading a *biblion*, the *biblion* in question is Isaiah (Lk. 4.17). Thus, for what it is worth, Luke's connecting of *biblion* with the prophet Isaiah has a precedent in his gospel.

In these texts, verbal similarity is minimal. However, it is worth noting:

Old Testament:
basileus...biblion...basilea...biblion...basilea...biblion...anegnō...basileus...biblion

New Testament:
basilissēs...aneginōsken ton prophētēn Ēsaian

Old Testament:
king...letter...king...letter...king...letter...read...king...letter

New Testament:
queen...reading Isaiah the prophet

Even though the word for reading, *anaginōskō*, is fairly common (LXX has around 60 occurrences; New Testament has 32), there are very few other instances in the Bible which speak of a king or royal official as actually reading. The clearest cases are Hezekiah (cf. 2 Kgs 19.14; Isa. 37.14) and Josiah (cf. 2 Kgs 22.2–23.2; 2 Chron. 34.14-30), and one might perhaps add a few other cases such as Ezra the scribe (cf. Neh. 8) and Jehudi, the messenger of Jehoiakim (cf. Jer. 36.21-23). Hence, as far as assessing whether similarities are coincidental or deliberate is concerned, there is considerable significance in the fact that the picture of a king or royal official as reading is found both in 2 Kgs 5 and Acts 8.

c. *Section 3. The Two Sendings which Lead to Knowing the Prophet and Something Other (2 Kings 5.8–10.15a; Acts 8.29, 26-27a, 30b, 34-35)*
Just at the point when Naaman may seem to be going nowhere, there is a double intervention on the part of Elisha: he sends to the king to tell Naaman to come to him; and then, as Naaman in his chariot stands at the door, he sends a messenger to tell him go wash in the Jordan. The two sendings, which are set up to some degree like parallels, create a tension that is rather mysterious. Naaman comes in order that, as Elisha says, he may know there is a prophet. But then, when he comes, he is sent away. Much to his angry puzzlement, he does not see Elisha, nor does the prophet touch him physically. Apparently, the prophetic power which he is to get to know is something other than what may be seen and touched, something other than the prophet himself. At any rate, there are two quasi-parallel sendings which suggest mystery and which bring the official from ignorance of the prophet to angry puzzlement about the prophet.

In the case of the Ethiopian, there are also two sendings: the Spirit tells Philip to come to the chariot, and the angel of the Lord had already told Philip to go down towards the desert. As in the Old Testament, the two sendings are set up, to some degree, like parallels.[8] And what they achieve is similar: they indicate, quite clearly, the presence of mystery, and they lead the Ethiopian official from not knowing what the prophet says to a calm puzzlement about the prophet: 'I pray you, of whom does the prophet say this: of himself, or of some other?'

In other words, what had been dimly implied in the Old Testament, that getting to know the prophet involves the presence of mystery, is dramatized vividly in the New Testament through the mystery-filled intervention of the Spirit and the angel of the Lord. And the Old Testament text's enigmatic indication that getting to know the prophet meant getting to know something beyond the prophet, something other, is stated in the New Testament as a clear question: Is the prophet telling me to focus on himself or on someone other? In both texts, the foreign official is led to knowing something else: in one case, the God of Israel (2 Kgs 5.15a); in the other, Jesus (Acts 8.35). Thus, the Old Testament cryptic suggestion

---

8. On the two sendings as variations on the basic idea of divine intervention, see, for instance, Haenchen 1971: 311; Schneider 1980: 501-502.

of a mysterious other is elaborated into vividly clear references to the presence of mystery and to another.

This procedure of rendering a text that is obscure into one that is vivid and clear was common in imitation and is found elsewhere in Luke, particularly in his reworking of the account of raising the widow's son.[9]

Looking at the texts in slightly more detail, it emerges that Luke's account of the two sendings involves a complex blend of careful continuity and considerable adaptation.

There is continuity between the Old Testament sending which brings Naaman in his chariot to Elisha's door in order that he might know the prophet (2 Kgs 5.8-9), and the New Testament sending which causes Philip to come to the Ethiopian's chariot in order to ask him if he knows the prophet's text (Acts 8.29, 30b). The focal point in both is the need to get to know the prophet or the prophetic word.

And there also appears to be continuity, but of a less obvious kind, between Elisha's sending of a messenger (*aggelos*) to tell Naaman to go down to the Jordan in order that he might be cleansed (2 Kgs 5.10), and the angel's sending of Philip down the elusive 'way' towards 'the desert' (Acts 8.26-27a). Both seem to suggest places of cleansing or renewal.[10] The fact that it turns out, against all odds, to be a place of water and baptism (Acts 8.36-38) lends further credibility to this idea. Thus, the sending of Naaman to wash in the Jordan is balanced by the sending of Philip to a place which, in some ways, is reminiscent of the Jordan.

In any case, what is certain is that in both texts there are two quasi-parallel sendings, and that the basic effect of these sendings is to lead the foreign official closer to knowing the prophet and to knowing something other than the prophet.

With regard to adaptations, the first and most basic has already been indicated: the sense of mystery is brought into the open and clarified.

Second, instead of having two sendings in immediate succession ('Elisha...sent... Elisha sent...'), the New Testament moves the later sending, the order to go down to the place of renewal, to the very beginning of the passage: 'But an angel of the Lord spoke to Philip, saying, "Arise..."' (Acts 8.26). The full reasons for this change may be quite complex, but one of them seems to be an extension of the reason already given: for greater clarity with regard to the presence of mystery. By putting the reference to the angel of the Lord at the very beginning of the text, the presence of a mysterious element is further highlighted, is made more vivid. A similar procedure may be observed in Livy. 'He... reorganizes the structural arrangement, and introduces new material to achieve more dramatic effects' (P.G. Walsh 1961: 190).

As for the fact that the order to go down is directed not towards the Jordan, but southwards, away from Jerusalem, this may be influenced by the fact that the general thrust of Acts 1–8, especially in ch. 8, is to move away from Jerusalem and towards even the most extreme parts of the earth.

What is essential is that the two rather cryptic sendings of the Old Testament are adapted to become two sendings in which the presence of mystery, the mystery surrounding the prophetic word, is much clearer.

There is a further rather subtle detail worth noting. In the Old Testament, Naaman's preoccupation with the prophet, and with a rather crude approach to him—to being touched by him—is broken by the servants' intervention. They ask a gentle question which leads

---

9. For further details on Luke's tendency towards dramatic clarity, and on the similarity of that tendency to the methods of Livy, see Chapter 29 on Lk. 7.11-17. On the place of brevity and vividness in ancient narrative, see Van Unnik 1979: 52-57.

10. In Lk. 3.3-4, the *way* in the *desert* is associated with washing in the Jordan. Thus, the connection has a precedent in the gospel.

Naaman away from his crude approach towards an approach which enables him to see beyond the prophet ('If the prophet had said...to you...?', 2 Kgs 5.13). The gentleness of this transitional question concerning what the prophet had said—this question through which the path is opened for the official to see further—to some degree accounts for the gentle, transitional question which opens the way for the Ethiopian to see further, to move from his concentration on the prophet Isaiah to someone else ('I pray you, of whom does the prophet say...?', Acts 8.34).

Despite the adaptations, the New Testament still has echoes of the Old Testament wording:

> Old Testament:
> *ēkousen...elthetō dē pros me...kai...gnōtō hoti estin prophētēs kai ēlthen...en...harmati*
>
> New Testament:
> *Proselthe...tō harmati...ēkousen...ton prophētēn...ginōskeis*
>
> Old Testament:
> *apesteilen...aggelon pros auton legōn Poreutheis*
>
> New Testament:
> *Aggelos...elalēsen pros Philippon legōn...poreuou*
>
> Old Testament:
> (Gentle transitional question): *elalēsen ho prophētēs pros se*
>
> New Testament:
> (Gentle transitional question:) *Deomai sou...ho prophētēs legei*
>
> Old Testament:
> He heard...let him come to me...and...let him know there is a prophet ...and he came...in...chariot
>
> New Testament:
> Come to...the chariot...he heard...the prophet...do you know?
>
> Old Testament:
> He sent...the messenger (*aggelos*) to him, saying, Go...
>
> New Testament:
> An angel spoke to Philip saying...Go
>
> Old Testament:
> (Gentle transitional question:) [If] the prophet had spoken to you...
>
> New Testament:
> (Gentle transitional question:) I ask you [about whom] the prophet speaks...

d. *Section 4. The Servant/s: Captive and Humble (cf. 2 Kings 5.2, 13; Acts 8.32-33)*
In relating the texts, one of the difficult judgments concerns the image of the servant/s. In the Old Testament text, a crucial but obscure role is played by the servants: the small maid who was *taken away captive*, and by the servants who implied the idea of doing something *humble*. In the New Testament a crucial role is played by the Servant, someone who is both captive and humble: 'As a lamb *led*... In his *humiliation*...'

It could be argued that the striking quotation from Isaiah is used to synthesize the two ideas of captivity and humility, and also to render the image of the servants into a form that is more explicit and vivid.

The difficulty is that neither the small girl nor the Isaian figure is explicitly called a 'servant'. Resolution of this difficulty would require an extensive discussion about the literary continuity, first, between the small girl and 'the servants', and, second, between the Isaian figure and Luke's explicit references to Jesus as servant (Acts 3.13, 26; 4.27, 30).

e. *Section 5. The Foreign Official Washes and is Renewed (2 Kings 5.14; Acts 8.38-39)*
As Naaman went down and washed seven times in the Jordan, so the Ethiopian, along with Philip, went down to the water and was baptized. As a result of the washing, Naaman was changed physically: his flesh became like that of a little child. For the Ethiopian, the change was internal, and it is reflected in the fact that, when he went on his way, he was 'rejoicing'.

The wording is worth noting:

Old Testament:
kai katebē...kai ebaptisato

New Testament:
kai katebēsan...kai ebaptisen

Old Testament:
and he went down...and washed

New Testament:
and they went down...and he washed

f. *Section 6. The Attempt to Exchange the Mysterious Gift for Money (2 Kings 5.15b-24; Acts 8.17-19)*
When Naaman returned to Elisha and offered him something, the prophet steadfastly refused. But Elisha's servant, Gehazi, felt that he must try to get some of what Naaman 'had brought'. So he ran after him and made up an excuse to ask for money and clothing. 'Give...a talent of silver', he said (2 Kgs 5.22). And the Syrian gave him what he asked.

In Acts 8, it is Simon who regards the gift of God as something to be exchanged for money. When he saw that the Spirit was given through the laying on of the apostles' hands, 'he brought' money to them and said, 'Give me also this power'.

But while Gehazi wants to sell the gift, to make money through it, Simon wants to buy it. In other words, while Gehazi is preoccupied with wealth, Simon is preoccupied with spiritual power. By focusing on this desire for spiritual power, Luke's text once again emphasizes what is internal.

The similarity of wording is limited but significant:

Old Testament:
enēnochen...dos dē autois...argyriou...argyriou... [v. 26, *to argyrion*]

New Testament:
pros-ēnegken autois chrēmata...dote... [v. 20, *to argyrion*]

Old Testament:
he brought...give them...silver...silver... [v. 26, the silver]

New Testament:
he brought to them money... Give... [v. 20, the silver/money]

One of the factors that needs further research is the use of hands: the way something is received through hands or through the laying on of (a) hand/s. On this question both texts imply a distinction between something good and something bad. In the Old Testament distinction, the process of receiving from people's hands is *bad* ('receiving' in or from 'the hand/s' is associated with giving or receiving money for the gift; cf. 2 Kgs 5.5, 15-16, 20, 23-24, 26). And the *good* (the free and authentic bestowal of the gift) is that which is given without hands (without the laying on of a hand; 2 Kgs 5.11). To put it simply: as far as the gift is concerned, the use of hands is bad. In the New Testament (Acts 8.15-19), the distinction is rather different: in the bestowal of the gift, there is a use of hands which is good (that performed by the apostles) and a use of hands which is bad (that desired by Simon). Luke's distinction keeps the essence of the Old Testament idea: it condemns a use of hands which exploits the gift for selfish purposes. But he does not condemn the basic idea of the laying on of (a) hands. Luke's salvaging of the idea of the laying on of hands should probably be seen, partly at least, as reflecting his general tendency in this part of Acts to speak of some process or other as involving the laying on of hands (cf. Acts 6.6; 9.12, 17; 13.3) (Coppens 1979).

As usual, Luke's wording is much more economical:

Old Testament:
[vv. 5, 11, *elaben en tē cheiri...epitithēsei tēn cheira*]...*labe...lēmpsomai...labein ek cheiros...lēmpsomai...labe...elaben...elaben ek tōn cheirōn autōn kai paretheto...*
[v. 26, *elabes...elabes*]

New Testament:
[v. 15, *labōsin*]...*epitithoun tas cheiras...kai elambanon...epitheseōs tōn cheirōn...epithō tas cheiras lambaanē*

Old Testament:
[vv. 5, 11, he took in the hand...lay the hand]... Take... I will [not] take...to take from the hand... I will take... Take...he took... And he took from their hands and laid...
[v. 26, you have taken...you have taken...].

New Testament:
[v. 15, that they might receive/take]... They laid the hands...and they received/took...the laying of hands...[that on whom] I lay hands may receive/take.

As well as speaking of Gehazi's attempt to get money, at this point, the Old Testament text also refers to Naaman's desire for true worship (2 Kgs 5.17-19). He wishes to have two mule-loads of the earth of Israel as a base for building an altar, and he apologizes that his duties involve him in other worship. This entire text, which is rather complex, appears to have been distilled into the note which says that the Ethiopian had come worshipping to Jerusalem (Acts 8.27c). In other words, the desire for an Israel-based worship has been abbreviated and updated to refer to Jerusalem-based worship:

Old Testament:
[*theos...en tō Israēl*]...*proskynēsai...proskynēsō...proskynein* (5.15)

New Testament:
proskynēsōn...eis...Ierousalēm.

Old Testament:
[God...in Israel]...to worship/bow down...I shall bow down...bowing down

New Testament:
worshipping...in...Jerusalem.

However, while the Old Testament puts this desire for contact with the traditional geographical center (Israel/Jerusalem) *after* the renewal, Luke puts it *before*, and, unlike the Old Testament text, does not give any indication that the renewed man retained any further relationship to Jerusalem. As in the case of the angel's directing of Philip to a road which leads away from Jerusalem, this adaptation, to some degree at least, probably reflects the tendency of Acts 1–8, and especially of ch. 8, to depict a general movement away from Jerusalem.

g. *Section 7. Confronting the One Who Commercialized the Gift (2 Kings 5.25-27; Acts 8.20-23)*

When Gehazi returns from his money-making expedition, he is first confronted and then irretrievably condemned. Simon also is confronted, but, in a typically Lukan twist, his condemnation is not irretrievable. He is given a chance to repent.

(1) *The confrontation, stage one (2 Kings 5.25-26a; Acts 8.20-21).* In making money from the gift, Gehazi took a deviant journey. Without telling Elisha, he went after Naaman. And when, on his return, Elisha asked him where he had been, he denied that he had taken any such journey, denied, as he put it, that he had gone 'hither or thither' (*entha kai entha*). But Elisha contradicted him by telling him that his own heart had been on the journey with Gehazi. In other words, *his heart* knew that Gehazi had, in fact, *gone hither and thither*.

In Acts, Peter confronts Simon by telling him that *his heart is not straight* before God.

Luke's text involves several adaptations. First, there is internalization. In place of a deviant journey—a process of going hither and thither—Luke depicts a deviousness or crookedness which is within.

Second, there is fusion. Instead of depicting a *heart* which is aware of *crookedness*, Luke speaks of *crookedness of heart*. (Obviously the two adaptations are closely interwoven. It is through the fusion, by bringing together the ideas of heart and crookedness, that Luke achieves internalization: crookedness of heart.)

Third, there appears to be word-play:

> Old Testament:
> *Ou pe-poreuetai ho doulos sou entha kai entha*
> *Ouchi hē kardia mou eporeuthē meta sou;*
>
> New Testament:
> *hē gar kardia sou ouk estin eutheia enanti tou theou*
>
> Old Testament:
> Your servant has not gone hither or tither (*entha kai entha*)
> Did not my heart go with you?
>
> New Testament:
> Your heart is not straight before (*eutheia enanti*) God

Thus, Gehazi's lie about his movements—he did not go *entha kai entha*—has apparently been adapted to describe the internal crookedness of Simon's heart: it is not *eutheia enanti* God. Similar word-play was seen in Luke's reworking of 2 Kgs 4.1-37.

A further detail needs to be noted. Here, as in the Naboth story, the distinction occurs between the source of Luke's *raw material* and the source of his *wording*. Luke's raw materials, his basic elements (the heart; deviousness) come from 2 Kings 5, but the wording which he employs ('your heart is not straight before God'), the wording through which he achieves fusion, internalization, and word-play, comes, to a considerable degree, from the Psalms (cf. Ps. 77.37 LXX: 'Their heart [is] not straight with him [God]'). Luke, of course, adapts the line, especially by changing 'straight with' (*eutheia met*), to 'straight before' (*eutheia enanti*), and it is through such changes that he maintains greater continuity with 2 Kings 5. The essential point, however, is that the text closest to Luke's wording is not necessarily a reliable guide to the origin of his raw material, to his basic source.

Apart from the three adaptations already noted, it should also be mentioned that while the Old Testament does not articulate the nature of Gehazi's crime—it simply describes it and leaves the process of articulation to the reader—the New Testament, through Peter's words, is much more clear and explicit: 'because you thought to buy the gift of God with money' (Acts 8.21).

Another noteworthy detail is difficult to evaluate. Gehazi brings his money to a place that is secret or dark (*eis to skoteinon*, 'to the dark', 2 Kgs 5.24). And Peter tells Simon and his money to go to perdition (*eis apōleian*, Acts 8.20). Given Luke's general practices, it could be argued that perdition is a kind of vivid internalization of the enigmatic dark place. But it is hard to be sure.

(2) *The confrontation, stage two (2 Kings 5.26c-27; Acts 8.22-23)*. In the final stage of the Old Testament confrontation, Gehazi is allowed to keep his ill-gotten gains, but he is told that Naaman's leprosy will cling to him and his seed forever.

In the New Testament scene, Simon is exhorted to prayerful repentance, and he is described as being in the grip of sin (literally, 'in the gall of bitterness and the bond of iniquity').

The text of Acts shows typical Lukan adaptations. Instead of allowing the culprit to persevere in his sinfulness (to keep the ill-gotten goods), Luke, who tends to emphasize the forgiveness of sins (see Fitzmyer 1981: 223-24), depicts an exhortation to prayerful repentance.

And instead of foreseeing a clinging malady which is physical ('the leprosy...will cling to you...forever'), Peter sees a gripping malady which is internal ('I see you as being in...the bond of iniquity').

It is worth noting that the idea of Elisha as a seer, as one who sees and foresees—an idea which in the Old Testament text is merely implied—is brought out rather more clearly in the New Testament text. Peter is depicted as one who sees ('I see you as being...').

Here again, incidentally, there is a distinction between the source of Luke's basic raw material and the source of his wording. The basic raw material—the idea of being in the grip of a powerful negative force—comes from 2 Kings 5, from the reference to the clinging leprosy. But to a considerable degree, Luke's wording concerning the gall of bitterness and the bond of iniquity, the wording through which he achieves a process of internalization, comes from fusing other Old Testament texts (cf. Deut. 29.17; Isa. 58.6).

h. *Section 8. The Chariot (cf. 2 Kings 5.8-9, 20-21, 26; Acts 8.28-30, 38)*
As already seen, most of the later part of 2 Kings 5 deals with Gehazi and has been used as source material for depicting the Simon episode. However, it contains two references to Naaman's chariot (Gehazi's running after it, and Naaman's returning from it to meet Gehazi), and these two references have been adapted not to the Simon text, but to the text concerning the Ethiopian. This causes a disturbance in the order of the correspondences between the texts, but it makes sense: the three references to the chariot are all adapted to the person most likely to have a chariot, the Ethiopian official.

Comparison of the two texts shows, not only that both refer three times to a chariot, but that—as already partly indicated—the surrounding contexts have significant similarities.

The Old Testament speaks of:
- approaching in a chariot and standing;
- running after a chariot and returning from it;
- returning from a chariot.

The New Testament refers to:
- returning in a chariot;
- approaching a chariot and running towards it;
- ordering a chariot to stand.

In effect, the three New Testament references consist largely of a reshaping of the three Old Testament texts. The similarity of wording is more evident in Greek:

Old Testament:
elthetō...pros...kai ēlthen...en...harmati kai estē (5.8-9)
dramoumai...kai...trechonta opisō autou (5.20-21)
kai epe-strepsen apo tou harmatos...autou
epe-strepsen...apo tou harmatos (5.26)

New Testament:
hypo-strephōn...epi tou harmatos autou (8.28)
pros-elthe...tō harmati...pros-dramōn (8.29-30)
stēnai to harma (8.38)

Old Testament:
come...to...and he came...in...[his] chariot and stood (5.8-9)
I will run...and...running after him, and he turned back from his chariot (5.20-21)
he turned back...from the chariot (5.26)

New Testament:
returning...on his chariot (8.28)
come to...the chariot...running (8.29-30)
[he commanded] the chariot to stand (8.38)

This verbal similarity has a number of unique features. First, though the word 'chariot', which occurs only four times in the New Testament (three times in Acts 8 and once in Rev. 9.9), is fairly common in the LXX (about 170 times), there is no other biblical passage in which the word occurs three times, and three times only, in the singular. (The one possible exception is 2 Kgs 10, but even there the first reference to 'chariot' [cf. 2 Kgs 10.2], though grammatically singular, is always understood to indicate a plural sense.)

Second, there is no other reference in the LXX to anyone in a chariot coming to a stand (or simply coming to stand). (The nearest thing to it are the references to Ahab remaining or standing [hestēkōs] in his chariot [1 Kgs 22.35; 2 Chron. 18.34].)

Third, there are no other references to returning in or from a chariot. (There is something close to it: Samuel turned his chariot [epestrepsen to harma, 1 Sam. 15.12], and Josiah did not turn aside in his chariot [ouk apestrepsen...epi to harma..., 1 Esd. 1.26].)

Fourth, there is no other reference to running towards or after a chariot. (There are three references to organized groups who run *ahead* of chariots [1 Sam. 8.11; 2 Sam. 15.1; 1 Kgs 1.5].)

Even if each of these features occurred, say, five or six times in both the Old Testament and New Testament, the fact that they all occur in the texts under discussion would link those texts in a very striking way. The fact that, for all practical purposes, none of them occurs anywhere else, means that the similarity is quite extraordinary.

4. Conclusion

In the texts under consideration there seems to be sufficiently strong evidence to indicate that Luke made direct use of 2 Kings 5. First, there is an extrinsic plausibility: Luke's kinship with rhetoric and rhetorical imitation, his special awareness of the Naaman story (Lk. 4, 27), and his previous use of other parts of the Elijah–Elisha narrative, particularly in the Stephen story. Second, there are the intrinsic similarities of the texts: from broad themes to tiny details, similarities which, in many cases, cannot be accounted for by coincidence. And, third, the dissimilarities, great though they are, are generally understandable. To a significant degree they may be accounted for through some of imitation's most basic and coherent processes of adaptation. Thus the pattern which emerges is so complex and coherent that deliberate artistry—direct literary dependence—seems to be the only way to account for it.

Luke's narrative does not depend on 2 Kings 5 alone. Several elements of his text seem quite independent of it. And at every stage, Luke is using vocabulary and concepts which reflect a specifically Christian background. Therefore, 2 Kings 5 provides not a complete explanation of Acts 8.9-40, but a starting point, a skeleton or foundation. It is one component.

Luke's use of 2 Kings 5 does not necessarily mean that his text contains no factual history. The presence of Simon alone, a rather well-known historical figure, is a reliable indication that elements of history have been woven into the text. But it does not seem possible, at least for the moment, clearly to distinguish those elements. In the case of the Ethiopian, for instance, account must be taken not only of the use of the Naaman story, but also of the fact that the text has been shaped so that it maintains fairly close narrative continuity with the Emmaus story. It is difficult in such a situation to unravel what is strictly historical. Therefore, it seems better at this point to say of the stories of Simon and the Ethiopian what J. Fitzmyer said of Luke 1–2: 'Whatever historical matter has been preserved...has been assimilated...to other literary accounts' (1981: 309).

Luke writes both as a Greco-Roman author and as a Christian narrator and theologian. As a Greco-Roman author, he has followed the widespread practice of grounding his composition on an ancient text. As a Christian narrator and theologian, he has re-examined part of his Old Testament heritage and expressed it in a way which is informed by Christian experience and thought, adapting the ancient text to a new age and stating its meaning with fresh clarity. Thus, he has followed the demands of rhetoric, but he has adapted those demands to the basic Christian idea that the Old Testament should not be destroyed, but fulfilled. In his own way, at a literary as well as a theological level, he has achieved part of the early Christian ideal of blending what was Greek and Jewish into one.

As for the long quest for the sources of Acts, this has consisted essentially of a search for specifically Christian sources originating in the first century, and the detection of Luke's use of some Old Testament texts leaves that central issue quite unresolved. But it casts light on it. It suggests, most obviously, that, in some areas of Acts the specifically Christian sources have been closely interwoven with an Old Testament foundation. It also suggests that those sources have been thoroughly reworked, adapted in accordance with some of the procedures of imitation. It further suggests that as far as sources are concerned, the stories of Stephen and Philip (Acts 6–8) are closely linked. At least they both use basic components from the Elijah–Elisha narrative. By the same token, Luke's use of the Old Testament raises a doubt about Harnack's distinction of sources, or at least about the fact that he assigned the Stephen story to the Antioch source, and the Philip story to the Jerusalem–Caesarea source.

Unit 10. Proto-Luke and Elijah–Elisha: The Damascus Attacker

Orientational Introduction to Chapters 40–43:
Upheaval and Breakthrough (2 Kings 6–13;
Paul and Peter, Acts 9–11), and Some Final Pieces

Ben-hadad's attack and escape (1 Kgs 20.22-43) is the only section of the Elijah–Elisha narrative prior to 2 Kings 5 that Luke has so far not used. This attack/escape text (1 Kgs 20) will be used later.

Following 2 Kings 5, eight chapters still remain: 2 Kings 6–13 tells largely of upheaval (war and murder, 2 Kgs 6–11), but the upheaval finally gives way to a positive breakthrough: to repair, resurrection, and restoration (2 Kgs 12–13). Most of these eight upheaval/breakthrough chapters have been condensed into Acts 9—an account which begins with Paul's tumultuous murder-related conversion (Acts 9.1-19a) and which finally switches from murderousness to positive action, especially to Peter's healing and raising (Acts 9.19b-43).

One major part of 2 Kgs 6–13 is not used in Acts 9, namely the story of the 'good-news lepers' (amid famine, lepers received good news, 2 Kgs 6.24–ch. 7). This story, while not appearing in Acts 9, contributes significantly to Acts 10–11, the account of the 'good-news outsiders' (how Cornelius and other Gentiles receive the Good News).

Ben-hadad's attack and escape (1 Kgs 20.22-43) is not forgotten. The attack (20.22-34) is integrated into Acts 9 (Paul's attack), and the escape into Acts 12 (Peter's escape). Thus the attack and escape serve to frame Acts 9–12.

This effectively concludes the *basic* or *major* pattern of the use of the Elijah–Elisha narrative in Luke–Acts, but three minor passages still need to be accounted for:

1. Amid famine, the prophets generate food (2 Kgs 4.38-44).
2. The trees and the restoring of the lost axe (2 Kgs 6.1-7).
3. A woman seeks justice (2 Kgs 8.1-6).

These three minor passages have been rearranged as minor components to suit the larger pattern. In the following outline of the contents of Chapters 40–43 of this volume, *minor* components are marked with an asterisk. The *basic* or *major* Old Testament references are in italics. The numbers on the left (40–43) refer to chapters of this volume:

	Attacks, Commissions, and a Commissioned Attacker (1 Kings 20.22-34; 2 Kings 6.8–9.13, Omitting 6.24–ch. 7; Acts 9.1-19a)	
40	Two attacks reversed (1 Kgs *20.22-34; 6.8-23*)	Paul's attack reversed…
	Two commissionings (2 Kgs *8.7–9.13*)	…and Paul is commissioned (9.1-19a)
	From Murderous Attacks to New Life (9.14–ch. 13; Acts 19b-43)	
41	Murderous attacks (Jehu…) (2 Kgs *9.14–ch. 11*)	Murderous attacks on Paul (9.19b-31)
	Repairs, resurrection, restoration (2 Kgs *12–13*)	Peter heals, raises (9.32-43; cf. 3.1-10)
	Good News for Outsiders (2 Kings 6.24–ch. 7; Acts 10–11)	
42	Famine: good news for lepers (*6.24–ch. 7*)	Peter hungry: good news for outsiders (chs. 10–11)
	* Famine: prophets generate food (*4.38-44*)	…and prophets deal with famine (11.27-30)

43	*Three Final Pieces (As Minor Components)*	
	Ben-hadad's escape (1 Kgs 20.35-43)	Peter's escape (Acts 12)
	* Tree; lost axe restored (2 Kgs 6.1-7)	Zacchaeus (Lk. 19.1-10)
	* Woman pleads for justice (2 Kgs 8.1-6)	The widow and the judge (Lk. 18.1-8)

Since the following chapters (40–43) deal mainly with just the final part of the Elijah–Elisha narrative—essentially with 2 Kings 6–13—they constitute a form of mopping up operation. Accordingly, their analysis of the texts is generally brief.

40

Struck Down, Temporarily Blinded, and Prophetically Commissioned: The Two Damascus-Based Attacks (1 Kings 20.22-34; 2 Kings 6.8-23) and the Two Commissionings (2 Kings 8.7-15; 9.1-13) as Components in Paul's Conversion from Attacker to Commissioned (Acts 9.1-19a)

The pertinent Old Testament texts deal largely with attacks and commissionings.

First the attacks.

The Elijah–Elisha narrative contains two accounts of Damascus-based attackers who fell into the power of Israel but found the defeat to be life-giving. The first account (1 Kgs 20.22-34) is the story of how Ben-hadad, having calculated that he would win if he fought Israel on the plain, nonetheless found that his army was massively defeated—struck down. But Ben-hadad was not lost: he did penance, his life was spared, and he was accepted by the Israelite king as a brother.

The second account (2 Kgs 6.8-23) is like a variation on the first. Again, the Syrian king engages in a calculating game about where to attack Israel, but when some of his army makes a move (against Elisha), it is again overpowered, this time by being temporarily blinded. Again, however, the overpowered people do well. Still blinded, they are led into the city (Samaria) where their lives are spared, and they are given food.

Both of these accounts have contributed to the description of the conversion of Saul at Damascus: how he was overpowered, temporarily blinded, led into the city, treated as a brother, found new life, and received food (Acts 9.1-19a).

Next the commissionings.

This later part of the Elijah–Elisha narrative recounts two commissionings: Elisha's commissioning of Hazael as king in Damascus (2 Kgs 8.7-15) and the commissioning of Jehu as king of Israel (2 Kgs 9.1-13). These two Old Testament commissioning accounts —somewhat like the two attack accounts (1 Kgs 20.22-34; 2 Kgs 6.8-23)—complement one another in various ways. They both begin by sending someone with something in his hand (a rich gift; an oil flask for anointing) in order to determine the future of a king (the fading Ben-hadad, 2 Kgs 8.7-8; the emerging Jehu, 2 Kgs 9.1-3). Then comes the central scene between the future king and the dread-filled prophetic appointer—a scene which lists the terrible things the new king will do (2 Kgs 8.9-13; 9.6-10). Finally, the still-unrevealed king-to-be emerges and, after briefly engaging in a deceptive conversation, he becomes more open; what was foretold begins to happen; cloth is spread (over the face of the fading king; under the feet of the emerging king); and a new person begins to be king—Hazael (2 Kgs 8.14-15), and Jehu (2 Kgs 9.11-13).

The commissioning of Hazael and Jehu may seem at first sight to be totally unrelated to the commissioning of Saul. Hazael and Jehu will be cruel. Yet their commissioning is no minor thing. In Elijah's encounter with God at Horeb, the first task listed by God is the commissioning of Hazael and Jehu: 'Go. Go back the same way to the wilderness of Damascus. And when you arrive, you shall anoint Hazael as king of Aram, and Jehu…as

Table 63. *The Damascus Attacker (1 Kings 20; 2 Kings 6–9; Acts 9.1-19a)*

	Attack Struck Down *1 Kgs 20.22-34*	Attack Temporarily Blinded *2 Kgs 6.8-24*	Commissioning (Prophetically) *2 Kgs 8.7-15, Hazael*	Commissioning (Prophetically) *2 Kgs 9.1-13, Jehu*	Attacker Commissioned Saul *Acts 9.1-19a*
1.	[Letters to the elders, 21.8] [Take women, children (20.3-8)]? Army threatens (20.27)	Army threatens (6.8, 24)			Saul breathes threats… Saul breathes threats… to lead men and women
2.	Knowing where to meet: on the plain (*euthu*, 20.22-26)	Knowing where, knowing even words in your room (6.8-13)			[Knowing he is on Straight (*eutheian*) Street, praying]
3.	You will know I am Lord. Many struck; wall fell; went into city (20.28-30a)				Paul, overwhelmed, falls. Who are you, Lord? Go into the city
4.		What will we do? Prayer. Servant does not see the vision. Army struck with blindness. Led them into Samaria	Elijah. went into Damascus		You will be told what to do. Men do not see [the vision]. Saul's eyes cannot see. And they led him into Damascus

5.		and Ben-hadad was sick. Will he live? (8.7)	and Ben-hadad was sick. And he was…not seeing for three days …he did not eat or drink
6.		Gift in hand, go…inquire (8.8)	Oil flask in hand, go…anoint (9.1-3)	Go…inquire. place (healing) hands (9.11-12)
7.		Elisha: I know how many evils… Hazael 'is…a dead dog'. The Lord has shown me you as king over Israel	The Lord has anointed you as king over Israel	Ananias: I heard how many evils… The Lord said, Saul 'is a chosen vessel' before kings and…Israel I will show him how many…
8.	Ben-hadad entered the house. Places cloth on body. Accepted as a brother and sent away	He went away and entered		Ananias went away and entered the house Places hands on him says, 'Saul, brother the Lord sent me. that you may see…'
	They entered Samaria.	Wet cloth over face. He began to reign	Garments under him: 'Jehu reigns'	Scales fell from eyes.
	Eyes were opened. Lives were saved. They ate and drank			Baptism, food, strengthens

king of Israel' (1 Kgs 19.15). And then God connects the work of Hazael and Jehu with the work of the prophet Elisha: whoever escapes Hazael will be put to death by Jehu, and whoever escapes Jehu will be put to death by Elisha (1 Kgs 19.17). Thus, the work of Hazael and Jehu, however terrible, is somehow important in the God-given prophetic mission. And as an important element in God's mission, it has a basic affinity with the commissioning of Saul.

But having an important role in God's mission is not the only link between these texts. Even Hazael's cruelty (1 Kgs 8.12), the factor which seems so distant from Saul, finds an exact echo in the New Testament account (Acts 9.13):

Elisha weeps:	Ananias objects:
'Because I know	'Lord, I have heard
how many evils (*hosa kaka*)	how many evils (*hosa kaka*)
you [Hazael] will do (*poiēseis*)	he has done (*epoiēsen*)
to the sons of Israel'.	to your saints in Jerusalem'.

Luke manages to turn around the reference to Hazael's evils so that it suits Saul. And the same is true of the Hazael text as a whole. The commissioning (including Hazael's apparent murder of the previous king, Ben-hadad, 2 Kgs 8.15) may appear highly negative, yet the fact that it is part of the prophetic mission indicates that it has its place, that there is something about it which is positive. Luke exploits this positive undercurrent, even if at times it means reversing aspects of the Old Testament text.

Luke's indebtedness to the second commissioning, that of Jehu (2 Kgs 9.1-10), is more difficult to trace, yet it is real; as often, Luke has combined two related texts.

One link between the Jehu and Saul texts is the decisive combination of hands and head: Elisha's prophetic representative carries in his hands a container or flask of oil and with that oil, he anoints the head of Jehu (2 Kgs 9.1, 3, 6)—a positive gesture which corresponds partly to Ananias's laying of his hands on Saul (Acts 9.12, 17). A further link is the idea of being specially chosen: Jehu is called 'from (*ek*) the middle of his brothers...from (*ek*) all' (2 Kgs 9.2, 5); Saul is a vessel 'of choice' (*ek-logēs*, Acts 9.15).

Whatever the full details, the basic picture which emerges is that the Elijah–Elisha narrative, with its various accounts of Damascus attackers and of commissionings, has supplied several components (or one complex component) for Luke's description of Saul's conversion. Luke distilled the various Old Testament accounts, and by fusing them into a flowing unity, embellished the picture of the event on the road to Damascus.

The outline (Table 63 above) lays out the approximate relationship between the texts.

1. *More Detailed Analysis*

a. *Section 1. Threats, and Deadly Letters from the Authorities (1 Kings 21.8 and 20.27; 2 King 6.24; Acts 9.1-2)*

When Luke was using the Naboth story to describe the killing of Stephen, there was one vivid factor which he omitted—the initial role played by letters, letters passed from the highest authority (in the king's name) to local officials (elders and nobles). It was these letters which caused Naboth to be led out to die (1 Kgs 21.8, 13).

But Luke does not omit this idea of deadly letters. Instead he gives them an initial role in the Saul story. At the beginning of the conversion account (Acts 9.1-2), the main clause tells how Saul went to the high priest for letters to be used against people in the Damascus synagogues. The relationship to the Old Testament action is close:

Old Testament:
King: letters > elders and nobles (orchestrated by Jezebel, to kill)

New Testament:
High priest: letters > synagogues (organized by Saul, breathing murder)

Luke has adapted the picture of civil authorities to fit the religious authorities of his own day—a procedure he had already used when writing the Stephen story. The connection with the Stephen story is clear in Luke; Saul is introduced as 'still breathing threats and murder'—a process which goes back to his role in Stephen's death (Acts 7.58; 8.1, 3).

Apart from using the Naboth account, Luke probably incorporated some echoes of the terrible threats from Damascus: the great armies which seemed as it they would overwhelm Israel (1 Kgs 20.22-27, especially 20.22, 27; 2 Kgs 6.24), and the threat to take the king's women and children (1 Kgs 20.3-8). This latter element—the effort to take the 'women and children' (to Damascus)—may, perhaps, have colored the picture of Saul's effort to lead 'men and women' (from Damascus) (Acts 9.2).

In any case, the account of the conversion of Saul begins, as do the accounts of the Damascus attacks (1 Kgs 20.22-27; 2 Kgs 6.8-14), with a sense of a great threat, and the instrument for implementing that threat is the same as in the Naboth story: deadly letters from the highest authority.

b. *Section 2. Knowing Where to Meet the Damascus Attacker—On the Plain/Straight; the Prophet(-like Person) Knows Best (1 Kings 20.22-26; 2 Kings 6.8-13; Acts 9.10-11)*

The two stories of Damascus-based attacks begin with a cat-and-mouse game: the king and servants in the mighty Syrian side are debating where to attack, but Israel's prophet knows the Syrian plans, and he knows in particular the location of the attacker (1 Kgs 20.22-26; 2 Kgs 6.8-13). Eventually, however, the Syrians think they can outwit Israel and its prophet. In one account, they decide to meet Israel on the plain (*kat' euthu*, 1 Kgs 20.23, 25), and in the other, they figure out the prophet's location: 'Behold (*Idou*), he is in Dotham' (2 Kgs 6.13). Needless to say, Israel's prophet will overcome these attackers.

Luke applies these accounts not to impending attacks but to an attack that has already been overcome. At the beginning of his next paragraph, he shows how the prophetlike Ananias, the man who sees in visions, knows the Damascus location of the would-be attacker: 'The street called Straight (*eutheian*)... Behold (*Idou*) he is praying' (Acts 9.11). Thus, the prophet's seeing of the would-be attackers, especially the attackers on the *euthu* (Old Testament), has become the prophetlike seeing of the would-be attacker on *Eutheia* Street a well-known street historically. Luke has domesticated the warlike setting to the streets of Damascus.

There is a further connecting detail: while the Old Testament prophet can see what one says in an inner room (2 Kgs 6.12), the prophetlike Ananias sees that Saul is praying—an activity which is even more internal than speaking in an inner room (Acts 9.11).

The verbs at the beginning of the two Old Testament accounts, *prosēlthen* ('he approached', 1 Kgs 20.22) and *ēn* ('he was', 2 Kgs 6.8), occur also at the beginning of these first two paragraphs of Acts 9—*prosēlthōn* ('[he] approaching', Acts 9.1) and *ēn* ('he was', Acts 9.10).

c. *Section 3. Struck Down: Knowing the Lord, and Going into the City (1 Kings 20.28-30a; Acts 9.3-6a)*

As the great army is about to attack, the Lord announces its defeat 'so that you may know that I am Lord (*egō Kyrios*)' (1 Kgs 20.28). And then, after a seven-day wait, the attackers are overwhelmed: 100,000 are struck down, and when the others go 'into the city', a wall 'falls' on them.

Aspects of this are reflected in the fate of the would-be attacker, Saul. As he approached Damascus, a light surrounded him; 'falling on the ground', he asked, 'Who are you, Lord (*Kyrie*)?', and the reply came, 'I am (*Egō eimi*)... Go into the city...' (Acts 9.3-6).

At this point, Luke's text is extremely dense and 1 Kings 20 is only one of many components. While it may have an oblique link with the striking and falling of 1 Kings 20, the image of 'falling on the ground' apparently takes its wording from the account of the conversion of the persecuting Heliodorus: 'Suddenly falling to the ground, he was enveloped in thick darkness' (2 Macc. 3.27).

Luke makes no mention of an army, still less of 100,000 men, but his description (Acts 9.3) contains an echo of the sudden appearance of the great army of heaven (Lk. 2.9, 13):

Lk. 2.9, 13	Acts 9.3
The glory of the Lord	Suddenly
shone about them...	a light
and suddenly there was	shone around him
a multitude of the army of heaven.	from heaven.

d. *Section 4. The Question of What to Do, the Two Forms of Blindness, and Leading Them to the City (2 Kings 6.15-19; Acts 9.6b-8)*

In the second attack account (2 Kgs 6.15-19), when Elisha and his servant are surrounded, the servant 'rises' and wonders 'what will we do?' (6.15).

And the Lord says to Saul, 'Rise...you will be told what to do' (Acts 9.6).

Then come the two forms of blindness. First, the day-to-day blindness of those who have ordinary sight but cannot see the heavenly dimension (the vision or light); and, second, the more acute blindness of those whose vision is physically impaired so that they cannot see even earthly things.

Elisha's servant cannot at first see the vision of the (heavenly) army which was around Elisha (2 Kgs 6.17), and in Acts the traveling companions did not see the light which shone suddenly from heaven around Saul (Acts 9.3, 7).

Then comes the more physical blindness: the attacking army is struck with blindness (2 Kgs 6.18), and when Saul opens his eyes, he sees nothing (Acts 9.8).

Finally, the blinded attackers are led into the city (into Samaria, 2 Kgs 6.19; into Damascus, Acts 9.8).

There is considerable similarity of detail. In the outline, Table 64 (from 2 Kgs 6.15-19; Acts 9.3, 6-8), verbal similarity in English reflects verbal similariy in Greek:

Table 64. *Opening the Eyes (2 Kings 6.15-19; Acts 9.3, 6-8)*

2 Kings 6.15-19	Acts 9.3, 6-8
—	The light shone around him.
Rising, the servant went out. Kyrios: Kyrie, what shall we do?	Rise and go in... You will be told what to do.
Elisha prays: Open his eyes.	Fellow travelers saw nothing.
The Lord opened his eyes and he saw the chariot of fire around Elisha.	—
The Lord struck them with blindness.	Saul, opening his eyes, saw nothing.
Come after me, I will lead you. And he led them to Samaria.	Leading him by the hand they led him into Damascus.

e. *Section 5. Coming to Damascus: Someone is Unwell, and is Even Overshadowed by Death (2 Kings 8.7; Acts 9.8b-9)*
In the account of how one Damascus king died and another began to reign (2 Kgs 8.7-13), the action begins with Elisha'a arrival into Damascus (*eis Damascon*) and with the news that King Ben-hadad was sick (the sickness which would bring death and a new king) (8.7).

When Saul was led into Damascus (*eis Damascon*), he was not well: 'he was three days not seeing, and he neither ate nor drank' (Acts 9.9). Furthermore, these three pre-baptism days of darkness and non-eating suggest—as in Jesus' case—a passage through death (Rom. 6.4 describes baptism as dying and rising with Christ).

Given the context, it seems that Luke has taken the sickness of the king and has used it as a starting-point for speaking of Saul's condition. The shadow of death which hangs over the king has given way to the idea of 'three days'—a phrase which, within the New Testament, is death-related but which is also strongly positive.

The final phrase, 'he neither ate nor drank', reinforces the suggestion of death and it also turns around a near-final phrase from the account of the second attack ('they ate and drank', 2 Kgs 6.23).

f. *Section 6. For the Sake of the One Who is Unwell: Go and Inquire, With a Gift in Your Hands (2 Kings 8.7-9; 9.1-3; Acts 9.11-12)*
The king tells Hazael to go to the man of God, saying to 'go...and inquire' if he will recover (*deuro...kai epi-zētēson*), and he sends lavish gifts 'in his hand' (*en tē cheiri*) to boost the chances of recovery (2 Kgs 8.8-9).

The Lord sends Ananias to Saul saying 'Go...and inquire' (*poreuthti... kai zētēson*), and the Lord tells how Saul has seen Ananias coming and 'placing his hands (*cheiras*) on him that he may see' (Acts 9.11-12).

Luke has kept the idea of going and inquiring, but he has changed the lavish gift in the hands (forty camel loads) into a gift which is more internal—the restoring of sight.

To some degree, Luke's idea (of using the hands) also incorporates the image from the Jehu scene of going to the person who is to be commissioned while bearing in one's hand an oil flask for anointing (2 Kgs 9.1-3).

g. *Section 7. The Debatable Appointment of a New Leader—His Many Evils and His Relationship to King/s and to Israel (2 Kings 8.10-13; 9.4-10; Acts 9.13-16)*
When Elisha is consulted, he grudgingly begins to declare that Hazael is to be the new king. He knows how many evils (*hosa kaka*) Hazael will commit, and Hazael says disparagingly of himself that he 'is a dead dog'. Yet the Lord has shown that Hazael will be king over Israel (2 Kgs 8.10-13).

Like Elisha, Ananias is God's instrument in appointing a new leader, and though he is not begrudging, he has doubts, for he has heard 'how many evils' (*hosa kaka*) Saul has committed.

But while the doubts about Hazael remain, those about Saul are dispelled. Hazael 'is...a dead dog' but Saul 'is a chosen vessel'—a typically Lukan reversal from negative to positive. And then the process of adaptation is continued:

> Old Testament:
> 'The Lord has shown' that Hazael
> will be 'king over Israel'.
>
> New Testament:
> Saul will carry the Lord's name 'before kings and before the sons of Israel';
> 'the Lord...will show' him how many things he must suffer.

Luke does not exclude suffering, but this suffering is set in the context of an appointment which is resoundingly positive. To some degree, the same was true of the sufferings implied in the Old Testament scene; the evils to be committed by Hazael had been foreseen by God, and, in that sense, had been incorporated into the divine dispensation—a positive context. But in Luke, the sense of the positive is much stronger and clearer.

Aspects of Luke's text, particularly the reference to kings and Israel (Acts 9.15) also connect with the commissioning of Jehu as king of Israel (2 Kgs 9.6). And like Jehu, Saul is chosen out (2 Kgs 9.2, 5; Acts 9.15).

h. *Section 8. The Final Episode: Entering to New Life—as Brother, as Seeing, as Eating, and also as Embarking on a New Mission (1 Kings 20.30b-34; 2 Kings 6.20-23; 8.14-15; Acts 9.17-19a)*

In three of the Old Testament texts, the final parts (1 Kgs 20.30b-34; 2 Kgs 6.20-23; 8.14-15) tell how someone from or in Damascus found new life. In the first (1 Kgs 20.30b-34), Ben-hadad put sackcloth on his loins and ropes on his head and was accepted as a brother. In the second (2 Kgs 6.20-23), the would-be attackers' eyes were opened, their lives were spared or saved, and they ate and drank. And in the third and enigmatic conclusion (2 Kgs 8.14-15), Hazael came to power as king. (He did so when he had placed a blanket dipped [*baptō*] in water on the face of the previous king, and the king died.)

Luke takes all three accounts of entering into new life and fuses them to help portray Saul's recovery. The idea of placing (*epitithmi...epi*) something (sackcloth, ropes) on Ben-hadad's body as a gesture of repentance and renewal (1 Kgs 20.31-32) is apparently one of the elements reflected in the placing (*epitithmi...epi*) of hands on Saul's eyes. Like Ben-hadad, Saul is accepted as a brother. And like the second group of attackers (2 Kgs 6.20-23), Saul's eyes are opened and he takes food.

It is more difficult to judge to what extent Luke has used the other conclusions concerning the coming to power of Hazael and Jehu (2 Kgs 8.14-15; 9.11-13). Some links are clear—most obviously the phrase 'he went away…and he entered' (2 Kgs 8.14; Acts 9.17). On the other hand, the similarity between dipping (*baptō*) the cloth in water (2 Kgs 8.15) and baptizing (Acts 9.18) may be coincidence, but it is difficult to be sure. What is certain is that at the end of the scenes, Hazael, Jehu, and Saul all emerge from relative obscurity and weakness into new strength.

2. *Conclusion*

The preceding analysis is incomplete; a full treatment of the texts would probably require a special study. The incompleteness is due in part to the nature of the account of Saul's conversion: particularly in its later stages (Acts 9.10-19a, especially 9.17-19a), it is a dense multi-layered synthesis of several texts.

What is important for the moment is that despite the incompleteness and the need for further detail and clarity, there is already a reasonable amount of evidence that the dramatic turnabout in Saul's life finds several partial precedents in the history of the ancient kings, particularly in those associated with Damascus. The way in which God once worked through kings—across the sweep of history—has found new expression in the development of the kingdom of God within a new more person-centered arena.

41

The (Attempted) Killings and the Restoration:
2 Kings 9.14–Ch. 13 as One Component of Acts 9.19b-43*

Proto-Luke used the remainder of the Elijah–Elisha narrative (2 Kgs 9.14–ch. 13) as one component for the remainder of Acts 9 (9.19b-43). The first part of the Old Testament text is largely negative—telling of the bloody coups by Jehu and Athaliah (2 Kgs 9.14–ch. 11) —and it has been used to describe Saul/Paul and the various attempts to kill him (Acts 9.19b-31). The second part is positive—telling of repairs, resurrection, and restoration (2 Kgs 12–13)—and this has been used to describe Peter's ministry of healing and raising (Acts 9.32-43).

1. *Introductory Analysis*

The final five chapters of the Elijah–Elisha narrative are like a long narrative of passion and resurrection. First, there are almost three chapters of 'passion'—chapters which tell of all the murders carried out by Jehu and Athaliah (2 Kgs 9.14–ch. 11). And then there are two chapters of 'resurrection'—positive accounts of repairs and restoration, even restoration from the dead (2 Kgs 12–13).

The idea of repairs and restoration needs further explanation. The repairs refer to the temple. When the new king, Jehoash, comes to power, he takes care of the temple, first by repairing it (2 Kgs 12.1-17), and then by saving it from Hazael; in fact, he saves all of Jerusalem (12.18-19).

The welfare of the temple is secured by using the *hagia* ('the holy [things]'), a reference to sacred dues or monies (2 Kgs 12.5, 19). Jehoash uses the *hagia* not only to pay for the repairs (12.5-17), but also—at the end of the chapter—to keep Hazael at bay (12.18-19).

The restoration refers to the events which followed Elisha's death (1 Kgs 13). There is indeed a sadness about the death of the prophet—the king goes down to him and cries— but there is also great energy and an outburst of multi-faceted life. The prophet helps the king to carry out a hope-filled ritual with a bow and arrow, a ritual suggesting a great victory (victory over Aram, 13.14-19); and when the prophet actually dies, the ritual gives way to a hope-filled reality with the raising of a man from the dead and the restoration of the captured cities (cities captured by Hazael of Aram, 13.20-25).

Thus the final emphasis is on victory and resurrection. True, the victory is not complete; Elisha's final outburst of anger (13.19)—somewhat like Jesus' anger as he approached the tomb of his friend (Jn 11.33)—is a reflection of the fact that even after the work of the greatest prophets, there remains an element of evil which causes distress, and anger.

Nonetheless, despite the cataclysm of the murderous coups (2 Kgs 9–11), the overall effect of the last two chapters of the Elijah–Elisha narrative is to emphasize the positive: the temple was repaired and saved (2 Kgs 12), and the prophet's death brought resurrection and restoration.

---

*   The material in this chapter is assessed in conjunction with the material in the next two chapters, at the end of Chapter 43.

Aspects of all these Old Testament events are reflected in the accounts of Saul/Paul (Acts 9.19b-31) and Peter (9.32-43).

Saul preaches in two cities—Damascus (9.19b-25) and Jerusalem (9.26-31)—but his preaching activity tends to be overshadowed by the atmosphere of fear and hostility. In Damascus, the Jews try to kill him, and in Jerusalem there is a similar attempt by the Hellenists. In the end, he is effectively driven out of both cities and is sent away to Tarsus.

Peter's activities are likewise concentrated largely in two cities: Lydda (Acts 9.32-35) and Jaffa (9.36-43). Unlike the case with Saul, however, the atmosphere around Peter, far from being one of fear and murder, is one of healing and resurrection. In Lydda he heals a paralytic, and in Jaffa he raises the dead Tabitha.

The broad continuity between the final chapters of the Elijah–Elisha narrative and Acts 9.19b-43 may be outlined as follows:

Murder (2 Kgs 9.14–ch. 11)	Attempted murder (Acts 9.19b-31)
Repairing the temple (12.1-11)	Healing the paralytic (9.32-35)
Works for temple Jerusalem/temple saved (12.12-19)	Tabitha worked for people
Elish'a death: resurrection; restoration (13.14-25)	she dies; is raised (9.36-43)

The Old Testament emphasis on the temple has been replaced, as elsewhere in Luke, by an emphasis on people—another aspect of moving the focus to what is within people, to what is more internal.

The Tabitha incident involves a combining of two texts: one about the temple and Jerusalem, the other about the events surrounding the death of Elisha.

Further details of the relationship between the texts may be seen in the outline (Table 65). By and large the succession of Old Testament events corresponds to the New Testament events. However, as the outline indicates, there seems to be no equivalent for the initial account of Paul's preaching in Damascus (Acts 9.19b-22); nor is it clear what Luke has done with some of the later killings (2 Kgs 10.12-27) and with the overthrowing of Athaliah (2 Kgs 12.13-16). It is also not clear how Luke used the ritual drawing of the bow and arrow (2 Kgs 13.15-19).

Table 65. *Death and Restoration (2 Kings 9.14–11.20; Acts 9.19b-31)*

MURDER AND SAUL: MURDER PLOTS OF JEHU AND ATHALIAH, AND THE PLOTS OF THE JEWS AND HELLENISTS AGAINST SAUL (2 KINGS 9.14–CH. 11; ACTS 9.19B-31)	
In Samaria/Damascus: Plotting...to Kill...to Kill *(2 Kings 9.14–ch. 10; Acts 9.23-25)*	
??	Paul preaches in Damascus (9.19b-22)
1. Jehu plotted (*syn-estraphē*) his (deadly) coup (9.14-16)	The Jews plotted (*syn-ebouleusanto*) to kill Saul (9.23)
2. The lookout on the tower and saw Jehu coming (to kill) (9.17-29)	They were watching the gates (*pulas*) to kill him (9.24)
3. They throw down (*kuliō*) Jezebel. Seventy royal sons killed: heads, brought in baskets (*en kartalois*), put at city gate (*pulē*) (9.30–10.11)	They let down (*chalaō*) Paul in a basket (*en spuridi*) (9.25)
More killings (10.12-27)	??

41. The (Attempted) Killings and the Restoration 431

	Back in Jerusalem: Saved from Attempted Murder (2 Kings 11; Acts 9.26-31)	
4.	Athaliah murdered all of royal stock but Jehosheba took the son and he was with her... ...and Jehoida took the officers and led them to him and made a covenant of the Lord with them involving going out and going in (11.1-11) (*elaben...auton...elabon... kai ēn met' autēs... kai apēgagen autous pros auton ekporeuomenos...eisporeuomenos ekporeuesthai.. kai...eisporeuesthai eisporeuomenous...ekporeuomenōn*)	In Jerusalem all feared Saul but Barnabas taking him led him to the apostles... and told how he saw the Lord and he was with them going in and going out...and... the Hellenists...tried to kill him (9.26-28) (*epi-labomenos auton ēgagen pros tous apostolous... kai ēn met' autōn eisporeuomenos kai ekporeuomenos*)
5.	He sent out (*exapesteilen*) the son, overthrew Athaliah (11.13-16) and led the son/king down (*katēgagon*) (11.12-19)	They led him down (*katēgagon*) to Caesarea ?? and sent him forth (*exapesteilan*) to Tarsus (9.30)
6.	All the people rejoiced, and city was at rest (11.20)	Whole church was at peace filled with the Holy Spirit (9.31)
	RESTORATION AND PETER: REPAIRING THE HOLY TEMPLE AND RAISING THE DEAD (2 KINGS 12–13)— PETER'S 'REPAIRING' OF AENEAS AND THE RAISING OF TABITHA (ACTS 9.32-43)	
	Repairing the Temple/Aeneas (2 Kings 12.1-11; Acts 9.32-35)	
7.	Use all the holy things (*hagia*) for all (*panta*) temple breaches, if any breach is found there (*heurethē ekei*, 12.5-6) In the 23rd year (*etei*) no repairs had been done (12.7-9) The priest located a chest for collecting money near the temple entrance (12.10-11)	Passing through all (*pantōn*) [places], Peter came to the holy ones (*hagioi*) at Lydda, and he found there a paralytic named Aeneas (*heuren ekei*) who had been eight years (*etōn*) lying in bed (9.32-33) [Healing, 9.34-35—recalling Acts 3.1-10] [Acts 3.2: They placed a begging lame man at the temple door.]
	Working for Temple; Raising the Dead/Tabitha (2 Kings 12.12–ch. 13; Acts 9.36-43)	
8.	Doing works for the temple doing...as many as were spent (*poiountōn ta erga... poiousin...hosa*, 12.12-13) No objects of silver or gold are to be given to the temple (12.14-17)	Tabitha: full of good works...which she did (*ergōn...hōn epoiei*, 9.36); ...as many as she had made (*hosa epoiei*, 9.39) [3.6: Peter gives no gold or silver]
9.	Elisha fell ill, the illness from which he died (*ērrōstēsten...autou...apethanen*, 13.14a)	Tabitha became sick and died (*astheneusen autēn apothanein*, 9.37)

King went down to him, wept (*eklausen*, 13.14b)		Peter…arising…came…all stood weeping (*klaiousai*, 9.39)
Ritual drawing of bow (12.15-19)		??
Elisha joins hands with king (12.16)		Giving her a hand,
10. Elisha's bones made the dead live and rise (*ezēsen kai anestē*) (12.20-21)		he raised (*anestē*) her, and calling the holy ones (*hagioi*)…presented her living (*zōsan*) (9.41)
Sending of holy things (*hagia*) saves the city from Hazael (12.18-19)	Lord takes mercy, reversing Hazael's work and restoring the cities of Israel (13.22-25)	New life of faith in Jaffa (9.42-43), culminating new life in the land and in other cities (cf. 9.31, 35)

2. More Detailed Analysis

a. *Section 1. Plotting to Kill (2 Kings 9.14-16; Acts 9.23)*
The Old Testament text begins by giving some details of the situation about how Jehu plotted (*synestraphē*) against Jehoram. (At the first opportunity, Jehu will send an arrow through Jehoram's heart.) The New Testament begins by saying more briefly that the Jews plotted (*synebouleusanto*) to kill Saul.

b. *Section 2. At the City Gates: Watching and Murder (2 Kings 9.17-29; 10.1-11; Acts 9.24)*
The Old Testament gives two scenes, each involving a strategic point of the city: first the watchtower from which the lookout sees Jehu coming (coming to kill, 2 Kgs 9.17-29), and then the gate where the murderers deposit the heads of the king's seventy sons (the heads had been brought in baskets, 10.1-10).

Luke combines the images of watchtower and gate, and thus he speaks of watching the gates—to kill.

c. *Section 3. Lowering Down the Murder Target (2 Kings 9.30-37, Jezebel; Acts 9.25, Saul)*
When Jehu arrives at Jezreel, he orders Jezebel's eunuchs to throw her down (*kuliō*) to her death. Luke reverses this: Saul, though likewise targeted for death, is lowered (*chalaō*) not to destruction but to safety. Luke also adapts a further detail from the account of the seventy sons: he says that Saul was let down 'in a basket'.

d. *Section 4. The Prestigious Escapee (the King's Son; Saul) Finds a Rescuer and Thereby Finds Strong Support (2 Kings 11.1-11; Acts 9.26-28)*
When the queen mother seizes power, she tries to kill the rest of the royal family, but a woman places the king's baby son, Jehoash, with his nurse, and thus he stays hidden in the temple. Six years later, he finds a powerful ally—Jehoida, the chief priest. And Jehoida organizes the commanders so that in their comings and goings they are committed to the welfare of the child.

Aspects of this Old Testament drama are reflected in the case of Saul. Like the king's son, he has escaped attempted murder, and for a while he experiences a form of exclusion (the child was hidden; Saul tried to join the disciples but they feared him, Acts 9.26).

But then an able ally (Jehoida; Barnabas) intervenes and takes charge, particularly by winning the support of the decisive leaders—the commanders (Old Testament) and the apostles (New Testament).

As the outline suggests, Luke has made quite a number of adaptations, but there are also several linguistic links between the texts.

e. *Section 5. Sending and Leading the Formerly Threatened Leader to a New Place of Greater Potential (2 Kings 11.12-19; Acts 9.30)*
The second part of 2 Kings 11 describes how they brought the king's son forth (literally, 'sent him forth', *exapesteilen*) to be proclaimed king, how Athaliah was overthrown, and finally how 'they led him down' (*katēgagon*) to the palace throne.

It is not clear what Luke did with the account of the overthrowing of Athaliah (11.13-16; her fate has some echoes of Jezebel, 2 Kgs 9.30-37), but the two main actions concerning the king's son—sending him forth (to be proclaimed), and then leading him down (to the palace throne)—are recaptured in Saul: they 'led him down (*katēgagon*) to Caesarea and sent him forth (*exapesteilan*) to Tarsus' (Acts 9.30).

Unlike the king's son, Saul is not immediately led and sent on his mission. That will come later. The next time Saul is mentioned, he is being 'led' to the breakthrough work in Antioch (Acts 11.22-30, especially 11.26), and the subsequent reference tells of his being sent on the first great mission (13.1-3).

f. *Section 6. All the People at Rest (2 Kings 11.20; Acts 9.31)*
Then both texts say that all the people enjoyed peace:

> Old Testament:
> And all the people rejoiced and the city was at rest.
>
> New Testament:
> The church throughout the whole of Judea, Galilee, and Samaria had peace...

Luke goes on to spell out the idea of peace: the church was built up, living in the fear of the Lord, and uplifted by the Holy Spirit. The context (but not the wording) suggests that Luke used the Old Testament text as a starting point for his own more elaborate picture of peace.

g. *Section 7. Repairing the Damage to the (Human) Temple (2 Kings 12.5-11, the Jerusalem Temple; Acts 9.32-35, Aeneas; cf. 3.2, the Lame Man)*
First of all these texts are connected by their framework—by a shared emphasis on the *hagia/hagoi* ('holy things/ones').

After the usual formulaic introduction to the new king (2 Kgs 12.1-5), the Old Testament tells how he had the temple repaired, particularly by his use of the *hagia* ('the holy [things]', i.e. sacred offerings or money). Instead of storing the *hagia*, the king took them out and used them for the good of the temple. This he did twice as recounted at the beginning and end of the chapter (2 Kgs 12). Having first used the *hagia* for repairs (12.5-6), he later used them to save the city altogether (he gave them to the attacking Hazael who then went away, 12.18-19). Thus—leaving aside the formulaic opening and closing (12.1-4, 20-22)—the references to the *hagia* form a precise frame for the main body of the chapter (12.5, 19).

In Peter's ministry (Acts 9.32-41) there is a similar phenomenon. If one leaves aside the closing comment (9.42-43), then the word *hagioi*, 'the holy [ones]', forms a precise frame to the entire account (9.32, 41). Luke has adapted 'holy [things]' to 'holy [ones/people]'. In other words, while keeping the sense of the temple and its holiness, he uses it not about external objects but about something more personal, something internal. Earlier, he had used the same adaptation—from the temple to the human person—on a massive scale, namely when adapting the Chronicler's account of the origin of the temple to his own account of the infancy of Jesus.

The double use of the plural *hagia/hagioi* is rare; it does not otherwise occur in the Elijah–Elisha narrative or in Luke–Acts. The added similarity of function—as a precise framework—makes the link all the more unique.

Apart from their frameworks, the texts are also connected by their central content—by an emphasis on repairing/healing.

The Old Testament account begins with the decision to use all the *hagia* to repair the temple, 'all [repairs], whatever gaps/repairs were found there' (*heurethē ekei*, 2 Kgs 12.5-6).

In the New Testament scene the suggestion is not of repairing the temple but of taking care of the church and its *hagioi*. Peter went through all areas (Acts 9.32), and when he came to the *hagioi* at Lydda and found there (*heuren de ekei*) a paralytic, he proceeded to heal him.

The actual healing (Acts 9.34-35) is like an abbreviated version of Peter's first healing, that of the lame man at the entrance to the temple (Acts 3.1-10). And, in fact, the picture of the man collecting money at the temple entrance is colored by the next part of 2 Kings 12: the account of how the priest placed a chest for collecting money at the temple entrance (12.10-11). Again Luke has changed from the picture of an object (the collecting chest) to the picture of a person (the begging man).

h. *Section 8. Doing Works for the (Human) Temple—But Giving it No Silver or Gold (2 Kings 12.12-17; Acts 9.36, Tabitha; cf. Acts 3.6, the Lame Man)*
The Old Testament account of repairing the temple goes on to tell of those 'doing the works' (*poiountōn ta erga*) and of paying them for all they were doing (*poiousin*), for all expenses, as many as (*hosa*) were incurred (2 Kgs 12.12-13).

The next character in the New Testament is Tabitha, who is introduced as 'full of good works and alms which she did' (*ergōn...hōn epoiei*, 9.36); and later there is a reference to the garments 'as many as she made' (*hosa epoiei*, 9.39). Thus, while the Old Testament works were for the temple, the New Testament works are for people.

Tabitha's giving of alms (9.36) has an echo of the only previous time that Acts spoke of alms—in the healing of the lame man (Acts 3.2, 3, 10)—and so the very next section of the Old Testament once again colors the account of the healing in Acts 3.1-10: just as those in charge of the Old Testament temple were not to 'give' it various objects, particularly 'gold and...silver' (2 Kgs 12.14-17), so Peter said: 'Silver and gold I have not, but what I have I give you...' (Acts 3.6).

i. *Section 9. Falling Ill, Dying, Crying, and Joining Hands (2 Kings 13.14-19; Acts 9.37-39)*
Apart from formulaic summaries (13.1-13), the final chapter of the Elijah–Elisha narrative (2 Kgs 13) consists of the account of the death of Elisha (2 Kgs 13.14-25), a text which is echoed in the death of Tabitha:

> Old Testament:
> And Elisha was sick with the sickness by which he died.
>
> New Testament:
> In those days she becoming ill she died.

Luke is more succinct. But he inserts 'In those days', a phrase which, insofar as it suggests a new beginning, recaptures something of the newness of 2 Kings 13.

The two accounts then go on to tell of weeping: the king wept for Elisha (2 Kgs 13.14) and the widows wept for Tabitha (Acts 9.39). And there is also a certain joining of hands: Elisha put his hands over the hands of the king (2 Kgs 13.16) and Peter gave Tabitha his hand (Acts 9.41).

The major puzzle in this account is the ritual drawing of the bow and arrow (13.15-19). It seems to be important in the Old Testament narrative, but it is not clear how Luke has used it.

j. *Section 10. The Raising of the Dead to New Life, and the Bringing of Salvation to the Cities (2 Kings 12.18-19; 13.20-25; Acts 9.41-43)*

After Elisha had died, a dead man who was thrown into his tomb revived: 'and he came to life and he arose' (2 Kgs 13.21). Thus the final episode in the Elijah–Elisha narrative is a form of resurrection from the dead.

Nor is this recovery an isolated event. In its closing verses, the narrative opens out. It recalls the covenant with Abraham, Isaac, and Jacob, and then, echoing Elisha's final words about victory over Aram, it recounts the recovery of the cities taken by Hazael (2 Kgs 13.22-25). Thus, the salvation which was illustrated so dramatically in the raising of the dead man was continued in another form in the saving of whole cities.

Aspects of this multi-faceted recovery are reflected in the Tabitha story, most obviously in the raising of Tabitha from the dead (note the wording in Table 65: Old Testament, *ezēsen kai anestē*; New Testament, *anestē...zōsan*).

Apart from recounting the vivid instance of a resurrection from the dead, both texts also record a further form of resurrection which is more suffuse and widespread: the recovery or new life in the cities of Israel. At the end of the two Old Testament passages (2 Kgs 12 and 13), there is an account of saving or restoring cities (Jerusalem is saved from Hazael, 12.18-19; and the cities taken by Hazael are recovered, 13.22-25). In the New Testament, after Tabitha's resurrection, there is new life in 'the whole of Jaffa' (more knowledge, more faith, and a suggestion of Peter being at rest, Acts 9.42-43). Furthermore, these indications of faith and rest are part of a larger pattern which includes earlier summary verses (9.31, 35) referring to 'the whole of Judea, Galilee, and Samaria' and to 'Lydda and Sharon'. Thus, the sense of new life in 'the cities of Israel' (these words, 'the cities of Israel', are the last words in the entire Elijah–Elisha) is echoed by a sense of new life in the land and cities of the New Testament. In the New Testament, the new life is primarily in the area of faith; it is more internal.

42

Amid Hunger and Famine:
Good News for Outsiders (Acts 10–11)

The account of the church's breakthrough first to Cornelius and then to Antioch (Acts 10–11) virtually begins and ends with images of hunger: Peter's initial hunger on the roof (10.10) and, later, the prophets' foretelling of world-wide famine (11.27-30).

These two images of hunger/famine reflect the use of two texts from 2 Kings. The extensive Cornelius account (Acts 10.1–11.18) depends on the prolonged drama of the Samarian famine and the lepers (2 Kgs 6.24–ch. 7). And the prophets' brief foretelling of famine (Acts 11.27-30) adapts the short account of prophetic miracles amid famine (2 Kgs 4.38-44). Thus:

Prophetic miracles in famine (2 Kgs 4.38-44)
Samarian famine, good-news (6.24–ch. 7)   Cornelius and Peter's hunger (Acts 10.1–11.18)
                                          Prophets foretell famine (11.27-30)

It is appropriate to deal first (Block A) with Cornelius, and then (Block B) with the prophets facing famine.

1. Block A. The Hostile Scattering of the Syrians (2 Kings 6.24–ch. 7) as One Positivized Component of the Friendly Gathering Around Cornelius (Acts 10.1–11.18)

When Luke reshapes the last great foreign attack of the Elijah–Elisha narrative—Syria's reduction of Samaria to starvation, and God's scattering of the Syrians (2 Kgs 6.24–ch. 7) —he does not reproduce the picture of God scattering the foreigners. Instead, following the essentially positive New Testament attitude towards foreigners (Gentiles), Luke positivizes the story, reversing some negative aspects. In the story of Cornelius (Acts 10.1–11.18), Luke uses God's miraculous rout of the Syrians to depict God's miraculous calling of the Gentiles.

a. *The Texts: Introductory Analysis*
(1) *The routing of the Syrians (2 Kings 6.24–ch. 7)*. The Old Testament account begins by telling briefly of Ben-hadad sending his camp or army against Samaria (2 Kgs 6.24). The resulting scene is vivid (6.25-31): as the king of Samaria walks upon the city wall, he is confronted by a hunger which is so bad that in the search for food, some people resort to cannibalism.

The story then moves to the house of Elisha: first, to the arrival of the messenger of the angry king (6.32), and, following the arrival of the king and his aide, Elisha's prophecy that the starving city will be saved; by the next day, it will have food in abundance (6.33–7.1). But the king's aide is cynical, saying that even if God opened floodgates (*kataractas*) of food from heaven, there would not be such abundance. So Elisha adds a second prophecy: when the abundant food comes, the aide will eat none of it (7.2).

The action then moves back to the original focus of the story—Ben-hadad's army or camp. Fleeing death and seeking life, four lepers approach the camp at night and, to their astonishment, find it empty. God had intervened miraculously, using the sound of a great army which caused the Syrians to flee for their lives, leaving an abundance of food (7.3-8). Before dawn, the lepers were announcing the good news (*eu-aggelia*) to the starving city (7.9-11).

Back in the palace, however, reaction was hesitant, even hostile. The king was skeptical, yet he agreed to send and see (7.12-16).

The people were saved, but in rushing for the abundant food, they trampled the cynical aide to death. As a consequence, he never ate any of the food—thus fulfilling what was foretold (7.16-20).

In varying degrees, modern authors would say that the Old Testament account is not ordinary history; rather, it uses history for purposes that are theological, didactic, or prophetic. Its primary interest is not in the story's externals but in a deeper level.[1]

This emphasis on something deeper or more internal—something prophetic—helps explain Luke's reworking of the Old Testament account. If the externals are not the primary interest, Luke is not bound by them. He can leave them aside and concentrate instead on distilling a message: a prophetic message which finds new form or fulfillment in another narrative.

(2) *The Gathering around Cornelius (Acts 10.1–11.18)*. The New Testament story begins not in the camp of the Syrians but in the camp of the Romans, among the Italica cohort at Caesarea. There, Cornelius has an angelic vision and so he sends three men, including a soldier, to Peter (Acts 10.1-8).

The next, vivid scene shows Peter on a roof, and, as he is feeling hungry, he sees a startling heaven-sent sight which encourages him to eat forbidden food (unclean animals) (10.9-16).

Then the messengers arrive at Peter's gate (10.17-23), and the next day the action moves back to the original setting in Caesarea with the army man, Cornelius.

When Peter arrives, he does not find the place deserted, but the opposite. There is a whole assembly of relatives and friends ('he finds many gathered together', *pollous syneleluthotas*); and Cornelius tells him about his extraordinary vision (10.23b-33).

Peter proceeds to preach, announcing the good news (*eu-aggelizomenos*) of Jesus, and telling how the word was handed on from John to Jesus to the preachers (10.34-43).

While he was yet speaking, there was an outpouring from heaven—'the Holy Spirit fell... poured out'—and so the people were baptized (10.44-48).

Back in Jerusalem, some reaction was hostile, but Peter told exactly what had happened, and he reminded them that the outpouring of the Spirit corresponded to what had been foretold (11.11-18).

Thus, in place of the wartime saga of scattering the Syrians and flooding the starving with food, Luke tells a peaceful story of gathering some Gentiles and flooding them with the Spirit. And in both accounts, this outpouring (of saving food; of saving Spirit) happens as foretold.

Further comparison shows further similarities, and so the literary dependence begins to emerge. Luke may have used many sources in composing this expansive narrative

---

1. Several scholars have wondered whether this dramatic Old Testament narrative is factual. De Vaux and Gray tend to regard it as historical, yet de Vaux (1958: 145) feels that there is something 'artificial' about the context in which the narrative is set, and Gray (1970: 465) regards the narrative as popular history. J.M. Miller (1966: 441-54) holds that all the accounts of war between the dynasty of Omri and Syria are contrived. The major studies of Schmitt (1972: 37-41) and H. Schweizer (1974: 309-407 [381-82]) conclude that the narrative is didactical rather than factual, and that the focus of the story is not on an ancient war but on the way God works through the prophets.

(36 verses), but one of these sources was the account of how God saved the people from the Gentile Syrians. In Acts, God does not save from the Gentiles; God saves the Gentiles themselves. By a series of adaptations, including some reversals, Luke has once again produced a text which is more positive, more universal, and more internal.

Table 66. *Good News amid a Foreign Army (2 Kings 6.24–7.20; Acts 10.1–11.18)*

	Sending the Soldier/s	
1.	Ben-hadad musters his (hostile) army against Samaria (2 Kgs 6.24-25)	Cornelius sends his (devout) soldier to Peter (Acts 10.1-8)
	On the Wall/Roof	
2.	The king on the wall, amid terrible hunger hears of taboo eating (6.25-31)	Peter, on the roof, feels hungry and is told to eat forbidden food (10.9-16)
	Men at the Door/Gate	
3.	While Elisha is in his house, the king sends a man. 'When the messenger (*aggelos*) comes, close the door; the voice (*phōnē*)...is behind him' (6.32)	While Peter is in his house, the men sent by Cornelius seek him —— and arrive at the gate calling (*phōneō*) for Peter, telling of Cornelius's *aggelos* (10.17-23a)
	Heavenly Outpouring—Giving Life/Baptism	
4.	'While still speaking...' '...flood gates in/from heaven...' Lepers: Why die? (6.33–7.4)	
	Among the Gentiles: A Wondrous Scattering/Gathering	
5.	Lepers arose, entered the Syrian camp. There was not a man —for the Lord had made a sound (6.5-8)	Peter arose, entered Ceararea. He found many —for Cornelius had seen a man, heavenly (10.23b-33)
	Announcing the Good News	
6.	The lepers announce the good news from the camp to the city walls to the king's house (6.9-11)	Peter tells of the good news from John to Jesus to the apostles (10.34-43)
4.		'While still speaking...' the Holy Spirit fell...poured out. Peter: Why not baptism? (10.44-48)
	Two Responses: Negative and Open-Minded	
7.	Back in the palace: king is negative about the good news A servant advises: send and see (7.12-16)	Back in Jerusalem: some are critical about sharing with the Gentiles Peter's story...of sending, seeing (11.1-14)
	Recalling the Floodgates/Outpouring	
8.	The aide who spoke of floodgates. As foretold, he died (7.17-20)	The Spirit fell [was poured out] as foretold, giving life (11.15-18)

As so often, Luke's text is also clearer. The Old Testament account has a complexity, including a complexity of characters, which tends to make it obscure. The lepers, for instance, are fascinating and pivotal—they discover the good news and announce it—but to some degree they intrude in the story; they are present only for the central section (2 Kgs 7.3-10). Luke leaves them out, assigning their role of discovering and announcing

42. Amid Hunger and Famine

to Peter, someone who is woven into the entire narrative. The result is that Luke's account has a more obvious unity, an even flow which is calm and clear.

The outline in Table 66 summarizes the texts approximately.

b. *More Detailed Analysis*

The following analysis does not attempt to unravel the full complexity of Luke's use of 2 Kgs 6.24–ch. 7. Rather, the purpose is simply to identify some of the main lines of dependence.

(1) *Section 1. The Gentile leader sends his soldier/s (2 Kings 6.24; Acts 10.1-8)*. The Old Testament account begins by telling, in one brief verse, how Ben-hadad gathered 'all his camp/army' (*pasan tēn parembolēn*) and lay siege to Samaria (2 Kgs 6.24).

The New Testament account, describing Cornelius and his angelic vision, is modeled largely on earlier parts of Luke (Zechariah's vision, and the friendly centurion who sent Jewish elders to Jesus, Lk. 1.11-22; 7.2-5), but it also includes elements which correspond to the Old Testament sending of an army camp. It describes an army camp (at Caesarea) and the sending of 'two household slaves and a devout soldier' (*stratiōtēs*) to Peter (Acts 10.7-8).

While Ben-hadad sent 'all' his camp in a hostile way, Cornelius, from his camp, sends well-disposed representatives to whom he explains 'all' (*hapanta*, 10.8). The 'all' adds to these missions—in the Old Testament by making it more hostile, and in the New Testament by making it more positive.

Thus, Luke has changed the 'all' into something which is not only more positive, but also more internal—something which the messengers and soldier carry within them.

(2) *Section 2. On the wall/roof: hunger and forbidden food (2 Kings 6.25-31; Acts 10.9-16)*. The accounts now switch to the destinations: Samaria and Peter. And immediately, in both texts, the scene moves to an elevated open-air position and to hunger: amid great hunger (*limos megas*), the king of Samaria is on the wall (*epi tou teichous*) (2 Kgs 6.25-26a); and Peter is on the roof (*epi to dōma*) feeling hungry (*prospeinos*) (10.9-10a).

Against this background of hunger, the scenes then change in startling ways and they speak of food, the preparation of food, and forbidden eating. The Old Testament is intensely negative: a woman tells of an agreement, already half-fulfilled, to cook and eat her child and the child of another woman (2 Kgs 6.26b-29). Luke also speaks of eating food which is forbidden: while a meal is being prepared, Peter is encouraged by a vision to eat all manner of animals, including those previously regarded as unclean (Acts 10.10b-14).

Thus, Luke uses the taboo surrounding cannibalism as a starting point for speaking positively of the taboo surrounding the eating of animals classified as unclean.

(3) *Section 3. The Men who are sent to the house come to the foor/gate for Elisha/Peter (2 Kings 6.32; Acts 10.17-23a)*. The Old Testament scene now moves to Elisha's house (*oikos*) and it tells how the angry king 'sent a man' (*apesteilen andra*) to this house. In the New Testament scene, attention switches to 'the men sent' (*hoi andres hoi apestalmenoi*) by Cornelius; they are inquiring about Peter's house (*oikia*).

The men who are sent are then described as coming to the door (Old Testament) or gate (New Testament). In the Old Testament they are accompanied by the sound (*phōnē*) of their master, and in the New Testament they call (*phōneō*). The Old Testament man is described as a messenger (*aggelos*), and the New Testament men tell that their master has seen an angel (*aggelos*).

Luke has taken the picture of the man sent by the hostile king and by giving it a positive turn has used it as one component to describe the arrival of the men sent by Cornelius.

(4) *Section 4. Following the outpouring from heaven, why can the outsiders not move towards life/baptism (2 Kings 6.33–7.4; Acts 10.44-48).* The Old Testament now gives two brief scenes: first, Elisha's promise about God-given food flowing in abundance (flooding down from heaven) (literally, 'floodgates in heaven', *kataraktas en ouranō*) (2 Kgs 6.33–7.2); and then the quite different scene of the lepers, who, in face of death, ask why they should not make a move towards a chance of life (2 Kgs 7.3-4).

It is fairly clear how Luke has used the scene of the flood of food from heaven. It has contributed to the surprising picture of how the Holy Spirit 'fell' and 'was poured out' on the Gentiles (Acts 10.44-46). In other words, both texts suggest pictures of salvation pouring out of heaven; but instead of food, Luke tells of a salvation which is more spiritual and more internal.

As for the second Old Testament scene when the doomed lepers make their courageous bid to move from death to life ('Why [*Ti*] sit here waiting for death…?', 2 Kgs 7.3-4), given the context, it would seem that Luke used this as a starting point for speaking of the life-giving rite of baptism and for asking why the Gentiles should not be baptized ('What [*Mēti*] is to prevent…?', Acts 10.47-48).

Apart from the affinity between the miraculous floodgates and the Spirit-filled outpouring, the texts contain verbal similarities:

Old Testament:	New Testament:
Eti autou lalountos (While still speaking)	*Eti lalountos tou* (While still speaking)
hypo-meinō (remain with; wait for)	*ta rhēmata tauta* (these words)
Akouson (Hear)	*Ēkouon* (They heard)
apekrithē (he replied)	*apekrithē* (he replied)
to rhēma touto (this word)	*Mēti*… (What…?)
Ti…(Why…?)	*epi-meinai* (remain with)

(5) *Section 5. Arriving into the camp of the Gentiles: the miraculous absence/presence of people (2 Kings 6.5-8; Acts 10.23b-33).* When the lepers arrived into the Syrian camp they found something miraculous—there was not a man there! God had made a sound of armies which had sent the Syrians fleeing.

Peter's arrival into Cornelius's 'camp' is just the opposite. Instead of making a hostile sound and sending people fleeing in panic, Cornelius had issued a friendly call and caused people to gather. Yet the sense of something miraculous is not lost; when Cornelius tells Peter about his vision (someone in shining clothing, Acts 10.30), the scene echoes the miraculous emptiness of the Syrian camp:

They rose	Rising
and entered into	he entered into
the Syrian camp.	Caesarea.
And behold there was not a man there (*kai idou ouk estin anēr ekei*).	—
For the Lord had made a sound… so they ran and…fled for their their lives.	But Cornelius called friends so when Peter entered, he found many gathered together…
—	And behold a man stood before me (*kai idou aner estē enōpion mou*).

Where the Old Testament told of a miracle of *scattering*, the New Testament tells of *gathering* and a miracle. The scattering involved a hostile gentile army, but the gathering involves an army man and his gentile friends.

(6) *Section 6. Announcing the good news—passing it on and on (2 Kings 7.9-11; Acts 10.34-43)*. Some time after arriving at the camp and experiencing its food and treasure, the lepers describe the day as one of good news: 'This day is a day of good news' (*eu-aggelias estin*') (2 Kgs 7.9), and then they decide to go and announce (*an-aggelō*) the good news to the palace (7.9). So they set off and announce (again *an-aggelō*) the news at the gate of the city. And the gatekeepers in turn announce (*an-aggelō*) the news within the palace.

Luke takes this picture of progressive *eu-aggelia*—announced from camp to gate to palace—and uses it as just one component for Peter's speech in Cornelius's house. Peter introduces the divine word as heralding the good news of peace (*eu-aggelizomenos eirēnēn*), and then, using *kēryssō* ('proclaim', 10.37, 42), and *par-aggelō* ('command', 10.42), goes on to speak of the passing on of the word—from John the Baptist to Jesus to Jesus' followers.

Despite the huge gap between the two kinds of announcing, Peter's testimony has echoes of the lepers' experience:

Old Testament:
The lepers entered...and ate and drank (7.8)
The lepers announce: 'We entered the camp and behold...' (7.10)

New Testament:
Peter: 'We ate and drank with him' (10.41)

(7) *Section 7. Two Responses to the good news: one negative, the other open-minded (2 Kings 7.12-16; Acts 11.1-14)*. When the lepers' news of peace and salvation reaches inside the palace, there are two contrasting reactions. The king is negative and cynical regarding the Syrians (2 Kgs 7.12); but the servant is open-minded, and advises that they 'send and see' (*apo-stellō*, *horaō*, 7.13). And they saw the miraculous situation, and announced it to the king (7.15).

And when the news about Cornelius reaches the apostles and others in Jerusalem, there are likewise two contrasting reactions. The circumcision party disputes against the idea of going in and eating with Gentiles (Acts 11.1-3); but Peter, in a matter-of-fact way which implies open-mindedness, recounts how the events had happened—how people had been 'sent' (*apo-stellō*) and how Cornelius 'saw' (*horaō*) the angel (11.4-13, especially 11.11, 13).

The result of sending and seeing was salvation. In the Old Testament, the starving people went out and found abundant food (2 Kgs 7.16). And in the New Testament, Peter recounts how his arrival meant that Cornelius and all his house were 'saved' (Acts 11.14).

(8) *Section 8. Recalling the Word of the Lord About the Outpouring From Heaven (2 Kings 7.17-20; Acts 11.15-18)*. The final Old Testament picture is negative: the aide who had made the cynical comment about the floodgates died, as the man of God had foretold. The final New Testament picture, however, is positive: the Spirit fell, as the Lord had foretold.

Thus, the closing episode in both stories goes back to the idea of the outpouring from heaven (Old Testament: floodgates of food from heaven; New Testament: the Spirit falling, poured out). Again the outpouring of food (Old Testament) is replaced by the more internal idea of the outpouring of the Spirit (New Testament). And in both cases, the outpouring involves a fulfilling of the word of the Lord. But instead of ending with death ('and he died', 2 Kgs 7.20), Luke ends with life ('God gave...life', Acts 11.18).

c. *Conclusion*

One could go into more detail in analyzing these texts, yet what has been given here is enough to draw a straightforward conclusion. When Luke was composing the Cornelius narrative he used the Samaria story as one component. There are great differences between the texts, but most of the differences can be accounted for. And there are also persistent similarities which are sometimes quite unusual, and which, by and large, occur in the same order.

2. *Block B. How the Prophets Dealt with the Famine*
(2 Kings 4.38-44; Acts 11.27-30)

The end of 2 Kings 4 recounts two brief famine episodes: one about providing soup (4.38-41), the other about providing loaves (4.42-44). Both episodes contain problems with the initial food supply: the quality of the soup is poisonous, and the quantity of the loaves is inadequate. But with great simplicity, Elisha resolves the problems. When he throws some meal into the soup pot the soup becomes drinkable, and when he insists on distributing the loaves they are more than adequate. He uses almost identical words about the soup and the bread: 'Pour [it] out to the people, and let them eat' (4.41); 'Give [it] to the people and let them eat' (4.43). The two episodes are like two parts of a single story.

The essence of the story—both parts—is a readiness, even in face of famine, to work in a spirit of trust with what is available. When Elisha says to put on the large pot, the prospects of filling it do not look good, given the famine. And, in fact, the available herbs, though abundant, are deadly (4.39-40). As for the loaves, though good, they are few (4.43). But Elisha has a prophetic approach to the problem; he is introduced as sitting with the prophets (literally, 'the sons of the prophets', 4.38), and at the end he quotes the word of God, 'They will eat and have some left' (4.44).

The most obvious connection between this story and the gospels occurs in the multiplication of the loaves (Mk 6.30-44; 8.1-10; and parallels. See Chapter 15, under 'Key Connections'). But there is also a connection with Proto-Luke.

Within the texts pertaining to Proto-Luke, the nearest equivalent is the account of how, after Spirit-led prophets came down from Jerusalem to Antioch and foretold a worldwide famine, the disciples responded with a calm sense of purpose; they decided quite simply that they would give what they could (Acts 11.27-30). In other words, instead of starting a mournful litany—the situation was impossible, and their resources were inadequate, and where was God—they decided to work with what was available. And the way in which they sent their contribution—to the elders through the Spirit-filled Barnabas and Saul (Acts 11.30; cf. 11.22-26)—suggests not only order but the presence of a spiritual reality which encompasses or overflows.

Thus, Luke retains the essence of the Old Testament passage: the idea of using whatever one possesses, and the implied presence of a God whose presence or providence encompasses all.

The link between the texts is strengthened by the fact that apart from 1 Kgs 18.2-4, these are the only texts in the Elijah–Elisha narrative and in the New Testament to speak of both prophets (*prophētai*) and famine (*limos*) (2 Kgs 4.38; Acts 11.27-28).

Luke has made several adaptations including abbreviation, modernization, and universalization, but the most basic change is a form of internalization. Having reproduced the basic idea of famine, he leaves aside all the Old Testament details about various kinds of food, and he places greater emphasis on the general method for responding to famine, especially the internal attitudes of generosity and trust—things which in the Old Testament were implied only dimly.

43

The Final Pieces of the Puzzle

A few passages in the Elijah–Elisha narrative have been omitted. They are not crucial to the reconstruction of Proto-Luke; Luke uses them in texts which can be reconstructed by other means (either they overlap with material from Judges, or they occur within Acts 1.1–15.35). Nonetheless, for the sake of completeness it is necessary to give at least a summary of how they were used. The passages are as follows:

1 Kgs 20.35-43:	The prisoner who escaped	cf. Acts 12, Peter's escape
2 Kgs 6.1-7:	The tree/wood that saved what was lost	cf. see Lk. 19.1-10, Zacchaeus
2 Kgs 8.1-6:	The woman pleading for justice	cf. Lk. 18.1-8, the widow and judge

1. *The Prisoner Who Escaped (Causing Others to Pay with their Lives), and the Man Who Was Struck Mysteriously for Not Respecting God's Voice (1 Kings 20.35-43; Acts 12)*

In the final part of 1 Kings 20, a prophet condemns Ahab for allowing Ben-hadad to escape. The condemnation begins with a curious episode. In order to condemn more effectively, the prophet wants to be wounded—apparently to look like one of those who had fought against Ben-hadad—and so he asks a man to strike him. But the man refuses, and for this refusal to listen to God's voice, the man himself is struck down by a lion (1 Kgs 20.35-36).

Having acquired his wound, the prophet poses as a combatant and tells the king a story: he, the combatant, had been entrusted with a prisoner whom it was his duty to guard under sanction of punishment. But he had been preoccupied by other things and the prisoner had escaped. The king, hearing the story, told the disguised prophet that he indeed deserved punishment. At that, the prophet pulled off the disguise and told the king that he, the king, was the culprit; he had Ben-hadad in his power but allowed him to escape and for that he would pay with his life (1 Kgs 20.37-43).

Luke used this text as one minor ingredient in the account of how Peter escaped from King Herod's prison (Acts 12). In both cases, a prisoner is to be guarded by a soldier or soldiers, and when the prisoner escapes, the king says that the guard/s should be condemned to die (1 Kgs 20.39-40; Acts 12.4, 17, 19).

Luke's literary dependence on this Old Testament text is clearest in his use of some of the details concerning the man who was struck for not attending to God's voice. In Luke's account, Herod is struck for not respecting God's voice, allowing his own voice to be confused with God's (Acts 12.22-23). The similarities are significant:

> Old Testament:
> The man (*anthrōpos*) would not strike him.
> Because you did not hear the voice of the Lord
> (*Anth' hōn ouk ēkousas tēs phōnēs Kyriou*)
> a lion will strike you.
> And as soon as he left him
> a lion struck him (*epataxen auton*).

New Testament:
The people cried out, 'It is the voice (*phōnē*) of a god
and not of a man (*anthrōpos*).
And immediately
an angel of the Lord struck him (*epataxen auton*)
because he did not give the glory to God
(*anth' hōn ouk edōken tēn doxan tō theō*).

The key offence in both texts is lack of respect for the voice of God. In the Old Testament, God sends a lion, but in the New Testament, God sends an angel, as frequently happens in Luke, and as had already happened in Acts 12.7.

2. *Jordan's/Jericho's Trees Add a Dimension to the House: The Finding of the Lost Axehead as One Internalized Component in the Saving of the Lost Zacchaeus (2 Kings 6.1-7; Luke 19.1-10)*

The housing was narrow where the prophets lived, so they went to the Jordan to cut trees for better housing; and they asked Elisha to come with them on this house-building expedition. So begins 2 Kings 6, and the brief episode which first seemed to be about narrow housing and trees then turns into a lost-and-found story. An axehead fell into the water—a borrowed one (due to be given back)—but Elisha sought out the spot where it fell, and with the help of a stick (literally a tree, *xylon*), raised up the lost axehead.

In dealing with this lost-and-found story, Luke has made one pivotal change: the focus changes from an object (an axehead) to a person (Zacchaus, Lk. 19.1-10). Instead of telling how the prophet first sought the place where the axehead fell and then used (part of) a tree to raise it and recover it, Luke shows Jesus as seeking out Zacchaeus, and Jesus speaks of himself as having come 'to seek and save what was lost' (Lk. 19.10). The lost-and-found story has been turned around to give a better idea of what is happening within human beings; it has been internalized.

Once account is taken of the central phenomenon of internalization, the other details begin to fall into place:

- The locations (Jordan, Jericho) are close to one another.
- The use of trees (to counter the narrowness of the housing and to raise the lost axehead) becomes the use of a sycamore to counter Zacchaeus's smallness, and ultimately to save him from being lost.
- The emphasis on the need for new housing (literally, 'dwelling', the verb *oikeō*, 2 Kgs 6.1-2) become the idea of saving the 'house' (*oikos*, Lk. 19.9).
- The prophets' invitation to Elisha to come 'with' (*meta*) them on the house-building expedition (2 Kgs 6.3-4) is turned around to become Jesus' request to Zacchaeus to stay in his house (Lk. 19.5-6). Thus, the notion of being 'with' someone gives way to the idea of abiding in someone's house.

There is much in the Zacchaeus episode which is not at all dependent on 2 Kgs 6.1-7. Yet, from Luke's opening reference to the location (Jericho) as far as the final word ('lost'), the two accounts show affinities which are persistent and consistent. The simplest way of explaining the data it to say that Luke has internalized the Old Testament story. The narrowness or smallness now applies not to a place or house but to a person. And what is sought and saved is not an iron axehead but, again, a person.

3. *The Woman Who Pleaded and Received Justice:*
The Story of the Shunammitess (2 Kings 8.1-6) as a Minor Component
in the Parable of the Widow and the Judge (Luke 18.1-8)

Finally, as a kind of epilogue to the story of the woman of Shunem, there is an account of how, after the end (*meta to telos*) of seven years of enforced exile, she came back to cry (*boaō*) to the king for the restoration of her house and lands. As it happened, just when the king was listening to Gehazi's account of how Elisha had once raised the woman's son, the woman herself arrived crying (*boōsa*, participle of *boaō*) for justice. And so, without any suggestion of a delay, the king saw to it that everything was restored to her.

This story has obvious similarities and dissimilarities with the parable of the widow who kept coming to the unscrupulous judge seeking justice or vengeance against her enemy. Both women take a long time to achieve justice: one because of her long seven-year absence, the other because the judge will not respond. But eventually, both are successful.

Luke's parable uses the Shunem story as one small component. His dependence is seen not only in the general similarity but also in some details. In the judge's complaint about the long time during which the widow keeps coming back, there are echoes of the long time of the Shunammitess's exile: 'He did not wish for a time, but after (*meta*) this he said to himself, "…I will avenge her lest in [the] end (*eis telos*)…"' (Lk. 18.4-5). And at the end of the parable Jesus tells how God will avenge those who are crying to him (*boōntōn*, participle of *boaō*) (18.7).

Orientational Conclusion to Chapters 41–43

The literary reworkings examined in Chapters 41–43 vary in quantity and clarity. In Chapter 41, regarding the use of nearly five Old Testament chapters (2 Kgs 9.14–ch. 13) in Acts 9.19b-43, there is a radical transition from a historiography which ranges over a major transition in the history of ancient Israel to a historiography which, as in other Lukan texts, is more oriented to a new kind of Israel where there is a more obvious emphasis on what is personal and internal. Consequently, the differences are great, but they are essentially intelligible; and the similarities are substantial (see Table 65 [pp. 430-32]).

Likewise in Chapter 42: the use of the two famine-related texts, especially 2 Kgs 6.24–ch. 7, while entailing radical change, also involves orderly substantial similarities. (Again, see the main outline, Table 66 [p. 438].)

In the case of Chapter 43, however, the similarities are generally neither as orderly nor as substantial. This does not make them insignificant, but it means that on their own, their claims to literary dependence would probably not survive. They are somewhat like the last recalcitrant pieces of a jigsaw puzzle: their place finally becomes clear, but only because so many other pieces are already in place.

Despite the weak claims of these last pieces, what is important is that the claims of the larger texts (the famine/siege in 2 Kgs 6.24–ch. 7, and the climactic 2 Kgs 9.14–ch. 13) are intelligible and substantial.

Unit 11. Proto-Luke and Judges

Orientational Introduction to Chapters 44–52:
Domesticated Wars—An Introduction to Luke's Reworking of Judges*

Unlike Judges, Luke–Acts does not recount colorful wars. Proto-Luke has domesticated the wars, internalized them (some would say spiritualized). A partly similar phenomenon occurs in some Qumran literature: war is largely internal, between light and darkness. In relatively simple scenes, Luke integrates images adapted from war: for instance, the fall of many in Israel (Lk. 2.34), the sword piercing the heart (Lk. 2.35), and the making of war on God (Acts 5.39). Even when he reproduces a classic element from war accounts—the sudden appearance of 'a great army (*stratia*)'—the army is 'an army of heaven praising God' (Lk. 2.13). Hence, Luke's focus in reworking Judges is not on the wars themselves, but on the deeper issues behind the wars, especially the drama of sin and divine mercy.

Luke's use of Judges is quite systematic. First, the opening (Judg. 1–3), mostly Israel's expansion, helps depict the gospel's expansion (Acts 12–14). Second, the highpoint, the Samson narrative (Judg. 13–16), opens to help form a frame (cf. Lk. 1–2; Acts 9–15). Third, the remaining chapters (Judg. 4–12 and 17–21) are spread across the gospel, generally in order:
- Judges 4–5, Deborah and Jael, contribute to Luke 1–2 (cf. especially Mary and Anna).
- Judges 6–12 and 17–18 help fill Jesus' journey (cf. Lk. 16.1–19.10).
- Judges 19–21, the painful finale, generally contributes to the passion narrative (Lk. 22–24).

Table 4 (p. 95) provides a fuller outline, following the order of Luke–Acts. However, in the following chapters (44–52), when actually comparing the texts, it seems better to follow the order of Judges (see table of Contents, Part III, Unit 11).

---

*   Among these nine chapters (44–52), the longest (Chapter 47) was published in *Journal of Higher Criticism* (1995).

44

The Mission to Gentile Territory:
Judges 1.1–3.6 as a Skeletal Framework for Acts 13–14

The opening chapters of Judges (Judg. 1–3) contain the double introduction (1.1–3.6) and a triad of judges (Othniel, Ehud, and Shamgar, 3.7-31). These texts have been used in Acts 12–14 as follows:
- The introduction's sense of mission—Israel's expansion into Gentile Canaan (Judg. 1.1–3.6)—has contributed to describing the church's missionary expansion among the Gentiles (Acts 13–14).
- The actions of the judges, especially Ehud, in overcoming tyranny (Judg. 3.7-31) have contributed to the overcoming of Herod (Acts 12).

This chapter concentrates on the diverse forms of expansion (Judg. 1.1–3.6; Acts 13–14).

1. *Two Accounts of Expansion (Judges 1.1–3.6; Acts 13–14)*

More than any other event of the early church, the missionary journey of Barnabas and Paul (Acts 13–14) constitutes the decisive breakthrough to the Gentile world. This major development had been prepared for in various ways, particularly by the ministry of Philip to Samaria and the Ethiopian eunuch (Acts 8), by Peter's baptizing of Cornelius (Acts 10), and by the development of the church in (Syrian) Antioch (Acts 11.18b-30). But it is the journey across the sea, first to Cyprus and then to (Pisidian) Antioch, which shows the new message as spreading indefinitely. By the end of the mission, five cities of Asia Minor have been evangelized—Antioch, three Lycaonian cities (Iconium, Lystra and Derbe) and, finally, Perga, near the sea—and with no stop in view, the message is already halfway to Athens.

The historicity and sources of this account are deeply controverted (Haenchen 1971: 400-404), but at least one source can be identified: the summary account, from the beginning of Judges, of how Israel had once spread into the Gentile land of Canaan (Judg. 1.1–3.6). Distilled to its essence, this ancient account has provided Luke with a skeletal framework, and around this framework he has added information from the first century and from the early church.

The beginning of Judges, one of the books which in ancient times were known as the Former Prophets, is very appropriate for Luke's purpose. If the church was to be considered as the new Israel and as the fulfillment of the prophets, then the development of the church should echo that of Israel. In particular, the spreading of the church into Gentile territory should echo and fulfill the spread of ancient Israel into the Gentile land of Canaan.

Judges 1.1–3.6 is not the first Old Testament text to tell of spreading into Gentile land. That event had already been spoken of in the book of Joshua, somewhat as earlier parts of Acts had already given intimations and indications of the spread of the church. But it is the beginning of Judges which supplies a summary of the process of settling in Canaan.

Recognition of the dependence of Acts 13–14 on Judg. 1.1–3.6 does not resolve the issue of historicity—an issue that would require distinguishing and evaluating Luke's other sources—but it underlines what others have often stated, namely that for Luke the events of Christian history needed to be set in the theological context of God's larger work, particularly as that work was experienced in ancient times.

Table 67. *Moving into New Territory (Judges 1.1–3.6; Acts 13–14)*

	Judges 1	Acts 13
1.	Embarking on the settlement of Canaan: the choosing of Judah, and of Simon (1.1-3)	Embarking on the Gentile mission: the choosing of Barnabas and Saul (13.1-3)
2.	First expedition (1.4-8): 'They found' Adoni-zedek, who cut hands, and cut his hands. (Then they conquered Jerusalem, 1.8)	Mission to Cyprus (13.4-13): 'They found' Bar-Jesus the magician, and left him groping for a guiding hand. (Then John returned to Jerusalem, 13.14)
3.	Southern expedition (1.9-16): —In Canaan: conquest of opponents —The woman in a drama of giving and asking —The 'ransom of water' * Moses' relatives go to the people	Mission to Pisidian Antioch (13.14-25): * Paul goes to the synagogue —Speech: Conquest of Canaan —The people in a drama of giving and asking —John's 'baptism of repentance'
4.	Destruction… following the words of Moses. The inhabitants of Jerusalem (1.17-21)	The inhabitants of Jerusalem, fulfilled the prophets by destroying Jesus (13.26-29)
5.	Luz: a story of rebirth, and of a promise which saved from doom (1.22-26)	The resurrection of Jesus, and the promise to save from corruption (13.30-37)
6.	Mingling with the foreigners (1.27-33)	Turning to the Gentiles (13.38-49)
7.	The Amorites react harshly The Amorite border (1.34-36)	The Jews react harshly Expulsion from the borders (13.50-52)
	Judges 2.1–3.6	Acts 14
8.	Future problems: You will make covenants with foreigners, and their gods will mislead you (2.1-5)	Problems in Iconium and Lycaonia: Jews form a plot with foreigners; crowds try to worship the apostles as gods (14.1-13)
9.	* Summary of a conclusion: * a generation went home, * lived a long time, * and knew the work of the Lord (2.6-7)	+ The apostles' quick reaction to idolatry: We are not gods. Turn to the God who allowed the nations to go their own way (14.14-18)
10.	From the death of Joshua to the raising up of judges (2.8-17a)	From the apparent death of Paul to the appointment of presbyters (14.19-23)
11.	+ Israel's quick reaction to idols: Israel regards idols as gods, and turns back from the way of God. God allows the nations to stay (2.17b–3.6)	* Concluding summary: * the apostles went back to their starting point, * made known the work of the Lord, * and sojourned not a short time (14.24-28)

2. Introductory Analysis

Judges 1.1–3.6[1] consists of two introductions (1.1–2.5 and 2.6–3.6). Both recount the process of settlement, but while the first emphasizes its progress, the second tells more of its problems, particularly the problem of idolatry—of worshipping pagan gods (2.17b–3.6).

Luke's account of the missionary journey is traditionally divided into two chapters (Acts 13 and 14), and while the first of these usually describes the journey's progress (the advance from Syrian Antioch, through Cyprus, to Pisidian Antioch), the second tells of many problems, including the problem of how Paul and Barnabas were almost worshipped as pagan gods (14.1-18).

By and large, Luke has used the two introductions as the basis, respectively, for Acts 13 and 14. The one exceptional text is the end of the first introduction (Judg. 2.1-5), a passage which, in preparation for the problems of the second introduction, speaks of problems, particularly that of being ensnared by pagan gods. When Luke is describing how the apostles were almost worshipped as foreign gods (Acts 14.1-18), he combines this early idolatry passage (Judg. 2.1-5) with the later one (2.17b–3.6). Thus, Judg. 2.1-5 becomes a source for part of Acts 14.

What Judg. 1.1–3.6 supplies is just one skeletal component. The great speech which Paul gives in the Antioch synagogue (Acts 13.17-41), for instance, does indeed incorporate the essence of part of Judges 1, but most of it, particularly concerning Jesus, is drawn from other sources. And the attempt at idolizing Paul and Barnabas, while it draws quite heavily on the idolatry passages in Judges, begins with a healing for which Judges apparently has no equivalent (Acts 14.8-10). Table 67 simplifies the relationship, but captures its essence.

3. More Detailed Analysis

a. *Section 1. Embarking on a New Mission: The Choosing of Judah and Simon (Judges 1.1-3) and of Barnabas and Saul (Acts 13.1-3)*

The book of Judges begins with a brief account of the Israelites asking God who should open the campaign against the Canaanites. God chooses Judah, who in turn chooses his brother Simeon as a partner. So Simeon sets off with him.

In Acts 13, the mission to the Gentiles begins as the Antioch church is worshipping, when the Holy Spirit chooses Barnabas and Saul for a special work, and the church sends them off.

The essence of both beginnings is the choosing of two people to lead a new mission. In both cases, the decision as to who will lead comes primarily from God, but there is also a human role. It is Judah who asks Simeon; and it is the church which sends forth Barnabas and Saul. This involves a significant change. In Acts, there is a direct choosing of two (rather than one), and the larger group (the church) retains a role in the mission of the two. Thus, in place of the Old Testament picture of an apparent concentration of power in one person (Judah), Luke portrays a scene in which power is more diffused and balanced.

At times, Luke's account is more elaborate than that of Judges—for instance, in the description of the church (Acts 13.1)—yet the texts seem to have several affinities:

---

1. The study of LXX version of Judges is complicated by the existence of two texts. For a review of the textual problems and the various editions, see Jellicoe 1968: 280-83; Bodine 1980a; 1980b; Satterthwaite 1991. This study takes account of both texts, but since the variations in the texts do not significantly alter the issue under discussion, it seems better not to undertake detailed analysis of the relative merits of specific readings.

The children of Israel asked the Lord: 'Who shall lead out (*aph-ēgoumenos*)?'	In Antioch…the church… was worshipping the Lord
And the Lord said, 'Judah… I have given the land into his hand. Judah: Come into my portion…'	The Holy Spirit said, 'Separate out (*aph-orisate*) for me Barnabas and Saul… for [my] work…'
And Simeon set out with him.	Then they laid their hands on them, And they sent them off.

The significance of some of the details is debatable, but the overall continuity is considerable. In particular, the giving over of land (into the hand) is replaced in the New Testament by giving over something more internal (through hands). In both cases, however, it is God who endows the hands.

b. *Section 2. The First Expedition into Gentile Territory (Bezek; Cyprus), and the Overcoming of the Leading Enemy (Adoni-bezek; Bar-Jesus, Judges 1.4-8; Bar-Jesus, Acts 13.4-13)*

The settlement of Canaan begins with an easy sweeping victory. The Lord simply delivers the Canaanites into Judah's hands, and without any apparent problem, he routs ten thousand men at Bezek (Judg. 1.4).

The mission to the Gentiles begins apparently with equal ease. Impelled by the Holy Spirit, there is an easy progression through Cyprus, announcing the word of God (Acts 13.4-6a).

But then the two missions meet strange opponents. The mission to occupy Canaan encounters Adoni-bezek (or Adoni-zedek), a chilling character. Under his table, scrambling for scraps, he had seventy kings with their thumbs and big toes cut off. The implication, for his regime as a whole, is a form of power which was both vast and horrific.

The man encountered in Cyprus, Bar-Jesus (Elymas), is initially less overpowering, but as a magician and false prophet he thinks he can manipulate the proconsul, the representative of the Roman Empire, and Paul describes him almost as if he were the source of all evil (Acts 13.6b-10).

But both opponents are overcome and, in their different ways, both are left groping. Having lost his own thumbs and big toes, Adoni-bezek is led to death in Jerusalem. And Bar-Jesus, struck with blindness, goes away looking for someone to lead him. In tentative outline:

Judges	*Acts*
Canaan: God-given success (1.4)	Cyprus: Spirit-sent preaching of God's word (13.4-5)
'They found Adoni-bezek' in Bezek (1.5)	At Paphos, 'they found Bar-Jesus' (13.6)
They cut his hands and big toes (1.6)	
Adoni-bezek had seventy kings with cut hands scrambling under his table (1.7)	Bar-Jesus tries to control the (Roman) proconsul. He is immensely evil (13.8-10)
	Paul: The hand of God is on you. And they leave Bar-Jesus groping for a hand to lead him (13.11)
They led him to Jerusalem, and they conquered Jerusalem (1.7b-8)	They sailed away…and John returned to Jerusalem (13.13)

44. The Mission to Gentile Territory

Without attempting a full analysis, one detail is worth noting. The reference to hands, which already appeared in the preceding passages (Judg. 1.1-3; Acts 13.1-3), reappears here in both texts in varied form.

c. Section 3. A Further Expedition into Gentile Territory (Southern Canaan; Pisidian Antioch) (Judges 1.9-16; Acts 13.14-25)

Following the clash with Adoni-bezek at Bezek, Judges recounts a southern advance which defeats the Canaanites and leads to a drama of giving and asking (Caleb gives his daughter Achsah to Othniel, and she embarks on a process of asking).

In Acts, the clash in Cyprus is followed by the mission to Pisidian Antioch, and in the synagogue there Paul speaks first of the conquest of Canaan and then of a drama of giving and asking (God gives judges, and then the people ask for a king).

Again, the old sacred history has provided a skeleton for the new. In simplified outline:

Judges 1.9-16	Acts 13.14-25
—	Those around Paul went to the Antioch synagogue and sat there (13.14-16a) (*ekathisan. Meta...ton laon*)
Judah conquered southern Canaan, and defeated various opponents (1.9-10)	God led Israel from Egypt to Canaan, and destroyed seven nations (13.16b-20a)
Caleb's 'giving' of daughter Achsah, and the 'asking' for a field (1.11-14a)	The 'giving' of judges, and the 'asking' for a king (13.20b-22)
Result: She cries for water (literally, 'a blessing...a ransom of water', 1.14b-15)	Result: Jesus, announced by John's 'baptism of repentance' (13.23-25)
Moses' relatives went up to the sons of Judah and dwelt with the people (1.16) (*katōkēsen meta tou laou*)	—

The water acquired by Achsah is quite different from the water of John's baptism, but it is vital to life ('a blessing...a ransom'), and its position at the beginning of Judges heightens its significance. Thus, for Luke, it provides an appropriate starting point for speaking of John's baptism.

The motif of the hands, though clear in Acts (to gain a hearing, Paul signals with his hand, 13.16), is much less certain in the Old Testament. A limited number of Hebrew manuscripts tell of Achsah clapping her hands as she asks for water (Judg. 1.14).

d. Section 4. Providential Destruction (Judges 1.17-21; Acts 13.26-29)

Judges now recounts two enigmatic passages, one dealing with thorough destruction (the ban, 1.17-21) and the other with surprising survival (the man from Luz, 1.22-26).

The destruction involves the Canaanite city of Zephath. It was delivered to the ban and renamed Anathema (or Destruction) (Judg. 1.17). Yet this barbaric episode is described as if it were part of a larger, positive process—a providence which, in accordance with the backing of Lord and the words of Moses, simultaneously guides and limits Judah in its struggle with the Canaanites (Judg. 1.18-21).

In Acts, Paul turns to the question of the death of Jesus, and even though his message is drawn from New Testament times, it is expressed with overtones of Judges—as a destructive process which nonetheless fulfilled the words of the prophets. Thus, Luke sees the providence which encompassed the evil of Jesus' death as forming a continuity with the providence which surrounded the evil of certain Old Testament events.

There is some linguistic continuity:

Old Testament:
anethema-tisan autēn kai exōlethreusen autēn…
tous katoikountas…
kai exēren…
ton katoikounta en Ierousalēm…ouk exēran

New Testament:
hoi katoikountes en Ierousalēm…anairethēnai auton

Old Testament:
they anathematized (*an-athematizō*) and destroyed it…
the inhabitants…
and drove out (*ex-aireō…*)
inhabiting Jerusalem…did not drive out (*ex-aireō*)

New Testament:
the inhabitants of Jerusalem…had him done away with (*an-aireō*)

Luke's single word, *an-aireō* ('to do away with/abolish/kill'), which he also uses elsewhere, is close in meaning to the Old Testament word *exolethreuō* ('to destroy utterly'). In addition, it reflects aspects of *an-athematizō* ('to place under the ban') and *ex-aireō* ('to drive out'), thus acting as a synthesis of three Old Testament verbs.

e. *Section 5. And Surprising Survival/Resurrection (Judges 1.22-26; Acts 13.30-37)*
In this next passages from Judges, the idea of destruction remains, but there is a change of tone, and the emphasis falls not on destruction, but on survival. The story concerns a forgotten name (Luz, the former name of Bethel) and an apparently doomed man (the nameless man who, having survived the destruction of Bethel, goes away with his clan and builds a city, naming it Luz). So the story is not only about the *destroying* of Bethel but even more so about the man who *escaped destruction* and a name which was *reborn* (1.23-26). It is a story which is associated with the tribe of Joseph (1.22).

Whatever the original meaning/s of this episode, Luke apparently uses it as a starting point for speaking of the resurrection—for an account of how, unlike others, Jesus escaped corruption (Acts 13.30-37). (Perhaps for Luke, as for some early church writers, Joseph evoked resurrection.)

In both accounts, the escape from destruction is promised in advance—by the Josephites to the otherwise doomed man (Judg. 1.24), and, through the Scriptures, promised by God to Jesus (Acts 13.32-35).

f. *Section 6. Breaking the Barriers: The Israelites Mingle with the Canaanites (Judges 1.27-33) and Paul Turns to the Gentiles (Acts 13.38-49)*
Judges now recites a litany of failures: five tribes, one after another, were unable to drive out the Canaanites, and so there was intermingling. It is said of the third tribe, Zebulun (at the center of the litany), that 'the Canaanites dwelt in the midst of them' (Judg. 1.30).

This intermingling or breaking of barriers seems to have provided Luke with a starting point for recounting how Paul also broke barriers by turning to the Gentiles. The essence of both accounts is that the breaking of the barriers is due, at least in part, to a failure on the part of the chosen group (Israel; the Jews). And, as a matter of detail, it is said in both cases that they 'were not able' (*ouk edynasthē*, Judg. 1.32; *ouk ēdyn ēthēte*, Acts 13.38) to accomplish full independence or self-sufficiency.

44. The Mission to Gentile Territory

g. *Section 7. A Harsh Reaction and a Reassertion of Boundaries (Judges 1.24-26; Acts 13.50-52)*

Having spoken of a process of intermingling, Judges switches briefly to a picture of confrontation and separation. The protagonists in this harsh process are the Amorites. First, they brought distress (*ex-ethlipsen*) on the Danites (Judg. 1.31), and later, there is a reminder of the Amorite border (*orion*, 1.36).

In Acts, also, the breaking of the barriers is followed by a brief scene of confrontation and separation. The Jews incited a persecution, and so people expelled (*ex-ebalon*) Paul and Barnabas from their boundaries (*orion*, 13.50).

Yet, between Judges and Acts there is a great difference in mood. While the reference to the border of Edom brings the account of Israel's campaign to a deflated stop, Paul uses expulsion from the borders of Pisidian Antioch as the occasion for a further journey to Iconium (Acts 13.51)

h. *Section 8. The Intensification of Problems, Particularly of False Covenants and Idolatry (Judges 2.1-5; Acts 14.1-13)*

When an angel speaks in Judges (2.1-5), its warning concerns two future evils: that Israel, forgetting the God who led the way out of Egypt, will form covenants with the Gentiles (2.1-2a); and that Israel will succumb to the attraction of pagan gods (2.2b-5).

Variations on these problems appear in Acts. While Paul's ministry in Iconium has echoes of the exodus from Egypt—it is accompanied by 'signs and wonders' (Acts 14.3; cf. 7.36, 'doing signs and wonders in the land of Egypt')—the Jews form a kind of deadly union with the Gentiles and they manage to drive the apostles out (14.1-7). And when Paul is in Lycaonia, there is the attempt to treat himself and Barnabas as false gods (14.8-13).

Judges 2.1-5	Acts 14.1-13
The Lord brought you up from Egypt (2.1a)	The Lord does signs and wonders (14.1-3)
Covenants with foreigners (2.1b-2a)	Jews join Gentiles in an assault (14.4-7)
?	Lystra: crippled man is healed (14.8-10)
Their gods shall be a scandal (2.2b-5)	Crowd regards the apostles as gods (14.11-13)

These latter texts concerning unreal gods (Judg. 2.2b-5; Acts 14.10-13; cf. 14.9-10) share a significant word cluster. (*eis*)*akouō, eipa/en, phōnē, hoi theoi, laleō, epēre/an tēn phōnēn autōn, kaleō, thuō* ('hear, say, voice, the gods, speak, raised up their voice, call, sacrifice').

i. *Section 9. A Concluding Summary (Judges 2.6-7; Acts 14.24-28): Going Home, Spending a Long Time, and Knowing the Work of the Lord*

The second introduction to Judges begins with a summary account which concludes the story of Joshua's generation. It tells how the people went to their homes, served the Lord for many days, and knew what God had done (Judg. 2.6-7). It is the end of their story and of their journey to Canaan.

Luke uses this summary to conclude the story of the apostles' journey to the Gentiles (Acts 14.24-28). In outline:

Judges 2.6-7	Acts 14.24-28
The people went to their homes (2.6)	The apostles returned to Antioch (14.24-26a)
They served the Lord many days (2.7a) As many (*hosa*) as knew all the great work (*to ergon*) of the Lord, as many things as he had done (*hosa epoiēsen*) in Israel (2.7b)	...the work (*to ergon*) which they fulfilled they made known [literally 'announced']... as many things as God had done (*hosa epoiēsen*) ...for the Gentiles (14.26b-27) They sojourned not a short time (14.28)

j. *Section 10. From the Leader's (Apparent) Death to the Appointment of Other Leaders (Judges 2.8-17a; Acts 14.19-23)*

After summarizing the end of Joshua's generation, Judges tells of the end of Joshua himself—how he died and was buried (Judg. 2.8-10). Then the story moves quickly to recount how the Israelites' situation became one of infidelity and distress (2.11-15), and how God raised up other leaders—judges (2.16-17a).

In Acts, there is a succession of events which, though very different at first sight, on analysis turns out on analysis to be radically similar. First, there is the apparent demise of the leader, Paul (left for dead by Jews who had stoned him, 14.19-20). Then, following an exhortation concerning fidelity and distress, there is the appointment of other leaders—presbyters. In outline:

Judges 2.8-17a	*Acts 14.19-23*
The death of Joshua (2.8-10)	The apparent death of Paul (14.19-20)
Israel abandons its God and so suffers distress (2.11-15)	Exhortation: Abide in the faith and come to God through distress (14.21-22)
The raising up of judges (2.16-17a)	The appointing of presbyters (14.23)

The negative-looking elements in Judges—particularly death and distress—are incorporated by Luke so that they are part of something positive. The stoning of Paul becomes a step to evangelization. Distress, instead of being a punishment from God, becomes a way of entering God's kingdom. And even the appointment of leaders, which in the Old Testament is surrounded by a sense of crisis, becomes in Acts a process which is calm and hopeful.

k. *Section 11. The Quick Reaction to Idolatry (Towards It, Judges 2.17b–3.6; Away From It, Acts 14.14-18)*

Judges describes the Israelites as quickly following the Gentiles and going their own way (literally, quickly leaving the way [*hodos*] of their fathers, 2.17b; cf. 2.19, 23)—with the result that God, in anger, allowed the nations to stay (2.20–3.6).

The apostles, however, quickly reject the movement towards idolatry ('they rushed into the [Gentile] crowd crying out…', Acts 14.14), and, while speaking of the kind providence which allowed the nations to go their own way, they call the crowd back to the living God. Thus, Luke keeps the idea of people tending towards idolatry and of God adapting to the situation, but his overall interpretation is more positive. The Old Testament momentum away from God becomes, in Acts, a momentum towards God.

The texts share several words: *hodos…poreuomai…autōn, poieō houtōs/tauta, apo/epistrephō…opisō/epi…theōn/theon, ethnoi, aphiēmi, panta(s) …panta(s), genea, akouō, didōmi* ('way…go…their, do thus/this, turn back/to…back/to…gods/God, nations, allow/leave, all…all, generation, hear, give').

4. *Conclusion*

At first sight, it may seem that there is no relation between the complex military conquest of ancient Israel (Judg. 1.1–3.6) and the missionary journey of Barnabas and Saul (Acts 13–14). Ultimately, however, both deal with the development of Israel: the establishment of the first Israel in Judges and the establishment of the new Israel in Acts. Once that overarching conceptual transition from *Israel* to a *new Israel* has already taken place—it occurs for instance in Paul (1 Cor. 10.18; Gal. 6.16; cf. Acts 1.6)—then the opportunity exists for making a corresponding transition between *the history of establishing Israel* and *the history of establishing new Israel*.

This opportunity—this implicit need to portray the establishment of a new Israel—provides part of the external plausibility for claiming Luke used Judges. In other words, given the idea of a new Israel, the 'renewing' or reshaping of Israel's history makes sense.

Luke's use of Judges is indicated, too, by similarities which are persistent and essentially in the same order. And, in the context, the differences are generally intelligible.

45

Escaping the Royal Guard:
Ehud's Overcoming of Eglon (Judges 3.7-31)
as a Framework for Peter's Escape from Herod (Acts 12)

Following its double introduction, Judges tells briefly of a triad of judges: Othniel, Ehud, and Shamgar (3.7-31). The focus of this triad is Ehud (3.12-30), the man who, having slain the tyrannical Eglon, escaped.

Luke uses this outwitting of Eglon to help describe the outwitting of another tyrant.

Among the opponents encountered by the developing Christian community, few appear more dangerous than Herod (Herod Agrippa, 10 BCE–44 CE). Without giving any reason, Luke reports that he laid violent hands on some church members and that he killed James, the brother of John (Acts 12.1-2). Then, finding that such murder gained some popularity, he turned his attention to Peter (Acts 12.3).

The account in Acts 12 contains three episodes:
1. Herod and James (12.1-2).
2. Herod and Peter (12.3-19).
3. Herod and the Tyrians and Sidonians (Herod's death, 12.20-23).

Though Herod is present in all three episodes, the person who emerges most clearly is Peter. Herod is like a dark background, someone whose hostility breaks out repeatedly but whose actual words never appear. On the other hand, Peter, despite his vulnerable status as an escaping prisoner, is involved in colorful conversations which show him increasing in strength (12.7-8, 11, 17: first the rescuing angel talks to him; then he talks to himself; and finally, among members of the church, he assumes a quiet authority).

The account of Peter's adventure is so memorable and complete that the other episodes —Herod's killing of James, and Herod's own death—may be viewed respectively as prologue and epilogue.

It is not known how much of Luke's account is historical, nor what sources he used in writing about Herod. Herod certainly did court popularity among the Jews, and Josephus' account of his death—he died suddenly during a public function (*Ant.* 19.8.2 §§ 343-54)— agrees in broad outline with that of Luke (Acts 12.20-23).

But much of Acts 12 seems to depend on factors other than exact history. Concerning the details of Herod's death, for instance, the account in Josephus suggests that he died of a ruptured appendix. But Luke says he was struck by an angel and was eaten by worms (12.23). What has happened, according to Weiser (1981: 284-86), is that in composing his account, particularly of Peter's rescue and Herod's death, Luke has drawn on literary traditions, especially on the literary conventions for describing rescues and deaths.

The purpose of the present chapter is to identify a further literary tradition in Acts 12: the entire chapter, with its three parts, depends in varying degrees on the account of the first three judges: Othniel, Ehud, and Shamgar (Judg. 3.7-31). In particular, the main episode, Peter's escape from Herod's armed power (12.3-19), builds on Ehud's termination of the power of Eglon (Judg. 3.12-30). As the Peter story is framed by a prologue and epilogue, the Ehud story is framed by the brief references to Othniel (Judg. 3.7-11) and Shamgar (Judg. 3.31). Othniel functions as a prologue, announcing the central theme of the subsequent episodes, and Shamgar serves, in practice, as a form of epilogue.

Table 68. *Escaping the Royal Guard (Judges 3.7-11; Acts 12.1-23)*

1. PROLOGUE (OTHNIEL; JAMES)	
Idolatry leading to anger [cf. Epilogue], and delivery into enemy hands (3.7-11)	Herod lays hands on the church and kills James with a sword (12.1-2)
MAIN EPISODE (EHUD AND EGLON; PETER AND HEROD)	
2. *Oppression and the Sword/Soldiery (Judges 3.12-18; Acts 12.3-6)*	
Further trouble (*prosethento*): Eglon oppresses Israel. Israel cries to the Lord (3.12-15a)	Further trouble (*prosetheto*): Herod imprisons Peter. The church prays to God (12.3-5)
Ehud and the sword (3.15b-18) (Ehud ties on the two-edged sword)	Peter and the soldiers (12.6) (Peter tied with chains between two soldiers)
3. *The Revealer Strikes (Judges 3.19-22: Acts 12.7-8)*	
The (false) revelation to Eglon: 'A word of God'	Revelation in prison: an angel of the Lord
So Eglon stands up, and Ehud puts the sword into his belly. He did not pull (*ex-espasen*) the sword from his belly	strikes Peter in the side and tells him to stand up. The chains fell (*ex-epesan*) from his hands
4. *The Escape (Judges 3.23; Acts 12.9-10)*	
Ehud went out past the appointed (guards), locked the doors, and went out	Peter went out, and passing the guards came through the (locked) gates, and went out
5. *The Scene at the Door (Judges 3.24-25; Acts 12.11-16)*	
The servants came and they realized that the doors were locked	Peter realized what happened and came and knocked on the door and a servant girl came
But they thought he was in the inner room and remained (outside). Nobody was opening the doors	But she ran in, and Peter remained (outside) knocking
So they took the key and opened, and behold, their lord, fallen dead	So they opened, and saw him, and were amazed
6. *The Further Escape (Judges 3.26; Acts 12.17)*	
Ehud escaped amid the tumult And no one noticed him And he escaped to Seirah	Peter, signals for quiet, tells of his escape And he had it announce And he went away to another place
7. *The Bloody Outcome (Judges 3.27-30; Acts 12.18-19)*	
The sounding of the horn, and the killing of the Moabites And Ehud judged Israel peacefully	Alarm among the soldiers, and the executing of the guards And Herod sojourned in Caesarea
8. EPILOGUE (SHAMGAR; THE TYRIANS AND SIDONIANS)	
Shamgar smote with an ox-goad (3.31)	Anger leading to idolatry of Herod [cf. Prologue] The angel of the Lord smote him (12.20-23)

But Peter is very different from Ehud. Ehud's victory, for instance, depends on the sword. In Acts 12, however, the sword is used not by Peter but by the deadly loser (Herod relies on the sword and soldiers). At the end, Ehud exacts punishment on ten thousand Moabites. Peter, at the end, exacts punishment on nobody, but Herod does when he turns on the guards. In other words, while Judges may seem to glorify the use of force, Luke is clearer about its dangers; he associates it with evil.

The extent of Luke's dependence on Judges 3 varies greatly. At times, the Old Testament text supplies some of Luke's details, but on other occasions it provides only a slender framework, little more than a starting point or suggestion. The peace of the final note, for instance, telling how Ehud judged Israel (3.30b), is no more than a starting point for Luke's closing note that Herod sojourned at Caesarea (12.19b). In other words, Luke has used the Old Testament idea of a relatively peaceful final note, but his basic information concerning the movements of Herod comes from other sources. Overall, however, as the simplified outline (Table 68) indicates, there is a consistent continuity between the texts.

In dealing with the prologue and epilogue, Luke has criss-crossed aspects of his source. In particular, one of the basic ideas of the Othniel prologue (idolatry leading to anger) reappears in varied form in the Acts epilogue (anger leading to idolatry, 12.20-23). And, partly because of that change, there is also a criss-crossing in quantity: while Judg. 3.7-31 has a relatively long prologue (3.7-11) and a short epilogue (3.31), Acts 12 has a short prologue (12.1-2) and a relatively long epilogue (12.20-23). Thus, the brief quantity of the Shamgar epilogue (Judg. 3.31) provides a rough model for the brief quantity of the prologue concerning James (Acts 12.1-2).

To some degree, this procedure is understandable. Prologues and epilogues tend to summarize aspects of the essence of texts, and for that reason they are partly interchangeable. Furthermore, it has been noticed elsewhere that in reworking texts Luke sometimes moves aspects of the conclusion to the beginning (e.g. when Lk. 9.51-56 reworks 2 Kgs 1.1–2.6, the image of being taken up [2 Kgs 2.1] is moved to the beginning of Luke's version [9.51]).

1. *More Detailed Analysis*

In the following analysis the emphasis falls on those aspects and details which occur in the same order. But Luke sometimes rearranges details. For instance, as already noted, he interchanges aspects of the prologue and epilogue. Rather than pursue every detail of rearrangement—a process which could be tedious and distracting—it seems better to concentrate on the central relationship between the texts.

a. *Section 2. Prologue (Othniel and James) (Judges 3.7-11; Acts 12.1-2)*
The most obvious resemblance between the Othniel and James episodes is in their function: both act as prologues. Other features of the James episode may, perhaps, have been colored by further aspects of Judges 3: the image of falling into the hands of a punishing king (*cheiras...basileōs/basileus*, Judg. 3.8; Acts 12.1), the use of the sword (*machaira*, Judg. 3.16; Acts 12.2), and the Shamgar epilogue, at least in its brevity (Judg. 3.31).

b. *Section 2. Oppression and the Sword (Judges 3.12-18; Acts 3–6)*
The prologue-like episodes opened the way to more trouble. The Israelites added (*prosethento*) to the doing of evil (Judg. 3.12). And Herod added (*prosetheto*) to the killing of James; he arrested Peter (Acts 12.3). Then, after a time of being militarily overpowered, there is a prelude to deliverance:

Oppression (Judg. 3.12-15a)	*Imprisonment (Acts 12.3-5)*
The Israelites added evil	Herod added the arrest of Peter
So the Lord strengthened Eglon to overpower Israel in various ways	He imprisoned him among four squads of soldiers and waited for Passover
And Israel served Eglon… eighteen years	So Peter was kept in prison
And Israel cried to the Lord	But the church prayed to God for him.
Prelude to Deliverance (3.15b-18)	*Prelude to Deliverance (12.3-6)*
When bringing gifts to Eglon, Ehud took a two-edged, span-long sword (*machairan distomon spathamēs*), and girded it to his thigh	When Herod was to lead out Peter, Peter was asleep between two soldiers (*metaxu duo stratiōtōn*), tied with two chains

The image of Israel as militarily overpowered in diverse ways has been reshaped by Luke—focused and modernized into the picture of Peter among four squads of soldiers. And the subsequent detailed description of Peter, as bound in metal (chains) between two soldiers, contains a reversal of the Old Testament account of Ehud tying the two-edged sword under his clothing to his thigh. Ehud encompasses the double edge of the metal sword, but Peter is himself encompassed by the metal and the sword (by the soldiers and the chains).

Luke's phrasing (*metaxu duo stratiōtōn*) may involve some play with words, or at least with syllables or first letters.

c. *Section 3. The Revealer Strikes (Judges 3.19-22; Acts 12.7-8)*
Ehud's claim to have a revelation ('a word of God') causes Eglon to stand and allows Ehud the chance to put the sword into Eglon's belly.

In Acts 12 there is a genuine revelation and a positive message: 'an angel of the Lord' strikes Peter in the side and tells him to stand. The word 'strike' (*patassō*, used in Judg. 3.29, 31) seems strong; as Haenchen (1971: 383) remarks, 'the angel is not particularly gentle with Peter'. In fact, the KJV said the angel 'smote Peter on the side'. But the angel's blow is generally understood as a strong prod, and it is altogether fitting as a positive variation on the way Ehud had struck Eglon.

The subsequent details are curious. While Ehud does not withdraw the sword but instead allows Eglon's fat belly to absorb the deadly metal, including even the haft, Peter has the opposite experience—the (metal) chains, which had enfolded him, fall from his hands. Again there seems to be some wordplay:

Old Testament:
He did not draw (*ex-espasen*) the sword from his belly

New Testament:
The chains fell (*ex-epesan*) from his hands

It seems difficult to say what, if anything, is the relationship between the brutal picture of the fat belly closing in around the haft and blade (Judg. 3.22) and the gentle picture of the angel telling Peter to wrap himself (Acts 12.8).

d. *Section 4. The Escape (Judges 3.23; Acts 12.9-10)*
Then both accounts tell of going out past the guards and through the doors. (The Old Testament text does not explicitly use the word 'guards', but that is what the Greek version seems to imply.) Ehud locks the doors, but in Luke's more miraculous description

the picture is of locked gates opening. Luke's account is more elaborate, but like the Old Testament passage it begins and ends with some form of 'and he/they went out' (*kai exerchomai*).

e. *Section 5. The Scene at the Door (Judges 3.24-25; Acts 12.11-16)*
The Old Testament story then tells of a straightforward, triple movement: the servants come to the doors, they wait (*pros-menō*), and finally they open the doors. Luke has the same essential drama (Peter comes to the door, he waits [*epi-menō*], and finally those inside open to him). But, again, Luke's account is more elaborate. In particular, while little is said about what is happening behind Eglon's door, Luke gives a colorful description of the animated discussion behind the door of the New Testament scene.

The end in both cases is dramatic but diverse. The opening of Eglon's door reveals death, and the opening of the door to Peter reveals someone who has been saved from death.

f. *Section 6. The Further Escape (Judges 3.26; Acts 12.17)*
Following the drama of the door opening, the Old Testament recounts how, amid the tumult, Ehud escaped. The New Testament also implies that there is a certain tumult (the scene of opening the door was confused; Peter has to signal for quiet), and against this background Peter narrates his escape, or rather his rescue.

Again Luke's account is more elaborate. And while no one notices Ehud, Peter, in what seems to be a direct contrast, gives orders to spread the news of his rescue. In other words, while using Judges 3, Luke adapts his source to the requirements of his own narrative, in this case the requirement that Peter, who originally was silent and unsure (Acts 12.7-9), gradually emerge as one who is in charge, someone who gives instructions.

Then Ehud and Peter move on:

Old Testament:
And he went by…and escaped to Seirah

New Testament:
And he went out and journeyed to another place

g. *Section 7. The Bloody Outcome (Judges 3.27-30; Acts 12.18-19)*
The result is noisy and murderous. Ehud sounded the horn and gathered a force which killed ten thousand Moabites at the Jordan. Peter's escape caused a great disturbance among the soldiers, and Herod ordered the guards to be killed.

At this point, the Old Testament text supplies only a framework and perhaps some general ideas such as that of soldiers killing each other. Much of Luke's description is from some other source.

Then, after the bloodletting, there is a note of calm: Ehud judged Israel in peace for eighteen years (Judg. 3.30b), and Herod went down to Caesarea and sojourned there (Acts 12.19b). Here, too, the influence of the Old Testament text is limited. It supplies framework and, to some degree, a mood. But Luke is also using other material.

h. *Section 8. Epilogue (Shamgar; Herod Dies before the Tyrians and Sidonians) (Judges 3.31; Acts 12.20-23)*
Finally, both texts give a kind of epilogue. The Old Testament tells how Shamgar smote (*epataxen*) the Philistines, and the New Testament tells how an angel of the Lord smote (*epataxen*) Herod.

Herod had been extremely angry (*thymo-machōn*), thus inducing the anxious Tyrians and Sidonians to idolize him (Acts 12.20-22). As mentioned earlier, the essence of this idea is found in the Othniel prologue: Israel's idolatry led God to anger (*orgisthē thymō*, Judg. 3.7-8). Thus, Luke's epilogue synthesizes aspects of both the Old Testament prologue and epilogue.

2. *Conclusion*

There are several factors in the similarity between Judg. 3.7-31 and Acts 12.1-23. First there is the broad framework: the sequence of prologue, main episode, and epilogue. Then there is the extraordinary similarity in the order of the events in the main episode. And, finally, the combination of themes and details which in diverse ways repeatedly link the texts. The scene at the door, for instance, in which those outside have to wait (*pros/epi-menō*) until it is opened to a startling sight, seems to be virtually without parallel in either the Old Testament or New Testament. (The nearest equivalents are parabolic, in Lk. 11.5-8 and 13.24-27.) The uniqueness is heightened by the fact that in each text the scene at the door is framed between two escape scenes. It seems reasonable, therefore, to conclude that Acts 12 has drawn on Judg. 3.7-31.

46

The Prophetess, the Fall and Piercing, and the Song: Judges 4–5 as One Component of the Infancy Narrative (Luke 1–2)

Apart from using Judges' initial picture of expansion (chs. 1–3) in Acts 12–14, Proto-Luke generally follows the order of Judges. Thus he uses the next major episode, Deborah and Jael (Judg. 4–5), in filling out the infancy narrative.

The essence of this idea is not new. Among the many Old Testament texts woven into Luke's infancy narrative it is generally accepted that one is the canticle of Deborah (Judg. 5) (Brown 1977: 342). Elizabeth's greeting to Mary (Lk. 1.42-45) is best regarded as building on the Old Testament poetic canticles, and her opening words ('Blessed are you among women', 1.42) are a close echo of Deborah's praise of Jael ('Blessed be Jael among women', Judg. 5.24).

The purpose of this chapter is to indicate *briefly* how Luke has used the larger Deborah story—not only Deborah's praise of Jael but the entire Deborah/Jael history, essentially all of Judges 5–6. The reason for the brevity is that for present purposes details are not necessary. What counts is the essential anchoring of the Deborah–Jael account within the infancy narrative.

The Old Testament text is vivid. Deborah is not alone in her fight against the oppressive Canaanites. In varying ways, she is helped both by Barak, the faint-hearted commander who relies on her prophetic insight, and by Jael, the woman who put a tent-peg through the temple of the Canaanite commander, Sisera.

The story of Deborah and Barak may be divided into three main sections:
1. The crisis role of Deborah, the prophetess (4.1-14a).
2. The fall of the enemy and the piercing of Sisera (4.14b-24).
3. The canticle (ch. 5).

Each of these sections finds a counterpart in Luke's infancy narrative, but in reverse order:

Judges 4–5	*Luke 1–2*
3. The prophetess Deborah (4.1-14a)	1. Canticles (Elizabeth, Mary) (1.42-55)
2. The fall of Israel's enemies, and the piercing of Sisera's head (and some of canticle) (4.14b–5.8)	2. The rise and fall of many, and the piercing of Mary's heart (2.34-35)
1. Canticle (Deborah, Barak) (5.9-31)	3. The prophetess Anna (2.36-38)

1. *More Detailed Analysis*

a. *The Song (of Deborah and Barak, Judges 5.9-31; of Mary, Luke 1.46-55)*
It is widely accepted that Mary's song, the Magnificat, involves a reworking of several Old Testament passages, particularly of the song of Hannah (1 Sam. 2.1-10; Brown 1977: 358-59). Closer analysis identifies a further component of the Magnificat, namely part of the canticle of Deborah. And, as mentioned earlier, part of Deborah's canticle is also used in the canticle of Elizabeth (Lk. 1.42-45).

The essence of the affinity between Deborah and Barak, on the one hand, and Mary and Elizabeth on the other, is that in the face of apparently unbeatable situations (virginity and Elizabeth's old age, Lk. 1.26-38; an iron-clad army, Judg. 4.3, 13), they discovered a whole other divine, dimension, and this discovery fills them with joy:

> Old Testament:
> My heart (*hē kardia mou*) beats for the command(er)s of Israel…
> Bless the Lord… (Judg. 5.9)
>
> Then his strength was glorified (*emegalunthē*);
> Lord, make lowly (*tapeinōson*)…those stronger then me (5.13, Codex Alexandrinus)
>
> Blessed among women be Jael…
> Above tent-dwelling women let her be blessed (5.24)
>
> New Testament:
> Blessed are you among women,
> and blessed is the fruit of your womb (Lk. 1.42)
>
> My soul (*hē psychē mou*) glorifies (*megalunei*) the Lord…
> because he has looked on the lowliness (*tapeinōsin*) (1.46, 48)

b. *The Fall and the Piercing (Judges 4.14b–5.8; Luke 2.34b-35)*
Deborah's command to Barak to rise up is followed immediately by two scenes—the fall of the enemy at the hands of Israel (Judg. 4.14b-16; cf. 4.23-24), and Jael's piercing of Sisera's head with a tent-peg (4.17-22). The subsequent song, the canticle of Deborah and Barak, begins (in the Greek) by speaking of revelation, of blessing, and of the rising up of Israel under Deborah (5.1-8, especially 5.2, 7).

In Luke's account, the appearance of the prophetess is immediately preceded by Simeon's blessing and his oracle to Mary: the child is set for the fall and rise of many in Israel, and a sword shall pierce Mary's soul. The effect of this rising and falling, and this piercing of the soul, is to reveal hearts.

The meaning of Luke's text is obscure and controverted (Fitzmyer 1981: 422, 429-30). Part of it seems to be that Jesus' searching message—about good and evil (implying a rise and fall in people's standing) and also about death (the sword)—will reveal what is deepest in people's hearts, their innermost values and fears. In any case, Simeon's blessing and oracle involve a process of rising, falling, piercing, and revealing.

The obscurity of Luke's text may be due in part to the obscurity of the Old Testament text, particularly the beginning of the song (5.1-8). Be that as it may, he has distilled the essence of the routing and piercing of Sisera (Judg. 4.14b–5.8). The more obvious elements of affinity of the texts may be outlined as follows:

Judges 4.14b–5.8	Luke 2.28-35
Simeon blessed them…	
Rise… Behold the Lord goes before you.	Behold, this [child] is set
Through the sword all fell.	for the rise and fall of many. in Israel…
The piercing of Sisera's head.	And a sword will pierce your soul also
A revelation was revealed in Israel…	so that thoughts may be revealed.
Bless the Lord…	
The rise of Deborah.	

Several words are shared: '(to) rise', 'behold', 'sword', '(to) fall', 'reveal', 'bless' (*anistēmi/anastasis, idou, rhomphaia, piptō/ptōsis, apokalyptō, eulogeō*). The piercing is expressed as 'driving through' (*diēlasen*, Judg. 4.21) and 'going through' (*dieleusatai*, Lk. 2.35).

c. *The Portrait of a Prophetess (Judges 4.1-14a; Luke 2.36-38)*

Against the background of Canaanite military power led by Sisera, Deborah emerges as a prophetess and a decisive leader. It is she who not only summons Barak to take action, but also stays with him on Mt Tabor so as to tell him when the time is right. Finally, the moment comes (Judg. 4.14): 'Rise', she says to Barak, 'for this is the day'.

The prophetess in Luke is a widow, Anna; and her strength is directed not so much at the social and military worlds, as at the spiritual. She spends her ascetical days not on Mt Tabor watching for the time of the liberation of Israel, but in the temple, attentive to God; and at the crucial moment of Jesus' presentation (Lk. 2.38), she breaks out in thanks and speaks to those who were waiting for the liberation (*lutrōsis*, 'ransom/redemption/release/liberation') of Jerusalem.

In comparison with Deborah, Anna's focus, while less impressive at one level, is ultimately deeper and broader. The liberation with which she is concerned will go engage the human soul and transcend boundaries (cf. Lk. 2.31-32, 34-35). Similarities are significant:

> Old Testament:
> And Deborah, a prophetess (*kai...prophētis*), the wife of Lapidoth—
> she (*autē*) judged Israel in that time,
> and she (*kai autē*) sat under the palm tree of Deborah (4.4-5)
>
> And she said to Barak, '...This is the day (*hautē he hēmera*)
> in which the Lord
> has...[liberated Israel]' (4.14a)
>
> New Testament:
> And...Anna, a prophetess (*kai...prophētis*), the daughter of Phanuel, of the tribe of Asher—
> she (*hautē*) was of a great age...
> and she (*kai autē*) was a widow...
>
> And coming at that very hour (*autē tē hōra*)
> she thanked God and spoke about him
> to all who were awaiting the liberation of Jerusalem

Explicit usages of the word 'prophetess' are rare, totaling seven: Miriam (Exod. 15.20), Deborah (Judg. 4.4), Huldah (2 Kgs 22.14; 2 Chron. 34.22), Isaiah's wife (Isa. 8.3), Anna (Lk. 2.36), and Jezebel (whose claim to prophecy was false, Rev. 2.20). Among these six, Deborah and Anna are the only cases where 'prophetess' is followed by a portrait of the woman. And, though Huldah comes close, they are also the only cases where 'prophetess' is followed by the peculiar repetitive phrasing ('she...and she...', [*h*]*autē...kai autē*). Thus the link between them is unique.

2. *Conclusion*

There is obvious plausibility to the idea that Luke's picture of the women in the infancy narrative employs the Old Testament, particularly Judges. The infancy narrative is visibly saturated with the Old Testament; and the opening annunciations (Lk. 1.5-38) have clear resonances of similar scenes in Judges (Judg. 6 and 13).

Apart from plausibility, there is significant similarity. Despite the brevity of the pertinent New Testament texts, some of the links are striking or unique.

While generally intelligible, the differences seem worthy of further research. Does the transition from the strong prophetess Deborah to the aged prophetess Anna imply that in the New Testament there is little room for strong prophetesses? Or had the Old Testament itself already ceased portraying new prophetesses, and was Luke merely reflecting the larger body of the LXX?

In any case, it is reasonable to conclude that Luke 1–2 draws on the women of Judges.

47

Judges 6–12 as One Component of Luke 16.1–18.8

Having traced Proto-Luke's use of Judges 1–5, including the use of Judges 4–5 in the infancy narrative, attention now moves to Judges 6–12. The present chapter seeks to show that much of Lk. 16.1–18.8 depends significantly and systematically on Judges 6–12 (the stories of Gideon, Abimelech, and Jephthah). For a summary, see Table 69.

Table 69. *Judges 6–12 as One Component of Luke 16.1–18.8*

	Judges 6–12	Luke 16.1–18.8
A.	TWO GIDEON STORIES (MOSTLY ABOUT POWER)	TWO RELATED PARABLES (ABOUT POSSESSIONS)
	Livelihood crisis; downing of symbols of power (6.1–8.3)	The steward's livelihood crisis; downing of bills/possessions (16.1-9)
	[Angel; night action;	cf. infancy narrative]
	Reversal: mean are punished; poor come to power (8.4-35)	The rich man and Lazarus (16.19-31)
B.	EVIL KINGDOM	KINGDOM OF GOD
	Deathly kingdom of Abimelech, with illustrative fable (ch. 9)	Kingdom of God, with illustrative healing (17.11-37)
C.	JUDGE AND VIRGIN	JUDGE AND WIDOW
	The maverick judge (Jephthah) and the defenseless woman (his daughter) (chs. 10–12)	The maverick judge and the widow (18.1-8)

1. *Presuppositions*

As well as presupposing Luke's use of the LXX, and the wider phenomena of imitation/emulation and rewritten Bible, it is useful to state some further presuppositions:

1. The Old Testament, in its reworking of texts, sometimes incorporate various elements of Egyptian literature (see especially Bryce 1979).
2. It has been widely recognized, ever since Gressmann's 1918 study, *Vom reichen Mann*, that the Lazarus parable contains significant resemblances to an Egyptian folktale. Among other things, the Egyptian story (found on the back of a Greek document dating from 47 CE)[1] tells about the relationship between conduct in this life and retribution in the next. It recounts how Osiris, the ruler of Amnte (the abode of the dead), sent Si-Osiris, someone who had been dead and who had been close to himself (Osiris) back to earth. One of the things done by Si-Osiris was to bring his father on a tour of the land of the dead and thus alert his father

---

1. For details, see Grobel 1963–64: 375. There are also affinities between Luke's parable and various rabbinic sources, but one cannot be sure these sources predated Luke.

to what happens after death. The father had seen two contrasting funerals: one of a rich man who was magnificently buried in fine linen, and the other of a poor man who was buried in misery. The father presumed that it would be better to die like the rich man. But Si-Osiris showed that in the abode of the dead, there was a reversal of roles: in one hall, the rich man was in torment (with a metal bar in his right eye socket), and in another hall, the formerly poor man was clad in fine linen and seated next to the enthroned Osiris. Si-Osiris then explains that the reversal of fortunes is due to the relative weight of the two men's good deeds. The similarity with the parable of the rich man and Lazarus is such that it would seem that, apart from its use of the Gideon story, Luke's text involves a reworking of some version of the Egyptian account.

3. The idea that Luke made some use of the Gideon story is not new. As a number of authors have partly indicated, there is evidence that God's two-part annunciation to Gideon (through the angel's message, Judg. 6.11-24, and through the subsequent reassuring sign, Judg. 6.33-40), has in some way served as a model for Luke's account of the angel Gabriel's annunciation to Mary (Lk. 1.26-38, an annunciation which concludes with a sign).[2] The two parts of the Old Testament text have been distilled, fused, and, together with other material, adapted to a new situation and to the requirements of a new narrative.

2. *The Key Outlines (Tables 70–73)*

The first set places the Gideon stories beside the two parables (Lk. 16). (It also includes an outline of an Egyptian folktale.) And the second set relates the Abimelech and Jephthah stories to Lk. 17.11–18.8. These four pages are dense—they need explanations involving themes and details—yet they act as a guide and provide some overall sense of how Judges 6–12 relates to Lk. 16.1–18.8. This chapter will now take the three Old Testament stories one by one: Blocks A, B, and C respectively.

Table 70. *Decisive Gideon and the Steward (Judges 6.1–8.3; Luke 16.1-9)*

A. THE PARABLES OF LUKE 16 (16.1-9, 19-31) AS REWORKINGS OF THE STORIES OF GIDEON (JUDGES 6–8)	
Gideon's Bold Decisions (About Power) Judges 6.1–8.3	*The Steward's Bold Decisions* (About Possessions) Luke 16.1-9
Sin Loses Livelihood	
1. *Crisis*: Israel's sins lead to Midian-mediated loss of the means of living (housing and food) (6.1-6)	*Crisis* and *confrontation*: Steward's dishonesty leads to loss of livelihood (16.1-3)

---

2. See Audet 1956: 352-72; Stock 1980: 461-65; De la Potterie 1988: 44. Close analysis shows that the New Testament annunciation (Lk. 1.26-38) involves a reworking not only of the initial call of Gideon (Judg. 6.11-24)—as indicated by the preceding authors—but also of the subsequent text (Judg. 6.33-40) in which Gideon is empowered (by the spirit of God and the army, 6.33-35) and in which he is further reassured by signs (6.36-40). The two texts (Judg. 6.11-24 and 6.33-40) are inherently connected. As Soggin (1981: 132) remarks, 'The proof which Gideon asks of Yahweh [6.36-40] is connected with his calling [6.11-24]'. Luke, in fact, has combined the two texts. The picture of Gideon as being strengthened by the spirit of God and consequently by *the army* (Judg. 6.33-35) has been filtered to portray Mary as receiving *the Holy Spirit* and *the power of the Most High* (Lk. 1.35). And the picture of Gideon as receiving confirming signs (Judg. 6.36-40) has been distilled yet more so that it colors the annunciation's concluding reference to a sign (Lk. 1.36-38): 'Behold...as you have said...let there be (*genēthētō/egeneto*)'; 'Behold... Let it be done (*genoito*)...according to your word'.

	Recalling Another House	
2.	Initial response to crisis (through a Moses-evoking prophet): God led you from *oikos* of slavery to their *oikos* (6.7-10)	Initial response to crisis: I will go from *oikonomos* to their *oikos* (16.4b)
	Angel and Sign	
3.	Angel and sign (6.11-24, 33-40)	[Angel, Mary and sign (1.26-38)]
	Decisive Reduction, Twice	
4.	The decisive action: Baal downed. Who did it? (6.25-32) Army reduced twice (7.1-8) (especially by lowering themselves, lapping like dogs, to take water on the tongue)	The decisive action: What to do? Down oil, wheat— two reductions (16.4a, 5-7)
	God's Wondrous Night	
5.	The night of: * the revelatory dream (7.9-15) * light-and-horns (7.16-22) *Confrontation*: 'What is this?…' (8.1-3)	[Night of light-and-song (2.8-20)] [Revelation to Simeon (2.25-35)]

Table 71. *Rags and Riches: Gideon (Judges 8.4-35), and Lazarus (Luke 16.19-31)*

Rich Man and Pauper (a story of reversed fortunes) Egyptian Folktale	*Gideon: Beggar to Gold* (with colorful details) Judges 8.4-35	*Rich Man and Lazarus* (reversed fortunes and colorful details) Luke 16.19-31
The Plight of the Poor/Hungry		
6. The rich man: at death is shrouded in fine linen and buried sumptuously	[Royal purple (8.26)]	A rich man is clothed in purple and fine linen, king-like (16.19)
The poor man: at death is wrapped in straw in a forlorn burial	Gideon and his 300 famished men are refused food (8.4-9) [The 300 had taken water with their tongues, lapping like dogs]	Lazarus, poor, pines for food, and is licked by dogs (16.20-21)
The Poor Man is Elevated		
7. Reversal: in Amnte (abode of dead) pauper is near to great god Osiris with fine linen and high rank. Elsewhere in Amnte rich man is in torment (a bar through his eye) so he prays and laments	Victory and reversal: 'refusers' punished, Gideon elevated (purple, kingly). Gideon 'died…and was buried' (8.10-17, 22-32)	Reversal: poor man dies and is carried to the bosom of Abraham. Rich man 'died…and was buried'. And in abode of dead, in torment, prays and asks for water on his tongue (16.22-24)
Explaining Reversal, and Remembering		
8. Si-Osiris explains the reversal (pauper had done better deeds)	Israel did not remember the good things Gideon had done (8.33-35)	Abraham explains the reversal: remember the good things of the past (16.25-26)

		Returning for the Sake of One's Family	
9.	Si-Osiris had returned from the dead to do the task which included alerting his father to the possible torments of the afterlife	[Gideon rises up to avenge his brothers (8.18-21)] [The Moses-evoking prophet; Israel did not hear (6.7-8, 10)]	Request that Lazarus return to warn the brothers in his father's house. Let them hear Moses and prophets or someone risen from the dead (16.27-31)

Table 72. *Reversal of Abimelech's Evil Kingdom (Judges 9; Luke 17.11-37)*

	Abimelech's Evil Kingdom (Narrow and Negative) Judges 9	The Kingdom of God (Positive and Universal) Luke 17.11-37
B.		
	Death and spoil (9.1-6): the death of the brothers, leaving one, and the 'gathering' to share the political spoil.	
	The Illustrative Story	
10.	Following the deaths: The illustrative story: Jotham's fable (9.7-21), showing Abimelech's deathly kingship [plus questions about diverse motives (9.16-21)]	As Jesus walks towards death: The illustrative story: the ten lepers (17.11-19), showing the nature of the kingdom of God in Jesus [plus questions about diverse reactions (17.15-19)]
	Retribution begins ('Deuteronomic') (negative): the brothers' death is to be punished (9.22-24)	
	The Initial Shock	
	Deathly camaraderie, eating, drinking (9.25-29)	
11.	The deathly kingdom's initial shudder (9.30-41):	The kingdom's initial unsettling approach (17.20-25):
	Reactions to (military) movements: (1) 'Look...'; (2) 'Look [in this direction]...Look [in that]'	Reactions to kingdom/Son of Humanity: Avoid; 'Look. here...Look there'. When they say, 'Look...Look...'
	Then Gaal went out (*ex-erchomai*)... And Abimelech pursued (*kata-diōkō*)	do not go off (*ap-erchomai*) do not pursue (*diōkō*)
	Abimelech's forces come with sunrise, from the mountains, in four directions	For the Son of Humanity will be like lightning flashing across the sky
	'Many' killed, and expelled	First he must suffer 'many' things, and be rejected
	The End	
		Positive camaraderie (universal: marrying, eating, drinking, buying, selling, planting, building)
12.	Three minor cataclysms (9.42-55): * killings in Shechem, in the 'field' (9.42-45) * burning in 'fire' of those in the 'house' (9.46-49) * killing by the 'woman' on the 'roof' (9.50-55)	Three universal-type cataclysms (17.26-32): * in the days of Noah, the flood killed all * in the days of Lot, the 'fire' killed all * in the day of the Son of Humanity...those on the 'roof', in the 'house', in the 'field'... Remember Lot's wife ('woman')

	The Principle of Retribution	
13.	Retribution concluded ('Deuteronomic', negative): The death of the brothers is punished (9.56-57)	Retribution (New Testament, universal) (negative and positive) (17.33)
14.		Death and spoil (universal) (17.34-37): The death of one, leaving one, and the 'gathering' of the eagles

Table 73. *The Maverick Judge and the Woman (Judges 10.1–12.7; Luke 18.1-8)*

C.	THE MAVERICK JEPHTHAH AND HIS DAUGHTER (THE WOMAN LOSES) JUDGES 10.1–12.7	THE MAVERICK JUDGE AND THE WIDOW (THE WOMAN WINS) LUKE 18.1-8
	The Protracted Crisis	
15.	Israelites plead repeatedly (10.6-18)	Always pray (*pros-euchomai*), and do not give up (18.1)
16.	Judges, their children and cities (10.1-5) Jephthah, the outlaw judge (11.1-3; 12.7)	The unscrupulous judge in a city (18.2)
17.	Gileadites plead with Jephthah: 'Fight the (attacking) Ammonites' (11.4-11)	Widow pleads with the judge: '*Avenge* me of my *adversary*' (18.3)
18.	Ammon is like Moab and Sihon of old—'not willing' to heed (11.12-28) Jephthah vows (*euchomai*, 11.29-31)	For a time he 'was not willing' (18.4a)
	The Troubled Resolution	
19.	Jephthah: 'My daughter, you have brought me deep trouble' Daughter: 'Do as you have spoken since the Lord has *avenged* you' (11.32-40)	The judge: 'This widow is causing me so much bother I will *avenge* her…' (18.4b-5)
	Epilogue (antithetical)	*Epilogue (synonymous)*
20.	The *adversary* (Jephthah) who cries…is saved by God (12.1-3), but for Ephraim, words bring death (12.4-6)	Will not God *avenge* those who cry to him? Yes, he will quickly *avenge* them (18.6-9)

3. *Block A. The Parables of Luke (16.1-9, 19-31) as Reworkings of the Stories of Gideon (Judges 6–8)*

a. *Introductory Analysis*

The Old Testament narrative begins with a crisis: because of their unfaithfulness, the Israelites are left with nothing to live on (the marauding Midianites deprive them of both shelter and food, Judg. 6.1-6). The Lord sends a prophet who, while evoking Moses, reminds the Israelites that God's original intention was just the opposite—not to remove the sustenance of life, but to provide it, bringing people into a nourishing land or dwelling (Judg. 6.7-10).

Then Gideon enters, and in two campaigns—two series of actions—he reverses the situation. First, in conjunction with God's angel and sign, he takes bold decisions: he both knocks down the prestigious altar of Baal (replacing it with an altar to God, Judg. 6.25-32) and cuts down drastically on the numbers in his army (from 32,000 to 10,000, and from 10,000 to 300, Judg. 7.1-8). His very name, 'Gideon', means 'to pull down' or 'cut down'. In the subsequent night action—a night of light and sound (torches and horns)—God causes the enemy to collapse and flee (Judg. 7.9-25).

In the second campaign (8.4-32), beyond the Jordan, there is a double climax. Not only does Gideon punish his enemies—including the mean-spirited men who refused to give bread to his famished army (8.4-21, the first climax)—but then the formerly famished Gideon rises to a position of great prestige and wealth (8.22-32, second climax) (Webb 1987: 147).

Finally, the narrative tells how when Gideon died, the people reverted to Baal and 'did not remember'... 'the goodness' of God and Gideon (8.33-35).

In Luke 16, the parable of the unjust steward (16.1-9)[3] praises the person who, instead of accumulating wealth, breaks free of it; he gives away his commission (Fitzmyer 1985: 1097). Thus, in his own way, he enters a new dimension, and his decisiveness serves as an example of the boldness and freedom which are necessary for gaining eternal life or eternal dwellings (16.9). However, the second parable, concerning the rich man and Lazarus (16.19-31), shows how the failure to rise above a wealth-centered life prevents a person from gaining everlasting life. Thus, the second parable complements the first and 'gives new meaning to the "dwellings that are everlasting" (v. 9)' (Fitzmyer 1985: 1127).

The structure of the second parable is 'two-peaked' (Fitzmyer 1985: 1126). An initial climax tells of the chasm between the rich man and Lazarus (16.26), and a second one highlights the failure of those who are wealth-bound to listen to the message concerning another dimension (vv. 27-31). Thus, the structure of the parables—two in number, the second being two-peaked—is essentially the same as the structure of the main body of the Gideon narrative.

Briefly stated, Luke has used the two Gideon campaigns as components for the two parables. Gideon's initial ability to break out of the normal cycle of thinking (his knocking of Baal, and his drastic reducing of the army) provides a basic ingredient for the parable of the decisive steward. And the later story, involving the refusal to give bread to the famished Gideon, has supplied one stratum of the account of the rich man's indifference to Lazarus.

Fitzmyer (1985: 1127) notes that some distinctive elements of the Lazarus parable (such as the dogs) find no parallel in the Egyptian text. But some such elements occur in Gideon's story. Thus, Gideon's story helps to fill the gaps.

Luke's concern about wealth or possessions may seem unrelated to Judges 6–8, for even though Judges 6–8 mentions various possessions, the concern in these Old Testament chapters is the larger question of relationships in general—relationships with God and

---

3. It is generally agreed that the varied sayings of Lk. 16.10-18 are in some way secondary to the two parables, and so this chapter concentrates just on the parables themselves (Lk. 16.1-9, 19-31). On the question of where exactly the first parable ends, it seems best to say 16.9; see, for instance, Marshall 1978: 621-22; Bossuyt and Radermakers 1981: 354. Fitzmyer (1985: 1096-1097), argues initially for concluding the parable at 16.8a, but, when commenting (p. 1105) on vv. 8b-9, Fitzmyer regards these verses as having been 'quickly associated with the parable itself', and as having come to Luke 'along with the parable itself'. In fact, as Fitzmyer suggests (pp. 1105, 1127), v. 9 is both an imitation of v. 4 and a preparation for the second parable. Thus, it is best to see it as integral to the two original parables. The fact that there is a very slight break before the end of the first parable (either before v. 8b or, more obviously, before v. 9) does not mean that (either of) these verses are secondary. Rather, the very slight break, particularly before v. 9, may be seen as an initial low-key form of something which, in the second parable, becomes a real division (at v. 27). In other words, the 'And I say to you...' (v. 9) is in narrative continuity with 'Then I ask you...' (v. 27). The two phrases are like the diverse sides of a coin, and the second is an intensification of the first.

people. But such also is the concern of Luke; he speaks of wealth or possessions symbolically to say something about larger issues and relationships.[4]

Luke has distilled and synthesized the Old Testament text. While keeping the basic structure of the two Gideon campaigns, he has rearranged some of the elements. And in combining the Old Testament story with a distinct Egyptian source, he apparently used other sources as well, some of them Christian.

b. *More Detailed Analysis*
The following analysis is incomplete, partly because the present writer has not been able to track all the details, and partly because a relentless presentation of every detail threatens to obscure the central thesis.

(1) *Section 1. The crisis and the confrontation: because of sinfulness, the* Kyrios *(Lord/ Master) takes away livelihood (Judges 6.1-6; 8.1-3; Luke 16.1-3),* The Gideon narrative begins by telling how, because of the Israelites' sinfulness, God (*kyrios*) deprived them of their livelihood, through the Midianites. The Israelites were driven to hide in clefts and caves, and, as for food, whatever they sowed was devoured; the Midianites 'left them with nothing to live on' (literally, 'they did not leave the substance of life [*hypostasin zoēs*]'). The beginning of the Lukan parable tells how, because of his steward's squandering, an owner (*kyrios*) decided to deprive the steward of his stewardship—in other words, of his livelihood.

Luke has made several adaptations. The sense of wrongdoing in general (as found in Judges) has been replaced by the more specific wrongdoing of squandering possessions—an adaptation which reflects Luke's overall concern with possessions. Other elements are similarly focused around the idea of possessions. The elaborate picture of Midian-mediated punishment has been distilled to its essence: the deprivation of the means of livelihood. And in place of the punishing Lord (*kyrios*) there is a master (*kyrios*) who is rich.

Luke has also employed a process of fusion. He has taken Ephraim's confronting of Gideon ('What is this you have done to us?...', Judg. 8.1-3), and adapted it to construct the confrontation between the master and the steward ('What is this I hear about you?...', Lk. 16.2).

Despite the changes, the parable retains echoes of the older text:

> Old Testament:
> The Ephraimites said to him:
> 'What is this you have done to us—not to call us?'
>
> And he said to them:
> 'What did I do...?
> And what have I been able to do...?'
>
> And their anger left them when he spoke this word (*logos*).
>
> New Testament:
> [The owner heard about the steward's abuse of his position]
> And having called him, he said to him:
> 'What is this I hear about you? Give an account (*logos*)...'
>
> Then the steward said to himself:
> 'What shall I do?...'

---

4. 'Luke uses the language of possessions symbolically...to express: a) the identity of God's people; b) acceptance and rejection in relation to God's people; c) authority over God's people...' (Johnson 1977: 126).

As often in using the Old Testament, Luke internalizes. In this case, a conversation which is purely external in the Old Testament, becomes, in part, a conversation which is within ('...said to himself').

(2) *Section 2. Initial response to the crisis: recalling the idea of changing from one house (*oikos*) to another (Judges 6.7-10; Luke 16.4).* In response to the cry of impoverished Israel, God sends a prophet who recalls the exodus —recalls how Israel moved from the house (*oikos*) of slavery and into a place where the people dwelt (*en-oikeō*) in the land of others. Thus it recalls a transition from one house to another.

In Luke, there is no prophet or exodus—the reference to the prophets and Moses is held over until the story of the rich man (Lk. 16.29-31)—but the essential transition is present: the steward calls to mind the idea of moving from his present house (his stewardship, *oikonomia*) to the houses of others. In other words, Luke has domesticated and internalized the Old Testament picture; the transition from one house to another has been brought down to fit the dimensions of a more domestic scene. And the process of calling the transition to mind has been placed *within* the impoverished person.

> Old Testament:
> I am he (*egō eimi*) who
> brought you up out of (*ek/ex*) Egypt
> and led you out from the house (*ex...oikos*) of slavery;
> and I delivered you from (*ek*) the hand of Egypt
> and from (*ek*) the hand of all who afflicted you
>
> and I cast them out before you
> and I gave you their land (*gēn autōn*).
> And I said, I am the Lord your God.
> Do not fear the gods of the Amorites
> among whom you dwell (*en-oikeō*) in their land (*en...gē autōn*).
>
> New Testament:
> I know (*egnōn*) what I will do so that,
> when I am removed from the stewardship (*ek...oikonomia*)
> they may receive me into their homes (*eis...oikous autōn*).

The similarity of *egnōn* to *egō eimi* looks like coincidence, but overall Luke's text appears to be an interiorized distillation of the Old Testament. The type of word-combination which is shared by these two texts (*ek/ex...oiko-...eis/en...oik-...autōn*) apparently does not occur elsewhere in the Bible.

(3) *Section 3. The angel and the sign (Judges 6.11-24, 33-40; Luke 1.26-38).* See Presupposition 3 (at the beginning of this chapter) and its footnote (n. 2).

(4) *Section 4. The decisive action—cutting down Baal and numbers (Judges 6.25-32; 7.1-8; Luke 16.5-7).* When Gideon takes action he does two distinct things. First (6.25-32), he takes the bold step of cutting down and pulling down the altar to Baal (his very name means 'he who cuts/pulls down'). And later (7.1-8) he reduces, twice, the number of his army (from 32,000 to 10,000, and from 10,000 to 300).

And when the steward takes action, he is equally decisive: he cuts down, twice, the commission he could have had in oil and wheat. In other words, while Gideon took decisive action against one form of idolatry (against Baal and imposing numbers), the steward took action against idolatry of a related kind (against numbers of oil and wheat).

In distilling the text, Luke used processes of domestication and fusion. Domestication refers to the change from ancient factors which are public (Baal and the army) to factors which are closer to daily life (oil and wheat). Fusion refers to the way in which Luke's single picture (of cutting down on the oil and wheat) seems to capture elements of both Old Testament actions: cutting down on oil and wheat is like a play on the picture of cutting down Baal (Baal is associated with oil and wheat; cf. Hos. 2.8-10), and the double reduction in numbers is a variation on the double reduction in the numbers of the army.

Details of the similarity are debatable. For instance, there may be a playful echo between the two decisive commands (Judg. 6.25; Lk. 16.6):

> Old Testament:
> 'Take (*labe*) your father's bullock
> …and pull down (*katheleis*) the altar of Baal'
>
> New Testament:
> 'Take (*dexai*) your [oil] bill
> and sit down (*kathisas*)…'

But other similarities are more striking. In the rest of the Bible there seems to be no other instance of people cutting down, twice, on the numbers which could have helped them. Hence, the link between the texts is unique.

(5) *Section 5. The revelation and the night of light and sound (Judges 7.9-25; Luke 2.8-20, 25-35).* Having reduced his army, Gideon first encounters a man with a revelatory dream, and then, with the help of light and sound (torches and horns), he embarks on a night action which routs the frightening enemy. In Luke, the corresponding episodes occur in Luke 2—the revelation to Simeon, and the night action which involves angelic light and sound (see Table 74).

Table 74. *The Night Action (Judges 7.9-25; Luke 2.8-20, 25-35):
Initial Summary Outline*

Judges 7.9-25	Luke 2.8-20, 25-35
That night: Do not fear the armed camp and its multitude (7.9-12)	At night: light and sound overpower those guarding their flocks: 'Do not fear' says one of the multitude, one of the army of heaven (2.8-14)
And behold a man with a dream about a fall (of Midian) and a sword (of Gideon) (7.13-14)	
When they heard this they returned and worshipped the Lord (7.15)	
Light and sound overpower those guarding, etc. (7.16-23)	
Messengers (*aggeloi*): Go to Bethbarah to deliver death (7.24-25)	When angels go: 'Let us go to Bethlehem' to see new-born life. All who heard wondered, and they returned praising God (2.15-20)
	And behold a man (Simeon) with a revelation about a fall and a sword (2.25-35)

The essence of Luke's transforming is the positivization of the image of an army. Instead of describing the divine overpowering of an evil army, he portrays the overpowering divine presence of a good army. Thus, what in the Old Testament was merely implied—

the supremacy of God's goodness—in the New Testament is described with unforgettable clarity. And instead of an army which in the night cries out about the sword ('A sword for the Lord...', Judg. 7.20), Luke portrays a heavenly army which cries out about peace ('Glory to God...and peace', Lk. 2.14). Furthermore, while the Old Testament spoke of administering death (to the evil-doers), Luke speaks of finding a life-giving newborn baby.

Luke's reworking also involves some internalization. For instance, the shepherds, as they talk to each other and absorb the event (Lk. 2.15-20), show a more explicit process of understanding, or internalizing, than Gideon and his companion (cf. Judg. 7.15). And the sword in Luke is one which pierces the internal heart rather than the body (Lk. 2.35; cf. Judg. 7.14, 22).

In addition, Luke uses various strategies of fusion or conflation. Not only does he conflate distinct passages of the Gideon story (see the initial summary, Table 74 above), but he combines the various elements of the Gideon story with other distinct sources. As seen earlier (Chapter 53), the account of the birth of Jesus (Lk. 2.1-20), for instance, involves a distillation of the Chronicler's account of the birth of the temple (1 Chron. 21–22). And these two texts—from Judges and 1 Chronicles—are but two components among many.

Luke's wording sometimes echoes or mirrors that of Judges (see Table 75, where the Old Testament text has been rearranged to facilitate comparison). As often, many details are debatable, but overall the similarity is significant.

Table 75. *The Night Action (Judges 7; Luke 2): A Closer Comparison*

Judges 7.9-25	Luke 2.8-20, 25-35
And it came to pass in that night that the Lord said, 'Stand up and go down to the [army] camp... And if you are afraid...' And Midian...was like a multitude ...a multitude (7.9-12)	And shepherds were in that land... guarding (*phylassontes*)...the night... And an angel stood above them... and the glory...shone (*peri-elampsen*)— 'Do not fear...' (2.8-12)
And he put...torches (*lampadas*)... 'And you shall sound the horn round the whole camp and you shall say...[having] roused the guards (*phylassontes*)... "A sword for the Lord and for Gideon"' (7.16-23)	And suddenly...a multitude of the army of heaven, praising God and saying, 'Glory to God... and...peace to people' (2.13-14)
And it came to pass (*kai egeneto hōs*) when Gideon heard the account... that he worshipped the Lord and returned...to Israel (7.15) And...he sent messengers (*aggeloi*) to all...Ephraim— 'Go...to (*heōs*) Bethbarah...' (7.24-25)	And it came to pass (*kai egeneto hōs*) when the angels (*aggeloi*) had gone— 'Let us go over to (*heōs*) Bethlehem' ...And they found...the baby... All who heard wondered and... they returned...praising God for all... (2.15-20)
...And behold a man recounted the dream... 'And behold...the tent fell... This is the sword of Gideon of Israel' (7.13-14)	And behold a person...Simeon... and it was revealed to him... 'Behold, he is set for the fall of many in Israel...and a sword shall pierce' (2.25-26, 34-35)

(6) *Section 6. The rich man and the poor man (Egyptian story; Luke 16.19-21; cf. lapping dogs and royal purple in Judges 7.5; 8.26).* The clear contrast between a rich man and a poor man has been adapted from the Egyptian account. The Egyptian text introduces the two at the moment of burial, but Luke introduces them in scenes which immediately precede the accounts of burial. By pushing the characters back into life, Luke achieves a more dramatic contrast, and he also builds greater narrative continuity with the earlier parable (16.1: 'There was a certain rich man...'; 16.19: 'Now there was a certain rich man...').

But while the essential contrast comes from the Egyptian text, many of Luke's details have been adapted from Judges. First, concerning the rich man. Gideon, who was close to being a king (Judg. 8.22-23, 31), received the purple clothing of the kings of Midian (Judg. 8.26). And the rich man, who apparently 'lived like a king' (Fitzmyer 1985: 1130), was dressed in purple.

Second, concerning the poor man. While Gideon's men had pined for bread (Judg. 8.4-9), the poor man desired the scraps or crumbs (Lk. 16.21). And while Gideon's men had been compared to lapping dogs (Judg. 7.5), the poor man was licked by the dogs (Lk. 16.21).

Further details remain elusive, particularly concerning Luke's possible use of Gideon's victory over Zebah and Zalmunna (Judg. 8.10-12). Yet the resemblances noted are significant. The word 'purple' (*porphyron/porphyran*), for instance, is rare. It does not otherwise occur in the Deuteronomic History (Judges–Kings) and, apart from Mk 15.17, 20, does not otherwise occur in the gospels. And the word 'dog' is not common. It does not otherwise occur in Joshua–Judges, and, apart from Mt. 7.6, does not otherwise occur in the gospels. The impression which emerges is that contrasting elements in the colorful history of Gideon have been used to develop the basic contrast between the rich man and the poor man.

(7) *Section 7. The reversal (Egyptian story; Judges 8.13-17, 22-32; Luke 16.22-24).* Here, too, the Egyptian story provides an initial framework for Luke's parable. The closeness of the former (Egyptian) pauper to the divine Osiris echoes in the closeness of Lazarus to Abraham, recipient of the divine promises. And the rich men, in contrast, are in torment.

But in the Gideon account, there is a form of reversal. Those who had refused to give food to the famished Gideon are punished, whereas Gideon is enriched and exalted. And again the Gideon account helps to fill out some of the details of the parable. As Gideon 'died...and was buried', so the rich man 'died...and was buried' (*apethanen...kai etaphe*, Judg. 8.32; Lk. 16.22). And as Gideon's men had been chosen by a process involving the lapping of water with the tongue (Judg. 7.5), the parable speaks of bringing a dipped finger-tip of water to the tongue (Lk. 16.24):

> Old Testament:
> ...whoever laps (*hos an lapsē*) the water with his tongue...
>
> New Testament:
> ...that he may dip (*hina bapsē*) his finger-tip in water...my tongue.

The similarities are hardly coincidence. Of the fourteen Old Testament occurrences of the direct phrase 'died...and was buried', seven are in Judges 8–12 (Judg. 8.32; 10.2, 5; 12.7, 10, 12, 14) and, apart from an indirect use in 1 Cor 15.3-4, the phrase never occurs elsewhere in the New Testament. Thus, the usages in Judg. 8.32 and Lk. 16.22 stand out—in Judg. 8.32 because it introduces a wave of further occurrences, and in Lk. 16.22 because it is essentially alone in the New Testament.

Simple though it is, the image of water on the tongue is otherwise virtually unknown in the Bible. (The only text really close to it is Isa. 41.17: 'The needy seek water and there is none, their tongue is parched...'). The curious occurrence of *lapsē* and *bapsē* (which in itself suggests a form of word-play) strengthens the similarity yet further.

(8) *Section 8. The explanation of the reversal (Egyptian story; Judges 8.33-35; Luke 8.25-26).* Once more the Egyptian account provides the basic framework. As Si-Osiris had explained the reversal of rich and poor, so Abraham explains it.

But again, Luke's adaptation is colored by the Gideon story. The account of how Israel did not remember the good things God and Gideon had done (Judg. 8.33-35) has been adapted to show the rich man as not remembering the good things he had received in his lifetime (Lk. 16.25-26):

> Old Testament:
> They did not remember the Lord...who rescued them from...all...and they did not act mercifully...according to all the good which he had done...
>
> New Testament:
> Remember that you received good things in your lifetime... And in all...

In both cases, there is a forgetfulness of the good, but Luke has adapted and synthesized the Old Testament passage. The idea of remembering the good(ness) is rare—two other references in the Old Testament (Sir. 11.25;[5] Ezek. 36.31) and none in the New Testament.

(9) *Section 9. Returning from the dead to warn one's kinsfolk (Egyptian story; Judges 8.18-21; Luke 16.27-31).* The Egyptian account supplies the essential idea of sending someone back from the dead to warn one's kinsfolk. Si-Osiris warns his father about the torments of Amnte, and Luke's parable speaks of the need to provide a similar warning ('Send [Lazarus] to my father's house').

But Luke's text has distinctive features—particularly about warning one's brothers (rather than one's father) and hearing Moses and the prophets.

Both of these features—care for one's brothers and the need to listen to the prophets—are found in alternate form in the Gideon story. When Gideon returns from crossing the Jordan, he goes and avenges his murdered brothers (Judg. 8.18-21). Luke has maintained the idea of care, even beyond death, for one's brothers' welfare, but he has directed that care towards the living rather than towards the dead. In other words, rather than avenge the dead he speaks of preserving the living. (The beginning of this parable showed a somewhat similar technique. Rather than introduce the two contrasting characters, rich and poor, as already dead—as in the Egyptian story—Luke pushes them back as it were into life.) The result, typical of Luke, is a dramatic text which is more positive, more hopeful, more domesticated.

There are some verbal affinities (Judg. 8.19-21; Lk. 16.27-28, 31):

> Old Testament:
> '...my brothers and sons of my mother... Rise... Rise'...arose (*anestē*)...
>
> New Testament:
> '...the house of my father...[my] brothers...should arise (*anastē*)...'

The idea of hearing Moses and the prophets (Lk. 16.29-31) is found at the beginning of the Gideon story—in the account of the prophet who, without explicitly mentioning Moses,

---

5. As in some other instances, Luke blends or weaves sources: while the *basic idea* of remembering the good seems to come from Judg. 8.33-35, Luke's *phrasing* appears to have been colored by Sir. 11.23-25 (*ta agatha...kakōn*).

recalls the Moses-led liberation from Egypt (Judg. 6.7-10). When first rewriting the Gideon story, at the beginning of the parable of the unjust steward, Luke did not make use of this reference to prophetic activity, but now, as a final element, he does use it. The reference to Moses becomes explicit, and the phrasing ('Moses and the prophets') is so shaped that it prepares the way for Luke's later post-resurrection phrasing ('Moses and all the prophets', Lk. 24.27). In fact, as Fitzmyer (1985: 1134) notes, Luke's phrasing is such ('should arise from the dead') that it contains an 'obvious...reference to Jesus' own death and resurrection'.

As ever, Luke seeks to be positive, tries to leave room for repentance. In the Gideon story, the incident concerning the prophet concludes with the picture of Israel not listening to the Lord (Judg. 6.10). But in the parable, the possibility of listening is kept open—listening to the prophets and to the risen Lord (Lk. 16.31).

c. *Summary of Block A*

Some aspects of the preceding analysis are debatable; some of the alleged links between the texts are weak or unclear. But, as always in presenting connecting evidence, the fact that some evidence is weak should not detract from the essential question: Is there evidence which is strong?

In this case there is:

1. *External plausibility (circumstantial evidence).* There is solid evidence not only that Luke generally adapted and imitated the LXX, but that he made specific use of the account of the angel's message to Gideon. Given this propensity, and the application of this propensity to part of the Gideon story, it is plausible that Luke also used the rest of the Gideon story.

2. *The range of the similarities.* While some similarities are weak or debatable, there is a wide range of similarities which are strong. Both texts (the Gideon story; the two parables) have the same unusual structure: two parts, the second of which is two-peaked. In the relationship between the first part of the Gideon story and the first parable, there is a pattern of similar incidents. Above all, there is a whole series of similarities of details or word-combinations, features such as otherwise rarely occur in the entire Bible: from the *oiko(nomo)s* into their *oikos*; two successive reductions in numbers; royal-like purple; dogs lapping/licking; 'died...and was buried'; lapping/dipping water with/on the tongue; remembering the good(ness).

3. *The coherence of the differences.* Great though the differences are, they are not a meaningless muddle. The main differences between the first parts of the texts (between Judg. 6.1-8.3 and Lk. 16.1-9) may be accounted for through coherent processes of imitation, of synthesis, and of adaptation to the requirements of Luke's own narrative. In the relationship between the second parts (between Judg. 8.4-35 and Lk. 16.19-31), the differences are far greater, but here, too, there is a basic coherence. Luke has used the Old Testament story not as a foundational element, but as a supplement to the framework which is supplied by the Egyptian story.

In the end, the evidence may be read in two possible ways. Either one is dealing with a series of coincidences that go beyond all known laws of probability, or, more simply, Luke, being a *littérateur* and being involved with the Gideon story, applied a literary method to that story.

The dependence of the parable of the unjust steward on the Gideon story helps to set the parable's strangeness in context. The Gideon story itself is strange. It has been said, for instance, that it illustrates the three main types of humor found in the Old Testament:

humor about human foibles, incongruity and irony, and word-play (Linton 1982). In fact, the entire book of Judges has been described as a triumph of irony (Linton 1982). Given such a background, it is appropriate that the parable itself should be unusually challenging.

4. Block B. The Deathly Kingdom of Abimelech (Judges 9) as a Foil for the Kingdom of God (Luke 17.11-37)

Israel's first kingship was that of the murderous Abimelech, a miserable three-year reign which ended in blood and flames. In this kingdom, God stayed in the background, except for framing notes which say that the kingdom's collapse was God's punishment (Judg. 9.22-25, 56-57).

The corresponding text in Luke is the account of the coming of the kingdom of God (17.11-37). The ending is equally dramatic: an apocalyptic evoking of flood and fire and brimstone which surpasses even the blood and flames of the Abimelech story. But the effect in Luke is quite different. The dramatic ending is not so much God's punishment as God's positive intervention.

Luke has taken the negative-sounding Old Testament story and used it to build a text which is more obviously positive. This dependence on Judges is limited; most of Luke's account is from other sources. Yet the link with the Abimelech story is important—it provides a form of background contrast, a foil.

It may seem negligent in dealing with Lk. 17.11-37 (especially 17.20-37) not to discuss its possible relationship to Mark 13, Matthew 24, and Q. Such discussion has its place, but not here. If introduced at this stage, it would prove frustratingly indecisive and ultimately quite distracting. For the present, it is necessary to allow the Proto-Luke hypothesis a chance to work. Attention, therefore, remains on Abimelech.

a. *Introductory Analysis*

Judges 9 contains two kinds of texts: the main account of the rise and fall of Abimelech's kingdom (9.1-6, 22-57), and Jotham's fable which, placed near the beginning of the story (9.7-21), uses imagery of a different kind to announce from Mt Gerizim (in Samaria) the evil nature of the kingdom.

Luke also uses two kinds of texts: the main discourse on the coming of the kingdom of God (17.20-37), and a preliminary episode which shows healing and God's glory (17.11-19). Like Jotham's fable, the healing of the lepers, especially of the Samaritan, intimates what is to come. Abimelech's kingdom will bring death, but the kingdom of God, inaugurated by Jesus, brings life and praise. In simplified outline:

Judges 9	*Luke 17.11-37*
Illustrative story: the fable	Illustrative episode: the cure
(the kingdom of the trees shows	(Jesus' healing of the lepers
the nature of Abimelech's kingdom)	shows the nature of God's kingdom)
The kingdom of Abimelech	The Kingdom of God and the days of the Son of Humanity

The dependence between the two illustrative episodes is quite limited. Jotham's fable does not account for the more historylike account of the healing. Yet, as will be seen, the fable does color the healing story.

The continuity between the healing (Lk. 17.11-19) and the kingdom (17.20-37) is sometimes overlooked. Even the kingdom text is sometimes divided into two essentially unrelated parts concerning the coming of the kingdom (17.20-21) and the revealing of the Son of Humanity (17.22-37).

But Marshall (1978: 648) regards all of 17.11–18.8 as a single block. And E. LaVerdiere (1980: 213-17), for instance, further underscores the unity of 17.11-37.

The core of this unity is the idea that the kingdom of God, however transcendent at one level, *functions within* people; it is 'within (*entos*) you'—an inner reality (17.21).[6] The essence of Luke's text, therefore, is the idea of God breaking through within humanity. It is an idea which may be expressed through the word 'kingdom', but it is a larger reality working within people in ways that are unpredictable.

This unpredictability is seen from beginning to end: in the way in which just one leper, a Samaritan, returns glorifying God (17.15-19), in the impossibility of limiting the kingdom and the Son of humanity to a specific time and place (17.20-23), and in the way in which one person is taken and the other is left (17.34-35).

What remains constant is the saving role of faith: 'On the day of the Son of Humanity, the faithful will be saved, like the Samaritan foreigner who returned to praise God in faith' (LaVerdiere 1980: 215).

The essential point is that Lk. 17.11-37 forms a unity, and the establishment of that unity opens the way for a closer comparison with the unified story of Israel's first kingship (Judg. 9).

b. *More Detailed Analysis*
(1) *Section 10. The illustrative story (the deathly fable and the life-giving cure) (Judges 9.7-21; Luke 17.11-19).* Jotham's fable about the trees choosing their king is overshadowed by death. It is told in the aftermath of the killing of Abimelech's brothers, and the tree which comes to power is the thorn bush, useful mainly as an incendiary device which destroys even the strong trees. Thus, the kingdom of the trees—normally a realm of thriving life—becomes a place of death.

Luke's episode is the very opposite. Jesus is on a path that leads to death (to Jerusalem, 17.11; cf. 9.51) and he is met by ten lepers—the complete number of the worst disease—but in this very situation, normally a scene of anguish, he opens the way to a realm of life. The fable portends a kingdom of darkness, but the cure announces a world of light.

Despite this contrast, there is continuity in important details:

Judg. 9.7-14;	Lk. 17.11-13
And he went (*kai eporeuthē*)	And as he was going (*kai...poreuesthai*)
and stood (*estē*)	ten lepers, men, stood (*andres...estēsan*)
atop Mt Gerizim	at a distance
and raised up his voice...	and raised their voices...
(*kai ep-ēran tēn phōnēn*)	(*kai ēran phōnēn*)
'Hear me, men (*andres*) of Shechem,	'Jesus, teacher, and God will hear you...
The trees...said [four times], "Rule over us"...'	Have mercy on us'

---

6. This traditional meaning of *entos*—found in the patristic interpretation and in the ancient translations—is sometimes said not to accord with other Lukan texts (see Fitzmyer 1985: 1161). But that depends on how one interprets the other texts. What is certain is that the idea of an inner reality accords well with the texts that are most decisive—those on either side of the word *entos*. The preceding account—the curing of the lepers and the recognition by one of them of the working of God—points to a reality which, however much it comes from God, works within people's efforts and perceptions (in the shouting, the walking, and especially in the seeing and believing, 17.13-15, 19). And the subsequent account, concerning the Son of humanity, speaks of deeply human things which effect Jesus and his disciples in their inner world: suffering, death, and the seeking or losing of one's life (17.25, 30-33).

The change from 'Rule over us' to 'Have mercy on us' reflects the essence of Luke's adaptation. Jesus is revealing a divine realm which, while it may be called a kingdom, is primarily a world of compassion or mercy.

Luke's account of the actual cure—how the lepers were cleansed as they went their way (Lk. 17.14)—is from another source, but the conclusion of the episode when Jesus raises questions about the lepers (17.15-19) seems to have been colored by the conclusion of the Jotham incident (Judg. 9.16-20). Jotham asked repeatedly about the motives of the men of Shechem, about whether or not they had done right ('If... If... If... If... But if not... And if not...'). And Jesus asks repeatedly about the lepers' reactions ('Were not ten...? Where...? Has none...?'). The essence of these questions is that in diverse ways they probe beneath the surface of human actions to ask whether or not there is an underlying goodness of faith present. It was not in the men of the kingdom of Shechem, but in the returned Samaritan: 'Your faith has saved you'. Thus the way is prepared for the subsequent drama concerning the external kingdom of violent power politics, and concerning the kingdom of God with its inner functioning.

(2) *Section 11. Initial commotions and sufferings (the commotion against Abimelech's kingdom, Judges 9.30-41, and the commotion caused by the coming of the kingdom of God, Luke 17.20-25).* When king Abimelech first learned that Gaal was plotting against him, the message began 'Look (*idou*)...' And when Gaal in turn stood beside the gate of the rebellious city at sunrise and saw Abimelech's armies coming down on him from the mountains (see Soggin 1981: 189) on four sides, his first words as he looked in different directions were 'Look... Look... (*idou...idou...*)'. Then Gaal 'went out' (*ex-erchomai*), and Abimelech 'pursued' (*kata-diōkō*) him.

In Luke's account of the coming of the kingdom and the days of the Son of Humanity (17.20-23), there is a similar sense of surprise and commotion: 'Look here...there, Look (*idou...idou*)... Look there... Look here (*idou...idou*)... Do not go off (*ap-erchomai*) or pursue (*diōkō*)'.

The crucial difference is that Luke is making a contrast. All the looking here and there, all the setting off and pursuing are to be avoided. The observable traits of the kingship of Abimelech are not those of the kingdom of God. The kingdom of God has a whole other dimension, and it is within.

The onslaught by Abimelech's forces has overtones of something overwhelming and universal. It comes with the sunrise, from the mountains, in four directions. But in the case of the Son of Humanity, the sense of something overwhelming and universal is explicit and greater: it is like lightening flashing across the entire sky.

The accompaniment of all this is much suffering. Abimelech inflicts many (*polloi*) deaths and expulsions (Judg. 9.40b-41), and the Son of Humanity has to suffer many things (*polla*) and be rejected (Lk. 17.25).

Understanding Luke's procedure is made more difficult by the problem of understanding the two texts in their own right. The Old Testament passage looks simple, but the simplicity of Judges is often deceptive. And Luke's passage is notoriously obscure.

It seems central to understanding Luke's adaptation that apart from the idea of kingdom, one of the key links between the passages is that of death. Abimelech's kingdom is deathly, and death also hovers increasingly over Jesus: in his destination (Jerusalem, 17.11; cf. 9.51), in his encounter with the lepers (17.12-19), and in his allusion to coming suffering and rejection (17.25). When Luke speaks of the coming of the kingdom and of the days of the Son of Humanity, apparently part of what he is doing is alluding to the way in which, often obscurely, death impinges increasingly on Jesus and his disciples.

Instead of rendering life meaningless, death is inherent in life; it is associated with the kingdom of God and with the revealing of the Son of Humanity. In other words, instead of making a mockery of God and of humanity (as it sometimes seems to do), death is an avenue through which both God and (the Son of) Humanity are revealed. If Luke's text is obscure, that is appropriate; so is the death-related process of which it speaks. And, despite all the obscurity, he has transformed the apparently meaningless tragedy of Abimelech's kingdom into a text which integrates the drama into the positive message of Jesus. He has set death in a new context.

(3) *Section 12. Camaraderie and three cataclysms (Judges 9.25-29, 42-55; Luke 17.26-32).* Abimelech's fall begins with conspiratorial camaraderie (including eating and drinking, 9.25-29) and ends with a form of triple cataclysm: first the killings in the field and in Shechem (9.42-45), then the burning of the leaders in the temple or house (9.46-49), and finally, at Thebez, the killing of Abimelech by a woman trapped on a roof (9.50-55).

Luke has taken these balancing elements—the camaraderie and the cataclysms—and has both interwoven them and expanded them. Luke's interweaving is easy to see: the cataclysms occur during the camaraderie while people are still eating, drinking, and so on.

Luke's expansion does not mean greater wordiness, but a wider vision. Thus, the camaraderie in Luke refers not only to negative pursuits, but to a whole range of pursuits which are positive: eating, drinking, marrying, buying, selling, planting, and building (a full range of human activities).

And instead of being of a limited kind, as in Judges, the cataclysms are in some way universal: the flood in the days of Noah 'destroyed them all' (Lk. 17.26-27); the fire and brimstone from heaven in the days of Lot likewise 'destroyed them all' (17.28-29); and the day of the Son of Humanity has implications for everybody (17.30-32).

The essence of Luke's transformation is that he has taken a text which seems narrow and negative, and, partly by blending it with other texts (especially from Genesis), has turned it into something universal and positive, something which applies to all people and which, despite its inclusion of negative elements (particularly catastrophe and death), implies a process which is ultimately positive—ultimately a manifestation of the kingdom of a merciful God. The God who rains floods and fire is the God who, in Jesus, healed the lepers, even though only one in ten recognized it. Thus, the evil kingdom of Abimelech is used as a starting point for describing an evil which is greater but which is nonetheless encompassed by the positive realm of God, a realm founded on mercy.

The main word-cluster shared by these texts (field, house, roof, fire, woman) does not occur anywhere else in the Old Testament or New Testament. Thus the link is unique.

(3) *Section 13. Retribution concerning death and life (Judges 9.22-24, 56-57; Luke 17.33).* The story of Abimelech's fall is framed neatly by two references to retribution: the fall was God's way of punishing Abimelech and his followers for the evil they had done, particularly for the murder of the seventy brothers (Judg. 9.22-24 and 56-57). This is classic Old Testament doctrine—Deuteronomic.

Luke also gives a classic doctrine of retribution: whoever seeks life loses it, but whoever loses life saves it (17.33). Instead of two balancing (framing) negative statements as in Judges, Luke's single statement has two parts which balance one another in a different way: one is negative and the other is positive. And instead of being worked out clearly in the external world of politics, the retribution takes place primarily within.

(4) *Section 14. Death (leaving one) and the gathering to share the spoil (Judges 9.1-6; Luke 17.34-37).* The deaths of the brothers (all except one), along with the subsequent sharing of the political spoil, occur at the beginning of the Abimelech story (Judg. 9.1-6). But it is inherently connected with retribution (one leads to the other) and for that reason, partly at least, Luke places his adaptation of it next to the principle of retribution—at the end.

What is essential is that the rather prolonged account of the process which killed the brothers, leaving only one, provides a partial background for Luke's neatly repetitive phrases about one being taken, and the other being left. And the subsequent picture, of the murderers gathering (*syn-ēchthēs-an*) to share the spoil (by installing their co-conspirator, Judg. 9.6) provides an important part of the background to Luke's final picture: the eagles gathering (*epi-syn-achthēs-ontai*) at the body (17.37).

Again, Luke's picture contains something more; it is broader and more positive. The image of the body, while it does indeed reflect evil (devouring a corpse), also evokes the positive image of the body of Christ (cf. especially 1 Cor. 11.24; 12.27; Lk. 22.19), an image in which evil (the evil overtones of the corpse) is absorbed into a world of goodness and harmony, an image which further modifies that of the kingdom of God.

c. *Summary of Block B*

The principles used in assessing the Gideon story apply here also. The data indicate either an incredible coincidence or a literary adaptation.

Meanwhile, Judges continues immediately with the story of Jephthah, and Luke continues immediately with the parable of the unscrupulous judge.

5. *Block C. The Lone Woman and the Maverick Judge: Luke 18.1-8 as a Radical Reworking of the Story of Jephthah (Judges 10.6–12.7)*

a. *Introductory Analysis*

The story of Jephthah (the outlaw judge) and his daughter is one of the harshest in the book of Judges. Jephthah's rash pronouncement (his 'vow' or 'oath'—noun, *euché*; verb, *euchomai*, Judg. 11.30, 39) leads him to killing his only child, his beloved daughter. Like him, she, too, succumbs to the power of his foolish word, and having grieved her virginity, she goes to her death.

Luke (18.1-8) tells a story which is radically different, yet strikingly similar. It is the account of a quietly powerful encounter between a maverick judge and a vulnerable woman (not a virgin, as in Judges, but a widow). The difference in Luke is that the woman wins. Her process of pleading is like that of praying (verb, *pros-euchomai*, Lk. 18.1), and it overpowers the judge.

The effect of both texts is to show the power of the word, particularly of the word which is solemn or related to God. The emphasis on the word is highlighted by the fact that the Jephthah story (in 11.12-28) offers 'the only example...in Judges...of diplomacy as a method of resolving disputes' (Hoppe 1982: 171). The word of the vow overpowers Jephthah and his daughter; and the persistent, prayerlike word overpowers the unscrupulous judge. Thus, the word has the power of life and death. But while the Jephthah story emphasizes the negative side of the word—its power to bring death—Luke looks at the other side of the coin, so to speak, and highlights the positive, the power of the word to induce the life-giving justice of God.

This does not mean that the two stories are completely one-sided. The Jephthah story is, in fact, aware that the outcome of the word can be positive, and so it begins largely with two persistent dialogues which have a positive outcome: the dialogue of the Israelites with

God (Judg. 10.6-16), and, to a lesser extent, the dialogue of the Gileadites with the outlaw Jephthah (11.4-11). But the subsequent effort to use the word—the entreaties to the Ammonites (11.12-28)—achieves nothing except refusal (see especially 11.17, 20, 29). And in the final episodes concerning the vow which killed Jephthah's daughter (11.29-40) and concerning the inability to say 'Shibboleth' (a word which killed 42,000 Ephraimites, 11.1-6), the emphasis falls resoundingly on the negative. Thus, the episode of Jephthah's deathly vow is part of a larger drama concerning the power of the word, a drama which moves increasingly from positive to negative.

On the other hand, the Lukan story, while it may be positive, also contains a negative dimension. The widow wants justice, but it will not necessarily be pleasant: 'Avenge me of my adversary' (Lk. 18.3).

Hence, in dealing with the ancient, complex drama of the powerful word, Luke has taken its most colorful episode, that of the deathly encounter between the outlaw judge and the defenseless woman, and he has turned it into a story where positive and negative are indeed both contained, but where the unlikely woman wins the struggle and where, correspondingly, the emphasis falls on the positive.

b. *More Detailed Analysis*
By and large, Luke keeps to the order of the Old Testament text. However, he has made a number of adaptations. As well as using the pleading scenes (Judg. 10.6-18, and one aspect of 11.4-11), his first verse, about always praying (18.1), depends also on the account of Jephthah taking the vow (11.29-31).

Furthermore, Luke's parable contains 'avenge' (*ekdikeō*) not just once, as in the Jephthah story (Judg. 11.36), but four times (Lk. 18.3, 5, 7, 8). There is a similar procedure elsewhere: in reworking 1 Kings 19, the single Old Testament reference to 'following' ('follow me', 1 Kgs 19.20) in the gospel becomes a recurring refrain (Lk. 9.57, 59, 61).

(1) *Section 15. Repeated human pleading, and pleading solemnly with God (Judges 10.6-18 [cf. 11.4-11]; 11.29-31; Luke 18.1)*. The beginning of the Jephthah story is dominated by two dialogues, two interrelated accounts of prolonged pleading. First, as the Ammonites and others attack, the Israelites as a whole plead with God (Judg. 10.6-18). Then, as the attack intensifies, the Gileadite leaders plead with Jephthah (Judg. 11.4-11). Initially, God and Jephthah will not hear such pleading, but gradually they become somewhat more responsive.

Later, at the beginning of the action when it is Jephthah's turn to plead (with God), he resorts to a certain brutalization of the word: he links his plea with vowing (*euchomai*) a deathly vow (*euchē*).

The beginning of Luke's parable also contains a form of pleading: it is always necessary to pray (*pros-euchomai*) and not give up (18.1). Thus, at one level Luke's text is like a simplified synthesis of the two Old Testament texts:

Old Testament:
repeated pleading; pleading with intense vowing (*euchomai*)

New Testament:
constant praying (*pros-euchomai*), and not giving up

But, on closer inspection, Luke's synthesis is not simple. He has made several careful adaptations. The idea of always praying is repeated, in variant form, in the 'not giving up', and this repetition captures something of the repetitive nature of the Old Testament texts. The move from *euchomai* to *pros-euchomai* maintains a certain continuity of content, but it also involves a form of word-play.

Thus, the number of elements behind Luke's text (about praying always, 18.1) is considerable. First of all, it depends on the Old Testament picture of the Israelites pleading to God (Judg. 10.6-18), and secondarily, on the repetitive aspect of the Gileadites pleading with Jephthah (11.4-11). It combines that basic picture of pleading to God with the episode of making the vow (9.29-31). And, as often in Luke, the actual phrasing may reflect another source—in this case, the New Testament tradition about praying (see 2 Thess. 1.11, 'we pray always'; cf. 1 Thess. 5.17).

While distilling the Old Testament texts, Luke avoids any impression that brutal vows are an appropriate method of dealing with God. Judges does not actually approve of such vows, but Judges can be misunderstood, and Luke wants to be clear.

(2) Section 16. The maverick judge (Jephthah, Judges 11.1-3 [cf. 10.1-5]; unnamed, Luke 18.2). Jephthah is a mighty man, but an outsider. Born of a prostitute, he is banished, and he lives apart, leading a force for whom 'might is right'. Yet, he is listed among the judges, and 'he judged (*krinō*) Israel' (cf. Judg. 12.7).

Luke's picture of a judge (*kritēs*) who neither feared God nor respected people (Lk. 18.2) reflects the portrayal of Jephthah. Jephthah lives by raw power; Luke's judge is unscrupulous. The essence of both is that each is a law unto himself. But Luke's adaptation is more domesticated.

Luke's judge was 'in a certain city', and the verses which precede the Jephthah story associate a judge with many 'cities' (10.1-5, especially 10.4).

(3) Section 17. Pleading with the judge to take action against one's enemy (Judges 11.4-11; Luke 18.3). The Gileadites 'come to' (*erchomai pros* + pronoun, twice) Jephthah and plead with him to 'fight the [attacking] Ammonites'—a phrase which occurs three times (Judg. 11.6, 8, 9). Similarly, in Luke, the widow 'comes to' (*erchomai pros* + pronoun) the judge and asks him to avenge her of her adversary.

Again, Luke has domesticated the Old Testament. Omitting the details of the Ammonite war, he has kept the central idea—being avenged of one's adversary.

Essentially the same two words, 'avenge' (*ekdikeō*) and 'adversary' (*antidikos*), are later found in the Jephthah story (Judg. 11.36, *ekdikeō*; 12.2, *anēr antidikōn*, 'an "adversarial" man'). Apart from Jer. 28.36 (LXX) and Judg. 6.31, such a word-combination does not occur in any other single story or passage in the New Testament or Old Testament.

(4) Section 18. The unwillingness to listen to the word (Judges 11.12-28; Luke 18.4a)
The plea to Jephthah is followed by appeals to the Ammonites, appeals which go back into history and which, in the telling, sound prolonged. But they achieve nothing. As of old, Moab and Sihon 'were not willing' (*kai ouk ēthelēsen*, twice, Judg. 11.17, 20), so now the king of Ammon 'did not listen to the words' (11.28) of Jephthah. In Luke (18.4a), the appeals are equally unsuccessful: 'And he was not willing (*kai ouk ēthelen*) for a time'.

The sense of passing time, which in the Jephthah story is achieved through prolonged negotiations and appeals to history, is communicated in Luke through a simple phrase: 'for a time' (*epi chronon*).

In Luke's simplified story, the adversary never appears but always stays in the background, and so, instead of being directed to the adversary (as in the Old Testament), the appeal is directed to the judge. This takes further liberty with the plot, but simplifying the plot clarifies the focus on the process of appealing and (not) listening, and thus more effectively brings out an essential part of the Old Testament story.

(5) *Section 19. Trouble linked to avenging: the decisive moment between the woman and the judge (Judges 11.32-40; Luke 18.4b-5)*. The returning Jephthah sees his daughter not as the victim of his own foolishness, but as someone who causes great trouble for him: 'Alas, my daughter, you have brought me deep trouble' (Judg. 11.35). But she tells him to keep his word since God has avenged (*ekdikeō*) him of his enemies (11.36). Thus the two elements—trouble and avenging—are connected; in fact, the avenging is seen as causing the trouble.

Luke links two similar realities—bother/trouble and avenging. But rather than the avenging causing the trouble, the trouble causes the avenging: 'This widow is causing me so much bother, I will avenge her' (18.5).

In both cases, there is a level at which it is the lone woman who causes the trouble, yet unlike the Old Testament where the trouble comes largely from a mixture of Jephthah's undue rigidity and his daughter's undue submissiveness, the trouble in the New Testament is a positive force which the woman deliberately maintains.

Here, as earlier, Luke simplifies the plot. Instead of being said by two different people (as in the Old Testament—by Jephthah and his daughter), the statements about trouble and avenging are both said by the judge.

(6) *Section 20. Epilogue (in parallelism): salvation and vengeance (Judges 12.1-6; Luke 18.6-9)*. Finally, there is a two-part epilogue concerning the hostile Ephraimites. In the first part (Judg. 12.1-3), Jephthah tells the assembled Ephraimites that when it came to crossing over against Ammon, his cries for saving help had been answered not by them but in effect by God. And in the second part (12.4-6), Jephthah's assembled Gileadites prevent the lying Ephraimites, when they want to cross over the Jordan, from saving themselves. The two parts balance each other in a prose form of antithetical parallelism. The first tells of a cry which is answered by God. And the second shows the reverse—a lie which leads to death.

Luke takes these two elements—the cry leading to salvation and the lie leading to death—and renders them into a parallel epilogue of his own: 'Will not God avenge his elect who cry to him…? Yes, he will avenge them quickly' (18.7-8a). Thus, instead of two parts where one is positive and the other negative, Luke gives two parts that are both essentially positive, but where both also include an allusion to something negative, to an evil which is to be overcome. Thus, both stories deal with evil, but while Judges may seem to suggest that evil is a runaway force—the final picture is of slaughtering the Ephraimites—Luke suggests an evil which is ultimately contained.

c. *Summary of Block C*

Once again, the data give a choice: either this is an extraordinary series of coincidences, or it is a literary imitation/reworking.

The Jephthah story can give offense, especially because of the killing of Jephthah's daughter and the 42,000 Ephraimites. Hence, there is justification, as Phyllis Trible indicates, for protest (1984: 64-87). It is arguable, however, that Judges does not approve of these killings. In fact, it implies condemnation, especially in the final line: 'In those days there was no king in Israel, and each man did as he pleased' (21.25).

But, condemnation notwithstanding, Judges is open to misunderstanding. For many readers, its stance is not clear. It is understandable, therefore, that Luke should rework the Jephthah story in a way which would develop the most basic issue—the relationship of the woman to the judge.

6. General Conclusion

Luke's adaptation of Judges 6–12 shows an extraordinary theological boldness. While being thoroughly imbued with the ancient scriptural tradition, Luke did not feel confined by it. Rather, he expressed his faithfulness to the ancient tradition by adapting it thoroughly to the insights of a new age, the insights of the Jesus tradition. In the spirit of that tradition, Luke wrote not to destroy, but to fulfill.

The use of Judges 6–12 in Lk. 16.1–18.8 forms a steady and distinctive pattern of dependence on the LXX. In itself, this does not prove that these Judges-based passages of Luke 16–18 belong to an earlier document, Proto-Luke. But it means that in some way they belong together, and that their togetherness comes from the LXX rather than from Mark. Thus, they add credibility to Feine's hypothesis concerning Proto-Luke, and they give it greater precision.

48

From the Infancy Narrative to the Final Gathering: The Story of Samson (Judges 13–16) as a Frame for Proto-Luke (Luke 1.5–2.52; Acts 9.32–15.21)

Having traced the use of Judges 1–12, the next narrative for examination is that of Samson (Judg. 13–16).

Among all the judges, Samson has a special place. He is climactically last, and his story has unusual length and personal detail. Here, more then elsewhere in Judges, there is the portrait of a life and its stages, a form of biography. It is a story which has inspired considerable art, including film.

It is generally recognized that Luke has drawn on the Samson story. The first chapter of the Lukan infancy narrative, with its double annunciation of birth (first to Zechariah and then to Mary, Luke 1, especially 1.5-38, 57-58, 80) builds significantly on the first chapter of the Samson account (Judg. 13; cf. Brown 1977: 156).

But the dependence goes further. Luke uses the larger Samson story as one of the devices for framing his entire account. The infancy narrative (Lk. 1–2, particularly in its opening and closing episodes) depends on the account of Samson's early years when he is still at home (Judg. 13–14). And the culminating section of Proto-Luke (Acts 9.32–15.35, particularly in its opening and closing episodes) depends on the later and final events of Samson's life (Judg. 15–16).

The idea of framing needs emphasis; the depth of the dependence is limited. In many of Peter's deeds and speeches (within Acts 9.32–11.26 and 15.6-21), for instance, the framework depends, in part at least, on the Samson story. But much of the content—for example, of Peter's speeches to Cornelius and to the Jerusalem assembly (Acts 10.28-43 and 15.7-11)—depends on other sources. The overall relationship is outlined below in Table 76.

The strength of the evidence for Luke's use of the Samson story varies considerably from episode to episode. The strongest evidence is at the beginning and end: in the annunciations (Lk. 1.5-38), and in the account of the Jerusalem assembly (Acts 15.1-21). These help to pin down clearly the fact and limits of its use.

Help in tracking it down is also provided by the angelic message to Cornelius (Acts 10.1-8). This is a relatively obvious variation on the annunciations to Zechariah and Mary, and so it provides an initial clue that the area around Acts 10 may be a worthwhile place to look when searching for the reworking of the rest of the Samson narrative.

But many of the connections are elusive, at least at first sight. There is probably no way, for instance, without the benefit of the context, that one would make a connection between Samson's partial revelations to Delilah (Judg. 16.4-14) and the tentative preaching of the word in Antioch (Acts 11.19-21).

Once the entire picture emerges, however—the whole pattern from Luke 1–2 to Acts 9–15—it assumes considerable strength and coherence. And at every stage, even in the supremely elusive Delilah–Antioch connection, are links of detail or language.

Therefore, it is necessary in weighing the evidence which is provided by the following analysis to take account both of the specific passage under consideration and also of its place within the larger pattern.

Table 76. *The Samson Story as a Frame*
(Judges 13–16; Luke 1–2; Acts 9.52–15.21)

Judges 13–14	Luke 1.5–2.52
1. Annunciations, birth, growing up (ch. 13)	Annunciations, births, growing up (Lk. 1.5-38, 80; 2.7, 21, 40)
2. Samson's youth: his involvement with a Philistine wife leaves his parents and others perplexed. Samson returns to his father's house (ch. 14)	Jesus' childhood: his excursion among the doctors of the Law leaves them and his parents perplexed. Jesus goes back with his parents to Nazareth (Lk. 2.41-52)
Judges 15–16	**Acts 9.32–15.21**
3. Samson's return to the Philistines brings death to a woman and her father. Then Samson dwelt in Etam (15.1-8)	Peter's presence among the Gentiles brings life to Aeneas and Dorcas. Then Peter abode in Jaffa (Acts 9.32-43)
4. The Philistines get Samson to come to them. He brings death (15.9-19)	Cornelius gets Peter to come to him. Peter brings (spiritual) life (Acts 10)
5. Samson is surrounded in Gaza but reveals (God's) awesome power (15.20–16.3)	Peter is confronted in Jerusalem but recounts God's supporting wonders (Acts 11.1-18)
6. Through Delilah, Samson's divine secret moves towards revelation (a threefold repetitive text) (16.4-14)	In Antioch, the revealing of God's word moves from reticence to proclamation (a balanced text, somewhat repetitive) (Acts 11.19-21)
7. Decisive breakthrough: Delilah reveals the divine secret to the Philistines (16.15-21)	Decisive reaction: the Jerusalem church approves open proclamation of the word to the Greeks (Acts 11.22-26)
8. The Philistine assembly: a finale which as never before reveals God's secret to the Gentiles. After two statements about what God has done, Samson brings down the house of the Philistines (16.23-31)	The Jerusalem assembly: a finale which brings to a new level the process of revealing God's word to the Gentiles. Two statements about what God has done culminate with a quotation about restoring the fallen house (Acts 15.6-21)

1. *More Detailed Analysis*

a. *Section 1. Annunciations, Birth/s, Growing Up (Judges 13; Luke 1.5-38, 80; 2.7, 21, 40)*
The similarities here are relatively easy to detect and have already been documented, at least in part. However, as Brown's analysis suggests (1977: 156, 270-71), Judges 13 is just one component among many.

Most of the reworking of Judges 13 occurs right at the beginning of the infancy narrative in the annunciations (Lk. 1.5-38). Only the closing verses (13.24-25, concerning birth and growth) are reflected at the center of Luke 1–2 (cf. 1.80; 2.7, 21, 40). Yet this final link (between the growing up of Samson and the growing up of Jesus, Judg. 13.24-25 and Lk. 2.40) is enough to set the stage for the next major connection concerning the first youthful episodes of Samson and Jesus (Judg. 14 and Lk. 2.41-50).

b. *Section 2. A Perplexing Youthful Episode, and a Return Home (Judges 14; Luke 2.41-50)*
As Samson begins to develop, the Judges narrative gives a vivid picture of his youthful exuberance: an excursion to Philistine territory leads to an infatuation and then to an adventure. He has no problem demolishing a roaring lion and raiding honey from a swarm

of bees—eating the honey from his hands as he walks along!—but, when it comes a clash of wits with the Philistines, to solving a riddle about lions and honey, he is mastered by the woman. However, the spirit of the Lord, which had first given him the strength to overpower the lion, also enables him to solve his dilemma with the Philistines and the woman. In fact, the entire adventure 'came from the Lord' (Judg. 14.4); it is part of the Lord's way of freeing Israel from Philistine power.

Samson's parents, however, do not understand. Like parents watching an unpredictable teenager, they first try to dissuade him from his involvement with the Philistines (Judg. 14.2-4), and even when they accompany him back to Philistine territory, they are left out of the secret of his God-given victory over the lion (14.5-6).

The adventure of the twelve-year-old Jesus in the temple is tame by comparison. Here there are no women, lions, or bees. Some might say it is not really an adventure at all. Yet it is a teenage excursion which leaves Jesus' parents confused, worried, and sad.

Luke has adapted the youthful adventure to the requirements of his own narrative, particularly to his focus on the temple. The problem is no longer oppressive Philistines, but the oppressive regime of the old Law, centered on the temple. So it is the doctors in the temple that Jesus engages. In his own way he, too, intimates to the representatives of the old regime that outside of themselves there is a further source of wisdom.

His parents, of course, do not understand. Like the parents of Samson who did not know that his adventure came from the Lord (Judg. 14.4), they do not know that he must be about his Father's business (Lk. 2.49-50). But at the end, Jesus, like Samson, goes home (Judg. 14.19; Lk. 2.51). The texts contain some similarities of detail:

Old Testament:
kai ho pater autou kai hē matēr autou ouk egnōsan (14.4)
kai katebē [cf. 14.1, 10, 19] *Sampsōn kai ho patēr autou kai hē matēr autou eis Thamnatha* (14.5)
kai epestrepsen meth' hēmeras (14.8)
idou tō patri mou and tē mētri mou... (14.16)

New Testament:
kai ouk egnōsan hoi goneis autou (2.43)
kai...epestrepsan...kai...meta hēmeras treis (2.45-46)
idou ho patēr sou kagō... (2.48)
kai katebē met' autōn...eis Nazareth (2.51)

Old Testament:
And his father and his mother did not know.
And Samson and his father and mother went down to Timna.
And he returned after [some] days.
Behold, [not even] my father and my mother...

New Testament:
And his parents did not know.
And...they returned...and...after three days.
Behold, your father and I...
And he went down with them...to Nazareth.

c. *Section 3. A Matter of Life and Death for the Man and the Woman (Judges 15.1-8; Acts 9.32-43)*

Apparently advancing in sensibility and technology, Samson seeks to return to his wife (bypassing her younger sister), and when the woman's father prevents him, he embarks on an ingenious plan of unleashing fiery pairs of foxes, thus spreading destruction through the land of the Philistines. The Philistines in retaliation burn the woman's house, thereby killing herself and her father. Samson responds by inflicting on the Philistine 'a great defeat'. Then he goes away and dwells in Etam.

The corresponding passage in Luke's work is the two-part account of how Peter, working near Jaffa (not far from traditional Philistine country), brought not destruction and death to that territory but faith and life (Acts 9.32-43). In particular, instead of being the occasion for the death of a father and a wife, Peter first heals a man (Aeneas, 9.32-35) and then restores life to a woman (Dorcas, 9.36-42).

At this point the Old Testament text has been thoroughly distilled. Here there are no fiery foxes and burning houses. The destructiveness has given way to the calm imparting of life. Destructiveness had its place, however, in the Old Testament story; though negative, it had a positive purpose—the combating of the deathly Philistine oppression. Luke renders this into a language which makes the positive purpose more obvious: combating deathly oppression becomes the communication of faith and life.

Most of Luke's text depends on other sources, and it has been adapted to fit the patterns and requirements of Luke's larger narrative, including the two-part pattern in Luke 7 (the centurion's servant, 7.1-10, and the widow's son, 7.11-17). The Samson incident provides only limited components—some coloring, and a slender framework. The shared framework is reflected in the opening and closing phrases of the two texts:

> Old Testament:
> Opening: *kai egeneto meth' hēmeras en hēmerais*... (Judg. 15.1)
> Closing: *kai katebē kai katōkei*
> *para tō cheimarrō*
> *en tō spēlaiō Ētam* (Judg. 15.8)
>
> New Testament:
> Opening: *egeneto de...* (Acts 9.32)
> Closing: *egeneto de hēmeras hikanas meinai*
> *en Ioppē*
> *para tini Simōni bursei* (Acts 9.43)
>
> Old Testament:
> Opening: And it came to pass after days on days [= after a time]...
> Closing: He went down and dwelt
> at (*para*) the wadi
> in the cave of Etam.
>
> New Testament:
> Opening: Now it came to pass...
> Closing: And it came to pass that he abode many days
> in Jaffa
> with (*para*) a certain Simon, a tanner.

As in other cases (for example, the relationship between Judg. 3.7-31 and Acts 12), there has been some criss-crossing of details between the opening and the closing. The 'days on days' from the Old Testament opening finds its equivalent, 'many days', in the New Testament closing.

And the sense of detail about where the protagonists went to dwell changes from an emphasis on geography or topography ('at the wadi in the cave of Etam') to an emphasis on a person ('in Jaffa, with a certain Simon, a tanner'). This accords with Luke's larger strategy of shifting the focus of the narrative to people (as for instance, in the shift from focusing on the temple to focusing on the person of Jesus).

d. *Section 4. The Gentiles Get Samson/Peter to Come to Them (Judges 15.9-19; Acts 10)*
Having told how Samson and Peter went to dwell in Etam and Joppa respectively, both texts then make an unusual move—they show the subsequent initiative as coming from the Gentiles. The Philistines come to Judah and demand to have Samson (Judg. 15.9-10). And Cornelius sends to Jaffa and asks that Peter come to him (Acts 10.5-8). This is the first time that the Philistines come in search of Samson, and the first time that Gentiles come in search of Peter.

The initial connection between the Cornelius episode and the story of Samson is relatively easy to see. Cornelius receives an angelic message (Acts 10.1-8) which is a variation on the annunciation to Zechariah (Lk. 1.5-20)—and thus a variation on the beginning of the Samson story (Judg. 13).

But the Philistine search for Samson is very different in character from Cornelius's quest for Peter. The Philistines come with an army. Cornelius, though he is a centurion, sends just two servants and one devout soldier. The relationship of the texts is a mixture of continuity and contrast. Some of the main points include:

Judges	*Acts*
The Philistines go up and encamp in Judah (15.9)	Cornelius sends a few people to fetch Peter (10.1-16)
The Judeans ask why they have come ('Why have you come up against us?') (15.10)	Peter asks why they have come ('What is the cause for which you are here?') (10.17-23, especially 10.22)
As the Judeans deliver Samson the Philistines run to meet him ('And he came...and the Philistines shouted on meeting him, and ran to meet him') (15.14)	As a group arrives with Peter Cornelius comes eagerly to meet him ('When Peter came in, Cornelius meeting him, fell at his feet [and] worshipped [him]') (10.25)

Both meetings contain two actions, one an intensification of the other. The Philistines shout and then run. Cornelius falls at Peter's feet and then worships. But the attitudes are different, and so is the subsequent action:

Judges	*Acts*
Samson slays the Philistines with the jawbone of an ass (15.15-17)	Peter's words bring new life to the Gentiles (10.26-43)
Samson receives water and his spirit revives (15.18-19)	The Spirit descends and Cornelius is baptized in water (10.44-48)

These final texts illustrate two of Luke's most basic procedures: contrast and christianization. Peter's imparting of life is a contrast with Samson's slaying. And the baptizing involves a christianization of Samson's use of water. In both cases, Luke maintains a certain continuity with the Old Testament, but he also makes changes and uses other sources.

e. *Section 5. From Being Surrounded/Confronted to Being Dramatically Strengthened (Judges 15.20–16.3; Acts 11.1-18)*
The next episode tells how Samson, when visiting a prostitute in Gaza, was surrounded by hostile Philistines who lay in ambush at the city gates. But in a display of power which completely overwhelmed his encircling opponents, Samson rose at midnight, took hold of the city gates, and walked away with them to a mountain top.

The next episode in Acts tells how Peter, when he returned from Cornelius to Jerusalem, was engaged in dispute by those insisting on circumcision. But Peter told of the dramatic events which had happened—the ecstatic visions and manifestations of the Spirit—and in this way he overcame the hostility of his opponents.

In comparison with the Old Testament episode, the New Testament account is prolonged and domesticated, and it certainly uses other sources. Yet both texts share a common theme: hostile opposition being overcome by a manifestation of a power which ultimately comes from the divine.

There is also some affinity of detail:

Samson went...to Gaza,	When Peter went up to Jerusalem
and seeing a prostitute went in to her.	those of the circumcision disputed with him
And it was announced...saying...	saying,
...they surrounded him to ambush him...	You went in to uncircumcised men...
in the gate of the city... (Judg. 16.1-2)	Peter explained, I was in the city... (Acts 11.2-5)

Both accounts also contain complementary images of peace—twenty years of judging (Judg. 5.20), and being peaceful (Acts 5.18; cf. Judg. 3.30 LXX). In the Old Testament text, the image of peace is at the opening, but in the New Testament, at the closing.

f. *Section 6. The Gradual Revelation (to Delilah/the Greeks): The Tension Between the Word Contained and the Word Spoken (Judges 16.4-14; Acts 11.19-21)*
The Samson story changes when, for the first time, it is said that Samson loves someone—Delilah. There is now a new personal intensity, as reflected in the threefold repetitive conversation between the couple (Judg. 16.6-14). The focus of this conversation is Samson's divine secret. For her own motives, Delilah wants to know what gives Samson his strength. The secret remains unknown, but the pressure is strong, and in the third conversation, when Samson refers to his hair (16.13-14), the divine secret is almost revealed.

In Acts, the scene changes to Antioch, and in the balanced, repetitive pictures of the comings and goings of the new church (Acts 11.19-20), there is a dynamic which reflects the essence of the Old Testament story. The word (*logos*), which initially is not spoken (11.19), is later revealed (11.20). Those going in one direction (to Phoenicia, Cyprus, and Antioch) 'spoke the word to no one' except to Jews (11.19), but those going in the opposite direction (from Cyprus and Cyrene to Antioch) 'spoke also to Greeks, proclaiming the good news of the Lord Jesus' (11.20). The same word for speaking or telling, *laleō*, is used twice in both texts (Judg. 16.10, 13; Acts 11.19, 20).

Luke has taken the idea of the divine secret, something which in the Old Testament is gradually being revealed to the Philistines through the struggles of Samson, and has adapted it to describe how, through the church's struggles, God's word is increasingly revealed to the Greeks.

g. *Section 7. Decisive Breakthrough: Further Revelation and Leading the Person (Samson/ Paul) Who Will Reveal Yet More (Judges 16.15-21; Acts 11.22-26)*
As the process of revealing develops, both texts tell of a decisive breakthrough. In the Old Testament story, Delilah finally wrests Samson's secret clearly from him, and in Acts, the authoritative Jerusalem church, which might have hesitated at widespread evangelization of the Greeks, instead gives its decisive support—'the word was heard' in Jerusalem—and they sent the wonderfully uplifting character of Barnabas ('for he was a good man, full of the Holy Spirit and of faith') to Antioch. It is as though, if it were possible, they had sent the Holy Spirit in person.

In both texts, the breakthrough is associated with a quality of the heart. Samson tells Delilah 'all his heart' and she tells it to 'all' (*panta... kardias...pantas*, Judg. 16.18). Barnabas exhorts 'all, that with purpose of heart they should stay close to the Lord' (*pantas... kardias...*, Acts 11.26). In other words, in both cases the truth of the secret resides in some way in the heart.

48. *From the Infancy Narrative to the Final Gathering* 495

Then the Philistines led Samson to Gaza (*ēgagon...eis Gazan*, Judg. 16.21), and Barnabas, in what may seems to be a surprising move, led Paul to Antioch (*ēgagen eis Antiocheian*, Acts 11.26). Thus, in different ways, preparation is made for future events: for Samson's final deed in Gaza, and Paul's mission from Antioch.

The texts conclude by giving diverse images of the fruitful passage of time. Samson's hair begins to grow (Judg. 16.22), and Paul and Barnabas spend a year developing the church in Antioch (Acts 11.26).

h. *Section 8. The Final Gathering which Reveals God to the Gentiles (Judges 16.23-31; Acts 15.6-21)*
The Samson story closes with a great assembly of the Philistines. Thousands of them, including all their leaders, gathered to offer sacrifice to Dagon, their god, and to mock the blinded Samson. But Samson, having prayed to God to remember him, brought the house down on them—thus manifesting to the Philistines, with cataclysmic force, the presence of a God who was truly overwhelming.

The corresponding Lukan episode is the assembly in Jerusalem, the final gathering which irrevocably cleared the way for the unhampered preaching of God to the Gentiles. Both accounts speak of God acting among the Gentiles, but there is a fundamental difference: the Old Testament God is revealed in a great act of judgment, but in the New Testament the emphasis is on God's compassion.

The Samson story, of course, is not Luke's only source for describing the Jerusalem assembly, but it has provided a certain framework. The relationship between the texts is a mixture of continuity and reversal (Table 77).

Table 77. *The Final Gathering (Judges 16.23-31; Acts 15.6-21)*

The Gathering	
The leaders of the Philistines assembled (*synēchthēsan*) to sacrifice to Dagon... and to rejoice (Judg. 16.23a)	The apostles and the elders assembled (*synēchthēsan*) to see about this word. After much disputing (Acts 15.6-7a)
The First Declaration (God's Action)	
And they said (*eipan*) 'Our God handed over (*paredōken ho theos hēmōn...*) Samson our enemy...' (16.23b)	Peter rose and said (*eipen*) to them 'Brethren...God chose among you...that... (*en hymin exelexato ho theos*) the Gentiles should hear the word...' (15.7b-11)
The Reaction to God's Deeds (Clamor/Silence)	
The people saw their god and they acclaimed him (16.24a)	The whole multitude was silent and they heard...what God had done... (15.12)
The Second, Complementary, Declaration (God's Action)	
And they said, 'Our God handed over (*paredōken ho theos hēmon*) Samson our enemy...' (16.24b)	After they were silent, James responded, 'Brethren, Simon described how... God visited... (*ho theos epeskepsato...*) the Gentiles to take...a people' (15.13-14)
The Fallen House	
Description of how, because of Samson, 'the house fell' (*epesen ho oikos*) (16.25-31)	Quotation from Amos about rebuilding the fallen dwelling (*an-oiko-domēsō...tēn peptōkuian*) (15.15-17)

Some reversals are clear: the clamor and silence; the house knocked down and the house rebuilt. Others are more subtle or debatable: the rejoicing and the disputing; Samson's enmity towards the Gentiles as opposed to the Jerusalem assembly's positive attitude towards them. And behind all these details is the larger reversal mentioned earlier: while the Old Testament episode shows God as implicitly judging the Gentiles, destroying their house, the New Testament shows God as working more compassionately to form Gentiles into a people so that through them God's former chosen house should be reconstituted.

2. *Conclusion*

No single character in Luke–Acts clearly reflects the raw Herculean dimensions of Samson. It may seem, therefore, that Proto-Luke does not use the Samson story.

But there are more dimensions or levels to the Samson story than raw heroics. Within the account of rough adventure lies a portrayal of great struggle, a God-related struggle which has inspired art and poetry, and it is this dimension/level that Luke has captured and had adapted to the emergence of the early church.

That Luke should so adapt the Samson story is externally plausible. Luke's infancy narrative, especially the annunciations, has obvious similarities to the beginning of the Samson story (Judg. 13). Having used part of the Samson story in so crucial an area—at the beginning—it is not surprising that Luke should use it further. It is particularly plausible, if Proto-Luke used the Samson beginning for his own beginning, that he should also use the Samson ending for his own ending (Acts 9.32–15.21).

The similarities (in Lk. 1–2 and especially in Acts 9–15) generally occur in the texts' frameworks rather than in the details of the plots—a role which accords broadly with the role of the whole Samson story as framing Proto-Luke. Because of this framing function, the similarities tend to be of a general natural. Yet they are significant, and not only by their content, but also by their order and the presence of shared details.

The huge differences between Samson's God-related heroics and the apostles' evangelizing become intelligible once allowance is made for Luke's tendency to internalize and for the broader tendency, from Hesiod to Virgil, of lessening the emphasis on heroics; Virgil's hero is indeed heroic; but he is also *pius*. (See Chapter 1, under 'Literary Imitation: The Practice'). Luke leaves the heroics aside and distills the God-related aspect, particularly the aspect of God's revelation, God's word.

It is reasonable, then, to conclude that the ancient picture of the hero who became the instrument of God's revelation (Judg. 13–16) has been adapted to form one element of the picture of God's later revelation.

49

The Search for a True Home (With God):
Zacchaeus's Search for Jesus (Luke 19.1-10) as 'A Diminutive Model' of the Danites' Marred Search for a Home with a Shrine (Judges 17–18)

Apart from using the Samson story (Judg. 13–16) to help build a general framework (Lk. 1–2; Acts 9–15; see Chapter 48), Proto-Luke now continues the sequential use of the rest of the Old Testament book: most of Judges 17–21 contributes to sections of Luke 19–24. First, Judges 17–18.

The account of how the Danites migrated to the north and set up a shrine (Judg. 17–18) —the infamous schismatic shrine of Dan—is a story of something which went terribly wrong. The original idea may have seemed good: having failed to receive an inheritance in the apportioning of the land, they decided to journey northwards in search of a home (18.1-2). And the subsequent decision to take a shrine with them (18.14-31) may have seemed even better. Now they could be at home with God, so to speak; they had found their true place.

But this quest for a home with God was fundamentally marred.

The rot at the center of the story is illustrated by the initial episode concerning the shrine of Micah (LXX: Michaias), the shrine which would eventually become the shrine of Dan (Judg. 17).

The Michaias episode begins with ominous pictures—a man stealing from his mother, and an abundance of cursed money (stolen, cursed, and later largely pocketed, though it was consecrated [Soggin 1981: 268]). And it is on the basis of these things, which are radically destructive of any home, that Michaias turns his house into a shrine of Yahweh. He makes an image and installs a priest, and though the priest appears to be in good standing as a Levite from Judah, he is little better than another of Michaias's images. The Levite replaces Michaias's son, and, living in Michaias's house, he is completely beholden to him (Judg. 17.11-13).

Michaias's name meant 'Who is like Yahweh' (or 'Yahweh the Incomparable'; see Boling 1975: 258), but in actual fact, from stealing his mother's money to making images to manipulating the priesthood, Michaias seems to have had no idea of anything outside himself, still less any sense of an incomparable God.

In the next chapter (Judg. 18), the same attitude shows up in the Danites—and with tragic results. In their search for a home and a shrine, they show no respect for the homes of others and no interest in whether their shrine is sanctioned by God. With the threat of force, they take Michaias's shrine with them, and then, with force unleashed, they wipe out a peaceful town and establish their home and shrine.

The entire account (Judg. 17–18) is like a reversal of the journey towards God. Yet at a certain level, it looks like a sincere quest with many of the trappings of a genuine search for a true home with God. In fact, the migration of Dan, with its journey and its establishing of a shrine, 'has been modelled on the pattern of the journey across the desert and the conquest, of which it forms a sort of diminutive model'.[1] But rather than being a copy of the episodes springing from the exodus, the migration of Dan is largely a contrast of those episodes. The shrine which emerges at the end of the Danites' migration does not have any of the divine sanction, or the challenging authority of the shrine which emerged from the exodus.

As Judges had once given a contrasting diminutive model of older events, so Luke in turn gives a contrasting diminutive model of Judges 17–18. The story of Zacchaeus (Lk. 19.1-10) distills and reverses much of the account of Michaias and the Danites. The Old Testament quest for a home with God, which in Judges 17–18 went so wrong, finds fresh expression in the brief account of Zacchaeus's desire to see Jesus. As in Judges 17–18, there is a certain amount of personal striving (his running ahead to climb the tree), yet the decisive turn comes from Jesus' invitation, 'Zacchaeus, hurry down…'. The shrine at the end of the New Testament account is not so much a specific religious building as a union with God within the home (Jesus, who is called 'Lord' goes in to 'abide' with Zacchaeus). A hand-made shrine has given way to a shrine of abiding togetherness, sanctioned by the Lord.

In reworking Judges 17–18 to help form the Zacchaeus account, Luke draws his framework largely from the Danites' history (Judg. 18) and uses almost all the initial story, the revealing account of Michaias (Judg. 17), as a single revelatory episode within that framework. It is the Michaias story, with its early emphasis on giving and returning silver money, which underlies much of Zacchaeus's revelatory exchange with Jesus about giving and returning goods (Lk. 19.8-9) (see Table 78).

Table 78. *Seeking a True Home (Judges 17–18; Luke 19.1-9)*

	Judges 17–18	Luke 19.1-9
1.	The man whose name was Michaias (17.1)	A man named Zacchaeus (19.1-2)
2.	Preliminary revelatory episode: the returning of money brings worship to the house (17.2-13)	—
3.	Dan seeks a place to live (18.1)	Zacchaeus seeks to see Jesus (19.3)
4.	Five Danites go ahead to see the desired place; then the others go up (18.2-12)	Zacchaeus runs in front and then goes up a tree to see Jesus (19.4)
5.	Danites invite Michaias's Levite to come and be with them (18.13-19)	Jesus invites Zacchaeus… so he (Jesus) can stay with him (19.5)
6.	The Levite is delighted (18.20)	Zacchaeus rejoices (19.6)
7.	Michaias shouts in protest (18.21-26)	On-lookers murmur (19.7)
		2. Revelatory exchange with Jesus: the returning of goods brings salvation to the house (19.8-9)
8.	Danites come to destroy (18.27-31)	Son of Humanity came to save (19.10)

---

1. Soggin 1981: 266-67; cf. Malamet 1971: 132, who argues that the account of the Danite migration 'seems to have been a sort of literary copy of a biblical narrative pattern evolved for portraying campaigns of inheritance (which pattern was followed on a much larger, pan-tribal scale, in the Exodus–conquest cycle').

49. The Search for a True Home

The procedure implied in the outline (Table 78), of moving the preliminary revelatory episode to a later position, occurs elsewhere in Luke. In the rewriting of 1 Kgs 17.1-16 and 2 Kgs 4.1-37, for instance, Luke uses curtain-raising episodes (1 Kgs 17.1-6 and 2 Kgs 4.1-7, episodes which intimate or reveal what is to come) as the basis for revelatory moments which, in the rewritten account, occur at a later stage (see Chapters 28 and 31, and their accompanying outlines).

This re-positioning of the revelatory episode helps explain one of its characteristics—the fact that within Luke's text Zacchaeus's exchange with Jesus brings a change of rhythm. In Fitzmyer's words (1985: 1219), 'Verse 8...disturbs the sequence'. In a sense the verse *should* disturb the sequence; it came from a distinct origin and has a distinct role.

1. *More Detailed Analysis*

a. *Section 1. The Man Named Michaias/Zacchaeus (Judges 17.1; Luke 19.1-2)*
The texts begin by introducing new characters into the respective accounts:

Judges	*Luke*
And there was a man	And entering he passed through Jericho.
from the mountains of Ephraim,	And behold there was a man,
and his name was Michaias (Judg. 17.1)	named Zacchaeus...a tax-collector...rich (Lk. 19.1-2)

For every element in the Judges story, there is a corresponding element in Luke—a new character, a name, and a geographic location (the mountains of Ephraim/Jericho). But Luke's account contains details and elaborations which suit his own narrative. In particular, the reference to passing through Jericho fits his continuing account of Jesus' journey towards Jerusalem. And the description of Zacchaeus as a rich tax-collector fits into the pattern of Luke's recurring emphasis on possessions. These elaborations are all the more appropriate because, more than Michaias, Zacchaeus is central to the subsequent account.

b. *Section 2. In the House: The Illustrative Episode (Judges 17.2-13; Luke 19.8-9)*
The Old Testament episode involves two incidents. First, Michaias gives money back to his mother, thus leading to the establishment within the house of a kind of shrine (Judg. 17.2-6). And later he gives money to a priest who is to live in his house and serve the shrine (17.7-13). Because Michaias returns the money, his house becomes a place of worship, and at the end, Michaias pronounces: 'Now I know that the Lord will do me good...'

As Zacchaeus speaks of giving and returning money, his house also becomes a place where the goodness of the Lord is present. Jesus is called 'Lord', and he makes a pronouncement about salvation coming to 'this house' (Lk. 19.8-9).

Luke has distilled the essence of the Old Testament account: giving and returning money opens the way for the Lord. But Luke has left out the details about installing a place of worship and has concentrated instead on worship's ultimate purpose: the building and expressing of a relationship with 'the Lord'.

Verbal links are considerable:

Old Testament:
[Michaias]...*eipen...idou...argyriou...par' emoi...kuriō
apedōken...argyriou...apodōsō...apedōken...edōken...
kai egeneto en tō oikō Michaia* (Judg. 17.2-6)

*kai eipen autō Michaias...
dōsō...argyriou...
kai...egenēthē...en to oikō Michaia* (Judg. 17.7-13)

New Testament:
Zachaios eipen pros ton kyrion Idou ta...mou
didōmi...apodidōmi
tō oikō toutō egeneto (Lk. 19.8-9)

Old Testament:
[Michaias] ...said '...behold the money/silver is with me'...'by/to the Lord'...
he gave back...money...I will give back...he gave back...he gave...
And it [the image/shrine] was in the house of Michaias...

And Michaias said to him...
And I will give you...money...
And he [the priest] was in the house of Michaias...

New Testament:
Zacchaeus...said to the Lord, 'Behold...my goods...
I give...and I give back...'
'...[salvation] has come to this house...'

c. *Section 3. Seeking One's Place with the Lord Despite the Crush of Others (Judges 18.1; Luke 19.3)*

The Old Testament describes the plight of Dan, the tribe which was seeking an inheritance to inhabit. Such an inheritance would normally have been a gift from the Lord (as apportioned in Josh. 13–19, especially 19.40-48), but no inheritance had fallen to Dan up to that day 'in the midst of the tribes of Israel'. The other tribes are not blamed for Dan's plight, but the fact remains that when the others have taken their share, there seems to be nothing left for Dan. (In the apportioning, Dan had been last on the list, Josh. 19.40-48.)

The plight of Zacchaeus was somewhat similar. He wanted to see Jesus, something to which he should have been entitled, but because of the crowd, he could not. (He was not last on any list, but he was short in stature).

The essence of Luke's transformation is that the quest for land has given way to a quest for vision—for seeing Jesus. In other words, the focus of the quest has been internalized.

Despite the great differences between the accounts, Luke retains some verbal details from the older text:

Old Testament:
The tribe of Dan sought (*ezētei*)
an inheritance for itself
because (*hoti*) an inheritance did not (*ouk*)...

New Testament:
[Zacchaeus] sought (*ezētei*)...
to see Jesus
but could not (*ouk*) because (*hoti*)...

d. *Section 4. Going Ahead to See, and Going Up (Judges 18.2-12; Luke 19.4)*

To find their inheritance, the Danites send a reconnaissance group which goes ahead through the mountains of Ephraim to see (*horaō*) the land (Judg. 18.2-10). And then the larger group of Danites begins to go up (*anabainō*) (Judg. 18.11-12).

The account in Luke is not of a whole tribe seeking land, but of one man seeking vision, and so the dimensions of the New Testament drama are smaller; it is a diminutive model. But the basic movements of the Old Testament account are all present. Zacchaeus is described as 'running ahead to the front', a phrase which is so repetitive as to be problematic (Fitzmyer 1985: 1224), but which makes sense when seen as echoing the process of long-distance scouting. And then he goes up (*anabainō*) a tree, to see (*horaō*) Jesus.

e. *Section 5. Arriving at the Place of Michaias/Zacchaeus: A Pressurized Invitation to Join with the One who is Journeying (Judges 18.13-19; Luke 19.5)*
When the journeying Danites arrive at the house of Michaias, they first deploy their forces and, having taken away the elements of the shrine with them, they invite the priest to come with them. It is an invitation which combines pressure and attraction: their forcefulness exercises pressure, and the idea of being with them (priest to a whole tribe) exercises attraction.

And when the journeying Jesus arrives to where Zacchaeus is, he asks Zacchaeus to join him, and in doing so, he both exercises gentle pressure ('Zacchaeus, hurry and come down...') and issues an attractive invitation ('for today I must abide in your house', Lk 19.5).

At this point, Luke has rearranged the characters and movements with considerable freedom, but he has kept the essence of the plot: the idea of a journey which, with pressure and attraction, invites someone to join in a process of worship or togetherness ('abide in your house').

The motif of looking or seeing which had been present in the preceding action (of going ahead to see) remains in both texts in modified form. It is the reconnaissance group, with its task of seeing more than the others, which takes the shrine and invites the priest to come with them. And as Jesus invites Zacchaeus, he too is described as seeing or looking ('Looking up, Jesus said to him...').

Luke seems to have varied resonances of the older text:

> Old Testament:
> *kai ēlthon heōs oikou Michaia...eis ton eikon Michaia*
> *kai ēspasonto auton...kai anebēsan...eisēlthon eis oikon*
> [Invitation:] *elthe meth' hēmōn, kai esē hymin...patera...hierea.*

> New Testament:
> *kai hōs ēlthen eis ton topon*
> *anaplepsas...eipen pros auton, Zakchaie, speusas katabēthi...*
> [Invitation:] *en tō oikō sou dei me meinai.*

> Old Testament:
> And they came to the house of Michaias...to the house of Michaias
> and greeted him...and they went up...and went into the house,
> [Invitation:] 'Come with us, and be to us a father and priest'.

> New Testament:
> And when he came to the place
> looking up...he said to him, 'Zacchaeus, hurry come down...
> [Invitation:] I must abide in your house'.

Many of the comparative details are debatable. For instance, does *speusas* ('hurry') echo something of *espasonto* ('greeted')? Do *anablepsas* ('having looked up', from *ana-blepō*) and *katabēthi* ('come down', from *kata-bainō*) echo *anebēsan* ('they went up', from *ana-bainō*)? Such connections would involve word-play.

f. *Section 6. The Invitation is Accepted with Joy (Judges 18.20; Luke 19.6)*
Michaias's priest was delighted when the Danites invited him to join them, and so he took the various parts of the shrine, 'and he entered the midst of the people' (Judg. 18.20). Zacchaeus was also glad to accept Jesus' invitation. The relationship between the texts constitutes a puzzle:

Judges	Luke
And the heart of the priest was glad,	And hurrying he came down,
and he took the ephod…and the image,	and he received him
and he entered the midst of the people.	joyfully.

The priest's taking of the shrine (ephod, image, etc.) finds an adapted equivalent when Zacchaeus accepts Jesus. (Elsewhere in Luke, Jesus replaces the temple; here he replaces the shrine.) In other words, in their different ways, both the priest and Zacchaeus accept the tangible signs of the divine presence (the shrine and Jesus). The more difficult question is whether or in what way the entry (into the people) is balanced by the descent (down to the house and Jesus).

In any case, what is essential in both instances is that there is an acceptance which seems unhesitating and joyful.

g. *Section 7. The Invitation is Protested (Judges 18.21-26; Luke 19.7)*
The joyful acceptance is followed in both texts by a protest. In a rather long-winded and repetitive scene, Michaias and the men with him shouted (*ekrazon*, from *krazō*—used three times, Judg. 18.22, 23, 24) against what was happening. And in Luke, all who saw murmured (*diegogguzon*, from *dia-gogguzō*, 19.7) because Jesus was with a sinful man. Apparently the long-windedness and repetiveness of the shouting scene have been distilled into the implied repetiveness of the murmuring.

h. *Section 8. The Final Contrast—Coming to Destroy (Judges 18.27-31) and to Save (Luke 19.10)*
The final scene in the Danites' story is one of climactic destruction and aberration: the Danites slaughter a peaceful people and then they set up an idolatrous shrine—the famous shrine of Dan which remained for centuries.

But while the Danites came for slaughter and sin (Judg. 18.27-31), the Son of Humanity came to seek and save what was lost (Lk. 19.10). As in the preceding incident (concerning the protest), Luke's text would seem to involve a distillation of account in Judges—in this case a positivized distillation—but, like the protest, it has been adapted to the flow of Luke's own phrasing and narrative.

2. *Conclusion*

Discussion of the evidence from this chapter (concerning Judg. 17–18) is deferred so that it can be set in the context of a broader discussion concerning the use Judges 17–21—appearing in the Orientational Conclusion to Chapters 49–52.

50

The Lonely Journey and the Knowing:
The 'Passion' of the Woman (Judges 19) as One Component
of the Passion Narrative (Luke 23.50–24.53)

Proto-Luke generally uses the end of Judges (chs. 17–21) for the end of the first part of his two-part work (thus, within Lk. 19–24), but he sometimes varies the order:

Judges	Luke–Acts
Dan's shrine (chs. 17–18)	Zacchaeus (Lk. 19.1-10)
Peace: death and love (ch. 21)	Last Supper (22.1-30)
A woman's Passion (ch. 19)	Passion, resurrection 23.50–24.53)
War (ch. 20)	Gamaliel's talk of war (Acts 5.33-42)

The present chapter concentrates on his reshaping of Judges 19.

Judges 19 is a gruesome account of how a woman, given over to gang rape by her Levitical 'husband', collapsed and met her death—thus awakening the Levite and all Israel to the horror of the sin.

The account begins with the Levite's enigmatic quest to seek the runaway woman and bring her home from her father's house (Judg. 19.1-5a). It is enigmatic because when the Levite approaches the father's house, the father gives him such a warm and prolonged welcome that the woman is lost sight of. During his visit to the father's house she is never mentioned. For three days it was as though she had disappeared.

Finally, however, the Levite insists on going home—a journey which will take him past Jerusalem to the mountains of Ephraim. This journey turns out to be extremely forlorn. But someone meets the Levite and the woman and as evening falls they have a heartwarming meal with the stranger (Judg. 19.4b-21).

Then tragedy strikes. The men of the town surround the house and demand to 'know' the Levite (sexually). The host pleads with them not to commit such a sin, but eventually the Levite takes the woman and leads her out to them. And so they 'know' her the whole night, thus preparing the way for her collapse and subsequent death (19.22-25).

At dawn, the woman came and fell at the doorstep.

In the morning, the Levite came out, saw her and said 'Arise, let us go'. It was only when she failed to answer that the Levite, who up to this point in the story had appeared to be only partly conscious, finally, in his own bizarre way, showed some awareness of the enormity of what has happened. (The Greek text says the woman was dead, but the original Hebrew leaves the reader wondering.) He carved her up and sent the pieces around to all the tribes of Israel, proclaiming that not since the time of the exodus had such a thing happened in Israel.

Luke has taken this tragic text, particularly its account of a forlorn journey which culminates in a knowing, and has used it as one component of his narrative of the passion and resurrection. The Old Testament journey which went past Jerusalem to Ephraim (Judg. 19.5b-21) has become one element in the account of the journey from Jerusalem to Emmaus (Lk. 24.13-35). And the tragic 'knowing' (verb *ginōskō*, Judg. 19.22-25) which

Table 79. *Passion and Death: A Reversal (Judges 19; Luke 23.50–24.53)*

The Quest for the Woman/Body	
1. The man from Ephraim and his quest to recover the woman …until morning (19.1-5a)	Joseph of Arimathea and the quest for the body of Jesus at morning (23.50–24.4)
From the Bowing Down to the Message	
	2. Morning continued: The women bow towards the ground; they confuse life with death. Then they spread the life-giving message (24.5-11)
The Journey	
3. The journey past Jerusalem to Ephraim (19.5b-21)	The journey from Jerusalem to Emmaus (24.13-35)
Knowing, Sin, and Suffering	
4. 'Knowing' the woman with its implied sin and suffering (19.22-25)	Knowing the risen Lord with its explicit relation to sin and suffering (24.36-53)
From the Falling Down to the Message	
2. At morning: The woman falls at the door. The Levite confuses death with life. Then he spreads the deadly message (19.26-30)	

would unleash a message to all Israel, has become one element in the 'knowing' (or recognizing) of Jesus—a knowing which would initiate a message to the whole world (Lk. 24.36-53; for the words 'recognize' and 'know', *epiginōskō* and *ginōskō*, see Lk. 24.16, 31, 35).

The contrasting meanings of 'knowing' are part of a larger contrast, part of a process whereby Luke has reshaped the tragedy so as to make it part of the positive message of Jesus' death and resurrection.

Such an association of the woman with the risen Lord may seem surprising, yet it accords with certain key factors. First, both texts (Judg. 19; Lk. 23.50–24.53) are passion narratives. Luke's account, while it speaks of the resurrection, does so within the context of the passion, and it contains repeated references to sin, suffering, and death (24.7, 20, 26, 46). And the suffering and death of the woman has been described as an 'extravagance of violence' (Trible 1984: 65). Trible's description is dramatic, but it accords with the proclamation that the crime against the woman was the worst thing that happened since Israel came up from Egypt (Judg. 19.31).

A further reason for associating the woman with the Lord lies in the affinity of Judges 19 with Genesis 19 (the destruction of Sodom)—a text in which some of the characters seem interchangeable with the Lord. (The most obvious link between Judg. 19 and Gen. 19 is the picture of a town crowd surrounding a house in order to abuse a guest sexually.) In Genesis 19, the guests look like men, but in fact they are angels (Gen. 19.1-2), and as such they represent the Lord (cf. Gen. 18.1-2, 16, 22). Thus the role of the woman (in Judg. 19) corresponds partly to the role of the threatened representatives of the Lord (in Gen. 19). At least, the two roles overlap sufficiently to be connected.

So, when Luke integrates the woman's suffering into the passion narrative of Jesus, he is not doing violence to the text. Rather, he is bringing out two inherent aspects of Judges 19—its role as a passion narrative in its own right, and its elusive relationship (seen through Gen. 19) to the Lord. In some sense, the attack on the woman is comparable to an attack on God's messengers—and thus to an attack on God.

Luke's text at this point is unusually dense; Judges 19 supplies just one component, one slender aspect.

1. *More Detailed Analysis*

The outline (Table 79) divides the texts into four main sections. In the longest of these sections—the journey (section 3)—the similarities are relatively easy to see, but in the others the connections are more limited or subtle. Hence, the overall relationship of the two texts is somewhat like that found in the Samson story: there are enough strong similarities to be sure Luke is using the Old Testament account, but the connection between some individual episodes is reduced or elusive.

By and large, Luke keeps the Old Testament order but he combines the beginning (Judg. 19.1-5a) and end (19.26-30) so that the two together form a basis for the beginning of his own account (for the burial and resurrection, Lk. 23.50–24.12). One reason for combining these texts is the fact that they both involve morning (Judg. 19.5a, 26). Luke has used both morning accounts to construct the account of the morning of the resurrection.

a. *Section 1. The Quest for the Woman/Body (Judges 19.1-5a; Luke 23.50–24.4)*
Whatever the ultimate origin of Luke's burial account, as it now stands the text has traces of the Levite's search for the woman (Judg. 19.1-5a). The burial account itself and its immediate sequel (the visit to the tomb) largely center around the quest for the body of Jesus (Lk. 23.50–24.4), and one element of this quest seems to have come from the search for the elusive woman. The relationship between the texts appears to be unusually subtle and complex, and the following outline involves considerable simplification:

Judges	*Luke*
The man from Ephraim and the woman (19.1-2)	Joseph of Arimathea and the Jews (23.50-51)
He went to her father for her; he went after her (19.3a)	He came to Pilate for the body. The women followed after (23.52-56a)
The father met him (19.3b)	
Lodged for three days. On fourth day rose early (19.5a)	Rested on sabbath day (23.56b) On first day of week came early (24.1-3)
	Two angels met them (24.4)

The man from Ephraim is new in Judges, as is Joseph of Arimathea in Luke. (Their names have a curious affinity: one is from Eph-ra-im and the other is Jos-eph of Ar-im…) Both characters are introduced by two short phrases, each beginning with *anēr* ('man'):

> Old Testament:
> And there was a man…and the man…
>
> New Testament:
> And behold a man…and [the] man…

It is difficult to say whether the Ephraimite's alienation from the woman (or rather, hers from him, Judg. 19.2) has anything to do with Joseph's disagreement with the Jews (Lk. 23.51).

Then, in both texts, there are two movements which are somewhat parallel: the repetitive description of the man going in search of the woman (*eporeuthē...eporeuthē*, 'he went...he went', Judg. 19.3a), and Luke's account of how, in their different ways, both Joseph and the women went in search of the body of Jesus. There even seems to be a linguistic echo: while the man 'went after' (*eporeuthē kat-opisthen*) the woman, the women 'followed after' (*kat-akoloutheō*)—a form of *akoloutheō* which, apart from Acts 16.17, does not otherwise occur in the New Testament.

The surprising and rather intrusive appearance of the father (*kai eiden*, 'And he saw...', Judg. 19.3b) seems to be balanced in Luke by the even more surprising appearance of the two angels (*kai idou*, 'And see/behold', Lk. 24.4). Interchanging a man or men with two angels becomes more likely in view of the way the (related) Sodom story interchanges men and angels (Gen. 18.16, 22: 19.1).

Finally, there is an intriguing affinity between the three-day time of relaxed lodging (Judg. 19.4-5a) and New Testament time of sabbath resting (Lk. 23.56b–24.3). In both cases, the quest has to wait: the man makes no progress in bringing the woman home; and the women have to wait before they can approach the body of Jesus. But later the quest is resumed, early (*orthrizō*, 'to get up early', Judg. 19.5a; *orthros*, 'early [morning]', Lk. 24.1). The absence of the woman—the strange failure of the narrative to mention her—is apparently matched in Luke by the perplexing absence of the body of Jesus.

Reviewing the entire texts (Judg. 19.1-5a; Lk. 23.50–24.4), it is easy to see a steady pattern of slight similarity. But what remains unanswered, at least in this analysis, is whether there is a further affinity which is more pervasive and profound.

b. *Section 2. As the Woman/Women Bow/s to the Earth, Life Mingles Overpoweringly with Death, and the Message Goes Out to All (Judges 19.26-30; Luke 24.5-12)*
When Luke joins the opening and closing morning scenes (Judg. 19.5a, 26), in order to describe the morning of the resurrection he also makes considerable use of other sources. Still, the influence of Judges 19 is significant—as can be seen from the affinity between the second morning scene (Judg. 19.26-30) and the continued account of the women's meeting with the two angels (Lk. 24.5-11[-12?]). The texts involve three basic actions:

The woman falls at the door (19.26)	The women bow to the ground (24.5a)
Not realizing she is (nearly) dead, the Levite tells her to arise (19.27-28a)	The angels: Why do you confuse the living with the dead? He is risen (24.5b-8)
He goes home and tells of this death to all the tribes of Israel (19.28b-30)	They go back and tell of this life to all the eleven and others (24.9-11)

The Levite's mistake is to seek life where there is death. The women's mistake, initially at least, is to seek death where there is life. Luke has taken the incredibility of the crime and, by turning it around, has used it as one element in describing the incredibility of God-given life.

c. *Section 3. The Journey Past/From Jerusalem to Ephraim/Emmaus (Judges 19.5b-21; Luke 24.13-35)*
In Judges 19, the quest for the woman is followed immediately by a difficult journey which, having left Jerusalem to one side, proceeds towards Ephraim (19.5b-21). The journey to Emmaus, which occurs shortly after the quest for the body, reflects several elements of the older journey:

	Judges	*Luke*
a.	Stay, it is late (Judg. 19.5b-9)	
b.	Jerusalem avoided; isolation (19.10-15)	
c.	Telling a stranger the plight (19.16-19)	Telling Jesus the plight (24.13-24)
d.	Stranger responds positively (19.20-21)	Jesus responds (24.25-27)
		Stay, it is late (24.28-32)
		Jerusalem accepted; company (24.33-35)

(1) *Element a. Stay, it is late.* Both texts contain distinctive accounts of pressing someone to stay and accept hospitality. The woman's father wants the Levite to stay with him in the house, and the travelers do not want Jesus to leave them. There are considerable linguistic links:

Old Testament:
...*kardian sou klasmati artou...poreuesthe*
kai biasato auton
heōs klinē hē hēmera
Idou dē eis hesperan keklinen hē hēmera
kardia...hodon (Judg. 19.5b-9)

New Testament:
...*eporeuonto...poreuesthai*
kai pare-biasanto auton
hoti pros hesperan...kai keklinen hēdē hē hēmera
arton...klasas [24.33: *klasei tou artou*]
kardia...hodō (Lk. 24.28-32)

Old Testament:
...[Strengthen your] heart with a fragment of bread...you shall journey
and he constrained him
until day declines
Behold the day has declined towards evening. [Lodge here,]
[let your] heart [rejoice]...[rise early for the] road.

New Testament:
...they were journeying...to journey
and they constrained him [saying, Stay with us,]
for it [is] towards evening...and the day has now declined
[Taking] bread...he broke [24.33: the breaking of bread]
[Did not our] heart [burn]...on the road.

(2) *Element b. Jerusalem avoided/accepted.* The pressing invitation to stay is followed immediately by a departure which leads to Jerusalem (Judg. 19.10; Lk. 24.31):

Old Testament:
He arose and went, and came opposite Jebus (that is Jerusalem).

New Testament:
And they rose up that same hour and returned to Jerusalem.

But the attitudes and results are different. The Ephraimite, who is accompanied by his traveling companion and the woman, cautiously avoids the strangeness of (Jebusite) Jerusalem and (with echoes of Lot, Gen. 19.15-22, 30-38) chooses instead to seek a place in a more familiar-sounding Israelite town of Benjamin (Judg. 19.11-13). The result (19.14-15) is that the sun sets on them and they become stranded in the middle of Gibeah—alone and in the dark.

The travelers to Emmaus, however, seek Jerusalem, and they do so despite the night, something which previously had made them so cautious ('Stay with us, for it is towards evening'). Now they face directly into the strangeness of the dark journey, and the result—in dramatic contrast to the miserable scene in Gibeah—is a vivid picture of togetherness and vitality: 'they found the eleven and those with them gathered saying, "The Lord is truly risen..." And they recounted how he was made known to them in the breaking of the bread.'

Obviously, most of Luke's description uses New Testament ideas and images, but it has been so constructed that it forms a contrast with the text of Judges. Behind both texts lies the central biblical idea, first illustrated at length in the contrast between Abraham and Lot that one cannot organize life or reduce it to familiar choices (Gros Louis (ed.) 1982: 53-70); fruitfulness and life are often to be found by facing the unfamiliar, including death.

(3) *Element c. Telling a stranger the plight.* The meeting with the stranger, which in Judges 19 occurs in the forlorn center of Gibeah (19.16-19), occurs in Luke at the beginning of the journey (24.1-24):

> Old Testament:
> And behold an old man...from...Ephraim.
> And he sojourned (*paroikeō*) in Gibeah...
> And raising their eyes they saw the man traveling...
> And the man said to them, 'Where...' Whence...?' (Judg. 19.16-17).
>
> New Testament:
> And behold two of them...journeying...to...Emmaus.
> And...and Jesus himself drawing near...journeyed with them...but their eyes were held...
> And he said to them, 'What...?'
> And one of them...replied, 'Are you sojourning (*paroikeō*)...in... Jerusalem' (Lk. 24.13-18)

The subsequent dialogue rapidly becomes a form of lament. The Levite tells his sad ironic story about a journey that has become isolated (even though he had organized it carefully and so has ample provisions) (Judg. 19.18-19). And the travelers to Emmaus, as they pursue their lonely journey, at some length tell the story of Jesus, a story which is even more sad and ironic (Lk. 24.19-24).

Again Luke's text draws heavily on Christian materials about Jesus, but he has adapted these materials so that they fit within the framework of the older narrative and suit the flow of his own account.

(4) *Element d. The stranger replies.* Finally the stranger replies, and his words are heartwarming. In a move that will gladden their hearts, the old man invites the Levite and those with him to come to his house; 'and they washed their feet and ate and drank' (Judg. 19.20-21). And, before joining his companions in the breaking of bread, Jesus speaks to their hearts about the life-giving words of the prophets (Lk. 24.25-27). Thus, in ways that are diverse but complementary, the forlorn journey is transformed.

d. *Section 4. The Knowing, the Sin, and the Suffering (Judges 19.22-25; Luke 24.36-53)*
The reception into the stranger's house had brought comfort to the travelers from Ephraim, and the gathering in Jerusalem had brought a wonderful change for the two who were journeying to Emmaus. But, before long, the happy scenes are interrupted:

> Old Testament:
> As they were being cheerful of heart (*autōn de agathunth-entōn*...),
> behold the men of the city, *evil-doers, surrounded* the house,
> ...and they said, 'Bring out the man that we may know him' (19.22)

New Testament:
As they were saying these things [about Jesus risen, made known] (...*de autōn lal-ountōn*),
he stood *in the midst* of them, and said to them, '*Peace* to you'.
...And he said, ...'See my hands and my feet that it is I...' (24.36-39)

Whatever the initial similarities of the scenes, they quickly develop into stark opposites. Jesus brings peace; the men of the town bring evil. Jesus is in the midst and so, by implication, is the Old Testament house (it is surrounded), and in both cases, those in the midst are to be known; but the ways of knowing are radically diverse. The knowing in the Old Testament scene (gang rape) involves profound evil; the knowing in the New Testament episode (group recognition of divinized humanity) involves the greatest good.

Apparently, Luke's procedure is to absorb even the greatest evil into a greater good. There are explicit suggestions of this in the later part of the New Testament scene when Jesus says that everything in the the scriptures finds fulfillment in him, his suffering, resurrection, and forgiveness of sins (Lk. 24.44-47).

And there are small linguistic indications in the fact that some of the most elevated moments at the end of the gospel (the promise of the Spirit and the journey to the ascension, Lk. 24.49-50) have traces of the wording of the rape scene. The rape continues 'until' (*heōs*) morning, and then they dismiss (*ex-apostellō*) her (Judg. 19.25); Jesus tells the disciples to wait until ('*heōs*') he sends (*apostellō*) the Spirit (Lk. 24.49). And, finally, Luke describes how Jesus 'led them out' (*exagō*) to Bethany. This is 'the word used in the LXX for Yahweh leading his people out of Egyptian bondage in the exodus' (Fitzmyer 1985: 1589). But it also echoes the tragedy of Judges 19:

Old Testament:
And he led her out to them outside [to be raped].
Kai exēgagen autēn pros autous exō. (Judg. 19.25)

New Testament:
And he led them out outside [to blessing and ascension].
Exēgagen de autous (exo). (Lk. 24.50)

2. *Conclusion*

See the Orientational Conclusion to Chapters 49–52 for a discussion of Judges 17–21.

51

The Civil War against Benjamin (Judges 20) as Part of the Background for Gamaliel's 'Anti-War' Speech (Acts 5.33-42)

The intervention of Gamaliel—the speech which saved the disciples from the wrath of the Sanhedrin—refers first to the movement led by Theudas and then, as something which occurred later, to the further movement led by Judas the Galilean (Acts 5.36-37). It is generally agreed, however, that in reporting on Gamaliel's speech, Luke has used considerable freedom. The Theudas movement, c. 45 AD, had not yet occurred when Gamaliel was giving the speech; and Judas the Galilean apparently came before Theudas, not after him. (See, for instance, Lampe 1962: 779j). However, as R.J. Dillon notes (1990: 41), the point of the speech is clear: 'Those leaders perished and their movements died with them, but that has not been the case with Jesus' following'.

This freedom on Luke's part coincides with another aspect of his procedure: in shaping Gamaliel's speech, he has reworked and absorbed Judges 20. He has distilled this account of the war against Benjamin so that it becomes one component of the account of the campaigns of Theudas and Judas.

The war against the tribe of Benjamin was caused by the crime of the Benjaminite city of Gibeah. The rest of Israel was so horrified by what the men at Gibeah had done that it demanded that Benjamin surrender the criminals. But Benjamin refused. For the purposes of this analysis, the account may be divided into three sections:

1. The gathering: all Israel considers the crime (20.1-7).
2. The decision (20.8-13).
3. The war (in two twofold parts, 20.14-28 and 20.29-48).

The first part of the war account (20.14-28) tells how, on two successive days, using the same tactics on both occasions, the Benjaminites inflicted heavy losses on the rest of Israel. But in the second part (20.29-48, describing the third day), Israel wins, virtually wiping out Benjamin. Like the first part, this second part is highly repetitive, but for a different reason. Instead of giving two accounts of two similar days (20.14-23, 24-28), it gives two accounts of a single day (20.29-36a, 36b-48). Whatever one makes of this perplexing repetition (two accounts of a single day, 20.29-36a, 36b-48)—whether one sees the text as badly edited or whether the apparent confusion is an appropriate literary reflection of the chaos of war and especially of the increasing chaos of kingless Israel—what is certain is that at a certain level the war narrative has a very tidy structure of two twofold parts.

When Luke is describing the gathering of the Sanhedrin to consider the apparent crime of the disciples (Acts 5.33-35), he uses the account of how Israel gathered to consider the crime of the Benjaminites (Judg. 20.1-7). And Gamaliel's account of the two campaigns of Theudas and Judas (Acts 5.36-37) depends partly on the twofold account of the war (Judg. 20.14-48). In outline:

51. The Civil War against Benjamin

Judges	Acts
1. The gathering of all Israel to consider the crime of the the Benjaminites (20.1-7)	The gathering of the Sanhedrin to consider the apparent crime of the disciples (5.33-35)
	The two campaigns of Theudas and Judas (5.36-37)
2. The decision: Israel commits itself to action. Benjamin refuses to cooperate (20.8-13)	The decision: Sanhedrin agrees to just warn the apostles. Disciples refuse to cooperate (5.38-42)
3. The twofold account of the war against Benjamin (20.14-48)	

1. More Detailed Analysis

a. *Section 1. The Gathering to Consider the Crime (Judges 20.1-7; Acts 5.33-35)*
The account in Judges 20 begins with the warlike gathering of all Israel—400,000 who wield the sword (20.1-2). The scene in Acts is closer to ordinary life (a meeting of the Sanhedrin), but the hostility is no less intense: 'And they, hearing it, were cut [to the heart] and they decided to kill them' (Acts 5.33). There are a number of detailed links:

> Old Testament:
> And the leadership of all the people (*pantos tou laou*)
> stood in the gathering (*estē...en tē ekklēsia*)...
> 400,000 that drew the sword.
> And the sons of Benjamin heard (*ēkousan*)...
> The Levite: ...'Sons of Israel [20.12....Israel men (*Israēl andras*)]
> give thought to yourselves (*dote heautois logon*)
> and counsel (*boulē*)'. (Judg. 20.1-2, 7)

> New Testament:
> And they hearing (*akousantes*)
> were cut and decided (*eboulonto*)
> to kill them.
> But there stood up in the Sanhedrin (*anastas...en tō synedriō*)...
> Gamaliel...honored by all the people (*panti tō laō*).
> Gamaliel: 'Men of Israel (*andres Israēlitai*),
> take heed to yourselves (*prosechete heautois*). (Acts 5.33-35)

b. *Section 2. The Decision about Taking Action, and the Defiance of Those who are Threatened (Judges 20.8-13; Acts 5.38-42)*
Given the problem of Gibeah's crime, the Israelites are decisive: 'All the people stood up as one man, saying...' (Judg. 20.8). And with some repetitive phrases, they said how they would organize themselves to take action against Gibeah (20.8b-10).

And Gamaliel, the man who is honored by all the people, is equally decisive. In stark contrast to the need to take action against the criminals at Gibeah, he tells the assembly to let the disciples be. And he uses phrases which are repetitive insofar as they are variously balanced or parallel. (Haenchen 1971: 253, refers to Gamaliel's '*parallelismus membrorum*...the traditional Jewish style of the Old Testament').

These decisions are effective. In a brief verse (20.11), Judges tells how all the Israelites gathered as decided. And, more briefly still, Luke tells how Gamaliel's decision took effect: 'And they obeyed him' (Acts 5.39).

While using other sources, Luke follows the structure of the Old Testament passage. The texts (Judg. 20.8-13; Acts 5.38-42) share the same general outline:

Judges	Acts
The decision by all the people, saying, ...'And now (*legōn...kai nun*) this is the thing we shall do to Gibeah...'	The decision by Gamaliel [the one honored by all the people]: 'And now I say... (*kai ta nun legō...*) let them be...'
The people follow the decision.	And they obeyed him.
'And they sent to...Benjamin' to be rid of the evil-doers.	And calling the apostles they warned them about Jesus.
But Benjamin would not listen.	But they went away rejoicing...

3. *Section 3. The Twofold Account of Warlike Campaigns (Judges 20.14-48; Acts 5.36-37)*
In distilling the prolonged war narrative (Judg. 20.14-48), Luke seems to draw first on its twofold structure. The two verses which describe the movements or campaigns of Theudas and Judas are like the two balancing parts of a single unit (Acts 5.36-37).

Apart from structure, Luke has also drawn on aspects of the Old Testament content. The only number in Luke's narrative is 400 (the number of those who attached themselves to Theudas). Josephus (*Ant.* 20.97), when reporting on Theudas, gives no numbers, and Haenchen (1971: 252) suggests that 'the figure of 400 may derive from some historical source'. In a sense, Haenchen is right: the 400 appears to be an adaptation of the 400,000 which is given twice in Judges 20 (at the beginning, 20.2, and in the account of the war, 20.17). In conjunction with 400, both texts (Judg. 20.2, 17; Acts 5.36) use *andrōn*, literally 'of men' (genitive plural):

> Old Testament:
> 400,000 men (*tetrakosioi chiliades andrōn*).
>
> New Testament:
> about 400 men (*andrōn arithmos hōs tetrakosiōn*).

Luke's account of how the campaigns of Theudas and Judas ended—how their followers were 'brought to naught' and 'scattered' (Acts 5.36-37)—corresponds closely to the ending of the war in Judges 20. The tribe of Benjamin was essentially annihilated (the numbers vary in the versions) and the few who did survive were scattered even into the desert (Judg. 20.35, 45-48).

2. *Conclusion*

See the Orientational Conclusion to Chapters 49–52 for a discussion of Judges 17–21.

52

Deathly Betrothal: The Conclusion of Judges (Judges 21) as One Component of the Last Supper (Luke 22.1-30)

In tracing Luke's use of Judges, perhaps the most difficult chapter is the last—the account of how the Israelites gave wives to the shattered Benjaminites (Judg. 21). Where, if anywhere, has Luke used this? He seems to have no major episode about getting wives.

However, there is one section of the Last Supper account which has a peculiar affinity with Judges 21: the preparation, whereby Jesus sends Peter and John ahead to meet a man carrying a pitcher of water and to prepare the room for the supper (Lk. 22.7-13). Attention to literary conventions shows that this perplexing passage is a variation on the conventional type-scene of a betrothal.

A betrothal scene usually involved a journey by the bridegroom or his surrogate to a foreign land, an encounter at a well with the betrothed-to-be, and finally the drawing of water, and a meal (Alter 1981: 52). It is a process which is seen clearly in the betrothals of Isaac and Jacob (Gen. 24 and 29), but as Alter indicates (pp. 47-62) it may undergo radical variation. One such variation—one which has considerable affinity with Lk. 22.7-13—is the case of Saul (see 1 Sam. 9–11, especially 9.11-12; Alter 1981: 60-61). The betrothal scene has been reduced to a minimum and has been adapted to intimate Saul's future history. The young women who figure so prominently in the Isaac and Jacob stories are virtually bypassed in Saul's case.

In Luke's episode they are bypassed completely. Instead of a woman, it is a man who carries water, thus indicating a betrothal process which is radically different in nature from the usual. What is in question, and what will be seen more easily in John's reworking of the betrothal scene (Jn 4.1-42), is a betrothal of faith, a giving of oneself to God's providence and to all that God's providence involves, including other people, and including (the shadow of) death.

The betrothal theme is not an isolated element in Luke. It sets the scene for one of the most central factors in the institution of the Eucharist (Lk. 22.14-23): the idea of giving one's body. Thus, the process described in Judges 21 of giving wives or spouses has a central affinity with the last supper's ideas of betrothal and of giving one's body. (A somewhat similar affinity was noticed earlier: the search for the woman [in Judg. 19] was rendered [in Luke's burial-and-resurrection account, 23.50–24.4] as part of the search for the body.)

This does not of course mean that Judges 21 is Luke's main source. Luke's primary affinity in describing the Last Supper is not with Judges, but with 1 Corinthians 11 (see Chapter 14; note Appendix 2; cf. Goulder 1989: 129-46), and this chapter presumes Luke's use of 1 Corinthians. But Judges 21 also is significant. Judges not only provides the key element of (a form of) betrothal, but it sets that betrothal in the context of (a form of) death—the apparent death of the tribe of Benjamin. It is necessary, therefore, to look at Judges 21 more closely.

Table 80. *Judges 21 as One Thread in the Last Supper Text (Luke 22.1-30)*

1. *The Shadow of Impending Death*	
One of the tribes is going to die.	The authorities seek Jesus' death.
Israel laments.	Judas emerges as a traitor.
Question: Who is a 'traitor'?	The authorities rejoice.
They had sworn not to give wives (21.1-7)	Judas sought to give Jesus over (22.1-6)
Who is a 'traitor?'	[Behold the traitor is here.
Behold, Jabesh is a 'traitor' (21.8-9)	Who is it? (22.21-23)]
2. *Forms of Betrothal*	
The sending of the 12,000	At the killing of the Passover,
to kill	the sending of the two to meet
and find marriageable women:	a man carrying a pitcher of water:
And they sent (*kai apesteilan*)	And he sent… (*kai apesteilen*…)
Go (*poreuthēte*)…	Go (*poreuthentes*)…and you will meet
and kill [all but virgins].	a man carrying a pitcher of water.
And they found (*heuron*) virgins	And they found (*heuron*) as he said
for Benjamin (21.10-14)	and prepared for the Passover (22.7-13)
3. *The Feast*	
At the feast of the Lord	At the Passover feast
the doomed come from the vineyards and seize	the doomed Jesus drinks from the vine
the dancing women (21.15-21)	and gives his body (22.14-20; cf. 1 Cor. 11.23-25)
4. *The Dispute (Gently Resolved) and the Togetherness*	
Dispute about the women:	Dispute about greatness:
to be resolved by mercy.	to be resolved by gentleness.
The men settle down and dwell	The disciples abided
with their wives.	with Jesus in his trials.
Israelites return to their tribes.	I give you a kingdom, judging
There was no king in Israel (21.22-25)	the twelve tribes of Israel (22.24-30)

Benjamin had seemed doomed. The few men who survived the battle had been scattered, ominously, to a place of stony desolation ('the desert, the Rock of Rimmon', Judg. 20.47; 21.13). Furthermore, all other Benjaminites (including all the women) had been killed (Judg. 20.48). Nor, apparently, could women be found; the other tribes had sworn an oath not to give their daughters to the Benjaminites (Judg. 21.1). For all practical purposes, Benjamin was dead.

It is with a sense of impending death, therefore, that the final chapter opens. The people gathered at Bethel, 'and there they sat until evening… and wept with a great weeping' (Judg. 21.2)—mourning the apparent death of one of Israel's tribes.

Then they realized that, paradoxically, their only hope lay in finding that one of their number was a kind of traitor. If there was a group which had broken ranks and had not taken the oath (about refusing to give their daughters to Benjamin), even though such a group would have merited death, they could be the source of new life—the source from which wives could be found. The Israelites discovered that there was such a group: the town of Jabesh-Gilead. And so they went out and killed everyone in Jabesh-Gilead—but not its marriageable women. These they brought home—400 of them—and the scene was set for recalling the scattered remnants of Benjamin from the desert (Judg. 21.5-14). Despite all the treachery and death, these women offered new life.

The later part of the chapter (Judg. 21.15-25) gives a more positive variation on the same theme: to provide wives for the remnants of Benjamin, the Israelites advised these Benjaminites to seize the daughters of Shiloh. At one level, this is as reprehensible as taking away the women of Jabesh-Gilead, but the overall mood of the passage is quite different: the women here are not so much bereaved survivors as dancers. There is no mourning or killing; on the contrary, the atmosphere is that of a feast, displaying well-intentioned advice, vineyards, dancing, a dispute being settled mercifully, rebuilding homes, dwelling together, and rejoining one's tribe (Judg. 21.19-24).

Overall, while drawing primarily on Christian sources, especially 1 Corinthians, Luke has used Judges 21 to develop some important elements of the Last Supper and also to give his account a certain framework.

The relationship between the texts is summarized in the simplified outline in Table 80. As the outline indicates, Luke uses the framework of Judges 21 but has reworked it into a shape which is clearer and more orderly. Thus, while the Old Testament references to the day of sacrifice and to a feast appear somewhat scattered (Judg. 21.4, 19), Luke takes such elements, and, combining them with Passover (cf. 1 Cor. 5.7), uses them as part of an orderly sequence of increasingly focused introductory indications of time (the approach of the feast, 22.1; the day [of sacrifice], 22.7; the hour, 22.14).

1. *More Detailed Analysis*

a. *Section 1. The Shadow of Impending Death (Israel Mourns, Judges 21.1-7; The Authorities Plot to Kill Jesus, Luke 22.1-6)*

The tearful sense of impending death (the death of one of the twelve tribes) which weighs so heavily at the beginning of Judges 21 has been radically transformed by Luke so as to become one component of the death threat which hangs over Jesus.

One aspect of this transformation is to render the older text into something clear and vivid. In place of the rather convoluted process whereby the ancient power and authority of Israel virtually wiped out one of the twelve, Luke portrays a much simpler picture of how, with the help of 'one of the twelve' (Judas, Lk. 22.3), the later authorities deliberately planned the betrayal and killing of Jesus.

The nature of this transformation is reflected particularly in one detail: the double reference about swearing or agreeing 'to give' (*didōmi*, Judg. 21.1, 7; Lk. 22.5, 6):

> Old Testament:
> Israel swore... A man shall not give (*dōsei*) his daughter...
> We have sworn...not to give (*dounai*) our daughters...
>
> New Testament:
> [The authorities] consented to give (*dounai*) him money,
> and he agreed...to betray (*para-dounai*) him...

In the circumstances, swearing not to give daughters as wives was the equivalent of a death sentence—which is what happens more clearly and simply in the authorities' plot against Jesus. In Luke, the balance between the two uses of 'swear' is replaced by the balance between the two interchangeable words 'consented' and 'agreed' (*syntithēmi* and *exomologeō*). And the fatal (not) giving of daughters is replaced, with typically Lukan emphasis, by the fatal giving of money.

A further detail of transformation highlights the deliberateness of the New Testament condemnation to death: where ancient Israel wept (Judg. 21.2), the later authorities rejoice (Lk. 22.5).

And the idea of a traitor, which in Judges 21 is expressed in a form which is rather negative and obscure (someone who by their refusal deserved death, Judg. 21.5), is expressed in Luke in a form which is clear and direct (someone who by his participation deliberately conspired to betray, Lk. 21.4).

The overall result, as so often in Luke's transformations, is a text which renders the obscurity and complexity of the ancient scripture into an account which, despite its depth, is clear and vivid.

b. *Section 2. Forms of Death and Betrothal (The Sending of the Twelve Thousand Killers to Find Wives, Judges 21.10-14; The Sending of Peter and John Luke 22.7-13)*

To find wives for the apparently doomed tribe, the Israelites send 12,000 strong men ('sons of strength') who, 'with the mouth of the sword', kill all the people of Jabesh-Gilead—except the virgin daughters. Then 'they led' these women back and gave them as wives to the survivors of Benjamin. As a process of espousal, it is unusually inhuman.

The radical nature of Luke's transformation becomes particularly clear in this episode. In place of an espousal which involves mass murder, he gives a form of espousal or betrothal which is deeply spiritual. As already mentioned, the sending of Peter and John to meet a man carrying water and to prepare the room for the meal, involves a radical reworking—a spiritualization or internalization—of the conventional type-scene of betrothal.

But this transformation does not mean that the idea of death, so powerfully present in the Old Testament scene, has been completely omitted. The sending of Peter and John is framed by four explicit references to the Passover (Lk. 22.7, 8, 11, 13), and the first of these speaks of the Passover as being 'sacrificed' (*thuō*), or as some translations say, 'killed', 'slaughtered'. Thus, the betrothal meal is also a memorial of death. Or, to phrase it as this episode suggests, the memorial of death is also a betrothal.

The relationship of death and love has challenged writers from Marvin Pope, commenting on the Song of Songs, to Rollo May, dealing with life in general (see Pope 1977: 210-29; May 1972: 98-121), and it is not summarized easily. What is reasonably clear, however, is that Luke also has engaged this enigmatic relationship. In the Old Testament scene, the combination of death and betrothal may seem bizarre. In Luke, however, death and love are blended into a flowing narrative which suggests that ultimately the two form a certain natural unity. The love aspect, the betrothal, is not terribly obvious, any more than it generally is when death hovers. But at a certain level of the text, and so at a certain level of reality, it is present and central.

c. *Section 3. The Feast (Judges 21.15.21; Luke 22.14-22)*

The second part of Judges 21 concerning the marrying of the dancers of Shiloh (21.15-25) may seem at first to be simply a doublet of the first part. It begins, somewhat as the first part had begun, by regretting that it is not possible 'to give' wives to the remnants of the threatened tribe (21.15-18; cf. 21.1, 7).

But the mood is different. And it changes even more when the previously doomed men are told of a forthcoming feast and of running away with a dancer (21.19-21). Now indeed they can begin to emerge from under the weight of imminent death.

Likewise in Luke, as the supper begins, there is a change of mood. Unlike the preceding episodes (the plot, and the sending of the two), both of which began by laying the emphasis on imminent death (the desire to kill, 22.2, and the killing of the Passover, 22.7), the supper begins with deep enthusiasm: 'With desire I have desired to eat this Passover with you…' (22.15). Jesus goes on to add 'before I suffer', and so there is no question of denying his coming death, but the emphasis has changed. Death or no death, there is a profound vitality within: desire and more desire.

The prospect of the forthcoming feast (Judg. 21.19-21) seems to have had considerable influence on how Jesus sees his forthcoming death (Lk. 22.14-18). However, the relationship between these two brief climactic passages (Judg. 21.19-21; Lk. 22.14-18) is unusually dense and subtle, and the analysis given here is very limited.

The texts begin by setting the scene: the annual feast (Judg. 21.19a), and the Passover supper (Lk. 22.14-15). Then in both texts, there is some repetition:

> Old Testament:
> ...saying,
> Go and lie in wait in the vineyards
> and, when the daughters who dwell in Shiloh come out to dance,
>
> then you shall come out of the vineyards
> and seize for yourselves a wife of the daughters of Shiloh
> and go away to the land of Benjamin.
>
> New Testament:
> For I say to you, I shall not eat it
> until it is fulfilled in the kingdom of God.
>
> Divide [this cup] among yourselves.
> For I say to you, from now on I shall not drink from the fruit of the vine
> until the kingdom of God comes.

In dealing with these hugely diverse texts, the central question is whether there is a relationship between the vitality of the marriage-related dance and Jesus' enthusiasm for the meal and the kingdom. At a later stage, Matthew will say that the kingdom of God is like a wedding feast (Mt. 22.1-14; cf. Lk. 14.16-24). In other words, has Luke taken all the vitality that is associated with a woman (including dancing and marriage) and transformed it into a picture of a vitality which is found in God, even in death?

Several details need examination. Does the taking of the women ('Seize for yourselves') have something to do with the taking of the meal ('Divide among yourselves')? And does the coming out of the dancers, and the subsequent action of coming out of the vineyards to seize them, have something to do with the fulfilling of the kingdom of God and with its coming? (It was seen earlier, for instance, in comparing Judg. 19.1-4 and Lk. 23.50–24.4, that the quest for the woman seemed to be reflected in the quest for the body. And aspects of the same woman–body association have appeared in this chapter—in the relationship between the 'giving' of the women in Judg. 21.1, 7, and the 'giving over' of Jesus in Lk. 22.6.)

Attention also needs to be given to the curious description of the location of Shiloh ('...north...eastwards...south', Judg. 21.19b)—as though its dimensions were related to the whole universe. (Like Jesus, when speaking of the coming kingdom, this description uses *apo...apo*, 'from...from'—Judg. 21.19b; Lk. 22.18). Does Shiloh somehow evoke a greater world, the world of God's kingdom?

Luke's subsequent text ('This is my body...', 22.19-20) is taken from 1 Corinthians, but the insertion of 'given' ('given for you', 22.19) may reflect the way Judges 21 (especially 21.18) uses 'giving' about the giving of the women.

The reference to the traitor ('Behold...', Who could it be?, Lk. 22.21-23) involves a reworking of the discussion about the conduct of Jabesh-Gilead (Judg. 21.8-9).

d. *Section 4. The Dispute (Gently Resolved), the Togetherness, and the Twelve Tribes of Israel (Judges 21.22-25; Luke 22.24-30)*
The taking of the women will lead to a dispute (literally, 'a judging') with their fathers and brothers (Judg. 21.22), and Jesus' giving of his body is likewise followed by a dispute

about who is the greater (Lk. 22.24-25). But both problems are to be resolved amicably, the first by mercy, and the second by a spirit of humility and service. Thus, instead of a dispute about women, Luke portrays a dispute which is of a more universal nature and which is more reflective of the spirit of the New Testament world, particularly of the contentiousness which is found in 1 Corinthians (11.16).

Then, as Judges speaks of the men dwelling with their wives (Judg. 21.23), Luke refers to the apostles abiding with Jesus through his trials (Lk. 22.28). In other words, instead of the stable togetherness of marriage, Luke depicts the stable togetherness of discipleship.

And, finally, as Judges tells how, in those pre-kingship days, the Israelites returned each to his own tribe (now restored to twelve) (Judg. 21.24-25), Jesus speaks to the apostles of a kingdom in which they will judge the twelve tribes of Israel (Lk. 22.29-30).

2. Conclusion

See the Orientational Conclusion to Chapters 49–52 for a discussion of Judges 17–21.

Orientational Conclusion to Chapters 49–52

It is clear, even at a cursory reading, that Luke–Acts does not have an exact equivalent for the horrors of Judges 17–21—the slaughter of a peaceful people (18.27-28) and the war-inducing gang-rape (chs. 19–20). The omission of such horrors, however, does not decide whether Luke used the text. Horrors are like the reverse side of heroics, and having omitted Samson's heroics, it is understandable that Luke should also omit the final horrors. The issue then is not whether Luke–Acts clearly mirrors Judges' dimension of horrendous crime, but whether it uses other features of Judges 17–21 that are ultimately more substantive.

The idea that Luke reworked Judges 17–21 receives its essential plausibility from Luke's general relationship to the LXX and from his tendency to use the LXX in a way that is systematic (Koet 1989: 141-43). If he makes systematic use of Judges 1–16, then it is plausible that he also uses Judges 17–21.

The similarities are difficult to trace. They generally occur in Luke's text not at the center of its plot, but as relatively small components—like distillations which have been reshaped for a new purpose. Yet there is a certain order in their occurrence. As already noted, the reflections of Judges 17–21 are largely concentrated within Luke 19–24:

Judges	Luke–Acts
Dan's shrine (chs. 17–18)	Zacchaeus (Lk. 19.1-10)
Peace: death and love (ch. 21)	Last Supper (22.1-30)
A woman's Passion (ch. 19)	Passion, resurrection 23.50–24.53)
War (ch. 20)	Gamaliel's talk of war (Acts 5.33-42)

Close examination of the similarities is even more taxing and time-consuming than usual in these matters, but it entails aspects of theme, plot, order, completeness, and detail. It leads ultimately to a dilemma that is familiar. Either some extraordinary coincidence occurred or, more simply, Luke had a copy of the older text and asked how it could contribute to the new history.

The great differences are essentially intelligible. In a move that complements the downplaying of heroics, Luke also reduces horrors. This is particularly understandable in an author who, by and large, emphasizes what is positive.

Unit 12. Proto-Luke and Chronicles, Ezra, Nehemiah

53

A New Temple and a New Law:
The Chronicler-Based Aspect of Luke 1.1–4.22a

Proto-Luke's infancy narrative (Lk. 1–2) is largely temple-centered; the temple is the location for its beginning (the angel's annunciation to Zechariah), for one of its later episodes (the presentation of Jesus), and for its end (the finding in the temple). Following this emphasis on the temple (Lk. 1–2), Luke then goes on to tell of a new beginning: the initial preaching of John and Jesus (much of 3.1–4.22a) is largely about a fresh start—a form of moral reconstruction.

These two features—the temple and moral reconstruction—find a precedent in the Chronicler's history (taking 'chronicler' broadly to include Ezra and Nehemiah). Chronicles (1 and 2) recounts Israel's history in a way that is temple-centered. And Ezra–Nehemiah recount Israel's post-exilic reconstruction.

The purpose of the present chapter is to indicate that Proto-Luke's account involves—as one component—systematic dependence on Chronicles/Ezra/Nehemiah.

Luke 1–4 omits use of 2 Chronicles 10–36—the part of the Chronicler's history that includes the description of the first temple's *decline and fall*. Luke does not omit these chapters altogether—he uses them in Acts 1–15 (see Appendix 3)—but at this early stage of his work he is, so to speak, carefully *constructing* something, and so he uses those texts which suit his theme: the account of the background and construction of the first temple (1 Chron. 1–2 Chron. 9), and the account of the reconstruction under Ezra and Nehemiah. Thus, he uses the account of the building of the Temple (1 Chron. 1–2 Chron. 9) as a base for his description of the living Temple which is Jesus (Lk. 1 and 2), and uses the picture of reconstruction found in Ezra–Nehemiah as a base for describing the moral reconstruction undertaken by John and Jesus (3.1–4.22a).

To understand more fully Luke's use of Chronicles, is it necessary to take account of the methods originally used by the Chronicler himself (see Myers 1965a: xv-lxiii; Cazelles 1961: 7-29). His first chapter, for instance (1 Chron. 1), consists of a radical re-presentation of 36 chapters of Genesis. Not only does the Chronicler thus drastically reduce Genesis, but he also changes its form: he neglects all its flowing narrative and simply strings together a chapter of genealogy. Furthermore, he proceeds to use this reduced and reshaped version of Genesis 1–36 for a purpose that seems different from its original purpose in the Pentateuch—as a foundation for his theme of the Temple. And so for ten chapters he reduces and re-forms the early books of the Bible, refashioning them into a single complex unit which serves as an introduction or preparation for his main interest—the Davidic Temple.[1]

When Luke was introducing his gospel (1.1-4), he did not say that he received his material from those who had been eyewitnesses and ministers of Jesus, but rather from those who 'from the beginning (*arché*) had been eyewitnesses and ministers of the word (*logos*)' (1.1)—a much broader designation, and one that fits very well with the idea that,

---

1. See the division of the text by Cazelles 1961: 31-70.

in writing his new work, Luke has made major use of the Old Testament. Luke is not speaking, as we might expect, of 'recent events' but of the 'things which have been fulfilled (*peplērophorēmenōn...pragmatōn*)'—again a phrase broad enough to refer to fulfillment of the Old Testament. And when he goes on to say (1.3) that he has followed (*parēkolouthēkoti*) everything from its source or start (*anōthen*) and is going to write an orderly account, we have further information which fits with the idea of systematic use of the Old Testament.

What Luke seems to have done is to take Chronicles to its fulfillment. Insofar as Chronicles had originally reshaped earlier books it was already an advance, but Luke brought the advance to a new stage. In fact, despite the vast differences between the two texts, Luke in many ways has followed closely the methods and text of the Chronicler.

Table 81. *Chronicles–Ezra–Nehemiah and Luke 1.1–4.22a: General Outline*

	Chronicles	Luke 1–2
1.	Preparation for David's reign (1 Chron. 1–10)	Preparation for Jesus' Davidic reign (1.1-25)
2.	Nathan announces David's reign (1 Chron. 11–12; 17)	Gabriel announces Jesus' 'reign' (1.26-38)
3.	The ark in the hills (1 Chron. 13)	Mary in the hill-country (1.39-45, 56)
4.	God gives David victory (1 Chron. 14; 18–20)	Mary's 'victorious' *Magnificat* (1.46-55)
5.	Priestly service, sons and song (1 Chron. 15–16)	Zechariah, his son and his song (1.57-80)
6.	Census, and the origin of the Temple (1 Chron. 21–22)	Census, and the birth of Jesus (2.1-20)
7.	The people, and piety of the Temple (1 Chron. 23–29)	People, and piety around Jesus (2.21-38)
8.	The building of the Temple (2 Chron. 1.1–5.1)	Jesus grows up (2.39-40)
9.	The Lord takes possession of Temple (2 Chron. 5.2–ch 9)	Jesus in the Temple (2.41-52)
	[Life and decline of the Temple (2 Chron. 10–36)]	[see Appendix 3, on Acts 1–15]
	Ezra–Nehemiah	Luke 3.1–4.22a
10.	The leading people: Persian, Israelite (Ezra 1–2)	Leading people, in Rome and Israel (3.1-2)
11.	Rebuild! (Ezra 3.1–6.18; Neh. 1–7, minus ch. 5)	Rebuild morally! (3.2c-6)
	[see Mt. 3.7-9]	[Brood of vipers (3.7-9)]
12.	Correction of social abuses (Neh. 5)	Correction of possible abuses (3.10-14)
13.	The people—purification and joy (Neh. 10–13)	The people—expectation and purification (3.15-18)
14.	Correcting marriages (Ezra 9–10 and Neh. 9)	Correcting Herod's marriage (3.19-20)
15.	Purification and celebration (Ezra 6.19-22)	Baptism of the Beloved (3.21-22)
16.	Ezra...son of...son of... (Ezra 7.1-10) [see Mt. 4.1-11]	Jesus...son of...son of (3.23-38)
17.	Ezra returns to Jerusalem (Ezra 7.11–ch. 8)	[The temptations (4.1-13)] Jesus returns to Galilee (4.14-15)
18.	Ezra reads Law; positive response (Neh. 8)	Jesus reads Isaiah; positive response (4.16-22a)

53. A New Temple and a New Law

Thus, just as the Chronicler had drastically reduced Genesis, so Luke in turn reduces ten chapters of Chronicles to 25 verses (1 Chron. 1–10; Lk. 1.1-25). Likewise, just as the Chronicler had squeezed the narrative life out of Genesis and reduced it to cultic dry bones, so Luke with equal freedom restores a living narrative, woven largely out of other Old Testament texts, to his introductory cultic scene. And just as the Chronicler had been so bold with Israel's history and traditions that he focuses them on the Temple, so Luke with equal theological adaptability uses the centrality of the Temple as a point of departure, a point from which he will build his theology of a new living Temple—the body of Jesus.

Such radical rethinking of the role of the temple was not new among New Testament writers. Already, in the epistles of Paul, the idea of the temple had been changed or spiritualized (Fraeyman 1947). The essence of Luke's transformation, therefore, is a variation on what had already been accomplished in the Pauline epistles.

1. *More Detailed Analysis*

The general outline (Table 81 above) shows the overall relationship of the texts. Luke usually follows the Chronicler's order, but occasionally he combines texts which have a shared theme. Thus, he brings together the separate texts on the establishment of David's reign (1 Chron. 11–12 and 17) and the separate texts on David's victories (1 Chron. 14 and 18–20). In dealing with the obscure sequence of Ezra/Nehemiah, he tends (as do modern researchers) to a greater degree of rearrangement.

Chronicles does not have comparable parallels for Lk. 3.7-9 and 4.1-13. These two texts have to be accounted for when dealing with later Luke's use of Matthew (see Chapter 25).

a. *Section 1. The Preparation for the Davidic Reign (1 Chronicles 1–10; Luke 1.1-25)*
As 1 Chronicles 1–10 prepares for the reign of David, so Proto-Luke's introduction and the story of Zechariah and Elizabeth (Lk. 1.1-25) prepare for the annunciation to Mary of the Davidic reign of Jesus. Though Proto-Luke uses several Old Testament sources, the basic outline of his text, and aspects of its content, are modeled on Chronicles (see Table 82 below).

Proto-Luke follows the basically positive mood of Chronicles, and when he comes to two very negative moments—the tragedy of Saul and the flight of the people (10.1-10)—he turns them into positive elements. In other words, he realizes that the Chronicler's narration of these sad events has a positive purpose, that the existence of great sorrow implies the existence of great joy, and so, rather than repeat, say, 'Woe to you rich' he can achieve much the same effect by saying 'Happy are you poor'. Thus he turns an Old Testament picture of sorrow into a New Testament picture of joy.

While Proto-Luke closely follows the outline of Chronicles, the extent to which he follows its content varies:
1. 1.1-4, Luke's idea of going back to the beginning (*arché*) of the word (*logos*), corresponds closely to the Chronicler's idea of building up from the very beginning of the Bible, and there is a correspondence too between the Chronicler's systematic genealogy and Luke's 'orderly' approach, yet the Old Testament raw material has been completely reshaped by being subjected to Luke's desire to produce an introduction similar to that of the Greek classics.
2. 1.5-10 contains a creative summary of the content of 1 Chron. 2.1–9.34—a summary that puts narrative life back into the text.
3. 1.11-25 uses 1 Chron. 9.35–ch. 10 as a framework, a starting-point from which to reach out and absorb a complex mesh of Old Testament texts (see Brown 1977: 270-82).

Table 82. *Preparation for the Davidic Reign (1 Chronicles 1–10; Luke 1.1-25)*

1 Chronicles 1–10	Luke 1.1-25
A genealogy from the very beginning of the Bible (ch. 1)	An orderly following of the word from the beginning (1.2-3)
Genealogies of Judah and its kings (chs. 2–4)	In the days of Herod king of Judea (1.5a)
Genealogies of the tribes, giving 'central place' to the priestly clans (chs. 5–8)[2]	Priest Zechariah of the Abijah line and Elizabeth, a descendent of Aaron (1.5b)
At 'the heart'[3] of the priestly genealogies two groups (6.16-32, 33-38, LXX) dedicated to God's service... (*ésan...enantion... dedomenoi eis pasan ergasian ...tou theou* (6.17, 33-34) and their sons (6.18-32, 35-38)	Both were upright before God following all commandments and ordinances... (1.6) (*ésan...enantion tou theou poreuomenoi en pasais tais entolais*) and they had no child (1.7)
'Jerusalem, the Holy City of Israel'[4]—all Israel and its relationship to the organization of the Temple worship in Jerusalem (9.1-34) (*pas Israél sul-loch-ismos dia-tetag-menai ephémeriai*, 9.1, 33)	All the people pray as Zechariah goes in to sacrifice according to the organization of the Temple worship (1.8-10) (*taxei...ephémerias e-lach-é pan to pléthos...tou laou*)
'Saul, David's Predecessor'[5] (9.34–ch. 10) The 'generation' of Saul (9.35-44) The tragedy of Saul (10.1-6) [Punishment of Saul was for not believing the word (10.13-14)]	John, Jesus' 'Predecessor' (1.11-25) Angel tells of John's 'generation' (1.11-13) The joy of John (1.14-19) Punishment of Zechariah for not believing the word (1.20)
Reactions: All Israel fled... (10.7-10) Gileadites took (*elabon*) the body and treated it with honor (10.11-12)	Reactions: The people waited... (1.21-23) Elizabeth conceived (*sun-elaben*) [a body] and was thus freed from shame (1.24-25)

b. *Section 2. The Annunciation of the Davidic Reign (1 Chronicles 11–12; 17; Luke 1.26-38)*

Chronicles continues by speaking of the establishment of David over all Israel in accordance with the word of the Lord through Samuel (1 Chron. 11.1-3), and the basic purpose of the many names and lists of the next two chapters (1 Chron. 11–12) seems to be the Chronicler's desire 'to present David as the one who gathers all the tribes under Yahweh ...as the one who gathers Israel together' (Cazelles 1961: 70n, 74n; Myers 1965a: 88). The chapters conclude by emphasizing again the establishment of David as king over all Israel (1 Chron. 12.39-41).

Luke might simply have composed an episode summarizing and updating the idea of establishing all Israel around a Davidic kingship as found in chs. 11–12, but instead he chose to use a procedure which is slightly more complex, but extremely logical: he takes these two chapters on the *establishment of all Israel around a Davidic kingship* in conjunction with 1 Chronicles 17, Nathan's prophecy on the *establishment of David's kingship forever*. Thus, while Luke, like the Chronicler in chs. 11 and 12, immediately refers to

2. Cazelles 1962: 41n. (see Myers 1965a: 35).
3. Cazelles 1962: 41n.
4. Cazelles 1962: 64.
5. Cazelles 1962: 67.

the house of David ('Joseph, of the house of David', 1.27), and seemed to allude to the gathering of *Israel around David* by telling us of the *virgin* (an image often used in the Old Testament to depict Israel; in this case the virgin espoused to *the Davidic Joseph*), yet, most of his narrative seems closer to the Nathan annunciation. As Brown (1977: 310) puts it: 'Gabriel's words in 1.32-33 constitute a free interpretation of...the promise of the prophet Nathan to David'. (Brown is referring primarily to the account of Nathan's promise in 2 Sam. 7, but his comments and analysis are equally valid of the account found in 1 Chron. 17.)

Furthermore, David's humble response in which he twice refers to himself as 'God's servant' (*doulos*, 1 Chron. 17.18, 20), appears mirrored in Mary's response: 'Behold the handmaid (*doulé*) of the Lord' (1 Chron. 17.18, 19, 23: *su ton doulon sou oidas, kai kata tén kardian su epoiésas... kai nun, kurie, ho logos sou...pisteuthéto*; Lk. 1.38: *idou hé doulé kuriou, genoito moi kata to réma sou*).

Thus, while Luke may have woven several diverse texts into the fabric of the annunciation scene, its basic framework and ideas follow closely the pattern of 1 Chronicles.

c. *Section 3. The Ark in the Hills (1 Chronicles 13; Luke 1.39-45, 56)*
The next chapter of Chronicles deals with the journey of the ark through the hills of Judah. And the next episode in Luke tells of Mary's visit to Elizabeth through the hill country of Judea. So much has already been written on the idea that Mary symbolizes the ark of the covenant[6] that rather than repeat the material, it seems better simply to outline the texts:

The ark moves through the hills of Judah	Mary sets off to the hill country of Judah
David dances	The child leaps
David wonders about bringing up the ark	Elizabeth wonders at the coming of Mary
The ark stayed three months (1 Chron. 13)	Mary stayed three months (Lk. 1.39-45, 56)

d. *Section 4. The Servant is Exalted and the Powers are Overthrown (1 Chronicles 14; 18–20; Luke 1.46-55)*
The next chapter of Chronicles (ch. 14) deals largely with David's victory over the Philistines, but since three later chapters (chs. 18–20) continue the same theme of victory over the Philistines and other enemies, Luke again takes the separate texts in conjunction. Thus, we have on the one hand the victories of David, and on the other, the glorious song of Mary, the *Magnificat* (Lk. 1.46-55). It might seem an odd combination, but as C. Westermann remarks (1977: 9): 'In the Bible, the course of the stars in the heavens and a child's laughter, the development of nations in history and a domestic quarrel which ends in peace, are equally important'. Thus, while there is little relationship *from the point of view of world news* between the building of an impressive empire, which is what David is doing, and the singing of a young woman, *from the point of view of God's activity* the two are closely related: God gave victories to David; God gave Mary victories that were spiritual or internal. The relationship is seen to be even closer when we realize that the essence of both texts is concerned not so much with distant wars or a distant song, as with expressing the identity and confidence of an existing community: the Chronicler's post-exilic community (Myers 1965a: xxxii) and Luke's Christian community. Victory in war or song of victory, both are based on what God has done for the Davidic people.

Furthermore, the two strophes of the song (1.46-50 and 1.51-55) correspond in a general way with the two separate texts of Chronicles. The first strophe shares with 1 Chronicles 14

---

6. The parallelism of the ark and Mary coincides with the observations of Lyonnet, Sahlin, Herbert, and Laurentin, and seems quite valid—despite the reservations of Brown. For discussion and references, see especially Brown 1977: 327-28, 344-45.

such basic themes as the exaltation of the servant (the Lord 'highly increased' David's kingdom, 1 Chron. 14.2), the image of the Lord as mighty, and the spread of the servant's name to all the earth (Chronicles), or to all generations (Luke). On the other hand, the more militant tone of the second strophe fits the more militant tone of 1 Chron. 18–20, especially ch. 20.

e. *Section 5. Priestly Service and Song (1 Chronicles 15–16; Luke 1.57-80)*
The Chronicler continues with the account of bringing the ark to Jerusalem, but he has elaborated the text of 2 Samuel so that the main emphasis is not so much on the *ark* as on the *Levites and priests* who are to carry and serve it. And while the Chronicler switches back from focusing on David to focusing on the priestly line, Luke similarly switches attention from the Davidic Mary back to the priestly family of Zechariah and Elizabeth. In both texts, the purpose of the priestly line is to prepare or make possible the way of the Lord. In Chronicles it is the priests, and the priests alone, who make it possible that the ark of the Lord should come to Jerusalem (1 Chron. 15.11-15); in Luke, it is the unique task of the one born into the priestly family, John the Baptist, to prepare the way of the Lord (Lk. 1.76).

There is an emphasis in the two accounts on the progeny of the priestly caste. In Chronicles we have a list of the various sons of Aaron and Levi (1 Chron. 15.3-10); in Luke, at long last, we have the birth of a son to Zechariah and Elizabeth (Lk. 1.57). Yet in both texts there is also the idea of a break with the past. In Chronicles it is a break which establishes the place of the priestly line: above the layman ('No…but the Levites', 1 Chron. 15.2 LXX). In Luke there is a corresponding break, but it is, typically, a break *away* from the established priestly tradition ('No, but he shall be called John', Lk. 1.60).

Table 83. *Priestly Service and Song (1 Chronicles 15–16; Luke 1.57-60)*

The priestly families who are to make possible the way of the ark of the Lord… …the sons… 'No…but the Levites' [indicating a break with previous practice—a break towards genealogical priesthood] (15.1-10)	The priestly family which is to prepare the way of the Lord… …the son… 'No, but he shall be called John' [indicating a break with established tradition—a break from genealogical priesthood] (1.57-60)
Repetition of the theme of a priestly break from previous practice ('…in the word of God according to the scripture'—*logó…graphé*) (15.11-15)	Repetition by Zechariah of the name which breaks from previous priestly tradition. ('He wrote saying'—*egrapsen legón*) (1.61-63)
The priestly cantors play tunes of joy (*euphrosuné*) before God's ark (15.16-24)	Zechariah breaks out in praise (*eu-logón*) of God (1.64)
The joy of all the people as the ark is brought up to Jerusalem (15.25–16.3)	The fear and wonder of all the people in the hill country of Judaea (i.e. the area through which the ark passed) (1.65-66)
The priestly song of praise (16.4-36)	Zechariah's canticle (1.67-79)
The priests serve God and are left waiting in the wings (until the Temple will be built) (16.37-43)	The boy grows in spirit and waits in the desert until his day of manifestation (1.80)

And then there is an outbreak of praise and wonder that spreads through the hills of Judea. On the one hand, there is the music and dancing by the priests and David as they bring the ark to Jerusalem (1 Chron. 15.16–16.3); on the other hand, there is Zechariah's sudden outburst of speech and praise and the spread of a sense of wonder through the hills of Judea (Lk. 1.63-66). Thus Luke's two references to some form of movement in the hill country of Judea (1.39, 65) correspond exactly to the Chronicler's two stages of the movement of the ark through those same hills (1 Chron. 13; 15.16–16.3).

Then both writers give a canticle of praise (1 Chron. 16.4-36; Lk. 1.67-69). While Luke's canticle reflects several Old Testament passages (Brown 1977: 386-89), its root inspiration seems to have been the complex canticle from the Chronicler.

Finally, there is a brief note which leaves the priestly line waiting in the wings: David left Asaph ministering patiently before the ark, and left Zadok offering sacrifice out at Gibeon (1 Chron. 16.37-43). It would be a while before they could minister in the coming Temple. Luke seems to have something similar in mind when he pictures the Baptist as growing (in *body and spirit* rather than in *cult*), and as biding his time in the desert (1.80). See outline (Table 83).

f. *Sections 6 and 7. Census Taking (1 Chronicles 15–16; Luke 1.57-80) and Piety (1 Chronicles 23–29; Luke 21–20)*
With sections 6 and 7 there is a transition. The narrative leaves those who wait in the wings (priests ministering out at Gibeah; John growing up in the desert) and moves to the central issue—the building of the Temple, or, in the New Testament, to the building of the living Temple which is Jesus.

Before building takes place, there is a complex prelude (1 Chron. 21–29; Lk. 2.1-38) (Cazelles 1961: 99n): first, the birth or siting of the Temple (Section 6); then, a survey of the people and piety of the Temple (section 7). The texts on the Temple's siting/birth (section 6) are akin and may be summarized simply by an outline (Table 84).

Table 84. *Prelude to a (New) Temple (1 Chronicles 21–22; Luke 2.1-20)*

1 Chronicles 21–22	Luke 2.1-20
David orders a census of all Israel (21.1-6), thus determining the site of the future Temple (21.15) (Census, i.e. complete counting, of all Israel)	Augustus decrees a census of the whole world, thus determining the site of the birth of Jesus (at Bethlehem) (2.1-7) (Fulfilling, i.e. complete counting, of the days of Mary and son).
The sword of the Lord and the fall of 70,000 in Israel (21.7-14)	(See below 2.34-35)
The angel instills dread but sacrifice brings salvation to David's Jerusalem, involving all the strangers in the country (21.15–22.4)	An angel causes fear but speaks of Christ the Savior 'in the city of David' to the shepherds in that land (2.8-11)
Introduction of tender-aged Solomon, child of great splendor and widespread peace (22.5-10)	Annunciation of the baby Jesus, a child of angelic praise and universal peace (2.12-14)
Solomon is to follow the commandments and ordinances of the Lord by building the Temple (22.11-16)	The shepherds follow the word of the Lord by going to the baby (2.15-17)
All the rulers of Israel enjoy peace, and are to devote heart and soul to seeking God and building his Temple (22.17-19)	The shepherds spread wonder and praise to all,
	and Mary guards all these things in her heart (2.18-20)

In section 7 the people and piety which surround the Temple/boy before it/he has been built up physically. The outline appearing in Table 85 provides a basic summary and comparison.

Table 85. *Temple People and Piety (1 Chronicles 23–29; Luke 2.21-38)*

1 Chronicles 23–29	Luke 2.21-38
Census/classification (= complete counting) of the priestly line (chs. 23–26)	Fulfilling (= complete counting) of the days for circumcision (2.21)
Classification (= a type of complete counting) of the lay organization (ch. 27)	Fulfilling (= complete counting) of the days for purification of woman, child (2.22-24)
David 'in Jerusalem' has his heart set on the future Temple and destiny of Israel but sees the need for a man of perfect heart (28.1-10)	Simeon 'in Jerusalem' awaits the consolation of Israel, a just and devout man (2.55)
David (before he died) had already envisaged the liturgy (*leitourgia*) (28.13, 20); he had a plan for the Temple in his spirit (*en pneumati autou*, 28.12) (28.11-21)	Simeon...would not see death until he had seen Christ (*Christon Kyriou*), and he came in the spirit (*en tó pneumati*) into the Temple (2.26, 27a)
David's prayer of self-dismissal and thanksgiving (29.1-20)	Simeon's prayer of self-dismissal and thanksgiving (2.27b-33)
(See above 21.7-14)	The fall and rise of many in Israel, and the piercing sword (2.34-35)
The people's prodigal service of worship (29.21-25) Summing up old David: his years at Hebron (seven) and in Jerusalem (29.26-28)	Anna's history of prodigal service of worship. Old Anna: her years of marriage (seven), and of Temple service.
The annals of the prophets announce the blessings of David's reign to all (29.29-30)	Anna, who is a prophetess, speaks of him to all (2.36-38)

Luke follows the order of Chronicles. The only exception is 2.34-35, on the piercing sword and the fall of many, which corresponds to 1 Chron. 21.7-14.

The Chronicler's initial mention of a census (1 Chron. 21.1-6) is carefully balanced in the gospel text by a similar idea (2.1-7), and there seems to be a connection also between the Chronicler's repeated theme of *census* and *classification* (1 Chron. 21.1-6; chs. 23–27, especially 23.1-6; 24.1-3; chs. 25–26; 27.1, 23-24) and Luke's recurring theme of the *census* and the *fulfilling of the days* (Lk. 2.1, 6, 21-22). This involves a twofold transformation. First, the notion of a census, which in Chronicles is a negative thing, a work of Satan (1 Chron. 21.1), becomes in the gospel something more positive. In other words, just as Luke's insistence on the positive image of the manger (2.7, 12, 16) appears to be a reversal of the Old Testament negative image of the manger (Isa. 1.3 LXX) (Brown 1977: 419), so also he has reversed the Old Testament negative image of the census. In the Old Testament, the census is a victory for Satan; in Luke, the census is associated with the victory for the woman and her child (see Gen. 3.15; Rev. 12.1-6). Second, the idea of counting all the people seems to be transformed into the idea of counting all the days of the woman and child. In other words, the depiction of the people through numbers (as in Num. 1–4) has been replaced by the picturing of the people through a woman and child (as in Gen. 3.15). And the counting of the people has become the counting of the days of the woman and child, or a counting of time. Even Luke's mention of the census is against the background of a double mention of time (1.80, 'until the day'; 2.1, 'in those days'). Already in the infancy narrative, Luke is emphasizing the importance of the development of time.

Luke's two uses of the title 'Christ' in the infancy narrative (Lk. 2.11, 26) correspond to the Chronicler's mention of the sacrifice or service (*leitourgia*) of the Temple (1 Chron. 21.6–22.1; 28.13, 20). And while the Chronicler had spoken of the altar/sacrifice or service 'to the Lord' or 'of the Lord' (1 Chron. 21.18, 22, 24-26; 28.13, 20, 21), Luke similarly associates the title 'Christ' with the Lord: the shepherds are told of 'Christ [the] Lord' (Lk. 2.11); Simeon is to see 'Christ [the] Lord' (2.26). Therefore, it would appear that just as the Old Testament related anointing with worship (e.g. Exod. 40.1-15; Lev. 8.10-12; Num. 7.1-3, 10, 84, 88), so Luke uses the term 'Anointed' (*christos*) in relation to worship, or as reflecting the Old Testament mention of worship.

The two prayers of self-dismissal and thanksgiving (David's in 1 Chron. 29.1-20, and Simeon's in Lk. 2.27b-33) have several points of similarity. In both cases, the prayer has an introduction and conclusion that involve other characters.

Introduction (1 Chron. 29.1-10a; Lk. 2.27b-28). Apart from the central figures, David or Simeon, each introduction mentions a child, Solomon and Jesus, and some general figures: the heads of the families and the leaders (1 Chronicles), and the parents (Luke). And apart from the similarity regarding the *dramatis personae* there is similarity in the action: the general figures (family heads and leaders of the people in Chronicles; the parents in Luke) have a sense of duty regarding the house of God, either by contributing to the Temple treasury (1 Chronicles) or by doing in the Temple what the Law demands (Luke). However, the central figures, David and Simeon, appear as manifesting not just duty, but love: David refers to the tender Solomon (who is to *build the Temple*) and to his love for the Temple (1 Chron. 29.1-5); Simeon takes the child in his arms *in the Temple* (Lk. 2.28a). And then, in this Temple–child–love situation, both David and Simeon suddenly begin to bless the Lord (1 Chron. 29.9b-10a; Lk. 2.28b).

The prayer (1 Chron. 29.10b-18; Lk. 2.29-32). The prayers have linguistic and thematic similarities (linguistic: *eulogeśan, pantón tón..., despozeis/despota, prosopon, ethnos, doxa, nun* plus vocative case; *eidon, Israél, laou sou*; thematic: praise to the Lord of all nations [1 Chron. 29.10b-12; Lk. 2.30-32a]; self-dismissal with a peaceful heart [1 Chron. 29.13-17ab; Lk. 2.29]; mention of 'Israel...your people' [1 Chron. 29.17c-18; Lk. 2.32b]).

Conclusion (1 Chron. 29.19-20; Lk. 2.33). Like the introductions, the conclusions broaden out from the central figures and include both the child and the broader group (the assembly; the parents). The assembly blesses the Lord; the parents are in wonder.

g. *Section 8. The Building of the Temple (2 Chronicles 1.1–5.1; Luke 2.39-40)*
The texts begin with references to wisdom and to some form of development—external or internal:

The wisdom of Solomon (ch. 1) and the building of the Temple (chs. 2–4)	Jesus grows in wisdom and in physical stature

These two texts about the building of the Temple/Jesus (2 Chron. 1.1–5.1; Lk. 2.39-40) seem to have several details in common:

1. The completion of everything regarding the Law of the Lord in the Temple (Lk. 2.39a) seems to reflect Solomon's completion of everything regarding the Temple (2 Chron. 5.1).

2. The note on the return to Galilee, to the city of Nazareth (Lk. 2.39b), seems to reflect Solomon's journey to Gibeon (2 Chron. 1.3-6). In association with Gibeon, the Chronicler mentions the departure of the ark from Kiriathjearim (2 Chron. 1.4) and on the other hand it was from Galilee that Luke had shown Mary, like the ark, setting out (Lk. 1.26.39). In other words, the journeys to Gibeon and Galilee reverse the ark journeys to Judea/Jerusalem.
3. 'And the grace of God was upon him' (Lk. 2.40b) seems to reflect 'And the Lord his God was with him and increased him greatly' (2 Chron. 1.1b).

h. *Section 9. The Lord Takes Possession of His Temple (2 Chronicles 5.2–ch. 9; Luke 2.41-52)*
When the Temple is finally ready, there is a feast to celebrate its inauguration, and the Lord appears to Solomon and speaks to him. Aspects of this inauguration are reflected, in domestic form, in the account of finding Jesus in the Temple (see Table 86).

Table 86. *Taking Possession of the Temple (1 Chronicles 5–9; Luke 2.41-52)*

1 Chronicles 5–9	Luke 2.41-52
The elders and all Israel go 'to Jerusalem…at the feast' (5.2-10)	The parents would go 'to Jerusalem for the feast' (2.41)
'And it came to pass that' (*kai egeneto*) all the priests [at the feast] sanctify themselves according to their arrangement, and sang, and * 120 played the trumpet (5.11-13a)	And when he was (*kai hote egeneto*) * 12 years old they went up according to the custom of the feast (2.42)
The Lord took possession of his dwelling (*oikon*)… (5.13b-6.2)… After so many days he is finally in Jerusalem (6.3-11)	At the completion of the days Jesus remained (*hyp-emeinen*) in Jerusalem (1.43a)
Solomon's prayer: let people in need turn back to the Jerusalem Temple (6.12-39)	The worried parents turn back to Jerusalem (2.43b-45)
The Lord's dramatic and powerful appearance in the Temple (6.40–7.6)	Jesus, after three days (connoting resurrection?), is found to be dramatically present in the Temple (2.46-48a)
Again, the theme of turning back from the way and seeking the Lord (7.7-22; cf. above, 6.12-39)	Mary's words ('sought thee sorrowing') repeat the theme of the anxious search (2.48b-50; cf. above, 2.43b-45)
Solomon subjects people (8.1-10)	Jesus is obedient to his parents (2.51a)
Holy things cannot bear the presence of a woman (8.11-16)	Mary kept all these (holy) things in her heart (2.51b)
The fame of Solomon's wisdom spreads… to the end of his days (8.17–ch. 9)	Jesus advances in wisdom and age (2.52)

The texts on turning back toward Jerusalem (2 Chron. 6.12-39; Lk. 2.43b-45) have some corresponding details: as well as referring to turning back (2 Chron. 6.37-38; Lk. 2.45), both mention the way or journey (*hodos*, 2 Chron. 6.16, 27, 30, 34, 38; Lk. 2.44) and knowing or not knowing (2 Chron. 6.29, 30, 33; Lk. 2.43c).

The question in Luke (2.48b-49: 'Why…?', 'Because…of my father') reflects 2 Chronicles (7.21-22: 'Why has the Lord done this…?', 'Because they forsook…the God of their fathers').

i. *Section 10. The Setting: The Leading People (Ezra 1–2; Luke 3.1-2b)*
The books describing the ministries of Ezra and Nehemiah begin largely with a list of names which set the scene. The ministries of John and Jesus are prefaced by a similar but more compact list. These names pertain both to the world scene, and the Israelite scene.

Table 87. *The Year, the Leaders*

Ezra 1–2	Luke 3.1-2b
The World Scene	
'In the first year of Cyrus King of Persia...' (Ezra 1.1-4)	'In the fifteenth year of the reign of Tiberius Caesar...' (3.1a)
The Israelite Scene: Secular	
The heads of the families of Judah...and the prince of Judah (1.5-11) The twelve men (2.1-2, connoting all Israel, twelve tribes) and the list 'of the people of Israel' (2.3-35)	The governor of Judea (3.1b), and the rulers of all the traditional land of Israel (3.1c)
The Israelite Scene: Cultic	
Those in the Temple/priesthood (2.36-70)	High priests: Annas and Caiaphas (3.2a)

In both texts these lists of names are brought to life by the vitality of the word of God: Ezra's list is based on the 'word of the Lord from the mouth of Jeremiah' (Ezra 1.1); and Luke's list is climaxed by 'the word of God' which 'came', prophecy-like, to John (Lk. 3.2b). In other words, the lists are alive with the power of the prophetic word.

j. *Section 11. Prepare for Rebuilding! (Ezra 3.1–6.18; Nehemiah 1–7, Omitting Ch. 5; Luke 3.2c-6)*
The two texts dealing with the rebuilding of Jerusalem (of its Temple, Ezra 3.1–6.18, and of its walls, Neh. 1–7, omitting ch. 5) can be taken in conjunction. Not alone are they complementary parts of the same reconstruction process, but they are both largely concerned with overcoming the opposition to rebuilding. Luke, in turn, through the words of Isa. 40.3-5, provides an image of building despite opposition—of constructing a straight way, a way of the Lord, despite all valley and hills.

Here Luke is blending: some of his basic material is from one source (Ezra); but his actual expression is from another, more poetic source (Isaiah). This blending of prose material with poetic expression has already been seen in earlier chapters.

Both of these pictures of construction-despite-opposition pertain to the post-exilic reconstruction of Israel, and in that sense they refer to the same basic reality. But, by putting the words of reconstruction on the lips of John the Baptist, Luke has changed their meaning so that they refer to a process of building that is not *material* but *moral.* In other words, with the help of Isaiah's poetry, the story of the physical rebuilding of post-exilic Israel has been transformed into the story of the spiritual rebuilding of New Testament Israel.

In addition, there are various connecting details:
1. The constructions begin with the notion of preparation: Ezra 3.3 has 'And they set up (literally, "prepared", *hetiomasan*) the altar on its foundation (literally, "preparation", *hetiomasian*)'; Lk. 3.4 reads 'Prepare (*hetiomasate*) the way of the Lord'.
2. Reconstruction begins against a background of virtual nothingness: Israel had come from exile, and Jerusalem was in ruins (literally, a desert, Neh. 2.17 [LXX, 2 Esd. 12.17]); John begins in the desert (Lk. 3.2c).

3. The description of John as coming and doing the round of the deserted Jordan area (Lk. 3.3a) seems to coincide with the picture of Nehemiah as coming, and as going all around 'deserted' Jerusalem (Neh. 1.1-3; 2.1-18).
4. In both cases, the reconstruction process is connected with, or geared towards, the removal of sin. The building of the Temple concludes with public sacrifice for sin (Ezra 6.13-18) and the building of the walls is preceded by Nehemiah's confession of sins (Neh. 1.5-11). Likewise, John's reconstruction is based on his 'proclaiming a baptism of repentance for the forgiveness of sins' (Lk. 3.3).

k. *Section 12. Correction of Social Abuses (Nehemiah 5; Luke 3.10-14)*

Toward the end of the Ezra–Nehemiah texts on rebuilding, there is a chapter (Neh. 5) on the correction of social abuses, a chapter which uses the abuses it corrects as a foil for presenting the idea of a compassionate and just society. Thus the Ezra–Nehemiah reconstruction movement is not only linked, as already seen, with the recovery from sin, but it is also linked with the construction of a just society. Similarly in Luke, the proclamation of John's building program—a way through the desert—is followed shortly after by John's correction of possible social abuses, and his corrections amount to a program for a just society. The elements of these two programs show a remarkable similarity:

Table 88. *Rebuilding Society*

Nehemiah 5	Luke 3.10-14
Regarding Basic Necessities	
To obtain corn they must pledge their children (5.2)	Let him who has two cloaks share with him who has none
To obtain corn they must pledge their property (5.3)	Let him who has food do the same
Regarding the Imperial Tax	
To pay the king's tax they must borrow money and sell their children (5.4-5) In solemn assembly Nehemiah corrects the officials (5.6-13)	Tax-collectors, exact no more than is appointed
Regarding the Use of Power	
As king's governor neither Nehemiah nor his kinsmen burdened or oppressed or took governor's allowance (5.14-19)	Soldiers, do not intimidate or extort and be content with your pay

Two aspects of Luke's text require comment: the content and the form. The content is a brief synthesis and adaptation of the entire chapter of Nehemiah. The repetition concerning food (Neh. 5.2-3) has been adapted slightly to become a repetition that affects both food and clothing. The role of Nehemiah as *authoritatively addressing* the great assembly (5.6-13) seems to be reflected in the title '*Teacher*' which the tax-collectors give to Jesus (Lk. 3.12). And the correction and repentance of the officials (5.6-12) is reflected in Luke's explicit note that the tax-collectors came to be baptized—implying repentance. Finally, the contrast between Nehemiah and his kinsmen, on the one hand, and the governors who preceded him and their minions, on the other hand (5.14-19), is summed up in John's exhortations to the military minions of the prevailing empire.

The form of Luke's text is based not so much on Nehemiah's entire chapter as on its opening verses (5.1-4). Just as these verses present three groups, so does Luke. But he has adapted the threefold form. What he seems to have done is transform the repetition of *tines... tines... tines* ('Some... More... Others') into *ti... ti... ti* (What?... What?... What?), and by changing the loud complaints into eager questions, he has speeded and compacted the action.

l. *Section 13. The People—Purification and Joy (Nehemiah 10–13; Luke 3.15-18)*
Thus far we have seen Luke's relationship to Nehemiah 1–7. The next two chapters (Neh. 8 and 9) appear to be 'Ezra material' (Myers 1965b: 152), so that by staying with the strictly Nehemiah material one comes to Nehemiah 10–13. And that is exactly what Luke has done: having rewritten Nehemiah 1–7, he moves on to Nehemiah 10–13.

Nehemiah 10–13 deals primarily with 'the people'. It gives various lists of the people and their priests, and it refers in particular to the cleansing (*katharizein*) of the people (chs. 10 and 13) and to their joy in celebrating the Dedication (12.27-47). The unity of chs. 10–13 seems assured by the fact that between chs. 10 and 13 there is a 'clear...relationship' (Gelin 1960: 100n), a careful balance (Myers 1965b: 175).

Correspondingly, Luke gives a compact four-verse picture of the people which opens and closes with balancing verses (3.15-18). Apart from these general elements of basic theme (the people) and broad layout (balance between beginning and end), there are other linking factors:

1. The bubbling joy of the people at the Dedication—literally, the Re*new*al (*Enkainia*, Neh. 12.27-47) would seem to correspond to the sense of *expectation*, of hearing the Good *News*, which Luke attributes to the people (Lk. 3.15, 18). But Luke has taken that sense of joy at what is *new*, which is in the middle of Nehemiah's text, and used it in his opening and closing verses in order to set the entire mood.
2. The notion of ritual purification of all (Neh. 12.30) finds a parallel in John's baptism with water (Lk. 3.16).
3. Nehemiah's emphasis on a drastic cleansing or purging (*katharizó*) of the people (the opening and closing chapters, especially 10.31-32; 13.1-9, 23-30) has been synthesized into a single verse in the middle of Luke's text ('The winnowing-fan...to cleanse [*diakathairó*]', 3.17).
4. In place of Nehemiah's lists of people, Luke simply refers to 'all' (3.15, 16).

m. *Section 14. From Correcting Unlawful Marriages to Being in Deep Trouble (Ezra 9–10, Nehemiah 9; Luke 3.19-20)*
Luke now turns back to rewrite one of the Nehemiah chapters which he had just skipped (Neh. 9), but just as some modern scholars (e.g. Gelin 1960: 92n) have noted that Nehemiah 9 seems to follow logically on Ezra 9 and 10, so Luke has treated these three chapters in conjunction.

Ezra's demand that the Israelites put away their unlawful wives (Ezra 9–10) is paralleled by John's condemnation of Herod's unlawful wife (Lk. 3.19a). And just as Ezra, in the context of referring to the unlawful wives, spoke of all of Israel's evil deeds (Ezra 9.6-15, especially 9.13), so John spoke of all of Herod's evil deeds (Lk. 3.19b).

Moving on to Nehemiah 9, what Luke does is to focus on the climatic point of that chapter (Neh. 9, especially 9.36-37: '[On top of all our long history of trouble,] Behold today we are slaves... We are in great distress') and he sums it up in the fate of John (Lk. 3.20: Herod 'added this also to everything else—he shut up John in prison'). In other words, just as the Ezra–Nehemiah texts on the problem of unlawful marriages (Ezra 9–10;

Neh. 9) come to a climax with a picture of the people as being '*slaves...in great distress*', so Luke's report on the correction of Herod's unlawful marriage comes to a climax with a picture of John being '*shut up...in prison*'.

Note also some linguistic affinities: *archontes* (Ezra 9.1) and *tetrarchés* (Lk. 3.19a); *pan...poiémasin...ponérois* (Ezra 9.13) and *pantón...epoiesén ponérón* (Lk. 3.19b); *epi pasi* (Neh. 9.33, 5 [19.33, 5 LXX]) and *epi pasin* (Lk. 3.20).

n. *Section 15. Purification and Celebration (Ezra 6.19-22; Luke 3.21-22)*
At this juncture, Luke has covered all of Nehemiah except ch. 8, but as regards Ezra, he has yet to account for two chapters (7–8) and a paragraph (6.19-22). He begins with the paragraph (6.19-22, the description of the Passover).

The Israelite feast of Passover described by Ezra is a mixture of purification and celebration. So is Luke's account of the baptism of Jesus. Not only does baptism parallel Ezra's notion of purification, but, insofar as it is through *water*, it also evokes the atmosphere of Israel's first Passover. On the other hand, Ezra's picture of a feast and joy (*euphrosuné*) is balanced by Luke's picture of love (the Beloved) and delight (*eu-dokésa*). In both texts, this happy mood is linked to a very concrete or physical manifestation of God's presence: God *turned the heart* of the king to them (*ep' autous*) to strengthen their hands; the Holy Spirit descended *in bodily form* on him (*ep' auton*). Furthermore, Ezra refers three times to those who celebrate as sons (sons of the exile...of Israel); Luke, on the other hand, shows Jesus as 'the Son', but this is said of Jesus after he emerges from among 'all the people'. In other words, Ezra's vague notion of the people as sons is so sharpened in Luke that the one who emerges from the midst of the people is the Son of God.

o. *Sections 16-18. Ezra and Jesus: Genealogy, Journey, and Public Reading (Ezra 7–8; Nehemiah 8; Luke 3.23-38; 4.14-22a)*
Finally, Luke gathers all the remaining material (Ezra 7–8 and Neh. 8) into a unit (as do some scholars: Pavlovsky 1957; Gelin 1960: 14 n. 89). It all pertains to Ezra and is remarkably similar to Luke's picture of Jesus:

Ezra 7–8 and Nehemiah 8	Luke 3.23-38; 4.14-22a
The setting out of Ezra, son of...son of... the hand of God was with him (Ezra 7.1-10)	The setting out of Jesus, son of...son of... son of God (3.23-38)
Ezra returns home with all, enjoying God's favor (7.11–ch. 8)	Jesus returns to Galilee enjoying the favor of all (4.14, 15)
Home in Jerusalem, Ezra reads the law and all are delighted (Neh. 8)	Home in Galilee, Jesus reads Isaiah and all approve (4.16-22a)

Luke combines sources. While systematically distilling Ezra–Nehemiah, he also quotes Isaiah. In later chapters there are variations on this procedure: for content, Luke sometimes uses his main source, but for wording he employs poetic expression from the prophets or Psalms.

2. *Conclusion*

There are massive differences between Luke (1.1–4.22a) and Chronicles/Ezra/Nehemiah but there are also solid indications that Luke used the old text.

First, there is external plausibility. Given general agreement that Luke used and imitated the LXX, it is particularly appropriate that as a historiographer he would pay special attention to the LXX's second major historiographical corpus—that formed by Chronicles/

53. A New Temple and a New Law

Ezra/Nehemiah. This second corpus was all the more instructive because it contained a reworking and interpretation of much of the older Primary History. And Luke, as well as being an historiographer, was engaged with the reworking of Scripture, with its interpretation and fulfillment.

Second, there are significant similarities. These include:
- *Motifs*: shared central themes, especially the temple and the Law.
- *Plot*: broadly similar actions, but with great 'historical' events adapted to personal or biographical events.
- *Language*: persistent links of verbal detail.
- *Completeness*: apart from 2 Chronicles 10–36 (used later), the Old Testament text is used completely.
- *Order*: Luke generally follows the Old Testament order; and his variations are understandable.

Third, the differences, huge though they are, are not a meaningless muddle; they are intelligible. They follow deliberate strategies or purposes, partly the shift of focus from the temple to the human person, and particularly the broad purpose of moving from an Old Testament narrative which is dominated by great sweeps of history towards a form of historiography which is more obviously person-oriented, closer to biography.

Consequently, unless one is to invoke an extraordinary phenomenon of coincidence, it is reasonable to conclude that Luke had access to the Chronicler's history and used it systematically. Just as the Chronicler had once rewritten Israel's history, leaving aside the previous emphasis on Israel's political and military status and focusing rather on the Temple and the Law, so Luke in turn has rewritten the Chronicler's history, moving the focus from the Temple of stone to a boy who is the living Temple of God, and replacing Ezra's reading of the Law with Jesus' reading of Isaiah's declaration of freedom and forgiveness. It is a new kind of Temple, and a new kind of Law.

While Luke's narrative contains several elements of history, it is clear that much of it is not based on history but rather on Scripture and theology. It is largely an artistic composition, a creative rewriting of Old Testament texts. Whether the infancy narrative's way of using the Old Testament should be termed a 'midrash' is disputed (Brown 1977: 560-61). What seems clear, however, is that the pervasive influence of the Old Testament—however one names it—is not limited to the infancy narratives.

54

Proto-Luke: Summarizing Argument 1—
The Distinctive Use of the Old Testament

As indicated in Chapter 10, especially in its final part, there are three key arguments for Proto-Luke:
1. Distinctive dependence on the LXX.
2. Unity of content and structure.
3. Subsequent verification.

Chapters 27–53 have concentrated on argument one—distinctive dependence, beginning in Luke 1–2.

Within the infancy narrative's dense reworking of the Old Testament are three threads which, in diverse ways, are particularly strong: the Elijah–Elisha narrative, Judges, and the Chronicler (see Chapters 27, 46, and 53). The passage influenced by the Elijah–Elisha narrative is brief (Lk. 1.5-17), but it is set at the beginning and appeals explicitly to the spirit and power of Elijah (Lk. 1.17).

After the infancy narrative the influence of these three threads does not stop. Rather, it recurs intermittently throughout the gospel, and continues into Acts 15.

The claim to the presence of these specific threads is not made lightly. It is based on three kinds of criteria: external plausibility, significant similarities (including theme, plot, motif, order, linguistic detail), and the intelligibility of the differences (for details, see Chapter 5).

Sometimes the threads overlap. This is true in the infancy narrative, and also true in some further passages. For instance, the parable of how the widow got her rights from the unjust judge draws considerably on the narrative of the maverick judge Jephthah (Judg. 10–12), but it also draws something from the account of how the woman of Shunem retrieved her property (2 Kgs 8.1-8).

This mixture of intermittent recurrence and overlapping forms a pattern that may be described as interwoven. (For a list of passages, see Table 6.)

What is essential is that the pattern of dependence is distinctive. The Lukan passages which incorporate the three Old Testament texts—the Elijah–Elisha narrative, Judges, and the Chronicler—stand out from the rest of Luke–Acts, through their systematic dependence. As indicated earlier, they comprise the following texts:

Annunciations/births:	Lk. 1.1-56//1.57–ch 2
Ministry: preaching/action:	Lk. 3.1-6, 10-38; 4.14-22a//7.1–8.3
Journey to Jerusalem:	Lk. 9.51–10.20; 16.1-9, 19-31//17.11–18.8; 19.1-10
Death/Resurrection:	Lk. 22.1-30; 22.66–23.49//23.50–ch. 24
Spirit promised/given:	Acts ch. 1//2.1-42
Ministry: action/preaching:	Acts 2.43–4.31//4.32–ch. 5
Leaving Jerusalem:	Acts 6.1–8.1a//8.1b–9.30
Breakthrough to Gentiles:	Acts 9.31–ch. 12//13.1–15.35

54. Proto-Luke: Summarizing Argument 1

The case for Luke 1–2 and much of 3.1–8.3 is clear. Luke 1–2 is a closely knit unit and in diverse ways depends systematically on all three pivotal sources. Likewise regarding 3.1–4.22a and 7.1–8.3: though these passages are now mixed with other material, especially from Mark, they stand out through their systematic dependence on the three sources (including Ezra–Nehemiah). Luke 7.1–8.3 is both unified in itself and solidly dependent on the Elijah–Elisha narrative.

Within 9.51–19.10—from departure for Jerusalem until Jesus meets Zacchaeus at Jericho—the pattern of systematic dependence is particularly intermittent. It omits a massive block (10.21–ch. 15) and parts of chs. 16, 17, and 18. Yet the intermittent texts themselves, beginning with Jesus' departure for Jerusalem (9.51-56), maintain the dependence at full strength—even if at times the manner of doing so is quite complex.

Within Luke 22–24, the evidence converges for including most of the Last Supper (22.1-30) but not the denials and night action (22.31-65). Aspects from most of the Last Supper (22.1-30), but not all of it, are dependent on both the center of Elijah–Elisha narrative (2 Kgs 2) and also on Judges 21. Dependence on the framework supplied by 2 Kings 2 resumes with the morning action (22.66) when Jesus is brought before the Sanhedrin, and this broad dependence on the center of the Elijah–Elisha narrative continues into Acts 2.

At various points, the inclusion of this material (Lk. 22.66–Acts 2) is confirmed by other factors. For instance, the appropriateness of including the bringing of Jesus before the Sanhedrin is confirmed by the narrative continuity between Jesus and Stephen, someone who was likewise brought before the Sanhedrin (Acts 6.9-14, especially 6.12) and whose account is modeled on the Elijah-related story of Naboth (1 Kgs 21). Elements of the account of Jesus' death reflect the departure of Elijah. And one component of 23.50–ch. 24 comes from Judges 19.

The inclusion of all of Lk. 22.66–ch. 24—rather than just parts of it—is further strengthened by the nature of the narrative at this point. It is essentially continuous, rather than episodic as in earlier chapters (for instance, Lk. 3–6). The shift from episodic to continuous—a shift which is frequent in biblical narrative (for instance, in Genesis, in the Elijah–Elisha narrative, and in Mark)—means that it is relatively easy to interject fresh material into the early chapters, but not into the later continuous narrative. Jesus' trial, death, and resurrection (22.66–ch. 24) is so continuous and close-knit that it is best seen as belonging together.

In the case of Acts, the stream of dependence (including occasional overlapping) runs almost unbroken—but only as far as ch. 15. The central framework, drawn from 2 Kings 2, extends into Acts 2.

The passages at the beginning and end of Acts 3–5 (the beggar at the temple, Acts 3.1-10, and Gamaliel's 'anti-war' speech, 5.33-42) depend variously on the Elijah–Elisha narrative and on Judges, and in doing so they draw the whole tightly knit block (Acts 3–5) into the pattern of dependence.

Likewise with the close-knit Stephen story (Acts 6–7). It is framed by dependence on the Elijah-related story of Naboth (Acts 6.9-14; 7.58). Acts 8–12 (especially chs. 8–9) draw heavily on the Elijah–Elisha narrative (for instance, the account of the Ethiopian on Naaman), and Acts 12.1–15.21 makes systematic use of Judges.

The subsequent narrative about writing the apostolic letter (Acts 15.22-35) at one level consists of an extended counterpart to the opening prologue (Lk. 1.1-4) and, as such, forms a fitting conclusion.

The texts in question—Septuagintal and extending intermittently from Luke 1–2 to Acts 15.35—form a distinctive body of material which corresponds significantly to the Feine-based theory of a Semitic Proto-Luke extending from Luke 1–2 to the center of Acts. As such, it adds credibility to the theory of Proto-Luke. For the moment, therefore, it is reasonable to use the theory of Proto-Luke as a working hypothesis.

Part IV

Appendices: Further, Exploratory Aspects of New Testament Intertextuality

Unit 13. Proto-Luke

Appendix 1

Proto-Luke:
Reviewing Aspects of the History of Research
and Rethinking the Arguments

In 1891 Paul Feine of Göttingen established a central hypothesis: Luke–Acts once existed in a shorter form, a form which was independent of the gospel of Mark (Feine 1891). The subsequent history of the idea[1] may be divided into three phases: Semitic Luke–Acts, Pre-Markan Luke, and Hebraic Luke–Acts.

1. *Paul Feine: Precanonical-Luke, Distinguished by its Jewish/Semitic Quality*

Feine's thesis started with a simple observation: Luke's work reflects two distinct strands, one thoroughly Jewish, the other decidedly Gentile. The Gentile strand was easily accounted for: it reflected the mentality of the evangelist Luke, someone who, though influenced by Paul, wrote as a Gentile. The Jewish strand, on the other hand, seemed to Feine so different from the Gentile strand that it required a distinct authorship. In fact, the only way to account for the Jewish material was to suppose that it came from a source which was older: 'I believe I can show…*that in certain parts both of the third gospel and of the Acts of the Apostles it is to be assumed as probable that there is a precanonical account*' (1891: iv).

Feine then went on to uncover those areas of Luke and Acts which, in his view, were distinguishable by their flavor of ancient Judaism, a flavor which was Hebraic. The infancy narrative, for instance, was pervaded by an ancient Jewish atmosphere, and so he reckoned that the precanonical account contained all of Luke 1–2, but not the Greek-sounding prologue of Lk. 1.1-4. Feine's final reconstruction consisted essentially of the following texts:

Luke 1.5–2.52;
3.10-14, 23-38; 4.14-30; 5.1-11; 6.20-49; 7.1-17, 36-50; 8.1-3;
9.51-56; 10.17-20, 25-42; 11.5-8, 27-28, 37-52; 12.13-21; 13.1-17, 31-33;
14.1-6, 16-24; 15.4-32; 16.1-13, 19-31; 17.11-37, 39-44; 18.1-14, 22-30; 19.1-17;
21.12-15, 37-38; 22.14-23, 31-71; 23.1–24.53;
Acts 1.3–8.24; 9.31–10.11; 10.18; 11.19-23; 12.1-24
(i.e. most of Acts 1–12, minus most episodes on Philip and Paul)

Feine concluded (pp. 233-35) that this precanonical document, Luke's distinctive source (*Quellenschrift*), was written by Jewish Christians in Jerusalem, around 67 CE, in Aramaic or Hebrew.

---

1. See, in particular, Taylor 1926: 2-32, 182-215; Page 1968: 2-35; Gaston 1970: 244-56; J.M. Harrington 1998: 4-557, especially 4-45, 98-200, 412-68.

2. Perry, Streeter, Taylor: 'Classic' Proto-Luke, Distinguished by Independence from Mark

Variations on Feine's hypothesis appeared soon afterwards in the works of other researchers (especially in Weiss, Spitta and, independently, in Burton of Chicago), but it was in the 1920s that the idea received a new form and that the *Quellenschrift* was explicitly named 'Proto-Luke'.

The starting-point now was not the Hebraic or Semitic quality of some of Luke and Acts but something quite different: (a) the relationship of Luke's gospel to the gospel of Mark, and (b) the particular relationship of Luke's passion narrative to that of Mark.

a. *Luke and Mark: The Relationship Between the Gospels*

The central point here is that if the four great Markan blocks (Lk. 4.31–6.11; 8.4–9.50; 18.15-43; 20.1–21.4) are removed from Luke one still has the essentials of a complete gospel, and so it may be argued that the Markan sections are later insertions, and that Luke's gospel first existed in a briefer form, Proto-Luke. In Streeter's words (1924: 207-208):

> Taken together [the non-Markan sections] are much larger in extent than the sections derived from Mark. From them comes the beginning, and from them comes the end of the gospel. Suppose then they all stood together in a single document—this would form something very like a complete gospel... We are on the verge of a conclusion of the first importance. At least we are compelled to test the hypothesis that *the non-Markan sections represent a single document, and to Luke this was the framework into which he inserted, at convenient places, extracts from Mark*.

The case for Luke's original independence from Mark was sometimes bolstered by the claim that, unlike the four clear-cut Markan blocks, the Q sections are interwoven with the specifically Lukan material (L), and this contrast (between interwoven sources on the one hand [Q and L] and large Markan blocks on the other) suggests two separate processes: one of detailed interweaving, and the other of the incorporation of large blocks. The distinction between the two processes confirms the hypothesis of two editions.

This latter argument involving Q is weakened by the uncertainty surrounding Q's origin and shape; but the more basic argument concerning the relationship to Mark can stand on its own.

b. *Luke and Mark: The Relationship Between the Passion Narratives*

What is true of the gospels of Luke and Mark is even more true of their passion narratives. Luke's account of the passion is such that, even when the Markan verses are removed from it, it still has a certain completeness, and so it is easy to envisage it as once having been independent of Mark.

Furthermore, the idea of Luke's independence is greatly strengthened by the order of Luke's episodes: Luke's order differs widely from that of Mark—a phenomenon which does not accord with Luke's practice elsewhere of incorporating great blocks of Markan material. Yet the specifically Markan verses follow Mark's own order as though they were inserted into an already existing narrative. The impression, therefore, is of two different authorial processes: an earlier one which was independent of Mark, and the present one which incorporates Mark.

As Proto-Luke was formulated in the 1920s, it generally began with the preaching of John (Lk. 3) and extended to the passion narrative. It did not include the infancy narrative or any part of the Acts of the Apostles.

Appendix 1. *Rethinking the Arguments* 543

3. Harald Sahlin: Proto-Luke, Distinguished by its Hebraic/Aramaic Quality

In the 1940s the theory of Proto-Luke was reformulated by Harald Sahlin of Sweden (Sahlin 1945; 1949). Sahlin's starting-point was the belief that C.C. Torrey, the man who claimed that much of the gospels and Acts were founded on Aramaic texts, was onto something, at least in some areas (1945: 7): 'It is my firm conviction that, as far as the Lukan writings are concerned, Torrey has hit on the right path; the start [which Torrey made] was correct, but it is necessary to go forward in a way which is simultaneously more careful and more radical'.

For Sahlin, the way forward was that of detailed analysis of Luke's text. He believed that by examining the third gospel and Acts closely enough with regard both to literary mode of expression and also to content or outlook, he could distinguish within Luke and Acts a level which he would call Proto-Luke (1945: 8). He reckoned that Proto-Luke was written in the fifties by a Jewish Christian, partly in Hebrew (Lk. 1.4–3.7a) and partly in Aramaic (from Lk. 3.7b onwards), and he regarded this early document as extending, with interruptions, from the infancy narrative (beginning in 1.5) all the way to Acts 15. But Sahlin never reached Acts 15, and never spelled out the full picture of what Proto-Luke looked like. He could not get a handle on the concept of Semitism. In fact, despite publishing two volumes, he got no further in his analysis than Luke 3. Thus the project faltered.

In recent decades, opinion on Proto-Luke has been divided. Fitzmyer (1981: 90) lists ten scholars who support it, and sixteen who oppose it; some of the sixteen opponents, however, 'would admit the hypothesis at least for the passion narrative' (Fitzmyer 1981: 90). Such dividedness of opinion is to some degree inevitable, for even when the arguments in favor seem strong it has not been possible to clinch them, at least insofar as it has not been possible to spell out the precise shape of Proto-Luke and the history of its role in relation to the development of Q and of the other gospels.

What is essential for the present investigation is that research into Proto-Luke has revolved around two types of arguments: those (of Streeter and Taylor) relating to Luke's use and non-use of Mark; and those (of Feine and Sahlin) invoking Luke's dependence on a source which was distinctly Jewish, Hebraic or Semitic. Of the two sets of arguments, it is those relating to Mark, particularly Mark's passion narrative, which have been stronger. The arguments concerning Luke's Semitic dimension have turned out, in practice, to be elusive.

4. Proposal: Adjust the Central Criterion: Not Semitism but Septuagintism

If scholars from Feine to Sahlin could not isolate the distinctive Semitic strand of Luke–Acts, why should it be possible now? It is possible because it is now recognized that Luke depends on the Septuagint (Fitzmyer 1981: 113; Koet 1989: especially 140-61; Sterling 1992: 363) and that his so-called Semitisms are essentially Septuagintisms—reflections of the Greek Old Testament (Fitzmyer 1981: 114). Consequently, what researchers such as Feine and Sahlin saw as Luke's Semitic strand can also be viewed as a Septuagintal strand. And since the Septuagint is clearly defined—a book which can be read and checked—the quest for the Semitic dimension becomes much more feasible. For instance, R. Dillon (1990: 8) can say, as if it were a commonplace, that in Acts 'the LXX mimesis is suspended after chapter 15'. If it seems clear to someone that the dependence on the Septuagint changes after Acts 15, then there is a good chance that close scrutiny will reveal much more about Luke's special Semitic/Septuagintal strand.

And so it works out. When the central criterion for judging Proto-Luke is adjusted and applied—when one searches for Septuagintism rather than Semitism (see Part III)—a distinctive strand does emerge, and it extends intermittently from Luke 1 to Acts 15, from the infancy narrative to the council of Jerusalem (Acts 15.35).

5. *Proto-Luke and Q: Aspects of Comparison*

In a comparison between Proto-Luke and Q, it may seem at first that Q has the advantage.[2] Q is immediately attractive. Details apart, it seems to solve problems with a minimum of effort. Proto-Luke needs more work and patience. Yet, in the final analysis the Proto-Luke hypothesis is more solid.

a. *The Logic of the General Argument*

At first it may seem that the claims of both hypotheses—Proto-Luke and Q—are equal. Each uses the similarity between two fixed texts to invoke a third. The similarity between Luke–Acts and the LXX is used to invoke Proto-Luke. The similarity between Matthew and Luke is used to invoke Q.

However, Q strains logic in a way that Proto-Luke does not. Proto-Luke is stable, fully present in Luke–Acts. In other words, Luke–Acts contains its entirety, unchanged. Q, however, is not fully contained either in Matthew or Luke, and so the reconstruction of its wording is extremely hazardous. It is therefore out of sight, hidden, in a way that Proto-Luke is not. It asks for forms of verses that have never been seen. This in itself does not discount Q, but it asks logic to go further, to claim more; and so, in comparison to Proto-Luke, it is weaker.

b. *The Logic of Specific Verses*

If a verse from Luke–Acts can be rooted either in the LXX or Q, priority goes to the LXX. Other things being equal, it is more logical, more credible, to attribute a text to a source that is certain (the LXX) than to a text that is hypothetical (Q). Again, therefore, in evenly balanced disputes about the parentage of verses, the LXX has the edge.

c. *General Background*

Proto-Luke has a specific verifable model (the Elijah–Elisha narrative); Q does not. (The role of the Gospel of Thomas as a model is problematic. It is not certain that Thomas or a Thomas-like text predated Q. And the genre of Thomas does not fit Q well. Thomas is simple—all sayings; Q is a more complex—sayings combined with narrative.)

d. *Structure*

Proto-Luke has a precise verifiable structure; Q does not.

e. *Effectiveness (*Brauchbarkeit*)*

In the long term, Proto-Luke works better. It accounts for almost all Q texts, either directly, indirectly (through its influence on Matthew and canonical Luke), or in conjunction with Matthew's *Logia*. And it accounts for far more gospel data, beginning with Mark's gospel. In other words, it solves more problems than Q and does so more comprehensively.

---

2. On Q research, see Robinson, Hoffmann and Kloppenborg 2000.

Appendix 2

1 Corinthians as One Component of Luke–Acts

As well as exploring Proto-Luke's use of the LXX, it is appropriate to indicate a further distinct source—the epistles. For reasons of space, this study limits itself to examining Proto-Luke's use of just one major epistle, 1 Corinthians.

The initial case for Proto-Luke's use of 1 Corinthians has already been made (Chapter 14). Luke's supper text (Lk. 22.14-30) was seen to involve a transformation of 1 Cor. 11.16-34. The purpose of this chapter is to indicate that Proto-Luke has similarly transformed the rest of 1 Corinthians. At times, the analysis is quite incomplete or tentative, but it is worth developing.

1. *The Texts: Introductory Analysis*

As the outline (Table 89 next page) indicates, Luke uses 1 Corinthians 1–10 with *order* and *completeness*: its parts are adapted, essentially in order, virtually all the way across Acts 1.1–15.35. There are two gaps, two areas in Acts 1.1–15.35, for which 1 Corinthians 1–10 provides no major equivalent. In the outline, the two gaps—essentially Acts 9 and 12—are marked by within angle brackets '< >' (ch. 9 is subdivided). 1 Corinthians 11–16 also is used *largely in order*, but *not continuously*:
- 1 Corinthians 11 and 15.1-7 underlie Lk. 22.1-30 and parts of Luke 24.
- 1 Corinthians 12–14 and 15.20-49 supplement Acts 2–5.
- 1 Corinthians 15.8-19, 50-58 and ch. 16 fill the two gaps, essentially in Acts 9 and 12.

The use of 1 Corinthians 12–14 and 15.20-49 to supplement Acts 2–5 means that Acts 2–5 conflates texts from the two ends of the epistle, from 1 Corinthians 1–5 and 12–15. This conflation strengthens another feature: the use of 1 Corinthians is generally heavier in Acts 1–5 than elsewhere.

Luke makes major changes in the material. The sense of an impending end gives way to a sense of ongoing history. Questions of sex and gender (especially in 1 Cor. 5–7) are distilled or adapted to illustrate what they imply about other issues. The account of the couple in 1 Corinthians 5, for instance—a case of incest—is adapted to provide one thread in the account of another couple, Ananias and Sapphira (Acts 5.1-11), a case concerned not with sex but with possessions. Luke seems to regard Paul's emphasis on sex/gender issues as secondary to the larger implications of the text. (Even Homer at his most colorful seems more interested in other issues. Havelock [1963: 61], argues that 'Homer is didactic, and that the tale is made subservient to the task of accommodating the weight of educational materials which lie within it'.)

For practical purposes, the subsequent analysis consists of three block:

Block 1: 1 Corinthians 1–5 and Acts 1.1–5.1-11: A Moderately Detailed Analysis
Block 2: 1 Corinthians 6–10 and Acts 5.12–15.35: A Summary Analysis
Block 3: 1 Corinthians 11–16 and Luke 22–24; Acts 2–5; Acts 9 and 12: A Summary Analysis

Table 89. *1 Corinthians as One Component of Luke 22.1–Acts 15.35*

1 Corinthians	Luke 22–Acts 15.35
	Eating, Eucharist, treachery, unlike kings, solidarity (staying) (Lk. 22.1-30) Suffering, rising as in scriptures (24.25-27, 44-48)
Division, two wisdoms, God's choice (ch. 1)	Unity, two apostles, God's choice (Acts 1)
Preaching, crucifixion, spirit (ch. 2)	Pentecost, Jesus, Spirit. *One spirit* (ch. 2)
People are a building…temple. No boasting—but all is yours (ch. 3)	The temple cure […you builders] (ch. 3) *No boasting; Christ restores *all*.
Apostles: judged and scorned. Yet enduring and positive (ch. 4)	Peter and John: judged ignorant. *Builders*. Yet confident and calm. *One heart* (ch. 4)
The man and the woman (a sexual sin) (ch. 5)	Ananias and Sapphira (a possessions-related sin) (ch. 5)
Disputes and courts (6.1-10)	Disputes; Stephen in court (chs. 6–7)
But you have been washed, sanctified in…the name of Jesus Christ…in the Spirit (6.11)	Conversion of Samaria to Christ …in the name of Jesus…in the Spirit (8.1b-25)
The body is not for fornication but for union with God, in spirit (6.12-20)	The Ethiopian is a eunuch but his baptized body rejoices (in God) (8.26-40)
	<Paul's conversion. Paul preaches Christ (9.1-30)>
	<Peter heals Aeneas; *raises dead* Dorcas (9.32-43)>
Man–woman relations, reflecting the end time (ch. 7)	Peter eats forbidden food (chs. 10–11)
	<Jerusalem collection; Peter's open door; house community; travel (chs. 11–12)>
Eating forbidden food (offered to idols) (ch. 8)	Mission: personal/ethnic relations: reflecting historical time (ch. 13)
Apostles (Paul/Barnabas): all things to all (ch. 9)	Paul/Barnabas: we are humans like yourselves (ch. 14)
Historical lessons and careful judgments (ch. 10)	Jerusalem council: history and new judgments (15.1-35)
Chapters 11–16	
Eating, Eucharist, guilty eater, unlike World, solidarity (waiting) (ch. 11)	
** *One spirit, one body, build up* (chs. 12–14) Christ died, rose, according to scriptures (15.1-7)	
<Appearance to Paul. Preaching Christ's resurrection (15.8-19)> * Resurrection—till God be *all in all* (15.20-49) <How the *dead rise* (15.50-58)> <Jerusalem collection; travel; open door; house community (ch. 16)>	
** Detail: One Spirit, many gifts…tongues…prophecy (12.1-11) One body…no need… love (12.12-31; ch. 13) (Distributing goods need not mean love) Prophetic speech…build up…order (ch. 14)	Spirit…many…tongues…prophecy (Acts 2.1-42) One heart…no need…care (2.43-47; 4.32–5.16) (Ananias/Sapphira share goods [5.1-11]) Prophetic Peter…builders…unity (4.1-31)

Appendix 2. *1 Corinthians as One Component of Luke–Acts* 547

2. Block 1. *1 Corinthians 1–5 and Acts 1.1–5.11: A Moderately Detailed Analysis*

As the general outline (Table 89) suggests, these texts involve a succession of chapters which, however inadequately, may be placed under five headings:
1. Unity; two ways and God's choice
2. Preaching Christ and the Spirit
3. The community and the building
4. Apostles under judgment
5. The sinful couple

Such simplification does not do justice to the texts, yet it helps to clarify the stage before proceeding to a more detailed examination.

It is also useful, before examining details, to give an initial sense of how Luke, in reworking 1 Corinthians 1–5, uses theological redesigning, and literary adaptation.

First, the theological redesigning. It may seem that the Jerusalem and Corinthian churches are poles apart: one riven by quarrels, the other a model of unity. But despite talk of divisions, 1 Corinthians is governed by 'the rhetoric of reconciliation' (Mitchell 1993), in other words, by a desire for unity. Unity was one of Luke's interests (Beker 1993: 514-15), and so he took the Pauline desire for unity and used it as one element in describing a unity that was exemplary. Furthermore, in constructing Acts 1–5, Luke used not only the tense scene in 1 Corinthians 1–5, he also used a much more harmonious part of 1 Corinthians, namely chs. 12–14 (see the discussion of Block 3 below). In thus conflating 1 Corinthians 1–5 with 12–14, Luke allowed the harmony or unity of 12–14 to prevail. At the same time, since he was interested in showing continuity with Israel (Beker 1993: 516-17), he located that unity in Jerusalem.

Further theological redesigning is seen with regard to the image of the building. When, in 1 Corinthians 3, Paul first speaks of the community as 'a building...temple' (*naos*, 3.9-17), Luke likewise begins to associate the Jerusalem community with a temple (builders, Acts 3.1-10; cf. 4.11; *topos*, 'place/temple', 4.31 and 6.14). But the temple in Acts is one which suits Luke's interests—the Jerusalem *hieron*. In other words, Luke incorporates the idea of the building/temple (including some of its details), but he adapts it to his own larger portrayal of the demise and replacement of the temple in Jerusalem.

Likewise, when the epistle suddenly switches to the sin of a man and a woman (the man with his father's wife, 1 Cor. 5), Luke follows suit; he switches to an account of a sinful couple (Ananias and Sapphira, Acts 5.1-11). But while he incorporates many elements of 1 Corinthians 5, he adapts the central offence from sex to possessions, in other words, to one of his own interests. Otherwise, he is just as severe with Ananias and Sapphira as Paul was in dealing with the incest.

With regard to broad literary strategies, Luke did not allow the epistle to dictate the shape of his own writing. Rather he adapted the epistle; he distilled its essence and used that essence as one component to enrich his picture of the early church.

Apart from distillation, Luke also made other changes, notably positivization and dramatization. Positivization is the turning of what seems negative in 1 Corinthians, especially its account of division, into something positive—the Jerusalem picture of unity. This is not a betrayal of 1 Corinthians. Rather, he articulates what the epistle implied: unity is crucial. Luke takes that idea and fills it out.

Dramatization is a further aspect of filling out—of putting historical detail and color into the epistle. In some ways, it is a process that is necessary. As scholars know too well, there is a huge vacuum in 1 Corinthians, a world of background which is largely missing, a community which Paul evokes but never clearly describes. Luke fills that gap. By using other sources, he provides his distillation of 1 Corinthians with a clear background (Jerusalem and its events), and his presentation of the community is orderly and relatively full. It is a procedure that corresponds broadly to what he suggests in Lk. 1.3—the idea of examining everything and giving an orderly account.

The following analysis does not attempt to be complete. Rather, its purpose rather is to highlight sufficient elements that the question of Luke's use of the epistle becomes worthy of attention. The analysis follows the general outline for Block 1 (see Table 90).

Table 90. *Block 1. 1 Corinthians 1–5 and Acts 1.1–5.11: General Outline*

	Gifted from Above; Waiting for the Revelation of Christ *(1 Corinthians 1.1-9; Acts 1.1-11)*	
1.	Prescript: Paul, called…an apostle of Jesus to the church of God… called to be holy: Grace…from God the Father (1.1-3, 13b-17)	Prologue: To Theophilus ('Friend of God'): Jesus chose the apostles… in the Holy Spirit… Await the promise from the Father (1.1-5) Baptisms: *a clear contrast* (1.5)
2.	You are enriched in everything… awaiting the revelation of Jesus… to the end…in the day of the Lord (1.4-9)	Not for you to know times, seasons; you will receive power. Ascension… This Jesus will come (1.6-11)
	Unity; the Two Wisdoms/Apostles and God's Call of the Unimpressive *(1 Corinthians 1.10-31; Acts 1.12-26)*	
3.	Avoid divisions among brothers. Be of one mind. Quarrelling (four names) (1.10-13a) Baptism: *implied contrast* (1.13-17)	Patient waiting (eleven names) All of one mind. Peter in the midst of the brothers (1.12-15)
4.	The two wisdoms, false and true: false wisdom is destroyed. True wisdom proclaims Christ (1.18-25)	Two apostles (false and true): the false, Judas, has collapsed. The true will witness to Jesus (1.16-22)
5.	God chose the unimpressive (1.26-31)	God chooses Matthias, not the impressive Joseph (1.23-26)
	The Powerful Preaching of Christ and the Spirit *(1 Corinthians 2; Acts 2.1-36)*	
6.	The power of Paul's preaching (2.1-5)	Pentecost and Peter's preaching (2.1-21)
7.	Announcing the preordained mystery of the crucifixion of the Lord —and God's unspeakable promise (2.6-9)	Hear about Jesus, preordained to crucifixion and resurrection —and the promise of not seeing corruption (2.22-28)
8.	God revealed the Spirit. The Spirit knows the Lord/Christ (2.10-16)	Prophetic David foretold resurrection, whence the Spirit. Jesus is known as Lord/Christ (2.29-36)
	Flesh Leads to Quarrels, Spirit Leads to Unity *(1 Corinthians 3.1-9; Acts 2.37-39)*	
9.	You are of flesh, not spiritual. The flesh leads to quarrelling. The community: a garden where people are one; God gives increase (3.1-9)	Repent…receive the Spirit. Baptism (Spirit) leads to sharing. The believers were together sharing; the Lord added to them (2.37-47)

	The Building/Temple—with Jesus as Foundation/Head *(1 Corinthians 3.10-23; Acts 3)*	
10.	The community as a building with Jesus as foundation; No foundation other than that laid; on top—gold, silver, stones. The work will become manifest. Your are God's temple (3.10-17)	In the temple Peter has no silver or gold, but Jesus becomes a man's 'foundation'. Peter: 'stone…builders…head… …no name other than that given'. The 'rebuilding' of the man becomes manifest (3.1-10; 4.10-12, 16)
11.	No claiming of false wisdom… no boasting. Yet all is yours: the world, life, death, all is yours/Christ's/God's (3.18-23)	In Solomon's portico: Peter disavows any special power or holiness. Speech: the prophets told of the restoration of all in Christ; you are the prophets' children (3.11-26)
	Apostles Under Judgment (1 Corinthians 4; Acts 4)	
12.	Apostles are to be faithful witnesses of Christ; human judgment does not count (4.1-5)	Peter and John preach Christ and induce faith; they are brought to human judgment (the sanhedrin, 4.1-10)
13.	The plight of the apostles (before pretentious Corinthians): 'fools…weak…without honor'; physically buffeted…unsettled. Yet blessing, enduring, positive (4.6-13)	The plight of Peter and John (before the sanhedrin): 'unlearned and ignorant'; threatened with punishment. Yet confident, calm, clear (4.13-22)
14.	Paul's sudden gentleness (4.14-21)	?? The community at home (4.23-37)
	The Man and the Woman: Remove the Evil from Among You *(1 Corinthians 5; Acts 5.1-11)*	
15.	The sexual sin of the man and the woman. Paul, absent in body but present in spirit, condemns. Satan's role (destroys flesh). Destroy the sinner's flesh. Let him be removed from you. Remove this evil from among you (ch. 5)	The possessions-related sin of Ananias and Sapphira. Peter, absent from the sin, condemns as if he had been present. Satan's role (poisons heart). Ananias and Sapphira die. They carry out Ananias. They carry out Sapphira (5.1-11)

a. *Section 1. Prescript/Prologue (1 Corinthians 1.1-3, 13b-17; Acts 1.1-5)*
Paul greets the Corinthians by speaking of his own call to be an apostle and their call to be holy (1 Cor. 1.1-3). Luke also begins by speaking of a call to apostleship and, implicitly, to holiness: 'Jesus chose the apostles in the Holy Spirit' (Acts 1.2). Luke has the two ideas (apostleship and contact with the holy) but in a form which combines them and which highlights one of his central themes—the Holy Spirit. Further comparison brings out more points of contact:

> 1 Corinthians 1.1-3, 13-17, 27-28:
> Paul, called to be an apostle (*apostolos*),
> to the church of God (*ekklēsia tou theou*)…
> to those made holy (*hagiazō*) in…Jesus, called to be holy (*hagioi*),
> from God the Father (*theou patros*).
> (1.13-17: Were you baptized? I baptized… You were baptized…
> [*ebaptisthēte…ebaptisa…ebaptisa…ebaptisa…ebaptisthēte*].)
> (1.27-28: God chose…chose…chose [*exelexato…exelexato…exelexato*].)

Acts 1.1-5:
To Theophilus (*theo-philos*, 'friend of God'),
about all Jesus did...commanding the apostles (*apostoloi*)
whom he chose (*exelexato*) through the Holy Spirit (*pneuma hagion*)...
saying...the kingdom of God (*theou*)...the promise of the Father (*patros*);
'John baptized... You will be baptized (*ebaptisen...baptisthēsesthe*)
in the Holy Spirit (*pneuma hagion*)...'

1 Corinthians is just one component—a transformed component—in Luke's more elaborate and vivid account. The first touch of vividness is the address not to a whole church of God (1 Cor. 1.2) but, building on Lk. 1.1-4, to an individual friend of God, Theophilus.

The rest of Luke's transformation shows a further tendency towards clarity and individuality. Where Paul had interwoven holiness with Jesus, and God with the Father ('made holy in Jesus'; 'from God the Father'), Luke adds distinctiveness and color. In place of two references to holiness ('make holy'; 'holy'), he speaks twice of the Holy Spirit. Instead of 'Christ Jesus', he shows Jesus doing specific things. In place of 'God', he speaks of the more earth-related 'kingdom of God'. And in place of the general wish of 'grace and peace from...the Father', there is a specific 'promise of the Father' to be given in Jerusalem before many days. Luke has added individuality and action. He has dramatized Paul, and vividly.

Concerning the repeated mention of baptism ('I baptized... You were baptized', 1 Cor. 1.13-17: 'John baptized... You will be baptized', Acts 1.5), it seems probable, given the context, that the references are connected. Apart from the linguistic affinity, both texts imply a contrast between a past ritual (Paul's previous baptizing; John's baptism) and a later process which is more spiritual (Paul's present evangelizing; baptism in the Spirit). But again, Luke's contrast is clearer and more colorful.

1 Corinthians 1 ends climactically with the idea of the divine choice:

> God chose...chose...chose (*exelexato...exelexato...exelexato*) (1.27-28)

Acts 1 uses this not as a climax, but as a framework:

> Jesus...chose (*exelexato*) through the Holy Spirit (1.1-2)
> Kyrie...show whom you have chosen (*exelexō*) (1.24)

b. *Section 2. You Have Received/Will Receive Power from Above, While Awaiting the Revelation of Jesus (1 Corinthians 1.4-9; Acts 1.6-11)*

The Corinthians, says Paul, are both gifted and receptive: God gave them much, and, as well, they receptively await the revelation of Jesus.

Luke has the same two ideas (giftedness, and receptivity towards the revelation of Jesus) but in a more vivid context. The giftedness is from the Spirit (yet to come). And waiting for the revelation of Jesus is linked with the account (drawn from other sources) of the ascension:

	Kyrie, in this time will you restore
	(*Kyrie, ei en tō chronō toutō*...).
	Not for you to know times, seasons,
The grace of God...is given to you;	But you will receive power when
you are enriched in everything...	the Holy Spirit comes on you,
—as the witness (*martyrion*) of	and you will be my witnesses
Christ was confirmed in you—	(*martyres*)...[Jesus ascends].

Appendix 2. *1 Corinthians as One Component of Luke–Acts*   551

…awaiting the revelation of our Lord Jesus Christ,	Why gaze into heaven? This Jesus will come as you saw him going.
who will confirm you to the end (*telos*), blameless in the day of the Lord (*en tē hēmera tou Kyriou*).	

Luke adapts the reference to eschatological time ('the end…the day of the Lord'): he sets it at the beginning of his passage, in the vivid context of a specific discussion about restoring the kingdom to Israel. Furthermore, he adds a corrective about trying to know the precise time.

Then he follows the flow of 1 Corinthians. The richness from God becomes the Spirit's power from above. The witness of Christ becomes the apostles' witnessing to Jesus. And, after the ascension, the awaiting of the revelation of Jesus becomes the memorable picture of the apostles who, instead of gazing after Jesus, accepted that he will return.

c. *Section 3. Unity: Desired (1 Corinthians 1.10-13a), Achieved (Acts 1.12-15)*
Paul now switches to the question of divisions and to the need for unity. Luke portrays unity as already achieved, and so at times his picture is the opposite of Paul's. There are three main elements:

1. Avoid divisions among brothers	3. Patient waiting (eleven names)
2. Be of one mind	2. All of one mind
3. Quarrelling (four names)	1. Peter in the midst of the brothers

Once allowance is made for the rearrangement, the interchange of the first and last elements, the texts follow one another closely:

1. I beseech you, brothers (*adelphoi*) by the name (*onoma*) of our Lord that all (*pantes*) speak the same (*to auto*) [with] no divisions in you (*en hymin*)	1. Peter…said in the midst (*en mesō*) of the brothers (*adelphoi*)—the crowd of names (*onomata*) in the place (*epi to auto*) was about 120
2. Be joined together (*ēte katērtismenoi*) in the same mind (*en tō autō noï*) and the same purpose (*en tē autē gnōmē*). For I was told brothers (*adelphoi*)…	2. All (*pantes*) were persevering (*ēsan proskarterountes*) with one mind (*omothumadon*) in prayer (*tē proseuchē*)… the women…brothers (*adelphoi*)
3. that there are quarrels (*erides*) among you…[four names]	3. In the upper room they were waiting (*ēsan katamenontes*) [eleven names]

The final reference (quarrels), again moved to the top, is turned around, thus showing its positive side (patient waiting). The names likewise are inverted, not four which arouse division (Paul, Apollos, Cephas, Christ), but eleven, suggesting harmony (the eleven).[1]

Luke then follows the rest of Paul's text closely, sometimes playing with the wording, and consistently adding vividness and detail. The idea, for instance, of all speaking the same (*to auto*, 1 Cor. 1.10) becomes part of the more vivid picture of all praying in the same place (*epi to auto*). And Luke elaborates: about 120 people were present.

d. *Section 4. The Contrasting Wisdoms (1 Corinthians 1.18-25) and the Contrasting Apostles (Acts 1.16-22)*
Paul now speaks of contrasting wisdoms—the collapse of the false wisdom and the proclamation of the true (Christ; God's wisdom). In Acts, Peter also implies a contrast, a

---

1. Paul's larger text (1.11-17) contains seven names, but the basic correspondence seems to be between the four and the eleven.

contrast not of wisdoms but of apostles, between the false apostle Judas who acted as guide (*hodēgos*) to those who arrested Jesus (Acts 1.16-20), and the need to find a true apostle, someone who will be a genuine witness to Jesus (1.21-22).

Both begin with the negative—the false wisdom and the false apostle. Here the process of adding elaboration and dramatic vividness reaches new intensity. Paul speaks of wisdom coming to nothing; Luke tells of how Judas the guide collapsed in a bloody outburst. Paul's general idea of a bankrupt wisdom which collapses finds graphic illustration in the account of the collapse of the impressive Judas, former apostle and guide to those who arrested Jesus (Acts 1.16-17). The fall of the wise has been illustrated by an account of the fall of someone who was knowledgeable.

Paul's text is no more than a starting point for Luke's distinctive account of Judas's fate, yet the epistle makes an important contribution. As well as providing the pivotal idea of a knowledge which is bankrupt or destructive, 1 Corinthians also furnishes a partial model for Luke's citation from scripture:

	It was necessary to fulfill the scripture which the Holy Spirit foretold through the mouth of David...
For it is written (*gegraptai gar*):	For it is written (*gegraptai gar*) in the book of Psalms:
'I will destroy the wisdom of the wise,	'Let his house become a wilderness, and let no one live in it' (Ps. 69.25),
and the cleverness of the clever I will set aside' (Isa. 29.14)	and, 'Let another take his office' (Ps. 109.8)

In place of parallel poetry from Isaiah, Luke gives a more complex use of parallel poetry from David/the psalms, an adaptation which prepares the way for the heavy use of David and the psalms in Acts 2 (2.25-35). And in place of the abstract ideas concerning wisdom and cleverness, Luke finds quotations which are more vivid. Instead of wisdom being destroyed (Isaiah), a house becomes a ruin, empty (Ps. 69); and instead of something (cleverness) being set aside (Isaiah), there is a picture of someone stepping in and taking over (Ps. 109) is offered. Again the images are vivid: the ruined house and the outsider's takeover.

These are the first explicit scriptural quotations in 1 Corinthians and Acts. And, 1 Corinthians and Acts are the only New Testament books which introduce their first scriptural quotation with *gegraptai gar*.

Having spoken of what is negative (the bankrupt wisdom; the doomed guide), both passages then go on to speak of what is positive—God's providence in 'our' preaching of Christ (1 Cor. 1.21-24; Acts 1.21-23). In slightly simplified form the texts are as follows:

It pleased (*eudokeō*) God	It is [providentially] necessary (*dei*)
to save through *our preaching* of Christ,	that someone become a witness [= *preacher*] with us,
Christ as crucified and	someone who was with Jesus from
Christ as God's power and wisdom.	the beginning until his ascension.

Luke keeps the opening ideas: providence; our preaching/witnessing. But in the proclaiming of Christ he has made a considerable change: Christ is no longer described in general terms as crucified and as power/wisdom; instead he is Jesus, a specific human whose life can be outlined (beginning from John's baptism until his assumption). Crucifixion and power are still implied, but within the context of a more complete life of Jesus. The result, once again, is more elaborate and more vivid.

e. *Section 5. God Chooses the Less Impressive (1 Corinthians 1.26-31; Acts 1.23-26)*
Both texts now continue by telling how God chose unimpressive candidates: the ordinary Corinthians (1 Cor. 1.26-31) and the simply named Matthias (who was chosen by lot, Acts 1.23-26).

Paul's description is ringing and repetitive, a multi-faceted contrast: 'Consider your call (*klēsis*)... Not many of you were worldly wise...[or] powerful...[or] well-born, but God chose (*exelexato*) the foolish...the weak...the lowly...so that all humans (*pasa sarx*) might not boast before God'.

Instead of a contrast with many facets (wise/powerful/well-born—foolish/weak/lowly), Luke gives a simple contrast between two candidates for apostleship: Joseph, called (*kaleō*) Barsabbas, with the added name (*epi-kaleō*) Justus, and Matthias.

Joseph's outward appearance (by name) was imposing; and by human standards it suggested being called. But it was the simply named Matthias whom God chose (*exelexō*, Acts 1.24, 26). Thus Paul's principle, that God's call does not follow worldly standards, is illustrated in Matthias.

Furthermore, while Paul had said that all humans (literally, 'all flesh', *pasa sarx*) should not boast before God, the prayer in Acts (1.24) gives a complementary truth: the Lord knows all human hearts (*kardio-gnōstēs pantōn*). In other words, both Paul and Luke put humans in proper relationship to God. But Luke has probed more deeply, more internally; he has gone to the root of not boasting: all humans should not boast before God because God knows the very heart of all humans.

f. *Section 6. In Spirit and Power: Preaching God's Word (1 Corinthians 2.1-5; Acts 2.1-21)*
Paul now turns the focus from the Corinthians to himself and his preaching. In one way, he seemed weak, and in preaching God he preached the cross. Yet there was nothing weak about his message; his word was 'in the showing of Spirit and power' (1 Cor. 2.4). In fact, this whole passage (2.1-5) has been entitled 'The Power of Paul's Preaching' (Murphy-O'Connor 1979: 17).

The next passage in Acts (2.1-21) might be entitled 'The Power of Peter's Preaching'. When the Spirit descends in fire, some see only drunkenness (a form of weakness?), but when Peter preaches, quoting the great vision of Joel, he does so like Paul—in Spirit and power.

Obviously the account of Peter's preaching is much more elaborate than the account of Paul's. For Luke, 1 Cor. 2.1-5 is little more than a starting-point; yet it helps to set the power-filled tone of Acts 2.

g. *Section 7. Announcing the Preordained Mystery of Crucifixion and Glory (1 Corinthians 2.6-9; Acts 2.22-28)*
Paul now turns from the power of his preaching to its content, the wisdom of God's preordained mystery, something unknown to those who crucified the Lord.

Luke takes this and follows it closely, but instead of separating the preordained mystery (or plan) from the crucifixion, he combines them. The preordained plan contains the crucifixion.

Both passages conclude by quoting scripture, but, as earlier (1 Cor. 1.19; Acts 1.16, 20), Luke switches from Isaiah to David's psalms and uses a more elaborate text. As often, Luke's picture is more vivid and detailed. Instead of speaking in a general way of crucifying the Lord of glory (1 Cor. 2.8), Luke tells of crucifying (literally, 'fastening' or 'nailing') Jesus of Nazareth (Acts 2.23). And instead of a cryptic scripture about something that has not entered human senses (eye, ear, heart), Luke's scripture is much clearer: the senses or body (heart, tongue, flesh) are positively involved and the promise is spelled out:

1 Corinthians:	Acts:
We speak a wisdom... (2.6)	Hear these words:
But we speak God's (*theou*) wisdom, in mystery hidden (*apo-kekrummenēn*) which God preordained before (*pro-ōrisen ho theos pro*) the ages (2.7), ...which the rulers did not know; if they had known (*egnōken...egnōsan*)	Jesus of Nazareth, a man designated by God (*apo-dedeigmenon...theou*) (2.22), he, given up by the ordained plan (*ōrismenē boulē*) and foreknowledge of God (*pro-gnōsei tou theou*)
they would not have crucified (*stauroō*) the Lord of glory (2.8).	you crucified (*prospēgnumi*)... (2.23), whom God raised...[from] death.
But as it is written (*kathōs gegraptai*),	Because (*kathoti*) he could not be held, for David says of him,
Eye (*ophthalmos*) has not seen, nor ear (*ous*) heard, nor was glad, has it entered the heart (*kardia*)... what God has prepared for those who love him (1 Cor. 2.9; cf. Isa. 64.4; 65.17)	I saw the Lord...so my heart (*kardia*) my tongue (*glōssa*) rejoiced, my flesh (*sarx*) will dwell in hope. For you will not abandon my soul in Hades, or let your holy one see corruption. You have made known to me the ways of life... You will make me full of joy with your face (Acts 2.24-28; Ps. 16.8-11)

In line with the tendency to be more clear and vivid, Luke also stresses what is positive and open. Where Paul had spoken of something hidden (*apo-kekrummenēn*, 1 Cor. 2.7), Luke refers to Jesus as manifested, designated (*apo-dedeigmenon*, Acts 2.22). And where Paul referred to the rulers who 'did not know' (1 Cor. 2.8), Luke looks at another side of the same reality, at the God who did know (God's foreknowledge, Acts 2.23).

h. *Section 8. Knowing God's Mystery from the Inside, through the (Prophetic) Spirit (1 Corinthians 2.10-16; Acts 2.29-36)*
Before analyzing these passages (1 Cor. 2.10-16; Acts 2.29-36), it is useful to set their three main elements in outline:

God revealed by the Spirit.	David foretold: God implied resurrection.
We received the Spirit.	The risen Christ received the Spirit for us.
The Spirit knows Lord/Christ.	Jesus is known as Lord/Christ.

The first main element is that of revealing or foretelling. Having spoken of God's preordained Christ-centered plan, it is necessary to explain how one knows about it. The answer, for both Paul and Luke, is revelation— revelation through the Spirit (Paul), and revelation through David (Luke). The relationship between the details of the texts is unusually complex:

To us (*hēmin*) God (*ho theos*) revealed through the Spirit— the Spirit knows (*oida*).	David's tomb is among us (*en hēmin*)... So he, being a prophet, and knowing (*oida*) that God (*ho theos*) swore..., foretold [= revealed] Christ's resurrection.

As Paul says, God revealed to us through the Spirit, and the Spirit knows (1 Cor. 2.10-11). But Luke has filtered that simple idea (of a special knowing) through the history of David

Appendix 2. *1 Corinthians as One Component of Luke–Acts* 555

(his prophesying and his tomb, Acts 2.30-31). He has also added a reference to the resurrection. Again Luke's text is more specific, more colorful, more elaborate.

Both writers then refer explicitly to the next main element, the Spirit. Paul says 'we have received the Spirit from God' (*hēmeis...to pneuma...elabomen...ek tou theou*, 2.12). Luke refers to the same phenomenon, but he inserts the role of Christ as mediator and refers to God as Father: 'We are witnesses...[Christ] having received the...Spirit from the Father, poured it out' (*hēmeis...tou pneumatos...labōn para tou patros*, 2.32-33,).

Finally, the third element: Paul makes a contrast between the natural person and the spiritual person (1 Cor. 2.14-16), and Luke makes a more tangible contrast between David and Jesus (Acts 2.34-36). The essence of the contrast is between those who attain the things of God in a special way and those who do not. The natural person does not receive the [gifts] of the Spirit of God (1 Cor. 2.14), and David did not ascend to heaven (Acts 2.34). In other words, in different ways both these natural persons do not attain the gift of heaven.

The spiritual person, however, and Jesus are both associated with a special knowledge. In the context of the spiritual person, Paul refers obscurely to knowing the mind of the Lord and having the mind of Christ (*egnō...kyriou...Christou*, 1 Cor. 2.15-16); and Luke gives the idea of knowing that Jesus is Lord and Christ (*ginōsketō...kai kyrion...kai Christon*, 2.36). Thus both Paul and Luke use the terms 'Lord' and 'Christ' in tandem and in the context of knowing. But, as ever, Luke is clearer.

Overall (1 Cor. 2.10-16; Acts 2.29-36), each writer tells of the revelation of the Christian mystery. However, while Paul gives the theological kernel, the Spirit's revelation of the mysterious divine depths, Luke unpacks the mystery, as it were; he shows how the revelation occurs in the concrete dimensions of time and space, in the circumstances of David and Jesus and Jerusalem.

i. *Section 9. Turn to the Spirit and Become One (1 Corinthians 3.1-9; Acts 2.37-47)*
Both writers now change focus from the central mystery to the disposition of the hearers. The Corinthians' disposition leaves much to be desired: essentially they are people not of spirit (*pneumatikoi*) but of flesh (*sarkinoi*).

The disposition of Peter's hearers is more complex (and reflects further sources), but it contains the same underlying problem: they need to change their way of thinking and become more spiritual: 'Repent (*metanoeō*)... and you will receive the gift of the Holy Spirit' (*hagiou pneumatos*, 2.38). The need to be spiritual (Paul) has become the need to receive the Holy Spirit (Acts).

The issue is not purely internal. What is at stake is unity. The lack of spirit leads the Corinthians to divisive quarrelling. In Jerusalem, however, acceptance of the Spirit leads to radical sharing. In outline:

1 Corinthians	*Acts*
You are not sufficiently spiritual; you are *sarkinoi* ('of flesh', 3.1-2)	Repent… receive the Spirit (2.37-40)
The flesh leads the Corinthians to quarrelling (3.3-4)	Baptism (Spirit) leads those who respond to sharing (2.41-42)
The community is like a garden where people are one, where God gives increase (3.5-9)	The believers were together sharing and the Lord added to them (2.43-47)

Some details need more careful scrutiny. It is not clear, for instance, whether the idea of leaving the flesh is echoed in Peter's final appeal: 'Save yourselves from this perverse generation (*genea*)' (2.40).

What is essential in the opening verses (1 Cor. 3.1-2; Acts 2.37-40) is that both texts indicate the need for the hearers to leave their present disposition and to become more spiritual. For Luke, however, the prospect of becoming more spiritual is nearer; the hearers are ready to receive the Holy Spirit. Luke manages, as usual, to be more positive.

Paul and Luke go on (1 Cor. 3.3-4; Acts 2.41-42) to show two sides of the same coin: lack of spirit (*pneuma*) leads to division (Paul); receiving baptism (and the Spirit) leads to unity (Acts).

Then Paul becomes more positive. He likens the community to a garden (or cultivated field, 1 Cor. 3.5-9) where there is a spirit of service; one waters and another plants, and both together form a unity (*hen eisin*, 'they are one', 3.8). Each does as God gives, and receives as God rewards.

Luke turns this horticultural unity into real life: having spoken of signs and wonders (indicators of God), he recounts how 'all the believers were together (*epi to auto*) and had everything in common (*koina*)...and they distributed according as anyone had need' (Acts 2.43-45).

For both, the increase comes from God (1 Cor. 3.6-7; Acts 2.41, 47):

> *1 Corinthians*:
> 'But God increased...but God who increases...' (*ēuxanen...auxanōn*).
>
> *Acts*:
> 'And there were added... And the Lord added' (*prosetethēsan...prosetithei*).

Thus, while Paul protests that spirit and unity are absent (3.1-9), Luke describes a community where the Spirit and unity are powerfully present (Acts 2.37-47).

j. *Section 10. Jesus Christ as the Only Foundation of the Living Temple (1 Corinthians 3.10-17; Acts 3.1-10; 4.11-12, 16)*

Paul now introduces new imagery: he compares the community to a building (*oikodomē, ep-oikodomeō*, 'build upon'; *naos*, 'temple). Within this building, Jesus Christ is the foundation (*themelion*), the one and only foundation that is laid.

Acts also switches to new images—first, the setting of the temple (*hieron*) where Peter heals a lame man in the name of Jesus Christ (Acts 3.1-10); and later (4.11-12) Peter's image of builders (*oikodomeō*). Within Peter's implied building, Jesus Christ is not the foundation but the head of the corner (*kephalē gōnias*), the one and only name that is given. For more detail, see Table 91.

Without attempting a full analysis, especially of the more debatable details, some central points stand out.

This is the first time that either 1 Corinthians or Acts focuses on a whole building. In both cases, the focusing is preceded, almost immediately, by a passing reference (to a building, 1 Cor. 3.9; to the temple, Acts 2.46). But then, suddenly, the references to a temple are multiple (1 Cor. 3.10-17; Acts 3.1, 2, 3, 8, 10).

The key idea behind the references to the temple is that the old stone building is giving way to a new temple formed of people. This is implied in Paul, at least insofar as he says that people form a temple (1 Cor. 3.16-17). And in Acts, where it emerges that the old temple is doomed (the old 'place', *topos*; see especially Stephen, 6.13-14; 7.48-49) the focus of prayer shifts to the new community, to their 'place' (*topos*, 4.31).

The idea of a shift from a physical building to people is seen particularly in Jesus. Within the diverse buldings envisaged by Paul and Peter, Jesus holds a key position: he is the foundation (1 Cor. 3.11); he is the head of the corner (Acts 4.11). In other words, instead of describing Jesus as the foundation (at the base), Luke gives a complementary image of leadership (at the top).

Appendix 2. *1 Corinthians as One Component of Luke–Acts*   557

Table 91. *Christ and the Temple Building*
(1 Corinthians 3.10-17; Acts 3.1-8; 4.11-12, 16)

1 Corinthians 3.10-17
You are God's building. According to God's grace given (*dotheisan*) to me... I laid the foundation (*themelion*)... Let each watch (*blepetō*) how he builds. For no other foundation can anyone (*allon oudeis*) lay except that laid (*ton keimenon*), which is (*hos estin*) Jesus Christ (*Iēsous Christos*). Whoever builds on the foundation with gold, silver, stones (*chryson, argyrion, lithous...*), their work will be made manifest (*phaneron genēsetai*) (1 Cor. 3.10-13)   If the work built...on [the foundation] remains, [there will be] a reward. If anyone's work is burned...they will be saved (*sōthēsetai*), but through fire (3.14-15)   You are God's temple (*naos*)... If anyone destroys God's temple (*naos*)... For the temple (*naos*) of God is holy (3.16-17)
Acts 3.1-8; 4.11-12, 16
Now Peter and John went up to the temple (*hieron*)... And a lame man was...by the door of the temple (*hieron*). Seeing Peter...about to enter the temple (*hieron*), he asked for alms (3.1-3)   Peter said, 'Look (*blepson*) at us... Silver and gold (*argyrion kai chrysion*) I have not, but what I have I give (*didōmi*) you... In the name of Jesus Christ (*Iēsous Christos*) of Nazareth, walk.' And...he raised him, and his feet and ankles were made firm, and leaping up, he stood... (3.4-8)   Peter to the Sanhedrin: 'The stone (*lithos*) rejected by you builders (*oikodomōn*) has become the head (*kephalē*) of the corner. And in no other (*allō oudeni*) is there salvation, nor is there (*oude gar estin*) any other name given (*to dedomenon*)... whereby we must be saved' (*sōthēnai*) (4.11-12)   Sanhedrin: 'That a notable sign has happened...is manifest (*gegonen...phaneron*) (4.16)

Yet Paul's idea of Jesus as the human foundation of a human temple is not lost in Acts. The healing of the lame man, while largely drawn from other sources, is described in a special way. Through 'the name of Jesus Christ' the man's feet and ankles (*baseis kai sphydra*) were made firm (*stereoō*, 'to make firm/solid', 3.6-7), a healing description which is unique in the New Testament, and one which, since it means that 'Jesus Christ' puts the man on his feet, corresponds to the idea that Jesus Christ becomes a person's foundation.

Thus, within the context of the old temple, a new foundation emerges—Jesus Christ, who not only establishes the man on his feet, but who, through him, attracts 'all the people' (3.9). The building of the new temple is under way.

k. *Section 11. From Disavowing Wisdom to Having Everything (1 Corinthians 3.18-23; Acts 3.11-26, Peter's Speech in Solomon's Portico)*
Paul's next words (3.18-23) may seem paradoxical. In effect he says: 'No false wisdom or boasting' (3.18-21a), 'but everything is yours' (3.21b-23). It is almost like saying: 'You have nought, you have all'.

The all is vast: 'All (*panta*) is yours—Paul, Apollos, Cephas, the world, life, death, things present, things to come; all (*panta*) is yours, and you are Christ's, and Christ is God's'.

The two parts of Paul's paradox would appear to have provided one small component for Peter's speech (Acts 3.11-26). As the miracle-working Peter stands in Solomon's portico, his first step is negative, to disavow any special power or holiness (3.11-12). Here, as in Paul, there is no false wisdom or boasting.

But then, having thus reduced himself, he gives a speech which in various ways encompasses everything, everything from Abraham, Isaac and Jacob to the prophets' idea of 'the restoration of all (*panta*)' (Acts 3.13-21). 'And', concludes Peter, 'you are the children of the prophets… It was for you God raised up his servant and sent him to bless you…' (3.25-26). As Paul would say, all is yours.

l. *Section 12. If Apostles are Faithful Witnesses, Human Judgment Does Not Count (1 Corinthians 4.1-5; Acts 4.1-9)*
Paul now speaks of the role of apostolic leaders (1 Cor. 4.1-5). If they are faithful servants (*hypēretai*, 'servants', but with the technical meaning of 'official witnesses' [Murphy-O'Connor 1979: 29]) it does not matter how they are judged humanly. What counts, then, is faithful witness, not human judgment.

In Acts 4.1-9, that same idea is one component in a vivid drama. Peter and John (two of them, thus constituting witness) teach the people about Jesus' resurrection, and the people believe (4.1-4). But then the apostles are brought before an imposing court of rulers, elders, scribes, high priests (4.5-6), and they are subjected to critical judgment (4.7-9). Despite the weight of the assembled critics, the clear implication is that the apostles are not guilty. They have been faithful witnesses, and ultimately this human judging does not count.

The word used here for judging, *anakrinō*, occurs ten times in 1 Corinthians, including three times in the present passage (1 Cor. 4.3-4). The only other New Testament occurrences are in Luke–Acts, including the present passage (Acts 4.9, the first occurrence in Acts).

m. *Section 13. The Plight of the Apostles (Before Seeming Rulers): Mentally Foolish-Looking and Physically Vulnerable (1 Corinthians 4.6-13; Acts 4.13-22)*
In face of the Corinthians, who seem to think they possess the eschatological kingdom ('You have come to your kingdom', 4.8), Paul describes the plight of the apostles: 'God placed us apostles last… We are fools…weak…without honor' (*mōroi…astheneis…atimoi*, 4.9-10). And there is also physical danger: 'We are hungry…beaten…defamed' (4.11, 13). Yet the apostles do not whine or cower: 'We bless…we endure…we speak positively' (4.12-13).

Many of the central elements of Paul's description of the apostles occur in adapted form in Luke's picture of Peter and John as they face the Sanhedrin. While the Sanhedrin has the appearance of power, the apostles seem unimpressive; they look 'unlearned and ignorant' (*agrammatoi kai idiōtai*, 4.13). They are also physically vulnerable. The Sanhedrin threaten (*apeileō*, 4.17) them, and even though they decide for the moment not to punish (*kolazō*, 4.21) them, it is clear they are in danger. Yet the apostles are neither offensive or cringing. Instead they speak with confidence (*parrēsia*, 4.13) and calm integrity (4.19-20).

n. *Section 14. ?? A Sharp Change to a Gentler (Household?) Setting (1 Corinthians 4.14-21; Acts 4.23-37)*
At the end of 1 Corinthians 4 Paul changes tone. He becomes gentle, speaking like a father to children and telling of significant visits, sending the beloved Timothy, and his own visit. (Paul's own visit, however, which depends on God, keeps a suggestion of explosive power.)

It is not clear, at least not to the present writer, what, if any, is the connection between Paul's sudden gentleness and the next passage in Acts, the description of community solidarity, both at prayer and in action:

Appendix 2. *1 Corinthians as One Component of Luke–Acts* 559

Suddenly Paul speaks gently to the Corinthians, as a father to children (1 Cor. 4.14-21).	??	Back at home: community solidarity in prayer and action (Acts 4.23-37).

Rather than insist on connecting these passages, it seems better to accept that they are not connected, or at least to leave the question open.

o. *Section 15. The Sin of the Couple: Remove the Evildoer! Powerful Judgment by an Apostle who was Physically Absent from the Crime (1 Corinthians 5; Acts 5.1-11)*

Now the tone changes again, drastically, and this time the affinity between the scenes is striking. Paul is suddenly dealing with a man's incestuous relationship with a woman (1 Cor. 5), and Peter is suddenly dealing with a man and woman who are cheating (Ananias and Sapphira, Acts 5.1-11). The cheating, however, is not sexual, as in Corinth, but has to do with one of Luke's central interests—possessions.

Luke indebtedness to 1 Corinthians 5, apart from his use of the Old Testament, is confirmed by several connecting details.

First, the picture of a couple (a man and a woman/wife) is not as common as it may seem. This is the first time that either 1 Corinthians or Acts refers to a couple or uses the singular *gynē* ('woman/wife'). Furthermore, in both cases the couple are deeply offensive to the community.

Second, the initial condemnation (by Paul and Peter) is done, in diverse ways, from a distance. Paul, 'absent in body, but present in spirit' (*pneuma*), has already pronounced judgment, as if present (1 Cor. 5.3). And when Peter meets first Ananias and then Sapphira, it is clear, though he was absent from the actual crime, that he already knew the crime, that in some sense he was present in spirit (Acts 5.3, 8-9). In other words, Luke has adapted the ideas of ready condemnation and being present in spirit to suit the case of Ananias and Sapphira. In fact, it is precisely on the basis of offending the Spirit (*pneuma*) that Peter condemns (5.3, 9). Again Luke has moved from the idea of spirit to that of the Holy Spirit.

Third, the punishment is lethal: 'the destruction of the flesh' (1 Cor. 5.5); death (Acts 5.5, 10).

Fourth, Satan is involved both in destroying the flesh (1 Cor. 5.5) and in filling the heart with lying (Acts 5.3). Thus, Satan's role in Acts is brought into line with Satan's role in Luke (Lk. 22.3, the misleading of Judas).

Finally, the evil ones are removed away from the community. Twice Paul speaks of removing the evil one (1 Cor. 5.2, 13; cf. Deut 13.6) and twice Luke gives a dramatic account of the sinners being removed, first Ananias and then Sapphira (Acts 5.6, 9-10).

3. Block 2. *1 Corinthians 6–10 and Acts 5.12–15.35: A Summary Comparison*

As indicated in the initial general outline (Table 89 above), the use of 1 Corinthians 6–10 runs, largely in order, from Acts 5 to 15, but with two gaps, essentially comprised of Acts 9 and 12:

In the following table the numbering of the correspondences, from 16 to 22 (on the left side), takes up from the detailed numbering in Block 1 (Table 90). As already mentioned, in this section (Acts 5.12–15.35) the use of 1 Corinthians is generally not as heavy as in much of Acts 1.1–5.11.

Table 92. *Block 2. Justice and Related Issues*

	1 Corinthians 6–10	*Acts 5.12–15.35*
16.	Disputes and courts (6.1-10)	Disputes; Stephen in court (5.12–ch. 7)
17.	But you have been washed, sanctified in…the name of Jesus Christ…in the Spirit (6.11)	Conversion of Samaria to Christ …in the name of Jesus…in the Spirit (8.1b-25)
18.	The body is not for fornication but for union with God, in spirit (6.12-20)	The Ethiopian is a eunuch but his baptized body rejoices (in God) (8.26-40)
		<Paul's conversion. Peter heals; raises the dead (ch. 9)>
19.	Man–woman relations, reflecting the end time (ch. 7)	Peter eats forbidden food (chs. 10–11)
		<Collection; Peter's escape (11.27–ch. 12)>
20.	Eating forbidden food (offered to idols) (ch. 8)	Mission: personal/ethnic relations: reflecting historical time (ch. 13)
21.	Apostles (Paul/Barnabas): all things to all (ch. 9)	Paul/Barnabas: we are humans like you (ch. 14)
22.	Historical lessons and careful judgments (ch. 10)	Jerusalem council: history; new judgments (15.1-35)

a. *Section 16. Disputes and Courts (1 Corinthians 6.1-10; Acts 5.11–Ch. 7)*
Paul's complaint about disputes and resorting to public courts finds a series of slender echoes in Acts:

1 Corinthians	*Acts*
Christians going before courts! (6.1-2)	Christians as a group apart (5.12-16)
Material disputes: appoint someone wise (6.3-6)	Distribution disputes: appointment of wise men (6.1-7)
Wrongdoers do not inherit the kingdom (6.7-10)	Speech involving not inheriting and wrongdoing (6.8–ch. 7)

The weakest link here is the third echo. Within Stephen's complex speech, the ideas of wrongdoing and inheriting are minor. Yet two details strengthen the connection:
- In both cases inheriting is used negatively: 'shall not inherit' (1 Cor. 6.9-10); 'did not give [Abraham] to inherit' (Acts 7.5).
- In both cases to do wrong/injustice (*adikeō*) is used twice, in rapid succession: concerning the internal dispute in Corinth (1 Cor. 6.7-8); and concerning Moses' intervention in the internal dispute among two Hebrews in Egypt (Acts 7.26-26; cf. 7.24).

b. *Section 17. Conversion in Corinth and Samaria: Made Holy…in Christ…and in the Spirit (1 Corinthians 6.11; Acts 8.1b-25, Especially 8.5, 12, 16-19)*
Paul's one-verse description of the conversion of the Corinthians (6.11) corresponds significantly to the coloring of some features of the conversion of Samaria. The Corinthians were 'washed…*made holy…justified… in the name of the Lord Jesus Christ* and *in the Spirit of God*'. And the Samaritan account, apart from emphasizing the *name* and the *Holy Spirit*, makes a distinction between baptism in *Christ* and receiving the *Spirit* (Acts 8.5,

12, 16-19). The Christ/Spirit distinction is not the same in both: what is merely distinguished in Paul is separate in Acts. And taken in isolation, the shared features would seem negligible. But in the context of the larger stream of similar elements, they are significant.

c. *Section 18. The Body (Especially in the Case of the Ethiopian Eunuch) is for the Lord to be One in Spirit (1 Corinthians 6.12-20; Acts 8.26-40)*
In contrast to prostitution's emphasis on the body as material, as forming a sexual/physical union, Paul indicates another aspect of the body: its union with the Lord, forming one spirit, the body being the temple of the Holy Spirit. To highlight this idea of the body in spiritual union rather than sexual union, Luke now introduces the Ethiopian eunuch, someone who, while incapable of sexual union, found spiritual union. Several aspects of the Ethiopian story emphasize the power of the Spirit or the spiritual world, even over the body. The Spirit sends Philip to the chariot (Acts 8.30) and later takes him away (8.39). The eunuch's body is given not to sexual union but to the waters of baptism, and he goes on his way rejoicing.

Here, as in using the incestuous couple to help portray Ananias and Sapphira (1 Corinthians; Acts 5.1-11), Luke omits the explicitly gender/sexual aspect and concentrates on a further or larger issue.

d. *Section 19. Inter-Personal/Ethnic Relations in a Changing Time (1 Corinthians 7, Man-Woman Relations; Acts 13, Mission and Inter-Personal/Ethnic Relations)*
Paul's chapter on marriage and virginity (1 Cor. 7) has major implications concerning the fate of the world: he indicates that time is running out, that the world is passing away (see especially 1 Cor. 7.29, 31). Within that context, he gives directions about gender relationships, and given the shortness of time, he tends to suggest that people not change their status.

In using 1 Corinthians 7, Luke again omits the gender element and concentrates on a larger issue—in this case, the fate of the world. But instead of suggesting, as 1 Corinthians 7 does, that time is ending, Luke shows time as ongoing, as forming a steady stream of history. This emerges particularly in Luke's account of the barrier-breaking mission of Paul and Barnabas (Acts 13). The whole mission is God's *ergon* ('work', Acts 13.3, 41), like a further stage of creation, and while the shape of the world may indeed be changing (as 1 Cor. 7.31 suggested), it is not passing away. On the contrary, it is advancing to a further stage. The missionary journey opens with an episode in Cyprus which summaries the Christian view of Judaism. The clash with Bar-Jesus intimates that Judaism will be blinded 'for a time' (Acts 13.4-12, especially 13.11), and the subsequent speech, in Pisidian Antioch, which sometimes spells out the number of years ('40 …450…40…'), gives a sense of the changing phases of Israel's history (Acts 13.17-41, especially 13.18, 20, 22). In essence, Luke has taken the difficult idea of a change in the shape of *the world* and has brought it down to earth—to the idea of a change in the shape of *world history*.

The link between the texts (1 Cor. 7; Acts 13) is confirmed by various details, including the following:
- Opening images of close-knit groupings (a couple; a church) who place someone apart during/for prayer (the couple stay apart for prayer, 1 Cor. 7.1-5; the church sets apart Saul and Barnabas, and then prays, Acts 13.1-3).
- Then, following a reference to Satan/the devil, a picture of someone in a close-knit group who turns back: the wife who separates (*apo…chōrizō*) from her husband (1 Cor. 7.5-11), and John, who turns back (*apochōreō*) from the mission (Acts 13.10-13).

- The pivotal emphasis on some form of steadfastness or remaining: the need to stay (*menō*) in one's God-given state (1 Cor. 7.20, 24), and the need to remain faithful (*pros-menō*) to God's grace (Acts 13.43).

Overall, Luke has taken inter-gender dynamics and adapted them to the dynamics between larger groups.

e. *Section 20. Avoiding Scandal When Eating Forbidden Food: Food Offered to Idols (1 Corinthians 8), or Food Shared with Gentiles (Acts 10.1–11.18)*
Paul's next major topic, the problem of food offered to idols (1 Cor. 8), reappears, explicitly in the decree of the Jerusalem council (Acts 15.20, 29), thus linking the two texts. However, there seems to be a further, broader connection, namely Paul's care, on the food issue, not to give scandal (1 Cor. 8), and it is this broader feature which Luke seems to have adapted when describing Peter and the issue of eating Gentile food. Peter does eat such food but he is very careful that his conduct is right before both God and humans (Acts 10.1–11.18).

However, this link needs testing. Many of the shared elements are quite general: eating, food, sacrifice, brother, plus summaries of the basic *kerygma* concerning God and Christ. In asserting the existence of a link, it is better, if possible, to identify a similarity that is more precise or unusual.

f. *Section 21. Portraits of Apostles: Paul and Barnabas (1 Corinthians 9; Acts 14)*
Paul's *apologia*, his account of himself and Barnabas as apostles (1 Corinthians 9), is reflected in Luke's account of the apostleship of Paul and Barnabas, and apostleship that extended from Iconium to Lycaonia and back to Antioch (Acts 14). Points of contact include:
- The identity of Paul and Barnabas as 'apostles' (1 Cor. 9.1-6; Acts 14.4).
- The role of Paul and Barnabas as 'evangelizing' (1 Cor. 9.16-17; Acts 14.7, 15, 21).
- The apostles making themselves like other people: Paul becomes 'all things to all' (1 Cor. 9.22), and, faced with receiving Lycaonian homage, Barnabas and Paul insist that they are like the Lycaonians, ordinary humans (Acts 14.15).

g. *Section 22. Dealing With the Ancient Traditions and Reaching Practical Solutions (1 Corinthians 10.1–11.1; Acts 15.1-35)*
Having finished the account of his apostleship, Paul turns to Mosaic history and the consequent need to move towards practical solutions. Luke does likewise. Having finished the account of Paul's missionary apostleship, he recounts a dispute about Mosaic tradition and the subsequent search at the Jerusalem meeting for practical solutions. The conclusion in both cases is very positive: there is a general spirit of freedom, but with attention to others' sensitivities, including sensitivity concerning meat sacrificed to idols (1 Cor. 10.14–11.1; Acts 15.19-35).

4. *Block 3. 1 Corinthians 11–16 and Luke 22–24; Acts 2–5; 9; 12— A Summary Analysis*

As already noted, the overall use of 1 Corinthians 11–16 is orderly, as follows:
- 1 Corinthians 11 and 15.1-7 underlie Lk. 22.1-30 and parts of Luke 24.
- 1 Corinthians 12–14 and 15.20-49 supplement Acts 2–5.
- 1 Corinthians 15.8-19, 50-58 and ch. 16 fill the two gaps, essentially in Acts 9 and 12.

Appendix 2. *1 Corinthians as One Component of Luke–Acts*

The more detailed outline below, adapted from the initial general outline, contains eight sections (23-30):

Table 93. *The Passover Mystery*

1 Corinthians 11–16	Luke 22–Acts 12 (Intermittent)
23. Covered head, drinking, eucharist, judging (ch. 11)	Carrying a jar, first cup, eucharist, judging (Lk. 22.1-30)
24. One Spirit, many gifts…tongues…prophecy (12.1-11)	Spirit…many…tongues… prophecy (Acts 2.1-42)
25. One body…no need…love (12.12-31; ch. 13) (Distributing goods need not mean love)	One heart…no need…care (2.43-47; 4.32–5.16) (Ananias/Sapphira share goods [5.1-11])
26. Prophetic speech…build up…order (ch. 14)	Prophetic Peter…builders…unity (4.1-31)
27. Christ died, rose…according to scriptures (15.1-7)	Suffering, rising—as in the scriptures (Lk. 24.25-27, 44-48)
28a. Appearance to Paul. Paul preaches Christ's resurrection (15.8-19)	Paul's conversion (Acts 9.1-30) Paul, risen in baptism, preaches Christ.
28b. How the dead rise (15.50-58)	Peter heals Aeneas, raises dead Dorcas (9.32-43)
29. Resurrection, until God be *all in all* (15.20-49)	Christ restores *all* (3.11-26)
30. Jerusalem collection, travel, open door, house church (ch. 16)	Jerusalem collection; Peter's open door; house community; travel (chs. 11–12)

a. *Section 23. Drinking, Eucharist, and Judging (1 Corinthians 11.2-34; Luke 22.1-30)*
As indicated in Chapter 14, the similarity of the supper texts (virtually identical in 1 Cor. 11.23-25 and Lk. 22.19-20) is part of a larger pattern. See Table 94 (next page).

The clear connection between the institution accounts (1 Cor. 11.17-26; Lk. 22.19-23) is generally attributed to a shared ritual, but it can also be accounted for by a shared text and by a sacramental mode of imitation which employs verbatim reproduction ('slavish precision', Hays 1989: 173-75 [173]).

However, apart from the sacramental mode, with its slavish verbatim repetition, imitation employs other modes such as the eclectic, heuristic and dialectical (Hays 1989: 173-74). The *eclectic* mode mingles several diverse texts. The *heuristic* mode focuses essentially on one text but rewrites and adapts it to a new situation. The *dialectical* mode engages an earlier text in a way that instead of transposing it completely to a new situation, sustains a tension between the two worlds of the two texts.

The difference between these modes, between sacramental/verbatim, on the one hand, and eclectic, heuristic and dialectical, on the other, helps to explain why Luke reworks Paul in diverse ways. Luke shifts modes according to the situation, according to the text in question and according to the requirements of his own narrative. While dealing with the basic eucharistic words, he imitates verbatim/sacramentally.

But he engages the rest of the supper account in ways which are closer to the other modes, especially to the heuristic. Instead of the Corinthian picture of acrimony, he portrays a last supper which emphasizes harmony and in which acrimony, even when it does occur, is contained with a larger positive context. While Paul, for instance, complains a manner of eating and drinking and drinking which is self-centered and gross (1 Cor. 11.20-22), Luke depicts a process of eating and drinking that is the opposite: not self-centered but altruistic; not gross but decorous (Lk. 22.14-17a).

Table 94. *The Supper Texts*

1 Corinthians 11	Luke 22.1-30
[Head covering, relationship to God (11.2-15)]	Betrayal; prepare (pitcher carrying, evoking betrothal?) (22.1-13)[2]
Problems: Contentiousness, divisions (11.16-19)	
1. Coming together to eat. Each for himself. Regarding the church of God as nothing. No praise (11.20-22)	Reclining together to eat. Desiring to eat with others. Fulfillment in the kingdom of God. Giving thanks (22.14-17a)
2. Eucharist. Do this…declaring the death of the Lord until he comes (11.23-26)	Eat this… I clearly imply my death 'until the kingdom of God comes'. Eucharist (22.17b-20)
3. Guilty eater. Examine yourself. Condemnation (11.27-29)	Treacherous table companion. Woe. Examining themselves (22.21-23)
4. Problems: Judgment: so as not to be like the world (11.30-32)	Problems: Contentiousness. Who is greater? Do not be like the kings (22.24-27)
5. Solidarity in waiting. Eating and not being condemned (11.33-34)	Solidarity in staying. Eating and judging (22.28-30)

b. *Section 24. Spirit, Tongues and Prophecy (1 Corinthians 12.1-11; Acts 2.1-42)*
Introducing his account of the Spirit and the Spirit's gifts, Paul looks back to the time when the believers were Gentiles/nations (*ethné*), and against that Gentile background, he speaks of the influence of the Spirit, one Spirit giving diverse gifts, including tongues and prophecy (1 Cor. 12.1-11). All these elements are present in Luke's account of Pentecost (Acts 2.1-42), a background of Gentile nations, Spirit, tongues, prophecy, and a transition from being passive Gentiles to being involved with the one Spirit. The primary result of the Spirit—the assertion that Jesus is Lord (1 Cor. 12.3)—is the climactic statement of Peter's Pentecost speech (Acts 36).

2. Paul's discussion of head-covering stresses 'the importance of the differences of the sexes' (Murphy-O'Connor 1990: 52). Yet, as usual in Paul's texts on gender-relations, there is a further issue: man–woman closeness is like the closeness of humanity with Christ/God; in a sense, one relationship flows into the other. (Eph. 5, speaking more clearly, compares man–woman love with Christ–church love.) To some extent, divine love (or Christ's love) is like human love, a central Old Testament theme. In adapting 1 Corinthians, Luke again omits the specific gender question (diverse head-covering) and focuses on the larger issue, on a divine–human closeness which is like man–woman closeness. The path to the Passover is marked by meeting someone carrying a pitcher of water, something which, carried on the head, formed a head covering. In Old Testament imagery—and the context is Old Testament (Passover)—such a meeting generally initiates some form of betrothal (Alter 1981: 47-63). Hence, Luke not only keeps a material head-covering, but a covering which implies some larger relationship. The full dimensions of this larger relationship are a matter for further investigation. For instance, is Luke's Passover account colored by the Song of Songs? Such an evoking of love would correspond significantly to the larger dimension of the Corinthian passage. In any case, both texts speak not only of a material covering of the head, but also of a covering which, in the context, evokes deep relationships.

c. *Section 25. One Body/Heart... No Need... Love/Care (1 Corinthians 12.12–Ch.13; Acts 2.43-47; 4.32–5.16)*
Having begun by speaking of the Spirit, Paul then turns his attention to the effect of the Spirit's gifts on the believers: the believers form one body so that one member does not say there is no need of another (1 Cor. 12.12-31); and the greatest is love (1 Cor. 13). These ideas recur in Luke's three summaries of the post-Pentecostal believers: they form one group, sharing all; there is no need among them; and they are characterized by love/care (Acts 2.43-47; 4.32-37; 5.12-16; note 4.32, 'one heart and mind'). Paul's principle that distributing one's goods need not entail love (1 Cor. 13.3) is illustrated in the case of Ananias and Sapphira (Acts 5.1-11).

d. *Section 26. Prophecy as an Instrument of Building Up and of Order/Unity (1 Corinthians 14; Acts 4.1-31; cf. 3.6-8)*
Paul's long chapter on spiritual gifts (1 Cor. 14) is primarily about the positive role of intelligible speech, especially of prophecy. The opening (14.1-5) uses *laleō* ('to speak'), seven times. The purpose of prophetic speaking is not to confuse but to build up (14.3, 17) and to promote order (14.26-40). Prophetic speech should be instructive even for the uninitiated (*idiōtēs*) (14.16, 23, 24).

Paul's chapter on prophetic speech is echoed in Luke's portrait of Peter—in the way his words build up the lame man (Acts 3.6-8), in his implied image of a building (4.11), and in the orderly or unified way the believers subsequently worship together (4.23-31). Peter's speech is seen as that of someone uninitiated (*idiōtēs*, Acts 4.13). Thus, while Paul envisaged prophetic speech as intelligible to the uninitiated, Luke turns the idea around: the uninitiated are capable of prophetic speech. Apart from one instance (2 Cor. 11.6), the only New Testament occurrences of the word *idiōtēs* are in 1 Corinthians 14 and Acts 4.

e. *Section 27. As You Received... Christ Died and Rose... As Scripture Said (1 Corinthians 15.1-7; Luke 24.25-27, 33-34, 44-48)*
Luke breaks 1 Corinthians 15 (comprising 58 verses) into smaller units and spreads them out to suit his own narrative. The first section, the basic account of Christ's death and resurrection (1 Cor. 15.1-7), lays the emphasis first and last not only on the actual events (death/resurrection) but even more on their context within tradition and scripture ('You received... I handed on...according to the scriptures'). This emphasis on reception and scripture helps explain why Luke uses this text not so much to describe the original events as to recount how these events were received, first on the road to Emmaus (Lk. 24.25-27), and later at the gatherings in or near Jerusalem (Lk. 24.33-34, 45-48). The texts share several elements: death, resurrection, appearances, reception, accordance with the scriptures, for (forgiveness of) sins. The discrepancies, for instance, an appearance not to the twelve (as in 1 Cor. 15.5) but to the eleven (Lk. 24.33)—may be accounted for largely through the requirements of Luke's own narrative (his next chapter, Acts 1, fills in the twelfth and allows for several appearances, such as those listed by Paul).

f. *Section 28. Paul: From Persecuting the Church to Preaching Christ and Resurrection (1 Corinthians 15.8-19, 50-58; Acts 9; cf. 8.1-3)*
Having recalled Christ's death, resurrection and appearance, Paul speaks of his own role. Though he persecuted the church, Christ appeared to him, and so he has become a preacher of Christ and of resurrection (1 Cor. 15.8-19). This basic sequence of events—persecution, appearance, preaching—occurs also in Acts (9.1-30; cf. 8.1-3). In Acts, the idea of resurrection (*anastasis*, 1 Cor. 15.12-13) recurs in adapted form: Paul's recovery evokes the resurrection: it follows three days of blindness and abstinence, and, accompanied by

baptism, it involves Paul's rising (*anastas*, Acts 9.18). Thus, rather than a picture of Paul preaching the resurrection (1 Corinthians), Luke tells how Paul, having been baptized into the resurrection, went on to preach.

The final part of 1 Corinthians 15, concerning the manner of the resurrection (15.50-58), finds a historicized equivalent in the final part of Acts 9 in the accounts of Peter healing Aeneas and raising Dorcas from the dead (Acts 9.32-43). The corresponding details include:

- A sense of secrecy: mystery (1 Cor. 15.51); Peter, alone, prays (Acts 9.40).
- Focus on the eyes: the twinkling of an eye (1 Cor. 15.52); Dorcas opens her eyes (Acts 9.40).
- Focus on clothing: resurrection involves being clothed anew (1 Cor. 15.53-54); Peter throws out those showing Dorcas's old clothes (Acts 9.39).

g. *Section 29. The Resurrection as Preparatory to a Universal Restoration (1 Corinthians 15.20-49; Acts 3.11-26)*

The center of 1 Corinthians is a dense section which describes Christ not only as risen, but as the beginning ('first-fruits') of a much larger process through which all things are eventually subjected to God, 'so that God may be all in all' (1 Cor. 15.28).

The essence of these ideas appears as one component in Peter's temple speech, wherein he speaks of the time of 'the restoration of all, which God [fore]told…' (Acts 3.11-26, especially 3.21). Both texts, concerning the subjecting of all (1 Corinthians), and the restoration of all (Acts), are preceded by 'it is [providentially] necessary…until' (*dei…archi*, 1 Cor. 15.25; Acts 3.21).

h. *Section 30. Jerusalem Donation; Travel; Open Door; House Community (1 Corinthians 16; Acts 11.27–Ch. 12)*

Paul's final chapter (1 Cor. 16), the collection for Jerusalem, which recounts his travel plans and final greetings, finds multiple echoes in the episode on combating famine (Acts 11.27-30) and especially in the account of Peter's escape (Acts 12). Shared elements include:

- Each person donates for the welfare of those in Judea/Jerusalem (1 Cor. 16.1-4; Acts 11.27-30).
- A door is open for Paul's work (1 Cor. 16.9) and for Peter's escape (Acts 12.6, 10).
- A house church/community: Paul sends greeting from the house church of Aquila and Prisca (1 Cor. 16.19), and Peter, prayed for by the church, visits those praying in the house of Mary, the mother of John Mark (Acts 12.5, 12).
- Traveling on: *while* planning visits, Paul gives an overall impression of travel which is onward and somewhat indefinite (1 Cor. 16.5-8); after his escape, Peter too travels away, without specifying the destination (Acts 12.17).

5. Conclusion

The preceding analysis is sometimes weak, yet it offers leads for further research. Its basic proposal, that Luke used 1 Corinthians, seems valid. First, there is extrinsic plausibility: in the context of communications in the early church, Luke could have sought a copy of 1 Corinthians. Second, there are many significant similarities. And third—though this is the weakest area of the analysis—the differences are generally intelligible. Overall, Luke adapts the epistle to a new purpose, and makes the text more full, more dramatic, and more vivid.

Appendix 3

The Use of 2 Chronicles 10–36 in Acts 4–15:
An Exploration

The books of Chronicles deal largely with the rise and fall of the temple. The rise (1 Chron. 1–2 Chron. 9) has been distilled and reshaped as part of the infancy of Jesus. In Acts, as he is bringing his work to a close, Proto-Luke comes back to the remainder of Chronicles, to the flourish and fall of the temple (2 Chron. 10–36). However, his way of using 2 Chronicles 10–36 is particularly elusive, thus making analysis difficult and tentative.

The Old Testament text (2 Chron. 10–36) is scattered throughout several chapters (Acts 4–15), as though Proto-Luke had rearranged it drastically to fit the final stages of his account.

Given this restructuring it is useful to divide the Old Testament text (2 Chron. 10–36) into two uneven sections which may be called the flourish (2 Chron. 10–28) and the fall (chs. 28–36).

1. *The Flourish (2 Chronicles 10–28)*

This material is quite in order. The history of the early church shows a sequence of events which follows almost exactly the order of events during the period when the temple was free and flourishing (2 Chron. 10.1–25.18). This sequence falls into four blocks.

a. *Block 1. The Schism and the Sadducees (2 Chronicles 10–13; Acts 5.17-42; also 4.34-36)*
Not long after the temple was built, a section of Israel broke away (2 Chron. 10). This separation from the true sanctuary is mirrored by Luke in his picture of the 'sect' of the Sadducees who search at a distance in confusion while the apostles teach in the temple (Acts 5.17, 24-25). The outlines of these two dramas coincide fairly neatly:
- Meeting the people (2 Chron. 10.1-5; Acts 5.17-21a).
- Consultation and confusion (2 Chron. 10.6-14; Acts 5.21b-23).
- Schism (2 Chron. 10.15-17; Acts 5.24-25).
- A question of stoning (2 Chron. 10.18-19; Acts 5.26).

Despite the schism, the country was given strong leadership and, after sinning, received forgiveness (2 Chron. 11–12). The apostles express the same basic ideas when they tell the Sanhedrin of the strong leadership of Jesus which gives forgiveness from sins (Acts 5.27-32). Again the ideas of the two narratives coincide:
- A human threat must give way to divine teaching and obedience (2 Chron. 11.1-4; Acts 5.27-29).
- Strength and leadership (2 Chron. 11.5-12, 18-23; Acts 5.30, 31a).
- Israel: sin and repentance (2 Chron. 12.1-4, 6; Acts 5.31b).
- Witness (2 Chron. 12.5; Acts 5.32a.
- God gives salvation to the receptive (2 Chron. 12.7-8; Acts 5.32b; on 2 Chron. 12.9-11, see Acts 5.18-21).

The action of the non-schismatic Levites in giving up their property to sacrifice at the temple in Jerusalem (2 Chron. 11.13-15) had been used earlier by Luke. It is reflected in the action of Barnabas the Levite who gave up his property and placed the proceeds at the feet of the apostles (Acts 4.34-37).

Later, in Chronicles, the schismatic tribes took to the field to destroy the men of Judah—at which point King Abijah gave a speech warning them not to fight against God (2 Chron. 13). When the apostles had spoken, the Sanhedrin intended to kill them—but the eminent Gamaliel gave a speech somewhat similar in substance to that of King Abijah (Acts 5.33-39; on 2 Chron. 13.13-23, see Acts 5.40-42).

b. *Block 2. Peter's Peace (2 Chronicles 14–20; Acts 9.31–11.18)*
For more than half a century, the land enjoyed considerable peace. Under the faithful guidance of Asa and Jehoshaphat, the country advanced in strength and instruction. This peaceful advance has been used by Luke to describe the ministry of Peter—how he worked throughout the land, and how he brought faith to the Roman Cornelius. The sequence of episodes in Acts follows that in 2 Chronicles:

(1) *Built up in peace (2 Chronicles 14; Acts 9.31-43)*. Under Asa 'the country was at peace...He rebuilt the towns' (2 Chron. 14.1-7). In Acts, 'the church throughout all Judea and Galilee and Samaria had peace and was built up', and Peter ministered in the towns (Acts 9.31-35). When invasion came, Asa turned it back by crying to the Lord (2 Chron. 14.8-14); when death came, Peter overcame it by prayer (Acts 9.36-43).

(2) *Seek and find (2 Chronicles 15.1–17.7; Acts 10.1-8)*. When Israel seeks the Lord (2 Chronicles 15; 17.1-6), the prophet proclaims the divine response (2 Chron. 16.7-9). When Cornelius seeks the Lord (Acts 10.1-2), the angel announces that his prayers are heard (Acts 10.3-4). In seeking to build up the land, the kings of Israel sent gifts from the house of the Lord and from the royal house (2 Chron. 16.1-6) and sent officers to give instruction in the law (2 Chron. 17.7). In seeking Peter, Cornelius sends two householders and a devout soldier 'having explained everything to them'.

(3) *Triple oracle (2 Chronicles 17.8–18.14; Acts 10.9-16)*. The history of Israel continues by telling about the 'ecstasy' that fell on neighboring kingdoms (2 Chron. 17.10), about the slaughtering of animals (18.2) and about the threefold prophetic exhortation: 'Go up and conquer' (18.4, 11, 14). Meanwhile, Peter has fallen into the ecstasy in which he sees all sorts of animals and in which he is told three times: 'Rise up, slaughter and eat'.

(4) *Searching for a shepherd (2 Chronicles 18.15-16; Acts 10.17-18)*. The uncertainty of the previous prophetic exhortations is swept aside by the outspoken Micaiah who draws a clear, sad picture of Israel as sheep without a shepherd, seeking home. In Acts, the scene changes from the puzzle of the ecstasy to the picture of the men sent by Cornelius standing at the gate 'inquiring for the house of Simon...who is called Peter'.

Sent from above (2 Chron. 18.18-22; Acts 10.19-21ab). Micaiah goes on to tell of a heavenly drama in which a spirit presents himself and is sent down to earth. In Jaffa, Peter is involved in a roof-top drama in which the Spirit sends him down to present himself to the messengers from Cornelius. (On 2 Chron. 18.23-27, see Acts 10.21c-23.)

(5) *Deception uncovered (2 Chronicles 18.28-32; Acts 10.23b-29)*. During the battle of Ramoth-gilead the enemy made the mistake of taking Jehoshaphat to be king of the northern kingdom. But a prayer to God shows them their mistake. As Peter enters the house of

Cornelius, the Roman officer makes the mistake of falling at Peter's feet. But Peter corrects this case of mistaken identity and misplaced subservience ('I too am a man'), and goes on to tell that God has shown him the mistake of dividing men into clean and unclean. (On 2 Chron. 18.33-34, see Acts 10.30-33.)

(6) *Conduct justified (2 Chronicles 19; Acts 11.1-12)*. Returning to Jerusalem after the battle, Jehoshaphat has to face questioning because of having given help to the northern king (2 Chron. 19.1-2), but his conduct justifies him. Peter, returning to Jerusalem after his speech to Cornelius, has to face questions about associating with pagans (Acts 11.1-3), but he justifies his conduct.

(7) *Saved by the spirit (2 Chronicles 20; Acts 11.13-18)*. When the whole assembly of Judah was in danger (2 Chron. 20.1-13), it was the intervention of the spirit (20.14-15) which changed the situation and led to joy and peace (20.26-30). Peter, in continuing to justify his conduct, tells how the whole household of Cornelius had been waiting to be saved (Acts 11.13-14), and about the decisive intervention of the spirit (11.15-17). When Peter recounted this, his questioners 'were put at peace and glorified God' (11.18).

c. *Block 3. Antioch's Anguish (2 Chronicles 21–24; Acts 11.19-30)*
The peace did not last. The next period was a time of assassination and idolatry. The Baal-worshipping Queen Athaliah was disastrous. Yet the temple recovered and regained its strength and status. This anguished recovery, from almost total neglect to full strength, has been used by Luke in describing the origin and growth of the Antioch church.

(1) *Painful beginnings (2 Chronicles 21; Acts 11.19-21)*. The murderous beginnings of Jehoram's reign (2 Chron. 21.1-7) lead to Edom breaking free of Judah (21.8-10) and causes God to lean hard on the unfaithful kingdom (21.11-20). The persecution surrounding Stephen (Acts 11.19) led some disciples to break out of the Jewish circle and speak to the Greeks at Antioch (11.20), 'and the hand of the Lord was with them'—not leaning on them but supporting them'.

(2) *Support from Jerusalem (2 Chronicles 22.1-9; Acts 11.22-24)*. One of the factors that helped to restore reverence for the Lord was the zeal against the idolators. In recounting this zeal, the Chronicler tells of the sympathetic visit of King Ahaziah who traveled from Jerusalem to boost the moral of his sick cousin. On the basis of these two men, of their sympathy and zeal, Luke depicts the visit of Barnabas who traveled from Jerusalem to encourage and strengthen the young Antioch church. (On 2 Chron. 22.7, see Acts 11.23.)

(3) *Surprise support (2 Chron. 23; Acts 11.25-26)*. The second factor that helped to restore the temple was the surprise emergence of a Davidic heir, suddenly brought out of hiding by the priests and Levites. And for the Antioch church, the second factor that lent support was the sudden emergence of Saul, brought out of his Tarsus seclusion by Barnabas the Levite. (On the original hiding of the heir, 2 Chron. 22.10-12, see the original secluding of Paul, Acts 9.29-30.)

(4) *Helping to strengthen a living temple (2 Chronicles 24; Acts 11.27-30)*. The final episode tells of the money collected by the priests and Levites to restore and strengthen the run-down Judean temple. And the final Antioch episode tells of the contributions carried by Paul and Barnabas to relieve the needy Judean community.

d. *Block 4. Kings under Control: Herod (2 Chronicles 25.1–28.15; Acts 12)*
Most of the Judean kings of the eighth century do not appear very bad. But the Chronicler makes one thing clear. In all they do, they are under the control of God who can punish or save, uphold or throw down (2 Chron. 25.8, 15, 20; 26.5; 28.8). Luke has reproduced this theme in his account of how Herod tried to imprison Peter and was soon struck dead. Some of the details of Luke's account reflect the Chronicler: the killing of James (Acts 12.2; 2 Chron. 25.3); the angel's solicitude for Peter's footwear and clothing (Acts 12.8; 2 Chron. 28.15); the sudden punishment of the king who offended the glory of God (Acts 12.23; 2 Chron. 26.19-20).

2. *The Fall (2 Chronicles 28–36)*

This section covers the century that finished the first temple, the final chapters of 2 Chronicles. On the basis of this section, Luke has depicted several aspects of Stephen and Saul (Acts 6–9).

But Luke has omitted the repentance–Passover material. In other words, at this stage of writing (Acts 6–9), Luke did not use four passages of Chronicles which deal with a process of repentance or Passover (2 Chron. 29.5-36; chs. 30, 33; 35.1-18). It will be necessary to come back to those at the end.

For the moment, the focus stays on Stephen and Saul, and on the main body of the final chapters of 2 Chronicles.

It is useful to regard these concluding chapters as centered around three basic dramas: the reform of Hezekiah; the reform of Josiah; and the final collapse.

a. *Drama 1. Hezekiah is Stephen (2 Chronicles 28.16-18; Acts 6)*
Luke's account of the emergence and role of Stephen (Acts 6) is based largely on the emergence of the good king Hezekiah (2 Chron. 28.16–32.33, omitting 29.5–ch. 30).

(1) *Crisis and convocation (2 Chronicles 28.16–29.4; Acts 6.1, 2a).* Ahaz neglected Judah in dealing with the temple goods (28.19-21, following MT numeration), and the situation became quite difficult, until finally Hezekiah called a crisis meeting. Luke tells us of a crisis in the early church because of the neglect of the widows in the daily distribution, until eventually a meeting was called.

(2) *Appointment of overseers (2 Chronicles 31; Acts 6.2-7).* As part of his reform, Hezekiah reorganized the priests and Levites so that they might devote themselves to the law (2 Chron. 31.4) and at the same time be appointed overseers to look after the temple distributions (31.11-15). The crisis in the early church was solved by allowing the apostles to concentrate on preaching, and by appointing seven other men, including Stephen, to supervise the distribution. Stephen's personal role is not always parallel to that of Hezekiah, but the drama that surrounds him sums up the history surrounding the king.

(3) *Strong attack, stronger defense (2 Chronicles 32.1-8; Acts 6.8-10).* The tranquility is shattered by the attack of Sennacherib on Jerusalem, yet with the Lord on his side, Hezekiah is stronger (2 Chron. 32.7-8). Stephen also is attacked, but his adversaries cannot withstand the wisdom and the spirit with which he speaks.

(4) *Two-pronged abuse (2 Chronicles 32.9-19; Acts 6.11-14).* Sennacherib sends his men to hurl blasphemies at the city and temple (2 Chron. 32.10-12), and then he himself adds further abuse (32.17-19). Stephen also has to face two waves of verbal abuse—mainly on the grounds that he had spoken against the temple.

(5) *The intervention of the angel (2 Chronicles 32.21; Acts 6.15).* When the temple seemed doomed, the Lord sent a delivering angel who destroyed the attacking forces. And as the accusing Sanhedrin looked at Stephen 'they saw his face like the face of an angel'. In addition, the prayer and mourning accompanying Stephen's death (Acts 7.60; 8.2) reflect Hezekiah's death (2 Chron. 32.24, 33). (On 32.18, see Acts 7.37; on 30.5-10, see Acts 7.51, 53.)

b. *Drama 2. Josiah is Saul (2 Chronicles 34; Acts 7.58–9.29)*
Of all the kings of Judea, Josiah was probably the most zealous in seeking to reform and maintain true worship. The first picture of him corresponds to the first picture of Saul: a young man who observes and promotes the destruction and death of whatever is seen as offending the temple (2 Chron. 34.1-7; Acts 7.58; 8.1, 3).

Josiah's next objective is to purify the land and temple. He goes to the high priest with money collected for temple repairs (2 Chron. 34.8-9). Paul is equally zealous. He too goes to the high priest, not bringing money collected for the temple but 'men and women, bound, to Jerusalem' (Acts 9.1-2). (On 2 Chron. 34.10, see Acts 9.21c; on 2 Chron. 34.11-13, see Acts 9.22a.)

Then comes the great discovery of Josiah's life: the book of the law which had lain hidden in the temple (2 Chron. 34.14-21). Paul's conversion brings a discovery that is equally soul-shaking, and soon he is engaged in proving to the Jews of Damascus that 'this is the Christ' (Acts 9.22).

Soon Josiah learns that disaster is imminent, but he escapes (2 Chron. 32.22-28). Paul also is threatened, but he escapes over the wall in a basket (Acts 9.23-25).

Finally, Josiah gathers all the leaders and people in Jerusalem. There they read out the contents of the discovery, and pledge their loyalty to the Lord (2 Chron. 34.29-33). Back in Jerusalem, Paul meets the disciples and apostles. Then they are told about his discovery on the road: 'After that Saul was with them...preaching boldly in the name of the Lord' (Acts 9.26-28). (On Acts 9.29-30, see 2 Chron. 22.10-12.)

c. *Drama 3. The Speech is the Collapse (2 Chronicles 35.19–36.21; Acts 7.1-60)*
Apparently, one elusive component of Stephen's speech, a speech directed in part against the temple, consists of a distillation of the Old Testament account of the collapse of the city and temple (following the LXX version, which includes four insertions from 2 Kings: after 2 Chron. 35.19, insert 2 Kgs 23.24-27; after 2 Chron. 36.2, insert 2 Kgs 23.31-33; after 2 Chron. 36.4, insert 2 Kgs 23.35; after 2 Chron. 36.5, insert 2 Kgs 24.1-4.)

An important element in the Old Testament account of collapse consists of the death of Josiah (2 Chron. 35.20-27). Partly on the basis of this text, Stephen speaks of Abraham (Acts 7.2-8a). Many details link the two texts, for example: Mesopotamia (2 Chron. 35.20; Acts 7.2); God spoke (2 Chron. 35.21-22; Acts 7.2-3); departure (2 Chron. 35.23; Acts 7.4); death...father (2 Chron. 35.24; Acts 7.4); hope (LXX 2 Chron. 35.26; Acts 7.5-7). But, as so often, Luke has gone far beyond one particular source, and his final formulation contains several quotations from other areas of scripture. Perhaps the most basic link between Josiah's death and Stephen's picture of the wandering Abraham is the theme of hope amid apparent failure; it is not the conquest or acquisition of this territory that really counts.

Josiah's successor was soon carried off to Egypt—thereby giving Stephen a good starting-point for the story of Joseph (2 Chron. 36.1-4; Acts 7.8b-16, insert 2 Kgs 23.31-33; cf. Wis. 10.13-14).

The last three kings of Judea may be reflected in the way Stephen divides Moses' career into three periods (2 Chron. 36.5-13; Acts 7.17-22; 7.23-29; 7.30-35). Finally, the speech tells of the people's reaction to the prophets (2 Chron. 36.14-16a; Acts 7.36-41), God's reaction to the people (2 Chron. 36.16b-17; Acts 7.42-43), and the final bankruptcy of the temple (2 Chron. 36.18-21; Acts 7.44-50).

3. *The Repentance–Passover Passages*

The passages of 2 Chronicles that have yet to be accounted for consist of those dealing with repentance and/or Passover. These four passages from the final chapters of 2 Chronicles have been used by Luke in the final section of his work (Acts 13–15).

The repentance of Israel under Hezekiah (2 Chron. 29.5-36) helps explain the reaction of Paul's audience at Antioch (Acts 13.38-49).

The repentance of Manasseh from idolatry (2 Chron. 33.11-20) has colored the account of how Paul prevented idolatry at Lystra (Acts 14.5-19).

The Passover celebrated under Josiah (2 Chron. 35.1-18) gives a picture of people and leaders gathered for worship, in many ways like the Antioch gathering that launched Paul and Barnabas on their missionary journey (Acts 13.1-3).

The Passover at the time of Hezekiah (2 Chron. 30) seemed problematic at first. Sections of the people had not fulfilled the ritual of purification and sanctification (20.17-18). But Hezekiah prayed for the Lord's mercy on every heart; and the Lord heard and healed the people (30.18-19), thus leading to heartfelt rejoicing. This Old Testament picture of vibrant peace has contributed to Proto-Luke conclusion. The whole Passover narrative (2 Chron. 30)—the decision by the assembly, the writing of letters, the sending of messengers, the freedom from legal requirements, the actual celebration—is reflected in Luke's account of the process of sending and celebrating that followed the Jerusalem council (Acts 15.22-35).

The last three verses of 2 Chronicles (36.21-23) in which the prophet looks forward to a new temple have contributed to the framework of the account of the council (Acts 15.7-21, especially 15.7, 12, 19, 21). However, it is Peter who speaks in place of the prophet; and the temple under discussion, which is being founded by Paul and Barnabas, is of a different kind. It is not a Jerusalem temple. It is spread across the world.

Appendix 4

The Trials and Death of the Just Man (Wisdom 1–5) as One Component of the Trial and Death of Jesus (Luke 22.66–23.49)

Several aspects of Proto-Luke's text, including important aspects the Passion Narrative, have not been accounted for. The purpose of this appendix is to indicate, by way of example, how some other of Proto-Luke's sources might begin to emerge. The example is Proto-Luke's use of the book of Wisdom.

It is quite plausible that Luke drew on the book of Wisdom. Written apparently in Alexandria around 30 BCE,[1] Wisdom had become part of the LXX, and, both in its aims and methods, it has affinities with Luke. In its aims, it sought to bridge the gap between Greeks and Jews.[2] In its methods, it distilled and reworked the Old Testament (see especially Skehan 1938; Larcher 1969: 85-103). Thus, for Luke—a Hellenistic writer who was engaged with the biblical heritage and who variously imitated the LXX—it provided at least a partial model.

The plausibility of Luke having used Wisdom is heightened by the broader connection between Jesus' sayings and the tradition or 'trajectory' of wisdom (J.M. Robinson 1971b; Jacobson 1978; Kloppenborg 1986). If the sayings of Jesus' were related to the wisdom trajectory, it makes sense that Luke should set Jesus' death also in that same wisdom context.

1. *The Texts: Introductory Analysis*

Several scholars regard Wisdom 1–5 as a unit, the first major section of the book.[3] It deals with human destiny, particularly the idea of immortal life with God, and it does so not in some vague philosophic way, but by linking a blessed destiny with a just life, and by contrasting the lives and destinies of the just with those of the wicked (Osty 1957: 31; Larcher 1983: I, 120). Its style is of a general moralizing kind, yet it implies a broad storyline: people who are wicked and death-oriented attack the just man and, in killing him, they seem to succeed. But in reality, the achievements of the wicked are illusory, and the just man, despite his death, is on the way to salvation. In the final reckoning at the judgment, they confess their sins and acknowledge the just man.

This implicit storyline has been taken by Luke and, with the help of other sources, has been rendered into a narrative that is powerfully vivid. Jesus is the just man who is subjected to trials and death. But it is clear to the reader that it is he and not the bystanders who is on the road to salvation. And at the end, particularly through the figures of the 'good

---

1. For opinions and discussion, see Winston 1979: 20-25, and especially Larcher 1983: I, 131-61.
2. See especially Larcher 1969: 179-236; Reese 1970. Note Wright 1968: 7: 'The author...attempts a synthesis between anthropocentric Greek humanism and theocentric Hebrew humanism'.
3. See F. Feldman 1926: 24-50; Osty 1957: 31-50; Maly 1962: 13-18; Larcher 1983: I, 120. Some authors include with chs. 1–5 all or part of 6.1-21 (see, e.g., Reese 1970: 34; Winston 1979: 151-56; Rybolt 1986).

thief' and the (crucifying) centurion, they confess their sins and he is acknowledged as a just man.

In Luke's adaptation, the final reckoning of sin and justice—a reckoning which Wisdom places in the eschatological future—is taken and rendered into the reality of history. Thus, Luke's reworking is both more vivid and more historicized.

To understand further what Luke has done, it is necessary to look more closely at the text. Unlike Wisdom 1–5, the unity of Lk. 22.66–23.49 is not immediately clear. In varied ways, both Fitzmyer and Neyrey, for instance, would connect 22.66 with what precedes (Fitzmyer 1985: 1452; Neyrey 1985: 69-107). Yet, whatever the strength of that connection, 22.66 represents some kind of beginning. In a gospel in which time is important, it moves from a prolonged night action to that of a new day; and as Caird, for instance, implies, it is the point at which a series of trials is inaugurated (Caird 1963: 245-48). As for 23.49, it obviously represents some kind of conclusion: it is the final death in the account of Jesus' death. Marshall regards it as a major point of division.[4] Though it is not unrelated to the account of the burial (23.50-56, especially 23.55-56), it is also quite distinct from it. The burial account intimates the dawning of a further new day (23.54); and, unlike those who surround Jesus during his trial and death, those at the burial approach Jesus with an attitude that for a long time has been positive.

In fact, a distinct feature of 22.66–23.49 is that, unlike most of what precedes and follows, it shows Jesus as alone, bereft of disciples. In 22.1-65, the disciples are emphasized, especially Judas and Peter. And in 23.50–ch. 24 beginning with Joseph of Arimathea, there is a further emphasis on people who are obviously disciples or are waiting in one way or another for Jesus. But in 22.66–23.49, despite a series of reactions that are increasingly positive (beginning with the forced reaction of Simon the Cyrenian, 23.26), none of the disciples is mentioned. In Luke's account, there is no clear evidence for calling Simon a disciple; all that is present is a potentiality.

It is only towards the end of 22.66–23.49, and especially in the reactions of the sympathetic onlookers (23.47-49), particularly that of those known to him and that of the women who had followed from Galilee (23.49), that the potentiality for discipleship is replaced by a picture of discipleship which is clear (see Fitzmyer 1985: 1520). While 22.1-65 tells of Jesus being surrounded by disciples, but shows those disciples as increasingly alienated (sleepy, treacherous, inclined to violence, flatly denying all knowledge of Jesus) and finally as giving way to a group blasphemers (*blasphēmountes*, 22.63-65), 22.66–23.49, while beginning with a picture of unrelieved hostility (22.66-71), Luke eventually begins to portray reactions that are increasingly positive, and finally comes to a picture of outright disciples (23.49).

Whatever the details, the essential point is that it is reasonable to see the account of the trial and death as forming some kind of unity. Even if that unity is denied, the case for the dependence on Wisdom 1–5 is not weakened; but the plausibility of that unity helps to make the nature of the dependence clearer.

One point is particularly clear. Luke, as well as being dependent, is also thoroughly independent. He may sift Wisdom 1–5 with systematic rigorous fidelity, adapting its various parts to the narrative about Jesus, but he rejects its suggestion of dualism—its impression of a clear-cut divide between the wicked and the just. In Luke's view, the disciples are capable of infidelity, and the wicked are capable of becoming disciples. He moves sinners not only from the eschatological future into the present, but also from the ranks of the condemned into the ranks of the saved.

---

4. Marshall 1978: 877. A. Büchele (1978: 59), while treating all of Lk. 23 as a unit, nonetheless regards 23.49 as a major dividing point.

Luke is faithful to Wisdom, but he is also challenging it, going beyond it and adapting it to the requirements of his own narrative and of his own Christ-centered vision of salvation.

2. *The Texts: A More Detailed Analysis*

The following analysis is incomplete and simplified. It is incomplete because it does not succeed in tracing all the points of connection between Wisdom 1–5 and Luke. The difficulty of tracing these connections is highlighted by Luke's use of Wis. 4.19 (the death of the unjust): Luke uses it not in the Passion Narrative, but in the account of the death of Judas (Acts 1.18-20). Thus, a full picture of the relationship of the texts may be much more extensive.

Table 95. *The Death of the Just Man (Wisdom 1–5; Luke 22.66–23.49):*
An Outline—Incomplete and Simplified

Wisdom 1–5	Luke 22.66–23.49
1. Seek the Lord in simplicity and trust, not in crookedness (1.1-5)	1. Interrogation of Jesus in perversity and distrust (22.66–23.5)
2. The Lord gets to know the words of the unjust (1.6-10)	2. Jesus sent by Pilate, gets to know the words of Herod, 23.6-9.
3. Avoid negative speech (1.11)	3. Jews' vehement accusations (23.10)
4. God creates, sin destroys (1.12-15; 2.21-24)	4. Herod sets Jesus at naught 23.11a)
	10. Jesus in a shining garment 23.11b)
5. Friendship with death (1.16b-e)	5. Friendship with death's agent (23.12)
6. The godless call for death, and for the death of the just (1.16a; 2.1-16, 19-20)	6. The Jews call for a murderer, and for the death of Jesus (23.13-25)
	9. Chastised, found guiltless (23.22)
7. Mockery of the just man (2.17-18)	
8. The just die into God's hands (2.16b; 3.1-3)	
9. Chastised, found worthy (3.4-6)	
10. The just will shine out (3.7)	
11. Those who trust find mercy (3.8-9)	
12. Sinners are pitiable… Blessed the barren. Sinners' future: like that of a shallow tree (3.10–4.6)	12. Weep for yourselves… Blessed are the barren. Your future: like that of dry wood (23.27-31)
13. The just man dies amid evil (4.7-14a)	13. Jesus dies amid evildoers (23.32-33)
14. People look (4.14b-18)	14. People watch (23.35a),
	7. and mock (23.35b-37)
15. The death of the unjust (4.19)	15. [Death of Judas (Acts 1.18-20)].
16. The just man is acknowledged (4.20–5.4)	
17. The unjust repent (5.3-16)	17. The 'good thief' repents (23.39-40),
	11. and finds mercy (23.42-43)
18. The earth made desolate (5.17-25)	18. Darkness over the earth (23.44-45)
	8. 'Into your hands…' (23.46)
	16. Jesus is acknowledged as just (23.47-49)

And the analysis is simplified because even when it does not accurately connect two texts, it does not always provide a full explanation of the nature of that connection. In the outline (Table 95 above) the nature of the connections is further simplified. Some connections are immediately plausible. Others, such as number 1 (Wis. 1.1-5; Lk. 22.66–23.5), appear conjectural, particularly when seen for the first time and when viewed in isolation. The process of comparison requires considerable patience.

a. *Section 1. Seek God in Faith, Not Perversely (Wisdom 1.1-4; Luke 22.66–25.5)*
The LXX text[5] exhorts people in power to seek God in simplicity and faith, and it warns that while simplicity of heart finds the Lord, self-centered skepticism and deception do not.

The New Testament is a two-part account of the interrogation of Jesus, first by the Jewish Sanhedrin (22.66-71) and then by Pilate (23.1-5). Pilate is trying to inquire honestly, yet both parts of the interrogation are dominated by Jewish perversity and deception.

Thus, while the LXX warns authorities in a general way that perversity fails to discern God, the New Testament shows a concrete example of perverse authorities who fail to discern God incarnate.

Obviously major aspects of Luke's text are not indebted to Wis. 1.1-5 and his greatest dependence is on sources that are Christian. But heavy dependence on Christian sources does not exclude a further limited dependence on Wisdom. And comparison of the texts shows the presence of significant elements which, conceivably, could have been adapted from the LXX: rulers inquiring about the down-to-earth reality of God (LXX: justice-oriented; New Testament: human-shaped); and the destructive role, within that quest, of perversity, disbelief and deception (cf. especially Lk. 22.67b-68; 23.2-5). There is reason to ask whether Luke has taken the LXX image of perversely approaching the Lord and adapted it to the vivid reality of the Jews perversely interrogating Jesus.

Verbal links are minimal:

LXX:
apisteō, theos

New Testament:
pisteuō, theos

b. *Section 2. The Lord Gets to Know the Unjust (Wisdom 1.6-10; Luke 23.6-9)*
God's spirit is friendly, says Wisdom, but not to the blasphemous or godless. The blasphemous man is scrutinized: the spirit of the Lord fills the inhabited world and knows all that is said; or, to put it another way, as does Wisdom, a report of the words of the blasphemer reaches the Lord. Thus, God's spirit goes out to examine the blasphemer and the blasphemer's words reach God.

In the New Testament, Jesus, apparently helpless, comes to Herod (he is sent by Pilate) and is present as the brutal ruler rejoices superficially, and hopes for a sign, and questions him with many words.

The relationship between the texts contains many subtleties. Wisdom had spoken of a report of the godless man reaching the Lord (Wis. 1.9), but Luke in effect tells that a report of the Lord (Jesus) had reached Herod (Lk. 23.8). And Pilate also, in hearing about Jesus and knowing about Herod (23.6-7), is subtly involved in the dynamic of Lord–blasphemer communication. But without attempting to unravel all the complexities, the basic point is clear. While the Old Testament warns authorities in a general way that their godless

---

5. The present analysis is based on the critical edition by Ziegler 1962. Differences from A. Rahlfs' *Septuaginta* are minor, but Ziegler's Wis. 3.19 has the equivalent of an extra line.

sentiments and words will not escape divine scrutiny, the New Testament shows a contrary example wherein, despite all appearances to the contrary, such scrutiny is quietly under way. The Jesus who had been able to assess the perversity of the Sanhedrin (22.67-68) will not have failed to detect the character of Herod.

Here, as previously, Wisdom's contribution is just one component.

Verbal similarity:

LXX:
akoustēs...gnōsin...logōn...akoē

New Testament:
akousas...epignous...akouein...logois

c. *Section 3. Negative Speech (Wisdom 1.1; Luke 23.10)*
Wisdom warns against various forms of negative speech: groundless complaining, defaming, and lying. Luke tells that the high priests and scribes stood there 'vehemently accusing' Jesus. Thus, while the LXX gives a general warning against destructive speech, the New Testament gives a concrete example of such conduct:

Verbal similarity:

LXX:
katalalias...katapseudomenon

New Testament:
katēgorountes

d. *Section 4. Sin (not God) Destroys (Wisdom 1.12-15; 2.21-24; Luke 23.11a)*
In both of these Wisdom texts, there is emphasis both on the positive power of God and on the negative force of sin. God brings things to be, but sin and the devil cause the death and destruction of the living.

The New Testament tells that Herod with his soldiers 'set (Jesus) at nought' (KJV), 'treated him with contempt' (RSV). The verb in question, *exoutheneō*, suggests a process of reducing to nothing.

While the LXX refers to the general process by which sinful forces destroy the living, the New Testament shows destructiveness in action. Jesus is not actually killed at this point, but the process of reducing him to nothing, particularly when done by Herod 'with his soldiers', suggests a thoroughgoing destructiveness that evokes the coming destruction in death.

There is some likelihood, therefore, that Luke blended these two texts and adapted them. In principle, such blending is plausible. Within the text of Wisdom, they are inherently connected both by content and by the fact that they frame the picture of life as the godless see it (1.16–2.20); and elsewhere, in reworking the LXX, Luke sometimes blends related texts.

Furthermore, in this adaptation, as in reworking the preceding passages of Wis. 1.1-11, what Luke highlights is the negative.

While a connection between these texts and Luke 23.11a seems warranted, Lk. 23.11a does not exhaust their meaning. Luke may have made further use of them elsewhere.

e. *Section 5. Friendship with the Forces of Death (Wisdom 1.16b-e; Luke 23.12)*
Wisdom sees the godless as friends of death, and as forming a covenant with death. Luke tells of Herod and Pilate, two leaders in Jesus' death, as forming a friendship with each other. (It is Herod with his soldiers who first set Jesus at naught, and it is Pilate's soldiers who will finally kill him.)

Luke's adaptation involves both blending and concretizing. The elements of *being friends* and *forming a covenant* have been blended or synthesized into the idea of *becoming friends*. And the general idea of a friendship with death has been concrete or vivid in the down-to-earth process of a friendship with someone who in some way represents death-at-work.

There is, of course, great irony in the text, for the gospel also has a very positive connotation: the death of Jesus brings reconciliation and friendship into the world. And this ironic overtone represents yet a further adaptation: turning what is profoundly negative into something positive. In fact, this is one of Luke's strategies. Though he is now emphasizing what is negative, his narrative as a whole is oriented towards the emergence of what is positive.

Verbal similarity:

LXX:
philon

New Testament:
philoi

f. *Section 6. The Godless Call for Death and for the Death of the Just Man (Wisdom 1.16a; 2.1-16, 19-20; Luke 23.13-25)*

With multiple images, Wisdom describes the godless both as calling for death and for a death-dominated mode of life for themselves (2.1-9; cf. 1.16a), and also as wanting to kill the just man (2.10-20).

In a text that is two-part (note the 'again' in 23.20), Luke describes the Jewish authorities first as demanding for themselves Barabbas, a murderer ('"release to us"…murder', 23.13-19), and then, with even louder shouts, as demanding the crucifixion of Jesus (23.20-25). To some degree, of course, both parts of Luke's text call for Jesus' death, but the initial emphasis is on the murderer, and it is only in the later part that the call for Jesus' crucifixion becomes explicit.

Those who are godless call for orientation-towards-death and for the death of the just man, and the Jewish authorities call for a murderer and for the death of Jesus.

Again, Luke has made the LXX images more down-to-earth. In place of the older general ideas and multiple images, he has given images which are synthesized and vivid.

Again, however, Wisdom provides just one component.

A few details are noteworthy. In Wisdom, justice is measured by the strength (*ischys*) of the godless who call for the death of the just man (2.11), and in Luke, the trial of Jesus is decided by the strength with which the Jewish authorities call for Jesus' death (*kat-ischuon*, 'and their voices prevailed', 23.23). Furthermore, Pilate also is subtly involved in the process of calling. It is with his calling of the Jewish authorities that each part of Luke's text begins (vv. 13, 20). Thus, despite his protestations, he, too, is an agent of death.

Verbal similarity:

LXX:
pros-kalesanto (1.16); *ischys* (2.11); [*thanaton…thanaton*, note 1.12-13]

New Testament:
syg-kalesamenos…thanatou…pros-ephōnēsen…thanatou…kat-ischuon

g. *Section 7. Mockery of the Just Man by His Murderers (Wisdom 2.17-18; Luke 23.35-37)*

In the course of describing how they will beset the just man and finally condemn him to a shameful death (Wis. 2.10-20), the wicked speak of mocking the just man's reliance on God: 'If the just man is God's son, [God] will *defend* him and *deliver* him' (2.17-18).

When Jesus is surrounded by enemies and is about to die, he too is mocked: 'Let him *save* himself, if he is the anointed of God'; 'If you are the king of the Jews *save* yourself'.

Luke's adaptation ('save...save' in place of 'defend...deliver') not only involves a vivid account of an actual mockery, but also an adaptation of that mockery to his central theme of Jesus as the Christ who saves, who brings salvation.

For verbal similarities, see section 14 below.

h. *Section 8. The Just Who Die are in God's Hands (Wisdom 2.16b; 3.1-3; Luke 22.46)*
According to Wisdom, the just man regards the end of life as blessed, and he relies on God as his father (2.16b). And when the actual death is recounted, it is preceded by the statement that the souls of the just are in the hand of God (3.1-2). Thus, death is preceded by the ideas of *relying on God as father* and of *the soul as being in God's hand*.

Jesus' death is preceded by 'Father, into your hands I commit my spirit'.

Most of Luke's *phrasing*, apart from the word 'father', is from Ps. 31.5, but the overall *content*, including the word 'father', is an accurate reflection of the Wisdom texts. The two general Old Testament ideas have been synthesized and made vivid in the account of the death of Jesus. This is not the first time that Luke uses diverse sub-texts for content and for phrasing.

Verbal links:

LXX:
2.16: *patera...theon*
3.1-2: *psychai en cheiri theou...tethnanai*

New Testament:
pater, eis cheiras sou paratithemai to pneuma mou...exepneusen

i. *Section 9. Chastised and Found Worthy of Life (Wisdom 3.4-6; Luke 23.22)*
The just who die are described as having been 'chastised' and 'found' worthy of life—immortal life with God.

In Jesus, Pilate 'finds' nothing worthy of death, and so he says he will 'chastise' him and let him go (Lk. 23.22; cf. 23.14-16).

Pilate's intention is to punish Jesus and release him, but in fact Jesus will die, and so Pilate's words have an ironic sense, one which reflects the ideas of Wisdom: in Jesus, there is nothing worthy of death and so after being 'chastised', he will be released into life with God.

Luke has adapted the notion of chastisement so that from Pilate's point of view it means something quite prosaic, but in the context of the larger account it refers to a chastisement that, like that in Wisdom, is life-giving.

Verbal links:

LXX:
athanasias...paideuthentes...heuren

New Testament:
thanatou heuron...paideusas

j. *Section 10. The Just Man Shines Out (Wisdom 3.7; Luke 23.11b)*
Not only does God accept the just; in God's searching presence they shine out ('like sparks among the stubble'). And Herod puts on Jesus 'a bright shining garment'.

In both texts the just man shines (LXX: *ana-lampsousin*; New Testament: *lampran*), but instead of the Old Testament image of shining sparks, Luke substitutes the image of a shining garment. This process, the substitution of images, was part of *imitatio*. (See Chapter 1, 'Literary Imitation: The Practice' [pp. 8-13].)

Jesus shines out almost in spite of Herod. Herod's purpose is to mock Jesus' guiltlessness, but again there is an ironic sense: amid the various rulers and accusers Jesus stands out as does the guiltless man in the presence of God.

k. *Section 11. Those Who Trust the King Find Mercy in Him (Wisdom 3.5-9; Luke 23.42-43)*
Having referred to the just as shining out, Wisdom goes on to speak of the just as *judging*, as having the Lord as *king forever*, as trusting the Lord, as *receiving grace and mercy*, and as going on to *live with the Lord in love*.

All of these elements are found in the account of the good thief. First he exercises judgment with regard to who is guilty and who is not. Then he trusts in Jesus as king ('Jesus, remember me...'). And finally he receives from Jesus abundant grace and mercy, a promise to be with him in paradise.

In Luke's adaptation, the LXX ideas are brought into a context which synthesizes them and makes them vivid. They flow into one another in a form that is highly memorable.

Verbal/phrasing links:

> LXX:
> *basileusai...en agapē prosmenousin autō*
>
> New Testament:
> *basileia...met' emou esē en tō paradeisō*

l. *Section 12. Pitiable are the Wicked; Blessed are the Barren (Wisdom 3.10–4.6; Luke 23.27-31)*
Contrasting the wicked and the just, Wisdom speaks of the wicked along with their wives and children as pitiable ('miserable...void...fruitless...worthless...foolish...depraved... accursed', 3.10-12) and of the just as blessed, even if they are barren or eunuchs (3.13-15).

In further contrasting the wicked and the barren, the LXX speaks of their respective futures: for the wicked and their children, there is nothingness and a hopeless day of reckoning (3.16-19), for the virtuous, even if childless, there is immortality (4.1-2).

Finally, the LXX compares the future prospects of the wicked and their children to that of a tree which is poorly rooted and which the storm will destroy (4.3-6).

The overall emphasis, apart from the idea of the blessedness of the barren, is on the wretchedness of the wicked and their children, now and in the future.

In the New Testament, as the people and the women lament over Jesus, he tells them that they and their children are worthy of pity ('Weep not for me, but weep...'), but that their future is doomed ('For behold the days are coming in which they will say "Blessed are the barren"... Then they will begin to say to the mountains...'). Finally, he suggests they are like wood which is due to be consumed.

In both texts there is a contrast: between the wicked and the virtuous; and between the people and Jesus. The people, including the women, follow current patterns of thinking, and see Jesus as pitiable, a young man dying before his time. But in a reversal which accords with the spirit of Wisdom, Jesus tells them that it is they who are pitiable. The women are referred to in the context of the people (23.27), and the people had been involved in the death of Jesus (23.13). They are not guiltless. As a people they have sinned, and their future is correspondingly negative.

Thus the LXX ideas that sinners are both pitiable and doomed are synthesized in Luke and rendered into a form which, once again, is strikingly vivid and memorable. And instead of having a separate text on the blessedness of the virtuous who die or are barren, Luke has integrated these ideas into the condemnation of the guilty people ('Weep not for me... Blessed...').

Part of Luke's *phrasing/wording* ('...to say to the mountains, "Fall..."') is from Hos. 10.8, but the underlying content, concerning future doom, corresponds to the text of Wisdom.

Finally, the image of the shallow tree which will be destroyed is adapted to that of the dry wood which will be consumed. As already mentioned (section 10), such substitution of imagery was a normal practice of rhetorical imitation.

Verbal links:

LXX:
gynaikes...tekna...genesis...makaria...steira...tekna...en hēmera... geneas... ateknia...tekna gennōmena

New Testament:
gynaikōn tekna....hēmerai en...makariai hai steirai egennēsan

m. *Section 13. The Just Man Dies Amid Evildoers (Wisdom 4.7-14a; Luke 23.32-33)*
In speaking of the untimely death of the just man, Wisdom says: 'Living among sinners he was taken up. He was carried away lest evil pervert his mind.'

Luke describes Jesus as going forth to death with two evildoers. Instead of fleeing their company as is implied in Wisdom, Jesus stays with them to the end.

Verbal links:

LXX:
kakia...akakon

New Testament:
kakourgoi...kakourgous

n. *Section 14. People Look On Not Understanding (Wisdom 4.14b-18; Luke 23.35a)*
Wisdom describes how, as the just man dies, people look on, not understanding, and not realizing what awaits the elect.

Likewise, when Jesus is crucified, the people stand and watch. Their lack of understanding is implied by their mockery; and they refer to Jesus as the elect.

What emerges is that Luke's account of the mockery (Lk. 23.35-37) involves a synthesizing of two pictures—of the people looking on uncomprehendingly as the just man dies (Wis. 4.14b-15), and of the godless who mock the man who is about to die (2.17-18; see section 7 above).

Verbal/phrasing similarity:

LXX:
hoi de laoi idontes...eklecktois
ei...estin ho dikaios hyios theou
antilēmpsetai autou kai rysetai auton

New Testament:
heistēkei ho laos theōrōn
sōsatō heauton
ei houton estin ho Christos tou theou ho eklektos
ei su ei ho basileus...sōson seauton

o. *Section 15. The Death of the Unjust (Wisdom 4.19; cf. 4.14b-18; Acts 1.18-20)*
Contrasted with the fate of the just is the fate of the unjust. Having scorned the just man who dies, these latter are themselves destined for a bad end: they shall become corpses, even dishonored corpses, objects of scorn. Worse still, the Lord '*will rend them... headlong...* And they shall be utterly *laid waste...* and their *memory shall perish.*'

The death of Judas is described in a similar vein. He became a repulsive corpse and worse: falling *headlong* his *entrails poured out*; his habitation became a *desert*, and his *charge was taken over by another*.

Part of Luke's text (cf. Acts 1.20) takes its phrasing from the Psalms but the basic content corresponds significantly to Wisdom.

Verbal links:

LXX:
prēneis [4.15-16: *episkopē...adikou*]

New Testament:
adikias...prēnēs...episkopēn

p. Section 16. *The Just Man is Acknowledged (Wisdom 4.20–5.4; Luke 23.47-49)*
In describing the final reaction of the wicked to the vindicated just man, Wisdom refers briefly to the moment when the oppressors, on seeing him, are *amazed at the unexpectedness of his salvation* (5.2b).

In Luke also there is a brief account of seeing and changing drastically: the centurion on seeing what had happened 'glorified God saying, "Indeed this was a just man"'. (Thus instead of 'the oppressors', the New Testament speaks of the centurion, presumably the one in command of the crucifying soldiers).

While maintaining the idea of a drastic change in the onlooking oppressor/s, Luke makes a basic adaptation: the unexpected salvation comes not so much to the just man as to the oppressor. Such is the implication of the centurion suddenly glorifying God. In place of Wisdom's clear-cut division between the wicked and the just, Luke once again—as in speaking of Jesus' relationship to the two evildoers (see section 13 above)—shows greater compassion and hope for the wicked. Jesus is a just man not merely for the sake of his own salvation; his justice and salvation are for others.

Having evoked the reality of salvation through the centurion, Luke then evokes two large groups—'all those who had assembled to see the sight' (23.48), and 'all' those known to him and the women who had followed from Galilee (23.49). These groups do not reflect Wisdom as closely as does the centurion. Rather, they are Luke's expansion of the sub-text, a way of suggesting that the salvation which came to the centurion goes forth to larger groups. A similar process of expansion is found in Luke's adaptation of the raising of the widow's son—in his references to the disciples, to the great crowd, and to the going forth of the word (Lk. 7.11, 17).

Verbal links, including, perhaps, word-play:

LXX:
dikaios...idontes...paradoxō tēs sōtērias...Houtos ēn...

New Testament:
idōn...edoxazen ton theon...houtos dikaios ēn

q. Section 17. *The Repentance of the Unjust (Wisdom 5.3-16; Luke 23.39-41)*
In a passage with a multiplicity of images, Wisdom describes how, in the final reckoning, the wicked confess their sins, and how, as they speak to one another in the presence of the just man and as they recognize his integrity, they repent (*metanoeō*, 5.3).

In Luke's text, one of the evildoers speaks to the other, and in doing so he both acknowledges that they have done evil, and he also recognizes that Jesus is innocent. And as he speaks further, he becomes even more repentant and turns to Jesus ('Jesus, remember me...').

Thus, Luke's full text concerning the good thief (23.39-43) involves a synthesizing of two pictures: that of the wicked coming to repentance (Wis. 5.3-16), and that of the just receiving grace and mercy (Wis. 3.8-9; see section 11 above). This instance of blending is particularly understandable: at one point the two Wisdom texts show an inherent connectedness or similarity (cf. 3.8-9 and 5.15-16).

When the repentant evildoer contrasts his own conduct and that of Jesus ('And we...But this man', Lk. 23.41) his words correspond echo the words of the contrast in Wisdom (5.4, 13):

LXX:
[5.2: *phobō*] *Houtos ēn...kai hēmeis*

New Testament:
phobē...kai hēmeis...houtos

As well as blending, Luke also dissects or divides. He uses some aspects of the repentance theme in Wis. 5.3-4 to depict the good thief, and other aspects to depict the centurion. And he makes a double or divided use of the word at the very beginning of the repentance speech, the dramatic *Houtos...* ('This man...'). Such processes, of blending and dividing, were part of imitation.

r. *Section 18. The Involvement of All Creation (Wisdom 5.17-25; Luke 23.44-45)*
Finally, and with multiple images, Wisdom tells that because of wrongdoing, God will cause creation to react against evildoers and so lawlessness will bring desolation on all the earth (*pasan tēn gēn*). More briefly Luke tells that during the crucifixion the sun was eclipsed and there was darkness over the whole earth (*holēn tēn gēn*).

3. *Assessing the Evidence*

The evidence presented here is preliminary in its nature and incomplete in its scope (it does not investigate Proto-Luke's possible use of the rest of Wisdom). Nonetheless, in broad terms it conforms to the three main kinds of criteria for judging literary dependence: external plausibility, significant similarities (some indeed are weak but others are striking); and intelligible differences (they can be accounted by Luke's broad purposes and strategies). There is sufficient evidence, therefore, to warrant further investigation.

Unit 14. The Triple Intertextuality of the Epistles

Appendix 5

The Triple Intertextuality of the Epistles: An Introduction

To avoid undue complexity, this volume has often given the epistles a secondary role. Yet, in the longer term, the epistles will be at the centre of discussions about the birthing of the New Testament.

The purpose of the present appendix is to highlight an idea that has been emerging in recent years, namely that a New Testament epistle is not an isolated document. Most epistles have at least three types of literary connection: with the Old Testament; with other epistles; and with the gospels.

At first, this idea may seem unlikely. Of the twenty-one epistles, many give the impression of being spontaneous responses to specific situations or occasions, and thirteen claim to have been written by one person, Paul. But these three basic features—Pauline, situational, spontaneous—are not to be taken at face value.

Pauline. The first feature to be questioned was Pauline authorship. Despite the thirteen letters' explicit claim to be from Paul—they all begin with Paul's name—nineteenth-century researchers concluded that not all could be from one person; and at one stage, in Tübingen, the number of genuinely Pauline letters was reckoned to be just four (Kümmel 1972: 250-51). Twentieth-century scholarship has generally reckoned at least seven (1 Thessalonians, Galatians, Philippians, Philemon, 1 and 2 Corinthians, and Romans) but even this careful calculation of authorship is further relativized by the use of secretaries, writers who sometimes functioned almost as co-authors (Murphy-O'Connor 1995: especially 6-8, 14-34). Neither Romans nor 1 Corinthians, for instance, were actually penned by Paul. Romans was written by Tertius ('Tertius, who wrote the epistle…', Rom. 15.22); and in 1 Corinthians, Paul simply signed his name (1 Cor. 16.21). To some degree, then, Paul is not so much the actual author of the epistles as their general source of inspiration. (In a somewhat similar way the Old Testament sometimes attributed complex bodies of writings to one person, particularly to Moses or David.)

Situational. As well as questioning the letter's source—its authorship—research also questioned its destination, namely the situation or occasion to which it was addressed. In the summary of Bailey and Vander Broek (1992: 29 [emphasis added]):

> It is often said that Paul's letters are one half of a dialogue. Paul is responding to the need and requests of specific Christian communities. His letters are 'situational' [or 'occasional']; they are real letters written to real churches… However, not all of the N.T. letters lend themselves easily to this situational interpretation. In the Pastorals, for instance, aspects of style, content and vocabulary indicate that they were certainly not written by Paul to Timothy and Titus. They are pseudonymous both in terms of author *and recipient*… In this case the interpreter should not take the letter form and what it indicates about a situation at face value.

As with the question of authorship, the Pastorals are the tip of an iceberg. They bring to the surface a problem which, on closer inspection, is much greater: to what extent do the implied situations in the thirteen Pauline epistles correspond to actual situations? Obviously, to some degree they do correspond. The letter to Titus, for instance, quotes a saying about Cretans that seems witheringly realistic (Tit. 1.12), and aspects of 1 Corinthians agree with what is otherwise known about the city. But if the portrayal of Pauline authorship is partly a pedagogical device, then, to a degree not yet determined, the same may be true of the portrayal of situations. For example, the diatribe—a rhetorical device used considerably by Paul—lends itself towards portraying an imaginary audience; it is 'a form in which the speaker confronts and debates an imaginary addressee' (Bailey and Vander Broek 1992: 38). To some degree, at least, the Pauline letters construct their readers.[1]

Spontaneous. Within this context—reassessing both authorship and situation—the question arises about the epistles' third basic feature, namely the spontaneity of their content. Whereas Adolf Deissmann, for instance, reckoned the New Testament epistles to be similar in nature to the spontaneous situational letters written on papyri—day-to-day correspondence (Deissmann 1927), very different in nature from the highly literary letters of authors such as Cicero and Seneca—later scholarship, while retaining Deissmann's basic insight that most New Testament letters, particularly those attributed to Paul, do have a down-to-earth flavor, has also emphasized that the epistles sometimes employ deliberate literary strategies.[2] Galatians, for instance, appears at first sight to be particularly spontaneous, but closer examination shows that it makes very deliberate use of rhetoric (Betz 1979). The letter to Philemon seems supremely occasional but it has a curious relationship to other epistles, especially Philippians, and particularly to the hymn on self-giving or self-emptying (Phil. 2.1-13). Paul's sending of the beloved Onesimus is like a giving of his own body ('he is my heart', Phlm 12), and the change of status from slave to beloved brother is like the exaltation of Onesimus (Phlm 15–16). What happened to Christ is being applied to a specific human life. The need to think twice in assessing the epistles is particularly well illustrated in Paul's autobiographical passages. These texts first appear thoroughly spontaneous and realistic, springing directly from his own personal experience, prime material for reconstructing history. But comparison with other ancient authors shows that Pauline autobiography is part of a larger literary practice and that the epistles deliberately use material which appears autobiographical for pedagogical purposes (Lyons 1985; cf. Gaventa 1986; Mahon 1989). As Lyons concludes (1985: 171, 224-26):

> Various strands of evidence come together to support the conclusion that Paul presents his 'autobiography' as a paradigm of the gospel of Christian freedom...
>
> The function one assigns to Paul's autobiographical remarks affects not only the interpretation of these sections of the letters but profoundly influences the generic conception of, and thus the interpretation of letters as a whole... The consensus approach to Paul's autobiographical remarks, the hypotheses which sponsor it, and the generally accepted interpretive technique, 'mirror reading', as applied to [the focus of this study,] Galatians and 1 Thessalonians is clearly a failure...
>
> Since we have only Paul's autobiographical remarks and not his opponents' accusations, which the consensus assumes provoked them, it is necessary to exercise restraint in asserting too confidently that specific charges actually existed, much less what they may have been. Even the existence of 'opponents' in the usual sense of the word is far from certain... What he says is determined by his rhetorical approach and not by his opponents' reproaches...
>
> Proper recognition of the rhetorical elements in Paul's autobiographical remarks provides a further challenge to existing approaches, which characteristically reach historical conclusions before the question of literary function has been adequately addressed.

---

1. '*Les lettres pauliniennes construissent leur lecteurs, du praescriptum au postscriptum*' (Aletti 1996: 49).

2. For introductions to the vast literary phenomenon of ancient letter writing, particularly in relation to the New Testament letters, see Doty 1973: especially 1-27; Stowers 1986; J.L. White 1988. White's essay includes an annotated bibliography (pp. 101-105). For clear summaries of basic Pauline forms and for further further annotated bibliography, see Bailey and Vander Broek 1992: 21-87.

Appendix 5. *The Triple Intertextuality of the Epistles* 587

Lyons's words touch a radical weakness in much New Testament research: the rush to historical conclusions, without first dealing adequately with literary questions.

The literary question of the epistles' intertextuality is the focus of the rest of this appendix. As already indicated, this question has three main aspects: (1) use of the Old Testament; (2) use of one another; (3) subsequent use in the gospels and Acts. Of these three aspects, the third has already been illustrated (Chapters 14, 18, 20, 21, and Appendix 2). Consequently, the focus here is on the first and second aspects.

1. *The Epistles' Dependence on the Old Testament*

Taken as a whole, the New Testament epistles show significant dependence on the Old Testament. It is not simply a question, as William G. Doty suggests in his otherwise excellent introduction to the epistles, of using the Old Testament as some form of adjunct—for instance, to buttress, to explain, to demonstrate, or to indicate continuity (Doty 1973: 54). Rather, the Old Testament text is at the heart of the Pauline epistle; it is constitutive (see the references to Koch and Hays in Chapter 13).

Rather than attempt to examine all twenty-one epistles, it is best, by way of appropriate sample, to concentrate on the leading four—Romans, 1 and 2 Corinthians and Galatians. Among these, 1 Corinthians has already been illustrated (in Chapter 13 above), so the focus here is on Romans, 2 Corinthians and Galatians.

a. *Romans (Especially Hays 1989)*

Romans shows significant indebtedness to the Old Testament: 'Romans contains a heavy concentration of scriptural quotations and allusions... Paul is seeking to ground his exposition of the gospel in Israel's sacred texts... [There is] an agglomeration of "holy texts" in this particular letter...' (Hays 1989: 34). As in the case of Jude, this dense use of the Old Testament is not haphazard. 'If...we attend carefully to Paul's use of the quotations, we will discover them spiralling in around a common focus: the problem of God's saving righteousness in relation to Israel' (p. 34). In Romans, as in 1 Corinthians, Paul's relation to the Old Testament varies: sometimes explicit, sometimes allusive and indirect (p. 34). In a sense, Romans flows from Scripture:

> This text [Romans] is most fruitfully understood when it is read as an intertextual conversation between Paul and the voice of Scripture, that powerful ancestral presence with which Paul grapples. Scripture broods over this letter, calls Paul to account, speaks through him; Paul, groping to give voice to the gospel, finds in Scripture the language to say what must be said, labors to win the blessing of Moses and the prophets. (Hays 1989: 35)

Hays (1989: 35) furthermore expresses a key feature of Paul's approach: to some degree, the epistle is more engaged with scripture than with a specific situation or occasion:

> To be sure, Paul is writing to his contemporaries at Rome, and no doubt has some practical purpose... Romans is, as J. Christiaan Beker has insisted, 'a profoundly occasional letter', which seeks to bring the gospel into a contingent historical situation... However, Paul tells us little about that situation. Once the conversation begins, the addressees recede curiously into the background, and Paul finds himself engaged with an older and more compelling partner.

Essentially, the same phenomenon occurs in 1 Corinthians, though in a different way: Paul sets out to engage a specific audience, and in 1 Corinthians he appears to keep them in focus, yet all the while he is engaging a further partner, Scripture, a factor which, on analysis, seems at times to govern the conversation.

b. *Second Corinthians (Especially Stockhausen 1989)*

An example of the relationship of 2 Corinthians to the Old Testament occurs not only in Hays (1989: 122-53) but especially in Carol Stockhausen, *Moses' Veil and the Story of the New Covenant: The Exegetical Substructure of II Cor. 3.1–4.6* (1989).[3] Particularly valuable are Stockhausen's conclusions concerning specific ways of using the Old Testament. She distinguishes five principles of Pauline exegesis:[4]

1. *The primary role of the Torah*:

> Paul's takes as the basis for his interpretative task the Torah; that is to say, narrative texts from the Pentateuch are usually (perhaps always) at the core of his arguments...[Paul] is usually (perhaps always) concerned with the stories themselves, that is, with plot line, character, narrative event and especially the inexplicable, unusual or unmotivated character or action.

2. *The complementary role of prophets/wisdom*:

> It is Paul's usual procedure to apply prophetic and occasionally sapiential texts to bring the Torah into the proper contemporary focus. These secondary interpreting texts are usually (perhaps always) linked to each other verbally and *linked to the fundamental Torah verbally*—forming a network of mutually interpreting texts which creates a new synthetic meaning at once scriptural and Pauline. (Emphasis added).

Having characterized principles 1 and 2 as 'fundamental', Stockhausen then distinguishes three further Pauline procedures:

3. *Focus on contradiction/disjunction*:

> A third favorite occupation of Paul's in relation to the Scripture, in particular the Torah, is the location and solution of contradictions or uneasily reconciled passages. As Dahl...and Beker remind...us there is a strong element of discontinuity in Pauline thought... This discontinuity is due, not only to the disjunction between Paul's way of life in the customs of his life and his new life in Christ, but to his tendency in response to locate and exegetically reconcile passages in his traditional Scriptures which express this conjunction. This sort of argumentation is present in 2 Corinthians 3, and might be illustrated with the antitheses of 2 Cor. 3.3...

4. *Attention to context—to the larger narrative.*
5. *Modernization—'the pesher-like contemporization discussed extensively by Dunn and others'.*

To some degree, principles 4 and 5 are extensions of principles 1 and 3 respectively. Principle 4, attention to the larger narrative, dovetails with the emphasis on Torah narrative as narrative (principle 1). And *pesher*-like contemporization (principle 5) builds on the process of contemporization often contained in the use of the prophets and wisdom (principle 3). The subsequent illustrations, therefore, concentrate on the most basic principles: numbers 1, 2 and 3. The illustrations begin briefly with 2 Corinthians and then move into Galatians.

To illustrate the first principle, that of building on the Torah and its narrative, Stockhausen (1993: 146-49) gives the example of the use of the Moses story in 2 Corinthians. In dealing with Moses, the epistle's interest is not just in occasional details of the Torah. Rather, 'Paul's concern [is] with extended narratives *as* narratives... [He] displays a serious and sustained interest in the narrative of the life of Moses. His interest peaks at the episode of the veiling of Moses' face, but it is not limited to that episode' (p. 146). In

---

3. For some further examples of the use of the Old Testament in 2 Corinthians, see, in Bieringer (ed) 1996, articles by S. Hafemann (pp. 277-303), D.A. Koch (pp. 305-24), M.E. Thrall (pp. 347-63: Old Testament-related literature), C.J.A. Hickling (pp. 367-76).

4. Stockhausen summarizes these principles in '2 Corinthians 3 and the Principles of Pauline Exegesis' (1993: 144-46).

particular, Paul includes 'the very early chapters...[and] the later Sinai events' (p. 147). In effect, Paul makes special use of the *beginning* and the *climactic middle*. Stockhausen does not investigate Paul's possible use of the end of the Moses story.

c. Galatians
One of the primary features of Galatians is 'a sustained interest in the Genesis Abraham narrative' (Stockhausen 1993: 149; cf. Hays 1989: 105-21). This 'sustained' quality means that the focus is on the story as a whole: 'Arguably...Paul has in mind and refers to the entire length of the story of Abraham through his brief citations and allusions. His references run *roughly in order* beginning from the beginning of Abraham's story to its end, *with emphasis on the beginning and end*' (Stockhausen 1993: 149 [emphasis added]). In practice, Paul also makes significant use of the middle of the Abraham story (Gen. 17–18, when Abraham receives another covenant and welcomes the appearance of the Lord/ messengers; Stockhausen 1993: 150, 159-61).

Thus, Galatians confirms what was seen in 2 Corinthians: that for Paul the sustained use of the Torah and its narrative constitutes a first principle.

To the general importance of Torah, particularly Genesis, in Paul's writings Hays adds an important emphasis: Paul makes special use of Deuteronomy (Hays 1989: 89, 94, and especially 162-68). Deuteronomy underlies central aspects of Paul's theology:

> The words of Deuteronomy become the voice of The Righteousness from Faith... Gerhard von Rad, arguing for theological continuity between Deuteronomy and the New Testament, highlights the Deuteronomist's emphasis on God's gracious initiative in covenant election, apart from Israel's merit... There is a deep structural affinity between the theology of the word in Deuteronomy and in Paul... Deuteronomy 32 contains Romans *in nuce*. (Hays 1989: 163-64)

The first principle then is well-established: Paul's scriptural basis is the Torah.

Moving ahead for the moment to the third principle articulated by Stockhausen—Paul's focus on contradictions/discontinuity/antitheses—it is necessary to mention a further feature. In Paul's sustained use of the Torah, whether in Romans, 2 Corinthians or Galatians or elsewhere, the primary mode of dependence is not one of verbatim repetition or explicit citation. Rather there is a constant tension with the Old Testament text: 'Paul is both like Moses and unlike Moses...both like and unlike Abraham' (Stockhausen 1993: 152).

Hays (1989: 173-78) is even more emphatic that Paul's primary mode of interacting with the Old Testament is not one of verbatim reproduction ('Sacramental imitation', a form of slavish precision) but one of dialectical imitation (pp. 176-77):

> Paul's fundamental reading strategies are profoundly dialectical. The word of Scripture is not played off as a foil...nor patronized as a primitive stage...nor regarded merely as a shadow... Paul's urgent hermeneutical project, rather, is to bring Scripture and gospel into a mutually interpretive relation... The dialectical strategy...allows the intertextual tension to remain.

One of the results of this third principle—this emphasis on dialectic or antithesis—is that dependence is not always easy to detect, at least the task is not more difficult than in tracing relationships between the Synoptic Gospels. Again, Stockhausen (1993: 152):

> It is true that...in Galatians 1 or 2...[Paul] does not cite the text of Genesis...[or] mention Abraham's name. However, it is also true that the story of Abraham is a remarkable parallel at its earliest poŞint to Paul's own story and to the pattern which the Galatians have followed and to which Paul writes to exhort them to remain constant. Both elements of this parallelism— place in the narrative sequence and similarity of content—are important for my purposes in much the same way that similar order and similar wording are important for the source critic working with the Synoptic Gospels, and as order and wording were important to my analysis of Moses traditions in 2 Corinthians 3–4.

Likewise concerning the use of Genesis 17 in Galatians 3 (Stockhausen 1993: 159-60):

> In the absence of citation modern critics demand unique repetition of vocabulary from the proposed source and similar usage such as I have outlined for 2 Corinthians 3. In defense then of my suggestion that Galatians 3 and 4 are primarily intended to reconcile within the Abraham narrative I would like to point out some preliminary lexical indicators of the presence of this pattern.
>
> It is remarkable, but not coincidental, how much of the key vocabulary of Galatians is to be found in the story of Abraham, and precisely as key terms in the older story... These terms represent [Paul's] theological concepts and these issues are historical for him *because* they are the key terms and ideas in Abraham's story.

What is essential is that, because Paul's relationship to Scripture is dialectical, the detection of his dependence is often not easy, and the criteria for establishing it differ from the criteria employed in dealing with other kinds of relationships.

Stockhausen's second principle of Pauline exegesis emphasizes the role of the prophets/wisdom as complementary to Torah and as contemporizing (1993: 144-45).[5] The principle may be illustrated by the use of Jeremiah.

The role of Jeremiah and the new covenant (Jer. 31.33-34) is present in 2 Corinthians (Hays 1989: 128-29; Stockhausen 1993: 154-58) but there is a further, noteworthy, use of Jeremiah in Galatians. It is as though the sovereignty of God's word in the life of Jeremiah provides broad inspiration for Paul's emphasis on his own supreme freedom under God. His call to preach, for instance, adapts that of Jeremiah.

Jeremiah 1.4-5	*Galatians 1.14-15*
* The word of the Lord came to me, saying,	* But when it pleased God
Before I formed you in the womb I knew you, before you came from your mother I consecrated you,	who chose me from my mother's womb and called me by his grace
	* to reveal his Son to me
I appointed you as a prophet to the nations.	that I might evangelize among the nations...

While the prophetic book then goes on to portray Jeremiah's apparently lone stand against corruption (Jer. 1.8, 11-14), Galatians goes on to tell of Paul's lone stand against similar hypocrisy (Gal. 2.11-14).

Even at his most passionate, he seems to be engaged with the text of Jeremiah (see Table 96).

Paul recasts the Old Testament text into another literary form, that of a diatribe with its questions (Martyn 1997: 281; cf. Betz 1979: 130); and he recasts the appeal to nature (controlling the sea, and giving rain and harvest) into an appeal to Christ (to crucifixion, and the giving of the Spirit and of miracles). Otherwise—without going into detail—the texts share either similarity or complementarity: a call for attention (Listen/O); senselessness in general; senselessness in more detail (eyes, ears, spellbound); a fundamental awesome reality (God's power over the sea; Christ's crucifixion); a challenging question about internal response (fear and trembling; faith); again, senselessness; a turning away (a turn-

---

5. Hays (1989: 162), rather than distinguishing between Torah and prophets/wisdom, uses the statistics of citation to name Paul's preferred Old Testament texts: Isaiah (28 citations), Psalms (20), Genesis (15) and Deuteronomy (15). Stockhausen's analysis, as well as suggesting some of Paul's preferred texts, spells out how these texts relate to one another: the Torah (though not cited as explicitly) is foundational; the prophets/wisdom (including the Psalms) are complementary.

ing from the Spirit to flesh); a failure to respond (the heart does not fear; experience makes no impact); the divine generosity (rain and harvest; Spirit and miracles); misuses of the law (Old Testament: by not acting on it; Paul: by relying unduly on it).

Table 96. *Confronting the Mindless (Jeremiah 5.21-25; Galatians 3.1-5)*

Jeremiah 5.21-25	Galatians 3.1-5
Now listen to this, stupid and thoughtless (*a-kardios*) people	O (*Ō*) mindless (*a-noētos*) Galatians
...they have eyes and do not see, they have ears and do not hear...	Who has put a spell on you? ...before whose eyes
	* Jesus Christ was depicted as crucified.
	This alone I wish to learn from you:
Do you not fear me, says the Lord,	Did you receive the Spirit by the works of the law
or tremble before me?	or by hearing with faith?
* I placed the sand as limit to the sea * an everlasting barrier which it cannot pass; * it storms but cannot prevail, * the waves roar but cannot pass beyond.	
But this people has a hearingless senseless heart (*kardia an-ēkoos a-peithēs*).	Are you so mindless? (*a-noētos*)
They have turned aside and gone away.	Having begun with the Spirit are you now ending with the flesh?
They do not say in their hearts, Let us fear the Lord our God	Did you experience so many things in vain? ...if it really is in vain.
* who gives the rain in its season, autumn rain, spring rain, * and keeps for us the weeks appointed for the harvest.	* Does he who supplies the Spirit to you, * and works miracles among you
Your lawlessnesses (*a-nomiai*) have turned those away,	do so by works of the law (*nomos*),
and your sins have kept the good things from you.	or by hearing with faith?

The account of Paul's confrontation with Peter (Gal. 2.11-14) is a further example of an apparently spontaneous text which turns out to be 'saturated with scriptural echoes, allusions and concepts', and an analysis of the surounding text—all of Galatians 1–2—shows a pervasive presence of Scripture (Ciampa 1998: especially 157-78, 296). Paul uses Scripture in 'redescribing his environment...himself...his opponents...the Galatians...the gospel...[and] the world in the image of scriptural prophets' (p. 295).

The basic conclusion concerning Galatians is essentially the same as that of Hays concerning Romans: while engaging a specific audience, Paul is also engaging specific writings. Furthermore, it often appears difficult or even impossible to distinguish what is historical from what is scriptural.

As one moves through the rest of the New Testament's twenty-one epistles the same phenomenon of dependence on the Old Testament emerges with varying degrees of clarity. Even the last, minuscule epistle, Jude, fits this pattern: 'The more closely Jude is studied, the more pervasive its allusions to the Old Testament are found to be... Such allusions belong to Jude's literary technique...and are largely deliberate' (Bauckham 1990: 136).

This deliberateness is seen also in the epistle's exegetical method, a method which was primarily Jewish: 'Though it has been rarely recognized, Jude's letter contains a peculiarly elaborate and interesting example of formal exegesis of Scripture in the style of the Qumran pesharim' (Bauckham 1990: 179). Jude's engagement with the Old Testament was deliberate and methodical.

The overall impression, from Romans to Jude, is that as a whole the New Testament epistles involve deliberate reworkings of the older Scriptures. They are not just occasional documents. In a basic, constitutive, way, their nature is scriptural—literary, in the most serious sense.

2. *The Epistles' Interdependence*

a. *From Four to Fourteen*

Most scholars agree that four epistles involve literary dependence on other epistles. Of these four, two bear Paul's name:

1. 2 Thessalonians, which copies from 1 Thessalonians.
2. Ephesians, which synthesizes aspects of several earlier epistles, especially Colossians.

The other two are:

3. 1 Peter, which has intricate affinities with several epistles, including Romans.
4. Jude, built largely on 2 Peter, especially 2 Peter 2.

There is no need here to spell out the details of these four patterns of literary dependence. The data are available elsewhere.[6] What is important is the basic principle: both among the epistles which bear Paul's name and among those that do not there are examples of literary dependence (in these cases, epistolary interdependence).

However, there are reasons to believe that these well-known four are the tip of the iceberg. Rainer Reuter, working partly on the basis of neglected nineteenth-century research and of Francis and Sampley's *Pauline Parallels* (1984 [1st edn 1975]), has initiated a long-term project to set forth schematically the instances of literary interdependence among the epistles (*Synopsis of the New Testament Letters*, Reuter 1997). The number he regards as literarily dependent on other epistles is not four but fourteen: six which bear Paul's name (2 Thessalonians, Ephesians, Colossians, the three Pastorals), and all eight epistles which do not have Paul's name (Hebrews, James, 1 and 2 Peter, 1, 2 and 3 John, and Jude). In effect, this omits just seven epistles (Romans, 1 and 2 Corinthians, Galatians, 1 Thessalonians, Philemon and Philippians). Introducing this project, Reuter explains aspects of its background and rationale (1997: 23 [emphasis added]):

> At first glance, the idea of writing synopses for the Epistles...may seem an unusual if not completely unnecessary project because...scholars only carry on synoptic work on the Gospels themselves... Theology students...only practice 'synoptic comparison' with reference to Mk, Mt and Lk and—derived from the last two—Q.

---

6. See especially, on 2 Thessalonians' use of 1 Thessalonians, Rigaux 1956: 133-59; on Ephesians' affinities with Romans, 1 and 2 Corinthians, Galatians, Philippians, Philemon, 1 and 2 Thessalonians: G. Johnston 1962: 110-11; on leading aspects of Ephesians' affinity with Colossians: Brown 1997: 628. To some extent, Ephesians is like a synthesis of important elements of the Pauline literature. On 1 Peter's affinities with several epistles: Selwyn 1961: 365-466. For an inadequate explanation of the 'very striking ...parallels' between 1 Peter and Hebrews, see the quotation (from Von Soden) in Selwyn (p. 464): 'The authors were contemporaries and breathed the same spiritual atmosphere'. On Jude as dependent on 2 Peter, see Reicke 1964: 189. On Jude as preceding 2 Peter rather than following it, see Bauckham 1990: 144-49, especially 146. Raymond E. Brown is exceptional; in all four cases, he deflects literary dependence or plays it down (1997: 592, 629 nn. 23/24, 716 n. 30, 748).

Appendix 5. *The Triple Intertextuality of the Epistles*

> Obviously this does not exhaust the possibilities for carrying on synoptic work on the New Testament because the same phenomenon apparent in the Synoptic Gospels also occur in the... Epistles: verbatim correspondence of large portions of text and the same sequence of text segments. This applies in particular to the wide-ranging parallels between Eph and Col, II Thess and I Thess, II Peter and Jude, which can be explained as literary reception.
>
> However, the relationship between Col and the genuine Pauline Epistles can also be described in a similar way as a relationship of *literary dependence, even though the reception is clearly quite different* from Eph, II Thess and II Pet.
>
> A synoptic presentation of the relationship between these writings is long overdue.

Reuter's reference to Colossians is particularly significant: it indicates a mode of dependence different from that of the more obvious cases. Once the principle is accepted that modes of literary dependence are diverse, then the search for literary connections becomes more open, more challenging, and in need of more careful criteria.

This basic idea that literary dependence appears to be quite widespread among the epistles is not new. Summarizing nineteenth-century research, Reuter (1997: 24-25) lists several instances of epistolary 'concordances...of such significance that they were often explained...as a result of literary dependence'.

But the nineteenth-century insights were not developed:

> These observations seem to have been largely forgotten today, hardly gaining a mention in contemporary exegetical literature. Nevertheless, these parallels cannot be denied and require renewed investigation... This means that all the Epistles of the New Testament need to subjected to a careful comparison. (Reuter 1997: 25)

Reuter's project suffers a key limitation: in judging relationships between texts, it relies unduly on one criterion: verbatim correspondence. Thus, it risks falling into the same trap as many gospel synopses: by focusing on one model of literary dependence—the obvious kind found in Matthew–Mark or some rewritten Bible—it often excludes more complex instances of dependence (as in John's use of Mark).

Nonetheless, Reuter's reference to Colossians's use of other epistles implies the acceptance in principle of diverse modes of dependence. Thus, in the long term, the way is open towards a fully inclusive method of research—towards more complex criteria and more complex models of dependence.

b. *Beyond Fourteen*

What remains to be investigated is whether some of the seven most basic Pauline epistles (Romans, 1 and 2 Corinthians, Galatians, 1Thessalonians, Philippians, and Philemon), apart from depending on the Old Testament, depend also on one another.

There are some broad affinities between these letters; this is particularly clear in the Francis and Sampley *Pauline Parallels* (1984). Unlike Reuter, the parallels of Francis and Sampley concentrate on the most basic epistles: all those with Paul's name, except the three Pastorals. And these ten share basic elements: 'In his letters, Paul echoes the structure of the common letter, he employs rhetorical devices, and he often repeats themes and images. The *Pauline Parallels*...is the analog for the Pauline letters of a gospel parallels' (Francis and Sampley 1984: xi).

But apart from general, formal features, these epistles also share content. It is broadly accepted, for instance, that Romans was written after Galatians and, at least in a general way, develops and clarifies the earlier epistle. More specifically, Romans contains multiple echoes of Paul's earlier letters. Fitzmyer gives a list of the connections, and sees Romans as 'an eirenic discussion of many of the topics that Paul had written about earlier, often in a more polemical or apologetic tone' (Fitzmyer 1992b: 73). What remains to be investigated is whether the list of echoes is the tip of a larger literary relationship.

A further example of a connection worth investigating is the curious affinity between the climactic kerygma of 1 Corinthians (1 Cor. 15.1-11) and the foundational kerygma of Galatians (Gal. 1). Both texts speak of:
- Death for our sins; resurrection from the dead (1 Cor. 15.3b, 4, 12; Gal. 1.1, 4a).
- Making known the gospel (1 Cor. 15.1-3a; Gal. 1.11-12).
- Revelation to Paul, involving: appearance/revelation of Christ; previous persecution of the church; allusion to Paul's manner of birth; his exceeding zeal; and the decisive role of God's grace (1 Cor. 15.8-10; Gal. 1.13-16a).
- Further appearances/revelations involving Cephas, James, and others (1 Cor. 15.5-7; Gal. 1.16-22).
- Brief reference to Paul's preaching of the faith (1 Cor. 15.11; Gal. 1.23).

The two epistles are generally dated to about the same period, but it is not certain which was written first. Besides, is it possible that the affinity is due to oral tradition?

But close analysis of the affinity may yet show that a literary explanation is more plausible than an oral one, and uncertainly about priority can sometimes be overcome. It was possible, for instance, through decades of patient literary sifting, to reach considerable agreement about priority between Matthew and Mark. The possible relationship between 1 Corinthians and Galatians may be complex, but need not be abandoned. If Galatians, amid all its apparent spontaneity, could engage Jeremiah, then, provided 1 Corinthians was already written, it could also engage 1 Corinthians, reshaping the earlier epistle as it reshaped the prophet.

What is important here is not to decide the specific issue, but simply to open the general quest: epistolary interdependence, having been partly discovered in fourteen epistles, is not to be excluded from many of the remaining seven.

The mode of dependence may vary from one case to another, as it does in Colossians' use of diverse epistles, and as it does among the gospels (John's use of Mark is unlike that of Matthew and Luke). There is no question, then, of claiming that all modes of epistolary interdependence are essentially the same. What is needed is open-minded exploration.

The New Testament epistles, no matter how literary, no matter how indebted to Scripture and one another, are ultimately informed by other, historical factors. Such factors include not only the social setting but also the more incalculable role of the Spirit among the spreading community. In the final analysis, it is this latter Spirit-led factor, rather than the letter of the Scripture, which most shapes the epistles (Hays 1989: 108).

3. Conclusion

The twenty-one New Testament epistles, when viewed as a single collection, give the impression of a body of literature which not only frequently employs ancient rhetoric, whether Hellenistic or Jewish, but also employs one of the key features of such rhetoric, namely the deliberate reworking and absorbing of existing writings. Consequently, no matter how spontaneous or occasional/situational these letters often seem to be, they have another dimension. They are engaged not only with a Spirit-led audience belonging to the present, but also with a writing tradition which grows out of the past and strikes a delicate balance between past and present. They are contemporary and historical; but they are also radically literary, *scriptural*.

Appendix 6

The Use of Daniel in 1 Corinthians: An Exploration

Daniel influenced the gospels and 'served as one of several models for the author of Revelation' (Yarbro Collins 1993: 90). This appendix seeks to indicate the same for an epistle: Daniel served as one of several models for the author of 1 Corinthians. This comparison is exploratory and is based on the text that seems closest to the epistle—the Old Greek ('OG'), the first, free Greek translation, sometimes placed within the Septuagint. Daniel is strongest in 1 Corinthians 1–4 and 15–16. In outline (designating the Susanna story, for convenience, as ch. 13, and Bel and the Dragon as ch. 14):

Table 97. *Episodes of Contrast and Conflict: The Judgment of the World*
(Daniel 1–6, 13, 14; 1 Corinthians 1–4)

		Daniel	1 Corinthians
1.	The opening contrast	1.4-21	1.3-21
2.	Abusive supper and new regime	1.1-16; ch. 5	11.17-19
3.	The crisis of mystery and death	2.1-24	2.6-8, 10
4.	The crisis resolved by the spirit	chs. 4, 5, 13	2.10-16
5.	Statue, stone and testing fire	2.25-35; ch. 3	3.10-15
6.	Grandeur and kingship: God's share	2.36-45; ch. 4	4.6c-8
7.	Order in the community	2.46-49; chs. 6, 14	14.25, 37

Table 98. *The Prophetic Visions of Building and Triumph*
(Daniel 7–12; 1 Corinthians 14–15)

		Daniel	1 Corinthians
8.	Prophecy: the quest for interpretation	7.15…8.13; 9.20	14.2-4
9.	Building the sanctuary	8.11; 9.2, 17, 25; 11.31	14.4-5, 12b-18
10.	Coping with sin	ch. 9	15.3b
11.	The triumph of one and all	chs. 7, 10-12	15.15b-28
12.	The secret	12.5-11	15.35-37

1. *Daniel 1–6*

The first half of Daniel (chs. 1–6) deals with the judgment of the world. This theme, which to some extent pervades the whole book, is brought out through a series of contrast and conflicts. The contrast between the young Israelites and the others involves a judgment of the world. The book contains considerable repetition and intensification: ideas that are first contained in chs. 1–2 are expanded in chs. 3–6 (and in chs. 13–14). Correspondingly, the author of the epistle often seems to have often taken the various elements of chs. 1–2 in conjunction with the various ideas in chs. 3–6 (and in chs. 13–14).

a. *Section 1. Opening Contrast: Godly Gifted and Worldly Wise (Daniel 1.4, 9, 17-21; 1 Corinthians 1.3-5, 20-21)*
Daniel begins by describing how God gives the faithful Israelites far greater knowledge and understanding than the wise men of the Babylonian empire. Paul rejoices over the wisdom and knowledge of the Corinthians, and then contrasts the wisdom of God with the bankruptcy of the wise men of the world. Both refer to wisdom, writing, understanding/ knowledge, grace, and (Dan. 1.17, 20; 1 Cor. 1.5) to being competent 'in every word'.

b. *Section 2. The Abusive Supper and the Night of the New Regime (Daniel 1.1-16; Ch. 5; 1 Corinthians 11.17-22, 23, 25)*
Daniel's first chapter speaks of the vessels of the temple (1.2) and the difficulty of partaking at the king's table (1.5) or supper (*deipnon*, 1.8). Later, the king brings out the vessels —at a supper (5.1-2, Belshazzer's last supper, with the writing on the wall). Paul uses both these episodes as components in depicting the Corinthians' abusive supper. Like Daniel's first meal crisis, the Corinthian supper refers to division (Dan. 1.1-2; 1 Cor. 11.18), a process of choosing and testing (Dan. 1.3, 5-16; 1 Cor. 11.19), and a lordly supper (Dan. 1.5-8; 1 Cor. 11.20). Like the later meal crisis, the Corinthian supper is a scene of abuse rather than praise (Dan. 5.1–4.23, involving abuse of the vessels of the temple; 1 Cor. 11.17, 22, involving contempt for the churches of God). While Daniel then recounts that on that same night the king was killed and a new regime established (Dan. 5.30-31), Paul immediately tells of the night when Jesus was handed over and established a new covenant 'after the supper' (1 Cor. 11.23, 25).

c. *Section 3. The Crisis of Mystery and Death (Daniel 2.1-24; 1 Corinthians 2.6-8, 10)*
None of the wise men of the Babylonian world can discover the mystery of the king's dream; but Daniel blesses the Lord as he receives special wisdom, a revelation of the depths of God (Dan. 2.19-23). Paul proclaims essentially the same idea. In both writers the mystery is linked to glory; failure to discover the mystery is linked to a shameful death (Dan. 2.4-6, the king promises glorification if they know the mystery, but public death or impaling or hanging if they do not; 1 Cor. 2.8, if they had known they would not have crucified the Lord of glory). (On light and dark, Dan. 2.22, see 1 Cor. 4.5. Note use of *deloō*, 'to make clear' [Dan. 2.5; 1 Cor. 1.11], and *logos* [Dan. 2.11, 1 Cor. 1.18].)

d. *Section 4. The Crisis Resolved by the Spirit (Daniel 4.1-3; 5.7-14; Ch. 13; 1 Corinthians 2.10-16)*
On other occasions of Daniel's intervention, his powers of discernment and judgment are attributed to the spirit. Paul sums up these episodes: he speaks of contrasting spirits (1 Cor. 2.12a) as the spirit in Daniel contrasts with the efforts of the Babylonian sages (Dan. 4.1-6 in Hebrew, or 4.4-9 in OG; see 1 Cor. 2.12b); and he speaks of contrasting ability to judge (1 Cor. 2.14-16) partly echoing the story of Susanna (Dan. 13). (Note specific words or roots: *psychē*, *mōria*, *anakrinō*, *nous*, 'soul, foolish, judge, mind', 1 Cor. 2.16b; see Sus. 63.)

e. *Section 5. Statue and Stone: The Day of Testing Fire (Daniel 2.25-35; Ch. 3; 1 Corinthians 3.10-15)*
The king's dream shows that in the final days a composite statue will be crushed by a stone; and when the king later makes a statue (ch. 3), it is challenged successfully by the

three fire-proven young men. Paul in turn makes a contrast between the foundation-stone, Jesus Christ, and the composite material that may be added. On the day (of judgment) the man who builds in such composite material will be tested by fire. (Other elements in both texts: wisdom given by God; make clear; reveal [Dan. 3; see 1 Cor. 4.9b?]; Paul is combining with another source.)

f. *Section 6. Grandeur and Kingship: Giving Due Recognition to God (Daniel 2.36-45; Ch. 4; 1 Corinthians 4.6c-8)*
In the interpretation of the king's dream, he is described as receiving from God a grandeur and a kingship that shelters all creatures but that is eventually replaced by God's kingdom; and after the next interpretation (Dan. 4), the proud king is in fact deprived of his kingdom so that he might learn that all kingship is from God. Addressing the Corinthians as kings, Paul give similar reminders: 'What can you boast of that you have not received?' (On the fate of the boastful king—removal for correction and departure from the world—see 1 Cor. 5.2ac, 4, 5, 10b; on his writing an epistle, Dan. 4.37b [longer LXX text], see 1 Cor. 5.9-10.)

g. *Section 7. Order in the Community (Daniel 2.46-49; Ch. 6; 1 Corinthians 14.25, 37b)*
After Daniel has given full disclosure of the king's mystery-dream, things fall into proper place: the king falls in prostrate worship; God is recognized; the gifted Daniel and his friends receive high rank in the kingdom. Later (ch. 6), this sense of order is threatened but is eventually reinforced. (Account should also be taken of some aspects of ch. 3, a text that begins with a coming together to worship and that runs somewhat parallel to ch. 6.) In general, Paul seems to have used this orderly material when depicting the new community (1 Cor. 12–15). More specifically, there are references to gifts (Dan. 6.1-5; 1 Cor. 12.3-5), worshipping acknowledgment of God (Dan. 2.46-47; 6.17, 21, 27; 1 Cor. 14.25), and recognition of the written decree of the Lord (Dan. 3.12; 6.11, 13-14, 26; 1 Cor. 14.37b). (Should the statue theme—composite, with limbs, with people gathered round it [Dan. 2.31-33; 3.7]—be linked to the body them in 1 Cor. 12? Compare Dan. 3.16-17 and 1 Cor. 12.5, 21; Dan. 3.28, 93 and 1 Cor. 13.3.) The idolatry idea from the statue theme recurs in the story of Bel and the Dragon (sometimes counted as Dan. 14). Here the pervading element is eating, which is a key to the idea of the body of Christ (1 Cor. 19.16-17). (On the sounds for worship [Dan. 3.4-5], see 1 Cor. 14.7-11[?]).

2. *Chapters 7–12*

The second half of Daniel narrates four prophetic visions. Their predominant theme is triumph—especially in the first (ch. 7) and the last (chs. 10–12)—but there is considerable emphasis in visions two and three (chs. 8 and 9) on building the sanctuary and on coping with *sin*. The four narratives are rather repetitious but Paul fuses them into a neat summary: he begins on the topic of *prophecy* (1 Cor. 14), and then he speaks of building, sin, and triumph (1 Cor. 14–15).

a. *Section 8. Prophecy: The Quest for Interpretation (Daniel 7.15-16, 19-20; 8.13-19, 27; 9.20-23; 1 Corinthians 14.2-4)*
Daniel now assumes the role of prophet, but his task is not simply to talk; there are visions to be interpreted; heavenly discourse (e.g. Dan. 8.13-14) must be translated for understanding by human minds. Paul tells of the mysterious discourse of the man speaking in tongues, 'speaking not to humans but to God...speaking mysteries' (1 Cor. 14.2). Paul calls for interpretation (14.5) so that the human mind may grasp the message (14.14-19).

This is precisely the advantage of prophecy—it speaks to the human mind and situation (14.3; see Dan. 9.1-2). (Within 1 Cor. 14 the influence of Daniel may be limited perhaps to 14.2-6, 13-19.)

b. *Section 9. Building the Sanctuary (Daniel 8.11-14; 9.2-3, 17-18, 25-27; 11.31; 1 Corinthians 14.4-5, 12b-18)*
Just as Daniel is concerned for the ruined sanctuary and sees the prophecy of Jeremiah as directed towards its rebuilding (Dan. 9.2), so Paul is concerned with the building of the church, and sees prophecy as accomplishing the task. These references by Daniel to prayer, the sanctuary or holy place, and sacrifice may perhaps have contributed to what Paul says concerning prayer, the place, and the difficulty of saying amen to the *eucharistia* or thanksgiving (1 Cor. 14.14-18).

c. *Section 10. Coping with Sin (Daniel 9; 1 Corinthians 15.3b)*
Daniel 9 has two sections. In the first (9.1-19), a long expression of contrition, Daniel peruses 'in the books' (*en tais bibliois*) or writings of Jeremiah and then prays in the name of the people and confesses 'our sins' (9.13, 16, OG). In the second (9.20-27), the angel Gabriel explains the scriptural text to show that this pervasion of sin will come to an end (9.24) when a *christed* leader comes and when a *christ* is cut off or destroyed (*christos*, 'anointed', 9.25-26). Paul expresses the essence of these elements in a single sentence: 'Christ died for our sins according to the scriptures'. Paul's indebtedness to Daniel at this point does not rule out other influences. Generally, Daniel supplies one component, not an entire formulation.

Just after this, Paul seems to have reached forward to the text that will be his next area of study, the fourth vision, the vision of triumph—the resurrection (Dan. 12.1, OG). Here, too, there is an angel, the archangel Michael, who stands over the people on the day of days: 'In that day all the people will be lifted up—whoever is found inscribed in the book (*en tō bibliō*)'. Apparently, this idea of resurrection for those 'in the book' contributed to Paul speaking of resurrection 'according to the scriptures' (1 Cor. 15.4). Thus, Paul's text, concerning Christ dying for sin and concerning resurrection (1 Cor. 15.3-4) has fused the climactic points of the third and fourth visions (Dan. 9.24-26; 12.1) and has expressed that fusion in memorable parallel phrases.

d. *Section 11. The Triumph of One and All (Daniel 7, 10–12; 1 Corinthians 15.15b-28)*
The two major visions of triumph, the first and fourth, are rather similar and complementary. Paul takes them together. He has already made use of a climactic point of the fourth vision (1 Cor. 12.1), and now he proceeds to rewrite that vision more systematically.

First, there is the process of witnessing to the apparition of the glorious man—Daniel's witness to the gleaming figure of white and light (Dan. 10.1-19), and Paul's witness to the glorious Christ (1 Cor. 15.15b-19). Though both writers bear witness to a central glorious figure (Dan. 10.1-6; 1 Cor. 15.15b), they also speak of how this figure affects themselves, lonely miserable men (Dan. 10.9, 11, 19; 1 Cor. 15.19) who need purification (Dan. 10.16; 1 Cor. 15.17) and who themselves go through a process of death and resurrection (Dan. 10.7-10, 17-19; 1 Cor. 15.16, 18).

Then Paul goes on to the later part of the vision, the resurrection of those who sleep, the transition from death to life (Dan. 12.2; 1 Cor. 15.20-22; cf. Dan. 12.1; 1 Cor. 15.4). But instead of trying to describe the risen (as Daniel does, 12.3, and as he himself does later, 1 Cor. 15.41-42), Paul for the moment (15.22-28) concentrates on the two ideas of death and life—death from the man Adam, life from the man Christ (see Sir. 25.24; 40.1). By thus emphasizing man/humanity, he connects with the first vision concerning the Son of Humanity (*ben adam*, Dan. 7.13-14).

Much of this vision (Dan. 7) is summed up by Paul in a few verses (cf. Dan. 7.9-27; 1 Cor. 15.23-28). First, there is the coming of the central figure (the Son of Humanity; Christ) who is linked, if not identified, with a larger group. His is the kingdom—a kingdom of all power and all time, right to the end, ultimately the kingdom of God (Dan. 7.13b-18; 1 Cor. 15.23-24; concerning the End, cf. Dan. 12.6-8). Second, there is an intermediate period of striving against enemies until all have been subjected to him (Dan. 7.22-27; 1 Cor. 15.25-27a). And third, there is the all-pervading sovereignty of the enthroned God who presides over the subjugation of all (Dan. 7.9-12, note the killing of the beast; 1 Cor. 15.27-28). Thus, the picture of divine sovereignty that was used in Daniel to *introduce* the visions is used by Paul to *conclude* 'that God may be all in all'.

As for Daniel's prolonged and complex account of beasts and fights (Dan. 7.1-8, 19-20; 8.1-10, 21-22; 10.20–11.45), Paul seems to have disposed of them all by recounting intriguingly that he fought with beasts at Ephesus (1 Cor. 15.32). Thus, he deflates the apocalyptic imagery and atmosphere of Daniel.

Reviewing the four prophetic visions, it emerges that Daniel has been brought down to earth. Abstracting from the complex heavenly images of Daniel, Paul has called for prophecy that communicates. Leaving aside the complex relationship between the different figures of Dan, Paul has taken one figure, the Christ, and grafted the other onto it. Omitting the rather cumbersome calculations of times and weeks and thousands of days, Paul refers to an intermediate period and to the end. Cutting through the heaviness of the contrition for sin, Paul simply and boldly proclaims that Christ died for our sins. As for the complex relationship between the one and the many in Daniel (the Son of Humanity is the saints), Paul expresses it through the idea that Christ is the first fruits of all humans (1 Cor. 15.23).

e. *Section 12. The Secret (Daniel 12.5-11; 1 Corinthians 15.35-37)*
Daniel ends in mystery (12.5-7). The answers to the basic questions of when (12.6) and how (12.8) are sealed and secret, unsolved parables. Apparently it is partly on the basis of this mysterious conclusion that Paul (fusing Sirach, especially Sir. 39.12–ch. 43, and other sources) writes the mysterious passage on the manner of the resurrection (15.35-58).

Finally, there is a blessing in peace. Daniel receives a parting word of blessed peace (12.12-13). Paul appears to have fused this picture of blessedness (*makarios*, 'blessed/fortunate') and peace with his portrait of the house of Stephanas (1 Cor. 16.15-18a). Stephanas's house is the first-fruits of Achaia, linked to the saints. Stephanas generally means 'crowned'; his associates are *fortunatus* and Achaicus. (Does this text—moving from *achaia* and 'the saints' to *achaicus*—deliberately interweave the one and the many, the individual and the collectivity?)

3. *Conclusion*

Whatever the details, the overall pattern indicates that, as in the case of the book of Revelation, 1 Corinthians used Daniel as one of several models. The author has distilled the narratives, prophecies and revelations of a profoundly Jewish work and has used that distillation as an important component of a letter that speaks to a wider world.

Appendix 7

The Use of Tobit in 1 Corinthians

Like Daniel, the book of Tobit provided one of several models for 1 Corinthians. The text of Tobit exists in slightly diverse editions or versions and it is difficult to be certain which is closest to the original. Overall, the evidence favors the Greek version found in a Sinai monastery about 1850, now designated 'S', and this also is the version that seems closest to 1 Corinthians. The S text omits two passages (Tob. 4.7-18; 13.3-10), but it alone contains many of the references given here. Tobit is indebted to Deuteronomy (Moore 1996: 20) so that, in the epistle, it is sometimes difficult to distinguish between the influence of Tobit and Deuteronomy.

While Daniel is a rather divisive book, cleaving the world with the ready sword of judgment, Tobit is more circumspect. Evil is indeed present in Tobit but the power of a good providence is always at work. The very names, Tobit and Tobias, suggest what is *tōb* ('good'), the word that highlights the goodness of creation (Gen. 1).

Tobit (1.2) begins with *the* classic problem—the suffering of the just man. The text gives two hints of a solution: despite the approach of death, the goods of which Tobit is deprived are being kept for him (1.19-22); and even when darkness closes in, there is reward (2.10-14a).

Paul links this solution to resurrection, so he holds it over until then (1 Cor. 15–16). In fact, almost the entire opening section dealing with Tobit (chs. 1–4) is held over to the end. Yet from these early chapters he makes use of two key features—the cross and the hidden plan.

The following table give the main links in outline.

Table 99. *The Story of Tobit*

		Tobit	1 Corinthians
1	The cross and the plan	2.3, 6, 14; 3.16-17	1.8-21; 2.9
2.	Journey and body/marriage	4.19-21; chs. 5–10	4.15-17; chs. 5–7
3.	The daily death	4.1-18	15.30-32
4.	Death to life: a new creation	11–12	15.35-58
5.	Generous journeying	1–3	16.1-12
6.	The universal house	13–14	16.13-24

1. Section 1. Tobit 1–3 (Initial Aspects)

a. *The Word of Death/the Cross (Tobit 2.6, 14c; 1 Corinthians 1.18-21)*
When told of a brutal death (Tob. 2.3; for hanging, see 3.10), Tobit remembers the prophetic word of sorrow, and later endures the ridicule of his wife: 'Where…? Where…?' ('Where are your alms? Where is your justice/righteousness/integrity [*dikaiosynē*]?'). This prevalence of death and sorrow, this uselessness of justice, is a challenge to all that Israel believes; it is a triumph for the wisdom of the world. Paul meets the problem squarely and

turns it around: the word of death is at the center of the message, and it is the wisdom of the world that is useless. And he quotes the prophetic word on the bankruptcy of wisdom and adds the taunt of 'Where...? Where...?' ('Where are your wise now? Where are your scribes?', 1 Cor. 1.20). Two prophetic quotes—from Amos (Tob. 1.6) and Isaiah (1 Cor. 1.19)—announce ominous endings (respectively of Israel's feasting, and of worldly wisdom). (Other details: knowledge, and faith, Tob. 2.14ac; 1 Cor. 1.21.)

b. *What God has Prepared: The Hidden Plan of Liberation (Tobit 3.16-17; 1 Corinthians 2.9)*
In Tobit and 1 Corinthians, the prevalence of death is interpreted in the light of the hidden plan of the God of glory.

2. Section 2. Tobit 5–10

The central section of Tobit—roughly chs. 5–10, dealing with the journey and marriage of young Tobias—fits largely into the center of 1 Corinthians (roughly chs. 5–7).

a. *The Fatherly Sending of Tobias and Timothy (Tobit 4.19–5.9; 1 Corinthians 4.15-17)*
While Tobit sends his only son Tobias accompanied by the faithful angel of God (Tob. 4.21; 5.4, 9), Paul combines son and angel to form the picture of Timothy, a beloved child, faithful to the Lord (1 Cor. 4.17). The child will remember the father (Tob. 4.19); the angel will show the child the ways (Tob. 5.10 S); Timothy will remind the Corinthians, Paul's children, of his ways (1 Cor. 5.15, 17). Other details of comparison: the name *timo-theos* recalls Tobit's exhortation to his son (Tob. 4.21; see also 1 Cor. 16.10); father–son imitation or obedience occurs in both texts (Tob. 5.1; 1 Cor. 4.15-16; see also the later sending of Tobias, 10.11-13).

b. *Recognitions, Greetings, Kisses, and Hand-Signatures (Tobit 5.3; 5.9–6.1; 7.1-9; Ch. 9; 1 Corinthians 16.18b-21)*
The atmosphere is fraternal and emotional, abounding in warm greetings and welcomes. Paul has condensed most of this into his concluding lines. In particular, the picture of the couple, Aquila and Prisca, appears to be modeled partly on Raguel and Edna (Tob. 7.1-9; 1 Cor. 16.19). Apart from the general atmosphere of fraternalism, greetings, and kisses, both couples extend much greetings, greetings that involve their houses (Tob. 7.1 S; 1 Cor. 16.19). In the house of Aquila and Prisca there is the church; and in the house of Raguel and Edna there is Sarah, the bride-to-be. Sarah and the church are associated with the greetings of the couples.

c. *Bodily Union: Abuses and Uses (Tobit 6; 1 Corinthians 6.12b-17)*
In both writers, the pervading idea is union. Again and again, the angel tells Tobias to take Sarah in a God-willed union of man and wife; and Paul speaks of the union effected by the body. But the crucial issue is the quality of the union. First, there must be control. Tobias is shown as mastering the great fish, a victory that provides the key to successful lovemaking (Tob. 6.2-8, 16-17). It is by the spreading incense of heart and liver—symbols of sacrifice and deep emotion?—that he will drive away the demon or evil spirit that invades the marriage-bed. And Paul also begins by saying he will not lose mastery of himself (1 Cor. 6.12b).

Second, there must be heart (heart, soul, or spirit). Both writers give contrasting examples of union without heart or spirit. Paul contrasts cleaving bodily to a prostitute with cleaving in spirit to the Lord (1 Cor. 6.16-17). Tobit contrasts the diverse ways of cleaving to Sarah: the seven dead husbands had simply attempted to enter her physically (Tob. 6.14

S); Tobias, however, sought the marriage in the context of God's people as a whole and his 'heart cleaved to her' before there was any physical contact (Tob. 6.19). (Other shared elements: food, Tob. 6.5-6; cf. 7.12; 1 Cor. 6.13; the book of Moses, Tob. 6.13; 1 Cor. 6.16.)

d. *Marriage (Tobit 7.9–8.21; 1 Corinthians 7.1-3)*

Tobit seems to account for some of the epistle's ideas on marriage: the power to give in marriage (Tob. 7.10; 1 Cor. 7.3; unlike Tobit, Paul shows it as a mutual process by the couple); coming together after prayers, despite Satan (Tob. 7.15–8.4; 8.9; 1 Cor. 7.5); the saving process in marriage (Tob. 6.18; 8.17; 1 Cor. 7.16, mutual in Paul); a marriage that is to last (Tob. 7.12; 1 Cor. 7.10). Tobit says the union is decreed by heaven according to the law of Moses, and he asks the Lord of heaven to bless it—which may be one reason why Paul says that the command not to separate comes from the Lord.

In different ways, the question of marriage involves writing (Tob. 7.14; 1 Cor. 7.1). But while Tobit (8.6) quotes Genesis, 'it is not good for the man to be alone', Paul says 'it is good for a man not to touch a woman' (1 Cor. 7.1), and to the unmarried and widows Paul advises 'it is good for them to remain as I am' (1 Cor. 7.8; contrast Tob. 7.7 and 1 Cor. 7.2). By appealing to Genesis, Tobit may have tightened up on the divorce procedure allowed by Deut. 24.1-3, but Paul seems to have decided to go beyond Genesis.

e. *Reckoning the Time (Tobit 9.1–10.7; 1 Corinthians 7.29-31)*

Time is running out, says Paul, and for the interim period gives advice to those with wives, those who cry, those who rejoice, those who buy. This picture partly parallels the Tobit story where the time of Tobias's return is preceded by wedding celebrations, business transactions (Tob. 9), and—when the time comes overdue—by tearful disillusion (10.1-7). (Tob. 10 contains a dramatic contrast between the repeated command of silence [10.6-7], and the triple request of the son to be sent forth by his father [10.8-9]. Should this be associated with the command of silence [1 Cor. 14.28.30, 34], which precedes the proclamation of death and resurrection [1 Cor. 15.1-3]?)

3. *Sections 3 and 4. Tobit 4 and 11–12*

The next section (Tob. 11–12) deals in effect with the re-creation of blind Tobit. Paul uses it to describe the resurrection of the body, the new creation of humanity (1 Cor. 15.35-38).

a. *The Death*

Old Tobit had been left as dead. His farewell to his son had been a death testament (Tob. 4.1-19a [S omits 4.7-18]), and it is summed up by Paul in a way that stresses the theme of death (1 Cor. 15.30, 31a, 34ab) (15.29, see Tob. 2.5, 9[?]).

b. *From Death to Life—A New Creation (Tobit 11; cf. 1 Corinthians 15.35-51)*

For the dead Tobit, the return of his son brings sight and new life through a process of handiwork and breathing that is reminiscent of the creation of humanity (Tob. 11.8, 11 S; Gen. 2.7). And the epistle, describing how the dead will rise (1 Cor. 15.35; see Tob. 11.2), speaks of a new creation, with Christ as a new life-giving Adam (1 Cor. 15.45-46). And just as Paul had earlier combined the figures of Tobias and the heavenly man Raphael to depict Timothy, so now he combines their roles to depict Christ, the new life-giving Adam, the man from heaven (Tob. 11.6; 12.1, 20; 1 Cor. 15.45-47). The revival of Tobit and the raising of the dead involves a dramatic change from weakness to strength (Tob. 11.16; 1 Cor. 15.43).

But as well as the revival of Tobit, there is the happy home-coming of the rescued Sarah, and joy for all (Tob. 11.17-19)—features that may help explain why Paul says 'we shall not all fall asleep; but we shall all be changed' (1 Cor. 15.51b), and there will be a different kind of body (Tob. 12.19-22; 1 Cor. 15.47-50). Obviously, the author of the epistle is also using other sources. Sirach, for instance, discusses creation (Sir. 39.12); Daniel 12, the raising of the dead. Tobit has both ideas. And the epistle has fused all.

c. *The Telling of the Mystery (Tobit 16.6-14; cf. 1 Corinthians 15.51-58)*
The dramatic return (Tob 11.6, 'Behold your son and the man') and the disclosure of the mystery (Tob. 12.6-8) are paralleled by Paul's 'Behold I tell you a mystery' (1 Cor. 15.51). Both texts speak also of sin (Tob. 12.10; 1 Cor. 15.56), thanksgiving (Tob. 11.14, 17; 12.6; 1 Cor. 15.57), rescue from death (Tob. 12.9; 1 Cor. 15.52); and the value of generous effort (Tob. 12.12-14; 1 Cor. 15.58).

d. *I Am...Sent...Not I, But the Grace of God...By the Will of God (Tobit 12.15-18; 1 Corinthians 1.1; 15.9-10)*
Paul's description of his mission is almost an exact reproduction of Raphael's.

4. *Section 5. Tobit 1–3 (Further Aspects)*

It is necessary now to return to the story of life, death, and liberation (Tob. 1–3). These early chapters had pictured the idea of a generous life that recovers its treasure (ch. 1), of a death that receives reward (ch. 2), and of a call for peace and liberation (ch. 3; peace, or freedom from scorn and fear, 3.1-5, 7-11; liberation or deliverance, 3.6, 12-15). Just as these themes had been depicted through the account of the generosity and journeying of Tobit, so Paul rewrites them by speaking of his own generosity and journeying (1 Cor. 16.1-12). (The account of Paul's journeying blends a subtle re-presenting of Tobit's life-and-death theme with complementary texts from Deuteronomy. Tobit itself echoes older scriptures.) This veiled drama of Paul's journeying, this miniature Pilgrim's Progress, may be summed up under the following headings: the generosity; the testing and treasuring; the crossing; and the journey

a. *The Generosity: From Gal...to Jerusalem (Tobit 1.3-14; 1 Corinthians 16.1-4)*
Tobit's care for the poor is paralleled by Paul's care for the saints. The content of the Tobit passage (paying tithes to the central sanctuary) is almost identical to part of Deuteronomy—which Paul has already been working on—and so he fuses the two into a single account. Hence, it may not be possible (or advisable?) to distinguish the two sources. But one difference may be noticed here. Deuteronomy (14.22) mentions no names; it simply says to bring one's offering from wherever one is to the place God chooses (14.22). But Tobit says that when he was in Galilee (*Galilaia*), he had brought offerings to Jerusalem (Tob. 1.5-6); and Paul says he has given instruction in Galatia (*Galatia*) about the collection that is to be brought to Jerusalem.

b. *A Time of Testing and Treasuring (Tobit 1.9-22; 1 Corinthians 16.1-4)*
Tobit, despite his generosity, loses everything. But the property, which had been put in the treasury of the kingdom, is returned to him; he is found worthy to return to Nineveh. In calling for generosity towards the saints, Paul colors his appeal with overtones of Tobit's experiences: each contributor is laying up treasure to himself (1 Cor. 16.2); those who are approved will journey—to Jerusalem (1 Cor. 16.3). (Direct literary dependence should probably be limited to Tob. 1.20-22 and 1 Cor. 16.1-4; in Greek, see the Tobit background to Paul's use of *log- di-etaxa, axion.*)

c. *The Crossing (Tobit 1.14; 1 Corinthians 16.5)*
Tobit journeyed to Media to the death (of the king); Paul will be crossing to Macedonia.

d. *The Journey to the Unknown—From Darkness to Light (Tobit 2; 1 Corinthians 16.6-8)*
Tobit 2 is a transition from a meal and a process of remaining (2.1-2) that is interrupted by various forms of death and darkness (2.3-10) to the reward of another meal (2.11-14a). In an extremely subtle piece of rewriting, Paul speaks of the transition from remaining or going through the winter (i.e. darkness) to the feast of Pentecost (1 Cor. 16.7-8). In different picturesque forms, both have presented the crisis of the crossing of death. For both of them, it is a journey to the unknown: after the sun sinks there is burial, and a journeying to blindness (Tob. 2.7, 10); after winter they will send Paul wherever he journeys (1 Cor. 16.6). By their use of dates (7 March, Tob. 2.12; Pentecost, 1 Cor. 16.8), both show a transition from darkness to light. Both refer to Pentecost and the time (Tob. 2.1, 11; 1 Cor. 16.7-8). (Tobit 2.2-3 provides complex background for Paul's use of *pros, tykon, idein*; for *ou, epitrepsē*; see also Tob. 2.8, 10. There is no space for extended analysis in the present study.)
(On 1 Cor. 16.9, see Tob. 3.11[?].)

e. *The Call for Peace and Liberation (Tobit 3; 1 Corinthians 16.10-12)*
The prayers of Tobit and Sarah are a call for peace and liberation. Their appeal for an escape from insult and shame (Tob. 2.1-5, 7-11) is reflected in Paul's plea that Timothy not be despised; let him be 'without fear', sent in peace (1 Cor. 16.10-11). Their call for liberation (*apoluō*) is reflected in the pending arrival of Apollos: 'He will come when the time is right' (1 Cor. 16.12).

5. *Section 6. Tobit 13–14*

The final section of Tobit (chs. 13–14) deals largely with the universal house—the house (temple/tent) for all the nations. The opening of Tobit's hymn, for instance (13.1-7, 11-12, S) gives a shining picture of unity and sharing. (See 1 Cor. 12[?] and Deuteronomy[?]).

a. *The Closing Combination*
The closing of Tobit's hymn apparently influenced the closing of Paul's epistle (Tob. 13.14-18; 1 Cor. 16.22-24). Each conclusion is a mixture—a blending of cursing and blessing (Tob. 13.14-16; 1 Cor. 16.22a, 23) and hope (Tob. 13.17-18; 1 Cor. 16.22b).

b. *The Fullness…of the Earth and the Union of the Houses (Tobit 14.4b-15; 1 Corinthians 16.15-20)*
Tobit looks to a time of fullness (*plēroō*, 14.5) when all the nations join with Israel to build the house of the Lord (14.4b-7), and when young Tobias went to live with Raguel his father-in-law 'he took possession of the house of Raguel and Tobit his father' (14.12-14). Paul depicts a fraternal union of Asia and Achaia and of the houses (Stephen's, Aquila's) in these diverse parts. The coming of Stephanas means a filling up of what the Corinthians lack (*plēroo*, 1 Cor. 16.17b). (Tobit speaks of Ahikar and Cyaxares, *Achikaros* and *Achiacharos*, 14.10-11, 15; Paul refers to *Achaias* and *Achaikos*, 16.15, 17.) Their actions lead Tobias and Paul to rejoice (Tob. 14.15; 1 Cor. 16.17) (Tob. 14.9, see 1 Cor. 16.15c, 16).

6. *Conclusion*

Details are often obscure or debatable, but the overall impression—taking Tobit as a whole—is that it has indeed provided a significant component for 1 Corinthians.

Appendix 8

Epistolary Interdependence: Proposal for Research—
The Case of 1 Thessalonians

None of the epistles carry dates, and so the order in which the epistles were written is usually decided on the basis of reconstructed history—by calculating, for instance, often with the help of Acts, what occasions led to the composition of 1 Thessalonians and 1 Corinthians (generally dated respectively to 51, and somewhere between 52 and 57). Such historical reconstructions, however, are hazardous, particularly since the degree of history in Acts is uncertain.

The proposal here is that the search for the order of the epistles be based not on reconstructed history but on literary comparison. This was done in gospel research. The relative order of Mark and Matthew was decided for most people not by reconstructing histories for the two gospels, but by prolonged comparison of the gospels' contents.

In the case of 1 Thessalonians and 1 Corinthians, for instance, one may ask whether, from a literary viewpoint, 1 Corinthians was first and was used by 1 Thessalonians. Such a hypothesis could be summarized as follows:

To a large extent, 1 Thessalonians is a free reshaping of 1 Corinthians. Much of the Corinthian drama, the human window-dressing, has been left aside, but most of the ideas and much of the language have been summarized and synthesized.

The opening chapter seems to peel off a layer of ideas that runs through 1 Corinthians: greetings of grace and peace (1 Thess. 1.2a; 1 Cor. 1.1-4a); giving thanks and making memory, that is, *eucharistein* and remembrance (1 Thess. 1.2-3; 1 Cor. 1.4; 11.24-26?); chosen by God—to power spirit and conviction, and to the imitation of the resilient Paul (1 Thess. 1.4-6; 1 Cor. 1.24-28; 2.4-6; 4.15, 20; 11.1); being a type for many others (1 Thess. 1.7-8; 1 Cor. 10.6, 11; for emergence of Macedonia and Achaia, see 1 Cor. 16.5, 15); turning from idols to the true God (1 Thess. 1.9; 1 Cor. 10.14, 20; 12.2); awaiting the risen deliverer from heaven (1 Thess. 1.10; 1 Cor. 7.20, 24, 29-31; 15.20, 28-30, 47-49?); knowing…our labor…is not in vain (1 Thess. 2.1; 3.5; 1 Cor. 15.10, 58).

The second chapter of 1 Thessalonians begins with a description of the apostles' zeal and suffering and care (2.1-12), a description that evokes much of what 1 Corinthians had said about Paul's preaching and apostleship (1 Cor. 2.6-7; chs. 3–4). Yet at this point 1 Thessalonians seems to use another source, the book of Wisdom, a move prompted perhaps by the emphasis on wisdom in 1 Corinthians (2.7-8). The picture of the apostles at work (1 Thess. 2.1-6) corresponds to the description of how wisdom operates (Wis. 1.1-6). Similar elements occur in both: making an entrance (Wis. 1.4a; 1 Thess. 2.1); chastisement or suffering (Wis. 1.4b, 5a; 1 Thess. 2.2); the exclusion of guile, error, and wrong-doing (Wis. 1.5; 1 Thess. 2.3); the uplifting character of the message; it is friendly, congenial… like a paraclete (Wis. 1.6a; 1 Thess. 2.3, *paraklesis*; cf. Acts 15.31); ideas of testing, trusting, speaking truly, quality of the heart (Wis. 1.1-3; 1 Thess. 2.4); God as witness (Wis. 1.6c; 1 Thess. 2.5); exclusion of the evils of mind and tongue (Wis. 1.6; 1 Thess. 2.5-6). (Compare Wis. 1.7-15 and 1 Thess. 1.8-10.)

The longer epistle (1 Corinthians) stresses the need to accept the true tradition that leads to faith (1 Cor. 11.23-24; 15.1-3, 11)—but despite its interest in the Jews it distinguished between such tradition and the practice of the Jewish race in general, 'Israel according to the flesh' (1 Cor. 11.23-24; 10.16-18). Thessalonians has a similar emphasis on tradition (2.13)—but it distinguishes harshly between the tradition of the Judean churches and the Jewish race (1 Thess. 2.14-16; see 1 Cor. 1.32–11.1; the objects of salvation, the Jews [1 Cor. 10.32-33], have become the obstacles to salvation [1 Thess. 2.16]). (Compare 1 Thess. 2.17-20; 1 Cor. 5.2-3, 5, 6a; 9.2, 15-16, 25; 3.13.)

1 Thessalonians 3 describes the mission of Timothy in a way that reflects and develops the Corinthian description of Timothy and others (1 Thess. 3.2, 6-8; 1 Cor. 4.18-21; 16.1-7).

The beginning of the fourth chapter (1 Thess. 4.1-8) sums up much of the Corinthian moral teaching on bodyhood and brotherhood (1 Cor. 5-7): the importance of conduct and of pleasing God (1 Thess. 4.1-2; 1 Cor. 7.17, 32-34; on tradition, see 1 Cor. 11.2-3, 23); God wants sanctification not immorality (1 Thess. 4.3; 1 Cor. 5.7-8; 7.14; cf. 5.1; 6.13, 18; 7.2); the proper approach to one's body or wife ('vessel', 1 Thess. 4.5 can mean body or wife; 1 Cor. 6.13–7.16); 'not in the passion of lust' (1 Thess. 4.5; 1 Cor. 5.10-13; 6.9-20); brotherhood and judgment (1 Thess. 4.6; 1 Cor. 6.1-8); called not to uncleanness but to holiness (1 Thess. 4.7; 1 Cor. 7.14); the indwelling spirit (1 Thess. 4.8; 1 Cor. 6.19-20). Developing the idea of brotherhood, 1 Thessalonians then makes use of some later Corinthian ideas of unity, gifts, and love (1 Thess. 4.9; 1 Cor. 12–13). (For 1 Thess. 4.10-12 see, perhaps, 1 Cor. 14; 4.12a.)

In the section looking forward to meeting the Lord (1 Thess. 4.13–5.1), many ideas resemble those found in 1 Corinthians (especially ch. 15): the Day of the Lord (1 Cor. 1.8; 3.13; 5.5); the coming of Christ (15.23); resurrection of the dead (15.20-22); and change in the twinkling of an eye (1 Cor. 15.5-57). Yet it is not immediately clear in 1 Corinthians how these elements are related to each another. The shorter epistle brings the loose ends together: the coming of the Day is the time of resurrection and of our being swept up to a new life (1 Thess. 4.13–5.2). Further, 1 Thessalonians discusses the place and time of this rendezvous with the Lord. The place is mid-air: 'the Lord will come down from heaven… and we will be swept up into the clouds to meet the Lord in the air' (1 Thess. 4.16-17). The time is more vague: 'like a thief in the night…suddenly' (1 Thess. 5.2-3).

Here too, in describing the coming, there is apparent use of the book of Wisdom—in particular, Wisdom's description of the final judgment and of the night of the exodus (Wis. 4.7–5.23; ch. 18). Both writers speak of assurance about death (Wis. 4.7; 1 Thess. 4.13); those who grieve without hope (Wis. 4.14–5.14; 1 Thess. 4.13); death-and-life (Wis. 4.10-14; 1 Thess. 4.14); spiritual armor (Wis. 5.17-22; 1 Thess. 5.8); being with the Lord forever (Wis. 5.15-16; 1 Thess. 4.17); the Lord or Word coming down from heaven (Wis. 18.15; 1 Thess. 4.16); a surprise coming in the quiet of the night (Wis. 18.14; 1 Thess. 5.30); light and darkness (Wis. 18.1-4; 1 Thess. 5.4-5). Some of 1 Thessalonians' other elements apparently come from Daniel: the archangel (Dan. 10.13; 12.1; 1 Thess. 4.16); clouds (Dan. 7.13, 18; 1 Thess. 4.17); times and seasons (Dan. 2.21; 7.12; 1 Thess. 5.1). The meeting with the Lord in the air (1 Thess. 4.17) seems to fuse aspects of the Word descending (Wis. 18.15) with the saints being brought on the clouds (Dan. 7.13, 18).

The final exhortations to the Thessalonian community (5.12-25) seem to be a summary of the extended Corinthian picture of the Christian community (1 Cor. 12–14). In particular, several snappy injunctions (1 Thess. 5.14d, 15-16, 23-24) apparently correspond to 1 Corinthians 13. Both epistles end with greetings, grace and holy kisses (1 Thess. 5.26-28; 1 Cor. 16.20, 23).

Such is the hypothesis. It is not proposed lightly, but, as in the case of Matthew using Mark, it needs repeated verification. If it is verified—or if some equally difficult case of epistolary interdependence is verified—then the literary development of the epistles should become easier to trace.

Bibliography

Achtemeier, P.
    1985   *Romans* (Louisville, KY: John Knox Press).
Adkins, A.W.H.
    1960   *Merit and Responsibility: A Study in Greek Values* (Oxford: Clarendon Press).
Aletti, J.-N.
    1996   'Paul et la Rhetorique', in Schlosser (ed.) 1996: 27-50.
Alexander, L.C.A.
    1992   'Schools, Hellenistic', in *ABD*, V: 1005-11.
    1993   'Acts and the Ancient Intellectual Biography', in *Acts' Setting*: I, 31-63.
    1996   'The Preface to Acts and the Historians', in Witherington (ed.) 1996: 73-103.
    1998   'Ancient Book Production and the Circulation of the Gospels', in Bauckham (ed.) 1998: 71-105.
Allison, D.C., Jr
    1993   *The New Moses: A Matthean Typology* (Edinburgh: T. & T. Clark).
    2000   *The Intertextual Jesus: Scripture in Q* (Harrisburg, PA: Trinity Press International).
Alonso-Schökel, L.
    1961   'Erzahlkunst im Buch der Richter', *Bib* 42: 143-72.
    1985   'Of Methods and Models', in J.A. Emerton (ed.), *Congress Volume, Salamanca 1983* (VTSup, 36; Leiden: E.J. Brill): 3-13.
Alter, R.
    1981   *The Art of Biblical Narrative* (New York: Basic Books).
    1985   *The Art of Biblical Poetry* (New York: Basic Books).
Anderson, W.S.
    1972   *Ovid's Metamorphoses: Books 6-10* (Norman, OK: University of Oklahoma).
Atkins, J.W.H.
    1934   *Literary Criticism In Antiquity* (2 vols.; Cambridge: Cambridge University Press).
Auerbach, E.
    1953   *Mimesis* (Princeton, NJ: Princeton University Press).
Aune, D.E. (ed.)
    1988   *Greco-Roman Literature and the New Testament: Selected Forms and Genres* (SBL, 21; Atlanta, GA: Scholars Press).
Arnold, B.T.
    1996   'Luke's Characterizing Use of the Old Testament in the Book of Acts', in Witherington (ed.) 1996: 300-23.
Audet, J.-P.
    1956   'L'Annonce A Marie', *RB* 63: 346-74.
Bacon, B.W.
    1918   *The Fourth Gospel in Research and Debate* (New Haven: Yale University Press).
    1930   *Studies in Matthew* (New York: Holt & Co.).
Badian, E.
    1966   'The Early Historians', in T.A. Dorey (ed.), *Latin Historians* (New York: Basic Books): 1-38.
Bailey, J.L., and L.D. Vander Broek
    1992   *Literary Forms in the New Testament: A Handbook* (Louisville, KY: Westminster/John Knox Press).

Bal, M.
- 1988 *Death and Dissytmmetry: The Politics of Coherence in the Book of Judges* (Chicago/ London: University of Chicago Press).

Baldwin, C.S.
- 1924 *Ancient Rhetoric and Poetic* (New York: Macmillan).

Balme, M.
- 1969 'Lyric Poetry', in Higginbotham (ed.) 1969: 24-62.

Barr, D.L., and J.L. Wentling
- 1980 'The Conventions of Classical Biography and the Genre of Luke–Acts: A Preliminary Study' (unpublished paper presented at the SBL/CBA regional meeting, Duquesne University, Pittsburgh, PA).

Barrett, C.K.
- 1957 *A Commentary on the Epistle to the Romans* (London: A. & C. Black).
- 1971 *A Commentary on the First Epistle to the Corinthians* (London: A. & C. Black, 2nd edn [1st edn 1968]).
- 1974 'John and the Synoptic Gospels', *ExpTim* 85: 228-33.

Barth, K.
- 1936 *Church Dogmatics*. I (Parts 1 and 2). *The Doctrine of the Word of God* (Edinburgh: T. & T. Clark).

Bauckham, R.
- 1990 *Jude and the Relatives of Jesus in the Early Church* (Edinburgh: T. & T. Clark).
- 1998 'For Whom Were the Gospels Written?', in *idem* (ed.) 1998: 9-48.

Bauckham, R. (ed.)
- 1998 *The Gospels for All Christians: Rethinking the Gospel Audiences* (Grand Rapids: Eerdmans).

Beker, J.C.
- 1993 'Luke's Paul as the Legacy of Paul', in *SBLSP*: 511-19.

Bellinzoni, A.J. (ed.)
- 1985 *The Two-Source Hypothesis: A Critical Appraisal* (Macon, GA: Mercer University).

Bergemann, T.
- 1993 *Q auf dem Prüfstand: Die Zuordnung des Mt/Lk-Stoffes zu Q am Beispiel der Bergpredigt* (Göttingen: Vandenhoeck & Ruprecht).

Bergler, S.
- 1988 *Joel als Schriftinterpret* (BEATAJ, 16; Frankfurt: Peter Lang).

Betz, H.D.
- 1979 *Galatians: A Commentary on Paul's Letter to the Churches in Galatia* (Hermeneia; Philadelphia: Fortress Press).
- 1995 *The Sermon on the Mount: A Commentary on the Sermon on the Mount, including the Sermon on the Plain (Matthew 5:3–7:27 and Luke 6:20-49)* (Hermeneia; Minneapolis: Fortress Press).

Bieringer, R. (ed.)
- 1996 *The Corinthian Correspondence* (BETL, 125; Leuven: Leuven University Press/Peeters).

Blenkinsopp, J.
- 1968 'Deuteronomy', *JBC* 6:
- 1990 'Deuteronomy', in *NJBC*, VI.

Blessington, F.C.
- 1979 *Paradise Lost and the Classic Epic* (Boston/London: Routledge & Kegan Paul).

Bloch, R.
- 1957 'Midrash', in *DBSup*, V: 1263-81.

Bloom, H.
- 1973 *The Anxiety of Influence: A Theory of Poetry* (New York: Oxford University Press).

Bock, D.L.
- 1987 *Proclamation from Prophecy and Pattern: Lucan Old Testament Christology* (JSNTSup, 12; Sheffield: Sheffield Academic Press).

Bodine, W.R.
1980 *The Greek Text of Judges: Recent Developments* (HSM, 23; Chico: Scholars Press).
1980 'Kaige and Other Recensional Developments in the Greek Text of Judges', *BIOSCS* 13: 45-57.

Boismard, M.-E.
1956 'Elie dans le Nouveau Testament', in *Elie le prophète, I: Selon les Ecritures et les traditions chretiennes* (Etudes Carmélitanes; Bruges: Desclée de Brouwer): 116-28.
1988 *Moïse ou Jésus: Essai de Christologie Johannique* (BETL, 84; Leuven: Leuven University Press/Peeters).
1994 *L'Evangile de Marc: Sa Préhistoire* (EBib, 26; Paris: J. Gabalda).
1997 *En Quête du Proto-Luc* (EBib, 37; Paris: J. Gabalda).

Boismard, M.-E., and P. Benoit
1965–72 *Synopse des Quatre Evangiles en Francais* (2 vols.; Paris: Cerf).

Boismard, M.-E., and A. Lamouille
1977 *Synopse des Quatre Evangiles en Francais*, III (Paris: Cerf).

Boling, R.G.
1975 *Judges*. AB, 6A; Garden City, NY: Doubleday).

Bonz, M.P.
1997 'Luke–Acts: A Narration of Christian Origins in Contemporary Epic Style' (unpublished dissertation, Harvard University).

Boomershine, T.E.
1985 Review of Kelber (ed.) 1983, *JBL* 104: 535-40.
1988 *Story Journey: An Invitation to the Gospel as Storytelling* (Nashville: Abingdon Press).

Bornkamm, G., G. Barth and H.J. Held
1963 *Tradition and Interpretation in Matthew* (Philadelphia: Westminster Press).
1983 'The Authority to "Bind" and "Loose" in the Church in Matthew's Gospel: The Problem of Sources in Matthew's Gospel', in G. Stanton (ed.), *The Interpretation of Matthew* (Philadelphia: Fortress Press; London: SPCK): 85-97 (first published in D.G. Miller [ed.], *Jesus and Man's Hope* [2 vols.; Pittsburg: Pittsburg Theological Seminary, 1970–71]: I, 37-50).

Bossuyt, P., and J. Radermakers
1981 *Jésus, Parôle de la Grace* (Bruxelles: Instut d'Etudes Theologiques).

Botha, P.J.J.
1993 'The Social Dynamics of the Early Transmission of the Jesus Tradition', *Neotestamentica* 27: 205-31.

Bouwman, G.
1969 'La Pécheresse Hospitalière', *ETL* 45: 172-79.

Bovon, F.
1989 *Das Evangelium nach Lukas (1:1–9:50)* (EKKNT, III/I: Zürich: Benziger; Neukirchen-Vluyn: Neukirchener Verlag) (ET *Luke I: A Commentary on the Gospel of Luke 1:1–9:50* [Hermeneia; Minneapolis: Fortress Press, 2002]).

Bowie, E.L.
1970 'Greeks and their Past in the Second Sophistic', *Past and Present* 46: 3-41.

Bowman, J.
1959 'The Samaritans and the Book of Deuteronomy', *OSTGU* 17: 9-18.

Bowra, C.M.
1945 *From Virgil to Milton* (London: Macmillan).

Boyarin, D.
1990 *Intertextuality and the Reading of Midrash* (Bloomington: Indiana University Press).

Brändle, R., and E.W. Stegemann
1998 'The Formation of the First "Christian Congregations" in Rome and the Context of the Jewish Congregations', in K.P. Donfried and P. Richardson (eds.), *Judaism and Christianity in First-Century Rome* (Grand Rapids: Eerdmans): 117-50.

Breytenbach, C.
- 1992 'Vormarkinische Logientradition. Parallelen in der urchristlichen Briefliteratur', *Four Gospels* 2: 725-49.

Brodie, T.L.
- 1978 'Creative [Re]writing: Missing Link in Biblical Research', *BTB* 8: 34-39.
- 1979 'A New Temple and a New Law: The Unity and Chronicler-Based Nature of Luke 1:1–4:22a', *JSNT* 5: 21-45.
- 1980 'Mark 10:1-45 as a Creative Rewriting of 1 Peter 2:18–3:17: An Abstract' *PIBA* 4: 98.
- 1981a 'Galatians as Art', *The Bible Today* 19: 335-39.
- 1981b 'Jacob's Travail (Jer 30:1-13) and Jacob's Struggle (Gen 32:22-32): A Test Case for Measuring the Influence of the Book of Jeremiah on the Present Text of Genesis', *JSOT* 19: 31-60.
- 1981c 'Jesus as the New Elisha: Cracking the Code [John 9]', *ExpTim* 93: 39-42.
- 1981d 'Luke the Literary Interpreter: Luke–Acts as a Systematic Rewriting and Updating of the Elijah–Elisha Narrative in 1 and 2 Kings' (unpublished dissertation, Rome, Pontifical University of St Thomas). Available through interlibrary loan from: United Library, Garrett-Evangelical/Seabury-Western Theological Seminary, Evanston, IL 60201; Pitts Theological Library, Emory University, 505 Kilgo Circle, Atlanta, GA 30322. Available from University Microfilms Inc. Tel (USA): (800) 521 3042. Chapter 6, section A (on Acts 8:1b-8) is wrong; otherwise the thesis is valid.
- 1983a 'The Accusing and Stoning of Naboth (1 Kgs 21:8-13) as One Component of the Stephen Text (Acts 6:9-14; 7:58a)', *CBQ* 45: 417-32.
- 1983b 'Luke 7:36-50 as an Internalization of 2 Kings 4, 1-37: A Study in Luke's Use of Rhetorical Imitation', *Bib* 64: 457-85.
- 1984a 'Greco-Roman Imitation of Texts as a Partial Guide to Luke's Use of Sources', in C.H. Talbert (ed.), *Luke–Acts: New Perspectives from the Society of Biblical Literature* (New York: Crossroad): 7-46.
- 1984b Review of Kelber (ed.), 1983, *CBQ* 46: 574-75.
- 1986a 'Towards Unravelling Luke's Use of the Old Testament: Luke 7.11-17 as an *Imitatio* of 1 Kings 17.17-24', *NTS* 32: 247-67.
- 1986b 'Towards Unravelling the Rhetorical Imitation of Sources in Acts: 2 Kgs 5 as One Component of Acts 8,9-40', *Bib* 67: 41-67.
- 1989a 'The Departure for Jerusalem (Luke 9:51-56) as a Rhetorical Imitation of Elijah's Departure for the Jordan (2 Kgs 1,1–2,6)', *Bib* 70: 96-109.
- 1989b 'Luke 9:57-62: A Systematic Adaptation of the Divine Challenge to Elijah (1 Kings 19)', in *SBLSP*: 236-45.
- 1990 'Luke–Acts as an Imitation and Emulation of the Elijah–Elisha Narrative', in E. Richard (ed.), *New Views on Luke and Acts* (Wilmington, DE: Michael Glazier): 78-85.
- 1992a 'Fish, Temple Tithe, and Remission: The God-Based Generosity of Deuteronomy 14–15 as One Component of the Community Discourse (Matt 17:22–18:35)', *RB* 99: 697-718.
- 1992b 'Not Q but Elijah: The Saving of the Centurion's Servant (Luke 7:1-10) as an Internalization of the Saving of the Widow and Her Child (1 Kgs 17:1-16)', *IBS* 14: 54-71.
- 1993a *The Gospel According to St. John: A Literary and Theological Commentary* (New York/Oxford: Oxford University Press.
- 1993b *The Quest for the Origin of John's Gospel: A Source-Oriented Approach* (New York/Oxford: Oxford University Press).
- 1993c Vivid, Positive, Practical: The Systematic Use of Romans in Matthew 1–7', *PIBA* 16: 36-55.
- 1994 'Again Not Q: Luke 7:18-35 as an Acts-Oriented Transformation of the Vindication of the Prophet Micaiah (I Kings 22:1-38)', *IBS* 16: 2-30.
- 1995a 'Luke's Redesigning of Paul: Corinthian Division and Reconciliation (1 Corinthians 1–5) as One Component of Jerusalem Unity (Acts 1–5)', *IBS* 17: 98-128.
- 1995b 'Re-Opening the Quest for Proto-Luke: The Systematic Use of Judges 6–12 in Luke 16:1–18:8', *Journal of Higher Criticism* 2: 68-101.
- 1996 'The Systematic Use of the Pentateuch in 1 Corinthians: An Exploratory Survey', in Bieringer (ed.) 1996: 441-57.

1997	'Intertextuality and Its Use in Tracing Q and Proto-Luke', in C.M. Tuckett (ed.), *The Scriptures in the Gospels* (BETL, 131; Leuven: Leuven University Press/Peeters): 469-77.
1999	'The Unity of Proto-Luke', in J. Verheyden (ed.), *The Unity of Luke–Acts* (BETL, 131; Leuven: Leuven University Press/Peeters): 627-38.
2000	*The Crucial Bridge: The Elijah–Elisha Narrative as an Interpretive Synthesis of Genesis–Kings and a Literary Model for the Gospels* (Collegeville, MN: Liturgical Press).
2001a	'An Alternative Q/Logia Hypothesis: Deuteronomy-Based, Qumranlike, Verifiable', in A. Lindemann (ed.), *The Sayings Source Q and the Historical Jesus* (BETL, 158; Leuven: Leuven University Press/Peeters): 729-43.
2001b	*Genesis as Dialogue: A Literary, Theological and Historical Commentary* (New York/Oxford: Oxford University Press).
2001c	'Genesis as Dialogue: Genesis' Twenty-Six Diptychs as a Key to Narrative Unity and Meaning', in A. Wénin (ed.), *Studies in the Book of Genesis: Literature, Redaction and History* (BETL, 155; Leuven: Leuven University Press/Peeters): 297-314.
2001d	'Towards Tracing the Gospels' Literary Indebtedness to the Epistles', in D.R. MacDonald (ed.), *Mimesis and Intertextuality in Antiquity and Christianity* (Harrisburg, PA: Trinity Press International): 104-16.
2002	*Proto-Luke: A Christ-Centered Synthesis of Septuagintal Historiography, and a Deuteronomy-Based Alternative to Q* (The Bible as Dialogue; Limerick: Dominican Biblical Centre).

Bronner, L.
1968   *The Stories of Elijah and Elisha as Polemics against Baal Worship* (Leiden: E.J. Brill).

Brooke, A.E. *et al.*
1930   *The Old Testament in Greek*. II, Part II. *1 and 2 Kings* (Cambridge: Cambridge University Press).

Brooke, G.J.
1989   'The Wisdom of Matthew's Beatitudes (4QBeat and Mt. 5:3-12)', *Scripture Bulletin* 19: 34-41.

Brown, R.E.
1961   'Incidents that are Units in the Synoptic Gospels but Dispersed in St. John', *CBQ* 23: 143-60.
1966   *The Gospel According to John I–XII* (AB, 29; Garden City, NY: Doubleday).
1971   'Jesus and Elisha', *Perspective* 12: 86-104.
1977   *The Birth of the Messiah* (New York: Doubleday).
1990   'Dead Sea Scrolls', in *NJBC*, LXVII.
1994   *The Death of the Messiah* (2 vols. Garden City, NY: Doubleday; London: Geoffrey Chapman).
1997   *An Introduction to the New Testament* (ABRL; Garden City, NY: Doubleday).

Brown, R.E., and J.P. Meier
1983   *Antioch and Rome: New Testament Cradles of Catholic Christianity* (New York/Ramsey: Paulist Press).

Bruce, F.F.
1954   *Commentary on the Book of Acts* (Grand Rapids: Eerdmans).

Brueggemann, W.
1997   *Theology of the Old Testament: Testimony, Dispute, Advocacy* (Minneapolis: Fortress Press).

Bryan, C.
1993   *A Preface to Mark: Notes on the Gospel in its Literary and Cultural Settings* (New York/Oxford: Oxford University Press).

Bryce, G.E.
1979   *A Legacy of Wisdom: The Egyptian Contribution to the Wisdom of Israel* (Lewisburg: Bucknell University Press; London: Associated University Press).

Büchele A.
1978   *Der Tod Jesu im Lukasevangelium* (FthSt, 26; Frankfurt: Knecht).

Bultmann, R.
- 1913 'Was lässt die Spruchquelle über die Urgemeinde erkennen', *Oldenburgische Kirchenblatt* 19: 35-37, 41-44 (ET 'What the Saying Source Reveals about the Early Church', in Kloppenborg [ed.] 1994: 23-34).
- 1926 'The New Approach to the Synoptic Problem', *JR* 6: 337-62.
- 1931 *Die Geschichte der synoptischen Tradition* (Göttingen: Vandenhoeck & Ruprecht, 2nd edn [1st edn 1921; 3rd edn with supplement 1958]).
- 1963 *The History of the Synoptic Tradition* (New York: Harper & Row) (ET of 1958 edn of *Die Geschichte*).
- 1967 'Der religionsgeschichtliche Hintergrund des Prologs zum Johannes-Evangelium', in E. Dinkler (ed.), *Exegetica: Aufsätze zur Erforschung des Neuen Testaments* (Tübingen: J.C.B. Mohr): 10-35.
- 1971 *The Gospel of John: A Commentary* (Philadelphia: Westminster Press).

Burkert, W.
- 1992 *The Orientalizing Revolution: The Near Eastern Influence on Greek Culture in the Early Archaic Age* (Cambridge, MA: Harvard University Press [German edn 1984]).

Burridge, R.A.
- 1992 *What Are the Gospels? A Comparison with Greco-Roman Biography* (SNTSMS, 70; Cambridge: Cambridge University Press).
- 1994 *Four Gospels, One Jesus* (London: SPCK).

Butterfield, H.
- 1981 *The Origins of History* (London: Methuen).

Byrne, B.
- 1986 *Romans* (Sacra Pagina; Collegeville, MN: Liturgical Press).

Byrskog, S.
- 1994 *Jesus the Only Teacher: Didactic Authority and Transmission in Ancient Israel, Ancient Judaism and the Matthean Community* (ConBNT, 24; Stockholm: Almqvist & Wiksell International).

Cadbury, H.J.
- 1920 *The Style and Literary Method of Luke* (HTS, 6; Cambridge, MA: Harvard University Press).
- 1927 *The Making of Luke–Acts* (New York: Macmillan).

Caird, G.B.
- 1963 *Saint Luke* (Harmondsworth: Penguin Books).
- 1976 'The Study of the Gospels: II. Form Criticism', *ExpTim* 87: 137-41.

Callebat, L.
- 1964 'L'Archaïsme dans les Métamorphoses d'Apulée', *REL* 42: 346-61.

Cameron, R.
- 1990 'What Have You Come Out to See? Characterization of John and Jesus in the Gospels', *Semeia* 49: 35-69.

Carlson, R.A.
- 1969 'Elie á l'Horeb', *VT* 19: 418-39.
- 1970 'Elisée—le successeur d'Elie', *VT* 20: 385-405.

Carlston, C.E.
- 1982 'Wisdom and Eschatology in Q', in Delobel (ed.) 1892: 101-19.

Carmichael, C.M.
- 1979 *Women, Law, and the Genesis Traditions* (Edinburgh: Edinburgh University Press).

Carroll, R.P.
- 1969 'The Elijah–Elisha Sagas: Some Remarks on Prophetic Succession in Ancient Israel', *VT* 19: 400-15.

Catchpole, D.
- 1993 *The Quest for Q* (Edinburgh: T. & T. Clark).

Cazelles, H.
- 1961 *Les livres des Chroniques* (La Sainte Bible; Paris: Cerf).

Cerfaux, L., and J. Dupont
    1953   *Les Actes des Apôtres* (La Sainte Bible; Paris: Cerf).

Childs, B.S.
    1980   'On Reading the Elijah Narratives', *Int* 34: 128-37.

Chomsky, N.
    1965   *Aspects of the Theory of Syntax* (Cambridge, MA: Harvard University Press).

Chouraqui, A.
    1975   'Une traduction de la Bible', *Etudes* 343: 447-62.

Christ, F.
    1970   *Jesus Sophia. Die Sophie-Christologie bei den Synoptikern* (AThANT, 57; Zürich: Zwingli Verlag).

Ciampa, R.E.
    1998   *The Presence and Function of Scripture in Galatians 1 and 2* (WUNT, 2/102; Tübingen: Mohr Siebeck).

Clark, D.L.
    1951   'Imitation: Theory and Practice in Roman Rhetoric', *Quarterly Journal of Speech* 37: 11-22.

Clifford, R.J.
    1990   'Genesis [1:1–25:18]', in *NJBC*, II.

Coleman, R.
    1969   'Pastoral Poetry', in Higginbotham (ed.) 1969: 100-23.

Collins, J.J.
    1997   'The Expectation of the End in the Dead Sea Scrolls', in C.A. Evans and P.W. Flint (eds.), *Eschatology, Messianism and the Dead Sea Scrolls* (Grand Rapids: Eerdmans): 74-90.

Conington, J.
    1963   *The Works of Virgil* (Hildesheim: Georg Olms).

Conroy, C.
    1996   'Hiel between Ahab and Elijah–Elisha: 1 Kgs 16,34 in its Immediate Literary Context', *Bib* 77: 210-18.

Conteneau, G.
    1966   *Everyday Life in Babylonia and Assyria* (New York: Norton).

Conway, R.S.
    1931   *Virgil as a Student of Homer* (Martin Classical Lectures, I; Cambridge, MA: Harvard University Press): 151-81.

Conzelmann, H.
    1972   *Die Apostelgeschichte* (HNT, 7; Tübingen: Mohr Siebeck).
    1975   *1 Corinthians* (Hermeneia; Philadelphia: Fortress Press).
    1987   *Acts of the Apostles: A Commentary* (Philadelphia: Fortress Press).

Cook, M.J.
    1980   Review of Gerhardsson, 1961, *Int* 34: 314-16.

Cooper, A.
    1979   Review of D.K. Stuart's *Studies in Early Hebrew Meter*, *BASOR* 233: 75-76.

Cope, O.L.
    1976   *Matthew: A Scribe Trained for the Kingdom of Heaven* (CBQMS, 5; Washington: Catholic Biblical Association of America).

Coppens, J.
    1979   'L'imposition des mains dan les Actes des Apôtres', in Kremer (ed.) 1979: 405-38.

Corley, B. (ed.)
    1983   *Colloquy [Fort Worth] on New Testament Studies: A Time for Reappraisal and Fresh Approaches* (Macon: Mercer University Press).

Cornford, F.M.
    1907   *Thucydides Mythistoricus* (London: E. Arnold).

Cox, A.
    1969   'Didactic Poetry', in Higginbotham (ed.) 1969: 124-61.

Cotter, W.J.
    1987   'The Parable of the Children in the Marketplace, Q(Lk) 7.31-35: An Examination of the Parable's Image and Significance', *NovTest* 29: 289-304.
    1989   'Children Sitting in the Agora: Q (Luke) 7:31-35', *Forum* 5: 63-82.

Craig, J.D.
    1927   'Archaism in Terence', *The Classical Quarterly* 21: 90-94.

Creed, J.M.
    1930   *The Gospel According to St. Luke* (London: Macmillan).

Cribbs, F.L.
    1979   'The Agreements that Exist Between John and Luke', in *SBLSP*: I, 215-61.

Crossan, J.D.
    1991   *The Historical Jesus: The Life of a Mediterranean Jewish Peasant* (San Francisco: HarperSanFrancisco).

Culler, J.
    1981   *The Pursuit of Signs: Semiotics, Literature, Deconstruction* (Ithaca, NY: Cornell University Press).

Culpepper, R.A.
    1975   *The Johannine School: An Evaluation of the Johannine School Hypothesis Based on an Investigation of the Nature of Ancient Schools* (SBLDS, 26; Missoula, MT: Scholars Press).

Dabeck, P.
    1942   'Siehe, es erschienen Moses und Elias', *Bib* 23: 175-89.

Dalton, J.F.
    1962   *Roman Literary Theory and Criticism* (New York: Russell & Russell).

Daniélou, J.
    1948   'Les Divers Sens de l'Ecriture dans la Tradition Chrétienne Primitive', *ETL* 24: 119-26.

Daube, D.
    1953   'Alexandrian Methods of Interpretation and the Rabbis', in *Festschrift Hans Lewald* (ed. Lewald's friends and colleagues; Basel: Helbring & Lichtenhahn): 27-44.

Dautzenberg, G.
    1992   'Elija im Markusevangelium', *Four Gospels* 2: 1077-94.

Davies, G.H.
    1962   'Deuteronomy', *PCB*: par. 231-44: 269-84.

Davies, P.R.
    1992   *In Search of 'Ancient Israel'* (JSOTSup, 148; Sheffield: JSOT Press).

Davies, W.D.
    1964   *The Setting of the Sermon on the Mount* (Cambridge: Cambridge University Press).

Davies, W.D., and D.C. Allison
    1988   *The Gospel According to Saint Matthew. I. Introduction and Commentary on Matthew 1–VII* (ICC; Edinburgh: T. & T. Clark).

De Jonge, M. (ed.)
    1977   *L'Evangile de Jean. Sources, rédaction, théologie* (BETL, 44; Leuven: Leuven University Press [2nd edn, 1987]): 73-106.

De la Potterie, I.
    1988   *Marie dans le Mystère de l'Alliance* (Jésus et Jésus-Christ, 34; Paris: Desclée).

De Vries, S.
    1978   *Prophet against Prophet: The Role of the Micaiah Narrative in the Development of Early Prophetic Tradition* (Grand Rapids: Eerdmans).

Deissmann, G.A.
    1910   *Light from the Ancient East: The New Testament Illustrated by Recently Discovered Texts of the Greco-Roman World* (London: Hodder & Stoughton [Ger. original 1908]).

Delobel, J.
    1966   'L'Onction par la Pécheresse: La composition littéraire de Lc., vii, 36-50', *ETL* 42: 414-75.

Delobel, J. (ed.)
 1982 *Logia: Les paroles de Jésus—The Sayings of Jesus: mémorial Joseph Coppens* (BETL, 59; Leuven: Leuven University Press/Peeters).

Denaux, A.
 1995 'Criteria for Identifying Q-Passages: A Critical Review of a Recent Work by T. Bergmann', *NovT* 37: 105-28.

Denaux, A. (ed.)
 1992 *John and the Synoptics* (BETL, 101; Leuven: Leuven University Press/Peeters).

De Roo, J.C.R.
 1997 'Is 4Q525 a Qumran Sectarian Document?', in S.E. Porter and C.A. Evans (eds.), *The Scrolls and the Scriptures: Qumran Fifty Years After* (JSPSup, 26; Roehampton Institute London Papers, 3; Sheffield: Sheffield Academic Press): 338-67.

Derrett, J.D.M.
 1970 *Law in the New Testament* (London: Darton, Longman & Todd).

Deutsch, C.
 1987 *Hidden Wisdom and the Easy Yoke: Wisdom, Torah and Discipleship in Matthew 11:25-30* (JSNTSup, 18; Sheffield: JSOT Press).

Dewey, J.
 1991 'Mark as Interwoven Tapestry: Forecasts and Echoes for a Listening Audience', *CBQ* 53: 221-36.

Dibelius, M.
 1919 *Die Formgeschichte des Evangeliums* (Tübingen: J.C.B. Mohr).
 1923 'Stilkritisches zur Apostelgeschichte', in Emil Balla *et al.* (eds.), *Eucharisterion: Studien zur Religion und Literatur des Alten und Neuen Testaments: Hermann Gunkel zum 60. Geburtstage* (2 vols.; Göttingen: Vandenhoeck & Ruprecht): II, 27-49.
 1956 *Studies in the Acts of the Apostles* (New York: Charles Scribner's Sons).

Dillon, R.
 1990 'Acts of the Apostles', in *NJBC*, XLIV.

Dodd, C.H.
 1937 *The First Epistle of John and the Fourth Gospel* (Manchester: Manchester University Press).
 1963 *Historical Tradition in the Fourth Gospel* (Cambridge: Cambridge University Press).

Dormeyer, D.
 1998 *The New Testament among the Writings of Antiquity* (The Biblical Seminar, 55; Sheffield: Sheffield Academic Press [Ger. 1993]).

Doty, W.G.
 1973 *Letters in Primitive Christianity* (Philadelphia: Fortress Press).

Douglas, M.
 1993 *In the Wilderness: The Doctrine of Defilement in the Book of Numbers* (JSOTSup, 158; Sheffield: Sheffield Academic Press).

Downing, F.G.
 1964 'Towards the Rehabilitation of Q', *NTS* 11: 169-81.
 1994 'A Genre for Q and a Socio-Cultural Context for Q: Comparing Sets of Similarities with Sets of Differences', *JSNT* 55: 3-26.

Draisma, S. (ed.)
 1989 *Intertextuality in Biblical Writings: Essays in Honour of Bas van Iersel* (Kampen: Kok).

Drury, J.
 1976 *Tradition and Design in Luke's Gospel* (Atlanta, GA: John Knox Press).

Dubois, J.D.
 1973 'La Figure d'Elie dans la Perspective Lucanienne', *RHPR* 53: 155-76.

Duke, R.K.
 1990 *The Persuasive Appeal of the Chronicler: A Rhetorical Analysis* (JSOTSup, 88; Sheffield: Almond Press).

Dumais, M.
 1976 *La langage de l'évangélisation: L'Annonce missionaire en milieu juif (Actes 13.16-41)* (Recherches de Théologie, 16; Montreal: Bellarmin).

Dundenberg, I.
    1994   *Johannes und die Synoptiker: Studien zu Joh 1–9* (AASF DHL, 69; Helsinki: Suomalainen Tiedeakatemia).

Dungan, D.L. (ed.)
    1990   *The Interrelationships of the Gospels (A Symposium Led by M.-E. Boismard, W.R. Farmer and F. Neirynck)* (BETL, 95; Leuven: Leuven University Press/Peeters; Macon, GA: Mercer University Press).

Dungan, D.L., and D.R. Cartlidge (eds.)
    1974   *Sourcebook of Texts for the Comparative Study of the Gospels: Literature of the Hellenistic and Roman Period Illuminating the Milieu and Character of the Gospels* (SBL Sources for Biblical Study, 1; Missoula, MT: Scholars Press, 4th edn).

Dunn, J.D.G.
    1986   Review of Kelber (ed.) 1983, *Int* 40: 72-75.
    1991   John and the Oral Gospel', in Wansbrough (ed.) 1991: 351-79.
    2003a   'Altering the Default Setting: Re-Envisaging the Early Transmission of the Jesus Tradition', *NTS* 49: 139-75.
    2003b   *Christianity in the Making. I. Jesus Remembered* (Grand Rapids: Eerdmans).

Dupont, J.
    1964   *The Sources of the Acts: The Present Position* (London: Darton, Longman & Todd).
    1980   'Le Pharisien et la pécheresse', *Communautés et Liturgies* 62: 260-68.
    1985   *Etudes sur les Evangiles Synoptiques* (BETL, 70A, 70B; 2 vols.; Leuven: Leuven University Press/Peeters).

Edwards, R.D.
    1976   *A Theology of Q: Eschatology, Prophecy, and Wisdom* (Philadelphia: Fortress Press).

Eliot, T.S.
    1944   *Four Quartets* (London: Faber & Faber).

Ellis, E.E.
    1957   *Paul's Use of the Old Testament* (Grand Rapids: Baker Book House).
    1978   *Prophecy and Interpretation in Early Christianity* (Grand Rapids: Baker Book House).
    1991   *The Old Testament in Early Christianity: Canon and Interpretation in the Light of Modern Research* (Grand Rapids: Baker Book House).

Ellis, P.
    1968   '1–2 Kings', *JBC* 10: 40.

Enslin, M.E.
    1970   'Once Again, Luke and Paul', *ZNW* 61: 253-71.

Euripedes
    1959   *The Complete Greek Tragedies* (trans. D. Grene; ed. D. Grene and R. Lattimore; Chicago: University of Chicago Press).

Evans, C.A.
    1994   'The Pharisee and the Publican: Luke 18:9-14 and Deuteronomy 26', in C.A. Evans and W.R. Stegner (eds.), *The Gospels and the Scriptures of Israel* (JSNTSup, 104; Studies in Scripture in Early Judaism and Christianity, 3; Sheffield: Sheffield Academic Press): 342-55.

Evans, C.A., and J.A. Sanders (eds.)
    1993   *Paul and the Scriptures of Israel* (JSNTSup, 83; Sheffield: Sheffield Academic Press).

Evans, C.F.
    1955   'The Central Section of Luke's Gospel', in Nineham (ed.) 1955: 37-53.

Exum, J.C.
    1976   'Literary Patterns in the Samson Saga: An Investigation of Rhetorical Style in Biblical Prose' (unpublished dissertation, Columbia University, New York).
    1980   'Promise and Fulfilment: Narrative Art in Judges 13', *JBL* 99: 43-59.
    1981   'Aspects of Symmetry and Balance in the Samson Saga', *JSOT* 19: 3-29.

Farmer, W.R.
    1976   *The Synoptic Problem: A Critical Appraisal* (Dillsbobo, NC: Western North Carolina Press).

Farmer, W.R. (ed.)
    1983   *New Synoptic Studies: The Cambridge Conference and Beyond* (Macon, GA: Mercer University Press).

Farrer, A.
    1955   'On Dispensing with Q', in Nineham (ed.) 1955: 55-86.

Feine, P.
    1891   *Eine vorkanonische Überlieferung des Lukas im Evangelium und Apostelgeschichte* (Gotha: Friedrich Andreas Perthes).

Feldman, F.
    1926   *Das Buch der Weisheit* (Bonn: Hanstein).

Feldman, L.H.
    1988   'Josephus' *Jewish Antiquities* and Pseudo-Philo's *Biblical Antiquities*', in L.H. Feldman and G. Hata (eds.), *Josephus, the Bible and History* (Leiden: E.J. Brill): 59-80.
    1994   'Josephus' Portrait of Elijah', *SJOT* 8: 61-86.
    1996   'Homer and the Near East: The Rise of the Greek Genius', *BA* 59: 13-21.

Fiorenza, F. Schüssler
    1994   'The Jesus of Piety and the Historical Jesus', *CTSA Proceedings* 49: 90-99.

Fischel, H.A.
    1969   'Story and History: Observations on Greco-Roman Rhetoric and Pharisaism', in D. Sinor (ed.), *American Oriental Society, Middle West Branch, Semi-Centennial Volume: A Collection of Original Essays* (Asian Studies Research Institute Oriental Series, 3; Bloomington: Indiana University Press): 59-88.
    1973   'The Uses of Sorites (*Climax, Gradatio*) in the Tannaitic Period', *HUCA* 44: 119-51.
    1975   'The Transformation of Wisdom in the World of Midrash', in Wilken (ed.) 1975: 67-101.

Fishbane, M.
    1985   *Biblical Interpretation in Ancient Israel* (New York/Oxford: Oxford University Press).

Fiske, G.C.
    1920   *Lucilius and Horace: A Study in the Classical Theory of Imitation* (Madison: University of Wisconsin Press [repr., Westport, CT: Greenwood Press, 1971]).

Fitzmyer, J.A.
    1962   'Memory and Manuscript: The Origins and Transmission of the Gospel Tradition', *TS* 23: 442-57.
    1971   *The Genesis Apocryphon of Qumran Cave 1: A Commentary* (BibOr, 18A; Rome: Biblical Institute, 2nd edn).
    1981   *The Gospel According to Luke I–IX* (AB, 28; Garden City, NY: Doubleday).
    1985   *The Gospel According to Luke X–XXIV* (AB, 28a, Garden City, NY: Doubleday).
    1990   'The Letter to the Romans', in *NJBC*, LI.
    1992a   'A Palestinian Collection of Beatitudes', *Four Gospels*: I, 509-15.
    1992b   *Romans: A New Translation with Introduction and Commentary* (AB, 33; Garden City, NY Doubleday).

Flender, H.
    1967   *St. Luke: Theologian of Redemptive History* (Philadelphia: Fortress Press).
    1992   'A Palestinian Collection of Beatitudes', *Four Gospels*: I, 509-15.

Flusser, D.
    1984   'Lukas 9,51-56—Ein hebräisches Fragment', in W.C. Weinrich (ed.), *The New Testament Age: Essays in Honor of Bo Reicke* (2 vols.; Macon, GA: Mercer University Press): I, 165-79.

Fohrer, G.
    1968   *Elia* (AThANT, 53; Zürich: Zwingli Verlag, 2nd edn).

Foley, J.M.
    1988   *The Theory of Oral Composition: History and Methodology* (Bloomington/Indianapolis: Indiana University Press).

Foucault, M.
    1966   *Les mots et les choses: une archéologie des sciences humaines* (Paris: Gallimard) (ET *The Order of Things: An Archaeology of the Human Sciences* [London: Tavistock, 1970]).

Fraeyman, M.
    1947   'La Spiritualisation de l'Idée du Temple dans les Epitres Pauliniennes', *ETL* 33: 378-412.

Francis, F.O., and J.P. Sampley
    1984   *Pauline Parallels* (Philadelphia: Fortress Press, 2nd edn [1st edn 1975]).

Frankemölle, H.
    1974   *Jahwe-Bund und Kirche Christi* (NTAbh, 10; Münster: Aschendorff).

Freedman, D.N.
    1963   'The Law and the Prophets', *Congress Volume, Bonn 1962* (VTSup, 9; Leiden: E.J. Brill): 250-65.
    1991   *The Unity of the Hebrew Bible* (Ann Arbor: University of Michigan Press).
    1992   'The Symmetry of the Hebrew Bible', *Studia Theologica* 46: 83-108.
    1995   'The Structure of Psalm 119', in D.P. Wright *et al.* (eds.), *Pomegranates and Golden Bells: Studies in Biblical, Jewish, and Near Eastern Ritual, Law, and Literature in Honor of Jacob Milgrom* (Winona Lake, IN: Eisenbrauns): 725-56.

Friedrichsen, T.A.
    1989   'The Matthew–Luke Agreements Against Mark: A Survey of Recent Studies', in F. Neirynck (ed.), *The Gospel of Luke* (BETL, 32; Leuven: Leuven University Press): 335-92.
    1992   'The Matthew–Luke Agreements Against Mark 1974–1991' (unpublished dissertation, 2 vols.; Leuven, Leuven University).

Funk, R.W., R.J. Hoover and the Jesus Seminar
    1993   *The Five Gospels: The Search for the Authentic Words of Jesus* (New York and Toronto: Macmillan).

Gabba, E.
    1981   'True History and False History in Classical Antiquity', *Journal of Roman Studies* 71: 50-62.

Gamble, H.Y.
    1995   *Books and Readers in the Early Church: A History of Early Christian Texts* (New Haven: Yale University Press).

Gardiner-Smith, P.
    1938   *Saint John and the Synoptic Gospels* (Cambridge: Cambridge University Press).

Gärtner, B.
    1955   'The Habakkuk Commentary (DSH) and the Gospel of Matthew', *ST* 8: 1-24.

Gast, F.
    1968   'Synoptic Problem', *JBC* 40.

Gaston, L.
    1970   *No Stone on Another: Studies in the Significance of the Fall of Jerusalem in the Synoptic Gospels* (Leiden: E.J. Brill).

Gaventa, B.R.
    1986   'Galatians 1 and 2: Autobiography as Paradigm', *NovT* 28: 309-26.

Gelin, A.
    1960   *Esdras et Néhémie* (La Sainte Bible; Paris: Cerf).

Gench, F.T.
    1997   *Wisdom in the Christology of Matthew* (Lanham, MD: University Press of America).

Gerhardsson, B.
    1961   *Memory and Manuscript: Oral Tradition and Written Transmission in Rabbinic Judaism and Early Christianity* (ASNU, 22; Lund: C.W.K. Gleerup).
    1964   *Tradition and Transmission in Early Christianity* (ConBNT, 20; Lund: C.W.K. Gleerup).
    1979   *The Origins of the Gospel Traditions* (Philadelphia: Fortress Press).
    1986   *The Gospel Tradition* (ConBNT, 15; Malmö: C.W.K. Gleerup).

Gils, F.
    1957   *Jésus prophète d'après les évangiles synoptiques* (Orientalia et biblica lovaniensia, 2; Louvain: Publications universitaires).

Goodenough, E.R.
    1940   *An Introduction to Philo Judaeus* (New Haven: Yale University).

Gordon, C.
1963 'The Mediterranean Factor in the Old Testament', in *Congress Volume, Bonn 1962* (VTSup, 9; Leiden: E.J. Brill): 19-31.

Goulder, M.D.
1974 *Midrash and Lection in Matthew* (London: SPCK).
1989 *Luke: A New Paradigm* (JSNTSup, 20; Sheffield: JSOT Press).
1992 'A Pauline in a Jacobite Church', *Four Gospels* 2: 859-75.
1993a 'Luke's Knowledge of Matthew', in Stecker (ed.) 1993: 143-62.
1993b 'Ruth: A Homily on Deuteronomy 22–25?', in H.A. McKay and D.J.A Clines (eds.), *Of Prophets' Visions and the Wisdom of Sages: Essays in Honour of R. Norman Whybray on his Seventieth Birthday* (JSOTSup, 162; Sheffield: JSOT Press): 307-19.

Grässer, E.
1976 'Acta-Forschung seit 1960', *ThR* 41: 141-94, 259-90.
1977 'Acta-Forschung seit 1960', *ThR* 42: 1-68.

Grassi, J.A.
1964 'Emmaus Revisited (Luke 24:13-35 and Acts 8:26-40)', *CBQ* 26: 463-67.
1968 'The Letter to the Ephesians', *JBC* 56.
1989 'Matthew as a Second Testament Deuteronomy', *BTB* 19: 23-29.

Gray, J.
1970 *I and II Kings* (OTL; Philadelphia: Westminster Press, 2nd edn).

Green, H.B.
1984 'The Credibility of Luke's Transformation of Matthew', in Tuckett (ed.) 1984: 131-55.

Greene, T.M.
1963 *The Descent from Heaven: A Study in Epic Continuity* (New Haven: Yale University Press).
1982 *The Light in Troy: Imitation and Discovery in Renaissance Poetry* (New Haven: Yale University Press).

Gressmann, H.
1918 *Vom reichen Mann und armen Lazarus: Eine literargeschichtliche Studie* (Abhandlungen der kaiserlichen preussichen Akademie der Wissenschaften, 7; Berlin: Königliche Akademie der Wissenschaften).

Grobel, K.
1963–64 'Whose Name was Neves', *NTS* 10: 373-382.

Gros Louis, K.R.R.
1974 'The Book of Judges', in *idem* (ed.) 1974: 141-62.

Gros Louis, K.R.R. (ed.)
1974 *Literary Interpretations of Biblical Narratives* (Nashville: Abingdon Press).
1982 *Literary Interpretations of Biblical Narratives*, II (Nashville: Abingdon Press).

Groves, J.W.
1987 *Actualization and Interpretation in the Old Testament* (SBLDS, 86; Atlanta, GA: Scholars Press).

Grunmann, W.
1961 *Das Evangelium nach Lukas* (THKNT, 3; East Berlin: Evangelische Verlaganstalt, 2nd edn).

Gundry, R.H.
1982 *Matthew: A Commentary on his Literary and Theological Art* (Grand Rapids: Eerdmans).

Gunkel, H.
1901 *Genesis, übersetzt und erklärt* (Göttingen: Vandenhoeck & Ruprecht [3rd edn 1910]).

Gusdorf, G.
1967 *Les Sciences Humaines et la Pensée Occidentale*. II. *Les Origines des Sciences Humaines* (Paris: Payot).
1974 'Humanistic Scholarship, History of', in *Encyclopedia Britannica, Macropaedia*, VIII: 1170-79.

Haenchen, E.
1971 *The Acts of the Apostles* (Philadelphia: Westminster Press).

Hafemann, S.
1996 'Paul's Argument from the Old Testament and Christology in 2 Cor 1–9', in Bieringer (ed.) 1996: 277-303.
Hall, D.R.
1994 'A Disguise to the Wise: METASCHĒMATISMOS in 1 Corinthians 4.6', *NTS* 40: 89-104.
Halpern, B.
1988 *The First Historians: The Hebrew Bible and History* (San Francisco: Harper & Row).
Halpern-Amaru, B.
1994 *Rewriting the Bible: Land and Covenant in Postbiblical Jewish Literature* (Valley Forge, PA: Trinity Press International).
Halverson, J.
1994 'Oral and Written Gospel: A Critique of Werner Kelber', *NTS* 40: 180-95.
Hamerton-Kelly, R.G.
1976 'Some Techniques of Composition in Philo's Allegorical Commentary with Special Reference to *De Agricultura*—A Study in the Hellenistic Midrash', in R. Hamerton-Kelly and R. Scroggs (eds.), *Jews, Greeks and Christians: Religious Cultures in Late Antiquity: Essays in Honor of William David Davies* (Leiden: E.J. Brill): 45-56.
Hanson, A.T.
1974 *Studies in Paul's Technique and Theology* (London: SPCK).
Haran, M.
1988 'On the Diffusion of Literacy and Schools in Ancient Israel', in J.A. Emerton (ed.), *Congress Volume, Jerusalem 1986* (VTSup, 40; Leiden: E.J. Brill): 81-95.
Hardie, C.G.
1970 'Virgil', in *OCD*: 1123-28.
Harnack, A.
1908 *Die Apostelgeschichte* (Beiträge zur Einleitung in das NT, 3; Leipzig: J.C. Hinrichs).
Harrington, D.J.
1986 'Palestinian Adaptations of Biblical Narratives and Prophecies. I. The Bible Rewritten (Narratives)', in R.A. Kraft and G.W.E. Nickelsburg (eds.), *Early Judaism and Its Modern Interpreters* (Atlanta, GA: Scholars Press): 239-47.
1990 'Mark', *NJBC*, XLI.
Harrington, J.M.
1998 'The Lukan Passion Narrative: The Markan Material in Luke 22,54–23,25' (3 vols., unpublished dissertation, Katholieke Universiteit Leuven).
Harrington, W.J.
1965 *Record of the Fulfilment: The New Testament* (Chicago: Priory Press).
Harriott, R.
1969 'Comedy', in Higginbotham (ed.) 1969: 195-222.
Hartin, P.J.C.
1988 'James: A New Testament Wisdom Writing and Its Relationship to Q' (unpublished dissertation, University of South Africa).
Hartmann, G.
1936 *Der Aufbau des Markusevangeliums* (NTAbh, 17/2-3; Münster: Aschendorff).
Havelock, E.A.
1963 *Preface to Plato* (Cambridge, MA: Harvard University Press).
1978 *The Greek Concept of Justice: From Its Shadow in Homer to Its Substance in Plato* (Cambridge, MA: Harvard University Press).
Havener, I.
1987 *Q. The Sayings of Jesus: With a Reconstruction of Q* (Wilmington, DE: Michael Glazier).
Hays, R.B.
1989 *Echoes of Scripture in the Letters of Paul* (New Haven/London: Yale University Press).
1993 'On the Rebound: A Response to Critiques of *Echoes of Scripture in the Letters of Paul*', in Evans and Sanders (eds.) 1993: 70-96.

1997	*First Corinthians* (Interpretation; Louisville, KY: John Knox Press).
1998	'The Conversion of the Imagination: Scripture and Eschatology in 1 Corinthians' (unpublished paper delivered at SNTS meeting, Copenhagen [forthcoming in *NTS*]).

Heidel, A.
    1951   *The Babylonian Genesis: The Story of Creation* (Chicago: University of Chicago Press).

Henaut, B.W.
    1993   *Oral Tradition and the Gospels: The Problem of Mark 4* (JSNTSup, 82; Sheffield: JSOT Press).

Hengel, M.
    1980   *Acts and the History of Earliest Christianity* (Philadelphia: Fortress Press).

Hess, R.S.
    1994   'One Hundred Fifty Years of Comparative Studies on Genesis 1–11: An Overview', in R.S. Hess and D.T. Tsumura (eds.), *'I Studied Inscriptions from before the Flood': Ancient Near Eastern, Literary, and Linguistic Approaches to Genesis 1–11* (Winona Lake, IN: Eisenbrauns): 3-26.

Higginbotham, J.
    1969   'Satire', in *idem* (ed.) 1969: 223-161.

Higginbotham, J. (ed.)
    1969   *Greek and Latin Literature* (London: Methuen).

Highet, G.
    1949   *The Classical Tradition* (New York/London: Oxford University Press).

Hodgson, R.
    1986   'On the Gattung of Q: A Dialogue with James M. Robinson', *Bib* 66: 73-95.

Hollander, H.W.
    1994   'The Testing by Fire of the Builders' Work: 1 Corinthians 3.10-15', *NTS* 40: 89-104.

Holst, R.
    1976   'The One Anointing of Jesus: Another Application of the Form-Critical Method', *JBL* 95: 435-46.

Holtz, T.
    1968   *Untersuchungen über die alttestamentlichen Zitate bei Lukas* (TU, 104; Berlin: Akademie Verlag).

Hooker, M.D.
    1993   'The Beginning of the Gospel', in A.J. Malherbe and W.A. Meeks (eds.), *The Future of Christology* (Minneapolis: Fortress Press): 18-28.

Hoppe, L.
    1982   *Joshua–Judges* (Wilmington, DE: Michael Glazier).

Horgan, M.P.
    1979   *Pesharim: Qumran Interpretations of Biblical Books* (CBQMS, 8; Washington: Catholic Bible Association of America).

Horton, F.L.
    1978   'Reflections on the Semitisms of Luke–Acts', in C.H. Talbert (ed.), *Perspectives on Luke–Acts* (Danville, VA: Association of Baptist Professors of Religion): 1-23.

Irvin, D.
    1977   'The Joseph and Moses Stories as Narrative in the Light of Ancient Near Eastern Narrative', in J.H. Hayes and J.M. Miller (eds.), *Israelite and Judean History* (Philadelphia: Westminster Press): 180-203.

Jacobson, A.D.
    1978   'Wisdom Christology in Q' (unpublished dissertation, Claremont Graduate School [see *Dissertation Abstracts* 39/6 (1978) 3653A]).
    1992   *The First Gospel: An Introduction to Q* (Sonoma, CA: Polebridge Press).

Jellicoe, S.
    1968   *The Septuagint and Modern Study* (Oxford: Clarendon Press).

Jeremias, J.
    1966   *The Eucharistic Words of Jesus* (New York: Charles Scribner's Sons).

Jervell, J.
1996 'The Future of the Past: Luke's Vision of Salvation History and its Bearing on His Writing of History', in Witherington (ed.) 1996: 104-26.

Johnson, L.T.
1977 *The Literary Function of Possessions in Luke–Acts* (SBLDS, 39; Missoula, MA: Scholars Press).
1991 *The Gospel of Luke* (Sacra Pagina, Series 3; Collegeville, MN: Liturgical Press).
1993 'The Social Dimensions of *Sótéria* in Luke–Acts and Paul', in *SBLSP*: 520-36.
1996 *The Misguided Quest for the Historical Jesus and the Truth of the Traditional Gospels* (San Francisco: HarperSanFrancisco).
1998 *Religious Experience in Earliest Christianity: A Missing Dimension in New Testament Studies* (Minneapolis: Fortress Press).

Johnston, G.
1962 'Letter to the Ephesians', in *IDB*, II: 108-14.

Jügling, H.-W.
1981 *Richter 19—Ein Plädoyer Für Das Königtum: Stilistische Analyse der Tendenzerzählung Ri 19,1-30a; 21,25* (AnBib, 84; Rome: Biblical Institute).

Jülicher, A.
1899 *Die Gleichnisreden Jesu* (2 vols.; Freiberg: J.C.B. Mohr [Paul Siebeck], 2nd edn).

Karris, R.J.
1990 'The Gospel According to Luke', in *NJBC*, XLIII.

Kelber, W.H. (ed.)
1976 *The Passion in Mark: Studies on Mark 14–16* (Philadelphia: Fortress Press).
1980 'Review of Gerhardsson, Memory', *JAAR* 48: 279-80.
1983 *The Oral and Written Gospel: The Hermeneutics of Speaking and Writing in the Synoptic Tradition, Mark, Paul and Q* (Philadelphia: Fortress Press).
1992 'Oral Tradition', in *ABD*, V: 30-34.

Kennedy, G.
1980 *Classical Rhetoric and its Christian and Secular Traditions from Ancient to Modern Times* (Chapel Hill: University of North Carolina Press).
1984 *New Testament Interpretation through Rhetorical Criticism* (Chapel Hill: University of North Carolina).

Kenney, E.J.
1972 'The Historical Imagination of Lucretius', *Greece and Rome* 19: 12-24.

Kettenbach, G.
1997 *Das Logbuch des Lukas: Das Antike Schiff in Fahrt und vor Anker* (EH, 23/276; Frankfurt/New York: Peter Lang).

Kieffer, R.
1992 'Jean et Marc: Convergences dans la Structure et dans les Détails', in Denaux (ed.) 1992: 109-25.

Kieweler, H.V.
1992 *Ben Sira zwischen Judentum und Hellenismus. Eine Auseinandersetzung mit Th. Middendorp* (BEATAJ, 30; Frankfurt: Peter Lang).

Kilgallen, J.
1976 *The Stephen Speech: A Literary and Redactional Study of Acts 7,2-53* (AnBib, 67; Rome: Biblical Institute).

Kilian, R.
1966 'Die Totenerweckungen Elias und Elisas—eine Motivwanderung', *BZ* 10: 44-56.

Kim, J.
1993 *The Structure of the Samson Cycle* (Kampen: Kok Pharos).

Klein, L.R.
1988 *The Triumph in the Book of Judges* (JSOTSup, 68; Sheffield: JSOT Press).

Kleinig, J.W.
1994 'Recent Research in Chronicles', *CRBS* 2: 43-76.

Kloppenborg, J.S.
    1985   'Bibliography on Q', in *SBLSP*: 103-26.
    1986   'The Formation of Q and Antique Instructional Genres', *JBL* 105: 443-62.
    1987   *The Formation of Q: Trajectories in Ancient Wisdom Collections* (Studies in Antiquity and Christianity; Philadelphia: Fortress Press).
    1988   *Q Parallels* (Sonoma, CA: Polebridge Press).
    1995   'Conflict and Invention: *Recent Studies on Q*', in idem (ed.), *Conflict and Invention: Literary, Rhetorical and Social Studies on the Sayings Gospel Q* (Valley Forge, PA: Trinity Press International): 1-14.

Kloppenborg, J.S. (ed.)
    1994   *The Shape of Q: Signal Essays on the Sayings Gospel* (Minneapolis: Fortress Press).

Kloppenborg, J.S. et al. (eds.)
    1990   *Q Thomas Reader* (Sonoma, CA: Polebridge Press).

Klotz, A.
    1907   'Klassizismus und Archaismus: Stilistisches zu Statius', *ALL* 15: 401-17.

Knauer, G.N.
    1979   *Die Aeneis und Homer: Studien zur poetischen Technik Vergils mit listen der Homerzitate in der Aeneis* (Hypomnemata, 7; Göttingen: Vandenhoeck & Ruprecht, 2nd edn [1st edn 1964]).

Knowling, R.J.
    1974   'The Acts of the Apostles', in W.R. Nicoll (ed.), *The Expositor's Greek Testament* (repr.; Grand Rapids: Eerdmans): 49-554.

Koch, D.A.
    1986   *Die Schrift als Zeuge des Evangeliums. Untersuchungen zur Verwendung und zum Verständnis der Schrift bei Paulus* (BHT, 69; Tübingen: J.C.B. Mohr).

Koenen, L.
    1994   'Greece, the Near East, and Egypt: Destruction in Hesiod and *the Catalogue of Women*', *Transactions of the American Philological Association* 124: 1-34.

Koester, H.
    1994   'Written Gospels or Oral Tradition?', *JBL* 113: 293-97.

Koester, H., and J.M. Robinson (eds.)
    1971   *Trajectories through Early Christianity* (Philadelphia: Fortress Press).

Koet, B.J.
    1989   *Five Studies on Interpretation of Scripture in Luke–Acts* (SNTA, 14; Leuven: Leuven University Press/Peeters).

Kolarcil, M.
    1991   *The Ambiguity of Death in the Book of Wisdom 1–6: A Study of Literary Structure and Interpretation* (AnBib, 127; Rome: Pontifical Biblical Institute).

Königsmann, B.
    1798   *De fontibus commentariorum sacrorum, quae Lucae nomen praeferunt* (Altonae).

Kremer, J. (ed.)
    1979   *Les Actes des Apôtres: Traditions, rédaction, théologie* (BETL, 48; Gembloux: Duculot).

Kugel, J.L.
    1981   *The Idea of Biblical Poetry: Parallelism and Its History* (New Haven: Yale University Press).

Kügler, J.
    1984   'Das Johannesevangelium und sein Gemeinde—kein Thema für Science Fiction', *Biblische Notizen* 23: 48-62.

Kuhn, T.
    1970   *The Structure of Scientific Revolutions* (Chicago: University of Chicago Press, 2nd edn).

Kümmel, W.G.
    1972   *Introduction to the New Testament* (Nashville: Abingdon Press).
    1994   *Vierzig Jahre Jesusforschung (1950–1990)* (BBB, 91; Weinheim: Beltz Athenäum).

Kurz, W.S.
    1980b   'Hellenistic Rhetoric in the Christological Proof of Luke–Acts', *CBQ* 42: 171-95.

1980c	'Luke–Acts and Historiography in the Greek Bible', in P.J. Achtemeier (ed.), *SBLSP*: 283-300.
1980a	'Farewell Addresses in Luke–Acts and the Greek Bible' (unpublished paper delivered at the Catholic Biblical Association Annual General Meeting, Duluth, MN).
1990	'Narrative Models for Imitation in Luke–Acts', in D.L. Balch, E. Ferguson and W.A. Meeks (eds.), *Greeks, Romans, and Christians: Essays in Honor of Abraham J. Malherbe* (Minneapolis: Fortress Press): 171-89.

Lacan, M.-F.
1957   'Le Prologue de Saint Jean: Ses thèmes, sa structure, son mouvement', *LumVie* 33: 91-110.

Lambert, W.G.
1960   *Babylonian Wisdom Literature* (Oxford: Clarendon Press).

Lambrecht, J.
1980   '"Are you the one who is to come, or shall we look for another?": The Gospel Message of Jesus Today', *LouvStud* 8: 115-28.

Lampe, G.W.H.
1962   'Acts', *PCB*: 882-926.

Lanci, J.R.
1997   *A New Temple for Corinth: Rhetorical and Archaeological Approaches to Pauline Imagery* (New York: Peter Lang).

Larcher, C.
1969   *Etudes sur la Livre de la Sagesse* (EBib; Paris: J. Gabalda).
1983   *Le Livre de la Sagessse ou La Sagesse de Solomon* (EBib; 3 vols.; Paris: J. Gabalda).

Lattimore, R.
1951   *The Iliad of Homer* (Chicago: University of Chicago Press).

Laurent, Y.
1947   'Le Charactère Historique de Gen. II–III, dans l'Exégèse Française au Tournant du XIXe Siècle', *ETL* 23: 36-69.

Laurentin, R.
1957   *Structure et Théologie et Luc I–II* (EBib; Paris: J. Gabalda).

LaVerdiere, E.
1980   *Luke* (Wilmington, DE: M. Glazier).

Le Déaut, R.
1971   'Apropos a Definition of Midrash', *Int* 25: 259-82.

Lechte, J.
1994   *Fifty Key Contemporary Thinkers: From Structuralism to Postmodernity* (London: Routledge).

Lee, G.
1981   'Imitation and the Poetry of Virgil', *Greece and Rome* 28: 10-22.

Légasse, S.
1992   'Scribes', in *DBSup* 12: 244-81.

Leipoldt, J.
1958   'Ein neues Evangelium: Das Koptisch Thomasevangelium übersetzt und besprochen', *TLZ* 83: 481-96.

Leishman, J.B.
1956   *Translating Horace* (Oxford: Bruno Cassirer).

Lemaire, A.
1981   *Les Ecoles et la Formation de la Bible dans l'Ancient Israël* (OBO, 39; Göttingen: Vandenhoeck & Ruprecht).
1992   'Writing and Writing Materials', in *ABD*, VI: 999-1008.

Lenchak, T.A.
1993   *'Choose Life!' A Rhetorical-Critical Investigation of Deuteronomy 28,69–30,20* (AnBib, 129; Rome: Pontifical Biblical Institute).

Lentz, J.C.
1993   *Luke's Portrait of Paul* (SNTSMS, 77; New York/Cambridge: Cambridge University Press).

Lesky, A.
1966 *A History of Greek Literature* (New York: Crowell, 2nd edn).
Lieberman, S.
1962 *Hellenism in Jewish Palestine: Studies in the Literary Transmission, Beliefs and Manners of Palestine in the First Century B.C.E.* (New York: Jewish Theological Seminary of America).
Lindars, B.
1965 'Elijah, Elisha and the Gospel Miracles', in C.F.D. Moule (ed.), *Miracles* (London: A.R. Mowbray; New York: Morehouse-Barlow): 63-79.
1976a 'The Place of the Old Testament in the Formation of New Testament Theology', *NTS* 23: 59-66.
1976b 'Word and Sacrament in the Fourth Gospel', *SJT* 29: 49-63.
Lindijer, C.H.
1978 'Two Creative Encounters in the Work of Luke (Luke XXIV 13-35 and Acts VIII 26-40)', *Miscellanea Neotestamentica* (2 vols.; NovTSup, 47/48; Leiden: E.J. Brill): II, 77-86.
Linton, C.D.
1982 'Humor in the Bible', in G.W. Bromiley (ed.), *International Standard Bible Encyclopedia* (Grand Rapids: Eerdmans): II, 778-80.
Lipiński, E.
1988 'Royal and State Scribes in Ancient Jerusalem', in J.A. Emerton (ed.), *Congress Volume, Jerusalem 1986* (VTSup, 40; Leiden: E.J. Brill): 157-64.
Loisy, A.
1920 *Les Actes des Apôtres* (Paris: Nourry).
1924 *L'Evangile selon Luc* (Paris: Nourry).
Long, B.
1973 '2 Kings III and Genres of Prophetic Narrative', *VT* 23: 337-48.
Lord, A.B.
1964 *The Singer of Tales* (Cambridge, MA: Harvard University Press).
1978 'The Gospels as Oral Traditional Literature', in Walker (ed.) 1978: 33-91.
Lubetski, M., and C. Gottlieb
1996 '"Forever Gordon": Portrait of a Master Scholar with a Global Perspective', *BA* 59: 2-12.
Luz, U.
1980 'Markusforschung in der Sackgasse?', *TLZ* 105: 641-55.
Lyonnet, S.
1990 *Etudes sur l'Epître aux Romains* (AnBib 120; Rome: Biblical Institute).
Lyons, G.
1985 *Pauline Autobiography: Toward a New Understanding* (SBLDS, 73; Atlanta: Scholars Press).
MacDonald, D.R.
2000 *The Homeric Epics and the Gospel of Mark* (New Haven: Yale University Press).
Mack, B.L.
1973 *Logos und Sophia: Untersuchungen zur Weisheitstheologie im hellenistischen Judentum* (SUNT, 10; Göttingen: Vandenhoeck & Ruprecht).
1993 *The Lost Gospel: The Book of Q and Christian Origins* (San Francisco: Harper).
Mahon, R.
1989 'Autobiography as Text-Work: Augustine's Refiguring of Genesis 3 and Ovid's "Narcissus" in his Conversion Account', *Exemplaria* 1: 337-67.
Malamet, A.
1971 'The Period of the Judges', in B. Mazar (ed.), *The World History of the Jewish People* (London/New Brunswick: Rutgers University Press): III, 129-63.
Malherbe, A.J.
1986 *Moral Exhortation: A Greco-Roman Sourcebook* (Library of Early Christianity; Philadelphia: Westminster Press).
1989 *Paul and the Popular Philosophers* (Minneapolis: Fortress Press).

Mally, E.J.
1968 'The Gospel According to Mark', *JBC* 42: 21-61.
Maly, E.H.
1962 *The Book of Wisdom* (New York: Paulist Press).
1979 *Romans* (NT Message, 9; Wilmington, DE: Michael Glazier).
Marshall, I.H.
1978 *The Gospel of Luke* (Grand Rapids: Eerdmans).
1999 '"Israel" and the Story of Salvation: One Theme in Two Parts', in Moessner (ed.) 1999: 340-57.
Martin, R.
1981 *Tacitus* (London: Batsford Academic and Educational Press).
Martyn, J.L.
1997 *Galatians: A New Translation with Introduction and Commentary* (AB, 33; Garden City, NY: Doubleday).
Mattill, A.J. Jr
1979 *Luke and the Last Things: A Perspective for the Understanding of Lukan Thought* (Dillsboro: Western North Carolina Press).
May, R.
1972 *Love and Will* (London: Collins).
Mayes, A.D.H.
1974 *Israel in the Period of the Judges* (SBT, 2/29; London: SCM Press).
McGiffert, A.C.
1920–33 'The Historical Criticism of Acts in Germany', in F.J. Foakes Jackson and K. Lake (eds.), *The Beginnings of Christianity, Part I: The Acts of the Apostles* (5 vols.; London: Macmillan): II, 363-95.
McKeon, R.
1936 'Literary Criticism and the Concept of Imitation in Antiquity', *Modern Philology* 34: 1-35.
McLaglan Wilson, R.
1979 'Simon and Gnostic Origins', in Kremer (ed.) 1979: 485-91.
McMahon, R.
1989 'Autobiography as Text-Work: Augustine's Refiguring of Genesis 3 and Ovid's "Narcissus" in his Conversion Account', *Exemplaria: A Journal of Theory in Medieval and Renaissance Studies* 1: 337-67.
McNicol, A.J. *et al.* (eds.)
1996 *Beyond the Q Impasse: Luke's Use of Matthew* (A Demonstration by the Research Team of the International Institute for Gospel Studies; Valley Forge, PA: Trinity Press International).
Meeks, W.A.
1967 *The Prophet-King: Moses Traditions and the Johannine Christology* (NovTSup, 14; Leiden: E.J. Brill).
Meier, J.P.
1976 *Law and History in Matthew's Gospel: A Redactional Study of Mt. 5:17-48* (AnBib, 71; Rome: Biblical Institute).
1980 *Matthew* (NT Message, 3; Wilmington, DE: Michael Glazier).
1991–2001 *A Marginal Jew: Rethinking the Historical Jesus* (ABRL; 3 vols.; New York: Doubleday).
Meyers, E.M.
1992 'Synagogue', in *ABD*, VI: 251-60.
Miles, G.
1976 'Glorious Peace: The Values and Motivation of Virgil's Aeneas', *California Studies in Classical Antiquity* 9: 133-64.
Miller, D., and P. Miller
1990 *The Gospel of Mark as Midrash on Earlier Jewish and New Testament Literature* (Studies in the Bible and Early Christianity, 21; Lewiston, NY: Edwin Mellen Press).

Miller, D.G., and D.Y. Hadidian (eds.)
    1971   *Jesus and Man's Hope* (Pittsburg Festival on the Gospels, 1970; Pittsburg: Pittsburg Theological Seminary).

Miller, F.J.
    1907   *The Tragedies of Seneca* (Chicago: University of Chicago Press).
    1927–28 'Ovid's *Aeneid* and Virgil's: A Contrast in Motivation', *Classical Journal* 23: 33-43.

Miller, J.M.
    1966   'The Elisha Cycle and the Accounts of the Omride Wars', *JBL* 85: 441-54.

Miller, J.M., and J.H. Hayes
    1986   *A History of Ancient Israel and Judah* (Philadelphia: Westminster Press).

Minette de Tillesse, C.
    1992   'Structure Theologique de Marc', *Four Gospels* 2: 905-33.

Mitchell, M.M.
    1993   *Paul and the Rhetoric of Reconciliation: An Exegetical Investigation of the Language and Composition of 1 Corinthians* (Louisville, KY: Westminster/John Knox Press).

Moessner, D.P.
    1989   *Lord of the Banquet: The Literary and Theological Significance of the Lukan Travel Narrative* (Minneapolis: Fortress Press).

Moessner, D.P. (ed.)
    1999   *Jesus and the Heritage of Israel: Luke's Narrative Claim upon Israel's Legacy* (Harrisburg, PA: Trinity Press International).

Mohrlang, R.
    1984   *Matthew and Paul: A Comparison of Ethical Perspectives* (SNTSMS, 48; New York/Cambridge: Cambridge University Press).

Montgomery, J.A.
    1951   *A Critical and Exegetical Commentary on the Books of Kings* (ICC; Edinburgh: T. & T. Clark).

Moo, D.J.
    1983   *The Old Testament in the Gospel Passion Narratives* (Sheffield: Almond Press).

Moore, C.A.
    1996   *Tobit* (AB, 40A; Garden City, NY: Doubleday, 1996).

Moran, W.L.
    1969   'Deuteronomy', *NCCHS*: 223-40.

Morgenthaler, R.
    1949   *Die lukanische Geschichtsschreibung als Zeugnis: Gestalt und Gehalt der Kunst des Lukas* (2 vols.; Zurich: Zwingli Verlag).

Mourlon Beernaert, P.
    1988   'Structure littéraire et lecture théologique de Marc 14,17-52', in M. Sabbe (ed.), *L'Evangile selon Marc: Tradition et Rédaction* (BETL, 34; Leuven: University Press/Peeters): 241-68.

Müller, P.
    1988   *Anfänge der Paulusschule: Dargestellt am zweiten Thessalonischerbrief und am Kolosserbrief* (AThANT, 74; Zürich: Theologischer Verlag).

Murphy-O'Connor, J.
    1967–68 'Miracles in Matthew', in *The Bible* (A Supplement to *The Furrow* 3 [1967]: 1-4; *The Furrow* 4 [1968]: 8-13; *The Furrow* 5 [1968]: 12-15).
    1979   *Acts of the Apostles: A Commentary* (Philadelphia: Fortress Press).
    1990   '1 Corinthians', in *NJBC*, XLIX.
    1992   'Qumran, Khirbet', in *ABD*, V: 590-94.
    1995   *Paul the Letter-Writer: His World, His Options, His Skills* (Collegeville, MN: Liturgical Press).

Murray, P.
    1991a   *The Absent Fountain* (Dublin: Dedalus).
    1991b   *T.S. Eliot and Mysticism: The Secret History of Four Quartets* (London: Macmillan).

Myers, J.M.
    1965a   *1 Chronicles* (AB, 12; Garden City, NY: Doubleday).
    1965b   *Ezra: Nehemiah* (AB, 14; Garden City, NY: Doubleday).
Neirynck, F.
    1974   *The Minor Agreements of Matthew and Luke against Mark, with a Cumulative List* (BETL, 37; Leuven: Leuven University Press).
    1976   'Q', in *IDBSup*: 715-16.
    1977   'John and the Synoptics', in De Jonge (ed.) 1977: 73-106.
    1978   'The Symbol Q (= Quelle)', *ETL* 54: 119-25.
    1982   'Recent Developments in the Study of Q', in Delobel (ed.) 1982: 29-75.
    1984   'John and the Synoptics: The Empty Tomb Stories', *NTS* 30: 161-87.
    1988a   *Duality in Mark: Contributions to the Study of the Markan Redaction* (BETL, 31; Leuven: Leuven University Press/Peeters).
    1988b   *Q Synopsis: The Double Tradition Passages in Greek* (SNTA, 13; Leuven: Leuven University Press/Peeters).
    1990a   'Introduction: The Two-Source Hypothesis', in D.L. Dungan (ed.), *The Interrelations of the Gospels* (BETL, 95: Leuven: Leuven University Press): 3-22.
    1990b   'Synoptic Problem', in *NJBC*, XL.
    1991   *Evangelica II: 1982–91: Collected Essays* (BETL, 95; Leuven: Leuven University Press).
    1992   'John and the Synoptics: 1975–1990', in Denaux (ed.) 1992: 3-62.
    1993a   'The International Q Project', *ETL* 69: 221-25.
    1993b   Review of *The First Gospel: An Introduction to Q* [by A.D. Jacobson], *ETL* 69: 177-79.
    1993c   Review of *Q-Thomas Reader* [by J.S. Kloppenborg *et al.*], *ETL* 69: 175-77.
    1996   'The Sayings of Jesus in 1 Corinthians', in Bieringer (ed.) 1996: 141-76.
Neirynck, F., and F. Van Segbroeck
    1982   'Q Bibliography', in Delobel (ed.) 1982: 561-86.
    1983–91 'Bibliography on Q', *ETL ElBib* 59: 214-15; 60: 197; 61: 212-13; 62: 215-16; 63: 219-20; 64: 222; 65: 237-38; 66: 257-59; 67: 255-56.
Neirynck, F., and J. Verheyden
    1992   'Bibliography on Q', *ETL ElBib* 68: 259-60.
Neirynck, F. *et al.*
    1992   *The Gospel of Mark: A Cumulative Bibliography 1950–1990* (BETL, 102; Leuven: Leuven University/Peeters Press [also published as CBRA, III; Brussels: Koninklije Academie]).
Nelson, P.K.
    1994   *Leadership and Discipleship: A Study of Luke 22:24-30* (SBLDS, 138; Atlanta: Scholars Press).
Neusner, J.
    1971   'The Rabbinic Traditions about the Pharisees before A.D. 70: The Problem of Oral Transmission', *JJS* 22: 1-18.
    1979   *Method and Meaning in Ancient Judaism* (BJS, 10; Missoula, MT: Scholars Press).
    1985   *The Memorized Torah: The Mnemonic System of the Mishnah* (BJS, 96; Chico, CA: Scholars Press).
Neyrey, J.
    1985   *The Passion According to Luke* (New York: Paulist Press).
Nielsen, E.
    1954   *Oral Tradition* (SBT, 11; London: SCM Press).
Nineham, D.E. (ed.)
    1955   *Studies in the Gospels: Essays in Memory of R.H. Lightfoot* (Oxford: Basil Blackwell).
Nodet, E., and J. Taylor
    1998   *The Origins of Christianity. An Exploration* (Collegeville, MN: Liturgical Press).
Nogalski, J.
    1993   *Literary Precursors to the Book of the Twelve* (BZAW, 217; Berlin/New York: W. de Gruyter).

Nordheim, E.V.
1978 'Ein Prophet kündigt sein Amt auf (Elia am Horeb)', *Bib* 59: 153-73.

North, R.
1990 'The Chronicler: 1–2 Chronicles, Ezra, Nehemiah', in *NJBC*, XXIII.

O'Brien, J., and W. Major
1982 *In the Beginning: Creation Myths from Ancient Mesopotamia, Israel and Greece* (Chico, CA: Scholars Press).

O'Day, G.
1982 'Hellenistic Romances and Early Christian Narratives' (unpublished paper delivered at the AAR/SBL regional meeting, Gainesville, FL).

Ogden, S.M.
1986 *On Theology* (San Francisco: Harper & Row).
1992 *The Point of Christology* (Dallas: Southern Methodist University Press).

Ong, W.
1971 *Rhetoric, Romance and Technology* (Ithaca, NY: Cornell University Press).
1977 *Interfaces of the Word: Studies in the Evolution of Consciousness and Culture* (Ithaca, NY: Cornell University Press).

Orton, D.E.
1989 *The Understanding Scribe: Matthew and the Apocalyptic Ideal* (JSNTSup, 25; Sheffield: JSOT Press).

Osty, E.
1957 *Le Livre de la Sagesse* (Paris: Cerf).

Otis, B.
1966 *Ovid as an Epic Poet* (Cambridge: Cambridge University Press).

O'Toole, R.F.
1983 'Philip and the Ethiopian Eunuch (Acts VIII 25-40)', *JSNT* 17: 25-34.

Page, A.F.
1968 'Proto-Luke Reconsidered: A Study of Literary Method and Theology in the Gospel of Luke' (unpublished dissertation, Durham, NC: Duke University).

Palmer, D.W.
1993 'Acts and the Ancient Historical Monograph', in *Acts' Setting*: I, 1-29.

Parry, M.
1971 *The Making of Homeric Verse: The Collected Papers of Milman Parry* (Oxford: Clarendon Press).

Pate, C.M.
2000 *The Reverse of the Curse: Paul, Wisdom, and the Law* (WUNT, 2/114; Tübingen: Mohr Siebeck).

Pavlovsky, V.
1957 'Die Chronologie der Tätigkeit Esdras: Versuch einer neuen Lösung', *Bib* 39: 436-39.

Pelling, C.B.R.
1980 'Plutarch's Adaptation of His Source-Material', *Journal of Hellenic Studies* 100: 127-40.

Perrin, N.
1974 *The New Testament—An Introduction: Proclamation and Parenesis: Myth and History* (New York: Harcourt Brace Jovanovich).

Pervo, R.I.
1987 *Profit with Delight: The Literary Genre of the Acts of the Apostles* (Philadelphia: Fortress Press).
1999 'Israel's Heritage and Claims upon the Genre(s) of Luke and Acts: The Problems of a History', in Moessner (ed.) 1999: 127-43.

Piper, R.A.
1989 *Wisdom in the Q Tradition* (SNTSMS, 61; New York/Cambridge: Cambridge University Press).

Plümacher, E.
1971 *Lukas als hellenistischer Schriftsteller* (SUNT, 9. Göttingen: Vandenhoeck & Ruprecht).

Plummer, A.
  1909   *An Exegetical Commentary on the Gospel According to S. Matthew* (London: Robert Scott).
Polag, A.
  1979   *Fragmenta Q: Textheft zur Logienquelle* (Neukirchen–Vluyn: Neukirchener Verlag).
Polanyi, M.
  1958   *Personal Knowledge: Toward a Post-Critical Philosophy* (Chicago: University of Chicago).
Pope, M.H.
  1977   *Song of Songs: A New Translation with Introduction and Commentary* (AB, 7C; Garden City, NY: Doubleday).
Porter, S.E.
  1990   'The Parable of the Unjust Steward (Luke 16:1-13): Irony *is* the Key', in D.J.A. Clines, S.E. Fowl and S. Porter (eds.), *The Bible in Three Dimensions: Essays in Celebration of Forty Years of Biblical Studies in the University of Sheffield* (JSOTSup, 87; Sheffield: JSOT Press): 125-53.
Porton, G.
  1979   'Midrash: Palestinian Jews and the Hebrew Bible in the Greco-Roman Period', in *ANRW* XIX, 2: 103-38.
  1985   *Understanding Rabbinic Midrash* (Hoboken, NJ: Ktav).
Praeder, S.M.
  1980   'The Narrative Voyage: An Analysis and Interpretation of Acts 27–28' (unpublished dissertation, Berkeley, CA: Graduate Theological Union).
  1981   'Luke–Acts and the Ancient Novel', in *SPLSP*: 269-308.
Preminger, A. (ed.)
  1975   *Princeton Encyclopedia of Poetry and Poetics* (Princeton, NJ: Princeton University Press, enlarged edn).
Preuss, H.D.
  1993   'Zum deuteronomistischen Geschichtswerk', *TRu* 58: 229-64, 341-95.
Przybylski, B.
  1980   *Righteousness in Matthew and his World of Thought* (SNTSMS, 41; Cambridge: Cambridge University Press).
Puech, E.
  1988a   'Les Ecoles dans l'Israel Préexilique: Données Epigraphiques', in J.A. Emerton (ed.), *Congress Volume, Jerusalem 1986* (VTSup, 40; Leiden: E.J. Brill): 189-203.
  1988b   'Un hymne essénien en partie retrouvé et les béatitudes: 1QH V 12–VI 18 (= col. XIII–XIV 7) et 4Q Béat', *RevQ* 13: 59-88.
  1991   '4Q525 et les Péricopes des Béatitudes en Ben Sira et Matthieu', *RB* 98: 80-106.
Quesnell, Q.
  1969   *The Mind of Mark: Interpretation and Method through the Exegesis of Mark 6:52* (AnBib, 38; Rome: Pontifical Biblical Institute).
Quintilian
  1960   *Institutio Oratoria* (trans. H.E. Butler; LCL; Cambridge: Harvard University Press, 1960).
Rad, G. von
  1962   *Old Testament Theology* (2 vols.; New York: Harper & Row).
  1966   *Deuteronomy* (Philadelphia: Westminster Press).
Reese, J.M.
  1970   *Hellenistic Influence on the Book of Wisdom and its Consequences* (AnBib, 41; Rome: Biblical Institute).
Reicke, B.
  1964   *The Epistles of James, Peter and Jude* (AB, 37; New York: Doubleday).
Reiff, A.
  1959   'Interpretatio, Imitatio, Aemulatio: Begriff und Vorstellung Literarischer Abhängigkeit bei den Römern' (unpublished dissertation, Cologne: Universität Köln).

Rese, M.
　1969　　　*Alttestamentliche Motive in der Christologie des Lukas* (Studien zum NeuenTestament, 1; Gütersloh: Gerd Mohn).

Reuter, R.
　1997　　　*Synopsis of the New Testament Letters*. I. *I. Colossians, Ephesians, II. Thessalonians* (StdRHEC, 5; 2 vols.; Frankfurt/New York: Peter Lang).

Reynier, C.
　1996　　　'Le Language de la Croix dans le Corpus paulinien', in Schlosser (ed.) 1996: 361-73.

Richard, E.
　1978　　　*Acts 6:1–8:4: The Author's Method of Composition* (SBLDS, 41; Missoula, MT: Scholars Press).
　1980　　　'The Old Testament in Acts: Wilcox's Semitisms in Retrospect', *CBQ* 42: 330-41.

Richardson, P.
　1987　　　'Gospel Traditions in the Church in Corinth (with Apologies to B.H. Streeter)', in G.F. Hawthorne with O. Betz (eds.), *Tradition and Interpretation in the New Testament* (Grand Rapids: Eerdmans): 301-18.

Rigaux, B.
　1956　　　*Les Epitres aux Thessaloniciens* (Paris: J. Gabalda).

Riley, H.
　1993　　　*Preface to Luke* (Macon, GA: Mercer University Press).

Riley, W.
　1993　　　*King and Cultus in Chronicles: Worship and the Reinterpretation of History* (JSOTSup, 160; Sheffield: JSOT Press).

Robbins, V.K.
　1994　　　*New Boundaries in Old Territory: Form and Social Rhetoric in Mark* (Emory Studies in Early Christianity, 3; New York: Peter Lang).
　1996　　　*The Tapestry of Early Christian Discourse: Rhetoric, Society and Ideology* (London/New York: Routledge).

Robinson, J.M.
　1971a　　'Kerygma and History in the New Testament', in Koester and Robinson (eds.) 1971: 20-70.
　1971b　　'"LOGOI SOPHON" On the Gattung of Q', in Koester and Robinson (eds.) 1971: 71-113.
　1975　　　'Jesus as Sophos and Sophia', in Wilken (ed.) 1975: 1-16.
　1992　　　'A Critical Text of the Sayings Gospel Q', *RHPR* 72: 15-22.

Robinson, J.M., P. Hoffmann and J.S. Kloppenborg
　2000　　　*The Critical Edition of Q* (Leuven: Peeters).

Rogerson, J.W.
　1974　　　*Myth in Old Testament Interpretation* (BZAW, 134; Berlin/New York: W. de Gruyter).

Rolland, P.
　1984　　　*Les Premiers Egangiles: Un nouveau Regard sur le Problème Synoptique* (LD, 116; Paris: Cerf).
　1992　　　'Marc, lecteur de Pierre et de Paul', *Four Gospels* 2: 775-78.

Roloff, J.
　1972–73　'Die Deutung des Todes Jesu', *NTS* 19: 38-64.

Rosner, B.S.
　1993　　　'Acts and Biblical History', in *Acts' Setting*: I, 65-82.
　1994　　　*Paul's Scripture and Ethics: A Study of 1 Corinthians 5–7* (AGJU, 22; Leiden: E.J. Brill).

Roth, W.
　1988　　　*Hebrew Gospel: Cracking the Code of Mark* (Chicago: Meyer-Stone).

Roudiez, L.S.
　1980　　　'Introduction', to Julia Kristeva, *Desire in Language: A Semiotic Approach to Literature and Art* (New York: Columbia University): 1-20.

Rybolt, J.E.
    1986   *Wisdom* (Collegeville, MN: Liturgical Press).
Sabbe, M.
    1991   *Studia Neotestamentica: Collected Essays* (BETL, 98; Leuven: Leuven University Press/Peeters).
    1994   'The Johannine Account of the Death of Jesus and Its Synoptic Parallels (Jn 19, 16b-42)', *ETL* 70: 34-64.
Sabbe, M. (ed.)
    1988   *L'Evangile Selon Marc: Tradition et Rédaction* (BETL, 34; Leuven: Leuven University Press/Peeters, 2nd edn).
Safrai, S.
    1987   'Oral Tora', in *idem* (ed.), *The Literature of the Sages—First Part: Oral Tora, Halaka, Mishna, Tosefta, Talmud, External Tractates* (CRINT, 2/1; Philadelphia: Fortress Press; Assen: Van Gorcum): 35-119.
Sahlin, H.
    1945   *Der Messias und das Gottesfolk; Studien zur protolukanischen Theologie* (ASNU, 12; Uppsala: Almqvist & Wiksell).
    1949   *Studien zum dritten Kapitel des Lukasevangeliums* (Leipzig: Otto Harrassowitz).
Sanders, J.A.
    1975   'From Isaiah 61 to Luke 4', in J. Neusner (ed.), *Christianity, Judaism and Other Greco-Roman Cults* (Leiden: E.J. Brill): 75-106.
    1978   Review of R.E. Brown's *The Birth of the Messiah*, *USQR* 33: 193-96.
Sarason, R.S.
    1981   'Towards a New Agendum for the Study of Rabbinic Midrashic Literature', in E. Fleischer and J.J. Petuchowski (eds.), *Studies in Aggadah, Targum and Jewish Liturgy in Memory of Joseph Heinemann* (Jerusalem: Magnes Press).
Sato, M.
    1988   *Q und Prophetie: Studien zur Gattungs und Traditionsgeschichte der Quelle Q* (WUNT, 2/29; Tübingen: J.C.B. Mohr).
Satterthwaite, P.E.
    1991   'Some Septuagintal Pluses in Judges 20 and 21', *BIOSCS* 24: 25-35.
    1993   'Acts Against the Background of Classical Rhetoric', in *Acts' Setting*: I, 337-79.
Scheid, J., and J. Svenbro
    1966   *The Craft of Zeus: Myths of Weaving and Fabric* (Cambridge, MA/London: Harvard University Press).
Schenk, W.
    1981   *Synopse der Redenquelle der Evangelien: Q-Synopse und Rekonstruktion in deutscher Übersetzung mit kurzen Erläuterungen* (Düsseldorf: Patmos).
    1992   'Sekundäre Jesuanisierungen von primären Paulus-Aussagen bei Markus', *Four Gospels* 2: 877-904.
Schillebeeckx, E.
    1979   *Jesus: An Experiment in Christology* (New York: Seabury).
Schleiermacher, F.D.E.
    1932   'Über die Zeugnisse des Papias von unsern beiden ersten Evangelien', *Theologische Studien und Kritiken* 5: 735-68.
Schlosser, J. (ed.)
    1996   *Paul de Tarse* (LD, 165; Paris: Cerf).
Schmid, H.H.
    1976   *Der sogennante Jahwist: Beobachtungen und Fragen zur Pentateuchforschung* (Zurich: Theologischer Verlag).
    1977   'In Search of New Approaches in Pentateuchal Research', *JSOT* 3: 33-42.
Schmidt, K.L.
    1919   *Der Rahmen der Geschichte Jesu: Literarkritische Untersuchungen zür ältesten Jesusüberlieferung* (Berlin: Trowizsch & Sohn).
Schmithals, W.
    1980   'Kritik der Formkritik', *ZTK* 77: 149-85.

Schmitt, H.-C.
    1972   *Elisa: Traditionsgeschichtliche Untersuchungen* (Gütersloh: Gerd Mohn).
Schneider, G.
    1980   *Die Apostelgeschichte: Erster Teil: Einleitung. Kommentar zu Kap. 1,1–8,40* (HTKNT, 5/1; Freiburg: Herder).
Schneiders, S.S.
    1986   'Theology and Spirituality: Strangers, Rivals, or Partners?', *Horizons* 13: 253-74.
    1989   'Spirituality in the Academy', *Theological Studies* 50: 676-97.
    1991   *The Revelatory Text: Interpreting the New Testament as Sacred Scripture* (San Francisco: HarperSanFrancisco).
    1993   'Spirituality as an Academic Discipline: Reflections from Experience', *Christian Spirituality Bulletin* 1: 10-15.
    1994   'A Hermeneutical Approach to the Study of Christian Spirituality', *Christian Spirituality Bulletin* 2: 9-14.
    1998   'The Study of Christian Spirituality: Contours and Dynamics of a Discipline', *Christian Spirituality Bulletin* 8: 38-57.
Scholer, D.M
    1986–93   'Q Bibliography', *SBLSP* 28: 23-37.
Scott, R.B.Y.
    1965   *Proverbs: Ecclesiastes* (AB, 18; New York: Doubleday).
Schulz, S.
    1972a   *Griechisch-deutsche Synopse der Q-Überlieferungen* (Zürich: Theologischer Verlag).
    1972b   *Q: Die Spruchquelle der Evangelisten* (Zürich: Theologischer Verlag).
Schürmann, H.
    1969   *Das Lukasevangelium, 1:1–9:50* (HTKNT, III.I; Freiburg: Herder).
Schweizer, E.
    1975   *The Good News According to Matthew* (London: SPCK).
Schweizer, H.
    1974   *Elischa in den Kriegen. Literaturwissenschaftliche Untersuchung von 2 Kön 3; 6,8-23; 6:24–7:20* (SANT, 37; Munich: Kösel).
Schwenk-Bressler, U.
    1991   *Sapientia Salomonis als ein Beispiel früjüdischer Textauslegung* (BEATAJ, 32; Frankfurt: Peter Lang).
Sellin, G.
    1983   'Das Leben des Gottesohnes: Taufe und Verklärung Jesu als Bestandteile eines vormarkinischen Evangeliums', *Kairos* 25: 237-53.
Selong, G.
    1971   'The Cleansing of the Temple in Jn 2,13-22, with a Reconsideration of the Dependence of the Fourth Gospel upon the Synoptics' (unpublished dissertation, Leuven University [abstracted in *ETL* 48 (1972)]: 212-13).
Selwyn, E.G.
    1961   *The First Epistle of St. Peter* (London: Macmillan).
Seneca
    1966   *Four Tragedies and Octavia* (trans. E.P. Watling; Harmondsworth: Penguin Books).
Senior, D.
    1983   *What Are They Saying About Matthew?* (New York: Paulist Press).
Shires, H.M.
    1974   *Finding the Old Testament in the New* (Philadelphia: Westminster Press).
Skehan, P.
    1938   'The Literary Relationship between the Book of Wisdom and the Protocanonical Wisdom Books of the Old Testament' (unpublished dissertation, Washington, DC: Catholic University).
Smend, R.
    1975   'Der Biblische und der Historische Elia', in G.W. Anderson *et al.* (eds.), *Congress Volume, Edinburgh 1974* (VTSup, 28; Leiden: E.J. Brill): 167-84.

Smith, D.M.
 1992 *John among the Gospels: The Relationship in Twentieth-Century Research* (Minneapolis: Fortress Press).

Snodgrass, K.R.
 1992 'Matthew's Understanding of the Law', *Int* 46: 376-78.

Soggin, J.A.
 1981 *Judges: A Commentary* (OTL; Philadelphia: Westminster Press).

Stanley, C.D.
 1988 'LXX and NT: A Review [of Koch, 1986]', *BIOSCS* 21: 3-9.
 1992 *Paul and the Language of Scripture: Citation Technique in the Pauline Epistles and Contemporary Literature* (Cambridge: Cambridge University Press).

Steck, O.H.
 1968 *Überlieferung und Zeitgeschichte in den Eliaerzählungen* (WMANT, 26; Neukirchen–Vluyn: Neukirchener Verlag).

Stegemann, H.
 1998 *The Library of Qumran: On the Essenes, Qumran, John the Baptist, and Jesus* (Grand Rapids: Eerdmans; Leiden: E.J. Brill [Ger. 1993]).

Steiner, G.
 1975 *After Babel: Aspects of Language and Translation* (New York/Oxford: Oxford University Press).

Stendahl, K.
 1954 *The School of St Matthew and its Use of the Old Testament* (ASNU, 20; Lund: C.W.K. Gleerup).

Sterling, G.E.
 1992 *Historiography and Self-Definition: Josephus, Luke–Acts and Apologetic Historiography* (NovTSup, 44; Leiden: E.J. Brill).

Stibbe, M.W.G.
 1992 *John as Storyteller: Narrative Criticism and the Fourth Gospel* (SNTSMS, 73; Cambridge/New York: Cambridge University Press).

Stipp, H.-J.
 1987 *Elischa-Propheten-Gottesmänner: Die Kompositionsgeschichte des Elischazyklus und verwandter Texte, rekonstruirt auf der Basis von Text- und Literarkritik zu 1 Kön 20.22 und 2 Kön 2–7* (ATS, 24; Erzabtei St Ottilien: EOS Verlag).

Stock, K.
 1980 'Die Berufung Maria', *Bib* 61: 457-91.

Stockhausen, C.K.
 1989 *Moses' Veil and the Story of the New Covenant: The Exegetical Substructure of II Cor. 3.1–4.6* (AnBib, 116; Rome: Pontifical Biblical Institute).
 1993 '2 Corinthians 3 and the Principles of Pauline Exegesis', in Evans and Sanders (eds.) 1993: 143-64.

Stowers, S.K.
 1986 *Letter-Writing in Greco-Roman Antiquity* (Library of Early Christianity; Philadelphia: Westminster Press).

Strecker, G. (ed).
 1993 *Minor Agreements: Symposium Göttingen 1991* (Göttingen: Vandenhoeck & Ruprecht).

Streeter, B.H.
 1924 *The Four Gospels: A Study of Origins* (London: Macmillan).

Stroumsa, G.G.
 1998 'The Christian Hermeneutical Revolution and its Double Helix', in L.V. Rutgers *et al.* (eds.), *The Use of Sacred Books in the Ancient World* (Contributions to Biblical Theology and Exegesis, 22; Leuven: Peeters): 9-28.

Stuhlmueller, C.
 1968 'The Gospel According to Luke', *JBC* 44.

Suggs, M.J.
 1970 *Wisdom, Christology and Law in Matthew's Gospel* (Cambridge, MA: Harvard University Press).

Swartley, W.M.
- 1994 *Israel's Scripture Traditions and the Synoptic Gospels: Story Shaping Story* (Peabody, MA: Hendrickson).

Sybel, V.
- 1924 'Die Salbungen', *ZNW* 23: 184-93.

Tacitus
- 1915 *The Histories of Tacitus* (G.G. Ramsay; London: John Murray).

Talbert, C.H.
- 1977 *What is a Gospel? The Genre of the Canonical Gospels* (Philadelphia: Fortress Press).
- 1978 'Oral and Independent or Literary and Interdependent? A Response to Albert A. Lord', in Walker (ed.) 1978: 93-102.
- 1986 *Reading Luke: A Literary and Theological Commentary on the Third Gospel* (New York: Crossroad).
- 1992 'Biography, Ancient', in *ABD*, I: 745-49.

Tannehill, R.C.
- 1984 'The Composition of Acts 3–5: Narrative Development and Echo Effect', in K.H. Richards (ed.), *Seminar Papers* (SBLASP, 23; Chico, CA: Scholars Press): 217-40.
- 1986 *The Narrative Unity of Luke–Acts: A Literary Interpretation.* I. *The Gospel According to Luke* (Philadelphia: Fortress Press).
- 1999 'The Story of Israel within the Lukan Narrative', in Moessner (ed.) 1999: 325-39.

Taylor, V.
- 1926 *Behind the Third Gospel* (Oxford: Oxford University Press).

Telford, W.R.
- 1992 'The Pre-Markan Tradition in Recent Research (1980–1990)', *Four Gospels* 2: 693-723.
- 1995 *Mark* (New Testament Guides, 2; Sheffield: Sheffield Academic Press).

Theron, D.J.
- 1957 *Evidence of Tradition* (Grand Rapids: Baker Book House).

Thiel, W.
- 1991 'Deuteronomistische Redaktionsarbeit in den Elia-Erzählungen', in J.A. Emerton (ed.), *Congress Volume, Leuven 1989* (VTSup, 43; Leiden: E.J. Brill): 148-71.

Thompson, C.L.
- 1979–80 'Cicero's Editing of Mythographic Material in the *De Natura Deorum*', *Classical Journal* 75: 143-52.

Thompson, M.B.
- 1998 'The Holy Internet: Communications Between Churches in the First Century Generation', in Bauckham (ed.) 1998: 49-70.

Thompson, R.J.
- 1970 *Moses and the Law in a Century of Criticism Since Graf* (VTSup, 19; Leiden: E.J. Brill).

Thompson, T.L.
- 1992 *Early History of the Israelite People: From the Written and Archaeological Sources* (SHANE; Leiden/New York/Köln: E.J. Brill).

Thompson, W.G
- 1970 *Matthew's Advice to a Divided Community* (AnBib, 44; Rome: Biblical Institute).

Thysman, R.
- 1966 'L'Ethique de l'Imitation du Christ dans le Nouveau Testament: Situations, Notations et Variations du Thème', *ETL* 42: 138-75.

Trible, P.
- 1984 *Texts of Terror: Literary-Feminist Readings of Biblical Narratives* (Philadelphia: Fortress Press).

Trocmé, E.
- 1975 *The Formation of the Gospel According to Mark* (Philadelphia: Westminster Press [Fr. 1963]).

Tuckett, C.M. (ed.)
- 1984 *Synoptic Studies: The Ampleforth Conferences of 1982 and 1983* (JSNTSup, 7; Sheffield: JSOT Press).
- 1996 *Q and the History of Earliest Christianity: Studies on Q* (Edinburgh: T. & T. Clark).

Turner, C.
1969 'History', in Higginbotham (ed.) 1969: 300-41.
Turner, N.
1959 'The Minor Verbal Agreements of Mt. and Lk. against Mk', in K. Aland *et al.* (eds.), *Studia Evangelica I* (TU, 73; Berlin: Akademie Verlag): 223-34.
Underhill, E.
1930 *Mysticism: A Study of the Nature and Development of Man's Spiritual Consciousness* (London: Methuen, 12th edn).
Utzschneider, H.
1989 *Künder oder Schreiber? Eine These zum Problem der 'Schriftprophetie' auf Grund von Malachi 1,6–2,9* (BEATAJ, 19; Frankfurt: Peter Lang).
Vaage, L.E.
1989 'Q and the Historical Jesus: Some Peculiar Sayings (7:33-34; 9:57-58, 59-60; 14:26-27)', *Forum* 5: 159-76.
Van Belle, G.
1975 *De Semeia-Bron in het Vierde Evangelie: Onstaan en groei van een hypothese* (SNTA, 10; Leuven: Leuven University Press).
1994 *The Signs Source in the Fourth Gospel: Historical Survey and Critical Evaluation of the Semeia Hypothesis* (BETL, 116; Leuven: Leuven University Press/Peeters).
Van Buren, P.M.
1998 *According to the Scriptures: The Origins of the Gospel and of the Church's Old Testament* (Grand Rapids: Eerdmans).
Van Ruiten, J.T.A.G.M.
1992 'The Intertextual Relationship Between Isa 11,6-9 and Isa 65,25', in F. García Martínez *et al.*, *The Scriptures and the Scrolls: Studies in Honour of A.S. van der Woude on the Occasion of his 65th birthday* (VTSup, 49; Leiden: E.J. Brill): 31-42.
Van Segbroeck, F.
1972 'Les citations d'accomplissement dans l'Evangile selon saint Matthieu d'après trois ouvrages récents', in M. Didier (ed.), *L'Evangile selon Matthieu: Rédaction et Théologie* (BETL, 29; Duculot: Gembloux): 107-30.
Van Seters, J.
1983 *In Search of History: Historiography in the Ancient World and the Origins of Biblical History* (New Haven/London: Yale University Press).
1992 *Prologue to History: The Yahwist as Historian in Genesis* (Louisville, KY: Westminster/ John Knox Press).
1994a *The Life of Moses: The Yahwist as Historian in Exodus–Numbers* (Kampen: Kok Pharos).
1994b 'The Theology of the Yahwist: A Preliminary Sketch', in Ingo Kottsieper *et al.* (eds.), *Wer ist wie du, HERR, unter den Göttern: Studien zur Theologie und Religionsgeschichte für Otto Kaiser zum 70. Geburtstag* (Göttingen: Vandenhoeck & Ruprecht): 219-28.
Van Unnik, W.C.
1979 'Luke's Second Book and the Rules of Hellenistic Historiography', in Kremer (ed.) 1979: 37-60.
Van Wolde, E.
1989 'Trendy Intertextuality?', in Draisma (ed.) 1989: 43-49.
Vaux, R. de
1958 *Les Livre des Rois* (La Sainte Bible; Paris: Cerf, 2nd edn).
1965 *Ancient Israel: Its Life and Institutions* (London: Darton, Longman & Todd, 2nd edn).
Vaux, R. de, *et al.*
1977 *Discoveries in the Judean Desert. VI. Qumrân Grotte 4/II. 1: Archéologie. II. Tefillim, Mezuzot et Targum (4Q 128–4Q 157)* (Oxford: Clarendon Press).
Vermes, G.
1973 *Scripture and Tradition in Judaism: Haggadic Studies* (Studia Post-Biblica, 4; Leiden: E.J. Brill, 2nd edn [1st edn 1961]).
1994 *The Dead Sea Scrolls: Qumran in Perspective* (London: SCM Press, rev. edn).
1997 *The Complete Dead Sea Scrolls in English* (London: Allen Lane/Penguin Books).

Via, D.O.
    1990   *Self-Deception and Wholeness in Paul and Matthew* (Minneapolis: Fortress Press).

Vielhauer, P.
    1968   'On the Paulinism of Acts', in L.E. Keck and J.L. Martyn (eds.), *Studies in Luke–Acts* (London: SPCK).

Vieweger, D.
    1993   *Die literarischen Beziehungen zwischen den Büchern Jeremia und Ezekiel* (BEATAJ, 26; Frankfurt: Peter Lang).

Viviano, B.T.
    1990   'The Gospel According to Matthew', in *NJBC*, XLII.

Volkmar, G.
    1876   *Marcus und die Synopse der Evangelien nach dem urkundlichen Text und das Geschichtliche vom Leben Jesu* (Zürich: Schmidt).

Von Stackelberg, J.
    1956   'Das Bienengleichnis', *Romanische Forschungen* 68: 271-93.

Walker, W.O. (ed.)
    1978   *The Relationships among the Gospels: An Interdisciplinary Dialogue* (San Antonio, TX: Trinity University).

Walsh, J.T.
    1982   'The Elijah Cycle: A Synchronic Approach' (unpublished dissertation, University of Michigan).

Walsh, P.G.
    1961   *Livy: His Historical Aims and Methods* (Cambridge: Cambridge University Press).

Wansbrough, H. (ed.)
    1991   *Jesus and the Oral Gospel Tradition* (JSNTSup, 64; Sheffield: JSOT Press).

Warner, S.M.
    1979   'Primitive Saga Men', *VT* 29: 325-35.

Watts, R.E.
    1997   *Isaiah's New Exodus and Mark* (WUNT, 2nd Series, 88; Tübingen: Mohr Siebeck).

Webb, B.G.
    1987   *The Book of Judges: An Integrated Reading* (JSOTSup, 46; Sheffield: JSOT Press).

Webster, J.
    1976   'Oral Form and Written Craft in Spenser's Faerie Queene', *Studies in English Literature* 16: 75-93

Wegner, U.
    1982–83   'Der Hauptmann von Kafarnaum (Mt 7,28a, 8,5 10.13 par Lk 7,1-10): Ein Beitrag zur Q-Forschung' (unpublished dissertation, Tübingen, Evangelisch-theologische Fakultät).

Wehrle, J.
    1987   *Prophetie und Textanalyse. Die Komposition Obadja 1–21 interpretiert auf der Basis textlinguistischer und semiotischer Konzeptionen* (ATS, 28; Erzabtei St Ottilien: EOS Verlag).

Weinfeld, M.
    1972   *Deuteronomy and the Deuteronomic School* (Oxford: Clarendon Press).
    1991   *Deuteronomy 1–11* (AB, 5; New York: Doubleday).
    1992   'The Phases of Human Life in Mesopotamain and Jewish Sources', in E. Ulrich *et al.* (eds.), *Priests, Prophets and Scribes: Essays on the Formation and Heritage of Second Temple Judaism in Honour of J. Blenkinsopp* (JSOTSup, 149: Sheffield: Sheffield Academic Press): 182-89.

Weiser, A.
    1981–85   *Die Apostelgeschichte* (ÖTK, 5/1-2; 2 vols.; Gütersloh: Gerd Mohn).

Wellhausen, J.
    1876   *Die Composition des Hexateuchs und der Historischen Bücher des Alten Testaments* (Berlin: Georg Reimer).

Welten, P.
    1973   *Geschichte und Geschichtsdarstellung in den Chronikbüchern* (WMANT, 42; Neukirchen–Vluyn: Neukirchener Verlag).

Wenham, D.
1984   *The Rediscovery of Jesus' Eschatological Discourse* (Gospel Perspectives, 4; Sheffield: JSOT Press).

Westermann, C.
1977   *The Bible: A Pictorial History* (A Crossroad Book; New York: Seabury).

White, H.O.
1935   *Plagiarism and Imitation during the English Renaissance* (Cambridge, MA: Harvard University Press).

White, J.L.
1988   'Ancient Greek Letters', in Aune (ed.) 1988: 85-106.

Wildemann, B.
1983   *Das Evangelium als Lehrpoesie. Leben und Werk Gustav Volkmars* (Kontexte, 1; Frankfurt/New York: Peter Lang).

Wiener, A.
1978   *The Prophet Elijah in the Development of Judaism: A Depth-Psychological Study* (London: Routledge & Kegan Paul).

Wilken, R.L. (ed.)
1975   *Aspects of Wisdom in Judaism and Early Christianity* (Notre Dame/London: University of Notre Dame Press).

Willi, T.
1972   *Die Chronik als Auslegung* (FRLANT, 106; Göttingen: Vandenhoeck & Ruprecht).

Williams, G.
1970   *The Nature of Roman Poetry* (London/New York: Oxford University Press).
1978   *Change and Decline: Roman Literature in the Early Empire* (Berkeley: University of California Press).

Wink, W.
1989   'Jesus' Reply to John. Matt 11:2-6/Luke 7:18-23', *Forum* 5: 121-28.

Winston, D.
1979   *The Wisdom of Solomon* (AB, 43; Garden City, NY: Doubleday).

Winter, B.W., and A.D. Clarke (eds.)
1993   *The Book of Acts in Its First Century Setting*. I. *Ancient Literary Setting* (Grand Rapids: Eerdmans; Carlisle: Paternoster Press).

Wire, A.C.
1991   'Gender Roles in a Scribal Community', in D.L. Balch (ed.), *Social History of the Matthean Community: Cross Disciplinary Approaches* (Minneapolis: Fortress Press): 87-121.

Witherington, B.
1994   *Jesus the Sage: The Pilgrimage of Wisdom* (Edinburgh: T. & T. Clark).

Witherington, B. (ed.)
1996   *History, Literature and Society in the Book of Acts* (Cambridge: Cambridge University Press).

Wolf, A.
1980   'H. Gunkels Auffassung von der Verschriftlichung der Genesis im Light mittelalterlicher Literarisierungsprobleme', *UF* 12: 361-74.

Wrede, W.
1971   *The Messianic Secret* (Cambridge: J. Clarke [Ger. 1901]).

Wright, A.G.
1968   'Wisdom', *JBC* 34.

Yahudi, J.
1982   *Hebrew is Greek* (Oxford: Becket).

Yarbro Collins, A.
1990   *Is Mark's Gospel a Life of Jesus? The Question of Genre* (Père Marquette Lecture in Theology, 21; Milwaukee, WI: Marquette University).
1992   *The Beginning of the Gospel: Probings of Mark in Context* (Minneapolis: Fortress Press).

1993	'The Influence of Daniel on the New Testament', in J.J. Collins, *Daniel: A Commentary on the Book of Daniel* (Hermeneia; Minneapolis: Fortress Press): 90-112.
1994	'From Noble Death to Crucified Messiah', *NTS* 40: 481-503.

Zeller, D.

1984	*Kommentar zur Logienquelle* (Stuttgart: Katholisches Bibelwerk).

Ziegler, J.

1962	*Sapientia Salomonis* (Septuaginta, 12/1: Göttingen: Vandenhoeck & Ruprecht).

Ziesler, J.

1989	*Paul's Letter to the Romans* (London: SCM Press; Philadelphia: Trinity Press International).

Zumwalt, N.

1977	'Fama Subversa: Theme and Structure in Ovid Metamorphoses 12', *California Studies in Classical Antiquity* 10: 209-22.

Index of Primary Biblical References

This index is essentially a guide to entire passages, not to the detailed contents within these passages. However, some noteworthy individual verses are included, as are references to entire biblical books.

Old Testament		15.9-10	245	4.14b–5.8	465
Genesis		15.11	246	5.9-31	464
entire book	51-55	15.12	246	6–12	467
1–15	29	15.13-15	246	6–8	468, 471
1.1–4.16	126, 128	17.6	244	6.1-6	473
17	590	18.9-22	117	6.7-10	474
		19.15	244	6.11-24	468
Leviticus		23–34	249	6.25-32	474
10.14-22	126	23–28	126, 127, 131	6.33-40	468
				7.1-8	474
Numbers		23.2	244	7.5	477
entire book	132	23.3	244, 249	7.9-25	475
10.1-13	126	23.18-19	249	8.1-3	473
11–17	135	24.14-15	249	8.4-35	469
		24.16-22	250	8.13-17	477
Deuteronomy		25.5-10	250	8.18-21	478
entire book	25-29, 67, 109, 589	26.16–ch. 28	117	8.22-32	477
		28.1-19	251	8.26	477
1	111-13, 130	29–34	111, 119	8.33-35	478
1.19	270	34	251, 271	9	470, 480
1.22-25	270			9.1-6	484
2–6	115	*Joshua*		9.7-21	481
2–4	132	7	385	9.22-24	483
2.1–4.40	133			9.25-29	483
2.1–4.32	115	*Judges*		9.30-41	482
2.1–4.31	112	entire book	32-38, 91	9.42-55	483
4.32–ch. 6	116	1.1–3.6	449, 451	9.56-57	483
5.1-22	111	1.1-3	451	10.1–12.7	471
5.22–ch. 6	117	1.4-8	452	10.6–12.7	484
6.5	271	1.9-16	453	10.6-18	485
7–11	111	1.17-21	453	11.1-3	486
7–9	133	1.22-26	454	11.4-11	486
7.1–10.11	112, 113	1.24-26	455	11.12-28	486
10.12–ch. 28	115	2.1-5	455	11.29-31	485
10.12–ch. 11	117	2.6-7	455	11.32-40	487
10.12–26.15	116	2.8-17a	456	12.1-6	487
12.1–26.15	111	2.17b–3.6	456	13–16	489
14–15	236	3.7-31	458	13	490
14.1-27	241	3.7-11	460	14	490
14.1-2	241	3.12-18	460	15.1-8	491
14.3-20	242	3.19-22	461	15.20–16.3	493
14.21	241	3.23	461	16.4-14	494
14.22-23	243	3.24-25	462	16.15-21	494
14.24-27	243	3.26	462	16.23-31	495
15.1-15	243	3.27-30	462	17–18	497
15.1-4	244	3.31	462	17.1	499
15.5-6	244	4–5	464	17.2-13	499
15.7-8	245	4.1-14a	466	18.1	500

Index of Primary Biblical References

18.2-12	500	21.1-3	386	5.1	405, 406
18.13-19	501	21.4	388	5.1a	405
18.20	501	21.5	388	5.2	411
18.21-26	502	21.6	389	5.3-5	405
18.27-31	502	21.7-16	389	5.3-5a	405
19	503	21.8-13	391	5.5b	406
19.1-5a	505	21.8-9	395	5.6-7	408
19.5b-21	506	21.8	424	5.8–10.15a	409
19.22-25	508	21.10a	396	5.8-9	415
19.26-30	506	21.10b	397	5.11-12	405
20	510	21.11	397	5.13	411
20.1-7	511	21.12	397	5.14	412
20.8-13	511	21.13b	398	5.15b-24	412
20.14-48	512	21.13c	398	5.20-21	415
21	513	21.13z	397	5.25-27	414
21.1-7	515	21.17-24	389	5.25-26a	414
21.15-21	516	21.25	386	5.26c-27	415
21.22-25	517	21.27-29	389	5.26	415
		22.1-38	312	6.1-7	444
Ruth		22.1-9	317	6.5-8	440
2	372	22.10-14	319	6.8-23	421
		22.16-19a	321	6.8-13	425
1 Kings		22.19b-23	322	6.15-19	426
16.29–17.1	284	22.24-25	319	6.20-23	428
16.29	39, 284	22.26-28	323	6.24–ch. 7	436
16.30-31a	286	22.34-35	319	6.24	424, 439
16.31b	286	22.36-38	321	6.25-31	439
16.31c-32	287	26.29–2 Kgs 13	39, 149	6.32	439
16.34	288			6.33–7.4	440
17.1-16	294	*2 Kings*		7.9-11	441
17.1-7	297	1.1–2.6	351	7.12-16	441
17.1	288	1.1-2a	353	7.17-20	441
17.8-9a	298	1.2b	354	8.1-6	445
17.10a	298	1.3	356	8.7-15	421
17.10b-11	298	1.4	353	8.7-9	427
17.14	300	1.5-6a	356	8.7	427
17.15-16	300	1.6b	353	8.14-15	428
17.17-24	302	1.7-14	356	9.1-13	421
17.17	303	1.15-17	353	9.1-3	427
17.18	299, 303	2.1-6	380	9.14–ch. 13	429
17.19-21	304	2.2-6	357	9.14-16	432
17.23	306	2.7-15	377	9.17-29	432
17.24	306	2.11	379	9.30-37	432
18	339	2.16–ch. 3	365	9.56	357
18.3-4	343	2.16-18	371	11.1-11	432
18.7-16	343	2.19-25	372	11.4-16	295
18.17-29	344	3	368	11.12-19	433
18.32b-39	344	3.1-3	373	11.20	433
18.40-46	343	3.8-14	374	12.5-11	433
19	359	3.18-19	375	12.12-17	434
19.1-8	362, 363	3.21-26	375	12.18-19	435
19.9-18	363	3.27	376	13	39
19.19-21	364	3.27b	374	13.14-19	434
20.1-21	385	4.1-37	325	13.20-25	435
20.1-12	386	4.1-7	330		
20.13-21	390	4.1-2	329	*1 Chronicles*	
20.22-34	421	4.8-11	332	entire book	24, 25, 87
20.22-26	425	4.12-16	332	1—2 Chronicles	9 92
20.27	424	4.17	333	1–10	523
20.28-30a	425	4.18-37	333	1	92
20.30b-34	428	4.22-33	372	11–12	524
20.35-43	443	4.38-44	442	13	525
21	385	5	402	14	525

15–16	526	8.27	597	New Testament	
17	524	9	598	*Matthew*	
18–20	525	9.2-3	598	entire book	68
		9.17-18	598	1–7	206
2 Chronicles		9.20-23	597	1–2	198, 210
entire book	24, 25, 87	9.25-27	598	3–4	198
5.2–ch. 9	530	10–12	598	3	211
9	92	11.31	598	3.7-10	264
10–36	92, 567	12.5-11	599	3.7-8	208
10–13	567	13	596	4.1-11	208, 264
14–20	568			4.3-4	212
28.16-18	570	*Habakkuk*		4.5-7	213
30	572	1.6a	29	4.8-10	213
33.11-20	572			4.12-17	213
34	571	Apocrypha/Deutero-		4.23–7.29	264
35.19–36.21	571	Canonical Books		4.23–5.2	202
		Tobit		5	201
Ezra		entire book	252, 600	5.5-9	109, 112,
entire book	87	1–3	603		113
1–2	531	4	602	5.17-48	109, 115
3.1–6.18	531	5–10	601	5.17-47	264
6.19-22	534	11–12	602	5.17-18	112, 115
7–8	534	13–14	604	5.20	214
9–10	533			5.21-44	116
		Wisdom of Solomon		5.45-48	117
Nehemiah		1–5	573	6.1-18	214, 252
entire book	87	1.1-4	576	6.19-24	215
1–7	531	1.1	577	6.25-34	216
5	532	1.6-10	576	7	216
8	534	1.12-15	577	8	198
9	533	1.16a	578	8.1–17.20	219
10–13	533	1.16b-e	577	8.1-4	223
		2.1-16	578	8.5-13	223
Proverbs		2.16b	579	8.14-17	223
24.23-24	122	2.17-18	578	8.18-27	224
30.1–31.9	122	2.19-20	578	8.28-34	224
		2.21-24	577	9.1-8	225
Jeremiah		3.1-3	579	9.9-17	225
1.4-5	590	3.4-6	579	9.18-26	226
5.21-25	591	3.5-9	580	9.27-31	226
31.31-34	119	3.7	579	9.32-34	226
		3.10–4.6	580	9.35-38	227
Daniel		4.7-14a	581	10	198, 265
entire book	595	4.14b-18	581	10.1-6	227
1.1-16	596	4.19	581	10.7-13	227
1.4	596	4.20–5.4	582	10.14-23	227
1.9	596	5.3-16	582	10.24-25	228
1.17-21	596	5.17-25	583	10.26-27	228
2.1-24	596			10.28-31	228
2.25-35	596	*Ecclesiasticus*		10.32-33	228
2.36-45	597	entire book	119-24	10.34-39	228
2.46-49	597	1–6	119	10.40-42	229
3	596	9.1-9	137	11–13	199
4	597	14.1-2	122	11.1-24	229
4.1-3	596	14.20-21	122	11.25-30	109, 119,
5	596	23.16-27	137		121, 229
5.7-14	596	24	109, 120	11.25b-30	119
6	597	25.13-26	137	12.1-8	230
7	598	38.24–39.11	137	12.9-14	230
7.15-16	597	42.9-14	137	12.15-21	230
7.19-20	597	51	120	12.22-37	231
8.11-14	598			12.38-42	231
8.13-19	597			12.43-45	231

Index of Primary Biblical References

12.46-50	231	6.14-29	154	2.40	490		
13	265	6.45–8.26	259	2.41-52	530		
13.1-52	231	7	160, 176	2.41-50	490		
13.53–18.35	200	7.24	152	3.1-6	104, 162		
13.53-58	232	7.31	152	3.1-2b	531		
14.1-2	232	8.1–9.1	160, 177	3.2c-6	531		
14.13-21	232	8.11–9.8	256	3.7-9	262, 264		
14.34-36	233	9.2-29	160, 179	3.7-8	267		
15.1-20	233	9.30-50	160, 180	3.10-38	104		
15.21-28	233	10.1-45	189	3.10-22	162		
15.22-33	232	10.1-31	161, 181	3.10-14	532		
15.29-31	233	10.1-2	192	3.15-18	533		
15.32-39	233	10.3-9	192	3.19-20	533		
16.1-12	234	10.10-12	192	3.21-22	534		
16.13-20	234	10.17-22	194	3.23-38	160, 174, 534		
16.21-23	234	10.24-31	195				
16.22-33	46	10.32-52	161, 182	4.1-13	264		
16.24-28	234	10.32b-34	191	4.2b-13	262		
17.1-8	235	10.32a	191	4.14-22a	104, 534		
17.7-13	235	10.35-40	194	4.14-15	162		
17.14-20	235	10.41-42a	191	4.16-22a	160, 174		
17.22–ch. 18	265	10.42b-43a	191	4.28-30	262, 264		
17.22–18.35	236	10.43b-45	191	4.31	267		
17.24-27	241	11–16	151	5.1-11	262, 267		
17.24-25a	243	11.1-25	161, 182	6.12-16	265		
17.25b-26	241	13	161, 185	6.17-49	264		
17.27b	242, 243	14	161, 185	7.1–8.3	97, 104, 159, 164		
18.15-35	243	14.26-72	259				
18.15a	244	15.1–16.8	161, 186	7.1-10	57, 155, 294		
18.15b	244	15.35-36	151	7.1	298		
18.16-17	244	16.7	152	7.3-4	298		
18.21-23	246	16.8	151	7.6b-7	299		
18.26-27	245			7.6b	303		
18.28-32	245	*Luke*		7.7b	303		
18.33-35	246	entire book	68	7.8	297		
19.3	249	1–2	104, 464	7.9	300		
19.9	249	1	162	7.10	300		
20 1-16	249	1.1–Acts 15.35	84-96	7.11-17	302		
21.28-32	250	1.1–4.22a	97, 159, 521	7.11-12	303		
22.1-14	250	1.1-25	523	7.13-14	304		
23–25	266	1.1-4	99	7.15	306		
23	200	1.5–2.52	489	7.16-17	306		
24.45–ch. 25		1.5-38	490	7.18-35	312		
28.16-20	251	1.5-17	284	7.18-20	317		
		1.5a	284	7.21-23	319		
Mark		1.6	286	7.26-28	321		
entire book	147-54	1.8	287	7.29-30	321		
1.1-20	159, 162	1.10-11	287	7.31-32	322		
1.1-16	156	1.13-17	288	7.33-35	323		
1.2	151	1.17b	288	7.36-50	161, 185, 325		
1.9	152	1.26-38	468, 524				
1.16-20	151	1.39-45	525	7.36	332		
1.21-45	157, 159, 164	1.46-55	464, 525	7.37	329		
		1.56	525	7.38	333		
1.21-28	155	1.57-80	526	7.39	332		
1.40-45	151	1.80	490	7.40-42	330		
2–7	155, 166	2.7	490	7.43	333		
2.1–3.12	160, 167	2.8-20	475	7.44-46	333		
3.13–4.41	160, 169	2.21	490	8.1-3	339		
4	60	2.25-35	475	8.2b-3	343		
5	160, 173	2.34b-35	465	8.4-15	265		
6	160, 174	2.36-38	466	8.25-26	478		
6.14–9.13	151	2.39-52	162	9.1-6	265		

9.46-48	265	18.1-8	445, 471,	24.13-53	179	
9.51–18.14	270		484	24.13-35	506	
9.51–10.20	98, 104	18.1	485	24.25-27	565	
9.51-58	160, 180	18.2	486	24.33-34	565	
9.51-56	159, 162, 351	18.3	486	24.36-53	508	
		18.4b-5	487	24.44-48	565	
9.51	353	18.4a	486	24.51	379	
9.52	354	18.6-9	487			
9.53	356	19.1-10	104, 161, 182, 444, 497	*John*		
9.54-55	356			entire book	68	
9.57-62	359			4.1-42	269	
9.57-58	362, 363	19.1-2	499	5–6	269	
9.59-60	363	19.3	500	7	269	
9.61-62	364	19.4	500	9	256, 269	
10.1-20	365	19.5	501	10	46	
10.1-11	160, 174	19.6	501	11.1-53	270	
10.1	371	19.7	502	17	138	
10.2-7	372	19.8-9	499	20.14-18	255	
10.8-11	372	19.10	502	21	267	
10.13-20	367	19.11-27	266			
10.13-16	160, 180	21.5-36	266	*Acts*		
10.13-14	373	21.34-38	271	entire book	68	
10.15	374	22–Acts 2	377	1	105, 169	
10.17a	374	22.1-30	105, 161, 185, 381, 513, 563	1.1–15.35	154	
10.19	375			1.1–5.11	547	
10.20	160, 180, 376			1.1-11	179	
		22.1-13	99	1.1-5	99	
10.23-37	264, 265	22.1-6	515	1.6-11	550	
10.25-37	270	22.1	381	1.9-10	379	
10.27	271	22.7-13	161, 182	1.12-15	551	
10.38-42	259	22.8	381	1.16-22	551	
11–12	298	22.14-30	139-43	1.18-20	581	
11.1-13	264	22.14-22	516	1.23-26	553	
11.37-54	266	22.24-30	160, 180, 517	2–5	315	
12.1-12	265			2.1-42	105, 564	
12.13-34	264	22.28-30	161	2.1-21	553	
12.35-48	266	22.31-65	259	2.1-4	339	
13.6-9	265	22.46	579	2.22-28	553	
13.18-30	265	22.65-71	161, 185	2.29-36	554	
14.25–ch. 15	265	22.66–25.5	576	2.34–5.11	161, 183	
15.11-32	310	22.66–23.49	105, 573	2.37-47	555	
16.1–18.8	467	22.66	381	2.37-38	389	
16.1-9	98, 104, 161, 181, 468, 471	23.1–24.12	161, 186	2.43–4.31	105	
		23.6-9	576	2.43-47	565	
		23.10	577	3–6	460	
16.1-3	473	23.11a	577	3.1–4.22	315	
16.4	474	23.11b	579	3.1-10	556	
16.5-7	474	23.12	577	3.2	433	
16.19-31	98, 104, 160, 180, 468, 469, 471	23.13-25	578	3.6-8	565	
		23.22	579	3.6	434	
		23.26-49	378	3.11-26	557, 566	
		23.27-43	161, 182	4–15	567	
16.19-21	477	23.27-31	580	4.1-31	565	
16.22-24	477	23.32-33	581	4.1-9	558	
16.27-31	478	23.35-37	578	4.1-4	161, 185	
17.1-2	265	23.35a	581	4.11-12	556	
17.11–18.18	104	23.39-41	582	4.13-22	558	
17.11-37	470, 480	23.42-43	580	4.16	556	
17.11-19	164, 481	23.44-45	583	4.23-37	558	
17.20–18.8	161, 185	23.47-49	582	4.23-36	344	
17.20-25	482	23.50–24.53	105, 503	4.23-31	160, 174, 339	
17.26-32	483	23.50–24.4	505			
17.33	483	24.4-9	343	4.32–5.42	105	
17.34-37	484	24.5-12	506	4.32–5.16	565	

Index of Primary Biblical References

4.32–5.11	161, 181	9.1-19a	421	13.38-49	572
4.34-36	567	9.1-8	161	13.50-52	455
5.1-11	385, 559	9.3-6a	425	14	562
5.1-2	386	9.6b-8	426	14.1-13	455
5.3-4	388	9.8b-9	427	14.4-28	160, 173
5.7	388	9.10-11	425	14.5-19	572
5.8	389	9.11-12	427	14.8-18	340, 344
5.12-16	160, 174	9.17-19a	428	14.14-18	456
5.17-42	567	9.18	185	14.19-23	456
5.17-21	161, 182	9.19b-43	429	14.24-28	455
5.26	161, 182	9.19b-31	430	15.1-35	160, 176, 562
5.33-42	510	9.19-30	161, 185		
5.33-35	511	9.23	432	15.6-21	495
5.33	161, 182	9.24	432	15.7-21	572
5.36-37	512	9.25	432	15.22-35	572
5.38-42	511	9.26-28	432	15.36–ch. 28	268, 269
5.9b-11	390	9.30	433	16.11-15	269
6–9	177	9.31–12.25	106	17	269
6	570	9.31–11.18	568	18.1–19.10	269
6.1–8.1a	105	9.31	433	20.1-24	269
6.9-14	389, 391	9.32–15.35	155, 166	21.1-26	270
6.9-10	395	9.32–15.21	489	27.1–28.15	273
6.11a	396	9.32-43	173, 430, 491		
6.11b	397			*Romans*	
6.12a	397	9.32-35	433	entire book	219, 587
6.12b	397	9.36	434	1.1-12	210
6.13-14	400	9.37-39	434	1.13-18	211
6.13b-14	398	9.41-43	435	1.19-23	215
6.13a	397	10	315	1.24-32	216
6.14	161, 185	10.1–11.26	160, 167	2.1-16	216
7.1-60	571	10.1–11.18	437, 562	2.17-29	233
7.1-51	161, 181	10.1-8	439	3.1-4	233
7.47-50	161, 185	10.9-16	439	3.5-8	233
7.58–9.29	571	10.17-23a	439	3.9	233
7.58	389, 398	10.23b-33	440	3.10-20	234
7.58a	391	10.34-43	441	3.21-31	223
8.1b–9.30	105	10.44-48	440	4.1-17	223
8.1-25	161, 185	11.1-18	493	4.6c-8	597
8.1b-25	560	11.1-14	441	4.18-25	223
8.1-3	565	11 15-18	441	5.1-11	224
8.9-40	402	11.19-21	494	5.12 21	224
8.9-11	405	11.22-26	494	6.1-14	225
8.15	389	11.27–ch. 12	160, 174, 183, 566	6.15–7.6	225
8.17-19	412			7.7–8.13	226
8.20-23	414	11.27-30	442	8.14-17	226
8.20-21	389, 414	12	154, 443, 458	8.18-30	226
8.22-24	389			8.31-39	227
8.22-23	415	12.1-2	460	9.1-5	227
8.25b	408	12.7-8	461	9.4-23	213
8.26-40	561	12.9-10	461	9.9-13	212
8.26-27a	409	12.11-16	462	9.24-29	213
8.26	389	12.17	462	9.30-33	213
8.27b	405, 406	12.18-19	462	10.2-23	214
8.28-30	415	12.20-23	462	10.14-15	227
8.29	409	13–14	449	10.16-21	227
8.30b-31a	408	13	561	11.1-4	228
8.30b	409	13.1–15.35	99, 106	11.5-10	228
8.31-39	161, 181	13.1–14.3	160, 169	11.11-12	228
8.32-33	411	13.1-3	451, 572	11.13-15	228
8.34-35	409	13.4-13	452	11.16-21	228
8.38-39	412	13.14-25	453	11.22-24	229
8.38	415	13.26-29	453	11.25-32	229
9	565	13.30-37	454	11.33-36	229

12.1-8	230	5	559	16.1-4	603
12.9-13	230	6–8	126	16.5	604
12.14-21	230	6.1-11	130	16.6-8	604
13.1-7	231	6.11	560	16.10-12	604
13.8-10	231	6.12–7.11	129	16.15-20	604
13.11-13	231	6.12-20	561	16.18b-21	601
13.14	231	6.12b-17	601	16.22-24	604
14.1-12	231	7	132, 561		
14.13	232	7.1-3	602	*2 Corinthians*	
14.14	232	7.10-11	136	entire book	588
14.15-21	232	7.17–8.6	133		
14.22–15.13	232	7.29-31	602	*Galatians*	
15.14	233	8	132, 562	entire book	71, 589
15.15-21	234	8.1-13	128	1	594
15.22-26	234	8.1-6	136	1.14-15	590
15.27-29	234	9	562	2.11-14	591
15.30	235	9.3-18	126, 137	3.1-5	591
15.31-33	235	9.3-12	137		
16	235	9.4-18	131	*Ephesians*	
		10	126	entire book	138, 256, 592
1 Corinthians		10.1–11.1	562		
entire book	595, 600, 605	11.2-34	563	1–3	155
		11.13	57	1.15–ch. 2	310
1–5	547	11.16-34	139-43	2	310
1.1-3	549	11.17-22	596		
1.1	603	11.23	596	*Colossians*	
1.3-5	596	11.23b	57	entire book	593
1.4-9	550	11.25	596		
1.10-13a	551	12.1-11	564	*1 Thessalonians*	
1.18-25	551	12.12–ch. 13	565	entire book	605
1.18-21	600	14	565		
1.20-21	596	14.2-4	597	*2 Thessalonians*	
1.25–2.5	133	14.4-5	598	entire book	592
1.26-31	553	14.12b-18	598		
2.1-5	553	14.25	597	*Philemon*	
2.6-9	553	14.37b	597	entire book	586
2.9	601	15.1-11	594		
2.10-16	554, 596	15.1-7	565	*1 Peter*	
2.10	596	15.3	57	entire book	592
2.68	596	15.3b	598	2.18–3.17	189
3.1–5.8	135	15.8-19	565	2.18-24	191
3.1-9	555	15.9-10	603	3.1-4	192
3.10-17	556	15.20-49	566	3.5-7	192
3.10-15	596	15.30	602	3.8-9a	194
3.18-23	557	15.31a	602	3.9b-12	194
4.1-5	558	15.34ab	602	3.13-17	195
4.6-13	558	15.35-37	599		
4.14-21	133, 558	15.50-58	565	*Jude*	
4.15-17	601	15.51-58	603	entire book	592
5–7	137	16	566		

Index of Select Subjects

This index is primarily a guide to some literary processes and to some literature-related people and institutions. It is not a guide to the entirety of this book's contents.

abbreviated   363
abbreviation   353, 363, 364, 442
action   45
Acts, sources of   402
actualization   30, 197
adaptation seems far fetched   154
adapting characters   404
antithesis   589
apocalyptic   371
art   33
art, Judges as an intricate work of   38
artistic composition   535

Beatitudes   261
beginning   119, 150, 154, 256, 263, 270, 341, 589
biographical   175
biography   390
blending   531, 577, 583

canon   279
canonicity   337
center   119
center of 2 Kings 2   377
center of Proto-Luke   377
Christian origins   278
christianization   308, 363, 364, 493
christianized   295, 324, 359, 363
clarification   197, 307, 309, 363, 364, 363
clarity   550
climactic middle   589
clues   45
coherence   46
combination   157, 165, 185, 473, 534
comedy   9
command and compliance   297
command-and-fulfillment   397
communication   73
compactness   162, 167
complementarity   307
complementary image   556
completeness   45, 519, 535, 545
component   125, 138, 159, 189, 359, 385, 391, 402, 421, 429, 464, 467, 503, 545
compression   10, 307, 309, 336
conceptual transition   456
condensed   601
conflation   10, 296, 331, 334, 476
conflict, sense of   167

conglomerate of materials   236
constitutive   125
contrast   308, 493
contaminatio   7

contemporization   30, 588
continuity   493, 495
copying   70
creative summary   523
credibility in narration   309
criss-crossing   460
criteria   43, 201

deuteronomized   237
dialectic   589
dialectical mode   563
diatribe   590
didactic poetry   9
differences   46
diptych   39, 101
dispersal   92, 156, 201, 266, 380
dissimilarities   336
distillation   339, 359, 502, 519, 547, 599
distilled   168, 473, 499
distilling   41, 132, 512
distills   224, 266
dividing   583
division   328, 336
domesticated   425, 474, 475, 486, 494
Double Tradition   260
doublets   200, 259
drama   15
dramatization   194, 307, 547

eclectic mode   563
Egyptian folktale   467
eight units   100
elaboration   10, 30, 250, 251, 307, 379, 499
emphasizing spirit   155
emulatio   261, 361
emulation   7
end   119, 150, 154, 256, 263, 341
ending   271
encyclopedic   23
epic   273
epic poetry   9
epistles intertextuality   587
epistolary interdependence   592

expansions 201, 237, 483
external plausibilities 44
explicitation 307

fiction 33
form-change 12
form criticism 51, 254
framework 458, 489, 498, 523
fulfill 488

fulfillment 42, 535
fusion 10, 296, 328, 336, 353, 363, 364, 406, 408, 414, 415, 473, 475, 476

genre 148, 149
geographic adaptation 307, 353
geographic structure 152
grafting 401
Great Omission 259
greater human involvement 164
Greco-Roman writing 3

healings 39
heuristic mode 563
historicized 574
historiography 13, 274
history, elements of past 32
(human) temple 433
humor 480

imagery, change of 170
imitation 6, 308
imitative historiography 311
immortality 41
incongruity 480
individuality 550
inner-biblical exegesis 27
institutions, adaptation of 76
institutional continuity 278
intensification 34, 287, 381, 397
intensifies 216
internal 427, 435, 446
internalization 11, 90, 241, 248, 294, 325, 336, 342, 390, 404, 408, 414, 442, 516
internalized 324, 339, 474, 496, 500
interpretation 241
intertextuality 74
interweaving 207, 483
inventive imitation 7
irony 480
isolation 73

language 535
legal exegesis 27
length 150
libraries 64
linguistic details 45
literary dependence 43
literary nature, essence of Judges 33
location 152
Logia 109, 197
lyric poetry 8

Mark does things by threes 156
méditation 24
metaphorical identification 30
middle 119, 150, 154, 256, 263, 341
midrash 24, 258, 311, 337, 399, 535
mimēsis 4, 256
Minor Agreements 260
modernization 248, 342, 363, 364, 408, 442, 588
modernized 241, 363
motifs 535
mystery/secrecy 155, 157

omission 259
Old Testament, normative 19
oral communication 5
oral tradition 18, 26, 48, 50, 254, 255, 337
oral transmission 258
order 45, 91, 165, 263, 270, 297, 485, 519, 535, 545, 567
Our Father 258

Papias 123
parabolic historiography 24
paraphrase 6, 399
pastoral poetry 9
Pauline autobiography 586
Pauline authorship 585
Pauline exegesis, principles of 588
personal, emphasis on what is 446
Pesharim 29
plausibility 206
playful echo 475
plot 45, 519
poetry 14
positive 206, 216, 324, 373, 456, 479, 483, 484
positivization 11, 90, 284, 308, 475, 547
practical 206
preGospel traditions 257
presentation 309
preservation 3
pre-sourcing 269
prolonged 494
prophecy 39
prophetic history 29
Proto-Luke 84-96, 154
Proto-Luke, history of research 541

Q 20, 88, 109, 111, 301, 312, 359, 544
quest for the historical Jesus 277
quest for the historical Paul 278
Qumran 29, 70, 122

reading 6
rearranged 501
rearranged drastically 567
recast 237
reduces 523
religious experience 76, 278
renewing 457
reorganizes the structural arrangement 309
repetition 34, 287, 373, 381, 386
re-positioning 499

Index of Select Subjects

re-presentation, radical 521
reshaping 457
reversal 90, 186, 287, 427, 436, 438, 495, 528, 530
rewording 307
rewriting 23, 234
rewritten Bible 29, 197, 256
rhetoric 5, 14
rhetorical imitation 336
roads 72

sacramental mode of imitation 563
satire 9
schools 63, 65
scribes 63
Semitism 88, 543
Septuagintism 88, 543
Sermon on the Mount 261
significant similarities 44
Signs Source 20
spirit, negative 164
spiritual experience 76
spiritualization 516
structural arrangement 410
structure 93
structure, variation in 155
structure, eightfold 98
substitution 11
substitution of images 579
succession 39
summarizes 225
synagogues 63, 66
synoptic problem 19
synthesis 10, 25, 27, 40, 92, 132, 149, 241, 248, 339, 358, 473, 478, 485, 578
synthesis, dense multi-layered 428

teaching, shift towards 157
temple, focus on 491
temple, spiritualized 523
theme 44, 519
theological redesigning 547
theory 6
tragic drama 9
transference 15, 90
transformation 8, 27, 41, 125, 126, 155, 212, 214, 256, 289, 312, 483, 500, 515, 523, 545
transformational strategies 324
transformed 399, 483, 508, 531
transforming 269, 361
transition, radical 446
transpositions 260
travel 72
triple intertextuality of the Epistles 585
Triple Tradition 260
type-scene of a betrothal 513

universal 373, 483
universalism 178
universalization 308, 442

verbatim correspondence 593
verbatim quotation 399
verbatim reproduction 563
verification 93
vivid 206

wording 399
word-play 247, 337, 356, 357, 406, 414, 478, 480, 485, 501
writers' network 69

zēlos 256

Index of Authors

Achtemeier, P.   207
Adkins, A.W.H.   12
Aletti, J.-N.   586
Alexander, L.C.A.   19, 61, 65-68, 70, 75
Allison, D.C., Jr   74, 236, 238
Alonso-Schökel, L.   33, 35, 50
Alter, R.   33, 34, 36, 56, 312, 337, 355, 395, 513, 564
Anderson, W.S.   10
Atkins, J.W.H.   17
Audet, J.-P.   468
Auerbach, E.   4

Bacon, B.W.   238
Bailey, J.L.   585, 586
Bal, M.   36
Baldwin, C.S.   5, 52
Balme, M.   8, 13
Barr, D.L.   19
Barrett, C.K.   57, 69, 126, 226, 254
Barth, G.   207, 219, 224
Barth, K.   18
Bauckham, R.   75, 591, 592
Beker, J.C.   139, 547
Benoit, P.   138, 198, 402
Bergemann, T.   43, 111
Bergler, S.   28
Betz, H.D.   71, 125, 201, 590
Bieringer, R.   588
Blessington, F.C.   335
Bloch, R.   24, 399
Bloom, H.   43
Bodine, W.R.   451
Boismard, M.-E.   138, 147, 189, 198
Boling, R.G.   497
Bonz, M.P.   273
Boomershine, T.E.   59
Bornkamm, G.   207, 219, 224, 236
Bossuyt, P.   472
Botha, P.J.J.   59
Bowie, E.L.   16
Bowra, C.M.   3, 12
Breytenbach, C.   189
Brodie, T.L.   3, 19, 21, 24, 27, 28, 39, 43, 47, 57, 59, 69, 70, 85-88, 99, 100, 104, 109, 138, 149, 150, 189, 201, 255, 256, 265, 269, 270, 291, 302, 369, 384, 393, 396, 448
Brooke, A.E.   284
Brooke, G.J.   122
Brown, R.E.   46, 61, 69, 70, 75, 101, 201, 254, 257, 303, 310, 311, 326, 336, 399, 464, 489, 490, 523, 525, 527, 528, 535, 592
Bruce, F.F.   385, 391

Brueggemann, W.   79, 124
Bryan, C.   56, 148
Bryce, G.E.   23, 24, 467
Büchele, A.   574
Bultmann, R.   18, 46, 51, 85, 109, 327, 402
Burkert, W.   74
Burridge, R.A.   148
Butterfield, H.   16
Byrne, B.   226
Byrskog, S.   50, 59

Cadbury, H.J.   15, 21, 398, 399
Caird, G.B.   58, 574
Callebat, L.   37
Cameron, R.   312
Carlson, R.A.   360
Carmichael, C.M.   26, 27
Cazelles, H.   521, 524, 527
Cerfaux, L.   392
Childs, B.S.   360
Chomsky, N.   48
Chouraqui, A.   28, 50
Ciampa, R.E.   125, 591
Clark, D.L.   4
Coleman, R.   9
Conington, J.   9
Conroy, C.   286
Conteneau, G.   37
Conway, R.S.   9-11
Conzelmann, H.   131, 139, 385, 391, 403, 408
Cook, M.J.   59
Cooper, A.   5
Cope, O.L.   68, 236
Coppens, J.   413
Cornford, F.M.   16
Cotter, W.J.   312
Cox, A.   9, 14
Craig, J.D.   37
Cribbs, F.L.   255
Culler, J.   74
Culpepper, R.A.   66-69

Dabeck, P.   302
Dalton, J.F.   5, 52
Daube, D.   311
Dautzenberg, G.   150, 151
Davies, G.H.   238
Davies, P.R.   28, 64, 68
Davies, W.D.   207, 238
De la Potterie, I.   468
De Roo, J.C.R.   122
De Vries, S.   312
Deissmann, G.A.   586

Delobel, J. 325, 337
Denaux, A. 43, 69, 111, 255, 267
Derrett, J.D.M. 330
Dibelius, M. 51, 68, 396, 403
Dillon, R. 167, 510, 543
Dodd, C.H. 58, 69, 254, 326
Dodds, R.E. 73
Doty, W.G. 586, 587
Drury, J. 310
Duke, R.K. 24, 28
Dumais, M. 310
Dundenberg, I. 69, 257
Dunn, J.D.G. 57, 59, 255
Dupont, J. 139, 337, 392, 402, 403

Eliot, T.S. 43, 279
Ellis, E.E. 47, 125
Enslin, M.E. 21, 138, 310
Evans, C.F. 270, 272
Exum, J.C. 33

Farrer, A. 260
Feine, P. 88, 541
Feldman, L.H. 73, 89, 573
Fischel, H.A. 311
Fishbane, M. 23, 27
Fiske, G.C. 4, 7, 9
Fitzmyer, J.A. 19, 29, 59, 99, 122, 139, 207, 228, 258-60, 267, 305-307, 311, 313, 314, 322, 325-27, 334, 337, 340, 349, 351, 353, 354, 357, 358, 368, 371, 375, 399, 400, 415, 417, 465, 472-77, 479, 481, 499, 500, 509, 543, 574, 593
Flender, H. 358
Flusser, D. 351
Foley, J.M. 53
Foucault, M. 3, 4
Fraeyman, M. 12, 523
Francis, F.O. 592, 593
Frankemölle, H. 237
Freedman, D.N. 25, 101
Friedrischen, T.A. 58, 260
Funk, R.W. 56, 57

Gärtner, B. 68
Gabba, E. 16
Gardiner-Smith, P. 254
Gast, F. 259
Gaston, L. 88, 541
Gaventa, B.R. 586
Gelin, A. 533, 534
Gerhardsson, B. 56, 58, 308, 337
Gils, F. 302
Gottlieb, C. 73
Goulder, M.D. 28, 70, 138, 189, 236, 260, 513
Grässer, E. 139, 404, 408
Grassi, J.A. 237, 251, 310, 407
Gray, J. 397, 437
Green, H.B. 258
Greene, T.M. 3, 4, 78
Gressmann, H. 467
Grobel, K. 467
Gros Louis, K.R.R. 36, 508
Groves, J.W. 26

Grunmann, W. 303
Gundry, R.H. 211
Gunkel, H. 51, 53, 54, 85, 326
Gusdorf, G. 12, 326

Haenchen, E. 19, 85, 139, 385, 391, 395, 398, 402, 407, 409, 449, 461, 511
Hafemann, S. 125, 588
Hall, D.R. 132
Halpern, B. 32
Halpern-Amaru, B. 89
Halverson, J. 50
Hamerton-Kelly, R.G. 311
Hanson, A.T. 126
Haran, M. 66
Hardie, C.G. 9, 43
Harnack, A. 402
Harrington, D.J. 29-31, 46, 154, 167, 181, 197, 233
Harrington, J.M. 541
Harrington, W.J. 190
Harriott, R. 9
Havelock, E.A. 12, 545
Hayes, J.H. 32, 33, 38, 85
Hays, R.B. 69, 78, 86, 125, 126, 132, 587-90, 594
Heidel, A. 23
Held, H.J. 207, 219, 224
Henaut, B.W. 60
Hengel, M. 13, 58
Higginbotham, J. 9
Highet, G. 335
Hoffmann, P. 544
Hollander, H.W. 136
Hooker, M.D. 149
Hoover, R.J. 56, 57
Horgan, M.P. 29
Horton, F.L. 19

Irvin, D. 23

Jacobson, A.D. 573
Jellicoe, S. 451
Jeremias, J. 325
Johnson, L.T. 76-78, 139, 294, 339, 385, 391, 473
Johnston, G. 592
Jüngling, H.-W. 34
Jülicher, A. 327

Karris, R.J. 313
Kelber, W.H. 55, 59, 254
Kennedy, G. 4, 5, 8, 13, 125
Kenney, E.J. 15
Kettenbach, G. 273
Kieffer, R. 255, 256
Kieweler, H.V. 23
Kilgallen, J. 391
Kim, J. 32, 33
Kleinig, J.W. 24
Kloppenborg, J.S. 544, 573
Klotz, A. 37
Knauer, G.N. 9, 10, 310, 328
Knowling, R.J. 396, 400
Koenen, L. 74
Königsmann, B. 402

Koch, D.A.   69, 78, 86, 125, 126, 132, 588
Koester, H.   50, 57
Koet, B.J.   59, 86, 89, 519, 543
Kügler, J.   55
Kümmel, W.G.   585
Kugel, J.L.   14
Kuhn, T.   20
Kurz, W.S.   5, 19, 52, 311, 337

LaVerdiere, E.   481
Lacan, M.-F.   355
Lambert, W.G.   3
Lambrecht, J.   312
Lampe, G.W.H.   510
Larcher, C.   573
Lattimore, R.   5
Laurentin, R.   310
Le Déaut, R.   311
Légasse, S.   64
Lechte, J.   74
Lee, G.   9
Leishman, J.B.   9
Lemaire, A.   64-67
Lenchak, T.A.   28
Lesky, A.   5, 15, 16
Lieberman, S.   331
Lindars, B.   69
Lindijer, C.H.   407
Linton, C.D.   480
Lipiński, E.   63, 64
Loisy, A.   327, 393, 396
Lord, A.B.   5, 18, 52, 53, 55
Lubetski, M.   73
Luz, U.   60
Lyonnet, S.   211
Lyons, G.   586

Mack, B.L.   111
Mahon, R.   586
Major, W.   23
Malamet, A.   498
Malherbe, A.J.   125
Mally, E.J.   259
Maly, E.H.   226, 573
Marshall, I.H.   84, 318, 322, 342, 351, 353, 375, 472, 481, 574
Martin, R.   14, 16
Martyn, J.L.   69, 590
Mattill, A.J., Jr   371
May, R.   516
Mayes, A.D.H.   32
McDonald   148
McGiffert, A.C.   402
McKeon, R.   4
McLaglan Wilson, R.   404
McNicol, A.J.   258
Meier, J.P.   117, 200, 206, 207, 225, 243, 252
Meyers, E.M.   67
Miles, G.   11
Miller, F.J.   9, 21
Miller, J.M.   32, 33, 38, 437
Mitchell, M.M.   125, 547
Moessner, D.P.   85, 132, 270

Mohrlang, R.   207
Montgomery, J.A.   326
Moore, C.A.   252, 600
Moran, W.L.   25
Morgenthaler, R.   337
Müller, P.   69
Murphy-O'Connor, J.   136, 139, 553, 558, 564, 585
Murray, P.   43
Myers, J.M.   521, 524, 525, 533

Neirynck, F.   43, 57, 69, 88, 148, 254, 255, 259, 260, 264, 267
Neusner, J.   5, 53, 59
Neyrey, J.   574
Nielsen, E.   54, 55
Nodet, E.   77
Nogalski, J.   28
Nordheim, E.V.   360
North, R.   24

O'Brien, J.   23
O'Day, G.   20
O'Toole, R.F.   408
Ong, W.   3, 5, 46, 52, 308, 337
Orton, D.E.   68
Osty, E.   573
Otis, B.   10

Page, A.F.   541
Palmer, D.W.   19
Parry, M.   5
Pate, C.M.   90, 124, 125
Pavlovsky, V.   534
Pelling, C.B.R.   13, 15, 16
Perrin, N.   254
Pervo, R.I.   84
Plümacher, E.   19, 85, 334
Plummer, A.   252
Polanyi, M.   20
Pope, M.H.   516
Porton, G.   24, 311, 399
Praeder, S.M.   20, 273
Preminger, A.   4
Preuss, H.D.   33
Przybylski, B.   206
Puech, E.   66, 122

Quesnell, Q.   155

Rad, G. von   14, 26
Radermakers, J.   472
Reese, J.M.   573
Reicke, B.   189, 592
Reiff, A.   4
Reuter, R.   592, 593
Richard, E.   358, 391-93, 395, 400
Richardson, P.   108, 124, 136
Rigaux, B.   592
Riley, W.   24
Robbins, V.K.   99, 148, 150
Robinson, J.M.   108, 109, 124, 136, 544, 573
Rogerson, J.W.   18, 54
Rolland, P.   138, 189

Index of Authors

Roloff, J.   190
Rosner, B.S.   19, 125
Roudiez, L.S.   74
Rybolt, J.E.   573

Safrai, S.   53
Sahlin, H.   543
Sampley, J.P.   592, 593
Sanders, J.A.   310
Sarason, R.S.   326
Satterthwaite, P.E.   19, 451
Scheid, J.   5
Schenk, W.   138, 189
Schillebeeckx, E.   18
Schmid, H.H.   28
Schmidt, K.L.   51
Schmithals, W.   18, 21
Schmitt, H.-C.   369, 437
Schneider, G.   139, 391, 392, 397, 409
Schneiders, S.S.   76
Schürmann, H.   302, 303, 306, 307, 310, 318, 325, 326
Schweizer, E.   211
Schweizer, H.   369, 437
Schwenk-Bressler, U.   29
Scott, R.B.Y.   24
Selong, G.   254
Selwyn, E.G.   592
Senior, D.   236
Skehan, P.   573
Smith, D.M.   254
Snodgrass, K.R.   207
Soggin, J.A.   497, 498
Stanley, C.D.   89, 126
Stegemann, E.W.   78
Steiner, G.   4, 6, 12, 16, 20, 43
Stendahl, K.   68
Sterling, G.E.   78, 85, 89, 274, 337, 543
Stibbe, M.W.G.   59
Stock, K.   468
Stockhausen, C.K.   78, 125, 588-90
Stowers, S.K.   586
Streeter, B.H.   69, 325, 542
Strousma, G.G.   78
Stuhlmueller, C.   101
Svenbro, J.   5
Swartley, W.M.   149, 270
Sybel, V.   325

Talbert, C.H.   13, 18, 19, 53, 56, 313, 314, 341, 372
Tannehill, R.C.   89, 314, 318, 355, 365
Taylor, J.   77, 78, 541
Taylor, V.   541
Telford, W.R.   147, 148
Thompson, C.L.   15
Thompson, M.B.   75
Thompson, R.J.   51
Thompson, T.L.   28, 64

Thompson, W.G.   238
Trible, P.   37, 487, 504
Trocmé, E.   147
Turner, C.   13, 16, 260, 310

Utzschneider, H.   63

Vaage, L.E.   312
Van Belle, G.   255
Van Ruiten, J.T.A.G.M.   28
Van Segbroeck, F.   236
Van Seters, J.   28
Van Unnik, W.C.   410
Van Wolde, E.   3, 43
Vander Broek, L.D.   585, 586
Vaux, R. de   122, 369, 392, 437
Vermes, G.   29, 122, 197
Via, D.O.   207
Vielhauer, P.   139
Vieweger, D.   28
Viviano, B.T.   233
Volkmar, G.   21
Von Stackelberg, J.   8

Walker, W.O.   18
Walsh, J.T.   297, 357
Walsh, P.G.   15, 296, 309, 410
Wansbrough, H.   51
Warner, S.M.   18, 54
Watts, R.E.   149
Webb, B.G.   33, 35-37, 472
Webster, J.   5
Wehrle, J.   28
Weinfeld, M.   26, 28, 67, 68, 256
Weiser, A.   458
Wellhausen, J.   51, 54
Welten, P.   24
Wenham, D.   147
Wentling, J.L.   19
Westermann, C.   525
White, H.O.   4, 7, 8
White, J.L.   586
Wildemann, B.   21, 189
Willi, T.   24
Williams, G.   37, 56, 309
Wink, W.   312
Winston, D.   573
Wire, A.C.   68
Wolf, A.   18
Wrede, W.   148
Wright, A.G.   573

Yahudi, J.   23
Yarbro Collins, A.   148, 595

Ziegler, J.   576
Ziesler, J.   207
Zumwalt, N.   21

www.ingramcontent.com/pod-product-compliance
Lightning Source LLC
Chambersburg PA
CBHW070156240426
43671CB00007B/467